Magill's
Cinema
Annual
2012

Magill's Cinema Annual 2012

31st Edition
A Survey of the films of 2011

Brian Tallerico, Editor

A VideoHound® Reference

GALE
CENGAGE Learning·

Detroit • New York • San Francisco • New Haven, Conn • Waterville, Maine • London

Magill's Cinema Annual 2012
Brian Tallerico, Editor

Project Editor: Michael J. Tyrkus

Editorial: Jim Craddock

Editorial Support Services: Wayne Fong

Composition and Electronic Prepress: Gary Leach, Evi Seoud

Manufacturing: Rhonda Dover

For product information and technology assistance, contact us at
Gale Customer Support, 1-800-877-4253.
For permission to use material from this text or product,
submit all requests online at **www.cengage.com/permissions.**
Further permissions questions can be emailed to
permissionrequest@cengage.com

While every effort has been made to ensure the reliability of the information presented in this publication, Gale, a part of Cengage Learning, does not guarantee the accuracy of the data contained herein. Gale accepts no payment for listing; and inclusion in the publication of any organization, agency, institution, publication, service, or individual does not imply endorsement of the editors or publisher. Errors brought to the attention of the publisher and verified to the satisfaction of the publisher will be corrected in future editions.

EDITORIAL DATA PRIVACY POLICY: Does this product contain information about you as an individual? If so, for more information about our editorial data privacy policies, please see our Privacy Statement at www.gale.cengage.com.

Gale, Cengage Learning
27500 Drake Rd.
Farmington Hills, MI, 48331-3535

ISBN-13: 978-1-55862-833-5
ISBN-10: 1-55862-833-9

ISSN: 0739-2141

Printed in Mexico
1 2 3 4 5 6 7 16 15 14 13 12

Contents

Preface

Magill's Cinema Annual 2012 continues the fine film reference tradition that defines the VideoHound® series of entertainment industry products published by Gale. The thirty-first annual volume in a series that developed from the twenty-one-volume core set, *Magill's Survey of Cinema,* the *Annual* was formerly published by Salem Press. Gale's seventeenth volume, as with the previous Salem volumes, contains essay-reviews of significant domestic and foreign films released in the United States during the preceding year.

The *Magill's* editorial staff at Gale, Cengage Learning, comprising the VideoHound® team and a host of *Magill's* contributors, continues to provide the enhancements that were added to the *Annual* when Gale acquired the line. These features include:

- More essay-length reviews of significant films released during the year
- Obituaries and book review sections
- Trivia and "fun facts" about the reviewed movies, their stars, the crew, and production
- Quotes and dialogue "soundbites" from reviewed movies, or from stars and crew about the film
- More complete awards and nominations listings, including the American Academy Awards®, the Golden Globes, and others (see the User's Guide for more information on awards coverage)
- Box office grosses, including year-end and other significant totals
- Publicity taglines featured in film reviews and advertisements

In addition to these elements, *Magill's Cinema Annual 2012* still features:

- An obituaries section profiling major contributors to the film industry who died in 2011
- An annotated list of selected film books published in 2011
- Nine indexes: Director, Screenwriter, Cinematographer, Editor, Art Director, Music Director, Performer, Subject, and Title (now cumulative)

COMPILATION METHODS

The *Magill's* editorial staff reviews a variety of entertainment industry publications, including trade magazines and newspapers, as well as online sources, on a daily and weekly basis to select significant films for review in *Magill's Cinema Annual. Magill's* staff and other contributing reviewers, including film scholars and university faculty, write the reviews included in the *Annual.*

MAGILL'S CINEMA ANNUAL: A VIDEOHOUND® REFERENCE

The *Magill's Survey of Cinema* series, now supplemented by the *Annual,* is the recipient of the Reference Book of the Year Award in Fine Arts by the American Library Association. Gale, an award-winning publisher of reference products, is proud to offer *Magill's Cinema Annual* as part of its popular VideoHound® product line, which includes *VideoHound®'s Golden Movie Retriever* and *The Video Source Book.* Other Gale film-related products include the four-volume *International Dictionary of Films and Filmmakers, Women Filmmakers & Their Films,* the *Contemporary Theatre, Film, and Television* series, and the four-volume *Schirmer Encyclopedia of Film.*

ACKNOWLEDGMENTS

The editor considers the talented team that makes up the writing staff of *Magill's Cinema Annual 2012* the most impressive yet assembled for this book with a diverse range of viewpoints and critical experience working together to create a comprehensive chronicle of the year in film. The writers continue to impress with their knowledge, dedication, and abilities. This year's edition is honored by the presence of eight members of the Chicago Film Critics Association, including three members of the Board of Directors, as well as one member of the Detroit Film Critics Society. The staff at Gale, Cengage Learning—Mike Tyrkus and Jim Craddock—deserve thanks for their continued efforts on behalf of the book as well. The editor must finally note that he would accomplish nothing in this movie-loving world if not for the support of his incredible wife Lauren, beautiful sons Lucas & Miles, and his entire network of family and friends who have supported him through the sometimes intense process of putting together this book. Projects this exhaustive cannot rest solely on the shoulders of one person and it is only through remarkable support that they can even be considered, much less accomplished.

We at *Magill's* look forward to another exciting year in film and preparing the next edition of *Magill's Cinema Annual.* As always, we invite your comments, questions, and suggestions. Please direct them to:

Editor

Magill's Cinema Annual

Gale, Cengage Learning

27500 Drake Road

Farmington Hills, MI 48331-3535

Phone: (248) 699-4253

Toll-Free: (800) 347-GALE (4253)

Fax: (248) 699-8865

The Year in Film: An Introduction

It is common for times of international stress in the real world to be reflected on the silver screen by journeys to a happier, more peaceful place. In 2011, that journey was into the past of the form itself as filmmakers used nostalgia in such highly acclaimed works as Woody Allen's *Midnight in Paris,* Martin Scorsese's *Hugo,* and Michel Hazanavicius' *The Artist,* all Oscar® nominees for Best Picture, Best Screenplay, and Best Director (and all winners of Academy Awards® with Scorsese's and Hazanavicius' taking home an amazing five apiece and dominating the evening's festivities). The nostalgia trip of American cinema was not just reserved for obvious examples like these three as many of the most-acclaimed works of the year also took place in other eras, whether it be the Disney-ifying of the Civil Rights Movement in *The Help,* Oscar®-nominated biopics of Marilyn Monroe (*My Week With Marilyn*) and Margaret Thatcher (*The Iron Lady*), or an attempt to recreate 1980s Spielberg magic in J.J. Abrams' *Super 8.*

The nostalgia was not just thematic. Old guard actors like Nick Nolte, Christopher Plummer, and Max Von Sydow all delivered performances that stood as some of the most acclaimed of their careers and the living legend that is Meryl Streep won her first Oscar® in three decades. The critically-beloved director Terrence Malick offered his first film in six years with the long-delayed *The Tree of Life,* which divided audiences who could not find their way into its dense, poetic narrative but critics placed it at the top of dozens of top ten lists, even winning the Chicago Film Critics Association Awards for Best Picture and Best Director of 2011 (it was also Oscar®-nominated in both categories but did not win a single Academy Award®). Alexander Payne offered his first screenwriting/directorial effort since *Sideways* (2004) and walked off with nearly as much acclaim and another Oscar®. Finally, Kenneth Lonergan unveiled his long-delayed *Margaret,* a film first considered a sophomore slump after the director's *You Can Count on Me* (2000) but was reassessed critically before the year even ended and considered a masterpiece in some circles. Today's film market eats itself so quickly that a film can become a critical cult darling between its bad initial reviews and its DVD release.

While storytelling seemed to be looking back, a number of the most important film-makers of all time chose to look forward in terms of their own craft. When critics proclaimed James Cameron's *Avatar* (2009) as a pioneering landmark in cinema, one wonders if they knew that perhaps its greatest impact would be to show incredible directors that 3D could be used as more than a mere gimmick. And so Martin Scorsese (*Hugo*), Steven Spielberg (*The Adventures of Tintin*), and even Wim Wenders (*Pina*) tried to use the technology to push their own creative envelopes with mixed results. The jury remains in deliberation on the creative viability of the form but it was notable that some directorial pioneers were experimenting with it.

In terms of box office, the year saw a whopping thirty films that broke $100 million at the domestic till (the exact same amount as 2010 and two less than 2009) and only seven films that broke $200 million (three less than 2010 and 2009). Once again, the top films of the year illustrated both a serious disconnect between critics and ticket buyers and a continued sense that there are no more original ideas in the world of the Hollywood blockbuster. The top nine films of the year were sequels and the tenth was based on a known property (*Thor*). Only two original screenplays even appear in the top twenty (*Bridesmaids* and *Rio*). Overall, three highly-anticipated sequels dominated multiplexes this year—*Harry Potter and the Deathly Hallows Part 2* ($381 million), *Transformers: Dark of the Moon* ($352 million), and *The Twilight Saga: Breaking Dawn Part 1* ($281 million). While critics admired the final film in the most profitable franchise of all time, they were not so kind to the other two sequels, giving them some of the worst reviews of their respective franchises.

The distance between ticket buyer and critic seemed notably immense in 2011 as the top ten most critically-acclaimed films of the year barely made a dent at the box office. If one takes the composite top ten project of *Movie City News* (which compiles over 200 top tens into one list) as a critical guide, most of the critically-beloved films of the year simply were not of interest to the average moviegoer. Some had small releases—*Melancholia, Certified Copy, Martha Marcy May Marlene*—but it is undeniable that others simply did not connect with their audience—*The Tree of Life, The Descendants,* and *Drive* were the top three on said list and none made a significant dent at the box office. In fact, *Bridesmaids* was the only film in both the top twenty of critical acclaim and box office, itself a notable achievement given the former theory that female comedies did not sell.

While it may be tempting to portray the critics vs. audiences dichotomy of 2011 as a trend in the making, it is more likely that it is merely a typical valley in this common debate. One needs only to look to 2010 to see a peak in the same argument, a year in which critics and viewers lined up as commonly as ever. It could easily return to a more unanimous cinematic world in 2012. And it is worth noting that the truly loathsome dreck of the year generally failed to connect with viewers as well as critics, such as with *The Darkest Hour, Hoodwinked Too: Hood vs. Evil, Shark Night 3D,* and *The Roommate.* And the most reviled purveyors of trash, Adam Sandler's Happy Madison, saw its gigantic bomb *Bucky Larson: Born to Be a Star* beaten out on worst of the year lists by almost-as-horrendous comedies *Jack and Jill* and *Just Go with It.* Happy Madison must be stopped.

Will the divide between critics and ticket buyers grow or shrink back again? Will filmmakers continue to look to the past to comment on the present? The nostalgia-heavy critical hits of 2011 may have been set in another time but they were very much a product of their day. Allen's trip through the prime of Parisian creativity can be seen as a clever lark or a commentary on the filmmaker's own propensity to live in the past. Scorsese's ode to the importance of film preservation could not exist without modern technology. And Hazanavicius' winner for Best Picture resonates more with the rose-colored glasses of the decades of movie history that have passed since the silent era. Even when cinema looks to the past, it continues to move in the only direction it can—forever forward.

Brian Tallerico
Chicago, Illinois

Contributing Reviewers

David L. Boxerbaum
Freelance Reviewer

Tom Burns
Publishing Professional

Dave Canfield
Professional Film Critic

Erik Childress
Professional Film Critic

Mark Dujsik
Professional Film Critic

Joanna MacKenzie
Freelance Reviewer

Matt Pais
Professional Film Critic

Locke Peterseim
Professional Film Critic

Matthew Priest
Freelance Reviewer

Steven Prokopy
Professional Film Critic

Brent Simon
Professional Film Critic

Peter Sobczynski
Professional Film Critic

Collin Souter
Professional Film Critic

Brian Tallerico
Professional Film Critic

Michael J. Tyrkus
Publishing Professional

Nathan Vercauteren
Freelance Reviewer

User's Guide

ALPHABETIZATION

Film titles and reviews are arranged on a word-by-word basis, including articles and prepositions. English leading articles (A, An, The) are ignored, as are foreign leading articles (El, Il, La, Las, Le, Les, Los). Other considerations:

- Acronyms appear alphabetically as if regular words.
- Common abbreviations in titles file as if they are spelled out, so *Mr. Death* will be found as if it was spelled *Mister Death*.
- Proper names in titles are alphabetized beginning with the individual's first name, for instance, *Gloria* will be found under "G."
- Titles with numbers, for instance, *200 Cigarettes,* are alphabetized as if the numbers were spelled out, in this case, "Two-Hundred." When numeric titles gather in close proximity to each other, the titles will be arranged in a low-to-high numeric sequence.

SPECIAL SECTIONS

The following sections that are designed to enhance the reader's examination of film are arranged alphabetically, they include:

- *List of Awards.* An annual list of awards bestowed upon the year's films by the following: Academy of Motion Picture Arts and Sciences, British Academy of Film and Television Arts Awards, Directors Guild of America Awards, Golden Globe Awards, Golden Raspberry Awards, Independent Spirit Awards, the Screen Actors Guild Awards, and the Writer's Guild Awards.
- *Obituaries.* Profiles major contributors to the film industry who died in 2011.
- *Selected Film Books of 2011.* An annotated list of selected film books published in 2010.

INDEXES

Film titles and artists are separated into nine indexes, allowing the reader to effectively approach a film from any one of several directions, including not only its credits but its subject matter.

- *Director, Screenwriter, Cinematographer, Editor, Art Director, Music Director,* and *Performer* indexes are arranged alphabetically according to artists appearing in this volume, followed by a list of the films on which they worked. In the *Performer* index, a (V) beside a movie title indicates voice-only work and an (N) beside a movie title indicates work as narrator.
- *Subject Index.* Films may be categorized under several of the subject terms arranged alphabetically in this section.
- *Title Index.* The title index is a cumulative alphabetical list of films covered in the thirty volumes of the *Magill's Cinema Annual,* including the films covered in this volume. Films reviewed in past volumes are cited with the year in which the film appeared in the *Annual*; films reviewed in this volume are cited with the film title in boldface with a bolded Arabic numeral indicating the page number on which the review begins. Original and alternate titles are cross-referenced to the American release title in the Title Index. Titles of retrospective films are followed by the year, in brackets, of their original release.

SAMPLE REVIEW

Each *Magill's* review contains up to sixteen items of information. A fictionalized composite sample review containing all the elements of information that may be included in a full-length review follows the outline on the facing page. The circled number following each element in the sample review designates an item of information that is explained in the outline.

1. **Title:** Film title as it was released in the United States.

2. **Foreign or alternate title(s):** The film's original title or titles as released outside the United States, or alternate film title or titles. Foreign and alternate titles also appear in the Title Index to facilitate user access.

3. **Taglines:** Up to ten publicity taglines for the film from advertisements or reviews.

4. **Box office information:** Year-end or other box office domestic revenues for the film.

5. **Film review:** A signed review of the film, including an analytic overview of the film and its critical reception.

6. **Reviewer byline:** The name of the reviewer who wrote the full-length review. A complete list of this volume's contributors appears in the "Contributing Reviewers" section which follows the Introduction.

7. **Principal characters:** Listings of the film's principal characters and the names of the actors who play them in the film.

8. **Country of origin:** The film's country or countries of origin and the languages featured in the film.

9. **Release date:** The year of the film's first general release.

10. **Production information:** This section typically includes the name(s) of the film's producer(s), production company, and distributor; director(s); screenwriter(s); cinematographer(s); editor(s); art director(s); production designer(s); music composer(s); and other credits such as visual effects, sound, costume design, and song(s) and songwriter(s).

11. **MPAA rating:** The film's rating by the Motion Picture Association of America. If there is no rating given, the line will read, "Unrated."

12. **Running time:** The film's running time in minutes.

13. **Reviews:** A list of brief citations of major newspaper and journal reviews of the film, including author, publication title, and date of review.

14. **Film quotes:** Memorable dialogue directly from the film, attributed to the character who spoke it, or comment from cast or crew members or reviewers about the film.

15. **Film trivia:** Interesting tidbits about the film, its cast, or production crew.

16. **Awards information:** Awards won by the film, followed by category and name of winning cast or crew member. Listings of the film's nominations follow the wins on a separate line for each award. Awards are arranged alphabetically. Information is listed for films that won or were nominated for the following awards: American Academy Awards®, British Academy of Film and Television Arts Awards, Directors Guild of America Awards, Golden Globe Awards, Golden Raspberry Awards, Independent Spirit Awards, the Screen Actors Guild Awards, and the Writers Guild of America Awards.

THE GUMP DIARIES ①

(Los Diarios del Gump) ②

Love means never having to say you're stupid.
—Movie tagline ③

Box Office: $10 million ④

In writer/director Robert Zemeckis' *Back to the Future* trilogy (1985, 1989, 1990), Marty McFly (Michael J. Fox) and his scientist sidekick Doc Brown (Christopher Lloyd) journey backward and forward in time, attempting to smooth over some rough spots in their personal histories in order to remain true to their individual destinies. Throughout their time-travel adventures, Doc Brown insists that neither he nor Marty influence any major historical events, believing that to do so would result in catastrophic changes in humankind's ultimate destiny. By the end of the trilogy, however, Doc Brown has revised his thinking and tells Marty that, "Your future hasn't been written yet. No one's has. Your future is whatever you make it. So make it a good one."

In *Forrest Gump,* Zemeckis once again explores the theme of personal destiny and how an individual's life affects and is affected by his historical time period. This time, however, Zemeckis and screenwriter Eric Roth chronicle the life of a character who does nothing but meddle in the historical events of his time without even trying to do so. By the film's conclusion, however, it has become apparent that Zemeckis' main concern is something more than merely having fun with four decades of American history. In the process of re-creating significant moments in time, he has captured on celluloid something eternal and timeless—the soul of humanity personified by a nondescript simpleton from the deep South.

The film begins following the flight of a seemingly insignificant feather as it floats down from the sky and brushes against various objects and people before finally coming to rest at the feet of Forrest Gump (Tom Hanks). Forrest, who is sitting on a bus-stop bench, reaches down and picks up the feather, smooths it out, then opens his traveling case and carefully places the feather between the pages of his favorite book, *Curious George.*

In this simple but hauntingly beautiful opening scene, the filmmakers illustrate the film's principal concern: Is life a series of random events over which a person has no control, or is there an underlying order to things that leads to the fulfillment of an individual's destiny? The rest of the film is a humorous and moving attempt to prove that, underlying the random, chaotic events that make up a person's life, there exists a benign and simple order.

Forrest sits on the bench throughout most of the film, talking about various events of his life to others who happen to sit down next to him. It does not take long, however, for the audience to realize that Forrest's seemingly random chatter to a parade of strangers has a perfect chronological order to it. He tells his first story after looking down at the feet of his first bench partner and observing, "Mama always said that you can tell a lot about a person by the shoes they wear." Then, in a voice-over narration, Forrest begins the story of his life, first by telling about the first pair of shoes he can remember wearing.

The action shifts to the mid-1950s with Forrest as a young boy (Michael Humphreys) being fitted with leg braces to correct a curvature in his spine. Despite this traumatic handicap, Forrest remains unaffected, thanks to his mother (Sally Field) who reminds him on more than one occasion that he is no different from anyone else. Although this and most of Mrs. Gump's other words of advice are in the form of hackneyed cliches, Forrest, whose intelligence quotient is below normal, sincerely believes every one of them, namely because he instinctively knows they are sincere expressions of his mother's love and fierce devotion. ⑤

John Byline ⑥

CREDITS ⑦

Forrest Gump: Tom Hanks
Forrest's Mother: Sally Field
Young Forrest: Michael Humphreys
Origin: United States ⑧
Language: English, Spanish
Released: 1994 ⑨
Production: Liz Heller, John Manulis; New Line Cinema; released by Island Pictures ⑩
Directed by: Robert Zemeckis
Written by: Eric Roth
Cinematography by: David Phillips
Music by: Graeme Revell
Editing: Dana Congdon
Production Design: Danny Nowak
Sound: David Sarnoff
Costumes: David Robinson
MPAA rating: R ⑪
Running time: 102 minutes ⑫

REVIEWS ⑬

Doe, Jane. *Los Angeles Times*. July 6, 1994.
Doe, John. *Entertainment Weekly*. July 15, 1994.
Reviewer, Paul. *Hollywood Reporter*. June 29, 1994.
Writer, Zach. *New York Times Online*. July 15, 1994.

QUOTES ⑭

Forrest Gump (Tom Hanks): "The state of existence may be likened unto a receptacle containing cocoa-based confections, in that one may never predict that which one may receive."

TRIVIA ⑮

Hanks was the first actor since Spencer Tracy to win back-to-back Oscars® for Best Actor. Hanks received the award in 1993 for his performance in *Philadelphia*. Tracy won Oscars® in 1937 for *Captains Courageous* and in 1938 for *Boys Town*.

AWARDS ⑯

Academy Awards 1994: Film, Actor (Hanks), Special Effects, Cinematography

Nomination:

Golden Globes 1994: Film, Actor (Hanks), Supporting Actress (Field), Music.

A

ABDUCTION

What if your entire life was a lie?
—Movie tagline

The fight for the truth will be the fight of his life.
—Movie tagline

They stole his life. He's taking it back.
—Movie tagline

Box Office: $28.1 million

The teenage secret-agent action thriller *Abduction* has at its center a paradox: It is a movie-movie, existing as an arch echo of a thousand other movies, informed only by the idea of being a movie. And yet it is simultaneously not much of a movie at all. At the heart of that mysterious center, and driving *Abduction*'s entire reason for being, is a similar illusion: Actor Taylor Lautner, who postures himself and is treated by both the film and the showbiz industry as a "star," and yet is not much of either an actor or a star.

In *Abduction,* Lautner plays Nathan, a handsome young high-schooler with a zest for crazy thrill seeking and a hatred of wearing shirts. Nathan's cool-kid world is turned topsy-turvy when he learns—in the best "I knew I was special!" tradition—that he is not just another teenage boy with attitude and unrequited crushes, but instead the orphaned child of secret agents, being raised not by his biological mother and father, but instead by (still loving and parental) CIA "keepers."

With a spin of the top-secret decoder ring, as soon as Nathan discovers his true identity his "keepers" are killed, and the bewildered young man finds himself on

the road and the run from various shadowy interests. Unknowingly having been trained all his life for self-defense and rugged spy craft, Nathan trades homework and pool parties for car chases and shootouts. At least he is able to bring along his would-be gal Karen, played with the genre's usual passive confusion and reluctant adoration by Lily Collins.

There's nothing wrong with making an illogical, lightweight, popcorn-chomper for teens, and in theory *Abduction* might serve such a purpose. As written by Shawn Christensen and directed by John Singleton, however, the film is long on illogical and lightweight and short on popcorn fun. Having once shown honest promise behind the camera, here Singleton directs the proceedings with a cynical apathy. Jumping through hoops seemingly dictated by marketing impulses and demographic demands, the director cannot find a point to it all—it is as if over the years his every filmmaking instinct has been sold and washed out.

With Singleton unable to exert any sense of style or cinema into it, *Abduction* exists only as a delivery system for bringing Lautner and his one-dimensional skills to, presumably, his adoring fans. Lacking even the simplest entertainment value, the film serves no purpose other than to crassly pander and cash in on Lautner's questionable and fleeting moment in the teen-beat sun.

Only Lautner himself feels fully committed to the endeavor as he smugly strikes action-hero poses in his leather jacket and jeans, hoping to seethe, sneer, and will himself into having a screen presence. The young man juts his jaw, flares his nostrils, and gives sullen, angry stares, as if continually overcompensating for his beady eyes and cute little cheeks. It all comes off laughable, especially when Nathan takes a stab at a big impassioned speech and ends up looking like a puppy trying to read a cereal box.

Real actors Sigourney Weaver and Alfred Molina are also on hand, but Weaver comes off as if her entire performance was emotionally over-dubbed, and between a few half-hearted lunges at putting teeth on the scenery, Molina looks much wearier than his character demands. Jason Isaacs and Maria Bello play Nathan's surrogate parents, but they are around just long enough for you to say, "Hey, is that…" before they are gone.

Meanwhile, *Abduction* sloppily dashes from plot point to plot point, from cool motorcycle to cool car to not-so-cool Amtrak, stopping now and then for a talkative character to pull it all together with expository stitching. With its Everyman (Boy) on the Run premise and big scenes on trains and at crowded ballgames, glancing bits of Hitchcock are sprinkled over the proceedings, but it all comes off too shallow to even be derivative—instead the film feels like a kid telling you all about a really cool movie they once saw. *Abduction* is so dedicated to serving what it thinks its audience wants that it ends up a teenage fantasy of a James Bond action thriller with a dreamy pin-up mannequin at its center; the cinematic equivalent of playing dress up.

Such a fluffy endeavor still might have worked if there were mildly authentic young actors grounding the silliness, but instead *Abduction* serves up lead characters as bland, blank videogame avatars—perhaps intended to make them easier for the viewer to project onto. Ultimately little more than a vanity project for Lautner, *Abduction* feels fake and lifeless—a flat and boring emptiness behind a shiny mirror.

Locke Peterseim

CREDITS

Nathan Harper: Taylor Lautner
Karen: Lily Collins
Frank Burton: Alfred Molina
Kevin: Jason Isaacs
Mara: Maria Bello
Kozlow: Michael Nyqvist
Dr. Bennett: Sigourney Weaver
Origin: USA
Language: English
Released: 2011
Production: Doug Davison, Ellen Goldsmith-Vein, Dan Lautner, Roy Lee, Lee Stollman; Lionsgate, Gotham Group, Vertigo Entertainment, Quick Six Entertainment, Mango Farms; released by Lionsgate
Directed by: John Singleton

Written by: Shawn Christensen
Cinematography by: Peter Menzies Jr.
Music by: Edward Shearmur
Sound: William R. Dean
Music Supervisor: Tracy McKnight
Editing: Bruce Cannon
Art Direction: Liba Daniels
Costumes: Ruth E. Carter
Production Design: Keith Brian Burns
MPAA rating: PG-13
Running time: 106 minutes

REVIEWS

Barker, Andrew. *Variety.* September 22, 2011.
Berardinelli, James. *ReelViews.* September 24, 2011.
Holden, Stephen. *New York Times.* September 22, 2011.
Lacey, Liam. *Globe and Mail.* September 22, 2011.
Mercer, Benjamin. *Village Voice.* September 24, 2011.
Rabin, Nathan. *AV Club.* September 24, 2011.
Smith, Kyle. *New York Post.* September 23, 2011.
Uhlich, Keith. *Time Out New York.* September 24, 2011.
Whipp, Glenn. *Los Angeles Times.* September 22, 2011.
Wilmore, Alison. *Movieline.* September 22, 2011.

QUOTES

Nathan: "They killed my parents."
Burton: "They weren't your real parents."

TRIVIA

Freema Aygeman, of *Law & Order: UK* and *Doctor Who,* filmed a cameo for the movie, but it was cut during editing.

AWARDS

Nomination:

Golden Raspberries 2011: Worst Actor (Lautner).

THE ADJUSTMENT BUREAU

They stole his future. Now he's taking it back.
—Movie tagline
Fight for your fate.
—Movie tagline

Box Office: $62.5 million

Phillip K. Dick has had more luck than most writers, too bad almost all of it came after he was dead. Out of his ten works adapted for the cinema, two emerged as bona fide masterpieces (*Bladerunner* [1992] and *A Scan-*

ner *Darkly* [2006]), while two others (*Total Recall* [1990] and *Minority Report* [2002]) are certainly fine adaptations. To that group add *The Adjustment Bureau*. Writer/Director George Nolfi has taken the heart and soul of Dick's tumultuous battle with the concepts of fate and free will, God and man, and brought to life a thrilling tale of why those things can and should inspire such passion in all of us. This is not a great film but it is a thought provoking, entertaining and occasionally transcendent one.

David Norris (Matt Damon) is a young career politician on the verge of winning a senate seat in New York. When a last minute scandal derails his campaign he sequesters himself in a hotel men's room to rehearse a prepared concession speech only to be surprised by a young woman (Emily Blunt) hiding from hotel security. Sparks fly immediately and even though she leaves before he can get her name he finds himself smitten, always in mind of her in the intervening years. A truly chance meeting on a bus three years later sets them up for possible romance until a group of mysterious suited figures hustle David into the "backstage of reality," informing him that he has deviated from "the plan." These men are The Adjustment Bureau, and it is their job to keep everything running accordingly. They inform David that he will forget that he ever met this woman or risk being "reset." What follows is a taut cat-and-mouse game in which David attempts to circumvent the constant manipulations of reality that predetermine his rise to political power and his separation from the woman of his dreams.

George Nolfi, making his directorial debut here, is a known primarily as a screenwriter having penned *Ocean's Twelve* (2004), *The Sentinel* (2006), and *The Bourne Ultimatum* (2007). He makes an even-more effective director than writer with nods to Hitchcock, mixed with a down-to-earth, real-world shooting style that constantly betrays viewers who might want to tell themselves that they are simply watching a movie. Nolfi gives few such handholds. He wisely eschews standard action sequences (there are few car chases, no explosions or gunplay etc.) in favor of using on-screen action as a way to mirror Norris' racing inner state and sense of urgency. This is a man at war with the universe, fighting to create his own future. Nolfi gets as much juice out of a tense cab ride or a solitary figure running down a rainy street as most directors get out of a Mexican standoff.

A word must be said here of the outstanding score here provided by Thomas Newman. It is a thing of subtlety and grace always working with the story, and the characters, always complimenting and supporting, helping to achieve goals rather than calling attention itself. Newman's resume is amazing. A brief listing of his best recent work would include *The Shawshank Redemp-*

tion (1994), *American Beauty* (1999), *The Green Mile* (1999), *Finding Nemo* (2003), *Little Children* (2006), and *WALL-E* (2008).

Matt Damon continues on a remarkable career path here. A standout turn as a heroin addict in *Courage Under Fire* (1996) along with an underdog Oscar® win for screenwriting and nomination for Best Actor for his contributions to *Good Will Hunting* (1997) led to portraying the lead character in Steven Spielberg's war opus *Saving Private Ryan* (1998). Since then he has appeared in a wide variety of films rarely failing to elevate even the least promising material. In good films, he shows a preternatural ability to make viewers forget he is Matt Damon simply becoming the character the story requires. Emily Blunt has logged under ten years in cinema and yet her career has been a wild mix of the forgettable and the sublime. Her role as Emily could have been a throwaway, but Blunt grabs hold of the script and wrenches solid believable emotionality out of her role as a woman struggling to believe in her own destiny.

Another neat trick is the manner in which the Adjustment Bureau itself is brought to life. Manipulators of reality, these are still not omniscient beings. Simple men in suits and hats, they go about their business without the aid of bombastic special effects. They themselves are subject to "The Chairman" and while the film offers Bureau member Thompson (Terrence Stamp) a wonderful monologue explaining the Bureau's influence in human history, the film goes out of its way to point out that people do have a choice in how they live, and that by taking a page out of the right book they may yet become trusted with greater authority. This message of taking responsibility for one's spiritual path is a refreshing one, the idea that it can be done hand-in-hand with a creator that loves his creations is a revolutionary one. In the extraordinary Wim Wenders film *Wings of Desire* (1987) angels observe the human race overcome with how much it is loved by their creator. The beings of *The Adjustment Bureau* skirt the title of angel as the movie reveals its scant cosmology, but they too are left a little in awe of man, perhaps a little jealous, as if they, in the end were merely the bureaucrats of Heaven and we, the great unwashed, the true heirs of destiny.

Dave Canfield

CREDITS
David Norris: Matt Damon
Elise Sellas: Emily Blunt
Harry Mitchell: Anthony Mackie
Richard: John Slattery

McCrady: Anthony Michael Ruivivar
Charlie Traynor: Michael Kelly
Thompson: Terence Stamp
Origin: USA
Language: English
Released: 2011
Production: Michael Hackett, Chris Moore, Bill Carraro, George Nolfi; Electric Shepherd Productions, Gambit Pictures; released by Universal Pictures
Directed by: George Nolfi
Written by: George Nolfi
Cinematography by: John Toll
Music by: Thomas Newman
Sound: Danny Michael
Editing: Jay Rabinowitz
Art Direction: Stephen H. Carter
Costumes: Kasia Walicka-Maimone
Production Design: Kevin Thompson
MPAA rating: PG-13
Running time: 106 minutes

REVIEWS

Chang, Justin. *Variety.* February 25, 2011.
Dargis, Manhola. *New York Times.* March 3, 2011.
Dendy, David. *New Yorker.* March 1, 2011.
Ebert, Roger. *Chicago Sun-Times.* March 4, 2011.
Giles-Keddie, Lisa. *Real.com.* March 2, 2011.
Hoberman, J. *Village Voice.* March 1, 2011.
Legel, Laremy. *Film.com.* March 4, 2011.
Longworth, Karina. *L.A. Weekly.* March 3, 2011.
McWeeny, Drew. *HitFix.* February 25, 2011.
Vaux, Rob. *Mania.com.* March 4, 2011.

QUOTES

David Norris: "All I have are the choices I make, and I choose her, come what may."

TRIVIA

The phone number given to Matt Damon by Emily Blunt in the movie ((212) 664-7665) is owned by Universal Studios and has been used in numerous films distributed by the company in an effort to avoid the much overused "555" prefix. If called, it will continue to ring indefinitely.

AWARDS

Nomination:
Screen Actors Guild 2011: Stunt Ensemble.

THE ADVENTURES OF TINTIN

This year, discover how far adventure will take you.
—Movie tagline

Box Office: $76.5 million

The Adventures of Tintin marks a first for director Steven Spielberg. Despite dabbling as a producer on several animated features including *The Land Before Time* (1988) and *Monster House* (2006), where he collaborated with George Lucas and Robert Zemeckis, respectively, *Tintin* is his first at the helm. A fascination with the Belgian comic strip character created by Georges "Hergé" Rémi goes back to his days filming the first of his Indiana Jones installments, to which the artist deemed Spielberg the perfect man for the job. After a suggestion by Peter Jackson that Tintin's likeness be best represented in animation, Spielberg agreed on a collaboration to bring the character to life through motion capture technology in a two-part series of movies where he would direct the first and Jackson the second. Though Tintin gets top billing here, the character's exploits are more familiarized in Europe where perhaps his bland personality can be forgiven as a catalyst to his grand, globe-trotting adventures. In America, Tintin is not as recognizable as Indiana Jones, but Steven Spielberg is, and it is his name and his talents that are the star of this otherwise average tale.

Tintin (voiced by Jamie Bell) is the kind of plucky amateur journalist/sleuth who often outwits the local police inspectors in solving the biggest of cases. Unwittingly, he comes upon a bidding war for a model ship called the Unicorn at a flea market. Tintin sees it as a unique decoration while an American named Barnaby (Joe Starr) and Sakharine (Daniel Craig) offer to buy it from him. Barnaby warns the kid he is stepping into danger by keeping the artifact, intriguing him further to look into the storied history of it full of treachery and curses.

Helped little by bumbling Inspectors Thompson & Thompson (Simon Pegg & Nick Frost), Tintin continues his quest aided by his even more inquisitive dog, Snowy. They discover that Sakharine has taken control of a steamer once commandeered by the permanently intoxicated Captain Archibald Haddock (Andy Serkis). Part of a long line of captains dating back to the days of pirates, Haddock joins Tintin on a daring escape in the hopes of reclaiming the legacy taken from his family by an all-too familiar face. This will take the trio from the ocean to the Sahara, from ships to airplanes and motorbikes in a race to and from Morocco.

Culled from a trio of Tintin adventures—"The Crab With the Golden Claws," "The Secret of the Unicorn," and "Red Rackham's Treasure"—adaptation duties fell to Brits Steven Moffat, Joe Cornish and Edgar Wright to cobble together Tintin's modern international coming out party. The Brits always seem to have a leg up on the

Americans when it comes to sophisticated slapstick and edgy humor. Perhaps restrained within the confines of PG-rated material, Moffat and Cornish (known mostly for their television creations) and Wright (who has found great fanboy appreciation for not just TV's *Spaced* but also *Shaun of the Dead* [2004], *Hot Fuzz* [2006], and *Scott Pilgrim vs. the World* [2010]) are left holding the bag to satisfy rather than reinvent it.

As detectives go, Tintin is hardly an inspirational figure for young boys eager to pick up a magnifying glass and read the fine print for a greater truth. Either he is finding exactly what he is looking for at just the right moment or stumbling upon the intrinsic details—with more than a little help from Snowy—that lead to the next mystery, giving him more in common with Inspector Gadget than Sherlock Holmes. Long the subject of young adult fiction and comic strips, kid detectives from Nancy Drew to Encyclopedia Brown were never up to the level of historically distinctive characters. It was more about the thrill of the hunt for younger readers to open up their minds into questioning true natures and playing simple lost and found. Since Tintin's villain is unveiled rather quickly, it becomes a matter of questioning motives rather than grand twists of the plot. Without the untapped supernatural ambiguities of Indiana Jones' hunts and his always-ready knowledge of historical connections to the present, Tintin's discoveries play second fiddle to how he is going to escape with his findings.

This is where Spielberg's touch takes on as great a significance as it ever has. Never a stranger to breaking new ground with elaborate action set pieces, seeing *The Adventures of Tintin* is akin to watching a child genius play with a brand new toy and showing you what makes it tick. Animation has progressed so fast over the last few decades that keeping up with it has led many to react negatively to some of its advances. More realistic 3-D animation has given way to those experimenting with the motion-capture experience, most notably one of Spielberg's early protégés, Robert Zemeckis. *The Polar Express* (2004) was the beginning of the "dead-eyed" argument when it came to translating fully-realized human characters instead of creatures like Gollum and King Kong brought to life by none other than Peter Jackson. The distraction often cited of some brand of emotional disconnect with animated humans continues to feel like more of an old excuse than recognizing the vast improvements in the technology.

Where there is little argument, however, is the manner in which action sequences have evolved within the format. While many of today's filmmakers over-edit close-ups of the effects rather than the causes of set pieces, animation has freed others to explore the realm of greater possibilities. From the climactic car chase in *Toy Story* (1995) to the assembly line pursuit of *Monsters, Inc.* (2001) to the barrier-breaking dimensions of battle in *Beowulf* (2007), all bets are off on where a director can place his camera and where the limitations of special effects fakery begin and end. Spielberg is having so much fun designing the action sequences here that one could practically see behind-the-scenes footage of him doing nothing but playing with action figures and smashing them into one another.

One set piece after another is spectacular enough to make one re-engage with the material immediately, beginning with several playfully exciting bits involving Snowy, a cat and traffic leading towards a fitfully amusing, but action-packed escape from Haddock's boat. These are just warm-ups though. As an appropriately realized recalibration of the Pirates of the Caribbean series — which in many ways became the surrogate of the long-dormant Indiana Jones series for a new generation — Spielberg delights in presenting his own version of a pirate flashback with ships literally locked and loaded for battle. That is still a mere prelude to his Pièce de résistance, a four-minute chase that evolves into a single unbroken shot through the Moroccan streets as our heroes interact with birds, bikes, tanks and broken dams. View it as a satiric wink to his elaborate Indiana Jones set pieces or simply as a director pulling out all the stops on his filmmaker colleagues like a kid on a playground who watches his friend kick the ball onto the roof, then says "watch this" and kicks one over it. This is all before another uniquely constructed climactic crane battle that puts the ultimate spin on the classic swordfight.

These signature Spielberg sequences may draw even further attention to just how lackluster the overall story is. Like all of the comic book heroes adapted to the big screen, there is the very delicate line between appeasing the longtime fans and opening up that appeal to a broader audience. This screenplay, unfortunately, does not fully inaugurate a need to actually want to follow these characters on another adventure the way we might an Indiana Jones, James Bond or Batman. Sure they show signs of life here and there, most notably the drunken Haddock playing the brash lout to Tintin's earnestness and whose hatred of the comic strip's famed opera singer is amusingly brought to life. But without the technical prowess of Spielberg — or, at least, a filmmaker of his ilk — behind it or some hidden adventure within Hergé's work that challenges us, Tintin never gets beyond a Saturday morning cartoon level. Peter Jackson is slated to take the helm for the second film in this series and hopefully afterwards we will look upon this first Tintin adventure as the decent, if unremarkable, origin tale that was just a warm-up for the mind-blowing next chapter.

Erik Childress

CREDITS

Tintin: Jamie Bell (Voice)

Red Rackham/ Ivan Ivanovitch Sakharine: Daniel Craig (Voice)

Captain Archibald Haddock: Andy Serkis (Voice)

Inspector Thompson: Simon Pegg (Voice)

Silk: Toby Jones (Voice)

Pedro: Sebastien Roche (Voice)

Tom: Mackenzie Crook (Voice)

Ben Salaad: Gad Elmaleh (Voice)

Origin: USA

Language: English

Released: 2011

Production: Steven Spielberg, Peter Jackson, Kathleen Kennedy; Hemisphere Productions, Amblin Entertainment, Wignut Films, Columbia Pictures; released by Paramount Pictures

Directed by: Steven Spielberg

Written by: Edgar Wright, Steven Moffatt, Joe Cornish

Music by: John Williams

Sound: Brent Burge

Editing: Michael Kahn

Art Direction: Andrew P. Jones, Jeff Wisniewski

MPAA rating: PG

Running time: 107 minutes

REVIEWS

Ebert, Roger. *Chicago Sun-Times.* December 21, 2011.

Koplinski, Charles. *Illinois Times.* December 28, 2011.

Levy, Shawn. *Oregonian.* December 20, 2011.

Lybarger, Dan. *KC Active.* December 21, 2011.

Morgenstern, Joe. *Wall Street Journal.* December 22, 2011.

O'Connell, Sean. *Filmcritic.com.* December 24, 2011.

O'Hehir, Andrew. *Salon.com.* December 20, 2011.

Phillips, Michael. *Chicago Tribune.* December 20, 2011.

Robinson, Tasha. *AV Club.* December 20, 2011.

Snider, Eric D. *EricDSnider.com.* December 21, 2011.

QUOTES

Captain Haddock: "You do know what you're doing, right?" Tintin: "Relax. I interviewed a pilot once!"

TRIVIA

Steven Spielberg originally planned on doing a live-action adaptation of Tintin, and called Peter Jackson to see if his VFX company Weta Digital would work on the film, in particular to create a CGI Snowy. Jackson, a longtime Tintin fan, convinced Spielberg that live action would not do justice to the books and that motion capture was the best way of representing Hergé's world. However, Snowy would still need to be CGI.

AWARDS

Golden Globes 2012: Animated Film

Nomination:

Oscars 2011: Orig. Score

British Acad. 2011: Animated Film, Visual FX.

ALBERT NOBBS

> *A man with a secret. A woman with a dream.*
> —Movie tagline
>
> *We are all disguised as ourselves.*
> —Movie tagline

Box Office: $2.4 million

To say that *Albert Nobbs* plays like a cross between *Gosford Park* (2001) and *Boys Don't Cry* (1999), minus all the violence and intrigue, is to still give director Rodrigo Garcia's movie a bit too much credit. A bland and generally suffocating period piece drama with a big gimmicky hook that pegs it as unabashed Oscar® bait, the film not so much tells a story as asks an audience to merely bask in Glenn Close's admittedly uncanny performance as a woman passing and working as a man in order to survive in 19th century Ireland.

Based on a very old short story, *The Singular Life of Albert Nobbs* by Irish novelist George Moore, this film is the definition of a passion project for Close, who starred in a 1982 stage production and would later spend more than a decade and a half trying to will it into existence as a movie. (Hungarian director Istvan Szabo retains a story credit from an earlier incarnation that fell apart in preproduction.) In addition to serving as a producer and co-writing the screenplay with John Banville and Gabriella Prekop, Close also co-wrote (with Brian Byrne) the Golden Globe®-nominated "Lay Your Head Down," sung by Sinéad O'Connor over the closing credits. All her devotion is unfortunately unmatched by psychological discernment, resulting in a chilly work that comes across as over-calculated and emotionally hollow.

A butler and steward at a modest hotel, title character Albert (Close) is a model of work ethic and mannered duty, standing at attention even when children pass her by in the hallway. She adopted the guise of a man long ago, and living the lie furnishes her a degree of autonomy. Living frugally and on site in an austere room, Albert's sexuality remains a secret to all those in the house, including young chambermaid Helen Dawes (Mia Wasikowska). When boxed into sharing her room with traveling housepainter Hubert Page (Janet McTeer), though, Albert ends up inadvertently coughing up her secret.

Albert is dumbstruck to learn that Hubert is a woman too, and even more so when Hubert explains an arrangement with Mary (Maria Doyle Kennedy) by which they enjoy a modest life together posing as a married couple. Already given to fanciful notions of opening a tobacco shop, Albert—more stirred from cautiousness than actually emboldened—gets it in her head that maybe she too can find some sort of sustaining companionship. An awkward courtship with Helen ensues, further complicated by the fact that she is already embroiled in lusty if not necessarily steadfastly committed clinches with new handyman Joe Macken (Aaron Johnson).

Almost everything that is right or connects in at least fitful fashion in *Albert Nobbs* can be traced back to the movie's twin gender-swap performances. Close is quite good—trading in understatement so subtle that it borders on subliminal. Her years of experience translate in this keen, clipped modulation, which has a viewer leaning forward in an effort to discern intent and sentiment that the script ultimately does not impart. McTeer, though, is a total blast of fresh air—guileless and free in all the ways that Close's rendering of her character is buttoned up. It is not necessarily a good sign when an audience wants to dance off with a supporting character into another film, but Albert and Hubert's charged, interesting scenes together indisputably form the spine of *Albert Nobbs*, to the point that it is palpably dispiriting when the narrative turns its attention elsewhere.

Most of Garcia's big screen work—from *Things You Can Tell Just By Looking At Her* (2000) and *Ten Tiny Love Stories* (2001) to *Nine Lives* (2005) and *Mother and Child* (2009)—tends to trade in grand if fuzzily defined themes, and deal with loosely tied together vignettes, often centering around women. Owing to this as well as other problems, most of his movies are also more interesting in theory than actuality.

While his previous work plumbing particularly feminine mindsets regarding loneliness, love, domestic life and societal hierarchy would appear to make Garcia an ideal candidate for this sort of story, he succeeds only in crafting an ornate, inscrutable framework—nothing that feels like a real, multi-dimensional world. Working with cinematographer Michael McDonough, production designer Patrizia von Brandenstein and costume designer Pierre-Yves Gayraud, Garcia constructs a film that feels of a piece, visually speaking, but one that is also oppressively dour, and engenders no audience identification.

On the surface this story would seem quite interesting, but its screenplay is full of diminishing touches. Albert, with the disposition of a church mouse, habitually talks to herself in the form of little asides of dazed reverie, particularly when dreaming of her precious tobacco shop and its accoutrements ("And a clock for the mantle!"). The romantic subplot with Helen seems superfluous at best, and any adrenalized charge of possibility that Joe's encouragement of Helen to extract from Albert as many material rewards as she can quickly fizzles when it becomes clear that the movie is not interested in such opportunistic and potentially dangerous games of discovery and blackmail. In his *Variety* review from the movie's Telluride Festival premiere, Peter Debruge characterized the film's narrative arc, not inaccurately, as the "slow-motion inevitability of looming misfortune."

Mostly, though, *Albert Nobbs* is sunk by just a massive, gaping expanse of unexploited territory regarding gender confusion and identity. The movie paints Albert as terribly naïve in both matters of the heart (she calculates an annual cost of courting Helen, and then immediately skips ahead to wondering if she should tell her of her secret beforehand, or "on our wedding night") and life in general. But the script is all about artifice, and does not scratch much beyond the surface of what would be extraordinarily profound psychological fences and problems, based on Albert's living of this sort of lie since she was 14 years old.

Neither does it substantively dig into other homosexual and transgender issues—Jonathan Rhys Meyers plays a viscount with same-sex predilections—which could potentially have rich comparative significance to the present day. At every point it approaches the precipice of something interesting and complex, *Albert Nobbs* blinks and backs away, content instead to marinate in its own specially formulated indistinctness.

Its failure to emotionally engage aside, *Albert Nobbs'* special prosthetic make-up work by Matthew Mungle, who won an Oscar® for his efforts on *Dracula* (1992), represents an impressive achievement, with seamlessly blended layers giving Close a beak-ish nose, yes, but also more rigidly defined cheekbones and a slightly squared jawline. And Close, as mentioned, commands one's attention. But she is playing a construct, absent any sort of meaningfully elucidated inner life. In its resolute presentation of a character who has so totally and completely submersed themselves in another persona that they no longer have anything real or true to say, *Albert Nobbs* perhaps hits the mark for which it was aiming. The fatal flaw in this design, unfortunately, is that the movie itself also ends up having nothing to say.

Brent Simon

CREDITS

Albert Nobbs: Glenn Close
Helen: Mia Wasikowska
Joe: Aaron Johnson
Hubert Page: Janet McTeer
Mrs. Baker: Pauline Collins
Polly: Brenda Fricker
Viscount Yarrell: Jonathan Rhys Meyers
Dr. Holloran: Brendan Gleeson
Sean: Mark Williams
Cathleen: Bronagh Gallagher
Origin: Ireland
Language: English
Released: 2011
Production: Glenn Close, Bonnie Curtis, Julie Lynn, Alan Moloney; Mockingbird Pictures, Parallel Films; released by Roadside Attractions
Directed by: Rodrigo Garcia
Written by: Glenn Close, John Banville, Gabriella Prekop
Cinematography by: Michael McDonough
Music by: Brian Byrne
Sound: Niall Brady
Editing: Steven Weisberg
Art Direction: Susie Cullen
Costumes: Pierre-Yves Gayraud
Production Design: Patrizia Von Brandenstein
MPAA rating: R
Running time: 113 minutes

REVIEWS

Berkshire, Geoff. *Metromix.com*. December 19, 2011.
Debruge, Peter. *Variety*. September 3, 2011.
Ellingson, Annlee. *Paste Magazine*. December 15, 2011.
Levy, Emanuel. *EmanuelLevy.com*. November 12, 2011.
Osenlund, R. Kurt. *Slant Magazine*. December 20, 2011.
Puig, Claudia. *USA Today*. December 20, 2011.
Schwarzbaum, Lisa. *Entertainment Weekly*. January 4, 2012.
Scott, A.O. *New York Times*. December 20, 2011.
Sharkey, Betsy. *Los Angeles Times*. December 22, 2011.
Travers, Peter. *Rolling Stone*. December 29, 2011.

QUOTES

Helen: "You are the strangest man I have ever met."

TRIVIA

The film was shot in in a mere thrity-four days on location in Dublin, Ireland.

AWARDS

Nomination:

Oscars 2011: Actress (Close), Makeup, Support. Actress (McTeer)

Golden Globes 2012: Actress—Drama (Close), Song ("Lay Your Heart Down"), Support. Actress (McTeer)
Ind. Spirit 2012: Support. Actress (McTeer)
Screen Actors Guild 2011: Actress (Close), Support. Actress (McTeer).

ALVIN AND THE CHIPMUNKS: CHIPWRECKED

Box Office: $130 million

There are some films that defy any sort of real necessity for critical analysis. Some films simply exist as a tent pole for quarterly profits and nothing more. There is no ambition on the part of the filmmakers or producers to elevate said product to the form of high art, nor is there any pretense that the product is nothing more than something to be marketed toward a certain demographic. To say that such a film is "critic proof" is almost beside the point. Usually, such films are a "Part 2 or 3" in a series and by the time films arrive in theaters, patrons have made up their mind about whether it will be worth the time and money. The *Big Momma's House* franchise fits this description, as do the *Garfield* movies. When one watches these kinds of films, it is hard not to let the mind wander to the absurdities that led to their existence. "Who decided it was a worthwhile endeavor for hundreds, if not thousands of people to get up every day at 5:00am for months on end just so that this film could get made, on time and on budget? Who decided the world could not live without this?"

Well, the box office numbers on the first two *Alvin and the Chipmunks* movies pretty much became a mandate for a third installment regardless of whether or not it was worth anybody's time and effort. The third film, *Alvin and the Chipmunks, Chipwrecked* does not exist to conclude a story arc that began with the first two. It exists as a placeholder in the nation's multiplexes, a celluloid babysitter for the laziest of parents and a waste of energy for all the talent involved. And there is talent here. Jason Lee, David Cross, Amy Poehler, Justin Long and Christina Applegate are just a few of the people who are all-too-generously lending their talent to these films for a second or third time with the simple hope that the paychecks clear.

The movie opens with, appropriately enough, a musical number involving the three main chipmunks, Alvin (voiced by Justin Long), Simon (voiced by Matthew Gray Gubler), and Theodore (voiced by Jesse McCartney), grooving to the Bangles' immortal hit

"Vacation." It is the sort of opening that stops a critic dead in their tracks with the simple thought of "I have nothing to say about this." There are also the three Chipettes from the last sequel, *Alvin and the Chipmunks: The Squeakquel* (2009). The Chipettes, Eleanor (voiced by Amy Poehler), Jeanette (voiced by Anna Faris), and Brittany (voiced by Christina Applegate), are all part of the Chipmunk family, headed by their human manager, Dave (Jason Lee).

Here, Dave and the Chipmunks decide to take a vacation aboard a cruise ship. Naturally, Dave wants them to stay put in their room and not come out and make a scene. One of the workers on this steam ship is a mascot in a pelican outfit who happens to be Ian (David Cross), the bitter former record executive who passed on signing the Chipmunks, Chipettes and Justin Bieber. Ian is a nemesis for Dave and who will do anything to see him and the chipmunks suffer.

A series of unfortunate and unfunny events lead the Chipmunks and Chipettes to hijacking a poor kid's kite and getting swept off the cruise ship and onto a deserted island. In an effort to find and rescue the Chipmunks and Chipettes, Dave and Ian end up going overboard and, using the pelican outfit as a floatation device, end up on the other side of the same deserted island. The Chipmunks and Chipettes adapt and make a new home for themselves with the help of a longtime island inhabitant, a former UPS delivery woman named Zoe (Jenny Slate), who has been living on this island for nine years and who has not one volleyball companion (in reference to the Tom Hanks film, *Cast Away* [2000]), but several volleyballs, tennis balls and basketballs, all with painted faces on them. David and Ian bicker and argue about how to get food, build a fire and so on. There appear to be no real villains here, not at first anyway.

The movie tries to be about the way in which parents distrust their kids a little too much. The Chipmunks and Chipettes are like children to Dave, who, it must be said, is probably the most tolerant father figure around, seeing as how he would have to look into every hamper and under every couch cushion before he would know if he had any real privacy. But because Alvin, the leader of the troublemakers in this high maintenance family, is always getting into trouble, Dave puts little trust in him. It is the bespectacled Simon who tells Dave "Sometimes kids will rise to the occasion if you show them a little trust." That is about the extent of an actual theme or food for thought for parents and kids to chew on.

It has often been said by industry insiders that the majority of Hollywood executives have no sense of humor or imagination and the arrival of *Alvin and the Chipmunks: Chipwrecked* is a testament to that. There have been many examples on how CGI technology and character rendering has helped to advance the state of modern storytelling, but films such as these make the case for where the technology went wrong. Why make a series of *Alvin and the Chipmunks* movies? Because they can. The best thing that can be said for *Alvin and the Chipmunks: Chipwrecked* is that it is not as bad as the obnoxious *The Smurfs* from the previous summer. Faint praise, indeed.

Collin Souter

CREDITS

Dave: Jason Lee
Daphne Snow: Alyssa Milano
Ian: David Cross
Captain Correlli: Andy Buckley
Alvin: Justin Long (Voice)
Simon: Matthew Gray Gubler (Voice)
Theodore: Jesse McCartney (Voice)
Eleanor: Amy Poehler (Voice)
Jeanette: Anna Faris (Voice)
Brittany: Christina Applegate (Voice)
Origin: USA
Language: English
Released: 2011
Production: Janice Karman, Ross Bagdasarian Jr.; Regency Enterprises, Fox 2000 Pictures; released by 20th Century-Fox
Directed by: Mike Mitchell
Written by: Jonathan Aibel, Glenn Berger
Cinematography by: Thomas Ackerman
Music by: Mark Mothersbaugh
Editing: Peter Amundson
Sound: Monique Salvato
Costumes: Alexandra Welker
Production Design: Richard Holland
MPAA rating: G
Running time: 87 minutes

REVIEWS

Adams, Derek. *Time Out*. December 13, 2011.
Brown, Joel. *Boston Globe*. December 15, 2011.
Lengel, Kerry. *Arizona Republic* December 15, 2011.
Lumenick, Lou. *New York Post*. December 16, 2011.
Markovitz, Adam. *Entertainment Weekly*. December 15, 2011.
Minow, Nell. *Chicago Sun-Times*. December 14, 2011.
Newmaier, Joe. *New York Daily News*. December 15, 2011.
O'Connell, Sean. *Washington Post*. December 16, 2011.
Rabin, Nathan. *AV Club*. December 15, 2011.
Schrager, Nick. *Village Voice*. December 17, 2011.

QUOTES

Alvin: "Guys, we're chipmunks! We're used to living in the wild!"

Brittany: "Correction: we're chipmunks that 'used' to be used to living in the wild!"

TRIVIA

The film's cinematographer, Thomas E. Ackerman, brought several of his students at the University of North Carolina School onto the production as interns.

ANONYMOUS

Was Shakespeare a fraud?
—Movie tagline

Box Office: $4.5 million

Soon after the release of *Anonymous,* a group of tourists shuffling past Shakespeare's grave reportedly stopped short in sheer terror when they heard the Bard's voice boom from the beyond, railing mightily against the film's director, Roland Emmerich. "Methinks thou art a general offence," the vexed spirit spat, "and every man should beat thee." Shakespeare was clearly restless in his resting place over Emmerich's bombastic big-screen assertion that alternative attribution is in order for the writer's towering achievements. The visitors understandably left the site feeling profound pity for the maligned, mouldering literary genius.

Okay, the above is utter nonsense that never actually happened but is useful in making a point, similar to so much of what is put forth in *Anonymous.* While everyone can agree that the source of the aforementioned quote is *All's Well That Ends Well,* some tenaciously continue to insist that all such works ascribed to William Shakespeare actually flowed from the pen of someone else. How, they ask, could a man of such common origins—a glover's son whose horizons were apparently never broadened by either higher learning or far-flung travel—be able to create plays and poetry of such uncommon, insightful brilliance? Thus, despite the fact that no one during Shakespeare's lifetime or for more than two hundred years after his death appears to have thought such attainment impossible, theories began popping up in the mid-1800s like peculiar, pernicious weeds, and have continued to flourish ever since despite the strenuous efforts of scholars to eradicate them. Proponents of Sir Francis Bacon, Christopher Marlowe, the 17th Earl of Oxford Edward de Vere, Queen Elizabeth I, and approximately seventy other personages have forcibly finessed facts and/or created outright (if imaginative) fictions, each group vying to convince the world to finally join them in singing the praises of the particular unjustly-unsung hero that they have proposed.

Now comes *Anonymous,* which is successful in making one point glaringly clear: Subtlety, thy name is not Emmerich. Having repeatedly laid waste to the globe with gusto in films like *Independence Day* (1996), *The Day After Tomorrow* (2004), and *2012* (2009), the director now stomps both purposefully and punishingly on poor Will in a manner similar to that employed by the titular terror of another of his productions, *Godzilla* (1998). Not content to simply add cinematic reinforcement to the theory that the Bard was a beard for de Vere, an aristocrat whose station chafingly-restricted his writing entertainments for the masses, Emmerich and screenwriter John Orloff have absolutely and gleefully ground their heels into Shakespeare's reputation. It is not merely asserted in *Anonymous* that the man from Stratford-upon-Avon is undeserving of his most-exalted place in literature's pantheon of greats. Shakespeare is quite thoroughly and mercilessly maligned as an illiterate, drunken, buffoonish, whoring, avariciously-blackmailing, murdering fraud. Both this character assassination and Rafe Spall's portrayal grate mightily.

Sharply contrasting with the lowly depiction of Shakespeare is the high-minded, noble earnestness of genteel de Vere (Rhys Ifans), who writes to quiet the voice heard in his head and bursts forth with swoony declarations like, "My poems are my soul!" Viewers are supposed to swallow that *A Midsummer Night's Dream* sprang from him years before his facial hair did. An orphan placed in the Puritanically-strict household of the Queen's close-but-untrustworthy advisor, William Cecil (David Thewlis), de Vere grows up to unwillingly enter into an unhappy marriage with Cecil's daughter Anne (Helen Baxendale), an untamed shrew who scornfully scolds him for committing the sin of writing plays and poetry. He deigns to secretly place works like *Henry V* and *Richard III* in the hands of Ben Jonson (an increasingly overwrought Sebastian Armesto), only to be disgusted when someone even further beneath him like loutish Shakespeare horns in to take credit for the masterpieces. Clearly, viewers are to feel sorry for painfully-unrecognized de Vere, but many left theaters instead feeling the most sympathy for sledgehammered Shakespeare.

Oxfordian is one thing; overboard is another. That alternative theory of authorship was first advanced by John Thomas Looney in his conclusively-titled 1920 book *Shakespeare Identified.* (The author's name, which never fails to make Shakespeare supporters snicker when encountered in print, is actually pronounced by rhyming it most enjoyably with baloney.) In particular, Looney pointed to elements of various Shakespeare works that he believed could be legitimately traced back to the Earl's own life experiences. Although many felt that it took the strenuous use of a shoehorn to make this Oxford fit, de Vere—well-travelled, educated, and connected—continues to be the most popular choice of those hunting for a secret scribe. Overheated, dizzy offshoots of this theory not only assert that Oxford and Elizabeth had an illicit love affair that produced Henry Wriothesley, 3rd Earl of Southampton, but also that de Vere himself was an earlier product of the Virgin Queen's unexpectedly-lively loins.

Many of those who embrace Oxford tend to shun these seamy, steamy spinoff theories, fearing their far-fetched nature will hurt the overall plausibility of the cause. However, Emmerich and Orloff have opted for an undiscriminating kitchen sink approach. Utilizing these suppositions, they not only can attempt to titillate, but also, after all sorts of less-than-intriguing intrigue concerning who will succeed Elizabeth, create a scenario that tidily (but by no means convincingly) explains how the anonymity of the "true genius" became cemented for centuries.

More than a few viewers emerged from theaters bewildered, as if they had just been made to navigate through the type of maze-like formal garden shown in the film. The path can certainly be hard to follow, with audience members being forced to repeatedly travel backwards and forwards between numerous time periods. The similar manner in which some male characters are coiffed and bearded also adds to the sense of confusion. (Edward Hogg as William Cecil's even more odious son Robert, all but twirls his particular mustache.) Having Joely Richardson and her real-life mother Vanessa Redgrave play younger and older versions of the Queen works well for continuity, but it is hard to connect Bower's Earl with that of the quite dissimilarly-visaged Ifans.

Unintentionally both comedy and tragedy, *Anonymous,* which was made on a budget of $30 million, grossed so little during a limited release that plans for a wider release were scrapped. Reviews were mixed. One can admire the production values, interior lighting that successfully recalls the paintings of Vermeer and de la Tour, and "helicopter shots" looking down on Elizabethan London that were created with cutting-edge CGI technology. What one cannot admire is Emmerich's steamroller surety and excess upon the screen and off, the latter including his outrageously-unbridled deriding of those who teach the traditional take on Shakespeare as "liars." It is his own take that is far more likely to be deserving of the label "improbable fiction." Those words are from *Twelfth Night* by William Shakespeare of Stratford-upon-Avon—and, unless better men than Emmerich prove otherwise, no one else.

David L. Boxerbaum

CREDITS

Earl Of Oxford: Rhys Ifans
Queen Elizabeth I: Vanessa Redgrave
Princess Elizabeth Tudor: Joely Richardson
William Cecil: David Thewlis
Young Earl Of Oxford: Jamie Campbell Bower
William Shakespeare: Rafe Spall
Earl Of Southamptom Henry: Xavier Samuel
Ben Johnson: Sebastian Armesto
Robert Cecil: Ed Hogg
Earl Of Essex: Sam Reid
Origin: United Kingdom, Germany
Language: English
Released: 2011
Production: Roland Emmerich, Larry J. Franco, Robert Leger; Columbia Pictures, Centropolis Entertainment, Relativity Media; released by Sony Pictures
Directed by: Roland Emmerich
Written by: John Orloff
Cinematography by: Anna Foerster
Music by: Harald Kloser
Sound: Hubert Bartholomae
Editing: Peter R. Adam
Art Direction: Stephan O. Gessler
Costumes: Lisy Christl
Production Design: Sebastian Krawinkel
MPAA rating: PG-13
Running time: 130 minutes

REVIEWS

Denby, David. *New Yorker.* October 21, 2011.
Ebert, Roger. *Chicago Sun-Times.* October 26, 2011.
Honeycutt, Kirk. *Hollywood Reporter.* October 5, 2011.
Hornaday, Ann. *Washington Post.* October 27, 2011.
Koehler, Robert. *Variety.* October 5, 2011.
Morgenstern, Joe. *Wall Street Journal.* October 27, 2011.
Morris, Wesley. *Boston Globe.* October 27, 2011.
Nicholson, Amy. *Boxoffice Magazine.* October 5, 2011.
Phillips, Michael. *Chicago Tribune.* October 27, 2011.
Pols, Mary. *Time.* October 27, 2011.
Puig, Claudia. *USA Today.* October 27, 2011.

QUOTES

Young Earl of Oxford: "How could you possibly love the moon when you have first seen the sun?"

TRIVIA

This is the first major full-length motion picture to be shot with the Arri ALEXA high-definition digital-video camera.

AWARDS

Nomination:

Oscars 2011: Costume Des.

ANOTHER EARTH

Box Office: $1.3 million

Science fiction, on the big screen, often finds the intrigue and moral intricacy of its big ideas pared down by Hollywood's tendency to conflate the genre's underpinnings with a need for action. The adapted works of author Philip Dick have often especially suffered in this regard. *Another Earth*, then, is a movie seemingly ripe with potential, built as it is around a simple but provocative concept: that there exists a second Earth, populated by parallel versions of all the same cities and individuals.

Unfortunately, director Mike Cahill's debut film for a while toes the line between understated and just not having much going on, before coming down with a thud on the latter side of the fence. A dewy romantic drama of grief and symbolic redemption co-written by Cahill and multi-hyphenate Brit Marling, *Another Earth* made its debut in early 2011 at the Sundance Film Festival, where it picked up a Special Jury Prize and was purchased for distribution by Fox Searchlight. Artfully constructed and peppered with a couple moments of genuine tenderness, *Another Earth* is nevertheless a wildly self-important melodrama, and an example of the fact that the absence of clamorous overstatement does not automatically confer insightfulness.

Out celebrating her college acceptance to MIT, high school student Rhoda Williams (Marling), driving home drunk and additionally distracted by radio news of the discovery of this new, fantastical mirror planet, plows through a car stopped at an intersection. In doing so, she kills the wife and young son of composer and college music professor John Burroughs (William Mapother), and puts him in a coma. Four years later, after serving out a prison sentence for vehicular manslaughter, a still-damaged Rhoda is working as a school janitor when she sets out to confess and apologize to John, who does not know her identity due to sealed juvenile records.

When she arrives on John's doorstep, though, Rhoda chickens out and pretends to be a maid, offering free housecleaning service. Over the course of the next several months, Rhoda returns and she and John develop first a cautious rapport and then the initial flickerings of a romance. She also enters an essay contest designed to select a civilian for space travel to the mirror Earth. When she wins, however, Rhoda is uncertain what to do, and whether whatever awaits on the planet that has been dubbed Earth 2 might be able to soothe John's emotional damage.

Another Earth's main problem is that its narrative seems steeped in indie movie clichés, and inadequately

worked out to boot. One of the quandaries with movies of this ilk, like *Monsters* (2010) or *Trollhunter* (2011), is that the smallest crack or flaw in the backdrop or canvas of the film's conceit can stick in the mind of a viewer like a kernel of popcorn stuck between one's teeth. Such is certainly the case with *Another Earth*. With the introduction of a second planet, let alone a reflected Earth, one would expect some of the constant background reportage that litters the movie to mention the effects of gravitational pull on the tides, for instance. But Cahill instead engages these issues only in haphazardly chosen fashion (it is brighter at night, but the seemingly increasing closeness of the orb does not much bother anyone), and in the most general terms. There is also the matter of the same fixed image, nipped from the 1969 Apollo 11 mission, always being used to represent Earth 2 hanging in the sky. These shortcuts and strokes of convenience reinforce the feeling that the movie is all a bunch of hooey.

The script's more Earthbound elements do not much help, either. A wise, blind janitor, Purdeep (Kumar Pallana), comes across as a wan and only slightly ethnically differentiated variation on the "Magical Negro," advising Rhoda, apropos of nothing, "Keep your mind clear." And pretentious, philosophizing voiceover from real-life scientist Dr. Richard Berendzen only further illustrates Cahill and Marling's difficulty at organically interweaving and grappling with the heavy thematic questions with which they wish to engage. Personality crisis and ethical dilemma spliced with low-fidelity sci-fi was achieved to much more enthralling effect in Duncan Jones' *Moon* (2009).

Watching *Another Earth,* one almost keeps waiting for a grander twist that never materializes. Instead, there is lots of narrative dawdling, and some montages; even the movie's one big putative cathartic moment, a monologue of confession that is well written in the literary sense, gets diced up and refracted through an arty lens. The ostensible universality of its examined grief matters not; the movie's stirred passions feel sprinkled on top like a seasoning, and not earned.

To the degree that *Another Earth* works, it has to do chiefly with Marling's presence. She has an unfussy natural beauty, as well as a sense of calm and centeredness that suits the material, inviting the audience to invest in her the qualities with which they most wish to identify. On the other hand, Mapother, who made an impression as an abusive scumbag in *In the Bedroom* (2001), is more problematic. Not to put too fine a point on it, but he has neither the transformative range nor, more directly, the visage necessary to pull off a character of scholarly depth. Exuding a kind of blue collar scruffiness, Mapother has wide-set eyes and an asymmetrical face, which slot him, rightly or wrongly, as a slightly untrustworthy figure. As a renowned composer or academic, he is simply not believable.

Cahill also serves as both editor and cinematographer on *Another Earth,* and, in layering in ambient music from duo Fall on Your Sword over nervous, handheld frames, makes a strange case for his talents laying elsewhere. Whereas many music videos are used as professional calling cards for young, would-be feature filmmakers, Cahill's collagist instincts seem to augur that his best work may be in that medium, or more experimental moviemaking. Precious, plodding and very pleased with itself and what it believes to be its profundity, *Another Earth* is an empty piece of hipster genre filmmaking. It wants to elicit questions from viewers, but it dredges up more frustration than anything else.

Brent Simon

CREDITS

Rhoda Williams: Brit Marling
John Burroughs: William Mapother
Kim Williams: Jordan Baker
Robert Williams: Flint Beverage
Purdeep: Kumar Pallana
Origin: USA
Language: English
Released: 2011
Production: Hunter Gray, Mike Cahill, Brit Marling, Nicholas Shumaker; Artists Public Domain; released by Fox Searchlight
Directed by: Mike Cahill
Written by: Brit Marling, Mike Cahill
Cinematography by: Mike Cahill
Music by: Fall on Your Sword
Sound: Michael Gassert
Editing: Mike Cahill
Art Direction: Brian Rzepka
Costumes: Aileen Diana
Production Design: Darsi Monaco
MPAA rating: PG-13
Running time: 92 minutes

REVIEWS

Biancolli, Amy. *Houston Chronicle.* August 12, 2011.
Burr, Ty. *Boston Globe.* July 28, 2011.
Chang, Justin. *Variety.* April 25, 2011.
Dargis, Manohla. *New York Times.* July 21, 2011.
Ebert, Roger. *Chicago Sun-Times.* July 28, 2011.
Honeycutt, Kirk. *Hollywood Reporter.* April 25, 2011.
Lane, Anthony. *New Yorker.* August 8, 2011.

Longworth, Karina. *Village Voice.* July 19, 2011.
Rozen, Leah. *The Wrap.* July 21, 2011.
Sharkey, Betsy. *Los Angeles Times.* July 21, 2011.

QUOTES

Richard Berendzen: "In the grand history of the cosmos, more than thirteen thousand million years old, our Earth is replicated elsewhere. But maybe there is another way of seeing this world. If any small variation arises—they look this way, you look that way—suddenly maybe everything changes and now you begin to wonder, what else is different? Well, one might say that you have an exact mirror image that is suddenly shattered and there's a new reality. And therein lies the opportunity and the mystery. What else? What new? What now?"

TRIVIA

The house used in the film at the one the Williams's live in, is actually director Mike Cahill's mother's house.

AWARDS

Nomination:

Ind. Spirit 2012: First Feature, First Screenplay.

APOLLO 18

There's a reason we've never gone back to the moon.
—Movie tagline

Box Office: $17.7 million

Not screened in advance for critics, this largely forgettable but fun-enough time-waster will be lost on all but the most forgiving viewers. It has a mildly interesting if somewhat silly premise that is rendered absolutely ridiculous by the end of the film's scant 86-minute running time. What might have made a chilling short story in an old paperback pulp collection is stretched out to feature length in what is one of the more disappointing horror films of the year. Hailed as an American breakout for director Gonzalo López-Gallego it is instead a misfire.

At the beginning of the film, viewers are informed that what they are about to watch has been culled together from approximately 84 hours of previously-unreleased footage of a top secret 1974 space mission. The main problem with this assertion from a dramatic standpoint is that, from this point forward, the film abandons almost all pretense of being anything other than a standard narrative rather than a found footage film, telling an almost moment-to-moment linear story. The way footage would play out if it really had been edited together as suggested is ignored. In short, viewers will feel as if they are simply watching another movie, rather than feeling immersed in an historical event. In real life, NASA has gone so far as to issue an official statement through liaison Bert Ulrich that "*Apollo 18* is not a documentar…ythe film is a work of fiction." thus underscoring the biggest problem a found footage film can have.

The film centers on three astronauts, Commander Nathan Walker (Lloyd Owen), Lieutenant Colonel John Grey (Ryan Robbins), and Captain Benjamin Anderson (Warren Christie) as they are informed that the abandoned Apollo 18 mission has been re-booted and is now a highly classified op aimed at placing ICBM detectors on the moon. The launch goes off without a hitch and while Grey remains in orbit, Anderson and Walker land and proceed with the mission, as well as collect samples. All goes according to plan until the astronauts are awakened that night by strange sounds outside the craft and monitors reveal strange, indistinct movements on the surface. Afterwards they find one of the rock samples loose on the floor of the ship, despite having been secured. The pair decide to investigate further, becoming more and more convinced that NASA officials have misled them about the true nature of the mission, especially when they find a devastated Russian lunar vessel and a dead cosmonaut.

Quickly finishing the mission, the pair attempt a launch back to Grey only to be thwarted by a mysterious accident. On inspection, decidedly non-human tracks are discovered outside the spacecraft and they find themselves unable to contact Grey or mission control. Desperate to find a way back home and unsure of who they can trust the pair must also contend the very real possibility that they have been infected by a form of extraterrestrial life that has made its way into the ship.

Almost everything about this movie feels perfunctory, as if a series of elements were strung together piecemeal simply for the excuse of getting a film title on a resume. This is probably overly harsh but it does speak to the general lack of character development. As astronauts, all three of these men play generally to type, which is to say they are as faceless as the moon itself, giving the characters the same sort of vanilla veneer one would expect from NASA PR footage. Cory Goodman's only other screenwriting credit is the equally bad but far more visually inventive *Priest* (2011).

The one area where the film excels is in the creation of the lunar landscape. Foreboding, the moon has always been an object of horror. From the earliest days of storytelling it has haunted the human mind with a sort of dark power that is well utilized here. Shadows loom, an eerie silence pervades, and a sense of otherness is neatly generated. When the astronauts are actually exploring the surface it becomes easy to imagine what might lurk in the inky corners and those scenes are a testimony to the power of film and found footage aesthetic in general.

But the special effects lack punch just when the film needs it most. After creating a solid lunar surface, the movie devolves into a series of completely unconvincing CGI monster effects. This is when *Apollo 18* loses a last chance to become anything memorable. The idea for the monster here is a goofy, if potentially fun one, but once the viewer figures it out (which they are likely to do early on) the film becomes downright boring, as it vainly tries to hide it's big "surprise."

The conspiracy angle of the film is a weak one not just from a logical but from a dramatic point of view. In the very suspenseful *Capricorn One* (1978) (and on countless real life web sites) viewers are asked to believe that the lunar landing happened in an earthbound studio, accomplished via special effects. In *Apollo 18* viewers are asked to believe that an actual lunar mission, complete with manned crew is kept secret under the auspices of a satellite launching mission. But even if viewers buy into that, the film goes a step further by creating a subplot involving a similar Russian expedition that will make any viewer shake their head. *Apollo 18* fails to dodge the meteoric filmmaking problems that it has in almost every department, emerging as something only die hard genre fans could possibly care about.

Dave Canfield

CREDITS

Benjamin Anderson: Warren Christie
John Grey: Ryan Robbins
Origin: USA
Language: English
Released: 2011
Production: Timur Bekamambetov, Michele Wolkoff; Bekmambetov Projects, Dimension Films; released by Weinstein Company
Directed by: Lloyd Owen, Gonzalo Lopez-Gallego
Written by: Brian Miller
Cinematography by: Jose David Montero
Music by: Harry Cohen
Sound: Darren Brisker
Editing: Patrick Lussier
Art Direction: Tyler Bishop Harron
Costumes: Cynthia Ann Summers
Production Design: Andrew Neskoromny
MPAA rating: PG-13
Running time: 90 minutes

REVIEWS

Faraci, Devin. *Badass Digest*. September 2, 2011.
Hale, Mike. *New York Times*. September 3, 2011.

Jones, Kimberley. *Austin Chronicle*. September 9, 2011.

Leydon, Joe. *Variety*. September 3, 2011.

Olsen, Mark. *Los Angeles Times*. September 3, 2011.

Robey, Tim. *Daily Telegraph*. September 5, 2011.

Snider, Eric D. *Film.com*. September 4, 2011.

Turner, Matthew. *ViewLondon*. September 9, 2011.

Vaux, Rob. *Mania.com* September 2, 2011.

Weinberg, Scott. *FEARnet*. September 2, 2011.

QUOTES

Nate: "Get it out. It's so cold. Get it out, Ben. Get it out, get it out! Damn it Ben get it out!"

TRIVIA

NASA's liaison for multimedia, Bert Ulrich, has gone on record stating that the filme "is not a documentary...the film is a work of fiction."

THE ART OF GETTING BY

(Homework)

The toughest lesson is love.
—Movie tagline

Everybody's got some.
—Movie tagline

Box Office: $1.4 million

Those fortunate enough to make the trek up to Park City every January are pretty familiar at the types of films they must choose from during the Sundance Festival. There are edgy relationship dramas, apocalypses on tiny budgets, experimental narratives, and revealing documentaries. What most of these films often have in common is the general mood brought by morose, dry, repressed emotional archetypes that occasionally have a snarky streak to clue viewers in that they are smarter than everyone else on-screen and probably them as well. Nothing makes a head spin more when such characters are exposed early on as being no more clever than the average teddy bear and nowhere near as cute. Gavin Wiesen's writing/directing first feature debuted under the title, *Homework*, at 2011's festival only to have its title changed later on to *The Art of Getting By*. Appropriately so, as this is one film that requires no heavy lifting and no need to take it home.

Teenage George Zinavoy (Freddie Highmore) has realized he is going to die someday. Not from any pressing recent diagnosis, just a general fact of life that most children learn before the limbo of middle school education. So he has decided that everything, especially his class assignments, are meaningless. This might be the fatalistic approach to someone without opportunities, but George lives with his mom (Rita Wilson) in upper Manhattan where therapy and medication are not a luxury, but a standard afterthought. For all of George's casual whining and indifference towards his existence, it takes all of ten minutes for a spark of interest to come into his life.

Her name is Sally Howe (Emma Roberts), the pretty girl in school he has noticed before but it is not until he saves her from a smoking rap that she thrusts her way into his life as some alternative reality thank you. George schools the girl with the floozy-boozy cool mom (Elisabeth Reaser) in his "art," a four-step process that ranges from cutting class to noodles with some random appreciation of culture thrown into the middle. It is a cliché that cinema's students disenchanted with the everyday curriculum are secret artists and George falls right into that cinematic archetype. In lieu of a suspension, he is awarded (or forced) by the principal (Blair Underwood) to chaperone an alumni of the school around during Career Day, Week or Month. His name is Dustin (Michael Angarano), now as successful as a young artist can be, and he will become both a mentor and a potential heartbreaker to George.

None of these relationships playing out over the course of roughly 79 minutes are particularly convincing. Worse than that, they are not even terribly interesting. Writer/director Gavin Wiesen does nothing to present his protagonist as anything but a dopey teenager that is presented as somehow above the fray because he wears an overcoat and discovered foreign films earlier than most contemporary sophisticates. Other than the requisite moment where the disillusioned homework flouter knows more about the assigned text than even his teacher (Alicia Silverstone) did, it is never proven that he is any more intelligent or better than any of the presumed phonies by which he is surrounded. One character is blander than the next and none of their motivations translate into anything that would be mistaken for thematic depth.

"You think too much, George," Sally screams at him after a particularly bad night out where she asks him to have sex with her only to rescind the offer seconds later since he is her only real friend and it would be weird. This single minute right in the middle of Wiesen's film would be highlighted with a marker in class as a representation of the phoniness that permeates everything that came before it and every place it is headed. It is an object lesson in the danger of having such a moment without properly establishing the key relationships burgeoning for attention. An audience is likely to be more familiar with Emma Roberts as the face that represents salvation for morose, conflicted misanthropes (See also: *Lymelife* (2008), *Twelve* (2010) and *It's Kind of a Funny Story* (2010) for further evidence) than this Sally person who keeps showing up in-between George's mood swings. Third wheel Dustin barely registers as a blip with his "mentoring" being little more than just a life-lesson of what can happen if one does not act on feelings immediately. The total miscasting of Angarano does not help matters since any other year he would be playing the Highmore role, minus the scruffy beard to represent his elder world-weariness.

Wiesen's debut is basically a collection of subplots for its lead character to look upon with smug insights while refusing to actually resolve any of them until a manipulative final act. The utter generic nature of the material might seem like a dime-a-dozen in a festival full of quirk and unobtrusive guitar solos. But it is something so unobtrusive, uninteresting and devoid of narrative functionality that makes a film like *The Art of Getting By* get under one's skin by the end. With nothing else to sell but an attractive cast and angst, it is sad that Fox Searchlight had no other choice but to market it as "from the studio that brought you *Juno* (2007) and *(500) Days of Summer* (2009)." To lump it in with those other exemplary tales of young love and a high-schooler with a voice all her own, is an insult to their creators.

Erik Childress

CREDITS

George Zinavoy: Freddie Highmore
Sally Howe: Emma Roberts
Dustin: Michael Angarano
Charlotte Howe: Elizabeth Reaser
Principal Bill Martinson: Blair Underwood
Ms. Herman: Alicia Silverstone
Jack Sargent: Sam Robards
Vivian Sargent: Rita Wilson
Origin: USA
Language: English
Released: 2011
Production: Jennifer Dana, Kara Baker, Gia Welsh, Darren Goldberg; Gigi Films, Goldcrest Pictures; released by Fox Searchlight
Directed by: Gavin Wiesen
Written by: Gavin Wiesen
Cinematography by: Ben Kutchins
Music by: Alec Puro
Sound: Mike Guarino
Music Supervisor: Linda Cohen
Editing: Mollie Goldstein

Costumes: Erika Munro
Production Design: Kelly McGehee
MPAA rating: PG-13
Running time: 84 minutes

REVIEWS

Burr, Ty. *Boston Globe*. June 16, 2011.
Ebert, Roger. *Chicago Sun-Times*. June 16, 2011.
Goss, William. *Orlando Weekly*. June 15, 2011.
Johanson, MaryAnn. *Flick Filosopher*. September 13, 2011.
Kenny, Glenn. *MSN Movies*. June 15, 2011.
Nusair, David. *Reel Film Reviews*. June 17, 2011.
O'Connell Scan. *Washington Post*. June 16, 2011.
Phillips, Michael. *Daily Film Fix*. June 16, 2011.
Sachs, Ben. *Chicago Reader*. June 16, 2011.
Snider, Eric D. *Cinematical*. February 4, 2011.

QUOTES

Dustin: "Women like being desired. Just throw her up against a wall and start kissing her. Chances are she'll kiss you back, and if she doesn't, at least you tried. You've got to do something or else you'll lose her."

TRIVIA

The film was shipped to theaters with the code name "Flunk."

ARTHUR

Meet the world's only loveable billionaire.
  —Movie tagline
No work. All play.
  —Movie tagline

Box Office: $33 million

The original 1981 *Arthur* remains a product of its time, but is still not without its charms. As the titular character, Dudley Moore's broad performance as the drunken millionaire was alternately over the top and (in its better moments) subtle and tender. Beneath the slurred speech and one-liners, there existed a real human being caught in a dilemma right out of a fairy tale. Marry the equally rich family friend and keep the fortune or throw it all away for real, true love? Moore's love interest was the equally charming Liza Minnelli, who added to the believability in the film's more sober scenes. In its day, *Arthur* was highly regarded and even earned Sir John Gielgud an Academy Award® for his portrayal as Arthur's loyal and openly snobbish servant Hobson. But not every movie can stand the test of time. Over the years, its status as a classic has faded, due in part to a lame sequel (*Arthur 2: On the Rocks* [1988]) and a *Simpsons* episode in which Homer laughs uncontrollably at Moore's drunken shenanigans while Lisa and Bart watch in utter confusion as to how anyone could find it funny.

The remake, however, will only help the original look like the classic many thought it would become. With Russell Brand in the title role, the newer Arthur is less controlled, less poignant and certainly less funny. No one should be surprised that there is a remake of *Arthur,* but the approach to the drunkenness in the current age should have given the makers some pause before following through on one. Most movies about drunken behavior are either tragic (*Everything Must Go* [2011]) or, at the very least, comedic cautionary tales (*The Hangover* [2009]). The original *Arthur* practically celebrated drunkenness, particularly with Moore's line "Not everyone who drinks is a poet. Some of us drink because we're *not* poets." It was a different time.

Brand is not lucky enough to have been given such prose. The story, for the most part, remains the same. Arthur Bach is a cheerful, drunken billionaire who has no hopes or dreams and does not appear to care what people think of his behavior. His family wants him to settle down once and for all and marry Susan Johnson (here played by Jennifer Garner), a cheerless socialite who wants to marry him for his name and not much else. Their marriage would be more of a business merger. To make matters worse for Arthur, Susan's father (Nick Nolte) is psychotic and intends to see this marriage happen, even if he has to threaten Arthur with construction tools.

Arthur, of course, inadvertently falls for someone of considerably less financial worth, an unlicensed New York tour guide named Naomi, played by Greta Gerwig (why her character's name is changed and no one else's remains a mystery). Arthur charms the pants off Naomi and she, in turn, hardly ever questions his erratic behavior. He promises he can take her on a date in an empty Grand Central Station, which, being a billionaire and all, he does. Their date would have been a great scene in another movie with different characters, but this movie never earns the sentiment for which it strives.

This is a problem throughout. The character of Hobson is replaced by a female, the always reliable Helen Mirren. As Hobson, she naturally brings a sense of dignity to the piece, but she is never given a scene that has an ounce of believability. It is a thoroughly wasted performance. The chauffeur Bitterman, who in the original was African American and is now an Hispanic played Luis Guzman, seems like he is in another movie altogether. Jennifer Garner gives an equally disposable performance and is given the unfortunate task of giving the movie one of many unnecessary moments of pure slapstick.

Then there is Brand. His Arthur is an inconsistent creation. There is never a sense of when he is drunk or when he is sober. With Moore, there was never any question. Brand plays the movie in one single note. Sometimes he has a drink in his hand, sometimes not. This character could not exist in real life and not have people despise him, which is why Mirren and Gerwig's performances look like they are just following the rules of the disjointed screenplay. Why would anyone fall for this guy and why would anyone go to so much trouble looking after him? Brand tries in the third act to convey sadness and loss, but it is too little too late.

Screenwriter Peter Baynham clearly knows the original approach to the story by the late Steve Gordon (who was nominated for an Academy Award® for his original screenplay) would not fly in this day and age. A film about a drunken billionaire during the recession would be in need of some changes if it is to connect with the financially-strapped American public. But the changes here feel forced, as if everyone is almost ashamed of the story they are trying to tell. Wedged into the storyline is a sub-plot borrowed from *Arthur 2: On the Rocks,* in which Arthur tries to get a job in a department store. And who really wants to see Arthur attend Alcoholics Anonymous? Even when the remake tries to honor the original by directly lifting some of its dialogue, it feels disingenuous.

Perhaps it is just a bad idea to try and earn an audience's sympathy for a drunken billionaire in this day and age. To try and stretch that idea out to an almost two-hour running time is an even worse idea. Director Jason Winer, who has done some solid television work, particularly with the sitcom *Modern Family,* lets too many unfunny scenes run too long. Just look at the scene where Nick Nolte as the domineering Burt Johnson comes dangerously close to seriously dismembering Arthur. Why is it necessary for this scene to go in this direction when Nick Nolte's intimidating presence should be enough for the scene to be believable and maybe even funny? For tedious scenes such as these, and there are many, one wonders if the creative minds behind this remake even bothered to watch the original, let alone learn from its strengths.

Collin Souter

CREDITS

Arthur Bach: Russell Brand
Naomi: Greta Gerwig
Susan: Jennifer Garner
Hobson: Helen Mirren

Burt Johnson: Nick Nolte
Vivienne Bach: Geraldine James
Alice Johnson: Leslie Hendrix
Bitterman: Luis Guzman
Origin: USA
Language: English
Released: 2011
Production: Chris Bender, Russell Brand, Larry Brezner, Kevin McCormick, JC Spink, Michael Tadross; Benderspink, Morra, Brezner, Steinberg & Tenenbaum Entertainment, Inc., Warner Bros., Langley Park Productions; released by Warner Bros.
Directed by: Jason Winer
Written by: Peter Baynham
Cinematography by: Uta Briesewitz
Music by: Theodore Shapiro
Sound: Jerry Ross
Music Supervisor: Dave Jordan
Editing: Brent White
Art Direction: Douglas Huszti
Costumes: Juliet Polcsa
Production Design: Sarah Knowles
MPAA rating: PG-13
Running time: 110 minutes

REVIEWS

Chang, Justin. *Variety*. April 8, 2011.
Ebert, Roger. *Chicago Sun-Times*. April 8, 2011.
Gleiberman, Owen. *Entertainment Weekly*. April 6, 2011.
Neumaier, Joe. *New York Daily News*. April 8, 2011.
O'Hehir, Andrew. *Salon.com*. April 8, 2011.
Puig, Claudia. *USA Today*. April 7, 2011.
Smith, Kyle. *New York Post*. April 8, 2011.
Snider, Eric. *Film.com*. April 8, 2011.
Stevens, Dana. *Slate*. April 8, 2011.
Tobias, Scott. *NPR*. April 8, 2011.

QUOTES

Arthur: "We shouldn't get married...we have nothing in common. You love horses. I don't trust them. Their shoes are permanent. Who makes that kind of a commitment to a shoe?"

TRIVIA

Kevin Smith was approached to direct the film at one point.

AWARDS

Nomination:

Golden Raspberries 2011: Worst Prequel/Remake/Rip-off/Sequel, Worst Actor (Brand).

ARTHUR CHRISTMAS

Ever wonder how 2 billion presents get delivered all in 1 night?
—Movie tagline

Box Office: $46.5 million

Some kids want the latest, highest-tech gadgets and toys for Christmas, even as their parents yearn for a quiet return to a charming holidays full of wooden tops and decked-halls. So it also goes for Christmas movies, which too often offer a choice between manic clamor and snooze-inducing sappiness. The computer animated *Arthur Christmas,* however, wonderfully serves both camps. Its story is about earnest heart trumping both modern Space-Age efficiency and old-time tradition, while the film itself is designed to entertain both gimmick-loving, short-attention tots and their older, world-weary guardians.

The brightly colored film is from Aardman Animation (the veddy British, veddy clever makers of the *Wallace and Gromit* films, *Chicken Run* [2000], and *Flushed Away* [2006]), and like many an animated Christmas special, it takes viewers behind the scenes at Santa's North Pole operation. According to *Arthur Christmas,* these days the one-night, world-wide delivery of presents is accomplished with a space-ship sleigh the size of a small town, battalions of commando elves, and a clockwork efficiency that would put both the military and an overnight delivery company to shame. Out in front of all this whip-crack dazzle is the latest in a long line of Santa Clauses, an oblivious, retirement-aged "non-executive figure head" (Jim Broadbent) who is content riding along behind the curve.

Keeping Christmas running smoothly from his massive North Pole Command Center is Santa's eldest son Steve (Hugh Laurie), a broad-chested, military fit go-getter and next in line for the red suit when the current Claus steps down. Nearly forgotten at the side is bumbling younger son Arthur (James McAvoy), a good-hearted soul dedicated to both the idea of Christmas magic and his idolized image of his father. It is a testimony to Arthur's cheerful Christmas purity and sense of tradition that the homebody son is more than happy tucked away in an office answering Santa's voluminous (even in the age of e-mail) letters.

Naturally *Arthur Christmas* unfolds on a Christmas Eve when all does not go according to Steve's air-tight planning. First Santa sidesteps his intended retirement, much to Steve's dismay; and second, a single child's gift is discovered undelivered—that it is one error out of billions of successes does nothing to assuage true-believing Arthur's own dismay over a present-less kid. So, Arthur sneaks out to deliver the package with the assistance of his irascible, politically incorrect Grandsanta (Bill Nighy) and an over-enthusiastic wrapping elf (Ashley Jensen). Fed up with Steve and Santa's reliance on modern gadgetry, Grandsanta hopes to reclaim past glories and relevance by taking the classic wooden sleigh and its eight reindeer out of mothballs.

As Arthur and company pinball over the world in the old-school sleigh (turns out Grandsanta's 70-year-old navigation methods are not wired for 21st-century globalization) co-directors Sarah Smith and Barry Cook and Smith's co-writer Peter Baynham keep the pace and fun and snappy, but never blindly frantic. *Arthur Christmas* sports a droll and dry British wit that mixes irreverent subversion with plenty of physical gags and a well-earned dollop of sentimentality.

The film pulls the balance off because it cares about its characters. This is still animated children's fare, but *Arthur Christmas* pays refreshing attention to the authenticity of the various Clauses and their motivations—their Christmas dinner together is an all-too familiar portrait of the passive aggressions and generational hierarchies surrounding any family run business. (Imelda Staunton oversees it all as Mrs. Claus). Especially well-drawn is Santa's fear of joining Grandsanta in retired obsolescence and his befuddled inability to know what to make of young Arthur. Even Steve with his smart phone and technocrat ambitions is fully sympathetic rather than a plot-device villain.

The filmmakers understand the best classic cartoon characters reflect real human behaviors and personalities rather than cardboard, utilitarian shtick that only serves the next sight gag. In *Arthur Christmas* the voice cast also serves the characters—McAvoy, Laurie, and Broadbent are all pleasantly uh-showy, and Jensen gets to ratchet up the enthusiastic silliness. And in his WWI-era army helmet and filled with Battle of Britain grit (not to mention a healthy dollop of sardonic English fatalism), Nighy's cranky and eccentric Grandsanta is hilarious.

Arthur Christmas may lean on its Yuletide context to hold it all together, and beyond the seasonal genre it may not have quite enough artistry and emotional depth to add up to an instant animated classic. However the film's smart humor and sweet-natured heart-tugging make it a holiday treat nearly everyone can delight in.

Locke Peterseim

CREDITS

Arthur: James McAvoy (Voice)
Steve: Hugh Laurie (Voice)
Santa: Jim Broadbent (Voice)
Grandsanta: Bill Nighy (Voice)
Mrs. Santa: Imelda Staunton (Voice)
Bryony: Ashley Jensen (Voice)
Origin: USA, United Kingdom
Language: English

Released: 2011
Production: Peter Lord, David Sproxton, Carla Shelley, Steve Pegram; Aardman Features, Sony Pictures Animation; released by Sony Pictures
Directed by: Sarah Smith
Written by: Sarah Smith, Peter Baynham
Music by: Harry Gregson-Williams
Editing: John Carnochan, James Cooper
Sound: Steve Zaragoza
Production Designer: Evgeni Tomov
MPAA rating: PG
Running time: 97 minutes

REVIEWS

Biancolli, Amy. *San Francisco Chronicle.* November 23, 2011.
Genzlinger, Neil. *New York Times.* November 22, 2011.
Orange, Michelle. *Movieline.* November 22, 2011.
O'Sullivan, Michael. *Washington Post.* November 23, 2011.
Phillips, Michael. *Chicago Tribune.* November 22, 2011.
Pinkerton, Nick. *Village Voice.* November 23, 2011.
Pols, Mary. *Time.* November 22, 2011.
Rodriguez, Rene. *Miami Herald.* November 23, 2011.
Russo, Tom. *Boston Globe.* November 23, 2011.
Savlov, Marc. *Austin Chronicle.* November 25, 2011.

TRIVIA

This is the second consecutive film written by Peter Baynham to have the name Arthur in its title, the first is *Arthur* starring Russell Brand.

AWARDS

Nomination:

British Acad. 2011: Animated Film
Golden Globes 2012: Animated Film.

THE ARTIST

Box Office: $28.1 million

Leading a nostalgic awards season with widespread critical acclaim, Golden Globe® wins, and ten Oscar® nominations, Michel Hazanavicius' *The Artist* was of the most surprising critical darlings of 2011 and even considered the frontrunner for the Oscar® for Best Picture. While some folks began a backlash against the film in an attempt to paint the work as a trifle, a pleasant diversion instead of an Oscar®-worthy achievement, the majority of people who "heard" the story of the perfectly-named George Valentin fell for this delightful, ambitious piece of filmmaking, a work that successfully redefines new millennium storytelling by unearthing an old-fashioned way to tell a tale.

The Artist is a silent film that opens with a shot of a man screaming and a title card that makes clear not only the high concept of the film but a crucial part of its plot—"I won't talk! I won't say a word!!!" That man is silent film era superstar George Valentin (Oscar® nominee Jean Dujardin) and his latest sure-to-be blockbuster is unspooling in front of a captive, adoring audience in 1927. When the film ends in a glorious shot of a plane flying into the great blue yonder, the audience bursts into applause as Valentin and his lovely co-star (Missi Pyle) hit the stage to soak it in and pump it up with a bit of soft shoe and physical humor. Almost immediately, the fact that one is watching a silent film fades away at the force of the storytelling on display. Visually inventive and driven by a stellar performance by Dujardin (and an equal one by co-star Berenice Bejo), the silent aspect of the filmmaking becomes a part of the fabric of the feature instead of merely a distraction or its only reason for existence. This is the greatest achievement of *The Artist*. It is a silent film and an ode to the era of silent film that does not rely on those elements as gimmick but merely uses its form as another weapon in the filmmaking arsenal, one that has not been properly explored in decades.

When the film opens, Valentin is on top of the world, starring in major hits for producer Al Zimmer (John Goodman), and becoming the icon that every man wants to be and every woman wants to be with. One of the lovely ladies who swoons whenever Valentin walks by is the also-perfectly-named Peppy Miller (Oscar® nominee Berenice Bejo), a gorgeous gal who Valentin literally bumps into after the show. The dashing leading man falls for the gal with the perfect smile and becomes a bit smitten with the obvious ingénue just before the rest of America does the same. As Miller's star rises, Valentin's plummets to Earth. Not only is the lovely Ms. Miller the pretty new face on the standee but she ushers in something far more devastating, the talkie. When Valentin refuses to give up on silent cinema, most of the people around him give up on Valentin. He becomes a relic, a symbol of old Hollywood in a time when new Hollywood is so alluring and captivating. He begins to finance his own pictures, one of which symbolically features the star sinking in quicksand. And it is not purely his career that begins to nosedive as his personal life falls apart as well. Before long, he is completely alone, an artist with nowhere to display his talent. Does George Valentin have another chance? Can his career be reinvigorated in the same way the film is attempting to prove the remaining vitality of silent cinema.

Like a silent film of the '20s, *The Artist* includes many of the broad emotions and melodramatic plot points required to keep an audience engaged in a film without audible dialogue. While it could have easily devolved into nothing but melodrama, Hazanvicius' script is so clever and so full of constant wit and imagination that it feels like much more than pure mimicry of a bygone era. Hazanvicius' Oscar®-nominated writing and directing (a category many were predicting he would win over living legends Woody Allen, Terrence Malick, Alexander Payne, Martin Scorsese) is both reverential of the era it is recreating and homage to it. This film would not and could not exist exactly as is in the 1920s and yet it feels completely loyal to it. It is a looking glass view of old Hollywood, a trip through the rabbit hole in which devices of silent film are used but with poignancy gained through hindsight. It drips with admiration and passion for the history of film and yet never loses the emotion of its story in egghead pretension. In fact, the low level of pretension in *The Artist* is what made it such a success and a possible Best Picture winner. Hazanavicius' smartest move was to not weigh his piece down in film references that would go over the head of most viewers but instead try and make a crowd-pleaser. *The Artist* proves that film has always been and will always be, a primarily visual medium. With so much modern screenwriting being overly heavy on expository dialogue (even blockbusters nowadays weigh down their bloated running times with unnecessary plot explanation), it is so refreshing to see a piece of cinema that conveys emotion, character, and theme through channels that have become increasingly underutilized.

Hazanavicius deserves every bit of the rapturous praise aimed at him by numerous awards-voting bodies, but the film simply would not have worked without the incredibly committed and daring performance by French superstar Jean Dujardin (considered by many a front-runner to win the Oscar®). He appears in nearly every scene and carries the film completely through humor, drama, and honest pathos. He is genuine while also being forced by the nature of the film to be incredibly broad. His remarkable charisma keeps the film going but it is the decisions he made, the refusal to go nearly as broad and mugging as many actors would have with the same material, that carry the film. More often than not, it is the little notes—the look on George's face when he overhears the girl who once captivated him dismissing his entire generation, the expression when he realizes that her film is opening at a much bigger venue than his own, or the way he seems incapable of moving past her as they try to shoot a dance number—that make this a truly stand-out performance. Most actors could have nailed the mugging. Dujardin realized it was the smaller moments that would separate his work, and the overall film.

Despite a bit of category confusion (BAFTA nominated her for Lead Actress while the Academy incorrectly chose Supporting), Berenice Bejo matches Jean Dujardin in every way. In many ways, she is the tipping point of the film, the stellar performance that takes it from good to great. It is a true breakthrough performance in every way. She not only plays a breakout ingénue. She is one. Peppy Miller could have become little more than a plot device, a way to comment on Valentin's spiraling fame, but Bejo never allows her to become merely that, matching her co-star in every possible way. And when they are on-screen together, it is when the film truly shines brightest.

Like many of cinema's most acclaimed films, *The Artist* is a tightrope act, a magic act that one watches, looking for the strings but falling for the tricks every time…until they stop looking for the strings. It is an ode to a time when most cinema historians feel movies were a bit more magical and the film's greatest accomplishment is that it makes the case that this is true not through commentary or recreation but by doing something far more difficult—by simply being a magical film in its own right.

Brian Tallerico

CREDITS

George Valentin: Jean Dujardin
Peppy Miller: Berenice Bejo
Al Zimmer: John Goodman
Clifton: James Cromwell
Doris: Penelope Ann Miller
Constance: Missi Pyle
The Butler: Malcolm McDowell
Peppy's Maid: Beth Grant
Peppy's Butler: Ed Lauter
Pawnbroker: Ken Davitian
Origin: France
Language: English
Released: 2011
Production: Thomas Langmann; La Petite Reine, Studio 37; released by Weinstein Company
Directed by: Michel Hazanavicius
Written by: Michel Hazanavicius
Cinematography by: Guillaume Schiffman
Music by: Ludovic Bource
Sound: Nadine Muse
Editing: Michel Hazanavicius, Anne-Sophie Bion
Costumes: Mark Bridges

Production Design: Laurence Bennett
MPAA rating: PG-13
Running time: 100 minutes

REVIEWS

Burr, Ty. *Boston Globe.* December 22, 2011.
Ebert, Roger. *Chicago Sun-Times.* December 21, 2011.
Gleiberman, Owen. *Entertainment Weekly.* November 23, 2011.
Jones, J.R. *Chicago Reader.* December 22, 2011.
Kohn, Eric. *IndieWire.* November 23, 2011.
Phillips, Michael. *Chicago Tribune.* December 22, 2011.
Pols, Mary. *Time.* November 23, 2011.
Rea, Steven. *Philadelphia Inquirer.* December 22, 2011.
Scott, A.O. *New York Times.* November 25, 2011.
Zacharek, Stephanie. *Movieline.* November 28, 2011.

QUOTES

George Valentin: "I won't talk! I won't say a word!"

TRIVIA

The role of Jack the dog was actually played by three matching Jack Russell Terriers: Uggie, Dash, and Dude. While the lead dog Uggie did the majority of scenes, all three dogs were colored before the filming began, made to look more alike.

AWARDS

Oscars 2011: Actor (Dujardin), Costume Des., Director (Hazanavicius), Film, Orig. Score
British Acad. 2011: Actor (Dujardin), Cinematog., Costume Des., Director (Hazanavicius), Film, Orig. Screenplay, Orig. Score
Directors Guild 2011: Director (Hazanavicius)
Golden Globes 2012: Actor—Mus./Comedy (Dujardin), Film—Mus./Comedy, Orig. Score
Ind. Spirit 2012: Actor (Dujardin), Cinematog., Director (Hazanavicius), Film
Screen Actors Guild 2011: Actor (Dujardin)
Nomination:
Oscars 2011: Art Dir./Set Dec., Cinematog., Film Editing, Orig. Screenplay, Support. Actress (Bejo)
British Acad. 2011: Actress (Bejo), Film Editing, Makeup, Sound, Prod. Des.
Golden Globes 2012: Director (Hazanavicius), Screenplay, Support. Actress (Bejo)
Ind. Spirit 2012: Screenplay
Screen Actors Guild 2011: Support. Actress (Bejo), Cast.

ATLAS SHRUGGED: PART 1

Who is John Galt?
    —Movie tagline

Box Office: $4.6 million

Atlas Shrugged: Part 1 sets out to adapt the late philosopher and novelist Ayn Rand's massive 1957 novel, which gave birth to and popularized her Objectivist moral philosophy of rational self-interest and helped create a devoted Rand following that while ebbing and flowing over the decades, experienced a resurgence of interest in the early 2010s.

The film adaptation is set in a dystopian 2016 from which all the great businessmen, scientists, industrialists, thinkers, and "prime movers" of American society are mysteriously vanishing, even as the government continues to squeeze to death the Great American Captains of Industry with odious, socialist-leaning laws and anti-monopoly regulations. Unknowingly caught in the middle are two gloriously laissez-faire capitalists, strangers brought together by the romance of making money: Dagny Taggart (Taylor Schilling) of the train company Taggart Transportation and Hank Rearden (Grant Bowler), maker of a new strong, lightweight metal. As adapted by writers John Aglialoro and Brian Patrick O'Toole, *Atlas Shrugged: Part 1* covers only the first third of Rand's novel and does so with leaden fidelity to the Rand's fiercely held doctrines and stylistic didacticism. Yet that somehow makes the film a deeply odd, stubbornly artless, but weirdly fascinating piece of failed cinema.

The thriller plot is driven by the mysterious phrase "Who's John Galt?" that keeps turning up around the disappearances, but all the whodunit is only there for Rand to hang her passionate pre-Objectivist philosophies on. (Come for the pot-boiling yarn, stay for the long sermons on the free market and the virtues of selfishness.) Rand believed literary characters should not be naturalistic but rather paragons of beliefs, and in their heightened perfection, the film's tough, intensely focused heroine Dagny and equally taciturn and dedicated hero Hank are Greek Gods in sharp business suits—almost every line of their dialogue is an economic treatise, a statement of personal creedo, or rote exposition. The lessons they mouth to each other are pure, distilled Randisms: The great joy is pride in the hard work you do for yourself, not others; and the only goal is to make money, to drive the engine of the economic world, and reward yourself with the luxurious homes, clothes, and meals all that money buys.

While their budding romance is fuelled by hot and heavy talk of unregulated industry and well-earned monopolies, Dagny and Hank are righteous, not robber barons—their old-timey, often family owned and run industrial companies bear no connection whatsoever to the complicated real world of global corporations and vast financial conglomerates. Instead the two of them talk rapturously about metals and trains, making deals, and building actual bridges, not metaphorical ones. Business is an art, and profit is beautiful: Hank stares lovingly out at his foundry floor—the glorious machinery of free-market capitalism churning along below his glass-office perch—and Dagny is taken to excitedly blurting out things like, "It's us who move the world," and "What we do is important!"

All this is pure pornography for Rand-style capitalists as the film's protagonists live and work the Good Life in their gleaming steel and glass towers and opulent mansions. (In this it is as much a fantasy as *The Lord of the Rings,* except few Tolkien fans view his Middle Earth as a working blueprint for how to run a perfect society.) However, for those not smitten with scenes that linger lovingly over the beauty of a well-laid railroad track and the thrill not of high-speed rail travel, but the earnings it represents, *Atlas Shrugged: Part 1*'s adorations can be a hard sell.

Its characters also echo Rand's bitter, angry stabs at those she considered the lickspittles of evil: The politicians and lazy lapdogs of big government, including the vile state agencies, guilds, and unions—Dagny all but spits on their "stupid altruistic urges" and the accompanying horrors of nationalization, collective needs, and shared burdens. Her sniveling brother James (Matthew Marsden) slithers in the pocket of such interests—he would twirl his mustache with villainous glee if only he were man enough to grow one.

Atlas Shrugged: Part 1 did not have a large budget, and as blandly directed by Paul Johansson, often its look, pacing, and tone seem more suited to a syndicated television show than a theatrically released feature. Still, to its credit the film gets an impressive amount of polish and serviceable production value (if no real visual richness) from its buck. The cast also does the best they can, and the uniformly stiff acting is not entirely the performers' faults. There is the sense that if films heroes showed any recognizable, relatable human emotion it would diminish their Randian perfection, and so Schilling and Bowler sometimes come off as if they are holding their noses while acting, like they have been given a particularly odious school assignment.

Despite moving at a steady clip (tossing out large hunks of plot as it goes), the film feels longer than its 90-minute running time thanks to the plodding cinematic ineptitude and the inert, emotionless polemics—plus there is its misguided love of board-room melodrama, and "This is important!" aversion to humor. However, there is that *Twilight Zone* style mystery tale at its center (Part 1 ends on a cliffhanger), and the dedication of the characters to their (that is, Rand's) beliefs makes Dagny and Hank feel like interesting zoo creatures with a penchant for urgent, declarative statements. There may be an old-fashioned blandness to its surfaces, but *Atlas Shrugged: Part 1* is so passionate in its proselytizing and such an archly self-serious screed against everything but rational self interest, that even viewers unimpressed with Rand's beliefs (if not outright dismissive of or disgusted by them) may find themselves strangely caught up in the stilted, low-budget, alien feel of it all.

Locke Peterseim

CREDITS

Dagny Taggart: Taylor Schilling
Henry "Hank" Rearden: Grant Bowler
James Taggart: Matthew Marsden
Eddie Willers: Edi Gathegi
Ellis Wyatt: Graham Beckel
Francisco D'Anaconia: Jsu Garcia
Orren Boyle: Jon Polito
Wesley Mouch: Michael Lerner
Phillip Rearden: Neill Barry
Lillian Rearden: Rebecca Wisocky
John Galt: Paul Johansson
Origin: USA
Language: English
Released: 2011
Production: Harmon Koslow, John Aglialoro; released by Rocky Mountain Pictures
Directed by: Paul Johansson
Written by: Brian Patrick O'Toole, John Aglialoro
Cinematography by: Ross Berryman
Music by: Elia Cmiral
Sound: David Holmes, Robert Sharkman, Dennis Grzesik
Music Supervisor: Steve Weisberg
Editing: Jim Flynn, Sherril Schlesinger
Costumes: Jennifer Soulages
Production Design: John Mott
MPAA rating: PG-13
Running time: 97 minutes

REVIEWS

Chocano, Carina. *New York Times*. April 28, 2011.
Ebert, Roger. *Chicago Sun-Times*. April 14, 2011.
Jenkins, Mark. *Washington Post*. April 15, 2011.
King, Loren. *Boston Globe*. April 15, 2011.
LaSalle, Mick. *San Francisco Chronicle*. April 15, 2011.
Persall, Steve. *Tampa Bay Times*. April 16, 2011.
Phillips, Michael. *Chicago Tribune*. April 14, 2011.
Rickey, Carrie. *Philadelphia Inquirer*. April 15, 2011.
Smith, Kyle. *New York Post*. April 14, 2011.
Tobias, Scott. *AV Club*. April 15, 2011.

QUOTES

Henry Rearden: "The next time you decide to throw a party, can you stick to your own crowd? Don't bother inviting people you think are my friends."

TRIVIA

Angelina Jolie, Charlize Theron and Maggie Gyllenhaal were among the actresses considered to play Dagny Taggart, with Brad Pitt being considered for the role of John Galt.

ATTACK THE BLOCK

Inner city vs. outer space.
—Movie tagline

Box Office: $1 million

An energetic combination of science-fiction, comedy, horror, and coming-of-age tale wrapped in a study of the hard-knock life of the impoverished class, *Attack the Block* also features one of the most unique and terrifying alien designs in recent memory. They are beasts about the size of a large dog with the broadness and gait of a gorilla ("bear-wolf-gorilla" monsters, as a couple of characters dub them, though the "monster" part is a bit more profane). They are, as one character puts it, of "the blackest black," blending seamlessly into the shadowy night of the bad part of South London, where gangs of hoodlums roam the streets and an egomaniacal drug dealer rules with illegal firearms and an army of thugs. Their teeth, which glow a sickly blue in the dark ("I don't think those are eyes," a character realizes with dread), are set in rows—jagged and razor-sharp. Their impulse to kill outweighs even their survival instinct.

They are, essentially, killing machines with which there is no negotiation or compromise, and these ferocious creatures provide the perfect opportunity to begin supporting the film's group of anti-heroes, who at first seem almost as instinctual as the aliens. The gang's life is also a cutthroat one, and their first appearances in the film are of robbing an innocent woman on her way home from work at knifepoint and chasing down a female specimen of the invading horde just to kill it. After they do, they heave its lifeless body in the air like a trophy. As nasty as the aliens turn out to be, there is something cruel in that image of the teenagers' bloodlust. Then again, though, they are just kids without a single, positive influence in their lives, and writer/director Joe Cornish finds the time in between the aliens' attacks to illuminate that fact.

Set in and around a public housing unit called Wyndham Tower (named after the science-fiction writer John Wyndham—the film's fictional locations are named after other writers in the genre), the story follows five teenagers who wander the streets of South London at night without any supervision. They are Moses (John Boyega), who is also the gang's leader, Pest (Alex Esmail), who smokes marijuana, Dennis (Franz Drameh), who is the group's resident daredevil (he wears a helmet), Jerome (Leeon Jones), who wears glasses, and Biggz (Simon Howard), who is separated from the rest of his friends in a garbage bin guarded by one of the aliens for most of the film.

Cornish's screenplay heavily incorporates colorful slang, which rolls trippingly off the young actors' tongues, into the gang's vernacular (Even before the film's United States premiere at the South by Southwest festival [popularly known as SXSW], rumors of the possibility of subtitles spread; thankfully, they never came to pass). The occasional mystery of the characters' meaning accompanied by their internal knowledge of what is being said adds to the sense of fraternity within the group (they constantly refer to each other lovingly as "fam"); this is their language, unique to them and only them.

During their first appearance, the gang mugs Sam (Jodie Whittaker), a nurse, on her way home to the same apartment complex where the teens live after work late at night. At the height of the robbery, a burning object crashes from the sky and into a nearby car. Sam escapes; the boys investigate the wreckage for any valuables in the vehicle. While doing so, a smaller version of the creatures that appear later in the story swipes at Moses, who determines to get revenge upon it by killing it. The teenagers return to the building in glory with their prize, and soon enough, the larger and far more vicious males of the species begin landing in the neighborhood. The gang is certain the rain of beasts is a hostile invasion and decide to protect their home turf.

The camera follows each individually as they enter their respective apartments to gather weapons (e.g., a baseball bat, a decorative samurai sword, a machete), and in these brief glimpses, Cornish reveals information about their family lives. The teens' apartments are either empty of other family members or contain inattentive ones, too caught up in their own lives or dismissive of the kids' activities to care much more than asking what they might be doing. All of them are able to sneak out with a weapon (despite the fact that possession of offensive weapon is a criminal offense in the United Kingdom, they are certain there is an exception to the law when faced with an alien attack) with no one to even question their reasons.

In spite of the backdrop of socioeconomic trouble, the malicious monsters, and the occasionally grotesque violence and gore (a creature crushes the head of one of the teens between its teeth, another rips apart a character's throat, and a group of aliens gives another character a grisly rhinoplasty), Cornish's aim is primarily comic. There are a few throwaway gags involving foreshadowing (the most clever one involves Pest shoving a baseball bat down the leg of his pants, causing him to fake a limp to slink out of his apartment without raising attention; later, after being bitten by an alien, he must, indeed, walk with a real hobble), but there are also some strong ancillary characters to add some flavor.

Stoners Ron (Nick Frost), who keeps a room full of marijuana in his apartment, and Brewis (Luke Treadaway), who deduces the reason for the aliens' knack for following Moses and his crew around after watching a nature special on television about pheromones, have an amusing scene outside of the main plot, and two young kids who insist they be called by their newly created street names Probs (Sammy Williams) and Mayhem (Michael Ajao) follow their local idols with their own plans of gaining notoriety. Most impressive is Jumayn Hunter as the block's infamous drug dealer Hi-Hatz, in a performance that manages to be equal parts menacing (covered in blood, he emerges from an elevator in which he has somehow survived a close-quarters encounter with an alien) and ridiculous (he is obsessed with listening to a rap song he recorded).

This is a solid film debut for Cornish. Outside of the effortless way the film glides between its genre trappings, *Attack the Block* finds resonance in its sense of responsibility to the community, observing how the unlikeliest group of compatriots can not only find common ground but also to respect each other—and not begrudgingly, either.

Mark Dujsik

CREDITS

Moses: John Boyega
Sam: Jodie Whitaker
Pest: Alex Esmail
Dennis: Franz Drameh
Jerome: Leeon Jones
Biggz: Simon Howard
Ron: Nick Frost
Brewis: Luke Treadway
Hi-Hatz: Jumayh Hunter
Origin: United Kingdom
Language: English
Released: 2011
Production: Nira Park, James L. Wilson; Big Talk Pictures; released by Optimum Releasing
Directed by: Joe Cornish

Written by: Joe Cornish
Cinematography by: Tom Townsend
Music by: Steven Price, Felix Buxton, Simon Radcliffe
Sound: Jim Greenhorn
Music Supervisor: Nick Angel
Editing: Jonathan Amos
Art Direction: Dick Lunn
Costumes: Rosa Dias
Production Design: Marcus Rowland
MPAA rating: R
Running time: 88 minutes

REVIEWS

Bradshaw, Peter. *Guardian.* May 12, 2011.
Brooke, Michael. *Sight & Sound.* May 17, 2011.
DeFore, John. *Washington Post.* August 19, 2011.
Ebert, Roger. *Chicago Sun-Times.* July 27, 2011.

Olsen, Mark. *Los Angeles Times.* July 29, 2011.
Orndorf, Brian. *BrianOrndorf.com.* June 1, 2011.
Rabin, Nathan. *AV Club.* July 28, 2011.
Rich, Katey. *CinemaBlend.com.* August 1, 2011.
Tallerico, Brian. *HollywoodChicago.com.* July 29, 2011.
Zacharek, Stephanie. *Movieline.* July 28, 2011.

QUOTES

Jerome: "This is too much madness to explain in one text!"

TRIVIA

Most of the young actors in the film were found through their schools and online open auditions.

AWARDS

Nomination:
British Acad. 2011: Outstanding Debut.

B

BAD TEACHER

She doesn't give an "F."
—Movie tagline

Box Office: $100.3 million

Considering how little effort seems to go into the Hollywood machine, it is actually surprising that there does not exist an entire franchise of films with titles beginning with "Bad" and ending with a typically friendly person or profession. Just think of it: *Bad Nurse. Bad Clown. Bad Philanthropist.* The scripts practically write themselves.

That does not mean that *Bad Teacher,* starring Cameron Diaz as exactly that, is totally without inspiration. In fact, Diaz is the hit-or-miss comedy's greatest, liveliest asset. Her performance as Elizabeth, a wildly inappropriate junior high teacher, demonstrates that the key to a lovably appalling comedic performance is not merely being extreme (Jack Black's annoying antics continually prove the opposite side of this coin in almost everything except *The School of Rock* [2003]). Rather, Diaz's perky, atrocious behavior remains objectionable yet mostly harmless, reminding viewers why people say it is good to be bad. There is something delightful and coolly detached in Elizabeth's shameless rebellion—not only is she the kind of person who carelessly tosses an apple toward a recycling bin, not a garbage can, but she barely musters the energy to get it in the basket. Obviously, she does not care when she misses.

Elizabeth is done with teaching until her rich fiancé Mark (Nat Faxon) breaks off their engagement, forcing Elizabeth to return to John Adams Middle School in suburban Illinois. It is a place where Principal Wally

Snur (John Michael Higgins) is very aware that the school's initials spell "J.A.M.S." and the golden teacher is Amy Squirrel (Lucy Punch), an overachieving irritant that kids in real life would almost certainly find as intolerable as Elizabeth does. In fact, positioning Amy, who schemes her way toward acquiring information about Elizabeth by grilling students seeking extra credit, as the villain helps Elizabeth become more sympathetic in viewers' eyes. Despite the fact that she wastes class time by showing movies and has much less interest in the students learning than she does in the breast implants she hopes to finance, now believing that this is her only sure-fire ticket to landing a man. Never mind that she is a tall, beautiful blonde whose endless legs inspire a widespread outburst of leering among kids' dads during a fundraising school car wash. From which Elizabeth, of course, pockets the nearly $7,000 in earnings.

Elizabeth's belief in the power of bigger boobs is further reinforced when she meets new substitute teacher Scott Delacorte (Justin Timberlake), whose family wealth makes him even more attractive to Elizabeth than his face. Scott just broke up with his giant-breasted girlfriend, so naturally that is the only type of woman he could want, Elizabeth thinks. She may come off as confident and powerful, but this teacher comes packed with insecurities. Only someone willing to call her on her issues has any chance of reforming her, and that is the goal of gym teacher Russell Gettis (Jason Segel), whose romantic intentions Elizabeth dismisses solely based on Russell's profession.

Other than Elizabeth and Amy, the script by *The Office* writers Lee Eisenberg and Gene Stupnitsky features far too many flimsy characters. Scott's defining characteristic is his unexpected awkwardness, and Timberlake never finds the right comic angle for him. Russell, meanwhile, is a nice guy who spends so much of the movie on the sidelines that he never feels appropriately integrated into the story. Most of *Bad Teacher* revolves around Elizabeth's foolish antics as she pursues her own agenda and manipulates others, whether it is feigning passion for the principal's strongest interest (dolphins) or using her sexuality to pose as a Chicago Tribune reporter and seduce/drug a state test representative (Thomas Lennon) and steal a copy of the test. People with a conscience would never consider sacrificing their own integrity and a barometer for children's educational status in order to guarantee that their class would achieve the highest scores and win their teacher $5,700 in prize money. Elizabeth is not one of those people with a conscience, though, so she could not be happier with her ruse that puts her much closer to a bigger bra and a better life.

Ultimately, the word for all of this is "innocuous". No student is ever in physical danger. Elizabeth never does anything truly shocking. Actually, every so often she does pay attention to the students and doles out harsh but ultimately helpful advice, such as when she levels with Garrett (Matthew Tiara) that he will never win the hot girl that he pines for and later helps him save face in front of his classmates. The best part of this sequence comes from Garrett's public declaration of love to Chase (Kathryn Newton), during which he recalls memories they shared together before she thought she was too cool for him. So often junior high kids want to act more stable than they are and pretend that nothing bad or embarrassing every happened, and Garrett effectively reminds everyone that beneath a thick outer shell is often something far more vulnerable.

With a less savvy actress than Diaz front and center, *Bad Teacher* would likely be forgettable and smug. She makes it work, though, with her falsely sincere delivery of lines like, "In a lot of ways, I think that movies are the new books." Or when she gestures to parents, who came to school to listen to the teachers talk about their classes, that they are welcome to enjoy snacks and drinks in the back of the room. All that Elizabeth has set out is a bag of Oreos and a container of water. It is a funny, appropriate image for her teaching style and attitude toward life: Do the bare minimum and get by on your charm and attitude.

This is also representative of *Bad Teacher*, which piles on forgotten characters and loose ends—multiple references are made to Amy's so-called major incident from 2008, which is never explained at all— while trying to coast on its largely inoffensive mean streak. That is good for a few laughs, but a more daring spirit and

even a better sense of place would have solidified the consequences of this bad teacher's behavior. Rather, this is a movie that suggests Elizabeth tried to pick up Chicago Bulls players by hanging out at the bars near their practice facility; anyone from the area knows that there are few bars near the Berto Center in north suburban Deerfield, and it is unlikely that the Bulls players would spend time in them anyway. Like much of Elizabeth's life and the movie about her, this joke displays little effort and little reward.

Matt Pais

CREDITS

Elizabeth Halsey: Cameron Diaz
Scott Delacorte: Justin Timberlake
Amy: Lucy Punch
Wally: John Michael Higgins
Carl Halibi: Thomas Lennon
Russell Gettis: Jason Segel
Origin: USA
Language: English
Released: 2011
Production: Columbia Pictures; released by Sony Pictures
Directed by: Jake Kasdan
Written by: Gene Stupnitsky, Lee Eisenberg
Cinematography by: Alar Kivilo
Music by: Michael Andrews
Sound: Joel Shryack
Editing: Tara Timpone
Costumes: Debra McGuire
Production Design: Jefferson Sage
MPAA rating: R
Running time: 92 minutes

REVIEWS

Berardinelli, James. *ReelViews*. June 23, 2011.
Dargis, Manohla. *New York Times*. June 23, 2011.
DeFore, John. *Hollywood Reporter*. June 18, 2011.
Ebert, Roger. *Chicago Sun-Times*. June 23, 2011.
Ogle, Connie. *Miami Herald*. June 23, 2011.
Phillips, Michael. *Chicago Tribune*. June 23, 2011.
Rabin, Nathan. *AV Club*. June 23, 2011.
Rea, Stephen. *Philadelphia Inquirer*. June 23, 2011.
Sharkey, Betsy. *Los Angeles Times*. June 24, 2011.
Weitzman, Elizabeth. *New York Daily News*. June 23, 2011.

QUOTES

Shawn: "LeBron is a better rebounder and passer."
Russell Gettis: "LeBron will never beat Jordan. Call me when LeBron has six championships."

Shawn: "That's your only argument?"
Russell Gettis: "It's the only argument I need Shawn!"

TRIVIA

Actor Bradley Cooper was at one time considered for a role in
  the film.

BATTLE: LOS ANGELES

Box Office: $83.6 million

The perfect B-movie is one that provides pure escapism for the audience. It has to succeed in spite of a bad
premise, forgettable effects, clunky performances or
dialogue. A great B-movie is, in the end, a triumph of
its own simple-mindedness, but it must also transcend it
to become something for the viewer that is more than
the sum of its parts. *Battle: Los Angeles* attempts to apply
this principle to the war film. This film is far too simple
to survive any sustained criticism. It is, in every sense,
fun escapist entertainment too concerned with spectacle
and rife with problems, but the one or two things that
viewers will find compelling about it are the things that
the film itself takes seriously.

A decade of American Military misadventures might
make *Battle: Los Angeles* easy to dismiss with a giant,
"Hoo-Rah!," followed by a raspberry, but this is clearly a
film made by someone who loves war cinema and more
importantly loves the high ideals of soldierly heroism. It
sticks solidly to the well dug by John Wayne long ago,
offering a bare-bones tale of soldiers in a non-stop
confrontation with combatants...who happen to be
aliens. Though heavily armed, the Marines are out-
gunned and outmanned and soon it becomes clear that
their most important weapon is the creed of the Marine
Corp itself, "Semper Fi." This is the most compelling
aspect of the film: It takes that creed seriously by
showcasing the teeth-gritting determination of fallible
human beings in the service of it.

Los Angeles-based Marine Staff Sergeant Nantz
(Aaron Eckhart) has handed in his retirement papers.
Feeling his age and back from a mission that cost others
their lives under his command, Nantz feels he can no
longer lead. When, almost simultaneously, a bona fide
worldwide alien invasion starts, he is quickly reassigned
to active duty behind a group of mostly-green recruits
who have heard the stories of his former failure. 2nd Lt.
Martinez (Ramon Rodriguez), the leader of the platoon,
is caught between his men's distrust of Nantz and Nantz
himself, who does his best to defer. Worse, one of the
recruits is the brother of one of the men who died under
Nantz's command. The platoon's three-hour mission, to

rescue civilians trapped in a police station in an alien-
controlled area, looks more and more like a suicide mission, and they soon find themselves fighting to simply
make it out alive before the air force bombs the area.

The film's weakest point is that the marines are
sketched out very broadly, given no character development beyond clichéd motivations. Nantz is the older
marine struggling to rise up after failure while other
sketchily-drawn characters have babies on the way, are
"the greenhorn," or "the tough chick." It is curious to
defend a film that has poorly-drawn characters as one
that nonetheless offers a weak-but-still-pulsing humanity.
Battle: Los Angeles gets the benefit of appealing to the
ideals of self-sacrifice, loyalty, forgiveness, and ingenuity
in the face of adversity. It is ham-fisted but certainly no
more so than the lives lived by many people who struggle
to transcend the mundane nature of their own lives.
Battle: Los Angeles aims low but it does celebrate the
simplicity of being a good soldier and a decent human
being. It is the one thing that saves it, the only thing
indeed that gives the film any emotional punch at all.

Jonathan Liebesman has yet to make a film that
convinces critics he should keep making them at all. His
short film on the direct-to-video *Rings* release is
considered a gem. But the badly-regarded box office
failure of *Darkness Falls* (2003) certainly did him no
favors. *The Texas Chainsaw Massacre: The Beginning*
(2006) is considered wrongly, by many, as just another
sequel money grab. The truth is it works very well as a
monster movie, giving Leatherface and the family a
somewhat-compelling back story to buttress their mythic
mojo.

Aaron Eckhart is easily the most important non
special effects element here. He has steadily risen through
the ranks to become a respected actor moving from
second banana roles to very solid upfront work in *In the
Company of Men* (1997), *Thank You For Smoking* (2005),
The Dark Knight (2008), and *Rabbit Hole* (2010).
Michelle Rodriguez has a deus-ex-machina role as a
take-charge soldier who helps save the day. Rodriguez
has managed to avoid doing anything that would help
her to transcend her "just-one-of-the-tough-guys" image.
Since her breakthrough in *Girlfight* (2000) she has appeared in a host of action flicks that basically demanded
her to look gorgeous and shoot guns and display exactly
the sort of grit called for here: *The Fast and the Furious*
(2001), *Resident Evil* (2002), *S.W.A.T.* (2003), and *Machete* (2010), among others. Of course, she is drop-dead
gorgeous and totally believable as a marine, but hopefully she will age gracefully into the depth she has occasionally demonstrated.

The aliens themselves are only mildly interesting to
look at. The viewer learns nothing of their culture and

clearly they are in the film so they can provide a backdrop to Liebesman's this-is-what-war-looks-like aesthetic. The special effects in general fail at points but work best when the action is up close and fast moving, which it almost always is. Less convincing are the initial explosions above L.A., although this is nitpicking. As a special-effects extravaganza *Battle: Los Angeles* works just fine. Once the marines start their mission the action is non-stop. No doubt this movie could have been shorter, but even at 116 minutes there is an audience that will end up putting this on the shelf and getting it out from time to time with their other favorite B-movies.

Dave Canfield

CREDITS

Staff Sgt. Michael Nantz: Aaron Eckhart
Tech Sgt. Elena Santos: Michelle Rodriguez
Michele: Bridget Moynahan
2nd Lt. William Martinez: Ramon Rodriguez
Jason Lockett: Cory Hardrict
Joe Rincon: Michael Pena
Cpl. Scott Grayston: Lucas Till
Hector Rincon: Bryce Cass
Cpl. Kevin Harris: Ne-Yo
Origin: USA
Language: English
Released: 2011
Production: Neal H. Moritz, Ori Marmur; Columbia Pictures, Relativity Media, Original Film; released by Sony Pictures
Directed by: Jonathan Liebesman
Written by: Christopher Bertolini
Cinematography by: Lukas Ettlin
Music by: Brian Tyler
Sound: Paul Ledford
Editing: Christian Wagner
Art Direction: Thomas Valentine
Costumes: Sanja Milkovic Hays
Production Design: Peter Wenham
MPAA rating: PG-13
Running time: 116 minutes

REVIEWS

Ebert, Roger. *Chicago Sun-Times*. March 10, 2011.
Lasalle, Mick. *San Francisco Chronicle*. March 10, 2011.
Lowry, Brian. *Variety*. March 9, 2011.
McWeeny, Drew. *HitFix*. March 10, 2011.
Newman, Kim. *Empire Magazine*. March 11, 2011.
Phillips, Michael. *Chicago Tribune*. March 10, 2011.
Savada, Elias. *Film Threat*. March 10, 2011.
Scott, A.O. *New York Times*. March 11, 2011.
Starnes, Joshua. *ComingSoon.net*. March 18, 2011.
Vejvoda, Jim. *IGN Movies*. March 11, 2011.

QUOTES

LCpl. Richard Guerrero: "So what's your take on this, specs?"
Cpl. Kevin Harris: "I don't know, extraterrestrial?"
Cpl. Lee Imlay: "You mean like from space?"
Cpl. Nick Stavrou: "No Imlay, from Canada."

TRIVIA

Aaron Eckhart broke his arm while filming a stunt and never missed a day of work because of it.

BEASTLY

It's what's underneath.
    —Movie tagline
Love is never ugly.
    —Movie tagline

Box Office: $27.9 million

On Kyle's (Alex Pettyfer) online profile, he identifies his interests as "anything bangable." His "about me" section notes, "Hate fattycakes." This is not the sort of guy that most people would say is full of heart and character.

Except the students at swanky New York high school Buckston Academy do not care that Kyle is a preening jerk who runs for president of the Green Committee simply because he wants the title on his transcript. He knows the student body, who look up to him as if he were a cult leader, will vote for him simply because he is rich, popular, good-looking, and the son of a TV news anchor (Peter Krause). It is the reason he walks around school like he owns the place, and it is why he thinks he has the right to call Kendra (Mary-Kate Olsen), a student whose face tattoo, gloomy expressions and preference for the color black make people think she is a witch, "self-mutilated tattooed Franken-skank." Fortunately for everyone who has come in contact with Kyle, Kendra really is a witch, and she will not stand for Kyle's shameless cruelty. Soon she has cast a spell—she calls out "Embrace the suck,"a reference to a senseless expression Kyle used in his Green Committee presidential campaign speech—that renders this once-pretty boy bald and covered in scars and tattoos of trees. Never mind that Kyle is still thin and muscular with plenty of strong features. He and his dad consider him hideous, so dad quickly gets a place outside NYC for Kyle to live until his condition goes away. (Obviously dad, whose motto is "People like people who look good; anyone who says otherwise is either dumb or ugly," is a big reason his son turned out to be such a prick.)

The only way Kyle will return to his blonde, insensitive self is if he can find a girl to love him within a year. (The film is adapted from Alex Flinn's novel, which attempts to modernize the *Beauty and the Beast* fairytale.) Luckily for him, Lindy (Vanessa Hudgens), a friendless, bookish outcast despite her obvious attractiveness and kindness, always thought that Kyle had substance underneath his perpetual malice. Even though he never, ever showed signs of having an interest in anyone outside of himself or the image looking back at him in the mirror. Anyway, she claims that she has long respected Kyle's willingness to call it like he sees it. This sounds like only the delusions of a girl with a crush on the most popular guy in school since Kyle was never fearlessly opinionated so much as he was brutally insulting and disgustingly egotistical. Unless anyone considers telling a classmate that she is an "ugly cow" to be a refreshingly honest statement.

Since Kyle mostly refuses to engage with anyone in the outside world (with the exception of a costume party that allows him to blend into the scenery while he feebly begs Kendra to lift her curse), the movie must concoct a way for Kyle and Lindy to spend more time together. Thus, in a sequence that elicits unintentional laughter, Lindy's drug-addict father (Roc LaFortune) has a gun pointed at him and his daughter by a drug dealer who wants money. Out of nowhere comes Kyle in superhero mode to disarm the attacker and save Lindy, insisting that he will go to the cops and turn in Lindy's dad for killing the dealer's brother if her dad does not agree to let Lindy stay with him. Soon Lindy moves into the house where Kyle lives with Jamaican maid Zola (Lisa Gay Hamilton) and blind tutor Will (Neil Patrick Harris), who have become like a surrogate mother and father to him. The unofficial guardians agree to refer to Kyle as Hunter, so Lindy does not know his true identity and Kyle—pardon, Hunter—can use information he gathered by secretly following Lindy around town to make her fall for him.

This would all be contrived garbage even if Pettyfer and Hudgens were capable of emoting, which they are not. They both look pained any time they are required to show any degree of natural human expression, and few things sink a movie faster than two bad actors playing off of each other. Well, actually, something that sinks *Beastly* faster than that is a complete cluelessness about how to express that idea that self-esteem and character come from within, not as a result of other people's perceptions. Kyle may be disfigured, but he is still clearly a good-looking person underneath his scars and tattoos, which some girls would probably consider badass. And he is never forced to challenge himself,

outside of the challenge to be a non-terrible human being. He merely has to hang out in a posh New York apartment (which he constantly refers to as Hell, by the way) and wait until he can manipulate someone who already liked him when he was still a jerk to say the words that will break his spell. Clearly Lindy is not as smart as she seems to think she is, however, as she does not even notice that Hunter's eyebrows spell the words "embrace" and "suck." Most girls would probably have a question or two about that.

High school emotions operate at an extremely high level, and logic does not always rule. (In Will's words: "High school unquestionably sucks ass.") Yet that is not an excuse to fill a movie with embarrassingly hokey choices (immediately after Hunter gives Lindy a letter that says he might be falling in love with her, a corny song kicks in singing about falling in love) and the sense that the characters' perspectives are not only phony but totally warped. On the phone, Lindy whines about her protective exile, "I know it's life or death, but I've been saving for that Machu Picchu trip for three years." That is a laughable statement from a girl who is supposedly smart and mature but clearly has no trouble brushing off the notion of her own death. Meanwhile, she and the rest of the folks at school, who at one point announce, "The Machu Picchu bus is leaving in five minutes," act as if the Peruvian landmark is only an hour's drive from New York. That is going to be one disappointed busload of kids who probably failed geography.

Matt Pais

CREDITS

Kyle Kingson: Alex Pettyfer
Linda Taylor: Vanessa Anne Hudgens
Kendra Hilferty: Mary-Kate Olsen
Rob Kingson: Peter Krause
Will Fratalli: Neil Patrick Harris
Sloan: Dakota Johnson
Origin: USA
Language: English
Released: 2011
Production: Susan Cartonis; Storefront Pictures; released by CBS Films
Directed by: Daniel Barnz
Written by: Daniel Barnz
Cinematography by: Mandy Walker
Music by: Marcelo Zarvos
Sound: Patrick Rousseau
Music Supervisor: Linda Cohen
Editing: Tom Nordberg

Art Direction: Isabelle Guay
Costumes: Suttirat Larlarb
Production Design: Rusty Smith
MPAA rating: PG-13
Running time: 86 minutes

REVIEWS

Cohen, Howard. *Miami Herald.* March 2, 2011.
Cordova, Randy. *Arizona Republic.* March 2, 2011.
Dargis, Manohla. *New York Times.* March 3, 2011.
Lumenick, Lou. *New York Post.* March 4, 2011.
Morris, Wesley. *Boston Globe.* March 3, 2011.
Orange, Michelle. *Movieline.* March 3, 2011.
Robinson, Tasha. *AV Club.* March 3, 2011.
Savlov, Marc. *Austin Chronicle.* March 5, 2011.
Schager, Nick. *Village Voice.* March 5, 2011.
Uhlich, Keith. *Time Out New York.* March 8, 2011.

QUOTES

Kyle: "I just was scared that you didn't love me. And I didn't think you could because of how ugly I am. I should've known better. That's not who you are. You took one look at me and still said you'd seen worse. And somehow, when I'm around you, I don't feel ugly at all."

TRIVIA

Actor Neil Patrick Harris wore opaque contact lenses so he would actually be sightless while filming the movie.

BEATS, RHYMES & LIFE: THE TRAVELS OF A TRIBE CALLED QUEST

Box Office: $1.2 million

Michael Rapaport, star of *True Romance* (1993), *Mighty Aphrodite* (1995), *Beautiful Girls* (1996), TV's *Boston Public,* and dozens more on-screen credits, turns his attention behind the camera to translate his passionate fandom of one of hip-hop's most important bands into a documentary that works for both fans who know A Tribe Called Quest and those who have never wondered if they left their wallet in El Segundo. The resulting film feels a little bloated and loses some traction as it tries and never really succeeds in determining exactly why one of the rap genre's most influential groups collapsed under the weight of its own egos, but it also firmly makes the case that Rapaport probably considers the most essential to its success—if one has not heard A Tribe Called Quest, they have not really heard rap. With five hit albums in eight years and an

influence that felt almost immediate, this was a rap band that mattered far more than any does today and if *Beats, Rhymes & Life* is little more than a love letter, it is a well-crafted and toe-tapping one.

The film results primarily from a series of interviews conducted while Rapaport was on tour with a reunited version of the band in 2008, a full decade after the release of their last CD, *The Love Movement.* Perhaps Rapaport sensed that any band that splits up at the peak of their fame is unlikely to have a tour that is all sunshine and roses when they reunite but the tensions rise quickly and he was there to capture some of what it must have been like to be in a band with too many leaders. The members of Tribe—Q-Tip, Phife Dawg, Ali Shaheed Muhammad, and Jarobi White—are candid and honest about their history, triumphs, and trials while Rapaport also takes the time to interview dozens of former collaborators and admirers including DJ Red Alert, Busta Rhymes, De La Soul, Beastie Boys, The Jungle Brothers, and Common. Like a lot of legendary bands, the formation of A Tribe Called Quest seems serendipitous as the right people happened to become friends and get their music heard at the right time. Tribe was a part of an explosive New York rap scene and they rode the wave, becoming overnight sensations in the right circles and really transforming the art from the gangster subgenre in the late '80s. They have regularly been ranked on lists of the best and most important rap bands of all time but, like so many great artists, they burned bright but briefly, only releasing albums from the 1990 to 1998, including the pedestal-placed *People's Instinctive Travels and the Paths of Rhythm* and *Midnight Marauders.*

Beats, Rhymes, & Life is most vibrant when it is chronicling those early days and the impact it would have on the form. It is best viewed as a piece about rap and its progression through the '90s, including the development of peers of Tribe's like De La Soul, than it is a piece about a specific band. Despite the candid nature of the interviews, one would still be somewhat hard pressed to state specifically why this band fell apart or why they continue to jump at each other's throats when they reunite. Hearing collaborators and colleagues like the members of De La Soul bemoan the fact that Tribe got back together in the first place because they do not convey the same sense of communal soul they once did due to their infighting is truly sad, but Rapaport almost takes too distanced of a directorial role, allowing Q-Tip and others to tell their stories without offering the narrative in which to place them. It almost feels as if the Tribe members themselves are too close both in relation and time to the dynamic to understand how a band so important simply falls apart.

If Rapaport's film does not quite work as chronicle of a band's dissolution; it certainly does work as a chronicle of a band's importance. It is often as vibrant and alive as A Tribe Called Quest itself, clearly the product of a documentary made by someone who was a hardcore fan of the band that he chose to profile. A Tribe Called Quest meant a lot to an entire generation of rap fans and future rap artists. They undeniably changed the form and if *Beats, Rhymes, & Life: The Travels of a Tribe Called Quest* makes more people aware of their influence, then it was a worthwhile venture.

Brian Tallerico

CREDITS

Himself: Q-Tip
Himself: Ali Shaheed Muhammad
Himself: Adam "MCA" Yauch
Himself: Phife Dawg
Himself: Jarobi White
Himself: Mike D
Origin: USA
Language: English
Released: 2011
Production: A Tribe Called Quest, Robert Benavides, Debra Koffler, Eric Matthies, Frank Mele; Rival Pictures, Om Films; released by Sony Pictures Classics
Directed by: Michael Rapaport
Cinematography by: Robert Benavides
Sound: Joe Dzuban
Music Supervisor: Gary Harris
Editing: Lenny Mesina, AJ Schnack
MPAA rating: R
Running time: 95 minutes

REVIEWS

DeFore, John. *Hollywood Reporter.* July 2, 2011.
Jenkins, Mark. *NPR.* July 8, 2011.
Morris, Wesley. *Boston Globe.* July 21, 2011.
Musetto, V.A. *New York Post.* July 8, 2011.
Olsen, Mark. *Los Angeles Times.* July 7, 2011.
Phillips, Michael. *Chicago Tribune.* July 14, 2011.
Sachs, Ben. *Chicago Reader.* July 14, 2011.
Schenker, Andrew. *Slant Magazine.* July 2, 2011.
Webster, Andy. *New York Times.* July 9, 2011.
Weiner, Jonah. *Slate.* July 13, 2011.

BEAUTIFUL BOY

To confront the truth, first they had to face each other.
—Movie tagline

Everything seemed perfect. Everything would change.
—Movie tagline

Beautiful Boy is a wrenching, gut punch of a movie that unflinchingly depicts the devastating aftereffects of an adult child's murder spree and suicide on his unfortunate parent's lives. The film succeeds as a grimly convincing document of that horrific experience and as a blistering acting showcase for Maria Bello and Michael Sheen. Beyond those two impressive achievements, however, *Beautiful Boy* fails to achieve any larger meaning.

That the film is pursuing such a meaning is obvious from the pretentious, creative Writing 101 voiceover which opens it. The narration is provided by college freshman Sam (Kyle Gallner) who is reading an excessively symbolic short story he has written about a family's trip to the beach. The family in Sam's short story is, of course, Sam's family: father Bill (Michael Sheehan) and mother Kate (Maria Bello). Bill and Kate's marriage has been on the rocks for a long time and it seems to finally be breaking up now that Sam is in college and out of the house. Bill surfs the internet at work for apartments to move into while Kate surfs the internet at home for a summer beach house for a family vacation that she hopes will heal their marriage. When Sam calls home the viewer is given a glimpse into the small family's dynamic. Bill appears to be the archetypical American father, uncomfortable with both emotion and communication. After a few friendly but perfunctory comments he begs off the call. Kate is much more involved in the call and seems have been far more engaged with her son's upbringing than Bill. Both parents, however, do not understand their son. Alarm bells should be going off in both of their heads when Sam launches into nonsensical mumbo jumbo about snowflakes having six sides but both end their conversations with their son with the mindless platitude "study hard."

Then comes the shocking news that there has been a shooting spree at their son's campus. As they frantically call Sam's cell phone over and over again, receiving no response, the doorbell rings. It is the police coming to announce what is unimaginable for any parent. But the unimaginable gets worse. Sam is not only dead but shot fourteen fellow students before turning the gun on himself. Reeling with shock, Bill and Kate flee to the home of Kate's brother Eric (Alan Tudyk) and his wife Trish (Moon Bloodgood). The remainder of *Beautiful Boy* will chronicle the devastating fallout of Sam's actions on Bill and Kate.

Beautiful Boy is essentially a play and as such its failure or success depends wholly on its script and acting.

Fortunately, writer/director Shawn Ku's script possesses the subtly its complex subject matter demands and in the formidable acting abilities of Sheen and Bello has two actors capable of conveying the range of raw emotions unleashed by Sam's act. Ku's minutely-observed script nails the small, day-to-day agonies of an unimaginable situation: how a suggestion from a boss not to come into work is really not a suggestion at all; how a kindly, seemingly even romantic, inquiry from a writer whose work Kate is proofreading, turns out to be a not so thinly veiled effort to do research into her son's death; how an angry public that does not understand the murders blames the parents who do not understand it any more than they do; how strangers and family alike do not know what to say to Bill and Kate and how often the things they do say to them are things that both they and Bill and Kate know they do not mean. "You are, of course, welcome to stay as long as you want,"says Trish after everything else she has said and done has made it abundantly clear that is absolutely not the case.

Sheen and Bello expertly convey the tortuous path of Kate and Bill's emotional journey from profound shock and crushing grief to the tremendous guilt they both wrongly place on themselves to the misplaced rage they eventually direct at one another. Each parent employs a different but equally dysfunctional coping strategy in response to these emotions. Bill initially tries to minimize what has occurred, to playact the illusion that he has not been affected. Kate compensates by trying to become the perfect mother to her brother's child Dylan (Cody Wai-Ho Lee), retroactively fixing her son through her nephew. Meanwhile, unaddressed white hot rage slowly builds beneath the surface of each spouse.

Bill and Kate's too-long suppressed rage comes to a head in the film's fantastic centerpiece in which they explode on one another in a hotel room. Up to this point Sheen's Bill has been the quiet, reserved, near-somnambulant character seen on the phone call with his son. Here he opens wide up, first in a funny sequence in which he serves Kate a tongue-in-cheek three-course meal of vending machine potato chips and cheap whiskey (demonstrating the qualities that presumably made him attractive to Kate in the first place) and then in an eruption of screaming verbal violence in which he claims to have felt trapped in his marriage with a wife that smothered both him and particularly their son with too much attention. Kate responds in kind, equally enraged at the audacity of his anger given his historic absence from the home. If she paid too much attention to her son, she screams, it was because she was doing the parenting of two people because he was never home. The entire film has been building to Bill and Kate's confrontation and their volcanic, cathartic exchange feels raw and authentic. Ku understands how spouses, owing to their intimate familiarity with one another, are uniquely able to make arguments that inflict the maximum amount of hurt on the other.

Beautiful Boy is a harrowing, emotionally draining experience that believably recounts a husband and wife's journey through the six stages of grief. It is a painful film to watch and it is supposed to be. Ku is to be admired for taking such a grim subject for his film and treating it with the realism and honesty it deserves. If the viewer seeks a small glimmer of what it might be like to experience an unimaginably painful event, *Beautiful Boy* delivers that experience. But other than as a brutally realistic document of that experience, *Beautiful Boy* does not provide any larger illumination of its subject. As it began, the film closes with the dead son's story book narration and the viewer is left with the impression that the film believes it has succeeded in being something more than a case study of agony. It has not.

Nate Vercauteren

CREDITS

Bill Carroll: Michael Sheen
Kate Carroll: Maria Bello
Sam Carroll: Kyle Gallner
Trish: Moon Bloodgood
Cooper: Austin Nichols
Origin: USA
Language: English
Released: 2010
Production: Lee Clay, Eric Gozlan; First Point Entertainment, Braeburn Entertainment, Goldrush Entertainment; released by Anchor Bay Entertainment
Directed by: Shawn Ku
Written by: Shawn Ku, Michael Armbruster
Cinematography by: Michael Fimognari
Music by: Trevor Morris
Sound: Joe Dzuban
Editing: Chad Galster
Art Direction: Abigail Potter
Costumes: Cynthia Ann Summers
Production Design: Gabor Norman
MPAA rating: R
Running time: 100 minutes

REVIEWS

Ebert, Roger. *Chicago Sun-Times.* June 9, 2011.
Fear, David. *Time Out New York.* May 31, 2011.
Holcomb, Mark. *Village Voice.* May 31, 2011.

Holden, Stephen. *New York Times.* June 9, 2011.
Leydon, Joe. *Variety.* May 29, 2011.
Lumenick, Lou. *New York Post.* June 3, 2011.
Morris, Wesley. *Boston Globe.* June 16, 2011.
Orange, Michelle. *Movieline.* June 2, 2011.
Rabin, Nathan. *AV Club.* May 5, 2011.
Rickey, Carrie. *Philadelphia Inquirer.* June 9, 2011.

THE BEAVER

He's here to save Walter's life.
—Movie tagline

Go ahead. Laugh. It is to be expected. The movie, after all, is called *The Beaver*. It is about Walter Black (Mel Gibson), who copes with depression by speaking in a Cockney accent through a beaver hand puppet that he affixes to his left hand and leaves on at all times—whether Walter is in the shower, at the office or having sex. The movie's name and plot generate all sorts of connotations, and none of them suggest what the film actually is: A delicately told, insightful drama about mental illness that stands as one of the biggest, best surprises of 2011.

Something that was not a surprise, however, is how few people found out first-hand what an unexpected marvel they were overlooking. Aside from its name and subject matter, *The Beaver* had another major road block in its box office outlook: Mel Gibson. So much of an actor's career relies on likeability (or at least the absence of unlikeability), and the Oscar®-winning actor did not help himself in that department by having numerous, widely-covered incidents that suggested he is an angry, homophobic Anti-Semite. Those characteristics have made some people want to have nothing to do with him or his work, no matter what the movie.

If people are ever willing to give Gibson another chance on-screen (he may not deserve one off-screen), *The Beaver* is the time to do it. Gibson gives one of his best performances as Walter, who opens the movie floating on a raft in a pool but does not look relaxed. Walter looks drained. This is not a man who has thrived in the two years he has worked as head honcho of his dad's toy company, since his father's suicide. He has been worn down by a job for which he was ill-prepared, and that has driven him to a state of depression which has alienated his sons Porter (Anton Yelchin) and Henry (Riley Thomas Stewart), and left his wife Meredith (Jodie Foster, who also directed) wondering if the man she loves will ever return to the way he used to be.

Cue the title character, a hand puppet that Walter spots in a dumpster and, for whatever reason, feels compelled to pick up and put on his hand. It does not

stop Walter from trying to hang himself from a shower rod in a hotel after he leaves his house, but, after that suicide attempt does not work, Walter's attempt to jump from his hotel room balcony is thwarted when the beaver talks to him. Of course, that is Walter talking for the beaver, who, in the aforementioned accent, tells Walter that he is here to save his "god-damn life." Foster's direction and Kyle Killen's script treat this very unusual situation with exactly the right tone: What begins with the slightest bit of humor, as Walter cheerfully speaks only through the beaver and Henry delights in spending time with both, quickly becomes far more serious and urgent as the family accepts that this is really happening. Some mild comfort comes from the index card that Walter provides, explaining that the beaver is actually a prescription puppet as recommended by a mental health professional in order to establish a psychological distance between Walter and negative aspects of his personality. Too bad the card is a lie, and Walter actually has not been to see doctor in more than a year.

As all of this is happening, Porter continues to chart the ways in which he is like his father in an effort to then eliminate them from his life. While many teenagers feel detached from and annoyed by their parents, Porter hates his father for the things that Porter hates about himself. This adds even more weight to Walter's struggle to regain his mental health and perhaps reestablish a bond with his first-born. Until then, Porter is occupied by his commissioned task to write a graduation speech for the valedictorian Norah (Jennifer Lawrence), who feels she does not know what to say or how to say it. The fact that she is beautiful certainly increases Porter's interest in helping her, even though she also agrees to pay him $500 for the job. Though some viewers may doubt the progression of Porter and Norah's relationship, it is actually an intelligently crafted dynamic between a girl with bottled-up emotions (largely due to tragedy in her past) and a guy who is bold and articulate enough to help her release a huge weight from her shoulders.

Perhaps it is a stretch that Henry's excitement about the beaver inspires Walter to develop a new, company-saving kid's toy, which in reality might not even be moderately successful. Walter's colleagues' lack of protest about their boss' new style also seems far-fetched. The achievement of *The Beaver*, however, is not necessarily in crafting an air-tight, realistic story. It is about chronicling the way that depression eats way at the self and that person's support system—this is reiterated in that the Blacks' house is literally falling apart, a metaphor that is a bit too obvious. One of the reasons depression can be hard to recognize is the same reason it is hard to portray on screen: This is an illness that is very hard to identify based on physical changes. Yet

Gibson and the film dare to acknowledge the anguished emptiness that comes from depression and the lack of easy answers. Meredith tells Walter she needs to know that his old self is going to come back, and she even shows him photos during their 20th anniversary dinner to try to help him remember how happy their lives used to be. The beaver, dressed in a tiny, custom-made tuxedo of his own, is not having it. He reminds Meredith that Walter does not have amnesia, he has depression. It is a sickness that can not be fixed by flipping a switch, but it is one that can be better understood through daring films like *The Beaver*, whose blissful last scene is a fantasy of the way a person with mental illness, or a person who loves a person with mental illness, dreams their lives might someday be again.

Matt Pais

CREDITS

Walter Black: Mel Gibson
Meredith Black: Jodie Foster
Porter Black: Anton Yelchin
Norah: Jennifer Lawrence
Henry Black: Riley Thomas Stewart
Jared: Zachary Booth
Origin: USA
Language: English
Released: 2011
Production: Steven Golin, Keith Redmon, Ann Ruark; Summit Entertainment, Participant Media; released by Summit Entertainment
Directed by: Jodie Foster
Written by: Kyle Killen
Cinematography by: Hagen Bogdanski
Music by: Marcelo Zarvos
Music Supervisor: Alexandra Patsavas
Sound: Michael Kirchberger
Editing: Lynzee Klingman
Art Direction: Alex DiGerlando, Kim Jennings
Costumes: Susan Lyall
Production Design: Mark Friedberg
MPAA rating: PG-13
Running time: 91 minutes

REVIEWS

Goodykoontz, Bill. *Arizona Republic*. May 19, 2011.
Lumenick, Lou. *New York Post*. May 6, 2011.
O'Hehir, Andrew. *Salon.com*. May 5, 2011.
Phillips, Michael. *Chicago Tribune*. May 5, 2011.
Puig, Claudia. *USA Today*. May 19, 2011.
Rickey, Carrie. *Philadelphia Inquirer*. May 12, 2011.

Robinson, Tasha. *AV Club*. May 5, 2011.
Scott, Mike. *New Orleans Times-Picayune*. June 24, 2011.
Taylor, Ella. *NPR*. May 6, 2011.
Zacharek, Stephanie. *Movieline*. May 5, 2011.

QUOTES

Norah: "I waited so long for this lie to come true, that I finally paid someone to tell the truth for me."

TRIVIA

At one point, both Jim Carrey and Steve Carell had been attached to play the lead character of the film.

BEGINNERS

This is what love feels like.
—Movie tagline

Box Office: $5.8 million

Mike Mills' *Beginners* tells the story of a 38-year-old man named Oliver (Ewan McGregor) whose father has just passed away. Four years ago and shortly after his mother died of cancer, his father finally came out and declared he was gay. He had been married to a woman since 1955. Suddenly, life as Oliver once knew it has changed. His father is not who he thought he was, but is still a kind and decent man. For the past four years, Oliver has had to try and adjust to a new idea of his father. The movie goes back and forth between this period and the time after his father's death, while also occasionally going back even further to when Oliver was a boy being raised by his no-nonsense mother who displays some unhappiness of her own. Oliver's father insists there was love between himself and Oliver's mother, but that he was not really around to see it.

Oliver's father is named Hal (Christopher Plummer) has just entered into his first homosexual relationship with a much younger man named Andy (Goran Visnjic), a nice man, but one who assumes everyone who is straight is uncomfortable being around gay people. Hal is also the proud new owner of a Jack Russell terrier, who inevitably ends up with Oliver after Hal dies. Hal goes to clubs and discovers "house music," wears fancier clothes and immerses himself in a group of gay friends. Oliver, meanwhile, tries to figure out if he really wants to be in a relationship with a woman he has just met while trying to come to grips with the fact that his parents were in a loveless marriage.

Beginners has a lot going on in terms of character conflict. The loss of a loved one brings with it a series of questions uneasy to answer and choices even harder to make. Oliver is in a state of re-tracing his steps throughout his life and is wondering if he is in fact repeating his father's ways of deception and/or denial about who he is and his mother's mostly cold disposition. Oliver falls somewhere in the middle of these two primary examples of adulthood making it almost impossible to achieve a level of intimacy with another human being. Consequently, his new relationship with Anna (Mélanie Laurent) is on-again, off-again.

Unfortunately, writer-director Mills employs all of this with too many overly precious gimmicks that seem to undermine the drama taking place. Anytime the movie shifts to another year, Mills displays iconic images from that year while Oliver narrates and tells the viewer what everything looked like back then. "This is 2003. This is the President. This is what the sky looked like. This is what happiness looked like." And so on. Of course, it is natural for Oliver to remember everything via pictures, many of which are too idyllic for words, but as a narrative device, it gets old rather quickly.

The same goes for the dog. The idea of giving the dog subtitles is just too cute and a little too cloying. When Oliver inherits the dog, he gives it a tour of his apartment as though it were a friend sleeping over. He talks to the dog and probably imagines the dog speaking back to him, much in the same way Tom Hanks talked to a volleyball in *Cast Away* (2000). The dog tells Oliver that he likes this Anna person and asks "Are we married yet?" There is no denying the dog is cute, but it is usually a sign of desperation from a director when there is a need to cut to a dog's reaction. This feels no different.

There is also the matter of the meet-cute between Oliver and Anna. They meet at a costume party. He is dressed as Sigmund Freud and sits at a couch most of the time while other costumed party-goers lay on it and tell him their problems. Anna shows up and has laryngitis and cannot talk. She writes everything down on a notepad and this is how they communicate for their first few scenes together. He is, naturally trying to hide his depression and she sees right through it and is drawn to him anyway. When they take off their facial costumes and really see each other for the first time, they are gratified.

There is nothing really inherently wrong with this scene, except that it is part of a bigger problem with the movie as a whole. It feels like a stereotypical "indie" film with all the earmarks of quirkiness that have become staples over the years. When men are at their most sullen, why do they suddenly meet an eccentric pixie girl whose job it is to draw them out of their shells? The subtitled dog and the repetitive narration are also symptoms of an indie film that strives for an innovative narrative approach, but instead feels like it's playing by prescribed rules of what a quirky indie/humanist comedy

should be. The result is a movie that has all the right story elements and actors, but falls victim to gimmicks that end up keeping the audience at an arm's length.

Still, *Beginners* is better than the sum of about half its parts. Mills is wise about his characters and while many of its narrative elements feel forced the overall sentiment of the piece does not. The performances are all terrific and worth seeing. Many people will see themselves in these characters and recognize and relate to their situations. Why do many filmmakers believe that this is not enough for a film? Mills earlier film *Thumbsucker* (2005) was equally quirky, but perhaps it benefitted from the time of its release when such conventions were more unusual.

Collin Souter

CREDITS

Oliver: Ewan McGregor
Hal: Christopher Plummer
Anna: Melanie Laurent
Andy: Goran Visnjic
Elliot: Kai Lennox
Georgia: Mary Page Keller
Young Oliver: Keegan Boos
Origin: USA
Language: English
Released: 2010
Production: Leslie Urdang, Dean Vanech, Miranda De Pencier, Jay Van Hoy, Lars Knudsen; Parts&Labor, Olympus Pictures; released by Focus Features Intl.
Directed by: Mike Mills
Written by: Mike Mills
Cinematography by: Kasper Tuxen
Music by: Roger Neill, David Palmer, Brian Reitzell
Sound: Susumu Tokunow
Music Supervisor: Robin Urdang
Editing: Olivier Coutte
Costumes: Jennifer Johnson
Production Design: Shane Valentino
MPAA rating: Unrated
Running time: 105 minutes

REVIEWS

Bayer, Jeff. *Scorecard Review.* June 12, 2011.
Brody, Richard. *New Yorker.* June 20, 2011.
Long, Tom. *Detroit News.* June 17, 2011.
Morris, Wesley. *Boston Globe.* June 9, 2011.
Phillips, Michael. *Chicago Tribune.* June 9, 2011.
Puig, Claudia. *USA Today.* June 2, 2011.
Rickey, Carrie. *Philadelphia Inquirer.* June 16, 2011.

Rogers, Nathaniel. *Film Experience.* June 5, 2011.
Sharkey, Betsy. *Los Angeles Times.* June 2, 2011.
Simon, Brent. *Shared Darkness.* June 3, 2011.

QUOTES

Oliver: "Six months later, my father told me he was gay. He
had just turned 75. I always remember him wearing a
purple sweater when he told me this but actually he wore a
robe."

TRIVIA

At 82 years of age, Christopher Plummer won an Academy
Award® for Best Supporting Actor for his work in this film,
thus becoming the oldest person to ever win an Oscar® for
acting.

AWARDS

Oscars 2011: Support. Actor (Plummer)
British Acad. 2011: Support. Actor (Plummer)
Golden Globes 2012: Support. Actor (Plummer)
Ind. Spirit 2012: Support. Actor (Plummer)
Screen Actors Guild 2011: Support. Actor (Plummer)
Nomination:
Ind. Spirit 2012: Director (Mills), Film, Screenplay.

BELLFLOWER

A love story with apocalyptic stakes.
—Movie tagline

In the Spring of 2011, as studios began trotting out
their advertising campaigns for Summer blockbuster
hopefuls, one trailer stood out dramatically. Making use
of a single, stationary camera and flickering, grindhouse
ambience, the hyper-stylized spot featured a souped-up
muscle car, sitting alone on a desert road, with the name
"Medusa" painted along its side in large, block letters.
After the inclusion of a few select press quotes,
incorporating choice words like "fire," "alcohol," and
"sex," a lone figure coolly emerges from off-screen, steps
into the vehicle, and starts it. Then, with flames erupt-
ing from its modified exhaust pipes, the car kicks up a
flurry of dirt and rocks and peels out in slow motion,
leaving everything obscured in a cloud of dust. At first
glance, this trailer seems to be little more than a buzz-
hungry "teaser." But upon seeing the film, it slyly reveals
itself to be a perfect, sixty second summary of all the
primal—if somewhat fleeting—pleasures *Bellflower* spews
about the screen and the feeling of confusion that
remains once they are gone.

Bellflower is the brainchild of first-time writer, director, producer and editor Evan Glodell, who also stars in

the film. And his uniform command over so many
aspects of the production suits it well; his character,
Woodrow, seeks desperately to gain control of the world
around him and it is through his singular, distorted,
pinhole perspective that the audience is meant to view
it. Woodrow's story is set in the time-forgotten town of
Bellflower, California, where he and his best buddy,
Aiden (Tyler Dawson), both live. Their camaraderie is
based, in large part, on a mutual admiration for the film
Mad Max II: The Road Warrior (1981) and its enigmatic
fiend, Lord Humungous. So they spend most days
preparing for a forthcoming, post-apocalyptic world
they have envisioned, which entails the construction of a
homemade flamethrower and the transformation of an
old Buick Skylark into the aforementioned "Medusa," a
fully tricked-out, mayhem machine. But their project is
temporarily suspended when Woodrow has a chance
encounter with a brash and sexy free-spirit named Milly
(Jessie Wiseman). There is an immediate connection
between the two of them, based on a shared hunger for
the occasional bout of recklessness to snap them out of
mundanity. In fact, their very first date evolves almost
instantly into a careless, booze-fueled road trip to Texas.
So they quickly fall for one another and before long,
Aiden and Woodrow are absorbed into Milly's social
circle, which includes Courtney (Rebekah Brandes), her
flirtatious, closest friend, and Mike (Vincent Grashaw),
her dour roommate (and presumed ex-boyfriend). For a
short time, they all seem comfortable with their roles in
this new arrangement. But once jealousy and infidelity
raise their ugly heads, the protagonists—despite their
supposed readiness for the impending end of civilization—find themselves entirely ill-prepared to deal with
the violent falling-out between a small group of friends.

Upon its release, much of the hype surrounding the
film was focused on the do-it-yourself manner in which
Glodell made it…and for good reason. Despite being
created on a staggeringly low $17,000 budget, from a
technical and aesthetic standpoint, *Bellflower* is a marvel.
A self-professed gadget geek, Glodell actually built many
of the items used in making the film himself. Along
with the modified vehicle and flamethrower at the center
of the film—both of which were fully-functional on and
off-screen—he also constructed the one-of-a-kind camera
with which the film is shot, using a combination of
vintage and modern parts. This invention, along with
the fine cinematography of Joel Hodge, gives the movie
a unique look that is bleary, wobbly, intensely saturated
and in-focus only in small selections of the frame. This
hazy, dream-like tone is *Bellflower*'s greatest achievement.
It is supplemented by the sound of the film—the
dialogue is often delivered half-heartedly and tough to
make out (earning the movie some charges of "mum-
blecore"), while the bulk of the background music is

gauzy and lo-fi, featuring vocals either muffled or distant. And as the story progresses and the characters' relationships become further complicated and entangled, its various elements begin melting together: day and night, sobriety and intoxication, reality and fantasy.

Early on in *Bellflower,* the relationships between Glodell's characters unfold quite naturally. Woodrow and Aiden share an affection and a loyalty that will feel very familiar to anyone possessing the sort of friendship whose longevity defies common sense. Likewise, Woodrow and Milly manage to find fleeting moments of tenderness and revelation that nicely capture the feeling of falling for someone. But Glodell also portrays the men of *Bellflower* as boys refusing to grow up. They belong to a generation weaned on a pop culture cocktail of sex, drugs and violence and find themselves with too much time on their hands to merely daydream about it. So enamored are they with the post- apocalyptic world presented in the aforementioned Mel Gibson film, that they seem almost unwittingly hell-bent on bringing it about themselves when it does not come to pass on its own. So it takes just a small amount of heartbreak to send them careening over the edge and when the film erupts suddenly into a senseless, fiery bloodbath, it should not come as any surprise to the audience. But just because it feels like a logical outcome for these characters, that does not mean it is a cinematically satisfying one. This abrupt change in the story smacks more of the filmmaker's own desires, rather than any instincts that would drive these characters, were they actual people. So it is disappointing to watch Glodell tear down so quickly everything he nurtured so carefully earlier in his film, simply for the sake of cheap, adolescent thrills.

Much has been written about the simplicity and carelessness with which *Bellflower*'s female characters are portrayed. Save for a few select scenes, in Woodrow and Aiden's world, the women seem to exist merely as either objects of desire or objects of destruction. But while one could certainly argue that approach makes the film's characters less engaging, it would be wrong to suggest that it gives rise to any inconsistency. Like the cloudy lens through which most of its footage is shot, *Bellflower* never asserts to present anything other than the skewed viewpoint of one man…be that Glodell or his character. And as a director, he manages to display such astonishing visual and tonal panache, that the audience is unlikely to turn away regardless. From the moment *Bellflower* emerged as the darling of the Sundance and South by Southwest Film Festivals, some began hailing Glodell as an original and important, new voice in independent cinema. And he is unquestionably talented in terms of his boldness, style and resourcefulness. But until he learns to create characters that ring true all the way through to the end of the film, viewers may want to observe from a safe distance.

Matt Priest

CREDITS

Woodrow: Evan Glodell
Aiden: Tyler Dawson
Milly: Jessie Wiseman
Mike: Vincent Grashaw
Courtney: Rebekah Brandes
Origin: USA
Language: English
Released: 2011
Production: Evan Glodell, Vincent Grashaw; Coatwolf Prods.; released by Oscilloscope Laboratories
Directed by: Evan Glodell
Written by: Evan Glodell
Cinematography by: Joel Hodge
Music by: Jonathan Keevil
Sound: Scott Casilas
Music Supervisor: Andrea von Foerster
Editing: Evan Glodell, Vincent Grashaw, Joel Hodge
Production Design: Team Coatwolf
MPAA rating: R
Running time: 104 minutes

REVIEWS

Abele, Robert. *Los Angeles Times.* August 4, 2011.
Biancolli, Amy. *San Francisco Chronicle.* August 18, 2011.
Ebert, Roger. *Chicago Sun-Times.* September 14, 2011.
Goodykoontz, Bill. *Arizona Republic.* August 25, 2011.
Jones, J.R. *Chicago Reader.* September 15, 2011.
O'Sullivan, Michael. *Washington Post.* September 8, 2011.
Phipps, Keith. *AV Club.* August 3, 2011.
Punter, Jennie Punter. *Globe and Mail.* September 29, 2011.
Schager, Nick. *Slant Magazine.* July 31, 2011.
Travers, Peter. *Rolling Stone.* August 4, 2011.

TRIVIA

Evan Glodell and Jessie Wiseman actually had to eat several live crickets during there scene in which their characters meet while competing in a cricket eating contest.

AWARDS

Nomination:

Ind. Spirit 2012: Cinematog., John Cassavetes Award.

A BETTER LIFE

Every father wants more for his son.
—Movie tagline

Box Office: $1.8 million

Concerned more with people than policy, *A Better Life*, from writers Eric Eason and Roger L. Simon and director Chris Weitz, approaches the hot-button immigration issue from a humanistic point of view. The drama is a gently crafted look into the lives of a father (the tremendous and surprisingly Oscar®-nominated Demián Bichir) working undocumented in Los Angeles and his antagonistic teenage son (José Julián).

Carlos (Bichir) is a gardener in Los Angeles, but when his boss offers to sell him his work truck and let him take over his clients, it puts the Carlos in a tricky spot. If the soft-spoken, carefully "invisible" man buys the truck, he puts his low legal profile at risk. If he does not, Carlos will likely be back on the street trying to scrape up random jobs. Either possibility—deportation or financial insecurity—threatens the father's entire reason for working as he does: to provide, as the film's title suggests, a better life for fifteen-year-old Luis (Julián).

For his part, the sullen teen is unappreciative—he sleeps comfortably in the sole bedroom of their small home, seemingly oblivious of his exhausted father sleeping on the couch each night, and asks for money with no real understanding of how hard Carlos works for it. Luis' own dreams are influenced by the drug-dealing gangs around him. The boy believes he is destined to be wealthy without having to strive: He naively wants either a mansion in Beverly Hills or exciting, cool gang credibility on the streets. But when Carlos does end up buying the work truck, a sudden crisis pushes the father and son together on a quest to right a wrong and preserve their suddenly tenuous way of life. Along the way there is the expected father and son bonding, but *A Better Life* also nicely maps the difference between Luis' lazy, inflated notion of "respect" and Carlos' idea of honor.

Though the film shows the stark contrast between Carlos' life and those of the clients whose lawns he tends to, *A Better Life* does not dwell on class separation. Instead, through both Carlos' hard work and Luis' vague aspirations, it focuses on the hope that the American Dream is still available—highlighted by a lovely scene in which Carlos takes an ethereal ride in the truck through the city streets at dusk, watching the comfortable lives of others drift by just out of reach.

Nor does *A Better Life* serve up lectures about racism and other social ills (even the gang members Luis idolizes are shown enjoying time with their families), and while it briefly explores the nature of the immigration legal process, it does so entirely from a personal not institutional point of view. The film is not a harrowing or shocking polemic, but it shows, on a level not often seen in mainstream films, the daily realities of other undocumented workers: the struggle to find and keep jobs, the hardware-store parking-lots and florescent-lit restaurant kitchens, the less-than-pleasant living arrangements, the money sent to families back home.

Weitz achieves all this with an attentive eye to daily details but also to hopes and fears, balancing an almost dreamlike tone at times with a more pragmatic essaying. But the director is also aided considerably by Bichir's warm and weary performance. The actor brings wonderful nuance to Carlos' quiet fortitude, earnest dignity, and patient pride. It is masterful character work—never once showy, but never less than powerfully layered and revealing. While highly-touted performances like Leonardo DiCaprio's in *J. Edgar* (2011) and Michael Fassbender's in *Shame* were overlooked, Bichir's work was resonant enough to earn arguably the most unexpected Oscar® nomination of the year.

The film, however, falls short of pulling all its observations together into a satisfying whole. As good as both Bichir and Julián are, their characters are simply defined, with much of their on-screen dimension coming from the performances. The plot also works both for and against itself. The crime mystery Carlos and Luis are caught up in propels the story and sets the stage for the son's greater understanding of his father, but Eason's script also lets the more overt threat take the place of deeper exploration of the characters' interpersonal conflicts.

So much in *A Better Life* is admirable and compelling, from the performances to the moments of honesty and verisimilitude. Ultimately, however, the film does not get as much traction as it could, considering its dramatic resources. The relationships are a little too neatly formed, with the father-son problems too easily resolved, and too often when it matters, Eason and the otherwise very capable Weitz fall back on big, easy drama that has a whiff of soap-opera about it. *A Better Life* is left feeling like a fairy tale documentary—gritty truths and honest human observation wrapped in a gauzy layer of artifice. It does not make the film bad—not at all—but disappointingly not as rich and affecting as it could be.

Locke Peterseim

CREDITS

Carlos Galindo: Demian Bichir
Luis Galindo: Jose Julian
Santiago: Carlos Linares
ICE Officer: Tom Schanley
Origin: USA
Language: English
Released: 2011

Production: Jami Gertz, Paul Junger Witt, Stacey Lubliner, Christian McLaughlin; Depth of Field, Lime Orchard Productions, McLaughlin Films, Witt/Thomas; released by Summit Entertainment

Directed by: Chris Weitz

Written by: Eric Eason

Cinematography by: Javier Aguirresarobe

Music by: Alexandre Desplat

Sound: Scott Hecker

Music Supervisor: Charles Martin Inouye

Editing: Peter Lambert

Art Direction: Christopher Tanden

Costumes: Elaine Montalvo

Production Design: Missy Stewart

MPAA rating: PG-13

Running time: 110 minutes

REVIEWS

Anderson, Melissa. *Village Voice.* June 22, 2011.
Baumgarten, Marjorie. *Austin Chronicle.* July 8, 2011.
Biancolli, Amy. *San Francisco Chronicle.* July 8, 2011.
Dargis, Manohla. *New York Times.* June 23, 2011.
Ebert, Roger. *Chicago Sun-Times.* July 6, 2011.
Hornaday, Ann. *Washington Post.* July 15, 2011.
Morris, Wesley. *Boston Globe.* July 15, 2011.
Orange, Michelle. *Movieline.* June 23, 2011.
Rainer, Peter. *Christian Science Monitor.* June 24, 2011.
Robinson, Tasha. *AV Club.* June 23, 2011.

QUOTES

Carlos Galindo: "This country is a land of dreams. It can be a hard place, a cruel place. But it's where I work, and I dream of a better place for my son."

TRIVIA

Director Chris Weitz likes to do perform all of the dangerous stunts in a script before asking his cast to perform them. "That is why," he told the audience at a SAG screening of this film, "in my films there are not many scenes that require stunt doubles."

AWARDS

Nomination:

Oscars 2011: Actor (Bichir)
Ind. Spirit 2012: Actor (Bichir)
Screen Actors Guild 2011: Actor (Bichir).

BIG MOMMAS: LIKE FATHER, LIKE SON

Momma's got back-up.
—Movie tagline

Box Office: $37.9 million

When the closing lines of *Big Momma's House 2* (2006) suggested to the family who was losing their federally-sponsored company that Big Momma "may be back" while Martin Lawrence looked back into the camera, it was less a solemn promise than a threat to the audience who just paid money to help keep this franchise going. That was also about the time that another black actor was introducing moviegoers to his own female fat suit. Turns out the world did not need Big Momma anymore now that Tyler Perry's Big Madea was cornering the market twice a year. Five Madea movies later, someone figured it was a bright idea to go get some of that Madea cash. The spotted red dress, blonde wig, fat suit and Martin Lawrence were dusted off to give it one more go. Thanks again, Tyler Perry.

When he is not donning the dress and makeup, Martin Lawrence is actually Malcolm Turner, an FBI agent who in the past had developed a reputation as a master of disguise. This character element is introduced for no other reason than to make it more palatable for an officer in the post-Hoover era to so quickly jump at the chance to dress in women clothing without any of that tricky sexual identity stuff. Malcolm got a wife and a stepson out of the deal, after all, and now his boy, Trent (Brandon T. Jackson), is on the verge of college. Except he would rather pursue his hip-hop ambitions and needs Malcolm to sign a contract to get around those pesky minor labor laws. When stepdad refuses, Trent ambushes him on the job where he is entrapping some bad guy with the pun-worthy (but never used) moniker of Chirkoff (Tony Curran). Though no one will ever confuse this scene with the blown wiretap sequence in *Blow Out* (1981), the deal goes bad, Malcolm and Trent are made, and believing there is a leak at the FBI, the pair go on the run.

The only way out of this without Bureau assistance is to seek out the missing flash drive that Malcolm's informant hid away for his protection. Naturally, it is at an all-girls school for the performing arts. Hidden in a music box that the witness' friend, Kurtis (Faizon Love) a security guard at the school, may know the whereabouts of, Malcolm gets a position as a house mother and Trent becomes Jasmine, a student. Following in his stepdad's footsteps (he still calls him Malcolm) in more ways than one, Trent develops a libido issue with the perky piano-playing Haley (Jessica Lucas). He even arranges a date for her with Jasmine's "cousin," thereby not having to hide the rise under his dress whenever they are together.

While this only further implicates the series' broad theory that black men (even, older supposedly mature ones) cannot control themselves in the presence of women in any state of undress, there is very little furthering for this trilogy to go. Malcolm inadvertently talks his way into posing semi-nude for an art class, supposedly to further the stereotype that women have bad eyesight and cannot notice that Rick Baker was not exactly Malcolm's makeup designer. This is the first film where Big Momma has actually been put into a position to interact with nothing but women. Instead of learning some feminine perspective the way Dustin Hoffman's Dorothy did in *Tootsie* (1982), Malcolm's experience on-campus leads to the rather shocking life lesson that "a real man wouldn't risk his life for some girl." Passed down from father-to-son at the 99-minute mark before likely heading off to jointly boo James Bond, every superhero ever and those flaky gentlemen of the Titanic.

Logic may not have any place in attempted farce, but considering the bad guys are not even close to being on their trail, why go through the charade when Malcolm could just show up at the school, flash a badge, find the music box and close the case? Not even the filmmakers appear concerned with the FBI's mole problem since it is never brought up again. If anything does strike as interesting viewing the desperation act of a forgotten franchise, it is that John Whitesell—director of the second film as well—comes fascinatingly close to turning this into a musical. Perhaps inspired by John Travolta's female fat suit turn in *Hairspray* (2007), Whitesell stops the film for no less than five song numbers — and a sixth over the end credits — that almost gives it a charm to match the only genuine presence on display in Jessica Lucas. One of her duets with Jackson may have resulted in the director having just watched *Once* (2007) the night before shooting. Unlike that wonderful music romance though, the guy leaves the pianist behind not to pursue his own musical career, but to…actually he just leaves and there is no resolution to their relationship.

More thought has probably already gone into the *Big Momma's House* than the original pitch eleven years ago. What started as a half-cocked blend of *Stakeout* (1987), *Kindergarten Cop* (1990) and *Mrs. Doubtfire* (1993) has led to little to talk about its existence other than initially being a surprise hit in the summer of 2000. From *Some Like It Hot* (1959) to *Norbit* (2007) in-between, men dressing up like women will likely always have a place in the wonder wheel of comedic outlines. *Big Momma's: Like Father, Like Son* may have hit upon the perfect metaphor in forcing viewers to watch Martin Lawrence and Faizon Love play a game of fat people twister. It is uncomfortable, there are only so many places one can go to make it entertaining and the whole thing can collapse if you make one too many moves.

Erik Childress

CREDITS

Malcolm Turner/Big Momma: Martin Lawrence
Trent/Charmaine: Brandon T. Jackson

Kurtis Kool: Faizon Love
Jasmine Lee: Portia Doubleday
Haley: Jessica Lucas
Mia: Michelle Ang
Isabelle: Emily Rios
Origin: USA
Language: English
Released: 2011
Production: David T. Friendly, Michael Green; The Collective, Friendly Films, New Regency Pictures, Regency Enterprises, Runteldat Entertainment; released by 20th Century-Fox
Directed by: John Whitesell
Written by: Matthew Fogel
Cinematography by: Anthony B. Richmond
Music by: David Newman
Sound: Kelly Oxford
Music Supervisor: Dave Jordan
Editing: Priscilla Nedd Friendly
Art Direction: Mark Garner
Costumes: Leah Katznelson
Production Design: Meghan Rogers
MPAA rating: PG-13
Running time: 107 minutes

REVIEWS

Gibron, Bill. *Filmcritic.com*. February 18, 2011.
Honeycutt, Kirk. *Hollywood Reporter*. February 18, 2011.
Johanson, MaryAnn. *Flick Filosopher*. February 16, 2011.
Leydon, Joe. *Variety*. February 18, 2011.
Olsen, Mark. *Los Angeles Times*. February 18, 2011.
Orndorf, Brian. *BrianOrndorf.com*. February 17, 2011.
Phipps, Keith. *AV Club*. February 18, 2011.
Putman, Dustin. *DustinPutman.com*. February 18, 2011.
Schager, Nick. *Village Voice*. February 18, 2011.
Snider, Eric D. *Cinematical*. February 18, 2011.

QUOTES

Big Momma: "Child, Like my Aunt Yorima used to say: Its better to be alone with yourself for the rest of your life, than to be together with bad company for a minute."

TRIVIA

The actor who portrays Trent in the film, Brandon T. Jackson, was actually a 26-year-old man portraying a 17-year-old boy.

AWARDS

Nomination:

Golden Raspberries 2011: Worst Actress (Lawrence), Worst Support. Actor (Jeong), Worst Support. Actress (Jackson).

THE BIG YEAR

Box Office: $7.2 million

It was not hard to identify the guttural call of the American Bored Moviegoer as it emanated from virtually every neck of the woods where *The Big Year* was being shown: after all, most people have heard snoring before. Birding can unquestionably be an enjoyable pastime, but it is challenging to look on for very long as others are doing it and keep giving a hoot. The film does indeed glide along gently, genially, and utterly inoffensively, periodically making faces smile and hearts warm with some sweet schmaltz. It just also makes eyelids rather heavy.

The Big Year itself does no mocking, affectionately featuring flocks of a mainly decent and likeable sort who incessantly, obsessively migrate back and forth across North America with eyes peeled and ready for rapture. There is camaraderie as well as competitiveness, the latter particularly evident with birders devoting themselves to a "Big Year," ornithologically one-upping each other over 365 days until someone ends up perched on top for spotting the most species. (It is amazingly all on the honor system, and the winner gets published recognition but no prizes.) Such avian ambitions can be quite detrimental to budgets and absolutely pulverize nest eggs, not to mention prove problematic if there are mystified and/or miffed loved ones with ruffled feathers back at the roost. However, the film itself aims to be as harmless as a dove, a compassionate coo of a comedy dealing with both human nature and Mother Nature that is uncommonly devoted to all things fowl instead of foul.

"Most people live their lives with the brakes on," observed Mark Obmascik, whose bestselling 2004 real-life chronicle *The Big Year: a tale of man, nature, and fowl obsession* is the basis for the film. "What happens when someone spends a year surrendering to the one thing he always wanted to do?" The answer is that perspective can fly right out the window. However, complications can lead to clarity and freneticism to fulfillment by the end of such an all-consuming, quirky, and quixotic quest to have the top tally. For each of these protagonists who love all things plumed, it is a big year indeed.

Success that amply fills one's pockets does not always satiate the soul, and thus, with decades of lucrative business-building behind him, Stu Preissler (Steve Martin) is looking to get out of the rat race and wholeheartedly chase birds. There are those back at his company (Kevin Pollack, Joel McHale) who are hoping to tug him back from the brink of retirement, but, as Stu's enthusiastic swooping down the ski slopes symbolically indicates, he is more than ready to push off and leave past pinnacles behind.

If Stu is facing the descending side of life, thirty-six-year-old Brad (Jack Black) has had an exceedingly tough time even getting a foothold to rise above his lowly, lonely existence. Unhitched from his wife due to his unbridled love of birding, cash-depleted office drone Brad must now reside with his sympathetic mother (Dianne Wiest) and an irascible lug of a father (Brian Dennehy) who denigrates his profound predominant interest as a mystifying waste of time. When, for example, Brad eludes to a comparison between himself and a beloved bird "that everyone underestimates" because of its outward ordinariness, the character comes off as rather endearing. Obviously longing to be lauded, Brad and his aural acumen (he has an encyclopedic knowledge of calls) embark on what promises to not only be a distraction but perhaps his salvation from demoralizing emptiness, inadequacy and anonymity.

Apparently no one in birding circles is likely to emit an owl-like "Who?" when the name Kenny Bostick (Owen Wilson) comes up, as he not only has won a Big Year competition but did so with a seemingly unattainable count of 732 species. The sly, smug, and sometimes unsportsmanlike building contractor is most often referred to solely by surname. While Stu and Brad initially refrain from letting on to each other that they are doing a Big Year, fearful of stoking an opponent's ambitiousness, neither man wants to stir and spur über-competitive Bostick to defend the remarkable record that defines him. While it can sometimes be hard in life to see the forest for the trees, *The Big Year* shows that it is even more difficult to do so when one's eyes are kept fanatically glued to them for glimpses of nature's winged wonders.

All the zealous zigzagging across the continent that ensues gets mighty repetitive, and the continual display of dates along with ever-increasing species totals made some increasingly impatient for December. By the film's end, Bostick has won another Big Year but lost a wife. (When he gazes contemplatively at a couple enjoying their child, the poignancy of the moment is decidedly undercut by what a ridiculous jerk he has been.) Though Bostick has beat them, both Stu, who becomes a contentedly-retired grandpa, and Brad, now reconciled (rather unconvincingly) with his father and blissfully attached to fetching fellow birder Ellie (Rashida Jones), gratefully conclude that they comparatively possess "more of everything."

Made on a budget of $41 million, *The Big Year* did little business. While *The Boston Globe* had described Obmascik's book as "superlative" and "ebulliently wonderful" with suspense that "ratchets up," most reviews of this cinematic adaptation were lukewarm at best. The majority of moviegoers expected the proceedings to be goosed-along more potently by the comedic likes of Martin, Black and Wilson. As in his 2008 hit *Marley & Me*, director David Frankel reveals and revels in people's life-enriching connection with beloved creatures, now feathered instead of furry. The scenery and birds depicted are indeed stunning, even if some of the creatures are rather distractingly computer-generated. *The Big Year* itself turns out to be most comparable to an ostrich, as it never takes flight. The film is so low-key and languidly-paced that it would have been of help if a crowing rooster had been included amongst the other birds appearing onscreen as the final credits roll.

David L. Boxerbaum

CREDITS

Stu Preissler: Steve Martin
Brad Harris: Jack Black
Kenny Bostick: Owen Wilson
Ellie: Rashida Jones
Annie Auklet: Anjelica Huston
Jessica: Rosamund Pike
Edith Preissler: JoBeth Williams
Raymond Harris: Brian Dennehy
Brenda Harris: Dianne Wiest
Crane: Jim Parsons
Barry Loomis: Joel McHale
Jim Gittelson: Kevin Pollak
Origin: USA
Language: English
Released: 2011
Production: Stuart Cornfeld, Carol Fenelon, Curtis Hanson, Karen Rosenfelt, Ben Stiller; Deuce Three, Fox 2000 Pictures, Red Hour Films, Sunswept Entertainment; released by 20th Century-Fox
Directed by: David Frankel
Written by: Howard Franklin
Cinematography by: Lawrence Sher
Music by: Theodore Shapiro
Sound: Paul Urmson
Music Supervisor: Julia Michels
Editing: Mark Livolsi
Art Direction: Michael Diner, Martina Javorova
Costumes: Monique Prudhomme
Production Design: Brent Thomas
MPAA rating: PG
Running time: 100 minutes

REVIEWS

Burr, Ty. *Boston Globe*. October 13, 2011.
Ebert, Roger. *Chicago Sun-Times*. October 12, 2011.
Gleiberman, Owen. *Entertainment Weekly*. October 12, 2011.
Hornaday, Ann. *Washington Post*. October 13, 2011.
Lowry, Brian. *Variety*. October 13, 2011.
Phillips, Michael. *Chicago Tribune*. October 13, 2011.

Pols, Mary. *Time*. October 13, 2011.
Puig, Claudia. *USA Today*. October 13, 2011.
Rainer, Peter. *Christian Science Monitor*. October 14, 2011.
Scott, A.O.. *New York Times*. October 13, 2011.

TRIVIA

Both Steve Carell and Dustin Hoffman were attached to star in the film at one point.

BILL CUNNINGHAM NEW YORK

Box Office: $1.5 million

Most profile documentaries showcase someone who is either at the twilight of their career, in the midst of turmoil or at the start of a journey that will take them into uncharted territories at great personal risk. Many are about a life fully lived, for better or for worse, from the cradle to the grave. There is almost always an overriding theme that is at the forefront of the story, usually involving failed relationships. Whatever the case, the life in question should be worthy of a feature length film and should give the audience a sense of a real journey through one's existence. But every once in a while, a group of documentary filmmakers drop in on a life that has already been well lived and shows no sign of stopping or slowing down. These are often characters who are bigger than life, have boundless enthusiasm, and/or are highly regarded amongst their peers and colleagues.

Such is the life of Bill Cunningham and such is the nature of the documentary *Bill Cunningham New York*. Here is a man very much alive and still very much in love with what he does. Cunningham is a fashion photographer, but one who does not spend his days in a photo studio surrounded by big lights, interns and technicians. He is out on the streets of New York, often riding his bicycle through the heaviest of traffic while on the lookout for anyone who is wearing the latest fashions and, most importantly, wearing them well. He is not afraid to just walk up to a person and take their picture with the intention of using it as part of the weekly fashion spread in the New York Times. Many people have become semi-famous for just walking down the street and catching Cunningham's eye on more than one occasion.

Cunningham is eighty years old and still uses real film in his camera instead of going digital. Most people would have retired by that age, but Cunningham seems as youthful and exuberant as he likely was when he first started out. His photographs have appeared in the original *Details* magazine (who have released issues devoted solely to Cunningham's photographs), *Women's Wear Daily,* and *Vogue.* He is a fixture at Paris and Manhattan social gatherings involving fashion even though he is not the least bit interested in celebrities. He has never owned a television and he rarely goes to the movies. For him, it is all about how these people present themselves. While he does co-mingle with other photographers, he is not considered "paparazzi." More often than not, he is ushered to the front of any VIP line by anyone important enough to notice him.

Bill Cunningham New York follows Cunningham around for what seems like a year, maybe less. At the start of the film, he lives in a studio apartment above Carnegie Hall in a rent controlled space that barely resembles a real apartment. The place is a maze of filing cabinets, desks and stacks of photographs that have yet to be filed. He lives alone in an office that has a bed mounted on milk crates. There is no sign of a kitchen anywhere. He eats only when he has to and usually as cheaply as possible. At his age, he still eats unhealthy breakfast sandwiches and pastries without a care in the world. "I've never cooked anything in my life," he says later in the film.

The closest thing *Bill Cunningham New York* comes to in terms of story or conflict is the apartment being taken over by those who want to use the space for more lucrative means. Carnegie Hall used to let artists live in these spaces, Bill being one of them. He shares the floor with another photographer who has been taking pictures of Hollywood celebrities for about as long as Bill has been taking pictures of fashion. There is camaraderie there and neither of them want to budge from their living spaces. But Cunningham would rather not dwell on these issues. Life is too precious to him to start worrying about bureaucracy and disappointment. He has carved a life for himself that works perfectly for him and as long as he can still do that, everything else will fall into place.

There is also an interesting passage of Bill's career where his photos were used as a punchline to some mean spirited observations involving the people in the photos. *Women's Wear Daily* took some of Cunningham's photos out of context and used them as a source of ridicule (not against Cunningham himself). Cunningham was so embarrassed by the piece, he vowed to never work with the magazine ever again. That is not to say Cunningham considers himself a real artist. He is just too nice a guy to want to be a part of something so mean. He is not out to laugh at fashion, no matter how outrageous it may seem. "If it isn't something a woman would wear, I'm not interested in it."

Director Richard Press clearly has a fondness for his subject in the same way Cunningham has a fondness for his subjects. Cunningham's life is not presented as some

kind of enigma. He comes from a regular, working class family and he was drafted into the military at one point (which might go to explain why he can afford the life he has, but the movie never truly investigates that). In an uncharacteristic and refreshing move for a documentary such as this, Press waits until near the end to ask two questions viewers will surely want to know while they watch the film: What role does spirituality plan in Cunningham's life? Did he ever have any romantic relationships?

The answers to these questions and how he answers them are very telling, but they are also diffused with laughter and self-effacement typical of Cunningham. This is a film about a guy who is content with where he wound up and is not about to spend any time with regret. It is this facet of his character that makes *Bill Cunningham New York* an accessible piece for those who have little to no interest in fashion or photography. Cunningham could be a garbage man and his outlook and attitude toward life would still be a fascinating thing to observe for ninety minutes. *Bill Cunningham New York* may lack tension, but it is a film much like the man himself: Happy to be here, in love with its subject(s) and fun to be around.

Collin Souter

CREDITS

Origin: USA

Language: English

Released: 2010

Production: Philip Gefter; New York Times, First Thought Films; released by Zeitgeist Films

Directed by: Richard Press

Cinematography by: Richard Press, Tony Cenicola

Sound: Philip Stockton

Music Supervisor: Brooke Wentz

Editing: Ryan Denmark

MPAA rating: Unrated

Running time: 84 minutes

REVIEWS

Chocano, Carina. *New York Times.* March 16, 2011.
Ebert, Roger. *Chicago Sun-Times.* May 19, 2011.
Holcomb, Marc. *Village Voice.* March 15, 2011.
Lacey, Liam. *Globe and Mail.* April 22, 2011.
Lumenick, Lou. *New York Post.* March 18, 2011.
Schwarzbaum, Lisa. *Entertainment Weekly.* June 14, 2011.
Tobias, Scott. *AV Club.* March 17, 2011.
Turan, Kenneth. *Los Angeles Times.* March 24, 2011.
Vognar, Chris. *Dallas Morning News.* April 7, 2011.
Weitzman, Elizabeth. *New York Daily News.* March 18, 2011.

AWARDS

Nomination:

Directors Guild 2011: Documentary Director (Press)
Ind. Spirit 2012: Feature Doc.

BLACKTHORN

> *Sam Shepard is Butch Cassidy.*
> —Movie tagline

When *Butch Cassidy and the Sundance Kid* (1969) rode onto screens there had never been anything quite like it before. Irreverent Westerns were plentiful but none with the star power that Paul Newman's and Robert Redford's teaming brought to the table. More than even star power though, the film was a masterpiece of wit, adventure and style. It has aged gloriously over the years. The idea of another film that supposes Cassidy made it out of the final showdown alive and hid out in Bolivia only to become homesick in later years, is a compelling one. Sadly, *Blackthorn* takes the character of Butch Cassidy into new, territory, without quite getting where it wants to go. Beautiful to look at, full of solid performances Blackthorn simply fails to live up to the promise of its concept.

Some twenty years after he was supposed to have died, Butch Cassidy, now going by the name James Blackthorn (Sam Shepard), learns he has a son back home in the United States and decides to risk leaving Bolivia and his companion Yana (Magaly Solier) to make one last trip home, taking the money he has saved, in hopes of starting a new life for himself and his new-found family. But that trip is fraught with danger and that danger springs to life in the form of would-be bandit Eduardo Apodaca (Eduardo Noriega) who ambushes him, losing Blackthorn's horse and money in the process, only to wind up needing the aging outlaw's help. He is on the run he explains and will be killed otherwise, and besides he has money having robbed a wicked mining boss. All Blackthorn has to do is get him safely to where the money is hidden. Blackthorn, seeing a chance to recoup his loss, reluctantly agrees and the two enter into an uneasy partnership. Pursued by the mining concern, they gun battle their way across the desert only to run into yet another problem in the form of ex-railroad employee and washed-up drunk, Mackinley (Stephen Rea), who has always maintained that Cassidy did not die and who could remake his own fortunes if he was able to bring in the old man now. Meanwhile, Cassidy is betrayed not unexpectedly, and comes to a crossroads between his old way of looking at the world and the new path he had hoped for.

Mateo Gil is best known as a solid screenwriter having penned both *Abres los ojos* (1997) and *The Sea Inside*

(2004) with longtime collaborator Alejandro Amenabar. His only other feature as director is *Nobody Knows Anybody* (1999) which also starred *Blackthorn*'s Eduardo Noriega, and his lack of directorial experience shows here. *Blackthorn* looks great, has an even tone, and takes full advantage of the scenery, but it feels tentative everywhere else. Its skeletal story structure feels weak, uninspired. There are some mildly interesting plot twists here and a few compelling notions to go along with the visuals but the overall impact of the film is just too laconic and easy going to make the eventual tragedy resonant and the film never really rises to the level of anything special much less bears comparison to George Roy Hill's masterpiece.

Performances are solid. Sam Shepard is predictably perfect for the role of Cassidy, who seems gruff and used up but is still plenty savvy and handy with a gun. The film derives most of its humor from his take-no-shit attitude and he has good chemistry with Noriega. Rea is very good as Mackinley, a man who is sorely tempted to think he can recapture the lost years by capturing the one man who eluded him.

One neat trick has the story jumping between Cassidy's present day and the events that led up to the Bolivian showdown. The device is well used here and gives Nikolaj Coster-Waldau as Young James and Padraic Delaney as the Sundance Kid the chance to invest the character of Blackthorn with some much-needed back story and motivation. But, in the end, it feels a little disconnected from the rest of the narrative.

Blackthorn ends plaintively enough, which is to say that it clearly sends a signal about the unimportance of being a myth vs. being a man. But viewers may well still find themselves longing for that final showdown that never comes. In Westerns, the showdown is where the man becomes larger than life. In *Blackthorn*, the showdown is mostly just a place that makes a man have to hide out in Bolivia, dagnabbit!

Dave Canfield

CREDITS

James Blackthorn/Butch Cassidy: Sam Shepard
Eduardo Apodaca: Eduardo Noreiga
Mackinley: Stephen Rea
Yana: Magaly Solier
Young Butch: Nikolaj Coster-Waldau
Sundance Kid: Padraic Delaney
Etta Place: Dominique McElligott
Origin: Spain, USA
Language: English, Spanish
Released: 2011

Production: Ibon Cormenzana, Andres Santana; Quickfire Films, Arcadia Motion Pictures, Aiete-Ariane Films; released by Magnolia Pictures

Directed by: Mateo Gil

Written by: Miguel Barros

Cinematography by: Juan Ruiz Anchia

Music by: Lucio Godoy

Sound: Marc Orts

Editing: David Gallart

Costumes: Clara Bilbao

Production Design: Juan Pedro De Gaspar

MPAA rating: R

Running time: 98 minutes

REVIEWS

Ebert, Roger. *Chicago Sun-Times* June 13, 2011.

Goss, William. *Film.com.* October 7, 2011.

Holcomb, Mark. *Village Voice.* October 4, 2011.

Hynes, Eric. *Time Out New York.* October 4, 2011.

JimmyO. *JoBlo's Movie Emporium.* September 27, 2011.

Long, Tom. *Detroit News.* October 28, 2011.

Lumenick, Lou. *New York Post.* October 7, 2011.

Savlov, Marc. *Austin Chronicle.* October 21, 2011.

Scheck, Frank. *Hollywood Reporter.* April 25, 2011.

Sealy, Shirley. *Film Journal International.* September 30, 2011.

QUOTES

James Blackthorn aka Butch Cassidy: "There are only two significant events in a man's life: when you leave home and when you go back. Everything else is just the middle."

BRIDESMAIDS

Box Office: $ 169.1 million

Annie Walker (Kristen Wiig) is a down-on-her-luck Milwaukee singleton who just found out that her best friend is getting married. Normally, Annie would be thrilled for her BFF, Lillian (Maya Rudolph), but Annie is going through a rough patch: The bakery she opened just a short time ago has fallen victim to the economy, she has had to move in with weirdo roommates and the man she is sleeping with treats her like little more than a call girl. Worse yet, she has been forced to take a job at a jewelry store hawking engagement rings to sickly sweet couples who ooze love. She wants to mope, but she is willing to pull herself up by her bootstraps and step up when Lillian asks her to be the maid of honor at her wedding. But try as she may, Annie just cannot nail that either. Any shower or bachelorette party-planning she does is outshone by Helen (Rose Byrne), a bridesmaid pick from Lillian's new life in Chicago where her fiancé

lives. Helen is an effortless "it" girl; she knows the right dress designers, can plan a knock-out party at the drop of a hat and does not balk at the insane price-tag of the top-of-the-line dresses Lillian has chosen for her wedding party. Between Lillian's engagement and Helen's wealth and togetherness, Annie is surrounded by reminders of her failed adulthood, and instead of resolving to get it together, it only drives her deeper into despair.

At face value, Annie does not seem like the kind of character that can hold a movie together and give the audience a hero to root for, but thanks to a smart turn by Kristin Wiig and a refreshing and clever script, Annie becomes a pitch perfect everywoman whose fall from grace is as touching as it is hilarious. Ultimately, this is where *Bridesmaids* succeeds, in its realness. Co-written by Wiig and Annie Mumolo it is the only movie in recent memory that nails what it is like to be a modern woman without any unrealistic fronting. Sure, Annie happens to look a bit too-well put-together for how disheveled she really is (how many shoes can an unemployed girl have?), but it is easy to forgive her that when she is so upfront about the awkward sex she has. From trying to look Hollywood perfect the morning after a one-night stand, to feeling like no matter how hard she tries she will never look as good as whichever woman she happens to be comparing herself to, all the while exploring the insanity that is female jealousy, biological clocks and the effects of mixing valium with alcohol, *Bridesmaids* hits on all the things that real life girlfriends dish about over cocktails, just with a Judd Apatow twist. The result is an estrogen-laced version of *The Hangover* (2009) that delivers non-stop laughs. The tropes may be the same as those found in any recent male-centered wedding comedy, such as the motley crew that assembles to make up Lillian's bridal party—which includes the show-stealing Melissa McCarthy as sexually confident and linebacker tough Megan— a disastrous trip to Vegas and a raunchy credit sequence, but Wiig and Mumolo did not just insert women into a *Wedding Crashers* (2005) set-up and rotate the camera for a different point of view. The result is decisively refreshing.

But the real success of the film is Annie herself. In Wiig's capable hands she is a perfect mix of delightful and desperate, funny and awkward. Of course, it is not surprising that Wiig can do funny—the *Saturday Night Live* star has a host of memorable sketch comedy characters to her credit. But what is surprising is how effectively she makes the transition to relatable heroine and romantic lead. As Annie, Wiig is warm, cute and charming and commands the screen effortlessly. But what really makes Annie such a winning presence is that she is always on the verge of losing it. Wiig adds a hint of desperation to Annie that somehow makes her that much more real. If one looks closely behind Annie's lemon smiles, her cute outfits, and sleepy-sexy hair there is a woman ready to crack and Wiig builds her desperation so well that when she finally does break she has every member of the audience rooting for her. Annie gets to say to the women who make her feel small, everything that anyone who has ever been outdone, outdressed and out-coiffed, would want to say, and to make it that much better, she also gets to throw some punches. But though *Bridesmaids* shows that girls can be just as gross and funny and drunk as boys, it does have one shortcoming: the movie canot seem to get away from the notion that all a woman needs is the love of a good man to make us feel whole. Sure, it is great that Annie gets her guy at the end of the movic (who would let the adorable Chris O'Dowd get away?), but female viewers would be even happier if she landed on an inspired career path and started feeling good about herself too.

Joanna Topor MacKenzie

CREDITS

Annie: Kristen Wiig
Lillian: Maya Rudolph
Helen: Rose Byrne
Megan: Melissa McCarthy
Rita: Wendi McLendon-Covey
Annie's Mom: Jill Clayburgh
Officer Nathan Rhodes: Chris O'Dowd
Ted: Jon Hamm
Becca: Ellie Kemper
Origin: USA
Language: English
Released: 2011
Production: Judd Apatow, Barry Mendel, Clayton Townsend; Universal Pictures, Relativity Media, Apatow Productions
Directed by: Paul Feig
Written by: Kristen Wiig, Annie Mumolo
Cinematography by: Robert Yeoman
Music by: Michael Andrews
Sound: George H. Anderson
Music Supervisor: Jonathan Karp
Editing: William Kerr, Michael L. Sale
Art Direction: Keith Cunningham
Costumes: Leesa Evans
Production Design: Jefferson Page
MPAA rating: R
Running time: 124 minutes

REVIEWS

Dargis, Manohla. *New York Times.* May 12, 2011.
Denby, David. *New Yorker.* May 23, 2011.
Ebert, Roger. *Chicago Sun-Times.* May 12, 2011.
Lumenick, Lou. *New York Post.* May 12, 2011.
Morgenstern, Joe. *Wall Street Journal.* May 13, 2011.
Phillips, Michael. *Chicago Tribune.* May 12, 2011.
Pols, Mary F. *TIME Magazine.* May 12, 2011.
Puig, Claudia. *USA Today.* May 12, 2011.
Sharkey, Betsy. *Los Angeles Times.* May 12, 2011.
Stevens, Dana. *Slate.* May 12, 2011.

QUOTES

Lillian: "Why can't you be happy for me and then go home and talk about me behind my back like a normal person?"

TRIVIA

Before he came to Hollywood, Jon Hamm, who plays Ted in the film, was a high school drama teacher at the John Burroughs School in Ladue, Missouri where one of his acting students was Ellie Kemper, who plays Becca.

AWARDS

Nomination:

Oscars 2011: Orig. Screenplay, Support. Actress (McCarthy)
British Acad. 2011: Orig. Screenplay, Support. Actress (McCarthy)
Golden Globes 2012: Actress—Mus./Comedy (Wiig), Film—Mus./Comedy
Screen Actors Guild 2011: Support. Actress (McCarthy), Cast
Writers Guild 2011: Orig. Screenplay.

BUCK

There's no wisdom worth having that isn't hard won.
—Movie tagline

Box Office: $4 million

Several generations ago horses were a fairly familiar part of the American experience even for those who grew up with no personal firsthand knowledge of the creatures—staples of the Western genre on both the small screen and in major motion pictures. As computer-generated special effects have both opened new narrative horizons and lowered the cost of creating big screen spectacle, Western's genre prominence has receded under the onslaught of fantasy, science-fiction and decidedly newfangled action behemoths. Hollywood's love affair with horses, though, has remained fairly steady, at least in terms of its dewy textures and fetishistic presentation.

If dogs are man's best friend, then horses are often like vessels for their dreams and the better angels of our nature, as showcased in movies like *Black Beauty* (1994),

Seabiscuit (2003), *Dreamer: Inspired By a True Story* (2005), *Secretariat* (2010), *War Horse* (2011), and, of course, *The Horse Whisperer* (1998). It is the latter movie that serves as a sort of reference point for Cindy Meehl's richly textured *Buck,* focusing as the quietly charismatic real-life horseman who helped inspire both the novel and Robert Redford's film. One need not be a horse enthusiast to appreciate this involving and rewarding nonfiction effort—a profound and moving portrait of channeling misfortune into something positive, and far and away one of the best documentaries of 2011.

Horses are majestic creatures, but known to have their own personalities, which often leads to training practices predicated on harsh punishments. Soft-spoken, middle-aged Buck Brannaman, who travels all over the country more than two-thirds of each year giving clinics to horse owners, instead preaches compassion and respect, and in doing so underscores how this unique animal-human relationship is in many ways a metaphor for the challenges of self-betterment, and life itself. As Brannaman explains early on regarding his business, many times he is not helping people with horse problems, but instead actually helping horses with people problems.

The delicate illumination of his incredible gift—just watching him work with animals, and forthrightly explain the reasoning and successful results of his methods to others—is fascinating in and of itself, but neophyte director Meehl shades her movie with plenty of Brannaman's personal story, which includes the death of his birth mother and a terribly abusive early childhood. The love of his incredible foster parents, including the wry aphorisms of his mother Shirley ("Blessed are the flexible, for they don't get bent out of shape"), seem to have penetrated a protective veneer all the way to Brannaman's core. In turn, they serve as a powerful example of the roles that adult care, choice and focus play in overcoming fundamental disadvantages. This narrative double helix, of shattered past and settled present, provides an emotional and captivating portrait of causality. It is a trite and often over-expressed notion, the saying that that which does not kill you makes one stronger. But in the case of Brannaman, his disposition and moral fiber is so clearly shaped by the tragedy and abuse of his adolescence, and in stark opposition to the character of his father, that the maxim holds true. Brannaman's adult talents could not have flourished from a place of psychological comfort and settledness.

Economical in word and deed alike, but also slyly funny (in perfect deadpan, he cops to a lesson learned from Oprah Winfrey), Brannaman is a figure of such understated charisma that one could just plant a camera on him and have an engaging, perfectly fine little movie. But *Buck* is not merely a film of homespun, feel-good

homilies. Its emotional expanse extends far beyond that, notably in an extended sequence in which a woman brings to one of Brannaman's clinics an ill-tempered, ungelded stallion deprived of oxygen at birth. When the tense hazard of the situation moves from potential to actual, Brannaman politely takes the woman to task for putting herself and others at risk by raising and taking care of her horse in an irresponsible fashion. In crisp shorthand, he diagnoses some of the traumas of her life, which are manifesting themselves through her relationship with this animal. The scene is breathtaking, and shattering in its unadorned poignancy.

Cinematographers Guy Mossman and Luke Geissbuhler capture the above scene and others with an unfussy aptitude. Some filmmakers might feel the need to overcompensate for the tranquil nature of the material by diving headlong into editorial dynamism, and loading up on style simply for style's sake. Meehl, though, doubles down on meditative rumination. The film presents itself in a manner that parallels the way its subject sees the world—straight on, and without the filter of any high-strung impulsivity. Meehl then bolsters her movie with sit-down interviews with some of Brannaman's friends, family and clients, as well as Redford.

Documentaries sometimes conform to the reputation of being thinly-sketched yarns, dependent on little more than the niche curiosity of their subject matter. *Buck,* though, is a deeply humanistic film, rendered with grace, compassion and intelligence. The feelings it elicits linger with one long after viewing. Its rhythms and life lessons swell the soul, making a compelling, persuasive and heartrending case for the boundless capability of human healing.

Brent Simon

CREDITS

Himself: Buck Brannaman
Himself: Robert Redford
Origin: USA
Language: English
Released: 2011
Production: Julie Goldman; Back Allie Productions, Cedar Creek Productions, Motto Pictures; released by Sundance Selects
Directed by: Cindy Meehl
Cinematography by: Luke Geissbuhler, Guy Mossman
Music by: David Robbins
Sound: Jacob Ribicoff
Music Supervisor: Liz Gallacher
Editing: Toby Shimin
MPAA rating: PG
Running time: 88 minutes

REVIEWS

Burr, Ty. *Boston Globe.* June 23, 2011.

Dargis, Manohla. *New York Times.* June 16, 2011.

DeFore, John. *Hollywood Reporter.* June 13, 2011.

Ebert, Roger. *Chicago Sun-Times.* June 23, 2011.

Greene, Ray. *Boxoffice Magazine.* February 5, 2011.

Harvey, Dennis. *Variety.* January 31, 2011.

LaSalle, Mick. *San Francisco Chronicle.* June 23, 2011.

Morgenstern, Joe. *Wall Street Journal.* June 16, 2011.

Schenker, Andrew. *Slant Magazine.* June 12, 2011.

Weitzman, Elizabeth. *New York Daily News.* June 15, 2011.

BUCKY LARSON: BORN TO BE A STAR

(Born to Be a Star)

> *There are no small actors. Just small parts.*
> —Movie tagline

Box Office: $2.5 million

There are certain phrases in the opening credits of a movie that should inspire fear, loathing and contempt from any intelligent moviegoer. "Tyler Perry Presents" is one. "Starring Katherine Heigl" is another. And of course, "A Happy Madison Production" is a no-brainer. The latter is Adam Sandler's production, with which he has helped finance many of his best friend's comedic undertakings. Buddies such as Rob Schneider, David Spade, and, now, Nick Swardson have benefited from Sandler's enormous success and have been able to get their own projects off the ground, such as *Deuce Bigelow: Male Gigolo* (1999), *The Master of Disguise* (2002), and *Dickie Roberts: Former Child Star* (2003), all of which have been granted the coveted green-light from the studios thanks to Sandler's pull and namesake.

There are many, many more comedies to mention that fall under this umbrella and any one of them could round out a list of the worst films of the last ten years, but it is quite possible that Sandler's production company has hit an all-time low after being in the game for roughly fifteen years with Nick Swardson's starring vehicle *Bucky Larson: Born To Be A Star.* Swardson co-wrote the script with Sandler and frequent collaborator Allen Covert. That three people could conceive of a project so witless, desperate and devoid of cleverness makes one wonder just how bad a script they would each come up with if left on their own.

Almost all of these Happy Madison comedies has a caricature of a protagonist instead of a person people can actually connect with, in this case a severely buck-toothed Iowa grocery store bagger with a bowl haircut.

He is, of course, a developmentally stunted man-child who has never seen anything remotely R-rated in his life. One night, he visits his friends next door who introduce him to the concepts of masturbation and pornography. Ever so curious, Bucky does as he is told, pulls down his pants, sits in front of the screen while his friends play an old porno movie and waits for something to happen down there. The movie they are watching, though, features actors who look familiar. They are, in fact, his parents (Edward Herrmann and Miriam Flynn).

Inspired by this notion that his parents were once "big stars," Bucky heads out west to seek his fortune in the porn industry, still not fully aware of all that will be expected of him if he were to actually get his foot (or whatever) in the door. When Bucky arrives, he meets a waitress named Kathy (Christina Ricci), a vacant non-character whose sole existence is based on helping Bucky feel special and worthy. Her only aspiration in life is to be a better waitress at a better restaurant. Eventually, after an audition for a commercial that goes horribly wrong, Bucky finds himself immersed in the porn world and is soon ready to make his first-ever feature.

After being laughed out of a party by one of porno's biggest actors, Dick Shadow (Stephen Dorff), Bucky is noticed by one of porno's biggest has-been directors, Miles Deep (Don Johnson). Miles takes on Bucky and gives him his first real shot. Bucky has a unique (for porn) physical attribute, that of microscopic genitalia. He is also prone to fits of spontaneous ejaculation just at the sight of a near-naked woman. Bucky never actually "performs" in these movies. Miles sees this as a new kind of porn video, one that can make insecure men actually feel better about their own lack of manhood. Bucky soon becomes an adored industry folk hero.

A good comedy rule is that anytime someone is visibly trying to be funny, they are probably not funny at all. Everyone here is trying really, really hard to be funny. This is one of those comedies that subscribes to the aesthetic that bigger and louder equals funnier. Just look at Kevin Nealon's performance as Bucky's obsessively angry roommate, Gary. Nealon has been funny in the past, but here he just looks desperate to steal every scene without having any tools at his disposal. Christina Ricci cannot decide if she wants to play her role with sincerity or as a gag. Swardson has rarely (if ever) been funny and his creation of Bucky is a testament to that. Just because a caricature is sweet-natured does not make him a real character.

This is a sad, sad comedy. There have been funny movies about porn before. Kevin Smith's sweet *Zack and Miri Make A Porno* (2008) and the little-seen, but very funny *The Amateurs* (2008) come to mind. Even in a juvenile comedy such as this, the writers cannot even come up with clever porn names or parody titles. That should be the most effortlessly funny part about making a comedy on this subject. Instead, the audience is stuck with unfunny actors all mugging for the camera while talented actors such as Edward Herrmann, Miriam Flynn, and Don Johnson wander aimlessly in the narrative, which has been haphazardly constructed in such a way that it becomes apparent that there really is no story here.

One could argue that a comedy such as this can get by on a loose and even clumsy storyline so long as the jokes are funny. Yes, a comedy can get by on jokes alone. It does happen. A comedy with a good storyline and good cast that is not funny is merely unfortunate. The worst kind of movie to sit through is a bad comedy. A bad drama, horror or thriller can at least be good for some *Mystery Science Theater*-like riffing. A bad comedy has nowhere to go. If a viewer cannot laugh "with" a comedy, there is no hope of laughing "at" it. *Bucky Larson: Born To Be A Star* has virtually nothing going for it. The good actors who appear in it win sympathy and concern for their well-being more than continued respect.

Collin Souter

CREDITS

Bucky Larson: Nick Swardson
Dick Shadow: Stephen Dorff
Kathy: Christina Ricci
Jeremiah Larson: Edward Herrmann
Miles Deep: Don Johnson
J. Day: Ido Mosseri
Gary: Kevin Nealon
Debbie Larson: Miriam Flynn
Origin: USA
Language: English
Released: 2011
Production: Barry Bernardi, Allen Covert, David Dorfman, Jack Giarraputo, Adam Sandler; Happy Madison Productions, Miles Deep Productions; released by Columbia Pictures
Directed by: Tom Brady
Written by: Nick Swardson, Adam Sandler, Allen Covert
Cinematography by: Michael Barrett
Music by: Waddy Wachtel
Sound: Elmo Weber
Music Supervisor: Michael Dilbeck
Editing: Jason Gourson
Costumes: Mary Jane Fort
Production Design: Dina Lipton

MPAA rating: R
Running time: 97 minutes

REVIEWS

Abele, Robert. *Los Angeles Times.* September 9, 2011.
Duralde, Alonso. *The Wrap.* September 9, 2011.
Gibron, Bill. *Filmcritic.com.* September 9, 2011.
Moore, Roger. *Orlando Sentinel.* September 9, 2011.
Rubin, Nathan. *AV Club.* September 9, 2011.
Scheck, Frank. *Hollywood Reporter.* September 9, 2011.
Scott, A.O. *New York Times.* September 9, 2011.
Sobczynski, Peter. *eFilmcritic.com.* September 9, 2011.
Staskiewicz, Keith. *Entertainment Weekly.* September 9, 2011.
Tallerico, Brian. *HollywoodChicago.com.* September 9, 2011.

AWARDS

Nomination:

Golden Raspberries 2011: Worst Ensemble Cast, Worst Picture, Worst Prequel/Remake/Rip-off/Sequel, Worst Actor (Swardson), Worst Director (Brady), Worst Screenplay.

BURKE AND HARE

No job too small. No body too big. No questions asked.
—Movie tagline

There was a time not that long ago when a dark comedy from John Landis, especially one that featured a talented ensemble of energetic actors, would be cause for international attention. How then does one explain the completely dead on arrival *Burke and Hare,* a film that made a reasonable (for a low-budget production) $4.3 million overseas but could not even pass the $5k mark in the United States? Never expanding past one theater in New York, where it bombed, this shockingly inert film is one that future viewers will stumble upon and be hard-pressed to shake the quizzical look from their face for its entire running time. How do so many talented people make a movie so stunningly lazy, so dramatically dull, and so shockingly disappointing?

A pair of notorious Scottish serial killers from the 19th century may not seem like the most positive starting point for a dark horror comedy but Landis has worked wonders with this kind of edgy material in the past. William Burke (Simon Pegg) and William Hare (Andy Serkis) were actual men in 1827 and 1828 who were caught killing locals in Edinburgh, Scotland, and selling them to a local doctor who needed relatively warm bodies for his teachings at the Medical College (played in the film version by the great Tom Wilkinson).

The adaptation's screenplay by Piers Ashworth and Nick Moorcroft adds a few supporting players to the body-selling drama, including a rival doctor (Tim Curry), Hare's wife (Jessica Hynes), and a prostitute named Ginny Hawkins (Isla Fisher), who Burke falls for and hopes to help finance her dreams of becoming an actress. Into this cluttered narrative falls the villainous Danny McTavish (Davis Hayman) and his henchman Fergus (David Schofield). McTavish wants a cut of the Burke and Hare business, as he does with most of the locals in town. Local law enforcement led by Captain Tom McLintock (Ronnie Corbett) begins to notice when so many townspeople start becoming medical college syllabus entries and eventually get to the bottom of what is happening with Burke and Hare.

Rarely has a film been produced with less genre focus. *Burke and Hare* can not accurately be called a comedy, a drama, or a horror film. It does not fulfill the requirements of any of the genres, finding shockingly few chances at humor or actual scares from the man who practically revolutionized the form with *An American Werewolf in London* (1981). He would return to horror with less-successful results with *Innocent Blood* (1992) but that film looks remarkably focused compared to this one. Neither scary nor funny, *Burke and Hare* turns talented actors into mouthpieces instead of giving them a chance to show off their undeniable skills. Simon Pegg and Andy Serkis are two wonderfully talented actors, especially when one considers their skills at physical comedy. Given the down-and-dirty plotline here, one would assume that Pegg & Serkis would be allowed broad comedy freedom but they are shockingly restrained, as are Wilkinson and Curry, two more actors who feel stifled by a production that does not know how to use them accurately. On paper, this cast, concept, and director should be a match made in Hollywood heaven, which makes the lackluster result all the more baffling. The film becomes even more frustrating in the final act when it appears that the lackadaisical attitude that impacted the production was conveyed to the editing booth as the plot becomes choppy and even hard to follow. In other words, the film starts boring and just gets frustrating. Landis reportedly wanted to make a British comedy not unlike *The Ladykillers* (1955) but he ended up with one that makes even the Coen brothers' remake of that beloved comedy classic look like a masterpiece.

Perhaps John Landis has simply lost his passion for the form. He was a part of a wave of maverick vanguard B-movie directors, most of who have lost their creative way (John Carpenter and Joe Dante being two that come to mind immediately). Landis' late-career sins may be the most egregious of the group with credits like *Beverly Hills Cop III* (1994), *The Stupids* (1996), and *Blues Brothers 2000* (1998) making the case that his early success may have been more a product of luck and collaboration than actual skill. And yet critics raised on films like *National Lampoon's Animal House* (1978) and *The Blues Brothers* (1980) still hold out hope that he will find that flicker of life again; the one that is so completely absent from this bafflingly dull work. Given the international response to *Burke and Hare* and IFC's wise decision to keep it as buried as possible from the public eye, one wonders how many more chances Mr. Landis will be given to reignite a flame that has been burned out for at least two decades.

Brian Tallerico

CREDITS

William Burke: Simon Pegg
William Hare: Andy Serkis
Dr. Robert Knox: Tom Wilkinson
Dr. Monroe: Tim Curry
Ginny: Isla Fisher
Lucky: Jessica Hynes
Captain McLintoch: Ronnie Corbett
Lord Harrington: Hugh Bonneville
Origin: United Kingdom
Language: English
Released: 2010
Production: Barnaby Thompson; Entertainment Films, Fragile Films, Ealing Studios; released by IFC Films
Directed by: John Landis
Written by: Piers Ashworth, Nick Moorcraft
Cinematography by: John Mathieson
Music by: Joby Talbot
Sound: Harry Barnes
Editing: Mark Everson
Art Direction: Nick Dent
Costumes: Deborah Nadoolman
Production Design: Simon Elliott
MPAA rating: Unrated
Running time: 91 minutes

REVIEWS

Bennett, Ray. *Hollywood Reporter.* August 29, 2011.
Burr, Ty. *Boston Globe.* December 1, 2011.
Gant, Charles. *Variety.* September 9, 2011.
Genzlinger, Neil. *New York Times.* September 8, 2011.
Goodykoontz, Bill. *Arizona Republic.* October 27, 2011.
Holcomb, Mark. *Village Voice.* September 6, 2011.
Lanther, Joseph Jon. *Slant Magazine.* September 4, 2011.
Rabin, Nathan. *AV Club.* September 7, 2011.

Smith, Kyle. *New York Post.* September 9, 2011.

Uhlich, Keith. *Time Out New York.* September 6, 2011.

QUOTES

William Burke: "Six years in the Army I don't get a scratch. Ten minutes as a grave robber I get shot in the ass."

TRIVIA

David Tennant was originally cast in the role of William Hare but had to drop out before filming began because NBC, for whom he had recently shot a TV pilot, refused to allow him to shoot the film for fear of scheduling problems if the pilot was picked up.

CAPTAIN AMERICA: THE FIRST AVENGER
(Captain America)

When patriots become heroes.
—Movie tagline

The first Avenger.
—Movie tagline

Box Office: $176.7 million

With the release each summer of several big-budget, heavily-hyped superhero movies, it is easy to get cynical about both the genre and the increasingly formulaic structure and shortcomings of its entries. Which makes *Captain America: The First Avenger* an even more pleasant surprise. *Captain America* still plays by the immutable laws of such movies: It includes an origin story, trailer-ready special-effects action shots, and a superfluous and chaste love interest—plus, for good measure it even throws in most of World War II. However thanks to writers Christopher Markus and Stephen McFeely, director Joe Johnston, and lead Chris Evans, the film manages to work in all the usual requirements while maintaining both storytelling cohesion and a good amount of square-jawed, comic-book fun.

Captain America: The First Avenger certainly has its star-spangled hands full. It simultaneously draws from Joe Simon and Jack Kirby's original 1940s two-fisted comic-book tales about World War II's shield-wielding Axis-basher, from Stan Lee and Kirby's resurrection of the character in the early 1960s to jumpstart the new line of Marvel superhero comics, and from an ongoing 21st-century effort by Marvel Studios to build a massive superhero film franchise around the superheroes who eventually form The Avengers (a super-group that were to get their own film in May 2012).

To its credit, the film gets all that in without—at least until its final act—feeling like an over-ratcheted assembly line. *Captain America* gets rolling in 1942 New York with scrawny, scrappy, perpetually 4-F Steve Rogers (Chris Evans) trying to enlist in the War Against Hitler. (To pull off Rogers' weakling physique, Evans' head is CGI imposed on a much thinner, shorter body—the visual effect works well enough that the viewer quickly forgets about it, though Evans' deep voice coming out of the diminutive frame is somewhat disconcerting.)

By luck the would-be volunteer gets into the Allies' top-secret "Super Soldier" program. On hand to guide or growlingly scoff at Roger's efforts during a basic training/testing sequence are British secret agent Peggy Carter (Hayley Atwell), Stanley Tucci as an ex-patriot German scientist, Dominic Cooper's Howard Stark, and, best of all, a perpetually perturbed Tommy Lee Jones as the obligatory skeptical Army colonel.

However once beanpole Rogers is zapped with super serums and "Vita-Rays" and turned into a strapping hunk of all-American muscle-bound might and Charles-Atlas wish-fulfillment, he is not shipped off to fight on a battlefield, but instead dressed up in a red-white-and-blue costume and sent on War Bonds propaganda tours across the nation. Meanwhile over in Nazi-land, renegade jack-booted German general the Red Skull (Hugo Weaving) and his not-quite-as-mad scientist (Toby Jones) are harnessing cosmic powers to fuel world domination plans.

It takes half the film's running time before Rogers actually leaps into action as Captain America, but Johnston has an easy touch with characters and tone and he never lets things sag. It helps that as the Star-Spangled Man, Evans keeps his chin up and the snark down—his Rogers is aw-shucks personable without being sappy, and his ramrod heroics never feel do-gooder corny.

In fact *Captain America* itself deftly handles its themes of patriotism and propaganda with a careful mix of irony and sincerity. The constant presence of newsreel updates, Roger's stint as a war-bonds "chorus girl," and war-effort posters over the credits are nods to Captain America's original comic-book role as a baseball, Mom, and apple pie wartime symbol (the hero's costume is literally wrapped in the American flag), but Johnston and Evans neatly keep the focus on Rogers the man and his personal values. (He says he does not *want* to kill anyone, but hates bullies.)

Most of all, Johnston understands the thrilling pulp heart of the film. He treats *Captain America,* with its super serums and villainous Alpine lairs (where Weaving mugs with relish as Wagner operas play) more like a 1940s pulp serial than a flashy modern super-hero movie. (At least until the end, when Cap and the film are clumsily recruited to set the stage for *The Avengers* film.) Johnston is a smoothly confident, sturdy director—by putting characters first over empty action and never treating their earnestness as a joke, he makes the potential clichés in *Captain America: The First Avenger* play out as old-fashioned movie fun.

Locke Peterseim

CREDITS

Steve Rogers/Captain America: Chris Evans
Peggy Carter: Hayley Atwell
Johann Schmidt/Red Skull: Hugo Weaving
James 'Bucky' Barnes: Sebastian Stan
Arnim Zola: Toby Jones
Howard Stark: Dominic Cooper
Col. Chester Phillips: Tommy Lee Jones
Abraham Erskine: Stanley Tucci
Dum Dum Dugan: Neal McDonough
Heinz Kruger: Richard Armitage
Nick Fury: Samuel L. Jackson
Origin: USA
Language: English
Released: 2011
Production: Kevin Feige, Amir Madani; Marvel Studios; released by Paramount Pictures
Directed by: Joe Johnston

Written by: Christopher Markus, Stephen McFeely
Cinematography by: Shelly Johnson
Music by: Alan Silvestri
Sound: Howell Gibbens
Music Supervisor: Dave Jordan
Editing: Robert Dalva, Jeffrey Ford
Art Direction: John Dexter, Chris Lowe, Andy Nicholson
Costumes: Anna Sheppard
Production Design: Rick Heinrichs
MPAA rating: PG-13
Running time: 121 minutes

REVIEWS

Ebert, Roger. *Chicago Sun-Times.* July 20, 2011.
Hornaday, Ann. *Washington Post.* July 21, 2011.
Levy, Shawn. *Oregonian.* July 21, 2011.
Longworth, Karina. *Village Voice.* July 20, 2011.
Phillips, Michael. *Chicago Tribune.* July 21, 2011.
Robinson, Tasha. *AV Club.* July 21, 2011.
Rodriguez, Rene. *Miami Herald.* July 20, 2011.
Scott, A.O. *New York Times.* July 21, 2011.
Turan, Kenneth. *Los Angeles Times.* July 22, 2011.
Zacharek, Stephanie. *Movieline.* July 21, 2011.

QUOTES

Abraham Erskine: "Whatever happens tomorrow you must promise me one thing. That you will stay who you are. Not a perfect soldier, but a good man."

TRIVIA

Jon Favreau was originally chosen by Marvel Studios to direct the Captain America film, but he decided to direct *Iron Man* insdtead. Similarly, Nick Cassavetes, who was also considered to direct this film, had also been set to direct *Iron Man* at one point.

CARNAGE

A new comedy of no manners.
    —Movie tagline

Box Office: $2.4 million

Yasmine Reza's award-winning play *God of Carnage* has been produced in multiple languages around the world on its way to what seemed like an inevitable film adaptation. Theatre pieces this dynamic and well-received always find their way to celluloid, but this piece seemed particularly challenging given the fact that the entirety of the drama takes place in one room between four characters. This has not stopped the movie-making machine in the past and there have been quality adaptations of small-cast plays from Mike Nichols' *Who's Afraid of Virginia Woolf?* (1966) to William Friedkin's *Bug* (2006), and dozens in-between. In fact, the Oscar®-winning and living legend director Roman Polanski has experience with adapting a limited-cast piece for the big screen with his well-received *Death and the Maiden* (2004), based on the play by Ariel Dorfman. Add his experience with stage-to-screen to the fact that he has long excelled at tense dramas with only a few characters (*Knife in the Water* [1962], *Cul-de-sac* [1966], and *Bitter Moon* [2002]) and *Carnage* seemed like a slam dunk, especially after the controversial filmmaker cast three Oscar® winners and threw them in a room with a fourth actor who had also been nominated for moviemaking's biggest award. With one of 2011's most pedigreed casts and one of the best living directors adapting one of Broadway's most beloved dramas, it was somewhat surprising how flatly *Carnage* was received by the movie-watching community. There are underrated elements here that work and flashes of the film that could have been, but they are off-set by a few crucial mistakes on every level, from some shallow character choices to a misguided prologue to even the sense that Polanski's heart was not completely in this production. After delivering one of the finest films of his amazing career just the year before in *The Ghost Writer* (2010), it was sad to see that the resurgence was short-lived.

Perhaps the most notable change that Reza made to her own source material (which she co-adapted with Roman Polanski) was that the previously-unseen action that incites the drama of the play is now seen, albeit in a long shot. A group of boys is playing in a park when one hits another with a stick, causing him to lose two teeth, viewers later learn. Seeing the violence of the act, however it may be explained or excused later, was a serious mistake. Whether or not the assault even happened is open to question in the original, but it is no longer in the film version, and closing the film with the kids in the park yet again was an equal mistake. A filmmaker could have chosen to open up the action of *God of Carnage* entirely, taking it to different locales, but the half-assed decision to provide nothing but prologue and epilogue merely highlights the theatricality of what comes in-between. It is the filmmaker's most egregious mistake on a screenwriting level.

The prologue ends, leading into the bulk of the piece—a parental conference between the parents of the stick-wielding child and his victim. The parents of the assaulter, Alan (Christoph Waltz) and Nancy Cowan (Kate Winslet) are at the New York apartment of the parents of the victim, Michael (John C. Reilly) and Penelope Longstreet (Jodie Foster). The Longstreets are naturally a bit perturbed that their son has been violently hit but the meeting between the two sets of parents

seems, at first, to be going off without a hitch. Sure, there is a bit of correction to the apologetic letter being drafted, but the Cowans are apologetic and the Longstreets make good hosts, even delivering some homemade cobbler on their well-organized coffee table. Tensions begin to rise when Michael reveals that he left his daughter's hamster in the streets of New York to die (which seems morally reprehensible to everyone, even his wife) and after Nancy throws up all over Penelope's beloved art books. It does not help that Alan is constantly answering work calls as if he is in his office while the other three people in the room basically stare at each other waiting for him to be done. There is clearly a disconnect between these New York couples and it is obvious to even those unfamiliar with the source material that the happy agreement about how to put this incident behind them is surely going to go sour.

How the détente turns into bickering is the art of the piece. There will be no grand plot twists or even excursions outside of the New York apartment and so the film relies heavily on the slowly increasing tension of people revealing how much they really do not like each other. However, viewers may be surprised at how slowly and, ultimately, inadequately, the tension rises. Whereas a piece like *Woolf* unearthed long-and-poorly-buried skeletons on one drunken evening, *Carnage* introduces viewers to two couples who would never interact if not for their fighting children and makes the case that they will probably never interact again. The overall dramatic purpose of the piece seems somewhat inert, especially for a director as typically vibrant as Roman Polanski, resulting in a film that exists almost purely as a performance piece.

Thankfully, an amazingly talented group of performers were assembled to pull it off. Perhaps most surprisingly, Waltz (Oscar® winner for *Inglourious Basterds* [2009]) steals the piece, finding the perfect rhythm (if not the perfect accent) for a businessman who barely cares about his wife and son much less the parents of one of his son's classmates. Where so many actors would have painted Alan Cowan as an archetypal yuppie, always chatting on his cell phone and distant even when he is pretending not to be, Waltz makes so many smart decisions here, including when he seems to find honest amusement in the increasingly drunken antics of the people around him. As played by Waltz, Alan does not think he is above what is going on in this middle-class apartment, because that would imply he cares enough to think anything about it at all. Jodie Foster (Oscar® winner for *The Accuses* [1988] and *The Silence of the Lambs* [1990]) makes smart decisions throughout as well, especially as her barely-covered insecurity begins to peek through and eventually cascade over the walls she has put up around her. Penelope Longstreet is relatively unstable, and loses all relativity when she starts drinking in the final act. One could argue that Foster is a bit over the top here, but she gives the piece its most life, offering a volatile counterpart to the acting decisions made by the other three performers.

As for Kate Winslet and John C. Reilly, the former does nothing at all to dismiss the idea that she is the best actress of her generation but is saddled with the most under-written role in the drama and the latter does his best with a role for which he does not seem naturally suited. Neither are particularly bad here but as the very-short piece (under 80 minutes) begins to wrap up, it is hard to shake the feeling that instead of a film in which all four actors felt equally involved, Winslet and Reilly took a back seat at some point in the production to the other two. In particular, it feels like Reza, Polanski, and Winslet never quite figured out this version of Nancy Cowan. She is a woman with an upset stomach, a violent son, and a distant husband, but she gets lost without much actual development of her own.

In the end, *Carnage* led most viewers to express surprise that Reza's play was as acclaimed and award-winning as it was on the stage. Given the strength of the performers who have brought these characters to life in front of an audience, there is something about the energy of seeing them work mere feet from the action that simply cannot be translated to the big screen. It is not like these four actors and their director are not capable of delivering powerful drama, but something about this one lost its deific power along the way.

Brian Tallerico

CREDITS

Penelope Longstreet: Jodie Foster
Nancy Cowen: Kate Winslet
Alan Cowen: Christoph Waltz
Michael Longstreet: John C. Reilly
Origin: France, Germany, Poland, Spain
Language: English
Released: 2011
Production: Said Ben Said; SBS Films, Constantin Film, SPI, France 2 Cinema; released by Sony Pictures Classics
Directed by: Roman Polanski
Written by: Roman Polanski, Yasmina Reza
Cinematography by: Pawel Edelman
Music by: Alexandre Desplat
Sound: Jean-Marie Blondel
Editing: Herve De Luze
Costumes: Milena Canonero
Production Design: Dean Tavoularis

MPAA rating: R
Running time: 79 minutes

REVIEWS

Kohn, Eric. *IndieWIRE.* October 4, 2011.
Lumenick, Lou. *New York Post.* September 30, 2011.
McCarthy, Todd. *Hollywood Reporter.* September 30, 2011.
Mondello, Bob. *NPR.* December 16, 2011.
Rabin, Nathan. *AV Club.* December 14, 2011.
Reed, Rex. *New York Observer.* December 14, 2011.
Rothkopf, Joshua. *Time Out New York.* December 13, 2011.
Stevens, Dana. *Slate.* December 16, 2011.
Turan, Kenneth. *Los Angeles Times.* December 15, 2011.
Zacharek, Stephanie. *Movieline.* December 15, 2011.

QUOTES

Alan Cowan: "I saw your friend Jane Fonda on TV the other day. Made me want to run out and buy a poster from the Ku Klux Klan."

TRIVIA

Director Roman Polanski makes a brief cameo as the neighbor who opens the door to see what is happening in the hallway.

AWARDS

Nomination:

Golden Globes 2012: Actress—Mus./Comedy (Foster), Actress—Mus./Comedy (Winslet).

CARS 2

Box Office: $191.5 million

It would be fair to say that for fifteen years Pixar Studios had a flawless track record, having produced not only one huge hit after another but hits that were unquestionably good-to-truly-great films. In that time period, their least regarded film had been *Cars* (2006), which did good business but failed to hold the attention of critics who faulted it as boring. It was a very curious assessment. *Cars* is a breathtakingly beautiful, very funny, and solidly heartwarming film, full of memorable characters that tells a solid story. To call *Cars* a weak link in the history of Pixar is to say hardly anything at all. Sadly the same is not true of *Cars 2,* which relies less on character and more on visual pyrotechnics to hold viewer attention and fails to do so.

The film starts out with an entirely new set of characters, all cars, involved in international espionage that could affect vehicles everywhere. Viewers meet Le-land Turbo (Jason Isaacs) desperately relaying a secret message to headquarters which is received by Finn McMissile (Michael Caine) who arrives too late and finds himself in a race to the death against a bunch of "lemons."

Meanwhile, Lightning McQueen (Owen Wilson), fresh off winning his 4th Piston Cup, arrives back in Radiator Springs for a visit only to find best friend Mater (Larry the Cable Guy) monopolizing every waking moment, especially the moments McQueen wants to share with Sally (Bonnie Hunt). During their conflict they catch a news report about Miles Axelrod (Eddie Izzard), a famous millionaire philanthropist who has developed a new fuel called Allinol, which may prevent the looming worldwide fuel crisis and which he plans to debut at his sponsored race The World Grand Prix. McQueen finds himself dragged into the race when Mater picks a fight with race car Francesco Bernoulli (John Turturro). Dragging the pit crew with them, McQueen and Mater find themselves in Japan prepping for the ultimate grudge match, fighting a media blitz, and suddenly unsure about how deep their friendship really runs.

About this time, Mater is mistaken for an agent by both the good guys led by McMissile and the mysterious lemons who pursue him in a series of high octane chases. Together with Agent Holly Shiftwell (Emily Mortimer), Mater uncovers a diabolical plot to use Allinol to destroy the fuel economy and blow up McQueen during the big race. Desperate to contact McQueen, who is no longer speaking to him, Mater must uncover the mysterious mastermind behind the lemon conspiracy or lose his friend forever.

The real problem here is the lack of a cohesive simple story. Viewers get a complicated spy yarn, the big race, and a coming-of0age story for Mater. Add in a couple of romances and the fact that *Cars 2* takes place over several continents, and nothing has a chance to gel into anything compelling. These problems, and a series of visually inventive (if too numerous) action sequences create a sense of hyperactive bloat. Though directors John Lasseter and Brad Lewis share story credit it should be remarked that Dan Fogelman is also story credited and Ben Queen is credited with the actual screenplay. A casual glance at both Queen's and Fogelman's resumes reveals some bad writing indeed. Queen has worked mainly in TV having created the show *Drive*. He does not prove himself ready to move on to bigger things here. Fogelman shares credit for the original *Cars* screenplay with fourteen other writers, which has to be some kind of record. His other credits include an equal number of misses and hits; the disappointing *Fred Claus* (2007) and *Bolt* (2008), the solid *Crazy, Stupid Love* (2011), and the very, very entertaining *Tangled* (2010). One thing *Cars* had going for it in spades was the amaz-

ing backgrounds and desert vistas. Whether that film was on the race track or presenting a beautiful sunset it was gorgeous to look at without seeming like it was trying too hard, it was almost 3D in its visual impact. *Cars 2*, which actually is in 3D, comes across as dramatically flat and paint by the emotional numbers, even as would-be thrilling visuals whiz by in spasms and flashes. Few of the action sequences have impact because the characters relationships are set in stone from the beginning. The irony is palpable, a movie about sentient cars in which characters have nowhere to go.

The voice cast here is fine. Larry The Cable Guy does a fine job as Mater but he simply has too much screen time in a movie that has no real surprises for what happens with his character. Owen Wilson is likewise forced to spin his wheels as Lightning McQueen. Everyone is forced to play directly and solely to type, not unforgivable in a children's film but far less satisfying an approach than viewers will have enjoyed in any previous Pixar film.

If the writing here is confused and convoluted and clichéd the direction is at least entertaining. The camera sweeps and swoops and provides ample opportunity for jaws to drop but it should be said that there is little of the sort of finesse on display that John Lasseter has evinced in prior directorial outings (*Toy Story* [1995] , *A Bug's Life* [1998]) which will likely leave viewers with the firm suspicion that co-director and co-writer Brad Lewis, who makes his directorial debut here, handled the bulk of the chores.

Finally, the conceit of a world populated only by cars seems far more strained than in the first film. Again, it is a deep flaw that is difficult not to attribute directly to the writing, which has the story taking place in such a wide variety of locales that almost any viewer will be distracted by questions about where the cars came from originally, what happened to the creators, etc. This would be nitpicking except that the film literally takes viewers all over the world from Radiator Springs to Japan and to Italy without ever exposing them to the actual functional society of the car-verse. It apparently just sprang into existence and is maintained via magic. In a film that told an original story or gave its characters room to breathe this might not be a problem but the whole of this film reduces itself to spectacle and simply fails to sustain the wonder one might feel at a world comprised entirely of self-aware machines.

Dave Canfield

CREDITS

Lightning McQueen: Owen Wilson (Voice)
Mater: Larry the Cable Guy (Voice)

Finn McMissile: Michael Caine (Voice)
Holly Shiftwell: Emily Mortimer (Voice)
Siddeley: Jason Isaacs (Voice)
Grem: Joe Mantegna (Voice)
Professor Zundalapp: Thomas Kretschmann (Voice)
Sally Carrera: Bonnie Hunt (Voice)
Ramone: Cheech Marin (Voice)
Luigi: Tony Shalhoub (Voice)
Chick Hicks: Michael Keaton (Voice)
Mack: John Ratzenberger (Voice)
Miles Axelrod: Eddie Izzard (Voice)
Francesco Bernoulli: John Turturro (Voice)
Origin: USA
Language: English
Released: 2011
Production: Denise Ream; Pixar, Walt Disney Pictures
Directed by: John Lasseter, Brad Lewis
Written by: Ben Queen
Music by: Michael Giacchino
Sound: Tom Myers
Music Supervisor: Tom MacDougall
Editing: Stephen R. Schaffer
Production Design: Harley Jessup
MPAA rating: G
Running time: 113 minutes

REVIEWS

Bray, Catherine. *Film4*. July 22, 2011.
Ebert, Roger. *Chicago Sun-Times*. June 23, 2011.
Goss, William. *Film.com*. June 24, 2011.
Lasalle, Mick. *San Francisco Chronicle*. June 23, 2011.
Lemire, Christy. *Associated Press*. June 21, 2011.
Luxford, James. *The National*. September 1, 2011.
Munro, Shaun. *What Culture*. July 22, 2011.
O'Hehir, Andrew. *Salon.com*. June 23, 2011.
Schager, Nick. *Village Voice*. June 21, 2011.
Scott, A.O. *New York Times*. June 23, 2011.

QUOTES

Finn McMissile: "My apologies, I haven't properly introduced myself. Finn McMissile, British intelligence."
Mater: "Tow Mater, average intelligence."

TRIVIA

The name the character voiced by Eddie Izzard, Miles Axlerod, is taken from one of Izzard's stand-up routines concerning the invention of the wheel and axle.

AWARDS

Nomination:
Golden Globes 2012: Animated Film.

CAVE OF FORGOTTEN DREAMS

Box Office: $5.3 million

Throughout his long and distinguished career as one of the world's boldest filmmakers, Werner Herzog has gone to extraordinary lengths, ranging from filming in locations as varied as the lip of a live volcano to the jungles of the Amazon to the South Pole to his mercurial collaborations with the late, great and borderline-crazy Klaus Kinski, to provide his viewers with the kind of unexpected sights and sounds that have become more and more infrequent in an increasingly homogenized society. With his latest documentary, *Cave of Forgotten Dreams,* he adds on an additional challenge to his usual mandate—can he make a film in 3D that justifies utilizing the increasingly hackneyed format in a way that works both aesthetically and artistically? And, as he has done before so many times in the past, he has come up with a fairly extraordinary piece of cinema and even manages to make the 3D gimmick seem like a legitimate artistic medium when placed in the right hands.

The subject of the film is the Chauvet cave system of southern France that was uncovered by mountaineers in 1994 after being hidden away for centuries and which was discovered to contain the remarkably well-preserved evidence of the oldest known cave paintings in history, estimated at being roughly 30,000 years old. Utilizing a tiny crew and adhering to the strict restrictions placed on those few individuals allowed into the cave in order to help preserve the find, Herzog manages to nevertheless hit upon a visual strategy that uncannily suggests what it might have been like to be in there thousands of years ago with nothing more than a couple of torches to light the way. The find allows Herzog to meditate on the notions of man, artistic expression and their respective places in the universe as a whole. And because it is a Herzog movie, after all, there are also plenty of oddball digressions that at first seem completely out of place, such as the revelation that one of the archaeologists in charge of the dig was previously employed as a circus clown and a finale involving the alleged discovery of mutant albino crocodiles courtesy of a nuclear generator located not far from Chauvet), but which afterwards feel like absolutely essential pieces of the puzzle that the film would be well neigh unimaginable without their presence.

After a couple of years of rapidly exponential growth, 2011 proved to be the year that the bloom departed from the rose that is 3D as the sheer overuse of the process combined with viewer apathy towards higher ticket prices and shoddy post-production conversions led many to believe that it might soon fade from view as quickly as it had during its previous incarnations in the 1950s and the 1980s. Ironically, this was also the same year that some notable directors, such as Wim Wenders (*Pina* [2011]), Martin Scorsese (*Hugo* [2011]), and Steven Spielberg (*The Adventures of Tintin* [2011], embraced the technology and utilized it as a specific tool in their arsenal to more fully enhance the particular stories that they were trying to tell instead of overusing it in order to provide audiences with one cheap thrill after another. Once again, it would be the always-innovative Herzog who would lead the way in this regard but even his most dedicated fans may have questioned whether he could make something out of the increasingly tiresome gimmick Amazingly, he manages to more than justify the format by utilizing the multi-dimensional aspect to further add to the effect by preserving the curves and protrusions of the surfaces on which the paintings were made. The end result is fairly stunning in the way that it manages to represent as closely as possible the experience of actually observing the paintings in their natural habitat. Despite the onerous conditions under which he was working, Herzog provides images so fascinating to behold that even the most vociferously anti-3D viewers will be forced to concede that this is one time in which the format more than justifies its existence.

Some critics of *Cave of Forgotten Dreams* have complained that it goes on a little too long for its own good and that it might have been more effective as a one-hour TV special than as a 90-minute movie. This, of course, is nonsense—between the stunning visuals from within the Chauvet system, the quirky portraits of the people and the various musings, mutterings and ramblings of Herzog, this is one of those rare films that could have gone on for double its running time without ever feeling like a drag for a moment. Although Herzog has long been considered one of the boldest and most audacious filmmakers working today, he has stepped up his game considerably in the last decade with a streak of top-notch filmmaking as strong and as varied as those of any of his contemporaries and if *Cave of Forgotten Dreams* is to be considered a minor effort, it would only be as the result of the company it is keeping. In the filmographies of practically anyone else, it would be considered a landmark work, the kind that one might hope would still be around to be rediscovered by whoever is roaming the planet thousands of years from now.

Peter Sobczynski

CREDITS

Herself: Dominique Baffier
Himself: Jean Clottes
Himself: Jean-Michel Geneste
Himself: Carole Fritz
Himself: Gilles Tosello
Werner Herzog (Narrated)
Origin: USA, Canada, France, Germany, United Kingdom

Language: English, German, French
Released: 2011
Production: Erik Nelson, Adrienne Ciuffo; Creative Differences, History Films, Ministere de la Culture et de la Communication; released by Sundance Selects, IFC Films
Directed by: Werner Herzog
Written by: Werner Herzog
Cinematography by: Peter Zeitlinger
Music by: Ernst Reijseger
Sound: Eric Spitzer
Editing: Joe Bini, Maya Hawke
MPAA rating: G
Running time: 95 minutes

REVIEWS

Chang, Justin. *Variety*. April 26, 2011.
Dargis, Manohla. *New York Times*. April 28, 2011.
Ebert, Roger. *Chicago Sun-Times*. April 28, 2011.
Hoberman, J. *Village Voice*. April 26, 2011.
Lane, Anthony. *New Yorker*. May 2, 2011.
Phillips, Michael. *Chicago Tribune*. April 28, 2011.
Tobias, Scott. *AV Club*. April 28, 2011.
Turan, Kenneth. *Los Angeles Times*. April 28, 2011.
Weinberg, Scott. *Cinematical*. September 18, 2010.
White, Armond. *New York Press*. April 27, 2011.

QUOTES

Werner Herzog: "In a forbidden recess of the cave, there's a footprint of an eight-year-old boy next to the footprint of a wolf. Did a hungry wolf stalk the boy? Or did they walk together as friends? Or were their tracks made thousands of years apart? We'll never know."

CEDAR RAPIDS

Today is the first day…of the rest of his weekend.
—Movie tagline

Box Office: $6.9 million

The set-up for the fish out of water comedy *Cedar Rapids* is reminiscent of a Frank Capra film: the attempted undoing of a charming—if not overly naïve—everyman by the realities of the big, bad city. The everyman in question is Tim Lippe (Ed Helms), a thirty-something insurance salesman who has never set foot outside of his small Wisconsin town. Tim is the kind of nice guy who actually believes that selling insurance is about helping people. He is, in fact, so sheltered that he does not even have to go as far as Capra's Washington D.C. to find a metropolis ready and willing to corrupt him. A weekend-long convention in Cedar Rapids, Iowa will do nicely. Of course society has come a long way since Mr. Smith went to Washington and the corruptible offences awaiting an aw-shucks Midwesterner have become raunchier. In the span of this one weekend Tim takes his first airplane ride, drinks alcohol, smokes pot, has a one-night stand, and almost loses his job. But because *Cedar Rapids* is a feel good butterfly comedy, Tim, despite his social awkwardness, emerges victorious with a new gig, new friends and new attitude. If the premise for this story sounds familiar, it is. Unfortunately, so is most of the plot. Still, like the quirky protagonist of the film, there is something about *Cedar Rapids* that is disarmingly charming and likeable.

Brevity works in favor of this tried and tested narrative. Clocking in at eighty-seven minutes, *Cedar Rapids* packs a lot into a short running time. But it is a testament to his writing skills that Phil Johnston's script feels perfectly paced. Devoid of any superfluous material, Johnston gets Tim into trouble quickly and repeatedly, but not repetitively. He does not overuse jokes or gags, knowing that doing so would potentially throw *Cedar Rapids* into schlocky territory, and would take away from the momentum of the film. At the same time, Johnston does not sacrifice any opportunity to be funny, managing to sprinkle a few sly winks and nudges into his script, such as the company name of Tim's Wisconsin insurance outfit, BrownStar, that go over well with audiences looking for extra laughs.

But the real reason *Cedar Rapids* works is Johnston knack for characters. He knows that in order for an awkward workplace comedy like this to really resonate and set itself apart, viewers have to want to root for the people on-screen, so he makes sure that his characters are more than standard archetypes. That is not to say that Tim and his crew do not fall into their own well-covered stereotypes, they do, but Johnston tries to layer them all with relatable, organic baggage. There is Ronald (Isiah Whitlock Jr.), another earnest do-gooder who keeps bobbing to the surface no matter how much life pushes him down, Dean (John C. Reilly), the rowdy troublemaker with a heart of gold, Joan, (Anne Heche) one of the few women of the Midwest insurance biz who looks to these weekend conventions to provide respite from her otherwise mundane life, and Bree, a hooker with good intentions. While there is nothing glamorous about this set of characters, in Johnston's hands their everyday-ness becomes a lively and worthy adventure.

It is easy to see that Miguel Arteta likes these characters as much as Johnston does because he does not let his actors skate by on their performances. Predictable scenarios like Tim getting carted off to a seedy house party where he unknowingly ingests many illegal substances, do not just come off as standard thanks to heartfelt turns by the actors. The cast each stands out in their own way, from Heche's surprisingly touching depiction of a tired mom looking for a vacation away from reality, to Sigourney Weaver as Tim's older, recently widowed girlfriend, doing so much with so little. Their full-on commitment to the project is catchy. Especially noteworthy is Ed Helms as Tim. A veteran of *The Office* and a member of *The Hangover* (2009) crew, Helms is not unfamiliar with raunchy comedy or playing the awkward dork. But he still makes Tim feel fresh and watchable by really investing in him. With Helm's wide-eyed smile, and Ned Flanders-esque outlook, Tim comes off as naive, but somehow understandably so. The result is a dorky lead whose virtues do not come off as farfetched, but somehow strangely admirable.

Still that is not to say that everything in *Cedar Rapids* goes off without a hitch. There are moments that feel more awkward than funny, the jokes rely heavily on gross-out humor, and it is hard to imagine today's tech-savvy, airport security conscious audience being able to fully wrap their heads around a character who does not know the 3oz-or-less rule. But if they take a page from Helms, let go of any preconceived notions, and really fall into what they are watching, they will be rewarded with a fun throwback.

Joanna Topor MacKenzie

CREDITS

Tim Lippe: Ed Helms
Dean Ziegler: John C. Reilly
Joan Ostrowski-Fox: Anne Heche
Ronald Wilkes: Isiah Whitlock Jr.
Bill Krogstad: Stephen Root
Orin Helgesson: Kurtwood Smith
Bree: Alia Shawkat
Roger Lemke: Thomas Lennon
Macy Vanderhei: Sigourney Weaver
Gary: Rob Corddry
Mike Pyle: Michael O'Malley
Origin: USA
Language: English
Released: 2011
Production: Jim Burke, Alexander Payne, Jim Taylor; Ad Hominem Enterprises, Dune Entertainment; released by Fox Searchlight
Directed by: Miguel Arteta
Written by: Philip Johnston
Cinematography by: Chuy Chavez
Music by: Christophe Beck
Sound: Thomas Varga
Music Supervisor: Margaret Yen
Editing: Eric Kissack

Art Direction: Rob Simons
Costumes: Hope Hanafin
Production Design: Doug Meerdink
MPAA rating: R
Running time: 86 minutes

REVIEWS

Hornaday, Ann. *Washington Post.* February 11, 2011.
Jones, J.R. *Chicago Reader.* February 11, 2011.
Lane, Anthony. *New Yorker.* February 28, 2011.
LaSalle, Mick. *San Francisco Chronicle.* February 10, 2011.
Morgenstern, Joe. *Wall Street Journal.* February 10, 2011.
Puig, Claudia. *USA Today.* February 10, 2011.
Roberts, Rex. *Film Journal International.* February 9, 2011.
Rooney, David. *Hollywood Reporter.* February 11, 2011.
Sharkey, Betsy. *Los Angeles Times.* February 10, 2011.
Zacharek, Stephanie. *Movieline.* February 9, 2011.

QUOTES

Dean Ziegler: "There's a separation between religion and
insurance. It's in the constitution."

TRIVIA

Although originally intended to be shot on location,
production was moved to Ann Arbor, Michigan when Iowa
shuttered its film tax credit program.

AWARDS

Nomination:

Ind. Spirit 2012: Support. Actor (Reilly), First Screenplay.

CERTIFIED COPY
(Copie conforme)

Box Office: $1.4 million

Abbas Kiarostami's brilliant *Certified Copy* can be examined and interpreted to death and yet it almost works better once the viewer divests themselves of typical expectations of character and plot. The film is about two people with a relationship dynamic that seems to shift and change as the story goes on. They seem at first to be strangers, but are they? They seem later to be intimately aware of each other, but are they? Why does it matter? Through much of Kiarostami's film, the two characters discuss the very nature of art as a copy. There is the obvious concept of copying in reference to art as discussed in the film, but in a sense is not film a copy of life at its very core? And, if so, is it not up the filmmaker to bend and shape that copy as they see fit, chang-

ing elements of it—even unexpected elements like character background—to fit thematic needs? Centered by a stunningly good performance from Juliette Binoche (one of the best of her lustrous career), *Certified Copy* is a riveting exercise in dialogue that works not unlike a trippier, French take on Richard Linklater's *Before Sunrise* (1995) and *Before Sunset* (2004).

Like those films, *Certified Copy* is a two-character piece with only minor supporting performance. The first is an author named James Miller (William Shimell, an inexperienced actor but leading British opera singer who proves himself an engaging male lead as well), who is in Tuscany promoting a book he has written. While there, he meets a woman credited only as "she" (Binoche) and the two take a day trip to a small Italian town. At first, they seem to be meeting for the first time. The film jumps around from English to French to Italian as the pair gets into some deep conversations about the subject of Miller's book, copying in art. The film could have easily succeeded if it was purely Miller and She speaking Kiarostami's brilliant dialogue.

Then the conversation turns. Do these people know each other? Could they even be married? Have they been to this beautiful Tuscan village before? On the surface, it seems that a woman mistakes the pair for an old married couple and they play along like any pair might do in the same situation. They come up with a shared back story and act as if they are married. But are they acting? They continue to keep up the back story and even seem to dig up honest emotional undercurrents between each other. Were they faking it as strangers or as old lovers? Does it matter?

Of course, they are faking it as all actors are simply by being in a film. Kiarostami is playing games with cliché and audience expectations of character. One thinks they know the very basic foundation of the relationship between the other two characters in his film and then they do not. And it is not coincidental that he has hired a non-actor as his male lead. It is someone pretending to be an actor pretending to be a character who may be pretending to be someone else altogether. And yet this piling on of thematic weight over honest character does not leave a cluttered film. In fact, the film only works if it has the opposite effect—pulling traditional expectations out of the viewer's mind and allowing one to appreciate the themes and the subject of conversation instead of who is having it. A very large portion of Kiarostami's script takes place as the characters are stationary (whether it is seated in an extended driving scene or two incredible dining scenes, one in a café and another in a restaurant). The writer/director wants one to focus solely on what these people are saying and the emotions they are expressing—do not ask if they are "true" to the characters but only if they are true to human experience.

Shimell is surprisingly good, especially when one considers his inexperience, but it the veteran here who really steals the piece. Juliette Binoche is stunning in every scene, giving one of the best performances of the year and one of the most notable of her increasingly impressive career. Looking stunningly beautiful, she is simply captivating, especially when it becomes clear that she is either taking the game they are playing very seriously or her emotions have overwhelmed the game they played in the first half and honest pain is coming to the surface. Whether or not her nameless character is a stranger, a wife, a lover, or something else altogether means nothing when the emotion is as purely and rivetingly presented as it is by Juliette Binoche. Her work transcends cliché and even basic plot. She defies expectations by proving them to be worthless in light of something even rarer in film—emotional truth.

Brian Tallerico

CREDITS

She: Juliette Binoche
James Miller: William Shimell
Origin: France, Italy, Belgium
Language: English, French, French
Released: 2010
Production: Marin Karmitz, Nathanael Karmitz, Angelo Barbagallo, Charles Gillibert; MK2, France 3 Cinema, BiBi Film; released by IFC Films
Directed by: Abbas Kiarostami
Written by: Abbas Kiarostami
Cinematography by: Luca Bigazzi
Sound: Olivier Hespel, Dominique Vieillard
Editing: Bahman Kiarostami
Art Direction: Lorenzo Sartor
Costumes: Marzia Mardone
Production Design: Giancarlo Basili, Ludovica Ferrario
MPAA rating: Unrated
Running time: 106 minutes

REVIEWS

Ebert, Roger. *Chicago Sun-Times.* March 17, 2011.
Gleiberman, Owen. *Entertainment Weekly.* March 9, 2011.
Hoberman, J. *Village Voice.* March 8, 2011.
Holden, Stephen. *New York Times.* March 10, 2011.
Kohn, Eric. *IndieWIRE.* March 7, 2011.
Nelson, Rob. *Variety.* May 17, 2010.
Phipps, Keith. *AV Club.* March 10, 2011.
Rainer, Peter. *Christian Science Monitor.* March 19, 2011.
Rea, Steven. *Philadelphia Inquirer.* March 31, 2011.
Stevens, Dana. *Slate.* March 12, 2011.

QUOTES

James Miller: "I didn't mean to sound so cynical, but when I saw all their hopes and dreams in their eyes, I just couldn't support their illusion."

THE CHANGE-UP

Who says men can't change?
    —Movie tagline

Box Office: $37.1 million

If at all possible (and it is always possible), a movie should avoid opening with a scene in which a young child projectile-poops into his father's mouth. In fact, that rule is a little limiting. Let the record show, now, that the first two minutes of *The Change-Up* have proven the unfunny grossness of such a scene, so no future film will need to do that.

In *The Change-Up,* Dave (Jason Bateman) is far from happy with his life as a highly paid, married father of three, and not just because one of his infant twins rockets feces into his mouth while Dave is stretching to reach a diaper. Though he is working on a merger that could make him a partner at his law firm and he has his beautiful, supportive wife Jamie (Leslie Mann) by his side, Dave has a bad case of "the grass is always greener." Maybe at one point he saw domestic and professional stability as the epitome of a fruitful adult life. Now, though, Dave looks at his longtime best friend Mitch (Ryan Reynolds), a ladies' man who earns pennies as an actor but has all the time in the world to smoke pot and sleep late, and envies a daily schedule without anything on it. (Not to mention the ability to have sex with anyone he wants; currently Dave struggles to contain his lust for his fun, fetching colleague Sabrina, played by Olivia Wilde). Mitch, meanwhile, admires Dave's big house full of food and warmth, which he certainly does not receive from the father (Alan Arkin) he is sure has been disappointed in him since Mitch dropped out of high school to become an actor.

That is not a bad set-up for a movie: Two men who have shared several decades of history and memories must each find a way to reconcile, to each other and to themselves, the notion that his best friend is in the exact opposite place in his life. Except *The Change-Up* is not a subtle drama about gaining perspective about adult priorities—the aforementioned poop-in-the-mouth scene probably makes that perfectly clear. No, this is yet another comedy in which the main characters swap bodies and discover what life is like in the other person's shoes. This happens when Dave and Mitch, drunkenly urinating in a fountain after a long night at the bar watching baseball, proclaim in unison, "I wish I had your life." Suddenly all of the lights around them go out, and the next morning Dave wakes up in Mitch's body and vice-versa, which does lead to a funny burst of honesty. "I'm a douchebag!" cries Dave from Mitch's body. "I'm a f**king tool!" screams Mitch, as Dave. Now these friends know what they really think of each other.

If the humor in *The Change-Up* was largely based in such spontaneous (if crass) truth, it could have been an amusing movie about one man learning to stop acting like a child all the time, and another man rekindling the youthful spirit that is still possible in a life of adult responsibilities. Instead, the script by Jon Lucas and Scott Moore greatly resembles their script for *The Hangover* (2009) in that *The Change-Up* often feels like a mean-spirited parade of sexist and racist jokes with an interest only in exploring its concept in a way that is painfully formulaic and juvenile. There are so many examples, so to name just a few: Mitch jokes that one of Dave and Jamie's kids looks "a little Down's-y," a horribly insensitive way to address that a child may have special needs; Dave, after becoming Mitch and arriving on an acting job only to find out that it is an adult film, must insert his thumb into a woman's butt and later kiss a man (Moore and Lucas do love their gay panic humor); Mitch, after becoming Dave and botching the merger, is told by his boss (Gregory Itzin) that he should, "Put on some proper clothes; you look like a Jew." This is one of many instances in which the writers of *The Change-Up* include a statement of bigotry in an attempt to be funny and salute stupidity, not to expose the character as a fool.

Other groan-inducing moments include Mitch, as Dave, instructing Dave's oldest daughter Cara (Sydney Rouviere) to solve all of her problems with violence and Dave, as Mitch, anticipating having sex with Mitch's regular Tuesday night partner Tatiana (Mircea Monroe) only to discover that she is nine months pregnant (and still eager to jump in the sack). In the midst of all these shenanigans is poor Jamie, who in numerous scenes cries (to a teenage babysitter or to Mitch, who is really Dave) about how miserable and unappreciated she feels. If Dave truly cared about his wife's happiness, he would be impacted enough to take responsibility for her feelings and play an active role in ensuring the safety of his children and the contentment of the woman he loves. Instead, since he is still in Mitch's body and wants to take advantage, he merely demands that his best friend shape up and work harder to live Dave's life for him while Dave tries to enjoy being Mitch and date/sleep with Sabrina. Ultimately (mini-spoiler alert!), Dave gets to sample the proverbial cake and eat it too, while his wife merely gets an apology that assumes she can now trust her husband and forgive all past indiscretions.

Aside from a few memorable laughs—the movie makes reference to hilarious, non-existent sexual positions with names like "The Pastrami Sandwich" and "The Wolfgang Puck"—*The Change-Up* will likely be remembered only as the film that ushered in a startling new concept: CGI nipples. While in late 2010 Jessica Alba was digitally presented as nude in *Machete* even though she was not naked during filming, *The Change-Up* takes it a step further by creating nipples for Wilde (seen only briefly, from the side) and digitally enhancing breasts for Mann, who did not actually film her scenes topless. Without even delving into the slippery slope that this practice creates (soon actors and actresses will need to stipulate in their contracts that not only will they not do nudity, they will not allow any naked body parts, real or digital, to be presented as theirs), it must be noted that this does not look natural on screen. Viewers can clearly tell that Mann's body has been digitally altered. However, when a film frequently incorporates CGI to show young children doing things such as banging their head against a crib or playing with a large knife, it is clear that reality and dignity are not anyone's concern.

Matt Pais

CREDITS

Dave: Jason Bateman
Mitch: Ryan Reynolds
Sabrina: Olivia Wilde
Jamie: Leslie Mann
Tatiana: Mircea Moore
Origin: USA
Language: English
Released: 2011
Production: David Dobkin, Neal H. Moritz; Big Kid Pictures, Original Film, Relativity Media; released by Universal Pictures
Directed by: David Dobkin
Written by: Jon Lucas, Scott Moore
Cinematography by: Eric Alan Edwards
Music by: John Debney, Matt Aberly
Editing: Lee Haxall, Greg Hayden
Sound: Tim Chau
Costumes: Betsy Heimann
Production Design: Barry Robison
MPAA rating: R
Running time: 112 minutes

REVIEWS

Chang, Justin. *Variety.* August 2, 2011.
Ebert, Roger. *Chicago Sun-Times.* August 3, 2011.

Goodykoontz, Bill. *Arizona Republic.* August 3, 2011.
Pols, Mary. *Time.* August 4, 2011.
Holden, Stephen. *New York Times.* August 4, 2011.
Moore, Roger. *Orlando Sentinel.* August 4, 2011.
Morgenstern, Joe. *Wall Street Journal.* August 4, 2011.
Persall, Steve. *St. Petersburg Times.* August 4, 2011.
Phillips, Michael. *Chicago Tribune.* August 4, 2011.
Stevens, Dana. *Slate.* August 6, 2011.

QUOTES

Mitch Planko: "So I can't sleep with my wife, I can't sleep with other women. What the hell is that?"

Dave: "Marriage."

TRIVIA

Most of the female nudity featured in the film is not real; computer-generated breasts were used for both Leslie Mann and Olivia Wilde.

COLOMBIANA

Revenge is beautiful.
—Movie tagline

Vengeance is beautiful.
—Movie tagline

Box Office: $36.7 million

With a production slate voluminous enough to put most actual studios to shame, the one-man filmmaking factory that is Luc Besson has cranked out an astonishing number of movies that he has worked on as writer, producer, director or, more often than not, some combination of the three. Although he has dabbled in unexpected genres from time to time—he helped to finance the contemporary western *The Three Burials of Melquiades Estrada* (2005) and directed the family-oriented trilogy *Arthur and the Invisibles* (2006), *Arthur and the Revenge of Maltazard* (2009) and *Arthur 3: The War of the Two Worlds* (2010)—he is most well-known for creating a string of outlandish thrillers featuring his patented blend of sexy stars, ultra-stylish visuals, weirdo humor, and wildly over-the-top action sequences that cheerfully defy such outmoded concepts as gravity and common sense in an effort to inspire popped eyes and dropped jaws in even the most jaded of viewers. Alas, even the most well-oiled production line coughs up a clinker and that is certainly the case with Besson's latest creation, *Colombiana,* a misfire that is such a total botch on virtually every imaginable level that if there was a cinematic version of the Consumer Protection Agency, they would be calling for its immediate recall on the basis that it posed an immediate danger to the intel-ligence of anyone unlucky enough to attempt to sit through it.

The film opens with a lengthy prologue set in 1992 in Bogota, Colombia, as the ten-year-old Cataleya (Amandla Stenberg) witnesses her parents being killed by Marco (Jordi Molla), the chief henchman of the fearsome drug dealer Don Luis. (It is barely noticed that her parents are apparently also in the drug trade as well and are armed to the teeth for their final standoff against Marco and his fellow flunkies.) Despite her youth and apparent inexperience, Cataleya still manages to stick a knife in Marco's hand, evade her pursuers through the streets of Bogota, and make it all the way to America, where she turns up on the Chicago doorstep of her Uncle Emilio (Cliff Curtis). Luckily for her, Emilio is also a criminal (going so far as to indiscriminately shoot up a street just to impart a valuable lesson) and when she vows to one day get revenge on the people who killed her parents, he agrees to teach her everything that she will need to know to become a top-notch assassin—provided that she stays in school, of course.

The story picks up years later with the grown-up Cataleya (now played by Zoe Saldana) demonstrating her abilities as a hired killer by knocking off a guy on heavy lockdown inside a prison via equal parts skill, strength, and the kind of utterly implausible coincidences that tend to get overlooked when a film of this type is working and that tend to stick out like sore thumbs when they are not. As it turns out, Cataleya is using all of these otherwise-unrelated murder-for-hire gigs as a way of flushing out the killers of her parents by decorating each of her victims with a drawing of the rare Colombian flower that she is named after (a fact that is mentioned in the dialogue approximately six zillion times in lieu of character development) in the hopes that when this information is released by the police, it will send the real bad guys her way. More or less confined to the sidelines during Cataleya's quest for justice is Ross (Lennie James), a singularly ineffectual cop whom she outwits at every turn, often without even trying, and Danny (Michael Vartan), the singularly ineffectual boyfriend who only gradually begins to find it strange that he knows absolutely nothing about his girlfriend or where she is constantly disappearing to despite having no apparent means of support outside of her frequently glimpsed undergarments.

On the surface, *Colombiana* may not sound appreciably different from any of the other action extravaganzas that Besson has unleashed over the years, but even his most ardent fans will have to admit that the execution of said material has been horribly bungled this time around. The screenplay by Besson and long-time collaborator Robert Mark Kamen is a tired rehash of material deployed far-more successfully in their previous outings tied together by a singularly unlikable and uninteresting central character—thoughtless, reckless, bloodthirsty and not nearly as clever as she would like to believe herself to be—and a story that is too silly to be taken seriously and too dull to work as the kind of live-action cartoon level of most of Besson's work. The direction by Besson protégé Oliver Megaton, whose previous effort was the redoubtable *Transporter 3* (2008), is similarly slack and plodding throughout, to the point where even the scenes that might have been instant classics in Besson's capable hands (such as an elaborate hit in which the corpulent target is eventually devoured by his own pet sharks) are ruined by dreadful and dreary execution that sucks all of the fun out of the proceedings at every turn.

And while Besson has managed in the past to create convincing action heroines out of the disparate likes of Anne Parillaud, Natalie Portman, and Milla Jovovich, he is unable to do the same here for Zoe Saldana. While she certainly looks great throughout, not even that is enough to make up for the listless and unconvincing performance that she turns in. As for the resoundingly uninteresting supporting cast, an assembly seemingly composed entirely of actors that only get hired when literally no one else in the SAG directory is available, all one can say is that this may be the first time in which Michael Vartan has appeared in a film in which he has not been the dullest person on the screen at any given point.

Absolutely lacking in wit, energy, excitement or any real reason to exist, *Colombiana* is the kind of film that seems to have been specifically designed to play in largely empty multiplexes during the generally lackluster period between the summer box-office derby and autumn's onslaught of Oscar® bait. Ordinary audiences will no doubt shrug it off as just another anonymous mess but for Besson's devoted fans, the sheer indifference and laziness of the entire exercise is almost like a kick to the head. If one wanted to put the best possible face upon the situation, it could be argued that Besson was so preoccupied with getting his Aung San Suu Kyi biopic *The Lady*(2011) up and running that he was unable to oversee this side project as diligently as he has with many of his previous productions. Even if that film turns out to be a masterpiece on every level, it will not take away from the fact that *Colombiana* is nothing more than a bitter bon-bon of a film that even the most undiscriminating of viewers will find virtually impossible to swallow.

Peter Sobczynski

CREDITS

Cataleya Restrepo: Zoe Saldana
Marco: Jordi Molla
Don Luis: Beto Benites
Special Agent Ross: Lennie James
Emilio Restrepo: Clifford Curtis
Danny Delanay: Michael Vartan
Young Cataleya: Amandia Stenberg
Special Agent Williams: Maximillian Martini
Fabio: Jesse Borrego
Warren: Graham McTavish
Richard: Callum Blue
Origin: USA
Language: English, Spanish
Released: 2011
Production: Luc Besson, Ariel Zeitoun; Europacorp, TF-1 Films, Grive Prods., TriStar Pictures; released by Stage Six Films, TriStar Pictures
Directed by: Olivier Megaton
Written by: Luc Besson, Robert Mark Kamen
Cinematography by: Romain Lacourbas
Music by: Nathaniel Mechaly
Sound: Frederic Dubois, Dean Humphreys
Editing: Camille Delamarre
Costumes: Olivier Beriot
Production Design: Patrick Durand
MPAA rating: PG-13
Running time: 107 minutes

REVIEWS

Edelstein, David. *New York Magazine*. August 29, 2011.
Gilchrist, Todd. *Boxoffice Magazine*. August 25, 2011.
Hale, Mike. *New York Times*. August 25, 2011.
Jenkins, Mark. *Washington Post*. August 26, 2011.
Morris, Wesley. *Boston Globe*. August 28, 2011.
Orndorff, Brian. *BrianOrndorff.com* August 26, 2011.
Snider, Eric D. *Film.com*. August 27, 2011.
Tallerico, Brian. *HollywoodChicago.com*. August 26, 2011.
Tobias, Scott. *AV Club*. August 26, 2011.
Weinberg, Scott. *Twitch.com*. August 26, 2011.

QUOTES

Cat-10: "I want to be a killer. Can you help me?"
Emilio Restrepo: "Sure."

TRIVIA

The film skipped theaters in Australia and went straight to DVD and Bluray.

CONAN O'BRIEN CAN'T STOP

In 2004, Conan O'Brien took over the coveted job hosting NBC's *The Tonight Show,* replacing a seemingly retired Jay Leno. O'Brien's version of the show ran for a good five months to less-than-stellar ratings. In 2009, the executives at NBC decided to experiment and bring back Leno for a one-hour primetime show. The experiment failed and NBC was left with two talk shows with low ratings. Soon thereafter, O'Brien was asked to have his show (which would still be called *The Tonight Show*) moved an hour back so that Leno could return to his old time slot. Not wanting to be the first host to have *The Tonight Show* technically air "the next day," O'Brien decided to step down altogether and give Leno back the show, knowing that that is what executives had hoped for all along. In the wake of this major disappointment, O'Brien was contractually obligated to not appear on any TV shows, radio broadcasts, or internet streams for six months.

To fill the time, O'Brien decided to get a show going that he could take on the road. It would be a big comedy and musical showcase with guest stars, a big back-up band and comedy centered on the well-publicized fights with NBC. It would not be a pity party, but a party for the fans who supported him across the country. The tour initially consisted of forty-four stops and was appropriately dubbed "The Legally Prohibited From Being Funny on Television Tour." Many shows sold out within minutes of being announced on Twitter and shows often had to be added in major markets.

The documentary *Conan O'Brien Can't Stop* is about that tour and the desired effect of just "having fun" as O'Brien tries to keep his sanity while meeting every possible obligation that being on the road demands. The film opens with a brief explanation of the NBC fallout then quickly jumps into the rehearsal process as O'Brien and his team of writers hash out the material. A pair of back-up singers called "The Coquettes" are hired and the show takes shape and is tested before being brought to the first stop in Eugene, Oregon. O'Brien has a wife and two kids whom he will not see for a few months.

This is not a process documentary, nor is it any kind of revenge piece for O'Brien. It is a backstage documentary about his kind of celebrity, the kind that just lost one of the most sought after gigs in show business. O'Brien claims he has never felt entitled to anything and that he is down to earth about everything, but he is entitled to be angry. Fair enough, and that anger does come across throughout the film. He puts a lot of pressure on himself to not come across as an arrogant jerk when meeting his countless fans. Instead he vents his frustration on his work staff, many of whom take his jabs in stride. O'Brien explains that while he often says things to his friends, family and co-workers that seem off-putting or outright rude, he insists that it not be taken too seriously and that it is simply his brand of humor.

To those who do not abide to that sort of subtle humor, O'Brien will often come across as unlikable and petty. One has to take into account, though, that he is tireless and that is his curse. Early in the film, he is asked why he "can't stop." O'Brien explains that he is happiest when he is performing for an audience. Yet, after each show, he sits alone and wonders how the show could have been better and why there is not a sense of camaraderie or celebration after any given performance for a job well done. O'Brien also makes every effort to meet and greet his fans before and after every show, sometimes to his annoyance, particularly at a stop where one of the back-up dancers brings in her whole family to meet with him. On the surface, O'Brien is cordial, accommodating and friendly. Once the room empties, O'Brien wonders aloud how is supposed to meet and greet so many people while maintaining his vocal cords for the next show.

There are plenty of celebrity walk-ons throughout the tour—Eddie Vedder, Jack White, Jim Carrey, Stephen Colbert and Jon Stewart all make appearances. O'Brien signs shirts, body parts and even helps fans get into the show who are in a tight spot. One fan casually makes an anti-Semitic remark, which puts O'Brien at unease while trying to help the guy out and being clearly offended by what the fan just said. The film shows parts of the show, but nothing in its entirety. O'Brien and his crew keep adding commitments throughout the tour, even on much-needed days off.

The question of why O'Brien "can't stop" is never really answered and the movie overall is a surface-level examination of this kind of celebrity status and the need for constant adulation. It is widely known that comedians are alternately insecure and attention starved. For those who are looking for a psychiatric examination into the mind of a troubled comedian, *Conan O'Brien Can't Stop* will disappoint. Director Rodman Flender is content with tagging along on the tour bus and occasionally getting some good backstage rants. In that regard, *Conan O'Brien Can't Stop* is an entertaining and funny enough road trip movie about a guy who, for whatever reason, clearly belongs on stage.

Collin Souter

CREDITS

Himself: Conan O'Brien
Himself: Andy Richter
Origin: USA
Language: English
Released: 2011
Production: Gavin Polone, Rachel Griffin; Pariah Production; released by Abramorama Films

Directed by: Rodman Flender
Cinematography by: Rodman Flender
Sound: Michael Clark
Music Supervisor: Paul DiFranco
Editing: Rodman Flender
MPAA rating: R
Running time: 89 minutes

REVIEWS

Burr, Ty. *Boston Globe*. June 23, 2011.
Childress, Erik. *eFilmcritic.com*. May 11, 2011.
Ebert, Roger. *Chicago Sun-Times*. June 23, 2011.
Goodykoontz, Bill. *Arizona Republic*. July 28, 2011.
Holden, Stephen. *New York Times*. June 23, 2011.
Howell, Peter. *Toronto Star*. July 6, 2011.
Kennedy, Lisa. *Denver Post*. July 24, 2011.
Long, Tom. *Detroit News*. June 24, 2011.
Schager, Nick. *Slant Magazine*. June 18, 2011.
Schwartzbaum, Lisa. *Entertainment Weekly*. June 22, 2011.

QUOTES

Conan O'Brien: "I'm like Tinkerbell; without applause, I die."

CONAN THE BARBARIAN

Box Office: $21.3 million

In *Conan the Barbarian*, the latest attempt to bring the legendary creation of the late writer Robert E. Howard from the pages of pulp fiction novels and comic books to the big screen, many enemies are crushed and driven before audiences—even closer than usual thanks to the miracle of 3D—but the only lamentations heard are the ones coming from fans of the character despairing at the sight of a seemingly sure-fire film franchise, one that started off beautifully with the classic *Conan the Barbarian* (1982) (featuring direction by wild-man filmmaker John Milius, a screenplay co-written with Oliver Stone, and a star-making lead performance by the largely unknown Arnold Schwarzenegger) and immediately self-destructed with the one-two punch of the inexplicably family-friendly *Conan the Destroyer* (1984) and the just inexplicable semi-spin-off *Red Sonja* (1985), once again stabbing itself in the foot with a mighty broadsword via a woefully unentertaining bore that pretty much kills off any hopes it might have had.

Ignoring the previous films, this iteration of *Conan the Barbarian* is another origin saga, and, to give it credit, it certainly starts off with a bang via a cheerfully insane opening bit in which the infant Conan is sliced out of the womb of his dying mother by his father (Ron Perlman) while a bloody battle rages around them. Ten years later, Conan, who is already demonstrating the kind of proficiency for lopping off the heads of his enemies normally seen in barbarians more than twice his age, is forced to witness dear old dad dying at the hands of Khalar Zym (Stephen Lang), an evil lunatic searching for the final piece of a magical mask that will complete merely the first half of a ritual that will revive the dead, grant him everlasting life and presumably inspire dogs and cats to live together. Twenty years later, the now-grown (and how) Conan (Jason Momoa) is still searching for Khalar in order to get all sorts of gory revenge against him. For his part, Khalar, along with his equally-twisted sorceress daughter (Rose McGowan), is still searching for the innocent and unknowing lass whose blood will allow him to finally complete that aforementioned ritual. These corpuscles turn out to be coursing through the veins of Tamara (Rachel Nichols), the comeliest cutie residing at the local remote monastery. Once she is discovered, the rest of the film consists of Conan rescuing the frequently distressed damsel (except for when she is rescuing herself via her own somewhat inexplicable fighting skills) and trying to avenge himself on Khalar in endless scenes featuring oily and muscle-bound dopes pounding each other with broadswords while gouts of CGI gore fly hither and non, mostly non.

The whole thing is ridiculous, of course, and while the same could be said about the first Conan film, the difference between the two is like the difference between night and a really weak and cheesy sword-and-sorcery extravaganza. One of the main reasons why the earlier *Conan the Barbarian* worked as well as it did was because John Milius treated the story seriously and offered viewers an unapologetically bloody and brutal saga in which good was Good, evil was Evil, men were Men and women were something else entirely. Alas, director Marcus Nispel—the man responsible for the patently unnecessary remakes of *The Texas Chainsaw Massacre* (2003) and *Friday the 13th* (2009)—has taken the opposite track and offers viewers an off-puttingly silly take on the material that includes deliberately ridiculous action sequences (including battles with sand demons and a giant octopus), copious amounts of bloodshed that have virtually no impact because of its blatantly computer-generated nature, and a villain so goofily over-the-top that he appears to have been trucked in from one of the Joel Schumacher *Batman* movies. Even Conan himself seems to be at odds with what the material needs in order to succeed. While Momoa more or less fills the role from a purely physical perspective, he lacks the dramatic heft, for lack of a better phrase, that Schwarzenegger brought to the part. In his take, Conan was a brute of few words who communicated almost entirely via action; the way one might expect a barbarian to behave. Here, in an apparent attempt to soften the character and possibly lure female audience members that might not necessarily spark to a film with "Barbarian" in the title, our barbarian is a reasonably happy-go-lucky type who is relatively loquacious (which, to be fair, is a little closer to the initial conception laid out by Howard), friendly, loyal and, after the inevitable gender-related banter, a gentle and considerate lover to the monk babe, even if the closest he get to something resembling foreplay comes when he remarks "Give her the leather and the armor."

Despite a couple of momentary bright spots—most of them contributed by the scenery-licking Rose McGowan (who was originally going to star in a now-defunct rebooting of *Red Sonja*) and none by the murkier-than-usual 3D photography—*Conan the Barbarian* proved to be a largely forgettable mess that was loathed by fans of the character and ignored by the mass audience in such massive numbers that it proved to be one of the most notable flops of the summer of 2011. While apologists might claim that the rejection of the film had less to do with its intrinsic qualities than it did with growing audience apathy towards 3D films in general (it was one of three such films to open on the same weekend, the others being the remake of *Fright Night* and the sequel/reboot *Spy Kids 4-D*, and all three were conspicuous flops), the painful truth is that it bombed because it was a tacky bit on nonsense that not only failed to live up to the lofty standards of the original film, it barely lived up to the less-than-lofty artistic heights of *Kull the Conqueror* (1997).

Peter Sobczynski

CREDITS

Conan: Jason Momoa
Marique: Rose McGowan
Khalar Zym: Stephen Lang
Corin: Ron Perlman
Tamara: Rachel Nichols
Origin: USA
Language: English
Released: 2011
Production: John Baldecchi, Boaz Davidson, Randall Emmett, Joe Gatta, Avi Lerner, Danny Lerner, Frederick Malmberg, Les Weldon; Nu Image Films, Millenium Films, Paradox Entertainment; released by Lionsgate
Directed by: Marcus Nispel
Written by: Joshua Oppenheimer, Sean Hood, Thomas Dean Donnelly
Cinematography by: Thomas Kloss
Music by: Tyler Bates
Sound: Selena Arizanovic

Editing: Ken Blackwell
Art Direction: James Steuart
Costumes: Wendy Partridge
Production Design: Chris August
MPAA rating: R
Running time: 113 minutes

REVIEWS

Dargis, Manohla. *New York Times*. August 18, 2011.
Debruge, Peter. *Variety*. August 17, 2011.
Dujsik, Mark. *Mark Reviews Movies*. August 18, 2011.
Ebert, Roger. *Chicago Sun-Times*. August 18, 2011.
Maltin, Leonard. *Leonard Maltin's Picks*. August 19, 2011.
McDonagh, Maitland. *Film Journal International*. August 18, 2011.
Orndorf, Brian. *BrianOrndorf.com*. August 18, 2011.
Phipps, Keith. *AV Club*. August 18, 2011.
Snider, Eric D. *EricDSnider.com*. August 24, 2011.
Tobias, Scott. *NPR*. August 18, 2011.

QUOTES

Corin: "When a Cimmerian feels thirst, it is a thirst for blood. When he feels cold, it is the cold edge of steel. For the courage of a Cimmerian is tempered: he neither fears death…nor rushes foolishly to meet it. To be a Cimmerian warrior, you must have both cunning and balance as well as speed and strength."

TRIVIA

Brett Ratner was originally attached to direct before being replaced by Marcus Nispel.

THE CONSPIRATOR

One bullet killed the President. But not one man.
—Movie tagline

Box Office: $11.5 million

At once emblematic of the types of noble, thematically resonant historical stories that Hollywood studios typically no longer produce, as well as the problems and pitfalls of adaptation and condensation so often associated with such productions, *The Conspirator* represents director Robert Redford's allegorical stab at the perils of extreme political and societal polarization, as viewed through the lens of the judicial aftermath of the Abraham Lincoln assassination. Ardent history buffs are apt to give *The Conspirator* an affirming nod, their recollections tilted to favor by a vague sense of narrative importance and a pair of scenes with rousing oratories.

Overwhelmingly, though, this is a stodgy, didactic tale to which the phrase "well meaning" is likely the kindliest adjective that could reasonably be applied.

Critical opinion was notably muted upon release, and general audiences were similarly not swayed. A soft mid-April opening slotted eleventh for its opening weekend, and the movie, which never expanded beyond nine hundred screens, ended up grossing only $11.5 million, far under its approximate $25 million production budget.

The Conspirator unfolds against the backdrop of post-Civil War Washington, D.C. With the country still reeling from the murder of President Lincoln, 28-year-old Union war hero and newly minted lawyer Frederick Aiken (James McAvoy) reluctantly accedes to the wishes of his mentor, Reverdy Johnson (Tom Wilkinson), and agrees to represent the lone woman, widow Mary Surratt (Robin Wright), charged in the assassination scheme. Surratt's crime, according to the government, is as an accessory, since she was the owner of a boarding house where John Wilkes Booth (Toby Kebbell) and others, including her own son, John (Johnny Simmons), met to plan simultaneous attacks to kill the president, vice president and other cabinet members.

The driving force behind the federal tribunal is Secretary of War Edwin M. Stanton (Kevin Kline), who is eager to relieve a nation's wounded psyche, and views across-the-board legal expediency as the easiest means to such an end. As he grapples with lead consul Joseph Holt (Danny Huston), Aiken comes to believe—through conversations with Mary's daughter Anna (Evan Rachel Wood) and others—that his client may be innocent, and being used chiefly as bait in an effort to lure out of hiding John, the only conspirator to have escaped a massive manhunt. Using various legal maneuvers, Aiken endeavors to save Mary's life, trying mightily to beat back overwhelming courtroom odds, crushing public opinion and a client that does not fully trust him.

There are certainly plenty of parallels between events portrayed in *The Conspirator* and the generally pervasive mood of fear, uncertainty and bubbling jingoism that has by and large marked the United States over the last decade. But the movie's examination of fear-mongering and guilt by association is tepid and one-dimensional. The screenplay, by James Solomon, from a story credited to he and Gregory Bernstein, never locates a consistent dynamic foil for Aiken, nor does it approach familiar scenarios in fresh ways.

This latter problem most plagues *The Conspirator*. Beat by beat, scene by scene, the film deploys the most recognizable and proverbial clichés in both dialogue and situation. In the process, it smothers the air out of its narrative, taking an event and era that by all accounts should be full of nervy energy and dark intrigue and instead making it leaden and inert. Short of a scene in which Aiken is physically beat up, every standard obstacle for the crusading protagonist is trotted out and touched upon, from snooty high-society types whispering behind his back and someone anonymously throwing a brick through Aiken's window to the expected scene where his courtroom adversary shouts, "Stand down counselor!" It is as if the off-screen social activism of Redford, in all its square-jawed righteousness, will not allow for creative dramatic staging.

The movie, too, struggles some with point-of-view. While Wright cycles through a litany of pained grimaces, the screenplay has trouble communicating the depth of Surratt's plight. Her character seems walled off, and never a reservoir of true audience sympathies. Frederick's arc establishes the putative narrative thrust as that of being a passionate defense of the tenets of law and justice, even and especially in times or war or other national duress. But a coda with John Surratt, in which he tells Frederick, "You were more of a son to her than I ever was," attempts to manipulatively foist a personal element upon the story that is not entirely convincing.

In parallel fashion, cinematographer Newton Thomas Sigel similarly complies with Redford's worst instincts, delivering a suffocating visual scheme that leans toward genre parody. The color palette is already gloomy and muted, perhaps aptly reflecting the clothes of the time, but dark rooms are illuminated by diffuse light streaming in from large windows, which seems paradoxical and stagey. Any chance to liven up the story and lend it a sense of either gritty reality or currency and immediacy goes out the window with this interpretation.

The Conspirator represents only the second film behind the camera for Redford in the past decade, and the other, *Lions for Lambs* (2007), reflects a similar interest in matters political. Whereas that movie had a few crackerjack spitfire exchanges on both moral and philosophical axes, though, *The Conspirator* has a lot more base-level anger and legal teeth-gnashing. It is merely a gussied-up, ploddingly paced procedural with a lot of extra characters. Only a spirited intellectual grappling between Johnson and Stanton, which serves as the movie's indisputable high point, stands out. But even that sequence underscores the movie's failings; it is never a good sign when a film's most memorable scene involves solely a pair of arguably secondary and perhaps tertiary characters.

Befitting a director with his sort of experience in front of the camera, Redford's touch with actors seems fairly hands-off, leading to a couple pockets of questionable demonstrativeness. Kline and Wilkinson do quite well, but Wood is given to a clipped and haughty manner that seems not of that period. McAvoy, meanwhile, expresses great passion and passable inner conflict, but his indeterminate accent seems to come and go.

The Conspirator does not look cheap, but neither is it extremely persuasive in its conveyance of time and place. Louise Frogley's costume design is suitable, but the movie overall lacks the visual grandeur and scope to breathe true life into this amazing plot—remembering again that Lincoln's assassination was but one piece of a larger anarchic plan. Even telling the aftermath of this story, and focusing on Mary's trial, should cast more of a spell, with swirling motivations and clashing personalities. Across the board, though, *The Conspirator* lacks the sort of basic vitality necessary for a big screen treatment of such a tale. Reading a book or firing up a History Channel special might be a better way to go for parties interested in learning more about the same story.

Brent Simon

CREDITS

Mary Surratt: Robin Wright
Frederick Aiken: James McAvoy
Secretary of War Edwin M. Stanton: Kevin Kline
Anna Surratt: Evan Rachel Wood
Judge Advocate Gen. Joseph Holt: Danny Huston
Nicholas Baker: Justin Long
Gen. David Hunter: Colm Meaney
Reverdy Johnson: Tom Wilkinson
John Wilkes Booth: Toby Kebbell
John Surratt: Johnny Simmons
Origin: USA
Language: English
Released: 2010
Production: Robert Redford, Greg Shapiro, Bill Holderman, Brian Peter Falk, Robert Stone; Wildwood Enterprises, American Film Consortium; released by Lionsgate
Directed by: Robert Redford
Written by: James Solomon
Cinematography by: Newton Thomas Sigel
Music by: Mark Isham
Sound: Richard Hymns
Editing: Craig McKay
Art Direction: Mark Garner
Costumes: Louise Frogley
Production Design: Kalina Ivanov
MPAA rating: PG-13
Running time: 122 minutes

REVIEWS

Anderson, John. *Newsday.* April 22, 2011.
Chang, Justin. *Variety.* April 14, 2011.
Goodridge, Mike. *Screen International.* April 13, 2011.
Kohn, Eric. *indieWIRE.* April 12, 2011.
Lane, Anthony. *New Yorker.* April 13, 2011.
Morgenstern, Joe. *Wall Street Journal.* April 14, 2011.
Phillips, Michael. *Chicago Tribune.* April 14, 2011.
Puig, Claudia. *USA Today.* April 17, 2011.
Scott, A.O. *New York Times.* April 14, 2011.
Sobczynski, Peter. *eFilmCritic.com.* April 14, 2011.

QUOTES

Mary Surratt: "Have you ever believed in something far greater than yourself?"

TRIVIA

This is the debut offering from the American Film Company; whose mission is to make historically accurate films about America's past.

CONTAGION

Don't talk to anyone. Don't touch anyone.
—Movie tagline
Nothing spreads like fear.
—Movie tagline

Box Office: $75.7 million

Since the age of Irwin Allen, the disaster film genre has seemingly been dominated by big-budget, bombastic directors like Michael Bay or Roland Emmerich, filmmakers who have typically received acclaim for their visuals and widespread disdain for their ability to tell a coherent story. Most directors of modern disaster movies have just regarded the disaster itself as the sole story requirement. "Earthquake," "Volcano," "Asteroid Headed Towards Earth," "End of the World"—in the disaster movie, those few words often count as fully fleshed-out story pitches.

So, when it was announced that acclaimed filmmaker Steven Soderbergh, one of the few directors working today who can easily vacillate between story-driven independent filmmaking (*Sex, Lies, and Videotape* [1989], *The Limey* [1999], Che [2008]) and big blockbuster ensemble pieces (the *Ocean's Eleven* series [2001, 2004, 2007]) was working on *Contagion,* a virus outbreak thriller, it definitely suggested a more interesting disaster film than most of the apocalypse scenarios that have cluttered the multiplexes.

Soderbergh's *Contagion* is, unquestionably, a disaster film, but it is one of the most gripping, cerebral disaster thrillers of the past two decades. And, possibly, the most interesting aspect of the film itself is how Soderbergh and screenwriter Scott Z. Burns both embrace and explode the typical genre characteristics of a disaster movie.

Case in point—it is not a spoiler to reveal that the world does not, in fact, come to an end in the closing moments of *Contagion*. The deadly virus does not sweep across the planet—like it did during the end credits of *Rise of the Planet of the Apes* (2011)—suggesting that humanity has finally sown the seeds of its own destruction. It is significant to note this distinction, the idea that *Contagion* is not about the actual end of the world, because so many modern disaster movies, in their desire to raise the stakes for their audience, have immediately jumped to the "global extinction event" option and, in doing so, have subtly moved into the realm of sci-fi and fantasy. The blaring rock soundtracks, eye-candy visual FX, and impossible technology in films like *2012* (2009) or *Armageddon* (1998) make it almost impossible to regard those movies as anything other than big-budget fantasies. The real world looks nothing like the visual worlds of Michael Bay or Roland Emmerich, so, when the Earth dies in their films, it is akin to watching the destruction of Middle Earth or Narnia.

Soderbergh, on the other hand, and perhaps in response to this trend, spends a huge amount of effort grounding *Contagion* in reality. He might use some of the same cinematic vocabulary and world-spanning backdrops of the typical disaster film, but the story itself feels almost achingly real, which makes *Contagion* seem that much more personal and completely terrifying.

Building on the headlines about recent real-world health scare—SARS, H1N1, or avian influenza—Soderbergh and Burns have created a procedural mystery around a viral outbreak that mystifies global medical authorities and threatens to endanger a large portion of the world's population. Structurally, *Contagion* most closely resembles Soderbergh's Oscar®-winning *Traffic* (2000), a film that examined the illegal drug trade by telling a series of interlinked stories that all presented different societal perspectives on the issue—the perspectives of traffickers, law enforcement, politicians, the families of users, etc. *Contagion* is set up in a similar fashion, showing the global impact of a vicious viral pandemic through the eyes of the victims of the disease, their families, the researchers trying to find the origins of the disease, the doctors desperate to find a vaccine, the journalists and the media, and so on.

Contagion opens with the personal impact of such a virus when a businesswoman, Beth Emhoff (Gwyneth Paltrow), returns from a work trip to Asia to her home in Minneapolis with the symptoms of what seems like a common cold. However, Beth's health quickly deterio-

rates and she mysteriously dies from her illness at a local hospital, both confusing and horrifying her husband Mitch (Matt Damon). The film cuts between several of the parallel storylines throughout, but Mitch's storyline is one of the movie's key emotional anchors. Damon plays traumatized grief extremely well—reminiscent of his performance in the similarly-structured *Syriana* (2005)—and, as he goes on the run with his daughter to escape the impact of the virus, particularly the paramilitary-style quarantine and expected rioting and violence, he really does convey the familial panic that such a scenario would inspire.

Meanwhile, as Mitch fights to protect his daughter, Soderbergh follows the global medical authorities as they discover the virus, quickly learn of its unprecedented virulence, and mobilize to find a vaccine and mitigate its damage. Dr. Ellis Cheever (Laurence Fishburne) at the Centers for Disease Control and Prevention sends Dr. Erin Mears (Kate Winslet) to Minneapolis, home of Beth Emhoff, to track down the origins of the U.S. outbreak, which places Mears in the unfortunate position of having to deal with the panic and military bureaucracy that is engulfing Minneapolis as the virus spreads across the city.

As Sears continues her investigation, the CDC and other political and scientific agencies explore various options for combating the virus. Once Beth Emhoff is identified as "patient zero," a World Health Organization scientist, Dr. Orantes (Marion Cotillard), travels to Hong Kong and China, following Emhoff's trip itinerary to hopefully find the origins of the virus. But Orantes is soon kidnapped and used as a bargaining chip for a village in China that wants first access to any potential vaccine. That vaccine in question is being developed at the CDC, thanks to a professor (Elliot Gould) and a CDC doctor, Dr. Hextall (Jennifer Ehle), who successfully identify the virus as Meningoencephalitis Virus One (MEV-1). And, with the virus identified, Hextall begins work on creating a vaccine, which comes with a whole host of ethical and scientific dilemmas.

Not satisfied with just showing the personal and procedural sides of the virus investigation, Soderbergh wisely also turns his gaze toward some of the uglier cultural side effects that an outbreak like this would inspire. The film is awash in moral gray areas—What are the ethics of human testing? Should CDC officials be punished for giving early warnings to family members to escape potential quarantine zones? Is it ethical to use the military to forcibly quarantine innocent American citizens to prevent the future spread of the disease? What is the responsibility of the media in a global pandemic situation? Is their only responsibility to report the facts or do they need to limit their reporting to help mitigate widespread panic?

This darker cultural side of the outbreak is exemplified by Jude Law's character, Alan Krumwiede, a freelance blogger who becomes one of the most outspoken media figures surrounding the pandemic. Krumwiede is a slick, intense conspiracy theorist, who stirs up outrage in the general population with a mixture of facts, spin, and misinformation. Krumwiede finds fame after accusing Dr. Cheever of warning his family to leave Chicago before a military quarantine began, and, most significantly, Krumwiede claims to have personally recovered from an MEV-1 infection thanks to a homeopathic cure. This causes a panicked nation-wide demand for the homeopathic remedy, which is further complicated when connections between Krumwiede and the company that produces the remedy are revealed.

A cure is discovered and the world is saved...this time. But Soderbergh makes *Contagion* much more subversive and insightful by using such a real-world, real feeling scenario to give a glimpse of how close humanity could come to succumbing to such a global outbreak. Soderbergh's cinematography and the look of *Contagion* are virtuoso-level on the technical side. The ways in which he shows the virus spreading across the world are alternately beautiful and terrifying. Watching *Contagion* in a packed movie theatre is a singular experience, because the movie itself takes everyday things like doorknobs, railings, or, say, a crowded room full of people and makes them ten times scarier than Michael Myers or Freddy Krueger.

While, yes, with a few exceptions (Damon, Ehle), *Contagion* could be described as an emotionally "cold" movie—there are far more tense investigation scenes than heart-wrenching tears for lost loved ones—the film does so much right and makes the outbreak feel so real and tangible that it makes *Contagion* a much more human experience than any other disaster film in recent or past memory. It was an extremely smart decision on Soderbergh's part to not turn *Contagion* into an "end of the world" movie. That would have made the film into something speculative, into a fantasy situation, into a cheap metaphor for the hubris of mankind finally catching up with it. Instead, Soderbergh creates a vivid, eerily plausible look at how a global health crisis—a painfully real scenario—could expose humanity to something very ugly, and, since he did not resort to the overdone apocalypse allegory, it is much harder for audiences to dismiss. *Contagion* is a rare strain of the disaster film virus—a strain that will stay with the viewer for days and weeks later, which is both a refreshing and scary development.

Tom Burns

CREDITS

Dr. Leonora Orantes: Marion Cotillard
Mitch Emhoff: Matt Damon
Dr. Ellis Cheever: Laurence Fishburne
Alan Krumwiede: Jude Law
Beth Emhoff: Gwyneth Paltrow
Dr. Erin Mears: Kate Winslet
Haggerty: Bryan Cranston
Ally Hextall: Jennifer Ehle
Roger: John Hawkes
Dr. Ian Sussman: Elliott Gould
Dr. David Eisenberg: Demetri Martin
Dennis French: Enrico Colantoni
Aubrey Cheever: Sanaa Lathan
Lorraine Vasquez: Monique Gabriela Curnen
Jory Emhoff: Luis van Rooten
Origin: USA
Language: English
Released: 2011
Production: Stacey Sher, Gregory Jacobs; Double Feature Films, Participant Media; released by Warner Bros.
Directed by: Steven Soderbergh
Written by: Scott Burns
Cinematography by: Steven Soderbergh
Music by: Cliff Martinez
Sound: Larry Blake
Editing: Stephen Mirrione
Art Direction: Abdellah Baadil, Simon Dobbin, David Lazan
Costumes: Louise Frogley
Production Design: Howard Cummings
MPAA rating: PG-13
Running time: 106 minutes

REVIEWS

Dargis, Manohla. *New York Times.* September 8, 2011.
Denby, David. *New Yorker.* September 12, 2011.
LaSalle, Mick. *San Francisco Chronicle.* September 8, 2011.
Longworth, Karina. *Village Voice.* September 6, 2011.
Morris, Wesley. *Boston Globe.* September 8, 2011.
O'Hehir, Andrew. *Salon.com.* September 9, 2011.
Phillips, Michael. *Chicago Tribune.* September 8, 2011.
Phipps, Keith. *AV Club.* September 7, 2011.
Schwarzbaum, Lisa. *Entertainment Weekly.* September 8, 2011.
Willmore, Alison. *Movieline.* September 8, 2011.

QUOTES

Dr. Ian Sussman: "Blogging is not writing. It's just graffiti with punctuation."

TRIVIA

Director Steven Soderbergh makes a brief cameo as the voice of Jon Neal in the first scene of the movie.

CORIOLANUS

Nature teaches beasts to know their friends.
—Movie tagline

It is not uncommon for acclaimed actors to jump at the chance to take a timeless Shakespearian character and pull him kicking and screaming into the modern era. Sir Ian McKellen did so with *Richard III* (1995) and Ethan Hawke took a hipster take with *Hamlet* (2000). Any film fan's list of the current actors who might be enticed by a similar project would almost certainly include Ralph Fiennes, a man who has copious experience playing legendary characters as diverse as Lord Voldemort (*Harry Potter and the Deathly Hallows: Part 2* [2011]), Hades (*Clash of the Titans* [2010]), Marcel Proust (*How Proust Can Change Your Life* [2000]), Heathcliff (*Wuthering Heights* [1992]) and even the voices of Rameses (*The Prince of Egypt* [1998]) and Jesus (*The Miracle Maker* [2000]). The title character in a William Shakespeare play seems like a slam dunk for this stellar actor and it makes perfect sense that he would choose a drama by the Bard as his directorial debut. Also unsurprisingly given the director's past, *Coriolanus* works best as a performance piece but falters a bit when its other elements are considered. As is often the case with actors turned directors, Fiennes draws stellar work from his cast. John Logan (*Gladiator* [2000], *The Aviator* [2004]) works admirably to adapt a play that has not really risen to the ranks of Shakespeare's most well-known works for a reason but *Coriolanus* is still a distant piece, one that never fully engages emotionally as much as it does as a very impressive acting exercise.

With little change to the actual dialogue (and Logan and Fiennes clearly relish the language as much as possible, choosing their set pieces and scenes as little more than ways to frame it), *Coriolanus* updates the Roman-set piece to an indeterminate time and place. While the language still refers to Rome, the setting looks similar to many of the wars of the last two decades. It could be Bosnia or even Kuwait with tanks, shaved heads, and graffiti-strewn walls. Wherever and whenever *Coriolanus* takes place is not relevant to the themes that Shakespeare embedded in the piece. It is about the gray area between heroes and villains; saviors and destroyers. In war, one side's victor is the other side's vanquisher. These themes are clearly timeless in nature and can apply to any generation or war-time setting but they are more interesting as intellectual talking points than as drama, which is why this play is not one of Shakespeare's most commonly staged.

The title character (Fiennes) is a victorious but not very well-liked leader. Coriolanus is the given leader name to Caius Martius, a Roman general who has recently defeated a wave of uprising Volscian enemies. To do so, he has made decisions that have not made him overly popular among the Roman people, who he clearly holds at arm's length for a reason. He is a leader on the battlefield but does not prevail at politics as he

does at warfare. When he returns from a battle and is dubbed Coriolanus, he runs for Consul of Rome and his general disdain for the people that live there is revealed. He lives to fight for the people but does not really like them. He is banished. Being a smart man who knows the value he could offer his former enemy, he teams with the Volscian Tullus Aufidius (Gerard Butler) to take back his city with violence. His mother Volumnia (Vanessa Redgrave) and wife Virgilia (Jessica Chastain) try to talk him out of returning the betrayal he feels with bloodshed. Of course, as in most of Shakespeare's war-set plays, *Coriolanus* ends with death.

While there are action set-pieces in Fiennes' film, it really comes alive when his actors are allowed to do what they do best and roll the timeless language around their mouths with glee. Butler has a little difficulty holding his own against legends like Fiennes and Redgrave, but he delivers more than his recent filmography might have suggested he would. As good as Fiennes is here as a sullen, brutal warrior, the film really belongs to Vanessa Redgrave, who delivers arguably the Best Supporting Actress performance of 2011, most notably in a stunning monologue late in the film in which she is absolutely mesmerizing. All flaws of the film fall away when Redgrave speaks. She finds that very rare ability to make Shakespeare's dialogue sound like it is coming from within her and not like it has been spoken by thousands of actresses for hundreds of years. The ubiquitous Chastain has a smaller part than in many of her notable 2011 works but she is solid here as well.

There is a reason that *Coriolanus* rarely pops up as a cultural example of William Shakespeare's work. Of course, a lesser play by the Bard is still worth staging in theatre or film, but the themes here seem relatively straightforward and even a little simplistic to attract a modern audience. There is not the depth of meaning or density of character that one finds in *King Lear, Hamlet, MacBeth,* or *Richard III.* Perhaps if Fiennes had picked one of those works as his first directorial effort than the expectations would have been too high given worldwide awareness of their themes. He picked a lesser Shakespeare play and delivered a piece that proves the timelessness of the most influential writer of all time by emphasizing the language and the talent of the people who speak it. Maybe next time he will go for *Lear.*

Brian Tallerico

CREDITS

Caius Martius Coriolanus: Ralph Fiennes
Tullus Aufidius: Gerard Butler
Volumnia: Vanessa Redgrave
Menenius: Brian Cox

Virgilia: Jessica Chastain
Sicinius: James Nesbitt
Cominius: John Kani
Brutus: Paul Jesson
Origin: United Kingdom
Language: English
Released: 2011
Production: Ralph Fiennes, John Logan, Gabrielle Tana; Hermetot Pictures, Kalkronkie, Icon Entertainment Media; released by Weinstein Company
Directed by: Ralph Fiennes
Written by: John Logan
Cinematography by: Barry Ackroyd
Music by: Ilan Eshkeri
Sound: Ray Beckett
Music Supervisor: Ian Neil
Editing: Nicolas Gaster
Art Direction: Rade Mihajlovic
Costumes: Bojana Nikitovie
Production Design: Ricky Eyres
MPAA rating: R
Running time: 122 minutes

REVIEWS

Ebert, Roger. *Chicago Sun-Times.* February 1, 2012.
Hynes, Eric. *Village Voice.* November 29, 2011.
Jones, J.R. *Chicago Reader.* February 2, 2012.
Neumaier, Joe. *New York Daily News.* December 1, 2011.
Puig, Claudia. *USA Today.* December 1, 2011.
Schager, Nick. *Slant Magazine.* November 28, 2011.
Sharkey, Betsy. *Los Angeles Times.* December 1, 2011.
Smith, Kyle. *New York Post.* December 2, 2011.
Stevens, Dana. *Slate.* January 19, 2012.
Zacharek, Stephanie. *Movieline.* December 1, 2011.

QUOTES

Caius Martius Coriolanus: "I'll fight with none but thee, for I do hate thee."
Tullus Aufidius: "We hate alike."

TRIVIA

The fight scene between Gerard Butler and Ralph Fiennes took two days to shoot.

AWARDS

Nomination:
British Acad. 2011: Outstanding Debut.

COURAGEOUS

Honor begins at home.
—Movie tagline

Four men, one calling: To serve and protect.
—Movie tagline

Box Office: $34.5 million

There have always been those who argue art (in this case, film) is at its best and best serves society and civilization when it is instructive—usually morally so. The problem with that highly questionable (and often reactionary) attitude, is that pumping a strong message into a film, or completely constructing a film entirely as a delivery method for a message, does not always make for the best, let alone most entertaining art. At least not for casual viewers outside the message's already devoted target audience.

Courageous is the latest in a series of films produced by and pointedly for Christians seeking moral guidance in their daily lives. As co-written, directed by, and starring Alex Kendrick, the new film is, like Kendrick's *Fireproof* (2008), exists only as a melodramatic delivery system for a sharply aimed moral message. Where *Fireproof* implored Christian couples to honor God and work hard at their marriage so He could help heal it, *Courageous* addresses a different issue: fatherhood. More specifically, raising good sons.

To that end, the film's plot follows four small-town sheriff's deputies (Kendrick, Ken Bevel, Ben Davies, and Kevin Downes) and a Hispanic friend of theirs (Robert Amaya) as the men struggle with fathering-based hardships and tragedies that function in the narrative purely as either turning points or tests. Naturally some of these hurdles are law-enforcement based (underscoring the need for the men to be as "courageous" in their parenting as they are on the mean streets of Albany, Georgia), but just as many are domestic, such as teaching daughters to date nice boys and connecting with sullen teenage sons.

Courageous is far from subtle. The family dramas the men face are big and broad, and the characters' soul-searching is shouted to the heavens with earnestly shaken fists. Even the cops-and-robbers element of the film feels informed not by actual experience or verisimilitude but by the filmmakers having watched a lot of cops-and-robbers shows on television. (More disturbingly, the drug-dealing, doo-rag-wearing, bad-guy thugs are one-note, African-American boogeyman stereotypes.)

Kendrick and his film, however, seem to wear their lack of cinematic sophistication like a badge of honor. The more someone might criticize *Courageous* for its clumsy, heavy handed drama and hammer-fisted sermonizing, the more that dismissal proves to the film's makers and supporters that any such critic has hardened his or her heart to the film's pure and true message. Messages this important, the film suggests, cannot be nuanced lest they miss their intended targets.

Not that the basic message is a bad one: Fathers, *Courageous* says, should be more involved and more responsible for the raising of their children. (Mothers, the film suggests by omission, come by this nurturing business naturally and need no such prodding and lecturing.) But that admirable lesson also comes wrapped in plenty of patriarchal Christian pulpit pounding. It is somewhat inaccurate to describe *Courageous* as "faith-based"—that implies a broader, vaguer focus. This is a *Christian* film, more specifically a Baptist one. The characters' behaviors are not changed by belief in a pan-religious, Judeo-Christian god or sense of moral spirituality—belief in Jesus alone redeems them as godly men. (One of the men scoffs agnostically at first at at the "religion stuff," but has come fully around by the end.)

Sodden with *After School Special* obviousness, as cinema *Courageous* is an earnest-but-clunky failure. It is overlong and wandering; its plot jumps from point to point, driven only by its lesson plan; and the plaintive, declarative dialogue and acting is hardly above the level of a church pageant. Again, its makers might say all that fancy movie stuff is beside the point: the film exists to guide and teach.

Yet even as instruction, *Courageous* is frustratingly misguided. Led by Kendrick's Adam Mitchell, the five men create and swear to a fathering Resolution that lists all the parental ideals they hope to embrace and follow. The Resolution is treated with great pride and reverence, but the film and its characters seem much more interested in its structured rules and rituals than concrete ideas about how to actually raise these desired manly, godly sons on a daily basis. Too often the only parenting tip or insight offered is to honor God, pray a lot, and let Him guide you.

One specific suggestion the film offers is for fathers to present their teen daughters with purity rings that symbolically bind the young women to both pre-marital abstinence and deference to their father's approval of any suitors. Once again substituting ritual for realistic instruction, it is a ceremonial gesture of jewelry giving that, when performed by Bevel and Taylor Hutcherson as his character's daughter, feels a little creepy.

Courageous is not all bad, not un-watchable, and not wrong in its intent, just its execution. Kendrick is a ploddingly semi-competent director, but shows some endearing charm. And while the shoehorning in of Amaya as the group's token Hispanic may feel cynically aimed at broadening the film's demographic appeal, the actor shows some comic timing—he and Kendrick have several genuinely amusing scenes together. There are also moments when, prodded by soaring horns on the soundtrack, the relentless earnestness of the film may produce a lump in a viewer's throat. After all, who does

not want to encourage and celebrate better parenting and stronger family ties?

Courageous, however, plays less like a work of affecting drama and more like a Sunday school workbook. For a film about the healing power of spirituality, it is utterly graceless.

Locke Peterseim

CREDITS

Adam Micthell: Alex Kendrick
Shane Fuller: Kevin Downes
David Thomson: Ben Davies
Nathan Hayes: Ken Bevel
Kayla Hayes: Eleanor Brown
Antoine: Matt Hardwick
Dylan Mitchell: Rusty Martin
Emily Mitchell: Lauren Etchells
Javier Martinez: Robert Amaya
Carmen Martinez: Angelica Nelsom
Origin: USA
Language: English
Released: 2011
Production: Stephen Kendrick; TriStar Pictures, Sherwood Pictures; released by Sony Pictures Entertainment
Directed by: Alex Kendrick
Written by: Alex Kendrick, Stephen Kendrick
Cinematography by: Bob Scott
Music by: Mark Willard
Sound: Rob Whitehurst
Editing: Alex Kendrick, Steve Hullfish, Bill Ebel
Costumes: Terri Catt
Production Design: Darian Corley, Sheila McBride
MPAA rating: PG-13
Running time: 130 minutes

REVIEWS

Brunick, Paul. *New York Times.* October 4, 2011.
Goldstein, Gary. *Los Angeles Times.* October 4, 2011.
Gonzalez, Ed. *Slant Magazine.* September 30, 2011.
Leydon, Joe. *Variety.* October 2, 2011.
Moore, Roger. *Orlando Sentinel.* September 28, 2011.
Rabin, Nathan. *AV Club.* October 1, 2011.
Russo, Tom. *Boston Globe.* October 4, 2011.
Schager, Nick. *Village Voice.* October 1, 2011.
Scheck, Frank. *Hollywood Reporter.* October 1, 2011.
Staskiewicz, Keith. *Entertainment Weekly.* October 4, 2011.

QUOTES

Pastor Hunt: "I have heard many people say, who have lost a loved one, that in some ways it is like learning to live with an amputation. You do heal, but you are never the same."

COWBOYS & ALIENS

Box Office: $100.2 million

Cowboys & Aliens is no laughing matter.

That is what was strenuously stressed by those responsible for this Western-Science fiction mashup, especially after audiences took its trailer the wrong way and guffawed when it was hoped they would gasp with excitement. However, one could hardly blame them, as the title alone created the expectation of an imaginatively-loopy and rousing romp of an adventure. Furthermore, with a plot that promises beings from outer space who suddenly settle out West and tangle with cowboys in the 1870's, it seemed like the filmmakers themselves were, at least in the tonal sense, also setting up camp. In actuality, they are straining to play things seriously straight, even as attacking alien craft put the boom back in boomtown for fizzled Absalom, New Mexican, and then snag comparatively backward, baffled frontier folk with long metallic lassoes and yank them skyward in a startling yet silly-looking (and implausibly-survivable) fashion. The anticipation was that viewers would find themselves acutely caught up as well in proceedings that had been sufficiently grounded, gripped by a visceral sense that, in short, stuff is truly at stake. However, more than a few moviegoers remained unmoved by it all, wishing they had instead witnessed something of captivating distinctiveness that had been leavened instead of made leaden.

Admittedly, the film initially intrigues. Having been briefly lulled by glimpses of still Southwestern sublimity, viewers are effectively roused by a grimy, hyperventilating man suddenly sitting up into the frame as if from a nightmare. Since he is played by Daniel Craig, most females in attendance felt that this manifestation added further rugged magnificence to the mise-en-sc?ne. While they might love to get their hands on the actor, the three outlaws who try to grab Craig's character in order to turn the presumed fugitive in for reward money do not even live long enough to regret their attempt, bested with swift, deadly skill. Thus, if this man's sudden appearance out of nowhere and in the middle of nowhere was not enough to arouse one's curiosity, there is also that impressive self-defense acumen, his amnesia (think Bourne bandit), the bleeding wound in his side, and that futuristic-looking cuff on his wrist.

While Absalom and vicinity seem devoid of gold to mine, there is certainly a treasure trove of Western character clichés there that provide some built-in genre predictability. There is Craig's solitary, enigmatic and shockingly-lethal stranger. (Circumstances will likely reveal his decency). Harrison Ford plays Colonel Woodrow Dolarhyde, the imperious cattle baron who has the struggling town by the pocketbook. (Events will bring him down off his high horse). Keith Carradine is the sheriff whose sworn duty puts him on a collision course with domineering Dolarhyde. (A confrontation is undoubtedly 'round the bend). Paul Dano portrays the tyrant's drunk, gun-wielding punk of a son Percy, who is used to darting out from his father's imposing shadow to bedevil with a frustrating impunity. (Comeuppance is surely ahead). One of his targets is Sam Rockwell's bespectacled saloon keeper Doc, a transplanted Eastern city dweller who needs to get tougher and shoot straighter in this especially wild West. (Viewers fully expect that both will happen before the credits roll). Adam Beach plays the noble Native American who has long wondered what it will take to garner the approval instead of the disdain of adoptive father Dolarhyde. (Get some hankies and a coffin ready). Neither last nor least is Noah Ringer as the sheriff's grandson, a character somewhat reminiscent of that portrayed by Brandon De Wilde in *Shane* (1953). (His eyes will not only be opened wide to things of this world but also another).

Even with stock characters that are scantily sketched and miles from being memorable, viewers might overlook such things as long as they remained sufficiently intrigued by The Man With No Name and No Memory, whose standing up to Percy makes him seem admirable until a wanted poster identifying him as criminal Jake Lonegren casts serious doubt. Just as a too-obviously-not-from-these-parts Ella (Olivia Wilde) is oddly intent on unlocking that memory, Jake himself is locked up and about to be carted off to a federal marshal along with Percy. (The loose cannon has inadvertently shot a deputy). Suddenly, Col. Dolarhyde arrives with his men and demands custody of both to do as he alone sees fit. Will this film's New Mexican lawman exhibit the same courage and integrity against formidable opposition as the one played by Gary Cooper in *High Noon* (1952)? Will Jake's guilt or innocence have the chance to be proven in court, and how can he defend himself without first being able to recall more than haunting mere flashes of the past? Most viewers were wanting to know—and then came the spaceship blitz, creating such a jolting, extreme, and absurd juxtaposition with the old West material that the web of believability in which many viewers had been successfully ensnared was destroyed even more thoroughly than Absalom by the aliens. What resulted for many is the exact degree of disengagement that director John Favreau said he had tried to avoid: "Oh, this is just a fantasy." The story had irrevocably lost its grip—with most of the film's overlong running time to go.

Orci, Kurtzman, Lindelof, Fergus, Ostby, Oedekerk, Hayter, Hauty, Boam, Evans, Donnelly and Oppenheimer is not the name of a law firm likely in need of more office space, but rather the surnames of those who worked at one point or another on the screen story and script for this loose adaptation of the 2006 graphic novel created by Scott Mitchell Rosenberg and written by Fred Van Lente and Andrew Foley. As for what they all came up with for the rest of *Cowboys & Aliens,* anyone who was on the edge of his or her seat was most likely there because a spring had uncomfortably given way toward the back of it. Icy, indispenibly-armed (or rather wristed) Jake and cranky-almost-to-caricature Dolarhyde form an uneasy alliance of necessity and head out to retrieve loved ones the audience either dislikes or has barely gotten to know, all the while accompanied by assorted others to which the audience also feels little connection. Wholly-expected run-ins with Jake's disgruntled old partners in crime and Native Americans already fed up with the white man's version of Manifest Destiny end up adding to the eccentric eclecticism of the posse. Triumphing over the derivative-looking aliens involves action that neither persuasively thrills nor potently chills. (Some are ridiculously felled by a mere punch.) After the beings are thunderously blown sky-high and reunions have left tear ducts unresponsive, Jake, redeemed through his heroism and now able to recall all, rides off toward a sun that set long ago on *Cowboys & Aliens.*

David L. Boxerbaum

CREDITS

Jake Lonergan: Daniel Craig
Col. Woodrow Dolarhyde: Harrison Ford
Ella: Olivia Wilde
Doc: Sam Rockwell
Nat Colorado: Adam Beach
Percy: Paul Dano
Sheriff Taggart: Keith Carradine
Alice: Abigail Spencer
Meacham: Clancy Brown
Hunt: Walton Goggins
Wes Claiborne: Buck Taylor
Origin: USA
Language: English
Released: 2011
Production: Johnny Dodge, Brian Grazer, Ron Howard, Alex Kurtzman, Damon Lindelof; DreamWorks SKG, Reliance

Media, Imagine Entertainment, K/O Paper Products, Fairview Entertainment; released by Universal Pictures
Directed by: Jon Favreau
Written by: Alex Kurtzman, Roberto Orci, Damon Lindelof, Mark Fergus, Hawk Ostby
Cinematography by: Matthew Libatique
Music by: Harry Gregson-Williams
Sound: Frank E. Eulner
Editing: Dan Lebental, Jim May
Art Direction: Chris Burian-Mohr, Daniel T. Dorrance
Costumes: Mary Zophres
Production Design: Scott Chambliss
MPAA rating: PG-13
Running time: 118 minutes

REVIEWS

Burr, Ty. *Boston Globe.* July 27, 2011.
Corliss, Richard. *Time.* July 28, 2011.
Dargis, Manohla. *New York Times.* July 28, 2011.
Ebert, Roger. *Chicago Sun-Times.* July 27, 2011.
Gilchrist, Todd. *Boxoffice Magazine.* July 24, 2011.
Gleiberman, Owen. *Entertainment Weekly.* July 27, 2011.
Honeycutt, Kirk. *Hollywood Reporter.* July 24, 2011.
Lane, Anthony. *New Yorker.* July 31, 2011.
Morgenstern, Joe. *Wall Street Journal.* July 28, 2011.
Phillips, Michael. *Chicago Tribune.* July 28, 2011.

QUOTES

Meacham: "Whether you end up in Heaven or Hell isn't God's plan, it's your own. You just have to remember what it is."

TRIVIA

Actor Daniel Craig was chosen partly because of his likeness to the legendary Steve McQueen.

AWARDS

Nomination:
Screen Actors Guild 2011: Stunt Ensemble.

CRAZY, STUPID, LOVE

This is crazy. This is stupid. This is love.
—Movie tagline

Box Office: $84.4 million

Somewhere, someone—maybe even a professor of profound literacy and Shakespearean insight—is writing about the topic of love in the most childish of terms. Maybe they are within the confines of love and their most base instincts to ogle the language in the most cutesy manner is overcoming them. Or they have fallen out of it and have resorted to the worst kind of name-calling and second grade adjectives to describe their heartbreak and spite the person responsible. Love is that unexplainable mystery that grabs all of us in some form or another. It could be for a couple of hours or an entire lifetime, but the feeling is unmistakable even if we do not fully understand it. Glenn Ficarra & John Requa's *Crazy, Stupid, Love.* does get it though and knows that the everyday confusion over how we define it can lead to decisions best described by the very adjectives it prefaces in its title turning us into cartoon characters who can only express themselves by holding up a picture of a screw and a ball.

Cal (Steve Carell) and Emily (Julianne Moore) have been married for over twenty years. But something has gone away and Emily announces at dinner that she wants a divorce. On top of that bombshell, she reveals she has slept with co-worker David Lindhagen (Kevin Bacon). Cal is devastated inside, but packs himself up quietly and leaves to drown his sorrows at an upscale bar where even his babysitter's father is forced to abandon him in the division of friends that comes when a couple splits. It is here where Cal meets a new friend in Jacob (Ryan Gosling), a smooth ladies' man who finds it pathetic that he has lost his way as a man. Jacob upgrades his look and gives him a few pointers in how to talk to women, a task Cal has never had to accomplish having found his "soul mate" at the age of fifteen.

At the same bar, the one person to actually reject Jacob's advances is law student Hannah (Emma Stone), more out of monogamy than the wanton primal desire to explore every inch of this natural charmer. Cal, meanwhile, begins to do just fine with the ladies, starting with clean and sober schoolteacher Kate (Marisa Tomei), who finds his honesty refreshing (even if honesty is against the advice of his new mentor). If only Cal's thirteen-year-old son Robbie (Jonah Bobo) had some to deal with the crush he has on family babysitter, Jessica (Analeigh Tipton), who is four years his senior and is crushing on somebody else. If Ashton Kutcher & Demi Moore can make it work, why not them he surmises. Perhaps they would be able to give some counsel to the adults here who are all equally confused by the dopamine guiding them to behavior that is outside their comfort zones.

Like another 2011 romantic comedy with aspirations of sidestepping conventions, *Friends With Benefits* (2011), Dan Fogelman's screenplay here ties in the subconscious obsession with looking towards movies to fill the collective blanks in an understanding of love. At first glance, Hannah's friend's assertion that her life is very "PG-13" may sound like a screenwriter's meta absolution to evade the issues in a real-world setting.

But movies still exist in that world and this one and can be used to woo a prospective mate as Jacob does in perfecting a signature move from *Dirty Dancing* (1987). When Emily takes time out during the final week of her marriage to go see the latest vampiric tween romance tale, is it purely for the sake of reference or because she was hoping to revisit that spark of young love? As an adult now, is she recognizing just how poorly told and fake those *Twilight* movies are or that the fantasy itself is "so bad?" Heartbreak is R-rated and dark, more like Ryan Gosling's last foray into divorce cinema, *Blue Valentine* (2010), but to laugh it off and move on while still clinging to the hope of a better tomorrow is a concept suitable for all ages, if not for maybe a little parental guidance.

Crazy, Stupid, Love. is a true ensemble piece front and center dealing with three primary relationships and then the assorted combos of crushes and one-night stands seeking to have more than they have been allowed. If Fogelberg's script resorts to the brand of sitcom conventions reserved for the dying laugh tracks of yesteryear, then it wields them as if it was the first to refine them from cinematic farce. This is a factor that does not come into play until the final act after Ficarra and Fiqua has set them up so precisely and if any disappointment results in somehow reducing the issues of upper middle class white people to an episode of *Three's Company*, just recall that *American Beauty* (1999) won five Oscars® doing just the same thing. These characters are not cartoonish by any definition and if backyard brawls and surprise revelations should not merely erase the carefully-plotted and naturally funny comedy that has been playing faithfully for ninety minutes.

Ensemble pieces tend to work on giving its characters equal weight throughout the story. In this respect, the film's men do edge out the women in both screen time and emotional resonance. Julianne Moore has her moments and Marisa Tomei certainly gets to sink her comedic chops into a role larger than expected, but it is really Emma Stone who, after a long absence in the middle returns for a desperate seduction scene that is equal parts sexy and sweet. She shares that extended dialogue scene with unquestionably one of the finest actors working today, Ryan Gosling. Ever since breaking through as the Jew-turned-skinhead in *The Believer* (2001), he has simply owned the screen as a sociopathic teen in *Murder By Numbers* (2002), then an idealistic teacher with a drug habit in his Oscar®-nominated turn from *Half Nelson* (2006), and the lonely guy who forms a relationship with a plastic sex doll in the wonderful *Lars and the Real Girl* (2007). Between those films and his stellar work in the gloomily realistic *Blue Valentine*, Gosling needed a comedy and he proves he is every bit as adept at when the situation is funny as to when it calls for dramatic depth. It is appropriate that Jacob is a character who is essentially living a life for two people and his seemingly impractical friendship with Cal is made all the more touching the more he lets his guard down.

Crazy, Stupid, Love. can definitely be referred to as an ipso facto direct follow-up to *The 40 Year-Old Virgin* (2005) which launched Steve Carell on his path to movie stardom. Both involve middle-aged men with little experience in the dating world who learn how to talk to women with a little help from those who claim to have all the answers. Cal even appears to use one of Andy Stitzer's old pick-up methods in re-asking questions. The common factor, of course, is Steve Carell, who, with his everyman charm and ability to effortlessly shift from goofy to solemn, is well on his way to taking on the modern mantle established by Tom Hanks.

This is a great movie that takes the position that no matter how hard we try to avoid it, love truly is all around us to paraphrase the theme song from the ever-appropriately titled *Four Weddings and a Funeral* (1994). If the situational awareness of its final act come off as a bit too contrived after the dedicated sincerity of its first two, consider the tactics used by Fogelman, Ficarra & Requa to build to that explosion of plot strands. As one searches for true happiness, anonymity can be just the distance needed to not fall for a false prophet. But when a real name is put on it, the result might seem disastrous at first, but can eventually lead to professions of love to an audience of strangers. Here is a movie where the audience should reciprocate that love.

Erik Childress

CREDITS

Cal Weaver: Steve Carell
Jacob Palmer: Ryan Gosling
Emily Weaver: Julianne Moore
Hannah: Emma Stone
David Lindhagen: Kevin Bacon
Kate: Marisa Tomei
Jessica Riley: Analeigh Tipton
Robbie: Jonah Bobo
Molly: Joey King
Richard: Josh Groban
Origin: USA
Language: English
Released: 2011
Production: Steve Carell, Denise Di Novi; Carousel Productions; released by Warner Bros.
Directed by: John Requa, Glenn Ficarra
Written by: Dan Fogelman

Cinematography by: Andrew Dunn
Music by: Christophe Beck, Nick Urata
Sound: Aaron Glascock, Curt Schulkey
Music Supervisor: Jason Ruder
Editing: Lee Haxall
Art Direction: Sue Chan
Costumes: Dayna Pink
Production Design: William Arnold
MPAA rating: PG-13
Running time: 117 minutes

REVIEWS

Berkshire, Geoff. *Metromix.* July 26, 2011.
Denby, David. *New Yorker.* July 25, 2011.
Ebert, Roger. *Chicago Sun-Times.* July 28, 2011.
Edelstein, David. *New York Magazine.* July 24, 2011.
Fine, Marshall. *Hollywood & Fine.* July 27, 2011.
Honeycutt, Kirk. *Hollywood Reporter.* July 21, 2011.
Longworth, Karina. *Village Voice.* July 26, 2011.
Novikov, Eugene. *Film Blather.* February 18, 2011.
Rocchi, James. *MSN Movies.* July 26, 2011.
Tobias, Scott. *AV Club.* July 28, 2011.

QUOTES

Jacob: "I'm going to help you rediscover your manhood. Do you have any idea where you could have lost it?"

TRIVIA

They offered a free iPad on set to whoever came up with a title for the film.

AWARDS

Nomination:

Golden Globes 2012: Actor—Mus./Comedy (Gosling).

CREATURE

Terror has teeth.
—Movie tagline

Creature, an unabashedly familiar slice of exploitative genre mayhem (its opening scene features a skinny-dipping girl getting her comeuppance in a lake), is the sort of project that even its makers (maybe especially its makers) would blanch at being called a film. It aspires to diversionary entertainment, nothing more. It is, in other words, a movie, through and through.

Still, this lack of greater manifest ambition need not immediately and automatically relegate a picture to critical derision. After all, movies like *Lake Placid* (1999) and the underrated *Slither* (2006), to name but a few, have located a sense of winking fun in their recycling of creature-feature genre tropes. This *Creature*, however, is both incompetently imagined and bungled in its execution, botching its single potentially interesting twist and then limping toward a jaw-droppingly inept finale.

The story centers on the requisite group of college-age friends making a road trip caravan—Oscar (Dillon Casey), his sister Karen (Lauren Schneider), Randy (Aaron Hill), and his girlfriend Beth (Amanda Fuller), and Niles (Mehcad Brooks) and his girlfriend Emily (Serinda Swan), who is also Randy's sister. Stopping off on the way to New Orleans to get gas in a backwaters burgh, the group comes across a collection of eccentric locals. These folks—inclusive of Chopper (Sid Haig), Bud (Wayne Pére), Jimmy (David Jensen), and Grover (Pruitt Taylor Vince), the town simpleton—relate the legend of an inbred man who lost his would-be bride to a monstrous albino alligator, and then, driven mad, hunted and consumed the beast, bringing about a transformation into a scaly, upright, flesh-eating monster known as Lockjaw.

Their curiosity piqued, the kids head out to a shuttered tourist trap, the dilapidated cabin which is supposedly the birthplace of the creature. They set up camp nearby, and soon discover both the truth of the legend and the fact that the aforementioned hillbilly yokels might be hiding another secret or two. Terror, in theory, ensues.

Highly derivative and brazenly ridiculous pieces of genre entertainment can be a lot of fun, unshackled from the self-serious burdens of character self-actualization and the like. Movies of this sort typically live or die based on three factors, however: the successful conveyance of a very singular tone; the eminence of their special effects work and/or gore; and the quality of their performances. *Creature,* alas, strikes out on all three counts.

Working from a script co-written with Tracy Morse, director Fred M. Andrews proves himself inefficient at eliciting tension or dread. One way for the movie to go would have been to embrace its rampant excesses in a manner akin to *Piranha 3D* (2010), *Snakes on a Plane* (2006) or *Anaconda* (1997), exploiting the inherently preposterous nature of its premise. Another way could have been to take a page from something like *Creature From the Black Lagoon* (1954), and make it a story of human invasiveness and overreach, lending the tale some allegorical heft or significance. *Creature,* though, opts for standard, middle-of-the-road scares, and the result is plodding and uninspired.

Given the fact that Randy and Niles are established as ex-military (the former a Marine, the latter a Navy SEAL), the movie would seem to set itself up to exploit these characters' putative physicality for a number of big, stalking, action set pieces. For the most part that does not happen, and when it finally does, the choreography is downright laughable. Without spoiling the specifics, *Creature*'s ending is improbably even more absurd, defying any kind of logical explanation in favor of something obviously predetermined to be visually arresting.

The story actually features one kinky revelation and another twist tied into that, but it crucially places these developments too close to one another within the narrative, missing a chance to plumb an audience's discombobulation, and then expounding upon the twists in a very nonsensical way. On a basic level, the explanation of the legend of Lockjaw is both needlessly complicated and not believable (an inbred hillbilly slaying and eating a ferocious killer alligator produces a hybrid creature?) given the relative lack of other fantastical elements within the story, and the specific mutation of the beast raises other questions, since said evolution apparently includes armpit hair, which would seem to be a distinct disadvantage for a swampy existence.

Visually, *Creature* is marked by pedestrian production value of the sort one might expect from a SyFy Channel small screen movie. The practical monster suit and other special effects are subpar. Wildly unrealistic stage lighting substitutes for outdoor and nighttime illumination, and cinematographer Christopher Faloona wastes any supplemental value of a Louisiana location shoot with static and unengaging compositions that do not take advantage of the natural surroundings. Andrews and editor Chris Conlee do not help matters with poor editing that often seemingly reflects a lack of coverage options; at one point a medium dialogue two-shot is swapped inelegantly for another medium two-shot, from another take.

Finally, *Creature* lacks any galvanizing, wonked-out performance that might mitigate its many problems. Horror veteran Haig, often cast as the creepiest figure on-screen, actually gives a restrained and fairly decent turn, but lapses back into vagaries when abandoned by the script. The actors playing the other locals—each conspicuously made up to highlight their lack of hygiene—all seem to be competing in an informal contest for Most Colorfully Accented Coot.

Brooks, Swan and Hill seem cast for their pretty faces, and obligingly give vacuous turns. Little is unfortunately asked of Fuller, who gave a shattering performance in *Red White & Blue* (2010), and is better than this material. A bit more is required of Schneider, who manages to make a solid if unspectacular impression. Of unfortunately special note, though, is

Casey, who is given uncomfortable leeway in crafting a talkative character driving the action (no matter the lack of sense this makes in relation to the movie's other presumably alpha male characters), and makes choices that consistently undercut any sense of tension.

A virtual cinematic grab bag of inanity, *Creature* is bad enough to make even a card-carrying PETA member reassess their commitment to that group's charter statement regarding animal cruelty. Do not indulge in the misery and boredom it bestows.

Brent Simon

CREDITS

Niles: Mehcad Brooks
Emily: Serinda Swan
Oscar: Dillon Casey
Karen: Lauren Schneider
Randy: Aaron Hill
Beth: Amanda Fuller
Bud: Wayne Pére
Jimmy: David Jensen
Grover: Pruitt Taylor Vince
Chopper: Sid Haig
Caroline: Rebekah Kennedy
Ophelia: Jennifer Lynn Warren
Origin: USA
Language: English
Released: 2011

Production: Bill Sheinberg, Jonathan Sheinberg, Sid Sheinberg; Bubble Factory, Lockjaw Productions; distributed by the Bubble Factory
Directed by: Fred Andrews
Written by: Fred Andrews, Tracy Morse
Cinematography by: Christopher Faloona
Music by: Kevin Haskins
Sound: Candice Baldwin
Editing: Chris Conlee
Costumes: Melissa Reed, Britany Viguerie
Production Design: Jakob Durkoth
MPAA rating: R
Running time: 93 minutes

REVIEWS

Beifuss, John. *Commercial Appeal.* September 16, 2011.
Genzlinger, Neil. *New York Times.* September 10, 2011.
Gilsdorf, Ethan. *Boston Globe.* September 10, 2011.
Hall, Corey. *Metro Times.* September 22, 2011.
Moore, Roger. *Orlando Sentinel.* September 9, 2011.
Olsen, Mark. *Los Angeles Times.* September 8, 2011.
Schager, Nick. *Boxoffice Magazine.* September 9, 2011.
Toppman, Lawrence. *Charlotte Observer.* September 15, 2011.
Weinberg, Scott. *FEARnet.com.* September 11, 2011.
Whitty, Stephen. *Newark Star-Ledger.* September 9, 2011.

TRIVIA

The film earned only $327,000 in its 1,507-theater opening weekend, setting the record for the worst opening weekend in more than 1,500 theaters.

D

A DANGEROUS METHOD

Based on the true story of Jung, Freud and the patient who came between them.
—Movie tagline

Box Office: $5.5 million

With *A Dangerous Method*, director David Cronenberg once again proves himself one of the more adventurous and interesting filmmakers working today. Along with exceptional performances from Michael Fassbender and Viggo Mortensen and a remarkably intelligent and classical screenplay, director Cronenberg has effortlessly crafted an engaging and thought-provoking look at the early days of psychiatry and, more succinctly, the birth of psychoanalysis. Like Cronenberg's more recent art house films (from *Eastern Promises* to 2002's *Spider*), there is still an element of the old Cronenberg film at work, though it's a more controlled and disciplined sensibility. As Ann Hornaday noted in the *Washington Post*, it is this restraint that "makes *A Dangerous Method* perhaps Cronenberg's most transgressive movie yet, one in which ideas—rather than their fetishistic signifiers—possess more energy and verve than the most calculated shock effect."

Based on the play *The Talking Cure*, the film chronicles the birth of psychoanalysis. As the film opens, a beyond hysterical woman named Sabina Spielrein (Keira Knightley) is hospitalized and put in the care of a very young Dr. Carl Jung (Michael Fassbender). Jung, as it turns out, has been studying the new "talking cure" being developed by fellow psychiatrist Sigmund Freud (Viggo Mortensen) and feels this form of treatment may

prove beneficial to Ms. Spielrein. Sabina ends up being a patient tailor-made for psychoanalysis as her problems, which include acute sexual anxiety and Sado-masochistic fetishes, stem primarily from an abusive father. Under the guidance of Dr. Jung, Sabina makes tremendous strides in identifying and dealing with her various afflictions and is ultimately revealed to be an intelligent and gifted individual, who aspires to be a psychiatrist herself someday.

Buoyed by his success with Sabina and the practice of psychoanalysis, Jung embarks on a journey to meet with Sigmund Freud. Since Freud has come to regard the younger doctor as his heir-apparent and the two men appear to be in sync with regards to psychiatry, they begin a quasi father and son relationship that will, as Hornaday writes, "shake and shape modern thought." Describing the interaction between Jung and Freud even further, Hornaday asserts that *A Dangerous Method* portrays their relationship as an "intellectual love story between [the] two men." This assessment is, of course, undeniably true and is made even more apparent when, upon returning home, Jung is propositioned by Sabina to embark on a sexual relationship, a wish he is incapable of reciprocating. As her doctor, he must refuse the invitation. That is, he must do so until the introduction of the wild, uncontrollable character of Otto Gross (played with unabashed glee by Vincent Cassel) arrives at the hospital to be treated by the good doctor. Claiming that "pleasure is simple until we decide to complicate it," Gross convinces Jung to reconsider the nature of his relationship with Sabina which ultimately leads to his theories diverging from Freud's—subsequently creating a rift between the two fathers of modern psychiatry within this bizarre psychological love triangle.

Screenwriter Christopher Hampton, superbly adapts his play *The Talking Cure*—which itself draws inspiration from the book *A Most Dangerous Method* by John Kerr. No stranger to angst-filled relationship triangles (*Dangerous Liaisons* and *Atonement* are among his credits), Hampton succeeds in crafting a story—one which Mortensen has called Cronenberg's Merchant-Ivory film—during which, as Roger Ebert observed in his review of the film, "we are learning, yet [we] never feel we're being taught." As Ebert further explains, the skill of the film lies within the flawless way that it "weaves theory with the inner lives of its characters." Overall, the script is, as Kenneth Turan noted in the *Los Angeles Times*, a "classically well-written" and that is why it succeeds in conveying a story that by all accounts should not be as riveting or accessible as proves to be.

All of the performances in *A Dangerous Method* are exceptional, but the standout here is Michael Fassbender (who has enjoyed a prolific 2011, with memorable turns in *Jane Eyre*, *Shame*, and *X-Men: First Class*). While Mortensen may do the better job of all three principle actors in capturing the nuances and mannerisms of his subject, it is through the eyes of Fassbender that the narrative unfolds and it succeeds based more on his ability to convey the loneliness and uncertainty of his character than anything else.

While some may claim that Keira Knightley's portrayal of Sabina, particularly in the early portions of the film, may be a bit too over the top or, as Kenneth Turan writes in the *Los Angeles Times*, may come "off as an actress acting crazy rather than a character going mad," it is her performances that is the narrative glue that ultimately holds the film together. That is, by beginning the film with her introduction, Sabina is being made the focal point from the onset. It is from her that all future action of consequence in the film will originate. While *A Dangerous Method* may ostensibly be about the relationship between Jung and Freud and their differing perspectives on psychoanalysis, there is an underlying theme that, according to Roger Ebert, suggests "psychoanalysis as a scientific system may have been harmed by the struggle between [Freud and Jung] and that Spielrein [having actually treated and examined her own mental state]…may have arrived at more useful conclusions than the two dueling male approaches." Furthermore, thrusting the viewer into the mouth of madness in this fashion is, as Wesley Morris put it in the *Boston Globe*, a "crucial declaration of priorities." By embracing chaos in such a way, *A Dangerous Method* begins, as Morris writes, "where other films hope to culminate."

But there is more at work in Croneberg's *A Dangerous Method* than the one-time horror director trying his hand at something new. Later era Cronenberg such as *Spider*, *A History of Violence*, and *Eastern Promises* has shown that he is capable of producing intelligent, thought-provoking drama and shedding the King of Venereal Horror moniker of his earlier films (*Shivers, Rabid, The Fly*). That does not mean however the new Cronenberg film has nothing in common with the old (he still employs pretty much the same crew, including cinematographer (Peter Suschitzky) and composer (Howard Shore), he has since the 1980s—giving his films a, more than likely, unintended uniformity). There is, in fact, something oddly familiar about *A Dangerous Method* when compared with his other films, the most obvious of which being the manifestations of sexual anxieties in the physical realm. From the sex slugs of *Shivers* and the revenge-seeking mutant children of *The Brood* all the way to the "mollusk" Sabina claims is pressing on her back when she masturbates, Cronenberg has always shown a fascination with the way sexuality figures into the human condition and what better way to discuss that than in a film about psychoanalysis? But here he does so with what Hornaday calls a "modulated, restrained style" rather than the more overt tactics he's used before. It's a style he has honed since *eXistenz* and one that shows promise for his future work. While it may be easy to claim that this show of restraint is dictated more by the fact that Cronenberg has not written the last four movies he has directed, that would be doing both the film and filmmaker a disservice. As Andrew O'Hehir notes on *Salon.com*, "even as it deals with sexual perversity and severe mental illness, *A Dangerous Method* is a restrained and elegant costume drama driven by characters, language and ideas, not violence or outré imagery." Or, should you approach the film as a inherently Cronenbergian creation, as Hornaday puts it, *A Dangerous Method* not only "feels like a movie Cronenberg was born to make…but with its primal urges swimming so close to decorous surface, it also feels like the movie he has been making all along."

Michael J. Tyrkus

CREDITS

Sigmund Freud: Viggo Mortensen
Carl Jung: Michael Fassbender
Sabina Spielrein: Keira Knightley
Emma Jung: Sarah Gadon
Otto Gross: Vincent Cassel
Origin: USA
Language: English
Released: 2011
Production: Jeremy Thomas; Recorded Pictures Company, Lago Film, Prospero Pictures; released by Sony Pictures Classics
Directed by: David Cronenberg
Written by: Christopher Hampton

Cinematography by: Peter Suschitzky
Music by: Howard Shore
Sound: Michal Holubec
Editing: Ronald Sanders
Art Direction: Anja Fromm
Costumes: Denise Cronenberg
Production Design: James McAteer
MPAA rating: R
Running time: 99 minutes

REVIEWS

Ebert, Roger. *Chicago Sun-Times.* December 14, 2011.
Edelstein, David. *New York Magazine.* December 27, 2011.
Hoberman, J. *Village Voice.* November 22, 2011.
McCarthy, Todd. *Hollywood Reporter.* October 24, 2011.
Morris, Wesley. *Boston Globe.* December 22, 2011.
Phillips, Michael. *Chicago Tribune.* December 15, 2011.
Scott, A.O. *New York Times.* November 22, 2011.
Stevens, Dana. *Slate.* November 23, 2011.
Turan, Kenneth. *Los Angeles Times.* November 22, 2011.
Zacharek, Stephanie. *Movieline.* November 22, 2011.

QUOTES

Carl Jung: "Sometimes you have to do something unforgivable…just to be able to go on living."

TRIVIA

Christoph Waltz was originally cast as Freud, but dropped out in favor of making *Water for Elephants.*

AWARDS

Nomination:

Golden Globes 2012: Support. Actor (Mortensen).

THE DARKEST HOUR

Survive the holidays.
  —Movie tagline
The invasion begins Christmas Day.
  —Movie tagline

Box Office: $21.3 million

The film lives up to its title for fans of science fiction. As far as apocalyptic alien invasion tales go, *Skyline* (2010) was the most current whipping child for genre aficionados. Now, Chris Gorak's *The Darkest Hour* certainly makes its play for yearly discussions of the worst of the worst. Movie fans will be huddled together during those talks, reminded of the very films where a group of survivors are the last hope for humanity's survival. A meaningful aside may occur as they wonder how they might react on their journey and how to fight

back if necessary. They may consider what they could have learned from previous remnants of a demolished society. The whole thing could eventually lapse into the deeper themes of how people respond when faced with either the principles of an invading species or confronting the very horror that humans are, indeed, the bad guy. Or it could be simply how cool the aliens looked and how awesome it was to see everything blow up real good. When those same movie fans discuss *The Darkest Hour* it will be only to frequently end the phrase, "well, it is not as bad as…"

Sean (Emile Hirsch) and Ben (Max Minghella) are best friends and business partners on their way to Moscow for a meeting involving their latest website venture. When they arrive, the Swede Skylar (Joel Kinnaman) has stolen their idea and quashed their plans. The fact that the whole explanation begins and ends with "you didn't get my e-mail" pretty much sums up just how this screenplay believes business is routinely conducted. With little left to do but get drunk and pick up chicks, the pair runs into another in vacationing gal pals Natalie (Olivia Thirlby) and Anne (Rachael Taylor). Then all the lights go out in Moscow.

Ever hear the one about the Swede, the Aussie, and the ugly American who try to survive an alien invasion armed with only the strength of their friends' pronounced eyebrows? Little orange globes of light begin falling from the sky. Pretty as they may be, a smart reaction might not be to poke it with a truncheon as one policeman decides and is quickly turned into dust and ashes for his attempt at inter-global communication. This becomes a habit for the aliens as they manage to wipe out most of Moscow and the world while the heroes have barricaded themselves in a storeroom for several days. When the sounds of despair have subsided and the food is gone, they finally venture out into the ravaged landscape in an attempt to get home. Such is the extent of their planning. Along the way, with help from a plucky teenager (Veronika Ozerova), a nutty electrician and some even wackier local survivalists getting a kick out of acting out either *The Road* (2009) or *The Road Warrior* (1982), they discover the aliens can be spotted through electricity. Despite the creatures having knocked out all the power, they can still be detected through close proximity with car headlights and uncorked light bulbs which these dim bulbs throw across the floor as the sound of broken glass fills the open space. No matter, they all still work.

The Darkest Hour needed to call a timeout on itself from the very opening as one of its potential heroes is smugly berating a flight attendant over his believed technological myth of electronic devices on airplanes. She smiles and he is immediately humbled over a power outage in mid-air so maybe he can be forgiven. What cannot though is the filmmakers creating a threat of such minimal visual terror that it is near impossible to create any sort of lingering suspense. The unknown in the darkness can be frightening. The invisible in plain daylight may cause panic in real life, but this is not *Contagion* (2011). It is a light show, literally as it turns out, with otherworldly creatures to run and hide from. There is nothing threatening about a partially obscured blur moving towards people. Unless you are a filmmaker that can maximize the suspense and drama of isolation under a budget that will only let you show the evil at your own convenience. Gorak is clearly not a filmmaker up to this task.

Gorak and screenwriter Jon Spaihts fail to provide the tiniest ounce of suspense, leaving so many open-ended opportunities that it nearly feels like someone just cut out all the payoffs. Much is made of a working radio isolated in a birdcage that Sean works with sweat-dripping intensity so as not to disturb its place. It turns out that it barely qualifies as the most intense game of Operation ever seen as Anne—who tries to qualify the suspense by being reluctant to cause noise—just grabs the radio when no one else is watching. Normally this would suggest a bad, selfish move in the future for poor Anne, but the radio is never mentioned or seen again. What is seen is the submarine. In the midst of all this carnage and no signs of life, a military sub has neverthe-less stayed alive to wait for survivors which they find at the first sight of water. "It's there," says one of the heroes before they are somehow blown halfway across town in need of rescue after falling into the river. The final Titanic survivors were not whisked away as far by the vortex of the sinking ship.

Steven Spielberg's *War of the Worlds* (2005) intro-duced viewers to dormant invaders ready to turn earthly inhabitants to dust from giant objects with horns loud enough to signal the rapture for neighboring states. *The Darkest Hour* just gives viewers the dust from golden globes that snatch their prey like the Balrog's whip-grabbing Gandalf. Even at 83 minutes, *The Darkest Hour* is too boring to make it worthy of Ed Wood-like status; no fool's passion for ambition or even a finale worthy of bringing more than four aliens out of hiding with which to do battle. Then again, once someone says to get the aliens "in the water and then fire the microwave gun," the film's place in bad-movie infamy has been perma-nently sealed.

Erik Childress

CREDITS
Natalie: Olivia Thirlby
Sean: Emile Hirsch

Ben: Max Minghella
Anne: Rachael Taylor
Skyler: Joel Kinnaman
Vika: Veronika Vernadskaya
Sergei: Dato Bakhtadze
Matvei: Gosha Kutsenko
Origin: USA
Language: English
Released: 2011
Production: Tom Jacobson, Timur Bekamambetov; New Regency; released by Summit Entertainment
Directed by: Chris Gorak
Written by: Jon Spaihts
Cinematography by: Scott Kevan
Music by: Tyler Bates
Sound: Stephane Albinet
Music Supervisor: JoJo Villanueva, Anastasia Brown
Editing: Fernando Villena, Priscilla Nedd Friendly
Art Direction: Ricky Eyres
Costumes: Varya Avdyushko
Production Design: Valera Viktorov
MPAA rating: PG-13
Running time: 89 minutes

REVIEWS

Anderson, Jeffrey M. *Common Sense Media.* January 7, 2011.
Brown, Joel. *Boston Globe.* December 27, 2011.
DeFore, John. *Hollywood Reporter.* December 26, 2011.
Drake, Grae. *Movies.com.* January 6, 2012.
Novikov, Eugene. *Film Blather.* December 25, 2011.
Olsen, Mark. *Los Angeles Times.* December 27, 2011.
Orndorf, Brian. *BrianOrndorf.com.* December 25, 2011.
Rabin, Nathan. *AV Club.* December 28, 2011.
Tyler, Joshua. *Giant Freakin Robot.* December 27, 2011.
Weinberg, Scott. *FEARnet.* December 26, 2011.

QUOTES

Sean: "Team work makes the dream work."

TRIVIA

Production was suspended for two weeks due to the extraordinary air pollution caused by heavy smoke from the wild fires surrounding Moscow in August 2010. Although it eventually resumed a few weeks later, smoke had still made it into a lot of shots and had to be digitally removed during post production.

THE DEBT

Every secret comes with a price.
—Movie tagline

Box Office: $31.2 million

John Madden's *The Debt* wants to be two things: a suspenseful cold war spy thriller and a cautionary tale about the emotional corrosiveness of lies. The film succeeds brilliantly in telling the first tale but not so much in the second. Madden's film opens with a pair of haunting sequences that encapsulate the two stories it is attempting to tell: An Israeli military transport plane sits on a Tel Aviv airstrip in 1966. Three young Mossad agents, a woman and two men, sit in the cargo hold. They exchange knowing glances as the hold door opens, bathing them in sunlight. They descend out of the hold on to the runway in slow motion with a half dozen men in black in front of cars applauding them. The look on the woman's face is not one of triumph. The second sequence is a passage from a book written by the woman's daughter in 1997 recounting the incident which allegedly brought the three agents to the hanger. The trio has abducted a Nazi war criminal in East Berlin. He has broken free of his bonds and viciously assaults the woman. As he flees, the bleeding woman drags herself to her windowsill and sends a fatal bullet into his back. Later in the film, the viewer sees this sequence again, with a crucial difference. This sequence is what actually happened and the woman has lied to her daughter and the world. Two versions of a single event: one reflecting what the participants in the events say happened, and one which reflects what actually happened. The gap between these two is what *The Debt* is about.

The Debt breaks its structure into two parts—1966 Berlin and 1997 Israel—to tell its two tales. In 1966, Israeli intelligence believes it has tracked down Nazi war criminal Dieter Vogel, the "Butcher of Birkenau," and has deployed two young Mossad operatives, Stephen Gold (Marton Csokas) and David Peretz (Sam Worthington), to confirm his identity, kidnap him, and smuggle him out of the country for trial in Israel. Since Vogel (played with slimy brilliance by Jesper Christensen) is a gynecologist, a female agent, Rachel Singer (Jessica Chastain) is added to the team. Rachel's reconnaissance trips as a patient to the gynecologist's office are both punishingly suspenseful and nauseating. The young agent must endure multiple office sessions with the not-so-good doctor, first to snap surreptitious photos of him to verify his identity and eventually to sedate and abduct him, all the while enduring the evil man probing around her most intimate spots and answering his faux innocent questions designed to ferret out imposters. The photos are developed and his identity is confirmed. The operation to extract him begins immediately. The night before the mission, a terrified Rachel seeks solace first with David (and then when refused) with Stephen. Thus an already complicated mission is complicated by a love triangle (though a mercifully minimal one).

The agents' mission to extract Vogel is both suspenseful and surprisingly plausible. For once, in an action thriller, the part of the plan that would not seem to work in the real world, a very risky East Berlin/West Berlin crossing involving trains that momentary block the view of patrolling East German guards, fails with near-disastrous results, forcing the trio to flee with their quarry, East German bullets zinging into the back of their van. Now, they find themselves stuck with Vogel with no ability to get him out of East Berlin. As they desperately try to figure a way to get him out, the doctor begins expertly manipulating his exhausted and frustrated captors, capitalizing on the love triangle he has detected, which leads to his eventual escape from his bonds and his attack of Rachel. The sequence which follows differs in a crucial respect from the sequence as depicted in Rachel's daughter memoir from the beginning of the film. This leads to a fateful decision on the part of the trio to lie about what happened. The 1966 portion of *The Debt* crackles with tension and is rich in atmosphere. Director Madden and screenwriters Matthew Vaughn, Jane Goldman, and Peter Straughan do an excellent job of keeping the viewer on the edge of his seat and of evoking the claustrophobic and unforgiving atmosphere of a Cold War Berlin, reminiscent of classics like *The Spy who Came in From the Cold*(1965). This section of the film is suspenseful, stylish and exciting.

The latter portion of the film, set in Israel in 1997, is decidedly less so, in part because it is going for something a little bit more ambitious; in part because it is harder to buy sexagenarian agents operating in the field (the climax overplays its hand a bit in this respect). While it continues the suspenseful events of thirty years ago (an unexpected development brings the events of 1966 to the present in a most unwelcome way for the trio), it is also attempting to convey the emotional consequences of living a lie for thirty years. Indeed, the characters motivations in 1997 turn on these emotional consequences. Stephen (Tom Wilkinson) is now a high level Mossad agent divorced from Rachel (Helen Mirren). Their daughter has just written a book about their 1966 exploits in Berlin. David, who has been absent from Israel and Stephen and Rachel's lives for three decades, abruptly returns looking haggard and haunted and after a discussion with Rachel in which he asks her for permission to reveal their lie to the world, permission which Rachel denies, decides to step in front of a semi truck.

The clear implication is that the corrosiveness of thirty years of lying to the world is what has destroyed Stephen and Rachel's marriage and causes David to be so tormented that he wanders the world for over half his life, killing himself finally out of despair. The problem is that this emotional aspect is too implied to be made real for the viewer. Little to nothing of the disillusion of Rachel and Stephen's marriage is depicted. Everything hinges on David feeling intolerably tortured by the three characters' shared lie but the script and the characters' 1997 cameo-length screen time do not succeed in conveying that feeling to the viewer. The 1966 David (played well by Sam Worthington) is a cipher (closed off to the world due to his rage and grief over being the only survivor in his family of the Holocaust) with generous screen time but no illumination of his character. The 1997 David is all illumination but no screen time. More is needed to bridge the gap between the characters who quickly agree to the lie in 1966 and the characters who have been so profoundly affected by that lie in 1997. The 1997 storyline is simply too truncated to make the viewer believe the characters would be affected in the way they have been.

This is not the fault of the actors whose work is uniformly excellent across the two eras (though the superb Ciarán Hinds' screen time as the modern-day David is disappointingly brief). Helen Mirren and Jessica Chastain shine as the young and old Rachel. David is played with charming ambition by Martin Csokas in 1966 and not-so-charming ambition by the always excellent Tom Wilkinson in 1997. And Christensen's cunning Vogel is the brilliant, rotten heart of the film. If the film had stuck solely with he and his abductors in 1966, *The Debt* might have been a classic of the genre. However, although *The Debt* works much better as a straightforward spy thriller than it does as a convincing cautionary tale about the perils of living a lie, it nonetheless is a most effective thriller worthy of viewing.

Nate Vercauteren

CREDITS

Rachel Singer: Helen Mirren
David Peretz: Ciaran Hinds
Stephan Gold: Tom Wilkinson
Young Rachel: Jessica Chastain
Young David: Sam Worthington
Young Stephan: Marton Csokas
Dieter Vogel/Dr. Bernhardt: Jesper Christensen
Sarah Gold: Romi Aboulafia
Origin: USA, United Kingdom
Language: English
Released: 2010
Production: Matthew Vaughn, Kris Thykier, Eitan Evan, Eduardo Rossof; Marv Films; released by Miramax Films
Directed by: John Madden
Written by: Matthew Vaughn, Jane Goldman, Peter Straughan

Cinematography by: Benjamin Davis
Music by: Thomas Newman
Sound: Peter Lindsay
Editing: Alexander Berner
Costumes: Natalie Ward
Production Design: Jim Clay
MPAA rating: R
Running time: 114 minutes

REVIEWS

Atkinson, Michael. *Village Voice*. August 30, 2011.
Baumgarten, Marjorie. *Austin Chronicle*. September 1, 2011.
Burr, Ty. *Boston Globe*. August 30, 2011.
DeFore, John. *Washington Post*. August 30, 2011.
Ebert, Roger. *Chicago Sun-Times*. August 30, 2011.
Mintzer, Jordan. *Variety*. August 30, 2011.
Rabin, Nathan. *AV Club*. August 30, 2011.
Rea, Steven. *Philadelphia Inquirer*. August 30, 2011.
Scott, A.O. *New York Times*. August 30, 2011.
Travers, Peter. *Rolling Stone*. August 31, 2011.

QUOTES

Stephan Gold: "I thought I'd been punished already."
Rachel Singer: "God doesn't plant car bombs."

TRIVIA

The plane seen landing in the background during the agents' arrival at the beginning of the movie is an Antonov An-26 of the Hungarian Air Force detailed with fake Israeli markings.

THE DESCENDANTS

Box Office: $75.6 million

Naturalistic humor and heartbreak commingle to winning effect in the justifiably lauded, Oscar®-nominated (for Best Picture, Best Actor, Best Adapted Screenplay, and Best Director) *The Descendants,* an examination and celebration of human imperfection that sketches the contours of anguish and rejuvenation with remarkable acuity and sensitivity. Smart, well-acted, and swollen with feeling, director Alexander Payne's Hawaiian-set fifth feature film, a definite companion piece to his earlier *About Schmidt* (2002), is a welcome treat for fans of adult contemporary drama that does not feel it necessary to baldly dictate sentiment to its audience.

Adapted by Payne, Nat Faxon and Jim Rash from Kaui Hart Hemmings' novel of the same name, *The Descendants* centers around Matt King (George Clooney), a lawyer and previously somewhat indifferent husband and father of two—the "back-up parent," he notes in voiceover—who is thrust into the bewildering role of chief caretaker when his wife is left in a coma and on death's door after a boating accident off of the coast of Waikiki. Nonplussed, Matt is uncertain how to cope with ten-year-old Scottie (Amara Miller), who projects an intact veneer but has started acting out in little ways, and freaked out her classmates and teachers by submitting a photo-journal school project documenting her mother's vegetative state. To help, Matt summons home his seventeen-year-old daughter Alex (Shailene Woodley) from school, and breaks the difficult news to her that her mother is not going to make it. Soon they will have to turn off her life support.

Matt wants Alex's help in looking after Scottie and telling the rest of the family, including Matt's father-in-law Scott (Robert Forster). Drafting her seemingly dim bulb stoner friend Sid (Nick Krause) for tagalong emotional support, Alex begrudgingly relents. But she also drops a bombshell on Matt that explains her recent disconnection from her mother—she caught her having an affair. Matt confirms the details via his wife's friends, Kai and Mark (Mary Birdsong and Rob Huebel), and sets out trying to learn a little bit more about the other man, real estate agent Brian Speer (Matthew Lillard).

As if all this were not stressful enough, as the presiding trustee amongst a group of cousins and other kin, Matt also holds the sole, controlling vote in an important, impending decision over to whom to sell a 25,000-acre parcel of land passed down from their ancestors, Hawaiian royalty and missionaries. It is a choice that carries enormous financial implications for those involved, as well as ecological repercussions for all islanders. While mulling this over and additionally making arrangements for his wife's impending death, Matt learns of Brian's whereabouts on the nearby island of Kauai and, with Sid and his daughters in tow, sets out to track Brian down and invite him to pay last respects to his wife. Not knowing what to really expect, when he comes across Brian's unaware wife Julie (Judy Greer), things get more complicated for Matt.

As with Payne's other films, comedy and tragedy abut one another in *The Descendants,* since it is through this lens of managed futility that Payne and his collaborators view the world. In sports, the cliché is that it is not the adversity that matters most, but rather how you deal with it. The same can be said of Payne's big screen protagonists, who in various ways each learn that lesson.

In *The Descendants,* Payne's focus shifts from extreme Type-A personalities, moral reprobates or otherwise gruff, abrasive or disagreeable characters, and

onto someone by no means pious but trying really quite hard to do good by those around him and make the best out of some very tough situations. It is for precisely this reason that the comedy in the movie seems so human. An audience can laugh at a character getting punched, or another's teary and very sincere profession of forgiveness, because the shock and awkwardness underpinning them is so astute. Other moments too—Matt's frantic, waddling run when he goes to neighbors seeking confirmation of his wife's affair, or the occasionally profane yet matter-of-fact outburst from Alex—have the weight of finely observed behavioral truth.

For some viewers, since its rhythms are considerably different than even other hybrid dramedies, these and other bits in the film may at first blush seem out of place, or a bit disorienting. Upon a second viewing, however, *The Descendants* not only holds up, but deepens appreciably. Payne and his collaborators place a light framework around the narrative via voiceover from Matt that sketches out his anxiety and uncertainty over presiding over a fractured family he deems an archipelago—part of the same whole, but distinctly apart. A lot of film narration these days is either redundant or expository spackle, but this voiceover provides nuanced and well articulated sentiment, lending voice to how disparate emotions can (and often do) coexist within each of us.

Screenwriters Payne, Faxon and Rash also pepper the script with hints of hereditary inclinations (Alex is away at boarding school to tame her rebellious spirit, and drunk when Matt first goes to pick her up), but do not overdraw matters. While the source material provides a rich springboard for Payne, the director also shrewdly knows to leave certain elements open-ended or ambiguous enough for audiences to establish their own connections to the material. (The issue of whether Alex and Sid are ever really dating, for instance, is never really concretely answered.) The film's accrued wisdom and emotional impact arrive a bit wryly and obliquely, and without fabrication.

Payne and cinematographer Phedon Papamichael, who also did fabulous work on Clooney's *The Ides of March* (2011), settle on a forthright approach for the movie's look. In widescreen location selections, *The Descendants* utilizes Hawaii's natural beauty and grandeur, but does not attempt to emotionally exploit it via sweeping technique or melodramatic connection. The visual scheme serves the story. Similarly, Payne and music supervisor Dondi Bastone's deft use of various native Hawaiian music helps root the movie, and give it a latent sense of fused melancholy and hopefulness—of certain things changing and slipping away but life also, by degrees, pointing upward.

In the run-up to *Sideways* (2004), in the process of casting it, Payne somewhat famously took a meeting with Clooney, who was a fan of both the script and his previous work, but then told the actor that he was not right for either of the male leads in that film, his movie star presence eclipsing even his ability to play rakish horndog Jack Cole. (Thomas Haden Church would end up being cast in that role, for which he would be nominated for an Academy Award®.) The pair's mutual admiration and respect would put Clooney at the top of Payne's call sheet for *The Descendants,* however, and it is a worthy match that embraces the actor's age and makes superb use of his off-screen profile. Clooney plays a guy who is well-off financially and kind of slightly patrician (or at least more cultured than some of his various cousins), but at his core fundamentally decent. Clooney wonderfully imbues the character with much grace, showcasing Matt's pain and vulnerability as well as his resolve.

Woodley has solid television experience, but in this, her feature film debut, she delivers a wonderfully nuanced and full-bodied portrait of teenage impatience. You see the wounds informing Alex's sharp-tongued insouciance and flashes of anger, as well as her clear love of her family. The two mindsets and behaviors are of course not mutually exclusive—a fact lost on many modern filmmakers, who peddle wan, dimensionless and inherently false characterizations of teens.

Payne rounds out his cast with a number of local nonprofessionals, but also some intelligent, counterintuitive choices of gifted performers often asked to do much less. Greer and Lillard are especially notable in this regard. They have each made a career largely though not entirely trading on their sunny charisma, and ably portraying wacky sidekicks and flighty best friends. Here they each get to play a couple different layers, and Brian and Julie's interactions (both individually and collectively) with Matt and Alex play out in delightfully unexpected but emotionally satisfying ways.

As rich as it is, regard for *The Descendants* probably owes something, too, to the seven-year-gap between the film and Payne's last release, *Sideways,* since so few contemporary American directors are focusing their attention on these sorts of intimate yet big-hearted tales of family loss, life and romantic yearning. Whereas many cinephiles, in a rotisserie reverie, might dream of Filmmaker X tackling a certain type of genre piece or Filmmaker Y getting a shot at a big-budget action movie, Payne seems not only utterly at home but very much built for films of this scale and scope, and not the broader fantastical realms of much of modern-day cinema. While he and his frequent writing partner, Jim Taylor, have undertaken various rewrite gigs—including screenwriting credits on *Jurassic Park III* (2003) and a draft of *I Now Pronounce You Chuck & Larry* (2007)—the "promotion" of a big studio directorial paycheck gig just for the sake of more frequent credits would be robbing audiences of perhaps the preeminent American big screen essayist working today. Here is to hoping Payne sticks with his own instincts, interests and vision.

Brent Simon

CREDITS

Matt King: George Clooney
Hugh: Beau Bridges
Scott: Robert Forster
Brian Speer: Matthew Lillard
Alexandra King: Shailene Woodley
Scottie King: Amara Miller
Elizabeth King: Patricia Hastie
Sid: Nick Krause
Julie Speer: Judy Greer
Origin: USA
Language: English
Released: 2011
Production: Jim Burke, Alexander Payne, Jim Taylor; Ad Hominem Enterprises, Little Blair Productions, Ingenious Film Partners; released by Fox Searchlight
Directed by: Alexander Payne
Written by: Alexander Payne, Nat Faxon, Jim Rash
Cinematography by: Phedon Papamichael
Sound: Jose Antonio Garcia
Music Supervisor: Dondi Bastone
Editing: Kevin Tent
Art Direction: Timothy "TK" Kirkpatrick
Costumes: Wendy Chuck
Production Design: Jane Ann Stewart
MPAA rating: R
Running time: 115 minutes

REVIEWS

Debruge, Peter. *Variety.* September 3, 2011.
Duralde, Alonso. *The Wrap.* November 15, 2011.
Ebert, Roger. *Chicago Sun-Times.* November 17, 2011.
Kennedy, Lisa. *Denver Post.* November 18, 2011.
McCarthy, Todd. *Hollywood Reporter.* November 18, 2011.
Morgenstern, Joe. *Wall Street Journal.* September 9, 2011.
Puig, Claudia. *USA Today.* November 15, 2011.
Scott, A.O. *New York Times.* November 15, 2011.
Stevens, Dana. *Slate.* November 17, 2011.
Tallerico, Brian. *HollywoodChicago.com.* October 14, 2011.

QUOTES

Matt King: "Don't be fooled by appearances. In Hawaii, some of the most powerful people look like bums and stuntmen."

TRIVIA

Actor George Clooney had wanted to play "Jack" in *Sideways*, director Alexander Payne's earlier film. Payne, however, turned him down, saying that he wanted someone less famous for the role.

AWARDS

Oscars 2011: Adapt. Screenplay

Golden Globes 2012: Actor—Drama (Clooney), Film—Drama

Ind. Spirit 2012: Screenplay, Support. Actress (Woodley)

Writers Guild 2011: Adapt. Screenplay

Nomination:

Oscars 2011: Actor (Clooney), Director (Payne), Film, Film Editing

British Acad. 2011: Actor (Clooney), Adapt. Screenplay, Film

Directors Guild 2011: Director (Payne)

Golden Globes 2012: Director (Payne), Screenplay, Support. Actress (Woodley)

Ind. Spirit 2012: Director (Payne), Film

Screen Actors Guild 2011: Actor (Clooney), Cast.

THE DEVIL'S DOUBLE

Play the part or suffer the consequences.
—Movie tagline

The 80's were brilliant, if you were in charge.
—Movie tagline

Money. Sex. Power. It's not enough.
—Movie tagline

Sex…power…too much money…what do you get a "Prince" that has everything?
—Movie tagline

Box Office: $1.4 million

For cruel and brutal despots, 2011 turned out to be anything but a banner year. Early in the year, the worldwide manhunt for Osama bin Laden came to an end with him being taken down by a Navy SEAL team within the walls of a compound he maintained in Pakistan. A few months later, following a popular uprising that saw him on the run from the people that he previously led with an iron fist for decades, Libyan president Muammar Gaddafi was captured in the wake of an attack by NATO warplanes and summarily executed. As it turns out, such people fared little better in reel life as well, as was demonstrated by the depiction of the notorious Uday Hussein in the rotten docudrama *The Devil's Double*. Uday, the son of former Iraqi despot Saddam Hussein, may have been a depraved and murderous degenerate to the nth degree but even *he* probably deserved a better movie to be the subject of than this one, a ridiculous and borderline repellent

example of bully-boy cinema that is less interested in telling what could have been a potentially fascinating story than in trying to outdo *Scarface* (1983) in terms of the amount of drugs, violence, profanity and macho swagger on display, albeit without any of the style or quiet dignity that Brian De Palma brought to that now-classic film.

Inspired by real events, the film tells the story of Latif Yahia (Dominic Cooper), a loyal Iraq and army lieutenant who possesses an uncanny physical resemblance to Uday Hussein (also played by Cooper). This genetic coincidence is brought to the forefront when he is summoned to the royal palace and informed that he is to serve as Uday's body double, or "fiday," in order to make public appearances as him when the situation is too dangerous for the real one to appear or, more often, when the actual Uday is too wasted from excessive amounts of sex, drugs and booze to pull himself together.

At first, Latif declines this dubious honor but when he is informed that his refusal to do so will condemn his entire family to death, he reluctantly accepts the position. From this unique vantage point, Latif gets to experience many of the perks of being Uday—incredible wealth, lavish parties and the favors of an exceptionally comely party girl Sarrab (Ludivine Sagnier)—but also gets a front-row seat to his increasingly unhinged behavior. To cite merely a few examples, he rapes a bride on her wedding day (a move that inspires her to commit suicide immediately afterwards), molests a school girl before having her body dumped on the outskirts of town after an overdose, and disembowels a rival with a knife while in line at a buffet. It eventually all becomes too much for Latif and he struggles to devise an escape for himself and Sarrab despite the danger it poses to himself and his family.

The trouble with *The Devil's Double* is not so much that it is crammed with amounts of drugs, gore and swearing so great as to rival anything ever put before a camera as it is that it fails to do anything with them except show them off in the crassest way possible in the hope of luring in the throngs that have made the aforementioned *Scarface* into a contemporary cult classic without recognizing the implicit critique of such behavior that existed in that film underneath the mountains of cocaine. An even bigger problem is that while it must be accepted that the film has no doubt taken certain dramatic liberties with Latif's actual story in order to make it more cinematic, it still never feels even vaguely authentic for a single moment and that robs the story of a lot of its potential power. Even if one were as crazy as Uday Hussein presumably was, would they go through the trouble of grooming someone to be their secret double and then repeatedly bring them along to big public functions with hundreds of people so that they can see the two of them together and no doubt notice the similarities between the two? Of course not, but the film continues to offer up one scene after another along those lines and it eventually begins to feel as though once-interesting director Lee Tamahori is less interested in presenting any real notion of what it might have been like behind the walls of the House of Saddam than in showing off his technically impressive but dramatically inert method for making it appear that Dominic Cooper is acting opposite himself.

In a dual performance aided by elaborate special effects allowing him to act opposite himself, Cooper gets to show off his blustery chops throughout but fails to infuse either character with enough personality to make them worth following for two hours. Uday is a portrait of wild excess while Latif is more restrained and human but the the characters are so opposite throughout that they may as well have been played by two different actors and when Latif is forced to play Uday, there is no sense of nuance as he shifts from one to the other—instead of coming across as Latif trying to play Uday, Cooper simply does the exact same stuff that he has been doing as Uday. For a performance like this to work, a certain degree of subtlety is required and that is one item that Cooper does not apparently have in his arsenal. In the only other performance in the film of note, the usually reliable Sagnier is not very convincing as the Iraqi sexpot and the film tries to compensate for her miscasting by having her disrobe frequently enough so that viewers will be otherwise distracted from her faulty accent and improbable presence.

There is, to be sure, an interesting and provocative film to be made about the subject of a man forced to impersonate a monster in order to save his life at the risk of losing his soul in the bargain. There is even one fairly brilliant scene here—a bit in which Latif is sent by Uday to meet with his father for a presumed dressing-down only to discover that he is actually talking to the double belonging to Saddam)—that suggests the complex head-spinner that it might have been if placed in the right hands. Alas, *The Devil's Double* is less interested in nuance than in throwing around so much gleeful ghastliness that it feels more like a celebration than a condemnation for most of its running time and by the time it finally ends, most viewers will have nothing on their minds than the stiff drinks and industrial-strength showers required to put the whole ugly experience behind them.

Peter Sobczynski

CREDITS

Uday Hussein/Latif Yahia: Dominic Cooper
Sarrab: Ludivine Sagnier
Ali: Mimoun Oaissa
Munem: Raad Rawi
Saddam Hussein/Faoaz: Philip Quast
Yassem: Khalid Laith
Qusay Hussein: Jamie Harding
Origin: Belgium
Language: English
Released: 2011
Production: Paul Breuls, Michael John Fedun, Emjay Rechsteiner, Catherine Bandeleene; Corsan Productions, Corrino Productions, Staccato Productions; released by Herrick Entertainment
Directed by: Lee Tamahori
Written by: Michael Thomas
Cinematography by: Sam McCurdy
Music by: Christian Henson
Sound: Tim Fraser
Music Supervisor: Mark Lo
Editing: Luis Carballar
Art Direction: Charlo Dalli
Costumes: Anna Sheppard
Production Design: Paul Kirby
MPAA rating: R
Running time: 109 minutes

REVIEWS

Childress, Erik. *.eFilmcritic.com*. February 3, 2011.
Debruge, Peter. *Variety*. January 24, 2011.
Ebert, Roger. *Chicago Sun-Times*. August 4, 2011.
Goss, William. *.Film.com*. August 9, 2011.
Morris, Wesley. *Boston Globe*. August 4, 2011.
Pais, Matt. *RedEye*. August 4, 2011.
Rabin, Nathan. *AV Club*. July 28, 2011.
Reed, Rex. *New York Observer*. July 27, 2011.
Scott, A.O. *New York Times*. July 28, 2011.
White, Armond. *New York Press*. August 3, 2011.

TRIVIA

A one point, director Danny Boyle was considered to helm the film.

DIARY OF A WIMPY KID: RODRICK RULES

Welcome to the next grade.
　—Movie tagline

Box Office: $52.7 million

Jeff Kinney's *Diary of a Wimpy Kid* books have remained hugely successful with kids and tweens since their debut back in 2007. It comes as no surprise that there would be a movie franchise, although their box office performance was probably thought to have been greater since the first film in 2010. Neither the original nor the sequel *Diary of a Wimpy Kid: Rodeick Rules* cracked the coveted $100 million mark domestically, but their modest success might still keep the franchise running, so long as the books keep flying off the shelves and the product is easy to sell. Unfortunately, that seems to be the unimaginative approach to this sequel: Just keep it light for the kids and do not mess with the formula. In fact, the sequel goes steps further to increase the level of obnoxiousness that kept the original from being a complete success.

Rodrick Rules again follows the misadventures of Greg Heffley (played again by Zachary Gordon), now in seventh grade and no longer at the bottom of the popularity totem pole. The film opens with a pre-credits sequence at a roller rink where Greg sees the new girl in town, Holly Hills (Peyton List), and instantly falls in love. Greg's older brother encourages Greg to ask her to skate with him during a slow song, a typically cruel prank that results in widespread humiliation with Greg's parents (Steve Zahn and Rachel Harris) adding insult to injury.

This film is more about Greg's relationship with his brother, Rodrick (Devon Bostick), whose relentless torments have finally irked their parents enough to give the two boys an incentive to try and be civil to one another: For every hour they spend together, they each earn a "mom buck," which they can cash in for real money at any given time. Rodrick, of course, does not take this seriously and eventually that plot point is dropped altogether. Rodrick has other things on his mind, such as participating in a local talent show with his band, Loded Diaper.

Greg, of course, dreams of being in another family altogether. With his best friend, Rowley (Robert Capron), they try to put together a seemingly spontaneous mishap on camera which they hope to upload onto YouTube as a way of becoming an instant internet sensation that will make them rich. It never really comes together and Rowley has other plans for putting together a magic act for the talent show, which Greg really wants nothing to do with. Meanwhile, after a disastrous incident at church, the Heffley parents have made the questionable decision to leave Greg and Rodrick home alone for the weekend as a means of punishment while they take their youngest brother to a water park. Naturally, Rodrick throws a wild party that eventually results in a huge mess to clean an hour before the parents get home, an episode that helps the bond between the two brothers.

Like the original, *Rodrick Rules* is episodic and only loosely rooted in a plot. Where the original film was about surviving a new school and environment, this film is about surviving a tormenting older brother. The parents seem clueless as to just how far Rodrick's cruelty goes. To make matters worse, the mom writes an advice column in which she not only names her kids outright (something no real columnist would ever really do), but chronicles their progress for the entire public to read.

The *Wimpy Kid* films are not entirely painful to sit through, but in the hands of more insightful writers and directors, there might have been something beyond a surface-oriented trifle that one expects to see after school on Nickelodeon or The Disney Channel. The books are cute and fun for kids to read and the movies aspire to be little more than easily digestible concoctions for their core audience. But there is a wealth of missed opportunities with these films. The insight into childhood is limited to the pencil doodles that permeate almost every page of the book and are often used to punctuate Greg's feeling in any given situation. There seems to be no room for real clarity or introspection with these characters.

It would be wrong to expect the level of sophistication that was evident in Spike Jonze's *Where the Wild Things Are* (2009), but *Rodrick Rules* is only occasionally willing to step outside its own cartoon world for something meaningful to grasp onto. The film has a couple of nice moments, particularly a scene between Greg and Holly late in the film, as they talk openly about the horrors about having an older sibling. But the movie too often blinks during such moments and feels the need to throw in a painful physical incident as a way of keeping the kids laughing instead of identifying. There is nothing wrong with making a comedy for kids, but there is also certainly nothing wrong with also giving that same audience a sense that the movie they are watching really understands them. Even *Ramona and Beezus* (2010) had the willingness to be about something.

Perhaps this goes toward explaining the slight box office drop from the first film to this new one. Parents have most of the control over what they take their kids to and maybe moms and dads out there decided to not take their kids to see a movie that would portray parents as buffoons, which this one does. Perhaps kids, too, maybe wanted a little more than just underwear jokes and broadly played situations that only ever exist on TV sitcoms. Who knows? As of this writing, there does not appear to be a third film in the making. Perhaps because the actors are getting older and the audience might be getting a little wiser.

Collin Souter

CREDITS

Greg Heffley: Zachary Gordon
Rodrick Heffley: Devon Bostick
Susan Heffley: Rachael Harris
Holly Hills: Peyton List
Frank Heffley: Steve Kahn
Bryce Anderson: Owen Best
Rowley: Robert Capron
Fregley: Grayson Russell
Patty Parrell: Laine MacNeil
Origin: USA
Language: English
Released: 2011
Production: Nina Jacobson, Bradford Simpson; Color Force, Dune Entertainment; released by 20th Century-Fox
Directed by: David Bowers
Written by: Jeff Judah, Gabe Sachs
Cinematography by: Jack N. Green
Music by: Edward Shearmur
Sound: James Kusan
Music Supervisor: Julia Michels
Editing: Troy Takaki
Art Direction: Shannon Grover
Costumes: Tish Monaghan
Production Design: Brent Thomas
MPAA rating: PG
Running time: 96 minutes

REVIEWS

Adams, Derek. *Time Out*. March 25, 2011.
Best, Jason. *Movie Talk*. March 25, 2011.
Cole, Stepehen. *Globe and Mail*. March 25, 2011.
Malcolm, Derek. *This Is London*. March 27, 2011.
Murphy, Kathleen. *MSN Movies*. March 25, 2011.
Neumaier, Joe. *New York Daily News*. March 25, 2011.
O'Sullivan, Michael. *Washington Post*. March 25, 2011.
Roeper, Richard. *RichardRoeper.com*. March 25, 2011.
Smith, Kyle. *New York Post*. March 25, 2011.
Zane, Alex. *Sun Online*. March 25, 2011.

QUOTES

Bill Walter: "Hey, no hard feelings, right?"
Rodrick Heffley: "Hey, Bill, you know what? After tonight, you're out of the band!"
Bill Walter: "What?"
Rodrick Heffley: "That's rock and roll, bro."

THE DILEMMA

Two best friends. Nothing could come between them...or could it?
—Movie tagline

The truth hurts.
—Movie tagline

Box Office: $48.5 million

It begins with one of those naively "deep" discussions into which a group of people can delve. "How well can you really get to know someone," is the question posed to the table of a group of four friends. Their answers are as obvious as the question. One says that it takes years of developing a relationship and being part of years of joys and struggles; another says it takes only a matter of seconds. Then, the man with the perfect name for a salesman (since he is one), Ronny Valentine (Vince Vaughn) gives his answer: A person can never *really* know another human being, giving the example of a man he heard about on the news who accidentally shot and wounded his wife with a crossbow after asking her to fetch him a glass of lemonade—only to do the same thing a second time and kill her.

Ronny's is probably the most sensible response, though the example he uses to illustrate it points to an inherently cynical disposition. Such is the nature of Allan Loeb's screenplay, which implements this prologue debate to foreshadow the broad strokes of the characters as much as to underline the movie's simplistic thematic point of trust, which is highlighted at almost every turn afterward. His best friend since college, Nick Brannen (Kevin James), who suggests knowledge of another person is almost instantaneous, is the romantic. Nick's wife Geneva (Winona Ryder), who states the process takes a decidedly longer period of time, is the realist. Ronny's girlfriend Beth (Jennifer Connelly), whom Loeb does not give an opportunity to answer, is not even a character unto herself; as a result, Loeb establishes her role as wholly subservient to everything happening around her, a function she continues to serve throughout the rest of the movie.

The script's subject of trust unfolds as Ronny learns that everyone important to him in his life has secrets, as though this is some sort of revelation. The shock begins when he spots Geneva with another man while he is assessing a botanical garden as a possible site for his proposal to Beth. Crawling through the flora, Ronny spies his friend's wife as she kisses Zip (Channing Tatum). After being startled by shouts of disapproval for venturing off the garden's path, Ronny must also succumb to a punchline as he falls face-first into a sampling of poisonous plants.

Thus is the first extraneous complication of many to accompany what Ronny believes is already a complicated scenario. It has little value as a joke, since the payoff is the symptom of "challenging urination," with Ronny stating to Beth he feels "challenged" and screaming in pain while making a stop in the bathroom. Plot-wise, the more important symptom is a telling rash on his face (and it is not the only injury to his countenance that Ronny experiences), the noticing of which begins his own pattern of lying and secret-keeping, which director Ron Howard shows in imagined flashbacks to events Ronny creates to sell his dishonesty.

This and the other impediments Ronny encounters only stall the resolution of the dilemma of the title: Whether or not he should tell Nick that Geneva is cheating. He makes up his mind fairly early that whatever repercussions may arise from a "kill the messenger" situation are worth being honest with his best friend. The major hindrance to implementing his decision is an important business deal Ronny and Nick have with a major automotive company to manufacture an electric motor that sounds and feels like the engine of a classic muscle car (Queen Latifah, in an embarrassingly pointless role, plays the supervisor assigned to their project, who uses sexual allusions to describe her excitement). Nick is anxious to the point of illness about the progress of his creation, and Ronny fears this news will only be a further detriment to his productivity.

From there arise other factors. Geneva threatens to reveal that she and Ronny had sex before she and Nick started dating and will lie to Nick that Ronny has been obsessing over her in the decades since to ward off the truth. Ronny learns Nick receives sexual attention at a massage parlor by following him late at night. He stalks Zip and Geneva back to Zip's apartment, where he takes pictures of the two in the throes of passion. It is no stretch to observe that Ronny's obsessive behavior and deceit are results of his addictive personality—he had a gambling problem for years but has not placed a bet in over a year—and it is also no stretch to find his conduct repellent (or to be annoyed by the way Loeb uses it so Beth fears her boyfriend has relapsed), particularly when he uses a toast at a party for Beth's parents' fortieth wedding anniversary to direct disguised criticism at Geneva.

The Dilemma comes to a head with a well-intentioned intervention for Ronny, featuring all the players, attempting further misfires at comedy, and employing one, final snag to his inevitable disclosure. The machinations of extending it, as they are through the rest of the movie, are shamelessly transparent.

Mark Dujsik

CREDITS

Ronny Valentine: Vince Vaughn
Nick Backman: Kevin James
Geneva Backman: Winona Ryder

Beth: Jennifer Connelly
Zip: Channing Tatum
Susan Warner: Queen Latifah
Thomas Fern: Chelcie Ross
Origin: USA
Language: English
Released: 2011
Production: Brian Grazer, Vince Vaughn; Imagine Entertainment, Spyglass Entertainment, Wild West Picture Show; released by Universal Pictures
Directed by: Ron Howard
Written by: Allan Loeb
Cinematography by: Salvatore Totino
Music by: Hans Zimmer, Lorne Balfe
Sound: Anthony J. Ciccolini III
Music Supervisor: Alexandra Patsavas
Editing: Dan Hanley, Mike Hill
Costumes: Daniel Orlandi
Production Design: Daniel Clancy
MPAA rating: PG-13
Running time: 111 minutes

REVIEWS

Beifuss, John. *Commercial Appeal* (Memphis, Tennessee). January 14, 2011.
Berardinelli, James. *ReelViews*. January 12, 2011.
Gibron, Bill. *PopMatters*. January 14, 2011.
Hewitt, Chris. *St. Paul Pioneer Press*. January 13, 2011.
Kenny, Glenn. *MSN Movies*. January 13, 2011.
Phillips, Michael. *Chicago Tribune*. January 13, 2011.
Putman, Dustin. *DustinPutman.com*. January 11, 2011.
Schrodt, Paul. *Slant Magazine*. January 13, 2011.
Scott, A.O. *New York Times*. January 13, 2011.
Sharkey, Betsy. *Los Angeles Times*. January 14, 2011.

QUOTES

Susan Warner: "I feel like I'm your Deep Throat. Have you seen that movie?"
Ronny Valentine: "All the President's Men?"
Susan Warner: "No, Deep Throat."

TRIVIA

Jennifer Garner was originally cast in the film but was eventually replaced by Jennifer Connelly after Garner dropped out.

DOLPHIN TALE

Inspired by the amazing true story of Winter.
—Movie tagline

Box Office: $72.3 million

Family films run the gamut of highs and lows in trying to appease their core audience. Like the toys designed with age limits on who is safe enough to play with them, films of this manner could just as easily come with the same pre-packaged warnings on who might just get the most enjoyment out of them. One normally fool-proof formula is to pair a child with an animal or creature of some sort and allow that bond to spill over until the humans in the audience cannot help but attach an interest in their journey. From *The Black Stallion* (1979) to *How To Train Your Dragon* (2010), a generation has learned about the best this particular genre has to offer and they now have another solid option in the subgenre in *Dolphin Tale*.

Sawyer Nelson (Nathan Gamble) is not exactly having the best summer. His poor studies have forced him to take classes. He appears to have no friends other than his cousin Kyle (Austin Stowell) and Kyle is headed into the Army. So, Sawyer spends his Florida days inside the garage tinkering with his toy helicopter. That is until riding his bike to school one morning he is sidetracked by the sight of a beached dolphin roped up in a crab trap. He helps cut it free and then watches as the local marine hospital, headed by Dr. Clay Haskett (Harry Connick Jr.), shows up to care for the creature with the severely injured tail.

Curious to know how the dolphin is doing, Sawyer sneaks into the converted sewage plant and meets Hazel (Cozi Zuehlsdorff), the precocious daughter of Dr. Clay. Soon he has an open invitation to come see Winter, as the dolphin is now called, and is ditching school much to the initial chagrin of his mom (Ashley Judd). The boy seems to have a special bond with Winter, who shows a will to survive only in his presence. Things look grimmer when her tail is amputated, presumably preventing any possibility for her to ever swim again. Though Winter does find a temporary solution, the long-term aggravation on her anatomy does not suggest any true long-term prospects. That is when Sawyer calls in the help of Dr. McCarthy (Morgan Freeman), a prosthetics expert who takes on the challenge of creating a new tale for the medical books.

Dolphin Tale is a film that continually threatens to go down the wrong path just as it is righting itself for the better. The sincerity of the film is never in question. It now becomes how the filmmakers choose to maintain it. Karen Janszen & Noam Dromi's screenplay invents one complication after another to keep the characters on their toes, but balances them in a way so viewers are not left with an onslaught of resolutions for the final act. Sawyer's school issues are solved with mom being more understanding than the usual movie parent who only finds clarity in the final minutes. Haskett's hospital is under threat of going under financially, but the board

discusses it as simple logic rather than a bunch of meanies threatening to sink Dr. Clay and his animals. Director Charles Martin Smith cannot help but introduce some comic relief for the kiddies involving a mischievous pelican and an out-of-control helicopter—the soundtrack of which will mean more to their parents—but avoids any scatological relief to garner cheap laughs or to mark villains.

Where the film treads on more sensitive territory, it is in by connecting the plight of Winter to the brave men and women who fight for our country. Based on true elements or not, the moment the champion swimmer with Olympic ambitions announces he is headed into service it seems likely that his dream will be dashed. Again, however, though it leads to moments of pride and a misplaced piece of realization by Sawyer that such injuries also affect others, it opens the doors on how inspiration can have that healing effect. Winter thus services not only as a parallel story for Kyle, but a beacon of light for children with disabilities beyond their control. Charles Martin Smith is careful not to exploit their plight for simplistic sympathy, casually introducing this element through their Winter wonderment rather than a blanket reassurance that everything is going to be OK in their world now.

The majesty of the dolphin world has been explored best in nature shows and documentaries that lend themselves to the high definition world of IMAX clarity and scope. The most disappointing aspect of *Dolphin Tale* is that any moment where Winter or her brethren can swim free, the film switches to CGI recreations that vastly cheapen the spectacle. Aerial and underwater photography are second only to animated features with the best potential for the modern 3-D surge, but when being constrained to rehabilitation in an above-ground swimming pool, a cheap conversion process after the fact looks even cheaper. Technical matters do run secondary to the story, however, and Charles Martin Smith, having had some experience in the animal world as the star of Carroll Ballard's *Never Cry Wolf* (1983) and behind the camera for some family fun in *Air Bud* (1997), keeps the material earnest without ever venturing into overtly heavy-handed miracle speak. The fact that Winter plays herself in the movie is miracle enough and families should still have a solid, emotional response to cheering on the recovery that led to an improbable starring role.

Erik Childress

CREDITS

Dr. Clay Haskett: Harry Connick Jr.
Lorraine Nelson: Ashley Judd
Dr. Cameron McCarthy: Morgan Freeman

Sawyer Nelson: Nathan Gamble
Reed Haskell: Kris Kristofferson
Hazel Haskell: Cozi Zuehlsdorff
Kyle Connellian: Austin Stowell
Origin: USA
Language: English
Released: 2011
Production: Andrew A. Kosove, Broderick Johnson, Richard Ingber; Alcon Entertainment; released by Warner Bros.
Directed by: Charles Martin Smith
Written by: Karen Janszen
Cinematography by: Karl Walter Lindenlaub
Music by: Mark Isham
Sound: Scott Clements
Music Supervisor: Deva Anderson
Editing: Harvey Rosenstock
Art Direction: Richard Fojo
Costumes: Hope Hanafin
Production Design: Michael Corenblith
MPAA rating: PG
Running time: 113 minutes

REVIEWS

Barker, Andrew. *Variety.* September 19, 2011.
Ebert, Roger. *Chicago Sun-Times.* September 22, 2011.
Hillis, Aaron. *Village Voice.* September 20, 2011.
Kenny, Glenn. *MSN Movies.* September 21, 2011.
McCarthy, Todd. *Hollywood Reporter.* September 19, 2011.
Orndorf, Brian. *eFilmCritic.com.* September 21, 2011.
Phillips, Michael. *Chicago Tribune.* September 22, 2011.
Rabin, Nathan. *AV Club.* September 22, 2011.
Schager, Nick. *Slant Magazine.* September 21, 2011.
Willmore, Alison. *Time Out New York.* September 21, 2011.

QUOTES

Hazel Haskett: "What does your dad do?"
Sawyer Nelson: "I don't know. He left like 5 years ago. We don't know where he is. He never calls, never writes."
Hazel Haskett: "Oh."
Sawyer Nelson: "So what does your mom do?"
Hazel Haskett: "She died when I was 7. Never calls, never writes."

TRIVIA

This marks the third picture that Ashley Judd and Morgan Freeman have made together.

DON'T BE AFRAID OF THE DARK

Box Office: $29.3 million

The remake of the horror film has become a standard, bi-monthly staple of the American cinematic landscape. Usually, the arrival of a horror remake is cause for skepticism if not outright scorn from die-hard fans. If any producer goes near a John Carpenter, George Romero or Wes Craven movie with plans of updating it for a new generation, the knives from fans come out before a single frame of film has been shot. Nothing is sacred in Hollywood anymore, and, for the most part, the studios never really looked at the genre as any kind of legitimate art form. To the modern producer (and even those of past generations), the genre exists to lure teenagers into the multiplexes, legendary status be damned. Curiously, someone actually had the idea to remake an obscure made-for-TV horror movie that was not very well executed and make it better and more interesting.

Don't Be Afraid of the Dark (1973) was the only kind of horror movie that kids were allowed to see back when it aired. If it ever was good, it certainly does not hold up today, but it is an interesting and probably enjoyable piece of nostalgia for those who may have seen it as a kid and who remember the fun in watching a scary movie on television. It was a haunted house movie at a time when a black cat still meant something and when a cone-headed, alien-like ghoul with one expression passed for creature make-up. It was a different time. Strangely, the storyline fit in with other movies from that era about oppressed, depressed middle-American housewives such as *The Stepford Wives* (1975) and George A. Romero's *Hungry Wives* (also titled *Season of the Witch*) (1972).

The original was about an average married couple who move into an old, creepy mansion in which the fireplace has been bricked off and the groundskeeper warns the couple to never, ever remove any of those bricks. Of course, he never says why and of course the wife breaks that rule. Soon, she starts hearing creepy little voices that speak of being "set free" and wanting her spirit. "We want you!!!" The husband has no idea why his wife is suddenly acting crazy, but clearly these creatures have a stranglehold on her psyche until she finally succumbs to their wishes.

The remake has added several new elements to that simple storyline, the most obvious being that the couple now have a child. Kim (Katie Holmes) and Alex (Guy Pearce) are a young couple with a nine-year-old named Sally (Bailee Madison). They move into the creepy mansion that has the same groundskeeper, Harris (Jack Thompson), who does not warn them about anything so much as hope they do not get too curious, particularly about the never-before-seen basement that houses all sorts of artifacts from the 1800s. As with most haunted house movies, the set-up is accomplished via a tour of the house in its calm state.

The weirdness begins when Sally discovers a cool hedge maze where she briefly disappears. She soon speaks of faeries and draws strange swirls. She believes that, through the creatures she discovered, she has found friends. At first, they seem harmless enough and she retreats to visit them, offering raisins for snacks. In the original, the creatures wanted a soul. Here, they want Sally's teeth, and they leave a strange silver coin under her pillow when she finally loses one. Eventually, she uncovers an old collection of rotted teeth in a dish. Suddenly, nothing seems right about these little gremlin-like creatures or their intentions.

The typical haunted house movie often has the tricky explanation as to why the family or couple choose to stay in the house even though they know something is inherently wrong with it. *Don't Be Afraid of the Dark* puts the burden on Alex, who is obsessed with getting his home renovation in *Architecture Digest*. Sally is his daughter from a previous marriage, and so Kim is a stepmom trying desperately to win a little girl's heart and approval, which is an uphill battle throughout most of the film. Kim identifies with Sally and her melancholic state, but is suspicious when she finds her dresses cut up with scissors. She immediately believes Sally did it. Sally's increasingly disturbing behavior is not lost on Alex, who brings in a psychologist to try and understand what his daughter is going through. Alex believes he has children figured out ("She's testing us. That's what kids do."). If the divorce and new surroundings have left Sally in a depressed and unstable state, it must be dealt with head-on with doctors and medicine. This leaves him certain that the house is not being haunted, and it just a figment of his troubled daughter's imagination. So why leave now when he is so close to a major accomplishment?

Don't Be Afraid of the Dark joins the ranks of recent in-name-only remakes, such as *Inglourious Basterds* (2009) and *Bad Lieutenant: Port of Call New Orleans* (2010), films that take only the bare essentials of their inspirations, but instead of copying them, they make the movies their own. Director Troy Nixey (making his feature debut) and writers Guillermo Del Toro and Matthew Robbins have turned the story from an examination of a middle-American housewife's mental state to that of a piece of childhood lore (the tooth fairy) that turns into a childhood nightmare. The movie maintains its tension by keeping most of the story grounded in Sally's point of view. The teddy bear that constantly reminds her "I love you" is more creepy than endearing and, even though the film's title suggests otherwise, there is plenty to be afraid of in the dark.

Collin Souter

CREDITS

Sally Hirst: Bailee Madison
Alex Hirst: Guy Pearce
Kim: Katie Holmes
Harris: Jack Thompson
Jacoby: Alan Dale
Origin: USA
Language: English
Released: 2011
Production: Guillermo del Toro; Gran Via, Miramax Films, Tequila Gang; released by FilmDistrict
Directed by: Troy Nixey
Written by: Guillermo del Toro, Matthew Robbins
Cinematography by: Oliver Stapleton
Music by: Marco Beltrami, Buck Sanders
Sound: Glenn Newnham
Editing: Jill Bilcock
Art Direction: Lucinda Thomson
Costumes: Wendy Chuck
Production Design: Roger Ford
MPAA rating: R
Running time: 99 minutes

REVIEWS

Bell, Josh. *Las Vegas Weekly*. August 24, 2011.
Ebert, Roger. *Chicago Sun-Times*. August 25, 2011.
Germain, David. *Associated press*. August 22, 2011.
Glieberman, Owen. *Entertainment Weekly*. August 24, 2011.
Honeycutt, Kirk. *Hollywood Reporter*. June 27, 2011.
Lafsky, Melissa. *New York Observer*. August 24, 2011.
O'Hehir, Andrew. *Salon.com*. August 25, 2011.
Rocchi, James. *MSN Movies*. August 22, 2011.
Tobias, Scott. *AV Club*. August 25, 2011.
Wilson, Chuck. *Village Voice*. August 23, 2011.

TRIVIA

Writer Guillermo del Toro makes a brief cameo appearance in the film as a passenger on the plane behind Sally.

THE DOUBLE

Keep your enemies close.
—Movie tagline

Michael Brandt's truly awful *The Double* could be compared to run-of-the-mill straight-to-DVD thrillers of the ilk that usually star fallen icons like Wesley Snipes or Val Kilmer (or both) but, to be honest, it is not really as accomplished as most of those films. The great irony of the film's title is that it could be taken as self-critical given how much of the film cribs from superior thrillers. It is a carbon copy, a double itself that has been severely faded and rendered useless in the reproduction. Writers Brandt and Derek Haas (who previously collaborated on

2 Fast 2 Furious [2003] and *Wanted* [2008], a comic book of a movie that looks downright logical compared to this mess) focus on all of the wrong elements of their overcooked story, forgetting to give it any personality much less an ounce of realism, and thereby produce a film that piles twist upon twist to the point that it feels like not just the audience but the actors on-screen have rolled their eyes and checked out artistically. And no one blamed them, especially not the distributors who chose to barely release the film at all, resulting in a measly $138k worldwide gross, the lowest total of star Richard Gere's career for any works released theatrically. Come to think of it, *The Double* practically is a straight-to-DVD thriller.

It is no spoiler to reveal (especially since the trailers gave it away as well) that the title refers to the character of Paul Shepherdson (Gere), a retired CIA agent brought back into service when the assassination of a Senator hints that the notorious Russian killer that Shepherdson infamously killed before packing up his desk may in fact still be alive. By the end of the first reel, Brandt & Haas reveal the first rock in a mountain of twists as the audience learns that Shepherdson actually was the mad Russian in question and it is he who has brought his alter ego back to life. His end game in doing so is never clearly defined by a script written by writers who never settled on how the viewer is supposed to feel about its central character. Should viewers root for the whiz kid Ben Geary (Topher Grace) to discover that the G-man legend with whom he is now working is also a legendary assassin? Or should they long for Shepherdson to complete whatever mission brought his alias out of retirement and quietly slip back into normal life with as little as collateral damage as possible? By never defining anyone's motivations or making clear why Shepherdson would have chosen such a bizarre cover as the CIA agent trying to catch him much less why he would risk capture again once his cover seemed stable (which is, to be fair, loosely revealed in the final act, although it is way too late to care), Brandt has made a film with no definable hero and a script nowhere near smart enough for that not to be a serious problem.

It does not help that Gere phones in a performance even more than he has in the last few years, which is truly saying something with drowsy turns in *Amelia* (2009), *Nights in Rodanthe* (2008), and *Bee Season* (2005) on the recent resume. He clearly saw that his writers and director were not interested in providing him with a believable character and so did none of the heavy lifting on his own. He is truly horrendous here, completely joyless and going through the motions for nothing more than a paycheck. Grace is woefully miscast (again…this once-promising actor needs a new agent) and even small roles like those played by Odette An-

nable, Stana Katic, and Stephen Moyer feel woefully out of place.

It would be unfair to place too much blame at the feet of the ensemble with a script this truly horrendous. If Brandt has been satisfied with one twist, his thriller could have been effective, but the least savvy viewers will know that if the identity of one double agent has been revealed in the first act, it must surely be because there are future twists waiting in the wings. Even with that awareness, the final act machinations of *The Double* are utter and total nonsense. Although the plot holes could have warranted it, perhaps the worst thing about *The Double* is that it fails even to approach B-movie, so-bad-it's-good stature due to the fact that it takes itself so damn seriously. Even mystery-of-the-week shows like *NCIS* do not take themselves this straight-faced seriously. And most of those at least endeavor to make sense. Well, at least as much as sense as a straight-to-DVD Val Kilmer movie.

Brian Tallerico

CREDITS

Paul Shepherdson: Richard Gere
Ben Gregory: Topher Grace
Tom Highland: Martin Sheen
Brutus: Stephen Moyer
Natalie Geary: Odette Yustman Annable
Amber: Stana Katic
Oliver: Christopher Marquette
Bozlovski: Tamer Hassan
Origin: USA
Language: English
Released: 2011
Production: Ashok Amritraj, Patrick Aiello, Derek Haas, Andrew Deane; Imagenation Abu Dhabi FZ, Hyde Park Entertainment; released by Image Entertainment
Directed by: Michael Brandt
Written by: Michael Brandt, Derek Haas
Cinematography by: Jeffrey L. Kimball
Music by: John Debney
Sound: Dennis Grzesik
Editing: Steve Mirkovich
Art Direction: Caty Maxey
Costumes: Aggie Guerard Rodgers
Production Design: Giles Masters
MPAA rating: PG-13
Running time: 98 minutes

REVIEWS

Abele, Robert. *Los Angeles Times.* October 27, 2011.
Henely, Kalvin. *Slant Magazine.* October 28, 2011.

Holden, Stephen. *New York Times.* October 27, 2011.
Hynes, Eric. *Time Out New York.* October 25, 2011.
Koehler, Robert. *Variety.* October 22, 2011.
Lumenick, Lou. *New York Post.* October 28, 2011.
Merry, Stephanie. *Washington Post.* November 3, 2011.
Reed, Rex. *New York Observer.* October 25, 2011.
Rooney, David. *Hollywood Reporter.* October 22, 2011.
Schenker, Andrew. *Village Voice.* October 25, 2011.

THE DOUBLE HOUR
(La doppia ora)

A romance. A robbery. A mystery.
   —Movie tagline
Nothing is what it seems.
   —Movie tagline

Box Office: $1.5 million

The "double hour" of the title refers to the time of day when the clock reads a dual number like 10:10 or 11:11. In the context of Giuseppe Capotondi's film it could also refer to double the storylines and double the crosses or twists. There are likely to also be a doubling of the school of thought in watching this film. Playing out amidst varying degrees of turns designed to take the audience along a wholly unexpected path, a film must be prepared to face the inevitable questions: Does the narrative play fair? Is the filmmaker juxtaposing some ambiguous thematic elements that overwhelm simple questions of psychological sanity? Most importantly, when dealing with characters faced with reality-based pickles, can a filmmaker ask an audience to care about their resolution when they have purposefully mislead them away from natural human feelings?

Ksenia Rappoport stars as Sonia, a hotel maid who opens the film cleaning the room of a young woman who will soon jump out the window. Many might be traumatized by such an event, but not Sonia who continues her nightlife ritual of speed-dating. After a string of uninspiring potential suitors, her last turns out to be Guido (Filippo Timi), a former police officer and current widower. It is he who explains the pertinence of the title, which "like a shooting star," should be wished upon whenever one notices it. This simple trifle is enough for Sonia to forget how late it is and go back to his place for what would appear to be a one-night stand. Guido's answer to giving her his number is to throw a bottle at the door. She is nevertheless smitten and he agrees to meet her again.

Working as a security guard at a palatial country estate, Guido takes Sonia up there for a romantic getaway. Instead they become the victims of an elaborate robbery and their worlds take a turn for the mysterious. Continuing her ability to just move on from distressing incidents, Sonia goes back to work. But she still carries a scar around from that day and Guido's policeman pal, Dante (Michele Di Mauro), is not convinced she has provided all the facts. Facts may be inconsequential to Sonia at this point as not only is the double hour appearing everywhere, but she may just be seeing ghosts on the hotel security cameras.

Lest one thinks any of this is worthy of a spoiler alert, take into account that this is roughly just the first half-hour of the film. And just like Sonia's attackers may not be done with her, Capotondi is not done messing with viewers yet either. *The Double Hour* fashions its narratives—plural—around a pair of major twists. One of which is rather simple to figure. The other, however, is a bit more jarring and while somewhat a screenwriting cliché these days actually reveals itself with not only a compliment of fair play and clues, but also allows a full act left on the clock to shift gears to almost another protagonist entirely.

The problem with this structure is also indicative of the problem with the screenplay by Alessandro Fabbri, Ludovica Rampoldi and Stefano Sardo in that there is little left to care for in the characters of Sonia and Guido. The more the film reveals about her, the less interesting she becomes, despite all evidence to the contrary. Finally, with Guido, Capotondi winds up with a movie that should be from his perspective but is instead thrust into limbo for the middle forty-five minutes and viewer sympathies are simply not built up to earn the conflicted ending. This is a relationship drama that turns into a crime film transported into a psychological thriller that then wants viewers to believe it was just spinning its wheels all along to bring them closer to the protagonists. That is where fairness takes a backseat.

Guido and Sonia's courtship is too rushed at the beginning to have any meaningful resonance once the film begins to fondly look back upon it. Their back stories do not provide the necessary built-up emptiness to declare the pair as instant soulmates thrust together and just as quickly flame out like the proverbial shooting star. *The Double Hour* would like to fool people into believing that it is really a story about people rather than crime, gimmicks and twists, but it really is just fooling itself.

Erik Childress

CREDITS
Margherita: Antonia Truppo
Riccardo: Gaetano Bruno

Bruno: Fausto Russo Alesi

Dante: Michele di Mauro

Marissa: Lucia Poli

Sonia: Kseniya Rappoport

Guido: Filippo Timi

Origin: Italy

Language: Italian

Released: 2009

Production: Nicola Giuliano, Francesca Cima; Medusa Film, Indigo Media; released by Samuel Goldwyn Films

Directed by: Giuseepe Capotondi

Written by: Alessandro Fabbri, Ludovica Rampoldi, Stefano Sardo

Cinematography by: Tat Radcliffe

Music by: Pasquale Catalano

Sound: Alessandro Zanon

Editing: Guido Notari

Costumes: Roberto Chiocchi

Production Design: Totoi Santoro

MPAA rating: Unrated

Running time: 95 minutes

REVIEWS

Antani, Jay. *Moving Pictures Magazine.* April 12, 2011.

Bell, Josh. *Las Vegas Weekly.* June 2, 2011.

Burr, Ty. *Boston Globe.* April 28, 2011.

Holden, Stephen. *New York Times.* April 14, 2011.

Murray, Noel. *AV Club.* April 14, 2011.

Phillips, Michael. *Chicago Tribune.* May 12, 2011.

Pinkerton, Nick. *Village Voice.* April 12, 2011.

Sachs, Ben. *Chicago Reader.* May 27, 2011.

Swietek, Frank. *One Guy's Opinion.* June 10, 2011.

Wilkinson, Ron. *Monsters and Critics.* May 24, 2011.

DREAM HOUSE

Once upon a time, there were two little girls who lived in a house.
—Movie tagline

Box Office: $21.3 million

A robustly unsatisfying psychological thriller, *Dream House* is the sort of movie that is not merely bad but actually leaves a viewer a bit angry, given the manner in which it mistakes—nay, embraces—meandering misdirection in and of itself for sly artfulness. On the surface, the film has a lot going for it, including an accomplished and awarded director and production team, as well as top-flight actors. In actuality, it is a flat-out disaster, a boring misfire that never flips the switch of eerie, sustained engagement in the fashion that it so desperately

wants. The presence of Daniel Craig, Rachel Weisz and Naomi Watts gave the movie enough juice for an $8 million opening weekend at the end of September, but generally deadly word-of-mouth resigned it to a $21 million domestic gross.

Burned out by the pace of his publishing firm job in New York City, Will Atenton (Craig) decides to retire, in order to remodel his quaint Connecticut home, spend more time with wife Libby (Weisz) and their two young daughters, Trish and DeeDee (Taylor and Claire Geare), and finally write that great American novel everyone seems to think he has in him. ("You have some great ideas in your head, let them out" says a colleague). As soon as he is unshackled from work, however, ominous things start happening. His youngest daughter believes she sees someone peeking through an outside window, while Libby is stricken by a vague but increasing sense of unease. After a group of Goth kids break into the house's basement and hold a séance, Will finds out that the prior tenant actually murdered his family.

This fact helps explain why everyone around town gives Will the stink-eye, but even his sole sympathetic neighbor, Anne Patterson (Watts), is unwilling to fully explain the events. As matters escalate, a panicked Will becomes convinced that the murderer (or someone else, a collaborator either corporeal or ethereal) is returning to his home, and trying to relive the crime by harming his family.

Jim Sheridan is a talented filmmaker, but the financial disappointments of *The Boxer* (1997) and *In America* (2003), both movies in which he had a personal stake, seemingly left him grasping nakedly at commercial relevance in the form of more specialized genre efforts. *Brothers* (2009), a remake of Susanne Bier's Danish film about fissures in a fraternal relationship opened by the return of one from the war in Afghanistan, seemed a brief creative retrenchment from this instinct, but the bloated *Get Rich or Die Tryin'* (2005), starring rap star 50 Cent, was a wholly undisguised attempt to capitalize on the fictionalized biography success of Eminem's similar *8 Mile* (2002), and a gross mismatch of director and material from the very beginning.

Dream House is even worse—a lame, recombinant haunted house/psychological thriller that loosely slots as some sort of gumbo concocted from leftover portions of *The Amityville Horror* (1979), *The Shining* (1980), *In Dreams* (1999), *Gothika* (2003) and *Shutter Island* (2010). Notwithstanding the fact that its poster does not even reflect an actual scene from the movie (part of a broader and fundamentally deceptive marketing campaign by distributor Universal that attempted to sell the movie as a supernaturally-inflected thriller, in an attempt to recoup what money it could theatrically),

Dream House simply has no conviction, or identifiable stamp of personal vision. Sheridan seems going through the motions, unconnected to the material. The pacing here is stodgy, and enlivened only in manic counterpoint by occasional scenes in which Craig flips out.

But it is the story itself that most condemns the film. As noted above, there is a pungent aroma of familiarity that comes off of *Dream House*. Nothing about screenwriter David Loucka's story feels particularly motivated by the actions that unfold within the confines of the screen. Instead, the entire narrative feels like a retro-engineered, overly whimsical response to the trending commercial acceptance of psychological thrillers. It is not entirely clear whether all of this heavy-handedness was present from the beginning, or there in trace amounts but exponentially exacerbated by studio-mandated editorial tinkering in an effort to refashion and reframe the movie as something it is not. (The film did sit on the shelf for quite a while after completion, and neither Sheridan nor any of his actors did press to support its release.) Either way, it is a mess.

It ruins nothing to say that *Dream House* is predicated upon a couple twists. Halfway through, a fairly easily ascertained revelation (still weirdly given away in pre-release trailers and TV ads) forces Will to confront the fact that the reality of his family life is not what he thought, and that he may in fact have a connection to the murderer. The specifics of this plot pivot point, which requires an out-of-hand dismissal of all sorts of laws, are ridiculous, but could be forgiven if the script actually substantively delved into the disorienting emotional and psychological impacts of Will's condition. The intrigue does not deepen, however. Instead, the movie only becomes more disjointed and implausible.

Cinematographer Caleb Deschanel's atmospheric frames are lit in just-so fashion, but go to waste in the service of a story with no grander hypnotizing spell. The actors fret and furrow their brows, and Craig pitches in with an energy that spikes a handful of scenes. But none of these things can rescue the material; plodding methodicism gives way to steeplechase shenanigans, but it is all unattached to any emotional feeling or investment. There is a cold, clinical quality to the narrative strings the film pulls, and there is nowhere near enough moody allure to make up for either the many flatly imagined second- and third-act set pieces or its harebrained final twist.

Other recent films have capitalized on a reawakened public appetite for spooky thrills, most notably the *Paranormal Activity* franchise and the low-budget *Insidious,* a $1.5 million production that ended up grossing just shy of $100 million worldwide. Some of these efforts have been good and others bad. None, though, have felt quite so crass and utterly uninspired as *Dream House,* a movie whose most notable and lasting attribute may well be in serving as the answer to a trivia question about on which production future husband and wife Craig and Weisz met.

Brent Simon

CREDITS

Will Atenton: Daniel Craig
Libby Atenton: Rachel Weisz
Ann Patterson: Naomi Watts
Jack Patterson: Marton Csokas
Hooded Man/Boyce: Elias Koteas
Dr. Greeley: Jane Alexander
Origin: USA
Language: English
Released: 2011
Production: James G. Robinson, David Robinson, Daniel Bobker, Ehren Kruger; Morgan Creek Productions; released by Universal Pictures
Directed by: Jim Sheridan
Written by: David Loucka
Cinematography by: Caleb Deschanel
Music by: John Debney
Sound: Tom Bellfort
Editing: Glen Scantlebury, Barbara Tulliver
Costumes: Delphine White
Production Design: Carol Spier
MPAA rating: PG-13
Running time: 92 minutes

REVIEWS

Berkshire, Geoff. *Metromix.com*. September 30, 2011.
Duralde, Alonso. *The Wrap.com*. September 30, 2011.
Gleiberman, Owen. *Entertainment Weekly*. October 1, 2011.
Grierson, Tim. *Screen International*. September 30, 2011.
Koehler, Bob. *Variety*. September 30, 2011.
Olsen, Mark. *Los Angeles Times*. September 30, 2011.
Rooney, David. *Hollywood Reporter*. September 30, 2011.
Snider, Eric D. *Film.com*. September 30, 2011.
Whitty, Stephen. *Newark Star-Ledger*. September 30, 2011.
Zacharek, Stephanie. *Movieline*. September 30, 2011.

TRIVIA

While making this film, actors Daniel Craig and Rachel Weisz met and fell in love, the relationship was made public months later. The two were later married. When asked about the movie, Craig has said: "The movie didn't turn out great. But I met my wife. Fair trade."

DRIVE

Some heroes are real.
—Movie tagline

There are no clean getaways.
—Movie tagline

Get in. Get out. Get away.
—Movie tagline

Box Office: $35.1 million

Nicolas Winding Refn's *Drive* is much like its unnamed central character in that the film is a force of nature more than a traditional drama. It is a film in which the style becomes an essential part of the substance. Drawing comparisons to Quentin Tarantino and Michael Mann's work, the film was easily one of the most acclaimed works of 2011 for good reason. Refn had made brief ripples in the international film scene with *The Pusher Trilogy*, *Bronson*, and *Valhalla Rising*, but *Drive* was a wave, a cinematic experience that knocked over anything in its way and instantly made the director one of the most interesting in his field today (and also won him an award at Cannes). Inspired by Grimm's Fairy Tales to create his own version of a knight saving a damsel in distress with a unique style that often seems inspired by '70s and '80s action dramas like those made by Walter Hill or William Friedkin, *Drive* is one of those instant classics, a modern take on timeless themes of heroism as filtered through the prism of fairy tale culture in the underbelly of the movie machine.

Only known as Driver (Gosling) both because it illustrates his single-minded focus and the character is meant to be more of a blank slate than a name might provide, the protagonist of *Drive* is purposefully meant to recall old-fashioned movie icons not unlike Steve McQueen, an actor notorious in no small part due to how cool he looked behind the wheel of a car. Driver works three inter-related jobs—his days are split between working at an auto body shop and doing stunts for Hollywood productions while his nights are spent serving as a getaway driver for criminals. In all endeavors, the driver has a laser focus, making sure his clients know that he will wait for them for five minutes, not a second more and not a second later. He does not want to know what they are doing in those five minutes. He does not want to have personal interaction. He will not get involved. For him, he is either acting or stationary. There is no in-between. He is either driving for a customer or he is not and it is this black/white mentality that informs all of the decisions he makes, especially some crucial ones late in the film. Like a classic hero, he is either on your side or he is not—there is no gray area.

The Driver makes a key decision when he makes contact with a sweet, beautiful single mother down the hall, a lovely girl named Irene (Carey Mulligan). While it sometimes feels like the Driver has very little personal interaction with the opposite sex before speaking to Irene, the two have an instant connection, in no small

part due to the fact that the gentleman takes to Irene's son. After a few chance meetings and help with her disabled vehicle, Driver almost seems to become a part of the family, replacing the father of Irene's son, Standard (Oscar Isaac), who sits in a jail cell.

Meanwhile, Driver is following his boss and friend Shannon (Bryan Cranston) into another misguided venture—a past decision left the mechanic shop owner with a noticeable limp and he is the kind of character who film fans immediately recognize as a bad guide through the underworld. Shannon wants to borrow money from Bernie Rose (Albert Brooks), a former movie producer who made films that were probably pretty bad but that critics called "European." Bernie has the cash that Shannon needs to buy a vehicle for Driver to race. This is a classic red herring in that most film goers would probably think that racing or the Driver's skills will then become the film's focus, but it is merely a way to display the power that Bernie has over Shannon and to introduce viewers to the businessman's muscle, an obnoxious pizza shop owner named Nino (Ron Perlman).

The race car loan arc is immediately discarded when Standard comes home carrying some baggage from his time behind bars. He owes some bad guys for the protection he received there and Driver stumbles upon a badly-beaten Standard after his jailhouse friends have come to threaten him into illegal action to repay his debt. When Driver feels like Standard & Irene's son is being threatened as well, he offers help. He will drive, Standard will do a simple pawn shop robbery, and a lovely woman named Blanche (Christina Hendricks) will come along for the ride. The job goes horribly awry, both Standard and Blanche end up dead, and Driver has what seems like a limited amount of time to make sure Irene is safe and vengeance is paid. He works well under pressure. In a series of scenes meant to make clear that the vengeful loner is not always as heroic as Hollywood has made him out to be—Driver often comes off more like Travis Bickle than a knight in shining armor—*Drive* turns brutal with extreme moments of violence framed in remarkable tinsel town style.

The first half of *Drive* is the set-up to the job. It is tantamount to Driver sitting in his car, observing so much of what is going on around him and planning his escape. As played perfectly by Gosling, Driver does not speak much. He watches the slimy gangsters, shifting allegiances, and lovely family down the hall. He takes it all in. And then he drives. The second half is the getaway. It is cut-and-dry—a tale of a good guy going after some very bad ones. There is never any doubt, any question of what should be done just as Driver does not question his client's motives or jobs. He just drives. In this case, he will make people pay. Viewers know that he will get from point A to point B. The only question is the route he will take.

Director Nicholas Winding Refn delivers a visually striking film that drew deserved comparisons to David Lynch, Michael Mann, and Quentin Tarantino. He is a filmmaker who finds poetry violence, lingering on shadows on the pavement, clenching fists, splashes of blood, or a man brutally kicking in another man's face in an elevator, scored to classic music, of course. With *Drive* he takes what could have so easily been nothing more than a no-brainer action vendetta piece and makes it into so much more; a film that feels downright instinctual. This is a work that does not feature much explanation, monologue, or clear motivations. It is about adrenalin, a visceral response to wrong-doing. By taking classic archetypes of Hollywood action and reducing them to their basic ingredients, Refn frees his work of all of the unnecessary baggage that usually comes with films like this one. He is far more interested in a music choice, a unique angle, a bloody jacket than he is in the standard tropes of the genre like the inevitable kiss scene between knight and damsel or the pre-death monologue by the bad guy. He includes those necessary ingredients but gets to those points in such a unique way that they feel new again. By doing so, he creates that very rare piece of work that can be valued as pure adrenalin-pumping action or as a work of art. Refn creates striking imagery but never loses the context, resulting in a film that is artistic without being pretentious. Even his music choices and the bizarre '80s font for his credits feels like something familiar but new.

The cast deserves credit for finding the same artistic wavelength as their talented director. Gosling continues to makes the case that he is one of the best actors of his generation by creating not just a character but in icon. Driver will surely achieve cult status in much the same way that Steve McQueen or John Travolta did in years past. Future generations of college dorm rooms will have his poster on their wall. And that might make his performance feel more surface-level than it actually is. Repeat viewing particularly points out the smart, internal, interesting decisions being made by Gosling here at every turn. This is a character who listens more than he speaks and Gosling never seems less than purely in the moment. He is ably matched by Albert Brooks, a man who gives his most memorable performance since *Broadcast News* (1987) and who was wisely being championed as a potential award winner for this work. He is beautifully subtle, never chewing the scenery like so many other actors would have with the same role. The whole cast works but the film belongs to Refn and Gosling, who championed the director and helped attach him to this work. It was Gosling's drive and that

which he saw in this relative unknown that resulted in one of the best films of 2011.

Brian Tallerico

CREDITS

Driver: Ryan Gosling
Irene: Carey Mulligan
Shannon: Bryan Cranston
Nino: Ron Perlman
Blanche: Christina Hendricks
Bernie Rose: Albert Brooks
Standard Gabriel: Oscar Isaac
Benicio: Kaden Leos
Origin: USA
Language: English
Released: 2011
Production: Marc Platt, Adam Siegel, Gigi Pritzker, Michel Litvak, John Palermo; Bold Films, Odd Lot Entertainment, Motel Movies; released by FilmDistrict
Directed by: Nicolas Winding Refn
Written by: Hossein Amini
Cinematography by: Newton Thomas Sigel
Music by: Cliff Martinez
Sound: Lon Bender
Music Supervisor: Brian McNelis, Eric Craig
Editing: Mat Newman
Art Direction: Christopher Tandon
Costumes: Erin Benach
Production Design: Beth Mickle
MPAA rating: R
Running time: 100 minutes

REVIEWS

Ebert, Roger. *Chicago Sun-Times*. September 15, 2011.
Hoberman, J. *Village Voice*. September 13, 2011.
Long, Tom. *Detroit News*. September 16, 2011.
Morgenstern, Joe. *Wall Street Journal*. September 15, 2011.
Morris, Wesley. *Boston Globe*. September 15, 2011.
Orr, Christopher. *The Atlantic*. September 16, 2011.
Pais, Matt. *RedEye*. September 15, 2011.
Puig, Claudia. *USA Today*. September 15, 2011.
Schager, Nick. *Lessons of Darkness*. September 12, 2011.
Travers, Peter. *Rolling Stone*. September 8, 2011.

QUOTES

Bernie Rose: "Here's what I'm prepared to offer. You give me the money, the girl is safe. Forever. Nobody knows about her. She's off the map. I can't offer you the same. So, this is what I would suggest. We conclude our deal. We'll shake hands. You start the rest of your life. Any dreams you have, or plans, or hopes for your future...I think you're going to have to put that on hold. For the rest of your life you're going to be looking over your shoulder. I'm just telling you this because I want you to know the truth. But the girl is safe."

TRIVIA

Hugh Jackman was originally cast in the role of Driver.

AWARDS

Nomination:

Oscars 2011: Sound FX Editing

British Acad. 2011: Director (Refn), Film, Film Editing, Support. Actress (Mulligan)

Golden Globes 2012: Support. Actor (Brooks)

Ind. Spirit 2012: Actor (Gosling), Director (Refn), Film, Support. Actor (Brooks).

DRIVE ANGRY

All hell breaks loose.
—Movie tagline

Box Office: $10.7 million

Drive Angry is the kind of film that should issue a fifth of Wild Turkey along with its 3D glasses. It knows exactly what it is, does not take itself seriously at all, and delivers delirious, over the top B-movie action. About two-thirds of the way through the film, scores of state troopers have set up a road block to try and stop Milton (Nicolas Cage), who they mistakenly believe has killed two of their own. Just as they are lining up their sights on Milton and his smoking hot female companion, the troopers detect a faint, but ever increasing noise…disco. Satan's henchman, The Accountant, (William Fichtner) is driving a hydrogen truck at top speed directly towards them. Inside the truck he is swaying and humming to the tunes of KC and the Sunshine Band's "That's the Way I Like It." The Accountant calmly steps out of the speeding truck onto the top of a nearby squad car. The truck slides toward the viewer in spectacular 3D, slamming through all of the squad cars and exploding but injuring none of the police, allowing Milton to escape. A less-imaginative and playful film would have had The Accountant simply kill everyone. The most refreshing thing about *Drive Angry* is that, in an era of increasingly pretentious big-budget fantasy films that take themselves way too seriously, it employs state of the art CGI and 3D technology to tell the straight-to-video story of dead man who has escaped from hell to save his grand-daughter from being sacrificed by a hillbilly devil worshiper.

Cage's daughter has been slain by one Jonah King (Billy Burke), the leader of a cult of Satanists who plans

to sacrifice his infant granddaughter on the next full moon to bring hell to earth. Cage figures Hell already has one member of his family too many already with him so he busts out (sadly off-screen) and back to the world of the living. His first stop is a small town diner where he inquires with his horny waitress (Christa Campbell) as to the ownership of the vintage 1969 Dodge Charger parked out back. *Drive Angry* is the kind of movie where waitresses look like porn stars and act a lot like them too. Within seconds of meeting him, she is propositioning him: "So, you gonna ask me what time my shift ends? It's a full moon tonight. I always feel randy on a full moon." Cage (looking weird these days, even on a good day), closing in on fifty and sporting one of worst haircuts and peroxide dye jobs in film history, looks like he has not slept or bathed in a week, but is nonetheless irresistible catnip to the twenty-something supermodel waitress. When Cage grabs her by the throat and gives her a wet, sloppy kiss full of tongue she is left shuddering with orgasmic delight, unable to speak having received the defining erotic experience of her life. Unfortunately for her, the Charger belongs to Piper (Amber Heard), her even hotter co-worker. Soon Milton and Piper are on the road, closing in on King and his armada of hillbilly followers (hilariously King's flagship is an RV). Hot on his heels is The Accountant, intent on bringing him back to Hell.

Nicolas Cage does fine work (no actor does deadpan better) but it is the film's two villains that make the film worth watching. Fichtner steals every scene he is in and ultimately the entire film. Fichtner is really only half a villain, more like Lee Van Cleef's vengeful bounty hunter temporarily teaming up with outlaw Clint Eastwood to take down a shared quarry in *For a Few Dollars More* (1965) than an out-and-out villain. The out-and-out villainy is provided by Burke who does a great job as the as the thoroughly evil King. With his leather pants, frilly silk red pirate shirt and sleepy delivery he is a cross between Jim Jones, Jim Morrison and Neil Diamond. Burke is so much fun to watch that one is actually sad to see him go when his time comes (and it comes in spectacular fashion).

If the road to Hell is paved with good intentions then the road out of hell is littered with spent whiskey bottles, steaming shotgun casings and dead hillbilly Satanists. *Drive Angry* delivers fun and imaginative action and, unlike a lot of 3D films, it was not filmed in 2D and then converted into 3D in the post production process. It was filmed in 3D and it shows in its deliciously over-the-top action. Its signature moment from an action perspective is a slow-motion tour-de-force in which Cage blows away half a dozen crazed hillbilly Satan worshipers while simultaneously continuing to engage in sex with a prostitute and drinking whiskey (he has a fifth of whiskey in one hand, a pistol in the other, and a moaning hooker in-between). The Satanists parade out one at a time to attack Cage and have cleaned out the tool shed to do it wielding respectively a crowbar, sledgehammer, hatchet, machete, scythe and cattle prod. (Only one ruins the party by bringing a shotgun but he fares no better than the rest). Cage dispatches them all with moves in which physics are not only an afterthought but a faraway dream. After dodging a thrown hatchet which slices off a lock of his hair, he shoots the attacker in the stomach which somehow knocks the assailant's legs behind him and then sends him, parallel to the floor, backward through a plate glass window. A very well placed bullet knocks his next attacker's machete blade into his skull (the hillbilly contemplates this development for a few cross eyed seconds before toppling to the floor dead). Only one attacker manages to make contact and when he cattle prods Cage its main effect is only to enhance the sexual experience of the hooker. Not slowed down in the least, Cage shoots him in the foot, pauses to take a deep pull on his whiskey, and then shoots the guy in the forehead when he hits the ground a few seconds later. Imagine the sensibility of B-movie classic *Road House* (1989) coupled with state of the art 3D and CGI action.

The three dimensions not only enhance the film's action but enable key, thematic subtext in a way only 3D can. The best scene in the film is a dialogue-free illustration of the emotional inner landscape of Milton and King. As Cage pilots the Charger through the darkness of night, the camera fixes on his face and his thoughts literally play across his face. Superimposed over his face and shooting towards the viewer in glorious 3D is the face of Jonah King, covered in blood, shuddering in over-the-top contortions with what appears to be an orgasmic revelation following the murder of cage's daughter with a straight razor. This, the most delightfully over-the-top sequence in a film full of such moments, is only made possible through 3D.

Drive Angry is the type of film in which the main character promises that he will drink wine out of the skullcap of the man who murdered his daughter and that is exactly what he does (tossing it aside like an empty Schlitz can when he is done). This is the kind of unpretentious B-movie absurdity one wishes Hollywood was making more instead of self-important superhero movies that approach their ridiculous premises with the seriousness of a Holocaust documentary. It is shame that *Drive Angry* did not make enough money to justify a sequel.

Nate Vercauteren

CREDITS

Milton: Nicolas Cage
Piper: Amber Heard
The Accountant: William Fichtner
Norma Jean: Katy Mixon
Roy: Pruitt Taylor Vince
Webster: David Morse
Jonah King: Billy Burke
Origin: USA
Language: English
Released: 2011
Production: Rene Besson, Michael De Luca; Millennium Films, Nu Image Films, Saturn Films; released by Summit Entertainment
Directed by: Patrick Lussier
Written by: Patrick Lussier, Todd Farmer
Cinematography by: Brian Pearson
Music by: Michael Wandmacher
Sound: Robert Shoup
Music Supervisor: Selena Arizanovic
Editing: Devin C. Lussier, Patrick Lussier
Art Direction: Zach Bangma, William Budge
Costumes: Mary McLeod
Production Design: Nathan Amondson
MPAA rating: R
Running time: 104 minutes

REVIEWS

Berardinelli, James. *Reelviews*. February 28, 2011.
Ebert, Roger. *Chicago Sun-Times*. February 25, 2011.
Jenkins, Mark. *Washington Post*. March 3, 2011.
Morris, Wesley. *Boston Globe*. February 26, 2011.
Nelson, Rob. *Variety*. February 25, 2011.
Savlov, Marc. *Austin Chronicle*. March 3, 2011.
Scott, A.O. *New York Times*. February 26, 2011.
Tobias, Scott. *AV Club*. February 25, 2011.
Travers, Peter. *Rolling Stone*. February 26, 2011.
Zachareck, Stephanie. *Movieline*. February 26, 2011.

QUOTES

The Accountant: "Wouldn't wanna be you when Satan finds out!"
Milton: "What's he gonna do, not let me back in?"

TRIVIA

The Latin inscribed on the god-killer's bullet reads *deus velox nex*, which loosely translates to "God's swift violent death."

AWARDS

Nomination:
Golden Raspberries 2011: Worst Actor (Cage).

DYLAN DOG: DEAD OF NIGHT

No pulse? No problem.
—Movie tagline

Living investigator. Undead clients. Zombie partner.
—Movie tagline

Box Office: $1.2 million

Once one gets past the holy trilogy of comic book heroes—Batman, Superman and Spider-Man—the pool of common knowledge becomes remarkably shallow. Those who show up every week to their neighborhood comic dealer notwithstanding, your average citizen can usually spot a superhero on sight by their costume, power, or some passing remembrance from their childhood or pop culture trivia. Though they may have missed the fact that films such as *Road To Perdition* (2002), *A History of Violence* (2005) and *Tamara Drewe* (2010) were originally written in the style of a graphic novel before receiving their big screen translations. Then again those were films mounted by acclaimed directors who had a lot more on their mind than pleasing fans of the original text. However, when an unknown director takes on a relatively-unknown property from abroad and the result is sold as "based on one of the world's most popular comics" it should be run from like a zombie plague. And with *Dylan Dog: Dead of Night,* one needs their best running shoes.

Tiziano Sclavi's hero, Dylan Dog (Brandon Routh), has given up his night job as a paranormal investigator. Once the so-called guardian of the undead, tragedy struck Dylan and now he makes his living in New Orleans as just a regular private eye. He is called into a case by Elizabeth (Anita Briem), whose "importer" father has just been killed by some monster. Hesitant to immerse himself back into the world of vampires and werewolves again, Dylan refuses. When his eager friend and partner Marcus (Sam Huntington) is attacked in their office and killed, Dylan is guilted back into the case of the exported importer.

Hair samples lead Dylan to the werewolf pack leader, Gabriel (Peter Stormare), whose own daughter may be directly involved. Despite the objections over being accused of murder, it is actually the local vampires who are taking a more active role in trying to keep Dylan off this case. Club owner Vargas (Taye Diggs), a vampire who owes his current elder status to Dylan, also denies involvement but is still curious about a missing artifact that could tip the balance of power to his kind. Any hopes for villainous credibility are pretty much dashed the moment he announces that "The human race is obsolete, y'all." While introducing Elizabeth to the world he was once entrusted to keep secret, Dylan must also deal with the reemergence of Marcus who is about to learn the lifestyle of the zombie, which, in his case, means being grossed out and cracking wise about it at every opportunity.

In a manner of speaking to the nature of the film's campy sensibility, Marcus lives up to the grand tradition of smart-alecky sidekicks who exist to either supply exposition, add comic levity to his partner's brooding nature, or simply just be killed. In Sclavi's comic, the sidekick was a Groucho Marx impersonator but was changed due to the production being unable to secure the rights to the likeness of the famed comedian. No excuse of permission issues were claimed in the absence of Dylan's other occasional aide, Inspector Bloch. Adaptations come with their varying roadblocks, but screenwriters Thomas Dean Donnelly & Joshua Oppenheimer—responsible for other disastrous revisions of Ray Bradbury's *A Sound of Thunder* (2005) and *Conan the Barbarian* (2011)—have created their own roadblock. Instead of establishing their surrogate sidekick as an already-undead ally, they continue to interrupt the central mystery with forays into Marcus' eating habits, personal grooming and zombie support groups. Then again, it is a red herring to blame these asides as the primary distraction from an already lifeless case.

Director Kevin Munroe, responsible for *TMNT* (2007), cannot stay focused on whether to inhabit the film with the distinctive trappings of film noir or dip it into the gooey campiness of a film in on its own joke. While humor and mythological creepiness has served television's *True Blood* quite well, this is a mash-up that can never serve the darker noir implications unless the filmmakers are serving up a true parody of the genre. *Dylan Dog: Dead of Night* is like the McDLT of adaptations, wanting to keep the hot side hot and the cool side cool, but like the fast food franchise keeps both sides under a warming lamp that rather defeats the purpose.

Dylan Dog, except for his clothing, has carried over almost none of the traits that he inhabited in the comics. "I thought I'd left my past behind. But sometimes it has a way of sneaking up and punching you square into the present," is not quite up to the standards of hard-boiled voiceover, but does accurately reflect how fans might react. As a detective story, monster tale or action film, *Dylan Dog: Dead of Night* possesses none of the excitement, fright or simple coolness that Munroe could have achieved through stylish cinematography, the absolute stamp on noirish underpinnings. Brandon Routh proved to be a stiff as the Man of Steel in *Superman Returns* (2006), but possessed some nice comic chops in smaller supporting roles in *Zack and Miri Make a Porno* (2008), *Scott Pilgrim vs. the World* (2010), and a recurring arc on TV's *Chuck*. A combination of his stiff mannerisms with his comic ability results in too much of the former and too little of the latter; an almost perfect limbo to which the film shall rest, hopefully, for all eternity until all its sins can be burned from memory.

Erik Childress

CREDITS

Dylan Dog: Brandon Routh
Marcus: Sam Huntington
Gabriel: Peter Stormare
Vargas: Taye Diggs
Wolfgang: Kurt Angel
Elizabeth: Anita Briem
Origin: USA
Language: English
Released: 2011
Production: Ashok Amritraj, Gilbert Adler, Scott Mitchell Rosenberg; Hyde Park Entertainment, Platinum Studios, Omni Lab Media Group
Directed by: Kevin Monroe
Written by: Thomas Dean Donnelly, Joshua Oppenheimer
Cinematography by: Geoffrey Hall
Music by: Klaus Badelt
Sound: Betsy Lindell
Editing: Paul Hirsch
Costumes: Caroline Eselin

Production Design: Raymomd Pumilia
MPAA rating: PG-13
Running time: 107 minutes

REVIEWS

Carr, Kevin. *7M Pictures.* August 25, 2011.
Duralde, Alonso. *Movies.com.* May 6, 2011.
Gilchrist, Todd. *Boxoffice Magazine.* July 26, 2011.
Goss, William. *Film.com.* April 29, 2011.
Levin, Robert. *Film School Rejects.* April 30, 2011.
Nusair, David. *Reel Film Reviews.* July 26, 2011.
Orndorf, Brian. *eFilmCritic.* April 29, 2011.
Phipps, Keith. *AV Club.* April 29, 2011.
Scheck, Frank. *Hollywood Reporter.* April 29, 2011.
Weinberg, Scott. *FEARnet.* May 2, 2011.

QUOTES

Dylan Dog: "See? That's just what this case needed. A seven-foot tall, flesh-eating zombie. Which begs the question, are there any actual people left in New Orleans?"

TRIVIA

One of the sleeper vampires is called Sclavi, which is a nod to Tiziano Sclavi, the author of Dylan Dog comic book.

E

THE EAGLE

Box Office: $19.5 million

About half way through Kevin MacDonald's *The Eagle*, the hero's sidekick asks him a very good question: "Why do you care so much about a piece of metal?" Unfortunately for the viewer, the hero and his film never come up with a compelling answer to that question.

The piece of metal is the Roman eagle standard of the Ninth Legion and the hero is centurion Marcus Aquila (Channing Tatum). In 120 A.D. the eagle disappeared along with the legion bearing it when Aquila's father unwisely led the legion to its doom in the mountains of Scotland. The loss of the standard is viewed as a national disgrace by the Empire and Aquila has made it his life's quest to reclaim the eagle and redeem the honor of his father. The film opens twenty years after the eagle's disappearance with Aquila, a newly minted officer, sailing down a haunting and unrecognizable Thames, its uninterrupted, untamed wilderness pressing out from either bank as the Nile would for conquerors of a later age.

Aquila's destination is the northernmost Roman outpost in Britain, the outpost closest to the great Roman wall (Hadrian's Wall) beyond which the eagle, his father, and his legion disappeared two decades before. At the outpost he meets Lutorius (the great Denis O'Hare), his second in command, who is skeptical of his green leader and his infamous last name. Aquila soon proves his chops, however, when the outpost is attacked by Celtic tribesmen who are understandably resisting the conquering invaders. After a well-directed sequence which demonstrates the strength of Roman formation tactics against superior numbers, Aquila succeeds in repelling the Celts and saving the garrison but is severely injured in the process. Fortunately, his wealthy uncle (Donald Sutherland) lives in Southern Britain and Aquila is taken there to recuperate. He is crushed when he learns he has been honorably discharged due to his injuries. In an effort to cheer him up, his uncle brings him to the local gladiator arena where, for no apparent reason (other than he has read the script), Aquila saves slave Esca (Jamie Bell) from death by persuading his fellow Romans to turn their thumbs up from down. Though the native Esca despises the Romans, he commits himself to Aquila's service for having saved his life. Aquila soon comes up with a reckless plan for the duo. Although he no longer has any troops at his disposal, he does have a native Brit who speaks the language and knows the land. He persuades the highly reluctant but nonetheless duty-bound Esca to accompany him beyond Hadrian's wall to search for the tribe that is rumored to have destroyed the legion and which may possess the eagle.

The eagle is a MacGuffin, a term coined by Alfred Hitchcock to describe an object that the protagonists of a film seek to obtain (for example the key in Hitchcock's *Notorious*[1946] or the Ark in Steven Spielberg's *Raiders of the Lost Ark*[1981]) and which propels the film's plot. There is nothing wrong with a MacGuffin and many a fine film has structured itself around one. However, the MacGuffin is merely a plot device and not enough, by itself, to make a film compelling if the viewer does not care about the character who is seeking it. To care about Aquila's quest, the viewer has to care about Aquila and *The Eagle* does not succeed in establishing that emotional partisanship. On the contrary, the viewer oftentimes finds himself rooting against Aquila.

The reason for this is that Romans are not inherently sympathetic characters. It is hard to sympathize with ruthless conquerors who have invaded a weaker society, enslaved its population and who routinely send the enslaved to gladiatorial arenas to watch them die for sport. Since the Ninth Legion headed north of Hadrian's Wall to butcher, rape and enslave the people who lived there, it is difficult to shake the notion that they deserved to get killed. Ridley Scott's *Gladiator*(2000) understood this and wisely made its protagonist's motivation old-school revenge that was easy to relate to: The hero was enslaved and his wife and child were murdered by the villain. In *The Eagle*, the *hero* is the one who orders Esca to kill a child—Pict, who has ineffectually attacked them—and then coolly slits the child's throat when Esca hesitates. Later in the film, it is only with the greatest reluctance that Aquila is persuaded not to kill a second child.

The one element that can make an unsympathetic character sympathetic, a nuanced script that plausibly distinguishes the characters from their culture, is not provided by screenwriter Jeremy Brock. Indeed, *The Eagle's* script's sole priority seems to be to convey only most basic, plot forwarding information in the most generic and obvious way possible. A hilarious example of this is Uncle Aquila's bringing his nephew to the gladiator arena. He looks down at the arena and then to Aquila and then simply says by way of explanation "fun." It is true that a gifted actor can sometimes make an underwritten, unsympathetic character interesting or even likable (Sutherland, a specialist in this area, did exactly that earlier in 2011 in *The Mechanic*). Unfortunately Tatum Channing is not a gifted actor and his single acting attribute, clenching his jaw to convey the entire range of human emotion, does little to overcome the viewer's disinterest in, and often active dislike of, his character.

The Eagle's failure to take flight is a bit baffling given that director Kevin MacDonald and screenwriter Jeremy Brock were responsible for the excellent *Last King of Scotland*(2006). MacDonald's direction is able and his action scenes, unlike *Gladiator's* split-second edits, intelligible (though intelligible does not equal realistic, at least with respect to the two main characters who, in complete contrast with the film's otherwise brutally realistic violence, each routinely cut down three to four opponents apiece in each battle like Arnold and Wilt Chamberlin in *Conan The Destroyer* [1984]). The acting, with the very notable exception of Tatum, is excellent. Bell does a good job (with not a lot to work with) of conveying a man torn between loyalty to his society and loyalty to the man to whom he owes his life.

Sutherland, given generic dialogue and an underwritten role invests his character with more humanity and likability than any other character in the film. Denis O'Hare and Mark Strong both do excellent work but in tiny roles that are little more than cameos. And the film's finest element is Anthony Dod Mantle's breathtaking cinematography which renders ancient Britain an exquisitely beautiful and mysterious place. Mantle's spooky Thames, murky, sun-dappled swamps, and glowing blankets of moss over Roman legionaries' bones (to name just a few of his striking images) are so mesmerizing that the film can almost be recommended on the basis of its sheer beauty alone. However, despite Mantle's incredible imagery and all the other elements listed above that the film gets right, *The Eagle's* generic script does not generate any emotional involvement with its protagonist and this results in a movie as bland and forgettable as its former Abercrombie and Fitch model star.

Nate Vercauteren

CREDITS

Marcus Aquila: Channing Tatum
Esca: Jamie Bell
Uncle Aquila: Donald Sutherland
Guern: Mark Strong
Lutorius: Denis O'Hare
Cradoc: Douglas Henshall
Origin: USA
Language: English
Released: 2011
Production: Duncan Kenworthy; Toledo Productions, Film 4, Focus Features Intl.; released by Focus Features Intl.
Directed by: Kevin MacDonald
Written by: Jeremy Brock
Cinematography by: Anthony Dod Mantle
Music by: Atli Orvarsson
Sound: Glenn Freemantle
Editing: Justine Wright
Art Direction: Peter Francis
Costumes: Michael O'Connor
Production Design: Michael Carlin
MPAA rating: PG-13
Running time: 114 minutes

REVIEWS

Baumgarten, Marjorie. *Austin Chronicle*. February 10, 2011.
Ebert, Roger. *Chicago Sun-Times*. February 9, 2011.
Edelstein, David. *New York Magazine*. February 14, 2011.
Hoberman, J. *Village Voice*. February 8, 2011.

Lowry, Brian. *Variety*. February 7, 2011.

Merrie, Stephanie. *Washington Post*. February 11, 2011.

Morris, Wesley. *Boston Globe*. February 10, 2011.

Rickey, Carrie. *Philadelphia Inquirer*. February 10, 2011.

Scott, A.O. *New York Times*. February 10, 2011.

Tobias, Scott. *AV Club*. February 10, 2011.

QUOTES

Marcus Aquila: "He's not a slave. And he knows more about honor and freedom than you'll ever know."

TRIVIA

The main character's name is Marcus Aquila; aquila is the Latin word for "eagle."

11-11-11

Mark the date. You can't stop what's coming.
—Movie tagline

The end is now.
—Movie tagline

Among the superstitious and those who study numerology a little too intensely for their own good, the arrival of November 11, 2011 or 11/11/11 for those who either still write checks or simply believe in the whole brevity thing was clearly fraught with portent and quite possibly an omen of bad tidings to come. Therefore, while most people commemorated the day by hitting "11" on their lottery tickets or watching *This Is Spinal Tap* (1984) in honor of 11-obsessed guitarist Nigel Tufnel or remembering that it was actually Veteran's Day and meant to recognize and honor those who have served in the Armed Forces, others were convinced that something grim and unpleasant was on the horizon. Although nothing particularly hideous wound up happening on a major scale, at least outside the immediate area of Penn State, it could be argued that the doom prophets were somewhat correct because the date did herald the release of *11-11-11,* an absolutely useless horror film that turned out to be as anticlimactic as Y2K and much less fun to boot. One of the dullest genre efforts to come along in recent memory, the film is a scare-free chunk of silliness so derivative and so utterly devoid of anything resembling a point that it makes that other numerology-inspired cinematic disaster *The Number 23* (2007) almost look competent by comparison.

The film stars Timothy Gibbs as Joseph Crone, a fabulously successful writer—imagine Stephen King in the glory days before *The Tommyknockers*—who has been in a tailspin since the death of his wife and child in a fire allegedly set by an obsessed fan. After surviving a major car accident with nary a scratch, Joseph is summoned by his estranged brother Samuel (Michael Landes), a priest who runs a small church, to return home to Barcelona and visit their dying father (Denis Rafter). Before long, Joseph, who professes to be an atheist, is haunted by strange occurrences and mysterious visions, many of which seem to correlate to the number 11, which he also seems to be seeing everywhere as well. As the date grows closer to November 11, 2011, the visions grow more and more powerful and Samuel suggests that the numbers 11-11-11 are a warning and that unless stopped, a powerful form of evil will be able to pass from its own dimension into ours on that date and destroy humanity. At first, Joseph thinks that this is nothing but asparagus but as things get weirder and weirder, he, with the help of newfound friend Sadie (Wendy Glenn) does what he can to stop the possible apocalypse but in doing so only finds himself sinking further and further into an unfathomable and fairly inexplicable trap.

11-11-11 was written and directed by Darren Lynn Bousman, best known for being the sure hand behind such classics as *Saw II* (2005), *Saw III* (2006), *Saw IV* (2007) and the weirdo would-be cult musical *Repo: The Genetic Opera* (2008), and in doing it, he seems to be striving to show that he can indeed make a film without relying entirely on severed limbs, hideous mutilations or the star power of Paris Hilton. The trouble is that while he has succeeded at making a physically bloodless horror film, he has also made one that is dramatically bloodless as well. There is just nothing at all for even the most indulgent viewer to grasp onto in order to develop any working interest in the proceedings. Bousman's screenplay is a complete disaster—the story is as hackneyed as can be (it plays like a lesser episode of one of the later permutations of *The Twilight Zone,* the characters are all charmless one-note dolts and the dialogue is so trite and clumsy that it makes the works of the late Ed Wood seem like poetry by comparison (this is the type of film in which the hero's loss of faith is subtly indicated by having someone mention it approximately once every three minutes)—. As for his direction, his work behind the camera is so clumsy and poky that it makes a film that clocks in at well under ninety minutes feel at least three times as long.

And the ending—dear God, the ending. Well, it is clearly designed to be one of those twist endings meant to pull the rug from out from under the feet of the viewers and send them out into the streets shocked and stunned beyond measure. They may indeed go out into the streets shocked and stunned but it will be based less on the quality of what they have seen and more on their amazement that Bousman actually thought he could rip-off the endings of so many other horror films—both classics and non-classics alike—and get away with it without anyone noticing. Then again, perhaps it was devised this way to prevent whatever viewers it managed to scrounge up (and to judge from its brief and abbreviated release, they were few in number) from wondering why the world failed to come to an end in all the other past years ending in 11—it must have really been something 2000 years ago when it actually was 11/11/11. They might even note that since the date consists of a two-digit number (that adds up to 2) repeated three times, it could be considered to be another example of that nonsense about the number 23 occurring everywhere. Of course, if they did that, it would mean that they were expending more thought on *11-11-11* than anyone actually involved in its actual production.

Peter Sobczynski

CREDITS

Joseph Crone: Timothy Gibbs
Samuel Crone: Michael Landes
Richard Crone: Denis Rafter
Sadie: Wendy Glenn
Sarah: Salome Jimenez
Origin: USA
Language: English
Released: 2011
Production: Wayne Allan Rice, Richard Heller, Loris Cursi, Christina Molina; Epic Pictures, Canonigo Films, Capacity Pictures; released by Rocket Releasing
Directed by: Darren Lynn Bousman
Written by: Darren Lynn Bousman
Cinematography by: Joseph White
Music by: Joseph Bishara
Sound: Jeremie Cuellar, Jordi Cirbian
Editing: Martin Hunter
Costumes: Toni Martin
Production Design: Mani Martinez
MPAA rating: R
Running time: 95 minutes

REVIEWS

Abele, Robert. *Los Angeles Times.* November 12, 2011.
Anderson, John. *Variety.* November 11, 2011.
Fear, David. *Time Out New York.* November 15, 2011.
Gibron, Bill. *Filmcritic.com.* November 11, 2011.
Harris, Mark. *About.com* November 11, 2011.
Lloyd, Jason. *Horrorphilia.* November 6, 2011.
Lowe, Justin. *Hollywood Reporter.* November 11, 2011.
Orndorf, Brian. *BrianOrndorf.com.* November 10, 2011.
Scythe, Ramius. *Horror Chronicle.* November 7, 2011.
Willmore, Alison. *Movieline.* November 11, 2011.

QUOTES

Joseph Crone: "What does it say about me that I find it much easier to believe in the Devil than I do in God?"

EVERYTHING MUST GO

Lost is a good place to find yourself.
—Movie tagline

Box Office: $2.7 million

As a comedian, Will Ferrell, whose fame has come from his tendency for wild, often random-seeming outbursts, has only achieved critical comic success when he is restrained, so it comes as no surprise that Ferrell's wholly submissive work in *Everything Must Go* is easily the actor's best performance to date. Ferrell has matured as a performer over the past decade, culminating in his work here.

Continuing that evolution, *Everything Must Go* might be the first time he plays an actual human being instead of a parody of one (as the villainous fashion designer in *Zoolander* [2001], a drunk attempting to relive his college days in *Old School* [2003], a television news star forced to reevaluate his career in *Anchorman: The Legend of Ron Burgundy* [2004], et al.), the construct of an overarching concept (as a human being raised as an elf at the North Pole in *Elf* [2003] or an Average Joe whose life is controlled by the whims of an omnipotent author in *Stranger Than Fiction* [2006]), or a broad comic foil (in the large majority of his roles, regardless of whatever else the character might entail). Ferrell's performance here sets the tone for the rest of the movie, which is quiet, subdued, and sympathetic to the self-ordained plight of its likeable loser of a hero. It is unfortunate, then, that writer/director Dan Rush, in his cinematic debut, is so adamant to put the pieces together in such an easily digestible and on-the-nose way.

Ferrell stars as Nick Halsey, a local executive for a major corporation who has risen through the ranks over the sixteen years in which he has worked for the company. His life's blood is salesmanship—the ability to know a product and the customer—and just after passing on some of the key rules he has learned over the years at a meeting, his boss (Glenn Howerton) fires him. The company has decided to make some changes, the boss tells Nick. His history of alcohol abuse has made him an unnecessary liability, most recently after a business trip to Dallas resulted in an investigation into possible sexual misconduct with a female colleague. Despite being sober for six months prior, there was alcohol involved then, too.

Nick is a functioning alcoholic. His first stop after losing his job (after puncturing the tire of his boss' car with the "generous" gift of a Swiss Army knife that the higher-ups thought was an acceptable severance present) is to a local convenience store where he picks out a twelve-pack of beer. After brief consideration, he returns for another six-pack, and on the drive home, he conceals his consumption by wrapping the can in a plastic bag. Upon arrival home, Nick finds that all of his belongings are piled up on the front lawn, the locks to his house have been changed, and a note from his wife with strict instructions: "Don't call me."

Inspired by a very short and far bleaker story by Raymond Carver called "Why Don't You Dance?," Rush's screenplay begins as a frank dissection of the extent of Nick's addiction. Each decision he makes, within the limited options available to him in this situation, is in some way related to his drinking; each new, additional obstacle that arrives (the company car he drives is repossessed, his credit cards are cancelled, and his wife has put a stop on their joint bank account) is only a detriment to his ability to obtain more beer. In the first of multiple visual metaphors to announce Nick's state of mind and character arc, he makes himself comfortable in his squalor, organizing his possessions for function and appearance. Most importantly, he finds his roosting spot—a reclining chair in the center of the lawn—and makes a convenient end table out of a mini refrigerator upon which to place his beer for easy access.

Supporting characters serve primarily as a springboard to extend Nick's development. Detective Frank Garcia (Michael Peña) is his sponsor from Alcoholics Anonymous who informs Nick that he can call his new living situation a yard sale and avoid going to jail; he also maintains that Nick must move on with his life, mainly in assuming that he and his wife will be able to reconcile. Nick's new and pregnant neighbor Samantha (Rebecca Hall) has just moved from New York to this small Arizona neighborhood where everyone seems to know everyone else's affairs. Later, Nick determines that her husband is also an alcoholic, which explains his absence. In a harsh scene that displays his awareness of his condition (and Rush's point that Samantha is a reflection of Nick's own wife), Nick berates her for staying with such a man. Finally, there is Kenny (Christopher C.J. Wallace), a young boy whose mother takes care of an elderly woman down the street from Nick's house. Nick hires him to help with the yard sale, paying him in commission and baseball lessons. Kenny's father—no longer part of the boy's life—used to play.

Nick's relationship with his own father haunts him, and, again, Rush relies on the obvious to point out this fact. Projected on Nick's garage door is a giant image of his father—beer in hand, yelling at the camera—from old home movies he finds, and his father's record collection is one of the few items Nick refuses to sell, even after deciding that, indeed, he must sell his things. "So you're letting some of this stuff go," Frank says, reinforcing the symbolism. The last, manipulative act of the movie forces revelation after revelation upon Nick (he might have been able to get back his own job, if only he had not stabbed his boss' tire; his wife requests a divorce through the mouthpiece of Frank, with whom she has been having an affair), testing his will to follow through with his new and sober outlook on life.

For a movie that has maintained a relatively bitter tone in showing its protagonist's desperation, the final act of *Everything Must Go* lets him off too easily. Certainly, there is room for redemption here, though when it is set to the tune of The Band's "I Shall Be Released," one cannot help but feel more than a tinge of doubt.

Mark Dujsik

CREDITS

Nick Halsey: Will Ferrell
Kenny Loftus: Christopher Jordan Wallace
Samantha: Rebecca Hall
Frank Garcia: Michael Pena
Delilah: Laura Dern
Kitty: Rosalie Michaels
Elliot: Stephen Root
Origin: USA
Language: English
Released: 2010
Production: Marty Bowen, Wyck Godfrey; IM Global, Nationlight EMG, Temple Hill Productions; released by Roadside Attractions, Lionsgate
Directed by: Dan Rush
Written by: Dan Rush
Cinematography by: Michael Barrett
Music by: David Torn
Sound: Trip Brock
Music Supervisor: Margaret Yen
Editing: Sandra Adair
Art Direction: Linda Sena
Costumes: Mark Bridges
Production Design: Kara Lindstorm
MPAA rating: R
Running time: 97 minutes

REVIEWS

Buckwalter, Ian. *NPR.org.* May 12, 2011.
Burr, Ty. *Boston Globe.* May 13, 2011.

Ebert, Roger. *Chicago Sun-Times*. May 11, 2011.
Edelstein, David. *New York Magazine*. May 8, 2011.
Hoberman, J. *Village Voice*. May 11, 2011.
Morgenstern, Joe. *Wall Street Journal*. May 13, 2011.
Murphy, Kat. *MSN Movies*. May 11, 2011.
Phillips, Michael. *Chicago Tribune*. May 12, 2011.
Schager, Nick. *Slant Magazine*. May 8, 2011.
Strout, Justin. *Orlando Weekly*. May 12, 2011.

QUOTES

Frank Garcia: "Do you know what the rate of success is for marriage when one person sobers up but the other one doesn't?"
Nick Halsey: "Is is higher than the suicide rate of cops?"

TRIVIA

Director Dan Rush sought the permission of Raymong Carver's widow, Tess Gallagher, before expanding upon the original short story "Why Don't You Dance?" which the film is based on.

EXTREMELY LOUD AND INCREDIBLY CLOSE

Box Office: $30.8 million

There really should be a rule: When invoking real-life tragedy, a movie must be honest. No exploitation. Simply a reflection on the past, with a depiction of the sadness and bravery involved as appropriate. That does not seem like too much to ask, does it?

For the past ten years, filmmakers have struggled with how to best turn the unthinkable tragedy of the September 11, 2011 terrorist attacks into something that can be called art. Almost unquestionably, the most successful example of a narrative film directly confronting 9/11 is Paul Greengrass' authoritative, moving *United 93* (2006). The low point is Oliver Stone's shallow, patronizing *World Trade Center* (2006). Well, until now. Again using real-life horror as a backdrop for an insincere, tangentially related story, director Stephen Daldry (*The Reader* [2008]) hits a new career low with *Extremely Loud and Incredibly Close*, one of the worst films of 2011 that somehow pulled a stunning and disappointing Oscar® nomination for Best Picture.

To be fair, *Extremely* comes from an extremely trite, offensively quirky source. Jonathan Safran Foer's 2005 novel of the same name overflows with false sentiment and an excruciating writing style that is not only difficult to stomach, but generates few vivid images that suggest an easy adaptability to the big screen. So perhaps

it is no surprise that Daldry's version, penned by sometimes-great, sometimes-awful screenwriter Eric Roth (*The Curious Case of Benjamin Button* [2008], *Munich* [2005], *The Postman* [2007]), ditches a gigantic chunk of the book because it simply cannot sensibly be translated visually. What remains is only the basics of a story that did not come close to working on the page and still, even when streamlined and simplified, becomes incredibly clunky and repulsive on the screen.

One year after 9/11, nine-year-old Oskar Schell (Thomas Horn) is still searching for a connection to his father Thomas (Tom Hanks), a jeweler who had a meeting on the 106th floor of the World Trade Center the day that America and the world changed forever. When Oskar discovers a key in his dad's closet, in an envelope labeled "Black," Oskar embraces the chance to unravel another mystery, much like the adventures in which Thomas often indulged him. So Oskar begins tracking down every person in New York with the last name of Black and asking them if they knew Thomas or something about the key. During the journey, Oskar notes that his diagnostic tests for Asperger's "weren't definitive", which is a cheap way of trying to draw charm from so-called quirks like requiring a tambourine to remain calm and asking a woman he barely knows if he can kiss her. Most of the time, Oskar is very self-aware, so much that he recognizes that his mission is an effort to maintain some semblance of a relationship with his father. He constantly makes statements that feel only like a script lazily trying to make a child's emotions as transparent as possible. When Oskar later notes in voiceover, "I wasn't getting any closer to my dad; I was losing him", it is one of many times that the film sacrifices narrative integrity in an effort to yank tears from the audience through contrived behavior.

In Foer's book, Oskar's search results in many episodic interactions with idiosyncratic folks in New York. In Daldry's film, Oskar's time at the homes of the many Blacks is largely reduced to a lesson-free montage. That is, except for when he visits Abby Black (Viola Davis), whose role in the story has gone from just-barely-believable to completely senseless. There, Oskar tells Abby that only humans, and especially not elephants, can cry tears, in dialogue that will remind some of young Ray Boyd (Jonathan Lipnicki) saying things like, "Did you know my neighbor has three rabbits?" in *Jerry Maguire* (1996). In Cameron Crowe's film, Ray is meant to be a cute, funny, and it works. In *Extremely Loud and Incredibly Close*, Oskar's precociousness is only used to simultaneously exploit a child's sadness and generate disingenuous entertainment from a boy that the movie implies is on the autism spectrum.

It is not inherently wrong to process 9/11 through the eyes of a child; the tragedy is so difficult for adults to understand that the perspective of kids, who were also forced to make sense of the unthinkable, can easily be forgotten. Yet *Extremely Loud and Incredibly Close* does not have such pure, noble intentions. Daldry manipulates viewers from the first moment, when a man falls through the air to the tune of Alexandre Desplat's twinkling score. It is not yet clear from what the man is falling; rather, Daldry just wants to create a moment of poetry out of real-life horror while ignoring the actual circumstances for the fall. This is despicable. Needless to say, people who jumped from the burning towers of the World Trade Center were not accompanied by the pretty sounds of a piano.

The stunning tastelessness only continues from there. This happens when Oskar's mom Linda (Sandra Bullock) stares at the towers from her office and pleads with her husband, who calls her from a tower after it has been struck, "You listen to me, you come home right now". (Daldry plays this and many other moments with crass, overdone intrusiveness, rather than the intimate truth of passengers on hijacked planes calling loved ones in *United 93*.) It happens when Abby Black's ex-husband William (Jeffrey Wright) confesses something to Oskar that is so unconvincing that perhaps it is only fitting that it results in a confession from Oskar that likewise has no business being delivered at this time. And the pointless manipulation really arrives in bulk in Oskar's relationship with the Renter (Oscar® nominee Max von Sydow), a man living with Oskar's grandmother (Zoe Caldwell).

Foer explains the dramatic tension involving the Renter by including decades-old letters that attempt to explain more about the history of the Schell family. As Daldry was unable to adapt these awfully written passages of the book, he cannot make any sense of why grandma is living with this man and why she wants to keep him away from her grandson. The Renter does not speak, which is only somewhat-better explained by the book and used purely for more forced sorrow and quirkiness in the film. Yet the greatest example of how the movie makes a bad character worse is how a sequence in the book, in which the Renter provides support for Oskar, has been changed so that the Renter now expresses agony as Oskar plays voicemail messages that his father left on 9/11. This causes the Renter to leave Oskar, whom he had accompanied on his search for the key's corresponding lock. The sequence has been orchestrated to make people cry, without any clarity or respect for the familial relationships that have preceded this situation.

The events of 9/11, of course, will always generate a huge emotional reaction simply by reminding viewers of what happened, though that does not give filmmakers a free pass to manipulate those feelings. However, the events can effectively serve as a backdrop for an explanation of a scary, uncertain world. Spike Lee achieved this masterfully in his *25th Hour* (2002), and Kenneth Lonergan's long-delayed *Margaret* (made in 2005, released in 2011) examines the inherent guilt of surviving a tragedy that claimed the life of another. That is why it is so unacceptable that *Extremely Loud and Incredibly Close* does not confront any of these feelings. The film serves only as an excuse for an intelligent, heartbroken child—whose use of imagination to block his sorrow works in the book and is largely ditched in the movie— to re-experience grief in an attempt to win awards. This plays with even less coherence as the story of a man who has lost his family on 9/11 in *Reign Over Me* (2007), and it is just as poorly judged as the outrageous invocation of 9/11 in *Remember Me* (2010), which used tragedy to add weight to a story without any. Similarly, the storytelling in *Extremely Loud and Incredibly Close* would be inept as ordinary drama, but it is vile as a supposed discussion of post-9/11 pain and recovery.

Perhaps some moviegoers will see the ads for *Extremely Loud and Incredibly Close* and assume that the presence of Hanks and Bullock guarantee a perfectly acted film that earns its tears. If nothing else, the 2011 calamity *New Year's Eve* and its 2010 predecessor *Valentine's Day* should have confirmed that just because a movie features big, award-winning stars does not mean that it is not hollow, hokey garbage. And while Hanks' performance in *Extremely Loud and Incredibly Close* registers as overly goofy, Bullock generates only melodrama. Sure, even the best actor in the history of movies could not lend truth to an absurd late-movie twist that explains why Linda did not mind Oskar's citywide journey. But when a movie interested only in superficial, Hollywood-ized tears cannot even deliver honest work from its leads, it is a sign of direction, writing and an overall project that should never have gotten off the ground.

There was plenty that needed to be changed about the novel *Extremely Loud and Incredibly Close*. Yet the movie simultaneously provides elements no one will understand if they have not read the book and new, insincere lessons whose additions make an exploitative tale even phonier. Acknowledging sadness is not the same thing as exploring it. The misjudgments of Daldry, Roth and Foer may be no more evident than when Oskar meets Abby. He insists on taking her picture as she cries and looks away. That is *Extremely Loud and Incredibly Close* in a nutshell: Invasively capitalizing on the tears without any consideration for the person.

Matt Pais

CREDITS

Oskar Schell: Thomas Horn
Linda Schell: Sandra Bullock
Thomas Schell Jr.: Tom Hanks
Oskar's grandmother: Zoe Caldwell
The Renter: Max von Sydow
Stan the Doorman: John Goodman
William Black: Jeffrey Wright
Abby Black: Viola Davis
Origin: USA
Language: English
Released: 2011
Production: Scott Rudin; released by Warner Bros.
Directed by: Stephen Daldry
Written by: Eric Roth
Cinematography by: Chris Menges
Music by: Alexandre Desplat
Sound: Danny Michael
Editing: Claire Simpson
Art Direction: Peter Rogness
Costumes: Ann Roth
Production Design: K.K. Barrett
MPAA rating: PG-13
Running time: 129 minutes

REVIEWS

Berardinelli, James. *ReelViews.* December, 22, 2011.
Lumenick, Lou. *New York Post.* December 23, 2011.
McCarthy, Todd. *Hollywood Reporter.* December 18, 2011.
Morgenstern, Joe. *Wall Street Journal.* December 22, 2011.
Osenlund, R. Kurt. *Slant Magazine.* December 22, 2011.
Pinkerton, Nick. *Village Voice.* December 20, 2011.
Pols, Mary. *Time.* December 22, 2011.
Puig, Claudia. *USA Today.* December 22, 2011.
Rothkopf, Joshua. *Time Out New York.* December 20, 2011.
Tobias, Scott. *AV Club.* December 22, 2011.

QUOTES

Thomas Schell: "If things were easy to find, they wouldn't be worth finding."

TRIVIA

James Gandolfini filmed scenes for the film as someone who meets Sandra Bullock's character at a grief counseling session, but they were cut due to a negative reactions from test audiences.

AWARDS

Nomination:

Oscars 2011: Film, Support. Actor (von Sydow).

F

FAST FIVE

Box Office: $209.8 million

If it is not already, *The Fast and the Furious* franchise (*The Fast and the Furious* [2001], *2 Fast 2 Furious* [2003], *The Fast and the Furious: Tokyo Drift* [2006], *Fast & Furious* [2009], *Fast Five* [2011]) is someday going to be studied by top people in Hollywood. Not by the creative folk who actually craft a film from the page to the final edit, but by the executive types who look at the nuts and bolts of what maximizes profits and keeps people coming back to a known property. It might take NASA scientists and physicists with their complicated math to breakdown how a throwaway film about street racing with unproven star power went on to be one of the biggest hits of 2001. Furthermore, how its sequels with their revolving returning cast members pulled off the same feat when they were generally regarded as subpar drive-in fare. For the fifth and potentially "one last job" entry into the series, for the first act at least, director Justin Lin appeared to take the bold step in fixing all the criticisms leveled at them. However, 130 minutes is a long ride in most vehicles and the drivers in *Fast Five* do not have the conversational skills to bridge the attractions for skeptical tourists.

Picking up where the fourth film left off, a daring open road prison break frees convicted thief, Dominic Toretto (Vin Diesel). Aided by his sister, Mia (Jordana Brewster), and one-time pursuer, ex-cop Brian O'Conner (Paul Walker), the trio moves down to Rio to lay low. Naturally, they immediately agree to a gigantic train heist. When the job takes a wrong turn, the pair are confronted with the architect, Rio businessman Reyes (Joaquim de Almeida), who was after a computer chip that conveniently lays out the locations of all of his money.

After escaping his clutches, Dom and Brian discover another adversary on their tail, F.B.I. Special Forces leader Hobbs (Dwayne Johnson) and his A-Team. Before splitting up for good, Mia announces that she is pregnant and they decide to weather the storm to take Reyes for all he is worth. This amounts to putting together the proverbial team; a concocted stew of supporting players from the previous films including Brian's partners from *2 Fast 2 Furious*, Roman (Tyrese Gibson) and Tej (Chris "Ludacris" Bridges), motorcycle hottie Gisele (Gal Gadot) from part four, and Vince (Matt Schulze), still carrying the scars of being on Dom's original crew in the first film.

The extended second act consists of everyone playing upon their specialty to infiltrate Reyes' securities and gather the resources necessary to take him. In the past these lunkheads and motormouths would simply show up, brag about their wheel proficiencies, spout some lame tough guy philosophy and then go really fast. Their entire plan to free Dom in the cold opening is to surround a prison bus with their cars and flip it. Fortunately for them, as a newscaster tells us, their gambit produced no vehicular fatalities.

These are street racers and low-tech thieves after all and in the two best sequences through five movies, they are best using their talents to entertain an audience when trying to hijack their targets at high speed. The climactic truck scene of the original was an unexpected highlight worthy of the *Mad Max* series and *Fast Five*'s first big gambit involving that speeding train is actually the kind of well-edited, practical stunt sequence that is too often missing in the era of computer-generated effects. Director Justin Lin either had a little marathon of *The Good, The Bad, The Weird* (2010) and Looney Tunes or was inspired just enough by the beginning of *Toy Story 3* (2010) to kick things off in such a way to actually get skeptics of the series on board. Even the foot chase that concludes the first act is an above-average piece of action filmmaking that suggests Lin, the helmer of the previous two entries was making a graduated effort to prove that well-regarded indie start-ups can be corrupted into making competent big-budget extravaganzas. (Both Lin and John Singleton, director of part two, got their starts with racially-themed crime dramas, *Better Luck Tomorrow* (2002) and *Boyz 'N' The Hood* (1991), and appear to have used a caldering iron to metaphor their melting pots with these films.) Well-executed action tends to have miraculous healing powers when it comes to threadbare plots, wooden characters and their even more wooden players. Unfortunately for *Fast Five,* there is a lot more of the latter.

As for the cast, Dwayne Johnson takes to the tough guy role with relish in his early scenes with lines comparing his good news/bad news to dessert and veggies, but even he must take a backseat to the charisma-challenged Diesel the longer the film goes on until he is barely a bookend for the destruction-laced finale. Instead the film spends too much time with the grating Tyrese Gibson, who mistakes volume for unforced charm, and the two bickering relatives (Tego Calderon & Don Omar), who henceforth owe royalties to Scott Caan and Casey Affleck who played virtually the same characters in Steven Soderbergh's Oceans' films.

As this chapter concludes, audiences can either gasp or wince at the contents of the big safe in the final sequence being akin to the worldwide grosses of these films while watching the characters laugh at the screen for giving it to them and then retiring into an epilogue of their riches.

Erik Childress

CREDITS

Brian O'Conner: Paul Walker
Dominic Toretto: Vin Diesel
Mia Toretto: Jordana Brewster
Luke Hobbs: Dwayne "The Rock" Johnson
Tej: Ludacris
Roman Pearce: Tyrese Gibson
Hernan Reyes: Joaquim Almeida
Vince: Matt Schulze
Han: Sung Kang

Gisele Harabo: Gal Gadot
Origin: USA
Language: English
Released: 2011
Production: Vin Diesel, Michael Fottrell, Neal H. Moritz; Universal Pictures, Original Film, One Race Productions; released by USA Network
Directed by: Justin Lin
Written by: Chris Morgan
Cinematography by: Stephen Windon
Music by: Brian Tyler
Sound: Peter Brown
Editing: Kelly Matsumoto, Fred Raskin, Christian Wagner
Art Direction: Thomas Valentine
Costumes: Sanja Milkovic Hays
Production Design: Peter Wenham
MPAA rating: PG-13
Running time: 130 minutes

REVIEWS

Bayer, Jeff. *Scorecard Review.* May 2, 2011.
Ebert, Roger. *Chicago Sun-Times.* April 28, 2011.
Hickman, Jonathan W. *Daily Film Fix.* April 29, 2011.
Howell, Peter. *Toronto Star.* April 29, 2011.
McGranaghan, Mike. *Aisle Seat.* April 29, 2011.
Morgenstern, Joe. *Wall Street Journal.* April 28, 2011.
O'Connell, Sean. *Washington Post.* April 29, 2011.
Roeper, Richard. *RichardRoeper.com.* April 28, 2011.
Snider, Eric D. *EricDSnider.com.* April 30, 2011.
Vaux, Rob. *Mania.com.* April 29, 2011.

QUOTES

Roman Pearce: "You know, I think I make a better special agent than you ever did."
Brian O'Conner: "I guess that depends on how you define 'special.'"

TRIVIA

The stunt involving the flatbed truck slamming into a moving train was filmed almost entirely without the use of miniatures or CGI and nearly derailed the train.

50/50

It takes a pair to beat the odds.
—Movie tagline

Box Office: $35 million

Some people probably do not think that it is possible, or reasonable, to make a comedy about cancer. Arguably the planet's nastiest, most difficult-to-treat disease, cancer is, obviously, no joke; it is a killer. Of course, everyone knows what they say about laughter being the best medicine. It is certainly a preferable one to grueling chemotherapy.

All that is a way of saying that *50/50,* a comedy about a healthy 27-year-old man who is diagnosed with a malignant tumor along his spinal column, succeeds surprisingly well as a funny diffuser of stress, even if the film consequently often remains at a certain emotional distance. Joseph Gordon-Levitt plays Adam, a very cautious employee of Seattle Public Radio who does not drive (it is too dangerous, he says) and will not cross the street when presented with a "Don't Walk" signal, even if there are absolutely zero cars around. (The film gets a meaningful opening chuckle from the sight of Adam, breaking from his jog and standing at a crosswalk, while another runner zooms by.) Adam does not drink. He does not smoke. He recycles! How could someone so good and so conscientious of himself and the world around him get cancer?

Well, because anyone can get it, regardless of age and health. Unfortunately, not all people with cancer are lucky enough to have a friend like Kyle (Seth Rogen). On the one hand, he is a goofy fountain of pop culture references that is happy to take advantage of the sympathy he receives from girls at bars (or bookstores, or wherever) once he tells them his best friend has cancer. On the other, Kyle is Adam's primary confidant and strongest provider of support—certainly more than Adam's girlfriend Rachel (Bryce Dallas Howard). At first she says that she wants to stay by Adam's side during his treatment but then buys him a dog (clearly to replace her as a source of comfort) and refuses to go inside the hospital, claiming that she does not want to mix that negative world with the positive world outside. Adam explains to his new friends (Philip Baker Hall, Matt Frewer), who are also receiving chemo, that the reason they have not met Rachel is an "energy thing." The guys feel that it is a "bullshit thing." They are right.

Aside for the evolving relationships in Adam's life, that is it for plot in *50/50.* That is a good thing. The movie does not try too hard to pull melodrama or tears from this situation; Adam, in fact, frequently seems numb to it. One of the movie's most significant flaws is that Gordon-Levitt's performance, until closer toward the end of the film when he allows more of Adam's fear and anger to seep through, spends so much time avoiding complex emotional terrain that he fails to tap into Adam's individual experience. (This may partially be a result of Gordon-Levitt being brought onto the project only a week before filming began, allowing him far less than the usual time to prepare.) Fortunately, Gordon-Levitt has such a strong rapport with every actor around him that the relationships between people compensate

for the lack of detail in Gordon-Levitt's individual turn. He and Rogen play off each other beautifully. They really seem like guys who have been best friends for many years, so that Adam tolerates Kyle's unbridled sense of humor—when Adam gets into Kyle's car after using Rachel's fruity-smelling shampoo earlier that morning, Kyle asks, "Did you sit in jam or something?"—and Kyle, despite mocking Adam for it, respects Adam's goodness that causes him to lead such a careful, calm lifestyle. If either guy was a duplicate of the other, they would probably hate each other. Their contrasts make them work as a team.

In addition, Anna Kendrick is immensely appealing as Adam's 24-year-old therapist Katie, who strives to maintain her professionalism as she works with Adam— even though her computer at work still has a screen saver that reads, "Katie's laptop.". That is not the most professional term to use for the computer of a woman working on her doctorate and trusted to open up a patient dealing with life-altering illness. (Adam is only her third patient, so she has time to fix that before her career gets off the ground.) Thanks to Kendrick's charm, the irresistible way that Katie refuses to take no for an answer when she offers Adam a ride to the doctor makes it obvious why he starts to see her as more than just his therapist. And Gordon-Levitt effectively expresses Adam's desire not to be babied or make those around him feel sorry for him as he retreats from his mother (Anjelica Huston), who is understandably very worried but demonstrates that in a way that, to Adam, is annoying rather than helpful.

Written by Will Reiser, the film is actually inspired by Reiser's real-life experiences; unfortunately, he was the Adam character, but fortunately, he survived. So while it is a bit disappointing that *50/50* does not suggest that Reiser obtained a large amount of new perspective from his life-threatening bout with cancer, it at least confirms that illness did nothing to hinder the sense of humor of this former producer of *Da Ali G Show.* (2000, 2003-2004) (And the film remains a more satisfying experience than Judd Apatow's comedy about cancer, *Funny People.* [2009]) The movie is stuffed with hilarious banter, such as Katie showing her age by not knowing who Doogie Howser is (she asks, "Does he work here?") and Adam insisting that Kyle's goal to get them laid is useless because, "No one wants to fuck me; I look like Voldermort." These lines are not just funny; they feel authentic to the characters. The same goes for Adam's mom's reaction when she learns her son has cancer. She immediately goes into Adam's kitchen to make him green tea, since she read that can reduce the risk of cancer by 15 percent. (Adam notes that he already has cancer, not really understanding what mom is going through.) *50/50* may not pull great drama out of comedy, but it works the other way around.

Matt Pais

CREDITS

Adam: Joseph Gordon-Levitt
Kyle: Seth Rogen
Katherine: Anna Kendrick
Rachael: Bryce Dallas Howard
Diane: Anjelica Huston
Origin: USA
Language: English
Released: 2011
Production: Evan Goldberg, Ben Karlin, Seth Rogen; Mandate Pictures, Point Gray; released by Summit Entertainment
Directed by: Jonathan Levine
Written by: Will Reiser
Cinematography by: Terry Stacey
Music by: Michael Giacchino
Sound: Robert C. Jackson
Music Supervisor: Jim Black, Gabe Hilfer
Editing: Zene Baker
Art Direction: Ross Dempster
Costumes: Carla Hetland
Production Design: Annie Spitz
MPAA rating: R
Running time: 99 minutes

REVIEWS

Berardinelli, James. *ReelViews.* September 28, 2011.
Goodykoontz, Bill. *Arizona Republic.* September 29, 2011.
Jones, J.R. *Chicago Reader.* September 29, 2011.
Jones, Kimberley. *Austin Chronicle.* September 29, 2011.
Mohan, Marc. *Portland Oregonian.* September 29, 2011.
Mondello, Bob. *NPR.* September 30, 2011.
Schwarzbaum, Lisa. *Entertainment Weekly.* September 28, 2011.
Stevens, Dana. *Slate.* September 30, 2011.
Tobias, Scott. *AV Club.* September 28, 2011.
Zacharek, Stephanie. *Movieline.* September 29, 2011.

QUOTES

Adam: "What were you doing when I called? Were you on Facebook?"
Katherine: "You know…umm…stalking my ex-boyfriend actually isn't the only thing I do in my free time."
Adam: "I wish you were my girlfriend."
Katherine: "Girlfriends can be nice. You just had a bad one."
Adam: "I bet you'd be a good one."

TRIVIA

Actor Joseph Gordon-Levitt actually shaved his head during filming. He and actor Seth Rogen were improvising in character while the cameras kept rolling since the scene was unscripted.

AWARDS

Ind. Spirit 2012: First Screenplay
Nomination:
Golden Globes 2012: Actor—Mus./Comedy (Gordon-Levitt), Film—Mus./Comedy
Ind. Spirit 2012: Film, Support. Actress (Huston)
Writers Guild 2011: Orig. Screenplay.

FILM SOCIALISME

Freedom doesn't come cheap.
—Movie tagline

When master filmmaker Jean-Luc Godard premiered his latest work, *Film Socialisme*, at the 2010 Cannes Film Festival amidst rumors that it might mark his final cinematic statement, the screenings were filled with people presumably expecting some kind of grand artistic summation along the lines of Ingmar Bergman's *Fanny & Alexander* (1983) or something equally conclusive. Not surprisingly, he instead presented them with an odd meditation of the current state of the world utilizing a free-wheeling blend of digital video ranging from the gorgeous to the grungy with a near-total disdain for even the most basic conventions of cinematic storytelling. Inevitably, the critical reaction was sharply divided between those who were convinced that they had seen a masterpiece and those who dismissed it as pretentious twaddle from a once-great director who had long sense taken leave of his artistic senses. While it certainly pales in comparison to the landmark works with which he first made his name in the 1960s, the film is a flawed-but-fascinating work that, if it turns out to be Godard's finale, concludes one of the most fascinating filmographies on an appropriately oddball note.

The film is divided roughly into three separate sections that deal more or less with Europe's dark, war-driven past and uncertain unification-driven future. The first and longest section takes place on a Mediterranean cruise filled with a cross-section of elite passengers as they blithely indulge in all the ship's comforts while the more ethnically diverse members of the crew quietly keep things moving along. The joke, of course, is that the passengers rubbing shoulders at the exercise classes and buffets are the descendants of ancestors who used to be at each other's throats and every once in a while, that history bubbles to the surface in the form of old World War II newsreel footage and the like that comes out of nowhere like a bad memory. The second part of the film is a more conventionally structured episode set in and around a remote gas station in the south of France where a now-conservative couple are questioned by their increasingly radical young children about their history in a manner meant to suggest that they represent all of Europe's political and historical failings as they stagnate while living off of the fruits of Third World resources. In the final movement, Godard returns to the more free-form approach of the first segment in which he briefly chronicles some of the grim failings of the West (slavery, war and democracy) via newly-shot footage juxtaposed with clips from films ranging from *The Battleship Potemkin* (1925) to the Steve Reeves version of *Hercules* (1959) before enigmatically concluding with a title card reading "NO COMMENT."

For most viewers, even those few who have kept up with Godard's output in the years since his initial artistic heyday in the Sixties, the mere experience of *Film Socialisme* will prove to be strange and occasionally frustrating. Having flirted with a return to straightforward storytelling (at least by his standards) with his last two features, *In Praise of Love* (2001) and *Notre Musique* (2005), Godard has returned to the frankly experimental narrative approach that has marked much of his work over the last couple of decades. To make things even more perplexing, the dialogue is spoken in a number of different languages and while there are subtitles to be had, they serve as yet another form of commentary by coming across as abstract condensations of what is actually being said and unless one actually speaks all of the languages, it is impossible to fully determine what is being said and further underlines Godard's uncertainty about how unity can occur between people who are set apart by the very languages they speak—in his eyes, even the seemingly universal language of art can separate more than unite. The closest thing the film comes to a non-enigmatic statement occurs when the first section concludes with the rueful statement "Poor Europe. Corrupted by suffering. Humiliated by liberty." and even that is kind of pushing it.

From an aesthetic standpoint, however, Godard once again demonstrates his ability to create rapturous symphonies of sound and vision. Visually, the look of the film, the first feature that Godard has shot entirely on digital video, veers wildly between lushly beautiful images featuring colors fairly ripe to bursting to shabby, artifact-riddled bits that appear to have cobbled from deteriorated VHS tapes or defective cell phones, but often just as beautiful to look at. In addition, there are numerous individual moments that are striking to behold as well—a young girl swimming in the shipboard pool while Madonna's "Material Girl" ethereally appears in the background and the young son from the gas station family cheerfully goofing off in the kitchen while his mother does the dishes are among the most touching

on display. There are even occasional bits of levity as well, such as the cuts during the second section to an eternally deadpan llama that almost suggest a strange homage to the blind camel in the immortal *Ishtar* (1987).

At an age when most filmmakers are either dead or worse—trapped on a never-ending awards circuit receiving Lifetime Achievement awards from industry colleagues who are perfectly content to offer up empty platitudes about past achievements but who would most likely blanch and the thought of helping to put together a new project—Jean-Luc Godard doggedly continues his reign as the world's oldest *enfant terrible* by continuing to create films that test the boundaries of what can be said and done with the tools of the craft and continuing to test the patience of even his most loyal supporters by challenging and provoking them and their ideas about cinema at every turn. In other words, he is somehow still making the films of a young man—works that are by turn energetic, earnest, pretentious and borderline silly—and even if they do not always work, there is still something about them that makes them more fundamentally interesting and intriguing than the efforts of a more mature talent whose sense of daring has dulled over the years. Godard may be one of the last living godfathers of the French New Wave but based on his work here, he is still a punk through and through, and while they may not always appreciate that the film world continues to be all the better for it.

Peter Sobczynski

CREDITS

Origin: Switzerland, France

Language: French

Released: 2010

Production: Ruth Aldburger, Alain Sarde; Vega Film; released by Lorber Films

Directed by: Jean-Luc Godard

Written by: Jean-Luc Godard

Cinematography by: Jean-Luc Godard, Jean-Paul Battaggia, Francois Aragno, Paul Grivas

Sound: Gabriel Hafner, Francois Musy, Renaud Musy

MPAA rating: Unrated

Running time: 102 minutes

REVIEWS

Ebert, Roger. *Chicago Sun-Times.* June 15, 2011.
Hoberman, J. *Village Voice.* May 31, 2011.
Jenkins, Mark. *NPR.* June 8, 2011.
Levy, Shawn. *Oregonian.* October 27, 2011.
Mintzer, Jordan. *Variety.* June 3, 2011.

Musetto, V.A. *New York Post*. June 3, 2011.
Phillips, Michael. *Chicago Tribune*. June 15, 2011.
Quinn, Anthony. *Independent*. July 8, 2011.
Scott, A.O. *New York Times*. June 2, 2011.
White, Armond. *New York Press*. June 2, 2011.

QUOTES

Rebecca: "You're absolutely right: I don't love any 'people.' Not French, not North American, not German. Not Jewish people, not black people. I love only my friends…when there are any."

TRIVIA

The cruise liner used in the film is the Costa Concordia, which was shipwrecked on January 13, 2012 off the coast of Italy.

FINAL DESTINATION 5

Death has never been closer.
　　—Movie tagline
This Summer, death decides how…fate decides when.
　　—Movie tagline
We all share a common destination.
　　—Movie tagline
Kill or be killed.
　　—Movie tagline

Box Office: $42.6 million

Contrary to the promise of its name, the *Final Destination* franchise shows no sign of coming to an end. Popping up every couple of years, the gore-heavy horror movies stick religiously to their formula: A group of a half-dozen or so young people avoid a deadly catastrophe only to find the Grim Reaper does not like a messy ledger book. So as Death comes to collect the unpaid bill, each survivor eventually dies in increasingly freakish (and bloody) accidents.

With five *Final Destination* films now out, that adds up to quite the collection of gruesome death scenes—a fact *Final Destination 5* reminds viewers of with opening and closing credits that trot out the franchise's dozens of previous kills with almost a whiff of nostalgia. That gives the latest proceedings even more of a ritualistic, snuff-film feel than before, and oddly (perhaps disturbingly) cultivates a sense of community among *Final Destination* fans who have loyally stuck around for over eleven years.

Sandwiched between this new film's bookending celebrations of a "Decade of Dismembering," there is yet another entire *Final Destination* plot. Another group

of young folks lined up for the slaughter (most of them employees at a paper company, perhaps a sly workplace nod to *The Office*); another oversized tragedy to kick things off (echoing the real-life disaster in Minneapolis a few years back, this time it is the collapse of an under-construction suspension bridge); another parade of subsequent deaths involving the impaling, electrocuting, burning, laser-ing, smashing, or otherwise slicing and dicing of the human body. (As many of these fatalities occur in workplaces or public areas, the entire *Final Destination* series plays out like the worst—or best—OSHA training film *ever*.)

Naming or describing the victims-to-be seems futile, as they exist only to die. Twice in fact: once in the film's early "premonition of disaster" fantasy sequence, then again later as their fatal destiny catches up with them. That doubling-down of deaths for each character further emphasizes not only the dark fatalism of the *Final Destination* films, but also their economical servicing of their audiences' lust for blood: Two-for-one night on gruesome demises!

The main protagonist (traditionally the one who sees the initial disaster coming, warns everyone away, and later is tasked with trying to understand why everyone is dying again) is played by Nicholas D'Agosto with a declarative blandness that erases his performance and character from the mind minutes after the final reel. (While it is standard to complain about the lack of character development and depth in such horror films, here having the leads take time out to discuss their rocky romantic relationship is deadlier than the film's executions.)

In fact, the only players who stand out are those who remind one of something else. Thriller fans may recognize the female lead as played by Emma Bell, who turned in much better work in the somewhat superior (relatively speaking, of course) *Frozen* (2010). Otherwise-talented comic actor David Koechner is on hand as one of the franchise's rare victims over twenty-five. And, as the group's young-professional alpha male, Miles Fischer clocks in the film's most memorable performance simply because he appears to have siphoned his look, mannerisms, and possibly life force from a 25-year-old Tom Cruise.

The executions of these cosmic lab rats are rolled out on a grim and gruesome assembly line, but this *Final Destination 5* lacks even the guilty pleasure kicks and morbid humor of previous installments. Helmed by James Cameron's former second-unit director Steven Quale, the movie feels dreary and dull, bled out, so to speak, of any thrills, style, or even base entertainment value.

Death's rigid rules of elimination are trotted out in part to give the characters something to talk about between splatters, but also because many horror fans cling to such metaphysical regulations as a way of enforcing order on all the bloody chaos. Meanwhile, the film's only running gag is the familiar *Final Destination* trick of playing coy about how a character will die—in the tension-free lead up to each death, more red herrings are juggled then at a busy fish market. Still, in the dark and depressingly banal world of *Final Destination 5*, even an impaling feels unsettlingly rote.

In the end, what viewers will recall about *Final Destination 5* are not late-inning attempts at cosmic plot twists or particularly gory deaths, but rather the disturbing feeling of having participated in a fetishistic death cult. As those credit montages underscore, these films are all (and any more, *only*) about "the awesome kills," and over the years their fans have come to celebrate them as such. Stripped bare and hollowed out of anything to recommend it other than the increasingly unimaginative ways it mangles human beings, *Final Destination 5* feels like a late-night infomercial for anti-life.

Locke Peterseim

CREDITS

Molly: Emma Bell
Sam Lawton: Nicholas D'Agosto
Isaac: P.J. Byrne
Candice: Ellen Wroe
William Bludworth: Tony Todd
Agent Jim Black: Courtney B. Vance
Peter Friedkin: Miles Fisher
Nathan: Arlen Escarpeta
Dennis: David Koechner
Olivia Castle: Jacqueline MacInnes-Wood
Origin: USA
Language: English
Released: 2011
Production: Craig Perry, Warren Zide; New Line Cinema, Practical Pictures, Jellystone Films, Parallel Zide; released by New Line Cinema
Directed by: Steven Quale
Written by: Eric Heisserer
Cinematography by: Brian Pearson
Music by: Brian Tyler
Sound: Dave McMoyler
Editing: Eric A. Sears
Art Direction: Sandi Tanaka
Costumes: Jori Woodman
Production Design: David Sandefur

MPAA rating: R
Running time: 92 minutes

REVIEWS

Childress, Erik. *eFilmCritic.com.* August 11, 2011.
Diones, Bruce. *New Yorker.* August 22, 2011.
Ebert, Roger. *Chicago Sun-Times.* August 11, 2011.
Gonzalez, Ed. *Slant Magazine.* August 11, 2011.
Hillis, Aaron. *Village Voice.* August 12, 2011.
Lacey, Liam. *Globe and Mail.* August 12, 2011.
Leydon, Joe. *Variety.* August 11, 2011.
Pais, Matt. *RedEye.* August 11, 2011.
Phillips, Michael. *Chicago Tribune.* August 11, 2011.
Tallerico, Brian. *HollywoodChicago.com.* August 11, 2011.

QUOTES

William Bludworth: "You were supposed to die on that bridge. You're not supposed to be here. You shorted death. So you let death have somebody else in your place, and you take their spot in the realm of the living. All the days and years that they have yet to live. And they take "your" place in death. Then the books are balanced."

TRIVIA

Many of the film's main characters are named after famous horror directors: Peter Friedkin is named after *The Exorcist* director William Friedkin, Candice Hooper is named after Tobe Hooper who directed *The Texas Chainsaw Massacre*, and Olivia Castle is named for William Castle who directed the original *House on Haunted Hill*.

FIREFLIES IN THE GARDEN

> *Sometimes a family must come apart before it can come together.*
> —Movie tagline

> *Having a son is not the same as being a father.*
> —Movie tagline

> *For one family, a chance to start again…*
> —Movie tagline

Dennis Lee's *Fireflies in the Garden* is a semi-autobiographical film that examines one family's pain, abuse, dislike, disrespect, disdain, and occasional love for one another through flashbacks, semi-incestuous moments, and maudlin self-expression. It obviously comes from a personal place, but the film itself lacks a personality to make it seem little more than a checklist of cathartic moments from the film's creator. This is not the first time a filmmaker has used the medium to explore his troubled relationship with his father and Lee will not be the last. It often requires quite a bit of bravery to lay everything bare and let the world into one's own pain. The trick is to not come off as self-indulgent or laughably melodramatic.

Fireflies in the Garden tells two stories of this family, one in present day and one in flashbacks. In the present day, Michael (Ryan Reynolds) is a successful mainstream novelist who is reluctantly returning home to join in celebrating his mother's college graduation. His mother, Lisa (Julia Roberts), and father, Charlie (Willem Dafoe), bicker and fight as usual in the car ride on the way to Lisa's sister Jane's (Emily Watson) house. Jane has two children, Christopher (Chase Ellison) and Leslie (Brooklyn Proulx), who are playing softball in the backyard while they wait for their aunt and uncle to show up. A series of events involving this game leads to Lisa and Charlie getting into a severe car accident that kills Lisa and leaves Christopher feeling responsible.

This is, of course, a dysfunctional family. Michael bonded with his Aunt Jane at an early age. There seems to be an entire generation in age between Jane and Lisa when the movie flashes back to Jane's visits with her sister. Michael has no kids and he is still a bit of a kid himself. He takes his cousins Christopher and Leslie out fishing via explosives and cheese, then asks the kids not to tell their mother. Michael has also just divorced an alcoholic (Carrie-Anne Moss), who turns up at Lisa's wake unannounced, which somehow turns into a moment of passion between them. There is much in the way of discontent, especially between Michael and his father, who is also a writer, but not a widely published one.

The flashbacks reveal the abuse Michael endured as a kid at the hands of his father. His mother protects him mostly with words and kindness, but ultimately seems helpless as Charlie has Michael stand for a long time while holding heavy paint cans. Michael tests Charlie's patience at almost every turn, almost wanting the abuse. His Aunt Lisa (played in the flashbacks by Hayden Panettiere) stays with the family while away from college and also offers to protect Michael as well as give him his first sensual, physical encounter with a woman, an act that goes unspoken about throughout the rest of the film. The final act of the flashbacks inevitably reveal more about infidelities that took place long ago as well as secretive relationships that took place in the present day.

Lee has assembled quite a roster of talent for this film, which has also been lovingly photographed by Daniel Moder. On the surface, it looks like a surefire piece of Oscar® bait, yet it sat on the shelf for three years before seeing the light of day in 2011. There are certainly enough names in here to lure in the curious, but the problems with Lee's film lie in the screenplay and the casting. The audience will be spending a lot of time trying to do the math in regards to age differences and just whom is related to whom and how. Hayden Panettiere and Julia Roberts should never be cast as sisters without any explanation in the narrative over how that is even possible. There is only so much young-age make-up an audience can ignore.

What is also hard to ignore is the level of artifice that takes place in many of the film's confrontational scenes, of which there are many. There is a scene at a dinner table so soon after Lisa's death in which Charlie is up to his old ways of provoking his son who takes the bait. This scene and many others feel as though these moments came out of thin air. There never seems to be any build-up to them or logical progression. Most jarring is a moment in the film that is meant to be lyrical and poetic as Michael, Christopher and Leslie go outside to catch fireflies. Its sole purpose is to be used as a transition to a flashback when Michael plagiarized a Robert Frost poem. If Christopher is so racked with guilt, as he is supposed to be in many scenes, how can he even think of doing something so fun and frivolous?

Lee's film means well and by the end, it is clear the film is Lee's letter of forgiveness for his father. But there is nothing that stays with the outside observer, save for a few nice shots of wheat fields and some good-as-usual performances. Films about dysfunctional families often benefit from not having flashbacks. With a cast as strong as this, it should have been easy to pull off. *Warrior* (2011), for example, does a masterful job of painting a picture of a family whose troubled past could be seen in their faces and through their tears. *Fireflies in the Garden* relies too heavily on recycled scenes from other movies like it and, as a result, feels more like a typical studio product loaded with star power than about one person's own genuine, cathartic journey.

Collin Souter

CREDITS

Lisa Taylor: Julia Roberts
Michael Taylor: Ryan Reynolds
Charles Taylor: Willem Dafoe
Jane Lawrence: Emily Watson
Kelly: Carrie-Anne Moss
Addison Wesley: Ioan Gruffudd
Ryne Taylor: Shannon Lucio
Jimmy Lawrence: George Newbern
Young Jane: Hayden Panettiere
Young Michael: Cayden Boyd
Origin: USA

Language: English

Released: 2008

Production: Sukee Chew, Vanessa Coifman, Marc Weber; Kulture Machine, Senator Entertainment Co.; released by Senator Entertainment Co.

Directed by: Dennis Lee

Written by: Dennis Lee

Cinematography by: Daniel Moder

Music by: Jane Antonia Cornish

Sound: Lesa Foust

Editing: Dede Allen, Robert Brakey

Art Direction: Timmy Hills

Costumes: Kelle Katsugeras

Production Design: Rob Pearson

MPAA rating: R

Running time: 89 minutes

REVIEWS

Ebert, Roger. *Chicago Sun-Times.* October 13, 2011.

Fear, David. *Time Out New York.* October 11, 2011.

Goss, William. *Film.com.* October 14, 2011.

LaSalle, Marc. *San Francisco Chronicle.* October 13, 2011.

Lumenick, Lou. *New York Post.* October 14, 2011.

Neumaier, Joe. *New York Daily News.* October 14, 2011.

Schager, Nick. *Village Voice.* October 11, 2011.

Smith, Neil. *Total Film.* May 29, 2009.

Sobczynski, Peter. *eFilmcritic.com.* October 14, 2011.

Willmore, Allison. *AV Club.* October 13, 2011.

TRIVIA

Co-stars Carrie-Anne Moss and Hayden Panettiere share the same birthday.

FOOTLOOSE

There comes a time to cut loose.
    —Movie tagline

Box Office: $51.8 million

In a time when the musical was all but dead, Herbert Ross' *Footloose* (1984) was part of the '80s revival of a bygone genre. There were expensive flops such as *Popeye* (1980), *Pennies From Heaven* (1981), and *The Pirate Movie* (1982), but also box office successes like *Annie* (1982), *The Best Little Whorehouse In Texas* (1982), and *The Blues Brothers* (1980), a wide variety of films aimed at kids and adults. Further sparked by the success of *Flashdance* (1983), it was the sound of feet rather than vocals that started to reverberate throughout cinema. Almost thirty years later, history seems to be somewhat repeating itself with similar successes and failures in the reinvigorated classic musical structure aimed at the younger generation within the trilogies created by *High School Musical* (2006) and *Step Up* (2006). In the case of Craig Brewer's *Footloose* remake though, history is more than just repeating itself. It is stuck in a Xerox machine that keeps charging.

Ren McCormack (Kenny Wormald) is being displaced from the big city to the small town of Bomont, Georgia after his long-suffering mom has passed away from leukemia. Moving in with his aunt and uncle Wes (Ray McKinnon), Ren soon discovers that there is even less to do in this place than he imagined. Due to a local tragedy after a high school gathering, Reverend Shaw Moore (Dennis Quaid) has imposed the town council to ban dancing and loud music; a lesson Ren learns after being pulled over for blasting Quiet Riot. The kid still has his looks though and they certainly attract the Reverend's daughter, Ariel (Julianne Hough), who has turned her Sunday best into rebellious jean shorts since her brother's death in the aforementioned tragedy led to the harmony prohibition.

Ren makes a friend in Willard (Miles Teller), a socially awkward kid who cannot even follow the instructions to line dancing let alone talk to a pretty girl. He also makes an enemy in Chuck (Patrick John Flueger), Ariel's boyfriend who tends to dance with his fists at the drop of a cowboy hat. Her pious papa is no supporter, seeing Ren as a bad influence, and wants his daughter nowhere near his antics. Ren just wants to dance though and, if he needs to, will bust his moves alone—under cover of barn, if necessary. Wanting to spread the joy of barn-dancing to his fellow classmates, Ren plans to organize a prom across city lines, but not without making his pitch through the word of God to his biggest opponent.

The original *Footloose* was a dim-witted affair that really offered the audience nothing but a peppy soundtrack. Its message of censorship and rebellion was not prominent enough to feel forced. Its dance moves were maybe one level above average square dance lessons in a grade school gym. Yet maybe it was this very simplicity that made it one of 1984's biggest hits. Certainly no one would accuse the recent *Step Up* films of being a profound examination of youth dance culture, so perhaps an updated *Footloose* would be uncharted territory for a new un-hip generation who could learn a thing or two from a cast that all look like they were held back about five years.

An experiment one could try is to make your dance partner close their eyes a half-hour into the original *Footloose*. Then splice in the 2011 version and see if they can spot the differences. The awkward hallway meeting of Ren and Willard—check. Ariel's dad gallantly tracking her down to give her money only to discover the riff-raff dancing at the drive-in—check. Ren's merciful plea to the city council to let the teens cut loose by comparing dance to celebratory Bible passages—check. Granted, there are subtle changes. What once was a drive-in restaurant is now a drive-in movie. The famed chicken challenge by Ariel's boyfriend now uses buses instead of tractors. Bomont is now in Georgia instead of Mormon-centric Utah. Those still closing their eyes will hear Wormald (an original Bostonian) drop his accent so often they may not even notice he has replaced Kevin Bacon unless they remember that his Ren was from Chicago. Just because the soundtrack (featuring remixes of no less than four of the original songs) shouts "Let's Hear It For The Boy" during the same dance training montage, there is no shame in shouting back, "he heard it already."

Footloose '84 was hardly Shakespeare. Still, it appears director Craig Brewer, in some disdain for signing on to helm the long-gestating remake (both Zac Efron and Chace Crawford were signed on as Ren in 2007 & 2009, respectively), decided to treat the material as such by leaving the text as is. This is all the more disconcerting considered that Brewer, in a brief career, directed two of the more interesting music-themed films of the past decade. *Hustle & Flow* (2005) and *Black Snake Moan* (2006) centered around music as a means of salvation for its characters from their unsavory and diminished life choices. It makes sense that Brewer would then take on the tale of music itself being branded the cause of a society's problems and the fight to take it back. It makes no sense why Brewer, even with PG-13 limitations, could not find a fresh way to make the material relevant for a new generation. Either the studio gave him the Reverend Moore treatment in suppressing his ideas or Brewer just took the paycheck (or maybe both). But if Brewer really wanted to inspire with a bit of WWRD (What Would Ren Do?) he would have gone before the studio brass and quoted Romans 12:2. "Don't copy the behavior and customs of this world, but let God transform you into a new person by changing the way you think. Then you will learn to know God's will for you, which is good and pleasing and perfect." Then kick off your Sunday shoes and hook up with a hot preacher's daughter.

Erik Childress

CREDITS

Ren MacCormack: Kenny Wormald
Ariel Moore: Julianne Hough
Rev. Shaw Moore: Dennis Quaid
Vi Moore: Andie MacDowell

Willard: Miles Teller
Chuck Cranston: Patrick Flueger
Wes Warnicker: Ray McKinnon
Origin: USA
Language: English
Released: 2011
Production: Gary Barber, Roger Birnbaum, Neil Meron, Dylan Sellers, Brad Weston, Craig Zadan; Paramount Pictures, Spyglass Entertainment; released by Paramount Pictures
Directed by: Craig Brewer
Written by: Craig Brewer, Dean Pitchford
Cinematography by: Amy Vincent
Music by: Deborah Lurie
Sound: Greg Hedgepath, Frank Smathers
Editing: Billy Fox
Art Direction: Chris Cornwell
Costumes: Laura Jean Shannon
Production Design: Jon Gary Steele
MPAA rating: PG-13
Running time: 113 minutes

REVIEWS

Ebert, Roger. *Chicago Sun-Times.* October 13, 2011.
Goss, William. *Film.com.* October 14, 2011.
Levy, Shawn. *Oregonian.* October 13, 2011.
Lybarger, Dan. *Moviemaker Magazine.* October 21, 2011.
McWeeny, Drew. *HitFix.* October 14, 2011.
Novikov, Eugene. *Film Blather.* October 14, 2011.
Orndorf, Brian. *BrianOrndorf.com.* October 12, 2011.
Rocchi, James. *MSN Movies.* October 11, 2011.
Roeper, Richard. *RichardRoeper.com.* October 14, 2011.
Scott, A.O. *New York Times.* October 13, 2011.

QUOTES

Willard: "You can stick a quarter in that girl's backpocket and tell whether or not it's heads or tails."

TRIVIA

Director Craig Brewer's boots can be seen dancing in the opening credits when the words "A Craig Brewer Film" appear on screen.

FRIENDS WITH BENEFITS

Box Office: $55.8 million

There are a few impossible things that *Friends With Benefits* asks its audience to take at face value: 1. That Jamie (Mila Kunis) is, despite her age, a successful and wealthy corporate headhunter that companies like *GQ* and Amazon would task with finding perfect, executive hires; 2. That Dylan (Justin Timberlake) is an uber-talented web designer worthy of attention from the above-mentioned companies; and 3. That these two young, hip and beautiful people are looking for a happily ever after. But what director Will Gluck knows is that if audiences do not have time to stop and over-analyze the set-up, they will fall for his smartly-cast, pop-savvy rom-com for the millennial generation hard and fast, so he comes at them like a toddler hyped up on candy. And it works. *Friends With Benefits* is a quick-witted, banter-driven movie that combines the "love letter to New York" feel of *Nick and Norah's Infinite Playlist* (2008) with a modern take on fairy tale romance a la *Love Actually* (2003).

It is not hard to come to terms with the first two items on Gluck's impossible list, even though Jamie and Dylan do not seem to actually ever do any work. No one works in movies set in New York, right? How could they when there are so many al fresco lunch opportunities to be had? And who would not want to be head hunted by Mila Kunis? In truth, there have been far-more-ludicrous scenarios for romantic comedies dreamed up by screenwriters and Hollywood execs, so a little suspension of disbelief over quality of employment and work ethic is no big deal. It is the fact that these two young and connected Manhattanites would rather sit at home watching movies than be out living it up—and hooking up—that is a little harder to swallow. As annoying as their un-*Sex And The City* approach to life is, it works to support the thesis of the film: that romantic relationship are best if they are built on friendship. And Kunis and Timberlake have spot-on BFF chemistry. They are comfortable enough to hang out in their underwear with each other, trade jabs like the oldest of frat brothers, and are on par professionally. Plus they are the perfect spokespeople for the savvy hipster way of life, which is as much a theme in Gluck's film as relationships are. When they first meet, Jamie, who is tasked with convincing Dylan to give up his laid-back Los Angeles way of life and move East, takes Dylan on an insider tour of the city that ends with a flash mob in the middle of Times Square. Dylan then incorporates a flash mob into an ad spot for GQ, attesting to the out-of-the-box thinking that makes him such a hot and in demand designer. Gluck seems to revel in the youthful, New York way of life: It is fast, it is hectic, it is quirky, and only those who know how to play it can really get ahead. And as much as the NY taxicab speed of the narrative keeps audiences from focusing on the impossible set-up of the story, Gluck also embraces it as a way to play to the sensibilities of today's plugged-in hipster crowd. As fabulously fake as Jamie and Dylan's huge apartment in midtown living is, they are immensely relatable as modern, young professionals whose jobs do not tie them to cubicles and who can walk and text effortlessly. It is their likeability and their modern realness that makes *Friends With Benefits* such a fun, engaging viewing experience.

But what is truly remarkable about *Friends With Benefits* is just how much Gluck can balance without it ever getting the better of him. A glittering and pitch-perfect supporting cast that ranges from Shaun White (as himself) to Jenna Elfman as Dylan's wacky sister, and from Patricia Clarkson as Jamie's less than stable mom to Woody Harrelson as Dylan's wacky co-worker is never undersold. Each character, no matter their screen time, is rounded, engaging and relatable, adding to Jamie and Dylan's storyline instead of taking away from it. Gluck also gives both Jamie and Dylan adequate restrictive baggage (she is emotionally damaged, he is emotionally unavailable) that delightfully results in tear-up worthy break-throughs, without it taking over the movie. They also have idiosyncrasies (Dylan is awful at math, but can still make it in the world!) that make them feel attainable to every viewing Tom, Dick and Harriett. The fact that Gluck manages to get in a meta jab at hokey Hollywood romantic comedies via the romantic comedy that plays on repeat on Jamie's TV, is just icing on a surprisingly delicious, satisfying cake.

Joanna Topor MacKenzie

CREDITS

Jamie: Mila Kunis
Dylan: Justin Timberlake
Lorna: Patricia Clarkson
Angie: Jenna Elfman
Parker: Bryan Greenberg
Mr. Harper: Richard Jenkins
Tommy: Woody Harrelson
Maddison: Rashida Jones
Sam: Nolan Gould
Quincy: Andy Samberg
Origin: USA
Language: English
Released: 2011
Production: Liz Glotzer, Will Gluck, Martin Shafer, Janet Zucker, Jerry Zucker; Screen Gems, Castle Rock Entertainment, Zucker Productions, Olive Bridge Entertainment; released by Screen Gems
Directed by: Will Gluck
Written by: Will Gluck, Keith Merryman, David A. Newman
Cinematography by: Michael Grady
Sound: Geoffrey Patterson

Music Supervisor: Wende Crowley
Editing: Tia Nolan
Art Direction: Bo Johnson
Costumes: Renee Ehrlich Kalfus
Production Design: Marcia Hinds
MPAA rating: R
Running time: 109 minutes

REVIEWS

Burr, Ty. *Boston Globe.* July 21, 2011.
Dargis, Manohla. *New York Times.* July 21, 2011.
Deburge, Peter. *Variety.* July 18, 2011.
Ebert, Roger. *Chicago Sun-Times.* July 21, 2011.
Gronvall, Andrea. *Chicago Reader.* July 21, 2011.
Phillips, Michael. *Chicago Tribune.* July 21, 2011.
Pols, Mary. *Time.* July 23, 2011.
Sharkey, Betsy. *Los Angeles Times.* July 21, 2011.
Stevens, Dana. *Slate.* July 23, 2011.
Tobias, Scott. *AV Club.* July 21, 2011.

QUOTES

Jamie: "Why don't they ever a make a movie about what happens after they kiss?"
Dylan: "They do it's called porn."

TRIVIA

Mila Kunis used a "butt double" for her character's nude scene despite the fact that she appears semi-nude in a handful of other scenes.

FRIGHT NIGHT

You can't run from evil when it lives next door.
—Movie tagline

Box Office: $18.3 million

The original *Fright Night* (1985) was greeted as an above-average vampire horror film that was refreshingly inventive and had a good sense of humor, a tall order in the horror genre back in the mid-eighties, when slasher films ruled the mainstream. At the time of its release, there were far too many films involving dimwitted teenagers going camping and getting hacked up one-by-one. *Fright Night* had a reverence for the old fashioned way of doing things. Not only had it gone back to a tried-and-true horror staple, it did so with a nod to old-time monster movies being shown on television with vampiric hosts whose time was sadly fading. The film spawned a less successful sequel, but the original is still considered a minor favorite amongst those who remember its release.

Time has not been entirely kind to Tom Holland's film. When watched today, it often feels more like a product of mid-eighties kitsch than a bona fide horror treasure. The hair, music, attitude and the inexplicable presence of the annoying Stephen Geoffreys make it look more and more like a relic with each passing generation. The storyline, by today's horror standards, also comes off a bit tired and predictable. There are no real surprises in the original *Fright Night*. Vampires were also not nearly as ubiquitous as they are in the 2010s. This generation has produced vampire stories for everyone: *Twilight* for the tweens, *True Blood* for the adults, *Cirque de Freak* for the kids, and the *Underworld* movies for whoever watches *Underworld* movies. A remake of *Fright Night* seemed unnecessary.

Thankfully, this remake has its own brand of cleverness and style for this day and age to match, if not surpass, the original's in its day and age. The basic storyline remains in place with the appropriate changes made. A young high school student named Charley Brewster (Anton Yelchin) is a typical teenager with a few nerdy friends, a cute girlfriend and a single mom. He lives in a quiet suburb out in Nevada where a mysterious, single and charismatic man named Jerry (Colin Farrell) has just moved in next door. Something about him seems a little odd, even though he comes off as a harmless, hunky construction worker who only works at night.

Charley's friend Ed (Christopher Mintz-Plasse) wants to investigate a little further. Their friend Adam has gone missing and he believes that Jerry might be behind it. In fact, he believes Jerry might be a vampire. Charley is reluctant to join Ed on his mission to break into Adam's house to try and get the full story, but Ed practically blackmails Charley by threatening to upload old, embarrassing home videos of the two of them onto YouTube for all of their high school classmates to see.

Eventually, it comes to light that Jerry is, indeed, a vampire and soon Charley must convince his mom (Toni Collette) not to ever invite him into the house. Jerry gets suspicious that Charley knows something, all the while trying to get in good with his next door neighbors. Jerry innocently asks if he can borrow a six-pack of beer from Charley to have on a date with a single, female neighbor who is on her way over. Jerry obliges and the two are at a bit of a standoff that neither of them can talk about. Charley will not invite him in, but how long can Jerry stand at the doorway before it becomes too awkward to bear?

Charley becomes obsessed with finding out how to get rid of Jerry, or at the very least keep him at bay. He does the usual with garlic and crucifixes in the windows, but just like in the original film, he needs reinforcements in the form of a real expert. The first *Fright Night* film had Roddy MacDowell as Peter Vincent, a TV horror movie host. The remake ingeniously changes this character into a flamboyant, celebrity magician/clairvoyant not unlike Christopher Angel. The Peter Vincent character (David Tennant) just happens to be doing a show in Las Vegas. Charley and his girlfriend Amy (Imogen Poots) head over there and find Vincent in his gargantuan hotel suite flanked by female hangers-on and surrounded by ancient artifacts that he bought on eBay.

The cast is clearly having a ball with the material. As Jerry, Colin Farrell has just the right touch of menace, smoothness and charisma to make Jerry a memorable screen villain and not just a run-of-the-mill vampire that the viewer is supposed to be attracted to as well as repelled by. Jerry is a character worthy of his own franchise. Likewise, David Tennant embraces the role of Peter Vincent as though he know he has been given a great gift. At once funny and downright idiotic, it is the kind of role that the wrong actor can easily make tiresome, but Tennant plays the role with just the right mixture of subtlety and swagger that when he joins in on the third act, the audience is eternally grateful to have him aboard.

Director Craig Gillespie (making his first foray into the horror genre) and screenwriter Marti Noxon (a former writer for TV's *Buffy the Vampire Slayer*) have wisely decided not to try and repeat the first film's horrific moments, but instead invent new ones. A brilliantly-staged sequence involving a car chase and a vampire who refuses to die recalls the kind of single-take craftsmanship seen in Steven Spielberg's *War of the Worlds* (2005) and Alfonso Cuaron's *Children of Men* (2006). The friendship between Charley and Ed is also given more depth this time around and Jerry's seduction of Ed carries more weight and gets right what the original film did not quite achieve.

Fright Night came out a week after the fifth installment in the *Final Destination* series. Both films were released in 3D and both adhered to the current mainstream 3D horror standards: The spikes, knives and spears come straight at the audience along with plenty of CGI gore and splatter. Both movies delivered the goods, but *Fright Night* would work no matter what. In fact, the 3D, at times, worked against the film, particularly with the darkly-lit scenes, and there are plenty. Gimmicks aside, this is a fun film that accomplishes the rare feat of surpassing the quality of the original and one that will still be fun to revisit twenty years from now.

Collin Souter

CREDITS

Charley Brewster: Anton Yelchin
Jerry Dandridge: Colin Farrell
Jane Brewster: Toni Collette
Ed Thompson: Christopher Mintz-Plasse
Amy Peterson: Imogen Poots
Peter Vincent: David Tennant
Mark: Dave Franco
Origin: USA
Language: English
Released: 2011
Production: Michael De Luca, Michael J. Gaeta, Alison Rosenzweig; Albuquerque Studios, DreamWorks SKG, Gaeta/Rosenzweig Films, Michael De Luca Films; released by DreamWorks SKG
Directed by: Craig Gillespie
Written by: Marti Noxon
Cinematography by: Javier Aguirresarobe
Music by: Ramin Djawadi
Sound: Mark Stoeckinger
Music Supervisor: Dana Sano
Editing: Tatiana S. Riegel
Art Direction: Randy Moore
Costumes: Susan Matheson
Production Design: Richard Bridgland
MPAA rating: R
Running time: 106 minutes

REVIEWS

Covert, Colin. *Minneapolis Star Tribune*. August 18, 2011.
Ebert, Roger. *Chicago Sun-Times*. August 18, 2011.
Goodykoontz, Bill. *Arizona Republic*. August 18, 2011.
Goss, William. *Film.com*. August 19, 2011.
Jones, J.R. *Chicago Reader*. August 18, 2011.
Rea, Stephen. *Philadelphia Inquirer*. August 18, 2011.
Scott, A.O. *New York Times*. August 18, 2011.
Smith, Kyle. *New York Post*. August 19, 2011.
Sobczynski, Peter. *eFilmcritic.com*. August 18, 2011.
Weinberg, Scott. *FEARnet*. August 19, 2011.

QUOTES

Jerry Dandrige: "What were you thinking, Charley? That you were just going to walk in here with your little crossbow and put to bed 400 years of survival? No, Charley. Not likely."

TRIVIA

Peter Vincent is named after two horror film icons, Peter Cushing and Vincent Price.

FROM PRADA TO NADA

A riches to rags story.
—Movie tagline

Box Office: $3 million

The ideas of taking the works of Jane Austen and adorning their solid and essentially timeless foundations with contemporary trappings is nothing new. Amy Heckerling scored a surprise hit and made a star out of Alicia Silverstone when she transformed *Emma* into *Clueless* (1995), Helen Fielding begat an entire cottage industry when she updated *Pride and Prejudice* with *Bridget Jones's Diary* (2001), and, more recently, numerous authors have made a minor mint by taking her stories, along with a number of other literary classics, and adorning them with zombies, vampires and other monsters. Therefore, the notion of taking Austen's masterpiece *Sense & Sensibility* and giving it a contemporary Latino spin is not an inherently awful one and in the right hands, it could have yielded a film that would be both entertaining and of a certain cultural value to a perennially under-served section of the movie-going audience. Unfortunately, *From Prada to Nada* is a film that is not so much *Clueless* as it is clueless in the way that it takes a classic story and reduces it into an indigestible mess of failed comedy and mawkish melodrama that plays more like a failed CW pilot than a major motion picture.

As the film opens, the Dominguez sisters—serious and studious Nora (Camilla Belle) and flighty party girl Mary (Alexa Vega)—are living in the lap of Beverly Hills luxury with their rich businessman father. Before long, however, their world comes crashing down among them when, in rapid succession, their father dies, they discover a half-brother, Gabriel (Pablo Cruz), that they knew nothing about and they learn that their father was bankrupt when he died. ("He wasn't prepared for the economic crisis.") After Gabriel buys up the house—largely at the insistence of his monstrous WASP fiancee (April Bowlby) so that she can make it even tackier than before—Nora and Mary are forced to leave. With nowhere else to go, they find themselves heading for East L.A. to stay with poor-but-proud Aunt Aurelia (Adriana Barraza) and her extended brood. While Nora at least makes an effort to adjust to her new situation—she drops out of law school to work at a legal firm while trying to learn more about a side to her culture to which she had never really been exposed—the frankly-embarrassed Mary spends all her time complaining about the food and limited transportation options and assuming that everyone in her new neighborhood is a gang member.

In developments that would feel inevitable even if they did not mirror such a well-known story, both sisters find romance as well. Nora, who has previously avoided such entanglements in the past in order to concentrate on her studies, finds herself falling for Edward (Nicholas D'Agosto), a friend of Gabriel and a lawyer at the firm where she works. Meanwhile, Mary shamelessly throws herself at her hunky TA (Kuno Becker) but also finds herself inexplicably attracted to a hunky local handyman (Wilmer Valderama). Beyond that, there are laughs, lovers, heartbreak and near-tragedies and without going into too many details, let it be said that by the time the film comes to an end, everyone involved has pretty much gotten exactly what they deserve.

Again, the basic concept of *From Prada to Nada* is solid enough but it has been handled in such a clunky and graceless manner that Austen's classic comedy of manners has been reduced to the level of a not-so-classic sitcom. The main problem is that neither the three credited screenwriters nor director Angel Gracia (making his feature debut after working in music videos and commercials) have any idea of how to update the Austen novel in a way that contemporizes the material in order to adjust to the times while still maintaining a degree of fidelity. Instead, they handle it in the crudest and clumsiest ways possible, such as presenting romantic complications that would have seemed unlikely on a lesser episode of *Love, American Style* and the equally tired concept that the only good and decent people out there are the ones who are steeped in their ethnic heritage to such a degree that they can bust out a lavish mural or a Frida Kahlo reference at the drop of a sombrero. Another considerable flaw is the inescapable fact that the two central roles have been hideously miscast. Although Nora is supposed to be the smart and soulful sister, Camilla Belle seems aloof and removed from the proceedings throughout and the romantic woes of the character ring especially hollow when coming from someone who goes through the entire proceedings looking like a supermodel and possessing what may be the best set of eyebrows since Brooke Shields or possibly Groucho Marx. Meanwhile, the flighty and often unlikable Mary is essayed by the eminently smart and likable Vega, and despite her efforts, she is equally unbelievable as well.

Then again, even if the filmmakers had realized that Belle and Vega were miscast and had them switch roles, it is unlikely that it would have helped *From Prada to Nada* to rise above the level of terminal mediocrity. (Even the title fairly screams of quiet desperation.) It feels as though it was specifically engineered to play in the dead of winter to small and indifferent audiences for a week or two before quickly slipping off to DVD. This is sad because with the right handling, this could have been a smart and entertaining film that might have even had the added benefit of inspiring the presumed tween target audience to go back and read the Austen novel. Instead, it turns out to be a variation of *Sense and Sensibility* that demonstrates precious little of those traits or much of anything else of note.

Peter Sobczynski

CREDITS

Nora: Camilla Belle
Mary: Alexa Vega
Aunt Aurelia: Adriana Barraza
Bruno: Wilmer Valderrama
Edward: Nicholas D'Agosto
Origin: USA
Language: English
Released: 2011
Production: Gary Gilbert, Linda McDonough, Gigi Pritzker, Chris Ranta; Gilbert Films, Gotham Music Placement, Lionsgate, Odd Lot Entertainment, Videocine Prods.; released by Pantelion Films
Directed by: Angel Gracia
Written by: Fina Torres, Luis Alfaro, Craig Fernandez
Cinematography by: Hector Ortega
Music by: Heitor Pereira
Music Supervisor: Dan Hubbert
Editing: Brad McLaughlin
Art Direction: Ricardo Davila, Carlos Lagunas
Sound: Michael J. Anastasi
Costumes: Naomi Crespo
Production Design: Anthony Rivero Stabley
MPAA rating: PG-13
Running time: 107 minutes

REVIEWS

Anderson, Jason. *Toronto Star*. February 11, 2011.
Grierson, Tim. *Screen International*. January 30, 2011.
Hills, Aaron. *Village Voice*. January 31, 2011.
Kenigsberg, Ben. *Time Out New York*. February 2, 2011.
Lane, Jim. *Sacramento News & Review*. February 11, 2011.
Orndorf, Brian. *BrianOrndorf.com*. May 9, 2011.
Punter, Jennie. *Globe and Mail*. February 11, 2011.
Robinson, Tasha. *AV Club*. January 31, 2011.
Savlov, Marc. *Austin Chronicle*. February 4, 2011.
Scheck, Frank. *Hollywood Reporter*. January 31, 2011.

QUOTES

Nora Dominguez: "I avoid relationships because I can't count on them."

THE FUTURE

There are arthouse films and there are art-*school* films, and writer-director-performance-artist Miranda July has proven increasingly adept at spinning the latter into the former. Her 2005 directorial debut *You Me and Everyone We Know* and now *The Future,* are certainly not everyone's cup of green tea—like July's on-screen persona (and quite a few other art-school students), the films are airily self-obsessed with their own twee non-conformism. Annoyance levels may vary depending on viewer tolerance for both creative, free-spirit flakiness and how carefully calculated that free-spirit flakiness may feel.

However, July's secret weapon is that she has genuinely profound and compelling things to, if not come right out and say, at least tumble awkwardly around. Pushing past her sometimes irritatingly odd persona and style actually becomes part of the viewing experience, as it makes the darker, heavier existential truths that lie ahead in her films resonate all the deeper. In that sense, July is the best sort of art-school flake— the kind who gets in her audience's heads, even if that audience is not sure it fully gets *her.*

That is certainly the case with *The Future,* the story of Sophie (July) and Jason (Hamlish Linklater), married, over-educated and under-employed thirty-somethings living mopey, inward lives in Los Angeles. He gives tech customer support over the phone, but feels he was meant for bigger things he never got around to doing. She teaches expressive dance to children, but dreams of sharing her own dances on a bigger stage: YouTube. They have matching thoughtfully careless hair and bored, monotone speaking voices.

The Future begins as Sophie and Jason face a frightening new commitment: adopting an ailing stray cat from a shelter. Whether the cat is a surrogate for parenthood or just a cat, the couple worries obsessively about the decision and each decide to spend the last twenty-eight days before they take possession of the feline freely exploring whatever life possibilities the universe might offer. For Jason that means quitting his job and going door-to-door on behalf of an environmental tree-planting organization. For Sophie it means quickly abandoning her plan of airing a new dance a day and instead backing tentatively, almost accidentally into an affair with an older man (David Warshofsky).

Ah, but if only that was all there was to it. It turns out *The Future* is narrated by Paw Paw, the frail, yearning cat healing up at the shelter while waiting for Sophie and Jason. (July provides Paw Paw's voice, pitched up a squeaky, scratchy octave.) If that sounds just too precious and precocious to tolerate, take heart: Paw Paw is a good measure of the film itself, as the cat conceit starts off eye-rollingly grating, but soon wins the viewer over, and eventually provides achingly moving insight and enlightenment in part because, not in spite of the fact they come from a talking cat. For all her thin, passive sensitivity and pixie-alien mannerisms, as a film maker and performer July's etherealness is sharply defined—she knows exactly what she's doing as she increasingly peppers the initial banal ordinariness of *The Future* with such magic realism as cats' inner monologues, crawling shirts, a talking moon, and one person's shocking (and then frightening) ability to stop time.

That all this quirkiness hovers between enchanting and irritating is the point of July's ingenious and visionary film making. She wraps very real human disconnect and self discovery in tangential whimsy and hypothetical worries, hiding much bigger issues inside her small deadpan focus. Though it examines the drowning of creativity in over awareness, *The Future* according to July is no loopy lark—it may float through life's whims and distractions on a stream of consciousness, but the film still tackles adulthood, sexuality, and loneliness with unflinching honesty and imagination.

Sophie finds a melancholy confidence with her illicit lover, as if the infidelity finally gave her purpose ("I'm wild," she cries in despair), while Jason becomes literally trapped in the long, dark teatime of the soul. Both are thrust unwillingly into the future, a place of responsibilities and consequences previously uncharted by all their hipster introspection. And as usual it is Paw Paw who puts it out there: the worst loneliness comes at night. Discovering the film to be filled with such harrowing sadness tucked inside what appears to be a goofy trifle can be jarring, leading some to reject *The Future* as fatalistic, pessimist, and defeatist, however Sophie and Jason suffer not from depression, but a slow deflation. The more you disconnect, the couple discover, the more you must face yourself.

The Future can be deceptively listless—at times it may not feel like its going anywhere, but some who see it will come away pleasantly surprised at where it so expertly and forcefully took them. Whether they like or hate *The Future*, or simply shake their heads in bafflement at its sliding parallel timelines and talking cats and moons, the film encourages viewer reflection either on its themes of life and its living, or simply on why July

and her film irritate—and to what extent that very irritation is part of the artwork's evocative message.

Locke Peterseim

CREDITS

Sophie: Miranda July
Jason: Hamish Linklater
Marshall: David Warshofsky
Gabriella: Isabella Acres
Joe: Joe Putterlik
Origin: USA, Germany
Language: English
Released: 2011
Production: Gina Kwon, Roman Paul, Gerhard Meixner; Razor Film, GNK Productions, Film 4; released by Roadside Attractions
Directed by: Miranda July
Written by: Miranda July
Cinematography by: Nikolai Graevenitz
Music by: Jon Brion
Sound: Patrick Viegel
Music Supervisor: Margaret Yen
Editing: Andrew Bird
Costumes: Christie Wittenborn
Production Design: Elliot Hostetter
MPAA rating: R
Running time: 91 minutes

REVIEWS

Burr, Ty. *Boston Globe.* August 5, 2011.
Ebert, Roger. *Chicago Sun-Times.* August 3, 2011.
Edelstein, David. *New York.* July 24, 2011.
Goodykoontz. *Arizona Republic.* August 18, 2011.
Groen, Rick. *Globe and Mail.* August 5, 2011.
Hoberman, J. *Village Voice.* July 27, 2011.
Hornaday, Ann. *Washington Post.* August 5, 2011.
Phillips, Michael. *Chicago Tribune.* August 5, 2011.
Schenker, Andrew. *Slant.* July 24, 2011.
Scott, A.O. *New York Times.* July 28, 2011.

G

THE GIRL WITH THE DRAGON TATTOO

What is hidden in snow, comes forth in the thaw.
—Movie tagline
Evil shall with evil be expelled.
—Movie tagline

Box Office: $101.4 million

As the pop culture cycle turns, it is common for a franchise to get to a point of complete saturation, in which it has in some way impacted nearly everyone who lives on the grid. Such is the case with Stieg Larsson's *Millennium Trilogy*, particularly the first book in it, *The Girl with the Dragon Tattoo*. Sold at book stores around the world to the point that it seemed to be required passage with a ticket on most forms of public transportation and adapted into a highly-acclaimed series of Swedish films that turned Noomi Rapace into an international superstar, it seemed inevitable that an American version of this pulp fiction would eventually hit celluloid. However, when the pedigree for the U.S. edition of Larsson's tale of misogyny and revenge was announced, it set most people back on their heels. One might have easily assumed that these lurid thrillers would have been easy pickings for a studio looking for a hack director-for-hire. The movies would likely be hits no matter who directed them. So when Sony announced that the critically-beloved David Fincher (fresh off his massive success for *The Social Network* [2010]) would try and bring this franchise the kind of pedigree than Jonathan Demme did to Robert Harris' Hannibal books with *The Silence of the Lambs* (1991), it became clear that the bar

had been set higher than either the book or the original adaptation hinted could be achieved. Some were skeptical. Most who knew Fincher's recent work were not. And when *The Girl with the Dragon Tattoo* was finally revealed (in most markets as late as possible for critics award consideration as Fincher was reportedly fine-tuning until the last minute), it delivered in every way. With mostly rapturous reviews, five Oscar® nominations, viewer approval to the tune of placement on IMDB.com's list of the top 250 films ever made, and a worldwide gross cresting above $200 million at the time of this writing, *Dragon Tattoo* is an undeniable smash, one of the most essential films of 2011.

The source material is, admittedly, still a bit flawed. It still runs too long, especially in a bizarre epilogue, but Fincher and writer Steven Zaillian (Oscar®-nominated the same year for his equally-stellar work on *Moneyball* [2011]) and it is still a relatively-predictable narrative. But it is what Fincher and his team do with that flawed material that makes the film remarkable. To say they made the best possible film that could have been produced from such a flawed novel is an understatement. They went beyond what one can presume even the sadly-deceased author ever thought possible, streamlining the source into a brutal, effective thriller with one of the best performances of the year and some of the most stunningly perfect technical elements of the last several.

The narrative actually takes some significant time before getting to its title character. The first act lead is undeniably Mikael Blomkvist (Daniel Craig), a journalist introduced in the center of a serious career crisis. Blomkvist was clearly set-up by a controversial subject of his latest journalistic investigation, resulting in a fake source slandering one of Sweden's most prominent businessmen. As the bad press swirls around Millennium Magazine, Blomkvist needs to take a break from his position until it blows over. He skulks off with his tail between his legs and is approached with an intriguing project during his time off by the ultra-wealthy Henrik Vanger (Christopher Plummer), the patriarch of a family so legendary that they essentially have their own island. Vanger (and his company) was forever impacted by the disappearance of the businessman's daughter Harriet decades earlier. Someone has been sending Vanger annual reminders of his daughter's disappearance and he needs someone like an investigative journalist to get to the bottom of what happened. Everyone in the family, including Martin (Stellan Skarsgard) and Anita (Joely Richardson), recognizes that the loss of Harriet and the questions surrounding her disappearance altered the course of one of their country's most important companies and forever changed the way its figurehead approached life. Can Mikael figure out what happened to her?

As Mikael is looking into the past in old-fashioned ways (leafing through photos, pasting notes on a bulletin board, conducting one-on-one interviews), Lisbeth Salander (Rooney Mara) is using modern investigative tools to look into him. She is a troubled, bisexual recluse with unique fashion style and an aggressive personality. While she may not be the first person a company hires to be their public face, she knows how to do her job when it comes to privacy. And so the Vangers use her to background check Blomkvist, given the access he now has to their family. Later, Salander is actually brought in to help Blomkvist as an assistant, and she already knows everything there is to know about him, even if she does so through illegal means. Lisbeth is the other side of the coin from Harriet, the missing girl. On the one hand, there is the girl who is the mystery at the center of the piece, the one for whom Mikael needs to learn all the secrets of to find, and behind him there is a woman who knows all the secrets about him. They could not be more different and yet they share one essential element of the story (especially when one considers the original title of the source, *Men Who Hate Women*)—they have both encountered truly horrendous men.

Lisbeth Salander is more than a mere heroine; she is a coiled force of nature. Mara is simply perfect here, having infamously beat out dozens of actresses for this highly-coveted part. She was heretofore pretty much unknown (outside of two key scenes in *The Social Network* and starring in the horrendous remake of *A Nightmare on Elm Street* [2010]). Mara is perfect here, almost seeming as if she is moving even when she is standing still. And she is absolutely fearless in the way she brings this complex character to life. Her Oscar® nomination was one of the more surprisingly perfect ones on the morning the Academy Award® favorites were revealed.

Craig, Skarsgard, and Plummer are all good here as well but, after Mara, the film belongs to David Fincher. His technical showmanship has been notable for years but it still has the power to overwhelm. He is simply at the top of his game in every way, working again with the great cinematographer Jeff Cronenweth to perfectly capture the danger of the snowy climate in which much of the film is set. Cronenweth's visual palette and the way he shoots so much of the film through windows or from low angles have a nearly-subconscious impact on the viewer. This film is as notably shot as any thriller in the last decade. The art direction, editing, Trent Reznor & Atticus Ross's score—every element clicks, assisting the tension and overall product as much as any actors in the ensemble.

But it is Fincher who guides it all with as confident and assured a hand as anyone in film today. After the success of *The Social Network,* it surprised some that he would go with such well-known material as Larsson's book. And yet this story fits in perfectly with his filmography as he has long been obsessed with rules and structure—the codes of *Zodiac* (2007), the Hitchockian riddles of *The Game* (1997), the biblical structure of *Seven* (1995), and what people are allowed to talk about that are in *Fight Club* (1999) are only a few examples. This is another film that is heavy with details on process—photos, emails, investigation, procedure. David Fincher finds a way to take what could be mundane in someone else's hands and reveal that it is true human drama that lies beneath these processes and not where so many lesser writers and filmmakers find it—in purely the result.

One can appreciate the film in context of Fincher's resume or pick apart the individual elements or one can ignore all of that and merely sit on the edge of their seat. This is a bullet train of a film, a work that still gets under the skin of viewers who have read the book or seen the Swedish original. Only a filmmaker as talented as David Fincher could take something this remarkably familiar, to the point of over-saturation, and make it completely new again.

Brian Tallerico

CREDITS

Mikael Blomkvist: Daniel Craig
Lisbeth Salander: Rooney Mara
Martin Vanger: Stellan Skarsgard
Henrik Vanger: Christopher Plummer

Erika Berger: Robin Wright
Annika Blomkvist: Embeth Davidtz
Anita Vanger/Harriet Vanger: Joely Richardson
Christer Malm: Joel Kinnaman
Dragan Armansky: Goran Visnjic
Frode: Steven Berkoff
Young Henrik: Julian Sands
Cecilia: Geraldine James
Det. Morell: Donald (Don) Sumpter
Wennerstrom: Ulf Friberg
Harald Vanger: Per Myrberg
Young Morell: David Dencik
Birger: Martin Jarvis
Bjurman: Yorick Van Wageningen
Plague: Tony Way
Trinity: Leo Bill
Young Martin: Simon Reithner
Gottfried Vanger: Jurgen Klein
Origin: USA
Language: English
Released: 2011
Production: Cean Chaffin, Scott Rudin, Soren Staermose, Ole Sondberg; Columbia Pictures, Yellow Bird Films; released by Sony Pictures
Directed by: David Fincher
Written by: Steven Zaillian
Cinematography by: Jeff Cronenweth
Music by: Trent Reznor, Atticus Ross
Sound: Bo Persson
Editing: Kirk Baxter, Angus Wall
Art Direction: Mikael Varhelyi
Costumes: Trish Summerville
Production Design: Donald Graham Burt
MPAA rating: R
Running time: 158 minutes

REVIEWS

Denby, David. *New Yorker.* December 5, 2011.
Ebert, Roger. *Chicago Sun-Times.* December 20, 2011.
Gleiberman, Owen. *Entertainment Weekly.* December 13, 2011.
LaSalle, Mick. *San Francisco Chronicle.* December 19, 2011.
O'Hehir, Andrew. *Salon.com.* December 19, 2011.
Puig, Claudia. *USA Today.* December 20, 2011.
Rodriguez, Rene. *Miami Herald.* December 20, 2011.
Tobias, Scott. *AV Club.* December 20, 2011.
Wise, Damon. *Empire.* December 16, 2011.
Zacharek, Stephanie. *Movieline.* December 20, 2011.

QUOTES

Lisbeth Salander: "He's had a long standing sexual relationship with his co-editor of the magazine. Sometimes he performs cunnilingus on her. Not often enough in my opinion."

TRIVIA

Johnny Depp, Viggo Mortensen, Brad Pitt, and George Clooney were all considered for the lead male role at one time.

AWARDS

Oscars 2011: Film Editing
Nomination:
Oscars 2011: Actress (Mara), Cinematog., Sound, Sound FX Editing
British Acad. 2011: Cinematog., Orig. Score
Directors Guild 2011: Director (Fincher)
Golden Globes 2012: Actress—Drama (Mara), Orig. Score
Writers Guild 2011: Adapt. Screenplay.

GLEE: THE 3D CONCERT MOVIE

Box Office: $11.9 million

There comes a time in every pop culture phenomenon where over-saturation takes hold and suddenly the novelty of what made it successful gets buried beneath the hype. Such is the case with the TV show *Glee,* a primetime series that cleverly took the aesthetic of the banal *High School Musical* movies and gave it a subversive edge. It became the next logical step for tweens who have outgrown the Disney Channel, but still want to see some quality singing and dancing. *Glee* was a big surprise in the annals of prime time television, which had not given a musical a serious shot at the big leagues since the abysmal failure of *Cop Rock* back in the '80s. But *Glee* worked. The show about a high school glee club showcased a winning cast of young actors, sharp writing and infectious musical numbers. Midway through its first season, it was clear that this series was going to be around a while, thanks to its legions of die-hard fans, affectionately known as "Gleeks."

Inevitably, there had to be a *Glee* movie of some kind. Sadly, the studios took the cheap and easy way out and simply filmed a concert movie in which the young actors performed the songs in front of screaming fans during the summer 2011 tour. People watched *Glee* for different reasons. For some, it was the writing and the absurd soap opera appeal. For others, it was the high energy musical numbers that had a hint of nostalgia. And for many of the younger viewers, particularly anyone who has ever felt like an outcast, it was the show's message about being a unique individual in the face of peer pressure and popularity contests that hit home. The concert movie is aimed primarily at the latter two groups. There is no witty banter or laughs here.

The adult actors, by and large, have stayed home or have had their scenes deleted.

Glee: The 3D Concert Movie is made up of on-stage performances, gushing audience testimonials and sidebar mini-documentaries about the show's fans and why the series means a lot to them. In other words, the movie exists as a commercial for the series and nothing more. It opens with the actors backstage exercising their vocal chords and cuts to fans outside the arena talking about their favorite characters. The *Glee* cast takes the stage with the show's opener—Journey's immortal "Don't Stop Believing"—and the movie shows its first signs of 3-D life by having a microphone coming at the audience.

Between the songs are more audience reactions and short documentaries that act as an attempt to draw out a story arc throughout the film's eighty-four minute running time. One is about a female dwarf who is a cheerleader at her school. She worries about prom, but is eventually asked out by an attractive, full-grown guy. Will they be awarded prom king and queen? Another tells the story of a gay teen who is outed at school. This story is told via reflection by the student. The third story is about a lonely teenage girl with Asperger's who makes friends with other fans of the show. It is safe to say that she is the show's most devoted fan.

While it is commendable that this particular concert film makes an attempt to validate its young fanbase by putting the camera on them and telling their stories, it does so in such a shallow and rushed manner that there is never any dramatic cliffhanger even as the movie tries to spread their stories out between songs. Is there any doubt that things will all turn out better in the end? Of course, these are stories about being a social outcast or being accepted in spite of physical abnormalities, something the show purports to be about every week. So, why have a musical number in which the wheelchair-bound character Artie (Kevin McHale) gets up out of his wheelchair to the tune of "Safety Dance" to enact his dream of being able to walk and dance on his own two feet?

The concert scenes are competently filmed, but never take full advantage of the 3-D effect. The cast perform in front of a giant video screen that could have easily been used to give the third dimension to the theatrical viewing experience, but those in charge of the process never get beyond the occasional close-up of a singer who looks right into the camera. There have been good 3-D concert films in the past (*U2 3-D* [2007] is a perfect example of how to utilize the gimmick in this setting). *Glee: The 3D Concert Movie* feels like an afterthought, an all-too-common trait amongst blockbusters looking to expand its box office performance in hopes of making *Avatar*-like grosses. All of the non-concert scenes are flat and visually uninteresting, so the added price to the ticket makes the movie an even bigger rip-off.

By the time *Glee: The 3D Concert Movie* hit theaters, the show and its success had reached its over-saturation point. As if the concert tour was not enough, there had been numerous CD releases and a waning interest in the show's storylines as it too often veered off into tribute shows (the Lady Ga-Ga show, the Madonna show, etc.) and focused less on the characters. The movie could have been an interesting examination of the phenomenon in the current pop culture landscape. Instead, the show that celebrates uniqueness and individuality has taken the most well-worn and tired road set forth by the innocuous likes of Hannah Montana, The Jonas Brothers and Justin Bieber.

Collin Souter

CREDITS

Quinn Fabray: Dianna Agron
Rachel Berry: Lea Michele
Holly Holliday: Gwyneth Paltrow
Blaine Anderson: Darren Criss
Kurt Hummel: Chris Colfer
Finn Hudson: Cory Monteith
Origin: USA
Language: English
Released: 2011
Production: Dante Di Loreto, Ryan Murphy; Ryan Murphy Productions; released by Twentieth Century Fox Film Corporation
Directed by: Kevin Tancharoen
Cinematography by: Glen MacPherson
Music Supervisor: Massimo Ruberto
Editing: Myron Kerstein, Jane Moran, Tatiana S. Riegel
Sound: Yann Delpuech
Costumes: Elizabeth Barrois
MPAA rating: PG
Running time: 100 minutes

REVIEWS

Barnard, Linda. *Toronto Star*. August 12, 2011.
Biancolli, Amy. *Huston Chronicle*. August 12, 2011.
Chaney, Jen. *Washington Post*. August 12, 2011.
Graham, Adam. *Detroit News*. August 12, 2011.
Kennedy, Lisa. *Denver Post*. August 12, 2011.
Kenny, Glenn. *MSN Movies*. August 11, 2011.
Neumaier, Joe. *New York Daily News*. August 12, 2011.
Schager, Nick. *Village Voice*. August 12, 2011.

Schwartzbaum, Lisa. *Entertainment Weekly.* August 12, 2011.
Smith, Kyle. *New York Post.* August 12, 2011.

TRIVIA

After the song "Teenage Dream" finishes, you can catch a glimpse of Damian McGinty from, *The Glee Project*, in the audience.

GNOMEO & JULIET

An epic tale on a tiny scale.
—Movie tagline

A timeless feud. A forbidden love. An epic battle.
—Movie tagline

Every day they sit and wait. But when we're away their adventure begins.
—Movie tagline

A little adventure goes a lawn way.
—Movie tagline

Box Office: $100 million

"This story has been told before. A lot," a garden gnome tells the audience at the start of the animated *Gnomeo & Juliet*. This version of *William Shakespeare's Romeo and Juliet* stars garden gnomes. They live in two backyards of two houses on Verona Dr. One set of gnomes are owned by the Capulets, the others by the Montagues. One house is red, the other blue. A fence divides them. When the adults leave, the gnomes come to life and get on with their daily routine. The rivalry is most overtly expressed through a lawnmower race between Gnomeo (voiced by James McAvoy) and Tybalt (voiced by Jason Statham), to the tune of Elton John's "Saturday Night's Alright For Fighting." The humans who own these houses also have a rivalry and believe that they are each vandalizing each other's backyards every time something is out of place.

The star-crossed lovers meet late one night while Gnomeo is out to tamper with his rival's lawnmower and Juliet (voiced by Emily Blunt) is out to steal an orchid that sits atop a greenhouse. He is dressed as though going out to fight in guerilla warfare; she looks like a ninja. When they meet, it is a but a mere misunderstanding followed by adorable flirtations with one another until they fall into a small pond that washes away their facial make-up and they see each other more truthfully. "She's red," he says. "Why, of all things, does she have to be red?" Juliet's confidant and servant Nanette (voiced by Ashley Jensen) cheerfully suggests that "a doomed love is the greatest love of all!"

As Gnomeo and Juliet try to keep their love a secret from everyone, the rivalry continues via (among other things) a psychotically powerful lawnmower called the Terrafirminator, ordered online by one of the house's owners. Juliet's father Lord Redbrick (voiced by Michael Caine) is, of course, the main obstacle in the storyline. He thinks she is too dainty and delicate to help out in the war between the Reds and the Blues. She is anything but and she demonstrates this while out on a date with Gnomeo in which they race lawnmowers together. Everything goes well for the both of them until an incident involving weed killer.

There are more than just gnomes in the film. There are lawn ornaments of all kinds, such as the fawn (voiced by Ozzy Osbourne) who assists Tybalt. Nanette is actually a plastic frog. During their date, Gnomeo and Juliet happen across a lawn flamingo. And there are plenty of tiny ceramic bunnies. Much like the toys in the *Toy Story* movies, whenever an adult is about to peek through the windows, everyone is aware of it and must get into character by freezing wherever they are and smiling.

Much of *Gnomeo & Juliet* is set to music by Elton John and is animated with the spirit and relentless energy of a Tex Avery cartoon. The meeting between Gnomeo and Juliet atop the greenhouse has a Rube Goldberg-like inventiveness to it, a scene that is meant to deflate the story of any real tragedy, much like their meeting later on when Juliet says the play's most famous line. *Gnomeo and Juliet* is not out to capture all the intricacies of Shakespeare's narrative, but to have fun with it and not take it too seriously.

The animation itself is quite wonderful. For something as surface-oriented as a garden gnome, the characters themselves are quite expressive without losing their ceramic texture, made all the more tangible by the clinking noise heard every time they touch an object or each other. It is a brightly colored and inventive world that is filled with all kinds of visual puns, most of which are for Shakespeare buffs and will likely go over kids' heads. The nine screenwriters it took to bring this thing together are careful not to let it get too bogged down into Shakespearean lore as to alienate the younger viewers, but it is nice to see some thought was put into entertaining the grown-ups in the audience as well.

It is almost impossible to dislike a movie that is almost all garden gnomes, especially one as playful as this. Still, with its British background and all-star British voice cast, there is a startling lack of real British humor in the film. It could do with a stronger dose of weirdness, especially given the limitless possibilities that animation brings. At times, it feels too confined by American standards of animation and storytelling that it often times feels compromised. It is a 3-D studio product and it is no surprise to find that nine screenwriters were brought in and something still feels amiss.

Still, there is enough charm, energy and all around good cheer to make this one slightly better than the average *Shrek* movie. Fairy tales have been done to death. With all the remakes still popping up on the cinematic landscape, it would not be surprising if Shakespeare were to become trendy again, even in 3-D.

Collin Souter

CREDITS

Gnomeo: James McAvoy

Juliet: Emily Blunt

Lord Redrick: Michael Caine

Tybalt: Jason Statham

Lady Bluebury: Maggie Smith

William Shakespeare: Patrick Stewart

Lady Montague: Julie Walters

Nanette: Ashley Jensen

Benny: Matt Lucas

Featherstone: Jim (Jonah) Cummings

Fawn: Ozzy Osbourne

Paris: Stephen Merchant

Terrafirminator V.O.: Hulk Hogan

Dolly Gnome: Dolly Parton

Origin: USA

Language: English

Released: 2011

Production: Baker Bloodworth, David Furnish, Steve Hamilton Shaw; Rocket Pictures, Miramax Films, Starz Animation, Touchstone Pictures; released by Touchstone Pictures

Directed by: Kelly Asbury

Written by: Kelly Asbury, Rob Sprackling, John R. Smith, Mark Burton, Kevin Cecil, Emily Cook, Kathy Greenberg, Andy Riley, Steve Hamilton Shaw

Music by: James Newton Howard, Chris P. Bacon, Elton John

Sound: Glenn Freemantle

Editing: Catherine Apple

Art Direction: Karen DeJong, Andrew Woodhouse

Production Design: Karen DeJong

MPAA rating: G

Running time: 84 minutes

REVIEWS

Barnard, Linda. *Toronto Star*. February 11, 2011.
Goodykoontz, Bill. *Arizone Republic*. February 9, 2011.
Holden, Stephen. *New York Times*. February 11, 2011.
Jenkins, David. *Time Out*. February 9, 2011.
Lacey, Liam. *Globe and Mail*. February 11, 2011.
Lumenick, Lou. *New York Post*. February 11, 2011.
Marks, Ken. *New Yorker*. March 7, 2011.

Minow, Nell. *Chicago Sun-Times*. February 11, 2011.
Robinson, Tasha. *AV Club*. February 10, 2011.
Turan, Kenneth. *Los Angeles Times*. February 10, 2011.

QUOTES

Featherstone: "He followed your scent all the way from the alley, and he doesn't even have a nose."

TRIVIA

The word "Capulet" is spelled out in International Maritime Signal flags on the front of Mr Capulet's house.

AWARDS

Nomination:

Golden Globes 2012: Song ("Hello Hello").

A GOOD OLD FASHIONED ORGY

A comedy about old friends in new positions.
   —Movie tagline

The sex comedy is an American staple. Though Hollywood attitudes may not be quite as liberating as international counterparts, it is still a necessity that most blue, white and red-blooded citizens reportedly thinks about every seven seconds. Why there has been a sudden explosion in recent years of films challenging the status quo as if the sexual revolution had been restarted is still one for the scholars to decipher. Free love notwithstanding, these films in their attempt to be humorous, have often ended up being about the cost of moving outside the marriage—even with permission. *The Freebie* (2010), *Hall Pass* (2011) and *Swinging with the Finkels* (2011) have already mined this territory in such a short period of time that the only question left is whether or not a really good film can actually be made from this premise. Take out the nuptial factor and the structure is not dissimilar to *When Harry Met Sally...* (1988), *No Strings Attached* (2011), and *Friends With Benefits* (2011) and their question of whether or not friends can have sex. Take out a sense of comic timing and a general lack of direction with the material and what would be left is the essence of *A Good Old Fashioned Orgy*.

Jason Sudeikis stars as Eric, the ringleader of a group of friends who spend most of their free time together, especially when it involves a theme party at his family's large beach home. His pals include McCrudden (Tyler Labine), his jobless, overweight shadow and Sue (Michelle Borth), who has secretly carried a little crush on Eric for years. Psychotherapist Sue (Lake Bell) overanalyzes every situation but cannot clarify her relationship with European bore Marcus (Rhys Coiro). Ever-more-insecure, in order, is workaholic Adam (Nick Kroll), recently slimmed-down Laura (Lindsay Sloane), and aspiring musician, Duquez (Martin Starr), whose girlfriend Willow (Angela Sarafyan), cannot even convince him to choose the right look for his album cover. About to leave the circle are Glen (Will Forte) and Kate (Lucy Punch) who attend their last "White Trash Bash" as a single couple.

Also expected to leave—at least from the family summer home turned party central—are Eric and his friends. It turns out that dad (Don Johnson) is putting it up on the market much to the chagrin of his son; unaware he even hit on one of the realtors, the spunky Kelly (Leslie Bibb), at his last party. Eric is not about to let the house go without sending it out in style. It is time for one big theme party to rule them all. But he has something a little more intimate in mind—no outside invitees; just the circle of friends at this one. Why not have an orgy? Having felt robbed of an entire period in their lives by the nominal threat of newly discovered diseases, Eric hopes to convince everyone that it is time to reclaim those years. After some initial hesitance, one-by-one, the group comes around to the idea. Now, if Eric can only hold off the sale of the house until Labor Day and manage his growing feelings for the pretty realtor unaware of his plans.

Killing time before the big party is not exactly tinged with any sort of suspense of how these relationships will inevitably play out. Co-directors and writers Alex Gregory & Peter Huyck show no interest in taking viewers down another path where regret and awkwardness are going to put a damper on the orgiastic fun. They just want to bring the funny, though that proves to be just as bumpy a road.

Ensemble-wise, the right players are in place. Sudeikis has been making the rounds away from his stint on Saturday Night Live as both a cinema scene-stealer in *The Rocker* (2008) and as a capable co-lead in *Horrible Bosses* (2011) and the aforementioned *Hall Pass*. Eric is hardly a stretch for him, aside from having less partners to carry the comic load. Labine showed great potential on TV's *Reaper* as a loyal comical oaf with a raging libido, and while he has the occasional moment here, his handlers never appear to have the proper strengths to mine the maximum potential of their front-and-center leads.

The surrounding support is handled spottily by actors given little to work with as characters. Trying to give equal time to an even dozen of odd characters with varying degrees of likability is daunting for any writer,

but lack of personalities by those portraying them further unbalances their humor input. The women of the story are more likely to be judged on their degree of hotness rather than their conversational skills, adding a further touch of unnecessary misogyny to a film dependent on satisfying urges rather than feelings. When the ladies get their brief moments away from the guys, the talk steers towards clichés of body types and insecurities rather than the idea that they are participating in this boy's fantasy for any true independence.

Sex comedies are not always dependent on depth as long as they are funny. Some modicum of credit is due for the filmmakers actually not chickening out at the last minute and going through with the orgy. It does spark a couple of the film's best laughs, particularly that of the underutilized Forte and Punch, whose characters crash the scene with a misinterpretation of the theme-within-a-theme. But Gregory and Huyck never push the limits into more dangerously taboo territory or explore the awkwardness of potential individual fetishes for the gang's pleasure. Perhaps that was what the side trip into an underground sex club was meant to satisfy because it certainly was not a longing to see David Koechner play another variation of his obnoxiously unappealing sex maniacs. For a country that boasts the same colored flag as the nation famed for the ménage a trois, American movies still have a ways to go to capture the same spirit of that particular bedroom party.

Erik Childress

CREDITS

Eric: Jason Sudeikis
Kelly: Leslie Bibb
Laura: Lindsay Sloane
McCrudden: Tyler Labine
Alison: Lake Bell
Kate: Lucy Punch
Dody: Lin Shaye
Glenn: Will Forte
Jerry Keppler: Don Johnson
Sue: Michelle Borth
Adam: Nick Kroll
Origin: USA
Language: English
Released: 2011
Production: James Stern; Fierce Entertainment, Aura Film Partnership, Endgame Entertainment; released by Samuel Goldwyn Films
Directed by: Peter Huyek, Alex Gregory
Written by: Peter Huyek, Alex Gregory
Cinematography by: John Thomas

Music by: Jonathan Sadoff
Sound: G. Michael Graham
Music Supervisor: John Houlihan
Editing: Anita Brandt-Burgoyne, Patrick J. Don Vito
Costumes: Leah Katznelson
Production Design: Alan Hook
MPAA rating: R
Running time: 95 minutes

REVIEWS

Covert, Colin. *Minneapolis Star-Tribune.* September 2, 2011.
Ebert, Roger. *Chicago Sun-Times.* September 1, 2011.
Fine, Marshall. *Hollywood & Fine.* September 1, 2011.
Jones, J.R. *Chicago Reader.* September 1, 2011.
Kaplan, Jeanne. *Kaplan vs. Kaplan.* September 2, 2011.
Keough, Peter. *Boston Phoenix.* August 31, 2011.
McWeeny, Drew. *Hitfix.* September 2, 2011.
Neumaier, Joe. *New York Daily News.* September 2, 2011.
Orndorf, Brian. *eFilmCritic.* August 31, 2011.
Whitty, Stephen. *Newark Star-Ledger.* September 2, 2011.

QUOTES

Adam: "This is the worst orgy ever. "

TRIVIA

Parties thrown by co-director/writer Peter Huyck in and around his southern Californian home were the inspiration for the film.

THE GREEN HORNET

Protect the law by breaking it.
—Movie tagline

Box Office: $97.8 million

The Green Hornet has been featured in a 1930s radio series, a 1940s serial and a 1960s TV show. Hornet comic books have come and gone since the 1940s. Despite the longevity implied by the near-century from the character's introduction to the 2011 film, this is a superhero that has simply never caught on like Batman, Superman, and Spiderman. In fact, The Green Hornet hardly bears mention at all alongside superhero icons of decidedly lesser stripe like Iron Man, Green Lantern, and Thor. While those characters have flourished in one medium, occasionally branching out into others, The Hornet has never even found a nest. His latest adventure will likely do little to change that. A lengthy and much troubled development process led to a film that generally looks good, has a few solid laughs, and slightly above average action/fight sequences, but a talky script, weak characters, and muddled motivations undermines these slight advantages at every turn.

The Green Hornet only tells a story in the sense that it hits certain well worn beats giving it a beginning, middle and end. There is little more to it beyond the basics. Britt Reid (Seth Rogen) is a troubled kid grieving the death of his mom and dealing with an overly stern father (Tom Wilkinson). Daddy dies, leaving a twenty-something Britt to run the family paper. Britt meets Kato (Jay Chou), the family mechanic, who turns out to be a tech-genius. Kato and Britt take the Black Beauty (it was just laying around) on a drunken joyride and run into some muggers. After beating up the muggers they look at each other and say, "Hey, wanna keep doing this?" They attract aggressive attention from local crime kingpin Chudnofsky (Christoph Waltz) leading to an inevitable showdown that also involves a corrupt DA (David Harbour). Along the way they hire blond eye candy (Cameron Diaz).

With nothing original or otherwise compelling to offer in story or character, all director Michel Gondry can do is wrestle with the screenplay, with the star, Seth Rogen, (who wrote it with longtime pal and co-writer, Evan Goldberg), and with his own uncertainty about how to bring his visual sensibility to the superhero genre. Gondry is best known for his surreal visuals and his loose approach to storytelling. This skill set worked well for the excellent *Eternal Sunshine of the Spotless Mind* (2004) and underrated *The Science of Sleep* (2006). But by *Be Kind, Rewind* (2008) Gondry seemed to be offering creative afterthoughts. Unfocused and too reliant on the skit-like antics of stars Jack Black and Mos Def, the film simply limped along. *The Green Hornet* suffers from exactly the same problem. No one seems to be at the helm.

Hornet screenwriter and star Seth Rogen (*Knocked Up* [2007], *Superbad* [2007], *Pineapple Express* [2008], *Funny People* [2009]) seems determined here to reinvent the Hornet franchise as a big budget action comedy. But his *Superbad*-style vulgarity hangs loosely on the character at best, never really seeming to fit and the film gives him little to do but act like a boorish fratboy. His badgering of Kato seems almost racist. Britt Reid is just a spoiled rich kid who rationalizes his vigilantism to have a good time. Kato in this film is basically a cipher with a quickly-discarded back story and an improbable skill set. Jay Chou (*Curse of the Golden Flower* [2006]) is great in the action scenes and manages to generate some minor energy with Rogen, but Kato never seems to be there for any other reason than to spice up the action or provide a convenient foil for lead character's barbs, too few of which are funny.

The same goes for poor Cameron Diaz (*The Mask* [1994], *Being John Malkovich* [1999], *Knight and Day* [2010]), who is predictably solid in her role as Lenore Case, office temp promoted to personal assistant. But all the movie gives her to do is project the image of a smart, capable, straight woman who has to fend off the romantic advances of Reid and Kato. By the time she becomes a meaningful part of the story viewers will wonder why she overlooks the opportunity for a sexual harassment lawsuit.

The other major player here, Christoph Waltz (*Inglorious Basterds* [2009], *Water for Elephants* [2011]), is well-cast as the menacing-but-paranoid and insecure old-school gangster Chudnofsky. But, as with the rest of the cast, the script demands barely anything of him beyond archetype. The one somewhat original idea, that of having Chudnofsky go through a mid-life crisis, is a promising one but not even the impressively gifted Waltz can generate comic energy out of his character's decision to change his name to *Blood*nofsky.

3D seems a complete afterthought here. Gondry does not use it to tell his story but simply to enhance the action sequences. Unfortunately, 3D robs the fights and crashes of brightness and punch. In 2D they feel far more alive but, as with Rogen's humor, the overall effect is of something somewhat viciously out of place. The Green Hornet and Kato finally emerge from the film as vigilantes in the worst sense, even killing a defenseless villain at the end of the film in a manner that suggests the most unpleasant sort of cinematic excess. If the movie had an ounce of brains or more heart it could have been a dark satire of the superhero genre like *Mystery Men* (1999), *Special* (2006) or *Super* (2011). Rogen has done some unexpectedly fine even somewhat subtle work. The criminally under-seen *Observe and Report* (2009) cast him as a mentally and emotionally disabled mall cop desperate to join the real police force. It was an intelligent-yet-brutal, darker-than-dark satire of the Mall of the American Dream that featured as many gasp-out-loud as laugh-out-loud moments. Comparatively, *The Green Hornet* is an empty time-waster bound to be seen by too many and forgotten shortly thereafter.

Dave Canfield

CREDITS

Britt Reid/The Green Hornet: Seth Rogen
Kato: Jay Chou
Lenore Chase: Cameron Diaz
Benjamin Chudnofsky: Christoph Waltz
Michael Axford: Edward James Olmos
Scanlon: David Harbour

Tupper: Edward Furlong
James Reid: Tom Wilkinson
Origin: USA
Language: English
Released: 2011
Production: Neal H. Moritz; Columbia Pictures, Original Film; released by Sony Pictures
Directed by: Michael Gondry
Written by: Evan Goldberg
Cinematography by: John Schwartzman
Music by: James Newton Howard
Editing: Michael Tronick
Sound: Nerses Gezalyan
Art Direction: Benjamin Edelberg, Chad S. Frey, Greg Papalia
Costumes: Kym Barrett
Production Design: Owen Paterson
MPAA rating: PG-13
Running time: 119 minutes

REVIEWS

Denby, David. *New Yorker.* January 24, 2011.
Ebert, Roger. *Chicago Sun-Times.* January 12, 2011.
Kois, Dan. *Washington Post.* January 13, 2011.
Miraudo, Simon. *Quickflix.* January 14, 2011.
Nusair, David. *Reel Film Reviews.* May 1, 2011.
Savada, Elias. *Film Threat.* January 16, 2011.
Scott, A.O. *New York Times.* January 14, 2011.
Starnes, Joshua. *ComingSoon.net.* March 22, 2011.
Stevens, Dana. *Slate.* January 13, 2011.
Vognar, Chris. *Dallas Morning News.* January 14, 2011.

QUOTES

Britt Reid: "Everyone knows, when you corner a hornet, you get stung."

TRIVIA

A poster for *The Lone Ranger* can be seen in Britt Reid's room. In the original radio program, Reid was the the Lone Ranger's grandnephew. His father rode with the Lone Ranger on some of his adventures and they shared the family name of Reid. Both radio programs were created by George W. Trendle and Fran Striker.

GREEN LANTERN

One of us…becomes one of them.
    —Movie tagline
In our darkest hour, there will be light.
    —Movie tagline

Box Office: $116.6 million

Sometimes a film simply needs time to be appreciated for whatever it is. *Green Lantern* is a perfect example. Dismissed by critics, the $200 million film has made a small profit but has already sunk into the background of a surprisingly bland series of 2011 big budget superhero outings that included *The Green Hornet, Thor, X-Men: First Class,* and *Captain America: The First Avenger.* Of these, only *The Green Hornet* was truly a bad film but one would never have known it from the exaggerated reviews of *The Green Lantern.* It certainly compares favorably with other less successful but solidly entertaining superhero outings like *The Shadow* (1994) and *The Phantom* (1996). Perfectly cast and visually spectacular, it also meets modest storytelling goals with a gee-whiz simplicity that makes critical nitpicking a bit like teasing the slow kid in class. *Green Lantern* is not a masterpiece, but it does have considerable charms for those who approach it looking for the chance to leap into the sort of wonder comic book superhero films can provide.

The film starts in the distant past, millions of years before the earth came into being. Present are the Guardians, a race of ultra-intelligent beings who use the essence of willpower (which is green) to form a universal police force which they call the Green Lantern Corps. Together they fight evil in all its forms, especially the being of yellow fear-essence Parallax (voice of Clancy Brown) who was imprisoned by Green Lantern Abin Sur (Temeura Morrison). For millions of years, Parallax has been held in check, only to escape in the present day, where he kills Abin Sur, who uses his final moments to crash land on earth commanding his ring of power to find a worthy successor.

Cut to test pilot Hal Jordan (Ryan Reynolds), who has overslept yet another mission. Jordan angers everyone around him with his irresponsibility and arrogance but skates by on his charm and piloting skills. When he crashes an expensive plane, putting a major military contract in jeopardy, he finds himself out of a job, until that is he comes upon the dying Abin Sur and is chosen by the ring to become the next Green Lantern. After a short interval, the ring whisks him away to the Lantern home base of Oa where a variety of other Lantern Corps members from countless other worlds begin the process of training him. Viewers meet the bird/lizard-like Tomar-Re (voiced by Geoffrey Rush) the massive Kilowog (voiced by Michael Clarke Duncan) and Sinestro (Mark Strong). Sinestro rejects the idea that a human , especially one as flawed as Hal Jordan, could ever be worthy to wear the ring of Abin Sur, and, discouraged, Jordan returns to earth, attempting to leave his destiny behind.

What no one in the Lantern Corps realizes is that a piece of Parallax has made it to earth in Abin Sur's body where it is being studied by Hector Hammond (Peter Sarsgaard), a scientist recruited by Hammond Sr. (Tim Robbins), his amoral father ,into government service. When Hector becomes infected by Parallax he quickly mutates into a grotesque monstrosity with psychic and telekinetic abilities becoming the agent wherein Parallax can invade earth. Jordan realizing the danger races back to Oa, where he attempts to enlist the aid of Sinestro and the other Lanterns to keep Parallax from destroying the planet. Rejected once more, he takes up the burden of protector and faces Parallax on his own terms.

Green Lantern is perfectly cast. Ryan Reynolds has been in more than his share of mediocre flicks, but every single one of them has been better off for his presence. In great films like *Buried* (2010) he has demonstrated surprising range. *Green Lantern* does give him limited opportunities to do more than display a likable charisma and his trademark sarcasm, but he rises to the challenge, giving Jordan an everyman quality.

Peter Sarsgaard virtually steals the movie as the tortured loser Hector Hammond, especially after he begins to transform into the agent of Parallax. Also a standout is Mark Strong as Synestro who manages to project beyond the dots glued to his face to portral a being of great moral strength who will someday be undone by his pride. Blake Lively plays Carol Ferris as a strong-minded, intelligent go-getter but it stills feels like type even if the role is more than eye candy. Tim Robbins is predictably effective as the wicked politico Hammond Sr. but one never gets the sense that his character is anything other than a caricature.

The real problem here is in the writing. This is basic origin/franchise introduction stuff, nothing to be ashamed of, but in the year of the superhero film *Green Lantern* hardly glows in the way it handles story arc, character development or relationships. For instance, for all its problems, *X-Men: First Class* sketches out a magnificently elegant take on the rivalry between Professor Xavier and Magneto. In *Thor,* the Gods seem very vested in one another, and, again, there is a central relationship between Loki and Thor that has some emotional weight. In *Green Lantern,* the relationships are set in stone as types from the very beginning and never budge an inch. Characters are either evil or good and there are hardly any shades between.

The real star here is the dynamic visual aesthetic of the film. The outstanding 3D explodes off the screen, into the screen, and is often used to help tell the story and put the viewer into a character's headspace. Whenever Jordan unleashes his green power to conjure a weapon the effect is dazzling. And the world of Oa seems endless, the repository of a universal series of epic heroic tales all waiting to be explored.

This brings to mind perhaps the most important observation that can be made about *Green Lantern*. "In brightest day/In blackest night/No evil shall escape my sight/Let those who worship evil's might/ Beware my power/Green Lantern's light." It is amateurish verse at best. Yet aesthetics aside it showcases the power of the superhero idea nicely. It is comforting to believe in simple good and evil and heroes that will defend that good. *Green Lantern* has a great lead, great villain, and great effects, but lacks the story to do more than be a simple fun time-waster for most viewers. But for the right viewers it may be a portal into real wonder.

Dave Canfield

CREDITS

Hal Jordan/Green Lantern: Ryan Reynolds
Carol Ferris: Blake Lively
Hector Hammond: Peter Sarsgaard
Thaal Sinestro: Mark Strong
Dr. Amanda Waller: Angela Bassett
Senator Hammond: Tim Robbins
Abin Sur: Temuera Morrison
Martin Jordan: Jon Tenney
Jessica Jordan: Amy Carlson
Carl Ferris: Jay O. Sanders
Tomar-Re: Geoffrey Rush (Voice)
Kilowog: Michael Clarke Duncan (Voice)
Parallax: Clancy Brown (Voice)
Origin: USA
Language: English
Released: 2011
Production: Greg Berlanti, Donald De Line; De Line Pictures, DC Entertainment; released by Warner Bros.
Directed by: Martin Campbell
Written by: Michael Goldenberg, Greg Berlanti, Michael Green, Marc Guggenheim
Cinematography by: Dion Beebe
Music by: James Newton Howard
Sound: Pud Cusack
Editing: Stuart Baird
Art Direction: Francois Audouy
Costumes: Ngila Dickson
Production Design: Grant Major
MPAA rating: PG-13
Running time: 114 minutes

REVIEWS

Dargis, Manohla. *New York Times*. June 16, 2011.
Ebert, Roger. *Chicago Sun-Times*. June 16, 2011.
Fry, Ted. *Seattle Times*. June 16, 2011.
Gleiberman, Owen. *Entertainment Weekly*. June 15, 2011.
McCarthy, Todd. *Hollywood Reporter*. June 15, 2011.
McWeeny, Drew. *HitFix*. June 15, 2011.
Moore, Roger. *Orlando Sentinel*. June 16, 2011.
Sexton, David. *This is London*. June 17, 2011.
Snider, Eric D. *EricDSnider.com*. June 17, 2011.
Turan, Kenneth. *Los Angeles Times*. June 16, 2011.

QUOTES

Hal Jordan: "In brightest day, in blackest night no evil shall escape my sight. Let those who worship evil's might, beware my power. Green Lantern's light."

TRIVIA

AT one point, director Quentin Tarantino was linked to the project.

THE GUARD

Box Office: $5.4 million

While the plot description may not convey it, *The Guard* is a not-as-interesting-as-it-might-seem exercise in mistaken identity. Comedic in spots, though hardly a farce, it is not the on-screen characters forced into confusion but the audience who may sense a burning familiarity with it all. The pairing of a scruffy white cop with a more authoritative black one is older than even the *Lethal Weapon* (1987-1998) series. The connection to the finale of *Tequila Sunrise* (1988) might escape some viewers who may be too wrapped up making the comparisons to the structure of *One False Move* (1992). Finally for those who might be excited to see the follow-up to the terrific *In Bruges* (2008), be sure to make note that its writer/director was Martin McDonagh and *The Guard* was created by John Michael McDonagh, his brother. John's resume is not nearly as thick as his playwright sibling and his directorial debut ultimately is just as thin.

Sergeant Gerry Boyle (Brendan Gleeson) is an Ireland police officer who practically sees the job as one big lark. Money and drugs from a crime scene are an added perk and he is prone to play dumb in the presence of authority despite carrying within him a keen knack for putting everything in perspective. When FBI agent Wendell Everett (Don Cheadle) comes to town on the trail of four drug dealers, he is stunned by Boyle's casual racism, but, before the officer can be suspended for interrupting further, he has already made Wendell's job simpler by connecting one of his own cases to the agent's.

There are three drug traffickers driving around in a car led by Francis Sheehy (Liam Cunningham) and his two underlings, Liam O'Leary (David Wilmot), and smart aleck loose cannon, Clive Cornell (Mark Strong). Boyle's wet-behind-the-ears partner (Rory Keenan) comes across the trio on a routine traffic stop and ends up paying the price. Not even a visit from the man's poor widow can snap Boyle out of taking his scheduled day off while Everett can get no cooperation from the locals. Boyle is by no means heartless as he is focused on keeping the final weeks for his dying mom (Fionnula Flanagan) as comfortable as possible and does not take kindly to one of his professional lady friends showing up with fresh bruises. Eventually, when he discovers there may be more to his partner's disappearance, he takes an active role in the investigation. Or as active as McDonagh's screenplay will let him.

There is a near-randomness to his structure that helps to satisfy his penchant for instilling every character in the region with the same quipster logic. For Boyle to be as unique a character as McDonagh may have envisioned, it would have helped a great deal for his surrounding company to not all be, seemingly, in on the joke. The three criminals all crack wise about their day-to-day jobs, pondering how useful every murder and payoff to the cops really are. There are superfluous rendezvous with an IRA contact and a kid, who each have something to say about killing Protestants and the mating habits of the MI-5. Even the epilogue is consciously self-aware of pointing out the little details that turned out to have greater consequences on the big details that make for a grandiose tale in the movies.

The best scenes within *The Guard* are the ones involving the tug-and-pull relationship between Boyle and Everett. Their contentious introduction is a nicely written setup that will define their time together, reminding one of the way Clint Eastwood prodded and poked Rene Russo during *In The Line of Fire* (1993), offending her every ideal but with a twinkle and a wink. When Everett remarks that he cannot figure out whether Boyle is "really smart" or "really dumb," it is left for the audience to decipher. Gleeson and Cheadle are terrific in these moments together. One of the *The Guard*'s greatest flaws is that this pairing is not on-screen enough. Though the percentage of the clock on the paltry 86-minute running time might prove otherwise, the gaps between their banter seem like the 24 hours Boyle suggests mean little to a crime investigation.

It is unfortunate that Cheadle's Everett is only around to call bull on Gleeson's Boyle when the rest of the cast sure could have used a little of the same. The familiarity of everyone's singularly snarky attitude plus the over familiarity of so many other crime films leaves

The Guard to distinguish itself purely on the strength of its accents.

Erik Childress

CREDITS

Sgt. Gerry Boyle: Brendan Gleeson
FBI agent Wendell Everett: Don Cheadle
Francis Sheehy: Liam Cunningham
Liam O'Leary: David Wilmot
Clive Cornell: Mark Strong
Aidan McBride: Rory Keenan
Eileen Boyle: Fionnula Flanagan
Gabriela McBride: Katarina Cas
Origin: Ireland
Language: English
Released: 2011
Production: Chris Clark, Flora Fernandez Marengo, Ed Guiney, Andrew Lowe; Reprisal Films, Element Pictures; released by Sony Pictures Classics
Directed by: John M. McDonagh
Written by: John M. McDonagh
Cinematography by: Larry Smith
Music by: Calexico
Sound: Robert Flanagan
Music Supervisor: Liz Gallacher
Editing: Chris Gill
Art Direction: Lucy van Lonkhuyzen
Costumes: Eimer Ni Mhaoldomhnaigh
Production Design: John Paul Kelly
MPAA rating: R
Running time: 95 minutes

REVIEWS

Bayer, Jeff. *Scorecard Review.* August 15, 2011.
Burr, Ty. *Boston Globe.* August 4, 2011.
Dargis, Manohla. *New York Times.* July 28, 2011.
Ebert, Roger. *Chicago Sun-Times.* August 4, 2011.
Levy, Shawn. *Oregonian.* August 11, 2011.
Lloyd, Christopher. *Sarasota Herald-Tribune.* August 31, 2011.
McWeeny, Drew. *Hitfix.* July 29, 2011.
Orndorf, Brian. *eFilmCritic.com.* August 24, 2011.
Phipps, Keith. *AV Club.* July 28, 2011.
Snider, Eric D. *Film.com.* July 27, 2011.

QUOTES

Sergeant Gerry Boyle: "I'm Irish. Racism is part of my culture."

TRIVIA

This film is the fourth collaboration between Irish actors Brendan Gleeson and Liam Cunningham.

AWARDS

Nomination:
British Acad. 2011: Orig. Screenplay
Golden Globes 2012: Actor—Mus./Comedy (Gleeson).

H

HALL PASS

Good for one week off marriage.
—Movie tagline

One week. No rules.
—Movie tagline

Box Office: $45.1 million

Hall Pass tells the story of a couple of long-domesticated guys who are given a chance to briefly revisit the ribaldry and raunchiness of their salad days and gradually discover to their horror that not only are they unable to tap into the giddy heedlessness that has been driving their memories of those cherished times, it gradually begins to dawn on them that they may never have possessed it in the first place. The trouble with the film is that it has been made by a couple of guys who are, based on the available evidence seen in the final product, more or less suffering from the same problem. Those guys are Bobby & Peter Farrelly, the fraternal filmmaking duo who caused a cinematic sensation with *There's Something About Mary* (1998), a film that demonstrated that blending outrageous gross-out humor with sweet-natured sincerity could, when handled correctly, yield results that were both hilarious and oddly heartwarming. In the years since then, the Farrellys have been steadily cranking out movies that have essentially followed that formula to one degree or another (though the lasting success of those efforts can be gleaned by the fact that nearly thirteen years down the line, they are still being referred to in the ads as the creators of *There's Something About Mary*) and *Hall Pass* is perhaps their most blatant attempt to date to follow in their own footsteps. While there are a few laughs scattered here

and there, the end result is mostly a tepid botch in which the sad desperation that the central guys display in front of the camera is outdone only by the sad desperation of the central guys behind it.

Owen Wilson and Jason Sudekis play Rick and Fred, a couple of guys who have long since abandoned their carefree days as randy lotharios for the day-to-day routine of suburban domesticity. Since this move involved marrying women embodied by the likes of Jenna Fischer and Christina Applegate, you would think that they would spend each and every day giving thanks to whatever deity was responsible for such good fortune but no, they spend all their time either blatantly checking out every single babe that wanders into their sightlines or jawing with their buddies about how many of them they would be bedding if only they were not married. Fed up with this nonsense and taking the advice of a pop psychologist (Joy Behar), the wives decide to nip it in the bud by offering their mates a "hall pass"—a one-week relinquishment of all the rules and obligations of marriage without any retribution or repercussions. At first, the guys are thrilled with the idea of a week of complete sexual freedom but after a number of false starts, mid-seduction stumbles, and some of the ickiest forms of interrupted potential coitus imaginable, it slowly begins to dawn on them just how good they really had it. And in a completely unexpected turn of events, their out-of-town wives find themselves pondering old maxims involving geese and ganders when they become the objects of desire of a couple of minor-league baseball players.

Throughout their careers, the Farrelly Brothers have never exactly been known for their graceful approach to the art of cinema and *Hall Pass* certainly will not inspire much in the way of critical revisionism to their work. Like their other efforts, it is so crudely made that they make Mel Brooks look like Terrence Malick by comparison, it runs on far too long for its own good and spends more time trying to invoke laughter through sheer outrageousness than with such once-common elements as wit or comedic timing. However, their earlier and more successful efforts, such as *There's Something About Mary* and especially *Kingpin* (1996) managed to overcome these handicaps by providing solid laughs amidst the sloppiness.

Unfortunately, like the vast majority of their recent output, *Hall Pass* pretty much fails at this one task throughout. For starters, the basic premise of the film is so arch and dated that it feels as though it would be more at home in an old and not fondly-remembered episode of *Love, American Style* than in a 2011 release, a sensation exacerbated by the inclusion of a long and staggeringly pointless set-piece in which our heroes and their pals eat a bunch of pot-laced brownies. Beyond that, the screenplay unfolds in painfully predictable ways—Rick meets his dream girl in a sexy Australian babe (Nicky Whelan) but loves his wife too much to seal the deal while Fred finds himself embroiled in increasingly raunchy hi-jinks culminating in a spectacularly gross and spectacularly unfunny sight gag (emphasis on "gag")—before stumbling on to the equally obvious conclusion in which marital bonds are restored, the joys of hearth and home are reaffirmed and annoyed audience members are left wondering why they blew ten dollars on a comedy so feeble that it takes two perfectly good comedic actresses like Fischer and Applegate and then ignores them for most of the running time instead of realizing that it might have come across as somewhat fresher and funnier if it had been presented from their perspective.

If one looks really hard and ignores the countless dead spots on display, there are a couple of amusing bits scattered throughout *Hall Pass*. Until they are reduced to mere buffoonery by the screenplay, Wilson and Sudekis do a pretty good job of meshing their differing comedic styles together and demonstrate enough amusing byplay to make one wish that the film had focused on that instead of on their separate misadventures. Even better, Farrelly Brothers regular Richard Jenkins pops up in the closing reels as an aging-but-still-skilled Lothario attempting to impart his wisdom upon his increasingly hapless charges and he provides enough of a comedic jolt during his brief appearance to make one wish that the film had been about him as well. If the Farrelly Brothers had only recognized and taken advantage of such bits of actual comedic inspiration literally standing before them, *Hall Pass* still might not have been a great

comedy but it probably could have at least turned out to be a reasonably decent one under the circumstances. Alas, by overlooking these elements in favor of once again rehashing their increasingly tired blend of slapstick and sentiment laced with toilet humor (literally at one point), *Hall Pass* winds up delivering all the laughter and gaiety of a detention slip.

Peter Sobczynski

CREDITS

Rick: Owen Wilson
Fred: Jason Sudeikis
Mandy: Alyssa Milano
Coakley: Richard Jenkins
Gerry: Tyler Hoechlin
Maggie: Jenna Fischer
Grace: Christina Applegate
Origin: USA
Language: English
Released: 2011
Production: Mark Charpentier, Bobby Farrelly, Peter Farrelly, Bradley Thomas, Charles B. Wessler; New Line Cinema, Conundrum Entertainment; released by Warner Bros.
Directed by: Bobby Farrelly, Peter Farrelly
Written by: Bobby Farrelly, Peter Farrelly, Pete Jones, Kevin Barnett
Cinematography by: Matthew F. Leonetti
Music by: Fernand Bos
Sound: Andrew Decristofaro
Music Supervisor: Manish Raval, Tom Wolfe
Editing: Sam Seig
Art Direction: Dan Morski
Costumes: Denise Wingate
Production Design: Arlan Jay Vetter
MPAA rating: R
Running time: 98 minutes

REVIEWS

Childress, Erik. *eFilmcritic.com*. February 25, 2011.
Denby, David. *New Yorker*. March 14, 2011.
Ebert, Roger. *Chicago Sun-Times*. February 25, 2011.
Goss, William. *Film.com*. June 16, 2011.
Jones, J.R. *Chicago Reader*. February 25, 2011.
Minow, Nell. *Beliefnet*. February 25, 2011.
Pais, Matt. *RedEye*. February 25, 2011.
Reed, Rex. *New York Observer*. February 25, 2011.
Snider, Eric D. *Film.com*. February 25, 2011.
Tallerico, Brian. *HollywoodChicago.com*. February 25, 2011.

QUOTES

Coakley: "Every loser in Vegas thinks they can do better! You know what winners do? They walk away from the table while they're up!"

TRIVIA

Amanda Bynes was cast in the rol of as Paige but had to drop out due to a conflict in scheduling.

THE HANGOVER PART II

The wolfpack is back.
—Movie tagline
Bangkok has them now.
—Movie tagline

Box Office: $254.5 million

The Hangover Part II is not so much a sequel to the 2009 smash hit, gross-out guy comedy *The Hangover* as it is a smeared carbon copy. Directed again by Todd Philips, *Part II* takes *The Hangover*'s characters, premise and narrative structure and plops them in Bangkok, hoping the audience will be satisfied with the film's sometimes leuder, nastier antics and fail to notice its glaring shortcomings.

Their Vegas bachelor party nightmare (which involved laced drinks, a prostitute's missing baby, and a crazy encounter with Mike Tyson and his pet tiger) now squarely behind them, the four friends of *The Hangover* reunite for another wedding. This time it is straight-laced dentist Stu (Ed Helms) who is tying the knot with Lauren, "an angel with a solid rack." She has chosen her native Thailand for the ceremony, which is lucky because it happens to boast a city notorious for debauchery. It also boasts Lauren's father, who is so anti Stu he compares the groom to watered-down white rice at the rehearsal dinner. What is Stu to do then, but prove to this future father-in-law, through repeated acts of poor-decision making, that he is anything but bland?

The shortcomings with the film start with the destination wedding set-up. It is easy to understand why Stu would invite Doug (Justin Bartha), the lost groom of *The Hangover* who spent the entirety of the first film, it turned out, locked on the hotel's roof, to his wedding, and to a certain extent why Phil (Bradley Cooper) would make the cut, even though the time between hangovers seems to have turned him into a more jaded and offensive version of himself, but how Stu is allowed to add Alan (Zach Galifianakis) to the guest list is inconceivable. Is Lauren so love-struck that she would allow a near stranger to crash her intimate wedding? Is Stu so masculine that he would just pull rank over his bride to be and invite Alan anyway? Flawed set-up aside, Stu is so easily bullied by Doug (who in turn gets bullied by his wife) to include the socially underdeveloped man-child, who believes that their time in Vegas has bonded them forever, that waking up in with amnesia in a seedy Bangkok hotel room with his friends, a gangster monkey

and a replica Mike Tyson tattoo on his face, miles from his ceremony site, are Stu's just deserts. As a side note, the fact that Doug is not among those hungover is disappointing. Having sat out for the entirety of the first film, it seemed only natural that Bartha should have the opportunity to join in the fun this time around.

In addition to the monkey and the tattoo, Stu, Phil and Alan find other clues from the previous night's black hole of bad behavior extravaganza: a severed finger in a bowl of melted ice and a coked-up Mr. Chow (Ken Jeong), who magically made the trip with them from Vegas. But that's not the worst of it. It turns out that the newest member of their crew (not Doug!), Teddy (Mason Lee), the bride's genius seventeen-year-old brother, is missing. The rest of the film unravels as one would expect, with the guys probing the depths of the Bangkok underworld trying to put the pieces of their collective lost memory back together. They bail out a Buddist monk from a Thai drunk tank, trace down the tattoo parlor responsible for Stu's new look, and visit a transsexual strip joint in the hopes of gaining a lead on Teddy's whereabouts. Over and over, however, they keep hearing that if the boy does not turn up soon, "Bangkok's got him." That is more of the trouble with this hangover; as much as Bangkok provides opportunity for new depths of depravity for the freaky foursome, the risks somehow seem more intense and therefore not as funny. Just as Chow is about to reveal the details of their blow-out night, he keels over of an apparent overdose. The severed finger is discovered to be Teddy's. One dead body and a potentially kidnapped, and severely injured, adolescent start the story at an emotional and comedic deficit. This *Hangover* also reaches beyond its means, groping for raunchy, racist fodder that lacks all comic integrity. Here the aim is to shock with kinky sex, full frontal nudity, and politically incorrect punch lines. The story recovers somewhat with funny lines throughout (mostly Galifianakis'), though nothing ever hits the insane and inappropriate, but somehow completely plausible, laugh out loud moment of the guys' discovering a baby in their Vegas penthouse. Though far from comic genius, there was a certain something about the first *Hangover* that grounded it in reality, making the gags resonate. This installment reeks of a blatant cash grab.

Joanna Topor MacKenzie

CREDITS

Stu Price: Ed Helms
Phil Wenneck: Bradley Cooper
Alan Garner: Zach Galifianakis
Doug Billings: Justin Bartha

Mr. Chow: Ken Jeong
Heidi: Juliette Lewis
Tattoo Man: Liam Neeson
Kingsley: Paul Giamatti
Teddy: Mason Lee
Lauren: Jamie Chung
Fong: Nirut Sirichanya
Origin: USA
Language: English
Released: 2011
Production: Daniel Goldberg, Todd Phillips; Legendary Pictures, Green Hat Films, Living Films; released by Warner Bros.
Directed by: Todd Phillips
Written by: Todd Phillips, Scot Armstrong, Craig Mazin
Cinematography by: Lawrence Sher
Music by: Christophe Beck
Sound: Peter Hliddal
Music Supervisor: Randall Poster, George Drakoulias
Editing: Debra Neil-Fisher, Michael L. Sale
Costumes: Louise Mingenbach
Production Design: Bill Brzeski
MPAA rating: R
Running time: 102 minutes

REVIEWS

Barker, Andrew. *Variety.* May 23, 2011.
Burr, Ty. *Boston Globe.* May 25, 2011.
Dargis, Manohla. *New York Times.* May 25, 2011.
Ebert, Roger. *Chicago Sun-Times.* May 24, 2011.
Lumenick, Lou. *New York Post.* May 25, 2011.
Phillips, Michael. *Chicago Tribune.* May 25, 2011.
Rickey, Carrie. *Philadelphia Inquirer.* May 25, 2011.
Sharkey, Betsy. *Los Angeles Times.* May 25, 2011.
Weitzman, Elizabeth. *New York Daily News.* May 25, 2011.
Zacharek, Stephanie. *Movieline.* May 26, 2011.

QUOTES

Mr. Chow: "What's the matter, you never do blow before? Sometimes your heart stop, it start up again. Read a book."

TRIVIA

Mike Tyson is said to have taken singing lessons in preparation for the scene in which he sings at Stu's wedding.

AWARDS

Nomination:

Golden Raspberries 2011: Worst Prequel/Remake/Rip-off/Sequel, Worst Support. Actor (Jeong).

HANNA

Innocence can be deadly.
—Movie tagline

Adapt or die.
—Movie tagline

Box Office: $40.3 million

In an age of soulless and unimaginative action films like *Transformers: Dark of the Moon,* Joe Wright's *Hanna* is a welcome breath of very fresh air. Wright, screenwriters David Farr and Seth Lochhead, and editor Paul Tothill deliver an exhilarating and innovative action tour-de-force that hits the viewer like a drop kick to the solar plexus from the film's titular heroine.

One of the most admirable things about *Hanna* is its dedication to defying the conventions of the action film genre. Its hero is a sixteen-year-old girl. Although on a mission of deadly revenge she takes time to befriend a family and go out on her first date. As much a coming-of-age story as a revenge thriller, *Hanna* is as interested in its protagonist's development as a person as it is in her kung fu-ing the bad guys. And, unlike most contemporary action films which view plot as an unavoidable necessity, a skeleton to hang the action on, the more basic and quickly dispensed with the better, *Hanna*'s plot is rich, intriguing and disturbing.

Hanna (Saoirse Ronan) has lived her entire life in uninhabited Finnish wilderness with her father, Erik, (Eric Bana) and has had no contact with the outside world since her birth. Their lives are quite primitive and the film opens with Hanna in bear skins stalking a deer with a bow and arrow. She dispatches the deer and then defends herself as her father abruptly appears and attacks her. This attack is a routine part of her existence as her father has been training her since birth for a single mission: to kill a woman named Marissa. He has done his work well. Although only sixteen, she is a master of hand-to-hand combat, long bows and firearms. On the downside, she does not know what electricity is and has never interacted with another human being other than her father. What would seem on the surface to be both insanity and unforgivable child abuse are necessary protective measures for when Hanna eventually joins the rest of the world, Marissa will become aware of her existence and do everything in her considerable power to kill her. The why of this is one of *Hanna*'s intriguing mysteries.

A chest in Hanna and Erik's home contains a homing device. Once Hanna flips its switch, Marissa and her agents will come. This confronts Hanna and the viewer with an intriguing dilemma. Is it preferable to live an isolated, primitive life of safety or in a modern world full of people, possibilities and extreme danger? For Hanna, as with all children, the outside world eventually becomes too tempting to resist and she activates the device, alerting Marissa to her existence.

Marissa is played to sinister perfection by Cate Blanchett, one of the finest actors working today. Blanchett (having a great time) invests Marissa with a Texas twang, a taste for immaculately tailored business suits, and the sweaty ruthlessness of a thoroughly psychopathic government operative trying to cover her tracks through any means necessary. If these means include torturing an entire family, murdering a teenage girl and shooting a grandmother in the back of the head, well, a girl's gotta do what a girl's gotta do. Marissa is aided in her bloody work by a former associate, Issacs (Tom Hollander), a demented sadist who runs a grotesque burlesque when he isn't murdering people. With his effeminate demeanor, bulbous frame, swollen lips, and jolly whistling (he literally whistles while he works, twirling a bloody crowbar like Fred Astaire twirling a cane) Hollander resembles Peter Lorre's child murderer from *M* (1931) channeling Hannibal Lecter. Marissa and Issacs are a pair of perverted scumbags for the ages, and it is a delight to see Blanchett and Hollander getting to go over-the-top and beyond with them while simultaneously wishing heartily for their speedy and fatal comeuppances.

After she triggers the homing device, Hanna and her father's stories diverge into two games of cat and mouse: Marissa, Isaacs, and their goons pursue Hanna while Erik pursues Marissa. When these characters inevitably come into contact, they clash in breathtaking action scenes which are the key reason to see the film. Early in the film, Hanna is captured by Marissa's agents and brought to an enormous and elaborate government facility in the American desert. Wright pours on the suspense as the viewer waits for Hanna, like a tightly coiled spring, to explode. When she does, she does so in spectacular fashion, killing an interrogator that Blanchett has sent in with her bare hands, flipping over the table to kill her armed guard and then spinning 360 degrees to shoot out the cameras that ring the circular room she is being held in, each camera blinking out as she pulls the trigger. Her escape from the facility is equally exciting, propelled by lightening quick edits and a pumping original soundtrack from the Chemical Brothers. Erik's storyline features an equally great scene in a parking garage when half a dozen agents try to take him out that is a masterpiece of choreography and direction. And when both father and daughter have their separate confrontations with Marissa, these scenes crackle with suspense and unpredictability (and in the case of Hanna's confrontation, a thrilling, slam-bang ending). *Hanna* features some of the best editing of any film in 2011 and Wright and Tothill pull off the impressive feat of making fist fights and shootouts, activities exhaustively depicted in film for over a century, fresh and exciting.

Hanna's charms are not confined simply to its amazing action, however. Contrasted against the monstrosity of Marissa and her evil minions is the innocence of the gentle family that takes Hanna in after she escapes from the facility. The film's best sequence does not involve shooting or stabbing but rather Hanna gazing longingly at the family in slow motion as Bowie's "Kooks" plays on the soundtrack. This haunting scene underscores the unconventionality of *Hanna* that makes it so memorable and even moving.

One one-hundredth of the people who saw *Transformers: Dark of the Moon* saw *Hanna*. That is a shame. With one one-hundredth of the budget of *Transformers*, *Hanna* delivers an action film experience with a thousand percent more imagination and emotional resonance. *Hanna* is one of the best and surprisingly affecting action films of 2011.

Nate Vercauteren

CREDITS

Hanna: Saoirse Ronan
Marissa Wiegler: Cate Blanchett
Erik Heller: Eric Bana
Isaacs: Tom Hollander
Johanna Zadek: Vicky Krieps
Origin: USA
Language: English
Released: 2011
Production: Marty Adelstein, Leslie Holleran, Scott Nemes; Ardustry Entertainment, Marty Adelstein Productions, Studio Babelsberg; released by Focus Features Intl.
Directed by: Joe Wright
Written by: Joe Wright, Joe Penhall, Seth Lockhead, David Farr
Cinematography by: Alwin Kuchler
Music by: Tom Rowlands, Ed Simons
Sound: Christopher Scarabosio
Music Supervisor: Ahmed Al-Ibrahim
Editing: Paul Tothill
Art Direction: Niall Moroney
Costumes: Lucie Bates
Production Design: Sarah Greenwood
MPAA rating: PG-13
Running time: 111 minutes

REVIEWS

Burr, Ty. *Boston Globe*. April 7, 2011.
Chang, Justin. *Variety*. March 30, 2011.
Dargis, Manohla. *New York Times*. April 7, 2011.
Ebert, Roger. *Chicago Sun-Times*. April 6, 2011.
Edelstein, David. *New York Magazine*. April 11, 2011.

Hynes, Eric. *Village Voice*. April 5, 2011.
O'Sullivan, Michael. *Washington Post*. April 7, 2011.
Rea, Steven. *Philadelphia Inquirer*. April 7, 2011.
Savloc, Marc. *Austin Chronicle*. April 5, 2011.
Tobias, Scott. *AV Club*. April 7, 2011.

QUOTES

Hanna: "I just missed your heart."

TRIVIA

According to Joe Wright, it was Saoirse Ronan who requested that the studio bring him on to direct the film.

HAPPY FEET TWO

Every step counts.
    —Movie tagline

Box Office: $63.9 million

With a resume as eclectic as any of his contemporaries, George Miller still remains a name that is often not checked off when film scholars compile their lists of the greats. Maybe because the best of his work is remembered with such fondness that film fans forget he actually only has seven feature films under his directing belt, not including his well-regarded short contribution to *Twilight Zone: The Movie* (1983). Those titles include his acclaimed debut, *Mad Max* (1979), and its follow-ups, along with *The Witches of Eastwick* (1987) and *Lorenzo's Oil* (1992). His role of co-writer and producer of the talking pig, *Babe* (1995)—which garnered seven Academy Award® nominations including Best Picture—led to Miller helming the sequel, *Babe: Pig In The City* (1998), that while widely praised became one of that year's more notorious box office failures. It took eight years for the director to take up the chair again with *Happy Feet* (2006), an animated feature that led to an Oscar® in that very category. Success breeds a necessity for more success though and the studio was wise enough to bring Miller back for a second go-round with the dancing penguins. Never one to rest on his creative instincts, however, Miller has again not just spun the same wheels for audience and financial expectations, and may have just cemented himself in the cinema books with a title all his own.

The hero from the first film, Mumble (voiced by Elijah Wood), is now happily together with his mate, Gloria (Alecia "Pink" Moore). Their young son, Erik (Ava Acres), is not quite as happy. His dancing skills are not up to par with the rest of the penguins in Emperor-Land and he goes off in search of his true purpose. Led by family friend, Ramon (Robin Williams) back to Adelie-Land, they are introduced to Sven (Hank Azaria) who has inspired penguin nation with his ability to fly. While Ramon is skeptical—given the whole physiological nature of their kind—Erik takes to Sven's words of encouragement and believes himself to now be capable of anything.

Meanwhile, a pair of Krill are having their own existential crisis. Will (Brad Pitt) has strayed from the swarm in the hopes of moving up the food chain, but his pal Bill (Matt Damon) would rather stick with the master plan and stay out of immediate danger. Their adventure will eventually cross paths with Mumble, who while in search of his son, is thrust into the role of reluctant hero again and again. First, when Bryan the Beach Master (Richard Carter), an elephant seal with self-image issues becomes trapped in a glacier crevice. Then an ever greater dilemma is created when the changing landscape traps nearly everyone in Emperor-Land with a diminished food supply and no foreseeable way out.

The *Happy Feet* films have been sold to audiences as lively musical spectacles with an emphasis on the penguin equivalent of a flash mob bursting out into spontaneous in-step choreography. Come for the singing and dancing, but then stay for ideas more profound. Again, on the surface, both films are structured around a very simple hero's journey. Mumble and his son found themselves as outcasts amidst a species who had all discovered their voice and stepped in line for the natural order. Their unique talents led them into the accompaniment of false prophets and "aliens" willing to exploit them for their own amusement and agendas. Ultimately, it was Miller's unique climax to the original that has set the tone for the greenlighters who may still be unaware of precisely what the director has accomplished. When he last left Mumble years ago, he had been captured by humans and imprisoned in a zoo for the entertainment of on-lookers still on a high from the Oscar®-winning documentary, *March of the Penguins* (2003).

Sven is a very different breed from his penguin publicist, Lovelace (also voiced by Robin Williams), the guru penguin featured in the original who professed the existence of entities beyond the humans. Each of them preached a similar implication, but Sven, while well-intentioned, is a purveyor of artificial optimism; a dangerous message sent to those resigned to their own helplessness. It may sound like Gandhi's "being the change you wish to see in the world," but it is a self-aggrandizing expectation for Erik and others to believe that very world has a plan to help the individual over the community. When Sven's true believers become backed into a literal corner of that world, there is a disturbing turn as the penguins' unawareness of their own limitations becomes a desperate attempt to live up to those very beliefs. It is a brave, stunning moment for the characters as well as for the real-life aliens behind their very existence who are all too aware that the circle of life is not all singing and dancing.

Where there is life though, there is hope, and *Happy Feet Two* stresses an ever more powerful message for kids in how all manners of a society must work together to achieve an ultimate goal. Relying on the hope and change that a single black-and-white penguin can provide may provide temporary relief, but it is the strength in numbers that can produce results and true optimism. Beach Master Bryan is a classic representation of those in power more concerned with maintaining an image for their own kind rather than venturing out to work for the common good. Will the Krill's determination to break from the swarm turns from an egocentric quest into an altruistic discovery that a single organism can change the world by becoming a leader rather than a follower. Finally, when all else seems lost, honoring Earth father in song to help save Mother Earth, is enough to inspire anyone. Especially when such a strong voice can produce a *Phantom of the Opera*-inspired aria from the smallest of mouths.

Happy Feet Two is the best kind of family movie, full of adorable funny protagonists in a rich, brilliantly-designed landscape that also touches upon deeper emotions and ideas for those capable of looking beyond the bright colors. One could absolutely walk into it with no fore knowledge of the first film and the backgrounds of the characters and still walk out with more food for thought than almost any original effort coming out of Hollywood these days. George Miller only has eight full-length features under his belt and remarkably, four of them are sequels. *The Road Warrior* (1981), *Mad Max Beyond Thunderdome, Babe: Pig in the City,* and, now, *Happy Feet Two,* all with more than just cheap product with name recognition. They are a continuation of inspiration that should find themselves on lists of the finest follow-ups ever made. As his latest draws to its climactic rallying cry, a familiar beat begins that should resonate with the elders in the audience. A pause may develop in their initial foot-tapping and thumb-snapping as they await for the lyrics to begin, unsure if they are being duped into the cheap imitation of a one-hit wonder whose title of *Ice Ice Baby* seems like an appropriate, if overtly obvious, fit to the film's setting. Alas, it turns into a cause for celebration as the anthem turns into the even more apropos David Bowie & Queen ditty, *Under Pressure,* uniting the audience into a tear-jerking finale set to the music of a time before those, unlike George Miller, believed that adapting meant just changing a few words and keeping the same rhythm.

Erik Childress

CREDITS

Mumbles: Elijah Wood (Voice)
Erik: Elizabeth Daily (Voice)
The Mighty Sven: Hank Azaria (Voice)
Ramon/Lovelace: Robin Williams (Voice)
Bad Bill: Ray Winstone (Voice)
Carmen: Sofia Vergara (Voice)
Noah: Hugo Weaving (Voice)
Gloria: Pink (Voice)
Will the Krill: Brad Pitt (Voice)
Bill the Krill: Matt Damon (Voice)
Origin: USA
Language: English
Released: 2011
Production: Doug Mitchell, George Miller, Bill Miller; Dr. D. Studios, Village Roadshow Pictures; released by Warner Bros.
Directed by: George Miller
Written by: George Miller, Gary Eck, Warren Coleman, Paul Livingston
Cinematography by: David Peers, David Dulac
Music by: John Powell
Sound: Wayne Pashley
Music Supervisor: Kim Green
Editing: Christian Gazal
Art Direction: David Nelson
MPAA rating: PG
Running time: 100 minutes

REVIEWS

Anderson, Jeffrey M. *Combustible Celluloid.* November 28, 2011.
Dargis, Manohla. *New York Times.* November 17, 2011.
Ebert, Roger. *Chicago Sun-Times.* November 17, 2011.
Goss, William. *Film.com.* November 18, 2011.
Levin, Robert. *Film School Rejects.* November 18, 2011.
Lybarger, Dan. *Moviemaker Magazine.* November 19, 2011.
McCarthy, Todd. *Hollywood Reporter.* November 18, 2011.
Phillips, Michael. *Chicago Tribune.* November 17, 2011.
Rocchi, James. *MSN Movies.* November 17, 2011.
Snider, Eric D. *EricDSnider.com.* November 19, 2011.

QUOTES

The Mighty Sven: "If you want it, you must will it. If you will it, it will be yours."

TRIVIA

Was delivered to theaters using the code name "Cold Package."

HAPPYTHANKYOUMOREPLEASE

Go get yourself loved.
—Movie tagline

Sitcom success typically affords its actors opportunities to parlay their small-screen recognition into hiatus passion-projects for the big screen. That was the case for Zach Braff with *Garden State* (2004), his directorial debut, and Jason Segel stepped out of the shadow of the Emmy®-nominated *How I Met Your Mother* with the raunchy, rangy *Forgetting Sarah Marshall* (2008), a semi-autobiographical comedy which he wrote and starred in. The same is the case with Segel's sitcom colleague Josh Radnor, who pulls multi-hyphenate duty in *Happythankyoumoreplease,* an unexceptional modern-day dramedy about a group of New York City friends.

Drawing heavily upon the chatty big-city ensembles of Ed Burns, Nichole Holofcener and others, but with a decided paucity of spark or memorable wit, Radnor's feature debut as both a writer and director demonstrates a nice touch with actors but little else to suggest the budding promise of a new auteur. After premiering to mixed reviews at the Sundance Film Festival in 2010, *Happythankyoumoreplease* received a cursory 2011 theatrical release via distributor Anchor Bay, grossing under $250,000 in an eight-week spring engagement before hitting DVD less than two months after closing.

On the way to an important meeting regarding his recently-completed work, aspiring novelist Sam Wexler (Radnor) runs into a young boy named Rasheen (Michael Algieri), who gets separated from his guardian on the subway. Upon finding out he is a product of the foster care system, Sam keeps Rasheen at his apartment and goes about his business for the rest of the week, including wooing Mississippi (Kate Mara), a cute bar hostess and would-be singer.

Intercut and occasionally overlapping with this story are the travails of two of Sam's best female friends. Annie (Malin Akerman), bald due a medical condition, attempts to escape the libidinal orbit of her ex-boyfriend, a sleazy rock 'n' roll bassist named Ira (Peter Scanavino), while slowly contemplating an unlikely romance with a coworker also named Sam (Tony Hale). Meanwhile, Mary-Catherine (Zoe Kazan) finds her relationship with longtime boyfriend Charlie (Pablo Schreiber) upset by the talk of a potential move to Los Angeles, which Mary-Catherine abhors.

Happythankyoumoreplease seemingly aims for some sort of generational statement, but only by way of the incidental fact that its characters are thirtysomethings contemplating life changes, as otherwise its dramatic conflicts are trite and its corresponding insights shallow. Notably, using a black child as a type of trigger and impetus for Sam's personal awakening feels like a particularly feeble and ill-considered socio-cultural marker, the sort of which many comedians rightly lampoon as condescendingly indicative of a well-meaning liberal's white guilt. That Radnor seems aware of this potential criticism (he pointedly includes a line

from Mary-Catherine addressing this fact) does not mean that it is in any way, shape or form adequately resolved. It is virtually inconceivable that anyone of sound mind would, under the guise of helping him or her, keep a lost kid without notifying other adults, but there Sam is, saying, "I don't know what else to do," and improbably succumbing—for no convincing reason other than narrative handiness—to Rasheen's plaintive stares when he makes a nominal effort to drop him off at a social services office.

Starting with this ridiculousness and moving forward, Radnor's movie seems to exist chiefly as a collection of poses and gimmicks. Annie has an Alopecia Awareness Party, which would seem a strange thing for an adult with a lifelong condition to do. Sam, meanwhile, gets drunk with Mississippi and proposes that instead of a one-night stand they have a three-night stand, meaning that she move in with him for three days. Mississippi is also far too flirty and accessible, especially for a small town transplant who is ostensibly trying to make her way in the hard-knock music business. Radnor attempts to mitigate the impracticable nature of this relationship by tossing in a few lines about how they are both "damaged," but it is a risible and unsatisfactory fix. As with virtually all the films of Eric Schaeffer, the main motivation here seems to be to give the actor-writer-director an excuse to kiss an attractive woman.

Radnor, who physically resembles the theoretical offspring of Jimmy Fallon and Keanu Reeves, has a charisma that does not translate especially well to the more relaxed rhythms of feature films. He is the wrong actor around which to build a film, and feels almost like the accidental star of his own movie—a matter not helped by the fact that Sam's professional strivings are essentially abandoned early in the first act.

Still, despite its general narrative failings and lack of engagement, Radnor somewhat acquits himself as a filmmaker. The movie evinces an impressive technical package for a low-budget debut feature—especially that of an actor turned director, where a coherent visual scheme is usually last on the long to-do list. Cinematographer Seamus Tierney conjures up a believable mood of charged possibility amidst a jumble of discrete locations, while costume designer Sarah Beers comes up with nice, smart looks that inform the characters' personalities, especially for Annie and Mary-Catherine.

Radnor also proves himself capable of working with other actors, as the movie in its third act delivers two emotionally robust sequences somewhat out of left field—Mary-Catherine sharing news of a possible pregnancy with Charlie, and Sam making a pitch to Annie that he can love her. Each of these scenes features one of *Happythankyoumoreplease*'s standouts. Hale, so comedically adroit on *Arrested Development,* finds nice nuance in the relative normalcy of his character. The real revelation, though, is the cherubic, 28-year-old Kazan. She has already had arresting lead turns in smaller films like *The Exploding Girl* (2010), but the ensemble nature of a movie like this really helps cast Kazan's superstar quality in starker relief. She is ever-present, and so smart and specific with her choices that the emotional weight and drive of her character overshadows Radnor's by far, and almost the rest of the entire movie. One would be happy, and say, "Thank you" for more of Mary-Catherine, if only they could slip off with her, into another film.

Brent Simon

CREDITS

Sam Wexler: Josh Radnor
Annie: Malin Akerman
Mary Catherine: Zoe Kazan
Rasheen: Michael Algieri
Charlie: Pablo Schreiber
Sam No. 2: Tony Hale
Mississippi: Kate Mara
Origin: USA
Language: English
Released: 2010
Production: Jesse Hara, Austin Clark; Paper Street Films; released by Anchor Bay Entertainment
Directed by: Josh Radnor
Written by: Josh Radnor
Cinematography by: Seamus Tierney
Music by: Jaymay
Sound: Michael Sterkin
Music Supervisor: Andy Gowen
Editing: Michael R. Miller
Costumes: Sarah Beers
Art Direction: Chris Trujillo
Production Design: Jade Healy
MPAA rating: R
Running time: 100 minutes

REVIEWS

Anderson, John. *Variety.* January 26, 2010.
Childress, Erik. *eFilmCritic.com.* January 31, 2010.
Grierson, Tim. *Screen International.* January 26, 2010.
Honeycutt, Kirk. *Hollywood Reporter.* January 26, 2010.
LaSalle, Mick. *San Francisco Chronicle.* March 10, 2011.
Mitchell, Elvis. *Movieline.* March 9, 2011.
O'Hehir, Andrew. *Salon.com.* March 4, 2011.
Rickey, Carrie. *Philadelphia Inquirer.* March 17, 2011.
Schwarzbaum, Lisa. *Entertainment Weekly.* March 2, 2011.
Tallerico, Brian. *HollywoodChicago.com.* March 11, 2011.

QUOTES

Annie: "Sadness be gone, let's be people who deserve to be loved, who are worthy, cause we are worthy."

TRIVIA

Even though Mary Catherine discovers she's pregnant during the film, it is never mentioned by her out loud. The only time she says anything about it, it is whispered an inaudible.

HARRY POTTER AND THE DEATHLY HALLOWS: PART 2

It all ends.
        —Movie tagline

Box Office: $381 million

The year 2011 saw the end of a movie franchise that was unlike any other. The *Harry Potter* movies have not only broken box office records during their ten-year run, but they have maintained a level of style, dignity and sophistication that only got stronger as the series went on. Several franchises during this time have come and gone, been rebooted or "re-imagined" and have fizzled after only two or three outings. But the team behind the *Potter* films managed to promise its audience the goods and, for the most part, they have always delivered on that promise. The series may have started out a bit shaky with the first two Chris Columbus-helmed films, but Columbus himself deserves a lot of credit for stepping down and bringing in a new fresh voice for the third chapter (*Harry Potter and the Prisoner of Azkaban* [2004], directed by Alfonso Cuaron) and from there, the series never looked back.

The most curious addition on the whole enterprise was that of director David Yates. With only some mini-series television work and a few small movies (most notably, the subtle and moving *The Girl in the Cafe* [2005]) to his credit, the choice was made to hand this unlikely candidate the rest of the *Potter* franchise. While many criticized the adaptation of *Harry Potter and the Order of the Phoenix* (2007) (the only Potter film not written for the screen by Steve Kloves), there was little doubt that Yates had the right sensibility for the project and the rest of the series. In hindsight, the choice makes perfect sense. Much of Yates' previous experience had been in miniseries form. He knows how to take characters and explore them over a long period of time.

Harry Potter and the Deathly Hallows: Part 2, the second half of a single-book adaptation, is as much a character study as anything else Yates has done. This film is not so much about Harry Potter (Daniel Radcliffe) or even Voldemort (Ralph Fiennes), but about Severus Snape (Alan Rickman), the cunning, monotone headmaster of Hogwarts' Slytherin house. When he was last seen in *Harry Potter and the Half-Blood Prince* (2009), he gave little doubt about his true allegiance when he ended up killing one of the most major characters in the series (Dumbledore). Here, the film opens with Snape looking down at what Hogwarts has become now that the dark Lord Voldemort has taken over: A joyless institution with students marching forlornly in unison with no sense of individuality. What could Snape be thinking?

The film gradually reveals Snape's motivations, his past deeds, his relationship with both of Harry's parents, and his standing with both Voldemort and headmaster Albus Dumbledore (Michael Gambon). His story becomes clearer, richer, and provides the series with one of its most emotionally heartbreaking moments (which is really saying something considering how many important, valiant characters have been killed off). Finally, the film ends (and this is not a giveaway) with Snape earning what he had always wanted: Recognition.

Of course, the film is also about Harry Potter, Ron Weasley (Rupert Grint), and Hermione Granger (Emma Watson) searching for the remaining Horcruxes (pieces of Voldemort's soul spread amongst several objects), which are scattered throughout England and/or Hogwarts. Their search began in *Harry Potter and the Deathly Hollows: Part 1*, perhaps the most grim and certainly the most melancholy of all the *Potter* films. At the start of *Part 2,* they have succeeded in finding and destroying two, with five more to go. Their search eventually leads them back to Gringott's Wizarding Bank where Harry was first shown how much money he really had (this was in *Harry Potter and the Sorcerer's Stone* [2001]).

The quest eventually brings the three main characters to Hogwarts where many of the supporting Hogwarts student characters from previous films have to keep together and out of the watchful eyes of Snape and any other headmaster working for Voldemort. Harry, Ron and Hermione tunnel under with help from Neville Longbottom (Matthew Lewis) and are greeted with applause and adulation from all his peers who wondered whether or not he was even alive. Harry informs them that they need to find an item in the Ravenclaw House, except he has no idea what it could be or where to find it.

With the help of fellow student Luna Lovegood (Evanna Lynch), Harry is put on the right path and is soon getting more help from the ghost Helena Ravenclaw (Kelly MacDonald). While Harry, Ron and Hermione search the school for Horcruxes, swords, and items from the Deathly Hollows (items which can help one achieve immortality), the entire school, led by Professor Minerva McGonagall (Maggie Smith), braces and prepares for battle against Voldemort and his army, who have just received word that Harry Potter is alive and well and in this school. Of course, during his search, Harry eventually encounters his boyhood nemesis Draco Malfoy (Tom Felton), a confrontation with a surprising conclusion.

By splitting J.K. Rowling's final book into two parts, Yates and screenwriter Kloves have the chance to let scenes breathe a little more, while still condensing moments in the book that went on a bit too long. All the right cuts were made. The final third of the film is the film's biggest improvement over the source material. The confrontation between Harry and Voldemort is not a spectator's sport this time as Harry explains to onlookers why Voldemort has no chance at winning. In the film, everyone at Hogwarts is attending to a deceased or injured loved one or trying to stay out of harm's way. Harry and Voldemort fight alone. When Harry returns from battle, he is not greeted with cheers and adulation as he was in the book. He is all but ignored by everyone. Not out of spite, but probably because with so much tragedy around, sometimes it takes time before things start looking pretty good again.

Deathly Hollows: Part 2 is the eighth theatrical release in the series. Many would argue that when joined with *Part 1* it is one singular film. It is no surprise to find than that much of the film works as one long, two-hour final act in which the stakes are at their highest and the action is revved up several notches. Where *Part 1* was morose and brooding (in a good way), *Part 2* often feels more like an Indiana Jones movie than a traditional *Harry Potter* film. The action set pieces are just as intense and inspired. It never feels bloated or drawn out. There is no "action for action's sake" here. There is plenty of time to breathe and catch up on where the characters are at and what they discover.

The arrival of *Deathly Hollows: Part 2* was a bittersweet moment for its fanbase and it is worth noting the uniqueness of this particular group of fans, particularly those who were Harry's age when the film series began. The Potter books and films have grown more sophisticated as its fans have gotten older. For those who have grown alongside the characters and actors who played them, it signifies the end of an era, perhaps the end of one's own youth. There was a collective feeling of "what now?" when this final film was released. The arrival of a new Harry Potter movie every year or so was like comfort food to which one could always look forward.

When revisited, from the very beginning to the very end, it becomes clearer that having a director such as Chris Columbus take on the first two films was actually the right choice, even though his films are often thought of as the weakest. Known primarily for innocuous populist entertainment with nary a trace of vision or style, Columbus is just the right sensibility for Harry Potter and friends as children. Alfonso Cuaron came just in the nick of time, though, with *Harry Potter and the Prisoner of Azkaban,* giving the Potter world a new look (more worn, less polished). Mike Newell, also known for making simplistic romantic comedies, finally brought a British touch to the series with *Harry Potter and the Goblet of Fire* (2005). Finally, Yates pushed *Potter* into adulthood and the series came to a graceful and satisfying conclusion.

But still, "now what?" The Harry Potter series—in book and film form—will likely remain timeless and shared with every passing generation, just as the *Star Wars* saga still is today. From the late nineties to the mid-'00s, the books changed the face of literature. Before their release, kids were not known to wait in line at midnight for a chapter book. The success of the films spawned countless forgettable imitators. *Harry Potter and the Deathly Hallows: Part 2* does not wallow in its finale, nor does it indulge in nostalgia. It ends just as the book did: With a coda which proposes that, yes, there could be more adventures at Hogwarts, but after such a long, meaningful journey, why spoil it?

Collin Souter

CREDITS

Harry Potter: Daniel Radcliffe
Lord Voldemort: Ralph Fiennes
Hermione Granger: Emma Watson
Ron Weasley: Rupert Grint
Rubeus Hagrid: Robbie Coltrane
Beatrix Lestrange: Helena Bonham Carter
Albus Dumbledore: Michael Gambon
Lucas Malfoy: Jason Issacs
Draco Malfoy: Tom Felton
Severus Snape: Alan Rickman
Remus Lupin: David Thewlis
Sirius Black: Gary Oldman
Aberforth Dumbledore: Ciaran Hinds

Filius Flitwick: Warwick Davis
Sybill Trelawney: Emma Thompson
Mr. Ollivander: John Hurt
Rufus Scrimgeour: Bill Nighy
Minerva McGonagall: Maggie Smith
Ginny Weasley: Bonnie Wright
Narcissa Malfoy: Helen McCrory
Origin: United Kingdom
Language: English
Released: 2011
Production: David Barron, David Heyman, J.K. Rowling; Heyday Films, Moving Pictures Company Ltd.
Directed by: David Yates
Written by: Steve Kloves
Cinematography by: Eduardo Serra
Music by: Alexandre Desplat
Sound: Stuart Wilson
Editing: Mark Day
Art Direction: Neil Lamont
Costumes: Jany Temime
Production Design: Stuart Craig
MPAA rating: PG-13
Running time: 131 minutes

REVIEWS

Burr, Ty. *Boston Globe.* July 13, 2011.
Childress, Erik. *eFilmcritic.com.* July 13, 2011.
Covert, Colin. *Minneapolis Star Tribune.* July 14, 2011.
Denby, David. *New Yorker.* July 15, 2011.
Ebert, Roger. *Chicago Sun-Times.* July 13, 2011.
Howell, Peter. *Toronto Star.* July 14, 2011.
Kennedy, Lisa. *Denver Post.* July 15, 2011.
Lumenick, Lou. *New York Post.* July 12, 2011.
Morgenstern, Joe. *Wall Street Journal.* July 14, 2011.
Turan, Kenneth. *Los Angeles Times.* July 13, 2011.

QUOTES

Harry Potter: "I never wanted any of you to die for me."

TRIVIA

Kate Winslet was reportedly offered the role of Helena Ravenclaw but her agent rejected the offer before she was able to consider it, believing that Winslet would not want to "follow suit with every other actor in Britain by being a part of Harry Potter."

AWARDS

British Acad. 2011: Visual FX
Screen Actors Guild 2011: Stunt Ensemble
Nomination:
Oscars 2011: Art Dir./Set Dec., Makeup, Visual FX
British Acad. 2011: Makeup, Sound, Prod. Des.

THE HELP

Change begins with a whisper.
—Movie tagline

Box Office: $169.7 million

At the beginning of *The Help*, Aibileen (Viola Davis), a black maid working in Jackson, Mississippi, gets asked if she ever wanted to do anything else with her life. She nods. She does not expound on any childhood dreams that fell by the wayside over the years, and as the silence surrounding her answer grows, so too does the realization that it does not matter what she would have rather done with her life, this was her only future. From the time she was fourteen years old, Aibileen has been working for white society ladies, cleaning their homes, preparing their meals, and raising their children. But now, something in Aibileen is breaking. The year is 1962 and a feeling of unrest has come to Jackson. Aibileen calls it a "bitter seed," planted in her by the untimely death of her son. To others watching, this seed is really the initial throes of the civil rights movement.

Just as the first African-American student, James Meredith, enrolls at the University of Mississippi, the fictional Skeeter Phelan (Emma Stone) returns to Jackson with a diploma from Ole Miss and dreams of being a writer. After being told by a New York editor that the only way she will get a break is to write about something that disturbs her, Skeeter decides to compile a selection of interviews with "the help," the maids who work for the women in Skeeter's country club social circle. She starts with Aibileen, who has worked for Skeeter's close friend Elizabeth for years. Because of the bitter seed, Aibileen is ready to talk. *The Help*, which is both the title of the film and the title of the manuscript Skeeter edits, is the story of not only of Skeeter's efforts to compile these testimonials, but also of the relationships between the African-American women who give their lives to the white families that employ them and the white women who run the homes in which they work. Adapted from the bestselling book by Kathryn Stockett, *The Help* is an almost perfect emotional movie full of heart and hope, but while the sparking ensemble cast and terrific performances warm the soul, the Hollywood-ization of the narrative leaves the experience lacking.

Though the novel is told from Aibileen, Minny (Octavia Spencer), another maid working in Jackson, and Skeeter's points of view, screenwriter and director Tate Taylor opted only for Aibileen to provide the voiceover for the film. The idea, no doubt, was to highlight the fact that no matter what, this is her story. But there is little this voiceover does that Viola Davis' astounding performance could not carry on its own. Davis is spellbinding as Aibileen, her calm exterior masking the storm of emotion brewing inside her. Often, the look in Davis' eyes conveys more than the dialogue being spoken as her performance transcends the clichéd screenwriting. The difficulty of her relationship with Elizabeth (Ahna O'Reilly) and Elizabeth's young daughter Mae Mobley (Eleanor & Emma Henry) is both heartbreaking and heartwarming, and Davis delivers an expansive and captivating performance.

To the director's credit, each time a new character is introduced it is as though they have stepped off the page and onto the screen. The pitch-perfect casting has much to do with this, but it is Taylor's ability to coax grounded and layered performances from this set of talented actors that makes *The Help* a stand-out film. As society queen bee Hilly, Bryce Dallas Howard's icy stare is paralyzing, Jessica Chastain as blonde bombshell outcast Celia Foote is right on the money and Sissy Spacek as Hilly's mom is beyond delightful. As Skeeter, Emma Stone strikes a lovely balance of earnest and naive. But it is Davis and Spencer that steal the screen. A ying and yang of personalities, Minny is boisterous where Aibileen is strong and silent. Their friendship is palpable and inspiring.

But time and again, as Aibilene's voice comes over the story, indicating that she is the one guiding the narrative; it is hard not to wonder why the film is spending so much time charting Skeeter's dating life. To his credit, Taylor does not aggrandize Skeeter as the savior of this film. As much as he can, he imbues her with a blinding naivety about the world around her: She asks the wrong questions of the women she interviews and expects honest answers; she does not fully understand why other maids will not help her in her endeavor. And Skeeter's touching relationship with her own maid (Cicely Tyson), the woman who raised her, allows her to stand out as more than just an interested, unfeeling bystander. But for all the emotional connection and the heart that Taylor gives Skeeter, he never really has her realize just how awkward and unjust her world is. In the same vein, he never really hits the same nail-biting tension as Stockett does in her novel (though some might say she never really gets deep enough either). There is a moment in the book where it dawns on the reader that what these maids are doing is illegal in the eyes of Mississippi law and could result in their death were they even found in the same room together. Though Tate has his characters worry about this, and talk about this, and exchange serious looks about this, the atmosphere of the film never reaches the level of fear that would truly get the audience thinking.

In one scene, on the night that Medgar Evers is gunned down in front of his home, Aibileen is forced off a bus by a nervous white driver and has to walk home alone. As she heads in the opposite direction from the police lights, the empty streets take on a menacing feel and she begins to run. Though the characters are fictional, this movie is trying to tell a real story about a real moment from our collective past. This feeling, the feeling of fear and anxiety that exists every time someone is striving for change, should exist for the audience every time Aibileen and Skeeter get together. But the reason it cannot is as much Taylor's doing as it is the result of the Hollywood machine. In Hollywood, Skeeter and Aibilene have to have a true, modern friendship. The film also has to be funny and ideally involve a romance to entice contemporary audiences.

It is not Tate's inability to grasp the gravitas of the subject matter, he tries to provide moments, like the one at the start of the film, for the audience to be challenged. And it is not the inability of the actors to really deliver thought-provoking performances, because they do. The film's flaws are the shortcomings of a movie production system that does not trust audiences to love a film that is challenging. And yet it would take a truly heartless person to not be moved when Aibileen gets to tell Hilly off. But though Skeeter's book makes a difference in the lives of the women she writes about, it is hard not to notice that she is the one who gets the big break, a job in New York, and a new beginning. And though Aibileen gets a personal victory when she sticks it to Hilly, it seems as though the movie is telling viewers not to question why it does not feel as sweet.

Joanna Topor MacKenzie

CREDITS

Aibileen Clark: Viola Davis
Eugenia "Skeeter" Phelan: Emma Stone
Missus Walters: Sissy Spacek
Minny Jackson: Octavia Spencer
Hilly Holbrook: Bryce Dallas Howard
Charlotte Phelan: Allison Janney
Stuart Whitworth: Chris Lowell
Johnny Foote: Mike Vogel
Robert Phelan: Brian Kerwin
Gracie Higginbotham: Dana Ivey
Celia Foote: Jessica Chastain
Constantine Jefferson: Cicely Tyson
Yule Mae Davis: Aunjanue Ellis
Elizabeth Leefolt: Ahna O'Reilly
Origin: USA
Language: English
Released: 2011
Production: Michael Barnathan, Chris Columbus, Brunson Green; DreamWorks SKG, Participant Media, Imagenation Abu Dhabi FZ, 1492 Pictures, Reliance Entertainment
Directed by: Tate Taylor

Written by: Tate Taylor
Cinematography by: Stephen Goldblatt
Music by: Thomas Newman
Music Supervisor: Jennifer Hawks
Editing: Hughes Winborne
Sound: Dennis Drummond
Art Direction: Curt Beech
Costumes: Sharen CQ Davis
Production Design: Mark Ricker
MPAA rating: PG-13
Running time: 137 minutes

REVIEWS

Dargis, Manohla. *New York Times.* August 9, 2011.
Denby, David. *New Yorker.* August 10, 2011.
Gleiberman, Owen. *Entertainment Weekly.* August 10, 2011.
Kennedy, Lisa. *Denver Post.* August 11, 2011.
Longworth, Karina. *Village Voice.* August 9, 2011.
Morgenstern, Joe. *Wall Street Journal.* August 11, 2011.
Phillips, Michael. *Chicago Tribune.* August 9, 2011.
Rickey, Carrie. *Philadelphia Inquirer.* August 9, 2011.
Sachs, Ben. *Chicago Reader.* August 11, 2011.
Stevens, Dana. *Slate.* August 11, 2011.
Zacharek, Stephanie. *Movieline.* August 10, 2011.

QUOTES

Aibileen Clark: "You is kind. You is smart. You is important."

TRIVIA

The book store featured in the film, Avent & Clark Booksellers, was named after Avent Clark, a production assistant on the film.

AWARDS

Oscars 2011: Support. Actress (Spencer)
British Acad. 2011: Support. Actress (Spencer)
Golden Globes 2012: Support. Actress (Spencer)
Screen Actors Guild 2011: Actress (Davis), Support. Actress (Spencer), Cast
Nomination:
Oscars 2011: Actress (Davis), Film, Support. Actress (Chastain)
British Acad. 2011: Actress (Davis), Adapt. Screenplay, Film, Support. Actress (Chastain)
Golden Globes 2012: Actress—Drama (Davis), Film—Drama, Song ("The Living Proof"), Support. Actress (Chastain)
Screen Actors Guild 2011: Support. Actress (Chastain)
Writers Guild 2011: Adapt. Screenplay.

HESHER

Sometimes life gives you the finger and sometimes it gives you...
—Movie tagline

Hesher is a character study about a character who would not last five minutes in a household without someone finally getting fed up and calling the authorities. It is a strange and interesting film, one that does not let such story problems get in the way of its otherwise strong narrative. It can be maddening at times and quite moving as well. It is mostly anchored in the realities of a family that is coming undone by tragedy, but the movie's center is a man who is anything but anchored. He is unlikable, unbelievable and unmerciful in his actions and words. Why any reasonable human being would let this guy sleep in their house or come in contact with their kids is anyone's guess, but *Hesher* tells that story anyway.

The film opens with a 12-year old boy named T.J. (Devin Brochu) riding his bike in pursuit of a beat-up car that is being towed away. This car carries a special significance that will become clearer later. During this pursuit, T.J. gets hit by a car. It is not the last time that this will happen. T.J. takes many beatings from automobiles throughout the story and the metaphor only becomes more potent. One day, in a fit of anger, T.J. throws a brick through the window of what looks like an abandoned home. It is, in fact, the shelter for a long-haired, unkempt man who goes by the name of Hesher (Joseph Gordon-Levitt). This leads to more physical altercations for T.J., who already has a junkyard bully after him at school. Soon, Hesher follows T.J. to school and finally to his house, where Hesher makes himself a new home.

T.J. lives with his father named Paul (Rainn Wilson) and Grandmother (Piper Laurie). It is a household that is coming to grips with the sudden death of T.J.'s mother. Paul takes anti-depressants, has stopped shaving and tries to get T.J. to join him on attending a grief support group. Hesher practically invades this home, mainly because he has nowhere else to go aside from his beat-up black van. He threatens T.J. about calling the police. When Paul comes home and finds Hesher, he is sitting on the couch in nothing but his underwear. He asks T.J., "Who is this?" A nervous T.J. replies "He's a friend of mine. He's washing his clothes." No more questions. Hesher then wonders aloud why they only have four channels on their television. He soon fixes their satellite so they can get more channels, but mainly porn, which he watches while T.J. and his father look on in bewilderment.

Hesher is soon a permanent fixture in the household, much to the delight of their grandmother, who often wonders who will go out for a walk with her in the morning. Hesher insists that T.J. go out with his grandmother "so she don't get raped." "Who would rape a grandmother?" she asks. "People do," he replies. Meanwhile, T.J. gets into another scuffle with the bully and is saved by a grocery store clerk named Nicole (Natalie Portman). T.J. is smitten by her and Hesher eventu-

ally involves himself in this little crush by offering such sage advice as "it's okay to want to poke her." Eventually, T.J., Nicole and Hesher become unlikely friends.

Hesher is exactly the kind of fearless and misanthropic character that actors love to play. Joseph Gordon-Levitt is clearly having a great time throwing himself into the physical and verbal extremities that make up this unusual person. Hesher talks matter-of-factly and openly about the most lewd sexual behavior as if he were talking about fixing a car. There are moments of rage, such as a scene in which he completely trashes his uncle's backyard, but writer/director Spencer Susser never reveals much. There are clues to Hesher's past and they are often spoken by him through metaphors, careful to keep those around him at arm's length.

The best performance in the film, however, comes from young Devon Brochu as T.J. It is a role steeped in sadness and a pent-up anger at everything around him. Brochu never crosses the line into childhood melodrama. It is a character who has seen enough to make him wiser than most adults around him. Rainn Wilson, who has finally been given another chance to give a strong dramatic performance after years of comedic roles, is subtle and believable as a father who knows there are choices to be made regarding getting through the grief process, but who cannot accept that his son wants to make those choices for himself.

The movie pulls off a lot and is worth seeing for the performances, but one thing it cannot do is convince the audience that the characters actually want Hesher around. Everyone seems to just accept this guy even though he does absolutely nothing to make himself acceptable. All he really does in the film is make a mess, talk rudely and wear out his welcome. Yet, nobody calls the police on him. In fact, he is not without someone willing to have sex with him. Look at the scene at the pool. When Hesher starts freaking out and wrecking the place, nobody in the scene gets a little scared or leaves. The script demands that these people care about him and want him around.

That is the hardest element to accept in an otherwise well made movie. Susser clearly empathizes with each of his characters, but Hesher himself is hard to get a hold of. Susser makes the strange choice early in the film to punctuate Hesher's dialogue with heavy metal guitar riffs, making him seem more like a caricature than a person with a soul. Yes, this is an extreme kind of character, but even bigger-than-life characters can have an earthiness to them that makes an audience and, more importantly, the characters on the screen want to invest their time. *Hesher* is most successful when it invests its time in the characters whose names are not on the poster.

Collin Souter

CREDITS

Hesher: Joseph Gordon-Levitt
T.J. Forney: Devin Brochu
Paul Forney: Rainn Wilson
Madeleine Forney: Piper Laurie
Nicole: Natalie Portman
Larry: John Carroll Lynch
Origin: USA
Language: English
Released: 2010
Production: Matthew Weaver, Lucy Cooper, Scott Prisand, Natalie Portman, Spencer Susser; Last Picture Co., Handsomecharlie Films, CatchPlay, DRO Entertainment, Corner Store Entertainment; released by Newmarket Films, Wrekin Hill Entertainment
Directed by: Spencer Susser
Written by: Spencer Susser, David Michod
Cinematography by: Morgan Susser
Music by: Francois Tetaz
Sound: Lee Orloff
Editing: Spencer Susser, Michael McCusker
Art Direction: Charles Varga Jr.
Costumes: April Napier
Production Design: Laura Fox
MPAA rating: R
Running time: 105 minutes

REVIEWS

Burr, Ty. *Boston Globe.* May 12, 2011.
Childress, Erik. *Cinematical,* February 5, 2010.
Ebert, Roger. *Chicago Sun-Times.* May 12, 2011.
Holden, Stephen. *New York Times.* May 12, 2011.
LaSalle, Mick. *San Francisco Chronicle.* May 12, 2011.
Morgenstern, Joe. *Wall Street Journal.* May 13, 2011.
Murphy, Kathleen. *MSN Movies.* May 11, 2011.
Nicholson, Amy. *Box Office Magazine.* January 26, 2010.
Smith, Kyle. *New York Post.* May 13, 2011.
Whitty, Stephen. *Newark Star Ledger.* May 13, 2011.

QUOTES

Mrs. Rosowski: "Life is like walking in the rain…you can hide and take cover or you can just get wet."

TRIVIA

Elephants make several appearances in the film. In one scene, Rainn Wilson's character is watching a TV show about elephants and we hear them in the background, in the scene with the car dealership a large pink elephant can be seen on the roof, and beside t.j's bed there is a figurine of yet another elephant.

HIGHER GROUND

Higher Ground is a nuanced, often moving, and deeply insightful film about a period of American religious history that has, as of yet, gone curiously unexplored in cinema. In her directorial debut, noted actress Vera Farmiga (*The Departed* [2006], *Up in the Air* [2009]), takes the high road, treating the 1970s era Jesus Movement as a place where faith collided with human absurdity to produce many, many worthwhile things and more than a few tragic ones.

Corinne (played as a child by Taissa Farmiga, Vera's sister and star of TV's *American Horror Story,* and later by the director herself) is a freewheeling teenager, desperate to escape the confines of her family and her romance with Ethan (Joshua Leonard) seems like a desirable enough alternative. But when an accident almost takes the life of their infant son she begins to seek out religion. Soon she and her husband have embraced newfound Christian faith in a small gathering of like minded younger people. The journey towards wholeness becomes complicated as culture and tradition collide.

The church seems to have a very limited place for women. Questioning anyone in authority is not encouraged and strange phenomena, like speaking in tongues, though seemingly beautiful and a source of great comfort to some, are just out of reach for Corinne, who begins to question the nature of her faith and faith community. What once seemed fulfilling now seems sparse and empty, especially after problems arise in her marriage. When Annika (Dagmara Dominczyk), a once high-spirited friend in the church is laid low by a paralyzing accident, Corinne finds herself at a crossroads. Leaving behind church and family she discovers an emptiness inside that neither secular or religious culture fills.

Higher Ground is most powerful when it is least strained embracing portrayals of people as they really tend to be rather than shaping characters into types that deliver whatever point the filmmakers wanted to make. The end result rambles a bit, but it does so in the manner of real life, with lots of open endings and questions resulting from the constant friction of spiritual yearnings and mundane realities. In one charming scene, Corinne is drawn into a discussion of the importance of keeping her and her husband's sex life spicy and tries following Annika's suggestion to draw pictures of her husband's privates. In another, viewers watch a group of extremely uncomfortable churchmen listening to a cheesy sex education tape. On the whole, the film is a marvel of awkward openness and loose revelation.

Farmiga is a wonder here, especially when Corinne's faith and intellect collide. Fragile, yet determined, Corinne clings not so much to doubt as to the idea that she must find a way to live beyond a stifling-if-well-meaning cultural expression of dogma. The character is in essence not an atheist, nor even quite an agnostic, but someone whose questions run so deep that they cannot be ignored or suppressed, even for the sake of human community. The sense of retreat is palpable but so is the sense that, given time, Corinne may well work this out and find a way to embrace the spirituality inherent in her journey.

That Farmiga can give such a powerful performance in the midst of directing the film, shows her to be what her most devoted supporters have always known she was: an actress of uncommon ability. Her directing skills show some choices that betray the unpracticed eye of a newbie, but, on the whole, this is a film that attempts to deal with the serious subject of spiritual longing without resorting to cliché or melodrama. In the best moments it has to offer, *Higher Ground* will take viewers on a virtual emotional tour of what has happened to the Jesus Movement itself. Characters splinter off into all sorts of theological and philosophical directions. Yet there is a sense that it is far from bankrupt, just not the exact path for everyone.

Special mention should be given to the performance of Dagmara Dominczyk as she brings a carefree sense of genuine *joi de vivre* to her role. Annika is no empty-headed doormat. She is a woman of conviction who pursues her role in the church with an optimistic open-minded zeal. She is an agent of change. Joshua Leonard too, makes the most of his role as Ethan, the would-be rock-n-roller-turned-Christian and family man. At one point, Ethan violently attacks Corinne only to collapse with regret shortly after. Through it all, Leonard manages to keep his character sympathetic and complex, despite the simplicity of thought Ethan is surrendered to.

Higher Ground had trouble finding an audience, partially because it refuses to pander to either those who seek an easy way out of spiritual unease or those who blissfully ignore life's biggest questions. By giving viewers a portrait of someone on the edge, the film encourages those on both sides towards an honest appraisal of belief, doubt, and the struggles common to anyone who has wrestled with religious conviction.

Dave Canfield

CREDITS

Corinne Walker: Vera Farmiga
Annika: Dagmara Dominczyk
Ethan Walker: Joshua Leonard
CW: John Hawkes
Mark: Ebon Moss-Bachrach
Pastor Bud: Bill Irwin
Bill: Norbert Lee Butz
Kathleen: Donna Murphy

Young Corinne: Taissa Farmiga
Wendy: Nina Arianda
Young Ethan: Boyd Holbrook
Origin: USA
Language: English
Released: 2011
Production: Claude Dal Farra, Renn Hawkey, Carly Hugo, Matthew Parker, Jon Rubinstein; BCDF Pictures, Group Entertainment, Ruminant Films; released by Sony Pictures Classics
Directed by: Vera Farmiga
Written by: Tim Metcalfe, Carolyn S. Briggs
Cinematography by: Michael McDonough
Music by: Alec Puro
Sound: James Demer
Music Supervisor: Levon Broussalian
Editing: Colleen Sharp
Art Direction: Lisa Myers, Shawn Carroll
Costumes: Amela Baksic
Production Design: Sharon Lomofsky
MPAA rating: R
Running time: 109 minutes

REVIEWS

Clifford, Laura. *Reeling Reviews.* August 26, 2011.
Ebert, Roger. *Chicago Sun-Times.* September 1, 2011.
Greene, Ray. *Boxoffice Magazine.* August 24, 2011.
Honeycutt, Kirk. *Hollywood Reporter.* January 25, 2011.
Lasalle, Mick. *San Fransisco Chronicle.* September 1, 2011.
Lumenick, Lou. *New York Post.* August 26, 2011.
Orange, Michelle. *Movieline.* August 25, 2011.
Robinson, Tasha. *AV Club.* August 25, 2011.
Scott, A.O. *New York Times.* August 25, 2011.
Snider, Eric D. *ErciDSnider.com.* August 24, 2011.

HOBO WITH A SHOTGUN

Delivering justice, one shell at a time...
—Movie tagline

In 2007, just before Quentin Tarantino and Robert Rodriguez were looking to re-introduce audiences to the exploitation cinema of the grindhouse era, a contest was started. Sponsored by the South by Southwest Film Festival, it was a chance for aspiring filmmakers to make their own version of a trailer that would fit right in with the genre steeped in revenge, bullets and wild, bloody mayhem. The winner was Jason Eisener, whose two-minute fake preview wowed the award show audience and became a YouTube sensation. Everyone who saw it wanted to see that goofy flick. A few years later, after another sparkling short film involving killer Christmas trees, Eisener got the chance to add another 80 minutes to *Hobo with a Shotgun*. Those who dabble in occasional excesses may remember the advice of another after-hours combatant in *Fight Club* (1999) who told viewers that one "can drink a pint of blood before you get sick." Eisener's trailer was the pint. His feature is a couple gallons.

Cult icon Rutger Hauer plays the unnamed hobo who arrives by train into the graffiti-renamed Scumtown. Though the palettes shine like Technicolor, the streets are paved with the homeless, those who would take advantage of them, and the roving psychos spawned literally by the crime boss known as The Drake (Brian Downey). His sons, Slick (Gregory Smith) and Ivan (Nick Bateman), delight in decapitating their own uncle while a bikini-clad streetwalker dances in the fountain of blood leftover. This is none of the hobo's business. Tired as he is, he just wants to save enough coins to buy a lawnmower and start a business that could earn him the green paper en route to a better life.

That is before he sees Slick harassing sweet-faced prostitute Abby (Molly Dunsworth), and steps in to enact a citizen's arrest. That is hard to do when all the cops are on the take, so the hobo is branded and thrown out a window for doing the right thing. As a robbery breaks out, he changes his purchase to a shotgun and begins a bloody reign of vengeance so fierce he dominates the headlines. "Hobo Stops Begging, Demands Change," is a particularly nice touch. Drake and sons though will have none of it and begin to push back in ever-more-unimaginable ways. It is a good thing that the Scumtown hero appears to have an unlimited supply of hobo ammo.

In no world or universe is an audience meant to take any of this seriously. That was entirely evident from the original trailer designed as a joke on the uber-violent exploitation of watching bad people getting blown away in the most graphic presentation possible. Filmmakers gleefully taking things over-the-top while their characters make pun-filled quips as the villains' last rites has been a staple of the best and worst action flicks over the years. Few things in cinema come as close to satisfying our inner frustrations with the injustices of the world than watching the representation of our worst enemies meet their bitter end on-screen. When the tables are turned, however, and little is left to our worst imaginations, the fun of it all is what meets a bitter end.

Even John McClane once had to turn away after stabbing a terrorist in the eye with an icicle. How might he react to seeing a school bus filled with children torched with a flamethrower? Not ten minutes after the hobo has finally begun to offer his supporters in the audience some payback to the debauchery of the first half-hour, does this unhilariously brutal act occur on-screen. Eisener's game is to hold every shot long enough to show the viewer every gory moment until skin and blood becomes bone. A man's head is crushed between two bumper cars. Another's foot is smashed apart in a feat-of-strength game. There are knife carvings, hangings, glass-chewing and shotgun castrations. If someone can think of it, Eisener and Co. have thought of something worse. Audiences prone to extreme violence, especially when played off as an over-the-top goof, should be able to ride it out for a while and laugh off the gore. The nastier it gets though, the mayhem that would cause your average moviegoer to look away may even produce wincing in the core audience enough to admit that this is too extreme.

Grounding it all is Rutger Hauer, who foregoes the winking stage and heads for a performance so perfectly straight that he almost brings depth to it all. His monologue to a delivery room full of babies is carried out with as much sincerity as his dying replicant's "tears in rain" speech in *Blade Runner* (1982). Eisener underscores the moment with a nice touch in having the babies' cries get louder with each pessimistic passing sentence. He is far from a director without talent. And maybe in the enthusiasm of letting it all hang out in a true American dream moment of reaping the spoils from a festival contest, Eisener forgot just when to pull back. Even a little proxy here and there of sound design over visual fury between the guiltless and the accountable would have gone a long way to sway public opinion. Robert Rodriguez and Frank Miller pulled off a similar level of gratuitous violence and shameless villainy in their *Sin City* (2005)—as well as in Rodriguez's Grindhouse feature, *Planet Terror* (2007)—but they always kept eyes glued to the screen beyond the stylish cinematography by knowing when violence can be funny. "They're gonna make a comic book out of my hate crimes," says one character in *Hobo with a Shotgun*. How happy he will be when discovering they did him one better and just made the movie.

Erik Childress

CREDITS

Hobo: Rutger Hauer
Abby: Molly Dunsworth
Drake: Brian Downey
Slick: Gregory Edward Smith
Ivan: Nick Bateman
Origin: USA
Language: English
Released: 2011

Production: Frank Siracusa, Niv Fichman, Rob Cotterill; Yer Dead, Whizbang Films, Rhombus Media, Alliance Films; released by Magnet Releasing

Directed by: Jason Eisener

Written by: John Davies

Cinematography by: Karim Hussain

Music by: Adam Burke, Darius Hobert

Sound: Zan Rosbrough

Editing: Jason Eisener

Costumes: Sarah Dunsworth

Production Design: Ewen Dickson

MPAA rating: Unrated

Running time: 86 minutes

REVIEWS

Burr, Ty. *Boston Globe.* March 18, 2011.
Fine, Marshall. *Hollywood & Fine.* May 4, 2011.
Gonsalves, Rob. *eFilmCritic.com.* April 18, 2011.
Goss, William. *Film.com.* May 11, 2011.
Levy, Shawn. *Oregonian.* May 19, 2011.
Murray, Noel. *AV Club.* May 5, 2011.
Nusair, David. *Reel Film Reviews.* April 1, 2011.
Rea, Steven. *Philadelphia Inquirer.* May 19, 2011.
Snider, Eric D. *Cinematical.* February 4, 2011.
Weinberg, Scott. *FearNet.* March 25, 2011.

QUOTES

Abby: "You can't solve all the world's problems with a shotgun."

TRIVIA

In the film, Slick and Ivan drive a Bricklin, a Canadian made car from the mid-1970s.

HOODWINKED TOO! HOOD VS. EVIL
(Hoodwinked 2: Hood vs. Evil)

Not all fairy tales go by the book.
—Movie tagline

Box Office: $10.1 million

With nearly eleven minutes of credits padding out an 85-minute running time, this film barely qualifies as a feature. Yet, even in that short amount of time, *Hoodwinked Too! Hood vs. Evil* fails to generate anything that would recommend it above even the direct-to-DVD herd (which is what most viewers will assume the film is given its $10 million domestic gross). Gone is the fast paced, delightful silliness of Hoodwinked (2004) and sadly present is a film that plays like a badly organized con job.

The sequel begins with Red (voiced by Hayden Panettierre, replacing Anne Hathaway from the original) on training leave from the H.E.A. (Happily Ever After) law enforcement team which is stationed outside a house made of candy in which Hansel (Bill Hader) and Gretel (Amy Poehler) appear to be held captive by a wicked witch. The operation led by Nicky Flippers (David Ogden Stiers) and Granny Pucket (Glenn Close) is botched by Wolf (Patrick Warburton) and Twitchy the squirrel (co-screenwriter Cory Edwards) leading to the kidnapping of Granny by Verushka the Witch (Joan Cusack). Red then interrupts her training with mountain-based martial arts and cooking camp Sisters of the Hood to rescue Granny before she is forced to divulge the secret ingredient to a truffle of awesome power. But before Red can succeed she must learn the important lessons of humility and patience.

Viewers will need patience and not just adult viewers. This tired mish-mash of uninteresting storytelling jettisons the original POV vignettes in favor of a more-or-less linear story and loses a lot in the process. The original *Hoodwinked* invited viewers to look for where stories would intersect each other, especially on repeated viewings. This pale imitation leaves behind almost all of the above in favor of an overly complicated story, too much exposition, by-the-numbers scoring, and characters whose primary function seems to be making constant pop cultural references that will likely make no sense to younger viewers at all. The creaky likes of *Goodfellas* (1990), *Happy Days,* and Hannibal Lecter all make appearances here, as do a host of other tired fart/poop jokes that, for the most part, give the film a slightly seamy quality. Most of it will probably go over youngsters' heads but this showcases the films major problem: the writing. This screenplay feels cobbled at best and the humor flows almost solely from one-liners that seem like constant asides rather than an integral part of the action or the storytelling.

When gags do work the film drives them into the ground through repetition. One bit has a character getting free of some predicament or vice only to be immediately killed by a falling object as they dance for joy. Once was reasonably funny, twice okay. But the film recycles this and other gags far too often. It also does the same with characters. Some of the characters like Twitchy and Japeth, the banjo playing doom-saying goat (Benjy Gaither), make welcome returns here but Boingo, the evil rabbit seems shoehorned in only so the writers could include those aforementioned Hannibal Lecter zingers, all of which are lame.

There are new characters as well. Wayne Newton has a good bit as a singing harp, Cheech Marin and Tommy Chong play a pair of the three pigs, and David Alan Grier voices Moss the Troll. But the characters serve little purpose and seem like filler. It is hard to blame the voice cast here. Everyone seems to be having a blast. Hader and Poehler pull way ahead of the pack as the evil twins, and there are some solid chuckles now and then despite the lameness of the material.

The animation seems a lot less lush here as well. Flatness abounds to the point of looking like animatic pre-visualizations rather than fully fleshed-out feature film animation. The 2D-ness of it all is especially ironic given that this is a 3D film. Some of the camera movement is nice, but, beyond that, the effect certainly lacks any connection to the storytelling at all. Even the score of the film is bad. The beginning of the film virtually rips off *The Incredibles* (2004) with its spy music theme and the rest of the music in the film is utterly forgettable.

The original *Hoodwinked* was funny, energetic and visually inventive. The sequel is all over the map. When looking at the great fairy tale comedies of the last ten or fifteen years names come up like *Shrek* (2001) and *Enchanted* (2007). What those films have in common is an aggressive vision of what they are. *Shrek* is a fairytale from the monster's point of view that, in the end, deals with ideas of the monstrous to deliver a surprisingly moving message about the nature of love and real beauty. *Enchanted* spoofs the Disney fairy tale films even as it sets about being one and celebrates the desire for the happily ever after. Of course, both those movies are also very, very funny, something which definitely cannot be said about *Hoodwinked Too! Hood Vs. Evil*.

Dave Canfield

CREDITS

Twitchy: Cory Edwards
Red Riding Hood: Hayden Panettiere (Voice)
The Big Bad Wolf: Patrick Warburton (Voice)
Granny: Glenn Close (Voice)
Nicky Flippers: David Ogden Stiers (Voice)
Boingo the Bunny: Andy Dick (Voice)
Kirk the Woodman: Martin Short (Voice)
The Giant: Brad Garrett (Voice)
Verushka the Witch: Joan Cusack (Voice)
Hansel: Bill Hader (Voice)
Gretel: Amy Poehler (Voice)
Mad Hog: Cheech Marin (Voice)
Stone: Thomas Chong (Voice)
Heidi: Heidi Klum (Voice)
Jimmy 10-Strings: Wayne Newton (Voice)

Origin: USA
Language: English
Released: 2011
Production: Maurice Kanbar, Joan Collins Carey; Blue Yonder Films, Kanbar Entertainment, Weinstein Company, HW Two; released by Weinstein Company, Anchor Bay Entertainment
Directed by: Mike Disa
Written by: Mike Disa, Cory Edwards, Todd Edwards, Tony Leech
Music by: Murray Gold
Sound: Karen Vassar
Music Supervisor: Mary Ramos
Editing: Tom Sanders, Robert Anich Cole
Art Direction: Ryan L. Carlson
Production Design: Ryan L. Carlson
MPAA rating: PG
Running time: 86 minutes

REVIEWS

Abele, Robert. *Los Angeles Times*. April 28, 2011.
Bates, Mack. *Milwaukee Journal Sentinel*. April 28, 2011.
Demara, Bruce. *Toronto Star*. April 28, 2011.
Nash, Scott. *Three Movie Buffs*. May 2, 2011.
Phillips, Michael. *Chicago Tribune*. April 28, 2011.
Puig, Claudia. *USA Today*. April 28, 2011.
Rea, Stephen. *Philadelphia Enquirer*. April 28, 2011.
Smith, Christopher. *Bangor Daily News (Maine)* April 29, 2011.
Smith, Kyle. *New York Post*. April 29, 2011.
Webster, Andy. *New York Times*. April 28, 2011.

QUOTES

Boingo the Bunny: "Why are you reading that book? Nobody reads books anymore! Movies are always better, especially sequels."

HOP

Big game, big ears.
—Movie tagline
Candy, chicks, and rock 'n' roll.
—Movie tagline

Box Office: $108.1 million

The movie industry is a business. For all of the legitimately talented directors and writers and actors that commit their lives to crafting quality products, there will always be studios churning out garbage that they expect to make money, whether or not it pleases audiences or represents anything close to intelligence or fun. After all, integrity cannot be cashed at the bank.

This approach surely must be held largely responsible for the recent influx of dreadfully mindless movies in which actors pretending not to be ashamed work alongside CGI versions of beloved childhood characters. *Alvin and the Chipmunks* (2007) is now a shrill, obnoxiously pop-culture drenched trilogy with no sign of slowing down commercially (it never had any creative energy to begin with). *Garfield* (2004) yielded two films that approximately no one over the age of seven enjoyed, and it could be a challenge to find youngsters who would testify to their own fandom anyway. *Yogi Bear* (2010) added another bad movie to the unfortunate filmography of talented comedian Anna Faris. And with *Hop,* even the Easter Bunny has now become fodder for a studio (in this case, Universal Pictures) to feebly inject desperate, rebellious attitude into something pure and hope it motivates parents to drop their dough on another stinker, merely for the sake of ninety minutes of questionable "entertainment for the kids."

If this sounds like a cynical, worn-out evaluation of this woeful mini-genre of family movies, that is fair. Of course, after sitting through junk after junk after junk it is difficult not to feel a sense of helplessness, especially when talking about a movie as fiercely, carelessly idea-free as *Hop.* Russell Brand voices the computer-generated bunny, who is the heir to the prestigious title of Easter Bunny but would much rather pursue his dream of being a rock 'n' roll drummer. So E.B., as he prefers to be called, escapes Easter Island and heads for California, where he connects with Fred (James Marsden), an unemployed dope who lives with his parents. In theory, Fred should be thrilled to encounter a talking rabbit who thinks he's Keith Moon. Instead, because this is the only reaction humans ever have in movies like this, Fred freaks out about E.B., and even after agreeing to help the little critter still labors to keep his new friend a secret. Dude, at least use the guy to make some money or pick up women or something. Do not just cause yourself unnecessary stress trying to keep E.B. hidden from everyone he knows.

Director Tim Hill, who also helmed *Garfield: A Tale of Two Kitties* (2006) and *Alvin and the Chipmunks* (2007), clearly believes that the mere mention of dreams and candy is enough to give young viewers what they want. *Hop* offers few jokes (and no laughs), and does not even embrace its many opportunities to have fun with its premise. Do talking bunnies find it odd that people eat chocolate bunnies for Easter? Or that the jelly beans that the bunnies poop are also eaten by people? The film passes on these comic chances and leans on lines like, after someone tastes a marshmallow, "Too much marsh, not enough mallow". Otherwise, the attempts at humor involve scenes like E.B. playing Rock Band to songs like Hole's "Celebrity Skin," which will

mean nothing to kids and only seems totally random to viewers old enough to know the song. Multiple renditions of "I Want Candy" further assert the extent to which the film commits to the obvious.

Poor Marsden, who appeared later in the year in another film (*Straw Dogs* [2011]) that does not have as much to do with animals as people may expect, struggles to avoid the sort of broadly mugging performance that often results from an actor taking a job to pay the bills and forced to act alongside a loudmouth animated creature. No actor could do anything with a guy like Fred, however, whose eventual interest in becoming the Easter Bunny himself appears not amusing and uplifting but just creepy. The guy is single and in his mid-30s. Aspiring to be the Easter Bunny is more likely cause for therapy, not celebration.

Brand's cinematic skills rest on his casually arrogant, bad-boy personality, so that he was chosen to voice E.B. is assumedly only a result of his being British. And that E.B. needed to have a British accent is merely another indication that *Hop* has nothing on its mind whatsoever, laboring in thinly thought-out ways to fill time and construct a story around the same template as so many other kids' movies: Someone wants to prove that they can do something that everyone else told them they could not do. Incorporating formulaic plotting into a film represents far less egregious laziness than corrupting a religious holiday for the purpose of commercialism. Much like *The Polar Express* (2004) makes kids think that Christmas functions primarily as a celebration of presents, *Hop* will make youngsters believe that Easter exists solely to salute the wonders of chocolate. Parents may take children to see the movie as an escape for everyone involved, but it may require more than an hour and a half for them to explain how much the flick gets wrong.

Despite a trailer that would be difficult to regard as anything but terrible, *Hop* still pulled in $108.1 million domestically plus another $75.9 million internationally. Perhaps the success is due to the likable pull of bunnies, or that movies with even vague religious connotations can strike a chord with a sizable audience. Not surprisingly, *Hop* was released right around Easter, reinforcing the studios' belief in the public's susceptibility to films about holidays, regardless of the holiday.

Matt Pais

CREDITS
Fred: James Marsden
Samantha O'Hare: Kaley Cuoco
Mrs. Beck: Chelsea Handler

Carlos/Phil: Hank Azaria
Henry O'Hare: Gary Cole
Bonnie O'Hare: Elizabeth Perkins
Himself: David Hasselhoff
Easter Bunny: Russell Brand (Voice)
Carlos/Phil: Hank Azaria (Voice)
E.B.'s Dad: Hugh Laurie (Voice)
Origin: USA
Language: English
Released: 2011
Production: Christopher Meledandri, Michele Imperato; Universal Pictures, Relativity Media, Illumination Entertainment; released by Universal Pictures
Directed by: Tim Hill
Written by: Cinco Paul, Ken Daurio, Brian Lynch
Cinematography by: Peter Lyons Collister
Music by: Christopher Lennertz
Sound: Richard L. Anderson
Music Supervisor: Julianne Jordan
Editing: Peter S. Elliot, Gregory Perler
Art Direction: Charles Daboub Jr.
Costumes: Alexandra Welker
Production Design: Richard Holland
MPAA rating: PG
Running time: 90 minutes

REVIEWS

Abele, Robert. *Los Angeles Times.* March 31, 2011.
Baumgarten, Marjorie. *Austin Chronicle.* March 31, 2011.
Gleiberman, Owen. *Entertainment Weekly.* March 30, 2011.
Moore, Roger. *Orlando Sentinel.* March 30, 2011.
Morris, Wesley. *Boston Globe.* March 31, 2011.
Phipps, Keith. *AV Club.* March 31, 2011.
Puig, Claudia. *USA Today.* March 31, 2011.
Schager, Nick. *Village Voice.* March 29, 2011.
Scott, A.O.. *New York Times.* March 31, 2011.
Scott, Mike. *New Orleans Times-Picayune.* April 1, 2011.

QUOTES

E.B.: "Fred, I think you and I got off on the wrong foot. You said some things, I flooded some things. Let's start over, okay?"

HORRIBLE BOSSES

Ever wish your boss were dead?
   —Movie tagline

Box Office: $117.5 million

A roguishly charming but consistently inconsistent dark comedy about a trio of bumbling pals who entertain a mutually advantageous murderous roundelay—think *Throw Momma From the Train* (1987) with no momma, no train and a third pair of victim and potential beneficiary—*Horrible Bosses* is frustrating and fun in almost equal measure, given some of the thoughts of what could have been that dance in one's head off to the side as the movie unfolds. There is little about the film that is original and the rate of its payoff is uneven, but there is certainly enough color and coarseness to more than satisfy fans of R-rated raunchiness, especially considering its high-profile cast.

Perhaps because of this star power but probably also owing to the fact that its central conceit is so easily translatable (everyone has or has had a boss they found repellent on some level), the film defied conventional Hollywood wisdom about R-rated comedies, grossing not only a better-than-expected $117 million domestically, but also a very robust $92 million abroad. For that reason, a sequel is being considered.

The film's story centers around three longtime friends: Nick (Jason Bateman), Dale (Charlie Day) and Kurt (Jason Sudeikis). Nick works as a mid-level office drone in a financial services company, where his rude, taskmaster boss Dave (Kevin Spacey) dangles a promotion just out of reach before finally deciding to absorb the position's salary and benefits for himself while passing off any extra work to his underlings. A dental assistant, Dale finds himself the victim of serial sexual harassment by his boss Julia (Jennifer Aniston), who threatens to tell Dale's fiancée Stacy (Lindsay Sloane) that they have had sex unless, well, he actually does agree to have sex with her. Kurt, on the surface, seems to have a lot going for him at the family-owned business where he has worked his way up the ladder. After his avuncular boss Jack (Donald Sutherland) passes away, though, Kurt finds himself having to fend off inane ideas from Jack's jealous, cocaine-addled son, Bobby (Colin Farrell).

Over drinks one night, their lives made increasingly miserable by these detestable overseers, the guys ponder the bliss that would result from simply having these folks out of their lives. Indeed, what if they murdered them? The colorfully named "Motherfucker" Jones (Jamie Foxx), an ex-con who sizes up the discomfited trio and decides to sell them his expertise in the field, provides a few general tips on how to avoid getting caught. From there, Nick, Dale and Kurt set about staking out one another's horrible bosses—a scheme that gets complicated when one of them dies and evidence arises linking some of the guys to the crime scene.

The movie's leads evince a nice chemistry with one another. Day imports his manic-chipmunk shtick from small screen cable hit *It's Always Sunny in Philadelphia,* while Sudeikis plays the bewildered yet upbeat Everyman (a character template with which he has much experience from *Saturday Night Live*) and Bateman ably deploys his ace touch with slow burn exasperation and deadpan humor. (In one of the film's few subtle jokes, Nick observes from afar amphetamine-freak Bobby's wild acting out and wonders out loud to himself, "Where does he get all that energy?" before pausing and then muttering, "Oh yeah.")

With considerable effort and force of will, Spacey, Aniston and Farrell also each make nice (if grotesque) impressions. Scene to scene, they are often quite funny—particularly Farrell, with his pot belly, receding hairline, hair-trigger impulsivity and sneering, half-witted retorts. But the fact is that these are each monstrous types—brutally uncaring supervisor, sexually rapacious harpy and the idiot who has failed upward. These supporting characters seem sketched from the outside in rather than the other way around; Bobby feels like a sitcom character (albeit an amusingly unhinged one) while Julia is a motivation-free sociopath. Dave, meanwhile, simply affords Spacey the chance to spin out a different iteration of his character from *Swimming With Sharks* (1994).

In short, the script—sold in 2005 by sitcom writer Michael Markowitz, and much tinkered with over the years, with John Francis Daley and Jonathan Goldstein finally also receiving screenplay credit—bears the marks of muddled intent and narrative vision. The basic idea of would-be white collar criminals who are essentially dopes, and terrible at law-breaking, recalls the brilliant *Office Space* (1999), but as one might surmise from the name of Foxx's character, *Horrible Bosses* is a more surface-oriented, less discerning and psychologically insightful treatment of the same concept. It settles for and delights in vulgarity when there could be a much deeper comedic exploitation of fundamental insecurities and pent-up anger.

Another comparable, more recent equivalent is the female-centric ensemble hit *Bridesmaids* (2011), co-written and built around Kristen Wiig. Whereas that film took some hits for its group diarrhea scene, it can be argued that said sequence served a utilitarian purpose, highlighting the planning ineptitude of Wiig's character, and further underscoring her increasing sense of separation from her best friend. Analogous scenes in *Horrible Bosses* are either unrealistic (lewd come-ons from Aniston's character that defy any sense of seduction however assertive) or laborious and awkwardly elliptical in their payoffs, as with a sequence involving Kurt placing various personal hygiene products of Bobby's in his pants, and thus leaving his DNA at Bobby's house.

If there is a standout element other than the film's engaging casting, it lies in the detailed work of director Seth Gordon, who first distinguished himself with the enormously entertaining documentary *The King of Kong: A Fistful of Quarters* (2007). Gordon here marshals a capable roster of below-the-line artisans, injecting the movie with a bouncy and vibrant tone and look (it is no coincidence that the movie's poster features day-glow hues of pink, blue and green) which pointedly contrasts with and reassuringly offsets the potentially dark subject matter.

Production design in relation to comedy is typically an afterthought, but Shepherd Frankel ably sketches distinct environments for each of the main characters' tormentors. Particularly effective is Bobby's bachelor lair (comically described as "a douchebag museum" by one character), which resembles the sort of weird "man cave" that a fan of hair metal, martial arts and Don "The Dragon" Wilson kickboxing flicks who came into money absent any real responsibility might actually concoct. More than the characters or actual story, it is these sorts of engaging background details, along with each lead's immense individual likeability, that sustain *Horrible Bosses*' perverse and mean-spirited wish fulfillment.

Brent Simon

CREDITS

Nick Hendricks: Jason Bateman
Kurt Buchman: Jason Sudeikis
Dale Arbus: Charlie Day
Jones: Jamie Foxx
Dr. Julia Harris: Jennifer Aniston
Bobby Pellit: Colin Farrell
Jack Pellit: Donald Sutherland
Dave Harken: Kevin Spacey
Rhonda Harken: Julie Bowen
Carter: John Francis Daley
Origin: USA
Language: English
Released: 2011
Production: New Line Cinema; released by Warner Bros.
Directed by: Seth Gordon
Written by: John Francis Daley, Jonathan M. Goldstein, Michael Markowitz
Cinematography by: Seth Gordon, David Hennings
Music by: Christopher Lennertz
Editing: Peter Teschner
Sound: Jeff Wexler
Costumes: Carol Ramsey
Production Design: Shepherd Frankel
MPAA rating: R
Running time: 98 minutes

REVIEWS

Berkshire, Geoff. *Metromix.com*. July 7, 2011.
Burr, Ty. *Boston Globe*. July 7, 2011.

Chang, Justin. *Variety*. July 6, 2011.

Ebert, Roger. *Chicago Sun-Times*. July 7, 2011.

Honeycutt, Kirk. *Hollywood Reporter*. July 5, 2011.

Lemire, Christy. *Associated Press*. July 6, 2011.

Longworth, Karina. *Village Voice*. July 5, 2011.

Phillips, Michael. *Chicago Tribune*. July 7, 2011.

Schwarzbaum, Lisa. *Entertainment Weekly*. July 6, 2011.

Stevens, Dana. *Slate*. July 7, 2011.

QUOTES

Dave Harken: "You can't win a marathon without putting some bandaids on your nipples!"

TRIVIA

At one point, both Frank Oz and Brett Ratner were attached to direct the film.

HUGO

Unlock the Secret.
    —Movie tagline

Box Office: $67.3 million

When it was first announced that the next film from Martin Scorsese, the man who has long been anointed as America's Finest Filmmaker, was going to be a an adaptation of the acclaimed children's book *The Invention of Hugo Cabret* many observers reacted to the news as if it were some kind of bizarre joke. After all, while Scorsese has long proclaimed that his own fascination with the cinema began when he was a small child, there was precious little in his filmography that one could actually show to the tykes without either boring or scarring the majority of them for life. Those fans will be relieved to know that *Hugo*, as it has now been dubbed, is neither a question mark nor a disaster. In fact, it is not even really a family film in the traditional sense of the word. What it is, in fact, is a Martin Scorsese film through and through and while the body count is close to nil, it still burns with the passion and intensity that has made his work so distinctive, not to mention the joy that he still gets in celebrating and paying homage to the art form that he has dedicated his life's work to pursuing. This time around, he goes back to its earliest days and presents us with a film that somehow works both as a love letter to the joys to be derived from the cinema, as spectator and creator alike, and as a marvelously engrossing and high-spirited adventure that is as enchanting as any of the Harry Potter movies and perhaps even more so because the magic that it is dealing with is the kind that is both real and that still has the power to enchant and amaze even after all of its secrets appear to have been revealed.

Set in 1931, the film takes place largely within the confines of Paris' Montparnasse train station and concerns a little boy named Hugo (Asa Butterfield) who literally lives within its walls. Like so many little boys in stories of this sort, Hugo has faced enormous tragedy at an early age. Once upon a time, he was a happy young lad who lived with his clockmaker father (Jude Law) and worked alongside him as he attempted to rebuild a mysterious automaton—a mechanical contraption designed to look like a person—that he discovered stashed away and unwanted in the museum where he worked a second job. Thanks to their combined skill and ingenuity, the contraption was nearly restored but before it could be completed, a terrible accident took Hugo's father's life and left him the hands of his drunken uncle (Ray Winstone), who lives in a long-forgotten apartment above the train station and who works at making sure that the station's elaborate clocks keep on ticking. With his uncle now missing, Hugo himself is secretly maintaining the clocks while trying to avoid being caught by the station's chief inspector (Sacha Baron Cohen), a goof with a mangled leg, zero personality skills and a grim determination to ensure that any stray kids that falls into his grasp goes straight to the orphanage if they commit even the most minor of transgressions. In his spare time, Hugo occasionally raids the decrepit little toy shop run by the tired and bitter Monsieur Melies (Ben Kingsley) for spare parts and gears that he can use to help restore the automaton.

One day, while Hugo is trying to snare some more parts, he is caught by Mr. Melies and when he is forced to turn out his pockets for the old man, he reveals a notebook filled with diagrams and specs regarding the automaton that his father made. For some reason, this discovery shocks Melies and he not only refuses to return the notebook but vows to burn it that very night, even after Hugo follows him out into the wintry night in the hopes of changing his mind. His appeals fail to register with Melies but Hugo's plight does attract the interest of his young goddaughter, the spunky and inquisitive Isabelle (Chloe Grace Moretz) and she promises to rescue the book for him. When the two meet the next day, she tells Hugo that not only did her godfather not burn the book, it seemed to upset him and his wife (Helen McCory) quite deeply. Needless to say, Hugo and Isabelle decide to delve deeper into uncovering the mystery, one that grows even more complex when it turns out that not only does Isabelle possess the key that makes the automaton run but when it does, it displays an even more inexplicable connection to the old man that may reveal who he once was and what made him what he is now.

For those with a certain knowledge about the history of the cinema, the name "Melies" may ring a bell or two and as it turns out, the old man turns out to be George Melies, one of the earliest pioneers of motion pictures and it is at this point that *Hugo* transforms from being merely an engaging children's story into a grand tribute to the formative years of the film industry from one of its most celebrated practitioners. As the story reveals Melies back story and his connection to the automaton, Scorsese offers up a fascinating history lesson on silent film that combines clips from some of its most famous images with recreations of how Melies achieved his then-revolutionary and still-impressive visual effects and he even manages to work in a firm but gentle plea for the importance of his pet cause of film preservation. On the surface, this may sound like it would only appeal to film fanatics of a certain age and certainly not anything that most kids would go for but Scorsese and screenwriter John Logan approach the material in such a magical and wide-eyed manner that it is virtually impossible to not get swept up in the story they are spinning. At a time when it appears that the notion of film being run through a projector and beamed upon a screen, even in the meager multiplex form that audiences have been forced to get used to in recent years, is being pushed aside for the cheaper and more convenient digital formats, *Hugo* serves as a stirring reminder of just how glorious and transformative the simple experience of seeing a film under the optimum conditions can be. At one point, when Melies is reunited with the work that he himself had assumed was lost and forgotten, he quietly remarks "I would recognize the sound of a movie projector anywhere," it is a notion that anyone who has ever fallen in love with the movies will instantly take to heart.

On the other hand, while movie buffs will obviously be the ones who will take the most from *Hugo* viewers with no particular grasp on the history of the cinema will find much to love here as well. Working from the Brian Selznick book (which, believe it or not, is based to a certain degree on real elements—Melies was a film pioneer who lost everything and worked in a toy store in Montparnasse until he and his films were rediscovered by a couple of cinema fanatics and he also apparently did build an automaton at some point), Scorsese and Logan have a fascinating tale to tell and do so without either dumbing things down in order to make them palatable to little kids (or, more often, their more easily abashed parents) or rushing things along in order to keep up with the frantic pacing that they have grown used to over the years. Instead, the film presents a lavish environment in which everything from the largest clocks to the tiniest gears to the freshest croissants

are presented in a manner that heightens the reality without making things cartoonish in the way that one might picture the events in their mind while reading them in a book. Adding immensely to this effect is the immaculate 3D photography by longtime Scorsese collaborator Robert Richardson, which is easily the finest example of the format to come along since *Avatar* (2009). While there are a couple of moments in which Scorsese cannot resist indulging in the essential silliness of the format by gleefully tossing a sword or two in front of the camera, he is more interested in using the format to both give extra detail to the intricacies of the enormous clockworks that Hugo live among and to properly illustrate the intricate multiple layers of trickery devised by Melies to pull off his movie magic.

The performances across the board are impressive as well. Relative newcomer Butterfield is a real find in the title role and Moretz, who has already gained a lot of acclaim over the last few years in such films as *Kick-Ass* (2010) and *Let Me In* (2010), solidifies her reputation as one of the most impressive young actresses working today (and will no doubt inspire numerous crushes to boot). Among the vets, Ben Kingsley gives one of his very best performances as Melies and proves once again that when given decent material, he can be one of our strongest actors. The supporting cast is filled with plenty of familiar faces, the best of the bunch being the legendary Christopher Lee as a librarian who helps Hugo and Isabelle on their quest while instilling a love of books in them as well and Sacha Baron Cohen as the goofy inspector with a performance that essentially represents the entire history of silent film comedy in only a few scenes and even he gets to deliver a moment or two of grace for his troubles in the end.

Hugo is a masterpiece, one of the very best films of 2011 and as personal and deeply felt as anything that Martin Scorsese has ever done. The question, though, is whether younger viewers will be interested in a film celebrating a type of art form that has been gone for nearly a century and of which they presumably have little to no real working knowledge. Admittedly, the one who only want to watch films that ask nothing of them than to watch bright colors for ninety minutes and then buy a lot of tie-in merchandise afterwards may not exactly spark to its more delicate charms. However, the ones who are bright and inquisitive and who like stories that engage rather than assault, they may well adore it and even develop an interest in cinema history as a result. Who knows—perhaps the next Georges Melies or Martin Scorsese will be among them and perhaps they will be inspired to one day conjure up something as wonderful as *Hugo*.

Peter Sobczynski

CREDITS

Hugo Cabaret: Asa Butterfield

Isabelle: Chloe Grace Moretz

Monsieur Labisse: Christopher Lee

Georges Melies: Ben Kingsley

Mama Jeanne: Helen McCrory

Monsieur Frick: Richard Griffiths

Uncle Claude: Ray Winstone

Lisette: Emily Mortimer

Station Inspector: Sacha Baron Cohen

Hugo's father: Jude Law

Madame Emile: Frances de la Tour

Rene Tabard: Michael Stuhlbarg

Origin: USA

Language: English

Released: 2011

Production: Graham King, Tim Headington, Martin Scorsese, Johnny Depp; Infinitum Nihil, GK Films; released by Paramount Pictures

Directed by: Martin Scorsese

Written by: John Logan

Cinematography by: Robert Richardson

Music by: Howard Shore

Sound: John Midgley

Music Supervisor: Randall Poster

Editing: Thelma Schoonmaker

Art Direction: David Warren

Costumes: Sandy Powell

Production Design: Dante Ferretti

MPAA rating: PG

Running time: 127 minutes

REVIEWS

Corliss, Richard. *Time Magazine*. November 22, 2011.
Dargis, Manohla. *New York Times*. November 22, 2011.
Debruge, Peter. *Variety*. November 18, 2011.
Denby, David. *New Yorker*. November 22, 2011.
Ebert, Roger. *Chicago Sun-Times*. November 22, 2011.
Goss, William. *Film.com*. November 22, 2011.
Orndorf, Brian. *BrianOrndorf.com*. November 23, 2011.
Phillips, Michael. *Chicago Tribune*. November 22, 2011.
Tallerico, Brian. *HollywoodChicago.com*. November 23, 2011.
Tobias, Scott. *AV Club*. November 22, 2011.

QUOTES

Hugo Cabret: "I'd imagine the whole world was one big machine. Machines never come with any extra parts, you know. They always come with the exact amount they need. So I figured, if the entire world was one big machine, I couldn't be an extra part. I had to be here for some reason."

TRIVIA

After screening the film, James Cameron called it a "masterpiece" and told Martin Scorsese that it was the best use of 3D he had seen, including his own films.

AWARDS

Oscars 2011: Art Dir./Set Dec., Cinematog., Sound, Sound FX Editing, Visual FX

British Acad. 2011: Sound, Prod. Des.

Golden Globes 2012: Director (Scorsese)

Nomination:

Oscars 2011: Adapt. Screenplay, Costume Des., Director (Scorsese), Film, Film Editing, Orig. Score

British Acad. 2011: Cinematog., Costume Des., Director (Scorsese), Film Editing, Makeup, Visual FX, Orig. Score

Directors Guild 2011: Director (Scorsese)

Golden Globes 2012: Film—Drama, Orig. Score

Writers Guild 2011: Adapt. Screenplay.

THE HUMAN CENTIPEDE II (FULL SEQUENCE)

100% medically inaccurate.
—Movie tagline

Viewers who enjoy extreme movies for their own sake might find a small place in their hearts for Tom Six's follow-up to his surprisingly-good *The Human Centipede* (2009), but it will be a small minority who knows deep in their heart that even giving the film credit purely for its excess is more than this sequel deserves. *The Human Centipede II (Full Sequence)* is a monument to excess that would make any mad scientist blush with shame. It is, in a word, disgusting, and succeeds at little else. The saddest thing is that the film has the makings of a first-rate satire of the exploitation film, offering a potentially compelling premise, solid casting, and a somewhat interesting visual aesthetic. But all of the above is utterly wasted by Six who quite literally uses every advantage these assets give him to virtually defecate on his audience.

Picking up immediately where the first film left off, the sequel starts with that film's closing credits, pulling back to show a portable disc player watched by an odd-looking man in a parking garage toll booth. Martin Lomax (Laurence R. Harvey) is a middle-aged, very short, blob-like asthmatic who is completely obsessed with *The Human Centipede* (2009) to the point of keeping a scrapbook detailing everything about it and the surgical procedures employed by the mad surgeon Dr Heiter (Dieter Laser in the first film).

Some of the reasons provided for Martin's obsession are shown early on in the film. He has been abused all of his life. First by his father who viewers hear raping him in voiceover, then by his mother, who hates Martin for the imprisonment of the father, and then by Dr. Sebring (Bill Hutchens), a vile old man who has been called in to help manage Martin's frail health. In addition to keeping the scrapbook, Martin also watches the original film at work, even masturbating to it with sandpaper wrapped around his penis. When not rewatching the film, Martin spies on the garage customers with his video surveillance cameras and takes care of the vicious centipede he keeps as a pet. But his unstable and sick existence is interrupted when his mother finds and destroys the scrapbook, triggering a rage in which he kills her. Martin then decides to embark on his ultimate statement of empowerment. He will build a human centipede out of not three, but twelve subjects. Gathering together the remains of his precious compendium and a handful of rusty tools and kitchen implements he rents a warehouse and sets about picking his victims.

They come from all walks of life and most are apprehended in the garage where Martin clubs them over the head with a crowbar (seen ad nauseum), cuts their Achilles tendons to prevent escape, and transports them to the warehouse bound and gagged, where they lay in their own filth while he gathers up the necessary number of participants for his experiment. Most of the people here are faceless, which sounds like a bad pun given the gross premise, but a few victims are highlighted by Six for special treatment. One, for instance, is pregnant. Another, a man who has foolishly berated Martin. In neither case do viewers find out enough about these people to care for them in any way. The cleverest moment comes when Martin is able to convince the lead actress from the first film to come to an audition for his new movie. But even the presence of Ashlynn Yennie (playing herself) fails to inspire Six to do anything with his semi-clever deconstruction of the first film's meta-narrative. The idea simply kneels like the second part of centipede waiting for the inevitable flow. By the time the actress shows up, the film goes into impossibly high gear. Teeth are hammered out with a chisel. Buttocks are rudely sliced open. Faces are stapled to asses. It seems endless, though, in reality, all of the above takes place in a little over an hour.

Due to the way the film constantly lavishes attention on his fevered brow, the only possible point of empathy is Martin himself. But the man is presented as an almost completely silent cipher. Viewers know he was abused but by the time he is literally conducting (complete with fart noises) his centipede through a mad digestive symphony of passing feces (the result of force feeding the head massive doses of laxative), there is no possible empathy to be had. Thus, scenes involving him being abused, beaten, clad only in his underwear, or worst of all, madly abusing himself, are simply part of the pointless carnage. When Martin breaks down in tears as his victims die seems simply de rigueur. This is a world where anyone could do these sorts of things to anyone else. All is chaos, there are no people.

Even then the film is far from finished when it comes to showcasing the worst images imaginable. Martin rapes the back end of the centipede after wrapping his privates in barbed wire. Martin chases a pregnant woman through the warehouse, into the parking lot, and into a car where she hemorrhages her baby into being only to stomp it to death as she plunges her foot onto the accelerator in order to make her getaway.

The film then ends on such a bald cheat that it would be worth mentioning, except that if, after reading this, viewers have any desire to see this film then there is really nothing more to say. Only the fact that this film is in black and white makes it viewable at all (without a barf bucket) although Six does go to the trouble of tinting the feces in the film brown as it spews from the clumsily knitted surgical seams of Martin's loathsome creation.

The first centipede film was all about restraint and, as such, was a fairly impressive accomplishment. True, the premise of a human centipede itself is so disgusting that even Six has spoken about the first film as merely a way of getting the audience used to the idea of the premise so that he could make the second. But the first film works. The second film does not, on any level. It is a film made only for people who are so cynical they can laugh at what should not be laughed at or so jaded they need to push themselves to new extremes. It is the cinematic equivalent of a Roman vomitorium.

Dave Canfield

CREDITS

Martin: Laurence R. Harvey
Miss Yennie: Ashlynn Yennie
Candy: Maddi Black
Karnie: Kandace Caine
Paul: Dominic Borrelli
Ian: Lucas Hansen
Dick: Lee Nicholas Harris
Greg: Dan Burman
Tim: Daniel Jude Gennis
Dr. Sebring: Bill Hutchens
Origin: United Kingdom
Language: English
Released: 2011

Production: Ilona Six, Tom Six; Six Entertainment Company; released by IFC Midnight

Directed by: Tom Six

Written by: Tom Six

Cinematography by: David Meadows

Music by: James Edward Barker

Sound: Eilam Hoffman

Editing: Nigel de Hond

Production Design: Thomas Stefan

MPAA rating: Unrated

Running time: 88 minutes

REVIEWS

Ebert, Roger. *Chicago Sun-Times*. October 8, 2011.

Faraci, Devin. *BadAss Digest*. October 7, 2011.

Koehler, Robert. *Variety*. September 29, 2011.

Larsen, Richard. *Slant Magazine*. October 2, 2011.

Lovell, Glenn. *CinemaDope*. October 16, 2011.

Morris, Wesley. *Boston Globe*. October 13, 2011.

Olsen, Mark. *Los Angeles Times*. October 6, 2011.

O'Sullivan, Michael. *Washington Post*. October 7, 2011.

Rothkopf, Joshua. *Time Out New York* October 5, 2011.

Savlov, Marc. *Austin Chronicle*. October 6, 2011.

TRIVIA

The film was originally shot in color but was switched to black and white when it was realized it was much scarier that way.

I

I AM

*What if the solution to the world's problems was
right in front of us all along?*
—Movie tagline

The shift is about to hit the fan.
—Movie tagline

Box Office: $1.6 million

Tom Shadyac made his career as a director of
raucous comedies, loosing small-screen star Jim Carrey
on an unsuspecting public by way of *Ace Ventura: Pet
Detective* (1994), and then helping to resurrect Eddie
Murphy's floundering career with *The Nutty Professor*
(1996). So the idea of Shadyac helming a documentary
about interconnectedness, the human spirit, and the
perils of unchecked materialism—just a few years after
overseeing the bloated *Evan Almighty* (2007), the most
expensive comedy ever made—would on the surface
seem to be a joke, the set-up for a mockumentary-type
exploitation of New Age, touchy-feely solutions and the
self-help shamans who peddle them.

And yet *I Am* is not a joke. Billed in its press notes
as "a prismatic and probing exploration of our world,
what is wrong with it and what we can do to make it
better," the film is unabashedly a work of reflective mid-
life crisis. And yet it is also a quite engaging and at
times terrifically moving, very personal repudiation of
not merely capitalistic excess, but the mindset and rooted
impulses which drive and fuel it. Improbable as it seems,
it took a comedian to make an entertaining and still
sincere movie about one of the wonkiest, most elusive
subjects imaginable—the science of human connection.

The seeds for *I Am* were planted when Shadyac suffered a significant bicycle trail accident in his native
Virginia in 2007. He broke a wrist and suffered other
scrapes and bruises, but far worse than the immediate
physical consequences was his diagnosis of post-
concussion syndrome. Even though he was wearing
a helmet, Shadyac was, for months, stricken with
debilitating headaches and acute sensitivity to light and
noise. No treatments seemed to help, and Shadyac claims
he even contemplated suicide, so unbearable were his
days.

It was against this backdrop of depression and
despair that he began to think about the separation of
humanity from the natural world, and the sort of
intrinsic loneliness hanging over American culture like a
cloud. The filmmaker did not "find Jesus" in quite the
traditional sense, but neither did he enter into this radical reevaluation and reorganization of priorities falsely.
Shadyac entirely funded the construction of a homeless
shelter in Charlottesville, Virginia, began living more
modestly, and divested himself of his 17,000-square-foot
Pasadena estate, moving into a beachside trailer park in
Malibu.

While there is a hint of back-patting, the film does
not much play up these personal changes in habit and
lifestyle as exemplars. Instead, it follows Shadyac as he
sets out to address possibly two of the broadest questions imaginable—what is wrong with the world (for
which the title offers up an answer) and what can we do
about it? Abetting him in this quest are various
philosophers, scientists, authors and even his father, who
for more than a dozen years served as the C.E.O. of

ALSAC/St. Jude, spearheading charitable fundraising for pediatric cancer research.

It can definitely be said that *I Am* has a rangy, scattershot energy and wide area of inquiry—as exemplified by its disparate slate of interview subjects, from David Suzuki, Noam Chomsky and Howard Zinn to Desmond Tutu, Lynne McTaggart and poet Coleman Barks. But if it is thematically similar to fellow "big picture" documentaries like *Imagine It!* (2009) and *What the Bleep Do We Know?* (2004), *I Am* has a lot more sharply defined personality than the former and a lot more grounded focus than the latter, which tried to link quantum physics and higher consciousness. Shadyac's own personal curiosity powers this movie, which may be a demerit to some but will prove fresh to a lot of viewers, given his affable disposition.

It is relatively easy to decry and assail greed, both individually and on a corporate level. Especially in the current depressed economy, examples abound of selfish and socially indifferent behavior. But Shadyac's film goes beyond stirred up oppositional passions or even pat solutions. It leans only nominally to the left politically, in its critiques of capitalism run amok, but it is not a polemic. Shadyac is instead interested in foundational notions, spanning time, of things like our relationship to material objects, and excessive and/or zero-sum competitiveness, where a person's gains must come at the expense of others.

Despite the self-indictment of its title, Shadyac's movie comes across as neither a lecture nor a bore. From red deer to honeybees, McTaggart and other interviewees elucidate the importance of consensus decision-making in animals, and how evolution is not merely survival of the fittest; in so doing, they make a compelling argument for the same actuality holding true with humankind. With this as its core theoretical/philosophical underpinning, *I Am*'s little digressive segments—about, variously, the intuitive nature of the heart, the evolutionary reinforcers (via surging endorphins) of compassionate behavior, how human emotional responses create electromagnetic fields that emanate from our bodies, and how Petri dish yogurt cultures respond to emotionality—are all fascinating vignettes.

Though surely a bit indulgent, and sometimes more than a bit reminiscent of the precocity of a college coffeehouse conversation, *I Am* takes a hearty swing at big ideas, and does so in a fairly charming fashion. If the film does not completely bowl one over on an emotional level, it is because Shadyac is extolling what he believes to be the base-level elements of solutions—compassion and cooperation—rather than any grand single set of resolutions. It may require an innate interest in this type of philosophical noodling, but any way you cut it,

however, even for general audiences, *I Am* is certainly more entertaining than *Evan Almighty.*

Brent Simon

CREDITS

Himself: Tom Shadyac
Himself: Noam Chomsky
Himself: Coleman Barks
Himself: Howard Zinn
Himself: Desmond Tutu
Origin: USA
Language: English
Released: 2011
Production: Dagan Handy; Flying Eye Productions, Homemade Canvas Productions, Shady Acres Entertainment; released by Paladin
Directed by: Tom Shadyac
Sound: Odin Benitez
Editing: Jennifer Abbott
MPAA rating: Unrated
Running time: 76 minutes

REVIEWS

Bell, Josh. *Las Vegas Weekly.* April 27, 2011.
Ebert, Roger. *Chicago Sun-Times.* April 21, 2011.
Honeycutt, Kirk. *Hollywood Reporter.* March 11, 2011.
Linden, Sheri. *Los Angeles Times.* March 10, 2011.
Morris, Wesley. *Boston Globe.* March 31, 2011.
Rickey, Carrie. *Philadelphia Inquirer.* April 28, 2011.
Schwarzbaum, Lisa. *Entertainment Weekly.* March 9, 2011.
Tallerico, Brian. *HollywoodChicago.com.* April 22, 2011.
Weitzman, Elizabeth. *New York Daily News.* March 18, 2011.
Whitty, Stephen. *Newark Star-Ledger.* March 18, 2011.

TRIVIA

Tom Shadyac described making this film with complete creative control as "freeing."

I AM NUMBER FOUR

Box Office: $55.1 million

The latest addition to the movies based on sci-fi young adult novels genre, *I Am Number Four* bargains that readers are ready to give up on the Edward versus Jacob debate of the *Twilight* movies and move on to a new kind of crush: aliens. Unfortunately, it also supposes that the readers who would buy a book about a hunted alien who falls in love with a humanoid girl would so desperately want a movie to be made of the book that they would not pay attention to the content. Admittedly, the blasé attitude which seems to surround the production of *I Am Number Four* is justified by a time where summer blockbusters are based on action figures as well as amusement park rides. *I Am Number Four* however does not possess a character with the charisma of Captain Jack Sparrow, as conceived by Johnny Depp in *The Pirates of the Caribbean* (2003), nor does it offer an escapist CGI explosion spectacular like *Transformers* (2007). Then there is the issue of a pretty savvy audience. The factor that the production team behind the book-to-movie project seemed to disregard was that readers—especially young readers—care about their literary heroes. Their on-screen embodiments have to tangibly exhibit all the crush-worthy characteristics that keep girls up late at night turning pages. This is where *I Am Number Four* falls short.

On the surface, *I Am Number Four* hits all the right tags: A good-looking teen outcast is on the run because he is truly different than all the other boys at school and it is the love of a sweet, confident, but slightly edgy girl that finally makes him realize that he has to stop running, stand up and fight. John (Alex Pettyfer) is an alien, part of a group of nine outcasts from his native planet, each one graced with a unique ability, that are now being hunted on earth. They look supermodel human and so can blend in easily with average high school kids, but each time one of them dies the remaining aliens are branded with a tattoo to remind them that their time is coming. Each one also has a handler that is tasked with keeping them safe and properly trained. John and his handler Henri (Timothy Olyphant) have moved around a lot, each time taking on a new identity in an attempt to outrun the aliens that are hunting them. But Paradise, Ohio is different. Sarah (Dianna Agron) is a soft-spoken photographer who immediately captures John's interest. It's their connection that jeopardizes John and Henri's whole set up and makes John confront his alien destiny.

The movie remains on the surface, never diving into the psyche of the characters, exploring what makes them tick, and answering the questions of how the aliens got to earth, why they look human (and why their hunters do not), what exactly their fight is all about and, most importantly, why anyone should care. The script, adapted by Alfred Gouch, Miles Millar and Marti Noxon, possesses the necessary scenes of John standing up to his handler and John falling for Sarah as he peruses her black and white (read: emotive) photographs, and it even has the right-sounding lines, such as John stating that on his home planet when one of his people falls in love that love is forever, but none of these seemingly-perfect notes are able to hit the intended audience where it counts: the heart. The distance is a result of two

things: some pretty mediocre acting and some lacking source material. Pettyfer, an actor-turned-model-turned-actor, possesses chiseled features that could give Robert Pattinson a run for his money, but he cannot pull off the lost, soulful gaze for which paranormal romantic heroes are known. The fact that he mumbles his lines without any feeling is also problematic. Fun to look at to be sure, Pettyfer just does not possess the screen presence demanded by the story. Agron tries to make up for it but the obvious lack of chemistry between the two is palpable.

No matter who would have embodied the homeless alien with a broken heart, it is hard not to wonder if the problems of this movie run through to its source material. The lore of vampires and werewolves are so ingrained into popular culture that their very mention already creates a picture in the mind of the viewer. Aliens however are a different matter. They have run the gamut from little green men, to insects wearing human suits, so a lot of world-building is needed for a movie based on them. *I Am Number Four* never takes time to do this. Instead the movie borrows from many other concepts, when they die, for example, the aliens turn to vampire-like dust and John's powers are akin to those possessed by mutants. The result is a jumble of known attributes that do not gel under the umbrella of this movie. Everything from the big issues (why are they aliens on earth and why/how does their fight impact humans?) to the smaller details (why does a hair dye job really work to throw off John's hunters and why is Henri so concerned with John's internet presence when the bad aliens never seem to use a computer?) are thrown together without a second thought. Overpowered by a hit soundtrack and governed by a camera that never seems to keep still during its relatively short running time *I Am Number Four* tries to make up for its loosely held together set-up with a few calculated chase scenes and carefully-placed explosions, hoping viewers will not have time to ponder what they are missing.

Joanna Topor MacKenzie

CREDITS

Number Four/John: Alex Pettyfer
Henri: Timothy Olyphant
Sarah: Dianna Agron
Mog Commander: Kevin Durand
Number Six: Teresa Palmer
Origin: USA
Language: English
Released: 2011
Production: Michael Bay; DreamWorks SKG, Reliance Big Entertainment, Bay Films; released by DreamWorks SKG

Directed by: D.J. Caruso
Written by: Alfred Gough, Miles Millar, Marti Noxon
Cinematography by: Guillermo Navarro
Music by: Trevor Rabin
Sound: Per Hallberg
Music Supervisor: Jennifer Hawks
Editing: Vince Filippone, Jim Page
Art Direction: Douglas Cumming, John B. Josselyn, Paul D. Kelly
Costumes: Marie-Sylvie Deveau
Production Design: Tom Southwell
MPAA rating: PG-13
Running time: 104 minutes

REVIEWS

Biancolli, Amy. *Houston Chronicle.* February 18, 2011.
Bowles, Scott. *USA Today.* February 17, 2011.
Burr, Ty. *Boston Globe.* February 17, 2011.
Catsoulis, Jeanette. *New York Times.* February 18, 2011.
Kenny, Glenn. *MSN Movies.* February 17, 2011.
O'Connell, Sean. *Washington Post.* February 24, 2011.
Pols, Mary F. *TIME Magazine.* February 17, 2011.
Rea, Steven. *Philadelphia Inquirer.* February 17, 2011.
Schwarzbaum, Lisa. *Entertainment Weekly.* February 19, 2011.
Sharkey, Betsy. *Los Angeles Times.* February 17, 2011.

QUOTES

Sam: "Did you see what just flew out of that truck? And your dog just shape-shifted into one of them. I thought he was gonna eat me."

TRIVIA

Sharlto Copley was originally cast as Henri, but had to drop out due to a scheduling conflict.

I DON'T KNOW HOW SHE DOES IT

If it were easy, men would do it too.
   —Movie tagline

Box Office: $9.7 million

In the wake of the near-universal disdain leveled at *Sex and the City 2* (2010), a film that even found devotees of the long-running HBO series recoiling in the face of its unbearably smug, obnoxious and self-absorbed manner, one might have assumed that Sarah Jessica Parker would have gone to great lengths to try to find a follow-up project that would put all memories of that disaster far behind her and demonstrate that she

could do more than simply play Carrie Bradshaw over and over again. And yet, *I Don't Know How She Does It* somehow manages to not only mirror all of the loathsome qualities of *SATC 2*, it often manages to exceed them. Deeply unfunny, resolutely shallow and jaw-droppingly unpleasant in its celebration of narcissistic behavior and unchecked materialism, this film could not have come across as a bigger insult to its female-centric target audience if Andrew Dice Clay had been the auteur behind it all and the best thing that can be said about it is that, in a welcome burst of common sense, audiences stayed away in droves and it turned out to be one of the biggest flops of the year.

Parker plays Kate Reddy, a Boston-based woman who finds herself struggling daily to find a balance between her professional and personal lives with nothing more than her pluck, her ingenuity, a high-paying job as a hedge-fund manager (portrayed here as the noblest occupation imaginable), a loving and supportive husband (Greg Kinnear) with a career as an architect, two young children who never seem to come up except for when they are required to help supply plot conflicts, an apartment with approximately the same square footage as many mid-sized museums and a support staff including a work-obsessed assistant (Olivia Munn), a nanny (Jessica Szohr) who is kind, efficient and always around (except for the times when the story requires her absence to advance the plot) and a best pal (Christina Hendricks) who only seems to exist to remind the audience of just how truly spectacular and special Kate is for her ability to juggle work and family unlike any other woman in the whole of history. Conflict arises when Kate's latest business proposal is hailed as a work of genius by the head honcho of her firm, Jack Abelhammer (Pierce Brosnan), and he immediately offers her a big promotion that will give her a sizable pay increase but which will require more work responsibilities including—gasp!—frequent out-of-town trips so that her utter brilliance is never too far away. For a while, Kate seems up to the challenge but when things get to be too much—of course, the only possible time that an all-important out-of-town business meeting can be held is on the morning after Thanksgiving—it appears that she may finally be forced to choose between her family and her job, both of which she dearly loves.

Although based—apparently quite loosely—on the 2002 chick-lit best-seller by Allison Pearson, *I Don't Know How She Does It* has clearly been designed by screenwriter Aline Brosh McKenna and director Douglas McGrath to resemble *Sex and the City* as closely as possible without incurring any lawsuits—everything from a running voiceover commentary from Kate to frequent side trips to New York City to a depiction of Kate's work life that stresses just how great she is at what she does without ever demonstrating what it is that she actually does that is so special in the first place. As irritating as that gets after a while (pretty much by the end of the first reel), what really sinks the film is the incredibly dated and retrograde attitude that it has towards the subject of working women trying to satisfy the demands of career and family. Here, that notion is such an incredible anomaly that the film practically canonizes her in every scene by having everyone remark on her remarkable ability to multitask ("You make complicated seem appealing" is one of the less subtle remarks in this vein.), though female viewers trying to juggle the same things without the same advantages that Kate flaunts will presumably be somewhat unimpressed with her accomplishments. They will probably be even less amused by the finale in which—Spoiler Alert!—Kate basically gets everything that she wants without actually having to do much of anything to achieve her goals. The only real voice of opposition comes from her mother-in-law (Jane Curtin), who shows up to remind Kate that back in her day, women simply stayed at home with the kids and that was that—viewers are presumably meant to take this speech as a measure of how far women have come since then but it is somewhat undercut by the inescapable fact that time she is describing would have been the 1970s and that she is apparently remembering the life of her own mother.

I Don't Know How She Does It is one of those movies where absolutely nothing works. As Kate, Parker delivers one of the most overtly preening and self-absorbed performances in recent memory (though to be fair, she is stuck with impossible-to-deliver lines as "Motherhood is like being a movie star in a world without critics") while the supporting cast ranges from the overtly bland (Brosnan and Kinnear) to the downright terrible (Munn) to the bewilderingly wasted (Hendricks). The direction by McGrath veers from limp comedy to hokey melodrama without demonstrating any feel for either approach and McKenna's screenplay is such an insult to the basic tenets of feminism that it makes one of the old ads for Virginia Slims look positively dignified by comparison.

Peter Sobczynski

CREDITS

Kate Reddy: Sarah Jessica Parker
Jack Abelhammer: Pierce Brosnan
Richard Reddy: Greg Kinnear
Allison Henderson: Christina Hendricks
Momo Hahn: Olivia Munn
Clark Cooper: Kelsey Grammer
Chris Burke: Seth Meyers
Maria Reddy: Jane Curtin
Wendy Best: Busy Philips
Janine LoPierto: Sarah Shahi
Lew Reddy: Mark Blum
Paula: Jessica Szohr
Origin: USA
Language: English
Released: 2011
Production: Donna Gigliotti; released by Weinstein Company
Directed by: Douglas McGrath
Written by: Aline Brosh McKenna
Cinematography by: Stuart Dryburgh
Music by: Aaron Zigman
Sound: William Sarokin
Music Supervisor: Dana Sano
Editing: Camilla Toniolo, Kevin Tent
Costumes: Renee Ehrlich Kalfus
Production Design: Santo Loquasto
MPAA rating: PG-13
Running time: 95 minutes

REVIEWS

Bayer, Jeff. *Scorecard Review.* September 20, 2011.
Edelstein, David. *New York Magazine.* September 12, 2011.
Holden, Stephen. *New York Times.* September 15, 2011.
Pais, Matt. *RedEye.* September 15, 2011.
Phillips, Michael. *Chicago Tribune.* September 15, 2011.
Puig, Claudia. *USA Today.* September 15, 2011.
Rickey, Carrie. *Philadelphia Inquirer.* September 15, 2011.
Robinson, Tasha. *AV Club.* September 15, 2011.
Snider, Eric D. *film.com.* September 16, 2011.
Stevens, Dana. *Slate.* September 16, 2011.

QUOTES

Momo Hahn: "I did have a fish once, but then he kept looking at me with these eyes, like, 'feed me!'—so I flushed him."

TRIVIA

Sarah Jessica Parker and Pierce Brosnan previously starred together in *Mars Attacks!*

AWARDS

Nomination:

Golden Raspberries 2011: Worst Actress (Parker).

I SAW THE DEVIL
(Akamreul boatda)

Evil lives inside.
—Movie tagline

Jee-woon Kim puts his audience in the quietest of spaces for the beginning of what is undoubtedly his most controversial film. Black screen, small white titles, no sound, and then a lilting, even romantic melody, joins a tranquil winter scene, a dark country road revealed through a car windshield whose rearview mirror is framed by the soft blue glow of a pair of plastic electric angel wings as the titles continue. Any revenge film is by default some sort of tragedy and here there is a palpable awareness of innocence and the ethereal beauty it brings into a dark world before it is extinguished. What follows is an almost indescribably visceral, graphic display of the worst behavior humans can inflict upon themselves and one another. The film is grotesque, disturbing, hyperviolent, sick and twisted for nearly all of its 142 minutes. But equally fair descriptors of *I Saw The Devil* would be—thematically complex, well-written, impeccably acted, beautifully lensed, and thought provoking.

After his fiancé is horribly murdered, Soo-hyun (Lee Byung-hun), a top secret agent, realizes the police will never catch the man responsible. He sets out not just to catch the killer, but punish him in a savage game of catch, torture, and release. After confronting and torturing various suspects, he discovers the killer, Kyung-chul (Choi Min-sik), a psychopath who has evaded police for years leaving behind a trail littered with the bodies of young women, children, and other innocent victims. Even when caught by Soo-hyun and savagely punished he does not change, but lashes out again when released, becoming more bestial. Soo-hyun follows the madman to the darkest corners of Kyung-chul's own life, from crime scene to crime scene. Rape, murder, and assault only strengthen both men's resolve. When the killer takes refuge with an old friend who is a serial cannibal, Soo-hyun, after rescuing the latest potential victim, dishes out more justice of the hard-to-watch variety, killing everyone in the house before catching and torturing the killer again. Finally, no longer caring if he is caught or not, Kyung-chul, having figured out Soo-hyun's method of tracking him, leads the secret agent to the site of his newest atrocity—the murder of his fiancé's father. Completely blind with the desire for revenge, Soo-hyun captures the psychopath one more time to deliver a final judgment only to make a startling discovery about himself and the nature of evil.

The most interesting aspect of the film is hinted at in the title. *I Saw The Devil* is a film, ultimately, about looking in the mirror. Just as Soo-hyun, the apparent protagonist believes he has seen the very personification of evil in the man that killed his fiancé so will the viewer. There is literally nothing redeemable about Kyung-chul who seems to kill for no reason except pleasure. He seems in every sense the opposite of what is good, a perfect foil for the most savage punishment a genre movie can devise. But in a devastating final turn Soo-hyun is finally forced to see himself as the weak and ineffectual child raging at an unfair world. His persecu-

tion of the killer has changed nothing, least of all evil itself, which has been content to infect him with precisely the same mad lust for chaos and destruction even as it itself is destroyed in the process. Kyung-chul may well be the Devil but Soo-hyun is no angel.

Matthew 10:28 says, "Do not fear those who kill the body but are unable to kill the soul; but rather fear Him who is able to destroy both soul and body in hell." Those plastic angel wings lighting the way down that country road at the start of film did not keep Soo-hyun's fiancé from being killed. That was not their function. Their function was to be a light, a comfort in a dark place. In the film, a policeman says, "Are we supposed to do all this just to save guys like this?" Tellingly, the officer is not talking about Kyung-hul, but another, more pathetic, villain in the film. *I Saw The Devil* makes a bold statement that, yes, people are not brought into the world to right every wrong or make the world perfect but bear witness to the way things should be, like a pair of ethereally beautiful glowing plastic angel wings. Whether or not viewers can accept the film as more than a loose pastiche of brutally violent scenarios may well have to do with the ability to receive that initial scene as an important part of what the film is trying to say.

Performances here are deceptive. On the surface, everyone plays to type. But those types are masterfully written and in support of an unusual story. As Kyung-chul, Min-sik Choi is in familiar territory. His stunning portrayal of Dae-su Oh, in the now classic revenge thriller *Oldboy* (2003), and Mr. Baek in *Lady Vengeance* (2005) already had him in the revenge movie hall of fame. This lifts him into a sort of luminary otherworld. As the vengeful fiancé Soo-hyun, Byung-hun Lee offers a character defined by stoic silence. But he moves through an arc here that challenges traditional notions of the hero even as he maintains composure through the heinous.

Director Jee-woon Kim has moved from genre to genre steadily throughout his career. His stopover into what could have been completely exploitive is instead a film head and shoulders above what 42nd street ever had to offer. He has created a film of near constant beauty in terms of composition and technique presenting a world that is utterly the outgrowth of his singular creative talent. Here Kim is no mere provocateur but a fair-minded moralist and a humble observer of the broken world.

Dave Canfield

CREDITS

Soo-hyun: Byung-hun Lee
Kyung-chul: Min-Sik Choi

Joo-yeon: San-ha Oh
Captain Jang: Kook-haun Chun
Detective Oh: Ho-jin Chun
Tae-ju: Moo-seong Choi
Je-yeon: Yoon-Seo Kim
Se-jung: In-seo Kim
Origin: Korea
Language: Korean
Released: 2010
Production: Hyun-woo Kim; Peppermint & Co., Siz Entertainment, Magnet Releasing; released by Magnolia Pictures
Directed by: Jee-woon Kim
Written by: Hoon-jung Park
Cinematography by: Lee Mogae
Music by: Mowg
Sound: Tae-young Choi
Editing: Na-young Nam
Costumes: Yoo-jin Kwon
Production Design: Hwa-sung Cho
MPAA rating: Unrated
Running time: 142 minutes

REVIEWS

Cabin, Chris. *Filmcritic.com*. March 3, 2011.
Catsoulis, Jeannette. *New York Times*. March 3, 2011.
Gibron, Bill. *PopMatters*. March 4, 2011.
Grady, Pam. *Boxoffice Magazine*. February 5, 2011.
Jenkins, Mark. *Washington Post*. March 18, 2011.
Long, Tom. *Detroit News*. April 15, 2011.
McWeeny, Drew. *HitFix*. March 1, 2011.
Olsen, Mark. *Los Angeles Times*. March 3, 2011.
Putman, Dustin. *DustinPutman.com*. February 28, 2011.
Singer, Matt. *IFC.com*. March 3, 2011.

QUOTES

Kim Soo-hyeon: "I will kill you when you are in the most pain. When you're in the most pain, shivering out of fear, then I will kill you. That's a real revenge. A real complete revenge."

TRIVIA

The Korea Media Rating Board forced a recut the film for its theatrical release, objecting to its violent content. Otherwise, the film would have gotten a "Restricted" rating, preventing any sort of release in theaters or on home video.

THE IDES OF MARCH

Box Office: $41 million

A meaty, complicated tale of hubris in which idealism hits the rocky shores of opportunity and expediency,

the political drama *The Ides of March* is multi-hyphenate George Clooney's fourth feature film as a director, and it again showcases his instinct for smart material with a special connection to the current zeitgeist. In chronicling the extinguishment of a flickering flame of naiveté, the movie baits its trap, and then artfully tightens the screws of moral and ethical compromise. It is specific in its setting, but the big thematic issues it explores—trust, loyalty, accountability and to what degree the means are justified by the nobility of a specific pursuit's end point—are timeless and universal, marking the film's titular tip of the cap to William Shakespeare's *Julius Caesar* as no matter of coincidence.

The Ides of March centers on the final laps of a Democratic presidential primary, in which the handsome, silver-tongued and unnervingly forthright governor of Pennsylvania, Mike Morris (Clooney), is locked in a fight with Arkansas Senator Ted Pullman (Michael Mantell) for the party's nomination. A true believer in Morris' soaring rhetoric and campaign of hopeful restoration for the United States, Stephen Myers (Ryan Gosling) is a young media consultant and upper-level campaign advisor who finds his idealism tested when a questionable decision puts him on the wrong side of Paul Zara (Philip Seymour Hoffman), Morris' campaign manager and Stephen's boss and mentor. Senator Pullman's campaign manager, Tom Duffy (Paul Giamatti), asks Stephen for a secret meeting, pitching him on coming over to their side by telling him that events are about to break against Morris. Stephen's confidence in his candidate is shaken but he refuses, and eventually tells Paul of the get-together.

While a North Carolina senator, Franklin Thompson (Jeffrey Wright), attempts to extract unreasonable concessions from both campaigns in exchange for his endorsement and pledged delegates ahead of a crucial and perhaps deciding vote in Ohio, Stephen tumbles into a casual sexual relationship with Molly Stearns (Evan Rachel Wood), a bright and charming intern with some secret troubles. When word of his clandestine meeting with Tom leaks out to *New York Times* reporter Ida Horowicz (Marisa Tomei), however, Stephen finds himself on the verge of being offered up as a sacrificial lamb, and pondering whether he can or even should use some of his crucial inside knowledge as leverage for professional advancement.

If Mike Nichols' screen adaptation of Joe Klein's *Primary Colors* (1998), a roman à clef of Bill Clinton's first presidential campaign, often seemed chiefly like a parade of impressions and colorful cameos, *The Ides of March* is a much more pessimistic and grounded thing, like a cross between *The Candidate* (1972) and various movies of political paranoia and backbiting, ranging from *The Parallax View* (1974) to *State of Play* (2009). Clooney's film, unlike those last two examples, does not tilt all the way to murder, but it does delve significantly into scandal and cover-up, all while never fully paying off its most salacious bits.

Because of this, *The Ides of March* is a film that suffers some in critical examination relative to both its ambitions, which outstrip the vast majority of modern Hollywood studio offerings, and lack of traditional cathartic release. In fact, criticism of it—which was the minority report from critics, but notably heavier from old guard veterans, who cumulatively rated it lower on Rotten Tomatoes, at 73 percent, than the 86 percent rating from all critics or even the 76 percent score from audiences—seems to often be as much about what the film deliberately lacks or is not rather than what it actually is.

Adapted by Clooney, longtime collaborator Grant Heslov and Beau Willimon from the latter's 2008 stage-play *Farragut North,* the film scrapes a thumbnail along the surface of the present-day American political scene, implicitly asking the question of whether the system as currently constituted can provide a platform for the rise of a true national leader when it systemically seems built to encourage and protect corrupt structures and compromised figures. The dialogue, peppered with colorful asides and industry-specific jargon, realistically reflects the movie's milieu, as well as the inner qualities and various levels of seasoning of its players. Still, in his review for the *Los Angeles Times,* Kenneth Turan lamented the film's plot proper, noting "the texture of reality and the sheen of fine craft disguise [its shortcomings] for a while, but not forever."

On the surface this and other criticisms like it are true, but *The Ides of March* is not, despite the juiciness of some of its second and third act twists, foremost and truly a plot-driven film. It is not about whether Morris wins the Democratic nomination, or suffers a downfall and humiliation. It is not about whether a specific secret is revealed. It is not even solely about Steven's fate, although he is undeniably the audience's emotional surrogate.

No, *The Ides of March* is fundamentally about the interior duality (some might say duplicity) of all of its characters—from the manner Ida shrewdly trades on her personal rapport with the campaign staffers she covers to how Paul brutally responds to a perceived slight and breach of trust—and how each of their individual make-ups and natures react to hard contact with suddenly introduced feelings of self-interest and self-preservation. At various moments, many characters seem not to be themselves so much as playacting a role they believe others want or need to see.

Some of the plot points on which the story pivots, including Tom's flattery of Stephen, are a bit thin; it is difficult to believe that a guy as smart as Stephen would fall for an opponent's vague pitch of shifting poll numbers and a secret campaign game plan. Similarly, Molly's motivations and decisions are a bit indistinct, and it seems especially doubtful that Ida or her editors would necessarily be as obsessed with a behind-the-scenes "process story" concerning campaign staffers in such a hotly contested election. But if the screenplay perhaps misses a chance to dig into some schemes a bit deeper and in a way that might wring from them some extra, devious delight, the essence and core of its characters are nicely fleshed out, and the movie continually presents rich, compelling scenes in which contrasting philosophies and competing goals are thrown up against one another, and forced to clash. Herein lies the movie's drama, in its individual battles for which personality and what sort of moral compass wins out.

Also, Gosling is a superb vehicle and conduit for audience sympathies. The young actor has a quiet, centered cool and steady, ever-present gaze that paradoxically hints at a restive soul. Gosling's rich touch with the conveyance of inner conflict—similarly put to grand use in *Fracture* (2007), in which he located the humanity in a slick careerist far more unappealing than his character here—highlights the latent yet powerful nature of Stephen's professional ambitions, notwithstanding his simultaneous desire to do good and affect change. All of the other supporting performances are fine, well crafted and of a piece, tonally, but Gosling is the sturdy peg on which *The Ides of March* entirely hangs.

Technically, the film is superb, as even its detractors seem to agree. Phedon Papamichael's evocative cinematography seems to reflect a setting winter's day sun, becoming chillier as the story darkens. Clooney's steady directorial hand and unfussy vision synch up nicely with the work of production designer Sharon Seymour and editor Stephen Mirrione, in a straightforward and very economical telling of the story. Replete with medium shots and close-ups that emphasize conversation over scenery, this is a campaign as viewed from the living room and basement, not an outside gate, with all the attendant pomp and circumstance. Alexandre Desplat's score, meanwhile, has a solemn, almost militaristic undertow, lending the proceedings an air of gravitas.

With its keen detail and a litany of pundit cameos (inclusive of Charlie Rose, Chris Matthews, Rachel Maddow and others), *The Ides of March* is political through and through, bearing ample evidence of Clooney's producing experience alongside Steven Soderbergh on the short-lived, Washington D.C.-set, corridors-of-power HBO series *K Street*. But it is not a polemic tract, and can certainly be enjoyed merely on the basis of its crisp writing and characterizations if one so desires, absent a grander or more specific emotional investment in the political aspects.

The most immediate narrative takeaway is that the people get the leadership they deserve, and therefore cannot reasonably expect behavior less self-absorbed and petty than what the electorate embodies. But in its canny presentation of American politics as an increasingly zero-sum game, in which societal gains are defined as wins for some and necessarily losses for others, *The Ides of March* also more broadly, allegorically makes the point that hypocrisy, smears and moral takedowns help beget and feed a culture that diminishes us all. If it is rather cynical and hard-hearted about this aspect of the human condition, *The Ides of March* is also never less than perceptive, smart and engaging.

Brent Simon

CREDITS

Gov. Mike Morris: George Clooney
Stephen Myers: Ryan Gosling
Paul Zara: Philip Seymour Hoffman
Ida Horowicz: Marisa Tomei
Tom Duffy: Paul Giamatti
Ben Harper: Max Minghella
Molly Stearns: Evan Rachel Wood
Origin: USA
Language: English
Released: 2011
Production: George Clooney, Grant Heslov, Brian Oliver; Exclusive Films, Smokehouse, Cross Creek Pictures; released by Sony Pictures
Directed by: George Clooney
Written by: George Clooney, Grant Heslov
Cinematography by: Phedon Papamichael
Music by: Alexandre Desplat
Sound: Elmo Weber
Music Supervisor: Linda Cohen
Editing: Stephen Mirrione
Art Direction: Chris Cornwell
Costumes: Louise Frogley
Production Design: Sharon Seymour
MPAA rating: R
Running time: 101 minutes

REVIEWS

Ebert, Roger. *Chicago Sun-Times*. October 6, 2011.
Gleiberman, Owen. *Entertainment Weekly*. October 5, 2011.
Kennedy, Lisa. *Denver Post*. October 7, 2011.
Lemire, Christy. *Associated Press*. October 5, 2011.
O'Hehir, Andrew. *Salon.com*. November 10, 2011.
Puig, Claudia. *USA Today*. October 6, 2011.
Rainer, Peter. *Christian Science Monitor*. October 7, 2011.
Scott, A.O. *New York Times*. October 6, 2011.
Stevens, Dana. *Slate*. October 6, 2011.
Turan, Kenneth. *Los Angeles Times*. October 6, 2011.

QUOTES

Tom Duffy: "All the reporters love you. Even the reporters that hate you still love you."

TRIVIA

Leonardo DiCaprio dropped out of the role of Stephen Meyers, but stayed on as executive producer through his company Appian Way. Chris Pine was then considered before Ryan Gosling was ultimately cast in the role.

AWARDS

Nomination:

Oscars 2011: Adapt. Screenplay
British Acad. 2011: Adapt. Screenplay, Support. Actor (Hoffman)
Golden Globes 2012: Actor—Drama (Gosling), Director (Clooney), Film—Drama, Screenplay.

IMMORTALS

The gods need a hero.
—Movie tagline

Box Office: $83.5 million

If David Lean were alive today his head would surely throb and his stomach surely turn if subjected to *Immortals,* a pseudo-historical epic that seems to exist for no other reason than the commercial grosses of similarly minded genre hits *300* (2007) and *Clash of the Titans* (2010), as well as the idea that November 11, 2011 was such a noteworthy date in history that it needed an action movie release. A pumped-up B-feature with wads of extra money thrown at it but none of the accompanying genuine sense of spectacle and imagination that go into the best sorts of unabashedly larger-than-life populist entertainment, *Immortals* represents perhaps the nadir of current mythology-infused Hollywood action spectacles, which is really saying something.

Healthy overseas returns (where the movie grossed over $100 million) and the theatrical surcharges for 3-D presentations helped make *Immortals* a box office winner for upstart distributor Relativity, but it is hard to imagine that the film engendered the sort of public goodwill generally necessary for a sequel.

A cooked-up gumbo of mystical and mythological components, *Immortals* unfolds in roughly 1230 BC, in a world where Zeus (Luke Evans) and other gods literally look down on humankind from their cool, cloudy perch of Mount Olympus. The gods' reign seems to be potentially endangered, however, by a ruthless and bloody campaign being waged by King Hyperion (Mickey Rourke). A scarred, snarling warrior on a personal vendetta, Hyperion seeks the Epirus Bow, a powerful and hidden weapon that will allow him to release a little cache of imprisoned fallen gods, the Titans, and thus destroy Zeus and the other gods who long ago failed to intervene and save Hyperion's family from sickness.

Zeus, then, remains hopeful that a young stonemason, Theseus (Henry Cavill), can grow some stones of his own and lead a proxy war to stop Hyperion. After his village is ransacked and his mother murdered by Hyperion, Theseus hooks up with thief Stavros (Stephen Dorff) and a couple other motley swordsman. Their paths cross with a quartet of clairvoyant Sybilline priestesses being sought by Hyperion, though only one, Phaedra (Freida Pinto), is the true oracle who might be able to reveal the location of the Epirus Bow. Battles ensue, a bit of the requisite romance between Theseus and Phaedra and, finally, a pyrrhic victory and nonsensical ascension.

Narratively, *Immortals* is a nonstarter, across the board. Ignoring the fact the almost comically imprisoned Titans, marching back and forth in their little cell, seem retro-engineered from the final level of a 1980s-era Nintendo game, the movie's most damning fault is that its characters are wafer thin and its dialogue mindless boilerplate. Still, *Immortals* violates even its own inane logic. By its end, Zeus' do-as-I-say-not-as-I-do dictum that Theseus "must come to the conclusion himself" to take down Hyperion becomes a personal exhortation to, "Prove me right—lead your people!"

One of the sub-textual through-lines would seem to be the desire of (certain) men to be gods and of gods to be men, but the script, by brothers Charles and Vlas Parlapanides, does nothing of substance with this contrast. Instead, in an effort to inject false profundity, a quotation from Socrates ("All men's souls are immortal, but the souls of the righteous are immortal and divine") is slapped up over the opening credits and then echoed again at the movie's conclusion. That is the type of film *Immortals* is—so bloated with myopic self-regard that it nudges its audience with a gloriously senseless quote just because it repeatedly underscores its title and, like, was from this famous philosopher guy.

The match of director Tarsem Singh Dhandwar (a renowned visual stylist who previously went by just his first name) and the 3-D format would seem to be a fit made in heaven, but the film underwhelms in even this regard. Whereas *Troy* (2004) was shimmery and lithe, as well as anchored by engaging performances, *Immortals* has some rapturous compositions and background detail, but seems uncertain of how to square all of this with its actors and action. In interviews at the time of the film's release, Singh cited the work of Italian Baroque painter Caravaggio as an inspiration, and it is true that he and cinematographer Brendan Galvin create tableaux that have an oftentimes luminous quality. They also use a heavily saturated palette (colorist Lionel Kopp even rates a title card and poster credit, which seems like a first for his sort of work) which gives the film a kind of otherworldly sheen. When the action unfolds, however, mechanical staging and editing instincts overwhelm the movie.

None of the performances take root in a viewer's imagination outside of the parameters of the screen. Cavill has a certain square-jawed earnestness that makes it easy to see why he was cast in the forthcoming *Superman* movie, but lacks the sorts of darker interior presence that perhaps could have lent the film gravitas. Pinto is a breathtaking beauty, but given precious little to do here. And perhaps understandably for a man who reached such depths, Rourke seems dead-set on converting his Oscar®-nominated lead turn in *The Wrestler* (2008) into as many lucrative studio paydays as possible, so he gets to indulge his growly instincts and again showcase those fantastically weird fingernails.

Gleefully eschewing even the pretense of any classic Greek outfittings, costume designer Eiko Ishioka's work is overblown, though at least keeping with the movie's inflated sense of its own importance. Costumes for Theseus and his cohorts work okay, but the body-conscious golden armor that the Olympians don for battle is risible, and of the same genus as the be-nippled *Batman and Robin* (1997) suits for which Joel Schumacher was so roundly mocked.

Worst of all, though, is composer Trevor Morris' pompously emphatic score. It more than just liberally echoes one of the signature motifs of *Inception* (2010); it so strongly recalls it that it actually comes across as a parody worthy of *South Park*, further undercutting the action by only serving to highlight the movie's comprehensively derivative nature.

If one yearns or needs to see Mickey Rourke theatrically eating pomegranates, *Immortals* satisfies that urge. Otherwise, this uninspired waste of time and money is destined to be just another "classical" movie that in fifteen years confuses plenty of middle school Latin and/or history students trying to escape required reading.

Brent Simon

CREDITS

Theseus: Henry Cavill
Phaedra: Freida Pinto
King Hyperion: Mickey Rourke
Stavros: Stephen Dorff
Athena: Isabel Lucas
Zeus: Luke Evans
Poseidon: Kellan Lutz
Apollo: Corey Sevier
Lysander: Joseph Morgan
Cassander: Stephen McHattie
Old Zeus: John Hurt
Origin: USA
Language: English
Released: 2011
Production: Mark Canton, Ryan Kavanaugh, Gianni Nunnari; Relativity Media, Virgin Produced, Roni Deitz, Atmosphere Entertainment, Hollywood Gang Productions; released by Relativity Media
Directed by: Tarsem Singh
Written by: Charles Parlapanides, Vlas Parlapanides
Cinematography by: Brendan Galvin
Music by: Trevor Morris
Sound: Paul Timothy Carden
Music Supervisor: Bob Bowen
Editing: Wyatt Jones, Stuart Levy, David Rosenbloom
Art Direction: Michele Laliberte
Costumes: Eiko Ishioka
Production Design: Tom Foden
MPAA rating: R
Running time: 110 minutes

REVIEWS

Berkshire, Geoff. *Metromix.com.* November 11, 2011.
Debruge, Peter. *Variety.* November 10, 2011.
Ebert, Roger. *Chicago Sun-Times.* November 11, 2011.
Gilchrist, Todd. *Boxoffice Magazine.* November 10, 2011.
Grierson, Tim. *Screen International.* November 10, 2011.
McCarthy, Todd. *Hollywood Reporter.* November 10, 2011.
Sharkey, Betsy. *Los Angeles Times.* November 10, 2011.
Smith, Kyle. *New York Post.* November 11, 2011.
Weitzman, Elizabeth. *New York Daily News.* November 10, 2011.
Whitty, Stephen. *Newark Star-Ledger.* November 11, 2011.

QUOTES

Theseus: "Stand your ground! Fight for order! Fight for the man beside you! Fight for those who bore you! Fight for your children! Fight for your future! Fight for your name to survive! Fight! For immortality!"

TRIVIA

Director Tarsem Singh has described the film as being like a "Renaissance painting style."

IN A BETTER WORLD
(Haevnen)

Box Office: $1 million

Screenwriter Anders Thomas Jensen's two-sided view of the world—that of the bullies and the bullied—raises far more questions than its simplistic moralizing attempts to answer. While setting forth with the best of intentions, *In a Better World* (originally *Hævnen* in its native Denmark, which is a more appropriate title given that the question of "revenge" is the crux of the story's thematic musing) suffers from loaded scenarios, easy resolutions, and misguided equivalence.

The philosophical battle is characterized by the difference between the viewpoints of a young, resentful, near-psychotic boy and a pacifistic, humanitarian, near-saintly man, only adding to the obvious nature of how Jensen weighs the dual options. That the latter turns out to be a hypocrite should, of course, be a point of contention to his philosophy, and Jensen ensures that no such doubt arises by pitting his change of heart against a foe that most sane and rational people would believe deserves whatever comeuppance might befall him. The more difficult path for both this heroic figure and Jensen's narrative is to battle evil without resorting (or, more specifically in his case, allowing others to resort) to violence, and in permitting the easy way out of a grim situation, Jensen also loses much of the dramatic potential of the fight.

The man in question is Anton (Mikael Persbrandt, in a performance that matches his character's rock-solid conviction), a doctor who routinely travels from his home in Denmark to a refugee camp in Africa to treat the displaced. His personal life is in shambles. He and his wife Marianne (Trine Dyrholm) are separated, after—based on the implication of a vague conversation between the two—Anton's affair with an unknown, unnamed woman. Their two sons Elias (Markus Rygaard) and Morten (Toke Lars Bjarke) live with Marianne at the family house and visit with Anton at their summer home when he returns from his trips.

The counterpoint to Anton's worldview is Christian (William Jøhnk Juels Nielsen), a boy in Elias' grade whose mother has recently died after an extended battle with cancer. He and his father Claus (Ulrich Thomsen) move from London to Christian's grandmother's (Elsebeth Steentoft) house in the same town where Anton's family resides.

Christian and Elias both, then, come from broken homes and, with Claus traveling back to London for business, have absentee fathers. Christian's background is further complicated by his relationship with his father, whom he believes is in some way responsible for his mother's death. He is closed off from Claus, and director Susanne Bier uses the repeated image of the father sitting alone at the kitchen table, further isolated and enclosed in helplessness by the frame of the door, waiting for a son who is too caught up in violent video games and Internet browsing to join his father.

Christian is angry with his dad and the world that took his mother away from him, and, no matter how blunt Jensen's screenplay may be in establishing the warning signs or—if one believes them to be such—mitigating factors of Christian's eventual decline into violent behavior, the script does address the division between father and son in a wholly sympathetic manner. Of particular honesty is a scene later in the movie when Christian finally tells Claus that he believes his father wished his mother to die, and Claus can only answer that, yes, once it became hopeless and she wanted to herself, he did indeed want her to die, if only so that her suffering might end. There is no processing this distinction within the mind of the grief-stricken 12-year-old.

An outlet for Christian's anger arrives in the form of the school bully Sofus (Simon Maagaard Holm), who, with a group of friends, taunts and pushes around his classmates as they make their way to the school building. After standing up to him in defense of Elias, Sofus throws a basketball in Christian's face, and, in retaliation, Christian viciously beats the tormentor with a pump for a bicycle tire and holds a knife to his throat. After the police and school officials intervene after the assault, Sofus' harassment stops. Jensen bypasses the most obvious query here—whether the bullying could be halted without resorting to physical violence through the intermediary of teachers and officials—by inserting a parent-teacher conference in which the teachers doubt that Sofus could be capable of such behavior. It is merely an obstacle meant to weigh the odds against Elias, who covers for his new friend's story that the attack was in self-defense, and Christian, thereby putting them into a transparently imbalanced situation where extraordinary measures seem necessary.

Anton is eventually faced with a similar situation in Africa. There, a brutal warlord known only as "Big Man" (Odiege Matthew) terrorizes the people in the outlying areas of the camp where Anton works. With a group of equally ruthless men, "Big Man" takes bets on the sex of the fetuses inside pregnant women's wombs; to determine who wins, he slices open their abdomens. Anton learns of this horror when a few women who survive arrive at the camp, and soon, he is face-to-face with "Big Man," who has an injured leg.

By this point, Anton has become the movie's moral center, lecturing his sons and Christian about dismissing the desire for violence (Claus makes a similar statement to his son after the beating of Sofus, stating that the cycle of retaliation is how wars start; "Not if you hit hard enough the first time," Christian responds, chastising his father's opinion). To prove his point, Anton visits the workplace of a man (Kim Bodnia) who slaps him in the face (for stopping a fight between their two young sons), insisting to the man's face that he is merely a "jerk" that finds power in bullying others. When the man begins slapping him again, Anton simply walks away, convincing his sons and Christian that the victory belongs to him and not the man. Christian doubts Anton's logic and begins a plan to destroy the man's van with a bomb made from fireworks. Elias conspires with him, though only to maintain his only friendship.

The convergence of the father and son's choices of allowing retaliation against the enemies of others (essentially and dishonestly putting the relatively harmless man who slaps Anton on the same level as "Big Man") is the movie's climax, and once their decisions have been made, Jensen drops the repercussions to smooth out the personal crises of the assorted characters. There is always another "Big Man" in the wings to take the place of his predecessor, and, for all its confused sermonizing, *In a Better World* seems eager to ignore reality.

Mark Dujsik

CREDITS

Anton: Mikael Persbrandt
Claus: Ulrich Thomsen
Marianne: Trine Dyrholm
Lars: Kim Bodnia
Elias: Markus Rygaard
Christian: William Johnk Nielsen
Origin: Denmark
Language: Danish
Released: 2010
Production: Sisse Graum Jorgensen; Swedish Film Institute, Zentropa Entertainment; released by Sony Pictures Classics
Directed by: Suzanne (Susanne) Bier
Written by: Anders Thomas Jensen
Cinematography by: Morten Soborg

Music by: Johan Soderqvist
Sound: Eddie Simonsen, Anne Jensen
Editing: Pernille Bech Christensen, Morten Egholm
Costumes: Manon Rasmussen
Production Design: Peter Grant
MPAA rating: Unrated
Running time: 113 minutes

REVIEWS

Blackman, Joshua. *FILMINK*. March 28, 2011.
Ebert, Roger. *Chicago Sun-Times*. April 14, 2011.
Edelstein, David. *New York Magazine*. March 27, 2011.
Gonzalez, Ed. *Slant Magazine*. March 27, 2011.
Hewitt, Chris. *St. Paul Pioneer Press*. April 14, 2011.
Rocchi, James. *MSN Movies*. March 31, 2011.
Schager, Nick. *House Next Door*. January 21, 2011.
Scott, A.O. *New York Times*. March 31, 2011.
Tallerico, Brian. *HollywoodChicago.com*. April 15, 2011.
Williams, Joe. *St. Louis Post-Dispatch*. May 6, 2011.

TRIVIA

The story that Christian reads at his mother's funeral is "The Nightingale" by Hans Christian Andersen.

AWARDS

Oscars 2010: Foreign Film
Golden Globes 2011: Foreign Film.

IN THE LAND OF BLOOD AND HONEY

As a generalized account of the horrors of the Bosnian War, which raged for over three years after the breakup of Yugoslavia without much international attention until word of ethnic cleansing and possible genocide spread (and even then it passed under many people's radars), *In the Land of Blood and Honey* contains scenes to set one's teeth on edge. A mother cradles her dead baby in her arms and contorts her face into a silent scream, so that the soldiers in the army of nationalist Bosnian Serbs may not hear it. Soldiers shoot down men in cold blood as they walk down the street.

They capture women and place them in a military barrack; after asking if the women can do menial chores, the soldiers pick one here and another there and rape them as the rest of the women watch on helplessly, knowing this torment will be their life for the foreseeable future. Among these female prisoners—some of them pregnant after constant sexual assaults—one lies awake sobbing in the night, wishing that she would die so that her husband might not know what has befallen her.

Writer/director Angelina Jolie, in her first work behind the camera for a narrative feature, arranges these horrific acts with bluntness and observes them with an impassive eye, unwavering except to survey the faces of witnesses realizing that they could be the next to be assaulted or killed. These are strong moments, imbuing the proceedings with a sense of resigned helplessness.

Paradoxically, it is when Jolie's screenplay converges on the specifics of its narrative that *In the Land of Blood and Honey* loses some of its power. The central arc is of a romance interrupted and the resulting power struggle between two former almost-lovers amidst the background of the strife (a group of women survivors in Bosnia and Herzegovina, thinking it was the story of a prisoner who falls in love with her rapist based on rumors, protested the movie at first, causing production to halt before it even started; the government retracted the decision after reading the script). The loss of the wider view is enough, in fact, for the movie ultimately to be an earnest but frustrating disappointment.

The two main characters are Ajla (Zana Marjanovic), a Bosniak (i.e., in simple terms, Bosnians who adhere to Islam and made up the slight majority of the population of Bosnia and Herzegovina at the time the conflict began) artist who has returned to her hometown after an unspecified absence, and Danijel (Goran Kostic), a Serb (i.e., the second most populace ethnic group in the country) and soldier in the Army. At the start of the movie in 1992, the two meet at a club for a date, dancing and gradually growing closer as the band plays until an explosion rocks the club.

Four months later, Ajla and her sister Lejla (Vanessa Glodjo), who has an infant son, are packing and preparing to leave their apartment and the country. A group of soldiers begins pounding on the doors within the apartment complex, directing everyone outside. After rounding up all the able-bodied men and executing them (Jolie keeps her shots focused on the women's faces as automatic rifle fire blares from around the corner), the soldiers choose some of the women, including Ajla, to be brought back to their compound. Danijel is one of the commanding officers of the unit and rescues Ajla before a soldier rapes her.

Danijel takes Ajla into his protection; he tells his men that no one else is allowed to touch her (When a soldier tests Danijel's loyalty to the cause by knocking down a tray Ajla is carrying and stepping on her hand as she attempts to clean up, Danijel walks away to save face; he and Ajla meet in seclusion to embrace afterwards). In the background during transitional scenes, radio and television broadcasts illuminate certain details, such as quoting then United States Secretary of State James Baker stating, "We don't have a dog in this fight;" in a similar way, such is the case with Ajla and Danijel. He is uncertain about the cause. His father (Rade Serbedzija), a general in the army, is a true believer in what he sees as an existential threat to the Serbs in Bosnia and Herzegovina from the growing Muslim population (He proudly cites a history of war, like so many nationalists are wont to do); Danijel protests to no avail that he recognizes these people—has grown up with them. She, a captive in a precarious state of safety, is too concerned with survival to fight.

An uncomfortable (at least on the part of the audience) romance blooms between the two captives—her physical and he ideological—until he is transferred to the front lines in Sarajevo. She escapes, reunites with her sister, and joins a band of Bosniak fighters.

The movie, populated with local actors speaking in the native Serbo-Croatian tongue and shot on location in Hungary with austere cinematography by Dean Semler, has the air of authenticity. Jolie's portrayal of the Serbs balances monsters like Danijel's father, who orders a mass execution—he manning a bulldozer to cover a mass grave—as an old friend of his begs for mercy, and ordinary men who do monstrous things for what they believe to be honorable reasons (in addition to Danijel's conflicted feelings, Darko [Nikola Djuricko], one of his friends and a fellow soldier, is convinced the present warfare will prevent his newborn child from having to fight in the future). A particularly harrowing scene follows a group of women as soldiers guide them through the forest to be used as human shields during a firefight.

The movie's final act, which brings Ajla and Danijel together again through a series of coincidences and ambiguous plotting (a vital scene regarding the Bosniak militia's plans and Ajla's own participation within them is edited in such a way that both are unclear until near the end of the movie), is easily its weakest. In it, Ajla and Danijel shift from lenses through which the audience sees the broader conflict to participants in their own comparatively melodramatic struggle. By the time the final text coda that states facts about Bosnian War arrives at the end of *In the Land of Blood and Honey,* the actual consequences of the war seem further away.

Mark Dujsik

CREDITS

Ajla: Zana Marjanovic
Danijel: Goran Kostic
Nabojsa: Rade Serbedzija
Darko: Nikola Djuricko

Mitar: Goran Jevtic
Nadja: Dzana Pinjo
Alexsander: Branko Djuric
Hana: Alma Terzic
Durja: Milos Timotijevic
Origin: USA
Language: Bosnian
Released: 2011
Production: Angelina Jolie, Graham King, Tim Headington, Tim Moore; GK Films; released by FilmDistrict
Directed by: Angelina Jolie
Written by: Angelina Jolie
Cinematography by: Dean Semler
Music by: Gabriel Yared
Editing: Patricia Rommel
Sound: Becky Sullivan
Costumes: Gabriele Binder
Production Design: Jon Hutman
MPAA rating: R
Running time: 127 minutes

REVIEWS

Coyle, Jake. *Boston Globe.* December 20, 2011.
Dargis, Manohla. *New York Times.* December 22, 2011.
Ebert, Roger. *Chicago Sun-Times.* January 4, 2012.
Macdonald, Moira. *Seattle Times.* January 5, 2012.
O'Hehir, Andrew. *Salon.com.* December 23, 2011.
Rabin, Nathan. *AV Club.* December 22, 2011.
Rea, Steven. *Philadelphia Inquirer.* January 5, 2012.
Rocchi, James. *MSN Movies.* December 19, 2011.
Turan, Kenneth. *Los Angeles Times.* December 23, 2011.
Willmore, Alison. *Movieline.* December 22, 2011.

TRIVIA

Marija Karan, Branko Tomovic, and Branka Katic were also considered for the lead roles at one time.

AWARDS

Nomination:

Golden Globes 2012: Foreign Film.

IN TIME
(Now)

Time is money.
—Movie tagline
Live forever or die trying.
—Movie tagline

His crime wasn't stealing time. He was giving it away.
    —Movie tagline

Tomorrow is a luxury you can't afford.
    —Movie tagline

Box Office: $37.5 million

Another science-fiction think piece from writer/director Andrew Niccol, *In Time* is a naïve allegory of the dangers of what one character dubs "Darwinian capitalism," which promotes the survival of the fittest, wherein the "fittest" are best defined as the richest and the economy is literally a system of survival. The currency of this dystopian future is time—not in a theoretical sense but in the urgent reality of months, minutes, and seconds of an individual's life.

The entirety of the population is genetically engineered to live out a normal life until the age of 25, at which time, physiological development ceases; no one physically ages past that point. At the same time, a clock on a person's left forearm begins counting down from one year; when the countdown reaches zero, the person dies. People can trade, borrow, earn, and steal time through almost any means necessary, and the gimmick provides Niccol with plenty of opportunities to implement the old standby of garnering tension: the ticking clock. The clock repeatedly runs low for multiple characters, and instead of exploring the instinctual terror of such a day-to-day, hour-to-hour, and second-to-second existence, Niccol instead finds comfort in the fight against an insane system—a fight that, by most of the characters' own admittance and basic common sense, is ultimately a losing one.

The hero is Will Salas (Justin Timberlake, who has shined in his pervious supporting roles but is unable to pass the scrutiny of a leading one), who has managed to live two years past his expiration date (people refer to their age by the number of years past 25) by working at a manufacturing company and through various loans that his mother Rachel (Olivia Wilde) has taken. They live in Dayton, a ghetto in comparison to the other "Time Zones" (neighborhoods divided by class), and death is a daily occurrence there. Bodies, with the thirteen zeros on their arm black instead of the eerie neon green of the living populace, lie in the streets—unmourned and barely noticed by others except in fleeting glances.

As intrinsically silly and implausible as the premise is (mostly for a lack of explanation of how and why this entire arrangement came to be and works), Alex Mc-Dowell's admirably restrained production design, which foregoes the typically elaborate blueprints of futuristic landscapes, keeps the material firmly planted in reality.

It instead focuses on the disparity between the poor and the rich, imagining Dayton as low-income suburb of the affluent neighborhood of a city that is New Greenwich—home of the wealthy and powerful. The only unique, contemporary technology accommodates the circulation of time—scanners for payment and metallic cubes for storage and distribution.

The plot begins after a short-lived introduction to the characters and the overall situation when Will encounters Henry Hamilton (Matt Bomer), a wealthy man with over a century on his clock, at a local bar, "slumming" it for a night. While there, a gang called the Minutemen, led by Fortis (Alex Pettyfer), approach the man, flaunting his time by buying the house drinks, with the intention of stealing his time. Will helps Hamilton escape, and the two spend the night in an abandoned warehouse, where they wax philosophical on the nature of the system. Hamilton, who has already lived for over a hundred years, is convinced that people need to die. He is also aware that there is plenty of time available to everyone; the upper classes are merely hoarding it to be immortal. As a last act, Hamilton gives Will all of his remaining time, save for five minutes so that he can find a quiet spot to die.

Rachel dies after an unjust scenario (She makes a loan payment, leaving her with only ninety minutes on her clock when the bus ride home costs two hours and the walk takes the same amount of time), and Will decides to make the wealthy of society pay for their heartless accumulation of time—time that could be better spent providing everyone with the chance to live a life without the constant fear of dying young. With his newly inherited capital, he travels to New Greenwich, where he meets bank owner Philippe Weis (Vincent Kartheiser) and his daughter Sylvia (Amanda Seyfried). Meanwhile, a devoted Timekeeper named Raymond Leon (Cillian Murphy) hunts for Will, whom surveillance cameras captured near Hamilton's body. After kidnapping her to evade the Timekeepers, Sylvia joins forces with Will, and the two become champions of the poor in the mold of Robin Hood—stealing from the well-to-do and redistributing time to the destitute.

With his barebones plot in motion, Niccol expends his concentration on the movie's style (which, with Colleen Atwood's monochromatic costumes, is considerable) and polish (which, with cinematographer Roger Deakins' spare use of light, is striking). Within the story, Niccol inserts a few action sequences of the generic variety—a few car chases and a pursuit across rooftops—that really only point to how determined Leon, in his Gestapo chic leather coat, is. An arm-wrestling match to the death (Time is transferred between people by grasping arms; the person whose arm is on top gains time from the other) between Will and Fortis loses whatever tension might have existed when Will foreshadows his strategy to Sylvia.

These are minimal issues, though, compared to the execution of the central metaphor. In between those action sequences, characters exist only to espouse very thinly veiled political statements ("No one should be immortal if even one person has to die," Will counters Weis) or obvious puns on the swap of time for money ("I'd say your money or your life," Will tells one of targets of his robbery). The concept of *In Time* is not nearly as intelligent as it supposes, and the implementation thereof leaves even more to be desired.

Mark Dujsik

CREDITS

Will Salas: Justin Timberlake
Sylvia Weis: Amanda Seyfried
Raymond Leon: Cillian Murphy
Philippe Weis: Vincent Kartheiser
Fortis: Alex Pettyfer
Borel: Johnny Galecki
Rachel Salas: Olivia Wilde
Henry Hamilton: Matt Bomer
Origin: USA
Language: English
Released: 2011
Production: Andrew Niccol, Marc Abraham, Eric Newman; Regency Enterprises, New Regency Pictures, Strike Entertainment; released by 20th Century-Fox
Directed by: Andrew Niccol
Written by: Andrew Niccol
Cinematography by: Roger Deakins
Music by: Craig Armstrong
Sound: Michael Babcock
Editing: Zach Staenberg
Art Direction: Priscilla Elliott
Costumes: Colleen Atwood
Production Design: Alex McDowell
MPAA rating: PG-13
Running time: 109 minutes

REVIEWS

Berardinelli, James. *ReelViews*. October 28, 2011.
Catsoulis, Jeannette. *NPR*. October 27, 2011.
Dargis, Manohla. *New York Times*. October 27, 2011.
Ebert, Roger. *Chicago Sun-Times*. October 26, 2011.
O'Hehir, Andrew. *Salon.com*. October 26, 2011.
Phillips, Michael. *Chicago Tribune*. October 27, 2011.
Robinson, Tasha. *AV Club*. October 27, 2011.
Schager, Nick. *Slant Magazine*. October 26, 2011.
Stevens, Dana. *Slate*. October 28, 2011.
Tallerico, Brian. *HollywoodChicago.com*. October 28, 2011.

QUOTES

Philippe Weis: "For a few immortals to live, many people must die."

TRIVIA

Many of the character names used in the film are those of famous, and not so famous, watchmakers.

INCENDIES
(Scorched)

The search began at the opening of their mother's will.
—Movie tagline

Box Office: $2 million

Based on the play by Lebanese-Canadian writer-director Wajdi Mouawad, *Incendies* has a lot in common with other great films about war. At times devastating and haunting, it transcends the grand-scale conflict of the Middle Eastern civil war it depicts (though no country is specified, all signs point to the action taking place in Lebanon) to present the personal, human side of years-long religious conflict. The film's director, Denis Villeneuve, elegantly transplants the story to the screen, maintaining a pulsing intensity throughout the narrative and touching on poignant themes that tug at the heartstrings. But when the central mystery finally reveals itself, instead of reeling in shock, viewers are left scratching their heads.

The opening of Villeneuve's adaptation is mesmerizing as young boys stand in a crumbling cement building, waiting to have their heads shaved. Something about the scene—the lost look in their eyes, the fact that no parents are around, the haunting Radiohead ballad playing in the background or the Western interpretation that this is how terrorists are made—suggests that these boys are bound for heartbreak. The next scene takes place half a world away, in present day Montreal. At the reading of their mother Nawal's (Lubna Azabal) will, twins Jeanne (Mélissa Désormeaux-Poulin) and Simon (Maxim Gaudette) are thrown a curveball when the notary hands them two letters—one intended for the absentee father they presumed to be dead and one for a brother they never knew they had. Their mother's instructions are simple: "Find them." Of course, the path to doing so is anything but simple. The audience can feel that Jeanne and Simon will somehow collide with the boys at the start of the film. And it is the wait for this collision that gives a tense immediacy to the film.

Leaving her brooding and doubtful brother behind in Quebec, Jeanne travels to the Middle East to retrace her mother's life. Her journey to find a father she never knew quickly turns into the discovery of her mother, whose life plays out in flashbacks. Villeneuve elegantly interweaves Jeanne's quest with scenes from her mother's life setting up powerful juxtapositions between the times the women literally walked the same paths, while also showcasing how deep the roots of culture and religion go. Nawal's story is wrought with suffering and brings forth some of the most powerful moments of the film, such as a haunting scene where a young Nawal tries to save a Muslim girl by claiming her as her Christian daughter. Needless to say it does not work. But as frightening, visceral and moving as Nawal's story is, the true impact comes with Jeanne in the present day. As she naively sets off to dig into her mother's past, Jeanne is thrown into a world that, in a sense, time forgot. The past is never buried here and her mother's sins are as fresh in the eyes of the people she approaches in her mother's village as they were years ago. When Simon finally joins his sister viewers are again shown just how deeply embedded the conflicts are in this part of the world. At one point, Simon is told that all it will take to finally access the information he is seeking is a spark. Once that spark ignites, the twins' worlds are thrown into a tailspin. As the plot arcs ever closer to an eerie right-wing prison torturer named Abou Tarek (Abdelghafour Elaaziz), the audience readies themselves for the final, monumental collision between Nawal's past and her children's present. But when the explosion hits, instead of a shocking reveal, it feels like one coincidence too far for comfort, causing the film to lose the opportunity of vital impact.

Until these last minutes, *Incendies* unravels as the story of a mother's strength and sacrifice for her children, of people doing what they must in order to survive in the most unimaginable circumstances and of residual guilt. There is a powerful metaphor here that Villeneuve works hard to embrace about the small twists that people who they are and about love and hate being just sides of the same coin. He also deftly explores the intangible and unalterable hold that religion and culture play in life and the ends to which they push people. But he never quite reaches the intensity of that fist scene, nor does he deliver on the pent-up, palpable anticipation it creates. Instead of a collision between past and present full of emotional gravitas the film spins into the realm of impossible melodrama and the result leaves viewers wanting.

Joanna Topor MacKenzie

CREDITS

Nawal Marwan: Lubna Azabal
Jeanna Marwan: Melissa Desormeaux-Poulin
Simon Marwan: Maxim Gaudette
Jean Lebel: Remy Girard
Abou Tarek: Abdelghafour Elaaziz
Maddad: Allen Altman
Chamseddine: Mohamed Majd
Fahim: Nadim Sawalha
Maika: Baya Belal
Origin: Canada, France
Language: Arabic, French
Released: 2010
Production: Luc Dery, Kim McCraw; MicroScope, TS Productions; released by Sony Pictures Classics
Directed by: Denis Villenueve
Written by: Denis Villenueve
Cinematography by: Andre Turpin
Music by: Gregoire Hetzel
Sound: Jean Umansky
Music Supervisor: Pascal Mayer, Sebastien Lepine
Editing: Monique Dartonne
Costumes: Sophie Lefebvre
Production Design: Andre-Line Beauparlant
MPAA rating: R
Running time: 130 minutes

REVIEWS

Burr, Ty. *Boston Globe.* May 12, 2011.
Edelstein, David. *New York Magazine.* April 19, 2011.
Gleiberman, Owen. *Entertainment Weekly.* April 19, 2011.
Holcomb, Mark. *Village Voice.* April 19, 2011.
Mondello, Bob. *NPR.* April 25, 2011.
Phillips, Michael. *Chicago Tribune.* April 28, 2011.
Robinson, Tasha. *AV Club.* April 21, 2011.
Sharkey, Betsy. *Los Angeles Times.* April 21, 2011.
Smith, Kyle. *New York Post.* April 22, 2011.
Williams, Joe. *St. Louis Post-Dispatch.* May 20, 2011.

QUOTES

Notary Jean Lebel: "To a notary, Mr. Marwan, a promise is a sacred thing."

AWARDS

Nomination:

Oscars 2010: Foreign Film
British Acad. 2011: Foreign Film.

INSIDIOUS

What's in that picture?
 —Movie tagline
We need to save Dalton...now!
 —Movie tagline

It's not the house that's haunted.
—Movie tagline

Box Office: $54 million

A slickly mounted and largely effective paranormal thriller, *Insidious* centers on Josh and Renai Lambert (Patrick Wilson and Rose Byrne), a young married couple who, shortly after a move with their three children to a new home, come to find their residence haunted by dark spirits. Young Dalton (Ty Simpkins) does not like his room, and hears strange noises in the attic. Things turn even more somber when he slips off the attic ladder and into a comatose state. Months later, he has still not recovered, but the Lamberts bring him home to care for him. After more troubling incidents, Renai insists on a move, and so they uproot their family once again.

Problems persist, however, and a nasty, demonic-looking figure pops up. Josh's mother, Lorraine (Barbara Hershey), believes Renai, and invites Elise Rainier (Lin Shaye), an old friend with experience in dealing with paranormal phenomena, to come and give the family a consultation. Along with her two seriocomic assistants, Tucker and Specs (Angus Sampson and Leigh Whannell), and their scientific equipment, Elise descends upon the Lambert home to observe Dalton. Her conclusion is that it was not their abode that was cursed, but rather their son. Dalton, Elise says, has the ability to astral project himself into parallel spirit worlds where, because of his youthful innocence, he is susceptible to a malevolent being that wishes to pry him from his mortal body and use it as a vessel into the world of the living. When Lorraine triggers memories of a similar knack in Josh, he tries to "trip" into this shadowy world and save his son.

The foundational moorings of *Insidious* may be somewhat shaky—it is in some ways the cinematic genre equivalent of a building constructed on sand, and not fully up to code for earthquakes—but that does not transmute the basic fact that director James Wan and writer-actor Whannell, after helping launch the gore and so-called torture-porn renaissance with their original entry in the *Saw* (2004) franchise, here demonstrate an inclination and ability to wring dread and scares out of scenes in a more elemental fashion. It is this against-the-popular-grain quality that helps *Insidious* stand out in the commercial marketplace against thematically similar competition, and was likely responsible for a good portion of its impressive $54 million domestic (and $92 million cumulative) theatrical haul, as well as its positive critical rating on aggregator sites like Rotten Tomatoes.

It certainly helps to have a game cast. Byrne, who is by and large relegated to much more buttoned-up work on the Emmy®-winning small screen legal drama *Dam-ages,* here showcases angst-ridden maternal concern and triggered fear. Wilson, too, delivers a solid performance. The movie sets up a quiet disconnect between the couple—hints of things they do not know about one another, or things of which they know, but do not recognize the full meanings and motivations—and then puts this to good effect in their reactions to Dalton's plight.

Mostly, though, *Insidious* reflects a smart assemblage of technical elements in streamlined service of a uniform goal: entertainment. The muted tones of David Brewer and John Leonetti's cinematography create a miasma of unease. And Wan's shot selection and editorial choices help build trepidation and anxiety—the spotlighting of a rustling tree in the deep-focus darkness outside of Dalton's room, for example, slowly brought into clarity. If there is disconnect or faltering in this regard, it is in the film's music. Given the movie's efficient and evocative early use of silences, it is both surprising and disappointing when the clanging and screeching strings of composer Joseph Bishara's efforts intrude on later scenes.

In its home stretch, *Insidious* also unravels a bit in its narrative. It feels as if Wan and Whannell, having set up the plot device of astral projection, feel compelled to stake out an audacious third act, yet are uncertain of where to take the story. The wrap-up of *Insidious* hinges greatly on this, obviously, and yet the presentation of a smoke-filled house and the vision of a ghastly family of murder victims seems informed by a ghoulish cartoon funhouse sensibility that is at odds with the rest of the picture, and only tenuously connected to either Dalton and/or Josh's past.

Having Josh trek into the beyond in pursuit of Dalton may read on paper as a heroic act and vicarious experience for viewers, but as rendered it is at once a divisive and somewhat known confrontation. The other cast members, meanwhile, are left to sit in the living room and sporadically shout and stroke a passed out Josh's leg while he completes this spirit-world steeplechase. For a film that has for the most part traded in careful doses of tone for the bulk of its running time, this final fifteen to twenty minutes feels like a compromise of that rather exacting construction. It may be the theoretical sizzle to sell the steak, but it basically turns out to be a lot of noisy sturm and drang.

That said, *Insidious* is overall a success, and cannot be completely marred by the relative conventionality of its conclusion. It is reminiscent in certain ways of *Drag Me To Hell* (2009), which marked Sam Raimi's return to the horror genre—both movies on a certain level acknowledge their goosing intent, but without any referential acts or winks from their characters—yet *Insidious* feels like even more of a discovery and pleasant treat for audiences, in large part to its much smaller budget. While Hollywood may throw more and more money at special effects and 3-D technology, there will always be something elementally cathartic about sharing darkness, some low-fi spookiness, nervous tension and a knowing laugh of release with an audience.

Brent Simon

CREDITS

John Lambert: Patrick Wilson
Renai Lambert: Rose Byrne
Dalton Lambert: Ty Simpkins
Elise Rainier: Lin Shaye
Foster Lambert: Andrew Astor
Tucker: Angus Sampson
Specs: Leigh Whannell
Origin: USA
Language: English
Released: 2010
Production: Jason Blum, Steven Schneider, Oren Peli; Haunted Movies, IM Global, Alliance Films; released by Alliance Films
Directed by: James Wan
Written by: Leigh Whannell
Cinematography by: David M. Brewer
Music by: Joseph Bishara
Editing: James Wan
Sound: Robert Cross
Art Direction: Jennifer Spence
Costumes: Kristen M. Burke
Production Design: Aaron Sims
MPAA rating: PG-13
Running time: 103 minutes

REVIEWS

DeFore, John. *Hollywood Reporter.* March 29, 2011.
Edelstein, David. *New York Magazine.* March 28, 2011.
Gleiberman, Owen. *Entertainment Weekly.* March 30, 2011.
Lemire, Christy. *Associated Press.* March 30, 2011.
O'Hehir, Andrew. *Salon.com.* March 30, 2011.
O'Sullivan, Michael. *Washington Post.* March 31, 2011.
Phillips, Michael. *Chicago Tribune.* March 31, 2011.
Puig, Claudia. *USA Today.* March 31, 2011.
Savlov, Marc. *Austin Chronicle.* April 1, 2011.
Tallerico, Brian. *HollywoodChicago.com.* April 1, 2011.

QUOTES

Elise Reiner: "It's not the house that is haunted. It's your son."

TRIVIA

The mask that Elise puts on to enter the dream world is the same as the one used by the the Sandman in the comic book series of the same name created by Neil Gaiman.

THE INTERRUPTERS

Every city needs its heroes.
—Movie tagline

Throughout the course of 2008, the total count of murders in the city of Chicago outnumbered the deaths of American soldiers in Iraq (509 to 314). In the summer of that year alone, the number of murders in Chicago almost doubled those of soldiers killed in the Iraqi war zone in the same period (125 to 65). Those statistics eventually made national news after a cell phone video capturing the brutal beating death of a 16-year-old boy on his way home from school spread around the Internet. At the time, director Steve James was following CeaseFire, a non-profit organization that serves as intermediaries within local communities struggling with violence. This group did not reach the same level of national attention, even though Attorney General of the United States Eric Holder is featured praising their efforts (at the press conference featured in the film, Holder calls CeaseFire "a rational, data-driven, evidence-based, smart approach to crime"). This disparity of coverage is just part of the ongoing story of the media's proclivity for following the old adage that, "If it bleeds, it leads."

CeaseFire's success within the neighborhoods in which the program has a presence is undeniable, as seen in a U.S. Department of Justice evaluation available through the organization's website, which shows, not only a reduction in violence, but also the group's work in helping clients find drug and alcohol rehabilitation, places to live, and education and job opportunities. Those, of course, get to the heart of some of the reasons for an increase in crime and violence in a community.

Documenting a year in the operations of CeaseFire, *The Interrupters* is not a film of statistics in the traditional sense. Even the aforementioned on that compares Chicago murders to deaths in Iraq is only featured in a short montage of news footage. A statistic here is one of the film's multiple subjects—the eponymous "interrupters" of retaliatory hostility—working at one crime scene only to hear about another shooting a few blocks away before he or she has completed their job at the first location. Data sets come from sources like the director of a funeral home recalling how many young people he has helped to recently bury. There are no charts or graphs, only collections of crosses, photographs, and mementos on sidewalks, street corners, and the sides of buildings that honor the lives of those whose deaths came too soon. James accompanies each shot of these makeshift memorials with the names and ages—most were in their teenage years—of the victims. With every turn, James never forgets the effects of violence on the community and the individual.

Dr. Gary Slutkin, Founder and Executive Director of CeaseFire, introduces the overarching concept of the organization. His experience lies in the treatment of infectious disease and the reversal of epidemics, both of which he considers violence to be. It is, in his estimation, a learned behavior that can be identified and changed over time. Meanwhile, Tio Hardiman, director of the Illinois branch, presents the unique role of the group's "Violence Interrupters," volunteers who themselves have left a life of crime and violent behavior to directly affect the lives of those who are still embroiled in a lifestyle that is destructive to themselves and others.

Three of these volunteers are the film's focus. Ameena Matthews is the daughter of the infamous gang leader Jeff Fort, currently serving a 155-year sentence in federal prison for murder and conspiring in domestic terrorism with Libyan officials. She was once caught up in a similar existence of dealing drugs and aggression. Her story echoes the other two primary subjects—Cobe Williams, whose father's murder started him down a path in and out of jail, and Eddie Bocanegra, who murdered a rival when he was seventeen. They have reformed for their own reasons—religious faith, children, and overpowering regret—and they are unafraid to speak honestly to James' camera about these experiences. James intercuts these personal interviews with photographs of their younger selves, from childhood innocence through their gradual descent into crime. Where one stops and the other begins is never clear. For Bocanegra, the act that now defines him was purely impulsive.

Slutkin's argument about the basis of violence is a compelling one, and James' decision to virtually ignore the indifference that comes with statistics in favor of a subjective view into The Interrupters' work only underscores the group's theory. An early encounter on the street sets the pattern for almost every other in the film. In it, a woman wields a butcher knife toward a group of people, one of whom earlier beat up her brother, as children stand by watching the potentially deadly scenario unfold. The event, as harrowing as anything this sometimes-excruciating film shows, summarizes every point Slutkin makes. Here is a woman who, out of a sense of honor, seeks to avenge a wrong perpetrated against a person about whom she cares; it is an example for the children in witness.

The cyclical nature of this sort of violence is its most distressing element. Hardiman, who started The Interrupters, realizes that the causes are far greater than any one group—let alone any one individual—can repair. The immediate goal for these volunteers is to lessen or eliminate the potential for one act of senseless violence to escalate into another. Matthews, Williams, and Bocanegra are fearless in their approach to their work, arriving at the scene of a crime where emotions—of key concern, the desire for retribution—are high.

In between times of on-site intervention, the three serve as mentors to at-risk individuals. Bocanegra teaches art therapy to children at local school (one of their teachers is shocked to hear some of the things her students have seen) and, in the most haunting image of the film, accompanies a family to the gravesite of their murdered young son as they hold a picnic there. Matthews sees some of herself in a teenage girl having difficulty adjusting to life with a mother whose drug addiction has essentially orphaned her. A scene at a park, in which Matthews grows increasingly frustrated with her inability to assist the girl, is a testament to James' ability to utilize *cinéma vérité* techniques to cull honesty from his subjects, while the encounters with one of Williams' contacts, a flamboyant man known only as "Flame," raises the eternal question posed by style of whether or not the presence of the camera drastically affects the conduct of the subject. The difference between his animated body language and comic manner and his final moments on-screen, when he is unaware that he is being recorded, is drastic.

Out of the pain and misery, *The Interrupters* finds hope in these relationships, and if James' coda seems to tie everything together too simply (the story of a mother afraid of her two sons' gang activity finds resolution with only one of the young men, ignoring the other), it comes at the end of a comprehensive exploration of a sensitive and imperative subject. It is a testament to courage and the possibility of redemption for the individual and society as a whole.

Mark Dujsik

CREDITS

Origin: USA
Language: English
Released: 2011
Production: Steve James, Alex Kotlowitz; Kartemquin Films, Rise Films; released by Public Broadcasting Service
Directed by: Steve James
Written by: Alex Kotlowitz
Cinematography by: Steve James
Sound: Zak Piper
Editing: Steve James, Aaron Wickenden
MPAA rating: Unrated
Running time: 125 minutes

REVIEWS

Anderson, Melissa. *Village Voice*. July 27, 2011.
Dargis, Manohla. *New York Times*. July 28, 2011.

Ebert, Roger. *Chicago Sun-Times.* August 10, 2011.

O'Hehir, Andrew. *Salon.com.* July 28, 2011.

Rodriguez, Rene. *Miami Herald.* August 26, 2011.

Singer, Matt. *IFC.com.* July 28, 2011.

Stevens, Dana. *Slate.* August 19, 2011.

Tobias, Scott. *AV Club.* July 28, 2011.

Turan, Kenneth. *Los Angeles Times.* August 26, 2011.

Wissot, Lauren. *Slant Magazine.* July 24, 2011.

TRIVIA

This film is Steve James' sixth feature length collaboration with his long-time filmmaking home, the non-profit Chicago production studio Kartemquin Films.

AWARDS

Ind. Spirit 2012: Feature Doc

Nomination:

Directors Guild 2011: Documentary Director (James).

INTO THE ABYSS

In the early months of 2011, celebrated filmmaker Werner Herzog released *Cave of Forgotten Dreams,* a spellbinding documentary that took viewers to a remote cavern system in France containing the earliest known cave paintings and presented them with evidence of some of the first attempts by primitive man to shed his primal nature and show glimmers of intelligence, beauty and the notion that there could be more to life without merely resorting to brute savagery to get along. As the year came to an end, he returned with another documentary, *Into the Abyss,* that took viewers to rural Texas and presented them with the story of evidence of a supposedly higher civilization that is perfectly willing to resort to savagery in an instant by killing its fellow members. Considering the sheer number of projects that Herzog has been working on over the last few years, the juxtaposition of the two films is most likely just a coincidence but it cannot be denied that *Into the Abyss* does serve as an intriguing companion piece to the earlier film. At the same time, however, it is a stunning work in its own right and one of the most powerful works to emerge Herzog's recent creative renaissance.

This time around, Herzog ventures to the prison in Huntsville, Texas and introduces us to two young men, Michael Perry and Jason Burkett, who decided one night to break into the house of a acquaintance and steal his red Camaro, a stupid and impulsive crime that quickly spiraled out of control and resulted in three people being murdered in the course of grabbing a car that they only managed to possess for a few hours before getting

arrested. Each insisted during their trials that the other one was primarily responsible for the killings but both were found guilty. However, while Perry was sentenced to death, Burkett got off comparatively easy with a mere 40-year sentence. Through interviews with the two killers, their families, the families of their victims, the criminal investigators and the people charged with carrying out Perry's execution, Herzog introduces viewers to a fascinating array of characters and paints an indelible portrait of how the lives of most of them were irrevocably changed forever all for want of a car that, in the end, is last seen moldering in a shabby impound lot.

Some people may go into *Into the Abyss* assuming that it will be something along the lines of *The Thin Blue Line* (1988), the landmark Errol Morris documentary that investigated the pleas of innocence of another prisoner slated for execution in Texas and uncovered new evidence that led to his exoneration, but that is not what Herzog has presented viewers with here. For one thing, there is no real doubt that the two prisoners were indeed guilty of their crimes. For another, Herzog makes it clear that while he is adamantly opposed to the death penalty under any circumstances, he is not one to be lulled into a sense of misguided sympathy as a result—when he meets Perry for the first time, a mere eight days before his scheduled execution, he coolly informs him that while he feels for him in the sense that he does not believe he should be executed, "It does not mean that I have to like you." Instead, Herzog is trying to do something different with this story by asking a far more complex and difficult question. Which is more preferable—a situation in which one person takes the life of another as the result of a stupid chain of circumstances that ends with someone dead for no good or coherent reason at all or a situation in which one person takes the life of another as the result of a meticulously conceived and executed plan designed to bring about some form of justice? The correct answer, of course, is that neither one is acceptable in a civilized society because no one has the right to take the life of another person under any circumstance.

Using a more subdued documentary approach that finds him staying behind the camera for virtually the entire film and asking question that are for the most part somber reasonable, Herzog pursues this idea through a series of interviews that find his subjects opening up in ways that neither he nor they could have possibly intended when they started. There is the prison chaplain who starts offering up the standard-issue homilies and then, after being prompted by Herzog to describe an encounter he once had with a squirrel, casts aside the hollow pieties in order to speak truthfully and movingly from the heart. There is the head of the prison guards who oversaw more than 100 executions before finally walking away from the job because he was finally convinced that the death penalty was wrong. There is Melyssa Thompson-Burkett, who met James Burkett in prison while working on his legal case and wound up marrying him and becoming pregnant with his child, though she is understandably coy about the details regarding the latter. In the most wrenching sequence, we meet Burkett's father, himself a convict whose failings as a father finally came through to him on the day when he, James and his other incarcerated son shared lunch together behind prison walls.

Into the Abyss is a film that tackles a difficult and complex subject that many people have passionate feelings about, and, as a result, it is one that is likely to raise the hackles of viewers on both sides of the question even before they actually see it. Those in favor of the death penalty will condemn it because of its obvious stance against it while those against it may wonder why Herzog did not choose to make his point about his opposition by focusing on either the perception of racial bias in terms of those being sentenced to die, the let-em-fry attitude that has been tacitly endorsed in Texas by Governors Bush and Perry via the sheer numbers of executions or by looking at a case in which there was some doubt about the guilt of the condemned prisoner. These might have made for intriguing films as well but with *Into the Abyss,* Herzog gives viewers something far riskier and far more rewarding in the long run—a film that will make anyone who sees it actually sit and contemplate their position on capital punishment at length, regardless of their current stance on the subject.

Peter Sobczynski

CREDITS

Himself: Richard Lopez
Himself: Fred Allen
Himself: Jason Burkett
Herself: Lisa Stotler-Balloun
Himself: Eddie Lee Sausage
Himself: Jeremy Richardson
Narrator: Werner Herzog
Origin: USA
Language: English
Released: 2011
Production: Erik Nelson; Creative Differences, Werner Herzog Filmproduction, Skelling Rock, Spring Hill; released by Sundance Selects
Directed by: Werner Herzog
Written by: Werner Herzog
Cinematography by: Peter Zeitlinger
Music by: Mark De Gli Antoni

Sound: Eric Spitzer
Editing: Joe Bini
MPAA rating: PG-13
Running time: 107 minutes

REVIEWS

Debruge, Peter. *Variety.* November 18, 2011.
Dujsik, Mark. *Mark Reviews Movies.* November 10, 2011.
Ebert, Roger. *Chicago Sun-Times.* November 10, 2011.
Phillips, Michael. *Chicago Tribune.* November 10, 2011.
Rainer, Peter. *Christian Science Monitor.* December 2, 2011.
Rea, Steven. *Philadelphia Inquirer.* November 17, 2011.
Scott, A.O. *New York Times.* November 10, 2011.
Tallerico, Brian. *HollywoodChicago.com.* November 11, 2011.
Tobias, Scott. *AV Club.* November 10, 2011.
Verniere, James. *Boston Herald.* November 11, 2011.

THE IRON LADY

Never compromise.
        —Movie tagline

Box Office: $24.7 million

"The Iron Lady" was a nickname given to Margaret Thatcher by the Soviet Defence Ministry newspaper *Red Star* in the seventies because of her tenacious opposition to Soviet expansion. What sounded like a backhanded compliment to Thatcher can also be likewise applied to this biopic, which despite an amazing performance by Meryl Streep, is pretty stolid and grey in tone like some cinematic monument that fails to rise to its necessary height. Worth seeing, but hardly definitive, *The Iron Lady* is Streep at her best and the history of Great Britain at its most cinematically staid. But, that said, the film does hold court on a fascinating individual mind even if it only manages to lightly touch on what made Margaret Thatcher who she was. Casual viewers are liable to walk away wanting to know more about Thatcher and her times and that is undoubtedly a good thing but anyone who appreciates good film is liable to walk away thinking that a really good film about Thatcher would have touched on their emotions in a deeper way.

Structurally, the film starts with Thatcher (Meryl Streep) retired and suffering the effects of old age. Her day-to-day activities are closely monitored by a group of well meaning but somewhat stifling care givers who serve primarily as reminders that she is slowly losing the ability to care for herself. Complicating matters are vivid memories and hallucinations involving all the events that helped shape her political and personal life. Most vivid are those involving her deceased husband Denis (Jim Broadbent), whose belongings still fill her house.

Moving back and forth through her life Thatcher gradually begins to take stock of where she finds herself in her autumn years trying to find the courage to accept her new role as elder statesman and let go of the past.

It would hardly be hyperbole to observe that Margaret Thatcher is one of the most reviled, revered and thus controversial political figures of her generation and it is here that the film falters, settling instead to hopscotch all the way through her life and career. The end result is a film that hits all the narrative high points but feels like Cliff Notes to a more interesting story. All the salient material is there: Young Maggie anxious for approval from distant parents, meeting Denis the love of her life, her struggles in the male dominated House of Parliament, her rise to power on a platform of conservative idealism, and her eventual isolation and resignation amidst intense civil unrest and class warfare.

It all seems somewhat distracting given that the one thing *The Iron Lady* does well is to show Thatcher's private desperation. Yet, even though the personal sacrifices she makes are somewhat glossed over, there are a number of fascinating scenes depicting Thatcher trying to come to grips with how she wound up alone in a house with the ghost of her dead husband, trapped by the reputation and influence she worked so hard to get.

Meryl Streep plays Thatcher in middle and old age and is simply breathtaking. It seems useless to make such observations but the subtlety she achieves completely subsumes her into the role. There is no notion of watching Meryl Streep, only of encountering this other person, who, used to getting her own way, is struggling under the weight of newfound limitations. Another scene in which she unjustly berates a loyal staff member will be difficult for anyone to watch who has ever had a boss turn on them in a meeting. Streep powerhouses her way through the role, tackling Thatcher in every mode and more the pity that the actress is stuck in a screenplay that fails to make the history around Thatcher, or the political intrigue, come to life.

Playing the younger Thatcher is a dreamy-eyed Alexandra Roach. She has a difficult job which she pulls off admirably making it easy to imagine how the younger, idealistic and ambitious Maggie Thatcher became the hardened conservative war hawk. Jim Broadbent also has a hard job. The Denis of Maggie's fugues is almost as much devil's advocate as a creature of nostalgia. One moment she is reminiscing about how they met, how they danced, fell in love, and the next she is bedeviled by him, harangued, mocked. Broadbent moves between approaches like a pro undermining any thought that the presence of Denis here is just a narrative device meant to provide sufficient pathos. The effect is both frightening and moving. Harry Lloyd plays the younger Denis with a goofy good-hearted but intelligent gentleness and again, as with Roach, offers his older counterpart solid ground upon which to build a characterization.

There are a handful of distinguished British actors here that in a better developed story would have been put to better use. Richard E. Grant plays advisor and eventual rival, Michael Heseltine, but, of the secondary roles, only Geoffrey Howe emerges as a real character. Played by Anthony Head, Howe moves from deep respect to heartbroken disillusionment with a subtle emotionality that should move anyone.

Director Phyllida Lloydi is best known for her work in opera but does have some feature work to her credit, most notably the enjoyable *Mamma Mia* (2008), which adapted the musical based on the songs of ABBA. For *The Iron Lady,* she is depending on an original screenplay written by Abi Morgan, whose work on the outstanding TV series *The Hour* (2011) was supplemented by a co-writing credit on *Shame* (2011). With Streep and Broadbent on board this should have been a knock out of the park but instead viewers miss the chance to get inside 10 Downing Street.

Dave Canfield

CREDITS

Margaret Thatcher: Meryl Streep
Denis Thatcher: Jim Broadbent
Geoffrey Howe: Anthony Head
Michael Heseltine: Richard E. Grant
Gordon Reece: Roger Allam
Francis Pym: Julian Wadham
Alfred Roberts: Iain Glen
Edward Heath: John Sessions
Young Margaret: Alexandra Roach
Young Denis: Harry Lloyd
Carol Thatcher: Olivia Colman
Airey Neave: Nicholas Farrell
Muriel Roberts: Victoria Bewick
Origin: United Kingdom, France
Language: English
Released: 2011
Production: Damian Jones; Pathe, Film 4, U.K. Film Council, DJ Films; released by Weinstein Company
Directed by: Phyllida Lloyd
Written by: Abi Morgan
Cinematography by: Elliot Davis
Music by: Justine Wright, Thomas Newman
Sound: Danny Hambrook
Music Supervisor: Ian Neil
Editing: Justine Wright
Art Direction: Nick Dent
Costumes: Consolata Boyle

Production Design: Simon Elliott
MPAA rating: PG-13
Running time: 105 minutes

REVIEWS

Levin, Rober. *The Atlantic.* December 30, 2011.
Morgenstern, Joe. *Wall Street Journal.* December 30, 2011.
O'Hehir, Andrew. *Salon.com.* December 29, 2011.
Putman, Dustin. *DustinPutman.com.* December 29, 2011.
Rainer, Peter. *Christian Science Monitor.* January 4, 2012.
Scott, A. O. *New York Times.* December 29, 2011.
Sharkey, Betsy. *Los Angeles Times.* December 29, 2011.
Snider, Eric D. *Film.com.* January 6, 2012.
Synnot, Siobhan. *Scotsman.* January 3, 2012.
Zane, Alex. *Sun Online.* January 6, 2012.

QUOTES

Margaret Thatcher: "Watch your thoughts for they become words. Watch your words for they become actions. Watch your actions for they become…habits. Watch your habits, for they become your character. And watch your character, for it becomes your destiny! What we think we become."

TRIVIA

Manchester Town Hall was used for the scenes shot in the offices and corridors of the Houses of Parliament.

AWARDS

Oscars 2011: Actress (Streep), Makeup
British Acad. 2011: Actress (Streep), Makeup
Golden Globes 2012: Actress—Drama (Streep)
Nomination:
British Acad. 2011: Orig. Screenplay, Support. Actor (Broadbent)
Screen Actors Guild 2011: Actress (Streep).

J

J. EDGAR

The most powerful man in the world.
—Movie tagline

Box Office: $37.3 million

There were few figures of the 20th century as complicated and loathsome as J. Edgar Hoover. All men have contradictions but the father of the FBI seems to have had more than his share. Ostensibly organized to fight crime, Hoover's FBI had a highly selective definition of who the criminals were. Hoover saw Communists everywhere but did not see the mafia at all, denying organized crime's existence long after its malignant presence was an established fact of American life. Although one of the FBI's principal responsibilities was to investigate civil rights violations, the FBI was the principal *violator* of the civil liberties of thousands of Americans, particularly civil rights activists, who Hoover, a through and through racist, despised with particular fervor. Animated by a pathological hatred for Martin Luther King and the SCLC, Hoover blackmailed attorney general Robert Kennedy into allowing him to illegally wire tap King and surveil his every move. He then sent sexually explicit recordings of King with his mistress to King's family to embarrass and threaten him. When King was assassinated in 1968, Hoover had to be forced by the attorney general to even investigate his murder. Professing to hate communists and communism, Hoover routinely employed the tactics of the secret police of communist and totalitarian countries to illegally monitor and blackmail American citizens guilty only of exercising their first amendment rights. Officially beholden to the authority of the executive, Hoover

blackmailed six presidents to stay in power for nearly thirty-seven years, dying in office in 1972. While the merest hint of homosexuality would result in an agent's instant expulsion, Hoover fashioned his FBI into a harem like organization in which all agents had to be white men possessing very specific physical attributes as formulated by the FBI director himself and conducted a nearly fifty year love affair with his Associate Director Clyde Tolson.

It is this fascinating last contradiction that is the principal (though sadly not sole) subject of Eastwood's film. Hoover's homosexuality is a refreshing focus given that past films featuring Hoover have either completely ignored this aspect of his character, marginalized it to irrelevance or cartoonishly exaggerated it (Bob Hoskins's beyond over the top caricature of Hoover in *Nixon* [1995] must be seen to believed). J. Edgar was a complicated man with a complicated private life and a long and complicated public life, which lasted nearly fifty years and included the creation of the FBI and key involvement in many of the twentieth century's most notorious crimes. It would be a tall order for a single film to cover even one of these lives, let alone both. Unfortunately, Eastwood and screenwriter Dustin Lance Black try to make a film about both Hoovers, and, in so doing, bite off more than they can chew with their 137-minute running time.

The cost of Eastwood and Black's attempt to try to pack an enormous amount of content into a relatively-trim running time is immediately apparent in the film's awkward and choppy opening. The viewer feels as though he or she has missed the first ten minutes of the film. The viewer is abruptly introduced to Hoover (Leonardo DiCaprio in terrible "old man" makeup) in the 1960s talking to a biographer. Before this scene has been adequately established, the film cuts to a flashback of Hoover's boss, attorney general Mitchell Palmer (Geoffrey Pierson), in 1919, surviving a Union sponsored bombing attack while Hoover provides a voice over to try and supply the event with historical context. The film then cuts to Hoover's awkward and unsuccessful attempts to woo his secretary, Helen Gandy (Naomi Watts) in the 1920s. The film eventually slows down, allowing for more sustained sequences in its various time periods, but, in general, *J. Edgar*'s narrative feels disjointed and chopped up as it hurries, hop scotches, and backtracks through its subject's 77 year long life. Freedom from chronology is, of course, one of film's great strengths and one of the aspects that distinguishes film from other mediums. The ability to play with time particularly suits biographical films, allowing filmmakers to flit back and forth from one point in the person's life to another. The problem is that *J. Edgar*'s fractured narrative does not feel like the product of a conscious artistic decision designed to serve the purpose of the film (as, for example, did the ingeniously splintered narrative of *Memento* [2000]) but rather the consequence of a three-hour movie chopped down to two in the editing room.

As a result, *J. Edgar* is a sprawling mess of a movie that, while containing some good (at times even electrifying) sequences, fails to adequately explore either the public or private life of its subject. Hoover's public life, which is essentially a history of the FBI, feels cursory. The creation of the FBI and its involvement in many of the most notorious cases of the twentieth century is a fantastic, through daunting, subject for a two-hour film. Hoover began working for the precursor to the FBI, the Bureau of Investigation, in World War I. He became that agency's director in 1924 and then invented the Federal Bureau of Investigation in 1935 and reigned as its undisputed monarch for nearly forty years. During his reign, the BI and FBI investigated or was involved in The Palmer Raids, the deportation of anarchist Emma Goldberg, The Lindbergh kidnapping, the Kansas City Massacre, the pursuit of John Dillinger, the arrest of Alvin Karpis, the surveillance of Martin Luther King and (if only begrudgingly) the investigation of his assassination, to name just a few. The film does a heroic job of attempting to dramatize these complex historical events, it's just that there are so many cases and so little time. The result of this is a "greatest hits" structure in which none of the events are explored in any depth. The Lindbergh kidnapping could be a film in itself. As depicted in Eastwood's film, it is not only hard to understand the FBI's role in the case and the kidnapping's nearly unimaginable impact on the public

at the time but even the basic facts of what occurred. Without some pre-existing background knowledge of the case, the viewer is unlikely to understand what is happening. And the Lindbergh kidnapping is the case which receives the most screen time of all the cases depicted in the film. *J. Edgar*'s stretched-thin coverage of too many cases makes the viewer appreciate the much more focused approach of Michael Mann's *Public Enemies* (2009), which wisely confined itself to the FBI's pursuit of one man.

Not only is this superficial survey of FBI history unsatisfying, it cuts into the time available for the *really* interesting story of J. Edgar's personal life. In 1927, Hoover made Clyde Tolson (Armie Hammer) his assistant director with little to no qualifications. He held the position (first at the BI and then at the FBI) for forty-five years until Hoover's death in 1972. During that time, they traveled to work together in the same car, took all their lunches and dinners together, and vacationed together with adjoining hotel rooms. Black's script convincingly presents this homosexual relationship as a highly repressed emotional bond that was physically platonic. Raised by an overbearing mother (a chilling Judi Dench) who possessed absolutely no tolerance for a homosexual son ("I'd rather have a dead son for a son rather than a lily for a son") in a society in which being gay was second only to being a Communist produces a man who cannot publically or privately acknowledge (even to the man he loves) his true self. This man becomes very good at blackmailing others because he understands how badly people want their secrets to remain secrets based on his own experience. The film does an excellent job of depicting the great cost of Hoover's inability to acknowledge his true self. Only in two brief scenes, one involving J. Edgar's invitation for Clyde to be his assistant (which is essentially an invitation to be his life partner) and another in which J. Edgar relishes his professional success with Clyde (the FBI's image has been placed on a Wheaties box) does Hoover allow himself any joy in being in a relationship with Tolson. The film has one great, exceptionally painful scene where Tolson tries to force Hoover to acknowledge their love and Hoover is unable to do so. The best Tolson can get, in an even sadder scene years later when they are both quite elderly, is a kiss on the forehead from Hoover. One of the casualties of *J. Edgar*'s overstuffed narrative is the character of Tolson. The viewer is left wanting to know much more about Hoover's lifetime lover and especially why he agreed to stay with a man only capable of giving him a kiss on the forehead after forty-five years of unwavering, loyal love. The scenes between Hoover and Tolson are fascinating and easily the best part of Eastwood's film. One simply wishes the entire film were about them.

DiCaprio and Hammer do a good job with very difficult (and, in the case of Hammer, underwritten) roles. Few things can be more difficult for an actor than to play a real historical figure, particularly one close enough in time that he is still seared into the national consciousness and can be seen and heard on film and television clips with just a quick mouse click. Judi Dench is spectacular as Hoover's sinister mother and the scene with her dancing without music with her middle-aged son in a hotel room is one of the creepiest in recent memory. As good as DiCaprio, Hammer and Dench are however, there are still some terrible, wince-inducing line readings, and Black succumbs a bit too much to the temptation to sentimentalize a man who does not deserve it.

In the end, however, J. Edgar is not undone by these shortcoming but by not having enough running time to adequately explore the life of its complicated subject. J. Edgar Hoover was a real man as complicated, contradictory and sinister as the fictional Tony Soprano. To be successful, *J. Edgar* needed either a much more limited scope or a much longer format such as a miniseries, multi-season cable series or even a non-fiction documentary series. Similarly to Martin Scorsese's flawed historical epic *Gangs of New York* (2009), *J.Edgar* contains some undeniably mesmerizing sequences but, overall, is a semi-coherent mess of a film due to too many sacrifices in the editing room.

Nate Vercauteren

CREDITS

J. Edgar Hoover: Leonardo DiCaprio
Helen Gandy: Naomi Watts
Clyde Tolson: Armie Hammer
Charles Lindbergh: Josh(ua) Lucas
Anne Marie Hoover: Judi Dench
Lela Rogers: Lea Thompson
Colonel Schwarzkopf: Dermot Mulroney
Robert F. Kennedy: Jeffrey Donovan
Agent Smith: Ed Westwick
Robert Irwin: Josh Hamilton
Emma Goldman: Jessica Hecht
Harlan Fiske Stone: Ken Howard
Mitchell Palmer: Geoffrey Pierson
Roberta Palmer: Cheryl Lawson
Dwight Eisenhower: Gunner Wright
Franklin Delano Roosevelt: David A. Cooper
Origin: USA
Language: English
Released: 2011
Production: Brian Grazer, Robert Lorenz; Malpaso Productions, Imagine Entertainment; released by Warner Bros.

Directed by: Clint Eastwood
Written by: Dustin Lance Black
Cinematography by: Tom Stern
Music by: Clint Eastwood
Sound: Jose Antonio Garcia
Editing: Joel Cox, Gary D. Roach
Art Direction: Gregory A. Berry
Costumes: Deborah Hopper
Production Design: James Murakami
MPAA rating: R
Running time: 137 minutes

REVIEWS

Burr, Ty. *Boston Globe*. November 10, 2011.
Dargis, Manohla. *New York Times*. November 8, 2011.
Debruge, Peter. *Variety*. November 4, 2011.
Ebert, Roger. *Chicago Sun-Times*. November 9, 2011.
Hoberman, J. *Village Voice*. November 8, 2011.
Lumenick, Lou. *New York Post*. November 9, 2011.
Rea, Steven. *Philadelphia Inquirer*. November 10, 2011.
Robinson, Tasha. *AV Club*. November 9, 2011.
Rothkopf, Joshua. *Time Out New York*. November 8, 2011.
Zacharek, Stephanie. *Movieline*. November 9, 2011.

QUOTES

J. Edgar Hoover: "What's important at this time is to re-clarify the difference between hero and villain."

TRIVIA

Judi Dench broke her toe while working on her previous movie but kept the injury to herself in order to avoid being replaced. Co-producer Robert Lorenz only found out after Dench finished filming her scenes.

AWARDS

Nomination:

Golden Globes 2012: Actor—Drama (DiCaprio)
Screen Actors Guild 2011: Actor (DiCaprio), Support. Actor (Hammer).

JACK AND JILL

His twin sister is coming for the holidays…and it ain't pretty.
   —Movie tagline

Box Office: $74.1 million

Otherwise-mature-of-taste film goers sometimes find themselves enjoying or at least tolerantly, perhaps inadvertently laughing at aggressively low-brow, slapstick, potty humor. There are even those who publicly admit to having a soft spot for the shamelessly silly and juvenile comedy films of Adam Sandler. So for Sandler's latest "family comedy" vehicle *Jack and Jill* to fail so miserably and relentlessly on nearly every level—even for the otherwise tolerant—is a dubious achievement of some notability.

In terms of both "film" and "funny," *Jack and Jill* is an excruciating misfire of such epic proportions that for years it will stand as a grim low mark by which all other cinematic, especially comedic, disasters are measured. What drags it to such depths? Is it the film's central premise of having Sandler play both halves of a set of paternal twins: Jack (Sandler's usual successful family man Everyman character) and Jill (Sandler again, crassly screeching in Ugly Sister drag)? Or the typical Sandler parade of bodily functions and all-inclusive bigotry? The shameless product placement? The lazy and gratuitous celebrity cameos? The artless and deferential direction by long-time Sandler hack Dennis Dugan?

Or is it that Sandler himself looks truly old and tired, seemingly filled with a self-loathing hatred of himself for still going through the motions and of his audience for still showing up. Through his Happy Madison production company, Sandler has made plenty of lowest-common-denominator comedies with director Dugan, including "family fare" such as *Big Daddy* (1999) and *Grown Ups* (2010) and more adult-oriented (in content, not sophistication) comedies like *Happy Gilmore* (1996), *I Now Pronounce You Chuck & Larry* (2007), and *You Don't Mess with the Zohan* (2008). None are masterpieces, but many of them at least partly amuse on a basic "too dumb not to laugh at" level.

Presumably over the years Sandler and Dugan and have developed a comfortable, no-fuss working relationship—but such collaborative familiarity can also breed complacency. There has always been a somewhat charming lackadaisical feel to these Happy Madison comedies, but lately loose and lackadaisical has become more contemptuous and lazy. Even those predisposed to this style of Sandler comedy will find *Jack and Jill* sloppy and disorganized—it is not just that the film feels underdeveloped and tossed together, it is that Sandler and his team do not seem to care at all at how shoddy it all ended up. Dugan has become more enabler than director.

Successfully transplanted from his Brooklyn roots, Sandler's Jack is a Los Angeles commercial director (making it all the easier to pile on the product placement) with a nice house and nice family (including trophy wife and film prop Katie Holmes). Jack is annually put out of sorts by a holiday visit from his still-New-York-City-rooted twin sister Jill, played in drag by

Sandler at a high pitch of braying neediness and neurotic pathos. The set-up has Sandler playing aggravated straight man to himself, but the "Sandler Everyman" has become so cynically dismissive of everything but his own safe little corner of success it is hard to feel any sympathy for his selfish frustration with Jill.

Not that Sandler's cartoon portrayal of Jill is a picnic. If Jack is unlikable, Jill is unbearable: all flatulence and fearful prejudices, she is presented as a horrible harridan, bereft of any redeeming qualities. There are hints that Jill is painfully lonely following the death of their mother, but *Jack and Jill* has no interest in humanizing any of its comedic targets. Which makes the film all the more grating when, as it crawls toward the finish, it wedges in the usual Happy Madison homilies about loving and appreciating your family.

And then there is Al Pacino as "Al Pacino." Unlike *Jack and Jill*'s numerous other celebrity cameos of varying star-power and effectiveness, Pacino has a full supporting role as a supposedly exaggerated version of himself. To say the venerable dramatic actor is the film's most consistently amusing element is damning with very faint praise indeed. As Jill's would-be suitor, Pacino broadly parodies his more bombastic, scenery devouring tendencies of the past 20 years, but his fictional ranting and raving for comedic effect is so similar to what the real-life Pacino already does on stage and screen, there is not much humorous dissidence.

Adding to *Jack and Jill*'s slapdash, tossed-off feel, entire scenes of connective plot tissue have been sliced away, presumably because their humor content did not meet even the film's lowly standards. Characters suddenly jump ahead to new days and locations, still referencing events now banished to the cutting room floor. Likewise, ideas with comic potential—like the made-up childhood "twin language" *Jack and Jill* share—are wasted away with the easiest, lowest-hanging jokes. "It is good enough for the fans who dutifully show up," appears to be the modus operati.

And kicking up the discomfort level from "annoying" to "offensive" is a running joke with Jack's Hispanic gardener (Eugenio Derbez) who also tries to woo Jill by shouting out self-deprecating ethnic and illegal-immigration clichés, only to supposedly negate them with a brown-face "I'm keeeeeding!" The filmmakers want to pass it off as ironic self-mockery, but the shtick is so shrill and graceless it ends up pandering to the worst audience reactions and playing out as plain old racism.

There is a sense that *Jack and Jill* is meant as Sandler's commentary on his own film career: that he craves respect for dramatic films like *Punch-Drunk Love* (2002), *Reign Over Me* (2007), and *Funny People* (2009), but cannot escape the no-brow crowd-pleasing schlock of films like *Jack and Jill* any more Jack can escape Jill. The fact, however, that this latest film was made with such scattershot disinterest from its star does little to resolve Sandler's inner struggle between his artistic ambitions and commercial temptations. Meanwhile, the viewer suffers mightily in the crossfire.

Locke Peterseim

CREDITS

Jack/Jill: Adam Sandler
Erin: Katie Holmes
Himself: Al Pacino
Sofia Sadlestein: Elodie Tougne
Gary Sadlestein: Rohan Chand
Felipe/Felipe's Grandma: Eugenio Derbez
Monica: David Spade
Todd: Nick Swardson
Office Worker: Tim Meadows
Origin: USA
Language: English
Released: 2011
Production: Todd Garner, Jack Giarraputo, Adam Sandler; Broken Road Productions, Happy Madison Productions; released by Sony Pictures
Directed by: Dennis Dugan
Written by: Steve Koren, Robert Smigel, Ben Zook
Cinematography by: Dean Cundey
Music by: Rupert Gregson-Williams
Sound: Russell Farmarco
Music Supervisor: Michael Dilbeck
Editing: Tom Costain
Art Direction: Alan Au, John Collins
Costumes: Ellen Lutter
Production Design: Perry Andelin Blake
MPAA rating: PG
Running time: 93 minutes

REVIEWS

Abele, Robert. *Los Angeles Times.* November 11, 2011.
LaSalle, Mick. *San Francisco Chronicle.* November 11, 2011.
Nicholson, Amy. *Box Office Magazine.* November 11, 2011.
O'Sullivan, Michael. *Washington Post.* November 11, 2011.
Phillips, Michael. *Chicago Tribune.* November 11, 2011.
Pols, Mary. *Time.* November 10, 2011.
Schager, Nick. *Village Voice.* November 9, 2011.
Schwarzbaum, Lisa. *Entertainment Weekly.* November 17, 2011.
Scott, A.O. *New York Times.* November 10, 2011.
Tobias, Scott. *AV Club.* November 11, 2011.

QUOTES

Jill Sadelstein (after breaking Al Pacino's Oscar®): "Oh my god, I'm sure you have others."
Al Pacino: "You'd think it, but oddly enough, I don't."

TRIVIA

Adam Sandler accidentally exposed his genitalia while playing Jill due to wearing a mini-skirt.

AWARDS

Golden Raspberries 2011: Worst Ensemble Cast, Worst Picture, Worst Prequel/Remake/Rip-off/Sequel, Worst Actor (Sandler), Worst Actress (Sandler), Worst Support. Actor (Pacino), Worst Support. Actress (Spade), Worst Director (Dugan), Worst Screen Couple (Sandler and Holmes, Sandler and Pacino), Worst Screenplay.

Nomination:

Golden Raspberries 2011: Worst Support. Actor (Swardson), Worst Support. Actress (Holmes).

JANE EYRE

Box Office: $11.2 million

Like any genre, period pieces (or "costume drama"), as well as film adaptations of literary classics, carry stereotypes and tropes that are either embraced by fans or rejected by those who see only petticoats, sideburns, and the stilted language of etiquette and stifled desires. So, it is cause for cinematic celebration when a costume drama and literary adaptation comes along that both plays to the genre's strengths and fills the screen with a thoughtful energy that wins over new converts. Director Cary Fukunaga's *Jane Eyre* takes on Charlotte Bronte's 1847 novel and does no harm to the source material so fiercely protected by fidelity-minded Bronte devotees. More importantly, it dares something even bolder: to be a great film in and of itself.

This latest version includes most of the characters and plot elements of Bronte's tale that make it so beloved (and so often filmed): Young orphan Jane Eyre (played as a child by Amelia Clarkson) is shuffled off to an oppressive girls school where she learns to stifle all her ideas and hopes and sublimate herself to a prospect-free life of being "poor, obscure, plain and little." Grown-up Jane (Mia Wasikowska) finds herself employed as the governess at Thornfield Hall, where she crosses paths and fates with the brooding, Byronic lord of the hall, Edward Rochester (Michael Fassbender). A tentative, sometimes tormented connection begins to form between the two, even as the mercurial Rochester's darker past knocks threateningly at the door.

One of the most important things Fukunaga and screenwriter Moira Buffini have done is use the last third of Bronte's novel—in which Jane is taken in by the missionary St. John Rivers and his sisters— as a framing device. The film opens with Jane fleeing across the moors from Thornfield and arriving at the Rivers home then uses that portion of the narrative as a stage from which the heroine reflects on her life, including the Rochester affair. That narrative decision solves one of the larger problems with adapting *Jane Eyre*: the last section with St. John simply is not as compelling and emotionally rich as the middle portion with Rochester. In fact some film versions—including the 1943 one with Orson Welles and Joan Fontaine—eliminate the missionary and his sisters completely. Those adaptations that do include the St. John portion earn points for fidelity, but lose narrative momentum as they wind down at home with the Rivers.

Fukunaga and Buffini's flashback structure not only deals with the "St. John problem," but also strengthens the Rochester plotline, juxtaposing St. John's pious, passionless altruism (finely tuned to benevolent obliviousness by actor Jamie Bell's restraint) with Jane's true, tumultuous love for Rochester. That latter thorny love story has always formed the heart of *Jane Eyre* adaptations, but here Wasikowska and Fassbender essay it with tight stillness and fiery repression. A fine, inward-folding actress in films like *The Kids are All Right* (2010) and *Alice in Wonderland* (2010), here Wasikowska's willowy fortitude perfectly creates a Jane whose outward humility and passivity masks a quietly alert strength. Her shyness revealed not as weakness but survival mechanism, at times this Jane seems shocked by the realization of her own fears and hopes, by her very existence.

Naturally, Rochester is the outward counterpoint to Jane. With bluffing intensity, Fassbender's Rochester is all sharply defensive belligerence to Jane's meekness; his bitter, blustering glare hiding his own self-loathing and doubts. But while his rugged face and piercing stare on screen feels like an accusation, daring you to challenge him, Fassbender is a too subtle an actor to lean entirely on passionate anger. For the connection between Jane and Rochester to work there has to be a sense of what these two very different people find of themselves in one another, and Wasikowska and Fassbender find and share that in their characters with a seeming effortlessness, their performances emotionally anchoring a love story that in the wrong hands has always risked wheeling into arch melodrama.

Tremendous acting aside (Sally Hawkins and Judi Dench are also on hand for supporting excellence), this *Jane Eyre* hums cinematically thanks to Fukunaga's unfussy naturalistic direction. Often shooting with an unobtrusive hand-held camera, he and his cinematographer Adriano Goldman revel in the shadows and light, finding pulsing texture in mist and mud as well as the candlelight and pale daylight—all without letting style overwhelm story.

Much of *Jane Eyre*'s subtext deals with the unseen, not just tales of forest spirits and haunted nightmares, but also Jane and Rochester's suppressed love for each other—as well as more worldly secrets hidden away. Fukunaga taps into that invisible world; winds whistling through heavy drapes, dark storms, and cold sunshine all map out a raw, repressed sensuality where spirit meets flesh. A look can burn, and a quarter smile feels like an explosion of joy.

Thanks to Fukunaga's cinematic honesty (and Bronte's timeless story), the muted colors and dim parlors never feel cheap or rote. *Jane Eyre* is much more than costumes and English locations, nor do the characters and plot feel taken down and dusted off from a book shelf. Driven by the same tension between passion and restraint that fuels the novel, Fukunaga and Buffini's film never feels overlong or overstuffed, but it does not skimp on the important themes or emotional heft of Bronte's book.

The result is a *Jane Eyre* everyone—devotees and neophytes, costume-drama fans and foes, and most of all those who appreciate terrific acting and filmmaking—can embrace and emerge from both enriched and entertained.

Locke Peterseim

CREDITS

Jane Eyre: Mia Wasikowska
Edward Rochester: Michael Fassbender
St. John Rivers: Jamie Bell
Mrs. Fairfax: Judi Dench
Blanche Ingram: Imogen Poots
Bertha: Valentina Cervi
Richard Mason: Harold Lloyd Jr.
Mrs. Reed: Sally Hawkins
Lady Ingram: Sophie Ward
Diana Rivers: Holliday Grainger
Mary Rivers: Tamzin Merchant
Grace Poole: Rosie Cavaliero
Mr. Brocklehurst: Simon McBurney
Origin: United Kingdom
Language: English
Released: 2011
Production: Alison Owen, Paul Trijbits; BBC Films, Ruby Films; released by Focus Features Intl.
Directed by: Cary Fukunaga
Written by: Moira Buffini
Cinematography by: Adriano Goldman
Music by: Dario Marianelli

Sound: Peter Lindsay
Editing: Melanie Oliver
Costumes: Michael O'Connor
Production Design: Will Hughes-Jones
MPAA rating: PG-13
Running time: 115 minutes

REVIEWS

Bayer, Jeff. *Scorecard Review.* March 28, 2011.
Burr, Ty. *Boston Globe.* March 17, 2011.
Denby, David. *New Yorker.* March 14, 2011.
Ebert, Roger. *Chicago Sun-Times.* March 17, 2011.
Long, Tom. *Detroit News.* March 25, 2011.
Phillips, Michael. *Chicago Tribune.* March 17, 2011.
Rickey, Carrie. *Philadelphia Inquirer.* March 24, 2011.
Scott, A.O. *New York Times.* March 10, 2011.
Stevens, Dana. *Slate.* March 11, 2011.
Zacharek, Stephanie. *Movieline.* March 10, 2011.

QUOTES

Rochester: "I offer you my hand, my heart. Jane, I ask you to pass through life at my side. You are my equal and my likeness. Will you marry me?"

TRIVIA

In order to create the gothic atmosphere present in the film, many shots were lit entirely by firelight or candlelight.

AWARDS

Nomination:

Oscars 2011: Costume Des.
British Acad. 2011: Costume Des.

JOHNNY ENGLISH REBORN

A little intelligence goes a long way.
　　—Movie tagline

One man. One mission. No chance.
　　—Movie tagline

Laugh at the face of danger.
　　—Movie tagline

Box Office: $8.3 million

At times when watching a mediocre comedy from a respected performer or filmmaker, the viewer is tempted to will the struggling thing across the finish line. The impulse is to turn a blind eye to obvious failings and give the miscued jokes and flat-falling gags as much latitude and forgiveness as possible—all in hopes of wringing some amusement from the time spent watching it.

That is the case with *Johnny English Reborn,* a sequel to the James Bond spoof *Johnny English* (2003). Though written and directed by different teams, both films feature the venerable British comedian Rowan Atkinson smugly mugging his way through a series of physical gags intended to mock not just spy film conventions but also English culture and post-imperial national pride and superiority—all while mining British comic traditions such as the broad physical buffoonery of Benny Hill and the "oh, how naughty" snickering of the *Carry On* movies.

Where the first film followed the bumbling agent English's accidental rise to the top of MI-7, this time the spy must save the world following his return from exile in Tibet (where he was training in the Zen art of slapstick while trying to shake off a mission gone bad). To observe that the film's plot hinges on a series of meaningless double-agent McGuffins would suggest there *is* much of a plot beyond a simple frame on which to hang a series of comedy sketches.

With that in mind, how well *Johnny English Reborn* works as entertainment depends entirely on how funny those sketches are. Atkinson is a masterful clown who has built a solid career and reputation on two television characters from opposite sides of the same sour-faced spectrum: The sharply cynical Captain Edmund Blackadder (quick to stab himself in the foot with his own rapier-like wit) and the nearly silent Mr. Bean (a bumbling malcontent who is the dark Anglo cousin to Jacques Tati's Monsieur Hulot). Atkinson's Johnny English stumbles somewhere betwixt the two: English has Blackadder's sneeringly misguided superiority and verbal pomposity and Bean's fearless dedication to gloriously silly sight gags.

That makes *Johnny English Reborn,* a parade of humor low, middling, and everywhere, in between. There are Bond-gadget jokes, jokes involving cars and women, and jokes that subvert all the other Bond-movie conventions, including a slow-motion helicopter race that is splendid in concept but eventually tiresome on screen. There is also an endless supply of jokes and stunts swinging at the most vulnerable symbol of macho-male delusion (and thus imperial power and authority): the testicles.

These comedy bits hit and miss with frustrating irregularity—sometimes within the course of a single scene. There is a semi-inspired bit of physical comedy with English raising and lowering a desk chair at a top-level meeting that gets at the heart of Atkinson's comedy: the higher the setting's stakes, the lower the comedy.

Finding such silly and simple joys amidst the self-important complexity of life's institutions and authorities is an admirable goal, but alas, as with so much of *Johnny English Reborn*'s humor, the malfunctioning chair bit never feels fully executed. The timing is slightly off and the joke is dragged out frustratingly past funny. The film's director Oliver Parker, helmed the two *St. Trinian's* films (*St. Trinian's* [2007] and *St Trinian's II: The Legend of Fritton's Gold* [2009]), which trafficked in shameless-but-shambling comic anarchy. Perhaps owing to that background or in deference to his star performer, here Parker seems unwilling to impose a unifying tone or more effective pace to the gags.

Atkinson must also shoulder some of the blame. Few comic actors today play a better buffoon than Atkinson—whether it is in a slow burn or stunned reaction, English's puffed-up twitch and blithering obliviousness are a wonder to behold as the actor's imposing eyebrows turn a simple wink into a grand endeavor. Paradoxical as it may seem, however, it is possible for a performer to simultaneously feel as if he is laboring intensely at making a gag work, and yet not fully committed to the endeavor—the effect is that of comic busy work. That makes the film feel like little more than a cash grab born of the same lazy cynicism Atkinson's characters once skillfully harpooned.

The rest of *Johnny English Reborn*'s game cast does their best to aid the cause, including Gillian Anderson as English's put-upon agency chief, Dominic West as a smoother fellow tuxedoed spy, Daniel Kaluuya as the earnest apprentice, Rosamund Pike as the obligatory "too-good-for-him" love interest, and Atkinson's old *Blackadder* cast mate Tim McInnerny in a riff on the Bond films' Q. They are all playing stock characters, but a film like this is out to celebrate not reinvent its genre.

Ultimately that decent support is only as solid as the center it is propping up, which is a series of "try anything" jokes that often start strong but end up going nowhere. Not every gag in a comedy film has to work, but enough of them need to succeed (that is, generate a spontaneous chuckle) in order to carry the rest of the also-rans along. If a few more of *Johnny English Reborn*'s amusing set ups paid off more effectively—or rather, were not slowly drained of all humor before they wrapped up—the film itself would be much easier to laugh at and enjoy. Instead, the film chugs along, intermittently amusing, but—no matter how much the viewer pushes and pulls at it—losing comic momentum with every scene. Comedy is infamously hard for performers, but it should not be such a chore for the audience.

Locke Peterseim

CREDITS

Johnny English: Rowan Atkinson
Pamela Head: Gillian Anderson
Simon Ambrose: Dominic West
Tucker: Daniel Kaluuya
Fisher: Richard Schiff
Origin: United Kingdom
Language: English
Released: 2011
Production: Tim Bevan, Chris Clark, Eric Fellner; Universal Pictures, Relativity Media, Studio Canal, Working Title Films; released by Universal Pictures
Directed by: Oliver Parker
Written by: Hamish McColl, William Davies
Cinematography by: Daniel Cohen
Music by: Ilan Eshkeri
Sound: Glenn Freemantle
Music Supervisor: Nick Angel
Editing: Guy Bensley
Art Direction: Paul Laugier, Mike Stallion
Costumes: Beatrix Aruna Pasztor
Production Design: Jim Clay
MPAA rating: PG
Running time: 101 minutes

REVIEWS

Abele, Robert. *Los Angeles Times.* October 21, 2011.
Baumgarten, Marjorie. *Austin Chronicle.* October 21, 2011.
Bowles, Scott. *USA Today.* October 21, 2011.
Holden, Steven. *New York Times.* October 20, 2011.
Mick LaSalle. *San Francisco Chronicle.* October 21, 2011.
O'Connell, Sean. *Washington Post.* October 21, 2011.
Rabin, Nathan. *AV Club.* October 20, 2011.
Russo, Tom. *Boston Globe.* October 21, 2011.
Taylor, Kate. *Globe and Mail.* October 21, 2011.
Zacharek, Stephanie. *Movieline.* October 20, 2011.

QUOTES

Johnny English: "You mean there's a mole and a vole?"

TRIVIA

Near the end of the film when Johnny English goes into spasm, he rops his pistol and you can briefly see "Tokyo Marui" sta,ped on the side. This is a replica BB gun and is mostly harmless.

JUDY MOODY AND THE NOT BUMMER SUMMER

Supermegatotally thrilladelic.
—Movie tagline

Box Office: $15 million

To be brutally honest right up front, there are only a certain amount of expectations that anyone whose age reaches into double digits can legitimately have in regards to a film like *Judy Moody and the Not Bummer Summer,* a project aimed squarely at the hearts, minds and allowances of kids who are a little too old for the likes of *Dora the Explorer* but a little too young for *Super 8* (2011). However, even the most lenient observer would suggest that even a film made almost exclusively for the younger set should at least attempt to avoid overtly irritating older viewers. *Judy Moody* violates that most basic rule of family filmmaking and the result is a garish mess that may briefly amuse younger viewers—provided that they have not already been previously exposed to movies of actual quality.

Judy Moody (newcomer Jordana Beatty) is an overly excitable third-grader (imagine Pippi Longstocking without the quiet dignity) who lives in mortal terror that her upcoming summer vacation is going to be boring. To that end, she devises an overly elaborate series of challenges for her and her three friends to undertake in order to score "thrill-points" that will result in the best summer ever. Perhaps as an indication of Judy's annoying nature, not only do two of her friends immediately hightail it to such exotic locales as circus camp and Borneo, her own parents take the opportunity to leave town as well and leave her and younger brother Stink (Parris Mosteller) in the hands of Aunt Opal (Heather Graham), whom she has not seen in years and who she assumes must be a harridan of incredibly fun-free proportions. In fact, she turns out to be a spunky and adorably flighty guerilla artist—the kind of wacky, free spirit who serves junk food to the kids and repeatedly endangers their lives with her questionable driving skills. With her inspiration, Judy and lone remaining friend Frank (Preston Bailey) try to earn their thrill-points with endeavors that involve tightrope walking, roller coasters, monster movie marathons and, yes, even a quest for Bigfoot thrown in for good measure.

Although it probably was not the intention of director John Schultz, *Judy Moody* is a throwback to those dark days between the death of Walt Disney and the release of *Star Wars* when live-action family films were noisy and idiotic constructions featuring shaggy district attorneys, place-kicking mules and anthropomorphic Volkswagens that at best placated younger viewers without actually entertaining or inspiring them, and, at worst, so put them off of the pleasures of art and the imagination that they single-handedly inspired several generations of business majors. While a certain lack of subtlety is to be expected in a film of this type, *Judy Moody* pitches things at such a hysterical level from the get-go that it feels as if the screenplay (co-written by Megan McDonald, the author of the book series that it

is based upon) must have been written entirely in capital letters—things are so overdone that a cameo from a banjo-picking Jaleel "Urkel" White turns out to be the most restrained element on display amidst the pratfalls, chases, screams and numerous jokes involving poop, barf, and chewed-up food. Adding to the artistic woes is one of the least appealing casts of kid actors to come along in recent memory led by Beatty, who delivers a performance so stridently obnoxious that the kids in *The Goonies* (1985) would have suggested that she tone things down. At certain points during the film, Schultz switches over to incredibly cheap-looking computer animation, presumably on the basis that things just were not cartoonish enough on their own.

Abysmal in so many ways that even younger viewers might find themselves feeling a bit insulted by how utterly juvenile the whole thing is, *Judy Moody and the Not Bummer Summer* is a true bummer through and through but if one digs deep enough, a couple of minor bright spots can be uncovered. For starters, it is not in 3D, thereby making it slightly easier for viewers who cannot take things anymore to gouge their eyes out. Then there is the unavoidable fact that Heather Graham looks as hot as ever and Schultz provides numerous shots of her jumping around or practicing yoga in what can only be a sop to dads shanghaied into taking the wee ones to an otherwise unrewarding journey to the multiplex. Finally, towards the finale, there is a scene at a circus in which Judy gets to be the girl sawed in half and if one leaves the theater at just the right moment, they can sort of convince themselves that the movie has a happy ending after all. For those who stay, there is the suggestion of a sequel in which Judy and Opal will take Paris by storm, a project that should have moviegoers from all around the world uniting in a single cry of "We Surrender!"

Peter Sobczynski

CREDITS

Judy Moody: Jordana Beatty
Stink Moody: Parris Mosteller
Aunt Opal: Heather Graham
Mr. Todd: Jaleel White
Frank Pearl: Preston Bailey
Mom: Janet Varney
Dad: Kristoffer Ryan Winters
Origin: USA
Language: English
Released: 2011
Production: Gary Magness, Sarah Siegel-Magness; Reel FX Creative Studios, Smokewood Entertainment; released by Relativity Media, 20th Century-Fox
Directed by: John Schultz

Written by: Kathy Waugh, Megan McDonald
Cinematography by: Shawn Maurer
Music by: Richard Gibbs
Sound: Edward Tise
Editing: John Pace
Art Direction: Valerie Green
Costumes: Mary Jane Fort
Production Design: Cynthia Charette
MPAA rating: PG
Running time: 91 minutes

REVIEWS

Baumgarten, Marjorie. *Austin Chronicle.* June 17, 2011.
Demara, Bruce. *Toronto Star.* June 9, 2011.
Ebert, Roger. *Chicago Sun-Times.* June 9, 2011.
Goss, William. *Film.com.* June 12, 2011.
Lowenstein, Lael. *Variety.* June 3, 2011.
Orndorf, Brian. *BrianOrndorf.com.* June 8, 2011.
Robinson, Tasha. *AV Club.* June 9, 2011.
Schrager, Nick. *Village Voice.* June 7, 2011.
Verniere, James. *Boston Herald.* June 14, 2011.
Webster, Andy. *New York Times.* June 9, 2011.

QUOTES

Judy Moody: "Can't, I'm busy on Tuesdays...from now, until always."

JULIA'S EYES
(Los ojos de Julia)

You can't hide in the dark.
—Movie tagline

In 2007, Juan Antonio Bayona's *The Orphanage* took the international arthouse scene by the throat and shook them with one of the best ghost stories of the last twenty years. Propelled by a stellar performance from the beautiful Belen Rueda and guided by the production of a man who knows horror incredibly well, as evidenced by his atmospheric direction of *Cronos* (1993) and *The Devil's Backbone* (2001), Guillermo Del Toro, the film was a critical smash and has garnered an appropriate following over the ensuing years. One senses it will soon be seen as the classic of the genre that it always should have been if the foreign film market were what it used to be stateside. Naturally, the reunion of Del Toro as producer and Rueda as star in Guillem Morales' *Julia's Eyes* (or *Los Ojos de Julia*) piqued the interest of fans of *The Orphanage,* but few were ever granted the chance to see it as IFC Films never released the film beyond New York and Los Angeles, letting it die a quick death at the

box office before shuffling it off to DVD before the end of the year. IFC Films has been a savior for many a foreign and independent film but even they make mistakes for *Julia's Eyes* should have been available to a larger portion of the arthouse market. It is nowhere near the incredible achievement of *The Orphanage* due to an over-long, expository first act, but Rueda shines yet again, giving another fearless, stellar performance and carrying the viewer into the film emotionally so its director can more effectively prove that there is good reason to be scared of the dark.

There is such a notable amount of safety that comes from vision. Plunge a heroine into blindness and a screenwriter has made her that much more vulnerable than an average protagonist. Surround her with potentially supernatural goings-on and a maniac and one has a pretty standard formula for horror. In the prologue, Sara (Rueda), a blind woman, screams at whoever (or whatever) keeps playing her least favorite song on the stereo before going into the basement and wrapping a noose around her neck. Before she has a chance to kill herself (and perhaps she was just threatening whoever was harassing her and never would have anyway), the stool is kicked out from underneath her. Months later, Sara's twin sister Julia (also Rueda) arrives with her husband (Lluis Hornar) and Sara's body is discovered. It is not long before Julia suspects foul play. Some of the blind women at a center that Sara attended claim that she had a boyfriend and ghostly activity seems to be tracking the living sister. Is there a ghost that haunted Sara until she killed herself? Or something far more dangerously human? The investigation is severely hampered when Julia herself starts to experience blindness symptoms and her husband hangs himself, leaving a note implying an affair with his wife's twin.

Clearly, this is complex material, made even more so when co-writer/director Morales reveals his hand long before the finale and the film turns into something closer to Giallo than a ghost story. At least it should have turned into that. Sadly, the occasional bursts of violence that should have dominated the storytelling in the final act, turning into a soap operatic gore-fest a la Dario Argento, are never quite artistically achieved. This is a film that features needles in eyes, a man in a freezer, and a head held up by the knife through its mouth, and yet Morales does not have the flair or style to quite pull off these extreme flourishes, allowing the final product to more closely resemble a straight-to-DVD thriller than an Argento film.

Lucky for him, he cast Belen Rueda. Once again, she is completely and totally committed to a physically and emotionally demanding role. In nearly every scene in the movie, thrown around the set, screaming, soaking wet—this is challenging material and she is more than up to it. One would hope that she could break through internationally as it appeared she might after her work in *The Sea Inside* (2004) and almost did again with the right audience after *The Orphanage.* She is extremely talented, making a thriller that hits a few too many generic beats like *Julia's Eyes,* pardon the pun, worth seeing.

Brian Tallerico

CREDITS

Julia Levin/Sara: Belén Rueda
Isaac: Lluis Homar
Angel: Pablo Derqui
Inspector Dimas: Fracesc Orella
Créspulo: Joan Dalmau
Soledad: Julia Gutiérrez Caba
Blasco: Boris Ruiz
Iván: Dani Codina
Lia: Andrea Hermosa
Origin: Spain
Language: Spanish
Released: 2010
Production: Juan Carlos Caro, Joaquín Padró, Mar Targarona, Guillermo del Toro, José Torrescusa; Antena 3 Films; released by IFC Films
Directed by: Guillem Morales
Written by: Guillem Morales, Oriol Paulo
Cinematography by: Oscar Faura
Music by: Fernando Velázquez
Sound: Oriol Tarragó
Editing: Joan Manel Vilasrca
Costumes: Maria Reyes
Production Design: Balter Gallart
MPAA rating: Unrated
Running time: 112 minutes

REVIEWS

Berkshire, Geoff. *Metromix.com.* August 25, 2011.
Edwards, David. *Daily Mirror* May 20, 2011.
Floyd, Nigel. *Time Out.* May 18, 2011.
Keller, Louise. *Urban Cinefile.* May 28, 2011.
Lee, Marc. *Daily Telegraph.* May 19, 2011.
O'Hehir, Andrew. *Salon.com* September 16, 2010.
Rose, Steve. *Guardian.* May 19, 2011.
Saito, Stephen. *Premiere Magazine.* August 24, 2011.
Smith, Anna. *Empire Magazine.* May 16, 2011.
Young, Graham. *Birmingham Post.* May 19, 2011.

JUMPING THE BROOM

> *Sometimes the only way to get past family drama…is to jump right over it.*
> —Movie tagline

Box Office: $37.3 million

After one-too-many failed one-night stands, Sabrina Watson (Paula Patton), a successful Manhattan lawyer makes a pact with God: She will not give up her "cookies" to anyone but her husband as long as God leads her to her soul mate. Not one to let a woman dwell in sexual frustration, God quickly plops Mr. Right (Jason Taylor, played by Laz Alonso) in front of Sabrina's car. She hits him, falls for him, and, after only five months, the two plan their wedding (not to mention their post-wedding cookie party). The trouble is that they have saved the family meet-and-greet for the wedding weekend and when her well-heeled, gigantic-compound-on-Martha's-Vineyard owning parents meet his Brooklyn postal worker mother, the sparks really start flying. At its core, there is something charming about this uptown-downtown romantic comedy, the trouble is that the charm is buried under layers of overly-manufactured drama.

From the get-go, it is hard not to notice that spirituality factors heavily into this narrative. This is not standard fare for most Hollywood romantic comedies, which tend toward the raunchy as a way to either enlist male viewers or to show-off their modern take on relationships. But in as much as *Jumping The Broom* swings the pendulum the other way, it does not wear any kind of agenda on its sleeve. The characters' relationships with God feel organic; their mentions of prayer, church and faith are not forced into the script—a testament to the co-writing efforts of Elizabeth Hunter and Arlene Gibbs. Unfortunately, not all elements in the movie work as seamlessly. From the over-the-top, never-ending parental drama to the lack of chemistry between the betrothed couple, there are a few too many kinks that get in the way of what works about this story.

Both Sabrina's parents and Jason's mother are quick to point out that the couple has not known each other long—even the officiant at their ceremony, Reverend James (a cameo by novelist and real life minister T.D. Jakes), makes a point to lecture them about how soul mate love often endures the hardest tests. Under normal romcom circumstances, it is these naysayers that would need to be proven wrong; these doubting Thomases that the audience would want to see eat their words. In *Jumping The Broom* however, they seem to be the voices of reason. Sabrina and Jason have not known each other long, but what is worse they do not give off that soul mate vibe. During their courtship, Hunter and Gibbs burden Patton and Alonso with stiff, awkward conversations about the many pleasant and exciting things to do in Manhattan, like the opera. Worse though is the fact that neither character displays any dimension. For a successful international lawyer, Sabrina lacks the confidence and poise that typically comes with the job. She is pouty and filled with doubt. Jason is a pushover for both his mom and his fiancé and not into his Blackberry enough for a Wall Street rags-to-riches success story. Their lackluster characterization aside, the real trouble is that Patton and Alonso do not have the chemistry needed by star-crossed lovers from different sides of the tracks to hint that they will survive.

There might have been more room to develop the Sabrina-and-Jason story if *Jumping The Broom* was not weighed down by an insane amount of subplots. Jason's mother has it in for Sabrina, Sabrina's mother has it in for her husband and Jason's mother, who in bad from showed up to the wedding with a number of uninvited, troublemaking guests, Sabrina's father is hiding something, her maid of honor is a notorious flirt, Jason's make-shift aunt is being wooed by a man old enough to be her son, there is tension between Jason and his cousin over Jason's financial success, oh and —spoiler alter— Sabrina's mom isn't really her mom. In a way, Hunter and Gibbs should get recognition for being able to balance all of these storylines without accidentally dropping one along the way. It is their ability to weave all of these quirky baggage-ridden characters together that gives the movie its watchable spirit.

In the end, there is too much weighty narrative. Some great performances by Angela Bassett as Sabrina's highbrow, judgmental mom and Valarie Pettiford as Sabrina's quirky, withdrawn aunt provide the film with some poignant moments. Even though their sisterly conflict takes the film into full on melodrama territory, the immensely watchable actresses make the unnecessarily complex story work. Though Loretta Devine as Jason's meddling mother lights up the screen as a misdirected desperate mom trying to hold on to her baby boy, the drama she stirs up is so outlandish and, truthfully, so unforgivable that it is her and not the made-it-to-the-altar happy couple that the audience is dwelling on as the credits roll.

Joanna Topor MacKenzie

CREDITS

Sabrina Watson: Paula Patton
Jason Taylor: Laz Alonso
Blythe: Meagan Good
Ricky: Pooch Hall
Mrs. Watson: Angela Bassett
Willie Earl: Mike Epps
Mrs. Taylor: Loretta Devine
Amy: Julie Bowen
Chef: Gary Dourdan
Sabrina Watson: Paula Patton
Origin: USA

Language: English
Released: 2011
Production: Tracey E. Edmonds, Elizabeth Hunter, T. D. Jakes, Michael Mahoney, Glendon Palmer; TriStar Pictures, Stage Six Films, Our Stories Films, Sony Pictures Entertainment, TDJ Enterprises; released by TriStar Pictures
Directed by: Salim Akil
Written by: Arlene Gibbs, Elizabeth Hunter
Cinematography by: Anastas Michos
Music by: Ed Shearmur
Music Supervisor: Kier Lehman
Editing: Terilyn Shropshire
Sound: Jay Nierenberg
Costumes: Martha Curry
Production Design: Doug McCullough
MPAA rating: PG-13
Running time: 107 minutes

REVIEWS

Anderson, Melissa. *Village Voice.* May 4, 2011.
Biancolli, Amy. *Houston Chronicle.* May 6, 2011.
Gleiberman, Owen. *Entertainment Weekly.* May 4, 2011.
Graham, Adam. *Detroit News.* May 6, 2011.
Kennedy, Lisa. *Denver Post.* May 6, 2011.
Lemire, Christy. *Associated Press.* May 5, 2011.
Orange, Michelle. *Movieline.* May 5, 2011.
Pais, Matt. *RedEye.* May 5, 2011.
Rickey, Carrie. *Philadelphia Inquirer.* May 6, 2011.
Willmore, Alison. *Time Out New York.* May 4, 2011.

JUST GO WITH IT

Sometimes a guy's best wingman…is a wingwoman.
—Movie tagline
Sometimes you need a girl, to get the girl.
—Movie tagline

Box Office: $103 million

Brooklyn Decker has large, impressive breasts. No one is disputing that, especially people who bought the Sports Illustrated Swimsuit Edition in 2010 with Decker on the cover. What everyone should dispute is the notion that this woman's body deserves an entire film that exists primarily to appreciate its first-time actress' figure as it jiggles in slow-motion.

In the often astoundingly moronic *Just Go With It*, Decker plays Palmer, who is just like any average woman…except the exact opposite. She is twenty-three but ready for a family of her own. She is a comfortably-employed teacher despite her apparent inability to process most of what anyone else says. And she is remarkably sweet and humble despite possessing the sort of looks that normally allow women to land any partner they desire. Not, for example, a guy like Danny (Adam Sandler), a pathological liar who makes fun of everyone and has no problem pushing women and children. For deeply mystifying reasons, Palmer immediately falls for Danny and has (off-screen) sex with him on the beach, only to wake up the next morning and find a wedding ring in his pants pocket. And to think, she thought she had met the man of her dreams in this shallow, immature, middle-aged plastic surgeon.

Actually, Danny is not married. He is just the kind of sleazebag that usually wears a wedding ring to pick up women, whom he tells that his wife is abusing him so, the morning after getting what he came for, he can leave notes saying things like, " P.S. Thanks for not beating me like my wife does." Since Palmer believes anything she is told, she does not suspect a thing when Danny claims that he is married to Katherine (Jennifer Aniston), a single mother of two who is actually Danny's assistant. Soon Danny and Katherine are caught in an elaborate hoax that brings Palmer, Katherine's kids (Bailee Madison, Griffin Gluck), and Danny's cousin Eddie (Nick Swardson), posing as a German "sheep shipper" named Dolph Lundgren who is also Katherine's boyfriend, on a Hawaiian getaway. It would be easy to question, among other things, how Palmer, a sixth-grade math teacher, can so simply drop everything and leave the mainland, but what would be the point?

Like so many of Sandler's comedies, *Just Go With It* is directed by Dennis Dugan and features crass misogyny that is constantly perpetuated by Sandler's character, who relentlessly mocks Katherine and takes no notice of her obvious beauty until she strips down to a bikini. Only then does Danny think that maybe what is under his nose—which, by the way, is gigantic in a shameless flashback that treats Jewish stereotypes as comic gold—might be able to compete with the twenty-something airhead who reads Seventeen Magazine and still laments the breakup of N'Sync. Other familiar Sandler favorites that return: Jokes about pooping and penises, and Sandler's perpetual condescension to everyone around him. This allows the actor to not so much act as just hang out and enjoy the scenery while he mocks everyone from homeless people to children with physical deformities. Rest assured, all it takes is one brief moment of Danny showing any amount of sweetness toward Katherine's kids and all of his incidents of verbal and physical cruelty are forgotten.

So many of the characters in *Just Go With It* are so foolish and irrational that most of the movie almost seems to exist in an alternate universe, in which normal standards of social behavior and critical thinking have not yet been developed. In the real world, Palmer would be at least a little scared off by the way that Danny yells at children, slaps Dolph in the face with a credit card, and ruthlessly degrades the woman he claims is his wife. Surely, in the real world, no Adam Sandler movie could possibly feature a married couple played by Academy Award®-winner Nicole Kidman (as Katherine's old college nemesis who just happens to be staying at the same Hawaiian resort) and musician Dave Matthews. (That the couple eventually competes against Danny and Katherine in a game that results in Ian [Matthews] lifting a coconut with his butt [while wearing pants, by the way]) only confirms that what is happening is not happening on Earth, and sure is not funny.) And only in Sandler's version of reality would a sweet woman like Katherine drag her kids around as part of a complicated ruse perpetrated by her boss so he can trick a hottie half his age into dating him.

Of course, at the beginning of the film, in 1988 Long Island, Danny has his heart broken when he overhears his fiancée, just before their wedding, admit to cheating and that she only wants to marry Danny because he is a doctor. Consequently his wedding ring scam is only meant to protect him from more pain and suffering. Perhaps a more sympathetic actor could have effectively conveyed this…actually, Sandler is plenty capable of being a sympathetic, wounded soul, as anyone who has seen *Punch-Drunk Love* (2002) knows. Unfortunately Sandler allows Danny no real vulnerability; he is too busy dishing out insults that, defense mechanism or not, just make him look like a jerk.

Aniston is a talented comedienne but can do nothing with material this awful, and Decker performs about as well as a woman needs to when her role specifies only a certain cup-size. Her contribution, at least, helped *Just Go With It* to be the only movie to have a clip included in a recent piece about America's obsession with breasts on NBC's *The Today Show*. In fact, the entire film probably could have been scrapped and released only as a five-second shot of Decker slowly emerging from the water in a bikini with its work cut out for it. That is obviously all that Sandler and Dugan expect their male teen audiences to care about. Not, for example, that the movie was adapted from the 1969 film *Cactus Flower* that originated as a French farce before becoming a Broadway play. This reviewer has not seen those points of origin but feels relatively confident in assuming they did not feature a character named Dolph Lundgren performing the Heimlich maneuver on a fake sheep.

Matt Pais

CREDITS

Danny: Adam Sandler
Katherine: Jennifer Aniston
Devlin Adams: Nicole Kidman

Ian Maxtone-Jones: Dave Matthews
Maggie: Bailee Madison
Palmer: Brooklyn Decker
Adon: Kevin Nealon
Eddie: Nick Swardson
Michael: Griffin Gluck
Kirsten: Rachel Dratch
Origin: USA
Language: English
Released: 2011
Production: Jack Giarraputo, Heather Parry, Adam Sandler; Columbia Pictures, Happy Madison Productions; released by Sony Pictures Entertainment
Directed by: Dennis Dugan
Written by: Adam Sandler, Allan Loeb, Timothy Dowling
Cinematography by: Theo van de Sande
Music by: Rupert Gregson-Williams
Sound: Elmo Weber
Editing: Tom Costain
Art Direction: Alan Au, John Collins
Costumes: Valerie Zielonka
Production Design: Perry Andelin Blake
MPAA rating: PG-13
Running time: 117 minutes

REVIEWS

Bowles, Scott. *USA Today.* February 10, 2011.
Hornaday, Ann. *Washington Post.* February 11, 2011.
LaSalle, Mick. *San Francisco Chronicle.* February 10, 2011.
Morris, Wesley. *Boston Globe.* February 10, 2011.
Persall, Steve. *St. Petersburg Times.* February 10, 2011.
Phillips, Michael. *Chicago Tribune.* February 10, 2011.
Phipps, Keith. *AV Club.* February 10, 2011.
Pols, Mary. *Time.* February 14, 2011.
Rea, Stephen. *Philadelphia Inquirer.* February 10, 2011.
Scott, A.O. *New York Times.* February 10, 2011.

QUOTES

Michael: "Mom, before we go can I make a Devlin?"

TRIVIA

Was shipped to theaters with the code name "Grounded Out."

AWARDS

Golden Raspberries 2011: Worst Actor (Sandler), Worst Director (Dugan)
Nomination:
Golden Raspberries 2011: Worst Support. Actor (Swardson), Worst Support. Actress (Kidman), Worst Screen Couple (Sandler and Aniston or Decker).

JUSTIN BIEBER: NEVER SAY NEVER

Find out what's possible if you never give up.
—Movie tagline

Box Office: $73 million

Less a concert film than a marketing campaign, *Justin Bieber: Never Say Never* exists primarily to reassure Justin Bieber's fans that he is exactly the normal, everyday kid of his public image. That Scooter Braun, the pop star's manager, and Antonio (a.k.a., L.A.) Reid, the executive of the record label to which the Bieber is signed, serve as producers for the movie (in addition to their appearances within it as, in the case of the former, part of the singer's entourage and, in the case of the latter, an interview subject) is all the evidence anyone needs to confirm that a cynical suspicion is sound. The participation of Anschutz Entertainment Group (AEG) Live (The company that produced the live tour upon which the movie focuses), which had been criticized for releasing the documentary *This Is It* (2009) so soon after the death of its subject Michael Jackson, only emphasizes the reasoning for skepticism.

Of course, this not an exception, as the same sort of criticism of focusing on the public relations aspect of artists over their output could conceivably be leveled at almost every aspect of the entertainment industry, especially in the music realm, where business models definitively conquered artistic concerns some time ago. From that perspective, too, there is nothing unique about the outline of Bieber's story—a talented kid rises to fame after being discovered by people who believe in him. That is the tale of almost every famous individual from the past and the present, and with the increase in television programs like *American Idol,* with both winners and losers going on to various levels of success, such stories are even more common. Even the baker's dozen of songs he performs throughout the movie are typical, overproduced modern pop ditties that fluctuate in quality from unfortunately catchy, repeated refrains ("Baby" and "One Less Lonely Girl") to entirely forgettable (the other eleven).

What is singular about Bieber is the way he is marketed. He began as a social media phenomenon when his mother Pattie Mallette posted videos of her son performing to the website YouTube, and, at the start of the movie, he is on a national tour only ten days from a performance at New York City's Madison Square Garden. As much a component of Bieber's success as his talent is Braun's mastery of social networking sites. An announcement on Twitter brings a mob of fans to a mall, where the fire marshal must announce that they must clear the area for safety concerns after the appearance has been cancelled. When Bieber is ill with a throat infection that causes one show to be postponed and threatens many others after, he sends out a single public message through the same site, resulting in a flood of his devotees' 140-character-or-less well-wishes that fill up the screen and keep increasing in a virtual pan across them.

Such instances are the only taste of the truly noteworthy part of Bieber's career. Perhaps director Jon M. Chu takes it as a given that the movie's core audience of Bieber admirers understand how his star rose. During cutaways to interviews with some of his fans awaiting a performance, they seem to know a lot of information about him, such as reciting the date of his birth in edited unison. He was born to a young mother, who raised him on her own in Stratford, Ontario, Canada, after his father left them when the son was ten-months old—the father Jeremy arrives to watch one show, tears filling his eyes, though the extent and nature of their relationship is left a mystery. By the age of eight, Bieber, with his natural sense of rhythm, accompanied a jazz band on the drums (there is a clip of a drum solo at a present day concert cut into this section, as further proof that he still plays), and it was videos posted online of his runner-up vocal performances at a Stratford theater that caught Braun's attention in the first place.

This biographical information is key to the marketed Bieber persona. On the massive screens on stage at venues where he plays, photos and videos of his early childhood and family appear in a slideshow format while he sings. The idea in this very public display of Bieber's private life is to show that, in spite of his newfound celebrity, he is still a perfectly ordinary 16-year-old. As a promotional tool, the movie does its job since Bieber does indeed come across as a regular teenager—or as normal of one as can be expected with a camera crew following him everywhere he goes, a full-time staff including a road manager/stylist and personal vocal coach, and a group of acquaintances that include Usher (who also serves as one of the movie's producers), Miley Cyrus, and Jaden Smith (son of Will Smith and Jada Pinkett Smith). After completing a show in Toronto, he returns home and goes out on the town with his friends, playing basketball at the local YMCA and stopping to tell a young girl playing a violin for money outside the theater not to give up on her dreams.

That clichéd story of meteoric success at a young age is like wish fulfillment for his fans. "Never say never," he tells the crowd, after proposing that people will say they can never live out their dreams. If Bieber can do it, so can they, the entire experience of *Justin Bieber: Never*

Say Never implies. It is odd, then, that his cheering, adoring fans rarely speak of their own personal passions except in terms of their beloved star. Instead of positing ambitions incorporating their own drives and talents, they espouse such goals as, "I'll be his first wife."

Mark Dujsik

CREDITS

Himself: Justin Bieber
Herself: Miley Cyrus
Himself: Ludacris
Themselves: Boyz II Men
Himself: Sean Kingston
Himself: Jaden Smith
Himself: Usher Raymond
Origin: USA
Language: English
Released: 2011
Production: Scooter Braun, Dan Cutforth, Jane Lipsitz, Usher Raymond, Antonio Reid; AEG Live, Insurge Pictures, Island Def Jam Music Group, MTV Films, Magical Elves Productions; released by Paramount Pictures
Directed by: Jon M. Chu
Cinematography by: Reed Smoot
Music by: Deborah Lurie
Sound: Tim Chau
Editing: Jay Cassidy, Jillian Twigger Moul, Avi Youabian
Costumes: Kurt and Bart
Production Design: Devorah Herbert
MPAA rating: G
Running time: 105 minutes

REVIEWS

Childress, Erik. *eFilmCritic.com*. February 11, 2011.
Edelstein, David. *New York Magazine*. February 11, 2011.
Eichel, Molly. *Philadelphia Daily News*. February 10, 2011.
Hartlaub, Peter. *San Francisco Chronicle*. February 11, 2011.
Koski, Genevieve. *AV Club*. February 10, 2011.
Macdonlad, Moira. *Seattle Times*. February 10, 2011.
Orndorf, Brian. *BrianOrndorf.com*. February 10, 2011.
Topel, Fred. *Screen Junkies*. February 11, 2011.
Tumas, Robert. *Slant Magazine*. February 11, 2011.
Whitty, Stephen. *Newark Star-Ledger*. February 11, 2011.

K

KABOOM

Blow your mind.
—Movie tagline

While still in his 30s making films like *Totally F***ed Up* (1993) and *The Doom Generation* (1995), the minor cult around writer/director Gregg Araki labeled him as a hipster artiste challenging the boundaries of independent film. Wink. But even Araki appeared to have left arrested development behind a little in his 40s with what many thought successfully tackled child molestation in *Mysterious Skin* (2004) and the all-day pot comedy, *Smiley Face* (2007), that was blessed with a wonderful comic performance by Anna Faris. Now, in his 50s, Araki may have regressed through a mid-life crisis back to the days of bizarro visual and plot fetishes of his yesteryear which resemble a Bret Easton Ellis novel filtered through a ten-year-old's world view of bisexual porn in *Kaboom*.

Smith (Thomas Dekker) is a college student struggling with his sexuality. He knows what he is, but it is never easy lusting after a straight roommate who looks like a mythological superhero. His best friend is the equally-disenchanted Stella (Haley Bennett), who listens to all his angsty nonsense and responds in kind by revealing just how disinterested she is in his stupid problems. Passing the time in-between, Smith hooks up with a no-strings-attached kind of girl in London (Juno Temple), who does not care if he is gay as long as he has a part that fits. Stella, meanwhile, is also enjoying sex with Lorelai (Roxane Mesquida), who dabbles in witchcraft and has the power to make body parts quiver and full

bodies cling to her company under penalty of violent spells.

There is a bigger problem on campus however, one that Smith may be having premonitions about through his dreams. They involve a red-headed girl, some dudes wearing animal masks and a dumpster. Before long, a red-headed girl (without a head) is found in a dumpster. Maybe it has something to do with Smith meeting a redhead the night before and running away from some guys in animal masks while a stoned-out watch guard known as the Messiah (Araki regular James Duval) roams the halls. Who has time for such real world problems when nude beaches and threesomes beckon? It is not like there is some inevitable apocalypse on the horizon or some other egregious metaphor of the like lurking out there or anything.

Metaphors for surviving the growth into adulthood that is the bridge of the college experience have been explored through literature and movies for years. From the fraternal satires of *National Lampoon's Animal House* (1978) and *Real Genius* (1985) to the harsher campus lessons of *The Paper Chase* (1973) and *Oleanna* (1994) it is a passage full of discovery, foolishness and all the fun and helplessness that comes with it. In Araki's hands though, there is carelessness in just branding his own mind's eye with a rhyme and reason associated with sending up collegiate clichés. *Kaboom* is more like his version of *Threesome* (1994), where college is an occasional distraction from feeding one's active libido, only Araki's is far less funny, much less honest and somehow ickier despite never pushing his usual boundaries of sexual depravity.

This is a film with a point of view only toward the outlandish. Like the setting itself, its plot is just background noise for a bunch of well-proportioned guys and gals to fetishize each other until it is time for the real world to come crashing in. If college was not already a rampant starting ground for adolescent satire, Kaboom might actually have something to say amidst its chaos. Lacking anything other than some occasional hipster dialogue, Araki's screenplay turns an audience into a group of bored philosophy students who have wandered into the wrong classroom. Juno Temple has a lively, sexy presence that invigorates here and there, clothes on or clothes off. Dekker's Smith makes for a less-than-compelling narrator and his frequent on-screen companion, Bennett, other than making pancakes somehow unappealing, is notable only for giving such a remarkably robotic performance.

If *Kaboom* was meant to be some dream-like hallucination passing for reality, than Araki the director hardly makes the case for it. A kaleidoscope of bright colors notwithstanding, the film does not warrant discussion for some alternative mindset when dream sequences are clearly labeled and otherworldly powers are produced without a speck of irony and just accepted. However frustrating the interpretations of works by David Lynch, Richard Kelly or Luis Bunuel (whose *Un Chien Andalou* (1929) is briefly referenced) might be, the least to be taken away from them is the variants of styles used to get under the gray matter and toy with concepts of reality. Between twin sisters, half-sisters, multiplied close-ups of regurgitations and all manner of conversation stoppers involving bodily waste removal, Araki has more or less made his version of *The Miracle of Life,* which every immature grade schooler can only remember for the graphic birth sequence. *Kaboom* is reaching more for the end of life, only by the time it reaches the countdown in the desperately manic final act, it is more like the end of the belief that Araki has grown up himself.

Erik Childress

CREDITS

Smith: Thomas Dekker
Stella: Haley Bennett
Lorelei: Roxane Mesquida
Thor: Chris Zylka
London: Juno Temple
Rex: Andy Fischer-Price
Hunter: Jason Olive
Oliver: Brennan Mejia
The Messiah: James Duval
Nicole: Kelly Lynch

Red-haired girl: Nicole LaLiberte
Origin: USA, France
Language: English
Released: 2011
Production: Andrea Sperling, Gregg Araki; Why Not Productions, Desperate Pictures; released by IFC Films
Directed by: Gregg Araki
Written by: Gregg Araki
Cinematography by: Sandra Valde-Hansen
Music by: Ulrich Schnauss, Mark Peters
Sound: Sean Madsen, Steve Utt
Music Supervisor: Tiffany Anders
Editing: Gregg Araki
Art Direction: JB Popplewell
Costumes: Trayce Gigi Field
Production Design: Todd Fjelsted
MPAA rating: Unrated
Running time: 86 minutes

REVIEWS

Cline, Rich. *Shadows on the Wall.* October 30, 2010.
Ebert, Roger. *Chicago Sun-Times.* February 17, 2011.
Edelstein, David. *New York Magazine.* January 31, 2011.
Goss, William. *Film.com.* June 6, 2011.
Honeycutt, Kirk. *Hollywood Reporter.* April 8, 2011.
LaSalle, Mick. *San Francisco Chronicle.* February 17, 2011.
Levy, Shawn. *Oregonian.* March 17, 2011.
Rea, Steven. *Philadelphia Inquirer.* March 17, 2011.
Scott, A.O. *New York Times.* January 27, 2011.
Utichi, Joe. *Cinematical.* May 28, 2010.

QUOTES

Stella: "You meet some guy on a nude beach and after five minutes you're downloading his hard drive in the back of a van. You're a slut."

TRIVIA

At one point Rooney Mara was considered for a role in the film.

KILL THE IRISHMAN

Based on the true story of Danny Greene the man the mob couldn't kill.
—Movie tagline

Box Office: $1.2 million

In the skies above suburban Lyndhurst, Ohio on October 6, 1977 were a few clouds, some flitting birds, and the severed arm of mobster Danny Greene as it hurtled in a ghastly arc from the blast that finally succeeded in killing him. Greene had been nicknamed "The Irishman" due to a profound, endlessly-expressed pride in his ancestry, but the frustrated, fuming Italians of La Cosa Nostra sputtered other, more colorful monikers each time their dogged competitor somehow managed to elude elimination. Indeed, coming up with a way to successfully slay this descendant of the Shamrock Isle turned out to be as difficult as finding a clover of the lucky, four-leaved variety. Luck had certainly not been a problem for Greene, however, dodging a bullet both figuratively and literally numerous times. A succession of bombs had either malfunctioned, been found and dismantled, or, most amazingly, reduced his residence to rubble from which he defiantly emerged with merely a cracked rib or two. The seemingly-invincible Greene, ironically ripped apart mere seconds after having a loose filling meticulously secured, is blown up in a way he would surely have much preferred in the lionizing *Kill the Irishman*. The interesting-but-flawed film boosts this admittedly-complicated criminal to lofty status as a sympathetic, hardscrabble hero for the little man.

Inexhaustibly determined, ferociously audacious, and bursting-forth with fearsome anger when set off, Greene was as explosive as any bomb. Thirty-six actual ones exploded in Cleveland during 1976 when a turf war began in earnest between him and the Mafia, resulting in the already-troubled municipality being labeled "Bomb City, U.S.A." As the film begins, Greene (Ray Stevenson) escapes one that has been planted in his car, emerging unscathed for the first of many displays of gutsinesss. "Is that all you got?" he bellows, his chest out, teeth bared, and eyes blazing. The flame-engulfed vehicle in the background fades even further into it with Greene roaring so in the fore. Thus, it is quickly established: This is a larger-than-life, seemingly-indestructible force of nature; a volcanic mountain of moxie the filmmakers clearly hope will fill the audience with admiration. The tone of *Irishman* has been set. He is the film's underworld underdog.

Showing a figure's fascinating complexity is different than resorting to magnification, distortion, and outright invention that impart an inaccurate, idolatrous portrait. Undoubtedly, Greene would have liked this likeness. Though charismatic, bright, often polite, religious, and routinely altruistic, Greene was also a tough-talking and corrupt union president, racketeer, and unbridled mob enforcer. He intimidated and murdered, even stooping so low as to threaten to kill one man's entire brood of children. Yet Ed Kovacic, then with the Cleveland Police Intelligence Unit and later the city's Chief, could not help but like Greene. (Kovacic and others on the force are combined into a single character played by Val Kilmer, a fact that could explain why he makes for such a corpulent cop.) "You're

different than all those idiots," one character states. More purposefully, a straight-talking, tough old bird of an Irishwoman (Grace O'Keefe) peers into "the eyes of a warrior" and pronounces that there is "something else: I see goodness." Director Jonathan Hensleigh, who rewrote a script by Jeremy Walters, obviously wishes viewers to do the same. Indeed, he takes great pains to make sure they do.

Thus, Greene is shown heroically coming to the aid and defense of a fellow dockworker who has swooned while forced to labor in excessive heat by a heartless, sneering, and thus starkly-contrasted boss/union president (Bob Gunton). Coitus interruptus is no sweat for Greene if it allows him to rush off and help a terrified friend in a jam. Greene is treated in such an acidly-dehumanizing manner by the aforementioned high-and-mighty lowlife that when he supplants the man after doling out some enjoyable-to-watch rough comeuppance, it feels like justice being served. When money that notorious kingpin Shondor Birns (Christopher Walken) requested from New York boss Tony Solerno (Paul Sorvino) gets intercepted, the fact that "The Irishman" is held responsible under penalty of death seems unjust and further aligns the audience's sympathies. (Birns, who always prided himself on being a dapper dresser, must surely be railing from down below about how Walken for some reason chose to portray him so scruffily.) Greene is shown to be violent but also a visionary, seeming much wiser than most wiseguys when he speaks with prescient caution about such things as the deepening quagmire in Vietnam, deficit spending, and high cholesterol. He is also shown magnanimously saving the aforementioned elderly lady from homelessness and chivalrously dashing to lead another in the opposite direction of one of his impending detonations. To prove he not only had a heart but a big one capable of breaking, the audience sees Greene crumple to the ground when hit with the departure of his wife (Linda Cardellini) and young kids. Added to all this is the extolling of how he used bad money to do a lot of good in his beloved neighborhood, earning the moniker "The Robin Hood of Collinwood."

What goes too far are two especially manipulative scenes of fictionalized content. In one, Greene tenderly and tearfully cradles a dying John Nardi (Vincent D'Onofrio), his last partner in crime. Worse is the outrageously-romanticized sequence in which Greene is stopped just steps away from death by a wide-eyed, worshipful boy who looks much like he must have in his own youth, and sagely stresses that any aspirations to be like him should definitely be ditched. He then beneficently bestows the necklace that had perhaps been responsible for keeping him so ceaselessly safe. Greene subsequently eyeing his executioner with fatalistic bravado is still more purposeful fabrication.

Shot in just thirty days on a shoestring budget of $12 million, Hensleigh's film earned mixed reviews and only $1.1 million during a limited release geared toward cities with larger Irish populations. Tax breaks and more-suitably-evident grit and decay necessitated today's Detroit standing in for Cleveland in the 1950's-1970's. (The director desaturates his visuals to help emphasize dilapidation.) Those who live where it all actually happened will howl at mispronunciations (especially "Collingwood"), misspellings (such as that of St. Malachi Church), and some strange alterations of dates (sometimes by mere days). Also, two of Greene's failed marriages and three of his children have been jettisoned from sight. Regardless, the film seemed to many viewers a succession of mob moments that they had seen done better before on both the big and small screens. Utilizing a laundry list of able actors who had appeared in those productions did not help to lessen this impression. Also, incessant, spectacular blasts begin after a while to lose their impact on the audience.

Nevertheless, the film is sufficiently absorbing, especially due to Stevenson's performance, even if he nails the requisite potency infinitely more than the charm. Rick Porrello, author of the 1998 book upon which *Irishman* is based, crowed that the production would end up standing next to classics like the *Godfather* trilogy (1972, 1974, 1990) and *Goodfellas* (1990). In actuality, however, the film is not deserving of being remembered so glowingly—and neither is Danny Greene.

David L. Boxerbaum

CREDITS

Danny Greene: Ray Stevenson
John Nardi: Vincent D'Onofrio
Tony Salerno: Paul Sorvino
Joe Manditski: Val Kilmer
Shondor Birns: Christopher Walken
Ray Ferritto: Robert Davi
Keith Ritson: Vinnie Jones
Jack Licavoli: Tony Lo Bianco
Mikey Mendarolo: Tony Darrow
Leo Moceri: Mike Starr
Mike Frato: Steve Schirripa
Joan Madigan: Linda Cardellini
Grace O'Keefe: Fionnula Flanagan
Ellie O'Hara: Laura Ramsey
Origin: USA
Language: English

Released: 2011
Production: Al Corley, Eugene Musso, Tommy Reid, Bart Rosenblatt; Anchor Bay Entertainment, Code Entertainment, Dundee Entertainment, Sweet Willaim Productions; released by Anchor Bay Entertainment
Directed by: Jonathan Hensleigh
Written by: Jonathan Hensleigh, Jeremy Walters
Cinematography by: Karl Walter Lindenlaub
Music by: Patrick Cassidy
Sound: Beau Williams
Music Supervisor: John Bissell
Editing: Douglas Crise
Art Direction: Gary Baugh
Costumes: Melissa Bruning
Production Design: Patrizia Von Brandenstein
MPAA rating: R
Running time: 106 minutes

REVIEWS

Abele, Robert. *Los Angles Times.* March 11, 2011.
Anderson, John. *Variety.* March 14, 2011.
Catsoulis, Jeannette. *New York Times.* March 11, 2011.
Feeney, Mark. *Boston Globe.* March 18, 2011.
Pinkerton, Nick. *Village Voice.* March 9, 2011.
Rooney, David. *Hollywood Reporter.* March 7, 2011.
Schwarzbaum, Lisa. *Entertainment Weekly.* March 18, 2011.
Toumarkine, Doris. *Film Journal International.* March 2011.
Wheat, Alynda. *People.* March 21, 2011.

QUOTES

Danny Greene: "Potato eater? Seeing as how the potato was the only source of nutrition in Ireland for 300 years and half the population including my ancestors died in the great famine, I'd say that term is insensitive."

TRIVIA

Val Kilmer joined the production after declining the opportunity to run for Governor of New Mexico.

KILLER ELITE

May the best man live.
—Movie tagline

Box Office: $25.1 million

The British Special Forces' selection process has much more to do with rejection, with over ninety percent of hopefuls reportedly falling short of that eminent military organization's towering standards. One thought of this when *Killer Elite*, which deals with the Forces' particularly-renowned Special Air Services unit, came before the public, as the film itself could not even measure up to the average moviegoer's infinitely less-rigorous requirements. While the story not only involves members of the stringently-selected SAS but also an ace assassin (Jason Statham) chosen for his supposedly-singular skills, it was almost as daunting a task as the division's fabled assessment trek across Brecon Beacons to find anything else here that one might call either first-rate or unique.

If one's satisfaction merely demands cacophonous gunplay, careening cars, billowing blasts, kinetically-cut fight scene confusion, spattering blood, and brutal bashes to the head, groin, and just about everywhere in-between, all goosed along by the testosterone-stirring throb of the soundtrack, then *Killer Elite* might indeed pass muster. Statham fans may be content with the actor only straying about as far from his tried-and-true screen persona as his omnipresent stubble protrudes from the surface of his scowling face. As tires screech during the early scene in which his deadly Danny Bryce and assorted cohorts attack a Mexican motorcade, viewers are given a hurly-burly heads-up that this will feel like something of a Statham retread, although with the added box-office allure of Clive Owen and Robert De Niro. *Killer Elite* does not limit itself to Statham sameness, however, as it also contains elements reminiscent of so many other—and better—films within the genre, and is riddled with almost as many cringe-worthily-clunky, cliché lines of dialogue as the casualties are with bullets.

There is certainly a concerted effort to make audiences feel for Danny, even though that would call for the uncomfortable embracing of a block of ice. This coldhearted killing machine has an immobilizing pang of conscience when his gaze is met by the terrified, gore-doused young son of his latest expertly-dispatched victim. Danny's consequential hesitation results in his being wounded, a sort of karmic tit that hardly cancels out his many terminal tats. As a close-up emphasizes, he both literally and figuratively has a great deal of blood on his hands, and viewers are meant to believe that his agony is deeper than his wounds. "I'm done," he asserts in a weak murmur. "I can't do this anymore."

Danny finds solace amidst the bosom of both the Australian outback's Edenic greenery and the honey-hued Eve named Anne Frazier (Yvonne Strahovski) whom he finds and falls for there. However, a letter and enclosed photograph reveal that Hunter (De Niro), the mentor for whom this hard man retains a soft spot, needs rescuing, and so a happily ensconced Danny must tritely boomerang back into action with a world-weary sigh and grudging snarl for one last job.

It seems that Hunter is in the clutches of a dying Omani sheik (Rodney Afif), whose demise must surely be hastened by the lung-punishing litany of expository information the character must spout. Three of the sheik's four sons were slain by SAS operatives during England's oil-conscious clandestine involvement in factional fighting within Oman. In order to free Hunter, Danny must exact retribution on the handful of men specifically responsible for the sheik's shrinking family, recording confessions before the onset of each seemingly-accidental death. With the help of two old associates, robustly-exuberant Davies (Dominic Purcell) and eerily-calculating Meier (Aden Young), Danny gets down to bloody business.

Opposing their efforts is Spike (Owen), a former SAS member doing the dirty work of The Feathermen, a group of powerful ex-SAS officers who in their own way are as shadowy as their tasteful but decidedly-dim lair. With a mustache best termed inadvisable and a blind eye perhaps symbolic of his inability to fully see the big picture (double-crosses abound), Spike's job is to loyally keep from harm those past and present SAS who courageously protected their country's interest and resultantly now need protecting themselves from Danny. Most viewers will likely disconnect from the film's overly-convoluted, fairly-incomprehensible covert geopolitical machinations, focusing instead on the showdown smack down between these two fiercely-determined antagonists. Except for Statham's pain-inflicting acrobatics while tied to a chair, what transpires is pretty standard stuff.

Executioner Danny's supposed humanity continues to be banged into the audience's heads throughout *Killer Elite*, as if repeatedly subjecting them to one scene's heavy-handed administering of a sizeable mallet. He endlessly voices his outraged repugnance for unnecessary collateral damage inflicted upon innocents, especially and most chivalrously when it comes to women and children. Danny starts to make a habit of gazing wistfully out airplane windows, bringing on flashbacks of his endangered idyllic existence with Anne in a sunny, verdant paradise on Earth which visually contrasts with shots of the hellish places to which necessity has now forced him back: scorched desert landscapes; grim blue/grey interiors; and the unsettling desolation of the Brecon Beacons during a nighttime snowstorm. However, there is very little to make one feel for him, to be emotionally invested in how things turn out for Danny or anyone else. (Watching De Niro's Hunter smilingly stuff cash into his pockets at the film's end, it is sadly hard to differentiate between the character and the now-coasting great actor.) By the time Danny and Spike finally part ways, they are both still struggling along with those watching to make sense of it all.

More intriguing than the film itself is the controversy surrounding its source material. Sir Ranulph Fiennes, widely-celebrated for his dashingly-courageous polar, Everest and other expeditions, has also been vilified for what many insist is absolute rubbish cagily masquerading as fact in his 1991 book entitled *The Feathermen*. Fiennes has remained irritatingly vague about the account's exact degree of authenticity, muddying things further by choosing to term its adaptation "pure fiction." In any event, *Killer Elite*, Gary McKendry's feature-film debut, was snuffed out by predominantly negative reviews, grossing merely a third of its $70 million budget.

David L. Boxerbaum

CREDITS

Danny Bryce: Jason Statham
Spike: Clive Owen
Hunter: Robert De Niro
Anne: Yvonne Strahovski
Davies: Dominic Purcell
Origin: USA, Australia
Language: English
Released: 2011
Production: Michael Boughen, Steve Chasman, Sigurjon Sighvatsson, Tony Winley; Omnilab Media, Ambience Entertainment, Current Entertainment, Film Victoria, International Traders; released by Open Road Films
Directed by: Gary McKendry
Written by: Matt Sherring
Cinematography by: Simon Duggan
Music by: Reinhold Heil, Johnny Klimek
Sound: Andrew Plain
Music Supervisor: Matt Biffa
Editing: John Gilbert
Art Direction: Tim Dickel, Aziz Hamichi, Richard Hobbs, Simon McCutcheon
Costumes: Katherine Milne
Production Design: Michelle McGahey
MPAA rating: R
Running time: 116 minutes

REVIEWS

Dargis, Manohla. *New York Times*. September 22, 2011.
Debruge, Peter. *Variety*. September 9, 2011.
Ebert, Roger. *Chicago Sun-Times*. September 21, 2011.
McCarthy, Todd. *Hollywood Reporter*. September 11, 2011.
Morris, Wesley. *Boston Globe*. September 22, 2011.
O'Sullivan, Michael. *Washington Post*. September 22, 2011.
Phillips, Michael. *Chicago Tribune*. September 22, 2011.
Pinkerton, Nick. *Village Voice*. September 20, 2011.
Rainer, Peter. *Christian Science Monitor*. September 23, 2011.
Schwarzbaum, Lisa. *Entertainment Weekly*. September 21, 2011.
Smith, Kyle. *New York Post*. September 23, 2011.
Travers, Peter. *Rolling Stone*. September 22, 2011.

QUOTES

Davies: "You don't trust that snake, do you? He's lying."
Danny: "Yeah? How do you know?"
Davies: "His lips were moving. "

TRIVIA

Robert De Niro is the only American born actor in this film.

KUNG FU PANDA 2

Prepare for the return of awesomeness.
    —Movie tagline

Box Office: $165.2 million

Putting an end to three years of wild speculation and whispered gossip, *Kung Fu Panda 2* finally revealed to both the moviegoing public and the titular character himself how an exuberant goof of a bear could have a dithering goose for a father: yes, it was indeed adoption after all. Geneticists everywhere may have responded with a resounding "Duh!" to this disclosure, but who really knew what to accept as possible amongst characters created by means of computer animation instead of biological procreation? Most fans of this film's 2008 surprise-hit predecessor starring Jack Black as lovable, portly panda Po had suspected the truth all along, but simply needed to hear it directly from the bill of Mr. Ping (excellent James Hong). Now knowing conclusively how a bambino more typically raised amidst a forest of bamboo wound up under the parentally-protective wing of a goose, everyone could at last stop wracking their noodles about the noodle-maker's dissimilarity from his son and simply accept him as Po's proud papa.

The panda's own curiosity is not fully satisfied by this revelation, however, and his angst-driven quest to learn about his life pre-Ping adds a surprising degree of often sobering emotional depth to the mix of comedy and explosive Kung Fu kinetics one expected to find in this satisfying sequel. In shedding light on Po's past, *Kung Fu Panda 2* includes some material that is quite dark and rather disturbing, such as nightmarish flashback glimpses of a panda genocide. As irresistibly-cute-and-cuddly cub Po is painfully parted from an adoring mother who must then dash off into the woods with death close on her heels, many adult viewers joined their tykes in tow in experiencing a disruption of the "inner peace" to which the film so often refers. Fortunately, just as full-grown Po's substantial heft fails to prevent him from coming out victorious in the end, *Kung Fu Panda*

2 avoids being adversely weighed-down by those components that are more somber and contemplative. Indeed, the continuing story of Po has not been encumbered but rather enriched.

It is hard not to think of the wildly-popular video game *Angry Birds* while watching *Kung Fu Panda 2,* as the film's plot is set in motion by a powerfully-peeved peacock motivated by wounded pride to reclaim what he feels is rightfully his—and then some. The fact that Lord Shen (an imperious, sinister Gary Oldman) was born without the normal breathtaking, multicolored beauty of his species might have been enough to make him assess his lot with resentfully-ruffled feathers. However, he was also profoundly hurt when his parents failed to appreciate his ingenuity in turning their ruling family's benign, festive fireworks into ominous, lethal firepower, and resultantly banished him. In addition, their breasts understandably failed to swell with pride when he committed the aforementioned mass extermination of pandas, Shen's response to the prediction of a Soothsayer (Michelle Yeoh) that his eventual power grab would be thwarted by " warrior of black and white." With weapons cunningly concealed amidst his plumage, a fierce army of hulking wolves at his disposal, and a new arsenal of massive cannon that seem certain to make Kung Fu resistance hopelessly ineffectual, Shen takes over Gongmen City and then, with devilishly-red-irised eyes burning with rapaciousness, sets his sights on all of China. With no anthropomorphic animal analysts around to help Shen deal with his festering parental issues, it is necessary for Dragon Warrior Po and the Furious Five—Tigress (Angelina Jolie), Monkey (Jackie Chan), Mantis (Seth Rogen), Viper (Lucy Lui), and Crane (David Cross)—to spring into action and keep the empire out of the peacock's treacherous talons.

It is during these defensive maneuvers that Po is detrimentally distracted by long-suppressed memories of his own parents that suddenly come flashing to the fore, creating an inopportune, gnawing need to know about his origins, of which Ping knows nothing. The desire to pry open the door to the past by this cherished child he raised clearly triggers the same, wholly-understandable sense of insecurity felt by other adoptive parents in such a situation, and his apprehension is both heartwarming and heartrending. The fact that Po will not only be seeking answers but also facing possible annihilation adds to Ping's tremulous trepidation, and one of the film's most memorable moments is the sweet one in which the goose takes a poignant last gander at a departing son he misses already. His Po thus goes off to formidably struggle on two fronts, one outside of himself and one within, and as long as his attention is divided because his soul is disquieted, the chances of besting Shen are, to put it mildly, not the best.

Cognizant of that fact, the devious bird who knows the truth purposefully fills in the blanks for Po with lies he cruelly hopes will cripple. As he mercilessly asserts that the panda's parents abandoned him due to a lack of love, the camera moves in on the resulting pain in the Dragon Warrior's eyes to maximize the audience's sympathy. The force of this devastating blow to the gut is immediately mirrored by the cannon blast to the belly that propels Po many miles away and nearly kills him. He is rescued both physically and emotionally by the Soothsayer (whom Shen has exiled in the interim), enabled to breach a long-standing, self-protective mental dam and let decidedly bittersweet recollections burst forth to finally set things straight and ameliorate. This onset of inner peace allows Po, like wise Master Shifu (Dustin Hoffman) before him, to catch a single droplet of water, roll it along his body, and gently set it down fully intact. This is both literally and figuratively a watershed moment, and Po himself is now fully intact, as well. As for viewers, they may find themselves falling apart to some extent during Po and Ping's moving reunification.

It is highly appropriate that the yin yang symbol pops up more than once during *Kung Fu Panda 2,* as the film itself possesses an ebbing and flowing of seemingly contrary elements that nonetheless complement each other to create a balanced whole. Amidst all this material that tugs at the heart are a sufficient number of moments that tickle the funny bone (usually involving endearing Po's overeager underachievement) and action-packed martial arts sequences designed to make eyes pop. It is quite humorous to watch Po operating in less-than-stellar "stealth mode", inaudibly and thus ineffectually throwing down the gauntlet to a distant and thus baffled Shen, or expressing confusion and skepticism concerning the Soothsayer's sex because of her goat beard. (There is also her insistent, instinctive nibbling on the robe of an increasingly-exasperated Shen). "Enough of this nonsense!" an impatient Shen declares at one point, but some expressed the wish that there had actually been more of it. Especially exciting is the heroic sextet's race to the top of Shen's towering palace and subsequent leap to safety as the structure topples to the ground. So is the scene in which Po once and for all halts Shen and his hellishly-glowing armada from spreading odiousness across China. As fireworks are once again used for something joyous, a yin yang symbol appears once again in the sky overhead, signaling that harmony has been restored.

Just as Po stuffs his mouth early-on with an impressive number of dumplings (which he then spits out but requests be saved to devour later), *Kung Fu Panda 2* boasts compositions that are often crammed with items upon which the eye can feast. Truly exquisite in the richness of both color and detail are the renderings of Shen's Tower of the Sacred Flame and other buildings throughout Gongmen City, as well as the varied vistas traversed by the characters or swooped over by the camera for a bird's-eye view. One appreciatively takes in the atmospheric mistiness of Shifu's Dragon Grotto, and the fiery reds and golden glows within Shen's diabolical foundry. Also well-done are the depictions of surfaces that gleam or feature reflections, the seemingly-touchable textures of fur and feathers, and the increased amount of expressiveness this time around of character's eyes. The film's 3D adds wonderful depth to the landscapes and further vitality to the action sequences. Also imaginative—and quite effective—is the switch to different animation styles during the prologue, nightmare and flashback sequences. While the closing credits seem almost as long as the film itself, the striking artwork that accompanies them is not to be missed.

Kung Fu Panda 2 is the directorial debut of Jennifer Yuh Nelson, who had served as head of story and director of dream sequences on *Kung Fu Panda*. Made on a budget of $130 million, the sequel received positive reviews and earned $165.2 million, making it the top-grossing film ever directed by a woman. As this is a production of DreamWorks Animation, the fact that the door is cracked open at the last second for a third installment is not surprising. What does give one pause is that there are plans for an eventual total of six films in the series. While *Kung Fu Panda 2* is a winning mix of vivacity and vulnerability like Po himself, it does not take the Soothsayer's foresight or Shifu's wisdom to know things will likely begin to sag at some point, like the belly of someone who has eaten more dumplings than was advisable.

David L. Boxerbaum

CREDITS

Po: Jack Black
Shifu: Dustin Hoffman
Tigress: Angelina Jolie
Monkey: Jackie Chan
Mantis: Seth Rogen
Viper: Lucy Liu
Crane: David Cross

Mr. Ping: James Hong
Lord Shen: Gary Oldman
Master Croc: Jean-Claude Van Damme
Master Thundering Rhino: Victor Garber
The Soothsayer: Michelle Yeoh
Origin: USA
Language: English
Released: 2011
Production: Melissa Cobb; DreamWorks Animation; released by Paramount Pictures
Directed by: Jennifer Yuh
Written by: Jonathan Aibel, Glenn Berger
Music by: John Powell, Hans Zimmer
Editing: Maryann Brandon, Clare De Chenu
Sound: Erik Aadahl, Ethan Van der Ryn
Art Direction: Tang K. Heng
Production Design: Raymond Zibach
MPAA rating: PG
Running time: 91 minutes

REVIEWS

Bowles, Scott. *USA Today*. May 26, 2011.
Corliss, Richard. *Time*. May 27, 2011.
Debruge, Peter. *Variety*. May 23, 2011.
Ebert, Roger. *Chicago Sun-Times*. May 25, 2011.
Gilchrist, Todd. *Boxoffice Magazine*. May 24, 2011.
Gleiberman, Owen. *Entertainment Weekly*. May 25, 2011.
McCarthy, Todd. *Hollywood Reporter*. May 23, 2011.
Morgenstern, Joe. *Wall Street Journal*. May 27, 2011.
O'Sullivan, Michael. *Washington Post*. May 25, 2011.
Page, Janice. *Boston Globe*. May 25, 2011.

QUOTES

Po: "My fist hungers for justice!"

TRIVIA

The character of Shen was originally created to serve as a devious mayor in *Kung Fu Panda*, but he was written of that film out before production started.

AWARDS

Nomination:

Oscars 2011: Animated Film.

L

LARRY CROWNE

Box Office: $35.6 million

Tom Hanks' directorial effort *Larry Crowne* is much like any one of the many Tom Petty songs that permeate much of the soundtrack: It is not terribly ambitious or deep, but it is catchy and infectious enough to make it easy to like. The film acted as a nice piece of summertime counter-programming to Michael Bay's headache inducing *Transformers: Dark of the Moon* (2011) during that crucial late June/early July opening. It is a relaxing, light breeze of a film that exists only to put a smile on the viewer's face for its quick ninety-nine minute running time. While it does deal with the subject of unemployment, its intent is not to make any grand statement on the economy or job loss. It keeps things light, but never dumb.

Larry Crowne (Hanks) is almost as Joe Average as it gets. He works at a K-Mart-type establishment and has been there for about thirteen years. He wears the uniform, wears the back brace and feels like he just might be getting Employee of the Month again, a feat he has accomplished more times than he can count. He likes his job and everyone likes him. But the meeting with his bosses goes in the complete opposite direction from what he expected. Larry is laid off in spite of being a good employee. His biggest mistake is not being ambitious or educated enough for advancement. Because of his lack of a college degree, he will never qualify for management.

After this crushing blow, Larry is forced to reassess everything in his life. He has a house, in which he used to live with his wife. He is still paying for the divorce.

He drives an SUV. As he is about to start collecting unemployment checks, he sees that everything in his life must eventually be downsized. He starts by having a yard sale, except that his neighbors across the street (Cedric the Entertainer, Taraji P. Henson) have a large, perpetual yard sale as a result of having blown all the money they won on a game show on frivolous items. But they are friends to Larry and are gracious enough to let him trade his flatscreen TV for the motor scooter just so he can stop spending $75 on a tank of gas for his SUV.

The most drastic move Larry makes is enrolling in a couple classes at East Valley Community College. Larry arrives for his first day on his scooter and wearing a polo shirt tucked in. This catches the eye of another student, Talia (Gugu Mbatha Raw), a younger, upbeat and free-spirited woman who first encourages Larry to not tuck his shirt in and, second, to join with her and the rest of her motor scooter gang. Larry decides to step out of his social comfort zone and join them. The leader is Talia's boyfriend Dell (Wilmer Valderrama), who warns Larry that everyone falls in love with Talia, but he better not.

Larry has two classes (or at least, the only two depicted in the film): Economics, taught by Dr. Matsutani (a perfectly cast George Takei), who is one minute unforgiving and intimidating, the next minute a jovial delight. His other is a speech class run by Mercedes Tainot (Julia Roberts), who provides the other narrative thrust in the storyline. Mercedes walks into class on the first day hoping she will have to cancel the class due to low enrollment. She always seems to get the bare minimum of students. Years of unfulfilling experiences teaching the same lessons to the same kinds of indifferent people have finally left her resentful and tired of everything, including her husband Dean (Bryan Cranston), who spends much of his days surfing for porn on the internet.

The reinvented Larry appears to be happier and freer. He has let Talia change his wardrobe and other members of the motor scooter gang come in and rearrange the furniture in his apartment. In class, Larry applies everything he learns to his situation. His economics class teaches him how to deal with the pushy lenders at the bank who try to talk him out of selling his house. Mercedes catches glimpses of Larry in non-classroom settings and comes to simultaneously resent and envy his transformation. She wants out of her current unhappy situation with her husband and job. Larry might not seem like the answer, but on one fateful evening he temporarily provides some much needed relief.

Larry seems to have a lot to deal with, but there is never a sense of real desperation on his part. He enrolls in these classes and buys new clothes, but it is never explained how he plans on paying for this stuff. Still, what *Larry Crowne* lacks in a storyline with real conflicts or urgency, it more than makes up for in charm and wit. This is not a movie about overcoming adversity, but about taking drastic steps to be a more well-rounded individual and to step out of one's comfort zone. Its screenplay (written by Hanks and Nia Vardalos) never belabors any of its thin storylines, nor does it resort to classroom clichés.

The cast helps a lot. Hanks, while giving a perfectly believable performance, is wise to stand aside and let the rest of the cast shine even more. Takei is an inspired choice for the economics professor and Wilmer Valderrama is perfectly subtle and very funny as Talia's boyfriend who repeatedly catches her and Larry in suspicious looking situations (again, the screenplay is smart to not dwell on these moments). But Roberts' performance is perhaps the most surprising. She has clearly thought this character out through and through and gives her best performance in many years. She picks just the right note and is consistent with it throughout. The viewer can see that Mercedes once had a passion for everything she taught, but has let her cynicism overtake her, since much of what she does offers no long-term reward.

This is Hanks' second big-screen directorial effort and it comes fifteen years after his last film *That Thing You Do* (1996) (with some television work in-between). That film was equally light on story, but long on charm. Hanks appears to enjoy telling stories about people whose successes are short-term and small scale in the grand scheme of things. They are small, personal and

ultimately gratifying successes and his directorial efforts can be described in much the same way.

Collin Souter

CREDITS

Larry Crowne: Tom Hanks
Mercedes Tainot: Julia Roberts
Lamar: Cedric the Entertainer
Dean Tainot: Bryan Cranston
B'Ella: Taraji P. Henson
Dr. Matsutani: George Takei
Frances: Pam Grier
Frank: Ian Gomez
Dell Gordo: Wilmer Valderrama
Talia: Gugu Mbatha-Raw
Wilma Q. Gammelgaard: Rita Wilson
Origin: USA
Language: English
Released: 2011
Production: Gary Goetzman, Tom Hanks; Universal Pictures, Vendome Pictures, Playtone Productions; released by Universal Pictures
Directed by: Tom Hanks
Written by: Tom Hanks, Nia Vardalos
Cinematography by: Philippe Rousselot
Music by: James Newton Howard
Sound: John Pritchett
Music Supervisor: Deva Anderson
Editing: Alan Cody
Art Direction: Carlos Menendez
Costumes: Albert Wolsky
Production Design: Victor Kempster
MPAA rating: PG-13
Running time: 99 minutes

REVIEWS

Holden, Stephen. *New York Times.* June 30, 2011.
Ebert, Roger. *Chicago Sun-Times.* June 30, 2011.
Lane, Anthony. *New Yorker.* July 18, 2011.
Long, Tom. *Detroit News.* July 1, 2011.
Lumenick, Lou. *New York Post.* July 1, 2011.
Rea, Steven. *Philadelphia Enquirer.* June 30, 2011.
Schwarzbaum, Lisa. *Entertainment Weekly.* June 29, 2011.
Sobczynski, Peter. *eFilmcritic.com.* June 30, 2011.
Uhlich, Keith. *Time Out New York.* June 29, 2011.
Whitty, Stephen. *Newark Star Ledger.* July 2, 2011.

QUOTES

Lamar: "I told you how to avoid divorce lawyers. You get married, and you stay married."

LIFE, ABOVE ALL

The phrase "grown up too soon" is a sort of vague, generic catch-all for the type of maltreatment of kids that perhaps stops short of actual physical or sexual abuse. Those acts (horrendous, certainly) are comparatively the subjects of many movies, whereas those focusing more on the latent parentalization of minors are aiming at a much smaller target. Oliver Schmitz's *Life, Above All,* which debuted at the 2010 Cannes Film Festival, is one such effort. A well-constructed, emotionally rich, issues-oriented drama that unfolds through the perspective of a determined young South African girl, the movie connects most readily with those who have some built-in emotional understanding and relationship to the unfortunately enduring topicality of many of the turbulent domestic issues with which its protagonist grapples.

Based on Allan Stratton's respected novel *Chanda's Secrets,* the film unfolds in a dust-ridden village on the outskirts of Johannesburg, where 12-year-old Chanda (Khomotso Manyaka) lives with her mother, Lillian (Lerato Mvelase), and two younger step-siblings. The death of Lillian's latest child, a newborn little girl, has stirred up old chaos, grudges and addictions. Chanda's alcoholic stepfather Jonah (Aubrey Poolo) has fallen off the wagon, convinced that Lillian's breast milk poisoned his "good seed," and killed their new baby. Already distraught and depressed, Lillian becomes quite sick.

Given Jonah's itinerant and philandering ways, Chanda fears that her mother might have contracted the AIDS virus. She tries to look after her and get her to seek medical attention, but is rebuffed. Then, on the advice of a local shaman, Lillian leaves town without her children. Already a de facto mother, Chanda is thrust into a scenario with no adult supervision or support network. Her neighbor, Mrs. Tafa (Harriet Lenabe), is initially helpful, letting Chanda use her phone and what not, but their relationship sours in the face of her increasingly judgmental nature, and is further complicated by Chanda's attempts to intervene in the troubles of her best friend Esther (Keaobaka Makanyane), who has turned to prostitution to make money.

Not entirely unlike Jennifer Lawrence's character in the critical darling *Winter's Bone* (2010), Chanda is forced into a situation whereby she must serve as a caregiver to younger half-siblings, while also attempting to modulate difficult circumstances further compounded by adults who have mentally or emotionally checked out, and abdicated any responsibility. The narrative here, however, is a bit less bleak than that film, and more constructed for a sense of audience-friendly uplift, even given the potentially dark nature of its subject matter.

As the title of its source material might suggest, the film unfolds fairly subjectively through Chanda's eyes, and in this important respect *Life, Above All* has a guide worth following—engaging and sympathetic, but untethered to any mannered formality. Depending a bit on the material, experience or technique is far less important with adolescent performers than merely a sense of them belonging within the greater framework of the story. It is much more the job and responsibility of the director to elicit the right struck notes of a child actor to then match the overall tone and aim of the piece. Schmitz succeeds quite capably in this regard. Befitting her nonprofessional status, Manyaka is naturalistic; she reasonably and realistically reflects the trauma that she is experiencing inward, never overplaying the emotions for cheap reaction.

In terms of its narrative trajectory, *Life, Above All* charts a fairly-expected path. Schmitz, though, is a South African-born filmmaker of German descent, and ergo has a somewhat unique connection to the material—a sort of fluid, insider's outside view, one might say—that helps keep the movie from tipping over into the maudlin or contrived. Cinematographer Bernhard Jasper's digitally-captured work favors natural lighting, and nicely captures the emotionally persuasive on-location settings, giving *Life, Above All* a true sense of rooted place. One also feels the setting's class and gender conflicts (including the damning opinions and double standards women impose specifically upon other women) without being hammered over the head with them.

If there is an accurate knock on *Life, Above All*, it might be that the film's earnestness and complete lack of narrative guile render it an overly programmatic journey, free of the intrigue and extra layer of audience absorption that often results from surprise. That said, the movie works perfectly fine as a series of pulled dramatic levers, and does not ring false in detail. Its allegorical underpinnings are real, too, since in the sub-Saharan reluctance to address the outbreak, spread or even in some pockets existence of the HIV virus, there certainly exists parallels to vocal, modern day American subgroups' disinclination to embrace scientific fact. Channeling universal feeling and experience through the specific, *Life, Above All* wins the implicit argued case of its title's preeminence.

Brent Simon

CREDITS

Chanda: Khomotso Manyaka
Esther: Keaobaka Makanyane
Lillian: Lerato Mvelase
Mrs. Tafa: Harriet Manamela
Jonah: Aubrey Poolo
Aunt Lizbet: Tinah Mnumzana
Iris: Mapaseka Mathebe
Soly: Thato Kgaladi
Dudu: Kgomotso Ditshweni
Aunty Ruth: Rami Chuene
Mr Pheto: Jerry Marobyane
Origin: South Africa, Germany
Language: Sotho
Released: 2010
Production: Oliver Stoltz; Dreamer Joint Venture Filmproduction; released by Sony Pictures Classics
Directed by: Oliver Schmitz
Written by: Dennis Foon
Cinematography by: Bernhard Jasper
Music by: Ali N. Askin, Ian Osrin
Sound: Sebastian Morsch
Editing: Dirk Grau
Art Direction: Tracy Perkins, Christiane Rothe
Costumes: Nadia Kruger
MPAA rating: PG-13
Running time: 100 minutes

REVIEWS

Burr, Ty. *Boston Globe*. August 4, 2011.
Ebert, Roger. *Chicago Sun-Times*. September 1, 2011.
Jones, Kimberly. *Austin Chronicle*. September 23, 2011.
Lane, Jim. *Sacramento News & Review*. August 31, 2011.
Mohan, Marc. *Oregonian*. September 16, 2011.
Moore, Roger. *Orlando Sentinel*. September 20, 2011.
O'Sullivan, Michael. *Washington Post*. August 5, 2011.
Rodriguez, Rene. *Miami Herald*. September 15, 2011.
Taylor, Ella. *NPR*. July 15, 2011.
Whitty, Stephen. *Newark Star-Ledger*. July 15, 2011.

LIKE CRAZY

> *I want you—I need you—I love you—I miss you.*
> —Movie tagline

Box Office: $3.4 million

One of the most memorable and promising feature film debuts of 2011 came in the form of a low-key, small piece about the follies of teenage romance called *Like Crazy*. Drake Doremus, working improvisationally with his talented young actors (Anton Yelchin, Felicity Jones, and Jennifer Lawrence), has crafted a film that fully understands that love is not absolute and that there may be no greater stress on young romance than distance and time apart. Young love often burns brightly and then fades away, but Doremus' film interestingly charts a love that has barely been given the time to burn and so is put on hold. What happens when a romance that should be passionate and explosive is forced to merely simmer? Does it grow stronger or fade out? Doremus wisely does not turn his tale of torn lovers into the soap operatic melodrama it could have been, choosing to tell his story in key incidents, almost as if the viewer is checking in on these two characters every few months and seeing the very subtle shifts in their relationship of which they may not even be fully aware. Most importantly, he puts almost all of the dramatic weight on the shoulders of his very talented lead actors, never cluttering the piece with too much directorial flourish or auteur commentary.

Jacob (Yelchin) and Anna (Jones) meet in Los Angeles but she is merely there on an exchange program and needs to go back to London when her student visa ends. The two fall so deeply in love that the thought of being split, even for a summer while Anna tries to get her paperwork in order so she return, drives them crazy. What could possibly happen if she stays? The young lovers have a great summer together but Anna has to go back across the pond for her family and she is denied re-entry into the United States when she tries to return. With Jacob waiting for her, Anna is put on a plane and sent back to London. The bureaucracy and red tape that come with trying to get back to the United States will dominate much of *Like Crazy* but the key to the film is how the distance begins to wear away at the initial love of these two characters. Jacob visits but he also starts his own design business in Los Angeles. Anna moves on as well, hiring an immigration lawyer to try to get her back to the man she loves, but also meeting someone new (Charlie Bewley). Jacob also has a beautiful new potential love interest in his life named Sam (Jennifer Lawrence) and the film becomes an interesting push-and-pull of audience expectations.

Should viewers want Anna and Jacob to get back together? Neither Simon nor Sam are presented as typically evil homewreckers like they would be in a traditional romantic drama. In fact, it starts to feel like Sam would make a better partner for Jacob than Anna. Maybe he should just move on. But how does one move on when it feels like their love story was cut off by red tape and never given the time it should have been to develop?

Sadly, Doremus never quite draws out a fully-formed character for Yelchin to play in Jacob. It is almost as if through his desire to present a film that never really takes sides or even presents a desired outcome for the viewer (at first, it is clear that the viewer should want them to get back together, but it almost seems inevitable as the film goes on that their love will not be the same even if they do) that Jacob came out a little undercooked. He almost feels more like a device, a sounding board or straight man for Anna, although this could simply be because Felicity Jones is simply stunning here. The newcomer is riveting in every scene, gloriously capturing screen charisma that one is most likely either born with or they are not. She has that "it factor" and she uses it perfectly here, capturing a young lady during some of her most key developmental years when she learns that love cannot always win out over injustice.

Like Crazy surely hits a few clichéd notes (the very title sounds clichéd) but the truth of Jones' performance (and Yelchin and Lawrence as well, even if they are not given as much to work with) make them feel genuine. One starts to believe in Anna's story and while the film could have been stronger if it was a story in which both halves of the arc were equally strong, it is nonetheless worthwhile simply for how delicately and heartbreakingly it portrays a young woman discovering that love is more complicated than movies like this one might lead girls to believe.

Brian Tallerico

CREDITS

Jacob: Anton Yelchin
Anna: Felicity Jones
Sam: Jennifer Lawrence
Simon: Charlie Bewley
Jackie: Alex Kingston
Bernard: Oliver Muirhead
Liz: Finola Hughes
Mike: Chris Messina
Ross: Ben York-Jones
Origin: USA
Language: English
Released: 2011
Production: Johnathan Schwartz, Andrea Sperling; Crispy Films; released by Paramount Pictures
Directed by: Drake Doremus
Written by: Ben York-Jones, Drake Doremus
Cinematography by: John Guleserian
Music by: Dustin O'Halloran
Sound: Stephen Nelson
Music Supervisor: Tiffany Anders
Editing: Jonathan Alberts
Art Direction: Rachel Ferrara

Costumes: Mairi Chisholm
Production Design: Katie Byron
MPAA rating: PG-13
Running time: 89 minutes

REVIEWS

Barker, Andrew. *Variety.* October 22, 2011.
Ebert, Roger. *Chicago Sun-Times.* November 2, 2011.
Fear, David. *Time Out New York.* October 25, 2011.
Hornaday, Ann. *Washington Post.* November 3, 2011.
Phillips, Michael. *Chicago Tribune.* November 3, 2011.
Pols, Mary. *Time.* October 31, 2011.
Puig, Claudia. *USA Today.* October 27, 2011.
Rainer, Peter. *Christian Science Monitor.* October 29, 2011.
Travers, Peter. *Rolling Stone.* October 27, 2011.
Turan, Kenneth. *Los Angeles Times.* October 27, 2011.

QUOTES

Jacob: "I don't feel like I'm part of your life. I feel like I'm on vacation."

TRIVIA

Director Drake Doremus screened a rough cut of this film to his former students at the Orange County High School of the Arts before it was submitted it to the Sundance Film Festival.

LIMITLESS

What if a pill could make you rich and powerful?
—Movie tagline

Box Office: $79.2 million

Bradley Cooper simply exudes jerkiness. It is not his fault, per se. It is just an incontrovertible fact. With his permanent tan, perfect smirk, and a kind of ineffable lack of gradation in his performances (he frequently seems at once insincere and also sort of charmingly unable to conceal his disingenuousness), Cooper looks like a glad-handing politician-in-training, a cross between an Abercrombie & Fitch model and the guy with whom your high school girlfriend cheated on you. One did not need his *Wedding Crashers* (2005) performance, as the unctuously named Sack Lodge, to verify that had he been born ten-to-fifteen years earlier Cooper would have gotten his start in Hollywood playing collar-popped preppy antagonists to John Cusack, Anthony Michael Hall, and other sympathetic nice guys.

If all this sounds like less a compliment than the beginnings of a rather nasty takedown, it is worth noting that it is precisely many of these aforementioned surface physical qualities that make Cooper such a unique and good fit for *Limitless,* a fairly heady and bewitching brew of paranoia, blackmail and good, old-fashioned physical imperilment based on Alan Glynn's 2001 novel *The Dark Fields.* The ease and grace with which Cooper occupies his lead character's slick playboy exterior creates a sense of inner conflict and tension in the dramatic, science-fiction-tinged thriller, in that the audience both pulls for his character and roots for a bit of dark comeuppance simultaneously. Audiences obviously agreed, as Stateside *Limitless* actually outperformed Cooper's much bigger-budgeted *The A-Team* (2010), and ended up pulling in $155 million worldwide at the box office, split almost equally between domestic and international receipts.

Suffering from a chronic writer's block, Eddie Morra (Cooper) has hit rock bottom, personally and professionally. Overdue on a novel, he has also been recently dumped by his girlfriend Lindy (Abbie Cornish), who is fed up with his general lack of life follow-through and success. It is in this run-down emotional frame of mind that Eddie crosses paths with Vernon (Johnny Whitworth), his ex-brother-in-law. After listening to Eddie unload his woes over a drink, Vernon slips him some NZT-48, a special designer and decidedly off-market drug meant to boost focus and cognition to almost superhuman levels by tapping into the "unused" portions of the brain.

Eddie takes it, and the effects are impressive, so he tracks Vernon down to ask for some more. Upon returning from an errand, however, he finds Vernon dead. Quickly rifling his apartment after phoning the police, Eddie locates Vernon's stash of the drug, along with some cash. He takes both, and flees.

Over the span of two short weeks, Eddie blossoms in just about every way imaginable. Able to pick up musical instruments and foreign languages in under an hour, he also leverages Vernon's nest egg into considerable stock market earnings via a series of micro-trades and highly intuitive pattern calculations. This earns Eddie the attention of a hard-charging energy baron, Carl Van Loon (Robert De Niro), who is locked in a potentially lucrative merger deal with a rival businessman, Hank Atwood (Richard Bekins). Carl brings Eddie on board as an advisor, and high-stakes financial gamesmanship ensues.

Also, as Eddie's supply of NZT-48 dwindles, his acuity and focus slip. The drug's more benign initial complications—a frenetic demeanor and some minor heart palpitations—become more and more pronounced, and a Russian thug named Gennady (Andrew Howard) stalks Eddie, searching for Vernon's stash. Meanwhile,

Eddie's ex-wife Melissa (Anna Friel) calls him and supplies a little more information about the drug, warning that further dabbling with it will only increasingly endanger his life. As the situation with Gennady escalates and becomes more violent and dangerous, Eddie tries to figure out a way to extricate himself from his overlapping predicaments.

Owing to Leslie Dixon's smart adaptation, *Limitless* succeeds in being both thought-provoking and enormously facile, which is no small feat. Director Neil Burger constructs, through smart editing and streamlined pacing, a movie whose cocksure biorhythms mirror the surging confidence of its protagonist as he undergoes his transformation. Yes, there is "science" here, but *Limitless,* much in a fashion akin to this year's *Source Code,* actually, makes sure it does not get too bogged down in wonky, scientific specifics. There is another story to be told here, and while it is informed by this speculative advance in medical technology, those elements are devices, and treated as such.

On a technical level, the film is a step up for Burger, who previously parlayed his debut low-budget curio *Interview with the Assassin* (2002) into *The Illusionist* (2006), which was followed by the competent but tonally jumbled and little-seen soldiers' road movie *The Lucky Ones* (2008). Here, Burger and cinematographer Jo Willems slip in lighting shifts, a few CGI elements, practical lens distortions and other warping techniques to give the movie a highly subjective bent during Eddie's dosed periods. It is a style that works, and fits the material, giving it a charged, vicarious liveliness.

Again, though, what mostly makes *Limitless* take flight, and gives it such an enjoyable vibe, are the performances. If his Southwestern accent is a bit rangy and free-form, De Niro at least seems engaged with the material. And the lurching Howard, with his slightly pronounced brow, comes across as believably dense but dangerous—a perfectly lug-headed foil who of course in the end is not necessarily Eddie's biggest problem. It is Cooper, though, that holds *Limitless* together, and imbues it with an abiding sense of pleasant watchability. One does not deeply and passionately care about Eddie's plight in the traditional sense, but for all the reasons previously mentioned, his dilemma remains a compelling one in which one feels an investment, however fuzzy and shifting underfoot.

The film's ending is a kind of middling thing, for reasons unrelated to its touch of ambiguity. Mainly, it is that its terminal point seems like it would have made an interesting second- or third-act pivot, since it is a chess move whereas some of ways in which *Limitless* chooses to spend its allotted running time are decidedly of the checkers variety. That said, if *Limitless* does not seemingly fully exploit some of the possibilities of its wild conceit that a viewer might dream up while watching, who is to say a more deeply intellectualized rendering of the same concept would pack quite as much pure entertainment punch?

Brent Simon

CREDITS

Eddie Morra: Bradley Cooper
Carl Van Loon: Robert De Niro
Lindy: Abbie Cornish
Vernon Gant: Johnny Whitworth
Pierce: Robert John Burke
Gennady: Andrew Howard
Melissa: Anna Friel
Kevin Doyle: Darren Goldstein
Morris Brandt: Ned Eisenberg
Mrs. Atwood: Patricia Kalember
Origin: USA
Language: English
Released: 2011
Production: Leslie Dixon, Scott Kroopf, Ryan Kavanaugh; Many Rivers, Boy of the Year; released by Relativity Media
Directed by: Neil Burger
Written by: Leslie Dixon
Cinematography by: Jo Willems
Music by: Paul Leonard-Morgan
Sound: Danny Michael
Music Supervisor: Season Kent, Happy Walters
Editing: Naomi Geraghty, Tracy Adams
Costumes: Jenny Gering
Production Design: Patrizia Von Brandenstein
MPAA rating: PG-13
Running time: 105 minutes

REVIEWS

Childress, Erik. *eFilmCritic.com*. March 18, 2011.
Ebert, Roger. *Chicago Sun-Times*. March 18, 2011.
Koehler, Robert. *Variety*. March 15, 2011.
Lemire, Christy. *Associated Press*. March 24, 2011.
Major, Wade. *Boxoffice Magazine*. March 17, 2011.
O'Hehir, Andrew. *Salon.com*. March 17, 2011.
O'Sullivan, Michael. *Washington Post*. March 17, 2011.
Puig, Claudia. *USA Today*. March 17, 2011.
Rainer, Peter. *Christian Science Monitor*. March 18, 2011.
Scott, A.O. *New York Times*. March 17, 2011.

QUOTES

Eddie Morra: "For a guy with a four digit IQ, I must have missed something. And I hadn't missed much. I'd come this close to having an impact on the world. And now the only thing I'd have an impact on was the sidewalk."

TRIVIA

Shia LaBeouf was originally cast as Eddie but had to drop out after badly injuring his left hand in July 2008.

THE LINCOLN LAWYER

Box Office: $58 million

The titular character in *The Lincoln Lawyer* has a reputation for constantly cracking a cocksure smile while never breaking a sweat, gliding smoothly from job to job with goals that appear to not be much loftier than the bottom line. It is no wonder they thought of casting Matthew McConaughey. The laid-back, golden-haired good ol' boy has too often seemed content to coast on his charismatic personality and chiseled physicality, snapping up easy paychecks for frothy and often forgettable fare that showed off a much greater interest in the development of his abdominal muscles than the stretching of his acting ones. However, bookending rote romantic comedies like *Fool's Gold* (2008) and *Ghosts of Girlfriends Past* (2009) are McConaughey's impressive portrayals in two admirable adaptations of crime novels: *A Time to Kill* (1996) and, now, *The Lincoln Lawyer*. Both projects, which feature the actor as a sorely-tested defense attorney in pursuit of justice, raised the bar for McConaughey and showed he could attract attention for more than merely being attractive. By no means does *The Lincoln Lawyer*, an entertaining, twisty thriller based upon the 2005 work by prolific author Michael Connelly, linger like the viscerally-provocative tale derived from fellow page churner, John Grisham. Still, those waiting for the Texas hunk to once again sink the blindingly-white teeth of that ingratiating smile into meatier material welcomed this performance, as it required exertion beyond the usual degree of ease.

It is said that most sharks remain in constant motion, and this legal one certainly falls into that kinetic category. The habitat of attorney Mick Haller (McConaughey) is the sprawling city of Los Angeles, which he crisscrosses while travelling from one courtroom to another in the chauffeured Lincoln Town Car that doubles as his office. Copies of Connelly's book that were printed to coincide with the film's release had a cover photo of McConaughey's Mick pensively perched upon the vehicle's hood. However, the work's original cover was far more fitting: A blurred image of the Lincoln shooting past as Haller tools about town, committing what purists like the prosecutor who once was his wife (Marisa Tomei) disparage as a ceaseless string of hit-and-run assaults upon idealized legal standards and practices. Haller swiftly and skillfully cuts the best deal he can for his lowlife clients (whose professions of innocence he regards with a cynically-dubious eye), but only after he has made the best monetary deal for himself. In the source material, his cautionary advice to prospective criminals is an avaricious twist on the famed theme song of television's *Baretta*: "Don't do the crime if you can't pay for my time." *The Lincoln Lawyer* tells the story of how this self-possessed, masterly manipulator-on-the-move—truly a "wheeler dealer"—is himself manipulated, causing things to spin perplexingly and dangerously out of control.

Haller may be relegated to the back seat due to a DUI-related license suspension (a glass is still quite often on the way to his lips), but in the figurative sense he is still very much in the driver's seat as the film begins. He is expeditiously sketched at the outset as an unflappable, rapacious and street-smart finesser, cajoler and flirt. Haller's eyes, which are repeatedly highlighted with close-ups, are constantly and effectively surveying and sizing-up, cannily looking for angles as well as still appreciatively assessing his ex's curves. One can almost see the dollar signs appear in those eyes in cartoon fashion when a co-conspiratorial bail bondsman (John Leguizamo) steers an unusually tony and clean-cut client his way, someone whose fervent and apparently-guileless declarations of innocence seem to promise a slam dunk in court as well as a big deposit in Haller's bank account. As the lawyer proceeds with his defense of petulantly-outraged and arrogant Louis Roulet (Ryan Phillippe), who is charged with horrifying assault and attempted murder of a prostitute (Margarita Levieva), it becomes increasingly evident that this client was not only born with a silver spoon in his mouth but also a forked tongue. Viewers notice that Haller's baby blues become blood-shot, weary and wary. "What am I missing here?" he asks, and as this strikingly calm, cool and collected finagler is introduced to uncertainty, seething frustration, and even agonizing desperation, the character's appeal deepens and sympathy for him rises.

Carrying forward the emphasis on peepers and perception, Haller has had a long-standing, underlying fear of becoming so jaded that he would no longer be able to recognize innocence when he sees it. He comes to the haunting realization that he had previously plea-bargained a man (Michael Pen~a) into a lesser prison sentence who actually deserved no time at all, as it was this blueblood of undetected cunning and brutality who had actually committed the crime. Many watching will see through Roulet's initial assertions of absolute candor (Phillippe telegraphs too much), and wonder why the hard-to-hoodwink lawyer is not more suspicious. Haller faces a daunting predicament: Roulet smugly admits he

committed both crimes, leaving the lawyer duty-bound to both try and get his client exonerated for the current crime and refrain from revealing what he has learned about the previous one due to attorney-client privilege. Thus, while the defense attorney's Lincoln still displays a license plate that reads "NTGUILTY," Haller himself now feels anything but that, and, as things become increasingly complex and precarious, he struggles to extricate himself from Roulett's web while simultaneously spinning a wilier one that will ultimately capture his comparably-nimble adversary. Haller will find a way for justice to be served and his own conscience assuaged, nailing Roulet and redemptively righting a wrong by garnering the release of the languishing, blameless convict. The screenplay repeatedly stutters on the way to finally communicating its ending. When a motorcycle gang reappears to lend a hand (among other things violently applied) to deflate puffed-up Roulet, the invented-for-film comeuppance scene strains credulity while also providing guilty pleasure.

Made on a budget of $40 million, *The Lincoln Lawyer* grossed just over a respectable $58 million, which was enough to start talk of a franchise and even spawned the development of a TV series based on the film. Most critics and moviegoers left theaters pleasantly surprised, having sufficiently enjoyed director Brad Furman's briskly-paced, gritty, and still-densely-plotted adaptation that kept most wondering how Haller would regain both the upper hand and his breezy equilibrium. McConaughey received the most praise, including from Connelly (who had envisioned someone like Andy Garcia for the role of the half-Mexican attorney). The actor is ably supported by Frances Fisher, Bryan Cranston, and, especially, William H. Macy, although the extent to which most secondary characters are fleshed out may best be described as skeletal. One cannot help but wonder if harsh realities would eventually have worn down fresh-faced, quixotic Jake Tyler Brigance of *A Time to Kill* into someone like pragmatic schemer Mick Haller. In any event, McConaughey truly and most fittingly does both of them justice.

David L. Boxerbaum

CREDITS

Michael 'Mick' Haller: Matthew McConaughey
Louis Roulet: Ryan Phillippe
Maggie McPherson: Marisa Tomei
Frank Levin: William H. Macy
Ted Minton: Josh(ua) Lucas
Val Valenzuela: John Leguizamo
Det. Lankford: Bryan Cranston
Heidi Sobel: Michaela Conlin

Jess Martinez: Michael Pena
Mary Windsor: Frances Fisher
Cecil Dobbs: Bob Gunton
Eddie Vogel: Trace Adkins
Carliss: Shea Whigham
Gloria: Katherine Moenning
Detective Kurlen: Michael Pare
Origin: USA
Language: English
Released: 2011
Production: Sidney Kimmel, Richard S. Wright, Scott Steindorff, Tom Rosenberg, Gary Lucchesi; Lakeshore Entertainment, Stone Village; released by Lionsgate
Directed by: Brad Furman
Written by: John Romano
Cinematography by: Lukas Ettlin
Music by: Cliff Martinez
Music Supervisor: Brian McNelis, Eric Craig
Editing: Jeff McEvoy
Sound: Steve Ticknor
Costumes: Erin Benach
Production Design: Charisse Cardenas
MPAA rating: R
Running time: 118 minutes

REVIEWS

Barker, Andrew. *Variety*. March 14, 2011.
Burr, Ty. *Boston Globe*. March 17, 2011.
Dargis, Manohla. *New York Times*. March 18, 2011.
Diones, Bruce. *New Yorker*. April 18, 2011.
Ebert, Roger. *Chicago Sun-Times*. March 17, 2011.
Hammond, Peter. *Boxoffice Magazine*. March 14, 2011.
Holcomb, Mark. *Village Voice*. March 15, 2011.
Honeycutt, Kirk. *Film Journal International*. April 2011.
Hornsday, Ann. *Washington Post*. March 17, 2011.
Pinkerton, Nick. *Sight & Sound*. May 2011.
Puig, Claudia. *USA Today*. March 17, 2011.
Schwarzbaum, Lisa. *Entertainment Weekly*. March 25, 2011.
Sharkey, Betsy. *Los Angeles Times*. March 17, 2011.
Travers, Peter. *Rolling Stone*. March 18, 2011.
Wheat, Alynda. *People*. March 28, 2011.

QUOTES

Mick Haller: "I checked the list of people I trust and your name ain't on it."

TRIVIA

Novelist Michael Connelly wanted Matthew McConaughey for the role of Mick Haller after seeing his performance in *Tropic Thunder.*

LOUDER THAN A BOMB

Largely ignored by the masses on its initial release after playing film festivals in late 2010 and arthouses in early 2011 (but embraced by almost every audience member lucky enough to stumble upon it), *Louder Than a Bomb,* the spectacular, inspirational documentary from Chicago directors Greg Jacobs and Jon Siskel started to finally build the following it will surely continue to unearth over the years after another Windy City legend, Oprah Winfrey, caught on to the film's quality and premiered it on her cable network, OWN. While the Winfrey label may cause some skeptical people to flee, fearing melodrama and overt manipulation, one hopes that her brand will help bring this documentary to a larger audience before it disappears like so many low-budget non-fiction films do every single year. The creative, passionate, talented voices that make up the body of *Louder Than a Bomb* not only offer perspective on how true art can come from unexpected places but have the force of the film's title by virtue of their remarkable honesty.

Directors Greg Jacobs and Jon Siskel tracked four teams of Chicago high school poets (from Steinmetz High School) competing in a local poetry slam with the same name as the title of the film. Instead of merely following their competitive arcs with a bit of background thrown in for each of the poets with the most vibrant personalities, Jacobs and Siskel turn the story into how people can take their personal stories and their imaginations and transform them into art. Documentaries that capture the creative process are one thing, but it is the truly exceptional entries in this subgenre that can convey the importance and power of individual artistic expression as inspiration instead of pure documentation of the creative process. The great documentaries on this subject are not merely about creation but about creativity. And there is a difference.

Jacobs and Siskel clearly found a few of the more interesting poets in their process as they began to document the annual competition and the poets who take it as seriously as young baseball players take the Little League World Series or the gawky rugrats in *Spellbound* (2002) took their spelling bee progression, and chose to focus on them. Most memorable are Nova Venerable, a beautiful young lady who speaks like an award winner as she eloquently turns her hopes and dreams into poetry, and Adam Gottlieb, a tornado of energy who seems to almost be so driven to express himself that he would explode if he had to keep it in. What Siskel and Jacobs so wonderfully capture about these two (and their other subjects) is that, while they are as talented as any poets their age, they are not necessarily unique. There could be a brilliant talent living on any street, riding the bus in any town, scribbling poetry on any train, or even inside the audience viewing this excellent film. And that is not meant at all to take away from the talents of Adam, Nova, or any of The Steinmenauts (the name for one of the groups from the school in the slam). On the other hand, some of the tear-inducing poetry in *Louder Than a Bomb* ranks among the best ever captured on film. But this is a work about more than just quality poetry. It is about expression—joy, anger, love, pain, conviction, concern—and how all of these emotions compete and even blend together, especially at an age when young people cannot distinguish between them from moment to moment…they just need to express it all.

One might be tempted to suggest that Siskel and Jacobs got lucky and that it is the poetry writers and pure talents of people like Gottlieb and Venerable that really make the film. That it is purely a case of being in the right place at the right time. This would be wrong. It would be underestimating how many hours of personal footage, poetry writing, and performances the directors had to craft into a coherent feature. And how the directors perfectly frame their themes not through over-emphasis but on reminding viewers of the key point of this competition through the oft-repeated mantra of the kids—"The point is not the points, the point is the poetry." This is a film that argues that winning is less important than expression. And it does so as well as any documentary in years.

Brian Tallerico

CREDITS

Origin: USA

Language: English

Released: 2010

Production: Gregory Jacobs, Jon Siskel; released by Balcony Releasing

Directed by: Gregory Jacobs, Jon Siskel

Cinematography by: Stephen Mazurek

Sound: John Mathie

Editing: John Fabrother

MPAA rating: Unrated

Running time: 99 minutes

REVIEWS

Burr, Ty. *Boston Globe.* June 5, 2011.

Ebert, Roger. *Chicago Sun-Times.* April 30, 2011.

Genzlinger, Neil. *New York Times.* May 17, 2011.

Hardy, Ernest. *Village Voice.* May 17, 2011.

Murray, Noel. *AV Club.* May 19, 2011.

Musetto, V.A. *New York Post.* May 18, 2011.

O'Sullivan, Michael. *Washington Post.* June 16, 2011.

Ramos, Steve. *Boxoffice Magazine.* May 21, 2011.

Uhlich, Keith. *Time Out New York.* May 17, 2011.

Weitzman, Elizabeth. *New York Daily News.* May 20, 2011.

M

MACHINE GUN PREACHER

Hope is the greatest weapon of all.
—Movie tagline

During the end credits of *Machine Gun Preacher*, photographs and video footage of the real-life players of the movie's story appear on the side of the screen. One clip is most telling. In it, the movie's subject Sam Childers asks the interviewer and, in turn, the audience a pressing question about his work: If it was their child that had been abducted, would they care how he managed to recover them?

The movie would have done well to put forward similar questions. The screenplay by Jason Keller presents only one character, a humanitarian doctor (Inga Wilson), who confronts the story's protagonist about his philosophy, which, when boiled down to its essentials, amounts to "Might makes right." The leader of the Lord's Resistance Army (LRA) Joseph Kony, she tells the fictional stand-in for Childers, had a similar effect on certain parts of the local population as he currently has. They once looked up to Kony and his mixture of self-stated Christian ideals and violent rebellion, and Sam, who at first comes to Eastern Africa to participate in harmless and constructive missionary activities (e.g., building homes), could be on track, the doctor says, to becoming a comparable figure. The Childers of the movie certainly has no qualms invoking a higher power or unloading various firearms in regards to his own mission.

Kony neither appears on-screen nor does he need to; his ragtag soldiers—burning down villages, killing innocent locals, and abducting children so as to shove rifles into their hands—do a fine enough job filling the movie's role of evil personified. The extreme nature of the faceless villains—in addition to being a fairly accurate reflection of the horrific human rights violations perpetrated by the LRA—is necessary as a way to ease the rough edges of Sam, who, as written by Jason Keller and played by Gerard Butler, is a clear-cut hero whose earlier transgressions are forgiven by a religious conversion and who is blameless for any later ones, as they are executed in the name of a greater good. That Keller seems unaware of the behavioral tie between Sam's two lives—pre- and post-conversion—is unfortunate, and the potential for a more complex character is left unrealized in favor of generic familial conflict and an unfocused attempt to raise the most basic awareness of intricate political issues.

After a prologue in South Sudan in 2003 that shows the LRA's brutality against a small village and its inhabitants (ending with forcing a young boy to kill his own mother), the movie opens in the early 1990s as Childers leaves prison. Keller loses no time in establishing Sam's nature, primarily the impulsive part thereof. Before they can reach their house, Sam and his wife Lynn (Michelle Monaghan) pull over on a side road off the highway to have sex in the front seat of the car. Almost immediately after arriving back at home, Sam is infuriated to discover that his wife has quit her job as a stripper (while he was in prison, she became a devout Christian), and his heated response—yelling, slamming his hands, and getting in uncomfortably close to Lynn while doing both—suggests the potential for violence.

The promise is fulfilled in the proceeding scenes, as Sam reunites with his old friend Donnie (Michael Shannon, a fine and woefully underutilized performance that serves as a tragic contrast to Sam's shift). The pair has an addiction to heroin, and it leads to two scenes that display Sam's capacity for violence. In the first, he and Donnie use shotguns to rob a drug dealer, and in the second, while driving home and under the influence of the narcotic, they pick up a hitchhiker (Mike Litaker) who threatens Donnie with a knife. Sam manages to gain the upper hand and viciously stabs the drifter; he and Donnie leave the man for dead on the side of the road.

With this action comes Sam's realization that his life is in need of a change, so he attends church services with Lynn and is baptized. After this, his life starts on the right track. He eventually opens his own construction firm and, after listening to a visiting minister (Bruce Bennett) speak about his own work in northern Uganda, takes a trip to Africa to help build homes for displaced locals. Curious about the talk of the LRA's atrocities, Sam follows Deng (Souleymane Sy Savane), a soldier in the Sudan People's Liberation Movement (SPLM), to South Sudan where he witnesses firsthand a migration of hundreds of orphaned children seeking refuge and the aftermath of an attack on a nearby village. Upon returning home, Sam has a vision and determines to build an orphanage in the middle of what everyone has dubbed a battlefield.

At first, Sam's bloodshed is in self-defense and for the protection of the orphanage and its residents. Director Marc Forster shoots the various assaults and ambushes with little finesse and an abundance of handheld-camera shots (that a number of the sequences take place at night is not helped by Roberto Schaefer's naturalistic cinematography), leading to needless confusion. The more straightforward scenes of carnage are at times chilling (One, in which the camera coldly watches as a young boy chases after a dog until an explosion sounds off-screen, is particularly so), though the occasional feeling of exploitation raised by the fact that this brutality is only the environment for the story of the movie's alien hero.

The focus of *Machine Gun Preacher* is always on Sam, and the difficulties he encounters are less about the people he tries to defend and more about his own dilemmas. He has trouble raising money for his efforts. His wife worries they will bring the family to financial ruin. His daughter Paige (Madeline Carroll) complains that her father cares more about "black babies" than her. Keller's screenplay is less a study of Sam's character than it is a melodramatic take on his situation. There is a fascinating persona here, especially in how he seems to reassign his old addictive and violent personality to this new obsession, and it is not until the movie shows the real-life subject during the credits—pumping and firing a shotgun with one hand like the star of an action movie—that the actual potential of the character reveals itself.

Mark Dujsik

CREDITS

Sam Childers: Gerard Butler
Lynn Childers: Michelle Monaghan
Donnie: Michael Shannon
Daisy: Kathy Baker
Deng: Souleymane Sy Savane
Paige Childers: Madeline Carroll
Bill Wallace: Peter Carey
Origin: USA
Language: English
Released: 2011
Production: Robbie Brenner, Marc Forster, Gary Sadfady, Deborah Giarratana, Craig Chapman; Safady Entertainment, Apparatus, GG Filmz; released by Relativity Media
Directed by: Marc Forster
Written by: Jason Keller
Cinematography by: Roberto Schaefer
Music by: Asche & Spencer
Sound: Marc Weingarten
Music Supervisor: Season Kent, Happy Walters
Editing: Matt Chesse
Art Direction: Jonathan Hely-Hutchinson, Paul Richards
Costumes: Frank Fleming
Production Design: Philip Messina
MPAA rating: R
Running time: 129 minutes

REVIEWS

Berardinelli, James. *ReelViews*. September 29, 2011.
Burr, Ty. *Boston Globe*. September 30, 2011.
Ebert, Roger. *Chicago Sun-Times*. September 28, 2011.
LaSalle, Mick. *San Francisco Chronicle*. September 30, 2011.
Phillips, Michael. *Chicago Tribune*. September 29, 2011.
Rea, Steven. *Philadelphia Inquirer*. September 30, 2011.
Robinson, Tasha. *AV Club*. September 22, 2011.
Rocchi, James. *MSN Movies*. September 21, 2011.
Scott, A.O. *New York Times*. September 22, 2011.
Shoard, Catherine. *Guardian*. September 13, 2011.

TRIVIA

Vera Farmiga was the first choice to play the character of Lyn, but dropped out due to her pregnancy and was replaced by Michelle Monaghan.

MAGILL'S CINEMA ANNUAL

MAGIC TRIP: KEN KESEY'S SEARCH FOR A KOOL PLACE

In July 1964, author Ken Kesey, coming off the success of both the publication and stage adaptation of *One Flew Over the Cuckoo's Nest* less than two years earlier, set off on a journey across the United States with a bunch of like-minded friends—a renegade group of communal acolytes and counter-culture truth-seekers known as the Merry Pranksters. The ostensible target or end-point destination of their journey was the World's Fair in New York City, but in truth this trip (pun embraced if not necessarily intended) was as much about the hedonistic experience of the open road as it ever was about merely getting to the other side of the country.

Poised somewhere between the beatnik and hippie generations, Kesey and his clan—which included Neal Cassady, the central figure immortalized in Jack Kerouac's *On the Road*—intended to make a documentary about their expedition. It never happened. But, more than four decades later, into the breach enters *Magic Trip: Ken Kesey's Search for a Kool Place*. A buzzed-about presentation at the 2011 Sundance Film Festival, the movie is a rangy, messy sort of snapshot memoir of that unfinished conjectural work, pieced together under a spate of new and collected interviews by filmmakers Alex Gibney and Alison Ellwood.

Narrated by Stanley Tucci, *Magic Trip* is most notable as a historic document, since as a stand-alone movie it mainly succeeds only in making one never want to do drugs. A graduate student at Stanford in 1959, Kesey volunteered to take part in what would later be revealed to be a CIA-funded study at the Menlo Park Veterans Hospital of psychoactive medications. Kesey would trip through LSD, Psilocybin, mescaline and alpha-methyltryptamines, among other substances, and some of the reel-to-reel audio recordings of those post-dosage discussion sessions (including one in which he pontificates in verbose fashion about the tape recorder's reel serving as its brain) make for a trippy, slurry delight. The build-up to the road trip, too, is interesting, as Kesey and his pals purchase a big school bus, dub it "Further," remodel the interior, deck it out in wild colors, and even retrofit it with an exterior storage appendage and a sort of pop-up turret.

After this preface, *Magic Trip* soon takes off, hitting the open road. Well…sort of. Kesey and company, total-ing about fifteen people in all, run out of gas at the end of his property, which is perhaps an inauspicious and somewhat telling opening to their voyage. They finally get going, though, and the 16mm footage of their progress is often wild and weird. Since no one on the trip really knew how to use their camera (or the sound equipment, which was eventually the chief reason that their planned documentary never happened), there is a decided lack of stuffy formalism or composition to the captured footage. It is wildly subjective, but in this amateurishness sometimes emerges quickening glimpses into the mindsets (and maybe even souls) of those operating the camera at any given moment—by zooming in on a fellow traveler's ample bosom (presaging the "free love" movement, there was plenty of partner-swapping along the way), a befuddled gas station attendant, or the swirling and oily detritus in a pool of nearby water.

Possessing a handful of these types of exceptional, unplanned moments, and a bit of quasi-expressionistic technique, *Magic Trip* connects intermittently as a fascinating piece of captured history, a sort of meandering, "prima facie" document of the cresting impulses that would eventually take form in the hippie movement of later in the 1960s and '70s. Overall, though, it is just a self-indulgent and kind of boring mess. There is a reason these home movies—no matter how famous some of the participants—never previously coalesced into something meaningful.

Ellwood, Gibney's editor on almost all of his work over the last half dozen years, takes a co-directing credit with him this go-round, no doubt instrumental to combing through the hundred-plus of hours of archival footage that finally saw the light of day in the wake of Kesey's 2001 death. But she and Gibney do not show their interview subjects, and while this tack sometimes works to the benefit of nonfiction material—most recently in the engaging *Senna* (2011), for one example—here it has a distancing effect. Since so many culled interviews are from participants we see on screen in the captured footage, failing to show them as they are now, in the present day, not only creates unnecessary muddle for younger viewers less familiar with Kesey and the Merry Pranksters, but also robs the movie of a chance to carve out more discrete personalities. This is undoubtedly an artistic choice on the part of Gibney and Ellwood, in an effort to preserve their film's air-quote textual authenticity. It is a grave miscalculation in terms of providing any contextual mooring, however.

As a unique slice of Americana, there is certainly some measure of value to *Magic Trip*. Mostly, though, it is just another artifact of boomer self-obsession, and a reminder of their generation's heavy hand in many of our current national predicaments. If there was much magic in Kesey's bus, it is no longer quite as readily apparent in this glimpse backward.

Brent Simon

CREDITS

Himself: Ken Kesey
Himself: Neal Cassady
Narrator: Stanley Tucci
Origin: USA
Language: English
Released: 2011
Production: Alex Gibney, Will Clarke, Alexandra Johnes; Imaginary Forces, Jigsaw Productions, Optimum Releasing, History Films; released by Magnolia Pictures
Directed by: Alex Gibney, Alison Ellwood
Written by: Alex Gibney, Alison Ellwood
Cinematography by: Alison Ellwood
Music by: David Kahne
Music Supervisor: John McCullough
Editing: Alison Ellwood
MPAA rating: R
Running time: 107 minutes

REVIEWS

Anderson, John. *Variety*. August 18, 2011.
Berkshire, Geoff. *Metromix.com*. August 4, 2011.
Feeney, Mark. *Boston Globe*. September 1, 2011.
Gleiberman, Owen. *Entertainment Weekly*. August 3, 2011.
Holden, Stephen. *New York Times*. August 4, 2011.
LaSalle, Mick. *San Francisco Chronicle*. August 4, 2011.
Olsen, Mark. *Los Angeles Times*. August 11, 2011.
O'Sullivan, Michael. *Washington Post*. August 19, 2011.
Rainer, Peter. *Christian Science Monitor*. August 12, 2011.
Weitzman, Elizabeth. *New York Daily News*. August 5, 2011.

MARGARET

A naturalistic and reconciliatory drama about a frayed adult sibling relationship, playwright Kenneth Lonergan's big screen directing debut, *You Can Count On Me* (2000), was a big success, netting Oscar® nominations for Laura Linney and its original script, and winning Best Screenplay prizes from both the Los Angeles Film Critics Association and the New York Film Critics Circle. Given that acclaim, one would reasonably expect a follow-up in short order.

In fact, though, Lonergan's sophomore effort, *Margaret,* has one of the more uniquely tortured backstories in modern studio film history, especially given the high profiles of its cast. The movie was originally shot in 2005; various slotted release dates came and went, with Lonergan being unable to deliver a cut that was satisfactory to all involved. Multiple breach of contract lawsuits were filed, further delaying matters, and in the interim producer Sydney Pollack and executive producer Anthony Minghella both passed away. Filmmaker Martin Scorsese and his longtime editor, Thelma Schoonmaker, then came in to work on a final cut, upon which Lonergan eventually signed off. Contractually obligated to give it a theatrical release if under 150 minutes (which Scorsese and Schoonmaker delivered, by one minute), distributor Fox Searchlight dumped the movie into a small handful of theaters with no marketing support. The result was a gross domestic theatrical haul of under $50,000, which certain mainstream blockbuster releases can pull from a mega-plex in a single day.

It would be most pleasant and convenient, then, to tidily report that *Margaret* was either an unjustly maligned new masterpiece or an unmitigated disaster. The truth, however, like life, is much more complicated. A manic, lurching drama in which various coming-of-age incidents and more conventional familial friction get loop-tied and melded to an unusual ethical dilemma that spawns a wrongful death civil suit, *Margaret* is not built for traditional catharsis or emotional engagement. But it is shot through with an uncommonly insistent energy—a movie with as much distinct, wide-eyed personality as it has little focus.

Despite its moniker, *Margaret* is not named for its protagonist, or even another character; its title actually comes from a 19th century poem "Spring and Fall: To a Young Child," by Gerard Manley Hopkins. Set in New York City, the movie centers on Lisa Cohen (Anna Paquin), an intelligent private school student who lives on the Upper West Side with her mother, Joan (J. Smith-Cameron, Lonergan's real-life partner), a successful stage actress, and younger sibling.

One day, Lisa distracts a bus driver, Jason (Mark Ruffalo), who then plows through a red light, striking and killing a pedestrian (Allison Janney). After some rumination, Lisa decides that Jason deserves a harsher judgment than the mere temporary administrative leave which he has been given, so she reaches out to the best friend of the deceased woman, Emily (Jeannie Berlin). Together they muddle through the process of retaining a lawyer and bringing a civil suit against Jason's employer, which in turn brings out of the woodwork an estranged relative who never had much contact with the victim, and ergo has a different set of aspirations for the resolution of the suit.

This in turn influences and impacts the trajectory of Lisa's more recognizable coming-of-age struggles.

While her mother entertains the attentions of a charming, foreign-accented gentleman suitor, Ramon (Jean Reno), Lisa contrives, in a very straightforward, dispassionate manner, to lose her virginity to bad boy Paul (Kieran Culkin) rather than embrace the advances of a classmate who is smitten with her. She also struggles at school and in relationships with her teachers (Matt Damon and Matthew Broderick), crossing the boundaries of appropriateness with one of the latter.

While its legal framework would seem to give *Margaret* a clearly defined narrative arc and spine, in reality Lonergan is only moderately interested in the actual lawsuit plotline. He engages it fitfully rather than procedurally, and instead seems more driven by exploring the interrelatedness of seemingly unconnected events. Literal tragedies—in the form of the inciting incident and also a couple spirited classroom debates about the September 11 terrorist attacks, and American foreign policy in the Middle East—both abut and give way to emotional heartbreak and calamity. It is in this metaphorical miasma that *Margaret* unfolds, assaying the interpersonal drift that such actions inspire. (In one unambiguous association that clearly informs Lisa's attitudes and choices regarding her burgeoning sexuality, Lonergan also stars as Lisa's biological dad, a well-meaning but unreliable telephonic presence in her life from the sunny West Coast.)

In a movie characterized by its solid supporting performances (including in particular Smith-Cameron and Reno), Berlin's shrill turn is problematic, and distasteful. It is partly a matter of function—when the movie seemingly arbitrarily decides it needs a more antagonistic presence, and someone to take Lisa to task, she transforms from sympathetic to strident—but it is annoying nonetheless, and undermines any accrued sense of realism in regards to Emily and Lisa's unusual partnership. *Margaret* is mostly a wild showcase for Paquin, though. In her livewire performance, a mix of fragility and hysteria, the Oscar®-winning actress robustly embodies both the difficulties of being a teenager and the thorniness that such precocity unleavened with life experience produces for those having to cope with said adolescent.

Lonergan's script, too, ably summons the tangled emotions of puberty, where certainty and insecurity rub right up against one another. The dialogue is often barbed or witty, and always thoughtful. If it is an utter mess in terms of proper plotting (multiple subplots could be reduced or removed, giving the movie a more streamlined perspective), *Margaret* is never false about Lisa's complicated, often conflicting white-hot feelings of entitlement and outrage that Lonergan puts under the microscope.

Unfortunately, there is just not enough of a sustained narrative hook or intensely disciplined thematic inquiry to lift the movie up to the mantle of "misunderstood masterpiece." The lived-in charm of *You Can Count On Me,* which came across as effortless and affectless, is largely absent here. That is not to say that *Margaret* feels false, just laboriously constructed and overstuffed, as well as frantic and needy. The fact that this cut of the film was approved by Lonergan but not executed or overseen by him further muddies authorial intent. If it were a song, Lonergan's film would be a grandiloquent descendant of Queen's "Bohemian Rhapsody," a spastic urban rock opera absent any unifying chorus. In cinematic form, this jumbled mass of conflicting impulses makes for a unique experience, but one with as many valleys as peaks.

Brent Simon

CREDITS

Lisa Cohen: Anna Paquin
Joan: J. Smith-Cameron
Maretti: Mark Ruffalo
Emily: Jeannie Berlin
Ramon: Jean Reno
Becky: Sarah Steele
Paul: Kieran Culkin
Origin: USA
Language: English
Released: 2011
Production: Gary Gilbert, Sydney Pollack, Scott Rudin; Fox Searchlight Pictures; released by Fox Searchlight Pictures
Directed by: Kenneth Lonergan
Written by: Kenneth Lonergan
Cinematography by: Ryszard Lenczewski
Music by: Nico Muhly
Sound: Jacob Ribicoff
Editing: Anne McCabe
Costumes: Melissa Toth
Production Design: Dan Leigh
MPAA rating: R
Running time: 150 minutes

REVIEWS

Chang, Justin. *Variety.* September 28, 2011.
Duralde, Alonso. *The Wrap.* September 29, 2011.
Edelstein, David. *New York Magazine.* September 26, 2011.
LaSalle, Mick. *San Francisco Chronicle.* October 7, 2011.
Linden, Sheri. *Hollywood Reporter.* September 28, 2011.
Long, Tom. *Detroit News.* October 7, 2011.
Morris, Wesley. *Boston Globe.* October 6, 2011.

O'Hehir, Andrew. *Salon.com*. September 28, 2011.

Scott, A.O. *New York Times*. September 29, 2011.

Sharkey, Betsy. *Los Angeles Times*. September 29, 2011.

QUOTES

Emily: "Because…this isn't an opera! And we are not all supporting characters to the drama of your amazing life!"

TRIVIA

The thetrical version of the film was edited by Martin Scorsese and Thelma Schoonmaker, not writer/director Kenneth Lonergan, who had demanded final-cut (although he did approve the edited version).

MARGIN CALL

Be first. Be smarter. Or cheat.
—Movie tagline

Box Office: $5.4 million

Since the big financial collapse of 2008, there have been several attempts by filmmakers to explain how it happened, who the main culprits were and how America would never be the same again. Through documentaries such as *Inside Job* (2010) and *Capitalism: A Love Story* (2009) as well as fictional narratives such as *Wall Street: Money Never Sleeps* (2010) and now with *Margin Call*, Hollywood and the independent studios have been looking to take the subject of America's new reality and boil it down to layman's terms while crafting it into conventional dramatic and thriller sensibilities. The results have been mixed, but there is an inherent fascination with watching the situation pile up as the viewer witnesses human nature at its least flattering while also waiting for those involved to be taken away in handcuffs.

Margin Call is the story of the 24-hour period that led to the downfall of America's financial stability. It takes place in an unnamed firm that could very well be Lehman Brothers, Fannie Mae or any other company that went belly up in 2008. The name does not matter and the characters are all fictional. At the start of the film, in the middle of a normal workday, layoffs take place in the risk management department of this large firm. Most notably, the head of this department, Eric Dale (Stanley Tucci), is laid off with a generous severance package. On his way out, he is consoled by one of his young employees, Peter Sullivan (Zachary Quinto). Eric decides to hand off a USB drive to Peter and asks him to take a look at it, but to "be careful."

As others go off to celebrate still having a job, Peter stays late, looks at what Eric handed him and notices that something is gravely wrong with the numbers and spreadsheets he is looking at. The numbers do not add up. Peter calls his friend and co-worker Seth (Penn Badgley) and his new boss Will (Paul Bettany) back to the office to confirm his conclusions. By midnight, their boss, Sam (Kevin Spacey), is called in to survey the potential damage that is about to unfold. By 2am, more bosses and bosses of bosses—headed by John Tuld (Jeremy Irons)—are called in to manage the crisis that will undoubtedly unfold.

There is no way out of the situation, it seems. There are no real golden parachutes for the firm as a whole even though some will get out of this with million dollar bonuses. Occasionally, a character tries to put a human face on the situation "Just look at all these people," Peter says in a cab ride, regarding the passersby on the street. "They have no idea what is about to happen." Sam must decide where his loyalty lies: With the firm or with John Tuld. Will is in charge of finding Eric Dale, whose cell phone has been terminated, and bring him back to the firm to try and explain and account for all the damage that has been done. It would appear that Peter and Seth, two guys in their mid-twenties, would be the first on the chopping block when the inevitable next round of lay-offs would occur. Seth seems obsessed with how much money everyone makes in a year and often uses it as a conversation starter. Another character, a senior executive named Sarah Robertson (Demi Moore), clearly has nowhere to go but down.

The meetings and decisions take place overnight and as the next day's trading bell sounds, the entire firm knows it will soon breathe its last breath of stability. The movie takes place mostly within the confines of the offices. The characters speak not with great urgency, but with quiet contemplation, as if they are all on their last evening before checking in with the authorities before their prison term. It is a grim time and the performances are more subtle and nuanced than usual, particularly from the likes of Spacey and Irons. There could easily have been a lot more in the way of rage, melodrama and desperation, but writer-director J.C. Chandor makes the right choice in taking a more direct, less obvious choice with the material. The movie has the elements of a thriller, but the tone is almost like that of a funeral.

Margin Call is not entirely successful with the human element. While these characters are not black and white in how they view the world, there never seems to be anything at stake for them if/when they do lose their jobs and livelihood. One could argue that that is the point: The people in charge of these numbers lose little in the grand scheme of things while the common man stands to lose it all. While the characters convey a sense of deep humility and fear over what is about to happen, the central elements of drama seem lost. The first thing Chandor tells the viewer about the Spacey character is that his dog is on the verge of death and that he has spent upwards of a thousand dollars a day on treatment for it. Chandor seems to be making the point that while it is easy to vilify the people within these financial institutions for their reckless behavior, there are still human beings there. A little more of that perspective would have helped.

Chandor makes a point time and again that the majority of the people who will see this film will have no idea how the markets work. Throughout the first half f the film, many characters demand that everything be explained to them in small words and layman's terms. The film is mostly successful in this regard. Occasionally, there are explanations that will sound like complete Wall Street gibberish to the average joe, but the performances by the cast help make it all go down rather smoothly.

The film was released in the fall of 2011 when the Occupy Wall Street protests were at their height of popularity not just in New York, but across the country. Many in the media seemed confused as to what the protesters wanted. Many understood that these people were not against America's system of capitalism, but against the greed and recklessness that it all entails. *Margin Call* does not give these people a voice, but for those who can never seem to quite articulate what it is that angers them, the film at least gives a good, simple perspective on how the country got to this point.

Collin Souter

CREDITS

Peter Sullivan: Zachary Quinto
John Tuld: Jeremy Irons
Sam Rogers: Kevin Spacey
Seth Bregman: Penn Badgley
Will Emerson: Paul Bettany
Jared Cohen: Simon Baker
Sarah Robertson: Demi Moore
Eric Dale: Stanley Tucci
Mary Rogers: Mary McDonnell
Ramesh Shah: Aasif Mandvi
Heather Burke: Ashley Williams
Origin: USA
Language: English
Released: 2011
Production: Joe Jenckes, Robert Ogden Barnum, Corey Moosa, Michael Benaroya, Neal Dodson, Zachary Quinto; Benaroya Pictures, Washington Square Films, Before the Door Pictures; released by Lionsgate
Directed by: J.C. Chandor
Written by: J.C. Chandor

Cinematography by: Frank DeMarco
Music by: Nathan Larson
Sound: Damian Volpe
Music Supervisor: Joe Rudge
Editing: Pete Beaudreau
Costumes: Caroline Duncan
Production Design: John Paino
MPAA rating: R
Running time: 107 minutes

REVIEWS

Covert, Colin. *Minneapolis Star Tribune*. October 20, 2011.
Ebert, Roger. *Chicago Sun-Times*. October 20, 2011.
Morris, Wesley. *Boston Globe*. October 20, 2011.
O'Hehir. Andrew. *Salon.com*. October 20, 2011.
Orr, Christopher. *The Atlantic*. October 21, 2011.
O'Sullivan, Michael. *Washington Post*. October 21, 2011.
Pols, Mary F. *TIME Magazine*. October 20, 2011.
Rea, Stephen. *Philadelphia Enquirer*. October 20, 2011.
Scott, A.O. *New York Times*. October 20, 2011.
Whitty, Stephen. *Newark Star Ledger*. October 21, 2011.

QUOTES

Eric Dale: "I run risk management…it just doesn't seem like a natural place to start cutting."

TRIVIA

Carla Gugino was attached for over a year to play the role of Sarah Robertson but was replaced by Demi Moore because of a scheduling conflict.

AWARDS

Ind. Spirit 2012: First Feature, Cast
Nomination:
Oscars 2011: Orig. Screenplay
Ind. Spirit 2012: First Screenplay.

MARS NEEDS MOMS

Mom needs a little space.
—Movie tagline

Box Office: $21.4 million

Most kids are too busy playing, avoiding responsibility and not eating their vegetables to get into nonsensical debates around the political and social issues inherent in family values. Parents to them are exactly what they appear to be—"Giant, summer-stealing, child-working, perfume-y garden goblins." At least that is according to Berkeley Breathed, author of the forty-page illustrated storybook now adapted into a motion picture by the same animation company that produced *The Polar Express* (2004) and *A Christmas Carol* (2009). Both of those films asked viewers to believe in the imagination of another world to rediscover the power of families, first suggested in classic tales many children grew up with. *Mars Needs Moms* was originally published in 2007 and while its message may be timeless, the movie adaptation is likely to be forgotten before the final credits end.

Young Milo (performed in motion capture by Seth Green and then later re-dubbed by Seth R. Dusky) is not exactly happy with all the chores thrust upon him by his mom (Joan Cusack). Take out the trash; clean his room; answer the phone; eat that broccoli. When mom discovers Milo has lied to her about that last task, she sends him to bed before he can watch his beloved zombie movie. That is when he callously hurts her feelings by announcing how much better his life would be if he did not have a mom at all. There is no such animosity for dad, delayed again from his business trip. Before Milo gets a chance to apologize, he watches as his mom is kidnapped by aliens and loaded onto a spaceship which he manages to hop aboard and end up on Mars.

Once there, Milo must avoid the laser-wielding guards ordered about by the nefarious Supervisor (Mindy Sterling) to intercept these human females. "She looks like the school lunch lady only with the power to execute you on site," says Gribble (Dan Fogler), a manic, overweight human who has been hiding about since being a part of Ronald Reagan's secret astronaut program, or so he says. Gribble knows firsthand the Martians' big plan, one that involves robbing the disciplinary skills of Earthbound mommies and transplanting them into the Martian children who grow out of the ground like plants. Sounds like it could be just what Milo ordered—a mom lacking the predisposition for demands—except when the procedure is complete, the mom is no more. And Milo will not let that happen.

Society can always count on the artists out there to plant the seeds of good parenting and where our childhoods would be without it. Rob Reiner's abysmal *North* (1994) notwithstanding, the highs of the fantasy worlds from *Where the Wild Things Are* (2009) and *A.I.: Artificial Intelligence* (2001) have taken audiences into alternate realities and broken down what fractured reality would be like without someone to tuck kids in at night. The endgame message is the easy part. Without the proper lesson to achieve that, however, is where *Mars Needs Moms* comes up way short.

The adaptation by Simon Wells & Wendy Wills would rather focus on the adventure aspects of the story. However, they do so not through the slick, colorful locales of Paul Verhoeven's Mars in *Total Recall* (1990) but through a dingy, trash-filled landscape that looks downright apocalyptic by comparison. This is not a pleasant-looking film in any dimension. Nor are there even scattered pleasures to enjoy with Milo on his journey. Gribble's antics are annoying even after discovering the pain behind his decades-long existence on Mars. The Supervisor's right-hand gal, Ki (Elisabeth Harnois), has a secret of her own inspired by American television, but her rebellion is a footnote and never concretely linked to an alternative ideology or what she is trying to accomplish with her art. Movie buffs might recognize some of the guards' padded outfits as a link to the grid world of *Tron* (1982), but more certainly the connection between the potential for Ki's story and the final revelations of Joe Dante's *Explorers* (1985). There too, did Dante draw the parallels of childhood revolt with the misleading images seen in movies, but did so by tapping into a deeper satire that is completely lost on the Wells'.

Mars Needs Moms is a surprisingly joyless film considering all the avenues of science-fiction, rescue missions and general wonderment of a boy traveling to another planet. Despite the involvement of Robert Zemeckis, who has pushed the boundaries of FX technology and a boy's relationship with his mother in *Forrest Gump* (1994) and *Back to the Future* (1985), the film's emotional undercurrent is flat and never sustains a drive in Milo's quest for success other than just getting to the end quicker. Simon Wells' formation of his version also lacks any of the inherent cynicism of Zemeckis, which could be a plus for a simple children's matinee, but it also drops the satiric edge that has been a staple of Berkeley Breathed's tales going back to his publication of the Bloom County comic strip. Wells' own pedigree as the great grandson of the legendary "father of science fiction," H.G. Wells is no doubt his own success cross to bear. (He is responsible for remaking the 1960 adaptation of H.G.'s *The Time Machine* for a 2002 Morlock audience.) Maybe that is why Milo's father is so absent from everyone's mind here that it might slip audiences' until he reappears in the end. Between Breathed, Zemeckis and great grandpa though, Simon Wells is unable to successfully channel the satire, technological storytelling or the awe of the unexplored, leaving viewers susceptible to the grande coffee the Martians lure mothers with in the original story; just to keep them awake.

Erik Childress

CREDITS

Milo: Seth Green (Voice)
Milo's Mom: Joan Cusack (Voice)
Gribble: Dan Fogler (Voice)

Ki: Elisabeth Harnois (Voice)
The Supervisor: Mindy Sterling (Voice)
Wingnut: Kevin Cahoon (Voice)
Milo's Dad: Tom Everett Scott (Voice)
Origin: USA
Language: English
Released: 2011
Production: Robert Zemeckis, Jack Rapke, Steve Starkey, Steven J. Boyd; Imagemovers; released by Walt Disney Pictures
Directed by: Simon Wells
Written by: Simon Wells, Wendy Wells
Cinematography by: Robert Presley
Music by: John Powell
Sound: William B. Kaplan
Editing: Wayne Wahrman
Art Direction: Norman Newberry
Production Design: Doug Chiang
MPAA rating: PG
Running time: 88 minutes

REVIEWS

Bell, Josh. *Las Vegas Weekly.* March 11, 2011.
Goss, William. *Cinematical.* March 14, 2011.
Keogh, Tom. *Seattle Times.* March 10, 2011.
Neumaier, Joe. *New York Daily News.* March 10, 2011.
Orndorf, Brian. *Sci-Fi Movie Page.* March 10, 2011.
Phillips, Michael. *Chicago Tribune.* March 10, 2011.
Phipps, Keith. *AV Club.* March 10, 2011.
Putman, Dustin. *DustinPutman.com.* March 10, 2011.
Roeper, Richard. *Hitfix.* March 10, 2011.
Snider, Eric D. *Film.com.* March 21, 2011.

QUOTES

Gribble: "Mars needs moms, so the aliens are stealing them from Earth to raise their own kids."

TRIVIA

Seth Green spent six weeks outfitted in a special sensor-equipped performance-capture suit while performing his lines in the role of Milo. During the post-production process, however, filmmakers noticed that while Green was able to imitate the physicality of a child, his voice sounded too mature. His voice was removed from the final print of the film and replaced with that of 11-year-old actor Seth Robert Dusky.

MARTHA MARCY MAY MARLENE

Box Office: $3 million

Martha Marcy May Marlene was a double winner at the 2011 Chicago Film Critics Association Awards, taking home prizes for Most Promising Newcomer and Most Promising Filmmaker. While the highly-praised drama was cited by several groups from its Sundance 2011 premiere through award season, this two-fer might be the most telling about the general response to the film. Not only did viewers leave the theater talking about what they had just experienced (and the film's controversial, very ambiguous ending) but everyone agreed that two names had to be added to the list of filmmaking people to watch—writer/director Sean Durkin and actress Elizabeth Olsen. Both of these talented young people made instant waves, winning awards with descriptions like "Most Promising" on the way to what many people think will be careers filled with trophies. And even if those Chicago career prognosticators are wrong and *Martha Marcy May Marlene* ends up being the peak for Mr. Durkin and Ms. Olsen, it will be quite an impressive peak.

The oft-mocked title of Durkin's film refers not only to the title character but to the lack of identity often found in lost young women and cult members. The protagonist is named Martha (Elizabeth Olsen) but her appellation is changed to Marcy May by the cult she joins after what seems to be like a few years adrift and growing distance from her friends and family. Marlene refers to the general name taken by cult members on the phone to avoid identification. She is essentially all four names in the film and it is merely one of many smart decisions by Durkin to underline this character's lack of focus or place in the world. She does not even have a consistent name, much less a consistent state of mind.

Martha is a character who tries to fit into two families but finds herself lost in both. In the film's harrowing opening, Martha escapes from an as-yet-undefined cult, working her way through woods, across roads, and to a pay phone, where she contacts her sister Lucy (Sarah Paulson). The sisters have not seen each other in two years (during the time one assumes Martha was in the cult) and it is soon clear that they had a strained relationship before they were physically split. The entirety of the film works in parallel threads as Martha tries to assimilate to life outside of the cult and flashes back to her time within it. Both halves of the film attain a dreamlike quality as the flashbacks play like buried memories of Martha's coming to the surface while the present-day material gains strength as Martha's paranoia increases over concerns that the cult members may be coming for her to forcibly take her back.

How Martha became attracted to and involved with a cult is never clearly underlined but Durkin does offer glimpses of a young lady who may have been missing a father figure. She found a truly-disturbing one in Patrick

(John Hawkes, someone who should have undeniably a bigger part of the year-end awards season conversation as he was for his Oscar®-nominated work in *Winter's Bone* [2010]), the leader of the unnamed cult who seduces young women through compliments and attention but uses them as essentially as a backwoods polygamist would, forcing them to clean, cook, and exist as objects for his sexual satisfaction. To anyone, Patrick would at first seem like a helpful, harmless leader, although Durkin wisely does not over-play that card, always keeping him as something of an enigma instead of a wolf in sheep's clothing. He is neither wolf nor sheep. He is something unique, especially to a young girl looking for a path through the world. Patrick leads people down dangerous ones, including training his followers aggressively to survive by any means necessary. It is a mindset that can only end in violence.

While the cult arc and its graphically violent climax could have easily resulted in a film about a girl coming "back to the real world" by dealing the horrors of the last few years, *Martha Marcy Mary Marlene* is daringly complex in the way that Durkin presents the "real world" as nearly-as-scary a place for his heroine to try and find happiness. Martha did not ever quite fit in during her time in Patrick's cult but she does not quite fit in with her sister and her new brother-in-law (Hugh Dancy) either. Durkin presents Lucy as a deeply flawed mother figure for Martha to off-set the deeply flawed father figure from which she just fled. Lucy is nowhere near as deadly as Patrick but the vast differences between Martha and Lucy make clear why she might have been attracted to the cult in the first place and why she is not exactly well-off now that she has left it. It does not help that Martha's increasing paranoia convinces her that the cult is coming for her before long. And she might be right.

What could have been a relatively straightforward drama becomes a haunting work in the hands of Durkin and Olsen. Hiring Jody Lee Lipes to shoot the film was an undeniably wise decision as the film has a mesmerizing visual palette, using the natural world in poetic ways. Durkin and Lipes focus on branches blowing in the breeze or waves lapping at the docks outside Lucy's house, adding a poetic tone to the piece that many other directors would have completely ignored. The slow, deliberate pace of the piece combined with the shots of nature add a sense of gravity to the overall tone of the film that cannot be under-appreciated.

But the true strength of the film is in Elizabeth Olsen's performance. It is, without question, one of the best performances of 2011, newcomer or otherwise. This is an incredibly challenging role that requires Olsen to portray a character at various stages of comfort and confidence without exaggerating her journey. Durkin

and Olsen wisely shot the two halves of the film—the cult farm and Lucy's house—but they realize that they need to constantly feel like the same girl instead of radically different dramas. Olsen makes so many smart decisions without ever feeling melodramatic. She listens when other actresses would have over-responded. She watches and thinks where other actresses would have failed to be as in-the-moment as this character requires. To be fair, she is balanced by the always-great John Hawkes, imbuing his character with just the right amount of malice and charm.

In perhaps his most-daring move (and arguably most-promising given the risky move it was as a screenwriter), Durkin ends his incredible drama with a question mark. There are no easy answers for Martha; for the Marcy Mays still in cults; for the Marlenes around the world. By recognizing that and treating his risky subject matter with respect, Sean Durkin has made a film that plays less like straightforward prose and more like a haunting piece of poetry, and one of the most promising cinematic poems in years.

Brian Tallerico

CREDITS

Martha: Elizabeth Olsen
Lucy: Sarah Paulson
Ted: Hugh Dancy
Patrick: John Hawkes
Watts: Brady Corbet
Origin: USA
Language: English
Released: 2011
Production: Josh Mond, Antonio Campos, Chris Maybach, Patrick Cunningham; FilmHaven Entertainment, Borderline Films, This Is That, Fox Searchlight, Cunningham & Mybach Films; released by Fox Searchlight
Directed by: Sean Durkin
Written by: Sean Durkin
Cinematography by: Jody Lee Lipes
Music by: Saunder Jurriaans, Danny Bensi
Sound: Micah Bloomberg
Editing: Zac Stuart-Pontier
Art Direction: Jonathan Guggenheim, David Tabbert
Costumes: David Tabbert
Production Design: Chad Keith
MPAA rating: R
Running time: 101 minutes

REVIEWS

Ebert, Roger. *Chicago Sun-Times.* October 26, 2011.
Hoberman, J. *Village Voice.* October 18, 2011.

Kohn, Eric. *Indiewire.* October 18, 2011.
Mohan, Marc. *Portland Oregonian.* November 3, 2011.
Moore, Roger. *Orlando Sentinel.* November 6, 2011.
Murray, Noel. *AV Club.* October 19, 2011.
Phillips, Michael. *Chicago Tribune.* October 27, 2011.
Rea, Steven. *Philadelphia Inquirer.* October 27, 2011.
Sharkey, Betsy. *Los Angeles Times.* October 20, 2011.
Travers, Peter. *Rolling Stone.* October 20, 2011.

QUOTES

Zoe: "There's no such thing as dead or alive; we just exist."

TRIVIA

Was shot over the course of twenty days.

AWARDS

Nomination:

Ind. Spirit 2012: Actress (Olsen), First Feature, Support. Actor (Hawkes), Producers Award.

THE MECHANIC

Someone has to fix the problems.
—Movie tagline

Box Office: $29.1 million

The sole feature that distinguishes Simon West's remake of *The Mechanic* from countless buddy action films is that in West's film one buddy has murdered the father of the other buddy and the other buddy may or may not know that. In theory, that twist is enough to elevate an otherwise routine action movie a step or two above the competition. Indeed, while the 1972 original was not a classic by any means, it did have a refreshingly unique resolution to this dilemma. Unfortunately, screenwriter Richard Wenk does not develop the intriguing relationship between the two main characters and abandons the unconventional resolution of the 1972 film, settling instead for a generic action film which borrows the title and basic premise of the first film while depriving it of the little originality that made it worth watching in the first place.

Jason Statham plays Arthur Bishop the titular mechanic/assassin and the film opens as he executes his latest spectacularly-implausible assassination. A South American drug lord returns to his guard-packed mansion and decides to take a swim. Bishop has managed to infiltrate the heavily-armed mansion, don scuba gear, enter the pool undetected, and wait underwater an indeterminate amount of time without being seen or his scuba bubbles alerting anyone. He then manages to drown the drug lord, hop out of the pool, change clothes and leave the mansion all without being detected or having the drug lord's death even recognized as an assassination.

Bishop receives what he calls his "assignments" from a shadowy organization that is never identified but, conveniently for Bishop's morality and the viewer's ability to root for him, thoughtfully only assigns him criminal targets (arms dealers, drug dealers, assassins, rapists etc) who have it coming. This changes when he is unexpectedly assigned to take out the closest thing he has to a friend, his mentor Harry McKenna (Donald Sutherland). When Bishop demands a meeting with his employers regarding this unwelcome assignment, he is informed that McKenna double-crossed a hit team in South Africa and is shown the grisly photos of the slain operatives to prove it. Bishop does some internet research and soul searching by way of a musical montage and reluctantly comes to the same conclusion.

Bishop confronts McKenna, who accepts his fate and seems to understand why it's happening. "South Africa," he asks resignedly before pulling out his trademark silver handled pistol to fire a few rounds into the side of Bishop's van to make it look like he put up a fight. "Why didn't you try to shoot me," Bishop asks. "They'd just send someone else," McKenna responds fatalistically before Bishop shoots him dead. This conversation lasts three minutes and is the most interesting part of the entire film.

Bishop thinks the matter is now closed but he has forgotten about McKenna's adult ne'er-do-well son, Steve (Ben Foster), who has had to be bailed out of trouble by his father his entire life. The kid soon contacts the assassin and tells him he wants to learn how to be a professional assassin just like his dad taught Bishop. The mechanic sensibly tells him to try his hand at something else and Steve jokes about killing a car-jacker to make himself feel better and then actually sets up a bait car to do exactly that. Feeling guilty, Bishop follows Steve and intervenes before he succeeds in murdering the car jacker. Guided by the same sense of guilt, he agrees to teach Steve how to be a mechanic and begins taking him along with him on his assignments.

The assignments form the bulk of the film and are fun and well-directed (an especially good scene involves a two way mirror and the administration of a fatal overdose of horse tranquilizer to a rotund, junky, sex-offending preacher) but nothing anyone who has seen a few action movies has not seen many times before. The action is conventional and surprisingly low rent, failing even to rise to the level of the standard genre action of

Statham's similarly budgeted *Transporter* films. One suspects that the action is purposely muted out of the misplaced view that this film is not simply an action movie but a suspenseful exploration of two men's complicated and unusual relationship.

The film is definitely not telling that story. The premise provides the opportunity to do so with its interesting juxtaposition between mentor and student: If Steve discovers what Bishop has done to his father, will history repeat itself or will Steve respect Bishop's actions given the context of the profession he has committed himself to? If confronted, will Bishop's response be similar to that of Steve's father for the same reason? But the dramatic potential of that juxtaposition is not explored in any depth because the characters do not have any depth.

Statham and Foster do as much as they can with a script that gives them little in the way of character. Statham plays essentially the same one-dimensional character of the *Transporter* films: A man of honor in a dishonorable profession, dispensing one-liners along with the exclusively bad people he is assigned to take out. Towards the end of the film, the script gives Foster a little speech where he declares that the new profession will be good for him because it will be an outlet for all the rage he has in him, but that eleventh hour speech cannot make up for the near total lack of character development which precedes it. Foster was excellent as a stone cold killer in the remake of the Western *3:10 to Yuma* (2007) but that film only required him to shoot people. With his short height, newsboy cap and goatee, Foster is very hard to take seriously as an assassin who, on his very first hit, is able to kill an experienced professional three times his size with his bare hands. The dearth of character development would be acceptable, indeed would be expected, if the film succeeded as an exhilarating action thrill ride but it does not. And the less said about the discarded ironic twist ending of the original film the better.

The Mechanic could have been a realistic study of the relationship between an assassin and his mentor and the psychological toll of killing people for pay over the course of a life time like *Panic* (2000). It also could have been an over the top, everything but the kitchen sink, action movie like the *Crank* series. *The Mechanic* fails to be either of these things, squandering the opportunity provided by its premise to comment on the nature of duty and loyalty in a very strange profession while simultaneously failing to deliver the over-the-top action that might have at least allowed it to succeed as an exciting action movie.

Nate Vercauteren

CREDITS

Arthur Bishop: Jason Statham
Steve Mckenna: Ben Foster
Harry Mckenna: Donald Sutherland
Kelly: Christa Campbell
Dean: Tony Goldwyn
Burke: Jeffrey Chase
Sarah: Mini Anden
Origin: USA
Language: English
Released: 2011
Production: Rene Besson, Robert Chartoff, John Thompson, David Winkler, Irwin Winkler, Rob Cowan, Marcy Drogin, Avi Lerner, William Chartoff; Millenium Films, Nu Image Entertainment GmbH; released by CBS Films
Directed by: Simon West
Written by: Richard Wenk, Lewis John Carlino
Cinematography by: Eric Schmidt
Music by: Mark Isham
Sound: David Esparza
Music Supervisor: Selena Arizanovic
Editing: T.G. Herrington, Todd E. Miller
Art Direction: Jason Hamilton
Costumes: Christopher B. Lawrence
Production Design: Richard LaSalle
MPAA rating: R
Running time: 100 minutes

REVIEWS

Anderson, John. *Washington Post*. January 28, 2011.
Dargis, Manohla. *New York Times*. January 27, 2011.
Ebert, Roger. *Chicago Sun-Times*. January 26, 2011.
Lowry, Brian. *Variety*. January 25, 2011.
Modell, Josh. *AV Club*. January, 27, 2011.
Pols, Mary. *Time*. January 28, 2011.
Rea, Steven. *Philadelphia Inquirer*. January 27, 2011.
Russo, Tom. *Boston Globe*. January 27, 2011.
Savlov, Marc. *Austin Chronicle*. January 26, 2011.
Travers, Peter. *Rolling Stone*. January 28, 2011.

QUOTES

Dean: "I'm going to put a price on your head so big, that when you look in the mirror your reflection's gonna want to shoot you in the face."

TRIVIA

The film was shipped to theaters with the code name "Money Maker."

MEEK'S CUTOFF

The archetypical structure and aesthetic character of the traditional cinematic Western has been long established. The landscapes are majestic and inviting. When death arrives—typically at the barrel of a gun—it is quick and justified by some moral or legal code. Most importantly, good and evil are clearly and cleanly defined.

Director Kelly Reichardt's *Meek's Cutoff* takes these trappings and turns them on their head and paints a wholly de-romanticized portrait of legends of blazing pioneers of the American West in the mid-19th century. Here, Reichardt and cinematographer Chris Blauvelt, using the same Academy ratio (1.37:1) of Hollywood's so-called Golden Age, frame the surrounding scenery as a seemingly endless wasteland towering above and descending below the characters (instead of to the sides, as results with widescreen photography), enclosing the picture in a confined box from which escape is impossible. The nighttime scenes are crushing in their darkness. Though it never comes for any of the humans during the course of the film, death is strongly suggested as a definite possibility for any number of these characters, and if one takes the historical event upon which screenwriter Jonathan Raymond establishes the story, it is more akin to an inevitable fact.

The distinction between good and evil is not the answer but the entire question. In a film that contains such clearly drawn dichotomies (the roles of men and women on the trail, the choice between decisions based in reason and those based on emotion, and, most pressing to the characters, life and death), Raymond's refusal to reveal the intentions and motives of the story's potential antagonists—let alone acknowledge their role as either a guide or a villain—is what haunts these lost souls, astray in an unforgiving terrain and—in quite the opposite fashion of standard tradition—slowly but surely dying as food and water grow scarcer with each passing day.

The film concerns three families traversing the desert of Oregon in 1845. Their destination is unspecified yet certain: West, to the promise of fortune. There are the Tetherows, Emily (Michelle Williams) and Solomon (Will Patton); the Gatelys, Millie (Zoe Kazan) and Thomas (Paul Dano); and the Whites, pregnant Glory (Shirley Henderson), William (Neal Huff), and their son Jimmy (Tommy Nelson). The families' guide is Stephen Meek (Bruce Greenwood, unrecognizable beneath a scraggly mane and beard), the historical frontiersman who led a disastrous wagon train expedition (Upon which the previously mentioned characters are based, though the numbers were greater in reality) down an uncharted path off the Oregon Trail that would eventually bear his name. This is where the Tetherows, the Gatelys, and the Whites are at the start of the film.

The introductory scenes set up the tone of uncertainty, the slogging routine of the trek, and Reichardt's minimalist technique. Using static shots and a simple pan, Reichardt keeps her camera back and simply watches as the party fords a river, immediately establishing the dynamic of the sexes as the men lead with the oxen-drawn wagons and the women linger behind carrying baskets and, in Millie's case, a birdcage over their heads. Soon, that separation is further solidified. As the women go about with habitual chores such as drying laundry and washing dishes, the men discuss plans for the journey out of the earshot of their wives. The scene is silent, save for the rushing water of the river that eventually gives way to the plodding of beasts' hooves and the constant squeaking of a worn-down wagon wheel. The direness of their situation is starkly set up when Thomas carves the word "lost" into the bark of a fallen tree.

Reichardt is infinitely patient with material. She allows for long, uninterrupted shots of the characters going about the business of their journey (The women rise early, prepare themselves for the day, and make simple greetings to each other while preparing for breakfast—lighting the fires and grinding coffee) or simply walking. A particularly striking transition (Reichardt also edited the film) observes the party exit the frame on the left only to reappear, as one shot gradually and almost imperceptibly fades into the next, in the distance from the right side of the frame; the effect is the contradiction of distance traveled while simultaneously suggesting that no progress has been made.

The considered pacing almost immediately demands that the audience begins questioning the circumstances of and around these characters. Their own doubts and concerns rise soon after. Unlike the other men in the group, who give their wives passing notice (Admittedly, similar moments between the other two pairings could happen off-screen, though based on what is presented, that seems unlikely), Solomon confides in Emily about his discussions with the other men.

Rumors, which Thomas thinks are important enough to mention to the other men, abound that influential people have paid Meek to keep emigrants from the territories to ensure that they do not become American simply because they contain enough American citizens. William, Solomon tells Emily, believes it worth giving Meek the benefit of the doubt. Emily, for her part, distrusts the braggart Meek, who enchants Jimmy with stories from his past. Raymond subtly shows Meek's own growing concern with the repetition of a phrase. "Hell's full of bears," he says to Jimmy after telling the boy the story of a bear attack. There are no bears in the area where they are, though, he assures him. Later, on two separate occasions, he informs the group that "Hell's full of" both "Indians" and "mountains" when he suspects there are the former and knows there are the latter where they are.

The turning point arrives when Emily, seeking firewood, encounters a Native-American man known only as "the Indian" (Rod Rondeaux, in a nuanced performance that gives nothing away while allowing for multiple readings of his character's possible aim or aims). Upon hearing the news, Meek tells the party horror stories about his past experiences with the strangers "heathen brethren," and only Solomon spares the Indian from death at Meek's hands when the two capture him afterward. Surely, Solomon rationalizes, this man, who has lived in the area his entire life, can lead them to water. The rest of the group agrees but with skepticism. Just as Meek, as Emily puts it, is either ignorant or evil, the Indian is either leading them to salvation or into a trap.

Meek's Cutoff offers no resolution to the frontiersmen and women's ordeal, instead ending on a note of nearly complete ambiguity. One of its final images is of a tree with a crown that is both dead and alive (The top half is bare; the bottom has leaves). Considering an earlier allusion to the Garden of Eden, it is an obvious metaphor but still a stunning sight, and perhaps the only way the film's play on dualities could close. Like the Biblical tree in the garden, it at once promises life and death (Is the tree here growing or dying?). No matter what lies ahead, they have decided for the first time to face the trial—to reap the benefits or shoulder burden—together.

Mark Dujsik

CREDITS

Stephen Meek: Bruce Greenwood
Emily Tetherow: Michelle Williams
Solomon Tetherow: Will Patton
Millie Gately: Zoe Kazan
Thomas Gately: Paul Dano
Glory White: Shirley Henderson
William White: Neal Huff
Jimmy White: Tommy Nelson
The Indian: Rod Rondeaux
Origin: USA
Language: English
Released: 2010
Production: Neil Kopp, Anish Savjani, Elizabeth Cuthrell, David Urrutia; Evenstar Films, Film Science, Primitive Nerd, Harmony Productions; released by Oscilloscope Laboratories
Directed by: Kelly Reichardt

Written by: Jonathan Raymond
Cinematography by: Christopher Blauvelt
Music by: Jeff Grace
Sound: Mandell Winter
Editing: Kelly Reichardt
Costumes: Victoria Farrell
Production Design: David Doernberg
MPAA rating: PG
Running time: 101 minutes

REVIEWS

Bradshaw, Peter. *Guardian.* April 14, 2011.
Burr, Ty. *Boston Globe.* May 6, 2011.
Ebert, Roger. *Chicago Sun-Times.* May 11, 2011.
Levy, Shawn. *Oregonian.* April 21, 2011.
O'Hehir, Andrew. *Salon.com.* September 16, 2010.
Phillips, Michael. *Chicago Tribune.* May 12, 2011.
Scott, A.O. *New York Times.* April 7, 2011.
Stevens, Dana. *Slate.* April 8, 2011.
Tobias, Scott. *AV Club.* April 7, 2011.
Zacharek, Stephanie. *Movieline.* April 7, 2011.

MELANCHOLIA

Enjoy it while it lasts.
—Movie tagline
It will change everything.
—Movie tagline

Box Office: $3 million

It is the end of the world and Lars Von Trier does not feel fine. The controversial and divisive director has suffered from intense, debilitating depression in the past and he reportedly used his film *Antichrist* (2009) as a way out of his own personal darkness. While that film was the work of a man running on pure emotion and sometimes suffered because of the lack of focus that comes from that production dynamic, his follow-up, *Melancholia* is the work of a master, easily one of the best films of 2011 and proof that when a talented filmmaker is willing to look inward it can produce the most amazing outward expression of art.

Split evenly into two halves, the first half of *Melancholia* feels nearly like an ode to Von Trier's former association with the Dogme genre (closely resembling Thomas Vinterberg's *The Celebration* [1998]) with its reliance on handheld cameras, actual light, and awkward human interaction. Well, not exactly. Before the film really begins, Von Trier presents a mesmerizing, haunting overture, in which he transforms the frame into barely-moving works of art, all of which seem to portend the apocalyptic action to come—A horse seems to be pulled into the ground, a woman runs across a golf course cradling her child, another floats down a stream. It is such a remarkable mood-setter that it cannot be understated or under-valued. From the very first reel, Von Trier is expertly playing with visual composition, score, and expectation. It lays a blanket of dread over the relatively straightforward hour that is to follow and injects the nuptials of Justine (Kirsten Dunst) and Michael (Alexander Skarsgard) with more than just cold feet.

Justine's wedding is not a pure disaster even if she does have an outdoor fling during it and fights with nearly every family member in attendance and yet it feels like the story of someone increasingly aware that something absolutely horrific is on the horizon. It is not coincidental that Justine is a character who has dealt with depression before. It is a mental illness that does not care if someone just got married and Von Trier is clearly using his overall science fiction arc as a metaphor for its often-unavoidable force. Yes, believe it or not, *Melancholia* is science fiction. Just as depression is about to creep back into Justine's life and destroy her chance at happiness, so is the planet Melancholia reportedly on a collision course with Earth. Von Trier uses the end of the world to examine that which is completely beyond human control.

Back to the wedding, where Von Trier also introduces Justine's sister Claire (Charlotte Gainsbourg), brother-in-law John (Kiefer Sutherland), father (John Hurt), and mother (Charlotte Rampling). Her family is supportive (as supportive as can be in a Von Trier film, which is one step above complete disaster) but they also are clearly frustrated by Justine, especially the less-patient John and her distant mom. Other guests at the wedding include Claire's boss Jack (Stellan Skarsgard) and his assistant (Brady Corbet) while great characters actors like Udo Kier and Jesper Christensen enhance the background in immeasurable ways. Much of the first half of *Melancholia* is surprisingly funny, as if Von Trier is noting the fact that humans will still act like the silly creatures they are even as the world is coming to an end. It is remarkably refreshing to see Von Trier having at least a little bit of fun after a few films that could only be described as dirges (*Antichrist, Manderlay* [2005]). He has not been this playful in some time and yet the emotional power of the overture combined with the subtle tones that Dunst hits in the first half make it clear that this is not a story that will be happy for too long.

While Justine stays a major character throughout, her sister Claire comes front and center for the second half of the film and Von Trier significantly ups the dread as he pares back on character. Most of the cast disappears, leaving Gainsbourg, Dunst, and Sutherland to watch as Melancholia heads straight for them. Or does it? Dunst's Justine seems resigned to the idea that the end of the world is nigh while her two relatives hem and haw over whether or not to say goodbye or keep on hoping. The metaphor grows deeper. Depression is not just a minor setback, it can suck in relatives and destroy basic humanity.

As he has before in his best films (*Breaking the Waves* [1996], *Dancer in the Dark* [2000], *Dogville* [2003]), Lars Von Trier both finds a way to use his more excessive directorial tendencies in favor of plot and draws a spectacular performance from his female lead. One could easily levy accusations of misogyny at Von Trier, although it feels notably turned down here for a refreshing change (especially when one considers the general idiocy of most of the men in the film). It helps that he cast an actress willing to give her all for the role. Kirsten Dunst is stellar here, especially in the way she goes from a vibrant woman who has just been married to a shell of a human being to someone who seems more resigned to the fate of the world than anyone around her. Dunst is ably assisted by the always-great Gainsbourg and legends like Hurt and Rampling.

As great as the ensemble is here (and Dunst should definitely be on any list of 2011 Oscar® snubs), this is a piece that supports the auteur theory through and through. It features not one shot, idea, or performance that feels out of place or not of the overall piece. He has always been a daring filmmaker who swung for the fences artistically but he seemed to lose the timing of his swing over the last few years. He may have had to hit emotional rock bottom to do so, but he found it again.

Brian Tallerico

CREDITS

Justine: Kirsten Dunst
Claire: Charlotte Gainsbourg
Michael: Alexander Skarsgard
Tim: Brady Corbet
Dexter: John Hurt
Gaby: Charlotte Rampling
Jack: Stellan Skarsgard
John: Kiefer Sutherland
Little Father: Jesper Christensen
Tim: Brady Corbet
Wedding Planner: Udo Kier
Origin: Denmark, France, Germany, Sweden
Language: English
Released: 2011
Production: Meta Louise Foldanger, Louise Vesth; Zentropa Entertainment, Memfis Film Intl., Slot Machine, Liberator Productions; released by Magnolia Pictures

Directed by: Lars von Trier
Written by: Lars von Trier
Cinematography by: Manuel Alberto Claro
Sound: Andre Rigaut
Music Supervisor: Mikkel Maltha
Editing: Molly Marlene Stensgard
Art Direction: Simon Grau
Costumes: Manon Rasmussen
Production Design: Jette Lehmann
MPAA rating: R
Running time: 135 minutes

REVIEWS

Corliss, Richard. *Time.* November 10, 2011.
Debruge, Peter. *Variety.* October 24, 2011.
Ebert, Roger. *Chicago Sun-Times.* November 9, 2011.
Edelstein, David. *New York Magazine.* November 7, 2011.
Newman, Kim. *Empire.* September 26, 2011.
O'Hehir, Andrew. *Salon.com.* November 11, 2011.
Phillips, Michael. *Chicago Tribune.* November 10, 2011.
Scott, A.O. *New York Times.* November 10, 2011.
Sharkey, Betsy. *Los Angeles Times.* November 10, 2011.
Tobias, Scott. *AV Club.* November 9, 2011.

QUOTES

Justine: "That I know things. And when I say we're alone, we're alone. Life is only on earth, and not for long."

TRIVIA

Penélope Cruz was originally cast as Justine, but instead opted to make *Pirates of the Caribbean: On Stranger Tides* and was replaced by Kirsten Dunst.

AWARDS

Nomination:

Ind. Spirit 2012: Foreign Film.

MIDNIGHT IN PARIS

Box Office: $56.6 million

Over his long and prolific career, Woody Allen has become so well known for his comedic/dramatic depictions of the lives and loves of neurotic New Yorkers that few have really noticed that he has also made a name for himself as one of the most consistently entertaining fantasists of our time. Of course, he hardly ever delves into the sort of expensive, effects-heavy blockbusters that are commonly associated with contemporary fantasy film-making but over the years, he has repeatedly demon-

strated a keen ability to come up with a nifty off-beat premise and explore it in a funny and fascinating manner, such as the contemporary doofus who wakes up 200 years in the future in *Sleeper* (1973), the examination of the strange life of a human chameleon in *Zelig* (1983), a movie character stepping off the screen and into real life in *The Purple Rose of Cairo* (1985), the nagging mother who magically appears over the Manhattan skyline to hector her son in the "Oedipus Wrecks" segment of *New York Stories* (1989) and any number of throwaway gags in many of his other films. With his latest film, *Midnight in Paris,* Allen once again comes up with an absolutely ingenious fantastical conceit and executes it brilliantly with a film that stresses a smart, witty and surprisingly thoughtful screenplay and wonderful performances over elaborate CGI gymnastics and is one of the most utterly beguiling films of 2011 as a result.

Owen Wilson stars as Gil, a successful screenwriter who yearns to make it as a serious writer but who is currently struggling to complete his first novel. While on vacation in Paris with fiancée Inez (Rachel McAdams) and her parents (Kurt Fuller and Mimi Kennedy), he succumbs to the romance and literary heritage of the city and idly begins to consider living there and being a full-time novelist. Inez is somewhat less impressed with both the city and Gil's daydreaming and begins spending more time hanging out with Paul (Michael Sheen), an old friend who is the kind of self-absorbed type who takes to lecturing the guides at the Louvre on the real history behind the art. One late night, after begging off going dancing with Inez and Paul, Gil goes for a walk to clear his head when an old-time Peugeot cab filled with mysterious partygoers arrives at midnight whisks him off to a swell soiree where he finds himself rubbing shoulders with a couple of fellow Americans named Scott and Zelda (Tom Hiddleston and Alison Pill). Yes, *that* Scott and Zelda and as the night progresses, he winds up in a cafe with none other than Ernest Hemingway (Corey Stoll), who makes the expected pronouncements about truth and beauty and then promises to show Gil's book to no less a figure than Gertrude Stein (Kathy Bates).

No, Gil has not gone crazy—through circumstances that Allen wisely leaves a bit vague, he has been taken back to the golden age of 1920s Paris, if only for a few hours before returning just as inexplicably to the present. The next night, he tries to return to the past with a confused Inez in tow but nothing happens until she stalks off just before midnight. Before long, Gil is back in the past and, while dropping off his manuscript with Gertrude, he makes the acquaintance of Picasso and, more significantly, Adriana (Marion Cotillard), a lovely and mysterious woman who is the past lover of the likes of Modigliani among others, the present lover of Picasso and, based on her reaction to hearing only the first few lines of his book, a possible future lover of Gil. If nothing else, the two clearly are kindred spirits, although Adriana cannot for the life of her understand how Gil can so highly venerate a period of time as dull and pedestrian as the one they are currently living in when the Belle Epoque was clearly so much more exciting and interesting. Meanwhile, in the present day, Inez and her parents are becoming increasingly irritated with Gil's frequent absences and his increasingly oddball behavior, even going so far as to hire a private detective.

On the surface, *Midnight in Paris* may sound like the kind of amusing little trifle that Allen might dash off for the pages of *The New Yorker* but it has far more going for than just a bunch of amusing literary in-jokes. Granted, how a viewer reacts to many of the specific jokes and references will be determined to a certain degree by how familiar they are with the various historical characters and their achievements—the most hilarious bit, for example, features Gil running into Luis Bunuel at a party and pitching him an idea that will sound very familiar to those with a working knowledge of his filmography. That said, even viewers whose sum knowledge of the lives of Hemingway and Fitzgerald is the fact that were famous people with those names once upon a time will still find much to delight here in the myriad ways in which Allen is able to come up with numerous and accessible riffs on what is essentially a one-joke premise. (There is one great moment where Gil is explaining his peculiar predicament to an audience consisting of Bunuel, Salvador Dali and Man Ray and when they find nothing particularly strange about his plight, he wistfully remarks "Yeah, but you're surrealists...") At the same time that Allen is demonstrating the pleasures to be had from the embrace of nostalgia, he also quietly but effectively shows the inherent perils of wallowing in the past as well. It may sound like a dream to live at the same time as the likes of Toulouse-Lautrec but what happens when you get sick and antibiotics have yet to be invented. As Gil himself notes, this is not exactly the most profound insight in the world but it cuts right to the heart of the matter with sufficient depth and surprising clarity.

Another one of the secrets to the success of *Midnight in Paris* is the smart casting choices that Allen has made this time around. At first glance, the notion of Owen Wilson taking on the kind of role that Allen himself most likely would have tackled if he had made the film a couple of decades earlier may seem like an epic mismatch and at first, hearing Allen's typically verbose dialogue delivered via Wilson's sheepish drawl is a bit disconcerting at first. As it turns out, Wilson and his laid-back manner is perfectly suited for the character,

especially when he is encountering his idols and is simply astonished by both his immense good fortune and by the fact that these heroic figures are friendly, approachable and perfectly willing to treat a general nobody like him as an equal. As the epitome of Jazz Age Paris who nevertheless also years for another era, Marion Cotillard is a delight throughout and her chops as a dramatic actress allow her to add a quiet but significant heft to both her character and the proceedings that might have gone overlooked in the hands of another actress. The supporting cast of familiar faces portraying familiar names contribute hilarious work in their brief performances, the funniest of the bunch being Adrien Brody's brief but decidedly Daliesque turn as—who else?—Dali himself. Of course, the most significant character of all on display here is Paris itself, depicted her in such ultra-Parisian terms that even the tour guide at the Louvre turns out to be played by French First Lady Carla Bruni. As seen through the ravishing cinematography of Darius Khondji, this film is as much of a love letter to the City of Lights as any number of his other classics have been to the Big Apple—by the end of the glorious dialogue-free prologue (one which overtly recalls the similar opening sequence from *Manhattan*(1979) of a typical day on the streets of Paris, even the most rabid xenophobes in the audience may find themselves mentally booking their own trips abroad.

Aside from a couple of tiny flaws—mostly concerning the relative weakness of the Inez character and a couple of clumsy one-liners about her arch-conservative parents that are especially jarring against the otherwise deftly handled proceedings—*Midnight in Paris* is an utter delight from start to finish that is smart, sweet and very, very funny indeed. Although many people—possibly even Allen himself among them—might argue that it is far easier to pull off a light fantasy like this than something heavier and more dramatic but I would suggest otherwise. A story like this is an incredibly delicate construct and if it isn't played with just the right touch throughout, the whole thing can fall apart in an instant and devolve into outright silliness. Happily, Allen never lets that happen and the end result is not only one of the best films of the year (and a multiple Oscar® nominee, including Best Picture, Best Original Screenplay, and Best Director) but one of the finest works of his entire career.

Peter Sobczynski

CREDITS

Gil: Owen Wilson
Inez: Rachel McAdams
Gertrude Stein: Kathy Bates

Salvador Dali: Adrien Brody
Adriana: Marion Cotillard
Paul: Michael Sheen
Zelda Fitzgerald: Alison Pill
F. Scott Fitzgerald: Tom Hiddleston
Ernest Hemingway: Corey Stoll
John: Kurt Fuller
Helen: Mimi Kennedy
Carol: Nina Arianda
Museum Guide: Carla Bruni
Origin: USA
Language: English
Released: 2011
Production: Letty Aronson, Jaume Roures, Stephen Tenenbaum; Gravier Productions, MediaPro, Television de Catalunya, Versatil Cinema; released by Sony Pictures Classics
Directed by: Woody Allen
Written by: Woody Allen
Cinematography by: Darius Khondji, Johanne Debas
Music by: Stephane Wrembel
Editing: Alisa Lepselter
Sound: Robert Hein
Costumes: Sonia Grande
Production Design: Anne Seibel
MPAA rating: PG-13
Running time: 100 minutes

REVIEWS

Childress, Erik. *eFilmcritic.com.* May 26, 2011.
Corliss, Richard. *Time.* May 12, 2011.
Debruge, Peter. *Variety.* May 11, 2011.
Denby, David. *New Yorker.* May 23, 2011.
Ebert, Roger. *Chicago Sun-Times.* May 26, 2011.
Longworth, Karina. *Village Voice.* May 17, 2011.
McCarthy, Todd. *Hollywood Reporter.* May 11, 2011.
Reed, Rex. *New York Observer.* May 18, 2011.
Scott, A.O. *New York Times.* May 19, 2011.
White, Armond. *New York Press.* May 18, 2011.

QUOTES

Inez: "You always take the side of the help. That's why Daddy says you're a communist."

TRIVIA

Director Woody Allen attempted to make the film in Paris in 2006, but abandoned the project as it proved too expensive.

AWARDS

Oscars 2011: Orig. Screenplay
Golden Globes 2012: Screenplay

Writers Guild 2011: Orig. Screenplay
Nomination:
Oscars 2011: Art Dir./Set Dec., Director (Allen), Film
British Acad. 2011: Orig. Screenplay
Directors Guild 2011: Director (Allen)
Golden Globes 2012: Actor—Mus./Comedy (Wilson), Director (Allen), Film—Mus./Comedy
Ind. Spirit 2012: Cinematog., Support. Actor (Stoll)
Screen Actors Guild 2011: Cast.

THE MIGHTY MACS

She dared to dream. They dared to believe.
—Movie tagline

Box Office: $1.9 million

At first glance, *The Mighty Macs* feels like something out of a time capsule rather than a contemporary feature film. After all, this is a G-rated live-action film that proudly espouses such time-honored values as faith and teamwork and even throws in a little bit of feminism—albeit in its most polite and non-threatening form imaginable—for good measure. That said, there is nothing inherently wrong with the notion of such a profoundly non-cynical film popping up in these resolutely cynical times as long as it is done reasonably well and this admittedly low-key affair does just that. It is no masterpiece and there is nothing on display that most viewers will not have seen before but it is presented with enough sincerity and charm to make it somehow work after all.

The film tells the true story of Cathy Rush (Carla Gugino) and how she took the basketball team at the all-girls Catholic university Immaculata College from obscurity to the national championships during their now-legendary 1971-1972 season. When Cathy first arrives at the school to take on the job, her first-ever coaching position, that sort of victory seems like a pipe dream at best after she discovers from the imperious Mother St. John (Ellen Burstyn) that the gym burned to the ground a few months earlier, the school literally has one ball and the only reason that the program still exists is to suppress the presumably raging hormones of the students. Despite a lack of support from both the college (which is in danger of being sold and dismantled at the end of the school year) and at home, where her NBA referee husband (David Boreanaz) complains that she is never around to make dinner, start a family or other wifely things, Cathy is determined to make something of the team—both to boost their self-respect and to make up for her own thwarted dreams of basketball glory—and with the aid of a spunky novice (Marley Shelton) dealing with her own crisis of faith, the team slowly begins to pull itself together and, through an improbable chain of events, finds themselves playing for the national championship.

Even if one goes into *The Mighty Macs* knowing absolutely nothing about the history of Rush, the team or women's college basketball in general, there is precious little in it that will come as much of anything resembling a surprise. (The closest thing it has to something resembling suspense involves a student who spends most of her time bragging about her engagement and that is only derived from whether her fiancée will perish in a terrible accident or simply straight-up dump her.) What the film admittedly lacks in complexity or suspense, though, it largely makes up for in genuine entertainment value. The film was clearly a labor of love for first-time writer/director Tim Chambers and while his work probably will not go down as one of the more auspicious directorial debuts of recent times, he does do a fairly good job of telling the story in a clean and efficient manner without succumbing to the mawkishness or cutesiness that might have overwhelmed the material in other hands. Another key to the success of the film is the performance from Carla Gugino as Cathy Rush. An always-winning performer who has too often been sidelined into wife/girlfriend roles that often relegate her to smiling and nodding at the antics of her various leading men, she gets a rare chance to take center stage here and even though the screenplay is not particularly challenging, the sheer force of her personality is enough to make the material somehow work even during its silliest moments (such as a bit in which she is forced to dress up as a nun in order to score a much-needed travel discount). Alas, the limited distribution of the film means that it will not do for her what the superficially similar *The Blind Side* (2009) did for Sandra Bullock but if nothing else, it certainly deserved to do so.

Like the sport that it celebrates, *The Mighty Macs* is a film that stresses the fundamentals over flash and while some viewers will no doubt deride it for its perceived squareness, others are likely to embrace it for precisely those very reasons. It shows that yes, a G-rated movie can indeed be made in this day and age without needing to be a cartoon (either literal or metaphorical) to get away with its lack of sex, violence or foul language. (That said, it is amusing to note that, according to one published account, Disney, that bastion of family filmmaking, offered to distribute the independently financed film at one point as long as just enough curse words were added to the soundtrack to ensure a more commercially viable PG rating.) Families with young daughters with an interest in sports should especially take to it for the way that it depicts female athletes without a lot of the condescension that often mars even the most otherwise well-intentioned attempts at that

particular sub-genre. *The Mighty Macs* may not be a cutting-edge masterpiece but from a dramatic standpoint, it hits more baskets than it misses and in the end, that is what really matters.

Peter Sobczynski

CREDITS

Cathy Rush: Carla Gugino
Ed Rush: David Boreanaz
Sister Sunday: Marley Shelton
Mother St. John: Ellen Burstyn
Mary Margaret O'Malley: Lauren Bittner
Sister Sister: Phyllis Somerville
Lizanne Caufield: Kimberly Blair
Trish Sharkey: Katie Hayek
Rosemary Keenan: Margaret Anne Florence
Colleen McCann: Kate Nowlin
Mrs. Ballard: Jesse Draper
Origin: USA
Language: English
Released: 2009
Production: Whitney Springer; Quaker Media; released by FreeStyle Production
Directed by: Tim Chamber
Written by: Tim Chamber
Cinematography by: Chuck Cohen
Music by: William Ross
Sound: Richard Murphy
Editing: M. Scott Smith
Costumes: Teresa Binder Westby
Production Design: Tim Galvin, Jesse Rosenthal
MPAA rating: G
Running time: 102 minutes

REVIEWS

Burr, Ty. *Boston Globe*. October 20, 2011.
Dujsik, Mark. *Mark Reviews Movies*. October 20, 2011.
Ebert, Roger. *Chicago Sun-Times*. October 20, 2011.
Goldstein, Gary. *Los Angeles Times*. October 20, 2011.
LaSalle, Mick. *San Francisco Chronicle*. October 20, 2011.
Leydon, Joe. *Variety*. October 18, 2011.
Pais, Matt. *RedEye*. October 20, 2011.
Phillips, Michael. *Chicago Tribune*. October 20, 2011.
Phipps, Keith. *AV Club*. October 20, 2011.
Rickey, Carrie. *Philadelphia Inquirer*. October 20, 2011.

MIRAL

Is this the face of a terrorist?
    —Movie tagline

That director Julian Schnabel's *Miral*—an adaptation of Rula Jebreal's 2003 autobiographical novel—

raises questions about how art subjectively approaches the Israeli-Palestinian conflict and the connection between the personal and propaganda underscores the film's power and its success as thought-provoking cinema. That Schnabel and Jebreal (who authored the film's screenplay) ultimately cannot find their way to any sure-footed examination or artistic resolution of those questions speaks to *Miral*'s failings as a complete and effective film.

Miral is a sometimes-fragmented historical journey from the founding of Israel in 1948 up to 1993's Oslo Declaration, moving through the Six-Day War of 1967 and with much of the narrative set during the start of the first Palestinian Intifada in 1987 and 1988. All this is shown through the often tragic lives of four Palestinian women. The first is the real historical figure Hind Husseini (Hiam Abbass) who founded the Dar al-Tifl al-Arabi (Arab Children's House) orphanage and school and whose dedication to education and peace had some call her "the Mother Teresa" of the Middle East. (Also on hand are Vanessa Redgrave and Willem Dafoe, playing American figures during the early days of Israel and Hind's orphanage.)

From "Mama Hind," the narrative zig-zags ahead twenty years to two other women—an imprisoned terrorist bomber named Fatima (Ruba Blal) and a fellow inmate, Nadia (Yasmine Elmasri). The final two-thirds of the film follow Nadia's young daughter Miral (Freida Pinto) who ends up in Hind's school and grows up to be a young educator herself. Fresh into her first teaching assignment in a West Bank refugee camp, Miral finds herself torn between Hind's non-violent philosophy and the Intifada's call to revolutionary arms—the latter expounded and personified by her new boyfriend Hani (Omar Metwally).

Creators' lives are sometimes held at arm's length during discussions of films' artistic merits, but in the case of *Miral* it is hard to avoid the personal context, especially when the film is so informed by it. Schnabel was romantically involved with Jebreal while making *Miral*, and the passion and affection the director feels for the writer and her story drives every frame of the film. Add in Schnabel's own background—his mother was the Brooklyn president of an American women's Zionist organization—and the result is a project that seethes with personal context.

The fact that an artist with a Jewish heritage made a film about the Israeli-Palestinian conflict from the perspective of his Palestinian girlfriend's story charges *Miral*. Schnabel and Jabreal's film does not endorse an agenda other than a vague quest for peace, but the seeming contradictions of its creators' backgrounds fuel its thematic tensions: optimism in the face of daunting

political reality, and between the creation of art and the striving for subjective truth.

Schnabel leapt to art-world fame in the early 1980s with big, daring works painted on broken dishware, and that use of art to draw hope from the sharp edges of brutality, destruction, and pain has infused his film making as well, including *Basquiat* (1996), *Before Night Falls* (2000), and most recently *The Diving Bell and the Butterfly* (2007). (This is the first of Schnabel's films that is not centered on a real-life creative individual.) With *Miral*, Schnabel is tackling a large, seemingly intractable issue that comes pre-loaded with controversy and volatility. That he and Jabreal dive in with blinders to the outside political landscape and their subject's daunting weight in order to focus on one young woman's story is perhaps foolhardy, but admirably ambitious in its foolhardiness.

Like much of Schnabel's film work, *Miral* is rich in vivid sound and vision, plugging the viewer in to the immediacy of its setting with alacrity and crackling with loud signifying moments like bombings, beatings, and the bulldozing of homes. The film works best as pure cinema, however, when pouring itself into spaces of silence, building a personal perspective and a national history a quiet moment at a time—a first-person point of view of a suicide by drowning is particularly effective and heartbreaking. From there, as he did in *The Diving Bell and the Butterfly*, Schnabel's imagery steadily juxtaposes an individual against place and time and perceives larger global issues through the prism of a self that cannot help but rub against the world around it and the past and present that shape it.

Unfortunately that same passionate dedication and eye toward seeing the conflict through Miral's microcosm so forcefully pushes the film ahead it loses the very depth of personality that should be fueling it. *Miral* is committed to its gritty, hard-earned hope, but it never truly breathes as an emotional story of one person's journey.

The film's flawed and complex protagonist has effective scenes with her religious and non-political father (Alexander Siddig, in a quietly moving performance), with Hani, and with her cousin's Jewish girlfriend (the director's own daughter Stella Schnabel) overall Miral feels disconnected from the vividly drawn world around her. Pinto is not to blame—she delivers a fine, unflinching performance—but too often Jabreal's declarative dialog reads more like political banners and pamphlet slogans than real people having conversations, and so the character feels less like a living individual and more like a marker or signifier of an ideal.

Specific events drift dreamlike through the sometimes nightmarish quagmire of history, and while Schnabel's camera and Jabreal's pen press in tightly against

Miral's world, the film never connects and pays off as a whole. Perhaps that is appropriate, if not inevitable, for a film that peers into half a century of the still-seething Middle East conflict and fumbles nobly for answers where there may be none readily available. By the time, however, *Miral* closes with the sudden and almost plaintive plea that "peace is possible," it feels as though the film has pushed and pulled the viewer into place.

Miral's makers feel and say so much, but lost in their fervor to raise hope from hardship and detached from a solid story and character that might have carried their banner, their film cannot offer any weightier artistic support for its cause than, "Wouldn't it be nice?" That's a fine sentiment and laudable goal, but it strands the cinematically-daring *Miral* short of its story's potential and the promise of its director's pedigree.

Locke Peterseim

CREDITS

Miral: Freida Pinto
Hind Husseini: Hiam Abbass
Hani: Omar Metwally
Eddie: Willem Dafoe
Miral's father: Alexander Siddig
Young Miral: Yolanda El Karam
Nadia: Yasmine El Masri
Fatima: Roba Blal
Eddie: Willem Dafoe
Bertha Spafford: Vanessa Redgrave
Lisa: Stella Schnabel
Origin: France, Israel, Italy, India
Language: English
Released: 2010
Production: Jon Kilik; Pathe, ER Productions, Eagle Pictures, India Take One Productions; released by Weinstein Company
Directed by: Julian Schnabel
Written by: Rula Jebreal
Cinematography by: Eric Gautier
Sound: Ashi Milo
Editing: Juliette Welfing
Costumes: Walid Maw'ed
Production Design: Yoel Herzberg
MPAA rating: PG-13
Running time: 106 minutes

REVIEWS

Chang, Justin. *Variety.* March 21, 2011.
Gleiberman, Owen. *Entertainment Weekly.* March 23, 2011.
Lemire, Christy. *Associated Press.* March 24, 2011.

Linden, Sheri. *Los Angeles Times.* March 24, 2011.
Long, Tom. *Detroit News.* April 1, 2011.
Morris, Wesley. *Boston Globe.* March 31, 2011.
O'Connell, Sean. *Washington Post.* April 7, 2011.
Pinkerton, Nick. *Village Voice.* March 22, 2011.
Puig, Claudia. *USA Today.* March 24, 2011.
Zacharek, Stephanie. *Movieline.* March 24, 2011.

QUOTES

Fatima: "Military occupation is a monster that kills your soul."

MISSION: IMPOSSIBLE—GHOST PROTOCOL

No Plan. No Backup. No Choice.
—Movie tagline

Box Office: $207.4 million

Brian De Palma's *Mission: Impossible* (1996) was a decidedly fun romp full of homage and wonderfully improbable adventure. *Mission: Impossible II* (2000) was a hugely expensive, stylistically bloated misstep from master director John Woo, turning up bad reviews and box office, that threatened to make producing another film in the franchise a mission impossible indeed. It was six years before J.J. Abrams' generally-excellent *Mission: Impossible III* (2006) hit screens and even then the series seemed in recovery rather than ramping up to more and bigger sequels.

In fact, at best, the idea of a fourth *Mission: Impossible* film seemed, well, meh. But *Mission: Impossible—Ghost Protocol* is easily the best film in the series. Director Brad Bird, known for his outstanding work in animated films (*The Iron Giant* [1999], *The Incredibles* [2004], and *Ratatouille* [2009]) has never had a problem bringing action sequences to vibrant life and here, on his first ever live action outing, he blows the doors off viewer expectations turning in some of the best action sequences in an American film in long time. From atop the world's tallest building to a gritty prison breakout, this is a movie filled with thrills, and a surprisingly light sense of humor.

The film opens in Budapest where IMF agent Trevor Hanaway (Josh Holloway) is assassinated, prompting team leader Jane Carter (Paula Patton) to organize an extraction of Ethan Hunt (Tom Cruise) from a Russian prison. Together with new-to-the-field agent Benji Dunn (Simon Pegg), Hunt leads a mission to infiltrate the Kremlin, and identify the assassin's employer, a mysterious entity named Cobalt who is up to no global good.

But when the Kremlin is attacked the IMF finds itself blamed and under Ghost Protocol. Completely disavowed, they also narrowly escape capture when their own secretary is assassinated, leaving them with systems analyst William Brandt (Jeremy Renner) in tow as they hunt the now identified Cobalt—Kurt Hendricks (Michael Nyqvist) a Swedish Russian bent on starting a Nuclear conflict to usher in humanity's next phase of evolution.

What follows is a series of fairly standard twist and turns with characters having the opportunity to exact revenge, pull together, repent for old misdeeds, and deliver quips and one-liners at just the right moments. Double crosses abound, crooked arms dealers surface. There is even an erstwhile Russian policeman trying to track down Hunt, convinced that he is the bad guy. It would all be fairly old hat if it was less than perfectly pulled off. Cast, director, and screenwriters are all at their peak here. The whole affair reeks of cheese whenever anybody talks in the damn thing but even then *Mission: Impossible—Ghost Protocol* is never less than a lot of fun.

As penned by Josh Appelbaum and André Nemec the implausibility factor almost takes the film over, introducing plot elements meant to render characters sympathetic but in reality they all they really do is keep reminding viewers what kind of movie they are watching. The character motivations here are mostly clichéd and the part of villain Kurt Hendricks is, unforgivably, almost dialogue free, giving Michael Nykvist little to do but run around. Appelbaum and Nemec come from a TV background having both worked on several excellent shows including *Alias* (2001), *October Road* (2007-2008) and the American version of *Life on Mars* (2008-2009), and they wear those influences on their sleeves. They create characters that are there to play to type and contribute little except a tight structure. What little character development there is lies in the hands of a top-notch cast. This is a well-written film but like so much cinema these days it plays like a curious hybrid begging the question of whether films are looking more like TV shows or TV shows are looking more like films. *Mission: Impossible—Ghost Protocol* plays almost exactly like a hugely expensive series finale wrapping up all the character turns in ways that would be almost unbearable if the cast were not better than the writing.

Cruise is almost a father figure here shepherding his team of mostly newbies as if Ethan Hunt were on track to become the new Jim Phelps. He fits the role surprisingly well and certainly has no problem with the action sequences but he also spends more time in the background giving other characters here plenty of face time. Simon Pegg delivers wonderfully as the nervous tech-rat though Paula Patton seems miscast as Agent Jane Carter.

Patton is a fine actress but she is utterly against type here, failing to project the toughness that would make her role seem a little less like window dressing. This is a nitpick. She does hold her own in the action sequences but not in a way that suggests this may break her out into bigger things. Jeremy Renner more than holds his own against Cruise even during the action sequences paying homage to the famous stunt from the first film that had Cruise suspended inches above danger.

The supporting characters are all fine here. Vladimir Mashkov as Anatoly Sidorov (policeman) seems just dangerous enough to make us wonder what will happen when he catches up to Ethan and President Omar Hassan (Anil Kapoor, well known to American audiences for his role as Prem, the game show host in the breakout hit *Slumdog Millionaire* [2008] and TV role on *24*) has a fun bit as a playboy billionaire.

But the real stars of *Mission: Impossible—Ghost Protocol* are the action sequences as directed by Brad Bird. Giant dust storms, thrilling chases, and an absolutely jaw-dropping sequence atop Dubai's Burj Khalifa Tower are supplemented with fabulous fight choreography and effects work to produce the blow-out flick that repositions the *Mission: Impossible* franchise as a viable tentpole property. But more importantly it positions Bird in the live-action arena. Bird never got the credit he deserved for the deeply heartfelt and thrilling *The Iron Giant* and this foray into what many will wrongly consider his first real film proves what those who have followed his work have always known, the man is a creative force of nature.

The importance of IMAX should be mentioned here. A few years ago, Roger Ebert called IMAX the future of the movies and it is an idea worth another look here. *Mission: Impossible—Ghost Protocol*'s IMAX sequences are mind-boggling, taking complete advantage of the format. It is telling that the film was not shot in 3D but in IMAX. It would hardly be a better film in 3D maybe not even as good. This is the closest thing viewers can get to the experience of the old Hollywood movie palace presentation. It punches in a way home theater never will and the same is not true of standard theater presentation anymore. *Mission: Impossible—Ghost Protocol* is more than just the future of a franchise but quite possibly the future of the viability of tent pole movie presentations. This is the mission of theater owners, should they decide to accept it.

Dave Canfield

CREDITS
Ethan Hunt: Tom Cruise
Brandt: Jeremy Renner

Benji Dunn: Simon Pegg
Jane Carter: Paula Patton
Trevor Hanaway: Josh Holloway
Luther Stickell: Ving Rhames
Kurt Hendricks: Michael Nyqvist
Anatoly Sidorov: Vladimir Mashkov
Sabine Moreau: Lea Seydoux
Brij Nath: Anil Kapoor
IMF Secretary: Tom Wilkinson
Origin: USA
Language: English
Released: 2011
Production: Tom Cruise, J.J. Abrams, Bryan Burk; Skydance Prods., Bad Robot; released by Paramount Pictures
Directed by: Brad Bird
Written by: Josh Applebaum, Andre Nemec
Cinematography by: Robert Elswit
Music by: Michael Giacchino
Sound: Michael McGee
Editing: Paul Hirsch
Art Direction: Helen Jarvis
Costumes: Michael Kaplan
Production Design: James Bissell
MPAA rating: PG-13
Running time: 133 minutes

REVIEWS

Biancolli, Amy. *San Francisco Chronicle*. December 16, 2011.
Dargis, Manohla. *New York Times*. December 15, 2011.
Ebert, Roger. *Chicago Sun-Times*. December 15, 2011.
Hornaday, Ann. *Washington Post*. Decemeber 16, 2011.
Howell, Peter. *Toronto Star*. December 16, 2011.
Kois, Dan. *Slate*. December 15, 2011.
Lloyd, Christopher. *Sarasota Herald-Tribune*. December 21, 2011.
Long, Tom. *Detroit News*. December 16, 2011.
Savlov, Marc. *Austin Chronicle*. December 15, 2011.
Turner, Matthew. *ViewLondon*. December 21, 2011.

QUOTES

Brandt: "That's it. Next time, I get to seduce the rich guy."

TRIVIA

As seen in the final shot of the film's second theatrical trailer, a missile flies over San Francisco and heads towards the Emeryville area—the location of Pixar headquarters.

MR. POPPER'S PENGUINS

Box Office: $185.8 million

People seemed surprised when *March of the Penguins* (2005) became the most successful documentary of its time. A part-nature, part-adventure educational G-rated film starring one of the most lovable and unthreatening species in the world was enough to make Chilly Willy return to join them, especially when it won the Oscar® for Best Documentary Feature. Less of a surprise was that a year later, the animated world would break-on through with a full-fledged penguin feature. The beautiful and wonderfully subversive *Happy Feet* (2006) from *Babe* (1995) director George Miller would go on to win the Best Animated Feature Oscar®. As the circle of life in Hollywood continued, the only surprise is that it took another five years for a live-action family feature to take advantage of the cuddly wobblers; ironically exploiting them in the manner that *Happy Feet* posed during its climax. Unfortunately for them, however, that while they still remain cute and perceptibly huggable, even the most adorable screen presences still need an environment in which to thrive.

Mr. Popper (Jim Carrey) thrives as a big New York property broker, grabbing buildings for the company at which he hopes to become full partner so they may break them down however they see fit. The now-successful businessman grew up with a father who was off most of his life exploring the world and sending back the occasional souvenir while communicating via radio signal. It could be the reason he became an absentee husband and father to his ex-wife, Amanda (Carla Gugino) and his young children, Janie (Madeline Carroll) and Billy (Maxwell Perry Cotton). One morning, Popper receives one last package from his passed-on father. What he believes is a frozen penguin statue springs to life and begins running around his fancy apartment.

Warding off the enforcement of his building's no-pet clause from a contemptuous neighbor (David Krumholtz) and a tip-hungry doorman (Desmin Borges) is the least of Popper's problems. No animal organization will take the penguin off his hands. They certainly will refuse to take the other five that arrive in what Popper believes is a return-to-sender box. The only person interested is the zoo handler (Clark Gregg) who may have bigger intentions in mind, but shows up at a time when Popper has finally made a connection with his children through the birds. Popper's new devotion leaves him less time to close the big deal with Tavern on the Green owner Mrs. Van Gundy (Angela Lansbury), but maybe opening up his family issues is a bigger deal to him for once.

This is fairly familiar material and yet entirely-unlike the 1938 children's book by Richard & Florence Atwater, which has only brought over the title and all that it entails. The closest thing Popper and his penguins come to a circus act is when he trains them to perform a small dance with him in a throwaway gag. There are plenty of circus-like gags on display though, if going to The Greatest Show on Earth means waiting for the performers to fall down, get injured in unfortunate places and clean up the inevitable poop. It is not exactly Oscar®-caliber material, though precisely what one might expect even at the PG-level from screenwriting duo Sean Anders & John Morris, responsible for low-rent raunchy comedies *Sex Drive* (2008), *She's Out Of My League* (2010), and *Hot Tub Time Machine* (2010).

What is solely missing from *Mr. Popper's Penguins,* aside from a steady dose of fart-less humor, is a healthy injection of wonderment. It is in this lacking where one can see the difference between a director with a sense of purpose and imagination and one moving things along as fast as he can through the least resistance to pick up a paycheck. Mark Waters had success not only with Lindsay Lohan twice in *Freaky Friday* (2003) & *Mean Girls* (2004) but had a lot of fun with *The Spiderwick Chronicles* (2008), a fantasy monster movie for kids that did not get nearly the kind of credit for being a throwback to the Amblin' productions of the '80s that J.J. Abrams' *Super 8* (2011) received this year. Waters had far less success with romantic ghost stories for adults in *Just Like Heaven* (2005) and *Ghosts of Girlfriends Past* (2009) and here is yet another film solely lacking the kind of spirit to which kids above the age of seven may have really responded.

Popper's transition into caring family man should also have him tapping into his father's sense as an explorer adapting to new environments. Instead of quickly packaging up a montage to bridge acts, Waters could have expanded Popper's efforts to turn his upscale apartment into a winter wonderland instead of merely presenting a brief overview of the finished product. When the film gets around to the penguin egg-laying the script fudges Popper's emotional connection to the birthing and instead reduces it to his determination to prevent tragedy and create faux sympathy. Unfortunately, the film also misses this opportunity to turn Gregg's zoo doctor into something more than just an inevitable villain used to break more than one family apart.

Somewhere, there is a child in all of us that will allow the occasional chuckle for a screeching penguin and maybe one well-timed expulsion of gas. Ophelia Lovibond does earn some smiles as Popper's assistant with a penchant for purposefully purporting her pleasure of "P" words, a running gag that Waters fails to properly put emphasis on each time. Though far from the climactic creativity of *Babe: Pig In The City* (1998), an extended party set piece is somewhat amusing, proving that the same setting in the lackluster *The International* (2009) has established that the Guggenheim might be

the new standard for action scene locales. Overall though, this is below the talent-level of someone like Jim Carrey who can single-handedly take control of a premise by putting the focus on his own reactive personality. He does get a moment or two to produce decent laughs but nothing up to the energy of something like *Liar Liar* (1997) or the Ace Ventura films. Through the last decade, Carrey has followed the same career path that Robin Williams and Eddie Murphy continue to wallow in, alternating attempts at drama with less-than-quality family fare. He found just about the perfect mix in *Lemony Snicket's A Series of Unfortunate Events* (2004). But book fans are more likely to put the adaptation of Mr. Popper's Penguins into the same category as the critically-reviled Carrey vehicles *How The Grinch Stole Christmas* (2000) and *A Christmas Carol* (2009).

Erik Childress

CREDITS

Tom Popper: Jim Carrey
Amanda: Carla Gugino
Mrs. Van Grundy: Angela Lansbury
Janie Popper: Madeline Carroll
Billy Popper: Maxwell Perry Cotton
Nat Jones: Clark Gregg
Pippi: Ophelia Lovibond
Mr. Gremmins: Jeffrey Tambor
Kent: David Krumholtz
Franklin: Philip Baker Hall
Origin: USA
Language: English
Released: 2011
Production: John Davis; Dune Entertainment, Davis Entertainment Company; released by 20th Century-Fox
Directed by: Mark S. Waters
Written by: Sean Anders, John Morris, Jared Stern
Cinematography by: Florian Ballhaus
Music by: Rolfe Kent
Sound: Danny Michael
Editing: Bruce Green
Art Direction: Patricia Woodbridge
Costumes: Ann Roth
Production Design: Stuart Wurtzel
MPAA rating: PG
Running time: 94 minutes

REVIEWS

Abrams, Simon. *Slant Magazine.* June 15, 2011.
Bell, Josh. *Las Vegas Weekly.* June 16, 2011.
Goodykoontz, Bill. *Arizona Republic.* June 15, 2011.

Honeycutt, Kirk. *Hollywood Reporter.* June 15, 2011.
Keogh, Tom. *Seattle Times.* June 16, 2011.
Koehler, Robert. *Variety.* June 15, 2011.
O'Hehir, Andrew. *Salon.com.* June 16, 2011.
Orndorf, Brian. *BrianOrndorf.com.* June 15, 2011.
Schager, Nick. *Village Voice.* June 14, 2011.
Williams, Joe. *St. Louis Post-Dispatch.* June 16, 2011.

QUOTES

Mr. Popper: "Hello! I have to send the penguins back."

TRIVIA

During the film, real penguins were used for certain shots and most of the scenes took place in a spacially refrigerated set.

MONEYBALL

What are you really worth?
—Movie tagline

Box Office: $75.6 million

Toward the end of *Moneyball,* Oakland Athletics' General Manager Billy Beane (Brad Pitt) lays back upon an emerald field of dreams that fell short and contemplates whether the grass might be at least figuratively greener for him at Boston's Fenway Park, where much-deeper pockets would facilitate instead of frustrate. The entire film, however, essentially—and quite intriguingly—has the man stretched out on a couch to undergo the audience's analysis, eliciting a nonprofessional but in all likelihood accurate diagnosis: A haunting, hard-earned aversion to failure leading not merely to a profound desire to succeed, but also an underlying need to both understand and prove his own worth.

In flashbacks, viewers see an eighteen-year-old Beane (Reed Thompson) nervously swallowing along with his parents at a life-determining fork in the road, being assured by scouts-with-no-doubts that he should detour away from a double-sport scholarship to Stanford and immediately embark instead toward supposedly-certain superstardom with the New York Mets. (They sing his praises to such an extent that actual playing almost sounds like it would be a superfluous waste of time on Beane's way to enshrinement amongst similar greats at Cooperstown.) Thus, one fully understands the bitter disappointment and lingering bafflement he felt after the latter path led to a dead end, his much-touted tools somehow only enabling him to attain major-league mediocrity. It therefore seems clear that the reason for Beane's eventual embracing of a radically-unconventional—but perhaps more accurate—means of evaluat-

ing talent and predicting future performance was probably two-fold: It enabled his cash-strapped A's to do more with less in the early years of the '00s, but its theories also helped to finally explain the puzzling and naggingly-painful reality of his own underachieving past.

How appropriate that Beane's office is adorned with a poster advertising the 1982 Oakland Coliseum concert of punk rock group The Clash, as those filing into that venue exactly two decades later bore witness to another subversive clash that involved Beane himself. Having been eliminated by the New York Yankees, baseball's monied monolith, in the 2001 American League Division Series, he frustratedly endeavored to somehow better a team that must press on without three star players or the funds necessary to purchase another triad as capable of leading them toward triumph. Necessity thus led Beane to step up to the plate, gustily grasping something with which he might lead his small-market team to win big anyway—or perhaps spectacularly whiff. He was willing to be fair game for (hopefully temporary) derision, which Beane certainly got from all sorts of outraged, scoffing skeptics as he endeavored to neutralize the richer teams' unfair advantage. He would attempt to outsmart his more-bankrolled competitors by turning a deaf ear to the subjective opinions of old-school big league scouts and listen instead to the revolutionary, revelatory statistics provided by an economics major fresh out of the Ivy League. As portrayed with deadpan, humorous hesitancy by a pre-trim Jonah Hill, Peter Brand is a portly portender of change. Who could help but root for a David as he daringly takes aim at more than one Goliath (perennial playoff achievers; obstructive, vociferous naysayers clinging to conventional wisdom; his own perceived failures at the sport) with a weapon of unproven utility handed him by his fat font of a sidekick?

Sabermetric statistical analysis had been around since the 1970's, first written about by Bill James in self-published works that garnered relatively few—but steadfastly fervent—followers. Once this incendiary idea finally finished its twenty-five-year slow burn and burst into full flame in Oakland, it was, as the film makes clear, all too easy for some to try and douse it with ridiculing references to James' job as a night watchman in a Stokely Van Camp pork and beans factory. However, while the plant may have been full of beans, the A's General Manager and his assistant bet that James himself was not. Thus, Beane and Brand began using James' alternative ways of perceiving usefulness, snapping up potentially productive assets at bargain prices because the rest of baseball was still sizing them up with the same old rigid yardstick The sabermetric slingshot Beane chose to put to the test can be complicated enough to make one's head hurt like that of a felled giant. Mindful of this, *Moneyball* nicely boils things down to basic concepts most will sufficiently grasp. The camera briefly scans pages of equations and charts of stats to simply suggest complexity without requiring the comprehension of what many might consider tedious, mind-taxing minutia.

A complexity audiences found both easy and enjoyable to embrace was that which is conveyed by Pitt's performance. On the one hand, viewers see a dynamic, adroit operator with a useful megawatt smile who shows a lot of guts while plowing ahead with unshakeable conviction. On the other, they also see a man who sits alone amidst silence and shadows, drained and deeply lost in thought, with guts one senses are anxiously churning as he at one point allows a "What the hell am I doing?" to escape. During one such solitary, subdued moment, a close-up guides one past this visionary's glazed gaze to glimpse what seems to be a queasy combination of stumped, dispirited desolation and contained, disgusted fury. Beane's frustration sometimes seeps to the surface in the form of fidgety toe taps, tightly-clamped lips, and impatience-revealing face rubbing, but also gushes forth in unnerving, volcanic bursts of temper. Contrasting sharply is the gentle, relaxed ease (and authentic-seeming sweetness) evident during the time he spends with his teen daughter, Casey (Kerris Dorsey). Pitt gives a compellingly-multifaceted portrayal of a fascinatingly-complicated man, work worthy of being remembered during awards season along with the actor's riveting appearance in Terrence Malick's *The Tree of Life* (2011).

It is not merely the telling use of metaphor when this possessor of tremendous drive who sets out to steer his team in an unpopular direction is endlessly shown behind the wheel of an otherwise empty car. The same goes for shots of a burdened Beane's intense efforts to lift weights. These meaning-filled images are also reflections of reality—part of Beane's strict policy of being anywhere else while a game is in progress, purportedly never trusting himself to refrain from the counterproductive unleashing of vehement emotion. However, viewers pick up on something further and even more fascinating: Beane may actually fear that the way hope has so often degenerated into disappointment in both his professional and personal lives (Robin Wright briefly appears as his ex-wife) could contagiously jinx the team.

Similar to how badly things initially went for the 2002 A's before their triumphant, struggle-justifying, major league record-setting winning streak (the film's climactic, uplifting field-action centerpiece), directors David Frankel, Steven Soderbergh and finally Bennett Miller all took their best swing at *Moneyball,* as did writers Stan Chervin, Steven Zaillian and Aaron Sorkin

(the latter also being responsible for the smart, crackling ialogue of 2010's *The Social Network,* another film about major informational innovation). In addition, a much more DePodesta-like Demetri Martin was replaced by Hill. Finally made on a budget of $50 million, *Moneyball* was a hit with audiences, critics, and Beane himself. Along with Pitt and Hill, Philip Seymour Hoffman also received particular praise for his abdominally-prominent portrayal of grumbling stumbling block Art Howe, the A's manager with a stubborn case of sabermetric-intolerance. The film is skillfully based upon the revealing, reverberatingly-influential 2003 bestseller by Michael Lewis (whose *The Blind Side* was adapted into a 2009 game-changer for Sandra Bullock's career).

While *Moneyball* presents both actual footage and recreations of important games (with sudden silences daringly used at times to intensify suspense and/or emphasize significance), its focus is not on play so much as portraiture. The film distinctly depicts a man who, in more ways than one, has something to prove. Ignored in the film is that it was actually Beane's predecessor, Sandy Alderson, who first introduced sabermetrics to the A's organization. Nevertheless, being the courageous individual who would fully put the theories into play and enable his underdog team to overachieve all the way to victory in the Fall Classic, would, for Beane, be both a personal and professional validating victory. Unfortunately, reality, shared in the film's final moments, has been much harsher. While integration of the so-called "Moneyball philosophy" has ended up putting World Series rings on fingers over in Fenway, Beane chose to stay in Oakland and has digits that remain devoid of any such adornment. It is not exactly the kind of stuff likely to lift moviegoers' spirits before they themselves hoist up everything else to leave the theater. Yet, especially thanks to Lewis' lionizing, Beane's exhaustive, exhausting and relatable bucking of the system with a hope of leveling the playing field has significantly impacted the business of baseball, a sport that has long been thought of as intractably traditional. It is hard, however, to stand tall for what you have accomplished when gnawed-at by what has agonizingly fallen short. Thus, Beane's precociously-perceptive and concerned daughter endeavors near the end of *Moneyball* to both impishly tweak and seriously teach him by singing a purposefully-altered rendition of Lenka's "The Show." (Nevermind that the girl is somehow covering a song that would not reach the public's ears for another half-decade.) The repeated, reworded line "You're such a loser, Dad!" is her own attention-getting, admonishing assessment, deserved, she feels, if he does not allow himself an assuaging adjustment of perspective. "Let it go," Lenka's lyrics advise not only the father Casey loves but also the rest of us, "and just enjoy the show."

David L. Boxerbaum

CREDITS

Billy Beane: Brad Pitt
Peter Brand: Jonah Hill
Art Howe: Philip Seymour Hoffman
Sharon: Robin Wright
Tara Beane: Kathryn Morris
Scott Hatteberg: Chris Pratt
Elizabeth Hatteberg: Tammy Blanchard
Ron Hopkins: Glenn Morshower
David Justice: Stephen Bishop
Ron Washington: Brent Jennings
Origin: USA
Language: English
Released: 2011
Production: Michael De Luca, Rachael Horovitz, Brad Pitt; Film Rites, Michael De Luca Productions, Scott Rudin Productions, Specialty Films; released by Columbia Pictures
Directed by: Bennett Miller
Written by: Aaron Sorkin, Steven Zaillian
Cinematography by: Wally Pfister
Music by: Mychael Danna
Sound: Ron Bochar
Editing: Christopher Tellefsen
Art Direction: Brad Ricker, David Scott
Costumes: Kasia Walicka-Maimone
Production Design: Jess Gonchor
MPAA rating: PG-13
Running time: 133 minutes

REVIEWS

Burr, Ty. *Boston Globe.* September 22, 2011.
Corliss, Richard. *Time.* September 22, 2011.
Dargis, Manohla. *New York Times.* September 22, 2011.
Debruge, Peter. *Variety.* September 9, 2011.
Denby, David. *New Yorker.* September 26, 2011.
Ebert, Roger. *Chicago Sun-Times.* September 21, 2011.
Gleiberman, Owen. *Entertainment Weekly.* October 21, 2011.
Honeycutt, Kirk. *Hollywood Reporter.* September 9, 2011.
Hornaday, Ann. *Washington Post.* September 22, 2011.
Morgenstern, Joe. *Wall Street Journal.* September 22, 2011.

QUOTES

Billy Beane: "There are rich teams, and there are poor teams. Then there's fifty feet of crap. And then there's us."

TRIVIA

Production of the film was supposed to begin in June 2009, but Columbia Pictures Studio co-chairman Amy Pascal axed

the movie after objecting to changes which original director Steven Soderbergh had made to Steven Zaillian's script.

AWARDS

Nomination:

Oscars 2011: Actor (Pitt), Adapt. Screenplay, Film, Film Editing, Sound, Support. Actor (Hill)
British Acad. 2011: Actor (Pitt), Adapt. Screenplay, Support. Actor (Hill)
Golden Globes 2012: Actor—Drama (Pitt), Film—Drama, Screenplay, Support. Actor (Hill)
Screen Actors Guild 2011: Actor (Pitt), Support. Actor (Hill)
Writers Guild 2011: Adapt. Screenplay.

MONTE CARLO

She's having the time of someone else's life.
—Movie tagline

Box Office: $23.2 million

Monte Carlo began life as *Headhunters,* a 2002 novel by Jules Bass about a quartet of Texas women who pose as heiresses while hunting for rich suitors in Monte Carlo and wind up meeting a quartet of gigolos pretending to be filthy rich playboy types. Although 20th Century Fox was initially so high on the project that they purchased the film rights a couple of years before the book was even published, it lingered in development hell for a few years until it was once again announced as an upcoming production, this time starring Nicole Kidman as one of three American schoolteachers who abandon their lame package tour of Europe and head for Europe where they pretend to be wealthy heiresses. After one final mutation, the film finally hit screens as a vehicle for young sensations Selena Gomez and Leighton Meester. Somewhere, there is probably a funny and scathing satire to be made about how one project can begin life as an adult-oriented project playing homage to the frothy likes of *Three Coins in the Fountain* (1954) and transmogrify into an utterly innocuous tweener epic. It would certainly be better than the film itself, a good-hearted but essentially feeble fable that will appeal only to twelve-year-old girls.

Gomez plays Grace, a sweet girl from Texas who, after graduating high school, is about to fulfill a lifelong dream by taking a trip to France accompanied by best friend Emma (Katie Cassidy). The first hitch in the plan occurs when Grace's stepfather insists that her older and not-particularly close stepsister, Meg (Meester), tag along as a chaperone and the second occurs when the tour group that they are part of is a third-rate endeavor complete with shabby accommodations and a schedule so rigid and jam-packed that their trip to the Louvre is rushed enough to give even the gang from *Band of Outsiders*(1964) pause. After getting separated from their group and caught in a rainstorm, the girls duck into a luxury hotel to dry off and discover that Grace is a dead ringer for snotty and scandal-plagued British heiress Cordelia Winthrop Scott (Gomez again). Inevitably, Grace is mistaken for Cordelia and she and the girls are instead swept away and taken to Monte Carlo where Cordelia is supposed to donate and model a million-dollar diamond necklace to be auctioned in order to help build schools in Romania.

Grace is forced to continue the hideous charade and things become more complicated when she finds herself falling for young aristocrat Theo (Pierre Boulanger) and cannot bring herself to tell him the truth. Meanwhile, party girl Emma, who has just rejected an exceptionally cloddish marriage proposal from longtime boyfriend Owen (Corey Monteith), gets swept up by a rich European. As for Meg, she continues to pout but starts to lighten up when she meets Riley (Luke Bracey), a hunky Australian drifter who survived a near-death experience and is now bumming around the world in order to live life to its fullest. Between the romantic entanglements and the repercussions of her initial fib, things grow steadily out of control for Grace and her friends and that is before the last-minute disappearance of the prized necklace and the last-minute arrivals of both Owen and the real Cordelia.

Considering the fact that *Monte Carlo* has nothing more on its mind than to be an instant staple at slumber parties—it practically arrived in theaters with potato chips and manicure kits crammed into the film cans—it seems a little harsh to apply the standard rules of critical analysis to it. And yet, it must be done because despite the candy-coated surface and vaguely empowering message about being yourself, the film as a whole is pretty much a washout even by its own admittedly innocuous standards. For starters, even viewers young enough to have somehow never encountered *The Prince and the Pauper* as is will undoubtedly recognize the basic premise from any number of sitcom episodes they have seen over the years and will also no doubt recognize that they have seen it deployed with more wit and style than has been utilized here. The comedic elements are flat, the dramatic elements are even more so, there is absolutely no discernible sense of logic on display and at 109 minutes, the paper-thin premise is stretched to the breaking point and beyond with all sorts of unnecessary subplots. Additionally, the film never quite overcomes the inherent problem that Monte Carlo as a whole just is not an inherently exciting place to visit unless you are a gambler or a decadent jet-setter—it seems strange that, amidst all the other changes that it underwent from its

initial conception to the final product, the screenwriters did not just contrive to keep the proceedings within the equally glamorous but more iconic surroundings of Paris. That said, the oddest aspect about the film is the strange lack of any discernible moral center. Consider the fact that by the time the film reaches its climax, the girls have, no matter how innocently it may have begun, technically engaged in fraud, impersonation, theft and even a bit of kidnapping before they are finally exposed in the most public manner possible—despite their admission of guilt and the presence of an internationally-known heiress hell-bent on pursuing a criminal complaint, the police refuse to press charges, essentially because they said they were sorry and that they had learned their lessons.

Of course, in the end, *Monte Carlo* is less a film than it is an extended referendum on the viability of Selena Gomez in transferring her skills from the tube to the big screen. In that regard, the film is slightly more successful because she is sweet and charming and likable enough to potentially make the leap provided that she gets a hold of better material than she has been given here. As for her co-stars, Katie Cassidy is pretty much a non-entity and that is only partially excused by the fact that her character is as well; her role is clearly another vestige from the original conception that inexplicably survived all the rewrites. As for Leighton Meester, she turns in the closest thing that the films has to an actual performance and while it has nothing on her always-priceless turns every week on *Gossip Girl* she does give her role a little more heft than it probably deserves

Peter Sobczynski

CREDITS

Grace/Cordelia: Selena Gomez
Meg: Leighton Meester
Emma: Katie Cassidy
Aunt Alicia: Catherine Tate
Owen: Cory Monteith
Robert: Brett Cullen
Riley: Luke Bracey
Pam: Andie MacDowell
Theo: Pierre Boulanger
Origin: USA
Language: English
Released: 2011
Production: Denise Di Novi, Alison Greenspan, Nicole Kidman, Per Saari, Rick Schwartz; Blossom Pictures, New Regency Pictures, Regency Enterprises, Walden Media
Directed by: Thomas Bezucha
Written by: Thomas Bezucha, Maria Maggenti, April Blair

Cinematography by: Jonathan Brown
Music by: Michael Giacchino
Sound: John Rodda
Editing: Jeffrey Ford
Costumes: Shay Cunliffe
Production Design: Hugo Luczyc-Wyhowski
MPAA rating: PG
Running time: 109 minutes

REVIEWS

Dargis, Manohla. *New York Times*. June 30, 2011.
Dujsik, Mark. *Mark Reviews Movies*. June 30, 2011.
Ebert, Roger. *Chicago Sun-Times*. June 30, 2011.
McCarthy, Todd. *Hollywood Reporter*. June 30, 2011.
Orndorf, Brian. *BrianOrndorf.com* June 30, 2011.
Pais, Matt. *RedEye*. June 30, 2011.
Phillips, Michael. *Chicago Tribune*. June 30, 2011.
Rickey, Carrie. *Philadelphia Inquirer*. June 30, 2011.
Tobias, Scott. *AV Club*. June 30, 2011.
Verniere, James. *Boston Herald*. July 1, 2011.

QUOTES

Grace: "I finally meet a guy who likes me for me. And I'm not even me."

TRIVIA

Nicole Kidman and Julia Roberts were the original stars of the movie, but producers decided to go with a more youth oriented cast.

THE MUPPETS

They're closer than you think.
—Movie tagline
Muppet domination.
—Movie tagline

Box Office: $88.1 million

When Jim Henson's *The Muppet Show* premiered on television in 1976, it took on the variety show format in a way that had not yet been done before. Today, the approach would have been something along the lines of parody or irony, but *The Muppet Show* was a sincere attempt at expanding the variety show format (popular in its day) and ingesting it with kid-friendly characters, adult celebrity guests, and a touch of weirdness that can only come from a production team possessed with some kind of genius. The show spent three seasons on the air delivering some of the most memorable songs and funniest antics on television while each episode introduced new characters who might only be seen once, but who all had some kind of unique personality unlike anything else on television at the time.

This inevitably would spawn a franchise of films over the next two decades or so, with varying degrees of success. The first three films, *The Muppet Movie* (1979), *The Great Muppet Caper* (1981), and *The Muppets Take Manhattan* (1984) were born out of the original creators' (Jim Henson, Frank Oz, et al) minds. After Jim Henson's untimely death in 1990 and the Muppets' name brand was purchased by Disney, the films retained some, but certainly not all of the charm that the original show produced. *The Muppet Christmas Carol* (1992), *Muppet Treasure Island* (1996), and *Muppets From Space* (1999), and various TV movies over the years, each had their moments, but fewer and fewer people turned out or tuned in for them. In spite of Kermit the Frog appearing as a commentator on VH1 specials about the '70s and '80s and even making a cameo in *Mr. Magorium's Wonder Emporium* (2007), it seemed the Muppets' time had passed.

Nobody could have predicted that someone from the Judd Apatow comedy team would be responsible for revitalizing the Muppet brand and giving it a modern reboot. In Jason Segel's romantic comedy *Forgetting Sarah Marshall* (2008), which he wrote and starred in, the main character is writing a stage version of Dracula for puppets. The end result is clearly Muppet-inspired and it only made sense that we would co-write (along with Nicholas Stoller) the next Muppet movie. In the months leading up to its release, a few online videos emerged, the most famous being the Muppets hilarious take on the classic Queen song "Bohemian Rhapsody." The video became an instant internet hit and, suddenly, the Muppets were on the public's radar again and the upcoming movie became more highly anticipated.

Segel's passion for the project is clearly on display in *The Muppets* with a screenplay that produces its fair share of Muppet mayhem, in-jokes, self-awareness, celebrity cameos and musical numbers on par with the original *The Muppet Movie* (still often considered the best of the Muppet movies). This is a big, happy movie made with pure love and reverence for what seems like a relic from a bygone era, something Segel and his team are keenly aware of from the very beginning. Why should anyone care about the Muppets in this day and age and why make another movie? Why not?

In this movie's world, there most certainly was a *Muppet Show* and in the last ten years or so, the Muppets have disbanded and gone their separate ways. The two main human characters, Gary (Segel) and Mary (Amy Adams), are a young couple on the verge of becoming engaged who live in a peaceful town called Smalltown. Gary lives with his best friend named Walter (voiced by Peter Linz), who happens to be a Muppet and a big fan of the original *Muppet Show*. Gary wants to take Mary to Los Angeles to propose marriage to her and who finds himself wanting to take Walter with them so he can take a tour of the *Muppet Show* studio. Mary would rather have some alone time with Gary, but agrees to it anyway.

The Muppet studios by now have decayed and look more like a haunted house than a place of wonder and nostalgia. Even the tour guide (hilariously played by Alan Arkin) is filled with despair at the thought of having to give such a tour. Walter wanders off and happens to overhear a conversation by a rich entrepreneur named Tex Richman (Chris Cooper), two of his large-size Muppet henchmen and the great critics of all things Muppet related, Statler (voiced by Steve Whitmire) and Waldorf (voiced by Dave Goelz). Tex has a plan to tear down this decrepit building so that he can tap into its oil that supposedly lurks beneath. The Muppets' day is over anyway and their contract to own the studio is on the verge of expiring and unless someone can pay him $10 million to stop it, the building will be his to do with whatever he wants.

Upon overhearing this, Walter makes it his mission to track down each and every Muppet to try and get them back together to put on a telethon, raise money to save the studio and revitalize the Muppet name. With Gary's help (while Mary gets some alone time), Walter and Gary first find Kermit the Frog who lives quietly in a mansion in LA with a mechanical 80's Robot (voiced by Matt Vogel). Kermit has accepted the idea of the Muppets being a relic from the past and after a heartfelt and moving musical interlude decides that it would be good to see his friends again. Gary, Mary, Walter, Kermit and '80s Robot hit the road in hopes of finding everyone else.

In their quest to "put the band back together," they discover Fozzie Bear (voiced by Eric Jacobson) in Reno playing with a way-below-par Muppets tribute band called The Moopets. Gonzo (voiced by Dave Goelz) is now a plumbing tycoon with his company Royal Flush. Animal (voiced by Eric Jacobson) is in an anger management therapy group along with Jack Black (playing himself). As a means of condensing the storyline, the characters all agree to cut to a montage and get the story going. They hit a snag when they realize they are missing one of their most prominent players: Miss Piggy (voiced by Eric Jacobson), who is living a life of luxury in Paris, France. Kermit and Piggy have always had an on-again, off-again relationship and after some serious cajoling from Kermit, Piggy reluctantly returns to the Muppets.

The storyline is appropriately simple. he "let's put on a show and save our place" plot is a popular one in the history of Hollywood musicals, making a cameo by Mickey Rooney here more than just a throwaway moment. The movie's gleeful embracing of such simplistic ideals is evident from the first musical number titled "Life's A Happy Song," a sentiment that is reprised later in the film. That is not to say that *The Muppets* is all about living in La-La Land. The movie has self-awareness that helps make it bridge a bit of a generation gap. What was funny on the show thirty years ago might not translate as well today, but Segel and company have somehow managed to make the Muppets grow up with the times while still maintaining their overall spirit of corny jokes and "hippie-dippy" idealism.

Purists will be happy to hear the voice actors ably stepping in and filling the shoes left vacated by both Jim and Brian Henson as well as Frank Oz. Eric Jacobson and Steve Whitmire (who have been giving their voices to these characters for years) do a commendable job at silencing any nay-sayers who feel the Muppets died with Jim Henson. Director James Bobin, known primarily for directing episodes of HBO's *Da Ali G Show* and the hilarious (and musical) *Flight of the Concords*, is a perfect choice the helm this project. The pace of the musical numbers and the comic timing compliments the lightning fast quips and punchlines, leaving little room for one joke to end and for the next one to get set up. This is a film audiences should see twice in order to see and hear all the jokes and gags.

Many have bemoaned Walt Disney Studios' acquisition of the Muppet brand name back in the early '90s and there seems to be a subtext in reference to that deal in *The Muppets* when there is talk about how they signed a contract with the evil Tex Richman. But nowadays, with Disney comes Pixar and *The Muppets* arrived in theaters packaged with a hilarious Pixar *Toy Story* short called *Small Fry*, in which Buzz Lightyear (voiced by Tim Allen) finds himself in a support group for abandoned fast food meal toys. Regardless of how one might feel about the Disney corporation, there is a perfect marriage here with Pixar and The Muppets. Both have a reverence for the way things used to be. Both appeal to kids as well as adults and both have a way of making an audience feel young again, no matter what their age.

Collin Souter

CREDITS

Gary: Jason Segel
Mary: Amy Adams
Tex Richman: Chris Cooper

Veronica Martin: Rashida Jones
Kermit/Statler/Rizzo: Steve Whitmire (Voice)
Miss Piggy/Fozzie Bear/Animal: Eric Jacobson (Voice)
Gonzo/Waldorf/ Dr. Benson Honeydew/Zoot: Dave Goelz (Voice)
Rowlf/Dr. Teeth/Swedish Chef/ Pepe the Prawn: Bill Barretta (Voice)
Scooter/Janice: David Rudman (Voice)
Origin: USA
Language: English
Released: 2011
Production: David Hoberman, Todd Lieberman; released by Walt Disney Pictures
Directed by: James Bobin
Written by: Jason Segel, Nicholas Stoller
Cinematography by: Don Burgess
Music by: Christophe Beck
Sound: Steve Cantamessa, Kevin O'Connell, Beau Borders
Music Supervisor: Bret McKenzie
Editing: James M. Thomas
Art Direction: Andrew Max Cahn
Costumes: Rachel Afiley
Production Design: Steve Saklad
MPAA rating: PG
Running time: 98 minutes

REVIEWS

Biancolli, Amy. *San Francisco Chronicle.* November 23, 2011.
Covert, Colin. *Minneapolis Star Tribune.* November 22, 2011.
Ebert, Roger. *Chicago Sun-Times.* November 23, 2011.
Goodykoontz, Bill. *Arizona Republic.* November 22, 2011.
Guzman, Rafer. *Newsday.* November 23, 2011.
Morris, Wesley. *Boston Globe.* November 22, 2011.
Phipps, Keith. *AV Club.* November 22, 2011.
Rea, Steven. *Philadelphia Inquirer.* November 23, 2011.
Schwartzbaum, Lisa. *Entertainment Weekly.* November 21, 2011.
Smith, Kyle. *New York Post.* November 23, 2011.

QUOTES

Tex Richman: "Maniacal laugh...maniacal laugh."

TRIVIA

Of all the actors and actresses making cameos in this film, Alan Arkin is the only one to have actually appeared on *The Muppet Show.*

AWARDS

Oscars 2011: Song ("Man or Muppet").

MY WEEK WITH MARILYN

Box Office: $13.7 million

In 1956, Marilyn Monroe was at the height of her popularity and yet few people knew who she really was.

There have been countless biographies, TV specials and movies made about this American icon whose death came all too quickly and who meant so many things to so many people. All of these biographers seem to agree on one thing: this was a truly troubled soul. The latest of these examinations into the life of the world famous diva is *My Week With Marilyn,* based on the memoir *The Prince, The Showgirl and Me* by Colin Clark, published in 1996. It is as sympathetic as anything else that has been filmed or written about Monroe and like all other films about her, the success of the piece depends greatly on the actress playing her. Michelle Williams took on the daunting task in not only evoking the glamorous movie star, but also the psychologically tortured and overly coddled human being.

Colin Clark's memoir is about his stint as a 3rd Assistant Director on the set of a film called *The Prince and the Showgirl* (1957), directed by and starring Laurence Olivier (Kenneth Branagh) and Marilyn Monroe. Colin (Eddie Redmayne) explains via voice-over "Everyone remembers their first job. This was mine." Colin dreams of working in Hollywood in any capacity and will sit in a waiting room as long as it takes before someone will hire him. He does just that in Olivier's film studio in England until nobody can say 'no' anymore. Olivier's film, originally titled *The Sleeping Prince,* is a light comedy vehicle for himself and Monroe. It stands to reason that the film should be a breeze to shoot, especially since Olivier has always been against the Method style of acting.

Monroe, on the other hand, has a strict acting coach named Paula Strasberg (Zoë Wanamaker), who insists on the Method style, by which Marilyn Monroe must immerse herself deeply into the character and almost become her throughout the shoot. These conflicting approaches to acting hold up the production for several hours and even days. Her prescription drug dependency only makes matters worse. She has pills to wake her up, pills to calm her down, pills to help her sleep and pills to calm her nerves. What should have been a quick and easy shoot ends up curing Olivier of ever again wanting to direct a movie (it would be thirteen years before he would direct another film). Only the film's co-star, Dame Sybil Thorndike (Judi Dench) shows any empathy, patience and understanding of the bigger picture here.

Colin, meanwhile, does what is asked of him in any situation while courting the head of wardrobe, Lucy (Emma Watson). They go out together and all seems well until Marilyn takes an interest in him as a bit of a temporary confidant. Marilyn was married to playwright Arthur Miller (Dougray Scott) at the time, who was gathering ideas for a new piece of literature, something unflattering and obviously inspired by his wife. This was her third marriage and it has often been noted that she had a thing for alpha-males, something Colin Clark was not. He was, however, what she needed at this particular time in her life and she makes the invite clear when she steps out of the bathroom naked and lets him off the hook by being so nonchalant about it.

The production bosses and Olivier dislike the notion of a mere 3rd Assistant Director getting such a privileged pass especially since the production has gone completely off the rails due to her behavior. Nevertheless, Marilyn and Colin take off one day to a remote area where they go skinny dipping. Marilyn suggests they make this a "real date," something that, for her, represents a time in her youth that was lost and that will provide a temporary fix. For Colin, it is as real as any love affair could be and he mistakes it as such. This eventually adds to the troubles her coaches and managers already have on their hands as Marilyn sleeps for days on end while losing sight of the job she was hired to do. Marilyn Monroe was notorious for being insecure in her acting abilities, but wanted to be taken seriously nonetheless. Olivier was always taken seriously as an actor, but he wanted to be a movie star as well. "This movie will help neither of you," Colin explains.

Such pointed observations help make *My Week With Marilyn* more of an enjoyable piece of insider Hollywood drama, which helps make the first hour move along at a brisk pace. Director Simon Curtis, who up until now has been primarily working in television features and miniseries, keeps the film moving along while giving the performances room to breathe, more so in the second half. Branagh is clearly having fun playing Olivier, something he was born to do, especially given their career parallels (both achieved success early in their careers for directing and staring in Shakespeare adaptations). Eddie Redmayne is a believable choice to play Colin Clark, not too good looking and not too put upon.

But the film belongs to Williams, who has to give so much of herself to Marilyn Monroe. Like many actors before her who have played iconic, bigger-than-life personas, she immerses herself in the role and manages to deliver on every facet of Monroe. This is not merely an imitation. It is a believable transformation. There is a real person here, one who was capable of being cordial and embracing of the press that surrounded her with their harsh flashbulbs as well as the enigmatic individual who never knew what to make of it all. Unlike so many actors who attempt to take on a larger than life persona, Williams never lets Monroe become a caricature.

My Week With Marilyn is a film perfect for its time. Monroe is still an often imitated and revered figure.

Madonna was famous for doing an imitation of Monroe in her Material Girl video as well as channeling her mannerisms for her role in Dick Tracy (1990). In the more current day and age, singer Lady Gaga is a Monroe-like spectacle, but without the engaging personality to go with it. Likewise, Lindsay Lohan tried her best to emulate Monroe in a nude spread for Playboy as another desperate attempt to revive her fledgling career. *My Week With Marilyn* takes the viewer back to a time when a person had to be uniquely qualified to be famous and to take on an iconic status. Unlike today's instant reality TV celebs and interchangeable starlets, Monroe had a charm and style that was unmatched and unmistakable.

Williams has the daunting task of going back and forth between the person and the persona at the drop of a hat while making it look effortless. She does just that. Better yet, it is not a great performance wasted in a mediocre film, as is so often the case. *My Week With Marilyn* is funny, heartbreaking and touching, not only in the way it depicts Monroe's tenderness and turmoil, but in the way it depicts a man's first true love. Who really knows if everything that happened in this movie is really true? Williams makes the viewer believe it very well could have happened. After all, she was only human.

Collin Souter

CREDITS

Marilyn Monroe: Michelle Williams
Colin Clark: Eddie Redmayne
Sir Laurence Olivier: Kenneth Branagh
Arthur Miller: Dougray Scott
Milton Greene: Dominic Cooper
Dame Sybil Thorndike: Judi Dench
Vivien Leigh: Julia Ormond
Lucy: Emma Watson
Sir Owen Morshead: Derek Jacobi
Paula Strasberg: Zoe Wanamaker
Sir Kenneth Clark: Pip Torrens
Hugh Perceval: Michael Kitchen
Vanessa: Miranda Raison
Cotes-Preedy: Simon Russell Beale
Arthur Jacobs: Toby Jones
Barry: Jim Carter
Roger Smith: Philip Jackson
Origin: USA, United Kingdom
Language: English
Released: 2011
Production: David Parfitt, Harvey Weinstein; Trademark Films, BBC Films; released by Weinstein Company
Directed by: Simon Curtis

Written by: Adrian Hodges
Cinematography by: Ben Smithard
Music by: Conrad Pope
Sound: Richard Taylor
Music Supervisor: Maggie Rodford, Dana Sano
Editing: Adam Recht
Art Direction: Charmian Adams
Costumes: Jill Taylor
Production Design: Donal Woods
MPAA rating: R
Running time: 99 minutes

REVIEWS

Burr, Ty. *Boston Globe.* November 22, 2011.
Childress, Erik. *eFilmcritic.com.* November 11, 2011.
Denby, David. *New Yorker.* November 22, 2011.
Ebert, Roger. *Chicago Sun-Times.* November 23, 2011.
Goss, William. *Film.com.* November 23, 2011.
Howell, Peter. *Toronto Star.* November 25, 2011.
Kennedy, Lisa. *Denver Post.* November 23, 2011.
Phipps, Keith. *AV Club.* November 22, 2011.
Schwarzbaum, Lisa. *Entertainment Weekly.* November 24, 2011.
Whitty, Stephen. *Newark Star-Ledger.* November 23, 2011.

QUOTES

Sir Laurence Olivier: "I think directing a movie is the best job ever created, but Marilyn has cured me of ever wanting to do it again."

TRIVIA

Ian Murray is the stand/by rigger for this movie. His adopted grandfather Jack Thompson was the stand/by rigger on *The Prince and the Showgirl.*

AWARDS

Golden Globes 2012: Actress—Mus./Comedy (Williams)
Ind. Spirit 2012: Actress (Williams)

Nomination:

Oscars 2011: Actress (Williams), Support. Actor (Branagh)
British Acad. 2011: Actress (Williams), Support. Actor (Branagh), Costume Des., Makeup, Support. Actress (Dench), Outstanding British Film
Golden Globes 2012: Film—Mus./Comedy, Support. Actor (Branagh)
Screen Actors Guild 2011: Actress (Williams), Support. Actor (Branagh).

N-O

NEW YEAR'S EVE

Box Office: $142 million

Following the formula that they rode to a surprise box-office success with *Valentine's Day* (2010), director Garry Marshall and screenwriter Katherine Fugate have come up with *New Year's Eve,* another star-studded spectacular following the misadventures of a group of disparate dopes during a holiday. Even those people who actually enjoyed *Valentine's Day* are likely to be stunned by the awful quality of this particular take on the subject. Ironically, the film winds up becoming a lot like the holiday that it celebrates—it is loud, obnoxious, over-stuffed with people trying too hard to have a good time, and, about halfway through, most viewers will find themselves wishing that they had just stayed home and watched some old Marx Brothers movies instead.

Switching coasts from Los Angeles to New York, the film follows the myriad adventures of a large group of familiar faces going through their equally familiar paces over the course of what feels like an endless December 31. Hilary Swank plays the official in charge of the ball drop in Times Square and is dealt a major setback when it breaks down a few hours before midnight. Michelle Pfeiffer is a frumpy secretary who quits her job and enlists brash bike messenger Zac Efron to help her complete her list of current resolutions before time runs out. Katherine Heigl is an up-and-coming caterer who gets her big break handling a lavish party only to discover that her ex, world-famous rock star Jon Bon Jovi, is one of the guests of honor. Ashton Kutcher is a lovelorn cartoonist who gets trapped in an elevator with starry-eyed back-up singer Lea Michele. Seth Mey-

ers and Jessica Biel are an expectant couple who find themselves competing with another couple, played by Til Schweiger and Sarah Paulson, to see who will deliver the first baby of the new year and win a $25,000 prize.

Meanwhile, Sarah Jessica Parker is a lonely divorcee who has to go into the city to chase down teenage daughter Abigail Breslin, who has slipped off to Times Square to get an all-important smooch from her would-be boyfriend. Josh Duhamel is trying to get into the city to show up for a date that he made the previous New Year's and is forced to drive in with a wacky family in a Winnebago. Robert De Niro plays a lonely dying man whose final wish is to go up on the roof of the hospital in order to properly see the fireworks and Halle Berry is the dedicated nurse who tries to make it happen for him. In addition, Sofia Vergara turns up as a large-breasted ethnic joke, Hector Elizondo fulfills his role of being to Garry Marshall what Dick Miller is to Joe Dante, and there are enough surprise cameos on display to fill out an entirely different and presumably better movie.

To be fair, even though *Valentine's Day* was mind-less fluff from start to finish, it sort of worked because the actors were likable enough to overcome the sitcom-style silliness of the screenplay and because Marshall did a decent job of keeping things moving along with the effortless precision of a genial party host who is constantly circling the room to make sure that none of his guests come away feeling slighted. This time around, however, the mood has soured considerably and virtually every character on display is either unlikable, uninterest-ing or both. To make matters worse, the situations that they find themselves enmeshed in are so trite and clichéd that one keeps hoping in vain that Marshall and Fugate will realize this and put some kind of spin on the material to mix it up a little bit. Another problem is the film's insistence on trying to insert poignancy into the proceedings in order to capture the sometimes bittersweet nature of the holiday. In theory, getting people misty-eyed on New Year's Eve is like shooting fish in a barrel but the film is so overly concerned with making audiences feel all warm and fuzzy in the end that most viewers will wind up feeling nothing other than a steadily building sense of resentment towards its hamhanded efforts. Of all the story lines, the only one that comes even vaguely close to being touching and funny is the one involving Michelle Pfeiffer and Zac Efron but the film is in such a rush to get to everyone else that their surprisingly effective screen chemistry winds up getting interrupted just when things threaten to get interesting.

With the exception of a couple of remarks from Marshall regular Larry Miller and an offhand Newark joke that is inserted into the proceedings for no reason, none of the allegedly comedic bits are funny in the slightest. However, that is not to say that *New Year's Eve* is not filled with laugh-out-loud moments but as it turns out, they are virtually all of the inadvertent variety. There is one cut from some form of silliness to De Niro lying on his deathbed that is so poorly deployed that it feels as if De Niro pissed off a member of the editing team and they decided to get back at him. There is the hilariously overwrought scene in which all the characters are linked in a moment of shared dramatic repose while Bon Jovi and Michele sing John Hiatt's "Have a Little Faith in Me" in what can only be described as a tone-deaf emulation of one of the key moments of the infinitely superior *Magnolia* (1999).

On the grand scale of New Year's-related movies, *New Year's Eve* is so utterly without merit that it makes *200 Cigarettes* (1999) look like *Ocean's 11* (1960) by comparison. This is one of those films that goes so bad so completely that it seem impossible that anyone involved with its production could have believed for a moment that it had any chance of working. At one point, Ryan Seacrest trots on, looks around at the chaos surrounding him and remarks "This never happened to Dick Clark." Sadly, truer words have never been spoken.

Peter Sobczynski

CREDITS

Stan Harris: Robert De Niro
Randy: Ashton Kutcher
Ingrid: Michelle Pfeiffer
Claire Morgan: Hilary Swank
Elise: Lea Michele
Laura Carrington: Katherine Heigl
Sam: Josh Duhamel
Ava: Sofia Vergara
Tess: Jessica Biel
Paul: Zac Efron
Kim: Sarah Jessica Parker
Jensen: Jon Bon Jovi
Hailey: Abigail Breslin
Kominsky: Hector Elizondo
Brendan: Chris Bridges
Griffin: Seth Meyers
James: Til Schweiger
Aimee: Halle Berry
Origin: USA
Language: English
Released: 2011
Production: Wayne Allan Rice, Mike Karz, Garry Marshall; New Line Cinema; released by Warner Bros.
Directed by: Garry Marshall
Written by: Katherine Fugate
Cinematography by: Charles Minsky
Music by: John Debney
Sound: Tom Nelson
Music Supervisor: Julianne Jordan
Editing: Michael Tronick
Art Direction: Kim Jennings
Costumes: Gary Jones
Production Design: Mark Friedberg
MPAA rating: PG-13
Running time: 118 minutes

REVIEWS

Anderson, Melissa. *Village Voice.*. December 6, 2011.
Barker, Andrew. *Variety.* December 6, 2011.
Ebert, Roger. *Chicago Sun-Times.* December 8, 2011.
Gleiberman, Owen. *Entertainment Weekly.* December 8, 2011.
Pais, Matt. *RedEye.* December 8, 2011.
Phillips, Michael. *Chicago Tribune.* December 8, 2011.
Puig, Claudia. *USA Today.* December 8, 2011.
Rabin, Nathan. *AV Club.* December 8, 2011.
Snider, Eric D. *film.com.* December 9, 2011.
Tallerico, Brian. *HollywoodChicago.com.* December 9, 2011.

QUOTES

Stan Harris: "Nothing beats New York on New Years Eve."

TRIVIA

Origianlly conceived of a as a sort of continuation for director Garry Marshall's *Valentine's Day*, the project eventually became its own entity, recasting many of the protagonists in different roles.

AWARDS

Nomination:

Golden Raspberries 2011: Worst Ensemble Cast, Worst Picture, Worst Actress (Parker), Worst Director (Marshall), Worst Screenplay.

NO STRINGS ATTACHED

Friendship has its benefits.
—Movie tagline

Box Office: $70.7 million

Woody Allen once so elegantly wrote in *Annie Hall* (1977) that relationships are like sharks. "It has to constantly move forward or it dies." Allen's beloved spin on the romantic comedy was more than thirty years ago, and, recently, the romantic comedy genre has sunk to new lows. There has been little creativity in structure, disbelief in character behavior, and almost no genuine comedy or romance. It has become so disheartening as of late that what the genre could be labeled "a dead shark." Most film writers cannot even be bothered to say the full name of the genre, speaking the term "rom-com." Even the once great Allen has fallen into a funk of mediocre monotony (with the possible exception of his 2011 hit *Midnight in Paris*). Thankfully, some voices from the old guard like James L. Brooks and Ivan Reitman are still around to prove that there is still some life in there even if it takes some creative CPR.

Adam (Ashton Kutcher) and Emma (Natalie Portman) have had an undefined relationship not unlike the leads in *When Harry Met Sally* (1989). From the uncomfortable response at camp to her belief that two people are not meant to be together forever to the awkward misunderstanding of a first date at college, it seems movie-appropriate that Adam would one day end up in a drunken stupor on her couch. What gets him there is the discovery that his dad (Kevin Kline), a famous former TV actor has taken to sleeping with his ex-girlfriend. A hunt for cheap, pathetic sex later and a night of innocence turns into a morning of satisfaction for both.

As Adam tries to gentlemanly pursue her, the intimacy-challenged Emma hits upon a better idea. They can "use each other for sex, day and night, nothing else." Just like the classic *Seinfeld* episode, the friends with benefits establish ground rules to keep this business-casual and to keep feelings out of it. Emma's pals, Patrice (Greta Gerwig) and Shira (Mindy Kaling) think

she is crazy for not pursuing a relationship with this obviously sweet guy that is into her. Adam's pals, Eli (Jake Johnson) and Wallace (Chris "Ludacris" Bridges) cannot believe he would want to jeopardize the situation by breaking Emma's clauses. And so grows the ever-twisting boundaries within the battle of the sexes.

Emma is an on-the-go doctor. When not at the hospital or some other work function the only times she is seen early on is grabbing a quick lunch or in her apartment where she sleeps. With the male as the heartbroken one, growing up in a family without a mom most his life, Meriwether has reversed the standard roles where women can be equally afraid of committing their precious time only to be truly surprised that there are still men left willing to open the door for them. This draws out a rather unique tension in which the viewer fears that Adam may be pushing at the borders around Emma's heart a little too hard.

For a genre that has been practically stripped entirely of its romantic and comedic roots, any film that can deliver just a mild touch of either successfully might be enough to recommend these days. *No Strings Attached* goes beyond the bare minimum, however, in large part to Elizabeth Meriwether's truly wonderful script. It explores the fundamental roots of the situation without grandstanding one point of view over another nor allowing its characters to fit within their traditional archetypal patterns. Both the men and the women are allowed to crudely announce their needs amongst their own, but are also good, respectful people as circumstances call for it. Rom-com plots are dependent on second-act shifts in mood and complications. One of the clever things about Meriwether's is that by removing the premeditated constraints of couplehood, the potential heartache of rival suitors and cheating is eliminated in traditional terms. Turning such age-old establishments of these films from mood-breakers into comedic possibilities is not just refreshing, but allows a closer connection to the true feelings of the protagonists.

Little of this would work had the two actors chosen for Adam and Emma not created such a palpable chemistry. Natalie Portman is one of the most charming, realistic presences in the movies today and she creates a reality for who her characters are that allows an instant connection. Rarely has she been given the chance to do comedy and, despite the emotional restraints on Emma, Portman has not been this loose since her memorable gal-pal in *Garden State* (2004). Ashton Kutcher, on the other hand, has never been one for garnering accolades for his film roles. He has generally portrayed the same loud goofball throughout his career in one overgrating pile of bad after another including *Dude, Where's My Car?* (2000), *What Happens In Vegas* (2008) and *Killers* (2010). A softer, more interesting side has been slowly emerging in Kutcher over the years though. Roles as a womanizing hustler who grows to love one woman in *Spread* (2009) and as the jilted florist who realizes he loves his best friend in perhaps the least cringe-worthy of the storylines in Garry Marshall's *Valentine's Day* (2010) may have just been warmups for Adam. Finally, he has the material worthy of the puppy dog-in-training and in *No Strings Attached* the match has produced the best screen performance of Kutcher's career.

Such is the cyclical nature of the movie business that the best ideas come around again in order to capitalize on success. The rom-com is such its own singular idea that the same basic formula can be used multiple times in the same year, sometimes even identically, as with *Friends With Benefits* (2011), which features the same basic concept and coincidentally Natalie Portman's *Black Swan* (2010) doppelganger, Mila Kunis, as well as Ivan Reitman's daughter, Catherine, in a small role. The dividing line between the two may come down to Meriwether's smart script here and the attachment of comedy-killing director Will Gluck of *Fired Up* (2009). Reitman's name is synonymous with some of the great comedies of the '80s and is responsible for proving Arnold Schwarzenegger was just as adept a comedic actor as an action star. But the director/producer has had some less-than-stellar efforts over the past couple decades culminating with the misguided high-concept of *My Super Ex-Girlfriend* (2006). While not exactly remembered for the romantic aspects of his films, an overlying goodness in his characters has always come to the forefront. That shines again in *No Strings Attached,* which is Reitman's best work since his presidential comedy *Dave* (1993). Between that assessment, the cliche-shedding romance hovering within *Bridesmaids* (2011) and Woody Allen also contributing his most enjoyably romantic work since the '90s in *Midnight In Paris* (2011), maybe this will be the year to remember as the one where the rom-com earned back its full name.

Erik Childress

CREDITS

Adam Kurtzman: Ashton Kutcher
Emma Franklin: Natalie Portman
Alvin: Kevin Kline
Patrice: Greta Gerwig
Dr. Metzner: Cary Elwes
Lucy: Lake Bell
Katie Kurtzman: Olivia Thirlby
Sandra Kurtzman: Talia Balsam
Wallace: Chris Bridges
Origin: USA

Language: English
Released: 2011
Production: Jeffrey Clifford, Joe Medjuck, Ivan Reitman; DW Studios, Handsomecharlie Films, Katalyst Films, Montecito Picture Co., Paramount Pictures; released by Paramount Pictures
Directed by: Ivan Reitman
Written by: Elizabeth Meriwether
Cinematography by: Rogier Stoffers
Music by: John Debney
Sound: Michael J. Benavente
Editing: Dana E. Glauberman
Art Direction: Gregory A. Berry
Costumes: Julie Weiss
Production Design: Ida Random
MPAA rating: R
Running time: 110 minutes

REVIEWS

Bell, Josh. *Las Vegas Weekly.* January 20, 2011.
Berardinelli, James. *ReelViews.* January 20, 2011.
Ebert, Roger. *Chicago Sun-Times.* January 20, 2011.
Goss, William. *Cinematical.* January 21, 2011.
McWeeny, Drew. *HitFlix.* January 19, 2011.
Montgomery, Karina. *rec.arts.movies.reviews.* March 18, 2011.
Morgenstern, Joe. *Wall Street Journal.* January 20, 2011.
O'Hehir, Andrew. *Salon.com.* January 20, 2011.
Putman, Dustin. *DustinPutman.com.* January 20, 2011.
Roeper, Richard. *RichardRoeper.com.* January 21, 2011.

QUOTES

Adam: "You know, I don't want to freak you out, but I'd love to hang out with you in the daytime sometime."

TRIVIA

The theatrical print of the film was shipped to theaters with the title *Dos.*

OF GODS AND MEN
(Des hommes et des dieux)

Box Office: $4 million

A very ruminative, serious drama about the unraveling of religious tolerance in the face of a rising terrorist threat during the Algerian Civil War, French film *Of Gods and Men* unfolds in a kind of gauzy, introspective haze. While charged with a few moments of violence, for better and worse, the movie mostly keeps the perspective of an outsider looking in, pondering the wisdom or duty of virtuous people to potentially sacrifice themselves merely in the name of service or obligation. After both opening the 2010 Cannes Film Festival and scoring its Grand Prize, the film went on to tremendous critical and native box office acclaim, pulling in over $40 million internationally, and winning France's Cesar® Award for Best Film.

Set in 1996, *Of Gods and Men* centers on a monastery in the remote town of Tibhirine, where nine Roman Catholic Trappist monks live peacefully amidst an otherwise overwhelmingly Muslim population. Their self-elected leader is Christian de Chergé (Lambert Wilson), and he oversees an austere regimen of prayer, beekeeping and community outreach. The medical arm of the latter is headed up by Luc (Michael Lonsdale), who treats the wounds of the destitute, and dispenses mended shoes to the youngest children and advice on life and love to those slightly older.

This coexistence is shattered by a sudden surge in Islamic fundamentalism, perpetrated by the Armed Islamic Group's war against what it views as a corrupt, inefficient and insufficiently spiritual government. Under the guidance of leader Ali Fayattia (Farid Larbi), these Algerian religious rebels one day swarm the monks' gated compound. Taking a bold stand, Christian turns away their demand to take Luc with them, to treat wounded soldiers, but knows that he has set in motion a chain of events which will imperil himself and his colleagues. For a while the monks treat sick and injured rebels as they would any other person seeking their help. But as the terrorist threat mounts, so too do pressures from crumbling government and Algerian army factions, none of whom wants the responsibility for protecting the monks if they choose to stay. With prayer and debate, the monks try to reach a consensus about what course of action to take, but eventually are confronted with a rebel group less willing than Fayattia to turn a blind eye to their religious differences.

Co-written by Etienne Comar and director Xavier Beauvois, *Of Gods and Men* feels sort of akin to Danis Tanovic's Oscar®-winning *No Man's Land* (2001), which centered on a pair of trapped soldiers from opposing sides of the 1993 war between Bosnia and Herzegovina. While the latter was a seriocomic work of historical fiction and the former is based much more strictly on a true story, each feels in significant ways like a moral construct, a theoretical dilemma generated for a classroom debate.

In fact, a handful of scenes of deliberation and conversation amongst the monks are largely compelling, spotlighting how uncertainty can absolutely coexist alongside faith. But as Roger Ebert pointed out in his March 11, 2011, *Chicago Sun-Times* review, *Of Gods and Men* does not seem to fully engage the fundamental questions which it raises—especially difficult but hugely important political considerations involving a tangled history between France and Algeria.

A couple scenes in which Christian discusses matters with a government official hint at some of this, but the film largely skirts sociopolitical specifics that would lend it a greater context, opting instead for a less opaque, more impressionistic tale of noble forfeit. The problem is that this tack requires an unassailable belief in the might of right and religious service, no matter the conditions—a belief, in short, that not every audience member might share. The opening twenty minutes of the movie, which are somewhat hard to track, is an especially notable offender in this regard, and continually interspersed sequences of Latin hymnal chanting extend far past the point of pious illumination, and eventually start coming across as captured Enigma outtakes, or parodies thereof.

Shot in Morocco, *Of Gods and Men* evinces an undeniable authenticity of place. Costumer Alice Cambournac and production designer Michel Barthélémy work together to craft a muted palette that is symbolically studded with splashes of hopeful color in the wardrobes of the local villagers, who are grateful for the monks' charity and fellowship, and desperate for them to stay. Meanwhile, Beauvois and cinematographer Caroline Champetier do a good job of locating small moments of realism to bolster the movie's lived-in credibility, as with the yawn of a small child during group prayers.

Tucked behind owlish glasses, Wilson gives a quiet, centered performance, at odds with some of the more outlandish genre films—inclusive of *The Matrix* sequels (2003), *Catwoman* (2004) and *Sahara* (2005)—that may mark his most familiar work among American audiences. A tall and typically rather dashing figure, he seems to shrink and reflect inward as Christian, personifying in contrasting fashion the enormous difficulty of the decisions he is often forced to make. The other supporting performances, too, are all dignified and of a piece. It is obvious that everyone was on the same page, and making the film Beauvois wished to make.

In the end, however, *Of Gods and Men* is an incredibly well-crafted film that plays to the innate strengths or emotional connectivity of its source material, but without fully delving into the situational specifics of its characters in a lasting, meaningful way. Foreign film arthouse audiences will no doubt find most reward here, and more generally fans of recent historical drama will also be able to appreciate the movie. Unfortunately, *Of Gods and Men* also illustrates that even compelling source material can render fallible finished cinematic product.

Brent Simon

CREDITS

Christian: Lambert Wilson
Luc: Michael Lonsdale

Christophe: Olivier Rabourdin
Celestin: Philippe Laudenbach
Amedee: Jacques Herlin
Jean-Pierre: Loic Pichon
Michel: Xavier Maly
Paul: Jean-Marie Frin
Bruno: Olivier Perrier
Rabbia: Sabrina Ouazani
Nouredine: Abdelhafid Metalsi
Omar: Abdallah Moundy
The terrorist: Adel Bencherif
Ali: Farid Larbi
Origin: France
Language: Arabic, French
Released: 2010
Production: Pascal Caucheteux, Etienne Comar; Why Not Productions, Armada Films, France 3 Cinema; released by Sony Pictures Classics
Directed by: Xavier Beauvois
Written by: Xavier Beauvois, Etienne Comar
Cinematography by: Caroline Champetier
Sound: Jean-Jacques Ferran
Editing: Marie-Julie Maille
Art Direction: Boris Piot
Costumes: Marielle Robaut
Production Design: Michel Barthelemy
MPAA rating: PG-13
Running time: 122 minutes

REVIEWS

Ebert, Roger. *Chicago Sun-Times*. March 11, 2011.
Honeycutt, Kirk. *Hollywood Reporter*. February 25, 2011.
Lane, Anthony. *New Yorker*. February 28, 2011.
Mintzer, Jordan. *Variety*. February 25, 2011.
Morgenstern, Joe. *Wall Street Journal*. September 11, 2010.
Schenker, Andrew. *Slant Magazine*. September 24, 2010.
Scott, A.O. *New York Times*. February 24, 2011.
Tallerico, Brian. *HollywoodChicago.com*. March 11, 2011.
Turan, Kenneth. *Los Angeles Times*. February 24, 2011.
Williams, Joe. *St. Louis Post-Dispatch*. March 25, 2011.

QUOTES

Christian: "Should it ever befall me, and it could happen today, to be a victim of the terrorism swallowing up all foreigners here, I would like my community, my church, my family, to remember that my life was given to God and to his country."

TRIVIA

This was the official French submission for the Foreign Language Film Award at the 83rd Academy Awards®.

AWARDS

Nomination:

British Acad. 2010: Foreign Film
Ind. Spirit 2011: Foreign Film.

ONE DAY

Twenty years. Two people.
　—Movie tagline

Box Office: $13.8 million

When a lorry runs down Emma Morley (Anne Hathaway) late in *One Day*, it briefly takes the audience's breath away while permanently doing the same to the poor protagonist. It was clearly hoped by those responsible for the film that this decisively-dealt deathblow would hit viewers almost as hard, but, for most, grief did not follow the gasp. The acutely-abrupt nature of the accident, coupled with a disturbingly-protracted shot of the corpse akimbo, were responsible for the impact on those watching, not the ripping-away of a dearly cared-for character. When ill-fated Em is poolside before departing on her bike ride to Kingdom Come, a sign glimpsed behind her reading "Shallow End" can unfortunately be read to indicate where David Nicholls' beloved bestselling story has been situated by his own frustrating adaptation.

The 2009 novel tickled funny bones and yanked at heartstrings as it creatively conveyed the relatable tale of Emma and Dexter Mayhew, supposed soul mates whose individual paths toward happiness and fulfillment repeatedly converge and diverge until a tragically-late matrimonial merging near the blindsidingly-bitter end. Each chapter enabled the tracking of the Brits' annual progress (or often lack thereof) over the course of two decades, taking stock each time the St. Swithin's Day anniversary of their initial connection rolls around. Looking in on—and, more importantly, looking into the minds and hearts of—the characters each year was telling and thus absorbing as the pages turned, but what the film version amounts to is a distancing and even irritating flitting from one depth-deficient snippet to another. Even those who especially enjoyed this cinematic retelling admitted there were times that greater understanding and emotional impact would have resulted if the proceedings had tarried a tad before once again skipping forward like a stone purposefully aimed to skim along the surface of deep waters. More than a few viewers grew downright cross waiting for Emma and Dexter (Jim Sturgess) to finally grow up and fess up so they could synch up, carping about this love's exceedingly slow burn.

Whether or not one's patience had been tried by these true friends, all recognized that they are put forth as an uplifting symbiotic confluence of yin and yang. (The symbol tattooed on Dex's ankle drives home the point.) When the two were virtual strangers graduating from college in 1988, full of youthful expectancy about both the future and an opportunity in the present to get carnally acquainted, they seem to have little in common beyond a shared surprise that their tryst turned out to be so utterly chaste. While Em possesses a low-maintenance, frumpy appearance, Dex is dashingly handsome and has, as it is put in the book, "a knack of looking perpetually posed for a photograph." She lacks self-confidence, while he is breezily devil-may-care. She is from the middle class, whereas he comes from a posh background that has kept money on that lengthy list of things about which he never worries. Emma is straitlaced, sensible, and has a definite point of view, while Dexter is a libertine more likely to have trouble seeing straight on the way to alcohol-induced insensibility. She can have a tart, quippy tongue, while he is usually quite a sweet talker. Emma is the type who conscientiously strives to stay on top of her class work, while Dexter more strenuously pursued being atop fetching classmates. Yet these opposites found themselves attracting in a manner neither had anticipated, durably bonding in a devoted if sometimes discordant special friendship through twenty years of eye-opening life lessons, all of which enabled them to finally recognize (or is it admit?) the true nature of their bond.

So *One Day* starts flipping through its album of cinematic snapshots. The audience sees Dexter encouragingly enthusing that aspiring writer Emma will be "the toast of London" within a year, at which point the film flashes forward to reveal she instead became stuck as a painfully-disillusioned drudge in a Tex-Mex restaurant, aka "the graveyard of ambitions." Eventually, she reclaims enough of her old gumption to leave guacamole behind, once again pressing on toward her dreams to become a teacher and then a successful author living in anything-but-prosaic Paris. In her personal life, Emma settles for rather aesthetically-displeasing Ian (Rafe Spall), a semi-sweet fellow restraint employee and profoundly-uninspired aspiring standup comic. Meanwhile, Dexter achieves celebrity as the host of television shows that descend further and further into cheesiness. In the face of embarrassingly high-profile ignominy, he resorts to increasing amounts of alcohol and drugs to maintain his buoyancy, which is clearly now a front with precious little left behind it. While his career arc is the inverse of Em's, Dex's being cuckolded by his shotgun-wedded wife Sylvie (Romola Garai) parallels her own woefully-unsatisfying, ill-fitting partnership.

Through it all, Dexter and Emma never let go of the often sorely-stretched lifeline that connects them to each other, even when it seems that perhaps they really should. These two who frolic also fight, sometimes look down on each other yet never gaze at anyone else so appreciatively. For each, the other often provides specifically-sought, unique validation, and stabilization. Viewers certainly get that the trials the pair goes through are fashioning them into pieces that will supposedly snap into place for an eventual perfect fit. However, being made to clearly understand something is not the same as being made to intensely feel it or care fervently about it, and most audience members simply watched an incremental, suspense-neutered, lacking march toward inevitability rather than rooted for any particular outcome.

Hathaway may have empathized with her character when the actress was bashed by many as an outrageous, too-unmousy miscast. Nicholls' English countrymen were further aghast that an American was cast to play "our Em." However, she is a capable performer who has previously portrayed more than one duckling on the uglier side who turned into a swan as Emma does before her demise. Hathaway can also do accents, although she unfortunately provides her character with more than one of them during *One Day*. Sturgess also acquits himself adequately, if not remarkably, excelling at being flirty, flip, and enthusiastically frolicsome while not possessing quite enough charismatic pull. His best scene is actually one in which Hathaway's Em is nowhere in sight, shared instead with Patricia Clarkson as Dex's concerned, cancer-ridden mother whom he carries up to bed with a revealing, affecting tenderness.

One Day was a disappointing follow-up to *An Education* for Danish director Lone Scherfig. Made on a budget of $15 million, the film had to struggle toward that figure due to underwhelming reviews. It was at the very end of the eighteenth chapter and with roughly fifty pages left to go that finesse was used by Nicholls to relate Emma accidents, her injuries not immediately revealed as life threatening. Through his prose, readers were able to be privy to thoughts that the bombshell final sentence revealed to be Emma's last. While fans of the book knew what was coming, there was a curious opting here for artless bluntness and some fairly heavy-handed foreshadowing. Emma sure gets clobbered again here, but, as with *One Day* in general, it was actually more powerfully and poignantly presented on the page.

David L. Boxerbaum

CREDITS

Emma: Anne Hathaway
Dexter: Jim Sturgess
Sylvie: Romola Garai
Ian: Rafe Spall

Callum: Tom Mison
Tilly: Jodie Whitaker
Alison: Patricia Clarkson
Marie: Josephine de la Baume
Origin: USA
Language: English
Released: 2011
Production: Nina Jacobson; Color Force, Film 4, Random House Films; released by Focus Features Intl.
Directed by: Lone Scherfig
Written by: David Nicholls
Cinematography by: Benoit Delhomme
Music by: Rachel Portman
Sound: Glenn Freemantle
Music Supervisor: Karen Elliott
Editing: Barney Pilling
Art Direction: Denis Schnegg
Costumes: Odile Dicks-Mireaux
Production Design: Mark Tildesley
MPAA rating: PG-13
Running time: 107 minutes

REVIEWS

Burr, Ty. *Boston Globe*. August 18, 2011.
Chang, Justin. *Variety*. August 17, 2011.
Ebert, Roger. *Chicago Sun-Times*. August 17, 2011.
Grady, Pam. *Boxoffice Magazine*. August 17, 2011.
Honeycutt, Kirk. *Hollywood Reporter*. August 17, 2011.
Hornaday, Ann. *Washington Post*. August 18, 2011.
Lane, Anthony. *New Yorker*. September 12, 2011.
Longworth, Karina. *Village Voice*. August 16, 2011.
Morgenstern, Joe. *Wall Street Journal*. August 18, 2011.
Puig, Claudia. *USA Today*. August 18, 2011.

QUOTES

Emma: "I'll only be a minute. No playing with yourself while I'm gone."

TRIVIA

While on location in Scotland, Anne Hathaway exposed her bottom to Jim Sturgess to set the mood for filming the film's skinny dipping scene.

OUR IDIOT BROTHER
(My Idiot Brother)

Everybody has one.
—Movie tagline

Box Office: $24.8 million

Define "idiot." Is a man with no career goals and an ability to live in the moment an idiot? Is a man who always tells the truth, even if it may get him into trouble, an idiot? Or are his sisters, who have busier lives but no shortage of problems for which they are at least somewhat responsible, actually more idiotic?

These are the questions posed by *Our Idiot Brother*, which has only simple answers in mind but provides plenty of easygoing laughs while getting to them. Paul Rudd stars as Ned, the sort of guy that would be easy to write off after noticing his lackadaisical attitude, casual attire (the guy wears shorts to a business meeting), and that he named his dog after Willie Nelson. Of course, Rudd, one of the world's most likable comedic actors, never underestimates his characters, and he never lets Ned become just an outrageous fool to be laughed at and mocked. Ned may have never had a real job and may willingly sell weed to a cop (Bob Stephenson) once the officer tells Ned that he had a "hard week," but Rudd presents this laid-back wanderer as a generous spirit with a good heart and an interest in marching to no one's beat but his own.

Ned's sisters, on the other hand, see him as an irresponsible nuisance. Miranda (Elizabeth Banks) prefers to focus on her first article for *Vanity Fair* about a person (not just moisturizer), wealthy British socialite Lady Arabella (Janet Montgomery). Natalie (Zooey Deschanel) is preoccupied by pathetic attempts at stand-up comedy, her girlfriend (Rashida Jones), and an artist (Hugh Dancy) that paints Natalie in the nude and suggests that she (and Ned) come with him to a life-coaching program. So, when Ned concludes his eight-month prison sentence—that cop really fooled him good—and finds out that his girlfriend Janet (Kathryn Hahn) no longer wants him as a boyfriend or a roommate on the farm where he lived, Ned follows a short stay with his mom (Shirley Knight) by moving in with his third sister, Liz (Emily Mortimer). Besides being a mother of two, Liz has the sort of relationship with her documentary filmmaker husband Dylan (Steve Coogan) that when she opens up her robe to reveal nothing underneath, Dylan, not at all aroused, simply responds, "Oh my god, what have you done to your vagina?" That is not exactly the intended result of a Brazilian wax.

In this way, *Our Idiot Brother* sets up a story without a plot, merely a group of characters and actors given a chance to interact at the normal speed of life. That allows for amusing detours like Ned's relationship with his parole officer Omar (Sterling K. Brown), who appreciates when Ned thanks him for his guidance but cannot ignore Ned when he admits to getting high again. (Ned likens his sessions with Omar to "free therapy," which is probably why he puts no limits on what he tells the man with the power to send him back to prison.) Ned's delightfully unsuspecting sensibilities are also reinforced when he is on the subway in New York and thinks nothing of handing a wad of cash to a stranger and asking, " Can you hold this?" The stranger looks at Ned in shock but does not steal the money; how many people with even a shred of a conscience would take advantage of someone so trusting? And the film's relaxed, character-driven pace also allows room for convincing scenes such as one in which Ned's three sisters initiate a conversation meant to come from a place of love and support only to have it spiral into an argument, during which Miranda and Natalie accuse Liz of putting no effort into her appearance, Liz condescendingly tells her sisters that they will understand how precarious family can be once they get their lives together, and Natalie is called out for supposedly using sex to drive her self-esteem. In this scene, Banks, Deschanel, and Mortimer excellently portray characters with lots of history between them, which causes conflict in the way that fights actually start between family members in real life.

Not all of *Our Idiot Brother* is so rich. Miranda's friends-and-maybe-more relationship with her neighbor Jeremy (Adam Scott), no matter how appealingly acted, feels uninspired, and the movie too strongly stacks the deck in favor of Ned's open-hearted idealism. There is certainly merit in the message that a busy life is not necessarily a better life, and that there are many different ways to pursue happiness that may or may not involve a steady job and a big house. However, *Our Idiot Brother* mostly lets Ned off the hook for his social blunders. Instead, he is presented as so incredibly likeable that he easily earns the admiration and trust of nearly everyone he meets (including Jeremy, Lady Arabella, and Billy [T.J. Miller], Janet's new boyfriend). On the contrary, Ned's sisters come off as judgmental and naïve about how their own selfishness and/or obliviousness has caused themselves the sort of stress Ned frequently avoids by confronting life from a slower, more giving perspective. As it turns out, the movie is not about Ned learning the error of his ways, but his sisters learning to love their brother and see that he is sometimes right.

So, even if *Our Idiot Brother* moseys to a contrived finale of mostly happy endings, its resolutions mostly feel like karma (despite Ned's contrived declaration to his sisters that it is time for him to move on and support himself, mostly because the movie ultimately needs him to show *some* kind of initiative). This is a movie about a man who believes in giving people the benefit of the doubt, and consequently the film itself favors posi-

tive results for those who do the right thing. Perhaps Ned, a guy who admits that people often think he is "retarded" (a line meant for laughs but instead makes a depressing, offensive statement about public perception) and boasts about winning "Most Cooperative Inmate" in prison, is not the usual icon for such good intentions. Yet the warmth and charm in Rudd's performance and the gently blended comedy and drama in the performances around him turn *Our Idiot Brother* from a film that could have felt silly and irritating into an appealing presence to hang out with for a while. Just like Ned.

Matt Pais

CREDITS

Ned: Paul Rudd
Liz: Emily Mortimer
Miranda: Elizabeth Banks
Natalie: Zooey Deschanel
Ilene: Shirley Knight
Dylan: Steve Coogan
Christian: Hugh Dancy
Cindy: Rashida Jones
Billy: T.J. Miller
Janet: Kathryn Hahn
Jeremy: Adam Scott
Lady Arabella: Janet Montgomery
Lorraine: Julie White
Origin: USA
Language: English
Released: 2011
Production: Anthony Bregman, Peter Saraf, Marc Turtletaub; Big Beach, Likely Story; released by Weinstein Company
Directed by: Jesse Peretz
Written by: Evgenia Peretz, David Schisgall
Cinematography by: Yaron Orbach
Music by: Nathan Larson, Eric Johnson
Sound: Joshua Anderson
Music Supervisor: Susan Jacobs
Editing: Andrew Mondshein, Jacob Craycroft
Art Direction: Michael Ahern
Costumes: Christopher Peterson
Production Design: Inbal Weinberg
MPAA rating: R
Running time: 96 minutes

REVIEWS

Chang, Justin. *Variety.* August 15, 2011.
Ebert, Roger. *Chicago Sun-Times.* August 25, 2011.
Morris, Wesley. *Boston Globe.* August 25, 2011.

Phillips, Michael. *Chicago Tribune*. August 25, 2011.

Pols, Mary. *Time*. August 25, 2011.

Puig, Claudia. *USA Today*. August 26, 2011.

Rabin, Nathan. *AV Club*. August 24, 2011.

Schwarzbaum, Lisa. *Entertainment Weekly*. August 24, 2011.

Scott, A.O. *New York Times*. August 25, 2011.

vkStevens, Dana. *Slate*. August 25, 2011.

QUOTES

Ned: "You know, he's just a little boy. Little boys fight. Doesn't mean he's going to grow up to be a frat-boy rapist."

TRIVIA

Elizabeth Banks and Paul Rudd, who play siblings in this movie, played a couple in *Role Models* and in *Wet Hot American Summer*.

P

PARANORMAL ACTIVITY 3

It runs in the family.
—Movie tagline

Discover how the activity began.
—Movie tagline

Box Office: $104 million

With its third installment (surely not to be the last, due to the almost-guaranteed financial strategy of a miniscule budget and exponential box office returns), the *Paranormal Activity* series falls into the same trap as so many horror franchises before it. Beyond being yet another retread of the same formula of the two previous movies (i.e., "found footage" of a family terrorized by a malevolent demon), *Paranormal Activity 3* continues to bring the series back in time to reveal more, essentially unnecessary details of the back story of its central characters and the cause of how and why—more or less—a demon has latched itself to two women for eighteen years.

Divulging the rationale of the supernatural is commonly the downfall of a horror series, and here, the movie follows the series' female protagonists to 1988, when they are children and first encounter the invisible demonic force that winds up striking fear into and ruining their lives in the future. The exposition of this history was one of the weaker elements of the inferior 2010 sequel, and as the focus of this one (screenwriter Christopher Landon penned both), it ultimately weighs down whatever return to form directors Henry Joost and Ariel Schulman (the directing team behind the

ingenious documentary *Catfish* [2010], making their fiction debut) manage to accomplish.

Whereas *Paranormal Activity 2* incorporated multiple cameras to capture extensive coverage of nearly every inch of the home that served as the setting (it was far too much, eliminating much of the tension and, with the number of cuts and camera selection of the editing, bringing into question the very premise of "found footage" gimmick), Joost and Schulman revert to the more minimalist approach of writer/director Oren Peli's 2009 original. There are only three cameras in play here, and the setup manages to reclaim some of the claustrophobic sensation of the audience being unable to see certain crucial areas.

The man setting up the cameras throughout his house is Dennis (Christopher Nicholas Smith), a freelance wedding videographer who lives with his girlfriend Julie (Lauren Bittner) and her two daughters Katie (Chloe Csengery) and Kristi (Jessica Tyler Brown). In a prologue that establishes the existence and mysterious disappearance of the resulting tapes, Katie Featherston and Sprague Grayden reprise their respective roles as the adult Katie and Kristi. Kristi has begun speaking to an imaginary friend she calls Toby, and Dennis begins to hear strange noises in the house—specifically the girls' upstairs alcove of a bedroom—when no one else is home.

While attempting to make a sex tape, Dennis and Julie are interrupted by an earthquake. In the resulting video, Dennis and his assistant Randy (Dustin Ingram) notice that the dust falling from the ceiling lands to form the outline of an otherwise invisible shape. To help him grasp a better understanding of what might be happening in the house, Dennis places cameras in his and Julie's bedroom and the girls' room; he rigs a third to an oscillating fan so that it pans back and forth between the kitchen and the living room.

The implementation of the premise remains the same as the previous movies. The cameras capture strange happenings in the house, as the footage fast-forwards from the house's occupants sleeping to a noise that startles someone out of bed. Kristi begins talking to Toby, who lives in a crawlspace that is conveniently off-camera, in the middle of night. Dennis checks the videotapes the next day of each occurrence, as Randy offers books from the library on demonology for his partner to research. Dennis insists that he cannot tell Julie about the incidents for fear that she might "freak out," though his biggest worry seems to be that she will stop him from carrying on his documentation. Dennis, like so many other protagonists in these "found footage" thrillers, lugs his camera around during even the most unlikely scenarios, and the oddity of that behavior is most notable during the movie's haunted-house style climax.

Joost, Schulman, and Landon take few chances with the material and instead continue to stage a series of parlor tricks. Julie walks out of the kitchen for a moment only to return to discover that everything—from small items to furniture—has disappeared; it soon drops from the ceiling. A babysitter (Johanna Braddy) mocks the idea of a ghost by wearing a sheet over herself when Katie asks for a bedtime story, and as she sits reading in the kitchen, a form underneath a sheet appears and disappears, leaving the sheet behind. This gag and a few others (e.g., the demon tormenting Randy and Katie when they attempt to play "Bloody Mary" and the appearance of a symbol on a child's toy during one nighttime episode) suggest that the demon has a sense of humor.

Paranormal Activity 3 is perhaps the most technically proficient movie in the series, yet it is also the weakest one. Familiarity with the material and a mistaken belief that it is the underlying mythology that is most important are major components of its overall deficiency, but the major fault is a basic one: The payoffs do not match the tension of the setups. The movie is one anticlimax after another.

Mark Dujsik

CREDITS

Dennis: Christopher Nicholas Smith
Katie: Katie Featherston
Young Kristi: Jessica Tyler Brown

Kristi: Sprague Grayden
Origin: USA
Language: English
Released: 2011
Production: Jason Blum, Oren Peli, Steven Schneider; Blumhouse Productions, Paramount Pictures; released by Paramount Pictures
Directed by: Lauren Bittner, Chloe Csengery, Oren Peli
Written by: Oren Peli
Cinematography by: Magdalena Gorka
Editing: Gregory Plotkin
Sound: Peter Brown
Costumes: Leah Butler
Production Design: Jennifer Spence
MPAA rating: R
Running time: 84 minutes

REVIEWS

Berardinelli, James. *ReelViews*. October 20, 2011.
Ebert, Roger. *Chicago Sun-Times*. October 19, 2011.
Kenny, Glenn. *MSN Movies*. October 19, 2011.
Kohn, Eric. *IndieWIRE*. September 29, 2011.
Moore, Roger. *Orlando Sentinel*. October 19, 2011.
Orndorf, Brian. *Blu-ray.com*. October 21, 2011.
Putman, Dustin. *DustinPutman.com*. October 20, 2011.
Schager, Nick. *Slant Magazine*. October 22, 2011.
Sobczynski, Peter. *EFilmCritic.com*. October 22, 2011.
Vaux, Rob. *Mania.com*. October 20, 2011.

TRIVIA

Most of the scenes in the trailers do not appear in the final cut of the movie, which angered many fans of the series.

PARIAH

Who do you become when you can't be yourself?
    —Movie tagline

It is an old story, that of the outcast teenager with a secret that he/she will eventually have to tell. It is the stuff of many novels, autobiographies, poems, songs, plays, mainstream and independent films. It is a tried-and-true formula and a universal rite of passage for many confused, scared and brave individuals. The secret is often that of sexual orientation. Despite the current age of media in which gay characters are seen and accepted in many mainstream movies and television shows, there remains deep seeded fear in many parents that their children will be gay. *Pariah* is about that fear and about that individual who has to see if there is any hope of reconciliation beyond that fear. Most likely, there is not, but the truth must come out sooner or later and everyone directly involved with the heroine of this tale will have to make a choice whether or not to accept it.

The character is Alike (Adepero Oduye), a teenager in Brooklyn who gets nearly perfect grades in high school and who has caught the eye of her poetry teacher. She could easily graduate early and start college in the spring if she wanted to. At night, she goes out to a lesbian nightclub with her friend Laura (Pernell Walker), who has yet to get her GED. When Alike (or Li) is at the club, she dresses freely in tomboy clothes. On her way home, she changes her shirts and puts on earrings to give off more of a feminine exterior. When she comes home after midnight and her mother (Kim Wayans) asks where she has been, she replies "the movies." It is not uncommon for Alike to come home to a new blouse purchased by her mother that bears no resemblance to Alike's fashion sense or personality.

Alike is in no real hurry, it seems, to get into a deep relationship with anyone. She collects many phone numbers while in the nightclub, but never calls any of them. She is a virgin and somewhat embarrassed by it, as most teenagers would be. At home, Alike's family life is a mixed bag of warmth and tension. Her father (Charles Parnell) often works late as a cop and the few times he is home, he can sometimes work in a little sarcastic humor at the dinner table, but is otherwise a no-nonsense individual. Her mother works as a clerk at a medical clinic and insists that Alike and her little sister Sharonda (Sahra Mellesse) attend church every Sunday morning. Both parents are in a state of denial over Alike's secretive sexual orientation.

After one of the church services, Alike finds herself fixed up, in a way, with a daughter of one of her mother's friends. Fearful that Alike does not have a school-based social life, her mother does what she can to keep Alike from hanging out with Laura. Alike's new friend Bina (Aasha Davis) is someone from school, whom Alike resents at first. She reluctantly forges ahead with the friendship anyway just so that her mother does not get suspicious. Much to Alike's surprise, the friendship is worth the effort and soon becomes something much deeper.

Pariah might sound like a predictable sort of hard-edged indie film with a no-name cast and an axe to grind, and in a way it is, but it also comes full of surprises and subtleties that make it a step above typical indie fare. The performances across the board are engaging and believable. Oduye is a real find as Alike. She conveys not only the tough exterior necessary for this character to navigate this kind of uneasy terrain, but also a warmth and vulnerability necessary to win over the film's audience. Charles Parnell and Kim Wayans as the parents are also wisely not made out to be hateful caricatures, but as rigid individuals whose lives have just been turned upside down and who have almost as hard a time navigating this new reality as their daughter.

The film was written and directed by Dee Rees and is based on a short film of the same name, which features many of the same cast members. The story clearly comes from a personal place and is infused with an authenticity that is often strived for in indie cinema, but not always easily achieved. Perhaps having some practice at making the short film helped, but Rees is clearly a director with a good instinct for achieving realism. The scenes with the parents are particularly strong. Rather than making them into one-sided, one-dimensional objects for the audience's scorn, Rees creates a pair of parents who are as much at odds with each other as they are with what is happening with their daughter. The father knows that something is up and when the inevitable happens, he is more fearful about his wife's reaction and actions that arise from it than anything else.

Cinematographer Bradford Young is not content with simply giving *Pariah* a "gritty" look to go with its Brooklyn landscape, but instead pulsates the frames with deep reds and blues while never really calling attention to it. It is not a stylistic film, but a well-made film with subtle stylistic flourishes. Likewise, with the screenplay, *Pariah* has the courage to actually arrive somewhere, whereas too many indie films these days appear to want to embrace the idea of the "ambiguous ending." *Pariah* could have easily fallen into the same trap, but Rees smartly takes the audience on her personal journey and is not about to leave them hanging or to fill in the blanks themselves.

Collin Souter

CREDITS

Alike: Adepero Oduye
Laura: Pernell Walker
Bina: Aasha Davis
Audrey: Kim Wayans
Arthur: Charles Parnell
Sharonda: Sahra Mellesse
Mack: Raymond Anthony Thomas
Candace: Shamika Cotton
Origin: USA
Language: English
Released: 2011
Production: Nekisa Cooper; Northstar Pictures, Aid + Abet, MBK Entertainment; released by Focus Features Intl.
Directed by: Dee Rees
Written by: Dee Rees
Cinematography by: Bradford Young

Sound: Jon Reyes
Editing: Mako Kamitsuna
Art Direction: Sarah White
Costumes: Eniola Dawodu
Production Design: Inbal Weinberg
MPAA rating: R
Running time: 86 minutes

REVIEWS

Biancolli, Amy. *San Francisco Chronicle*. December 28, 2011.
Brody, Richard. *New Yorker*. December 26, 2011.
Fear, David. *Time Out New York*. December 20, 2011.
Holden, Stephen. *New York Times*. December 27, 2011.
Lumenick, Lou. *New York Post*. December 28, 2011.
Neumaier, Joe. *New York Daily News*. December 29, 2011.
Pols, Mary F. *TIME Magazine*. December 28, 2011.
Sharkey, Lisa. *Los Angeles Times*. December 28, 2011.
Snider, Eric D. *Cinematical.com* February 4, 2011.
Whitty, Stephen. *Newark Star-Ledger*. December 28, 2011.

QUOTES

Mika: "Yeah I like girls. But I love boys."

AWARDS

Nomination:
Ind. Spirit 2012: Actress (Oduye).

PASSION PLAY

Between Heaven and Hell is fear.
—Movie tagline

Love is stronger than death.
—Movie tagline

The directorial debut of screenwriter and producer Mitch Glazer, *Passion Play* is a film that, on the surface, should have a certain cult/indie cineaste appeal, given its out-there premise and intriguing cast: Mickey Rourke, Bill Murray, Megan Fox and Rhys Ifans. In reality, though, nothing about this misguided guys-and-doll drama merits much attention. At once self-consciously eccentric and entirely self-serious, *Passion Play* attempts to peddle a story of redemption and trade in meaningful metaphor, but instead comes across as merely grandiloquent, silly, and wearying. After debuting to negative notices at the 2010 Toronto Film Festival, the movie received a courtesy May theatrical release by distributor Image Entertainment in limited markets, with a quiet home video debut shortly thereafter. All in all, it is a case of deserved marketplace disregard.

Wringing his re-ascendant, Oscar®-nominated lead turn in *The Wrestler* (2008) for all its worth, Rourke stars as washed-up jazz musician and recovering heroin addict Nate Poole, who finds himself on the wrong side of a grudge and debt with gangster Happy Shannon (Murray). After escaping Happy's ordered hit in a bizarre turn of luck, Nate flees across the desert and stumbles across a strange traveling circus run by Sam (Ifans). The outfit's star freak attraction is Lily (Fox), a pretty but sad young girl who has real, honest-to-goodness wings sprouting from her back, yet insists she is no angel. Nate is not so sure, and instantly smitten.

Like addicts almost wordlessly finding one another in a crowded bar, Lily and Nate are drawn together by their damaged pasts. Lily is convinced Sam will give chase if she leaves, but she intercedes when Sam tries to hurt Nate, and so the pair strike out together. With Happy's minions closing in, Nate at first tries to make a bargain that will save his life. In Lily, though, Happy sees only dollar signs. Chastened, Nate tries to break Lily free from Happy's restrictive custody.

Outwardly, *Passion Play* has the appearance of something darkly mysterious, quirky and fun, but in reality it is leaden and gloomy. The characters do not so much react to one another and exist in the same plane as they do just make statements and deliver occasional absolutes. The screenplay is itself a longtime passion project—reportedly a bottom-drawer spec effort dating back to the 1980s, and held onto by Glazer to avoid sullying it with creative compromise foisted upon it by the Hollywood studio system. Ergo, while Glazer (married to Kelly Lynch, who also appears here in a small role) amply conveys a sense of his own personal investment in the material, he unfortunately does not develop any of his characters in interesting ways. They remain the grungy loser, the mobster and the girl, and that is all.

Additionally, beyond its own assured self-seriousness, *Passion Play* never locates a convincing tone. While there are questions to be answered, it is not a mystery, per se, and Rourke and Fox are not the sort whose chemistry sparks feelings of being swept up in a grand romance. Instead, the film labors to convince an audience of its artfulness, thus draining any wild, just-go-with-it energy that the premise could conceivably otherwise enjoy. As it winds its way inexorably toward the most clichéd ending possible, there is neither any otherworldly comedy nor the comparable, noir-gone-mad insanity of something like *Wild at Heart* (1990), which has a similar lovers-on-the-lam conceit.

In fact, *Passion Play*'s most fascinating and amusing moments consist almost entirely of sub-textual entertainment. The interplay between Happy and Nate seems to mirror the detached bemusement one might think, off-screen, Murray would hold for Rourke. And when they first meet, Lily says to Nate, "You were famous, and handsome—what happened?," summoning memories of Rourke's old, first-go-round heyday.

The varying pitches of the movie's performances signal a director not particularly well versed in working with actors. If Murray seems bored, Ifans is amped up, almost like he is playing an action movie villain. Rourke, meanwhile, is somewhere in between—heavy on the brooding, but also given to big flashes of emotionalism. Somewhat interestingly and perhaps surprisingly, the best performance might well belong to Fox. Whether the result of trading down in scale from working with Michael Bay, tapping into the correlative constraints of being perceived as a sex bomb starlet, or just sheer dumb luck, with her rather melancholic turn Fox actually finds and communicates hidden reserves of pain within Lily that the script never really attempts to more deeply elucidate.

On a technical level, *Passion Play* gives evidence of at least a stab at concerted moodiness—and given the ham-fisted directness of some of its dialogue of confrontation, one feels it could benefit from long passages of silence, to play up its atmosphere and inject more of a sense of ambiguity. The overarching problem is one of means and the experience or ability to pull off such a design, as *Passion Play* is riddled with various production shortcomings and editorial glitches. Glazer and cinematographer Christopher Doyle frequently deal in close-ups in an attempt to encourage subjective identification, but the trade-off is too-tight compositions which indulge Rourke in some terrible mock trumpet-playing. In another scene, night inexplicably turns to day—the obvious result of shoddy neophyte filmmaking which, in the editing bay, painted Glazer into a corner from which he could not escape. *Passion Play*'s narrative pitfalls and traps, meanwhile, were baited a long time ago.

Brent Simon

CREDITS

Nate Poole: Mickey Rourke
Lily the Bird Girl: Megan Fox
Happy Shannon: Bill Murray
Harriet: Kelly Lynch
Sam: Rhys Ifans
Origin: USA
Language: English
Released: 2010
Production: Daniel Dubiecki, Megan Ellison; Annapurna Prod., Coridel Prods.; released by Image Entertainment

Directed by: Mitch Glazer
Written by: Mitch Glazer
Cinematography by: Christopher Doyle
Music by: Dickon Hinchliffe
Sound: Tim Chau
Editing: Billy Weber
Art Direction: Gustav Alsina
Costumes: Lisa Jensen
Production Design: Waldemar Kalinowski
MPAA rating: R
Running time: 92 minutes

REVIEWS

Anderson, John. *Variety*. September 16, 2010.
Bennett, Ray. *Hollywood Reporter*. September 13, 2010.
Gleiberman, Owen. *Entertainment Weekly*. May 11, 2011.
Holden, Stephen. *New York Times*. May 6, 2011.
Morgenstern, Joe. *Wall Street Journal*. May 5, 2011.
O'Hehir, Andrew. *Salon.com*. May 8, 2011.
Rothkopf, Joshua. *Time Out New York*. May 3, 2011.
Smith, Kyle. *New York Post*. May 6, 2011.
Tallerico, Brian. *HollywoodChicago.com*. May 6, 2011.
Whitty, Stephen. *Newark Star-Ledger*. May 6, 2011.

TRIVIA

Toby Kebbell was originally cast as Happy Shannon but dropped out and Bill Murray came on to replace him.

PAUL

> There were many sights they planned to see. This
> was not one of them.
> —Movie tagline
>
> Who's up for a close encounter?
> —Movie tagline
>
> Fugitive, celebrity, slacker, joker, alien.
> —Movie tagline
>
> Only girls phone home.
> —Movie tagline

Box Office: $37.4 million

The frame of the road trip movie is really a vehicle for the writers of *Paul* to spew forth a series of references to popular culture. As unfair as it might be to the movie, it is nearly impossible to view *Paul* outside of the context of *Shaun of the Dead* (2004) and *Hot Fuzz* (2007). All three films star Simon Pegg and Nick Frost as outsiders who perfectly understand each other while some form of chaos breaks out around them, and Pegg serves as a co-screenwriter for the trio of movies. (This time, Frost is the second writer, while in the other two, Edgar Wright co-wrote and directed). The key difference is that while the previous efforts managed to find a perfect harmony of jovial and sincere homage, *Paul* comes across as an extended in-joke for the genre conscious (making the comparison even more unjust for the earlier films).

After a prologue set in Wyoming in 1947 in which a young girl (Mia Stallard) witnesses a UFO crash into her pet dog (the glowing light under the doorway to her home echoes *Close Encounters of the Third Kind* [1977], the first of many callbacks to that film), the story moves to present-day San Diego, as Graeme Willy (Pegg) and Clive Gollings (Frost), best friends and partners in graphic novel development (Graeme illustrates and Clive writes), approach the Mecca of geek culture: San Diego's Comic-Con. The event brings with it a tone of polite self-ridicule from the start, as when the two chuckle in mockery at a collection of people dressed as Orcs before they themselves partake with cheerful abandon in multiple video game previews, comic book signings, and tables selling equally nerdy costume pieces.

The idea is that Graeme and Clive are more skeptical of the fantasy element of the costumes, as opposed to the wearing of costumes on its own, since they are quite taken by the multiple women attired in metallic bikinis that echo the iconic outfit from *Star Wars: Episode VI—Return of the Jedi.* (Clive is drawn to a woman in an Ewok costume from the same film, an attraction that is explained later by his admission that his last sexual encounter was with a woman in similar dress). When tourists stumble across them recreating a scene from the television series *Star Trek,* they scurry away in shame.

The duo's plan is to rent an RV and travel to famous UFO hotspots across the western United States, from Area 51 in Nevada to Roswell, New Mexico. At a stop at the "black mailbox," a spot outside of a mysterious military base where UFO seekers gather, Graeme and Clive witness a car flip off the highway, and upon investigating the crash, find themselves face to face with Paul (voiced by Seth Rogen), the same extraterrestrial whose craft fell on the dog in the opening scene. He is a generic-looking alien (a big head about half the height of his short body with a dull green hue), though, in one of the movie's more inspired comic thoughts, Paul explains the familiarity of his appearance is part of a massive conspiracy by the government to use popular culture—such as some of Graeme and Clive's beloved comic books and movies—to gradually acclimatize people to his image in case anyone were ever to encounter him. The special effects to create Paul are seamless, though his character is ultimately as standard as his appearance.

Paul is sarcastic, smokes (tobacco and military-grade marijuana), and is laid-back; his powers include healing (which he passes on as an idea to Steven Spielberg [making a vocal cameo] to use for his alien in *E.T.: The Extra-Terrestrial* [1982] while being locked up in an Army warehouse identical to the one in Spielberg's own *Raiders of the Lost Ark* and *Indiana Jones and the Kingdom of the Crystal Skull* [2008]), camouflage (like the creature in *Predator* [1987]), and passing on information through telepathy. He uses the last to convert a fundamentalist Christian named Ruth Buggs (Kristen Wiig), whom the trio must take with them after Paul reveals himself to her to win an argument about evolution, into a rather tame hedonist. Ruth is the movie's funniest character on a conceptual level, and even though Pegg and Frost's script provides little for her to do beyond awkward, failed attempts at cursing, Wiig's enthusiastic delivery makes the character work better than it should.

Her father (John Carroll Lynch), whose weapons are a shotgun and a Bible, is one of many characters on the trail of Paul and his new human friends. Three agents from an unnamed government agency are the key pursuers. Zoil (Jason Bateman) takes on the aid of Haggard (Bill Hader) and O'Reilly (Joe Lo Truglio), a pair of incompetent rookies. Their actions veer into broad, Three Stooges-like physical comedy quickly, though Bateman's deadpan delivery gives the gags some grounding. Their boss is known only as "The Big Guy," and, since she is played by Sigourney Weaver, it is a foregone conclusion that someone will quote her character's defiant, climactic line from *Aliens* (1986). The only questions are who will say it and when.

The chase and blunt homages of *Paul* gradually reach a level of monotony as the climax once again culls from *E.T.* and *Close Encounters* with the battle to earn a return trip home for Paul taking place at Devils Tower. Once they have been established, the movie's plot and joke structures take on a sense of inevitability, and director Greg Mottola's constantly ironic tone does not aid in making the stream of allusions seem anything less than cynical pandering.

Mark Dujsik

CREDITS

Graeme Willy: Simon Pegg
Clive Gollings: Nick Frost
Special Agent Lorenzo Zoil: Jason Bateman
Ruth Buggs: Kristen Wiig
Haggard: Bill Hader
Pat Stevens: Jane Lynch
Adam Shadowchild: Jeffrey Tambor

Moses Buggs: John Lynch
The Big Guy: Sigourney Weaver
Tara Walton: Blythe Danner
Gus: David Koechner
Jake: Jesse Plemons
Young Tara: Mia Stallard
O'Reilly: Joe Lo Truglio
Paul: Seth Rogen (Voice)
Origin: USA, United Kingdom
Language: English
Released: 2011
Production: Nira Park, Tim Bevan, Eric Fellner; Working Title, Big Talk Productions, Relativity Media; released by Universal Pictures
Directed by: Greg Mottola
Written by: Simon Pegg, Nick Frost
Cinematography by: Lawrence Sher
Music by: David Arnold
Sound: Peter Kurland
Music Supervisor: Nick Angel
Editing: Chris Dickens
Art Direction: Richard Fojo
Costumes: Nancy Steiner
Production Design: Jefferson Sage
MPAA rating: R
Running time: 104 minutes

REVIEWS

Corliss, Richard. *Time.* March 17, 2011.
Dargis, Manohla. *New York Times.* March 17, 2011.
Ebert, Roger. *Chicago Sun-Times.* March 16, 2011.
Levy, Shawn. *Oregonian.* March 17, 2011.
Morris, Wesley. *Boston Globe.* March 18, 2011.
O'Hehir, Andrew. *Salon.com.* March 17, 2011.
O'Sullivan, Michael. *Washington Post.* March 18, 2011.
Phillips, Michael. *Chicago Tribune.* March 17, 2011.
Vaux, Rob. *Mania.com.* March 18, 2011.
Wilonsky, Robert. *Village Voice.* March 16, 2011.

QUOTES

Clive Gollings: "Agent Mulder was right!"
Paul: "Agent Mulder was my idea!"

TRIVIA

Bill Hader was originally cast in the role of Paul, but producers felt that Seth Rogen better embodied the physical antithesis of the character and went with him instead.

PEARL JAM TWENTY

As much as it chronicles the remarkable staying power of one of the most notable rock bands of the last two decades, the incredible rock documentary *Pearl Jam Twenty* also illustrates the close connection its award-winning director had with the band and the music scene in Seattle. The best documentaries are often personal stories and while this tribute to the band who wrote "Alive," "Jeremy," and "Black" could have easily come off as an extended episode of VH1's *Behind the Music,* it is the commitment of Cameron Crowe to the material that helps to truly elevate it. With amazing archival material expertly edited together by someone who truly knows the band along with engaging, revealing interviews with everyone in Pearl Jam and many inspired by it, *Pearl Jam Twenty* aspires for more than a mere fan piece. It is such an accomplished piece of filmmaking it could easily convert those unfamiliar with the band altogether. In other words, it even works for those living under a rock.

The director of *Jerry Maguire* (1996), *Almost Famous* (2000), and *We Bought a Zoo* (2011) moved to Seattle at just the right time, tapping into the music scene that was just then blossoming in the city but was about to take over the international rock world. Some of the earliest archival material in *Pearl Jam Twenty* features footage that includes Crowe himself or was shot by the director. Crowe, always a music fan, became struck by what arguably separated this scene from the others around the country—an honest sense of community between the men who would soon become household names like Chris Cornell of Soundgarden, Kurt Cobain of Nirvana, and Andy Wood of Mother Love Bone. That final young man never lived up to his potential, dying way too young, just as he was on the verge of superstardom. The resulting dissolution of Mother Love Bone sent two of its members—Stone Gossard and Jeff Ament—seeking a new lead singer. A demo track of lyric-less music was sent and a troubled kid named Eddie Vedder sent back what would become "Footsteps" (and, in the film's notable fashion, that first demo tape is actually included in the film). Pearl Jam was born.

That first demo, black-and-white footage of the second time that Pearl Jam ever played on a stage, a haunting clip of Vedder and Cobain dancing backstage at the MTV Video Music Awards—rarely has a documentary assembled more notable archival footage. It is accompanied by reflections on the history of the band by not just its own members but other contemporaries (mostly Cornell, an incredibly well-spoken artist who perfectly gets what Crowe is going for as an interviewer. He makes a great subject). How did a bunch of kids playing guitar in their basement go to headlining Lollapalooza few years later and riding the wave of grunge, which would undeniably change the entire music landscape in the early '90s?

While the film features several stellar performances, Crowe has higher aspirations than mere concert film. He often uses the band's music as commentary, drawing connections between Vedder's lyrics and life. Instead of merely telling the story chronologically, he often bounces back and forth, weaving their entire career into one piece that transcends pure rock and roll. For example, a current performance of "Release" could be used to talk about the importance of the songwriting process to a young Vedder. Despite singing it for twenty years, the song still has resonance for the lead singer and will always mean more than just another track on a set list. That is why the band has survived and even thrived outside of the spotlight of the early days of grunge—by not losing sight of what mattered to them: expression.

Pearl Jam Twenty is a long rock documentary that somehow still feels a bit truncated in the second half of the band's career. The last ten years, as the band settled into a groove outside of Billboard appearances and Ticketmaster controversies, are somewhat skipped over, probably due to the fact that Crowe himself probably fell out of the music scene compared to where he was during the band's first ten years (even making a film with them, 1992's *Singles*). But it is a minor complaint for a major film. When Cameron Crowe got to Seattle twenty years ago, he was smart enough to see what was going on around him and not just watch it but actually help propel it into the spotlight. In much the same way Martin Scorsese's passion comes through in his music films (*The Last Waltz* [1978], *Shine a Light* [2008]) and Jonathan Demme feels a close tie to his subjects in his best non-fiction work (*Stop Making Sense* [1984], *Neil Young: Heart of Gold* [2006]), Cameron Crowe becomes a part of this love letter to his favorite band and makes the case they should be everyone's favorite in the process.

Brian Tallerico

CREDITS

Himself: Cameron Crowe
Himself: Edward Vedder
Himself: Stone Gossart
Himself: Jeff Ament
Himself: Matt Cameron
Himself: Mike McCready
Himself: Chris Cornell
Origin: USA
Language: English
Released: 2011
Production: Cameron Crowe, Morgan Neville, Kelly Curtis, Andy Fischer, Barbara Mcdonough; Tremolo Prods., Vinyl Films; released by Public Broadcasting Service
Directed by: Cameron Crowe

Written by: Cameron Crowe
Cinematography by: Nicola Marsh
Music by: Pearl Jam
Editing: Chris Perkel, Kevin Klauber
Sound: Eric R. Fischer, Kevin Klauber, Chris Perkel
MPAA rating: Unrated
Running time: 109 minutes

REVIEWS

Dixon, Guy. *Globe and Mail.* September 22, 2011.
Linden, Sheri. *New York Times.* September 22, 2011.
Murray, Noel. *AV Club.* September 21, 2011.
Rea, Steven. *Philadelphia Inquirer.* September 22, 2011.
Rose, Joseph. *Portland Oregonian.* September 20, 2011.
Rothkopf, Joshua. *Time Out New York.* September 20, 2011.
Schager, Nick. *Slant Magazine.* September 20, 2011.
Smith, Kyle. *New York Post.* September 23, 2011.
Stevens, Dana. *Slate.* September 24, 2011.
Webster, Andy. *New York Times.* September 22, 2011.

TRIVIA

When asked how he felt about the film, bassist Jeff Ament claimed he felt uncomfortable with how often he used profanity on camera.

THE PEOPLE VS. GEORGE LUCAS

Any objections?
    —Movie tagline

The title of Alexander O. Philippe's documentary is one of the most misleading of the year. It gives the impression that the purpose of the film is antagonistic, presenting the case against one of cinema's most influential filmmakers. While Philippe certainly set out to chronicle the tumultuous relationship that has formed since George Lucas began updating his most beloved films and directing the prequels that even diehards thought would probably never get made, he does so from the perspective of someone who is clearly a fan of the universe that this filmmaker created. It is not a "hatchet job" that many people might assume from the title. Instead, it is an affectionate love letter to the people who have built their lives around *Star Wars* (1977) and the machine of films, toys, games, conventions, costumes, TV specials, and world views that followed. Philippe wisely realizes and portrays the fact that it is the love of this series that makes perceived artistic slights and the general ego of Mr. Lucas harder to take. It is a clever, fun documentary of the type that perfectly captures the sensitivity that comes when people love a film series so much that they consider it their own.

The structure of *The People vs. George Lucas* is a clever one in that Philippe turns much of it over to the allegedly-aggrieved fan base, assembling interviews with fan-submitted contributions sent in via the internet while the movie as being made. The first act of the film is a relatively straightforward adoration piece about the first three films—*Star Wars: Episode IV—A New Hope, Star Wars: Episode V—The Empire Strikes Back* (1980), and *Star Wars: Episode VI—Return of the Jedi* (1983)—and the incredible influence they had not just on the form but on the very concept of fandom. People did not just love these movies, they took to them like people take to religion, memorizing the lines, collecting the toys, and turning the concept of The Force into a way to live their lives. It is the fact that people became so immersed in the original "Holy Trilogy" that would make what happened to the franchise later such a hot button, divisive topic for so many people. Many directors would have leapt right into the meet of the "vs" part of their title but the main reason that Philippe's film works as well as it does is because of how lovingly he sets up the connections that fans felt had been betrayed.

It starts with the Special Editions, the re-releases of the first three films with new special effects and even some significant alterations to the storytelling. Ask any movie fan over twenty-five if Greedo shot first and watch them start to twitch. The most notorious bit of character revision in history completely changes the set-up of one of the most beloved icons in the history of film. Han Solo was an anti-hero, the kind of guy who would shoot someone who he felt might do him harm, even if that someone did NOT shoot first. The decision to go back and put an awkward version of Jabba the Hutt in the first film was misguided at best but the decision to change the set-up of Han Solo felt like actual betrayal of the entire series. People started to doubt everything they thought about George Lucas and their favorite movies. And it was not going to get any easier with the prequels (*Star Wars: Episode I—The Phantom Menace* [1999], *Star Wars: Episode II—Attack of the Clones* [2002], *Star Wars: Episode III—Revenge of the Sith* [2005]). Philippe goes through every bit of evidence in his titular case from the refusal to make the original films accessible to fans to the prequels and the realization that Mr. Lucas, especially through the character of Jar Jar Binks, was making movies for kids and not his adult fans.

One should not write off this film as purely about a film about artistic disagreements between a filmmaker and his fans as there is a much more interesting key question at the foundation of *The People vs. George Lucas*: Does the public have the rights to the materials that have defined its culture? Is Lucas doing something wrong by not recognizing that changing and rewriting the history of his films is also rewriting the history of his fans? Philippe presents both sides with interesting interview subjects like Neil Gaiman making the case that, since Lucas created it, he has every right to do with it what he will. And the filmmaker wisely points out that, despite the many message boards that exist purely because people needed a place to vent about Jar Jar Binks, the prequels were massive hits worldwide. The scariest thing for true fans of the original series is probably this fact: Their kids are going to love Jar Jar Binks.

Brian Tallerico

CREDITS

Origin: USA

Language: English

Released: 2010

Production: Alexandre O. Philippe, Vanessa Philippe, Kerry Deignan Roy, Robert Muratore, Anna Higgs; Quark Pictures, Exhibit A Pictures; released by Wrekin Hill Entertainment

Directed by: Alexandre O. Philippe

Written by: Alexandre O. Philippe

Cinematography by: Robert Muratore

Music by: Jon Hegel

Sound: Robert Muratore, Philip Lloyd Hegel

Editing: Chad Herschberger

MPAA rating: Unrated

Running time: 97 minutes

REVIEWS

Cline, Rich. *Shadows of the Wall.* May 26, 2011.

Fear, David. *Time Out New York.* May 4, 2011.

Goldstein, Gary. *Los Angeles Times.* May 14, 2011.

Hale, Mike. *New York Times.* May 5, 2011.

Jones, J.R. *Chicago Reader.* May 27, 2011.

Keizer, Mark. *Boxoffice Magazine.* May 9, 2011.

Kennedy, Lisa. *Denver Post.* June 17, 2011.

Longworth, Karina. *Village Voice.* May 4, 2011.

Neumaier, Joe. *New York Daily News.* May 6, 2011.

Smith, Kyle. *New York Post.* May 6, 2011.

QUOTES

Jay Sylvester: "George Lucas may be the brainchild behind Star Wars; he may have come up with the story and a lot of the characters, but everyone who participated in making those films had some type of creative input. I mean they won an Oscar® for best special effects. Some of those effects are stripped out and replaced with CGI enhancements, if you wanna call them that. I think that that's really disrespectful to the people who worked on those models and did those shots."

The Hot Docs DVD was released on September 13, 2011, the same week the Star Wars trilogies were released on Blu-ray. Although additional changes were made to the films, this documentary explores the previous changes made to the original trilogy.

THE PERFECT HOST

Dinner parties are a dying art.
—Movie tagline

Make sure he doesn't serve you your last supper.
—Movie tagline

The thriller genre has a long history of cat-and-mouse games in which the filmmaker reveals that the mouse has some claws of its own but even within that niche subgenre, *The Perfect Host* stands out as a unique entry. Director Nick Tomnay guides Clayne Crawford and David Hyde Pierce to stellar performances, elevating the piece above some of the significant tonal inconsistencies within its screenplay. Like many of these films, one quickly realizes that watching a cat catch a mouse is no fun at all and that the rodent must therefore turn the tables. Once that obvious revelation comes to the surface, *The Perfect Host* does not have many places to go and gets a bit repetitive and even slightly annoying before its final act. Forcing a character into the world of a madman presents a tricky line for a filmmaker since viewers must go along on the journey and this nut job is particularly grating. However, Pierce and Crawford offer enough character quirks to keep it engaging until near the end of the party.

John Taylor (Crawford) is injured and on the run. He has clearly just committed a crime, the details of which will become clear through flashback and investigation on the part of Detectives Morton (Nathaniel Parker) and Valdez (Joseph Will). The urgent fact is that John needs to stop the bleeding and get away from the convenience stores blaring his image as a wanted man. After one failed attempt at sanctuary, he stumbles to the doorstep of Warwick Wilson (Pierce), grabbing a postcard and using it to pretend to be an acquaintance of Wilson's friend Julia in Australia. While Taylor at first seems in total control of the situation, the radio soon reveals that he is a fugitive and it appears that Wilson will be taken hostage. It is hard to take a crazy man hostage. Since his arrival, Wilson has been telling Taylor that he is hosting a party that evening. He is but there will be no other guests. As Taylor soon learns after he is drugged and tied up, he will be the only real person at the party even if Wilson will be dancing, partying, flirting, fighting, and even having graphic sex with the people in his head.

Watching Wilson dance with imaginary friends to "Car Wash" is more annoying than tension inducing. Clearly, Wilson is a very special kind of crazy, as he has imaginary party conversations with people who are not there and shows Taylor a series of photographs of a victim and a home movie of him brutally slicing his own chest with a knife. As Wilson's insanity gets ratcheted up, Tomnay makes a crucial mistake of releasing the tension by taking viewers into flashbacks that essentially make Taylor a noble criminal. Why feel the need to make the lead more likable? Were writers Tomnay and Krishna Jones actually concerned that people might root for Warwick to mutilate his houseguest if he was just an actual bad guy? The decision to avoid what could have grown theatrical with two men in an L.A. apartment may have seemed wise on paper but it drains the natural tension of the piece. Viewers should be stuck with John Taylor and Warwick Wilson for the majority of the running time of *The Perfect Host,* instead of constantly getting breaks from the brewing insanity through flashbacks and detective investigations (that culminate in the kind of coincidence that can sink a movie like this one if it is thought about for even a few seconds).

Screenwriting flaws aside, Crawford and Pierce are quite good here, even to the point that they can iron out a few of the kinks in the screenplay and their performances warranted a larger theatrical release than the one granted the film by Magnolia (which resulted in a measly $49k in theatrical box office). Crawford is aggressive enough to be believed as a criminal but also likable and engaging enough as a lead. The Emmy-winning Pierce perfectly tweaks his buttoned-up persona in a way that turns his Niles Crane character from *Frasier* into something malevolent. One could imagine Niles ending up at this short pier of craziness were his whole family to die in a car accident before his eyes. Warwick Wilson still serves wine, still wants to entertain his party guests (imaginary and Taylor), and tries hard to keep his worldview in place (including dissuading a neighbor played by Helen Reddy from calling the police). He is an anal lunatic. Although one should not assume that this was an easy role for Pierce merely because this one has commonalities with his most well-known character. He finds something new and interesting here, playing to his strengths at the same tim.

In the end, *The Perfect Host* does not take enough risks to be seen as more than a performance piece for its talented leads. It should have been tenser, darker, and more unpredictable. Despite two strong lead turns, it is a piece about a criminal and a madman that feels remarkably by-the-numbers and sane.

Brian Tallerico

CREDITS

Warwick Wilson: David Hyde Pierce
John Taylor: Clayne Crawford
Detective Martin: Nathaniel Parker
Cathy Knight: Helen Reddy
Simone De Marchi: Megahn Perry
Origin: USA
Language: English
Released: 2010
Production: Stacey Testro, Mark Victor; Stacey Testro International, Mark Victor Productions; released by Magnolia Pictures
Directed by: Nick Tomnay
Written by: Nick Tomnay, Krishna Jones
Cinematography by: John Brawley
Music by: John Swihart
Editing: Nick Tomnay
Sound: Kelly Cabral
Costumes: Cynthia Herteg
Production Design: Ricardo Jattan
MPAA rating: R
Running time: 93 minutes

REVIEWS

Abele, Robert. *Los Angeles Times.* June 30, 2011.
Gleiberman, Owen. *Entertainment Weekly.* June 29, 2011.
Harvey, Dennis. *Variety.* June 26, 2011.
Keizer, Mark. *Boxoffice Magazine.* June 26, 2011.
Kohn, Eric. *IndieWire.* June 30, 2011.
Lowe, Justin. *Hollywood Reporter.* June 26, 2011.
Murray, Noel. *AV Club.* June 30, 2011.
Musettto, V.A. *New York Post.* July 1, 2011.
Orange, Michelle. *Movieline.* June 30, 2011.
Travers, Peter. *Rolling Stone.* June 30, 2011.

QUOTES

Warwick Wilson: "You can't kill me, I'm having a dinner party."

TRIVIA

The film was shot in only seventeen days.

PIRATES OF THE CARIBBEAN: ON STRANGER TIDES

Box Office: $241.1 million

In the annals of Hollywood studio filmmaking—a place with no small history of dimwitted notions—the idea of a movie based on a Disney World theme park ride at one point seemed like an especially creatively bankrupt move, a crass admission that evaluating original screenplays and actually developing unique new stories had become just too burdensome a task for well-paid executives. But, perhaps owing in part to diminished expectation, *Pirates of the Caribbean: The Curse of the Black Pearl* (2003) was an unexpected delight—a spry and wickedly engaging sea-set adventure anchored by an immensely entertaining performance from Johnny Depp, for which he was nominated for a Best Actor Oscar®. Three sequels on, the thrill is gone.

A heavy sense of obligation weighs down *Pirates of the Caribbean: On Stranger Tides,* a bloated piece of semi-anonymous corporate entertainment that cinematically approximates the consequences of an all-you-can-eat dessert buffet. While it represents a slight uptick from the dreadful *Pirates of the Caribbean: At World's End* (2007), it is still a film of ever-diminishing returns; its luster of enjoyment fades noticeably as it slogs through 137 minutes, and even more as one reflects upon it after its conclusion. Whereas the first film in the franchise—and the best action films in general—have some sense of expansiveness outside of their frames, *On Stranger Tides* just feels distended. Every nook and cranny is stuffed with movement, and the action sequences are not so much plot-motivated thrills as giant exercises in masturbatory kinetic excess.

Audiences lapped it up, of course, to the tune of over a billion dollars worldwide (and its end credits hint at the possibility of yet more movies), but the undeniably downward-charting critical response and filmgoer enjoyment seem to indicate that a point of critical mass is near, and a rethink soon necessary if the *Pirates of the Caribbean* franchise is to survive at a level commensurate with its established production and marketing costs.

On Stranger Tides unfolds some time after *At World's End.* Intent on getting back his beloved ship, the Black Pearl, jaunty rogue pirate Captain Jack Sparrow (Depp) is captured attempting to rescue his first mate, Gibbs (Kevin McNally). Shortly thereafter, however, he escapes from the custody of King George II (Richard Griffiths), who is dead set on Great Britain reaching Ponce de Leon's perhaps not so mythical fountain of youth in the New World before ships from rival Spain can claim it. Jack's old nemesis, Captain Barbossa (Geoffrey Rush), has quit his pirating ways to become a privateer to the British king, and he sails for His Majesty.

Jack's curiosity in the fountain of youth is boosted by tales from his father (Keith Richards, in a cameo appearance), however, and even more so when he finds out someone has been trying to raise a crew by impersonating him—an impostor that turns out to be Angelica

(Penelope Cruz), an old flame of Jack's who may or may not be the daughter of the fearsome and notorious Blackbeard (Ian McShane). Soon Jack finds himself an unwitting passenger of Angelica, Blackbeard and the latter's zombified crew on the Queen Anne's Revenge, racing toward the cherished prize.

Along the way there is a cabal of bloodsucking mermaids, which feels like a studio-note sop to the surging pop cultural popularity of vampires. It turns out that two chalices once belonging to de Leon must first be gathered before drinking from the mystical fountain; when utilized simultaneously, the person drinking from a cup containing a mermaid's tear has their life extended, while the other person dies, their remaining years "donated" to the other. Thus, one of the mermaids, Syrena (Spanish actress Astrid Bergès-Frisbey, making her English language debut), is taken prisoner by Blackbeard, who is determined to proactively turn back a prophesied death at the hands of a one-legged man. Along the way, a naïve young missionary Philip (Sam Claflin) develops a crush on Syrena.

It is true that there is functional delight in some of the movie's set pieces. Director Rob Marshall, taking over for previous helmer Gore Verbinski, certainly evinces an experience with elaborately choreographed set pieces. On stage he is a six-time Tony Award® nominee, and his work on *Chicago* (2002) and *Nine* (2009) obviously involved highly technical staging. That same sense of captured movement characterizes *On Stranger Tides*. Even if some of its frames are at times a bit too dark, Marshall and cinematographer Dariusz Wolski favor wide shots over close-ups in action scenes, trying to give the film more of a sense of open space.

There is a pinch of spitfire repartee in at least a few of the dialogue exchanges, too. When Angelica notes with a sigh that Jack has not changed, he retorts, "And that implies a need?" Still, these are characters as convenient poses, not fleshed out, multi-dimensional roles with possibly competing agendas. It is not merely that *On Stranger Tides* is the cinematic equivalent of fast food, as so many studio summer films are these days, designed foremost to provide cacophonous spectacle rather than an emotionally engaging narrative. The chief problem is that the franchise's DNA has been fatally compromised. No longer does a spirit of joyful playfulness drive the *Pirates* series. Returning scribes Ted Elliott and Terry Rossio's screenplay, even though it is suggested by a novel by Tim Powers which gives the movie its designated subtitle, leans mightily on (presumed) affection for recurring characters and programmatic plot twists instead of really taking its audience on an adventure journey where it feels like anything might happen. Even what should ostensibly be surprise twists come off as yawningly contrived herein.

Then there is the clear, overarching mandate from producer Jerry Bruckheimer and his studio cohorts, which seems designed to banish the notion of more than eight consecutive seconds of stillness or rumination. This sense of puffed-up grandiosity informs everything about the movie's basic template, to the point where, even on a first viewing, it almost feels like *On Stranger Tides* should be background noise to checking email or some other mundane multitasking. Because there is so much action, the specifics of any given gambit or stunt lose meaning and impact. Ten different companies were used for visual effects work on the movie, which includes more than 1,100 augmented shots, and while the cumulative effect is impressive as a general reel-type showcase for Hollywood marvel, there are not special moments that stick out in one's memory like the bullet-time of *The Matrix* (1999), the sinking ship of *Titanic* (1997) or the liquid-metal rejuvenation of *Terminator 2: Judgment Day* (1991). The violence is also consequence-free. When one man leaps impulsively into the fray only to be cut down, Jack quips, "Someone make a note of that man's bravery."

The movie's performances cannot save it either. Depp minces about and deploys his by now characteristically effete mannerisms to slightly amusing effect, but the story damningly does not foist upon him situations that significantly expand his rendering of the character. The audience is subjected to a greatest-hits package, in essence. Cruz, meanwhile, is a beauty capable of wicked charisma, but is hamstrung here by a character that is poorly conceived. She and Depp previously costarred together in *Blow* (2001), so there is a certain rooted rapport between the pair, but many of their scenes together also have a slapdash, thrown-together quality, as if the mere sight of two movie stars together was supposed to thrill, and spackle over any story incongruities.

Hans Zimmer's punchy, memorable music again gives the movie an active sense of spirit, providing its swashbuckling and derring-do with an important sense of aural underpinning. Still, it is not for nothing that the film ends with a post-credits tag on an island. *On Stranger Tides* is less than the sum of its already damaged and uninspired parts, a prime exhibit of creative ambition and inspiration drained by the trappings and comfort of success. Its makers and distributor, however, are cut off from this opinion, and so will continue to deliver more of these movies as long as they feel there is money to be made.

Brent Simon

CREDITS

Captain Jack Sparrow: Johnny Depp
Angelica: Penelope Cruz

Blackbeard: Ian McShane

Captain Hector Barbossa: Geoffrey Rush

Joshamee Gibbs: Kevin McNally

Philip: Sam Claflin

King George II: Richard Griffiths

Tamara: Gemma Ward

Cameo: Judi Dench

Origin: USA

Language: English

Released: 2011

Production: Jerry Bruckheimer; Jerry Bruckheimer Films, Walt Disney Pictures; released by Walt Disney Pictures

Directed by: Rob Marshall

Written by: Ted Elliott, Terry Rossio

Cinematography by: Dariusz Wolski

Music by: Hans Zimmer

Sound: Shannon Mills, George Watters

Music Supervisor: Bob Badami, Melissa Muik

Editing: David Brenner, Michael Kahn, Wyatt Smith

Art Direction: Drew Boughton, John Chichester, Robert Cowper, Zack Grobler, Thomas Voth

Costumes: Penny Rose

Production Design: John Myhre

MPAA rating: PG-13

Running time: 136 minutes

REVIEWS

Barker, Andrew. *Variety*. May 12, 2011.
Bennett, Ray. *Hollywood Reporter*. May 11, 2011.
Berardinelli, James. *ReelViews*. May 19, 2011.
Ebert, Roger. *Chicago Sun-Times*. May 19, 2011.
Hornaday, Ann. *Washington Post*. May 20, 2011.
LaSalle, Mick. *San Francisco Chronicle*. May 19, 2011.
Morgenstern, Joe. *Wall Street Journal*. May 20, 2011.
Phillips, Michael. *Chicago Tribune*. May 19, 2011.
Scott, A.O. *New York Times*. May 19, 2011.
Sharkey, Betsy. *Los Angeles Times*. May 19, 2011.

QUOTES

Jack Sparrow: "You know that feeling you get when you're standing in a high place...sudden urge to jump? I don't have it."

TRIVIA

Jerry Bruckheimer gave strict casting instruction to casting directors that actresses auditioning for the mermaid roles had to have natural breasts.

POETRY
(Shi)

In the opening sequence of *Poetry*, the latest work from acclaimed South Korean filmmaker Lee Chang-dong, viewers are treated to an initially pastoral view of a group of small children playing by the side of a river that slowly and quietly turns darker as the camera eventually turns towards something in the water that turns out to be the body of a young girl. This sequence is a stunner by itself but it also serves as a perfect summation of the film as a whole in the way that it brings both the fragile beauty and the harsh reality of the world together in surprising and emotionally devastating ways. The end result is a film that may sound on the surface like the most potentially depressing thing ever and transforms it into a truly affecting movie-going experience.

After that opening, viewers are introduced to Mija (Yun Jung-hee), a woman of a certain age who works as a part-time maid for an elderly stroke victim, is raising her insolent teenaged grandson Wook (Lee David) while his mother, her daughter, is away and whose gentle, caring and empathetic manner is far removed from the generally self-absorbed people around her. In her first appearance, she is going to an appointment with her doctor and while she does not seen to fully grasp it at first, it is pretty much apparent that she is entering the early stages of dementia. After this visit, she impulsively chooses to sign up for a poetry class where each member is assigned to write a poem by the end of the semester and admonished to remain open to the world around them for inspiration. At first, she tries, finding said inspiration in the usual places—flowers, fruit and the like—but nothing seems to be happening and it is then that things take a turn for the bleak. It turns out that the girl found in the opening sequence was a sixteen-year-old schoolgirl who committed suicide after being the victim of a string of repeated gang rapes at the hands of six of her classmates and, according to the girl's diary, Wook was one of her attackers.

Mija learns these details when she is summoned to a meeting with the parents (well, the fathers) of the other five boys, all of whom are desperate to cover up the incident and the complicity of their children. In the most casual manner possible, the well-to-do men decide that the best thing to do is simply pay off the girl's mother, a poor widowed farmer with another child she is trying to raise, a move that is also endorsed by the school administrators, who want to put the matter behind them before word gets out to the press. Mija is stunned by the news of the crime, shocked by the cold-hearted reactions of the other parents to the monstrous acts of their children, and unable to confront Wook directly about what he has done and struggles to process what is going on, even going so far as to quietly attend the funeral for the girl, where she even steals a framed photograph that she later places in front of Wook while he eats in a desperate attempt to inspire him to come clean. Eventually, it becomes clear to Mija that her poetic inspiration will not be coming from the usual sources—her poem will take the form of an elegy to the young girl whose sad life and tragic demise has almost gone unnoticed in the effort to smooth things over and act as if nothing ever happened.

With a plot that involves aging, dementia, artistic discovery and the discovery of the reprehensible acts of a close family member, *Poetry* may sound like an absolutely unbearable descent into the most mawkish melodrama imaginable but it only takes a few minutes to realize that Lee (whose previous film was the well-received *Secret Sunshine* [2007], which also dealt with people trying to come to grips with tragedy) is not going to resort to soap-opera histrionics. Instead, he has chosen an approach that takes the harsh and decidedly unpleasant details of contemporary life and handles them in a delicate and thoughtful manner that is, yes, rather poetic to behold and not at all the sentimental slop that it might have become in lesser hands. The delicacy of what Lee has done here as writer and director is echoed by the equally subtle and beautifully detailed central performance by Yun, the celebrated veteran of more than 300 Korean films who came out of a sixteen-year-long retirement to take on the role of Mija. As the character tries to figure out a way of coming to terms with the devastating upheavals in her life while looking for the artistic voice that she presumably hopes will allow her to present her thoughts to the world before she is cruelly robbed of them, Yun never hits a false note or goes for an easy tear-jerking moment, despite all the opportunities provided by such a role, and her work is all the more devastating as a result.

On first glance, some viewers may find Lee's pacing a bit too restrained and laid-back for its own good, especially in conjunction with its 139-minute running time, and may think that some elements, such as the visits to local poetry readings, segments in which Mija's classmates are seen discussing the most beautiful moments of their lives, and the details of the relationship between Mija and her employer, are on the extraneous side. In fact, these elements add additional shading to the material and do so in such a way that the film would be almost unthinkable without them. In the end, *Poetry* is a powerful work that reconfirms Lee as one of the more significant voices on the international film scene today. Ironically, this film that deals in part with the eradication of memory, either by disease or deliberate dismissal, is one that will haunt viewers for a long time to come.

Peter Sobczynski

CREDITS

Mija: Jeong-hieYun
Jongwook: Da-wit Lee
M. Kang: Hira Kim
Kibum's Father: Nae-sang Ahn
Heejin's Mother: Myeong-shin Park
Origin: Korea
Language: Korean
Released: 2010
Production: Jun-dong Lee; UniKorea Pictures; released by Kino International
Directed by: Chang-dong Lee
Written by: Chang-dong Lee
Cinematography by: Hyun Seok Kim
Editing: Hyun Kim
Costumes: Choong-yeon Lee
Production Design: Jeom-hui Sihm
MPAA rating: Unrated
Running time: 139 minutes

REVIEWS

Chang, Justin. *Variety*. May 19, 2010.
Dargis, Manohla. *New York Times*. February 10, 2011.
Ebert, Roger. *Chicago Sun-Times*. February 25, 2011.
Edelstein, David. *New York Magazine*. February 7, 2011.
Lee, Maggie. *Hollywood Reporter*. October 14, 2010.
Orndorf, Brian. *BrianOrndorf.com*. May 4, 2011.
Pais, Matt. *RedEye*. February 25, 2011.
Phillips, Michael. *Chicago Tribune*. February 24, 2011.
Turan, Kenneth. *Los Angeles Times*. May 5, 2011.
White, Armond. *New York Press*. February 9, 2011.

POM WONDERFUL PRESENTS: THE GREATEST MOVIE EVER SOLD

(The Greatest Movie Ever Sold)

He's not selling out, he's buying in.
—Movie tagline

The title for Morgan Spurlock's *POM Wonderful Presents: The Greatest Movie Ever Sold* might be the first of its kind. Right there, telling the viewer up front what corporation is responsible for the film they are about to see, is a brand name. Movies are and always have been filled with product placements. They are a major force of revenue in Hollywood, and, while Spurlock himself is a Hollywood outsider, he is here trying to play the Hollywood filmmaking game in the most absurd and extreme manner possible. He pulled such a stunt with his 2004 documentary *Super Size Me,* in which he acted as his own guinea pig by eating nothing but McDonalds for thirty days straight. It was a gimmick through which Spurlock dissected the state of the nation's health and diet.

Here, Spurlock is attempting a new kind of gimmick. By wanting to make a documentary about advertising, Spurlock attempts to get the entire movie funded entirely by way of product placement. "What will the movie be about?" ask the curious CEOs and heads of advertising. "Well, it's being made right now. *This* is the movie," Spurlock replies. The "plot" of the film is to see if he can indeed fund an entire production by willing corporations and companies who want their products featured prominently in the film. The company that pays $1 million for their product placement in the film will have their product displayed above the title.

Unlike his contemporaries, Spurlock is not overly opinionated about his subject, just mainly curious and willing to expose the facts via a stunt or two. He is not much of a provocateur or undercover journalist, but rather a charming and likable host and participant, which in some ways is much harder to pull off. Unlike Michael Moore, Spurlock's version of the "everyman" seems more genuine and he is the right person to approach this subject without being pretentious or self-righteous about it (unlike, say, the stuffy and condescending 2004 documentary, *The Corporation*).

While *Greatest Movie* might not actually *be* a "great" movie, it is an entertaining one. Nothing he reveals is particularly shocking or startling, but it does give the viewer pause as to how much advertising is out there and in how many different forms. It is said that $412 billion a year is spent on advertising. The goal of this movie, Spurlock tells the audience, is transparency. The viewer is there to see every meeting Spurlock has with these companies, many of whom laugh him out of the room and express great disinterest in participating in what looks like a scheme to make such companies look like fools. This is not an unwise decision for these companies to make, since Spurlock is known mostly for making McDonalds, one of the world's biggest corporations, look like the main culprit in a worldwide crime spree.

It comes as no surprise then that the company that ponies up the most money is a health food drink. POM Wonderful is 100% pomegranate juice and ends up being featured sitting on a table in almost every scene after the deal is made. It is appropriate because a brand, it is said, is like a personality. The brand being advertised must fit the personality of the bigger work in which it is being featured. There are many seemingly convoluted ways of measuring a person's "brand," but of course Spurlock is game enough to have his personality tested. The result has little more substance than that of a streetside fortune teller telling someone they are going on a long journey, but it is interesting that people get paid to conduct such tests.

There are other gimmicks spread throughout the ninety minutes. Spurlock promises commercial breaks within the film to the companies that pay more. Indeed, the movie has commercials in it, all of them made by Spurlock. Companies such as Jet Blue Airlines, Hyatt Hotels and Old Navy give Spurlock permission to use their brand names in his film. Even the band OK Go is recruited to compose the theme song. There are rules to follow, of course. Spurlock is given many contracts to sign, many of which contain such absurd stipulations such as "you must not say anything disparaging about Germany in the film."

Spurlock does take some time away from the corporate offices of Manhattan where he lives and looks to other parts of the country for extremes in advertising. A portion of the film is spent looking at a public high school where many outside areas are used for advertising, a measure approved by the school board so that revenue can keep coming in. Spurlock also makes his way to Sao Paolo where advertising on the streets is banned. If there is anything startling in *Greatest Movie,* it is the sight of a street in a major city without a single billboard. Merchants are forced to talk up their businesses without the luxury of big, attention-getting images.

The overall feel to *Greatest Movie,* though, is that it exists more for the gimmick than for the examination of the subject. The snake-eating-its-tail aspect of the project feels slightly like an elaborate prank, but perhaps it is just as well. Advertising is inherently absurd and more and more people are becoming savvy to the nature of it. Spurlock should have also looked back to a time many years ago when someone thought it would be a great idea to have gigantic, lit-up billboards far up into the sky, an idea that was thankfully squashed. Apparently, there are limits.

Collin Souter

CREDITS

Narrator: Morgan Spurlock
Origin: USA
Language: English
Released: 2011
Production: Jeremy Chilnick, Morgan Spurlock, Keith Calder, Jessica Wu, Abbie Hurewitz; Snoot Entertainment, Warrior Poets; released by Sony Pictures Classics, Stage Six Films

Directed by: Morgan Spurlock
Written by: Morgan Spurlock, Jeremy Chilnick
Cinematography by: Daniel Marracino
Music by: Jon Spurney
Sound: Abe Dolinger, Timothy Dutton
Music Supervisor: Jonathan McHugh
Editing: Thomas M. Vogt
MPAA rating: PG-13
Running time: 86 minutes

REVIEWS

Childress, Erik. *eFilmcritic.com.* May 11, 2011.
Ebert, Roger. *Chicago Sun-Times.* April 21, 2011.
Goodykoontz, Bill. *Arizona Republic.* April 21, 2011.
Holden, Stephen. *New York Times.* April 21, 2011.
Lemire, Christie. *Associated Press.* April 20, 2011.
Lumenick, Lou. *New York Post.* April 22, 2011.
Neumaier, Joe. *New York Daily News.* April 22, 2011.
O'Sullivan, Michael. *Washington Post.* April 22, 2011.
Schwarzbaum, Lisa. *Entertainment Weekly.* April 22, 2011.
Strout, Justin. *Orlando Weekly.* May 4, 2011.

TRIVIA

The soundtrack includes Moby's "Run On" from the album *Play,* which is the first album ever to have all of its tracks licensed for use in movies, television shows, and commercials.

POTICHE

France, 1977: Women's Liberation is in the air.
 —Movie tagline

The trophy is coming off the shelf.
 —Movie tagline

Box Office: $1.6 million

Something is seriously lost in translation in this retro battle of the sexes flick based on the eponymous play from the 1970's. Despite sporting a winsome cast, including French veterans Catherine Deneuve and Gérard Depardieu, and the appropriate quirky comedy beats, *Potiche* does not come off as a witty, worthy commentary about gender inequality. Rather, the film feels tired and dated—and not in a kitschy or clever and ironic way.

Roughly translated, "potiche" means trophy wife. In this case, the potiche is Suzanne Pujol (Deneuve), the dutiful wife to Robert Pujol (Fabrice Luchini), the gruff manager of the umbrella factory that she inherited. Mrs. Pujol is the ideal housewife: She jogs, writes trite poetry, keeps the house and staff organized, lets her husband

make all the financial decisions for the family, and turns a blind eye to his infidelity. But when he is kidnapped by the factory union who demand swift changes to their working conditions, Mrs. Pujol does an about face and decides to take charge. Encouraged by the union's leader, Babin (Depardieu), who turns out, quite randomly, to be Mrs. Pujol's ex, she decides to give running the factory a go. Despite a few bumps, she proves to be a more-than-capable manager, increasing productivity and engaging her children (who were otherwise estranged from their father) in the family business. When her husband returns following a recuperation vacation, Mrs. Pujol faces a possible return to the old status quo. Inspired by what she was able to achieve at the factory, however, she decides to take her life into her own hands and best her husband once and for all.

Potiche sets itself up to be a deft social comedy about the war of the sexes in 1970's France. Pitting the longtime married couple against one another aims to be funny as is illustrates just how little one can know about the person one shares a bed with. Mr. Pujol is a man's man, forceful, entitled and a skirt chaser (leave it to French cinema to really go for the skirt chasing in R-rated fashion), while Mrs. Pujol is, for all intents and purposes, a sit-on-the-sidelines kind of a wife, as likely to sing along with the striking union's chants because they are catchy, as she is to do think to do something about them. He would never think that a woman could outsmart him, and, until recently, she would never think to try. He thinks he knows everything about her, but she has got a few feisty skeletons in her closet. Their head-butting is meant to be the meat of the narrative and the audience is supposed to get a kick out of watching her get the better of him.

Unfortunately, unlike Mrs. Pujol, *Potiche* never quite finds its footing. Its theatrical roots get in the way as characters muse deeply and at length about their lives, their memories, and their current situations. On stage, these quasi-monologues might let actors flex their thespian muscles, but on-screen it plays out as too much telling and not enough showing—and in this instance, also as too much subtitle reading. The predictable plot twists would be easy to forgive if *Potiche* embraced its setting or its genre conventions more. As it stands, the film loses points for not being self-referential enough, instead begging the question "Why bother with a period setting if it is not going to be used to its full advantage?" *Potiche* does not embrace or revel in the wacky, full of social satire possibilities decade it is depicting. Other than the butterfly collars and lack of cell phones, the era barely registers. To top it off the characters are too flat to be funny and the actors seem to lack all comedic timing. But the film is not played straight either. There are moments of earnestness such as Mrs. Pujol's daughter coming to her looking for marital advice, or her son really feeling he has a place at his family company. These however, are paired with outlandish moments, like Mrs. Pujol flashing back to her sepia-tinged tryst with Babin. When her son confesses that he only has room for one woman in his life: his mother, it is hard to tell if we are to feel sorry for him for deciding on a life as a mommy's boy or if he is making an attempt at humor. The whole narrative seems to live in this awkward in-between land of not quite comedy and not quite drama. The result is a confusing time-warp gender-bender that does not cross cultures.

Joanna Topor MacKenzie

CREDITS

Suzanne Pujol: Catherine Deneuve
Maurice Babin: Gerard Depardieu
Robert Pujol: Fabrice Lunchini
Nadege: Karin Viard
Joelle: Judith Godreche
Laurent Pujol: Jeremie Renier
Genevieve: Evelyne Dandry
Andre: Bruno Lochet
Origin: France
Language: French
Released: 2010
Production: Eric Altmayer, Nicolas Altmayer; Mandarin Cinema, France 2 Cinema, Mars Films, Wild Bunch, Scope Pictures; released by Music Box Films
Directed by: Francois Ozon
Written by: Francois Ozon
Cinematography by: Yorick Le Saux
Music by: Philippe Rombi
Sound: Jean-Paul Hurier
Editing: Laure Gardette
Costumes: Pascaline Chavanne
Production Design: Katia Wyszkop
MPAA rating: R
Running time: 103 minutes

REVIEWS

Ebert, Roger. *Chicago Sun-Times.* April 16, 2011.
LaSalle, Mick. *San Francisco Chronicle.* March 31, 2011.
Levy, Shawn. *Portland Oregonian.* April 21, 2011.
Longworth, Karina. *Village Voice.* March 22, 2011.
Phillips, Michael. *Chicago Tribune.* April 16, 2011.
Reed, Rex. *New York Observer.* March 22, 2011.
Scott, A.O. *New York Times.* March 24, 2011.
Weitzman, Elizabeth. *New York Daily News.* March 25, 2011.
Young, Deborah. *Hollywood Reporter.* March 21, 2011.
Zacharek, Stephanie. *Movieline.* March 24, 2011.

TRIVIA

A trailer for this film is used in British cinemas as part of the "Don't let mobile phones spoil your film" campaign. The

English subtitles have been replaced with new phone-related dialogue and the music with a ringtone version.

AWARDS

Nomination:
British Acad. 2011: Foreign Film.

PRIEST

The war is eternal. His mission is just the beginning.
—Movie tagline

Box Office: $29.1 million

In 2010, director Scott Stewart and actor Paul Bettany teamed up to bless the moviegoing community with *Legion,*,a spectacularly silly apocalyptic thriller featuring goofy-looking monsters, ridiculous action sequences, and some of the most laughable theological arguments in recent cinematic memory. The results were dire and aside from those who treasured it for its inadvertent camp value, it was quickly forgotten by those who managed to catch it during its brief appearance in the marketplace. In the wake of something that grisly and unrewarding, one might expect that Stewart and Bettany would simply shake hands and go their separate ways for the mutual benefit of their careers and the sanity of moviegoers but instead, little more than a year later, they joined forces again to present *Priest,* yet another spectacularly silly apocalyptic thriller featuring goofy-looking monsters, ridiculous actions sequences and theological material so utterly goofy that it makes *Legion* look perfectly sound from an eschatological standpoint by comparison.

Based on the graphic novel series by Min-Woo Hyung, *Priest* posits an alternate history of Earth in which mankind has been locked in a centuries-old battle with vampires with the fate of humanity at stake, no pun intended. Eventually, the tide turns in favor of humans thanks to an elite squad of vampire hunters, developed under the aegis of the Catholic church and known as Priests, who do battle with the creatures with an awe-inspiring array of martial arts skills. Eventually, the vampires are all but decimated, the Priest squad is disbanded and forced to integrate with normal society, something that they are ill-suited for, and what remains of humanity now largely resides within the walls of an oppressive cityscape that is architecturally straight out of *Blade Runner* (1982) and *Brazil* (1985) and ruled with an iron grip by the church, complete with public confessionals on the streets where the phone booths presumably used to be. The fragile truce between humanity and the hoary underworld is shattered when a horde of bloodsuckers under the thrall of the evil vampire king known as Black Hat (Karl Urban) attacks a remote farm and make off with the sweet-and-innocent Lucy (Lily Collins). When word of this gets to her uncle, a former priest known only as Priest (Paul Bettany), he, along with the girl's hot-headed boyfriend (Screen Gems stalwart Cam Gigandet) and a fellow renegade Priestess (Maggie Q), defies the church leaders (headed by none other than Christopher Plummer) and goes off to reduce the vampires into a collection of 1's and 0's before Black Hat can transform her into a vampire and take over the world.

With its bizarre combination of vampires, spaghetti western iconography and martial arts mayhem, *Priest* feels at times as though the projectionist in a grindhouse theater of old drunkenly decided to randomly splice together reels of different exploitation movies that he happened to have on hand with him up in the booth. For a certain strain of trash film aficionado, such a creation might seem to be a delightfully cheesy way of killing eight-seven minutes but as anyone who actually attempts to watch it will quickly discover, those minutes die as slowly and painfully and grotesquely as anyone or anything does on the screen during them. Even by junk movie standards, *Priest* is a stinker for the ages that comes complete with uninteresting characters, ponderously action set-pieces, an incredibly convoluted screenplay that never once makes sense on a basic scene-for-scene basis and, thanks to the addition of post-production 3D to the proceedings, a decision presumably made approximately five seconds after *Avatar* (2009) made a bazillion dollars, a visual style that is so murky that it practically seems to be daring viewers to watch it without either tossing the glasses away in sheer frustration or simply fleeing the theater altogether.

Priest is total junk from beginning to end and is pretty much worthless on every possible level—too silly to work as a straightforward action-horror hybrid, too unspeakably boring to make it as camp and the only good news for the actors is that their contributions are so forgettable that most people will never recall them having been in it in the first place. (The film even somehow manages to make the endlessly charismatic Maggie Q come across like just another faceless drone here.) Lucky for them, few viewers actually made it out to the multiplex to see it when it debuted at the beginning of the summer—most having decided instead to either see *Thor* (2011) again or simply not go to the movies at all—and it disappeared from theaters even quicker than *Legion* had the previous year and hit DVD soon thereafter.

Peter Sobczynski

CREDITS

Priest: Paul Bettany
Priestess: Maggie Q
Hicks: Cam Gigandet
Lucy: Lily Collins
Black Hat: Karl Urban
Aaron: Stephen Moyer
Salesman: Brad Dourif
Monsignor Oreleas: Christopher Plummer
Shannon: Madchen Amick
Origin: USA
Language: English
Released: 2011
Production: Michael De Luca, Josh Donen, Mitchell Peck; Screen Gems, Michael De Luca Films, Stars Road Entertainment, Tokyopop, Buckaroo Entertainment; released by Sony Pictures
Directed by: Scott Stewart
Written by: Scott Stewart, Cory Goodman
Cinematography by: Don Burgess
Music by: Christopher Young
Sound: Martin Lopez
Music Supervisor: Thomas Milano
Editing: Lisa Zeno Churgin, Rebecca Weigold
Art Direction: Andrew Max Cahn, A. Todd Holland, Christa Munro
Costumes: Ha Nguyen
Production Design: Richard Bridgland
MPAA rating: PG-13
Running time: 87 minutes

REVIEWS

Feeney, Mark. *Boston Globe.* May 16, 2011.
Felperin, Leslie. *Variety.* May 9, 2011.
Gibson, Bill. *Filmcritic.com.* May 15, 2011.
Hale, Mike. *New York Times.* May 13, 2011.
Neumaier, Joe. *New York Daily News.* May 13, 2011.
Olsen, Mark. *Los Angeles Times.* May 13, 2011.
Orndorf, Brian. *Sci-Fi Movie Page.* May 13, 2011.
Rabin, Nathan. *AV Club.* May 13, 2011.
Schrager, Nick. *Slant Magazine.* May 13, 2011.
Snider, Eric D. *Film.com.* May 13, 2011.

QUOTES

Priest: "You would have made a good priest."
Hicks: "Thanks!"
Priest: "Don't let it go to your head!"

TRIVIA

Gerard Butler and Steven Strait were originally cast as the leads of the film.

PROJECT NIM

Human beings have long-abused their position at the top of the natural kingdom. They are, by their very nature, egotistical and power-hungry. Despite what nature preservation groups might want people to believe, there is simply no way around the fact that people have lorded their power over lesser species since cavemen discovered they could use wild animals for sustenance, shelter, and warmth. The problems that naturally come with control and manipulation of another species is disturbingly chronicled in James Marsh's *Project Nim,* a documentary about the rampant egotism of man's manipulation of another species. Even the desire to learn about another species' relation to our own and the expressed teaching purpose at the beginning of Marsh's documentary are merely disguises for control. And the truly frightening story at the core of the film is how much the people involved in this project abused their subjects not just physically but psychologically as well. Chimps may be like humans, but it takes great ego to think that something like us is exactly the same as us. While that may seem an obvious truth, it certainly does not hurt to be reminded of it by *Project Nim.*

Man's fascination with primates seemed more prominent than ever in 2011 with a talking gorilla in *Zookeeper* (2011) and the rebellion at the core of *Rise of the Planet of the Apes* (2011). The fact that these creatures are so much like humans and yet also unique in important ways is the foundation of *Project Nim.* Marsh chooses to focus heavily on the title character, bringing his tragic arc to life, but fails a bit to give the larger piece context within the greater story of animal experimentation or man's clearly-continuing obsession with the closest species to them on the evolutionary spectrum. His film is very-focused and truly interesting but it falls just short of the greatness it could achieved by placing this bizarre true tale in the entire fabric of man's relation to primate.

The anthropomorphizing of the chimps has led generations to believe that they are just like humans without the voice boxes or the upbringing. Such beliefs have led to teaching them sign language for communication and experimenting with how they are raised in an effort to learn more about their potential as a species. As if a chimp who could talk and was tucked in bed every night by a loving mother would somehow be just like a hairy human child. This is the deeply-flawed logic behind Project Nim, a study that starts in the '70s and was designed to prove that chimps would communicate effectively with humans if they were given the same developmental process and nurturing as children. A chimp named Nim was taken from his mother and given to a family of self-described hippies, who took him in without question and basically assimilated him into their family as if they had adopted a child. They talked to him like the other kids in the family, breast-fed him, taught him sign language, and even gave him alcohol and drugs in an effort to allow him to experiment like an adult human.

Lost in all of this silliness was the fact that Nim was not a human. Marijuana and signing for milk was not going to change that simple truth. In fact, the differences between Nim and his "siblings" and "parents" became more pronounced, not less, the more time he spent with his human family. The study was deeply flawed at its core but it was even more destined for failure because no one involved had anything resembling a scientific plan. The family that Nim was first placed with (there would be multiple families) did not bother to keep any records and clearly misunderstood the entire purpose of the experiment, if there ever really was one. Nim gets older, transfers from caretaker to caretaker, and his story goes from an interesting one to a stunningly tragic one. There may be no more truthful line in the film than "You can't give nurturing to an animal that could kill you."

The way that James Marsh edits and assembles his film one can clearly tell that he knows that Project Nim was doomed from the start. He fully captures the flawed people at the core of "Project Nim" and the mistakes they made but he never finds the greater context for what they did. Some of the most interesting segments in the documentary include talk show appearances and a fascinating *New York Magazine* cover story, but the story here is so bizarre that it sometimes feels like it takes place in another world. What happened to Nim feels so secluded from reality but even just the summer movies of 2011 make clear that man's obsession with primates played a role in how something like this could happen in the first place and the logic that allowed it to go so horrendously as an experiment. *Project Nim* is one of those films that documents something that one would like to think could never happen again but the horrifying truth is how much it so easily could.

Brian Tallerico

CREDITS

Lab Tech: Bob Angelini
Dr. William Lemmon: Bern Cohen
Stephanie LaFarge: Reagan Leonard
Origin: United Kingdom
Language: English
Released: 2011
Production: Simon Chinn; Red Box Films, Passion Pictures, BBC Films; released by Lionsgate, HBO
Directed by: James Marsh
Cinematography by: Michael Simmonds
Music by: Dickon Hinchliffe

Sound: Steven Robinson
Editing: Jinx Godfrey
Art Direction: Gonzalo Cordoba
Costumes: Kathryn Nixon
Production Design: Markus Kirschner
MPAA rating: PG-13
Running time: 93 minutes

REVIEWS

Burr, Ty. *Boston Globe.* July 14, 2011.
Ebert, Roger. *Chicago Sun-Times.* July 7, 2011.
Jolin, Dan. *Empire.* August 8, 2011.
Orange, Michelle. *Movieline.* July 7, 2011.
Phillips, Michael. *Chicago Tribune.* July 7, 2011.
Rickey, Carrie. *Philadelphia Inquirer.* July 21, 2011.
Scott, A.O. *New York Times.* July 7, 2011.
Smith, Kyle. *New York Post.* July 8, 2011.
Stevens, Dana. *Slate.* July 9, 2011.
Tobias, Scott. *AV Club.* July 7, 2011.

AWARDS

Directors Guild 2011: Documentary Director (Marsh)
Nomination:
British Acad. 2011: Feature Doc.

PROM

Who are you going with?
   —Movie tagline

Box Office: $10.1 million

The opening credits of *Prom,* which maneuver from photograph to photograph of various scenes of the main characters in the ensemble in a tableau of exposition, hint at the sort of scrapbook mentality of Katie Wech's screenplay and Joe Nussbaum's direction. Each character's major personality trait or quirk is cemented. All of their interpersonal relationships are firmly established. Even the narration from the primary character bluntly states the movie's central, naïve theme—that prom is a life-changing event in the lives of its attendees. Theoretically, there is nothing wrong with cutting to the chase; the problem that arises from this straightforward origin is that every conflict between or problem for the characters is as cleanly resolved (or left decidedly unresolved, as is the case in one of the movie's many subplots) as the script plainly establishes it.

Likewise, the characters themselves are essentially archetypes of the high school experience as defined by decade after decade of television shows and movies about the subject. They exist, not even to complete obvious character arcs, but to ensure that all bases are covered in the preordained spectrum of what constitutes the entertainment industry's perception of the high school life (or, on a cynical level, to reach as much of potential adolescent audience as possible).

The de facto leader of the cast of characters is Nova Prescott (Aimee Teegarden), a generically ambitious over-achiever who—in addition to her constant studying, serving as student council president, and securing a "full-ride" scholarship to Georgetown University—has volunteered to organize the nuts and bolts of her school's prom. Hers is a romantic view of the night in question, and the sappiness of her point of view is only surpassed by the imprecise nature of the words she chooses to describe it (starting off with the innocuously skeptical yet vaguely cheerful opening line: "High school: It happens to everyone").

After the shed containing all of the decorations burns down, her committee separates, assuming there is no way they will be able to replace the destroyed ornaments in time for the dance. Instead of investigating the cause of the fire (it is also subtly unnerving that the student responsible for the blaze not only does not confess to the accident but also seems blissfully unaware of the fact that he caused it), the principal (Jere Burns), in his last act in a screenplay that drops characters and consequences when they have either served their purpose or might result in an appearance in juvenile court, assigns the school's rebel with a heart of gold Jesse Richter (Thomas McDonell) to aid Nova so that he "might even learn something about hard work and dedication." The irony, of course, is that Jesse knows plenty about these things (and he skips class but only to walk his younger brother [Robbie Tucker] home from school, since their father left the family), and it is up to Nova to realize that it is actually he and not the milquetoast Brandon (Jonathan Keltz) who is her romantic interest.

Interspersed throughout this central plot, which might be the least involving of the multitude, though that is a tough competition, are the trials of insipidly interconnected classmates. Jordan (Kylie Bunbury) is dating the unrepentant shed-burner and varsity football star Tyler (DeVaughn Nixon), who is having an innocent tryst with sophomore Simone (Danielle Campbell), who is the object of affection of independent-music aficionado Lucas (Nolan Sotillo), who is friends with the equally socially ostracized Corey (Cameron Monaghan). Then there are the comparatively unconnected characters: Long-term couple Mei (Yin Chang) and Justin (Jared Kusnitz), nerdy wallflower Lloyd (Nicholas Braun), and scattered others (only Ali [Janelle Ortiz] and Rolo [Joe Adler] have much screentime, as she tries to unravel what she believes to be a lie about his girlfriend who conveniently lives in Canada).

The most dramatic potential comes from the unspoken conflict between Mei and Justin, with the latter convinced that they will be attending college together in Michigan even though she has eyes on a school in New York, though, since the script leaves the problem silent, whatever dialogue could arise between the two is substituted for muted tension. Lloyd, on the other hand, is here solely for comic relief, as his grand attempts to ask assorted girls to prom (e.g., a note on a locker and a banner hanging from an overpass) are thwarted (The note is creepy, and the banner is seized by a passing truck). The salvation for Lloyd's dateless prom comes from a character who has only one scene prior, even though Lloyd has a brief connection with another girl named Betsy (Allie Trimm) in a library—a scene that winds up having the singular purpose of making a tortured allusion to Edith Wharton's *Ethan Frome*. That Wech would dismiss the obvious setup in favor of treating another of her characters as a Chekov's gun only further demonstrates the screenplay's apathy toward its characters.

The movie cannot even bring itself to acknowledge the secondary argument of Nova's opening thesis about the school-ending dance—that the cliques which have defined students throughout their high school career mean little to nothing at prom. Once the event finally arrives, these characters are still too busy dealing with their own various dilemmas to even consider anyone in the peripheral. The interlaced stories lead to an even greater fundamental issue with *Prom*: The division of the characters that comes from the episodic narrative counters the very idea of unity.

Mark Dujsik

CREDITS

Nova Prescott: Aimee Teegaarden
Jesse: Thomas McDonell
Mei: Yin Chang
Tyler: DeVaughn Nixon
Simone: Danielle Campbell
Sandra: Christine Elise
Lloyd: Nicholas Braun
Kitty Prescott: Faith Ford
Principal Dunnan: Jere Burns
Origin: USA
Language: English
Released: 2011
Production: Ted Griffin, Justin Springer; Rickshaw Productions, Walt Disney Pictures; released by Walt Disney Pictures

Directed by: Joe Nussbaum
Written by: Katie Wech
Cinematography by: Byron Shah
Music by: Deborah Lurie
Sound: Odin Benitez
Editing: Jeffrey Werner
Costumes: Shoshana Rubin
Production Design: Mark White
MPAA rating: PG
Running time: 109 minutes

REVIEWS

Angulo Chen, Sandie. *Washington Post*. April 27, 2011.
Barnard, Linda. *Toronto Star*. April 28, 2011.
Gonzalez, Ed. *Slant Magazine*. April 27, 2011.
Jones, Kimberley. *Austin Chronicle*. April 29, 2011.
Kenny, Glenn. *MSN Movies*. April 28, 2011.
Legel, Laremy. *Film.com*. April 29, 2011.
McKiernan, Jason. *Filmcritic.com*. April 28, 2011.
O'Hehir, Andrew. *Salon.com*. April 28, 2011.
Pinkerton, Nick. *Village Voice*. April 27, 2011.
Putman, Dustin. *DustinPutman.com*. April 29, 2011.

QUOTES

Lloyd Taylor: "The prom is like the Olympics of high school. You wait four years, three people have a good time and everybody else gets to live on with shattered dreams."

PUNCTURE

Madman. Genius. Playboy. Friend. Fool. Lawyer.
—Movie tagline

Mike Weiss (Chris Evans) and Paul Danziger (co-director Mark Kassen) are hometown boys who made good with their own independent law practice. They specialize in insurance cases for those who cannot afford more lucrative representation and their settlement profits help cut into the debt they are on the verge of putting in their rearview. They are turned on to a case involving a nurse (Vinessa Shaw) who was accidentally stuck with a contaminated needle while serving a hospital patient. A family friend of hers, Jeffrey Dancort (Marshall Bell), has designed a revolutionary hypodermic which retracts upon a single usage, preventing potentially dangerous re-use. Since the medical supply industry is already making millions off the more traditional—and cheaper to produce—needle, Dancort's innovation has been suppressed for years.

Mike sees the value in a case like this even if his partner is more realistic in the time-and-money department in what it takes to research and fight the team of attorneys waiting for them. They are led by Nathaniel Price (Brent Cullen), a condescending gent who smiles while trying to convince Mike and Paul that this is a losing venture. Never one to be intimidated, Mike presses on with his investigation looking for the proof needed to sway a jury that big business has once again squashed the little guy and possibly killed countless millions in the wake of their own arrogance and greed. Oh, and let the record show that Mike is also quite the habitual drug user himself.

Parallels between a recreational needle addict willingly injecting himself with poisons and the tragic infection of those trying to get healthy through them might seem like an obvious irony though it's unsure whether screenwriter Chris Lopata ever recognized that connection. More time is spent on the damage that their key witness does to the case than anything Mike does on the job to stifle progress. At their first big meeting with the opposition it is Dancort's impatience with pointless questions—the most on-point being the initial "Why so grumpy?"—that derails things far more than Mike's drug-induced oversleeping. Genre fans familiar with Marshall Bell's work as an always-welcome heavy or crazy person will recognize that aspect of his persona more than the revolutionary innovator he is supposed to be here. In relation, Dancourt's unpredictable demeanor becomes a far greater influence and setback to the case than Mike's reckless behavior.

Easily the most telling moment of the film is when Mike is hospitalized and it is only then that his best friend of many years—and co-worker to boot—is first clued into his dangerous habit. This telling and unfathomable fact about Paul's inattention to detail collapses the drama into such a state of disbelief that it is reasonable to question how legitimately the drama actually corresponds with real life. *Puncture*'s final act spins out-of-reality with each passing scene particularly when the identity of a mystery man (Michael Biehn) who has been following Mike around is revealed. Then it is reasonable to wonder how much of these climactic meetings are pure writer's invention or meant to invoke a fictitious fantasy in Mike's psyche of how he wishes he got his final licks in.

Like all philanthropic films trying to introduce dialogue to a culture that may have missed the story in-between gossip and sports, *Puncture* has its heart in the right place but needs a serious dose of Epinephrine to get it pumping. Mike Weiss is a flawed character but a potentially fascinating one and Chris Evans does a fine enough job in making us believe he cares. The problem is that this is a film that refuses to make his struggles relatable. It is a story about personal demons and extracurricular distractions that could prevent a man

from honestly making the world a better place. He is never meant to be Erin Brockovich, the crusading single mom brought to vivid life by Steven Soderbergh and Julia Roberts. Mike is more in line with Jan Schlichtmann, portrayed by John Travolta in Steven Zaillian's *A Civil Action* (1998). He, too, was a man reaping the personal benefits of large settlement cases only to damn his firm's partners into debt by believing in one case that affected more people than the few that first presented it to him.

The Kassen brothers fail to capture what made those compelling films drive through their familiar narratives to arrive at conclusions, not just about a corrupt profit system but about the strength and stubbornness of the crusaders who fought them. *Puncture* is a film that should be getting under the skin rather than retracting every time that the viewer wants to know more than the usual clichés.

Erik Childress

CREDITS

Mike Weiss: Chris Evans
Paul Danzinger: Mark Kassen
Vicky: Vinessa Shaw
Nathaniel Price: Brett Cullen
Red: Michael Biehn
Daryl King: Jesse L. Martin
Senator O'Reilly: Kate Burton
Jeffrey Dancort: Marshall Bell
Jamie Weiss: Tess Parker
Sylvia: Roxanna Hope
Origin: USA
Language: English
Released: 2011
Production: Adam Kassen, Mark Kassen; Cherry Sky Films, Kassen brothers Production, LikeMinded Pictures; released by Millennium Entertainment
Directed by: Mark Kassen, Adam Kassen
Written by: Chris Lopata
Cinematography by: Helge Gerull
Music by: Ryan Ross Smith
Sound: Eric Milano
Music Supervisor: Jim Black
Editing: Chip Smith
Art Direction: Yvonne Boudreaux
Costumes: Kari Perkins
Production Design: Christopher Stull
MPAA rating: R
Running time: 100 minutes

REVIEWS

Catsoulis, Jeannette. *New York Times*. September 22, 2011.
Douglas, Edward. *Comingsoon.net*. September 23, 2011.

Ebert, Roger. *Chicago Sun-Times*. October 6, 2011.
Gilsdorf, Ethan. *Boston Globe*. October 24, 2011.
Gronvall, Andrea. *Chicago Reader*. October 13, 2011.
Keough, Peter. *Boston Phoenix*. October 18, 2011.
MacDonald, Moira. *Seattle Times*. November 3, 2011.
O'Sullivan, Michael. *Washington Post*. October 21, 2011.
Phillips, Michael. *Chicago Tribune*. October 6, 2011.
Singer, Matt. *Time Out Chicago*. October 6, 2011.

QUOTES

Nathaniel Price: "I bet you spent your whole life believing that you, you were born to do something great, make a difference, do something special. Important. But Michael, it's the most ordinary thought anybody ever had."

TRIVIA

The movie is based on a true story and received the blessing of the real-life Weiss and Danziger.

PUSS IN BOOTS

Live for danger. Fight for justice. Pray for mercy.
    —Movie tagline

Looking good never looked so good.
    —Movie tagline

Nine lives. One destiny.
    —Movie tagline

Rebel. Lover. Hero.
    —Movie tagline

He's been a bad kitty.
    —Movie tagline

Box Office: $149 million

In 2001, the first *Shrek* movie came out and was a surprise success at the box office, taking in roughly $265 million. It was a traditional storybook fantasy for the kids with a little bit of edge for the adults. In the decade that followed, three more *Shrek* movies came out. *Shrek 2* (2004) and *Shrek the Third* (2007) each grossed more at the box office than the movie that spawned them. Somehow, Cameron Diaz, the voice of Princess Fiona in all the films, reportedly became the highest paid voice actor of all time (she did little more than show up to say her lines). It was not until the fourth offering, *Shrek Forever After* (2010), that the series started to lose its steam. The film grossed $238 million, which in *Shrek* terms is considered a disappointment.

Still, the *Shrek* franchise was considered a cash cow for DreamWorks Animation and it should probably come as no surprise that a spin-off was necessary to keep the brand going. Enter *Puss In Boots,* a film solely dedicated to the Zorro-like, swashbuckling titular character voiced with great finesse by Antonio Banderas. Puss did not enter the *Shrek* world until *Shrek 2* and in doing so ran away with the entire movie. It is a wonderful creation. By taking off his hat and bugging out his impossible-to-resist pussy cat eyes, the orange tiger-striped feline could get anybody to do anything he wanted. Puss is all about style and panache, but still likes to do cat-like things like lick himself all over and sip milk with a rapid tongue.

Puss is an outlaw, and, in true Western movie fashion, he enters the town as a Cat with No Name, entering a saloon and turning all heads of all the human characters that inhabit it. Puss insists he is not here for trouble, just looking for a score. He is informed of Jack and Jill, murderous outlaws in possession of magic beans that could give him a beanstalk of wealth and riches. Jack (voiced by Billy Bob Thornton) and Jill (voiced by Amy Sedaris) are a couple who travel by night and are, strangely enough, in the throes of a domestic squabble in which Jack wants to settle down and have a family and Jill wants to keep running. Puss tracks them down at a hotel and makes a plan to steal the beans.

His plan is thwarted by the presence of another thief in disguise who is also after the beans. The thief turns out to be another cat, Kitty Softpaws (voiced by Salma Hayek). A chase and fight ensues and soon Puss is in an underground lair populated by cats who have a weekly dance fight. After a spirited dance-off, Puss learns of Kitty's true identity and follows after her as she disappears into the night. Instead of finding her, he finds an old friend from the past who betrayed him, Humpty Alexander Dumpty (voiced by Zach Galifianakis), who is (as expected) a large egg. Humpty and Kitty are a team working together who have orchestrated a plan to lure Puss into their plan to steal the magic beans.

A flashback reveals Puss meeting Humpty in an orphanage where Humpty specializes in planting and nurturing magic beans as well as constructing hang gliders. He talks about his dreams of finding a golden goose who lays golden eggs. They never do find the beans. Humpty and Puss remain friends until Humpty gets Puss involved in a bank robbery against his will, which leads to a chase and Humpty being imprisoned. Thus began Puss' life as an outlaw. Humpty and Kitty manage to convince Puss to join them in their plan, provided Humpty understands that their friendship is still over and this is just business.

Puss In Boots makes virtually no mention of the *Shrek* movies or their characters. A smart move is made by the film's creators to distance the material from the original inspiration and make *Puss In Boots* its own movie with its own voice. It resists any opportunity there might have been to get snarky with the audience or make a clever in-joke about its chosen genre, something that was a staple in the *Shrek* franchise. There are no movie gags or contemporary pop music in the film's arsenal. It stays true to its western and fairy tale roots while still going for the laughs, though not quite as often as one would hope. Banderas and Hayak are a solid off-screen voice couple and the characters are engaging enough to make the overall plainness of the movie not feel like a chore to sit through.

Still, the movie loses a bit of energy once the quest kicks into gear. Aside from a wondrous middle section on the beanstalk that might have been inspired by Terry Gilliam, *Puss In Boots* gets too bogged down in a conventional storyline with little in the way of surprises and not enough tension to warrant any real excitement. Younger viewers will likely still be enchanted by the film, but grown-ups might find themselves wondering where they have seen all of this before. The film goes down easily enough for its ninety-minute running time, but by the time it is over, there leaves little desire for another full-on franchise.

Collin Souter

CREDITS

Puss in Boots: Antonio Banderas (Voice)
Kitty Softpaws: Salma Hayek (Voice)
Humpty Dumpty: Zach Galifianakis (Voice)
Jack: Billy Bob Thornton (Voice)
Jill: Amy Sedaris (Voice)
Imelda: Constance Marie (Voice)
Origin: USA
Language: English
Released: 2011
Production: Joe M. Aguilar, Latifa Ouaou; DreamWorks Animation; released by Paramount Pictures

Directed by: Chris Miller
Written by: Tom Wheeler
Music by: Henry Jackman
Sound: Richard King
Editing: Eric Dapkewicz
Art Direction: Christian Schellewald
Production Design: Guillaume Aretos
MPAA rating: PG
Running time: 90 minutes

REVIEWS

Gleiberman, Owen. *Entertainment Weekly*. October 27, 2011.
Goss, William. *Film.com*. October 28, 2011.
Holden, Stephen. *New York Times*. October 27, 2011.
Kenny, Glenn. *MSN Movies*. October 25, 2011.
Lumenick, Lou. *New York Post*. October 28, 2011.
O'Sullivan, Michael. *Washington Post*. October 28, 2011.
Robinson, Tahsa. *AV Club*. October 27, 2011.
Sobczynski, Peter. *eFilmcritic.ciom*. October 28, 2011.
Turan, Kenneth. *Los Angeles Times*. October 27, 2011.
Whitty, Stephen. *Newark Star Ledger*. October 28, 2011.

QUOTES

Humpty Dumpty: "I'm not a person. I'm not a bird. I'm not even a food. I don't know what I am."
Puss in Boots: "You are what you have always been, my brother."

TRIVIA

Antonio Banderas participated earnestly in a viral marketing event upon the film's release by posing for photos surrounded by cats.

AWARDS

Nomination:

Oscars 2011: Animated Film
Golden Globes 2012: Animated Film.

R

RAMPART

The most corrupt cop you've ever seen on screen.
—Movie tagline

It must be of incredible frustration for real-life police officers to watch themselves portrayed on screen. The rookies are usually dim bulbs, too wet behind the ears to make a difference and often screwing something up…or being killed. Action films occasionally elevate the heroics while ignoring the boring everyday tactics of procedure and extensive paperwork. Then there are the corrupt cops that expose the worst fears about those who chose to wear a badge in order to feed their greatest inebriation of power and control. Lining their pockets alternates from "earning" the scratch left behind by the bad guys they arrest to being on "the take" to serve and protect society's underbelly from incarceration. It almost certainly leads to a fascinating moral study of characters representative of the very demons that ordinary citizens wrestle with in less extreme fashions every day. Oren Movermen's *Rampart* gives cops another face they would rather distance themselves from, but ultimately is a film which comes up short when trying to connect his behavior to the grand social dynamics of corruption and scapegoats.

Set during 1999 when Los Angeles' rampart scandal involving police brutality was in full bloom, Dave Brown (Woody Harrelson) is a cop who believes it is just another political witch hunt designed to diminish their ability to enforce the law. Dave is hardly the holiest of officers however. Constantly investigated by the department, he has even earned himself the nickname of "Date Rape," referring to a past case where he may or may not

have gone Dirty Harry on a perp he knew to be guilty. He lives with his sister ex-wives—not in a polygamist manner, they are actual sisters (Anne Heche & Cynthia Nixon)—and the daughters from each marriage. When he cannot get a nostalgic bedroom romp at home, Dave makes his ways to the bars for casual one-night stands that end with him smoking and no conversation.

Trouble seems ready for Dave to find it, as when a random motorist plows into his squad car. After the driver tries to flee, Dave runs him down and beats him, in full view of spectators with video cameras. This turns the spotlight back on him with an assistant D.A. (Sigourney Weaver) who does her best to cut through Dave's brand of compromised legalese and a rising politician (Steve Buscemi). Never one to cool off from the prevailing heat coming down on him, Dave seeks out an old friend of his father's (Ned Beatty)—a retired cop—who has his ears tuned into the latest underground scores that men in blue can exploit. Date Rape Dave also carries on a new relationship with a lawyer (Robin Wright Penn) whom he is actually willing to talk to, provided it is about sex or details that may help his case.

As you might be able to tell, *Rampart* is in no shortage of subplots. But like leads that produce no arrests, each of them never follows through to a substantial conclusion. They are little more than vignettes that do nothing but reinforce what even the rookie detectives in the audience can deduce after one or two scenes with Dave. This is a bad guy, a casual racist (though he claims to "hate everybody"), and a misogynist who bullies a female colleague to finish her food like a stepdad trying to mark his authoritative territory. He does try to maintain cordial relationships with his daughters, but teenager Helen's (Brie Larson) rebellious phase is representative of a problem he cannot solve, lest he is able to use deadly force.

Rampart's screenplay was co-written by James Ellroy, the well-praised crime novelist whose works have been turned into the unforgettable *L.A. Confidential* (1997) and one which everyone would like to forget in *The Black Dahlia* (2006). The writer has dabbled in other screenplays, including *Street Kings* (2008), another hard-boiled action picture about police corruption and the little seen *Dark Blue* (2002) with Kurt Russell in basically the Dave Brown role set just before the Rodney King riots. *Rampart* is meant more to be a character piece than a sprawling tale of big city corruption and it when Moverman loses sight of that the audience can be quickly distracted into believing a larger ensemble is going to bring everything to a head. Sigourney Weaver is great in a pair of scenes, but she disappears too quickly. Steve Buscemi has more screen time in the opening credits of HBO's *Boardwalk Empire*. Ben Foster is unrecognizable as a wheelchair-bound homeless snitch who offers little other than to remind viewers that he too worked with Moverman on his first film, *The Messenger* (2009). By the time Ice Cube shows up late as another investigator on Brown's case, he is just the final name on a list of celebrities contributing cameos to a story that amazingly wants to have a level of ambiguity about it in the end.

The one place where *Rampart* succeeds, and overwhelmingly so, is in creating a vehicle for Woody Harrelson to really grit his teeth into. Summoning both his casual charm and a restrained menace reminiscent of his turn in *Natural Born Killers* (1994), Harrelson—even through his outbursts—feels like a man completely in control of his own philosophy and enjoys toying with his superiors. Dave's arrogant insistence of remaining on the job, despite all efforts to force him out, suggests his one-way (or stalled) story is headed for a redemptive sadness and isolation, rather than a full-blown forgiveness. Except the film never quite gets there. Moverman is too insistent on being restrained in his presentation of one-man-as-the-city and then bursting into flashes of larger schemes. A moratorium must be placed on filmmakers using the underground sex club as the rock bottom of an anti-hero's perilous personal journey. In the end, the problems of one cop are not enough to condemn a city's ideology nor cast general aspersions against the men and women out there on the job every day. Nor is that cop interesting enough to have viewers wondering where his next radio call will take him past the open-ended conclusion, even if the implication is hell.

Erik Childress

CREDITS

Dave Brown: Woody Harrelson
Linda Fentress: Robin Wright
Joan Confrey: Sigourney Weaver
Kyle Timkins: Ice Cube
Hartshorn: Ned Beatty
Bill Blago: Steve Buscemi
Barbara: Cynthia Nixon
Catherine: Anne Heche
Helen: Brie Larson
General Terry: Ben Foster
Margaret: Sammy Boyarsky
Origin: USA
Language: English
Released: 2011
Production: Lawrence Inglee, Clark Peterson, Ben Foster, Ken Kao; Lightstream Pictures, Waypoint Entretainment, Third Mind Pictures; released by Millennium Entertainment
Directed by: Oren Moverman
Written by: Oren Moverman, James Ellroy
Cinematography by: Bobby Bukowski
Music by: Dickon Hinchliffe
Sound: Lisa Pinero
Editing: Jay Rabinowitz
Art Direction: Austin Gorg
Costumes: Catherine George
Production Design: David Wasco
MPAA rating: R
Running time: 108 minutes

REVIEWS

Berardinelli, James. *Variety.* December 1, 2011.
Corliss, Richard. *Time Magazine.* September 15, 2011.
Dargis, Manohla. *New York Times.* November 22, 2011.
Fine, Marshall. *Hollywood & Fine.* November 21, 2011.
Goss, William. *Film.com.* November 22, 2011.
Honeycutt, Kirk. *Hollywood Reporter.* November 21, 2011.
Longworth, Karina. *Village Voice.* November 22, 2011.
Nusair, David. *Reel Film Reviews.* September 20, 2011.
Roeper, Richard. *RichardRoeper.com.* December 2, 2011.
Swietek, Frank. *One Guy's Opinion.* December 27, 2011.

QUOTES

Dave Brown: "I don't cheat on my taxes...you can't cheat on something you never committed to."

TRIVIA

To achieve his character's appearance, Harrelson sought advice from Christian Bale who told him to eat very little and run as fast as possible.

RANGO

Box Office: $123.5 million

Since the release of *Shrek* in 2001, most animated films have made an attempt to throw in snarky pop culture references within their narrative, either as throwaway jokes to wink at the audience. The purpose, presumably, is to use these references as a way of keeping adults entertained while their kids can enjoy the characters and everything else that they do understand. But often there is too much winking and one gets the feeling that the authors would rather joke about the story than actually tell it with sincerity. While there is certainly nothing wrong with going for an easy laugh, the exercise can be somewhat cumbersome when a younger and less hip viewer is trying to watch a movie and keep grasp of the storyline while being assaulted with gag after gag after gag.

Not all animated films fall into this trap. Some have great respect for their chosen genre and the conventions that come with them. *Rango* is such a film. Without a trace of a wink, the film is an all-out Western and, perhaps most miraculously, it is its own Western. It does not simply run down a checklist of Western cliches, but rather draws its storyline more from *Chinatown* (1974) than something by John Ford or Clint Eastwood (although there are references to their work as well). It is a movie that loves movies and, most of all, loves the fun of them.

The story is introduced via a four-piece mariachi band of owls in the desert. They speak of a folk hero, who they say will die in this story. The Stranger (voiced by Johnny Depp), as he is first referred to, is at first a pet chameleon suffering from an existential crisis. He thinks of himself as "undefined." He is a wannabe actor trying to act out a scene with some inanimate objects that reside in his cage with him. The cage itself sits in the backseat of a crowded station wagon driving through the Mojave Desert. An accident causes the cage to fall out of the back window and in the middle of nowhere, leaving the pet chameleon on his own.

He first meets a wise sage in the form of an armadillo (voiced by Alfred Molina) who suggests that the lizard not journey into the desert. But water must be found in order for anyone—or anything—to survive. "If you want to find water," the armadillo says. "You must first look for Dirt." The chameleon eventually finds a town that is actually named Dirt. It is a town straight out of a classic movie western and the chameleon is the Lizard With No Name. He first ventures into a saloon where he is laughed at for ordering water. The bartender instead gives him a prickly bottle of cactus juice. When asked his name, the lizard looks down at the bottle labeled Durango and realizes this is his chance to start anew, with a new name and new identity; the ultimate acting challenge. The bottle gives him the idea to name himself Rango.

Rango adopts a new persona for himself, that of a fearless gunslinger who, as he tells it, shot down seven villainous brothers with one single bullet. The lie takes him deeper, of course, but soon he has won the adulation of the townsfolk who assume every word he says is true. Of course, there are other forces that bring fear to the town, particularly a giant hawk that touches down every once in a while to hunt for an edible critter or two. Rango, who has already had one run-in with the feathered creature before he arrived in Dirt, manages to outsmart it yet again, convincing the town once and for all that he is a force with which to be reckoned.

Rango eventually assumes the role of town sheriff. The Mayor (voiced by Ned Beatty), a turtle in a wheelchair, informs Rango of a water shortage that has the whole town feeling desperate. Some suspect that water is being thrown out into the dessert. But why? The only water that remains in the water bank is what appears to be a gallon or so at the bottom of a giant water dispenser jug. Meanwhile, Rango does his best at acting the role of sheriff, making many mistakes along the way, most notably giving three bank robbers a permit to tunnel underground for the purposes of mining. When the water in the bank goes missing, Rango must put together a posse to retrieve it and bring the three bank robbers to justice.

This sets in motion one of the best action sequences in the last few years, animated or otherwise. Rango and his posse ride small birds as horses, a couple of which pull a carriage (it is a Western, after all) while the robbers ride bats through the sky resulting in not only a classic desert chase scene, but also an aerial dogfight. It is one of the many big, inventive pieces in the film. Another unexpected moment of high originality comes when Rango first witnesses a water dance. The townsfolk line up side by side every Wednesday to try and divine the water from out of a drain. This is done by dancing in unison, with determination and dedication. It never works, of course, but it is certainly worth trying.

The conspiracy over the water supply is inevitable, but *Rango* never lets itself get bogged down by it. It retains the freshness of its premise by introducing its audience to new and interesting characters while also maintaining a fast-paced, comedic zest that keeps the tone light and enjoyable. Depp's delivery is so fast that it can be hard to keep up, but this works in the character's favor, since the idea is for him to try and stay one step ahead of everyone else, lest he be discovered as being just an ordinary lizard in an extraordinary circumstance.

But the casting of Depp is a curious one. It is a natural choice, of course, because Depp has worked extensively with director Gore Verbinski on the first three *Pirates of the Caribbean* movies, but the length to which the screenplay puts this lizard in an existential dilemma over his identity makes one think about actors such as Depp who are, in fact, able to disappear so far into a role that they become unrecognizable. Depp has made a career out of creating some of the most iconic and memorable characters of the last twenty years that it is rare to see him play a character that is not in full make-up. Depp must feel a kinship with the character of Rango. It is not snarkiness for the sake of it when the movie throws in references to Depp's characters in *Fear and Loathing in Las Vegas* (1998) and *Don Juan DeMarco* (1994).

Verbinski has gone out of his way to create a fully imagined animated movie that has a palpable human quality to it. During production, Verbinski had his voice cast also act out the movie on a soundstage so as to give the animators a reference point not just in visual terms, but emotional terms as well. The characters in *Rango* do not behave like animated movie characters, but like real life movie characters. Every facial movement and nuance of a performance is captured in a way that is seldom seen in an animated movie. The viewer forgets that these are animals. Credit is also due, of course, to the animated team that rendered an increasingly popular form of photorealistic animation. Also, cinematographer Roger Deakins was once again brought in as a visual consultant to help make the cameras for *Rango* move like a real movie. Deakins has been doing similar work on Pixar's movies, most notably *WALL*E* (2008).

There are many eye-popping, exciting and visually breathtaking moments in *Rango*, yet it was a bit of an anomaly when released in theaters because it was not released in 3D. By this time, it was unheard of to release an animated movie in a 2-D-only version. This is both refreshing (parents no longer have to deal with the choice of paying more for a kid's ticket) and a little frustrating. Many animated films, such as *Cars 2* (2011), have no business being in 3D, but the studios demand it anyway. *Rango*, on the other hand, would have looked great in the format. But as always, the test of a great movie is whether it works either way and *Rango* works better than just about any live action or animated 3D movie out there.

Collin Souter

CREDITS

Rango: Johnny Depp (Voice)
Rattlesnake Jake: Bill Nighy (Voice)
The Spirit of the West: Timothy Olyphant (Voice)
Tortoise John: Ned Beatty (Voice)
Beans: Isla Fisher (Voice)
Priscilla: Abigail Breslin (Voice)
Bad Bill: Ray Winstone (Voice)
Roadkill: Alfred Molina (Voice)
Doc/Merrimack/Mr. Snuggles: Stephen (Steve) Root (Voice)
Balthazar: Harry Dean Stanton (Voice)
Origin: USA
Language: English
Released: 2011
Production: John Carls, Graham King, Jacqueline M. Lopez, Gore Verbinski; Industrial Light & Magic, Blind Wink, GK Films, Nickelodeon Movies; released by Paramount Pictures
Directed by: Gore Verbinski
Written by: John Logan
Music by: Hans Zimmer
Sound: Addison Teague
Editing: Craig Wood
Art Direction: John Bell
Production Design: Mark McCreery
MPAA rating: PG
Running time: 107 minutes

REVIEWS

Burr, Ty. *Boston Globe.* March 3, 2011.
Childress, Erik. *eFilmcritic.com.* March 4, 2011.
Corliss, Richard. *TIME Magazine.* March 4, 2011.
Diones, Bruce. *New Yorker.* March 14, 2011.
Ebert, Roger. *Chicago Sun-Times.* March 2, 2011.
Howell, Peter. *Toronto Star.* March 4, 2011.
Kennedy, Lisa. *Denver Post.* March 4, 2011.
Schager, Nick. *Village Voice.* March 1, 2011.
Scott, A.O. *New York Times.* March 3, 2011.
Witty, Stephen. *Newark Star Ledger.* March 4, 2011.

QUOTES

Rango: "I will blow that ugly right off your face!"

TRIVIA

The first cat that Beans talks to in Dirt is a nod to staple western actor Pat Buttram.

AWARDS

Oscars 2011: Animated Film
British Acad. 2011: Animated Film

Nomination:
Golden Globes 2012: Animated Film.

REAL STEEL

If you get one shot, make it real.
—Movie tagline

Courage is stronger than steel.
—Movie tagline

Champions aren't born. They're made.
—Movie tagline

Box Office: $85.5 million

There is a nearly foolproof simplicity to a movie about boxing robots that is both supporting and limiting. *Real Steel* is no masterpiece of science fiction or even science schmaltz, but it does not have to be much more than it is: A clanking, cliché-fueled entertainment about a father and son who reconnect and giant robots that punch each other. It is out to thrill and entertain while tugging on a few heart wires, and that it does on a level not one millimeter above average expectations.

Real Steel is set in 2020, conveniently not so far in the future that fashion, transportation, or communication have changed, but enough that the sweet science has been replaced by the science science: Ten-foot-tall remote-controlled robots now battle it out in boxing arenas rather than humans. The suggestion is that people's desire for more and more vicious carnage in the ring eventually led to the use of the stand-in automatrons, but this is not the kind of science-fiction film that slows to examine what that—or a video-game detachment toward violence—says about modern society and culture.

As written by John Gatins, Dan Gilroy, and Jeremy Leven, and directed by Shawn Levy, *Real Steel*'s world is no dark dystopia, but instead a brightly lit truck-and-beer-commercial version of America, complete with country roads and rodeos, long-haul trucking, and a down-home gear-head's love of nuts and bolts. Hugh Jackman plays Charlie Kenton, a once-near-great boxer now roaming the country (especially the Southwest) with a broken-down collection of robot boxers, hustling up fights for a buck, and always looking for the big score while staying a highway or two ahead of debt collectors.

Charlie's rock-'em sock-'em vagabond life is interrupted by his sudden custody of Max (Dakota Goyo), an estranged eleven-year-old son Charlie initially sees as another cash asset he can leverage to stay in the boxing game. There follows a typical father-son journey of discovery and bonding, with young Max literally digging

up and making a project out of an old-school boxing robot he calls Atom. Scratched and dented Atom turns out to be a natural, and soon the boy, his robot, and his ersatz dad are on the road toward a showdown with the world champion 'bot, Zeus.

All this is served up with plenty of pre-programmed "give the little guy a chance" *Rocky*-isms and can-do, underdog spirit. Zeus was created by a chic and sullen Japanese video-game guru for a rich and snobby Brazilian boxing family, and by the time Max, Charlie, and Atom square off in the championship ring against such international and corporate domination, the film's "Made in America" theme is as obvious as its numerous product placements.

Jackman may be Australian, not American—and a dancer, not a boxer—but that matters little. The easily likable actor is here to provide enough winking charm to help audiences overlook that Charlie is initially a cynical, deadbeat dad. The character is a collection of con-man, heart-of-gold clichés, and Jackman does not reach for anything deeper than redemption-ready gruffness. Like Jackman, Goyo also acquits himself adequately with minimal effort.

The film's most intriguing character however is Atom. Not because the hulking, blank-faced robot is interesting—it is not. Rather what's fascinating is how Gatins' script and Levy's direction use Atom not just as an in-ring sporting proxy, but an emotional stand-in for both Charlie and Max. Atom has no artificial intelligence—he is nothing more than a remote-control toy—so the human father and son must project all the robot's on-screen personality onto it. Yet Atom's boxing career is also the mechanism by which Charlie and Max find each other. *Real Steel* cheats that tricky balance: When necessary, it treats Atom as a living, breathing character, but when not needed, the robot is set aside like a convenient stack of circuit boards and servos.

Real Steel is loosely based on a short science-fiction story by Richard Matheson, but Matheson's "Steel" is a melancholy tale of a washed up (childless) human fighter pushed to desperate and life-threatening lengths in the world of robo-boxing. The film version holds no such grim pessimism—it is a bright, feel-good film that rivets the visual kick of impeccably rendered and choreographed CGI robots punching each other to an equally artificial dose of sports-movie hope and dysfunctional-family heart.

Levy is a shameless journeyman director of middle-of-the-road fare, and at no point here does he punch above his clean, well-lit weight class. But with Steven Spielberg producing, Levy's film never fails land its punches. The fight scenes are suitably exciting without being memorable, while a sure-fire way to drum up a crowd-pleasing scene is to show lots of pleased and cheering crowds. Those viewers interested in real science fiction ideas or honest tales of human relationships might wish *Real Steel* was not so relentlessly formulaic, but Levy knows how to work that formula. Plus, there are those big, boxing robots.

Locke Peterseim

CREDITS

Charlie Kenton: Hugh Jackman
Max Kenton: Dakota Goyo
Ricky: Kevin Durand
Bailey Tallet: Evangeline Lilly
Finn: Anthony Mackie
Deborah Barnes: Hope Davis
Marvine Barnes: James Rebhorn
Tak Mashido: Karl Yune
Origin: USA
Language: English
Released: 2011
Production: Don Murphy, Susan Montford, Shawn Levy; 21Laps Entertainment, Reliance Big Entertainment; released by DreamWorks SKG
Directed by: Shawn Levy
Written by: John Gatins
Cinematography by: Mauro Fiore
Music by: Danny Elfman
Sound: Steve Cantamessa
Music Supervisor: Jennifer Hawks
Editing: Dean Zimmerman
Art Direction: Seth Reed
Costumes: Marlene Stewart
Production Design: Tom Meyer
MPAA rating: PG-13
Running time: 127 minutes

REVIEWS

Baumgarten, Marjorie. *Austin Chronicle.* October 7, 2011.
Ebert, Roger. *Chicago Sun-Times.* October 5, 2011.
Holden, Steven. *New York Times.* October 6, 2011.
Phillips, Michael. *Chicago Tribune.* October 6, 2011.
Pinkerton, Nick. *Village Voice.* October 5, 2011.
Pols, Mary. *Time.* October 7, 2011.
Sharkey, Betsy. *Los Angeles Times.* October 7, 2011.
Tobias, Scott. *AV Club.* October 6, 2011.
Wickman, Forrest. *Slate.* October 6, 2011.
Zacharek, Stephanie. *Movieline.* October 6, 2011.

QUOTES

Charlie Kenton: "What do you want from me?"

Max Kenton: "I want you to fight for me! That's all I ever wanted!"

TRIVIA

Michigan was chosen as the location for this movie by director Shawn Levy because he was blown away by the Model T Automobile plant in Highland Park near Detroit. No other location he visited in New Mexico, Los Angeles, or Georgia came close.

AWARDS

Nomination:
Oscars 2011: Visual FX.

RED RIDING HOOD

Who's afraid?
  —Movie tagline
Believe the legend. Beware the wolf.
  —Movie tagline

Box Office: $37.7 million

Red Riding Hood opens in the Middle Ages in the small, European mountain village of Daggerhorn. Its inhabitants seem to get the finest Medieval hair and skin care available, but such an unblemished and sexy physical state requires a sacrificial pig. Literally. It seems that for generations the Daggerhornians have been plagued by the occasional predatory werewolf, held at bay by said sacrifices. Unfortunately, as the film begins, the mysterious wolf is no longer satisfied with scrawny livestock and has begun feasting on the village's crop of nubile young women.

It is near-impossible to separate *Red Riding Hood* from the recent spate of dark-fantasy romances aimed with terrifying precision and determination at a very specific target audience: mostly female, mostly young, seeking dark-and-sexy fairytales about angst-ridden young women and the Byronic man-boy-monsters with whom they cannot help fall in love. A spin on the Brothers Grimm premise, the latest entry in this subgenre's mix of dark-outside fears and darker-inside secrets might have yielded a rich, Gothic bouquet of (not-so) repressed desires and blood-red chills. Instead, *Red Riding Hood* is a stupefying slog through tired teen-romance clichés that lacks even a hint of invigorating irony or at least enjoyable camp.

The film's heroine is Valerie (Amanda Seyfried), a good-but-headstrong girl who finds herself facing a fate worse than being devoured by a hungry wolf: Her parents (Billy Burke and Virginia Madsen) have arranged for her to marry the village rich boy (Max Irons) instead of the bad-boy woodcutter (Shiloh Fernandez) whose dark and dangerous ways have ensnared her heart. Lukas Haas plays a man of the cloth trying to do the right thing, while Julie Christie keeps a respectable distance as Valerie's woods-dwelling grandmother. Soon Gary Oldman drops in as a church inquisitor/wolf hunter, dusts off his old Carpathian accent from *Bram Stoker's Dracula* (1992), and proceeds to gnaw on the scenery with great relish.

The rest of *Red Riding Hood* plays out as a "Who's Afraid of the Big Bad Wolf" mystery with little red herrings popping up at every turn as the viewer struggles to care about the creature's identity. Nor is the beast itself kept cloaked for long in the shadows. CGI marvels—even cheap, fake-looking ones—must be trotted out, so *Red Riding Hood*'s werewolf, complete with the usual computer-generated sheen of unreality, is seen early and often, neatly erasing any potential viewer dread.

Meanwhile, swept away by hormones and wolfen paranoia, the village's young men posture and threaten, while the young women titter and backstab as if they spend half their time reading *The Crucible* (1953) and the other half watching *Gossip Girl*. There is a festival celebration by bonfire (the medieval equivalent of a homecoming dance, complete with gloomy 21st-century goth dream-pop tunes), literal rolls in the hay, and plenty of adolescent-yearning hearts and hairy palms.

Seyfried, normally a fine actress capable of rich variety, comes off unsure what to do with all this over-ripe, slo-mo, teen melodrama, so she plods dutifully along with a languid acquiescence. Her male co-stars do not fare so well. Irons seems to have inherited a mouth-breathing gene that skipped his actor father Jeremy, while Fernandez becomes the first young performer who cannot spark some chemistry with the beautiful Seyfried.

While tales like this of dark, young love have been around for millennia, in their current incarnation the PG-13 *Ur*-text is *Twilight*, (2008) a film *Red Riding Hood*'s director Catherine Hardwicke is well-versed in, having helmed the first entry in the highly profitable film series. Working from a script by David Johnson, Hardwicke fills *Red Riding Hood* with *Twilight* touches: A young woman straining against the mores of her community, forbidden love expressed with endless sullen glances, squabbling rival suitors, and lots of strolls in moody forests. She even hauls along *Twilight*'s Burke to once again play the heroine's disapproving father.

Hardwicke serves all this up amid the sun-dabbled trees and windmills with an arch, faux naturalism that is intended to feel like a dark fantasia, complete with the pseudo-sexual themes that have always accompanied the tale of Little Red Riding Hood. However, the director, who authentically explored the modern teenage girl's heart and habits in her first feature, *Thirteen*, (2003) brings no similar honesty to *Red Riding Hood*. (Nor is the one-time production designer able to gussy up the film's look with anything striking or visually pleasing.) This film feels carefully and slavishly constructed by committee to sell directly to the teen female viewers; there is no room left for an original touch or intriguing quirk. No one—from Hardwicke, through the actors, down to the pig wrangler—appears creatively committed to the endeavor, so they listlessly go through the motions in pursuit of what they think young female viewers want to see.

Tied so tightly to its formula and driven only by unyielding demographic desire, none of *Red Riding Hood* makes much sense, and matters even less. Its bland pandering leaves it so hollow it is hard to imagine even its target audience finding much to enjoy. Gothic portent and eye-rolling romance renders the film too silly to take seriously and too leaden to enjoy. Dull even by the light of its crimson moon, *Red Riding Hood* ends up often laughable but never any fun.

Locke Peterseim

CREDITS

Valerie: Amanda Seyfried
Peter: Shiloh Fernandez
Henry: Max Irons
Father Solomon: Gary Oldman
Grandmother: Julie Christie
Adrien Lazar: Michael Shanks
Cesaire: Billy Burke
Suzette: Virginia Madsen
Father Auguste: Lukas Haas
Origin: USA
Language: English
Released: 2011
Production: Jennifer Davisson Killoran, Julie Yorn, Leonardo DiCaprio; Appian Way; released by Warner Bros.
Directed by: Catherine Hardwicke
Written by: David Leslie Johnson
Cinematography by: Mandy Walker
Music by: Brian Reitzell, Alex Heffes
Sound: Michael McGee
Editing: Nancy Richardson, Julia Wong
Art Direction: Don MacAulay
Costumes: Cindy Evans
Production Design: Thomas E. Sanders
MPAA rating: PG-13
Running time: 100 minutes

REVIEWS

Childress, Erik. *eFilmCritic.com*. March 10, 2011.
Dargis, Manohla. *New York Times*. March 10, 2011.

Denby, David. *New Yorker.* March 28, 2011.

Dujsik, Mark. *Mark Reviews Movies.* March 10, 2011.

Ebert, Roger. *Chicago Sun-Times.* March 11, 2011.

Fendelman, Adam. *HollywoodChicago.com.* March 10, 2011.

Pols, Mary F. *TIME Magazine.* March 10, 2011.

Puig, Claudia. *USA Today.* March 10, 2011.

Reed, Rex. *New York Observer.* March 16, 2011.

Roeper, Richard. *RichardRoeper.com.* March 11, 2011.

QUOTES

Suzette: "If you love her, you'll let her go."

TRIVIA

The film was shipped to theaters with the code name "Fangs of Affection."

RED STATE

Fear God.
— Movie tagline

Love thy neighbor.
— Movie tagline

Box Office: $1.1 million

Writer/director Kevin Smith combines David Koresh's group of Branch Davidians and the Westboro Baptist Church (a character makes a passing reference to "Phelps in Kansas" to avoid confusion) to create a portrayal of evil that is admittedly haunting during the course of one scene. The group is called the Five Points Trinity Church, led by Abin Cooper (Michael Parks), and Smith first introduces them protesting the funeral of a murdered gay teenager. Cooper stands off to the side, sipping a cup of coffee, as his followers hold up hateful signs and chant vitriol about the young man and the state of his eternal soul. The sight of the demonstration, sadly, is familiar, though in the picture of Cooper's calm and content demeanor, *Red State* suggests that the real face of evil is a casual one.

That outlook changes into a far more simplistic one over the course of the movie, which shifts gears from teen sex comedy to horror and from a bureaucratic comedy of errors to a violent standoff. It is difficult to imagine such an erratic narrative working in the context of the movie's solemn subject matter. The credits of the movie divide the characters into three castes that are generally considered topics to avoid in polite conversation: Sex, religion, and politics. And with the screenplay's continually wavering perspectives it seems as though Smith is uncomfortable doing much more than merely flirting taboo. As a result, *Red State* is ultimately like the

awkward chuckle from an embarrassed participant in a conversation that has veered outside of his comprehension.

The script's first focal point is Travis (Michael Angarano), a student at the local high school who watches the Five Points Church's protest as his mother (Anna Gunn) drives him to class. Conveniently enough, his teacher (Deborah Aquila) happens to be giving a lesson on the First Amendment to the Constitution, which leads perfectly into a little bit of exposition on the church: They have made a laughing stock of the entire state, do not even have the support of "ultra-conservatives," and are completely within their rights to practice the First Amendment as long as they stay away from the Second Amendment. That is, as they say, all the foreshadowing that is necessary.

Travis' friend Jarod (Kyle Gallner) has been browsing online personal ads looking for an anonymous sex partner, and he has found one who will take himself, Travis, and their friend Billy Ray (Nicholas Braun) at the same time. The trio sneaks off into the night in Travis' family car to a trailer in the middle of nowhere, sideswiping the parked car of the town's sheriff Wynan (Stephen Root), who is in the midst of a clandestine meeting for oral sex from another man. Wynan, a married law enforcement officer who is later torn between doing the right thing and keeping his sexuality a secret, would be an intriguing character, though Smith reduces him to bouts of drinking and sobbing. The sheriff only exists as a plot device to send his deputy (Matt Jones) in search of the car that struck his own so that the confrontation with the Five Points Church, which has an arsenal of assault rifles in the cellar, can begin.

Smith is similarly apathetic toward the large majority of the movie's characters. The teenagers, whom Sara (Melissa Leo), a member of the church, drugs so that the church can hold them captive and execute them for their intent to break "God's law" against fornication, are ironically and solely defined by their sex drives. The twenty or so people in Cooper's congregation (all related by blood or marriage) are blind disciples to their leader, and the federal agents that eventually surround the church's compound, led by Joseph Keenan (John Goodman), are blind adherents to orders. Only one believer named Cheyenne (Kerry Bishé) and one federal agent named Harry (Kevin Alejandro) question their respective positions. Cheyenne wants only to protect the children inside the church from what she suspects will be a massacre, and Harry has doubts about being part of what he knows will be a massacre. In a cruel moment of misanthropy, Harry suppresses his hesitation just as Cheyenne might succeed, and Smith's script dispatches a few other vital or dramatically viable characters in an equally matter-of-fact way.

The only time Smith's screenplay maintains its focus—incongruously enough—is when the movie first enters the belly of its beast. After switching the focal point from Travis to Jarod, who is locked in a dog cage with a piece of cloth over it, Smith once again changes the position of his figurative spotlight to Cooper once inside the Five Points Church and allows the mad, murderous preacher an extended monologue—a sermon of hatred and hellfire. Parks' relatively subdued performance and Smith's close-ups of Cooper and his admiring followers (not to mention the additional weight of the length of the speech) give far more credence and legitimacy to the character's words than they deserve.

The narrative is a bedlam of tone and construction (bursts of violence and chaos mixed with chatty exposition), and *Red State* cannot even find the courage to follow through on the seemingly inevitable climax of the story, which, after arriving at a stalemate, hints at a literally Apocalyptic outcome. Instead, Smith takes the conservative route and confirms the nagging suspicion that he sees the whole affair as one, big joke.

Mark Dujsik

CREDITS

Abin Cooper: Michael Parks
Joseph Keenan: John Goodman
Sheriff Wynan: Stephen Root
Travis: Michael Angarano
Jarod: Kyle Gallner
Billy-Ray: Nicholas Braun
Sara: Melissa Leo
Origin: USA
Language: English
Released: 2011
Production: Jonathan Gordon; Harvey Boys; released by Smodcast Pictures
Directed by: Kevin Smith
Written by: Kevin Smith
Cinematography by: David Klein
Sound: Glen Trew
Editing: Kevin Smith
Art Direction: Susan Bolles
Costumes: Beth Pasternak
Production Design: Cabot McMullen
MPAA rating: R
Running time: 88 minutes

REVIEWS

Alter, Ethan. *Film Journal International.* September 21, 2011.
Gonsalves, Rob. *EFilmCritic.com.* September 5, 2011.

Goss, William. *Film.com.* September 23, 2011.
O'Hehir, Andrew. *Salon.com.* October 19, 2011.
Orndorf, Brian. *Blu-ray.com.* September 1, 2011.
Rabin, Nathan. *AV Club.* September 22, 2011.
Rich, Katey. *CinemaBlend.com.* January 23, 2011.
Schager, Nick. *Boxoffice Magazine.* September 30, 2011.
Scott, A.O. *New York Times.* September 22, 2011.
Willmore, Alison. *Movieline.* September 22, 2011.

QUOTES

Joseph Keenan: "People just do the strangest things when they believe they're entitled. But they do even stranger things when they just plain believe."

TRIVIA

Writer/director Kevin Smith wrote the part of Abin Cooper specifically for Michael Parks and went so far as to says that if Parks had not agreed to appear in the film, the project would have been dropped entirely.

RESTLESS

Who do you live for?
—Movie tagline

Like a hip band playing in a coffee house while someone plays bongos and another smokes clove cigarettes in time with spoken word poetry, Gus Van Sant's *Restless* undeniably sets the twee meter to red. It is as subjective as performance art, so weighed down with self-aware plot elements in and a hipster tone that it made skin crawl for some critics. However, it is also, thanks in no small part its talented lead actress and accomplished technical team, remarkably consistent in its vision. It has a unique world view and sticks to it, like a poet who may use a different rhythm than his peers but does so confidently and consistently enough line after line. In the end, a bit more grounding might have made the final product more emotionally resonant, but Van Sant's direction and the work by Mia Wasikowska warrant a look.

Restless is a poetic piece about a common subject for the form: death. It is about two people for whom it is not an abstract or an inevitability as it is for most viewers but a part of their daily existences—one as a survivor and one as a too-soon victim. On one level, *Restless* is not unlike a hipster take on themes Hollywood has been exploring for years through the over-populated and typically manipulative "love through terminal illness" subgenre. It clearly reflects themes that have been explored before but Jason Lew tackles them from a unique angle, incorporating cancer, funerals, survivor's guilt, and even the ghost of a WWII pilot into his narrative.

For the tragically-named Enoch (Henry Hopper, who bears such a strong resemblance to his father Dennis that it almost feels like the late great actor is haunting the film himself), death is in the rearview mirror. He is the survivor of a horrible car accident that took his parents and sent him to live with his distant Aunt Mabel (Jane Adams), who Enoch partially blames for the accident happening in the first place. Enoch was dead for a few minutes and awoke to find a new friend in his world, the ghost of a WWII Kamikaze pilot named Hiroshi (Ryo Kase). Whether or not Enoch is being haunted or just has a very vivid imaginary friend (or perhaps even just is not playing with a full deck) is never fully answered. Regardless, the hero of *Restless* plays Battleship with a long-dead Japanese pilot. It is easy to see why most critics and audiences turned off from what Lew and Van Sant were attempting before the end of the first act.

Enoch is not just accompanied by a reminder of death, he is obsessed with it, going to funerals to listen to the eulogies of complete strangers; he wanders morosely through graveyards; he has become alienated from all of his peers. At one of the memorials, Enoch runs into a sweet girl named Annabel (Mia Wasikowska), who seems to be the first person to have actually seen Enoch in months. It is as if everyone else looks right past or even through the young man. Surely, Enoch and Annabel will fall in love and their commitment is tested when the Enoch learns that his first real girlfriend has but a few months before terminal cancer will take her. *Restless* is not really about fighting the inevitable death but more exists to suggest that there can still be beauty in the final days, even if those days come way too young.

There is an unforced, almost peaceful tone to *Restless* that can be often captivating. Shattering that peace more than any other element of the production is Hopper's overly-mannered and self-conscious performance, one that calls attention to itself too often to fit in the fabric of the piece. However, every other element, particularly Danny Elfman's score and the great Harris Savide's striking cinematography works together to challenge the typical tropes of the terminal illness love story genre. This is a piece without many emotional peaks (and it is the few over-cooked scenes that impede the success of the film above all else) and the attempt to make a film that approaches the end of death more like a peaceful blanket of snow than an impending thunderstorm is notable.

Finally, the great Mia Wasikowska adds an admittedly-lesser piece of evidence to the case that she is one of the best actresses of her young generation. Her stellar work on HBO's *In Treatment* (2008) and in films like *The Kids Are All Right* (2010) and *Jane Eyre* (2011) have made her a part of any such conversation. She is a fascinating young actress, always seeming completely in the moment and someone who makes unique, complex acting decisions every time. She is let down a bit by elements of *Restless* and the inconsistent choices made by her co-star but she is a true artist, and perhaps the fact that her talent can shine through even in a near-miss like this makes that case even more strongly than the more prominent films in her resume.

Brian Tallerico

CREDITS

Annabel Cotton: Mia Wasikowska
Enoch Brae: Henry Hopper
Hiroshi Takahashi: Ryo Kase
Elizabeth Cotton: Schuyler Fisk
Mabel: Jane Adams
Rachel Cotton: Lusia Strus
Origin: USA
Language: English
Released: 2011
Production: Brian Grazer, Bryce Dallas Howard, Ron Howard; Imagine Entertainment, Columbia Pictures, 360 Pictures; released by Sony Pictures Entertainment
Directed by: Gus Van Sant
Written by: Jason Lew
Cinematography by: Harris Savides
Music by: Danny Elfman
Sound: Robert C. Jackson
Editing: Elliot Graham
Art Direction: Benjamin Hayden
Costumes: Danny Glicker
Production Design: Anne Ross
MPAA rating: PG-13
Running time: 91 minutes

REVIEWS

Ebert, Roger. *Chicago Sun-Times.* September 21, 2011.
Hornaday, Ann. *Washington Post.* September 29, 2011.
Linden, Sheri. *Los Angeles Times.* September 17, 2011.
Phipps, Keith. *AV Club.* September 14, 2011.
Puig, Claudia. *USA Today.* September 15, 2011.
Rothkopf, Joshua. *Time Out New York.* September 13, 2011.
Schwarzbaum, Lisa. *Entertainment Weekly.* September 15, 2011.
Scott, A.O. *New York Times.* September 15, 2011.
Travers, Peter. *Rolling Stone.* September 15, 2011.
Zacharek, Stephanie. *Movieline.* September 12, 2011.

QUOTES

Annabel Cotton: "About the hospital. I don't work there. I am a patient."

TRIVIA
Schuyler Fisk is the daughter of Sissy Spacek.

RIO

This turkey can't fly.
—Movie tagline

1 out of every 8 Americans is afraid of flying. Most of them don't have feathers.
—Movie tagline

He's going to the wildest, most magical place on earth...home.
—Movie tagline

Box Office: $143.6 million

There is a love-scene gag in *Rio* involving a disco ball and the 1985 prom-dance ballad "Say You, Say Me." "Lionel Richie," says a character hoping to spark some avian romance, "works every time." Overall, *Rio*—the computer-animated tale of two very different birds of a feather trying to survive and maybe find love in Rio de Janeiro, Brazil during carnival—takes a similarly pleasing, pop-fluff approach to kids' cinematic diversion. Like Lionel Richie crooning a shallow love song, *Rio* entertains on a sappy, colorful surface level because that is exactly what it was carefully designed to do. And little else.

Rio makes its "let us entertain you" intentions clear right away, opening to a Busby Berkeley routine performed by flocks of brightly colored, singing and dancing Amazonian birds. "Song, dance, color, and movement" is *Rio*'s operating message—almost as if it was tested on infants to gauge their sensory perceptions. Which it may well have been.

All of this in-flight spectacle is interrupted by mean human poachers capturing and caging the fancy free performers. Their captives include a young blue macaw who is shipped off to the never-ending cold of Minnesota and raised by a mild-mannered bookstore owner (Leslie Mann) to become a domesticated brainy bird named Blu. That grown-up Blu is voiced with jabbering neuroses by Jesse Eisenberg, fresh off his triumph as Mark Zuckerberg in *The Social Network* (2010), only underscores the point: Blu has a big head, but an underdeveloped heart. Nor can he actually fly. In true animated family film fashion, Blu has lessons to learn.

The film does nothing with its initial, traumatic premise: That young Blu is ripped from his family and sent thousands of miles north figures only as a plot device, not any source of emotional depth. It has been sixty-nine years since *Bambi* (1940) and, unfortunately, today many "kids movies" like *Rio* are not about to

pause for any sort of "alienating downer." The movie is resolutely devoted to hollow entertainment: There are songs to sing and slapstick to shuck out.

Blu and his owner Linda soon wind up in Rio de Janeiro, where a dutifully wacky Brazilian ornithologist (Rodrigo Santoro) hopes to mate the male blue macaw with one of the few remaining females of his rare species: an escape-minded firecracker named Jewel (Anne Hathaway). (This is where the Lionel Richie comes in.) Of course, nothing goes as planned, and the mismatched, differently-tempered Blu and Jewel are bird-snatched by smugglers (aided by a preening, malicious cockatoo named Nigel, voiced by Jermaine Clement).

The rest of *Rio* is parade of primary colors and celebrity voice performances, as Blu and Jewel—chained together *Defiant Ones* style—roll through jungle, beach, and carnival, having adventures while learning to dance and love. And, of course, fly. George Lopez, Jamie Foxx, and The Black Eyed Peas' will.i.am are on hand as new-found bird pals, and Tracy Morgan voices a drooling bulldog with his usual gonzo vulnerability.

Rio is relentlessly pleasing and lightly entertaining, with something for everyone: action, humor (both broad for the kiddies and wry for the adults), international flavor (sans the city's wretched favelas, naturally), a monkey versus bird battle, and some very un-Minnesotan "tushy-shaking." There are feathers and sequins, pretty views of *Rio* from the air, and even a little spirituality—if circling the giant Christ the Redeemer statue a few times counts. (Please pay no racially-conscious mind to the mildly uncomfortable fact that the villainous monkeys break dance to hip-hop, wear lots of bling, and steal from tourists.) And it all feels so very test-marketed and demographically-shaped.

Rio may slap on a flimsy message about trusting your heart not your head, but the film itself feels very carefully calculated—it is all head, no heart. To complain about *Rio*'s lack of genuine emotion or character development (beyond serving the dictates of the conveyor-belt plot) would be akin to complaining about the lack of such nuances in a toy commercial. Early on the freedom-fearing Blu whines that he loves the safe predictability of his cage, and that is what *Rio* provides for viewers: Clean and polished entertainment marketing to drop children into for ninety minutes of bright and shiny babysitting. Never mind that every scene, every joke, every celebrity voice may initially amuse or divert but ultimately feels flat and soulless.

Produced by Blue Sky Studios and directed and co-written by Carlos Saldanha—the same crew that created the similarly amusing-but-empty *Ice Age* franchise, there is little to openly dislike in *Rio*, but not much to fully embrace, either. Devoid of rich emotional or visual texture, the movie is well enough made and holds together solidly for its running time, but all its above-average quality feels driven not by a desire to excel as animated art but rather to be cross-platform, over-seas-friendly product. "Song, dance, color, and movement"—it works every time. Just ask Lionel Richie.

Locke Peterseim

CREDITS

Blu: Jesse Eisenberg (Voice)
Jewel: Anne Hathaway (Voice)
Linda: Leslie Mann (Voice)
Rafael: George Lopez (Voice)
Fernando: Jake T. Austin (Voice)
Pedro: Will I Am (Voice)
Nico: Jamie Foxx (Voice)
Origin: USA
Language: English
Released: 2011
Production: Bruce Anderson, John C. Donkin; Blue Sky Studios, 20th Century-Fox; released by 20th Century-Fox
Directed by: Carlos Saldanha
Written by: Carlos Saldanha, Don Rhymer, Todd R. Jones
Cinematography by: Renato Falcao
Music by: John Powell
Sound: Randy Thom, Gwendolyn Yates Whittle
Editing: Harry Hitner, Randy Trager
MPAA rating: G
Running time: 96 minutes

REVIEWS

Corliss, Richard. *TIME Magazine.* April 14, 2011.
Hornaday, Ann. *Washington Post.* April 15, 2011.
Lacey, Liam. *Globe and Mail.* April 15, 2011.
Long, Tom. *Detroit News.* April 15, 2011.
Lumenick, Lou. *New York Post.* April 15, 2011.
Morgenstern, Joe. *Wall Street Journal.* April 14, 2011.
Phillips, Michael. *Chicago Tribune.* April 14, 2011.
Puig, Claudia. *USA Today.* April 14, 2011.
Sharkey, Betsy. *Los Angeles Times.* April 14, 2011.
Travers, Peter. *Rolling Stone.* April 21, 2011.

QUOTES

Jewel: "Aw, this is great. I'm chained to the only bird in the world who can't fly! Is there anything else I need to know?"
Blu: "Yes. I can't fly, I pick my beak, and once in a while I pee in the birdbath!"

TRIVIA

Early story art reveals that Nigel originally had a metal talon.

AWARDS

Nomination:

Oscars 2011: Song ("Real in Rio").

RISE OF THE PLANET OF THE APES
(Rise of the Apes)

Evolution becomes revolution.
—Movie tagline

Box Office: $176.8 million

The original *Planet of the Apes* (1968) was such an influential phenomenon of a movie that it transcended its origins, becoming a pop culture touchstone that spawned four sequels, a TV show, toys, games, and a twist-ending structure that was mimicked as often as it was mocked. The franchise died out as quickly as it came to life in the mid-'70s, only to get one seemingly final nail in its coffin when Tim Burton released a critically-reviled reboot in 2001 that made some decent cash but failed to reignite the dead series. Consequently, expectations for Rupert Wyatt's reboot ten years later in the form of a prequel titled *Rise of the Planet of the Apes* were pretty low. It stands as one of the greatest film surprises of 2011 that Wyatt's work is easily the best piece of filmmaking to exist within the franchise, notching rave reviews around the world and grossing almost half a billion dollars worldwide. With a landmark performance from Andy Serkis, stellar direction from Wyatt, and an underrated screenplay that perfectly connects the dots for both fans of the original film and newcomers to the concept, *Rise of the Planet of the Apes* was the perfect August capper on a summer season filled with a surprising amount of quality work.

By now, the cultural influence of the original film, which was actually based on a 1963 book by Pierre Boulle, is so complete that writers Rick Jaffa and Amanda Silver know that not much retread is needed for modern viewers. They perfectly balance a few in-jokes/references that will play well to the hardcore faithful but never fail to provide a foundation that will appeal to younger viewers who do not know Charlton Heston outside of the N.R.A. The title is really all the foreshadowing/recap needed for either audience: This is how humans became the minority on their own planet. And it turns out that the end of human dominance started in San Francisco with an eager-and-idealistic scientist named Will Rodman (James Franco). Rodman has been working on a cure for Alzheimer's disease, which afflicts his father, well-played by the great John Lithgow, adding a bit of emotional weight to what could have been a perfunctory first act. Instead of the typical wheel-spinning of most blockbusters in which it is crystal clear that everyone involved is merely waiting for the big CGI set pieces, the relationship between Rodman and his father creates emotional investment on the part of the viewer, who gets to know Rodman, his dad, and, most importantly, Caesar (Andy Serkis, in motion capture, much the same way he did in *The Lord of the Rings: The Two Towers* [2002] and *The Adventures of Tintin: The Secret of the Unicorn* [2011]), as fully-defined characters.

Rodman's experiments to find a cure have led to testing on apes and, after the first signs of success backfire horribly, the scientist is forced to shut down the program but not before rescuing from the facility an offspring of the first generation of experimented-upon apes, a pet/child/friend named Caesar. It turns out that the experimentation on Caesar's mother has had its effects amplified in the next generation. Caesar is not an average simian. He learns sign language quickly. He develops an intense range of human emotions, including sympathy for Rodman's father and even love for his owner/father. He is expressive, loving, and needy. He also feels rage and betrayal. When his protective animal nature gets the best of him, Caesar is forced into an ape habitat, ripped from his family and those he thought loved him.

The second act of the perfectly-structured script for *Rise of the Planet of the Apes* plays not unlike a prison escape movie (and it seems not coincidental that Wyatt's previous directorial credit was the break-out movie *The Escapist* [2008]) in that Caesar is forced to deal with habitat employees (including a warden-like character played by Brian Cox and an abusive guard played by Tom Felton) and to rally his fellow prisoners to revolt. Not only is Caesar smart enough to turn the tables on his captors, he figures out how to give his gift of intelligence to his fellow habitat-dwellers, resulting in the most remarkable final act in an action movie this year. As apes overrun the city of San Francisco, the entire piece builds to a remarkable crescendo on the Golden Gate Bridge, a sequence that will stand the test of movie time when it comes to fantastic action set-pieces. Freida Pinto co-stars are Rodman's love interest and a fellow scientist, but she almost purely exists to explain plot details and character motivations. She is a beautiful woman and has displayed some interesting range in the right material but her supporting character here is the film's greatest weakness. It was very smart of the writers to force all humans to take a back seat to the ape characters at a certain point, but Pinto could have used a bit more development.

Rise of the Planet of the Apes is, first and foremost, spectacular entertainment, an old-fashioned rollercoaster ride of a film that tries above all else to keep viewers engaged. It is sci-fi escapism built on ideas and characters instead of built around new ways to market video games, children's toys, or an animated TV spin-off. One of its most remarkable achievements is how that old-fashioned sense of storytelling has been told by special effects artists using the most revolutionary new toys. And there is no more notable technical achievement in film in 2011 that that of Caesar, a completely genuine, completely believable creation from the amazing WETA, the studio Peter Jackson used for the *Lord of the Rings* (2001-2003) trilogy. This is the most remarkable single character in the history of CGI. There is not one shot in *Rise of the Planet of the Apes* in which Caesar feels anything less than real and in-the-moment. It is no mere cartoon or added effect and, in many ways, it is a more notable and history-making achievement than *Avatar* (2009). Even viewers usually attuned to "looking for the strings" when it comes to special effects found themselves fully engaged in the accomplishments of Andy Serkis and his amazing team.

The underrated script and landmark special effects might have made for an above-average summer blockbuster, but *Rise of the Planet of the Apes* goes beyond that thanks to the stellar direction from Rupert Wyatt. He may be relatively new to the game, but he could teach a few veterans how to make a piece of escapist entertainment (he certainly delivered a more accomplished example of it in 2011 than the former master of the form, Steven Spielberg, and the maestro made two movies this year). The pacing of *Apes* is a thing of beauty. The rollercoaster metaphor may be overused when it comes to summer blockbusters but it is appropriate here when one considers the importance of pacing to a film like this one. Movie goers, like rollercoaster riders, subconsciously want perfectly-designed tracks without too many peaks or valleys that go on too long. *Rise of the Planet of the Apes* has some cheesy bits and some undefined supporting characters, but they are quickly forgotten in favor of what works. With incredible editing and stellar cinematography (from regular Peter Jackson collaborator Andrew Lesnie, perfectly using the trees and architecture of San Francisco), Wyatt does not weigh his piece down with exposition and tells his story visually in ways that most other filmmakers would never even dare attempt. *Rise of the Planet of the Apes* is such a strong example of visual storytelling, the backbone of film, that one could watch it silently and still enjoy it.

Rise of the Planet of the Apes reminds one of the days when big summer movies were not just retreads of things seen (or read) before. The season used to be about one thing above all else: Showing viewers something that they had never seen before. It was about wonder instead of the over-emphasis of the familiar that has dominated the season over the last two decades. *Rise of the Planet of the Apes* brings back the wonder.

Brian Tallerico

CREDITS

Will Rodman: James Franco
Caroline: Freida Pinto
Caesar: Andy Serkis
Franklin: Tyler Labine
Charles Rodman: John Lithgow
Hunsiker: David Hewlett
John Landon: Brian Cox
Robert Franklin: Tom Felton
Origin: USA
Language: English
Released: 2011
Production: Peter Chernin, Dylan Clark, Rick Jaffa, Amanda Silver; Dune Entertainment, 20th Century-Fox, Chernin Entertainment; released by 20th Century-Fox
Directed by: Rupert Wyatt
Written by: Amanda Silver, Rick Jaffa
Cinematography by: Andrew Lesnie
Music by: Patrick Doyle
Sound: Chuck Michael
Music Supervisor: Maggie Rodford
Editing: Conrad Buff, Mark Goldblatt
Art Direction: Helen Jarvis
Costumes: Renee April
Production Design: Claude Pare
MPAA rating: PG-13
Running time: 105 minutes

REVIEWS

Corliss, Richard. *TIME Magazine.* August 4, 2011.
McCarthy, Todd. *Hollywood Reporter.* August 4, 2011.
Morgenstern, Joe. *Wall Street Journal.* August 4, 2011.
Neumaier, Joe. *New York Daily News.* August 4, 2011.
Newman, Kim. *Empire Magazine.* August 8, 2011.
Pinkerton, Nick. *Village Voice.* August 4, 2011.
Puig, Claudia. *USA Today.* August 4, 2011.
Rea, Steven. *Philadelphia Inquirer.* August 4, 2011.
Stevens, Dana. *Slate.* August 4, 2011.
Turan, Kenneth. *Los Angeles Times.* August 4, 2011.

QUOTES

Dodge Landon: "Take your stinking paws off me you damn dirty ape!"
Caesar: "No!"

TRIVIA

The head of the research department, Steven Jacobs, is named after Arthur P. Jacobs, the producer of the original Planet of the Apes franchise.

AWARDS

Nomination:

Oscars 2011: Visual FX
British Acad. 2011: Visual FX.

THE RITE

You can only defeat it when you believe.
—Movie tagline

Box Office: $33 million

Can demonic possession be boring? Surprisingly, yes it can. This earnest but less-than-compelling possession tale has little to recommend it to anyone but horror completists and those interested in following the cinematic trail left behind by director William Freidkin's seminal 1973 adaptation of William Peter Blatty's novel *The Exorcist.* That trail has, of late, been marked by some good films—*Dominion: Prequel to the Exorcist* (2005), *The Exorcism of Emily Rose* (2005), *Requiem* (2006), *Paranormal Activity* (2007), *Paranormal Activity 2* (2010), and *The Last Exorcism* (2010). These were, by turns, scary, thoughtful and/or simply entertaining. *The Rite* is barely any of these things except by default. More importantly, it fails to make viewers care much about the titanic struggle of good and evil it attempts to showcase.

Michael Kovacks (Colin O'Donoghue) is a young man enduring a crisis of faith, having entered the priesthood primarily to satisfy (and get away from) his father (Rutger Hauer). On the eve of his resignation from seminary, his mentor (Toby Jones) persuades him to enroll in a specialized exorcism course in Rome, Italy. He reluctantly agrees only to find the course produces more questions than answers. Sent by the instructor, Father Xavier (Ciaran Hinds), to observe a practicing exorcist, Father Lucas (Anthony Hopkins), the student becomes even more troubled. As his skepticism about Lucas's methods and eccentricities grows, so does the urgency of the Father's practice, resulting in a dangerous situation for a young pregnant woman who may be possessed or simply the victim of abuse. Soon tragedy upon tragedy threatens to crush both men until the issue of Kovack's belief is put to the ultimate test when Lucas himself becomes the object of the demonic possession.

When possession stories fail (*Exorcist II: The Heretic* [1977], *The Manitou* [1978], *Exorcist: The Beginning* (2004), *Insidious* [2010]) the reason often has to do with an over-reliance on booming voices, spinning heads, levitation, and pretty young things screaming obscenities. *The Exorcist* (1973) itself is a good example. The effects in it have aged only moderately well but the movie is understood to be a classic because of its complex take on faith in crisis. *The Rite* too makes an attempt to be a faith-in-crisis film, but ultimately settles for being effects-driven genre fare offering none of the subtlety that would allow its characters to speak with more authority about the point the film tries to make.

It would be easy to blame the source material. The film is based on a book by Matt Baglio which chronicles the real life journey of Father Gary Thomas, an Exorcist in the Roman Catholic Church. But Thomas, in the few interviews he has given, is anything but sensational in his talking about what he does. A closer look at the screenwriting credits reveals the presence of Michael Petroni, a writer who has always specialized in watering down decent source material, having produced the screenplays for *Queen of the Damned* (2002) and *The Chronicles of Narnia: The Voyage of the Dawn Trader* (2010). Subtlety is hardly his trademark.

Anthony Hopkins is no stranger to the horror genre. Beyond his devastating turns as Hannibal Lecter in *Silence of the Lambs* (1991), *Hannibal* (2001) and *Red Dragon* (2002) he has turned in marvelous work in *Audrey Rose* (1977) and *Magic* (1978), but he has also saved his worst performances for the genre. His take on Van Helsing in *Bram Stoker's Dracula* (1992) was so ham-fisted it can only be described as embarrassing and his turn in *The Wolfman* (2010), while fun at times, had a decidedly phoned-in quality. His take on Father Lucas is a misstep. There is almost nothing to like about the character, and thus there is no investment when he gets possessed. Lucas is an unfocussed mass of hypocrisies and eccentricities. When he does finally get possessed, Hopkins is predictably electric. By then, it is too little, too late.

Far more problematic than Hopkins' performance is the vanilla turn of lead Colin O'Donoghue. *The Rite* gives Kovacks the same faith crisis issues that plagued Father Damien Karras in *The Exorcist,* but without the same sense of what is at stake. As played by O'Donoghue, Kovack's unbelief is simply weightless, a borrowed tragedy, and O'Donoghue, who is known primarily for middling TV work, seems unable to bear the burden of cynicism the role seems to initially require.

Director Mikael Håfström first came to the attention of American audiences when his film *Evil* (2003) was nominated for an Academy Award® for Best Foreign Film. But his subsequent efforts have been little more than entertaining. *Derailed* (2005) was a standard action thriller and while *1408* (2007) was a lot of fun it also did little more than fill in the genre blanks. More interesting was *Shanghai* (2009), a 1940's noir thriller starring Chow Yun Fat and John Cusack.

Possession stories work most powerfully when they connect with a desperate instinct that viewers have about evil. By definition, possession stories put a face, however featureless, on evil, rendering it as a personality that can be directly hated and feared. More importantly, evil becomes something that can be confronted even if it proves too elusive to perfectly defeat. This is the final comfort of such filmic encounters, they sketch an order out in a universe that seems mostly indifferent to suffering, struggle and the injustice of life by also outlining a greater design in which spirituality is the ultimate arbiter of reality.

Dave Canfield

CREDITS

Michael Kovak: Colin O'Donoghue
Father Lucas: Anthony Hopkins
Angeline: Alice Braga
Father Xavier: Ciaran Hinds
Father Matthew: Toby Jones
Istvan Kovak: Rutger Hauer
Origin: USA
Language: English
Released: 2011
Production: Beau Flynn, Tripp Vinson; New Line Cinema, Contrafilm, Flecther & Company; released by Warner Bros.
Directed by: Mikael Hafstrom
Written by: Michael Petroni
Cinematography by: Benjamin Davis
Music by: Alex Heffes
Editing: David Rosenbloom
Sound: Dave Whitehead
Art Direction: Stuart Kearns
Costumes: Carlo Poggioli
Production Design: Andrew Laws
MPAA rating: PG-13
Running time: 112 minutes

REVIEWS

Bray, Catherine. *Film4*. February 22, 2011.
Brenner, Jules. *Cinema Signals*. May 19, 2011.
Brown, Renn. *CHUD*. January 28, 2011.
Ebert, Roger. *Chicago Sun-Times*. January 27, 2011.
Floyd, Nigel. *Time Out*. February 23, 2011.
Holden, Stephen. *New York Times*. January 27, 2011.
Lemire, Christie. *Associated Press*. January 26, 2011.
Miska, Brad. *Bloody Disgusting*. January 28, 2011.
Parker, Trevor. *Fangoria.com*. January 27, 2011.
Pinkerton, Nick. *Village Voice*. January 25, 2011.

QUOTES

Father Lucas Trevant: "Be careful Michael, choosing not to believe in the devil doesn't protect you from him."

TRIVIA

The film was delivered to theaters using the code name
"Denial."

THE ROOMMATE

> *2,000 colleges. 8 million roommates. Which one*
> *will you get?*
> —Movie tagline
>
> *Nothing tests a friendship like murder.*
> —Movie tagline
>
> *She's cute…loyal…and a psychotic. No one's*
> *perfect.*
> —Movie tagline

Box Office: $37.3 million

Take one premise stolen pretty much entirely from
another, better film (albeit one just old enough so that
the target audience of easily entertained teens hopefully
will not recognize it), remove virtually all traces of skin,
gore and other things that might push it out of the
commercially viable PG-13 rating and into a less desirable R, no matter how much the story cries out for
them. Throw in a bunch of familiar faces who are
recognizable enough from television but not so recognizable to bump up the budget and add a pinch of Billy
Zane for seasoning. Sprinkle it with a number of
instantly forgettable tunes on the soundtrack and serve
on a cold February weekend when the competition
consists almost entirely of holiday holdovers and other
studio castoffs. The result is *The Roommate,* a half-baked
thriller that seems to promise a tasty soufflé of trashy
thrills but offers up only a sad array of leftovers that
even the most lenient viewers will find virtually impossible to swallow.

Sarah Matthews (Minka Kelly) is a fresh-faced co-ed
from Des Moines who has just arrived in Los Angeles to
study fashion design at that most august hotbed of learning, the University of Los Angeles, an educational
paradise where the dorms are closer to hotel rooms,
every student appears to have stepped off the cover of a
fashion magazine and the only apparent adult on campus
is lecherous fashion teacher Billy Zane (and you can tell
he is a professor because he uses the word "juxtaposition" in a sentence at one point). Almost immediately
upon arrival, Sarah takes possession of a trampy dorm
mate in Tracy (Aly Michalka), a hunky musician
boyfriend in Stephen (Cam Gigandet) and, most
unbelievably, a cart to carry her stuff up to her room.
After a night of partying, Sarah returns to find that her
roommate, Rebecca Evans (Leighton Meester) has
arrived. The two instantly become friends but before
long, the film begins to subtly insinuate that all is not

right with Rebecca—after all, she prefers staying in or
museum visits to drunken parties and would rather be
called Rebecca instead of Becky. It turns out, of course
that Rebecca really is a bona-fide psycho who has gone
off of her meds and will stop anyone who comes between
her and her new (and only) BFF, be they tramp, be they
a slimy teacher, or be they adopted kitten that winds up
getting a ride in a clothes dryer in the film's most notorious scene. When the crazy finally gets to be a little too
much for her, Sarah leaves and goes to stay with Stephen,
naturally neglecting to report Rebecca's obvious
problems to either her family or school officials. Rebecca
does not take to this development very well and the
whole thing leads to a semi-Grand Guignol climax filled
with guns, knives, last-minute rescues, people dangling
outside windows and pithy quips delivered with killing
blows.

If you are old and learned enough to be reading this
book, you are no doubt old and learned enough to realize that *The Roommate* is pretty much a top-to-bottom
steal from *Single White Female* (1992), Barbet Schroed-
er's agreeably pulpy thriller in which wacko Jennifer
Jason Leigh threatened to take over the life of roomie
Bridget Fonda, with a smidgen of psycho perennial *Fatal
Attraction* (1987) tossed into the mix for good measure.
The problem with *The Roommate* is not the fact that it
is not very original but the fact that it fails to properly
exploit a premise that could have resulted in an agreeably juicy bit of exploitation junk in the right hands.
Instead, the screenplay by Sonny Malhi is pretty much a
non-starter throughout—aside from the aforementioned
bit involving the kitten and the abrupt removal of a
belly ring, nothing interesting ever happens as the story
just drags on endlessly. By the time it finally arrives at
the long-awaited catfight climax even that is hardly
enough to rouse the enterprise from the torpor in which
it has settled. Likewise, the direction from Christian E.
Christiansen is equally lackluster—his efforts are so
blandly unmemorable that it seems as though he might
be the rare feature film director who is using his work as
a calling card to get work in the television industry
instead of vice versa. As for the leads, they are all attractive but none of them make much of an impression on
the proceedings. This is actually a bit surprising since
both Kelly and Meester have had considerable success
on television (on *Friday Night Lights* and *Gossip Girl,*
respectively) but you would hardly know that based
solely on the negligible-to-nonexistent performances that
they turn in here.

Too silly to work as a genuine thriller, too boring to
make it as camp, and with a depiction of mental illness
that would be borderline offensive if it were not as cartoonish as everything else on display, *The Roommate* is
the kind of film that is so absolutely undistinguished in

every aspect that it almost seems unfair to review it and therefore enter it into the permanent record instead of simply allowing it to drift off into the cinematic ether where it belongs. While it did make a few bucks at the box-office and on home video, that is less a testament to its artistic strengths as it is to the fact that some teenagers will sit through virtually anything as it is marketed heavily enough on their favorite shows and in their favorite magazines. One day, however, they and their tastes will mature and when that happens, junk like this will be instantly and completely erased from their minds, at least until that fateful day when they finally come across *Single White Female* and think "Hey, wait a second…"

Peter Sobczynski

CREDITS

Rebecca: Leighton Meester
Sara: Minka Kelly
Stephen: Cam Gigandet
Tracy: Alyson Michalka
Irene: Danneel Harris
Jason: Matt Lanter
Alison Evans: Frances Fisher
Jeff Evans: Tomas Arana
Professor Roberts: Billy Zane
Origin: USA
Language: English
Released: 2011
Production: Doug Davison, Roy Lee, Irene Yeung; Screen Gems, Vertigo Entertainment; released by Sony Pictures Entertainment
Directed by: Christian E. Christiansen
Written by: Sonny Malihi
Cinematography by: Phil Parmet
Music by: John (Gianni) Frizzell
Sound: Anthony J. Ciccolini III
Music Supervisor: Michael Friedman
Editing: Randy Bricker
Costumes: Maya Lieberman
Production Design: Jon Gary Steele
MPAA rating: PG-13
Running time: 91 minutes

REVIEWS

Catsoulis, Jeanette. *New York Times*. February 4, 2011.
Hall, Peter. *Cinematical*. February 4, 2011.
Hornaday, Ann. *Washington Post*. February 7, 2011.
Koplinski, Charles. *Illinois Times*. February 10, 2011.
Mitchell, Elvis. *Movieline*. February 4, 2011.
Orndorff, Brian. *BrianOrndorff.com*. February 4, 2011.
Pais, Matt. *Metromix.com*. February 4, 2011.
Pols, Mary F. *Time*. February 7, 2011.
Snider, Eric D. *EricDSnider.com*. April 4, 2011.
Uhlich, Keith. *Time Out New York*. February 4, 2011.

QUOTES

Alison Evans: "Rebecca is doing really well?"
Sara Matthews: "She's doin' good."
Alison Evans: "She's taking her medication?"
Sara Matthews: "Medication?"

THE RUM DIARY

One part outrage. One part justice. Three parts rum. Mix well.
—Movie tagline
Absolutely nothing in moderation.
—Movie tagline

Box Office: $13.1 million

The late, great Hunter S. Thompson wrote his first and only novel, the loosely autobiographical *The Rum Diary*, in the early 1960s, long before he would become one of the most celebrated writers of our time, and when it failed to find any interest among publishers at the time, it went into a drawer and would only see the light of day in 1998, supposedly because he needed the money. However, when people finally got a chance to read this fabled manuscript, which was penned before Thompson had fully developed the singular voice that made his prose so exciting to read, they discovered that it was a typical first novel—sincere and well-meant but fairly weak overall—and without his subsequent name recognition to give it a boost, it would have continued to languish in obscurity. Now, after years of false starts, *The Rum Diary* has finally hit the big screen in a version starring Johnny Depp (a close friend of Thompson's who brilliantly played his alter ego, Raoul Duke, in Terry Gilliam's stunning adaptation of *Fear & Loathing in Las Vegas* [1998]) and the end result is pretty much the same thing—a fairly ordinary story that has a few amusing moments but one which most likely would have never attracted the likes of Depp or director Bruce Robinson, the auteur of the Thompson-esque cult classic *Withnail & I* (1987) had it been penned by anyone else.

Depp plays Paul Kemp, a semi-ambitious journalist with an already-heroic capacity for alcohol who arrives in Puerto Rico circa 1960 to work for a third-rate newspaper alongside harried editor Lotterman (Richard Jenkins), drunken photographer Sala (Michael Rispoli), and Moburg (Giovanni Ribisi), a flat-out degenerate whose journalistic skills pale next to his ability to make 470-proof rum out of filters stolen from the local distillery. At first, Paul is stuck on such unrewarding assignments as doing horoscopes and covering the bowling beat but before long, his talents catch the eye of sleazy American land developer Sanderson (Aaron Eckhart), who wants to exploit those gifts by convincing Paul to write some pieces that will help pave the way for a massive land grab that will make him and his fellow investors millions while forcing thousands of locals from their homes. For a while, Paul sort of goes along with the plan, seduced by the presence of easy money and Renult (Amber Heard), Sanderson's seemingly easier fiancée, but eventually his sense of righteous anger is touched and he does what he can to bring the greedheads down. That is, at least during the brief periods of time when he is not soused on rum or dabbling in a strange new thing known as LSD.

With the potentially volatile combination of Thompson, Depp and Robinson, fans would not think that anything they could come up with could possibly be dismissed with an indifferent shrug and a "meh" and yet, that is precisely the case with *The Rum Diary*. The basic story is not especially fresh or exciting—it is just the standard tale of a semi-innocent torn between easy temptation and doing the right thing—there are too many subplots and supporting characters thrown into the mix and then largely abandoned and the ending is literally spelled out for viewers via a series of title cards instead of actually showing what happened. Although it is nice to see Bruce Robinson return to helm his first film since *Jennifer 8* (1992), his screenplay and direction are both curiously flat and fail to properly convey even the trace beginnings of Thompson's voice in cinematic turns in the way that Gilliam did with *Fear & Loathing*. As yet another Thompson alter ego, Depp is good but all he is doing is essentially giving us a dialed-down version of his previous turn and the sight of him playing a younger version of the writer despite the passing of more than thirteen years since that initial performance is downright distracting at times, and although it was his clout that finally got the film made in the first place, it might have been more effective if someone else had taken the part and he instead grabbed one of the other ones instead. As for those supporting roles, Eckhart is effective as the blandly manipulative Sanderson, Heard is saddled with a character that only has her going through some poorly motivated motion while looking gorgeous, and Ribisi chews the scenery so thoroughly that he seems to be under the mistaken impression that *he* is supposed to be playing Hunter S. Thompson.

It is difficult to recommend *The Rum Diary* by any means—the material is just too familiar and insubstantial for its own good and its brief attempts at emulating Thompson's later weirdness simply do not work very well. That said, it is never exactly boring and it does contain enough amusing moments to keep it from sliding away into complete disposability. For those who are not already devoted fans of Thompson and his work, there is not much of anything here that has not already been done before and done better. As for those devoted fans, they may get a little more out of it because while they too will have seen nearly all of it before, it almost seems appropriate since they will presumably have plenty of experience with flashbacks.

Peter Sobczynski

CREDITS

Paul Kemp: Johnny Depp
Chenault: Amber Heard
Sanderson: Aaron Eckhart
Lotterman: Richard Jenkins
Bob Sala: Michael Rispoli
Moberg: Giovanni Ribisi
Donovan: Marshall Bell
Segurra: Amaury Nolasco
Origin: USA
Language: English, Spanish, German
Released: 2011
Production: Christi Dembrowski, Johnny Depp, Graham King, Anthony Rhulen, Robert Kravis; GK Films, Infinitum Nihil, FilmEngine, Dark & Stormy Entertainment; released by FilmDistrict
Directed by: Bruce Robinson
Written by: Bruce Robinson
Cinematography by: Dariusz Wolski
Music by: Christopher Young
Sound: Mark A. Mangini
Editing: Carol Littleton
Art Direction: Dawn Swiderski
Costumes: Colleen Atwood
Production Design: Chris Seagers
MPAA rating: R
Running time: 110 minutes

REVIEWS

Burr, Ty. *Boston Globe*. October 27, 2011.
Corliss, Richard. *Time*. October 27, 2011.
Dujsik, Mark. *Mark Reviews Movies*. October 27, 2011.
Ebert, Roger. *Chicago Sun-Times*. October 27, 2011.
Edelstein, David. *New York Magazine*. October 31, 2011.
Orndorf, Brian. *BrianOrndorf.com*. October 28, 2011.
Pais, Matt. *RedEye*. October 27, 2011.
Scott, A.O. *New York Times*. October 27, 2011.
Snider, Eric D. *Film.com*. October 28, 2011.
Tobias, Scott. *AV Club*. October 27, 2011.

QUOTES

Sala: "Do not confuse love with lust, nor drunkenness with judgment."

TRIVIA

Benicio Del Toro was attached to direct and star in the the film and one point.

S

SANCTUM

(James Cameron's Sanctum)

The only way out is down.
—Movie tagline

Box Office: $23.2 million

In the wake of the overwhelming popular success of *Avatar* (2009), James Cameron's sci-fi epic that utilized the most technologically advanced and elaborate iteration of the old promotional standby known as 3D, Hollywood decided that there was gold in them there multidimensional hills (hills that had already been mined when the fad briefly came and went in the Fifties and later in the Eighties) and set about releasing as many movies in the process as they possibly could, either by legitimately filming them in 3D or, more often than not, by taking movies that were shot normally and then reconverting them after the fact via new computer technology. Perhaps unsurprisingly, the same basic flaws surfaced that killed the format during its previous incarnations—cruddy movies and cruddier effects, especially in regards to the retrofit titles—and while the format initially flourished with the popularity of such films as *Alice in Wonderland* (2010) and *Clash of the Titans* (2010), audiences began to grow increasingly weary of the gimmick, especially once they began to realize that the additional box-office surcharge (ostensibly lobbied to help theater owners pay for converting to 3D) meant that they were paying at least three dollars a head for a noticeably-darker picture and images that failed to pop off the screen as distinctly as had been promised by the ads. By the time 2011 rolled around, the bloom was off the rose to such a degree that not even a film like *Sanctum* could make much of a dent at the box-office despite being presented by James Cameron himself (whose name was more prominent in the ads than any of the actual filmmakers or actors) and utilizing the 3D camera rigs he developed for *Avatar*. Then again, perhaps it is unfair to blame *Sanctum* for tanking because of audience apathy towards 3D because it is such a boring and pedestrian ride from start to finish that it is difficult to imagine people going for it even when the gimmick was at its absolute peak.

The film tells the story of a group of walking clichés who have gathered together in a remote area in Papua, New Guinea in order to venture into a vast underwater cave exploration site financed by rich jerk Carl Hurley (Ioan Gruffudd) and mapped out by dashing adventurer/lousy father Frank McGuire (Richard Roxburgh). Joined by Josh (Rhys Wakefield), Frank's resentful teenage son, Victoria (Alice Parkinson), Carl's inexperienced fiancée, and several others who turn up long enough to up the body count, the expedition is about to begin when a tragic accident leads to the death of one member of the team, an incident for which Josh blames his father despite the fact that he is actually equally culpable, if not more so, than the old man. Before the blame game can continue much further, a freak storm overtakes the site that cuts off all communication with the surface and collapses the only known means of escape. With dwindling supplies and no other choices to be had, the group presses on into the unexplored area of the cave system in the hopes of finding a new exit before it becomes totally flooded by the steadily rising waters. Despite racing against the clock, however, they still manage to find the time to stop the action to indulge in fruitless arguments, engage in heartfelt banter and do exactly what they have just been told not to do so that they can perish according to schedule.

Considering the fact that most people would probably rank the various horrors connected with cave diving depicted here—with drowning, falling, and getting crushed, among others—as exceptionally grim and unpleasant ways to meet their respective makers, it would seem as though a film along the lines of *Sanctum* would not have to do too much in order to freak them out and have them vowing never to ever again explore any remote cave systems. And yet, *Sanctum* pretty much fails at that task for a number of reasons. For starters, the screenplay by co-writers John Garvin and Andrew Wight is a mess throughout with a story that drags when it should be moving along at a rapid clip so as to suggest the pressures of the time limit that the characters are working under and which is jammed with so many lines of overly clichéd dialogue (including the likes of "Who the hell do you think you are?," "I know I haven't been anything like a father to you," and "You remind me of me") that it almost feels as if Garvin and Wight were having a private contest to see who could get the most of them in. The characters on display run the gamut from the banal to the blatantly unlikable and are portrayed in such a generic manner throughout by the ultra-bland cast that it is impossible to work up any rooting interest in their survival. Then again, the film itself barely seems to have any interest in its own survival. With most of the action taking place either in low-lit caves or in the even-more under-lit depths of the rising water, it is often difficult to make out who is who or what is going on at any given time even without the added dimness provided by the miracle of the three-dimensional process. (It is possible to shoot in 3D in a cave system and come up with beautiful imagery, as Werner Herzog proved conclusively in his haunting documentary *Cave of Forgotten Dreams,* but, at the risk of sounding painfully redundant, director Alister Grierson is no Werner Herzog.)

Those who do further reading into the behind-the-scenes story surrounding *Sanctum* will soon discover that co-writer Andrew Wight was once an underwater cave explorer and that the film was loosely inspired by an expedition that he took part in that was also beset by a freak storm that forced him and his party to seek another way out of the system they were trapped in. In the right hands, such a story could have been made into a gripping and tension-filled documentary along the lines of *Touching the Void* (2003) and what it might have lacked in the increasingly redoubtable thrills of 3D would have been more than offset by the simple act of hearing such a tale from the mouths of the survivors themselves. Instead, it has been transformed into a visually murky and dramatically inert tale of pseudo-daring-do destined to be seen by few and remembered by fewer. Then again, if its failure to attract audiences turns out to be the hoped-for first nail in the coffin of the current version of 3D, it could well wind up finding a place in the hearts of true movie lovers—the type who do not require goofy goggles to fully experience a film—after all.

Peter Sobczynski

CREDITS

Frank McGuire: Richard Roxburgh
Josh McGuire: Rhys Wakefield
Carl Hurley: Ioan Gruffudd
Victoria: Alice Parkinson
George: Daniel Wyllie
Origin: USA
Language: English
Released: 2011
Production: Ben Browning, James Cameron, Ryan Kavanaugh, Michael Maher, Peter Rawlinson; Great Wight Productions/Osford Films, Universal Pictures, Relativity Media, Wayfare Entertainment, Sanctum Australia; released by Universal Pictures
Directed by: Alister Grierson
Written by: Andrew Wight, John Garvin
Cinematography by: Jules O'Loughlin
Music by: David Hirschfelder
Sound: Paul Pirola
Editing: Mark Warner
Art Direction: Jenny O'Connell
Costumes: Michael Davies
Production Design: Nicholas McCallum
MPAA rating: R
Running time: 108 minutes

REVIEWS

Dargis, Manhola. *New York Times.* February 3, 2011.
Ebert, Roger. *Chicago Sun-Times.* February 3, 2011.
Gonsalves, Rob. *EFilmcritic.com.* February 7, 2011.
Goss, William. *Cinematical.* February 4, 2011.
Gronvall, Andrea. *Chicago Reader.* February 4, 2011.
Koplinski, Chuck. *Illinois Times.* February 10, 2011.
McDonagh, Maitland. *Film Journal International.* February 3, 2011.
Orndorf, Brian. *BrianOrndorf.com.* June 9, 2011.
Pais, Matt. *Metromix.com.* February 3, 2011.
Robinson, Tasha. *AV Club.* February 3, 2011.

QUOTES

Dex: "Josh is his own man. He doesn't take after his dad much."

Josh: "What, you mean I'm not an emotional shutdown Nazi a**hole?"

TRIVIA

Co-writer John Garvin wrote the role of Jim Sergeant with himself in mind (he is an accomplished diver), with the hope that director Alister Grierson would let him play the part.

SCREAM 4
(Scre4m)

New decade. New rules.
    —Movie tagline

Box Office: $38.2 million

Give credit where credit is due: More than a decade after the *Scream* horror franchise seemed to have run out of bloody steam, *Scream 4* director Wes Craven and screenwriter Kevin Williamson have returned to impressively craft a sequel that deftly, relentlessly folds into itself like an M.C. Escher drawing of a ball of snakes eating their own tails. It is almost impossible to tell where *Scream 4*'s ironic self-awareness starts or ends, or whether terms like "good," "bad," or "necessary" even apply any longer.

Scream 4's self-reflective meta-mania starts early with a series of sharply clever prologues, but soon things are back in place for the usual *Scream* film story. While the past decade and a half has added cell phones, texting, Facebook, and video-cam blogging to the average teenager's daily existence, the plot mechanics of this funhouse of horrors do not deviate far from the formula Williamson and Craven created with the first *Scream* film in 1996: Someone is tormenting poor, put-upon, professional Scream survivor Sidney Prescott (Neve Campbell) by dressing up in the now-iconic Ghostface costume—complete with Bowie knife—and stabbing everyone around her (primarily attractive teenagers now almost a generation younger than Sidney).

Other regular series characters have returned: In addition to Sidney, there is more career climbing from Gail Weathers (Courteney Cox) and more bumbling from the Worst Police Department in the Country, now headed up by Sheriff Dewey Riley (David Arquette). New faces lined up for the slaughter include Anthony Kennedy, Adam Brody, and Allison Brie, plus a fresh crop of teens led by Emma Roberts, Rory Culkin, and Hayden Panettiere.

In addition to the killings and hyper-attention to the ever-changing "rules" surrounding them, a *Scream* film also means a parade of red herrings and narrative head fakes. Despite, however, all the narrative hand-wringing over who is doing the stabbing, the not-so-secret secret of the franchise is that for all the mystery tale tricks and twists, it doesn't matter who is under the Ghostface mask or what petty issues and jealousies drove him or her to get so homicidal. The series' enduring face of fear is a cheap Halloween costume, itself a self-congratulatory wink at Edvard Munch and the threatening, taunting voice on the line still belongs to Roger Jackson.

By now, the franchise's hook has become its own existence—the gimmick is that characters in this fictional universe are aware of the *Scream*-like film franchise (called *Stab* in the film's world) that is based on the "real-life" events in their world. As a result, where the first *Scream* film reflected on horror and slasher film tropes, *Scream 4* is all about the *Scream* movies, including itself. The new film's characters acknowledge that Ghostface and the *Scream/Stab* franchise is now part of the pop-cultural landscape and therefore more of a punch line than a scary movie—it lost some of its dark power as it became celebrated, not feared. After all, Sidney is returning to her hometown on a book tour for her "survivor" memoir, and one of *Scream 4*'s central themes (aside from people getting killed) is that today's media-centric youth crave fame and celebrity more than sex or cheap thrills.

Williamson and Craven lead the film deeper into a funhouse maze of mirrors, having its too-clever-by-half teens discuss not just horror-film rules, but the fact that they are discussing them. By the time characters end up making meta comments on how "meta" it all is, the film starts to feel like its own DVD commentary track. There are times all this clever meta-whatever threatens to make *Scream 4* more entertaining to talk about than watch. As a slasher film, *Scream 4* is old-school familiar, coming up short on new ways to kill teenagers; and if (according to one of the film's teen horror mavens) "unexpected" is the new cliché, then even the inevitable unexpected reveal of the killer's identity cannot help but feel somewhat ho hum.

However, what the film makers lack in snappy, cutting-edge innovation, they make up for with well-honed skill. A genuine horror-film legend, Craven is still a master at using lighting, framing, and editing to build tension and execute, so to speak, jump-jolt scares with precise and pleasing payoffs, and Williamson's script sports a solid scene and story craft often missing from the cinematic teen-horror landscape. All that professionalism makes *Scream 4* more solidly entertaining than it has a right to be. The gory navel gazing may not fully make the case for the franchise's continuation, but it gooses a decent amount of fun out of a film (and a genre) frighteningly obsessed with itself.

Locke Perterseim

CREDITS

Sidney Prescott: Neve Campbell
Gale Weathers-Riley: Courteney Cox
Sheriff Dewey Riley: David Arquette
Jill Roberts: Emma Roberts
Kirby Reed: Hayden Panettiere
Charlie Walker: Rory Culkin
Trevor Sheridan: Nico Tortorella
Judy Hicks: Marley Shelton
Kate Kessler: Mary McDonnell
Detective Hoss: Adam Brody
Deputy Perkins: Anthony Anderson
Rachel: Anna Paquin
Chloe: Kristen Bell
Origin: USA
Language: English
Released: 2011
Production: Wes Craven, Iya Labunka, Kevin Williamson; Dimension Films, Corvus Corax Productions, Outerbanks Entertainment, Midnight Films; released by Dimension Films
Directed by: Wes Craven
Written by: Kevin Williamson
Cinematography by: Peter Deming
Music by: Marco Beltrami
Sound: Donald J. Malouf
Music Supervisor: Liza Richardson
Editing: Peter McNulty
Art Direction: Gerald Sullivan
Costumes: Debra McGuire
Production Design: Adam Stockhausen
MPAA rating: R
Running time: 103 minutes

REVIEWS

Corliss, Richard. *Time.* April 15, 2011.
Goodykoontz, Bill. *Arizona Republic.* April 13, 2011.
Hale, Mike. *New York Times.* April 15, 2011.
LaSalle, Mick. *San Francisco Chronicle.* April 15, 2011.
Levin, Josh. *Slate.* April 15, 2011.
Morris, Wesley. *Boston Globe.* April 15, 2011.
O'Hehir, Andrew. *Salon.* April 13, 2011.
Rabin, Nathan. *AV Club.* April 14, 2011.
Rodriguez, Rene. *Miami Herald.* April 13, 2011.
Sharkey, Betsy. *Los Angeles Times.* April 15, 2011.

QUOTES

Chloe: "There's something really scary about a guy with a knife who just…snaps."

TRIVIA

In an effort to make their acting more intense, Wes Craven didn't allow the actors to meet who was on the other end of the phone line when Ghost Face contacted them.

SEASON OF THE WITCH

Not all souls can be saved.
—Movie tagline

Box Office: $24.8 million

In *Season of the Witch,* Nicolas Cage stars as a 14th century crusader who, along with his fellow brother in arms Ron Pearlman, goes AWOL after the victims of his uncannily awesome and deadly swordsmanship start haunting his dreams. Their desertion does not last long however and the two are ultimately apprehended at the first town they come to on their journey home. Lucky for them there is a get out of jail free card: the town has fallen victim to the plague and the local clergy believe that a witch is responsible. If the ex-soldiers agree to accompany the suspected witch to a trial at a distant monastery (the idea being that if she is found guilty of witchcraft and killed, the plague would immediately stop), they will be released. Propelled by a new distaste for what they perceive to be the church's various rash actions, they accept the mission, vowing to provide the haunting, eerie, and beautiful girl (played by Claire Foy) with a fair trial. Along the way the assembled team, which in addition to the ex-crusaders includes a thief turned trail guide and a priest, encounters vicious werewolves, a precarious rope bridge and an endgame that does not go exactly as planned.

Season of the Witch is one of those all too common Hollywood occurrences: a seemingly well-cast, well-CGI'ed blockbuster action movie that ultimately falls flat in its delivery. In a sense, the movie's shortcomings can be summed up in the fact that there are not actually any witches in *Season of the Witch*. There are demons and possessed zombies, to be sure, but no witch in sight. This blatant lack of focus permeates throughout the movie, from the writing to the casting, and the result is a distorted and contrived cinematic experience.

It is easy to imagine that, at some point during the developmental stages of the project, someone pitched *Season of the Witch* as *Robin Hood: Prince of Thieves* (1991) meets *The Transporter* (2002). *Season of the Witch* is filmed in the same pre-storm grey that dominated *Robin Hood* and takes a page from Luc Besson's dangerous human cargo road trip set-up. It feels as though Behmen (Cage) and his faithful, sacrificing right-hand man

Felson (Perlman) walked the same hazy, rolling countryside as Robin (Kevin Costner) and Azeem (Morgan Freeman) after they left the crusades. It would not have been surprising if the duo stumbled upon Locksley castle. Furthermore, Cage attempts to channel Costner throughout the film, opting for a quiet, monotone delivery of all of his lines with the hope that it translates to a boiling-beneath-the-surface intensity. The idea behind the almost-whispered delivery is to portray Behmen as a reserved warrior, so that when he does yell to make a point about the senseless carnage he witnessed during his time at war, it is clear that he means it. Cage's take lacks all the charisma that Costner brought to post-crusader trauma. Both Cage and Costner sport the same awkward, stringy long hair, but gone is Costner's commanding screen presence and the warmth that made him a likeable lead. In Cage's hands, Behmen comes off as a dubious, uncomfortable knight, one that lacks the confidence necessary to possess the mad skills the script purports he has.

It is actually quite surprising that Cage does not gel in this role, especially since he has so many action roles to his credit. But Cage simply does not seem comfortable in medieval garb wielding a sword. The costume looks awkward on him. Perhaps he was hindered by Bragi F. Shut's inconsistent script, which in addition to mashing old-English with modern phrases and jokes, jumps genres and storylines without a second thought. In an attempt to infuse something new into a predictable narrative, Shut changes up story lines faster than the audience can keep track of them. One minute he is exploring *The Transporter* storyline and developing a strange, but intriguing relationship between Behmen and the accused witch (is she bad or just misunderstood?), the next he plants Behmen firmly into a zombie movie, even having him call out the all too well-known command of "You have to cut off their heads!" Finally, just when it seems like there cannot possibly be any more twists, Behmen performs an exorcism and battles a dragon-esque demon who possesses a deep, auto-tuned voice. Of course, it does not help that director Dominic Sena decided not to take any period detail too seriously, allowing the cast's sparkling chiclet teeth to blind the audience and to have them forgo any accents altogether (nothing screams crusades like a bunch of Americans in Europe), making *Season of the Witch* feel more like a filmed medieval role playing game than a grounded story.

Joanna Topor MacKenzie

CREDITS

Behman: Nicolas Cage
Felson: Ron Perlman
Eckhardt: Ulrich Thomsen
The Girl: Claire Foy
Debelzaq: Stephan Campbell Moore
Hagamar: Stephen Graham
Origin: USA
Language: English
Released: 2010
Production: Alex Gartner, Charles Roven; Atlas Entertainment, Relativity Media; released by Lionsgate
Directed by: Dominic Sera
Written by: Bragi Schut Jr.
Cinematography by: Amir M. Mokri
Music by: Atli Ovarsson
Sound: Scott Martin Gershin
Music Supervisor: Happy Walters
Editing: Dan Zimmerman, Bob Ducsay, Mark Helfrich
Art Direction: Kai Koch
Costumes: Carlo Poggioli
Production Design: Uli Hanisch
MPAA rating: PG-13
Running time: 95 minutes

REVIEWS

Barker, Andrew. *Variety.* January 6, 2011.
Bowles, Scott. *USA Today.* January 7, 2011.
Ebert, Roger. *Chicago Sun-Times.* January 7, 2011.
Gleiberman, Owen. *Entertainment Weekly.* January 7, 2011.
Honeycutt, Kirk. *Hollywood Reporter.* January 6, 2011.
Howell, Peter. *Toronto Star.* January 6, 2011.
Lemire, Christy. *Associated Press.* January 6, 2011.
Olsen, Mark. *Los Angeles Times.* January 6, 2011.
Rich, Katey. *CinemaBlend.com* January 6, 2011.
Schager, Nick. *Slant Magazine.* January 6, 2011.

QUOTES

Debelzaq: "We're going to need more holy water."

TRIVIA

Claire Foy's character is simply called "The Girl" in the credits.

AWARDS

Nomination:

Golden Raspberries 2011: Worst Actor (Cage).

SENNA

The legend of the greatest driver who ever lived.
 —Movie tagline

No Fear. No Limits. No Equal.
 —Movie tagline

Box Office: $1.6 million

Religion and politics often divide folks quite nastily, so it is frequently another great pastime, sports, that serves as a unifier of especially pluralistic societies. In particular, sports heroes can serve to unite and uplift people, especially if their field of competition is international, and therefore allows for a degree of nationalistic fervor to creep into play. Such was certainly the case with Ayrton Senna, a fiery and hard-charging Formula One racing star who rose to prominence and a certain level of domination in the sport in the 1980s and early 1990s, serving as a sterling beacon of pride and hope for his homeland of Brazil. A new documentary bearing his surname—as well as the stamp of Audience Award prizes at both the Sundance and Los Angeles Film Festivals—tells his story, in a unique and interesting way that does not require a previous or abiding interest in racing.

Actually, while its title may indicate the star of the show, *Senna* is also in significant ways about French-born racing star Alain Prost, the man whom a young Senna would first compete against, then team with, and ultimately supplant as World Champion. The film chronicles their rivalry and eventual uneasy alliance under the McLaren Racing Team banner, and how any detente they had would finally shatter in the crucible of competition, perhaps owing as well to their native personality differences. Known as "The Professor," Prost was (if such a thing can exist) a cautious racer, more than willing to pay heed to overall points standings and not jeopardize his overall position late in the season by pressing to finish any higher than he needed to in a given, specific race. He was also a skilled glad-hander and navigator of the sport's political mechanisms, perhaps aided, the film implies, by a shared nationality with longtime Formula One president Jean-Marie Balestre.

Senna, on the other hand, came from a well-to-do family, but seemingly drove with a sort of chip on his shoulder that one might typically associate with someone with a much more disadvantaged socioeconomic background. Bearing witness to his annoyance with unspoken Formula One protocol about how to pass competitors, and even less patience for its off-the-track obligations and niceties, it is easy to imagine Senna a sort of real-life forerunner to Ricky Bobby, Will Ferrell's fictional lead of *Talladega Nights* (2006), vacuumed free of the blithe obliviousness, but gripped by the same tunnel-visioned mantra: "I wanna go fast!" When he got in his car, Senna drove to win, period. His competitive streak, meanwhile, was matched, and probably informed, by an uncanny skill for flourishing even further in the sort of rain and inclement weather that would cause most drivers to ease off the throttle just a bit. In this context, Senna seems not so much a crazed or reckless

daredevil as just a competitor increasingly emboldened by the growing sample size of his own successes.

Working from a framework script by Manish Pandey, director Asif Kapadia eschews the default nonfiction presentation of talking heads, and instead layers interview footage from racing reporters and broadcasters actually under a lot of footage from races, which is a smart and savvy choice that gives *Senna* a much more streamlined and theatrical feeling than many documentaries. Even though some of the footage is dated and degraded (it is comprised of various film stocks and video, with some even taken from YouTube), the visual absence of present-day subjects preserves a certain amount of suspense for those who may be unfamiliar with Senna's story, and also serves to underscore his rivalry with Prost.

Even more exciting is a considerable amount of point-of-view material presented from inside the cockpit of Senna's vehicles. This helps give viewers a charged and pulse-quickening emotional investment in the proceedings. Kapadia and editors Gregers Sall and Chris King also make reflective editorial use of slow motion to channel the manner in which many top-level athletes describe their field of vision narrowing, and the basket or net becoming bigger, in moments of extreme pressure. This is then pointedly, nicely contrasted with off-the-track material which seems to further highlight the frustrations Senna had for the political elements of his sport. Most emblematic of this is an amazing sequence in which a group of Formula One drivers contentiously debate safety and pit stop measures with organization president Balestre.

If there is a knock on *Senna*, it is that it lacks the same drive and burning ambition of its subject. In not quite digging deep enough into his personal life to match and marry the trials and tribulations of his amazing career to what he was going through off the track, the film delivers a portrayal that is not entirely complete. This disappointment is relatively minor, but cast into starker relief both by the movie's stylistic engagement and other successes as well as the fact that this is Kapadia's fourth feature film.

Senna ably communicates what the driver—with both his philanthropic efforts and the manner in which he comported himself—meant to Brazil as a whole, at a time when so many of its poor had no hope for economic self-betterment. And it reveals the importance of both Senna's faith and his family to him; his sister and mother are among the interviewees, and there is also a good bit of family home video vacation footage. But, watching these amazing exploits and the manner in which he almost literally made his car dance around the edges of Monte Carlo's winding streets, say, there is less of a sense of Senna the man than one would want from a movie like this. Kapadia's film humanizes a legend, absolutely, but it also remains at a certain remove.

Brent Simon

CREDITS

Himself: Ayrton Senna
Himself: Richard Williams
Himself: Pierre van Vliet
Himself: Reginaldo Leme
Himself: John Bisignano
Himself: Alain Prost
Himself: Frank Williams
Origin: United Kingdom
Language: English
Released: 2011
Production: Tim Bevan, Eric Fellner, James Gay-Rees; Studio Canal, Working Title Films, Midfield Films; released by Universal Pictures
Directed by: Asif Kapadia
Written by: Manish Pandey
Cinematography by: Jake Polonsky
Music by: Antonio Pinto
Sound: Stephen Griffiths, Andy Shelley
Editing: Chris King, Gregers Sall
MPAA rating: PG-13
Running time: 106 minutes

REVIEWS

Clifford, Laura. *Reeling Reviews*. August 18, 2011.
Ebert, Roger. *Chicago Sun-Times*. August 18, 2011.
Hartl, John. *Seattle Times*. August 25, 2011.
Lane, Anthony. *New Yorker*. August 22, 2011.
McCarthy, Todd. *Hollywood Reporter*. February 8, 2011.
Morgenstern, Joe. *Wall Street Journal*. August 11, 2011.
Schager, Nick. *Slant*. August 7, 2011.
Singer, Matt. *IFC.com*. August 12, 2011.
Stevens, Dana. *Slate*. August 18, 2011.
Turan, Kenneth. *Los Angeles Times*. August 11, 2011.

QUOTES

Jean-Marie Balestre: "The best decision is my decision!"

TRIVIA

Despite being given a limited release, it set a UK box office record for a documentary during its opening weekend.

AWARDS

British Acad. 2011: Feature Doc., Film Editing
Nomination:
British Acad. 2011: Outstanding British Film
Writers Guild 2011: Best Doc. Screenplay.

A SEPARATION
(Nader and Simin, a Separation)
(Jodaelye Nader az Simin)

Ugly truth, sweet lies.
    —Movie tagline
Lies may lead to truth.
    —Movie tagline

Box Office: $2.1 million

Asghar Farhadi's *A Separation* is one of the most emotionally devastating cinematic experiences in years, a film that truly transcends language and culture to tap into something universal about the complexity of human relationships in which there are no easy decisions and no one to blame but a string of bad luck and a societal system that allows it to happen. Unlike most Hollywood representations of it, divorce rarely has a clear-cut good guy and a bad guy. More often than not, there are issues of blame on either side. Understandably, that gray area of life is incredibly difficult to capture in the medium of film, which often demands a protagonist and antagonist within a three-act structure. Viewers need someone to root for, someone to blame, someone they want to see get custody and find happiness. The dissolution of an actual marriage and the collateral damage caused by the people around it is infinitely more complicated than it is often represented in fiction, especially film. The brilliant, shattering, Oscar®-nominated screenplay for *A Separation* (the movie was also nominated and considered the presumptive favorite to win Best Foreign Language Film) does not ever resort to melodrama but taps a much-deeper vein of sadness, the true cost of making decisions for which there is no easy answers.

A Separation opens with a legal hearing between Nader (Peyman Moaadi) and Simin (Leila Hatami) asking for adjudication in a situation that can leave neither party truly happy. Emotions are heated from the very beginning as both characters seem to address the viewer directly with the camera serving as the judge. The effect is remarkable, turning the viewer into a participant who will hear the stories of these two people and, one assumes, judge their behavior. What follows is not so easy to judge.

Simin wants to leave Iran and she wants to take her smart, sweet daughter Termeh (Sarina Farhadi) with her. Nader cannot leave because he needs to take care of his very-ill father (Ali-Asghar Shahbazi), a man so deep into senility and Alzheimer's Disease that he not only does not speak any more but cannot make it to the bathroom in time to relieve himself. Understandably, Nader does not want to leave his father and does not want his wife to take his daughter. In fact, he will not grant her request to do so. After expressing what Simin interprets as apathy regarding whether or not they get a divorce, she makes up her mind that she cannot return to the home, but the judge forces them to figure out their daughter's fate on their own. Will Nader grant approval for Simin to take her daughter and leave? Will Simin leave without her? She packs a bag and heads to her mother's to consider the options.

Simin's absence forces Nader to hire a woman to watch and care for his father while he is at work. From her first appearance, Razieh (Sareh Bayat) seems simply exhausted. She has to commute hours to get to this job that does not pay enough to justify the workload or the religious and social issues that arise when she has to change an elderly man's pants for him. She clearly cannot handle the job and it is not only because she is in her second trimester and bringing her daughter Somayeh (Kimia Hosseini) with her to the apartment. She tries to pass the job along to her husband Hodjat (Shahab Hosseini) but she has not told him she took it in the first place and her home life seems tumultuous at best. Hodjat is being regularly arrested by his creditors and probably would not look kindly on his wife changing an adult man's pants. Despite her exhaustion, she keeps coming to work.

A few days into the job, Nader and Termeh come home early to find an absolute nightmare. Nader's father has been tied to the bed from which he has fallen out and lies next to on the ground, seemingly unconscious. Razieh and Somayeh are nowhere to be found. The caretaker and her daughter arrive back at the apartment and Razieh tells Nader that she had to go out for an emergency and knows that his father usually sleeps at this time. He should have stayed asleep. They should have been back before Nader. *A Separation* is a masterpiece of little beats, the moments that turn people in one direction or another and change fate. In the heat of the moment, Nader not only is faced with the near-death of his father but some money that appears to be missing from a room that Razieh was not supposed to enter. He does not pay Razieh, assuming she took the money and therefore needs no more and an altercation ensues after he accuses her of taking it, an unimaginable accusation for an honorable woman who cannot handle the claims of thievery. In a heated moment, he pushes her out the door and she falls on the stairs. Or does she? The actual fall is unseen other than when Nader looks and sees her getting back up. Did she fall on her own from exhaustion? Or from the water required to clean up after her daughter inadvertently left garbage on the stairs? Or could the tragedy that befalls Razieh have happened somewhere else altogether? And will Nader

turn blame back to Simin? For if she had not separated with him, Razieh never would have been there in the first place.

Farhadi does not answer all of these questions. He is more concerned about the impact of questions than their answers. When a couple separates, there are always unanswerable questions of blame and fault. And a separation has a ripple effect that often encompasses family members in its wake. It is not coincidental that the most heartbreaking victims of the impact of what occurs after Nader and Simin separate are the elderly and the young—the innocent who get so easily trapped up in the decisions of others. The children in *A Separation* are not traditionally torn in a Hollywood sense between mother and father but they are forever impacted by the drama caused by the separation at its core.

Issues of honesty seem to have a bit more impact due to the honor of Iranian culture (a few lies here and there would have drastically changed the action and American audiences may wonder why being accused of thievery or being asked to swear to something n a Quran has the dramatic impact they would in the States) but one of the most remarkable things about Farhadi's incredible script, very arguably the best of 2011, is its universality. The minute that one starts to blame Nader or Simin or Razieh or Hodjat, Farhadi brilliantly twists the story a degree and presents the character and their motivations in a slightly different light. Hodjat may be a dangerous hothead but given the immense tragedy he recently faced, who can blame him? Nader may have gone too far in pushing out Razieh but given the state he had just found his father in, who can blame him? Farhadi never places blame, allowing the action to unfold organically, believably, and emotionally.

It helps immensely that his cast is simply spectacular. Being relatively unfamiliar with Iranian cinema, most viewers probably will not be able to discern if actors like Moaadi or Hatami are really stretching far beyond their real-life personas but that takes nothing away from the realism they bring to this piece. It is the kind of film for which the acting is so strong that one does not even notice it. These people simply feel real. Their story rings true. And their truth is devastating.

Brian Tallerico

CREDITS

Nader: Payman Moaadi
Simin: Leila Hatami
Tarmeh: Sarina Farhadi
Razieh: Sareh Bayat
Hodjat: Shahab Hosseini

Origin: Iran
Language: Persian
Released: 2011
Production: Asghar Farrhadi; released by Sony Pictures Classics
Directed by: Asghar Farhadi
Written by: Asghar Farhadi
Cinematography by: Mahmoud Kalari
Music by: Sattar Oraki
Sound: Mohammad Reza Delpak
Editing: Hayedeh Safiyari
Costumes: Keyvan Moghadam
Production Design: Keyvan Moghadam
MPAA rating: PG-13
Running time: 123 minutes

REVIEWS

Corliss, Richard. *Time.* January 3, 2012.
Edelstein, David. *New York Magazine.* January 7, 2012.
Jones, J.R. *Chicago Reader.* January 26, 2012.
Kohn, Eric. *IndieWIRE.* December 26, 2011.
Mondello, Bob. *NPR.* December 30, 2011.
Morgenstern, Joe. *Wall Street Journal.* December 29, 2011.
Phillips, Michael. *Chicago Tribune.* January 26, 2012.
Stevens, Dana. *Slate.* January 4, 2012.
Tobias, Scott. *AV Club.* December 29, 2011.
Turan, Kenneth. *Los Angeles Times.* December 29, 2011.

QUOTES

Nader: "What is wrong is wrong, no matter who said it or where it's written."

TRIVIA

This is the first to ever win three Bears from the Berlin International Film Festival.

AWARDS

Oscars 2011: Foreign Film
Golden Globes 2012: Foreign Film
Ind. Spirit 2012: Foreign Film
Nomination:
Oscars 2011: Orig. Screenplay
British Acad. 2011: Foreign Film.

SHAME

Box Office: $3.7 million

Steve McQueen's *Shame* turned out to be one of the most discussed and divisive films of 2011, a work that ended up on nearly as many worst of the year lists

as best of the year compendiums. Michael Fassbender and Carey Mulligan's emotionally (and often physically) bare performances earned them critical citations from the Toronto Film Festival through the end of the year but both were left off the list when Oscar® nominations were announced in favor of more obvious, less-inspired choices (Fassbender topped most lists of the greatest snubs of the year). The unique, daring directorial style of McQueen combined with the bleak, depressing story pushed the film out of an awards season dominated by feel-good fare like *The Artist* (2011) and *Hugo* (2011) but history will be kind to this film, a drama that works as more than mere performance piece or titillating provocation. Like most films as controversial as *Shame,* this is dark, confrontational material of the kind that too few major filmmakers are even willing to consider producing much less able to bring to life in such a mesmerizing, haunting manner. It may have ridden a rollercoaster of critical returns when it played in theaters but future generations will wonder how there was ever a question of its immense quality.

Like a lot of addicts, Brandon (Fassbender) hides his problem in carefully-constructed routine. He rarely lets people into his life. He does not return his sister's phone calls. He does not seem to date much or have much of a social life beyond a friend (James Badge Dale) at work who essentially seems to use him as a wingman for happy hour pick-ups. There is a possible love interest (Nicole Beharie) at work as well but it seems doomed from the start not due to any fault of hers but because Brandon is not an average suitor. He is a sex addict. His addiction brings him little joy. He masturbates, watches porn, engages in online interactions with naked women, and even has one-night stands, but none of these activities bring him any perceptible joy. They simply define his existence as routine does for most people. The problem is that Brandon's routine has deepened to the point that no one can invade it or risk toppling his system. This is why the arrival of his sister Sissy (Mulligan) creates such problems for him.

Sissy has her own problems (and there is a dark shared past hinted at for the siblings). While Brandon's dark past may have led to his sexual addiction, it has made Sissy something of a flighty personality. She breaks Brandon's routine in half—using his shower, sleeping with his co-worker, and discovering some of his secrets. It forces Brandon deeper into his own problems, culminating in a trip into the sexual underworld at just the time that Sissy needs him most. Brandon does not understand someone needing someone for anything other than sexual release. His failure at a romantic relationship and his inability to help his sister proves this character deficiency. And yet McQueen's film is not a standard "descent to rock bottom" addiction piece.

First and foremost, Brandon is not a typical pervert. He does not wear a raincoat or have sweaty palms. He is a very handsome man in his thirties who betrays none of his addictions in public. When his co-workers find a copious amount of porn-related viruses on his computer, they assume that someone else did it. Brandon is too "normal."

Much was made of the NC-17 rating given the film by the MPAA but the flesh on display, much of it belonging to Fassbender and Mulligan, is there to de-sexualize it. Both characters/actors are introduced completely naked with full-frontal nudity (Brandon getting out of bed in the morning and Sissy in the shower). Before he has even spoken, Brandon is seen urinating. His body is presented as functional, not sexual. However that does not mean it was easy for the actors. McQueen and co-writer Abi Morgan wrote a screenplay that would have understandably terrified most actors and actresses who might consider the roles of Brandon and Sissy. So much is asked of the two actors that play these two characters, including complete physical and emotional vulnerability. There is no cliché here, only daring and memorable drama. Luckily for McQueen, he found two actors who seem incapable of playing pure cinematic archetype, instead finding the truth in every role they play, even if the truth is as raw as it is here. Fassbender never plays Brandon as the monster he could have so easily become in a lesser actor's hands. It is an extremely internal performance, daring in its small beats, until the final act when the actor is forced to lay it all on the line in a series of daring scenes. While people were commenting on Fassbender's physical endowments, the key to his performance actually lay further up—in Brandon's deep, sorrowful eyes. And Mulligan matches him at every turn, finding the emotional rawness that Fassbender does more physically. If Brandon is introverted, Sissy is the extrovert. She sings, sleeps around, and seems almost be like a wanderer, someone without a home. Once again, like Fassbender, Mulligan never plays the cliché.

McQueen and his talented cinematographer Sean Bobbitt brilliantly turn New York City into the third central character in the film, shooting through skyscraper windows and down barren city streets populated with nothing but streetlights. Not only does the cinematography lend the piece an air of voyeurism, it deepens the theme through a timeless motif of how people can be so solitary in a crowded city. As McQueen and Bobbitt track Brandon jogging down a desolate street, it raises the expected questions—What is going on behind those doors? What is happening one room from the window through which we gaze? One of the keys to the success of *Shame* is that McQueen and Morgan never present it as a unique story. It takes something as extreme and

salacious as sex addiction and makes it feel strikingly common in a city the size of New York. The brilliance of McQueen's film is that he has taken situations that will not be familiar to most viewers and made them feel relatable, understandable, and genuine. Perhaps the film was divisive because it hit too close to home for some viewers.

Brian Tallerico

CREDITS

Brandon: Michael Fassbender
Sissy: Carey Mulligan
David: James Badge Dale
Marianne: Nicole Beharie
Origin: United Kingdom
Language: English
Released: 2011
Production: Iain Canning, Emilie Sherman; See Saw Films, FilmFour, U.K. Film Council; released by Fox Searchlight
Directed by: Steve McQueen
Written by: Steve McQueen, Abi Morgan
Cinematography by: Sean Bobbitt
Music by: Harry Escott
Sound: Ken Ishii
Music Supervisor: Ian Neil
Editing: Joe Walker
Art Direction: Charles Kulsziski
Costumes: David Robinson
Production Design: Judy Becker
MPAA rating: NC-17
Running time: 101 minutes

REVIEWS

Chang, Justin. *Variety.* November 8, 2011.
Ebert, Roger. *Chicago Sun-Times.* November 30, 2011.
McCarthy, Todd. *Hollywood Reporter.* November 8, 2011.
O'Hehir, Andrew. *Salon.com.* November 8, 2011.
Puig, Claudia. *USA Today.* December 1, 2011.
Rickey, Carrie. *Philadelphia Inquirer.* December 8, 2011.
Tobias, Scott. *AV Club.* December 1, 2011.
Turan, Kenneth. *Los Angeles Times.* December 1, 2011.
Uhlich, Keith. *Time Out New York.* November 29, 2011.
Zacharek, Stephanie. *Movieline.* December 1, 2011.

QUOTES

Sissy Sullivan: "We're not bad people. We just come from a bad place."

TRIVIA

Actor Michael Fassbender has said that he actually urinated on camera when a scene required him to do so.

AWARDS

Nomination:

British Acad. 2011: Actor (Fassbender), Outstanding British Film

Golden Globes 2012: Actor—Drama (Fassbender)
Ind. Spirit 2012: Foreign Film.

SHARK NIGHT 3D

Terror runs deep.
—Movie tagline

Box Office: $18.9 million

There are two types of moviegoers in the world those who would never dream of wasting their time and money on going to see anything entitled *Shark Night 3D* on the basis that it sounded like idiotic and irredeemable trash and those who would rush out to the local multiplex on opening night to see it precisely on the basis that it sounded like idiotic and irredeemable trash. Sadly, the film pretty much fails to live up (or down) to such lofty expectations as it squanders a seemingly irresistible B-movie premise on a paint-by-numbers programmer that turns out to be little more than a slightly-more-expensive version of the low-budget water-based campfests that the legendary Roger Corman now produces for cable television's SyFy Channel (featuring such inexplicable creatures as DinoSharks and MegaPiranhas) with, of all things, a heaping help of *Straw Dogs* (1971) randomly tossed into the mix. As shark-infused thrillers shot in an increasingly questionable multi-dimensional format go, the good news is that it is indeed better than *Jaws 3D* (1983), a film so infamously bad that it was one of the main culprits of the death of the brief 3D revival in the 1980s. The bad news is that it turns out to be not *that* much better in the long run.

As the film begins, a group of Tulane University students—blonde sweetheart Sara (Sara Paxton), hunky nerd Nick (Dustin Milligan), horny nerd Gordon (Joel David Moore), cheerful tramp Beth (Katherine McPhee), vain douchebag Blake (Chris Zylka), basketball prospect Malik (Sinqua Walls) and Maya (Alyssa Diaz), the longtime girlfriend of the latter—head off to spend the weekend at the lavish and remote lake house in the Louisiana Gulf owned by Sara and her family. It transpires that this is the first time Sara has returned home in three years following some harrowing, if initially unspecified, trauma involving old local boyfriend Dennis (Chris Carmack) but that is quickly forgotten once the gang arrives at the house and strip down to their bathing suits for the impending revelry. The bacchanal is soon interrupted when Malik goes into the water while water-skiing and emerges missing an arm and an initial attempt to get him to safety ends with Maya getting chewed up as well. It turns out that the lake is positively teeming with sharks and the others are left to struggle through their long shark night of the soul while waiting for help to arrive. Of course, one might think that their chances of survival would be pretty good as long as they stay out of the water but the only thing that the screenplay by Will Hayes & Jesse Studenberg works harder at than trying to contrive ways to toss them back into the drink is to contrive ways to keep them from changing out of their swimsuits into more sensible outfits once the carnage kicks in.

As can easily be surmised from the title alone, *Shark Night 3D* is an incredibly dumb movie through and through and it would be well nigh impossible to mount a credible complaint about the lack of intelligence, logic or coherence without sounding like a fool. For a movie like this to succeed, however, it needs to supply viewers with the kind of stupidity that is cheerfully and knowingly moronic enough to work as camp entertainment without pushing things so far that it begins to insult the intelligence of even those expecting nothing more than ninety minutes of nonsense. At first, the film seems to be obeying that rule by kicking things off with a cheerfully blatant copy of the opening scene of *Jaws* (1975) and setting up both the premise and the central characters, all of whom are portrayed by actors who were clearly hired for their abilities at filling their Speedos and bikinis (in this regard, former *American Idol* finalist McPhee takes top honors), in a reasonably breezy and efficient manner. However, once the sharks start snacking, the whole thing quickly goes downhill into a morass of wooden acting, muddled plotting and murky attack scenes (once again, the combination of 3D, night photography and the water proves to be virtually unwatchable) and aside from the occasional moment of delightful lunacy—such as the bit in which one of the characters wanders out into the water in order to single-handedly kill a shark with nothing but a spear and his misguided machismo—it becomes an absolute chore to sit through. And yes, the screenplay does offer an explanation as to why a seemingly normal lake—even one filled with salt water—would become the habitat for enough sharks to fill a year of *Shark Week* but said explanation is so moronic and nonsensical—even by shabby B-movie standards—that if the writers of *Scooby-Doo* had dared to present it as the solution to an episode, they would have been forced to hang their heads in shame.

That said, most trash movie fanatics might have been willing to overlook the sloppy screenwriting, dead-end direction and lackluster performances of *Shark Night 3D* as long as it delivered on its unspoken promise of providing viewers with plentiful doses of mostly naked people being gruesomely chomped to death by giant sharks in the same way that *Piranha 3D* did the previous summer. Alas, in one of the more inexplicable moves in recent cinematic memory, perhaps inspired by the well-publicized failure of director David Ellis' previous animals-amok epic, the decidedly R-rated *Snakes on a Plane* (2006), the film was released with a PG-13 rating that minimized those elements to such a degree that it calls the entire existence of the enterprise into question.—even the television edits of the *Jaws* films contained more gore than is seen here. This was presumably done in an effort to expand the potential audience pool but it wound up backfiring badly as those not necessarily inclined to see something entitled *Shark Night 3D* stayed away in drove while the horror fans took one look at the rating, realized that it would clearly be missing all the good stuff and also kept their distance. In other words, despite the large amount of underwater predators on the screen, the only thing about *Shark Night 3D* that actually bites is the film itself.

Peter Sobczynski

CREDITS

Sara: Sara Paxton
Maya: Alyssa Diaz
Nick: Dustin Milligan
Dennis: Chris Carmack
Gordon: Joel David Moore
Blake: Chris Zylka
Beth: Katharine McPhee
Malik: Sinqua Walls
Red: Joshua Leonard
Sherrif Greg Sabin: Donal Louge
Origin: USA
Language: English
Released: 2011
Production: Mike Fleiss, Lynette Howell, Chris Briggs; Sierra Pictures, Incentive Filmed Entertainment; released by Relativity Media
Directed by: Daniel R. Ellis
Written by: Jesse Studenberg, William Hayes
Cinematography by: Gary Capo
Music by: Graeme Revell
Sound: Steve Aaron
Music Supervisor: Joe Rudge
Editing: Dennis Virkler
Art Direction: Craig Jackson
Costumes: Magali Guidasci
Production Design: Jaymes Hinkle
MPAA rating: PG-13
Running time: 95 minutes

REVIEWS

Abele, Robert. *Los Angeles Times*. September 2, 2011.
Catsoulis, Jeannette. *New York Times*. September 3, 2011.
Gibron, Bill. *Filmcritic.com*. September 2, 2011.
Jones, Kimberley. *Austin Chronicle*. September 9, 2011.
Michel, Brett. *Boston Herald*. September 9, 2011.
Morris, Wesley. *Boston Globe*. September 5, 2011.
Orndorf, Brian. *BrianOrndorf.com*. September 2, 2011.
Pinkerton, Nick. *Village Voice*. September 7, 2011.
Robinson, Tasha. *AV Club*. September 2, 2011.
Weinberg, Scott. *FEARnet*. September 2, 2011.

TRIVIA

Director David R. Ellis had wanted to release the film with the title "Untitled 3D Shark Thriller."

SHERLOCK HOLMES: A GAME OF SHADOWS

Box Office: $185.4 million

One of the most popular characters in the history of modern storytelling, Sherlock Holmes has been fodder for every conceivable kind of cinematic re-imagining. Some of the best films that riff on the great detective include *The Private Life of Sherlock Holmes* (1970), *They Might Be Giants* (1971), and *Young Sherlock Holmes* (1985). These very different films (one is largely a comedy examining the less savory aspects of the detective, one has a lovable madman adopting the persona of Holmes, and one is an adventure film tracking Holmes' movement from gifted teenager to reclusive genius) all hold in common an ability to hang on to the essence of the things that make Holmes special while plugging him into new adventures. With his modern hit franchise, Guy Ritchie re-imagines the great detective and his erstwhile partner Watson as action heroes but sadly fails to give them a story to act upon, choosing instead to create a thin, visually dynamic, pastiche of all things Holmesian to serve as a showcase for action set pieces and broad comic moments. From a storytelling standpoint, *Sherlock Holmes A Game of Shadows* is likable and often very entertaining, but also a complete mess.

Ritchie's approach to the Holmes franchise is, in effect, a spoof of all things that have become associated with Sir Arthur Conan Doyle's beloved series. Kieran & Michele Mulroney's loose approach to the plotting and ham-fisted comic sensibility seems based on an utter confidence that viewers will have fallen in love with the characters by now. They have made a relatively safe bet. Robert Downey Jr. and Jude Law fire on all cylinders bringing the well known duo to hilarious life. The tone is always playful but also juvenile—elementary, indeed. The irony is that the story is only as messy as the detective himself as portrayed by Robert Downey Jr.

The film starts with Holmes (Robert Downey Jr.) as he is in the process of linking together a number of outwardly unrelated crimes that have taken place across Europe. He believes they are the work of a single criminal mastermind, one Professor James Moriarty (Jared Harris), renowned mathematics genius and respected academic. Moriarty, sensing that Holmes is on to him, forces a meeting, warning Holmes to cease his investigations unless he wants his loved ones to suffer the consequences. Falling directly into the cross-fire are Holmes' one true love, Irene Adler (Rachel McAdams), and the soon-to-be wed Dr. Watson (Jude Law) and his betrothed Mary Morstan (Kelly Reilly). Desperate to outrace Moriarty's vast army of criminal underlings, Holmes rushes to the aid of his friends, finding it necessary to stage daring rescues, plan Watson's bachelor party with his brother Mycroft (Stephen Fry), and invade a honeymoon in drag. Assisting him for part of his adventure is one of Moriarty's intended victims, a gypsy girl named Sim (Noomi Rapace). A fierce game of cat and mouse leaves bodies in its wake and Holmes evading the deadliest of Moriarty's allies, the incredible marksman, Colonel Sebastian Moran (Paul Anderson) while he tries to figure out and thwart Moriarty's hidden plan.

Any further or more detailed a plot description would rob the film, not of the few surprises that work, but give the impression that one event leads to another more or less logically. There are no real surprises that will matter to most viewers and the order of events is anything but logical. Instead, whenever the story needs to progress somebody simply blows something up, or tries to kill someone or inexplicably discovers a clue that will lead them on to the next place the plot demands. It is too simple of a story for Doyle or the classic character.

Another major weakness is an over-reliance on what does initially work for the film. Viewers will remember the voiced-over slow-motion visuals signaling Sherlock's deductive thought processes from the first film. It has always mattered far less whether the audience believes Holmes can actually do the things he does than it matters how badly they want to watch them being done. Holmes is, in effect, a mental magician who constantly cheats but puts on a dynamite show. Ritchie's device worked very well in the first film and works well here precisely because it is as fascinating as it is improbable. But *Sherlock Holmes: A Game of Shadows* repeats it ad nauseum. Ritchie even includes a moment where Moriarty uses it. The moment is meant to be funny but it is robbed of its effect by repetition.

Likewise, the bickering between Holmes and Watson grates over time. The pair (like most narrative same-sex duos) has often inspired gay humor but what starts off very funny here, goes nowhere except on and on and on, providing no insight into the characters even if it does give Downey and Law a chance to riff, often hilariously. The climax of this device is reached early on in a riotous scene where Holmes, in drag, ends up wrestling with Watson in a train car. But sadly, even after a moment this broad, Ritchie and cast keep hitting the one note, albeit a tad softer, for the rest of the film.

Some will find fault with Ritchie's heavily stylized visuals but they do wonders here. Victorian London is always a fun place to visit cinematically and Ritchie's muted palette contributes to the dingy atmosphere that viewers associate with it. His use of slow motion is the real bone of contention for many, and while it is used a great deal in the film, it is generally fascinating to watch, and quite beautiful rendering the action sequences in incredible detail that can be appreciated more fully.

As mentioned, Downey Jr. and Law are uniformly excellent in their roles and supported by an outstanding cast, most notably Jared Harris who dominates in the role of Moriarty thought the script gives him nothing but clichés with which to work. Rachel McAdams as Irene Adler and Eddie Marsan as Inspector Lestrade are spot on and embody those characters well but they have precious little screen time. The striking and talented Noomi Rapace is unforgivably wasted in the do-nothing role of Sim the gypsy and sadly there is no secondary character to compare with the giant Dredger played by Robert Maillet in the previous installment.

The first *Sherlock Holmes* (2009) offered impressive style but also a little substance with Ritchie utilizing his opportunity to recast the Holmes mythos in his signature visual style. *Sherlock Holmes A Game of Shadows* plays like a feature length if solid gag reel from that first film. The film does have an absolutely fabulous ending that in a better movie would have added a grace note onto the roaring finish but instead viewers are liable to feel a little wistful, wishing that they could remember any of the movie that preceded it.

Dave Canfield

CREDITS

Sherlock Holmes: Robert Downey Jr.
Dr. John Watson: Jude Law
Inspector Lestrade: Eddie Marsan
Professor James Moriarty: Jared Harris
Mycroft Holmes: Stephen Fry
Simza Heron: Noomi Rapace
Irene Adler: Rachel McAdams
Mary Morstan Watson: Kelly Reilly
Mrs. Hudson: Geraldine James
Col. Sebastian Moran: Paul Anderson

Origin: USA

Language: English

Released: 2011

Production: Joel Silver, Lionel Wigram, Susan Downey, Dan Lin; Silver Pictures, Wigram Productions, Village Roadshow Pictures; released by Warner Bros.

Directed by: Guy Ritchie

Written by: Kieran Mulroney, Michele Mulroney

Cinematography by: Philippe Rousselot

Music by: Hans Zimmer

Sound: Chris Munro

Editing: James Herbert

Art Direction: Niall Maroney

Costumes: Jenny Beavan

Production Design: Sarah Greenwood

MPAA rating: PG-13

Running time: 129 minutes

REVIEWS

Demara, Bruce. *Toronto Star*. December 16, 2011.

Ebert, Roger. *Chicago Sun-Times*. December 15, 2011.

Leupp, Thomas. *Hollywood.com*. December 16, 2011.

Kennedy, Lisa. *Denver Post*. December 16, 2011.

O'Hehir, Andrew. *Salon.com*. December 15, 2011.

Russell, Mike. *Oreegonian*. December 15, 2011.

Savlov, Marc. *Austin Chronicle*. December 15, 2011.

Scott, A.O. *New York Times*. December 15, 2011.

Velez, Diva. *TheDivaReview*. December 17, 2011.

Yamato, Jen. *Movieline*. December 15, 2011.

QUOTES

Professor Moriaty: "People have an innate desire for conflict. So what you are fighting is not me, but rather mankind. War, on an industrial scale, is inevitable. I'm just supplying the bullets and bandages."

TRIVIA

Actors Brad Pitt, Gary Oldman, Daniel Day-Lewis, Sean Penn, and Javier Bardem were all considered for the role of Professor Moriarty.

THE SITTER

Worst. Babysitter. Ever.
—Movie tagline

Need a Sitter?
—Movie tagline

Box Office: $30.4 million

At least Noah Griffith (Jonah Hill), the slacker protagonist of *The Sitter*, acknowledges and apologizes for the fact that he has placed the lives of children in danger throughout the course of the movie. It is more than can be said of screenwriters Brian Gatewood and Alessandro Tanaka, who have generated a screenplay that is entirely dependent on the concept that the children in question are precocious and/or rebellious enough to be prepared for peril or obnoxious enough to somehow deserve it. In general, child endangerment for dramatic purposes is a cheap, manufactured excuse for heightening conflict; used for comedy, it can be reprehensible.

Fortunately for the screenwriters and director David Gordon Green, whose odd career trajectory from independent, character-driven films about real people (*George Washington* (2000], *All the Real Girls* [2003], *Undertow* [2004], and *Snow Angels* [2007]) to hit-or-miss, crude high-concept comedies in which the characters exist solely to serve the gags (*Pineapple Express* [2008], which hits more often that it misses, and *Your Highness* [2011], which misses the large majority of the time) reaches its nadir with this movie, the placement of its child characters in situations that would traumatize even the toughest of adults is the least of the sins of *The Sitter*. Unfortunately, the major problem lies at a more basic level of simple function: It simply is not funny.

The minimal story follows Noah, an unemployed young man in his early twenties who has no foreseeable prospects in his life. His "girlfriend" Marissa (Ari Graynor) has pictures of her ex-boyfriend, a professional kickboxer named Ricky Fontaine (Jack Krizmanich) who appears later in the movie just so that there might be a physical confrontation, adorning her bedroom. To establish Noah's status as a perennial loser, the movie opens with him performing oral sex on Marissa and hinting to no avail that he wants her to reciprocate.

Soon after, he rides a bicycle home (a character mentions that he had been arrested recently for drunk driving), where his mother (Jessica Hecht) sketches out the rest of Noah's minimal character traits (that he is unemployed and his wealthy father [Bruce Altman] has moved on from their lives) and the plot: She could be going out on her first date in a while but her friends' babysitter has cancelled. For the date to go through and to give his mother a chance at some happiness, Noah begrudgingly agrees to watch her friends' children for the night.

The three children have their broad quirks. Slater (Max Records) is anally retentive and suffers from extreme anxiety. Blithe (Landry Bender) fancies herself a budding beauty queen and type of celebrity that is only famous for partying. Their adopted brother Rodrigo (Kevin Hernandez) has a fondness for fighting (watching kickboxing matches constantly), destroying things (especially with cherry bombs), and running away (the family has tagged him with a GPS tracking system).

Early in the evening, Marissa calls Noah from a party she is attending with a request and an offer: If he brings her cocaine, she will have sex with him. Without a second thought, Noah brings his wards with him to buy cocaine from a temperamental and insecure drug dealer. His name is Karl, and, as played by Sam Rockwell, the character and his performance are at least funny on a conceptual level, which is more than one can say about any other element of the movie. The eventual through line of the plot arrives when Rodrigo steals a decorative egg containing $10,000 worth of cocaine, and the contents spill out when Noah and the boy wrestle for possession. Karl gives Noah until the end of the night to pay him back.

In between the screenplay's few key plot points, the dynamic between Noah and the children undergoes an equally simplistic reversal. At first, they do not like each other. Blithe attempts to convince a pair of employees at a clothing store (where Noah stops with the girl after she loses control of her bowels) that he is a sexual predator that has kidnapped her (the two clerks and a visit to a bar bring up the at least questionable portrayal of the movie's African-American characters, who—save for Roxanne [Kylie Bunbury], a former college classmate of Noah's who becomes the inevitable love interest—are either quick to anger, eager to brawl, or both). Rodrigo escapes to a fancy restaurant, where he destroys a toilet. Only the melancholy Slater is sympathetic at face value, though the way the script treats his repressed sexuality gives the impression of ridicule in the guise of understanding.

The rest of the movie plays out predictably, as Noah learns to tolerate and even care for the children (and vice versa), has compulsory confrontations with his foes (including his father, Marissa's ex-boyfriend, and Karl), and learns something or other about responsibility (a lesson that, given the movie's overall lack of maturity, comes across as phony). Though chaos governs the comic moments, the characters and situation of *The Sitter* are entirely routine.

Mark Dujsik

CREDITS

Noah Griffith: Jonah Hill
Kart: Sam Rockwell
Marissa Lewis: Ari Graynor
Julio: JB Smoove
Jacolby: Method Man
Slater: Max Records

Rodrigo: Kevin Hernandez
Blithe: Landry Bender
Jim Griffith: Bruce Altman
Sandy Griffith: Jessica Hecht
Origin: USA
Language: English
Released: 2011
Production: Michael De Luca; Dune Entertainment, Rough House Pictures; released by 20th Century-Fox
Directed by: David Gordon Green
Written by: Brian Gatewood, Alessandro Tanaka
Cinematography by: Tim Orr
Music by: David Wingo, Jeff McIlwain
Sound: Christof Gebert
Music Supervisor: Mark Wike
Editing: Craig Alpert
Art Direction: Matthew Munn
Costumes: Leah Katznelson
Production Design: Richard Wright
MPAA rating: R
Running time: 81 minutes

REVIEWS

Andersen, Soren. *Seattle Times*. December 8, 2011.
Berardinelli, James. *ReelViews*. December 10, 2011.
Dargis, Manohla. *New York Times*. December 8, 2011.
DeMara, Bruce. *Toronto Star*. December 8, 2011.
Ebert, Roger. *Chicago Sun-Times*. December 7, 2011.
Osenlund, R. Kurt. *Slant Magazine*. December 8, 2011.
Phillips, Michael. *Chicago Tribune*. December 8, 2011.
Sobczynski, Peter. *EFilmCritic.com*. December 9, 2011.
Tallerico, Brian. *HollywoodChicago.com*. December 9, 2011.
Tobias, Scott. *AV Club*. December 8, 2011.

QUOTES

Noah Griffith: "My name's Noah Jaybird. Ca caaa! What's your name?"
Soul Baby: "They call me Soul. Soul Baby."
Noah Griffith: "Soul Baby?"
Soul Baby: "Yeah."
Noah Griffith: "Keep it in control baby. Tears, no fears man."
Soul Baby: "Is that right?"
Noah Griffith: "Respect it, don't neglect it. Treat it, don't beat it."

TRIVIA

This is the last film to feature Jonah Hill's rotund physique before his dramatic weight loss.

THE SKIN I LIVE IN
(La piel que habito)

Box Office: $3.2 million

Although Pedro Almodovar has tripped thorough any number of increasingly wild and wooly generic tropes throughout his career, *The Skin I Live In* marks his first outright foray into the horror genre and is far more out there in terms of its narrative and tone than he had allowed himself to be in recent years with such relatively sedate works as *Volver* (2006) and *Broken Embraces* (2009). Reuniting with Antonio Banderas, who first came to international prominence through appearances in his early films, for the first time since *Tie Me Up, Tie Me Down* (1990), is an agreeably depraved excursion into pure weirdness with a plot so cheerfully deranged and kinky that it would seem equally at home in the most elite arthouses of today as well as the sleaziest grindhouses of yore. In both cases, however, this is a film that definitely would have sent even the most jaded viewers reeling out into the streets after it ended looking fairly pole-axed over what they had just experienced.

In the film, Banderas plays Dr. Robert Lesgard, a brilliant plastic surgeon who, equally haunted and inspired by the tragic death of his beloved wife twelve years earlier in the aftermath of a fiery car wreck, has become obsessed with developing a highly advanced form of synthetic skin utilizing a radical breakthrough in transgenic mutation involving the combination of human and animal genetic material. Because such experimentation is frowned upon by the medical community as madness, Lesgard carries out his experiments from within the confines of his lavish and remote estate which is equipped with such necessities as a fully appointed lab and operating room, a discreet housekeeper in Marilia (Marisa Paredes) and his very own test subject in Vera (Elena Anaya), a beautiful young woman who spends her days in her room doing yoga and reading while clad in nothing but a flesh-colored bodysuit. Although Lesgard's work is progressing by leaps and bounds, Vera is a little less thrilled with the arrangement—she is essentially a prisoner, her every move is constantly monitored by Lesgard and Marilia and she has attempted suicide multiple times.

This would seem to be enough plot to fuel two or three different movies but in this case, it is all a mere backdrop to the actual narrative. That arrives violently when Zeca (Roberto Alamo), a jumpy weirdo clad in a Gaultier-designed tiger suit, turns up on Lesgard's doorstep one day when the doctor is out and demands to be let in. Without giving away too many details about what happens next, let it be said that his arrival instigate a series of astonishing and terrifying events and revelations involving rape, murder, infidelity, secrets, lies, betrayal, suicide, forbidden lust and outright weirdness. It also inspires the revelation of another key incident in Lesgard's tragic and twisted past from six years earlier, one involving his shy but lovely daughter Norma (Ana Mena), a lavish garden party in which she finds herself succumbing to the seduction of young rake Vincente

(Jan Cornet) and the tragic misunderstanding that finally pushed him over the scientific demarcation line separating "ambitious" and "mad". Somehow, all of these seemingly disparate elements manage to tie into one another in a climax that will have even those viewers expecting to see something unusual with their jaws on the floor out of sheer disbelief over what they have just witnessed.

Although based, apparently quite loosely, on a novel by Thierry Jonquet, *The Skin I Live In* is clearly a Almodovar experience through and through in the way that he has taken classic movie tropes—including structural elements from Alfred Hitchcock's *Vertigo* (1958) bits and pieces from any number of mad scientist epics like the Georges Franju classic *Eyes Without a Face* (1959) and a generous sampling from the decidedly outré output of fellow countryman Jess Franco—and mixed them together with his own penchant for kinky sexuality, dark humor, shameless melodrama and extremely stylized surroundings into the kind of salacious cinematic stew of the kind that only he would be brave and/or foolhardy enough to even attempt in the first place. Unlike *Volver* and *Broken Embraces,* both of which contained their fair share of strange elements but which were otherwise reasonably straightforward from a dramatic perspective, *The Skin I Live In* is just as flat-out insane as his earlier films but instead of using an overly mannered approach in order to distance himself from the real emotions bubbling under the candy-coated surfaces and jokey manner, he plays things relatively straight here and it is all the better for it. After all, considering the fact that this is a horror film—although one more interested in unnerving viewers instead of making them nauseous—a silly take on the material would have been disastrous because this is not the kind of take on the genre that lends itself easily to laughter and while he could have easily made it into one big joke, what he has done here is more of a challenge and, in the end, far more rewarding. (That said, it may have been exactly this cool and reserved tone that inspired the lukewarm reviews that it garnered after premiering in Cannes earlier this year but if it had arrived bearing the name of David Cronenberg—whose early work it most often suggest at times—there is a very good chance that it would have been hailed as genius.)

Adding immeasurably to the success of the film is the presence of Antonio Banderas in a performance that goes a long way towards keeping the film from spinning off into all directions. In the years since he last worked with Almodovar, Banderas has become an enormously popular star around the world and it is that very movie star mystique that is deployed here in such effective ways. Face it, Dr. Lesgard is pretty much a monster through and through, especially as more is revealed about him, and in the hands of most other actors, trying to transform such a character into someone worth following into the depths of his depraved obsessions would be next to impossible. Here, Almodovar utilizes Banderas' star appeal in much the same way that Hitchcock did when he hired Jimmy Stewart to play the equally dark and twisted lead in *Vertigo*—he allows the actor's natural appeal to shine through in the early going so that by the time that the weird stuff begins kicking up in earnest, viewers have already been lured into their web and continue to stay there by virtue of Banderas' exceptional work. As for Ayana, who previously worked with Almodovar in *Talk to Her* (2004), her work is equally impressive in the way that she takes what, with the extended scenes of her lounging around in either a form-fitting flesh-colored bodysuit or nothing at all, could have easily been little more than an extended modeling job and instead turns it into an equally complex and effective turn that becomes all the more rewarding once the hidden depths of her character are revealed as well.

Dark, demented and oddly tender at its admittedly bleak center, *The Skin I Live In* is one of those films that viewers will either love or loathe in equal measure. Regardless of where they stand on the issue, anyone who does go to see it will come away with the sensation that they have indeed truly seen something that they will not forget for a long time, no matter how much they may want to do so. Granted, it is not the easiest film to embrace and those who prefer their entertainment to be more on the safe and predictable side should probably give it a pass for fear that it may be a bit too much for them. However, for fans of Almodovar—those in long standing and newly minted alike—and those whose tastes are more on the adventurous side, *The Skin I Live In* is, in the end, a cut above the rest, among other things.

Peter Sobczynski

CREDITS

Dr. Robert Ledgard: Antonio Banderas
Marilia: Marisa Paredes
Vera: Elena Anaya
Norma: Blanca Suarez
Vicente: Jan Cornet
Origin: Spain
Language: Spanish
Released: 2011
Production: Agustin Almodovar, Esther Garcia; El Deseo; released by Sony Pictures Classics
Directed by: Pedro Almodovar
Written by: Pedro Almodovar
Cinematography by: Jose Luis Alcaine

Music by: Alberto Iglesias
Editing: Jose Salcedo
Sound: Pelayo Gutiérrez
Costumes: Paco Delgado
Production Design: Antxon Gomez
MPAA rating: R
Running time: 117 minutes

REVIEWS

Corliss, Richard. *Time Magazine.* October 13, 2011.
Dargis, Manohla. *New York Times.* October 13, 2011.
Dujsik, Mark. *Mark Reviews Movies.* October 20, 2011.
Ebert, Roger. *Chicago Sun-Times.* October 20, 2011.
Edelstein, David. *New York Magazine.* October 10, 2011.
Goss, William. *Film.com.* October 14, 201.
Longworth, Karina. *Village Voice.* October 11, 2011.
Newman, Kim. *Empire Magazine.* August 22, 2011.
Reed, Rex. *New York Observer.* October 12, 2011.
Rothkopf, Joshua. *Time Out New York.* October 11, 2011.

QUOTES

Marilia: "The things the love of a mad man can do."

AWARDS

British Acad. 2011: Foreign Film
Nomination:
Golden Globes 2012: Foreign Film.

SLEEPING BEAUTY

Sleeping Beauty is not, like the 1959 Disney film based on the Brothers Grimm fairytale, a family friendly story about an innocent woman saved from a curse of eternal slumber by a handsome prince. It is far from it. In 2011, *Sleeping Beauty* covers something far more challenging, controversial and adult: Writer-director Julia Leigh's feature debut positions a beautiful, naked, sleeping woman as non-sexual currency, onto which the rich, old white men who pay for her company can project either admiration or anger as long as they do not penetrate her. By the way: The girl has been drugged, so there is no chance of her waking up and wondering why somebody's grandfather is licking her face.

That role probably does not seem like a job many women would covet, despite being paid no less than $250 an hour. In fact, Lucy (Emily Browning) surely would not have considered it were she not so in need of funds that she already works four part-time jobs to pay her college tuition. She works a mindless office job, an equally unfulfilling job at a restaurant, participates in laboratory studies and, when time allows, prostitutes herself at bars. So perhaps it is not a huge step when Lucy finds out, for the large aforementioned wage, she can work as a "Silver Service" waitress, requiring her to strip to her underwear and serve brandy to wealthy senior citizens who consider beluga caviar to be a standard menu item. After doing this a few times, Lucy moves on to the next level: allowing herself to be drugged so she can sleep soundly while some of the men she has served can join her naked in bed. Lucy's superior Clara (Rachael Blake) requires these men to agree not to have sex with Lucy, but there is no other person or surveillance in the room while the guys do things like kiss her and burn her with cigarettes. So it is not as if the sleeping beauty's safety is guaranteed.

Obviously, this is an abnormal storyline, and plenty of viewers will recoil at the sight of a young woman subjecting herself to this sort of indignity. Yet Leigh is not looking to shame Lucy and the other women who participate in this unusual, secret world, which Clara tells Lucy comes with very heavy penalties if Lucy breaches her trust. Of course, Clara also tells Lucy, "Your vagina will be a temple." With no hesitation, Lucy replies, "My vagina is not a temple." Some may perceive this as Lucy suggesting that her body does not represent as much value as Clara claims. Others may simply see Lucy as a sexually active college student who does not label her most private parts with such extreme, sacred language. Surely she is glad that she will not have to have sex with any of the people old enough to remember watching Elvis on TV, but Lucy also does not want to be seen as some holy object.

Similar questions of value and challenges to the perceived meaning of words, objects and more occur throughout the movie. Lucy asks a few different guys if they will marry her, as if the question is as casual as, "Nice weather we have been having, huh?" After her first big payday, Lucy stares at the money, only to burn one of the bills, admiring her earnings and then refusing to let them control her. Her roommates are as concerned about Lucy's late rent payment as they are about her failure to properly clean the grout in the bathroom. Lucy determines if and when she will sleep with guys at the bar based on a coin toss—or maybe she is just making them think that the coin has the power, when she knew she would sleep with one no matter what. Lucy pours vodka into the cereal of her friend Birdmann (Ewen Leslie), something that might be a normal breakfast for some alcoholics but clearly has added significance here. Each time Lucy and Birdmann spend time together they engage in small-talk pleasantries, ironically and implicitly suggesting that their relationship is simpler than it actually is. A man at the bar tells Lucy that rather than faking his own death, he has faked his life (one of Lucy's clients expresses a similar sentiment to Clara in a heartbreaking monologue about discovering that he never really appreciated the important people in his life; he merely went through the motions).

Still, perhaps no interaction highlights this world in which serious things are taken lightly and absurdities are taken seriously more than when Lucy is commanded to apply lipstick that is the same color as her labia. When she does not check the color of her own labia before applying lipstick, she is told, "It's not a game." Her lipstick is wiped off, and a new shade is applied. Lucy clearly cannot believe this request. What she does not yet realize is that when young women are seen as non-living art, every color choice matters.

The point is that people frequently fail to make the distinction between surviving and really living, and that beauty matters in some situations but not all. (The knockout final shot puts an unforgettable stamp on the challenge of determining from a distance when someone is sleeping or dead.) The eerie quiet of *Sleeping Beauty* often feels ice cold, and it is hard not to be reminded of Stanley Kubrick's *Eyes Wide Shut* (1999) when group nudity is presented as, among other things, an exclusive privilege for the wealthy.

Sleeping Beauty is not without its own original pulse, however. At one point, Lucy awakens in the middle of the night, naked in her own bed. Though she is alone, she goes to put on her underwear, a sign that even though she is unconscious during her work, deep-down she feels uncomfortable with her newfound vulnerability, whether she understands it or not. Lucy's numbness does not shield her from the reality of the situation; if anything, the more familiar she becomes with what she is doing, the more curious she grows to want to know what happens to her while she sleeps. Part of life is realizing that people cannot control what happens while they sleep, a state of both purity and vulnerability. Lucy, however, starts to realize she misses the freedom to choose when she sleeps, and how.

Matt Pais

CREDITS

Lucy: Emily Browning
Clara: Rachael Blake
Man 1: Peter Carroll
Birdmann: Ewen Leslie
Man 2: Chris Haywood
Man 3: Hugh Keays-Byrne
Origin: Australia
Language: English
Released: 2011

Production: Jessica Brentnall; Screen Australia, Magic Films; released by IFC Films

Directed by: Julia Leigh

Written by: Julia Leigh

Cinematography by: Geoffrey Simpson

Music by: Ben Frost

Sound: Ben Osmo

Editing: Nick Meyers

Art Direction: Annie Beauchamp, Jocelyn Thomas

Costumes: Shareen Beringer

MPAA rating: Unrated

Running time: 104 minutes

REVIEWS

Berardinelli, James. *ReelViews.* November 2, 2011.

Cabin, Chris. *Filmcritic.com.* October 27, 2011.

DeBruge, Peter. *Variety.* October 10, 2011.

French, Phllip. *Observer (UK).* October 16, 2011.

Jenkins, David. *TimeOut.* October 11, 2011.

Mowe, Richard. *Box Office Magazine.* October 10, 2011.

O'Hehir, Andrew. *Salon.com.* October 10, 2011.

Rooney, David. *Hollywood Reporter.* October 10, 2011.

Smith, Anna. *Empire.* October 10, 2011.

Tallerico, Brian. *HollywoodChicago.com.* October 14, 2011.

TRIVIA

Emily Browning replaced Mia Wasikowska who had dropped out to do *Jane Eyre.*

THE SMURFS

Smurf happens.
—Movie tagline

Adventure doesn't get any bigger.
—Movie tagline

Box Office: $142.6 million

It has been twenty-eight years since the tiny blue creatures known as the Smurfs hit the big screen with a feature-length adventure. At the time, they were at the peak of their popularity on Saturday morning television and despite not containing the same voice affectations and feeding upon the original mythology, *Smurfs and the Magic Flute* (1983), was put into theaters for the holidays. For six more years the Smurfs would live out their days on television, growing in village numbers if not ratings and they were left to become another footnote in cartoon history collecting dust. Taking advantage of the advances in animation two decades-

plus later, not to mention the roundabout nature of nostalgia, Sony Pictures decided to give Peyo's little folk a chance at a comeback. Haste to make a few million bucks has resulted in a cinematic endeavor so creatively lazy and devoid of effort that even children will recognize its failure.

Narrator Smurf does not so much get viewers up to speed on what the little guys have been up to over the years, just what they have always been doing—singing, searching for Smurfberries and living up to their very names. Papa Smurf (voiced by Jonathan Winters) and his ninety-nine sons—and one created daughter, Smurfette (Katy Perry)—have always had to hide their brethren from the evil alchemist Gargamel (played in human form by Hank Azaria), who has sought out Smurfs as the key ingredient to creating gold. Though this Rumpelstiltskin-like obsession is never referred to in the film, the hunt is still on in full force and during their escape, Papa and five of his Smurfs are sucked through a portal into present day New York City.

Here the Smurfs end up in the home of a forthcoming papa and ad wizard, Patrick Winslow (Neil Patrick Harris). Naturally stunned to have these clearly animated things pitter-pattering their little feet around their house and talking to them, Patrick and his pregnant wife, Grace (Jayma Mays), grant them shelter until they can find a way back home. This will not occur until the next blue moon, giving the Smurfs plenty of time to wreak havoc at Patrick's office and experience the joys of playing Rock Band. Gargamel has also made his way to the Big Apple though and has made a makeshift laboratory that requires any DNA strand of the Smurfs to capture their essence and make old women look young again. At least that is what it does in one scene in the hopes of perhaps tricking the audience that they too can feel like a kid again just by hearing the word "Smurf" over and over and over again. More likely it will have the reverse effect.

As a TV show, *The Smurfs* covered the standard ground of ten-to-twelve-minute comic adventure stories meant to convey a lesson for watching youngsters. As a film director, Raja Gosnell has specialized in films nine times as long, each with a singular lesson—never go see another Raja Gosnell film again. Since debuting with the Macaulay Culkin-less *Home Alone 3* (1997), the former film editor has littered cinema's landscape with Martin Lawrence in an old-lady fat suit, two Scooby-Doos, and a talking Chihuahua film. Not once in his seven previous features has Gosnell ever displayed a knack for the simplest of slapstick comedy timing or an appreciation that the gamut of ages attending his films might have a brain.

Instead of finding a way to craft, at the very least, a more colorful tale set within the Smurf world, it took four screenwriters to focus on just six Smurf characters and separate them from their brethren into a world with pure product placement—a billboard for Sony's 2011 upcoming animated holiday feature, *Arthur Christmas,* can even be seen, making the film little more than a commercial for another one. Aside from Papa and Smurfette, the writers chose as their central Smurfs: Brainy (Fred Armisen), Grouchy (George Lopez), Clumsy (Anton Yelchin), and Totally Invented Smurf, aka Gutsy (Alan Cumming). The film's one truly amusing moment comes as Patrick wonders whether they are given their names at birth or are monikered after they develop a specific trait. If only there were a gag about an Interesting, Funny, or Action-Packed Smurf rather than the Passive-Aggressive one left behind, it would at least explain why this Smurf adventure lacked anything of the sort.

Brainy never does anything annoying enough to get his signature kick out of the film—an absolute miss of an opportunity for a 3D format that adds the usual little to a film of this type. Clumsy's mission is to stop living up to his name and getting everyone into trouble, another missed chance to explore whether or not a Smurf can change their birthright. George Lopez contributes some of the worst voice work in a near century of the medium, turning Grouchy's scowling aesthetic on and off with a disappearing accent. As far as Gutsy Smurf is concerned, unless there has been some Scottish uprising in the last few years that contractually demands animated films to have one Braveheart-like warrior amongst their ranks, what is the point of introducing a new strong and brave smurf when Hefty and his heart tattoo was already a prominent star of the TV show? Especially when Hefty makes a cameo during the climactic battle with Gargamel that might have kids wanting to learn more about Martin Scorsese's *Gangs of New York* (2002) than pretending to be interested in who is actually winning.

Shots of Smurfs on taxis up against ads for Blue Man Group and Blu-ray discs is about the level of cleverness in store for adults who might still be clinging to a little childhood nostalgia. Those with children now may not be ready to explain the kind of lessons to their youngsters that their Smurf adventures hardly prepared them for; lessons such as the insecurity over an unintended pregnancy and what it means when Katy Perry's Smurfette says "I kissed a Smurf and I liked it" and Gargamel telling Azrael, "I wish I could quit you." When the Muppets got their first shot at a feature film in 1979, they attracted the likes of Steve Martin, Richard Pryor, and Orson Welles amongst a bevy of others to contribute celebrity cameos. The Smurfs are reduced—in a single scene, no less—to the likes of Joan Rivers (with the only line of dialogue), and gossip columnists Michael Musto and Liz Smith to delight the kiddies. Neither a sincere effort nor a meta snarkfest at The Smurfs' history and questionable lineage, the four credited screenwriters fail to commit to either and instead borrow their moral message from the mouth of Ferris Bueller when Grace tells her husband, "if you don't stop to see that for just one minute, you're going to miss it." Wherever parents and their kids have an opportunity to buy a ticket, Blu-ray or cable package to see *The Smurfs,* "stop and miss it" is the best advice one can give.

Erik Childress

CREDITS

Patrick Winslow: Neil Patrick Harris
Grace Winslow: Jayma Mays
Hefty Smurf: Gary Basaraba
Henri: Tim Gunn
Papa Smurf: Jonathan Winters (Voice)
Gusty Smurf: Alan Cumming (Voice)
Grouchy Smurf: George Lopez (Voice)
Brainy Smurf: Fred Armisen (Voice)
Clumsy Smurf: Anton Yelchin (Voice)
Gargamel: Hank Azaria (Voice)
Odile: Sofia Vergara (Voice)
Smurfette: Katy Perry (Voice)
Jokey Smurf: Paul (Pee-wee Herman) Reubens (Voice)
Azrael the Cat: Frank Welker (Voice)
Greedy Smurf: Kenan Thompson (Voice)
Handy Smurf: Jeff Foxworthy (Voice)
Narrator Smurf: Tom Kane
Origin: USA
Language: English
Released: 2011
Production: Jordan Kerner; Columbia Pictures, Sony Pictures Animation, Kerner Entertainment Company; released by Columbia Pictures
Directed by: Raja Gosnell
Written by: J. David Stern, David N. Weiss, Jay Scherick, David Ronn
Cinematography by: Phil Meheux
Music by: Heitor Pereira
Sound: James Sabat
Editing: Sabrina Plisco
Art Direction: Chris Shriver
Costumes: Rita Ryack
Production Design: Bill Boes
MPAA rating: PG
Running time: 103 minutes

REVIEWS

Burr, Ty. *Boston Globe.* July 28, 2011.
Chang, Justin. *Variety.* July 28, 2011.

Gonzalez, Ed. *Slant Magazine.* July 28, 2011.

Hickman, Jonathan W. *Daily Film Fix.* July 29, 2011.

Johanson, MaryAnn. *Flick Filosopher.* July 26, 2011.

Kenny, Glenn. *MSN Movies.* July 28, 2011.

McWeeny, Drew. *Hitfix.* July 28, 2011.

Minow, Nell. *Chicago Sun-Times.* July 29, 2011.

O'Connell, Sean. *Washington Post.* July 29, 2011.

Robinson, Tasha. *AV Club.* July 28, 2011.

QUOTES

Grouchy: "Where the Smurf are we?"

Gutsy: "Up the smurfin' creek without a paddle, that's where!"

TRIVIA

Wallace Shawn and John Lithgow were both considered for the role of Gargamel.

SNOW FLOWER AND THE SECRET FAN

Box Office: $1.3 million

Wayne Wang's *Snow Flower and the Secret Fan*, which is based on the best-selling novel by Lisa See, tells three stories at once: One is present day, one is flashback of the recent past and one is a story that takes place over a century ago. All three stories involve two female friends who come from different class backgrounds and who have two different destinies, but each event in their lives is something that puts their friendship to the test. Little mysteries and parallels lurk within each narrative while customs of centuries' past are examined, which ultimately contrast sharply with those of today.

The main story takes place in present day. A young woman in Shanghai named Nina (Bingbing Li) has a job that has just promoted her to be in charge of operations in New York. On the night of her promotion, she gets a call in the middle of the night. Her best friend Sophia (Gianna Jun), whom she has not seen in months, has just had a bad accident and is now in a coma. Nina puts off going to New York so she can attend to Sophia, whom she has known since childhood. Nina is driven to investigate what Sophia has been up to in the past six months. Nina eventually uncovers a manuscript written by Sophia marked "Untitled." It becomes quite obvious that the story is meant to parallel Nina and Sophia's real lives.

The fictional story takes place in 1839 in Hunan. During that time, there was a customary marriage of sorts between two women called the Laotong. In a world dominated by men, two female children could be bound

together in lifelong friendship and communicate secretly, presumably as a means of survival. In this story, the girls, Snow Flower (also played by Gianna Jun) and Lily (also played by Bingbing Li), are bound together in spite of their class differences. Their proximity of their astrological signs binds them together. A far more cruel practice of the day is that of feet binding. During these times, it was common for women to have their feet bound and tightened at such a young age so as to be more attractive to men. This becomes the basis of an art exhibition in the present day story.

As Nina reads this story, the film flashes back to 1997 when Nina and Sophia signed their own Laotong, which really is no more significant in the present day than getting a tattoo that says "(Best friend's name) Forever!" Nevertheless, they see it as an eternal bond. Much like in the novel Sophia is writing, Nina and Sophia's parents threaten to dismantle the friendship due to class differences and the fact that they listen to rock music instead of "nice" music. Sohpia and Nina carry on their friendship in spite of these obstacles, much like Lily and Snow Flower carry on theirs. In the story, Nina and Sophia send a secret fan back and forth, writing to each other in a secret Laotong language that only they know.

Other parallels come into play. Sophia decides to marry a dashing Australian (Hugh Jackman) against the advice of Nina, which sets off a fierce argument between them. In Sophia's story, Lily marries an abusive butcher while Snow Flower is married off and is expected to give birth to a son (there is disappointment when a daughter is born). In the story, a Typhoid epidemic breaks out and many suddenly die, while one of the girls' father in the present day dies unexpectedly after making poor investments in the stock market. In both stories, the girls' friendship starts to dissolve and thy grow more and more distant until a major tragedy brings them back together.

Director Wayne Wang is returning to his roots, in a way, with this film. In 1993, his filmed adaptation of Amy Tan's novel *The Joy Luck Club* brought him international recognition as a major filmmaking talent. Since then, his career has been a strange roster of hit-and-miss mainstream titles, ranging from the good (*Smoke* [1995], *Anywhere But Here* [1999]) to the God-awful (*Maid In Manhattan* [2001], *Last Holiday* [2006]). *The Joy Luck Club* had a similar playbook by telling the stories of Chinese-Americans both in flashback and in present day. It was a moving film with a similar narrative structure that worked. The problem with the adaptation of *Snow Flower and the Secret Fan* is that the adaptation itself yields little purpose. See's novel only told the story of Snow Flower and Lily. Wang and his screenwriters Angela Workman, Ronald Bass and Michael K.

Ray have added in the contemporary story of Sophia and Nina.

The result is a movie that feels more fractured than tightly knitted together. It bounces back and forth through time and completely removes whatever dramatic tension that might have been palpable with just one story or the other. The viewer is often way ahead of everything as the film slowly reveals the parallel stories. The stilted dialogue and one-dimensional characters do not help. Its lovely score by Rachael Portman and sumptuous cinematography by Richard Wong go a long way toward making the film easily digestible, but ultimately the narrative offers little in the way of surprises and the movie seems interchangeable with others of its kind.

Collin Souter

CREDITS

Lily/Nina: Bingbing Li
Aunt: Vivian Wu
Snow Flower/Sophia: Gianna Jun
Sebastian: Archie Kao
Arthur: Hugh Jackman
Anna: Coco Chiang
Mrs. Liao: Jingyun Hu
Bank CEO: Russell Wong
Butcher: Jiang Wu
Origin: USA
Language: English
Released: 2011
Production: Wendi Murdoch, Florence Sloan; IDG China Media; released by Fox Searchlight
Directed by: Wayne Wang
Written by: Ronald Bass, Angela Workman, Michael Ray
Cinematography by: Richard Wong
Music by: Rachel Portman
Sound: Christopher Quilty
Editing: Deirdre Slevin
Art Direction: Molly Page
Costumes: Man Lim Chung
Production Design: Man Lim Chung
MPAA rating: PG-13
Running time: 120 minutes

REVIEWS

Bernard, Linda. *Toronto Star*. July 15, 2011.
Dargis, Manohla. *New York Times*. July 14, 2011.
Ebert, Roger. *Chicago Sun-Times*. July 21, 2011.
Goss, William. *Orlando Weekly*. July 27, 2011.
Long, Tom. *Detroit News*. June 29, 2011.
Longworth, Karina. *Village Voice*. July 12, 2011.
Merry, Stephanie. *Washington Post*. July 21, 2011.
Morgenstern, Joe. *Wall Street Journal*. July 14, 2011.
Staskiewicz, Keith. *Entertainment Weekly*. July 13, 2011.
Whitty, Stephen. *Newark Star-Ledger*. July 15, 2011.

QUOTES

Nina: "The world is always changing. Every day it's changing. Everything in life is changing. We have to look inside ourselves to find what stays the same, such as loyalty, our shared history and love for each other. In them, the truth of the past lives on."

TRIVIA

Rupert Murdoch personally asked Fox Searchlight to release this film in North America.

SOMETHING BORROWED

It's a thin line between love and friendship.
—Movie tagline

Box Office: $39 million

Six years ago in law school, meek and brainy Rachel (Ginnifer Goodwin) fell for her gorgeous study partner, Dex (Colin Egglesfield), but even though it was obvious that he liked her back, Rachel stood idly by as Dex was snatched up by Darcy (Kate Hudson), Rachel's bombastic, sexy, but not so clever, life-long best friend. Now, weeks before their wedding, Rachel lets it slip that she has always had feelings for Dex and the two consummate their crush. This sets Dex and Rachel on a rollercoaster of guilt—the intricacies of which are pointed out by their moral compass, third wheel friend Marcus (John Krasinski)—but it is alright because Darcy has secrets of her own (read: it is ok to cheat on her). Adapted from the novel by Emily Griffin, *Something Borrowed* is a romantic comedy that rests on some shaky ground by proposing that cheating is morally allowed as long as the cheaters really love one another. The only saving grace of this unnecessarily complicated flick is the fact that Rachel and Dex possess actual chemistry.

Something Borrowed is cursed from the get-go because it is a movie about cheating, which means that, in addition to the expected conventions of characters falling down comically and proclaiming their love to one another in the rain, a lot of screen time is spent justifying the illicit affair taking place. Screenwriter Jennie Snyder proposes that what Rachel and Dex are doing is acceptable because Dex and Darcy are so very mismatched. Darcy is wild, whimsical and not very articulate, so it is obvious that Dex would be better off with Rachel, who Snyder proposes, matches Dex both in intellect and temperament (but not to worry, Rachel still has a fun side, as evidenced by the retro dance routine she and Darcy perform). Opposites do not attract in Snyder's world, in fact they should be spared lifetime together by any means necessary.

To substantiate that claim, director Luke Greenfield has Hudson play Darcy as a spoiled, superficial Manhattanite whose main personality fault is that she is not at all interested in acting her thirty-something age. For example, Darcy likes to drink, and when she drinks, she likes to dance on the bar. This is an embarrassment to her straight-laced lawyer best friend and straight-laced lawyer fiancé—that is until they get home and have loud (and presumably very satisfying) sex.

Hudson, as always, is fun to watch, but her cluelessness gets exhausting. It is hard to believe that someone so with it would be so blind to what is going on around her. It is no wonder that she looks so tired for most of the film. Darcy, like all wild girls, is no angel, which is why the audience is supposed to think that Dex is better off with Rachel. And to a certain degree, Snyder and Greenfield succeed in making a credible case for the cheating couple. Rachel and Dex are relaxed and comfortable around one another and they have a solid connection rooted in friendship. Then there is the chemistry between Goodwin and Egglesfield. When they are on-screen together, it is hard not to want them to end up together, Darcy be damned. The one problem with this is that Dex, as handsome as he is, comes off as a complete jerk. Viewers may be able to concede that calling off an engagement is difficult (and Snyder gives Dex a controlling father who he has to stand up to), but the way in which Dex strings Rachel along throughout the majority of the film is downright frustrating. Instead of a confused, love-struck hero trying to do right by the women in his life, he rolls like a typical frat-boy player.

Then there is Marcus, who, at the start of the narrative seems to be playing the part of the "guy that Rachel is really supposed to end up with but just does not know it yet," but whose storyline and character just get dropped midway through the film. Granted, his role might have been more clearly defined if Goodwin and Kasinski came across as anything other than siblings on screen. Though his wit and comedic timing is missed when his character initially jets off to London, as the Rachel-Dex-Darcy triangle unravels, it starts to feel like maybe Marcus just made a lucky escape.

Despite the strikes against it, *Something Borrowed* is pleasant enough to watch. The laughs are consistent and Hudson and Goodwin possess a believable friendship. The movie also deserves credit for embracing the

disastrous fallout once Rachel and Dex are discovered. Cheating, *Something Borrowed* ultimately concedes, is messy business. Still, it would have been a significantly more satisfying film if both women kicked Dex to the curb and instead embraced their friendship.

Joanna Topor MacKenzie

CREDITS

Rachel: Ginnifer Goodwin
Darcy: Kate Hudson
Dex: Colin Egglesfield
Ethan: John Krasinski
Marcus: Steve Howey
Claire: Ashley Williams
Origin: USA
Language: English
Released: 2011
Production: Broderick Johnson, Andrew A. Kosove, Aaron Lubin, Pamela Schein Murphy, Molly Smith; 2S Films, Alcon Entertainment, Wild Ocean Films; released by Warner Bros.
Directed by: Luke Greenfield
Written by: Jennie Snyder Urman
Cinematography by: Charles Minsky
Music by: Alex Wurman
Sound: Avram D. Gold
Music Supervisor: Dave Jordan
Editing: John Axelrad
Costumes: Gary Jones
Production Design: Jane Musky
MPAA rating: PG-13
Running time: 112 minutes

REVIEWS

Debruge, Peter. *Variety.* May 2, 2011.
Hammond, Pete. *Box Office Magazine.* May 4, 2011.
Honeycutt, Kirk. *Hollywood Reporter.* May 2, 2011.
LaSalle, Mick. *San Francisco Chronicle.* May 5, 2011.
Lumenick, Lou. *New York Post.* May 6, 2011.
Ogle, Connie. *Miami Herald.* May 12, 2011.
Rickey, Carrie. *Philadelphia Inquirer.* May 5, 2011.
Scott, A.O. *New York Times.* May 5, 2011.
Sharkey, Betsy. *Los Angeles Times.* May 5, 2011.
Tobias, Scott. *AV Club.* May 5, 2011.

QUOTES

Ethan: "The Hamptons are like a zombie movie directed by Ralph Lauren."

TRIVIA

Emily Griffin, the writer of the novel *Something Blue* (the sequel to *Something Borrowed,* can be seen sitting on a bench next to Rachel and Marcus reading the novel.

THE SON OF NO ONE

Serve. Protect. Lie.
—Movie tagline

Dito Montiel's *The Son of No One* marks the third collaboration between the author/filmmaker and his friend/muse Channing Tatum after 2006's highly-lauded *A Guide to Recognizing Your Saints* and 2009's significantly-less-lauded *Fighting*. After their first work together earned raves on the festival circuit, it looked like the two could have forged a partnership to rival Martin Scorsese and Robert De Niro, but the depressing, repugnant *The Son of No One* further disproves that hypothesis by presenting a misguided, poorly-edited mess of a thriller; a film that thinks it is a gritty statement on the ghosts of New York's finest but is actually a borderline incoherent mess. Tatum does reasonably engaging work, proving yet again that his most common collaborator brings the best out in him, but he is let down by a horrendous screenplay, misguided production decisions, and some supporting cast members too complacent not to fall back on the clichés of roles they have played numerous times.

One of the most prominent flaws of Montiel's screenplay, based on his own book, is a structure that is constantly jumping back and forth between 1986 and 2002. In the former time period, the focus lies squarely on a frightened child nicknamed "Milk" (Jack Cherry), who is trying to grow up in the projects, surrounded by drugs and violence. In the opening scene of the film, the terrified young boy cowers in a bathroom as a drug-addled maniac tries to break in. The fact that he shoots him would not surprise anyone nor convict him in any court of law and yet it is the inciting incident for the entire film. Milk committed justifiable homicide and then later killed another scumbag in a completely understandable, accidental manner and those two incidents are the basis for the dark secrets at the heart of *The Son of No One,* and it is a foundation that never allows anything to grow. First, the idea that a reporter (Juliette Binoche) in 2002 would have the slightest concern or interest in the fact that two ne'er-do-wells died in the projects sixteen years earlier is ludicrous beyond all comprehension, especially given the stories that would have dominated most reporters daily schedules in the year after 9/11 in New York. Second, the belief that Milk's story, when told to anyone, would cause any sort of serious repercussions is similarly silly. And yet, Detective Charles Stanford (Al Pacino), the former partner of Milk's father, covers it up, assuming that the dead men were not worth much anyway and that it might be smart for the police to have someone on their side on the inside of the increasingly crime-ridden projects.

Sixteen years later, Milk has grown up and joined the force as Officer Jonathan White (Channing Tatum). Of course, as only happens in fiction, he is assigned his old stomping grounds and forced to deal with the ghosts of the past while fighting crime in the present. As his Captain (Ray Liotta) becomes more concerned about the potential newspaper article being prepared, White becomes more unhinged (but never enough so for the movie to get interesting), while his partner (James Ransome) and wife (Katie Holmes) exist purely as plot devices. In the script's most embarrassing turn of events, White's one friend (Tracy Morgan) from childhood who stood by him and kept his secrets is now a deeply-damaged adult.

None of the too-talented-for-this-material cast does anything notably wrong here but Montiel's script is simply one of the worst of the year, a work awash in clichés when it endeavors to make any sense at all. The potential for a gritty Sidney Lumet-esque NYC drama about hidden pasts and the increasingly-dark days of the new millennium in the Big Apple is clearly there and Tatum actually does some decent acting work here, proving that he could deliver for the right director in the right material. He found neither here despite his friendship with a man once considered the next big voice in independent cinema and now facing a career edging closer to straight-to-DVD.

As for the supporting cast, one could do much worse than Liotta, Pacino, and Binoche, but the two gentlemen play into their stereotypes, sleepwalking through roles that they have found meatier in the past, while the lovely Binoche is just wasted, especially when one considers the award-worthy performance she gave this year in *Certified Copy* (2011). Viewers have come to expect some lackluster fare from Liotta and Pacino, but it is disheartening to see an actress as talented as Binoche get sucked into something this horrendous.

And yet, it is the decisions made by Montiel that deserve most of the blame, not a cast that was clearly uninspired by the material. The structure of the script and its constant jump-cutting through time destroy any chance of pace or rhythm, something desperately needed in a film such as this one. Even Montiel's production decisions are misguided, such as his over-use of an awkward score by Jonathan Elias & David Wittman or his guidance of shaky, inconsistent cinematography by Benoit Delhomme. Even the editing seems off. Ultimately, it call comes back to a laughable script that ends in a rooftop shootout that defies all logic, something viewers would be wise to use in avoiding this disaster.

Brian Tallerico

CREDITS

Jonathan "Milk" White: Channing Tatum
Charles Stanford: Al Pacino
Lauren Bridges: Juliette Binoche
Capt. Marion Mathers: Ray Liotta
Young Milk: Jake Cherry
Kerry White: Katie Holmes
Vincent Carter: Tracy Morgan
Young Vinnie: Brian Gilbert
Charlotte "Charlie" White: Ursula Parker
Officer Thomas Prundenti: James Ransone
Loren Bridges: Juliette Binoche
Origin: USA
Language: English
Released: 2011
Production: John Thompson, Holly Wiersma, Dito Montiel; Millennium Films, Nu Image Films; released by Anchor Bay Entertainment
Directed by: Dito Montiel
Written by: Dito Montiel
Cinematography by: Benoit Delhomme
Music by: Dave Wittman, Jonathan Elias
Sound: Bryan Dembinski
Music Supervisor: Selena Arizanovic
Editing: Jake Pushinsky
Art Direction: Michael Ahern
Costumes: Sandra Hernandez
Production Design: Beth Mickle
MPAA rating: R
Running time: 95 minutes

REVIEWS

Abele, Robert. *Los Angeles Times.* November 4, 2011.
Anderson, John. *Wall Street Journal.* November 3, 2011.
Hazelton, John. *Screen International.* November 4, 2011.
Holden, Stephen. *New York Times.* November 3, 2011.
Lumenick, Lou. *New York Post.* November 4, 2011.
Pais, Matt. *RedEye.* November 3, 2011.
Rainer, Peter. *Christian Science Monitor.* November 4, 2011.
Rea, Steven. *Philadelphia Inquirer.* November 3, 2011.
Rich, Katey. *CinemaBlend.com.* January 29, 2011.
Zacharek, Stephanie. *Movieline.* November 3, 2011.

QUOTES

Loren Bridges: "Tampered evidence is wasted evidence."

Officer Thomas Prudenti: "Yeah…you realize it's not actually evidence untill someone gives a f**k about this?"

TRIVIA

Robert De Niro was originally cast as Detective Stanford, but was replaced by Al Pacino.

SOUL SURFER

When you come back from a loss, beat the odds, and never say never, you find a champion.
—Movie tagline

Box Office: $43.9 million

Inspirational true stories generally do not have to work too hard to poke the emotional core of an audience. These films may begin badly but are certainly destined for an achieved goodness. Even with a paint-by-numbers script, a filmmaker can stay the course and easily reach forty percent of their viewers as long as they stay within the lines and keep the subject matter flowing with a universal appeal. Sports, civil injustice, and family are three good places to start. Religion is a trickier subject, however, just as politics: The two things never brought up at the dinner table because the alienation risk is too high even if only one person does not subscribe to the shared viewpoint. The risk is ever greater for a film since the larger disaffection at play is whether or not the true believers will want to associate with such a hokey, clichéd, guffaw-inducing tale as the dramatization presented of surfer Bethany Hamilton in *Soul Surfer*.

AnnaSophia Robb plays the real-life Hamilton who, at the age of thirteen, was already a competitive surfer living in Hawaii with her parents, Tom & Cheri (Dennis Quaid & Helen Hunt), and her two older brothers. She surfs alongside her best friend, Alana (Lorraine Nicholson), and her worst rival, Malina Birch (Sonya Balmores), who taunts her in and out of the water. When not surfing, the Hamilton family is deeply involved with their local church which allows Bethany a chance to go straight from the ocean into the tent setup on the beach for prayer and song. Her group leader, Sarah Hill (Carrie Underwood), is disappointed that Bethany has chosen surf training over helping kids out in Mexico. She probably doubts that choice as well the next morning, with her left arm dangling in the Pacific after a shark attacks and takes it from her.

Bethany survives but now finds a new set of challenges ahead of her. Preparing lunch becomes an exasperated chore with only one arm to lean on, let alone the prospects of getting on a surfboard again with fractured aerodynamics. The media are all over her story, as they usually are for tales involving sharks and tragedies to blonde, white girls. Afternoon tabloid journalists, *Inside Edition,* offer to spring for a prosthetic arm in exchange for an exclusive interview. Determined not to just feel sorry for herself—or for the sponsorships she is losing—Bethany labors with her dad on a way to make the elements work for her so she can get back up on that board for the next big competition.

The screenplay by four writers (including director Sean McNamara) cobbled together from the screen story by seven writers adapted from the biography it took three people (including Hamilton) to fashion tries, at a fault, to be earnest at every turn of Bethany's journey. The addition of the religious overhead to what would be just an average underdog sports tale brings with it a set of complications that now puts added weight on an audience's perception of this story. They are now being asked to believe in not just the potential power of Bethany's determination but the higher power that may be adjusting the wind and giving her the extra arm of push she needs until all that self-fortitude is no longer her own to claim.

Soul Surfer does not thrust the boundaries of metaphysics in such a way to actually show her Lord riding shotgun on the back of her surf equipment. But it does so in a far more ham-handed way to suggest the influence of a heavenly presence if Bethany follows a more righteous path. Is it a coincidence that the shark attack occurs almost immediately after turning down a philanthropic opportunity to Mexico in place of selfish pursuits? Or that when Bethany appears to have given up for good, she takes up Sarah on a relief effort to a Thailand tsunami and finds her faith in surfing and the world restored? The way real-life tragedy is shoved in to make everyone feel guilty about rooting for Bethany runs counterproductive to the very impetus behind telling it. And, boy, do the writers tell it.

Soul Surfer needed to concentrate more on adapting viewers to the pleasures and complications of surfing than to its philosophy of believing in a higher power. Through some really atrocious special effects, Robb's head is plastered onto the body of another during the more challenging scenes and it is distracting enough to focus away from the potential grace and near-mystical qualities of becoming one with nature. Cutting the head off to spite the digitally-removed arm is almost a perfect metaphor for the ongoing battle between scientific fact—which surfers use to strengthen their ride—and spiritual faith, which one must believe in when seeing the actress standing atop a board missing an appendage.

Director Sean McNamara—who creepily appears twice on screen as a dialogue-less sponsor smiling at the young girls—has not exactly raised the bar for tween cinema as a producer for direct-to-video sequels to *Legally Blonde, Bring It On,* and *Into the Blue*—perhaps a training ground for making films about pretty blonde protagonists, fringe sports and water—and director of the live-action adaptation of *Bratz* (2007), a doll line turned into an offensively-crafted film where teenage individuality was stressed in-between montages of the latest fashion trends. McNamara is more sincere here in playing towards the larger base, but it does not take a part-time theologian familiar with the King James collection of poetry to recognize the hackneyed nature of the writing and filmmaking here. *Soul Surfer* is a parable for people who have only read one book and seen none of the films that embrace faith and spirituality as a metaphor that truly inspires an audience rather than trying to bite it into them.

Erik Childress

CREDITS

Bethany Hamilton: AnnaSophia Robb
Tom Hamilton: Dennis Quaid
Cheri Hamilton: Helen Hunt
Sarah Hill: Carrie Underwood
Alana Blanchard: Lorraine Nicholson
Holt Blanchard: Kevin Sorbo
Dr. Rovinsky: Craig T. Nelson
Malia Birch: Sonya Balmores
Noah Hamilton: Ross Thomas
Origin: USA
Language: English
Released: 2011
Production: David Brookwell, Sean McNamara, Douglas Schwartz, David A. Zelon, Dutch Hofstetter; Enticing Entertainment, Brookwell-McNamara, Island Film Group, Life's a Beach Entertainment, Mandalay Vision; released by Sony Pictures, FilmDistrict, TriStar Pictures
Directed by: Sean McNamara
Written by: Sean McNamara, Michael Berk, Deborah Schwartz, Douglas Schwartz
Cinematography by: John R. Leonetti
Music by: Marco Beltrami
Sound: Daniel Pagan
Music Supervisor: Julia Michels
Editing: Jeff W. Canavan
Art Direction: Rosario Provenza
Costumes: Kathe James
Production Design: Rusty Smith
MPAA rating: PG
Running time: 105 minutes

REVIEWS

Anderson, John. *Wall Street Journal.* April 7, 2011.
Ebert, Roger. *Chicago Sun-Times.* April 8, 2011.
Gronvall, Andrea. *MSN Movies.* April 7, 2011.
Hillis, Aaron. *Village Voice.* April 6, 2011.
Honeycutt, Kirk. *Hollywood Reporter.* March 28, 2011.
Minow, Nell. *Beliefnet.* April 7, 2011.
Nelson, Rob. *Variety.* March 28, 2011.
Orndorf, Brian. *eFilmCritic.* April 6, 2011.

Rich, Katey. *CinemaBlend*. April 7, 2011.
Rothkopf, Joshua. *Time Out New York*. April 6, 2011.

QUOTES

Bethany Hamilton: "Surfing isn't the most important thing in life. Love is. I've had the chance to embrace more people with one arm than I ever could with two."

TRIVIA

The dog featured in the movie is actually Bethany Hamilton's own dog Hana.

SOURCE CODE

Make every second count.
—Movie tagline

Box Office: $54.7 million

Boasting a very talented cast at the top of their game, *Source Code* races through a scenario that could have been a forgettable episode of TV's *The X-Files* or a cheap genre flick, but this race through time and space tells an uncommonly moving story that leaps past an inevitable breakdown in sci-fi logic to land squarely in the ranks of the best science fiction thrillers ever made.

U.S. Army helicopter pilot Colter Stevens (Jake Gyllenhaal) wakes up on a crowded Chicago commuter train with no memory of having ever gone to sleep. The last thing he remembers is being in the air over Afghanistan. Now he finds himself disoriented, sitting across from a beautiful young woman named Christina (MIchelle Monaghan), who calls him by another name. After looking at his reflection with wonder, he realizes that he has somehow assumed the identity of someone else. An explosion suddenly rips through the train killing him and all others on board. Stevens then awakens to find himself in a pod device communicating with a fellow officer named Goodwin (Vera Farmiga), who, along with scientist in charge Rutledge (Jeffrey Wright), informs him that he has been placed in a "time reassignment state" that allows him eight minutes per jaunt to access the physical past and discover the identity of the bomber so that authorities can try to prevent a larger secondary attack. As time runs out in one reality, Stevens must race repeatedly through the alternate possibilities of the past. During one such race he realizes there may be away to save everyone on the train if only he can get the disbelieving Goodwin and Rutledge to send him back one more time.

Director Duncan Jones first made himself known with his astonishing debut, *Moon* (2009), which told the story of a worker on the lunar surface who discovers he is a clone designed to live and die there. Emotionally rich and visually minimalist, *Moon* was hugely reminiscent of *2001:A Space Odyssey* (1968), offering a sort of hyper-reality in which a tale of survival edges out into the stuff of spirituality. *Source Code* provides Jones with a more complex visual tapestry, and though he bends his camera to the demands of genre he does so in the service of everything that makes *Source Code* a story worth telling and watching. This is a film that revels in genre, a primer in achieving cinematic suspense, but it also offers a story in which a man fumbling his way toward transcendence, chooses hope, arriving at a good end not just through the chicanery of genre mechanics or deus ex machina plotting, but because that is where the story of that particular man would end.

Jones has a great partner in composers Chris Bacon and Gad Emile Zeitune who provide a score that can only be described as thrilling. Yet it should be remarked that this is film music that never gets in the way. It is, like the rest of the film, an awful lot of fun and always compliments the emotional territory, being less about cuing the audience how they should feel than about effectively underscoring what Jones and his team of actors and technicians have already accomplished.

Sole credited screenwriter Ben Ripley (*Species III* [2004], *Species: The Awakening* [2007] *The Watch* [2008]) has certainly never done anything to suggest he would turn out a script this smart, or witty, or finely emotionally tuned. *Source Code* offers plotting, dialogue and character development that must have made casting easy. Any actor reading this script would want to be part of the project. The casting here is certainly impressive.

Jake Gyllenhaal lends the main character of Colter Stevens an energetic, completely believable, and harried air. Gyllenhaal remains one of his generation's most interesting actors. A dynamic performance in Joe Johnston's marvelous *October Sky* (1999) and boldly offbeat lead characterization in Richard Kelly's massive cult hit *Donnie Darko* (2001) cemented him as someone to watch. Though he has had some missteps, attempting to recast himself as a modern action hero by appearing in forgettable fodder such as *The Day After Tomorrow* (2004) and *Prince of Persia: The Sands of Time* (2010) he has continued to do remarkable complex work in fare such as *The Good Girl*(2002), *Brokeback Mountain* (2005), and especially David Fincher's masterfully chilling *Zodiac* (2007). With this film, he finally breaks through to action hero status...providing he can find another project of this quality. Michelle Monaghan has the least difficult role in the piece as Christina Warren, the young woman who finds herself dragged across destiny, but she and Gyllenhaal have great chemistry and she does exude a certain girl-next-door leading lady charisma hinting at what she could bring to the right part. Vera Farmiga finds herself in familiar territory here, having appeared in quirky genre fare before like *Dummy* (2002), *Joshua* (2007) and *Orphan* (2009). Jeffrey Wright is known for playing officious types and makes a great mad scientist in Rutledge, even if his character is the one that comes closest to stereotype. He carries the part along, offering an all-too-real and highly disturbing portraiture, calm and collected in his scientific work yet betrayed as anti-human when crossed. Dr. Rutledge has no people in his inner dialogues, only results, career, and the ends of his bureaucratic means.

Of course, there is a point where the central sci-fi conceit of *Source Code* breaks down. But so effortless does the film seem in the way it handles human elements that most viewers will need a second screening to figure out where. This is genre full, to the brim, of honestly come-by romance, intrigue, humanity and enough expertly-managed sci-fi fodder to start anyone down the path of figuring out just how much of what it says about space and time is potentially real.

Dave Canfield

CREDITS

Captain Colter Stevens: Jake Gyllenhaal
Christina: Michelle Monaghan
Colleen Goodwin: Vera Farmiga
Dr. Rutledge: Jeffrey Wright
Derek Frost: Michael Arden
Origin: USA
Language: English
Released: 2011
Production: Mark Gordon, Philippe Rousselet, Jordan Wynn; Mark Gordon Company, Vendome Pictures; released by Summit Entertainment
Directed by: Duncan Jones
Written by: Ben Ripley
Cinematography by: Don Burgess
Music by: Chris P. Bacon
Sound: Tom Bellfort
Editing: Paul Hirsch
Art Direction: Pierre Perrault
Costumes: Renee April
Production Design: Barry Chusid
MPAA rating: PG-13
Running time: 94 minutes

REVIEWS

Bumbray, Chris. *JoBlo's Movie Emporium.* March 31, 2011.
Cole, Stephen. *Globe and Mail.* April 1, 2011.
Dargis, Manohla. *New York Times.* March 31, 2011.
Ebert, Roger. *Chicago Sun-Times.* March 31, 2011.
Goss, William. *Film.com.* July 29, 2011.
Greydanus, Steven D. *Christianity Today.* April 1, 2011.
Hoffman, Jordan. *UGO.* March 14, 2011.
Mitchell, Elvis. *Movieline.* March 31, 2011.
Turan, Kenneth. *Los Angeles Times.* March 31, 2011.
Williams, Kam. *NewsBlaze.* April 4, 2011.

QUOTES

Colleen Goodwin: "The program wasn't designed to alter the past. It was designed to affect the future."

TRIVIA

At one point, Topher Grace was considered for the lead role in the film.

SPY KIDS: ALL THE TIME IN THE WORLD IN 4D

Saving the world is their idea of family time.
—Movie tagline

Box Office: $38.5 million

Most genre directors forge their way into movies by focusing their skills or passion on one particular type of filmmaking. Robert Rodriguez has somewhat separated himself away from those one-trick ponies in that he has focused on a whole two. Since launching his career with the legendary low-budget action picture, *El Mariachi* (1992), Rodriguez continued to honor the grungy aesthetic of the grindhouse tradition with subsequent bullet-laden efforts while exploring the effects-laden possibilities of digital cinema. This led to his most hailed achievement, his adaptation of Frank Miller's comic noir series, *Sin City* (2005). Though it also led to him exploring affordable effects work for a younger crowd and, as it turned out, both *Spy Kids* (2001) and *Spy Kids 2: Island of Lost Dreams* (2002) were very entertaining family films that also found ways to pay tribute to the youthful influences of many cinephiles. Rodriguez then doubled down on the technology at his disposal and, while out in front of the current theatrical revolution with *Spy Kids 3-D: Game Over* (2003), the film itself was a disposable eyesore that also fronted the worst of the filmmaker's more manic tendencies. Eight years have now passed, 3D is an unfortunate cinema staple, and Rodriguez appears to have nowhere left to take audiences with this series other than another worthless gimmick.

Gregorio and Ingrid Cortez are no longer the adult protagonists of the series as duties have been shifted over to a relative of theirs in the spy business, Marissa Wilson (Jessica Alba). She is introduced in the final hours of her pregnancy, just as she is still on the job chasing down and capturing the notorious Tick Tock (Jeremy Piven), a henchman for another baddie known as the Timekeeper. Marissa vows to give up the business for good to settle in with her new family, including her reality-TV star husband, Wilbur (Joel McHale), and his two kids, Rebecca (Rowan Blanchard) and Cecil (Mason Cook). Rebecca is no fan of her new stepmom and delights in booby-trapping her into messy situations. Marissa, while keeping her past a secret, has also streamlined the home into a last line of defense to keep everyone safe.

The Timekeeper is still on the prowl and he needs a sapphire necklace of Marissa's to complete his master plan of speeding up the world's time. As the necklace has changed hands now to Rebecca, the kids are now in danger and when the baddie's goons attack, they discover mom's true identity (as well as their pet, Argonaut, who is really a mechanical watchdog with a sarcastic streak supplied by Ricky Gervais). Cecil and Rebecca are thrust into the brief history of the OSS' Spy Kids chapter by their cousin Carmen (Alexa Vega), who along with her "retired" brother Juni (Daryl Sabara), were the precocious original world-savers. Together, they are all activated into service by OSS boss Danger D'amo (also played by Jeremy Piven) to stop the Timekeeper and uncover his diabolical plan for Armageddon before he can spell it out for them.

Most kid adventure films—even *The Incredibles* (2004) and *Spy Kids* wannabe *Agent Cody Banks* (2003)—are not as ambitious in plot as this fourth chapter, but Rodriguez has either restrained himself in making its time-related paradoxes too complicated or was just too lazy to have any real fun with it. There is not an idea on display here that is maximized for its full potential aside from the "butt bombs" produced by Argonaut (literally) and the newborn baby (intestinally). Assembling the varying connections between the past, present and future could certainly be daunting for kids not yet versed in *Back to the Future* (1985), but the Timekeeper's plan is already so thickly convoluted that it hardly seems to matter. Maybe "adults overthink everything" as one character says, but even a five-year-old should be able to recognize Jeremy Piven with a goatee and dark glasses.

That is unless they are too distracted by having to look down at their scratch-and-sniff cards. While there is the usual extra surcharge for the 3D experience, the purported fourth dimension of "Aroma-scope" is free even in 2D. Guided by Pavlovian numbers on the screen, a viewer can then rub the corresponding number on their card and be treated to eight scents of both the edible and unpalatable variety. Most of the card smells

tend to blend together, leaving the only positive of the gimmick as a way to gauge how much longer one has to get to the end; an additional tie-in to the Timekeeper's plan that Rodriguez probably never intended. The bad news being that viewer watches do not speed up the way they do in the movie.

The only momentary pleasures to be found throughout are in the occasional quips by Gervais who gets the added bonus of mocking the characters—and the effort in general—after the fact. "You should have a competition to see who is the most annoying," Argonaut says to the kids well after viewers have already made that judgment. Annoying is certainly a step up from the monosyllabic expressionless acting viewers have come to expect from Jessica Alba. Though as Rodriguez's self-implied muse for this series reboot, she is certainly an ample reflection for the direction his career has taken. Though getting a chance to have some over-the-top fun as part of the actual *Grindhouse* (2007) experience with *Planet Terror* (2007), he is being more recently remembered for his failed spinoff, *Machete* (2010) and his practically-forgotten supplemental kids efforts, *Shorts* (2009) and *The Adventures of Sharkboy and Lavagirl* (2005), inspired by an idea by his own kids. Even they have probably outgrown these films by now and are ready to move into the world of daddy's ultra-violent cinema.

Erik Childress

CREDITS

Marissa Cortez Wilson: Jessica Alba
Timekeeper/Danger D'Amo: Jeremy Piven
Wilbur Wilson: Joel McHale
Carmen Cortez: Alexa Vega
Juni Cortez: Daryl Sabara
Uncle Machete: Danny Trejo
Cecil Wilson: Mason Cook
Rebecca Wilson: Rowan Blanchard
Gregorio Cortez: Antonio Banderas
Argonaut: Ricky Gervais (Voice)
Origin: USA
Language: English
Released: 2011
Production: Elizabeth Avellan, Robert Rodriguez; Dimension Films, Troublemaker Studios, Spy Kids 4 SPV; released by Dimension Films, Anchor Bay Entertainment
Directed by: Robert Rodriguez
Written by: Robert Rodriguez
Cinematography by: Jimmy Lindsey
Music by: Carl Thiel
Sound: Ethan Andrus

Editing: Dan Zimmerman
Costumes: Nina Proctor
Production Design: Steve Joyner
MPAA rating: PG
Running time: 89 minutes

REVIEWS

Barker, Andrew. *Variety*. August 19, 2011.
Cline, Rich. *Shadows on the Wall*. August 22, 2011.
Johanson, MaryAnn. *Flick Filosopher*. August 19, 2011.
McCarthy, Todd. *Hollywood Reporter*. August 19, 2011.
Minow, Nell. *Chicago Sun-Times*. August 20, 2011.
Orndorf, Brian. *eFilmCritic*. August 19, 2011.
Rabin, Nathan. *AV Club*. August 19, 2011.
Schaefer, Stephen. *Boston Herald*. August 20, 2011.
Schager, Nick. *Village Voice*. August 22, 2011.
Willmore, Alison. *Time Out New York*. August 24, 2011.

TRIVIA

The genesis for this film came from an incident on the set of *Machete* when star Jessica Alba had her then one-year-old baby Honor Marie on set when the child's diaper exploded. While watching Alba change the diaper and trying not to get anything on her costume, director Robert Rodriguez began to think "What about a spy mom?"

STAKE LAND

The most dangerous thing is to be alive.
—Movie tagline

Stake Land is a very good film with a terrible title. Meant to convey a sense of apocalypse (and to identify itself as a vampire film) it sounds instead like a rip-off of another great movie, *Zombieland* (2009). But though *Stake Land* does stake out some territory familiar to the zombie meta-narrative, showcasing characters in the fight for survival against a ravenous monster hoard and each other, it emerges as far more than a simple recasting of genre mechanics. Just as the best zombie movies tend to have some sort of social commentary going on, *Stake Land* is rife with rich subtext, presenting apocalypse drenched in political and spiritual commentary.

A vampire epidemic has destroyed America from within. A few humans manage to cobble pockets of society together while armed vigilantes roam the countryside hunting and killing the infected. One such hunter named Mister (Nick Damici) rescues Martin (Connor Paolo), a teenager, from being slaughtered with the rest of his family during a vampire attack. Taking the boy under his wing, they hit the road and rescue a nun named Sister (Kelly McGillis) from an attack by

members of The Brethren, a cult like sect run by Jebediah Loven (Michael Cerveris), who believes the vampires are working in God's service to judge the sins of man and cleanse the earth of the unrighteous. Arriving in a nearby safe town, they meet and befriend Jamie Lloyd (Danielle Harris), a young, very pregnant woman who escapes with them just as the town is overrun in a vamp attack instigated by The Brethren. Taking to the foothills they find themselves in as much danger from the elements as from vamps and cult members.

Writer/director Jim Mickle and co-writer Nic Damici are no strangers to the horror genre. They made a great little horror film, *Mulberry Street* (2006), in which an apartment building becomes a refuge for survivors of a plague that turns people into rat monsters. The obviousness of the people-as-rats-in-urban-America metaphor aside, *Mulberry Street* (an obvious nod to the famous *Twilight Zone* episode "The Monsters Are Due on Mulberry Street") was a well-written and well-mounted film that mined concerns about urban economic and social poverty for a wealth of dramatic and horrific impact. Just as *Mulberry Street* examined urban social dysfunction *Stake Land* shows us rural America as inhabited ghost town, offering a sprawling shabby geography that seems haunted by the foreclosure headlines and economic ruin of today. The monster stuff seems almost like an afterthought.

If the film has a central weakness it lies in the character of Jebediah Loven. *Stake Land* is far from an anti-religious film. In fact the film goes out of its way to present a sensitive and intelligent portrait of spiritually in the character of Sister, the nun. But it is a film that fails to make the extremism of The Brethren believable. They seem mostly like characters from a movie here, perhaps a *Mad Max* (1979) knock-off, though Micheal Cerveris does his best with a part that saddles him with little opportunity for subtlety. A genuinely chilling lead up to the final confrontation reveals the cult leader to have mutated into an uber-vamp who retains his intelligence. The obvious conclusion is that a statement of some sort is being made about the dangers of the religious right but it seems ham-fisted at best.

As mentioned, though this is ostensibly a vampire film, it functions more like a zombie or monster movie. The vampires work as well-executed special effects, but, like zombies or infection monsters, are simply too rabid to have much in the way of personality. They jump, crawl, or lurch into frame surrounding whichever hapless actor is due for an attack and then are dispatched. There are some awfully ghastly/fun genre moments, including one in which flaming vamps are tossed from helicopters into a settlement in what has to be the most creative vamp attack in film history, but this is in keeping with a movie that expertly balances the tension between horror, humor and heart.

The tight screenplay gives the actors much with which to work. Veteran actor Nick Damici hits a career high point with his characterization of Mister, expertly evoking the energy of macho screen icons without descending into self-parody. Big screen newcomer Connor Paolo more than holds his own as Martin, lending the character a sense of nervous energy as of a character that sees his break through coming and wants to lunge for it. Also welcome is the presence of genre stalwart Danielle Harris who first made her mark in *Halloween 4: The Return of Michael Myers* (1988), and *Halloween 5* (1989) in the role of Jamie Lloyd. The name of Kelly McGillis (*Witness* [1985], *Top Gun* [1986], *The Accused* [1988]) will be recognizable to anyone who grew up in the eighties. McGillis was always a capable actress and, here, she exits the story far too early.

There are so many little indie horror films out there with big ambitions and so few that manage to achieve them. *Stake Land* succeeds on nearly all counts coming dangerously close to being a great film. It is hardly difficult to imagine a time when future generations hold revival screenings of it to talk about its significance as an important American film. The best compliment is that *Stake Land* nearly goes, and in moments does go, far beyond the borders of genre into those of simple compelling drama, calling to mind other great post apocalyptic efforts like *Time Of The Wolf* (2003) and *Threads* (1984).

Dave Canfield

CREDITS

Martin: Connor Paolo
Mister: Nick Damiki
Sister: Kelly McGillis
Belle: Danielle Harris
Jebedia Loven: Michael Cerveris
Willie: Sean Nelson
Origin: USA
Language: English
Released: 2010
Production: Derek Curl, Larry Fessenden, Adam Folk, Brent Kunkle, Peter Phok; Glass Eye Pix; distributed by Dark Sky Films
Directed by: Jim Mickle
Written by: Nick Damici, Jim Mickle
Cinematography by: Ryan Samul
Music by: Jeff Grace
Sound: Tom Efinger
Editing: Jim Mickle
Costumes: Elisabeth Vastola

Production Design: Daniel R. Kersting
MPAA rating: R
Running time: 98 minutes

REVIEWS

Catsoulis, Jeannette. *New York Times.* April 21, 2011.
Ebert, Roger. *Chicago Sun-Times.* April 28, 2011.
Floyd, Nigel. *Time Out.* June 15, 2011.
Glasby, Matt. *Total Film.* June 7, 2011.
Larson, Richard. *Slant Magazine.* April 25, 2011.
Longworth, Karina. *Village Voice.* Apil 19, 2011.
McDonaugh, Maitland. *Film Journal International.* August 19, 2011.
Tobias, Scott. *NPR.* April 22, 2011.
Vaux, Rob. *Mania.com.* April 22, 2011.
White, Julian. *Little White Lies.* June 16, 2011.

QUOTES

Martin: "I've seen things you wouldn't believe. Things a boy shouldn't see. I was like any other kid. I didn't believe in the boogeyman. Then the world woke up to a nightmare."

TRIVIA

The football helmet that Martin puts on at the beginning of the film is a Daniel Boone helmet, a reference to directer Jim Mickle's high school.

STRAW DOGS

Everyone has a breaking point.
—Movie tagline
We take care of our own.
—Movie tagline
Don't let them in.
—Movie tagline
I will not allow violence against this house.
—Movie tagline

Box Office: $10.3 million

Sam Peckinpah's *Straw Dogs* (1972) was a savage, methodical, and visceral (especially for its time) examination of a meek, American everyman pushed to his limit when his wife and home are threatened. It was not so much a revenge movie, but a story of self-discovery. The central character, a mathematician (Dustin Hoffman), looks easy to intimidate and he is throughout most of the story. But in the film's unrelenting second half, he finds himself stubbornly trying to do what is right by his home, his victimized wife and his own nature, which appears to be splitting him in two. By defeating the monsters outside his door, he must think like one and become one. By doing so, he finds himself capable of committing heinous acts of violence, but in a way that completely out-smarts the thugs trying to make his life a living hell.

Rod Lurie's remake follows most of the same playbook as the original, but with some very noticeable changes. Instead of a mathematician, the character of David Sumner (James Mardsen) is a Hollywood screenwriter. Instead of England, the story takes place in rural Mississippi. Most of the story remains the same. David and his wife Amy (Kate Bosworth), an aspiring actress, retreat from the glitz of Hollywood to a simpler, more remote location so he can concentrate on finishing a screenplay. The town happens to be Amy's childhood home. They meet old friends of Amy's in a bar, one of which is an old high school boyfriend named Charlie (Alexander Skarsgard), who sizes up David pretty quickly as someone who will be easy to push around, even subtly.

Charlie tries to be amicable and to fit in with this new scene, but is clearly uncomfortable with trying to be something he is not. The men see right through him. These are the same guys who got hired to work on the roof of David and Amy's farmhouse. They arrive bright and early for the first day, which prompts David to ask them with trepidation if maybe they could come a little later from now on so as not to wake them. The men help themselves to beer in their fridge without asking and play their music as loud as they want. There are only so many times that David can ask them to alter their behavior.

Amy has different issues with this situation. She goes running every morning in skimpy running shorts and a tank top, not exactly a sight these guys are used to seeing out in the backwoods of Mississippi. As expected, they constantly have their eyes on her, which she resents. David suggests maybe toning down the sexiness and try to be more modest, a suggestion that offends her deeply. As a way of secretly taunting David and openly taunting the workers, she stands at her window and stares right at them while almost revealing her naked upper half. It is an act of defiance, but little does she know she has awakened a few sleeping giants.

Charlie's friends convince David to come out hunting with them. Things seem a little suspicious when Charlie and one of the other guys do not show up. David goes hunting with the other guys anyway while Charlie pays Amy a surprise visit when she is at her most vulnerable. The original *Straw Dogs* was infamous for its prolonged rape scene and excessive violence. Lurie's version is more in a hurry to get the scene over with and the undertones of the dynamic between the two characters are not nearly as layered. It is no more

pleasant to watch, of course, but the overall effect of the scene throughout the rest of the movie is somewhat lost.

There is a subplot involving a mentally-challenged young man named Jeremy (Dominic Purcell) and his supposed affections of the cheerleader daughter of a gruff and hateful football coach (James Woods). In this film, this character feels forced into the narrative as a convenient means to an end. If the film were not a remake, but instead its own piece, it would still come off as contrived and awkwardly placed. Jeremy is the device that gets the rest of the thugs in town (all of who were former football players) to rally together and unleash all of their violent tendencies on anyone weaker than them, whether they are innocent or not.

On its own, separate from the shadows of Peckinpah's work, Rod Lurie's *Straw Dogs* works for about the first hour. Lurie tries to emulate the original in spots by paying cinematic homage, usually through obvious means, such as one shot that has Charlie's muscular physique dominating the front of the frame, hands on hips, with David's face in the middle, almost in a virtual headlock. Lurie's pacing is obviously different to suit today's attention spans and, as its own thriller, it is never dull. Among the cast, only Skarsgard brings the movie alive. He has just the right amount of menace behind the facade he creates while giving David a false sense of security.

The problem with the remake is that it is just too clumsily written. The bear trap, a recurring motif that was introduced right off the bat in the original, is wedged into a scene in the middle of Lurie's remake. Even the title gets an explanation this time, something that did not seem necessary in the older version. David explains how he sees these guys as "straw dogs," as if he just read the explanation in a sidebar paragraph from a textbook. The final act, truly scary and full of dreadful silences in the original, feels as though it is trying to quickly satisfy the bloodlust of the audience. The original was meant to question that bloodlust, both of David and anyone who kept watching the movie even as it provoked the viewer into walking away from it.

Times have changed since 1972, of course, and Peckinpah's masterpiece is still just as unsettling, but maybe today's audiences would not think so. One has to wonder why Lurie felt compelled to try and up the ante on the remake while also dumbing it down. It may not be fair to always compare a remake with its original source and there is certainly more than one way to do a great remake of a great film. But Lurie's version lacks purpose. Even changing the character to a Hollywood screenwriter smacks of laziness. Peckinpah's film leaves a viewer contemplating their own violent tendencies and capabilities. The remake leaves a viewer thinking "Oh, sure, they just happen to have a bear trap lying around."

Collin Souter

CREDITS

David Sumner: James Marsden
Amy Sumner: Kate Bosworth
Charlie: Alexander Skarsgard
Jeremy Niles: Dominic Purcell
Deputy John Burke: Laz Alonso
Daniel: Walton Goggins
Coach Stan Milken: Anson Mount
Janice Heddon: Willa Holland
Tom Heddon: James Woods
Chris: Billy Lush
Origin: USA
Language: English
Released: 2011
Production: Mark Frydman; Screen Gems, Battleplan; released by Sony Pictures
Directed by: Rod Lurie
Written by: Rod Lurie
Cinematography by: Alik Sakharov
Music by: Lawrence Nash Groupe
Sound: Steve Aaron
Editing: Sarah Boyd
Costumes: Lynn Falconer
Production Design: Tony Fanning, John P. Goldsmith
MPAA rating: R
Running time: 110 minutes

REVIEWS

Covert, Colin. *Minneapolis Star Tribune.* September 15, 2011.
Ebert, Roger. *Chicago Sun-Times.* September 15, 2011.
Gleiberman, Owen. *Entertainment Weekly.* September 15, 2011.
Howell, Peter. *Toronto Star.* September 15, 2011.
Jones, J.R. *Chicago Reader.* September 15, 2011.
O'Sullivan, Michael. *Washington Post.* September 16, 2011.
Phipps, Keith. *AV Club.* September 15, 2011.
Rickey, Carol. *Philadelphia Inquirer.* September 15, 2011.
Smith, Kyle. *New York Post.* September 16, 2011.
Weizman, Elizabeth. *New York Daily News.* September 16, 2011.

QUOTES

Charlie: "Oh you want your glasses, go ahead put them on, I want you to see what's coming."

TRIVIA

The famous quote from the film "I will not allow violence against this house" is not in the theatrical version of the remake.

SUBMARINE

A comedy that doesn't let principles stand in the way of progress.
—Movie tagline

In this age of instant cinematic gratification—when audiences crave big thrills, big laughs, and big drama up front—it is rewarding to find a smaller film whose off-beat charms please more over time, one that grows richer on repeated viewings. *Submarine,* the directorial debut of British playwright and comic actor Richard Ayoade is just such a low-key film. A precocious and deadpan funny coming-of-age story, at first it can feel smothered by its stylish self-reflection, but as the viewer eases into and gives in to its ironically earnest textures, *Submarine* reveals itself as a wry comedy of adolescent confusion and yearning.

Fifteen-year-old Oliver Tate (Craig Roberts) lives in Swansea, Wales (by the sea, of course), but most of his time is spent in his own mind, a precise and pretentious place where he sees his life as a New Wave foreign film with himself as the ennui-ridden hero on an existential journey. Out in the real world of classroom embarrassments and schoolyard bullies, Oliver has two primary goals: to be the best boyfriend he can to the sullenly alluring Jordana (Yasmine Paige), and help save the moribund marriage of his parents (Sally Hawkins and Noah Taylor).

Ayoade is adapting Joe Dunthorne's 2008 novel, but has moved the time frame back to a vague point in the mid-1980s, though the writer-director wisely avoids drenching *Submarine* in pop-culture period kitsch. (The only tip offs are the lack of cell phones, Internet, CDs, and DVDs.) Instead, Oliver has decorated his worldview (and his room) with *Catcher in the Rye,* Woody Allen, Carl Theodor Dreyer, French crooners, and Nietzsche. So tightly wound in his own self-defeating cleverness, at least the young man is up front about his pretensions as a means to discovery. He thinks life is a puzzle to be solved, a mystery to be cracked—if he can only follow the right clues, drop in the right intellectual references, and analytically classify everything into the right columns, the answer to "Who am I?" will appear neatly in the final tally.

At first Oliver can seem off-puttingly self-centered, with his arch introspection leaning toward cruel obliviousness. But thanks to Ayoade's writing and direction and Roberts' performance, Oliver's confused sensitivity and vulnerability soon seep through. The film eventually spends enough time in Oliver's over-thought head for the viewer to peel away the jaded posing from the scared teen angst it hides. Roberts also does a fine, forthright job of making Oliver sympathetic despite the boy's affectations, nicely portraying the wide-eyed and weary worries of someone who has nothing to worry about.

As Oliver's parents, Hawkins neatly folds her usual extroversion inward, bundling it in hovering neuroses, while Taylor matches her understatement as Oliver's marine-biologist father, a man surrendered to depressed banality and analytical repression. Together they form a portrait of resigned-but-functional marital sadness. The only time Ayoade lets go the reins and indulges in outright comedy is at the expense of Oliver's new neighbor, Graham (the excellent Paddy Considine) a pompous, mulleted "mystical ninja" (that is to say, a post-punk twit) who hawks New Age books and tapes. It does not help Oliver's cause that Graham was once his mother's own teen love and her marital ennui may be leading her back under his sway.

Meanwhile on the "first girlfriend" front, Paige's smolderingly pragmatic and apathetic Jordana not only ignites Oliver's teenage hormonal urges, but introduces him to a messiness of the heart that he both craves and cannot properly comprehend. There is the first kiss, the heady rush of early love, and the obligatory (though off screen and hi-jink-free) loss of virginity, and Ayoade captures it all with filmic moments that are both warmly familiar and coolly detached, and yet fresh and evocative. Though he and Jordana tell themselves they are anti-romance, Oliver's pose is contrived while Jordana's is a defense against the harsh world—Oliver fusses over his parents' moribund marriage, but Jordana exposes him to actual loss and family crisis. Naturally the melodramatic but still emotionally underdeveloped Oliver does not deal well with real-world tragedies that are much less aesthetically pleasing than those in his philosophy books and French cinema. His careful efforts to be worldly only reveal how little he really knows at age fifteen about people and life.

The film's title refers to Oliver's realization that people can be frustratingly, frighteningly unknowable—each locked away underwater in their own little submersibles, only connecting through vague, easily misunderstood sonar signals. It also represents the even darker side of such emotional isolation—the slowly sinking depression that can drag someone down to the bottom of the ocean. (Which Oliver's father helpfully reminds students is about six miles deep.) And while the world of Oliver's parents is aggressively dull brown, his own romantic and existential yearnings are often set against the sea at dusk. With Erik Wilson's cinematography filling the screen with deep dark blues, and Andrew Hewitt's aching original score peppered with melancholy nouveau New Wave songs from Alex Turner of The Arctic Monkeys, *Submarine* sometimes feels deliciously lost in a bittersweet haze.

At first it is tempting to dismiss *Submarine* as a promising first try, a film so dense with stylistic conceits that it works only as a series of film-school exercises, faking meaning with empty method. Except that in adeptly melding his over-thought film style with Oliver's over-thought inner life, Ayoade succeeds in filling both with an oddly moving sincerity. If the director's style and his protagonist's excessive self-analysis threaten to turn dreary, luckily the film is layered with dry, subversive humor, and—despite the faux-jaded protestations of Oliver and Jordana—achingly romantic. For those willing to dive past the surfaces, that makes *Submarine* one of the year's most delightful discoveries.

Locke Peterseim

CREDITS

Oliver Tate: Craig Roberts
Jordana Bevan: Yasmin Paige
Lloyd Tate: Noah Taylor
Jill Tate: Sally Hawkins
Graham Purvis: Paddy Considine
Origin: United Kingdom
Language: English
Released: 2010
Production: Mary Burke, Mark Herbert, Andy Stebbing; Warp Films, Film 4, Film Agency for Wales, Red Hour Films; released by Weinstein Co.
Directed by: Richard Ayoade
Written by: Richard Ayoade
Cinematography by: Erik Wilson
Music by: Andrew Hewitt
Sound: Martin Beresford
Editing: Nick Fenton, Chris Dickens
Art Direction: Sarah Pasquali
Costumes: Charlotte Walker
Production Design: Gary Williamson
MPAA rating: R
Running time: 96 minutes

REVIEWS

Corliss, Richard. *Time.* June 3, 2011.
Ebert, Roger. *Chicago Sun-Times.* June 8, 2011.
Michael Phillips. *Chicago Tribune.* June 9, 2011.
O'Sullivan, Michael. *Washington Post.* June 10, 2011.
Punter, Jennie. *Globe and Mail.* June 10, 2011.
Rabin, Nathan. *AV Club.* June 2, 2011.
Savlov, Marc. *Austin Chronicle.* June 17, 2011.
Scott, A.O. *New York Times.* June 2, 2011.
Stevens, Dana. *Slate.* June 3, 2011.
Turan, Kenneth. *Los Angeles Times.* June 3, 2011.

QUOTES

Oliver Tate: "My mother is worried I have mental problems. I found a book about teenage paranoid delusions during a routine search of my parents' bedroom."

TRIVIA

Each of the film's main characters has a color which is refelcted in their clothes and possessions. Oliver is blue, Jordana is red, Jill is yellow, Lloyd is brown, and Graham is black. As Oliver grows closer to Jordana, more red can be seen sneaking into his palette.

AWARDS

Nomination:

British Acad. 2011: Outstanding Debut by a British Writer, Director, or Producer.

SUCKER PUNCH

You will be unprepared.
—Movie tagline

Box Office: $36.4 million

Nearly forty years after the release of *Pong*, the modern video game is now taken seriously as an art form, prompting the sort of critical discourse previously reserved for more traditional mediums. And increasingly, the most acclaimed games are the ones cited as approaching the quality of motion pictures, both in narrative and appearance. It is curious then that film director Zack Snyder seems so intent on accomplishing the reverse, crafting movies that approximate the experience of playing a video game. If the most notable of his previous films—*300* (2007) and *Watchmen* (2009)—were jabs in that general direction, then *Sucker Punch* is his attempt at a knockout blow: A hyper-stylized assault on the senses that looks and feels like a video game designed by a gang of over-sexed, over-caffeinated teenage boys at a sleepover.

Sucker Punch opens with what essentially amounts to a very expensive "cut scene" (a non-playable, cinematic section within a video game that forwards the story). The doe-eyed, porcelain-faced protagonist—appropriately referred to only as Baby Doll (Emily Browning)—experiences a series of dramatic events, set in dialogue-free slow motion, along with a techno-goth revamping of The Eurythmics' "Sweet Dreams." Within the first five minutes, her mother dies and leaves a fortune to her two daughters, which enrages their stepfather and drives him to take it out on the younger sister, who is killed just as a gun-wielding Baby Doll arrives to defend her. The stepfather then frames Baby

Doll for the murder, labeling her a lunatic in the wake of her mother's death, and bribes the head of an insane asylum, Blue Jones (Oscar Isaac), to commit her. By the ten-minute mark, the audience has learned that Baby Doll's captor plans to render her lifeless by lobotomizing her in just five days' time. She spends the remainder of the film trying to escape that fate. But the hasty manner in which all of that exposition and character motivation is crammed into the first few minutes should alert the audience that Snyder has no plans of revisiting such "trifles" later on in the film.

Once the basics have been conveniently dispensed with, *Sucker Punch* does not waste any time getting down to business, which at its core, is an attempt to stimulate pleasure centers for both sex and violence simultaneously. Rather than limit himself to the confines of the asylum, Snyder (who wrote the screenplay with Steve Shibuya) has determined that Baby Doll's *mind* will serve as a better location for his outrageously unrestrained action sequences. So he assigns her a coping mechanism that allows her to withdraw deep into her own psyche, rather than face the horrors of her physical situation. Unfortunately, the world she imagines there is only slightly better. It is a turn-of-the-century brothel, in which she plays an erotic dancer in pigtails and a schoolgirl's uniform, whom Blue—the sinister overseer in this setting as well—aims to prostitute. So anytime Baby Doll is forced to dance, she retreats even further into her mind and lands in one of a number of alternate realms, including Feudal Japan, the trenches of World War II and the surface of an extraterrestrial planet somewhere in the future. But wherever she travels, Baby Doll is joined by four fellow inmates from the asylum, each of them absurdly attractive and equally underdressed: Sweet Pea (Abbie Cornish), Rocket (Jena Malone), Blondie (Vanessa Hudgens), and Amber (Jamie Chung). And under the direction of a mysterious sage (Scott Glenn, channeling the late David Carradine), Baby Doll hatches a plan reminiscent of many a video game in which they must secure four objects from the various worlds in order to ensure their escape in the "real" world. But unlike films such as *Inception* (2010) or *Flatliners* (1990), which carefully defined the relationships between their competing realities, as well as the stakes and consequences within each, *Sucker Punch* messily fails to do so and the viewer eventually loses his bearings.

Though the movie does not succeed in many areas, fans of Snyder's will be pleased to learn that its action sequences often deliver. There are four in total and between them, the ladies visit wildly different locales, make use of nearly every weapon and vehicle imaginable and fight off an impressive array of enemies, including steampunk Nazis, fire-breathing dragons and laser-packing robots. But despite this kitchen sink approach, Snyder's increasingly recognizable visual style creates a consistency. Much like *300* (2007), nearly all of the backdrops are entirely digital, but rendered with beautiful details and desaturated colors resembling those of an oil painting. And his liberal use of slow motion and zoom is effective in alternating the viewer's focus between the physicality of specific, dramatic actions and the chaos of the battles overall. The fight choreography (by Damon Caro, of *The Bourne Trilogy* [2002, 2004 and 2007]) is also noteworthy; it seems to subscribe to real world physics and delivers the kind of visceral impact one feels in the gut.

But little else about the film works. The bulk of the soundtrack, for example, consists of classic songs by artists like The Beatles, The Smiths and Pixies updated unnecessarily by arranger/producers Marius De Vries and Tyler Bates into glitzy, over-produced versions. Many of these are so invasive, that the scenes in which they are used feel more like music videos than anything else. And the film is so geared towards its action sequences that the passages of dialogue in between them come across like mere placeholders. Neither the writing nor the delivery of the words is convincing; only Cornish and Isaac occasionally manage to rise above their lines and lend any tangible drama to the proceedings. This makes most of the downtime in *Sucker Punch* feel like a slog. So by the time the fourth—and supposedly most important—action sequence rolls around, the audience is more than ready call it a day.

Sucker Punch's biggest problem is that in its go-for-broke attempt to sexualize its violence (a dicey proposition for any film), it ends up objectifying and victimizing anyone and everyone on the screen. There simply is not enough evidence to suggest that Snyder respects and cares for his main characters. He certainly works hard to ensure they *look* good, especially as they are mowing down legions of faceless, soulless adversaries in the imaginary worlds. But when it comes to their existence in the "real" world, he gives little insight as to what makes them tick, then later, seems to revel in brutally tearing them down. When not facing impending lobotomy, the women are either being thrown into walls, pinned to tables, threatened with rape, stabbed or shot. So Snyder's idea of sexiness is revealed to be at best, reductive and adolescent, or at worst, creepy and misogynistic. And without a fundamental understanding of such a central concept, he fails. Watching someone else play a video game can be enjoyable—even mesmerizing—as long as that player continues to demonstrate a level of mastery. But once it becomes clear that Snyder

cannot do so in his own film, it is only a matter of time before the viewer begins asking for the controller back.

Matt Priest

CREDITS

Babydoll: Emily Browning
Rocket: Jena Malone
Blondie: Vanessa Anne Hudgens
Amber: Jamie Chung
Sweet Pea: Abbie Cornish
Blue: Oscar Isaac
Madam Gorski: Carla Gugino
High Roller: Jon Hamm
Wise Man: Scott Glenn
Origin: USA
Language: English
Released: 2011
Production: Deborah Snyder, Zack Snyder; Legendary Pictures, Cruel and Unusual; released by Warner Bros.
Directed by: Zack Snyder
Written by: Zack Snyder, Steve Shibuya
Cinematography by: Larry Fong
Music by: Tyler Bates, Marius De Vries
Sound: Michael McGee
Editing: William Hoy
Art Direction: Grant Van Der Slagt
Costumes: Michael Wilkinson
Production Design: Rick Carter
MPAA rating: PG-13
Running time: 109 minutes

REVIEWS

Corliss, Richard. *Time*. March 28, 2011.
Debruge, Peter. *Variety*. March 24, 2011.
Jenkins, Marchk. *Washington Post*. March 27, 2011.
Jones, Kimberley. *Austin Chronicle*. March 31, 2011.
Lumenick, Lou. *New York Post*. March 25, 2011.
O'Hehir, Andrew. *Salon.com*. March 24, 2011.
Phillips, Michael. *Chicago Tribune*. March 24, 2011.
Rabin, Nathan. *AV Club*. March 24, 2011.
Scott, A.O. *New York Times*. March 24, 2011.
Sharkey, Betsy. *Los Angeles Times*. March 24, 2011.
Travers, Peter. *Rolling Stone*. March 25, 2011.

QUOTES

Wiseman: "For those who fight for it, life has a flavor the sheltered will never know."

TRIVIA

Pink Floyd's *Dark Side of the Moon* and *Sucker Punch* sync in a compilation titled, "Dark Side of the Sucker Punch." A fan discovered the connection and has revealed all details including the compilation itself through the internet.

SUPER

Shut up, crime!
  —Movie tagline

When his drug-addict girlfriend gets seduced by a strip club owning dealer, Frank (Rainn Wilson,) an unassuming fry cook, hits rock bottom. Life has not exactly been fair and this is the final straw. While zoning out watching a Christian cable channel, Frank is inspired by a schlocky TV caped crusader who uses his super powers to spread the good word to teens. Since bad guys ruined his life, he reasons, he will ruin some of theirs. He stitches together a costume, decides on a name (The Crimson Bolt), arms himself with a wrench and goes hunting for crime. The set-up for this film reads like a revenge-fueled noir comedy, but as audiences learned with last year's cult hit *Kick Ass* (2010), self-made superheroes do not have it easy. Their obvious lack of otherworldly powers leaves them vulnerable when confronted with real life, gun-wielding criminals. Screenwriters and directors can try to spin it in many ways, with potty mouthed side-kicks and awkward fight scenes, but real world violence, as *Super* points out, is no laughing matter.

An indie *Kick Ass* for the adult market, *Super* ratchets up the violence that made *Kick Ass* fans wince while toning down the likeable characters that made last year's feature so winning. Wilson, best known for his role as Dwight in TV's *The Office,* plays Frank like a lost, put-upon puppy. In many ways, he is the perfect candidate for superhero-ness: he is jilted and completely unnoticeable, deriving any and all courage from his costume. But Frank has not been bitten by a spider nor does he have access to cutting edge weapons technology. The only thing he has going for him is the fact that he certifiably mad. He has hallucinatory visions that he interprets as directives from the universe. He has a warped sense of power and is as ready to inflict crippling beatings on muggers and rapists as he is on the innocent jerk who butts in line at the movie ticket window.

Arguably less stable than Frank is Libby (Ellen Page), a comic book store clerk who curses a blue streak and insists Frank take her as his sidekick. Libby dubs herself Boltie, gets a tight fitting costume and then repeatedly tries to seduce The Crimson Bolt. Her enthusiasm ("We could get claws!") is probably the only part of *Super* that comes close to being charming —and to delivering genuine laughs. It is hard to know if writer-director James Gunn is trying to make a comment on the personality traits of someone who would blatantly put themselves in the line of fire for kicks or if he is simply going for an absurdist comedy angel. If it is the former then *Super* does make a point: you would have to be nuts to want to go out and confront criminals on a daily basis, in which case Frank and Libby fit the bill. If it is the latter, unfortunately, any laughs are the result of uncomfortable nervousness as Frank exacts his revenge fantasies. *Super* is so excessively violent it is hard to want to laugh at anything on-screen. Watching Frank pummel a man with a wrench in broad daylight is scarring, not funny. After a pretty drab opening, the film does gain some momentum as The Crimson Bolt and Boltie gear up for their final battle, but all of that stops cold when Boltie's head is graphically blown off.

Granted, without a level of gore *Super* would have read more like a sad middle-aged meltdown drama. But even with the violence, the film is still more depressing than entertaining or funny. When Frank is introduced, he is so very pathetic that it is hard to imagine him ever having a girlfriend at all. Maybe Gunn was trying to say something about what makes superheroes turn to vigilante justice, namely despair and the drive for revenge. If that is the case, he forgot about the other side of the equation: the hope and love that keep comic book heroes human. Sure, it is great to see bad guys get their just deserts, but it is the emotional connection that keeps fans coming back for more. It is the relationships, however weird and tenuous, that made *Kick Ass* more than just an action flick. And though Frank is driven by his love for his girlfriend, *Super* is too weighed down by its midlife-crisis-with-weapons angle to ever rebound from his walk on the dark side. The result is a confusing and awkward film that is not tight enough to be an action comedy and not kitschy enough to be camp.

Joanna Topor MacKenzie

CREDITS

Frank D'Arbo/ The Crimson Bolt: Rainn Wilson
Libby/ Boltie: Ellen Page
Sarah Helgeland: Liv Tyler
Jacques: Kevin Bacon
The Holy Avenger: Nathan Fillion
Det. John Felkner: Gregg Henry
Abe: Michael Rooker
Hamilton: Andre Royo
Sgt. Fitzgibbon: William Katt
God: Rob Zombie (Voice)
Origin: USA
Language: English
Released: 2010

Production: Miranda Bailey, Ted Hope; This is That
 Productions, Ambush Entertainment; released by IFC Films
Directed by: James Gunn
Written by: James Gunn
Cinematography by: Steve Gainer
Music by: Tyler Bates
Sound: Gary J. Coppola
Music Supervisor: Liz Gallacher
Editing: Cara Silverman
Costumes: Mary Matthews
Production Design: William Elliot
MPAA rating: Unrated
Running time: 96 minutes

REVIEWS

Abele, Robert. *Los Angeles Times.* March 31, 2011.
Burr, Ty. *Boston Globe.* March 31, 2011.
Ebert, Roger. *Chicago Sun-Times.* April 7, 2011.
Gleiberman, Owen. *Entertainment Weekly.* March 30, 2011.
Gronvall, Andrea. *Chicago Reader.* April 7, 2011.
Holden, Stephen. *New York Times.* March 31, 2011.
Longworth, Karina. *Village Voice.* March 29, 2011.
Mitchell, Elvis. *Movieline.* March 31, 2011.
Phillips, Michael. *Chicago Tribune.* April 7, 2011.
Tobias, Scott. *AV Club.* March 31, 2011.

QUOTES

Jacques: "You really think that killing me…stabbing me to
 death is going to change the world?"
Frank D'Arbo: "I can't know that for sure, unless I try."

TRIVIA

Near the end of the movie when Liv Tyler's character is in a
 rehab group session, she can be heard stating "f**ked up,
 insecure, neurotic, and emotional." This is a reference her
 father Steven Tyler's song "FINE" which is an acronym for
 the same line.

SUPER 8

It arrives.
 —Movie tagline

Box Office: $127 million

J.J. Abrams' *Super 8* is a brilliant distillation of
everything that its creator found inspirational in the '70s
and '80s works of its producer, Steven Spielberg. Rather
than make a pure homage or ode to a bygone era,
Abrams dared himself to prove that a Spielbergian
blockbuster could still find an audience, still hit an
emotional chord, and still inspire future filmmakers.

The result was a film that did reasonably well (nearly
$260 million worldwide) but fell a bit short of high
expectations and divided viewers as it played in theaters
(although its Blu-ray release seemed to already be spawn-
ing an eventual re-appreciation). History will be very
kind to *Super 8,* much like the influential blockbusters
that planted the initial kernel for its existence in the
brain of a child who dreamed someday about being a
director himself.

Set in the early '80s, *Super 8* could have been
released in the same string of Spielberg hits that
produced *Jaws* (1975), *Close Encounters of the Third
Kind* (1977), *Raiders of the Lost Ark* (1981), and *E.T.:
The Extra-Terrestrial* (1981)—which is not, in any way,
meant to intimate that Abrams' film is of the same
caliber as those undisputed classics, merely that it is cut
from the same cloth. Like *E.T.* and *Close Encounters,*
Super 8 focuses on an alien arrival in a small town (not
unlike the sleepy burg awakened in *Jaws*) and the film
features a group of adventurous young people who could
have been inspired by the Spielberg-produced *The Goonies* (1985). And what separates Abrams' film from others
that try to mimic the work of the Oscar®-winning director is his keen understanding that it is not the alien or
the shark that matters but the people facing it. *Super 8*
is not as much of an "alien movie" as it is a film about a
child dealing with loss, a father coming to terms with
his grieving son, and even first love. It is about childhood exploration of a dangerous world and the realization that figures of authority, from teachers to deputies
to the military, may not be what they at first seem.

Instantly displaying his deft gift with visual storytelling, *Super 8* opens with a series of shots, including a
newly-updated factory sign making clear that an accident had happened yesterday and a boy sitting on a
swing holding a clearly-important locket, that make
clear that a young man has just lost his mother. The boy
in question is named Joe Lamb (Joel Courtney) and his
father Jackson (Kyle Chandler) is the Deputy in a small
town. Joe's friends are headlined by aspiring director
Charles (Riley Griffiths), a gregarious young man who
seems to know the entire oeuvre of George A. Romero
by heart and has been inspired by him to make his own
zombie flick (the character who makes a movie inspired
by his hero in much the same way Abrams is doing one
inspired by Spielberg is a clever in-touch that never feels
overly underlined). The supporting friends in this filmmaking friendship crew include Cary (Ryan Lee), Martin
(Gabriel Basso), and Preston (Zach Mills). Everything
changes the night that Charles asks the lovely Alice (Elle
Fanning) to play a key role in his movie, for which Joe
is doing makeup (and, of course, playing a small role).
Joe has long-had a totally understandable crush on Alice
and struggles to keep a straight face near her without

going all doe-eyed. Complicating matters is the fact that Alice's father (Ron Eldard) is a drunkard for whom Joe's mother filled in on the morning of her death. One can assume that were Alice and Joe to form a long-term relationship, dinner with the in-laws might be tense.

The action of the piece kicks in fully when the gang is filming an expository scene at a train station only to witness an amazingly detailed and disturbing derailment. One of their teachers drives on the track and hits a train straight-on. The ensuing chaos looses a car from which something escapes and leaves a series of white cubes on the landscape. Joe takes home one of the cubes while the town becomes a hotbed of military activity looking for whatever launched itself from the derailed car. As people, car engines, and dogs go missing, Joe's father attempts to get to the bottom of it all while the kids at first see the action around them as mere production value for their film before realizing the interstellar drama underneath it all.

With his script for *Super 8,* Abrams plays with timeless themes that are often associated with his inspiration. The alien activity, the small-town environment, the purity of adolescence, and, yes, a heavy dose of sentimentality are all included here but they are woven together in such an expert way that some critics and too many viewers undervalued the accomplishment. What could have been just another summer alien blockbuster becomes so much more with some of the best genre writing, directing, and acting in years.

To start, there is the cast assembled by Abrams and his team. Courtney has a perfect every-kid quality, never pushing the sentimental envelope to the point of manipulation and actually giving a more subtle turn than most gave him credit for giving. He is not quite a straight man, but also nowhere the exaggerated hero viewers have come to expect in not only summer action films but ones headlined by teenagers. He is forced to carry quite a bit of exposition and emotional weight in Abrams' script—;oss of a mother, first love, saving the world from alien attack—and he does so with ease, never in a way that feels manipulative. The rest of the cast is strong, especially Mr. Chandler, but, in many ways, the film is stolen by future star Elle Fanning. From her very first scene, lit by the interior of a car, to two of the most genuine star-making moments in years—one just before the derailment and another as she watches old movies of Joe's mother—Fanning captivates. She has that rare combination of young beauty, intelligence, and screen presence that comes along every few years, reminding one of teenage performances from Jodie Foster and Kate Winslet.

Perhaps Abrams' most notable accomplishment is in how he has made an alien film in which the extraterrestrial takes a back seat in the memory banks to the people involved. He, of course, employs the Spielberg-patented trick of not showing the creature to the viewer until well into the film, at which point some were disappointed by his design. Yes, the creature looks familiar to sci-fi fans, but he almost should, in the same sense that the kids model their zombies after the Romero dead-star, open-mouth, cocked-neck look. If the alien looked markedly "new" then that would break the mood and dominate the conversation. J.J. Abrams has made an alien film that is not really about the alien (and only those who understood that appreciated the lack of action in the end while others bemoaned the absence of a typical blockbuster set piece). It is a film about letting go and dealing with loss. All of Abrams' work has spun itself around issues with parents and children (even *Star Trek* [2009] and TV's *LOST*) and it is a truly amazing achievement that this great filmmaker took what interests him now and filtered it through the film view of what made him a director in the first place. *Super 8* is a monumental achievement, summer blockbuster entertainment that proves that critics who have bemoaned the lack of quality in the warmer season are not wrong. If only they could all be this good.

Brian Tallerico

CREDITS

Jackson Lamb: Kyle Chandler
Alice Dainard: Elle Fanning
Louis Dainard: Ron Eldard
Nelec: Noah Emmerich
Jen Kaznyk: Amanda Michalka
Charles: Riley Griffiths
Joe Lamb: Joel Courtney
Origin: USA
Language: English
Released: 2011
Production: J.J. Abrams, Bryan Burk, Steven Spielberg; Paramount Pictures, Amblin Entertainment, Bad Robot; released by Paramount Pictures
Directed by: J.J. Abrams
Written by: J.J. Abrams
Cinematography by: Larry Fong
Music by: Michael Giacchino
Sound: Ben Burtt, Matthew Wood
Music Supervisor: George Drakoulias
Editing: Maryann Brandon, Mary Jo Markey
Art Direction: David Scott
Costumes: Ha Nguyen
Production Design: Martin Whist
MPAA rating: PG-13
Running time: 112 minutes

REVIEWS

Childress, Erik. *eFilmCritic.com.* June 1, 2011.

Corliss, Richard. *TIME Magazine.* June 2, 2011.

Ebert, Roger. *Chicago Sun-Times.* June 8, 2011.

Edelstein, David. *New York Magazine.* June 6, 2011.

Lemire, Christy. *Associated Press.* June 7, 2011.

McCarthy, Todd. *HollywoodReporter.* June 6, 2011.

Pais, Matt. *RedEye.* June 8, 2011.

Phillips, Michael. *Chicago Tribune.* June 8, 2011.

Roeper, Richard. *RichardRoeper.com.* June 9, 2011.

Travers, Peter. *Rolling Stone.* June 9, 2011.

QUOTES

Cary: "Stop talking about production value, the Air Force is going to kill us."

TRIVIA

Director J.J. Abrams named the town the film is set in Lillian, Ohio, after his grandmother.

T

TABLOID

People often return to familiar places as they age. Creative people are no different. In fact, they are, if anything, even more liable to return to what has worked for them in the past. In many cases, such journeys are undertaken in an attempt to rediscover something that was lost. But in the case of documentarian Errol Morris the opposite is true. He got his start doing documentaries about quirky people such as *Gates of Heaven* (1978) and *Vernon, Florida* (1981) and never really stopped. Over the course of nine features and a TV series (*First Person* [2001]), he has managed to build not just a career but a genuine legacy, redefining the documentary form in ways that infuriates purists and making some of the most compelling oddball portraits in the history of film. *Tabloid* deconstructs his audience's fascination with lurid stories even as it presents one mother of a lurid story. The end result is in a league with his best (if not his most urgent) work, feeling less in rank with *Fog of War* (2003) or *The Thin Blue Line* (1988) and more with *Mr. Death: The Rise and Fall of Fred Leuchter Jr.* (1999) or *Standard Operating Procedure* (2008).

Tabloid tells the story known round the world as "The Case of The Manacled Mormon." Kirk Anderson, a young missionary with the Mormon Church goes missing in the late seventies only to return with a wild tale of having been chained to be a bed, seduced, and, finally, repeatedly raped by Joyce Bernann McKinney, a former Miss Wyoming World. But as police and journalists across two continents sort through the facts the details that emerge paint a different story then either side tries to pass off as the truth.

These are only some of the particulars. The story of how the two met, and what constituted the true nature of their relationship is unveiled by Morris one startling revelation at a time. It is his particular genius to endear the characters to viewers even as they become increasingly strange. All along, the viewer senses that the director has chosen this story not just because of its participants but because of how his audience will react to them, and the opportunities those participants will provide for the audience to re-humanize the whole affair. In short, to get beyond tabloid sensationalism and see these people as people.

This is quite similar in many respects to Morris' last feature *Standard Operating Procedure* (2008), in which the U.S. soldiers featured in the famous Abu Gharib snapshots were finally brought out into something approximating an undistorted view. But, here, Morris is back in the land of whimsy that spawned his amazing pet cemetery debut *Gates of Heaven,* his hilarious and heartwarming *Vernon Florida,* and his quirky but insightful *Fast, Cheap & Out of Control* (1997). This is Morris reminding his audience that at any moment they might find the camera turned on them, exposing their quirks, making them look foolish or at least gloriously un-self-aware.

The bottom line to getting Morris is understanding that his chief joy has always been sticking it to those who think they can judge a book by its cover. Morris is hardly content with the cover, choosing instead to get deep into the story of his subject's lives, looking for the core themes that would otherwise be obscured by surface details, however colorful and interesting those details may be at first glance. He has plenty of players to choose from here. On the surface, all of these people are successful members of their community. Joyce McKinney was a successful model and beauty pageant winner; Kirk Anderson was on a fast track in the Mormon Church community where success in religion and business go hand-in-hand. The monolithic and fast growing Mormon Church itself seems unshakable by something as mundane and tawdry as a lower-level member sex scandal. As to the journalists reporting on the story and the audience who weighs their words, they are simply observers, right? Morris goes the easiest on his audience, but no one with a conscience will be able to consider this tale without a pang of self-recognition. Greed, lust, meanness, glibness, self-righteousness, and outright dumbness are in ample display. But so is whimsy, honesty, emotional rawness, psychological brokenness, and other traits that should trigger empathy.

Tabloid ranks among Morris's greatest works precisely because it takes a story that seems utterly throwaway and reveals within the tawdriest bits of it a group of living, breathing, broken, wonderful, awful people. McKinney who is the focus of the piece seems full of joie de vivre even as she also seems out of her mind. In an interesting post-script to the tale, viewers find out that McKinney is the woman recently made famous for having her dog cloned. Her desperate need for attention is made clear long before that, but listening to her talk about her beloved deceased pet and insisting that the new one is in fact that same pet is an introduction to a special kind of mania where every wish in life comes true, everyone's story is interesting, and everything reported by the media is truthful. Perhaps this single coda is the film's greatest achievement. *Tabloid* knows that the devil is in the details and so are the things that make life worth living, and dreams worth having. There is an uneasy relationship between faith and fear here, and Morris boldly leaps into the fray trying to determine who said what to who to create a definitive history. Luckily for viewers, as a documentarian, he is interested in so much more.

Dave Canfield

CREDITS

Herself: Joyce McKinney
Origin: USA
Language: English
Released: 2010
Production: Julie Bilson Ahlberg, Mark Lipson; Air Loom Enterprises, Moxie Pictures; released by Sundance Selects
Directed by: Errol Morris
Cinematography by: Robert Chappell
Music by: John Kusiak

Sound: Bruce Perman
Editing: Grant Surmi
Production Design: Steve Hardie
MPAA rating: R
Running time: 88 minutes

REVIEWS

Denby, David. *New Yorker*. July 24, 2011.
Ebert, Roger. *Chicago Sun-Times*. July 14, 2011.
Hoberman, J. *Village Voice*. July 12, 2011.
Jones, Kimberley. *Austin Chronicle*. August 5, 2011.
Kendrick, James. *Q Network Film Desk*. July 27, 2011.
Keough, Peter. *Boston Phoenix*. July 13, 2011.
Lasalle, Mick. *San Franscisco Chronicle*. July 14, 2011.
Miller, Prairie. *Newsblaze*. July 11, 2011.
Munro, Shaun. *What Culture*. February 10, 2011.
Scott, A.O. *New York Times*. July 14, 2011.

TAKE ME HOME TONIGHT
(Kids in America)

Best. Night. Ever.
—Movie tagline

Box Office: $6.9 million

For the last four years, Matt Franklin (Topher Grace) has been ruing the day he let Tori Frederking (Teresa Palmer) get away. She was his high school crush and he never had the guts to ask for her number. Now, one MIT degree later, Matt finds himself working in a mall video store under the auspice of trying to figure out his life and still pining for the girl that got away. The year is 1988, which is why video stores exist, and with them come all the vestiges of the '80s that those who came of age during the decade would relish remembering: back-combed bangs, shoulder pads and the term "awesome." When Tori walks into Matt's store during one of his shifts, he does the only thing any like-minded, embarrassed, video store guy would do: He takes off his uniform, ducks out the back, pretends to bump into Tori, and lies about a job with Goldman Sachs. She buys it, asks him to a party and the rest of *Take Me Home Tonight* unravels in the vein of other much more memorable "best night of our lives" party movies, like *Can't Hardly Wait* (1998) or *Superbad* (2007). Though it possesses the required amount of boozing, mishaps and raunch that the genre requires, in the end *Take Me Home Tonight* lacks any catchy teen spirit.

True to form, the movie is full of stock characters that are meant to evoke the relatable, nostalgic feelings from the audience. Matt is the everyman, dorky wallflower with potential who does not get just how awesome he is. His sister, Wendy (Anna Faris), is an aspiring writer wasting her time with the ex-high school jock who has not grown up. And then there is Matt's sidekick, Barry (Dan Fogler), the over-the-top loser who just realized he is wasting his life in a dead-end job. The trouble is that none of them come across as remotely interesting. As best-friend material, Fogler is all wrong. He is loud, obnoxious, without any trace of lovability, and more annoying than funny. Sure, he is the necessary character foil meant to raise Matt's stock with the audience, but in this instance it has the opposite effect. Instead of looking better standing next to Barry, Matt loses credibility for having such a best friend.

Faris as Matt's sister is disappointingly underdeveloped and underused, especially since her arc is far more watchable than her brother's. She has bigger risks to take and is actually attempting to take them. Faris is known for her comic timing, yet here she is a shell of herself, awkwardly balancing drama with comedy and not being given the room to really develop either angle. And then there is Grace, whose Matt is too average for his own good. Matt comes off as a slacker and the night never feels like an all-or-nothing opportunity for him. There is no urgency to the character or the situation. Then there is the issue of his MIT degree. In the '80s, it might have been trouble to be "MIT smart," but in this day and age of hipster dork it is hard to understand why anyone would lie about working for Goldman Sachs when they have an instant street cred engineering degree from MIT.

There are just enough moments of raunch and debauchery to elicit a few giggles and fulfill the sex quota of best night of your life party genre, but it is not enough to cause the audience to rehash plot points with friends once the credits roll. Rather, they are more likely to ask the following question, "Why the 80's?" Sure, it is a funny decade, thanks to acid wash and hair scrunchies, and, to that end, the parties Matt visits are peopled with your requisite head bangers, break dancers, and Goths. But other than giving Matt an awkward opportunity to espouse on the wrongness of sexual harassment in the workplace, nothing about the time period feels necessary. The '80s atmosphere does not contribute to the film save for the soundtrack and allowing characters to explore retro dress. The film would have been better served if director Michael Dowse and the writing team of Jeff and Jackie Filgo gave more thought to the characters and their conflicts instead of the time period. They also did not take into account that setting a movie in the '80s would inherently draw comparisons to films of that decade. Unfortunately for this film, some of the best teen movies were made in the '80s.

From *The Breakfast Club* (1985) to *Say Anything* (1989), the decade essentially dominated the market with relatable teen angst and drama. *Take Me Home Tonight* would really have had to step it up to give these classics a run for their money. And in the end, it did not even come close.

Joanna Topor MacKenzie

CREDITS

Matt Franklin: Topher Grace
Wendy Franklin: Anna Faris
Barry Nathan: Dan Fogler
Tori Frederking: Teresa Palmer
Kyle Masterson: Chris Pratt
Bill Franklin: Michael Biehn
Ashley: Michelle Trachtenberg
Pete Bering: Michael Ian Black
Shelly: Lucy Punch
Carlos: Demetri Martin
Trish Anderson: Angie Everhart
Origin: USA
Language: English
Released: 2011
Production: Ryan Kavanaugh, Jim Whitaker, Sarah Bowen; Imagine Entertainment, Relativity Media; released by Universal Pictures
Directed by: Michael Dowse
Written by: Michael Dowse, Jackie Filgo, Jeff Filgo
Cinematography by: Terry Stacey
Music by: Trevor Horn
Sound: Lisa Pinero
Music Supervisor: Kathy Nelson
Editing: Lee Haxall
Art Direction: Elliott Glick
Costumes: Carol Oditz
Production Design: William Arnold
MPAA rating: R
Running time: 98 minutes

REVIEWS

Burr, Ty. *Boston Globe.* March 3, 2011.
Gleiberman, Owen. *Entertainment Weekly.* March 2, 2011.
Honeycutt, Kirk. *Hollywood Reporter.* March 2, 2011.
Lowry, Brian. *Variety.* March 2, 2011.
Phillips, Michael. *Chicago Tribune.* March 3, 2011.
Pinkerton, Nick. *Village Voice.* March 2, 2011.
Pols, Mary F. *TIME Magazine.* March 3, 2011.
Rea, Steven. *Philadelphia Inquirer.* March 3, 2011.
Sharkey, Betsy. *Los Angeles Times.* March 3, 2011.
Simon, Brent. *Screen International.* March 2, 2011.

TRIVIA

The number Tori gives Matt at the end of the film, 818-404-7327, is an out IOC service number to NBC/Universal studios.

TAKE SHELTER

Box Office: $1.7 million

Take Shelter is a quietly devastating film that chronicles either a man's descent into paranoid schizophrenia or his selection as the harbinger of a coming apocalypse. Watching the man attempt to determine which of these two terrifying possibilities applies to him is one of 2011's most suspenseful and heartbreaking experiences.

The man is Curtis LaForche (Michael Shannon). Curtis and his wife Samantha (the ubiquitous Jennifer Chastain starring in her *seventh* role of 2011) live in rural Ohio with their hearing-impaired six-year-old daughter. He is a construction worker, she a homemaker, and they live the kind of ordinary, realistic lives that these days only seem to exist in the realm of independent film. Indeed, much of the pleasure of writer/director Peter Nichol's film consists of simply basking in his refreshingly realistic and recognizable world, a world rarely seen in contemporary Hollywood film. The LaForches exist in the real world, living paycheck to paycheck, mortgaged to the hilt, their health insurance (upon which their daughter's upcoming cochlear implants depend) only as reliable as Curtis's continued employment. As with millions of Americans today, they are just one or two patches of bad luck away from catastrophe.

One day Curtis is out doing some yard work when he sees a flock of black birds swirling together in an organized and ominous fashion. The sky erupts into forked lightning, deafeningly loud thunder and thick syrupy rain. No one else sees the birds, hears the thunder or feels the rain. Curtis tries to ignore these visions but they get worse. In one vision, he and his daughter are attacked by shadowy figures. In another Curtis's home is struck by some invisible force, his furniture floating in the air as if a silent bomb has detonated. Eventually the visions involve both his wife and co-worker, Dewart (Shea Wigham), trying to kill him. These mysterious visions are extremely well done by Nichols and his special effects team. Whether divinely inspired or products of schizophrenia they are as terrifying as a brick through a bedroom window at midnight.

However, despite what the previews might suggest, Curtis's visions are not the central conceit of the film. They are in fact a small part of the film. Nichols is not so much concerned with the visions themselves but their effect on the man who is having them and those around him. Frequent Nichols collaborator Michael Shannon does excellent, Oscar®-worthy work, in a film which requires him to be in nearly every scene. The true pleasure of the film is the process of watching Shannon's rational, reasonable man trying to cope with frightening visions that he cannot explain. Do the visions portend a coming apocalypse that he must protect himself and his family from? Or are the visions generated by his diseased mind and it is *he* that his family must be protected from? Curtis visits his mother (Kathy Baker, excellent in a very sad role) in an assisted living facility who began having symptoms of schizophrenia when she was around Curtis's age to determine if he has inherited her symptoms. He consults his family doctor who refers him to a psychiatrist in bigger city. Because he cannot afford a psychiatrist, he goes to the library to research schizophrenia himself and then goes to a public health counselor. The counseling does not help and, with the assistance of Dewart, Curtis begins building an underground tornado shelter with money he does not have and construction equipment "borrowed" from work.

The hallmark of Nichols's film is its absolute dedication to realism and the humanity of his characters. Curtis responds to his visions, and those around him respond to Curtis's behavior, in a way that is completely believable and authentic. As he tries to both determine the nature of the visions and prepare for a coming apocalypse, Curtis keeps all of his fears locked inside himself. This is a very understandable (and male) response for someone who is afraid he might be going insane but this causes problems as his inconsistent behavior ripples across the tiny community he lives in. Jennifer Chastain does superb work as a patient, understanding wife who is trying to be supportive of her husband but is justifiably terrified by her husband's strange, unexplained behavior. Wigham is excellent as well as Curtis's loyal friend who, not understanding what his friend is going through, feels betrayed and, in turn, betrays his friend. Following a vision in which Dewart tries to kill him, Curtis asks his boss Jim (Robert Longstreet) to switch Dewart to a different work crew. Since he fails to explain his reasoning to Dewart, Dewart understandably feels betrayed and, in retaliation, informs their boss of their borrowing without permission the equipment from work to build Curtis's shelter. Angered, Jim fires Curtis, resulting in the loss of his health insurance. A more conventional film would make Curtis's boss, and the town as a whole, into a one dimensional villain. However, Jim is not an evil man, but a small business man who justifiably worries about the insurance risk of workers using his equipment without his authorization which could bankrupt him. The town, as a revealed in an explosive scene in a cafeteria where most of its citizens have gathered for a Friday night fish fry, is not comprised of Archie Bunker bigots but normal people who are simply trying to understand a man who is telling them that a storm is coming like Noah warning of the flood. "You think I'm crazy? Well, listen up, there's a storm coming like nothing you've ever seen, and not a one of you is prepared for it."

Nichols's admirable commitment to realism coupled with Shannon's subtle acting and presence in nearly every scene in the film combine to create a character the viewer really cares about and generates a great deal of suspense about his fate and the fate of those around him. These elements coalesce in a climax of nearly unbearable suspense when a real tornado forces Curtis and his family into the shelter he has constructed and Curtis, certain that the apocalypse awaits outside, does not want to let them out the next day. As Samantha pleads with her husband to let her out, the viewer feels her claustrophobia and trembles at the very real possibility that Curtis will not open the door.

Take Shelter is an independent film in the best sense of the word.: Unpretentious; unfurling at its own, slow pace; its writing, directing and acting absolutely dedicated to depicting real people responding to real world problems in a completely authentic way. Most films are about what happens to people. Nichols film is about how what happens to people affects them and those around them. He offers no easy answers and the film is the better for it. *Take Shelter* is one the most intriguing, haunting and emotionally devastating films of 2011.

Nate Vercauteren

CREDITS
Curtis LaForche: Michael Shannon
Samantha LaForche: Jessica Chastain
Dewart: Shea Whigham
Nat: Katy Mixon
Kyle: Ray McKinnon
Kendra: Lisa Gay Hamilton
Jim: Robert Longstreet
Sarah: Kathy Baker
Hannah LaForche: Tova Stewart
Origin: USA
Language: English

Released: 2011
Production: Tyler Davidson, Sophia Lin; Grove Hill Productions, Strange Matter Films, Hydraulx; released by Sony Pictures Classics
Directed by: Jeff Nichols
Written by: Jeff Nichols
Cinematography by: Adam Stone
Music by: David Wingo
Sound: Will Files
Editing: Parke Gregg
Art Direction: Jennifer Klide
Costumes: Karen Malecki
Production Design: Chad Keith
MPAA rating: R
Running time: 124 minutes

REVIEWS

Anderson, Melissa. *Village Voice.* September 27, 2011.
Burr, Ty. *Boston Globe.* October 20, 2011.
Chang, Justin. *Variety.* September 25, 2011.
Ebert, Roger. *Chicago Sun-Times.* October 5, 2011.
Lumenick, Lou. *New York Post.* September 30, 2011.
Murray, Noel. *AV Club.* September 28, 2011.
Rea, Steven. *Philadelphia Inquirer.* October 20, 2011.
Scott, A.O. *New York Times.* September 29, 2011.
Uhlich, Keith. *Time Out New York.* September 27, 2011.
Zacharek, Stephanie. *Movieline.* September 29, 2011.

QUOTES

Curtis: "You think I'm crazy? Well, listen up, there's a storm coming like nothing you've ever seen, and not a one of you is prepared for it."

AWARDS

Ind. Spirit 2012: Producers Award
Nomination:
Ind. Spirit 2012: Actor (Shannon), Director (Nichols), Film, Support. Actress (Chastain).

TERRI

We've all been there.
—Movie tagline

Calling someone an outsider implies that there is a clear-cut group of people who can be called insiders. As many (and ideally all) adults know, one of the biggest lessons of growing up is realizing that social status is often in the eye of the beholder. The insightful drama *Terri* does an excellent job of combining so-called outsiders with perceived insiders and showing that everyone is part of the same human category, trying to figure out the world as best as they can.

In a lovely, subtle feature debut performance, Jacob Wysocki stars as overweight fifteen-year-old Terri, who is frequently tardy for school because he is just not that eager to get there. That is not to say that Terri's home life is much better. Having no idea where his parents are, Terri lives with his uncle James (Creed Bratton), who dips in and out of lucidity and tells Terri that the teenager lives "a prince's life" in James' house. Most people would disagree with the statement, but Terri does have the basics necessary for living even if the standard meal he and his uncle enjoy is beans on toast.

Terri's tardies and refusal to participate in classroom activities lands him the office of assistant principal Mr. Fitzgerald (a great John C. Reilly), a friendly guy who hides neither his disdain for teenage foolishness nor his sympathy for certain adolescent woes. Fitzgerald takes an interest in Terri—who wears pajamas to school, claiming that they are comfortable but certainly, on some level, preferring to distract from his large figure—and establishes a weekly meeting on Monday mornings for them to talk. At first Terri appreciates the gesture; unlike most high school students, he does not feel embarrassed to spend time with an administrator whom he calls a friend. When Terri later discovers that the only students Fitzgerald meets with weekly are all kids with physical or mental disabilities or behavioral problems, Terri tells Fitzgerald, "I'm a part of a group of monsters." This leads to another attempt by the elder man (who has his own problems with his wife at home) to connect with his latest project, which again leads to a feeling of broken trust and proof that the man may be as unsure as the boy about how to navigate his role in life.

While some may call *Terri* episodic, writer Patrick Dewitt (crafting a script from a story conceived with director Azazel Jacobs) shows a keen understanding of both the stubborn routine and casual unpredictability of teenage life. For a short time, Terri's mission to kill mice in the attic leads to a fixation on the rare control he possesses when setting traps. A particularly poignant moment finds Terri arranging the dead mice so that even in death they are not alone, their tails touching in the center of the circle as the bodies like motionless in traps. Soon Terri sets the traps in the woods and finds that birds, too, are susceptible to the temptation of free food, prompting brief joy in Terri and, later, shame in Uncle James when he sees what his nephew has done. Terri is not hiding from his actions; he brings his uncle to see what he has done because he has not fully processed what has happened and how he feels about it. (Another reflection of Terri's in-progress sense of self comes when Fitzgerald tells him there are good-hearted students and bad-hearted students and Terri, questioning which one he is, admits, "I don't know if I know.")

While Terri is occasionally a target for bullies, he is not ostracized from his entire class. The girls that make up his home economics group seem to like him. Yet Terri is a loner, often an emotionless straight line in an environment constantly throbbing with emotional peaks and valleys that do not involve him. So it is a considerable shift in Terri's schedule when he strikes up an off-balance friendship with Chad (Bridger Zadina), another one of Fitzgerald's students (though the assistant principal demonstrates far less affection for Chad and his constant, crass trouble-making). However, Terri is surely less surprised by the time he spends with Chad than the friendship that develops between he and Heather (Olivia Crocicchia), a pretty (and, assumedly, consequently popular) girl whose reputation and social status are ruined after a sleazy classmate persuades her to allow him to finger her during class. After Terri defends Heather to Fitzgerald and later deflects attention from Heather during class, the petite, once-lively girl now finds support in the large boy who clearly has warmth to offer to someone interested in receiving it. These developing friendships lead to a wonderful climactic scene in which Chad crashes a planned get-together between Terri and Heather. In the course of an evening and more alcohol than any of them have had before, the scene displays a great deal about teenagers' simultaneous eagerness to grow up and frequent lack of readiness to actually experience the rites of passage that lie between youth and adulthood. The scene is acted beautifully, especially by Wysocki, taking in what Terri sees without totally feeling a part of it, and Crocicchia, showing how quick decisions and the reactions they cause around her may continue to greatly impact Heather's life from now on.

Terri trails off at the end, unable to find a satisfactory final moment for many of the highly resonant scenes that come before, and a scene of Terri, Chad and Fitzgerald attending the otherwise empty funeral of the school secretary feels contrived, rather than a natural accumulation of struggling individuals. Yet there are many moments, large and small, that exemplify a sensitive understanding to life's many challenges. When other students spot what is being done to Heather in class, one guy calls out "Stud!," articulating in one word the gender-based double standard about sex as the expression on Heather's face sours from pleasure to agony. Elsewhere, in Fitzgerald's office, the assistant principal tells Terri that he once knew a kid who tied flaming tennis balls to the tails of cats. That kid grew up to be a cop. In other words, people are capable of a wide variety of actions (which speak particular volumes when no one else is watching), and what Terri is today has no bearing on what he will be in the future. What makes *Terri* such a rewarding experience is the awareness of how difficult it can be to figure out a planet in which everyone often feels that sense of uncertainty.

Matt Pais

CREDITS

Mr. Fitzgerald: John C. Reilly
Terri: Jacob Wysocki
Uncle James: Creed Bratton
Heather Miles: Olivia Crocicchia
Chad: Bridger Zadina
Origin: USA
Language: English
Released: 2011
Production: Alison Dickey, Hunter Gray, Lynette Howell, Alex Orlovsky; Verisimilitude, Silverwood Films; released by ATO Pictures
Directed by: Azazel Jacobs
Written by: Patrick DeWitt
Cinematography by: Tobias Datum
Music by: Mandy Hoffman
Sound: Eric Thomas
Music Supervisor: Joe Rudge
Editing: Darrin Navarro
Art Direction: Nicholas Kelley
Costumes: Diaz
Production Design: Matthew Luem
MPAA rating: R
Running time: 105 minutes

REVIEWS

Ebert, Roger. *Chicago Sun-Times.* July 20, 2011.
Hornaday, Ann. *Washington Post.* July 14, 2011.
Murray, Noel. *AV Club.* June 30, 2011.
Phillips, Michael. *Chicago Tribune.* July 21, 2011.
Rickey, Carrie. *Philadelphia Inquirer.* Aug. 4, 2011.
Rothkopf, Joshua. *TimeOut New York.* June 28, 2011.
Scott, A.O.. *New York Times.* June 30, 2011.
Scott, Mike. *New Orleans Times-Picayune.* Aug. 26, 2011.
Weber, Bill. *Slant Magazine.* June 29, 2011.
Wilson, Calvin. *St. Louis Post-Dispatch.* Aug. 4, 2011.

QUOTES

Mr. Fitzgerald: "I knew this kid growing up who tied flaming tennis balls to cats' tails and loved every minute of it. I think he's a cop now."

AWARDS

Nomination:
Ind. Spirit 2012: First Screenplay.

TEXAS KILLING FIELDS

Once in…there's no way out.
—Movie tagline

"Inspired by true events" is often a bad omen at the start of a thriller, as ironically it is usually a pre-excuse for baroque flights of unrealistic fancy. In the case of *Texas Killing Fields*, the "fields" exist—they are an actual stretch of swampy, abandoned oil fields along a Texas highway between Houston and Galvenston where over the decades dozens of women's bodies have been found, presumably dumped there by various murderers.

It is the desolate tragedy and unsettling eeriness of that real-life location—not accompanying case details—that director Ami Canaan Mann and writer Don Ferrarone mine for creepy atmosphere in this fictional crime film. As for the baroque flights of unrealistic fancy, Mann keeps them mostly contained to her and cinematographer Stuart Dryburgh's roving camera. In terms of narrative, *Texas Killing Fields* is going for a more prosaic, procedural feel (no raving speeches in grotesque lairs from megalomaniac serial killers), though Mann's primary cinematic interest is in laying on as much grimy, sweaty atmosphere as possible.

The story unfolds in the fictional Texas City (standing in for the real League City, Texas) as women's butchered bodies are turning up in the nearby swamp and a new pair of mismatched detective partners (Sam Worthington and Jeffery Dean Morgan) work to solve the murders. That means murky nighttime scenes illuminated only by the rolling lights of roadside patrol cars and daylight hours spent knocking on the trailer-trash doors of the impoverished local residents. *Texas Killing Fields* starts out concerned with forensic details and interrogation-room posturing, but Mann's attention is drawn to the rot-yellow florescent lighting and spirit-crushing banality of small-town sleaze as the film's tough, damaged cops get in the faces of smugly scummy criminals.

If that eye for gritty visual detail sounds familiar, it should be noted Mann is the daughter of film maker Michael Mann, and takes after her father when it comes to approaching dark-souled crime tales with highly stylized realism. (There is even a well-done car chase and cop-criminal shoot out that naturally invites comparisons with her father's *Heat* [1995]). *Texas Killing Fields* has a hyper-naturalism—gloomy lingering shots of trees and grass as well as the man-made textures of overpasses, factories, and run-down offices are framed with a strong aesthetic eye. The film has a washed-out, poorly lit documentary verisimilitude, complete with Texan jangly steel guitars and Southern drawls; but Mann's camera rarely rests, whirling around its subjects as though the director cannot bring herself to let go of her cinematic gimmicks. She is after a portentous atmosphere, languid with secrets—at one point an almost other-worldly mist drifts through the town like something out of a horror film.

In front of the camera, things are more rote. Playing Detective Sounder, a grumbling local-boy cop, Worthington once again proves that his greatest strength as an actor is the ability to pass his stony lack of charisma off as inexpressive gravitas. As his partner Heigh—a transplanted New York City cop who did not leave his gruff, blunt emotionalism behind in the big city—Morgan gives off the requisite damn-the-rules, kick-in-the-door world-weary swagger. While neither performance is bad, too many of Morgan and Worthington's scenes play out like a parody of laconic hard-boiled cops blustering at one another instead of talking.

Jessica Chastain is a cop in the next jurisdiction over, who also happens to be Sounder's ex-wife. However, as she pursues similar cases in her territory, Chastain's character drifts in and out of the film with no apparent rhyme or reason other than to occasionally bust up the boys' testosterone fests and artificially give Worthington's character a vague back story. Also doing more than the script expects with an underwritten "stray dog" character is teenage Chloë Grace Moretz. Her Little Ann is a wayward girl whose imperilment drives the second half of the plot and gives Heigh someone for whom to fight the good fight.

Over the course of the film, Heigh's emotions take over both the law-enforcement process and the narrative as the mysterious woman killer begins to taunt and target the cops themselves, and *Texas Killing Fields* tosses aside crime scene investigations for cynical-cop crusades and their accompanying clichés. Though Mann is going for a deconstruction of both police procedurals and self-destructive police dramas, at times the film becomes so minimalist, so enraptured with details, it loses its purpose, drifting along on atmosphere and style without making much narrative sense. Following the plot and characters can be frustrating, as it often feels like pieces of story have been left out—perhaps intentionally to echo the protagonists' confused fumblings in the dark, or part of a failed effort to cobble something like a cohesive tale out of Mann's over-active style.

The filmmaking on display is admirably artistic and compelling, at least in its intentions, but the storytelling and flattened character arcs are frustratingly muddled. All the pieces are here for a gritty cops-and-crime noir, but in the end they do not fit together into a larger picture. Without any character depth, resonance, or evocative motivations on either side of the increasingly familiar mystery, the visually gripping *Texas Killing Fields* only adds up to a whole lot of very pretty ugliness.

Locke Peterseim

CREDITS

Mike Souder: Sam Worthington
Brian Heigh: Jeffrey Dean Morgan
Little Ann Sliger: Chloe Grace Moretz
Pam Stall: Jessica Chastain
Rule: Jason Clarke
Rhino: Stephen Graham
Origin: USA
Language: English
Released: 2011
Production: Michael Jaffe, Michael Mann; Anchor Bay Films; released by Anchor Bay Films
Directed by: Ami Canaan Mann
Written by: Donald F. Ferrarone
Cinematography by: Stuart Dryburgh
Music by: Dickon Hinchliffe
Sound: Ron King, Richard Schexnayder
Editing: Cindy Mollo
Art Direction: Jonah Markowitz
Costumes: Christopher Lawrence
Production Design: Aran Reo Mann
MPAA rating: R
Running time: 105 minutes

REVIEWS

Allen, Boo. *Denton Record-Chronicle.* October 20, 2011.
Berkowitz, Lana. *Houston Chronicle.* October 20, 2011.
Corliss, Richard. *Time.* October 14, 2011.
Ebert, Roger. *Chicago Sun-Times.* October 19, 2011.
Goodykoontz, Bill. *Arizona Republic.* October 20, 2011.
Kohn, Eric. *IndieWire.* October 13, 2011.
Mottram, James. *Total Film.* October 26, 2011.
Schager, Nick. *Slant.* October 9, 2011.
Sharkey, Betsy. *Los Angeles Times.* October 14, 2011.
Zacharek, Stephanie. *Movieline.* October 14, 2011.

QUOTES

Det. Mike Souder: "I'm sorry, Levon. I'm sorry we're stopping you from your day job, as what, a f**king rocket scientist?"

TRIVIA

In preparation for their roles, actresses Sheryl Lee and Chloë Grace Moretz spent time in a rehabilitation center for drug addicts.

THE THING

It's not human. Yet.
—Movie tagline

*In a place where there is nothing, they found
   something.*
   —Movie tagline

Box Office: $16.9 million

When John Carpenter released *The Thing* (1982), his remake of the horror classic *The Thing from Another World* (1951) (both of which were adapted from the 1938 John W. Campbell short story *Who Goes There?*), his grisly tale of a group of men at an isolated research station in the Antarctic fighting off an alien intruder with the ability to replicate them perfectly hit theaters a mere two weeks after another cinematic visitor from outer space—a far warmer and fuzzier thing known as E.T.—had begun enchanting the world. Needless to say, the movie pretty much tanked at the box-office, but, over the years, it began to amass a large cult following (not unlike what happened with *Blade Runner* (1982) which came out on the exact same day) that embraced it for the incredible amount of suspense and tension that Carpenter was able to generate from such a theoretically familiar conceit and, of course, the gloriously grotesque special effects, courtesy of Rob Bottin, that still astonish and repulse three decades later. In fact, the reputation of *The Thing* has grown so considerably over the years, even among many of those who initially dismissed it at the time, that it would receive that most dubious of honors—its very own remake.

Technically, *The Thing* is actually a prequel to the events of the Carpenter version instead of being an outright remake, though the differences between the two are so negligible that perhaps it should be dubbed a "requel." Again set in Antarctica during the winter of 1982, the film opens as a trio of scientists from a Norwegian outpost stumble upon what appears to be a spaceship and an alien creature embedded in the ice. The crew, headed by the imperious Dr. Sandor Halverson (Ulrich Thomsen) and consisting of taciturn helicopter pilot Carter (Joel Edgerton), recently arrived American paleontologist Dr. Kate Lloyd (Mary Elizabeth Winstead), and a bunch of Norwegian guys who are either named Lars or who should be, brings the block of ice holding the creature back to base for study and inadvertent thawing. The creature quickly breaks out of the ice and begins running amok through the confines of the base and decimating anyone unlucky to come into its space with an astounding array of pincers, claws, teeth, and other assorted menacing mandibles. Not only that, it has the amazing ability to replicate its victims so perfectly that it is able to hide in plain sight amongst the others until the time comes for it to messily jump from one meat ship to the next as it struggles to escape from the base and move on to greener—okay, redder—pastures.

Like most prequels, *The Thing* is hobbled by the fact that since it has to tie in properly to an already existing narrative, its ability to offer up new and surprising twists and turns is curtailed significantly because it can really only end in one particular fashion. In this case, that is an even bigger problem because the story elements are so necessarily limited—a close-knit group of isolated scientists, a frigid locale, a creature who can assume the form of any of the other cast members—that there is not really much of anything that a filmmaker can do to mess things up in an exciting manner. As a result, debuting director Mattihijs van Heijninse Jr and screenwriter Eric Heisserer are forced to attempt little more than what Carpenter did thirty years ago. While Carpenter treated his story as a slow-burning fuse by slowly creating a palpable sense of tension and paranoia amongst his already-edgy characters in the first half before going for the more visceral shocks in the second, this version pretty much does away with any noticeable amount of suspense in order to shoehorn in as many big "BOO!" moments as possible in which something or some Thing suddenly pops up out of nowhere to either throw a false scare into the proceedings or to tear apart another cast member like fresh bread. At first, this approach does inspire some jolts among the more skittish members of the audience, even if their response is based more on simple reflex action than anything else, but after a while, even the most tightly wound viewers will pick up on the repetitive rhythms and find the tension slackening at just the point when it should be at its tightest.

Then again, those who are interested in seeing *The Thing* simply for the gross-out material are also likely to come away from it feeling very disappointed as well. Rob Bottin's original conception of the monster is one of the all-time great designs in creature feature history and part of the reason why it remains so effective is that it was done with practical effects that, no matter how outlandish they became, maintained a certain palpable sense of weight and gravity because they were actual things that people were actually responding to both on the screen and in the audience. Inevitably, the effects this time around, although based on what Bottin created, are largely handled by CGI and as a result, there is a certain detachment between the creature and its surroundings that, while not overly blatant, is nevertheless noticeable and the kind of thing that can help damage material like this that already requires a certain suspension of disbelief if it is to have any hope of working in the first place.

Like the Carpenter version, *The Thing* tanked at the box office with the general public while critics and fanboys decried the filmmakers for having the audacity to tamper with such a beloved classic. However, the comparisons between that film and this new iteration pretty much end there because this *Thing* is a total bore from start to finish that is little more than the world's most expensive piece of mediocre fan fiction in that it does little more than offer up ideas and conceits that have already been used without any of the creativity that made them so memorable in the first place. In the end, *The Thing* ironically becomes the very thing that it is trying to depict on the screen—a soulless creature that more or less knows how to mimic authentic human behavior and personality but is undone by its constitutional inability to generate such things completely on its own

Peter Sobczynski

CREDITS

Kate Lloyd: Mary Elizabeth Winstead
Braxton Carter: Joel Edgerton
Derek Jameson: Adewale Akinnuoye-Agbaje
Adam Goodman: Eric Christian Olsen
Dr. Sander Halvorson: Ulrich Thomsen
Origin: USA
Language: English
Released: 2011
Production: Marc Abraham, Eric Newman; Morgan Creek Productions, Strike Entertainment; released by Universal Pictures
Directed by: Matthijs van Heijningen Jr.
Written by: Eric Heisserer
Cinematography by: Michel Abramowicz
Music by: Marco Beltrami
Sound: Scott Hecker
Editing: Peter Boyle, Julian Clarke, Jono Griffith
Art Direction: Patrick Banister
Costumes: Luis Sequeira
Production Design: Sean Haworth
MPAA rating: R
Running time: 103 minutes

REVIEWS

Catsoulis, Jeannette. *New York Times*. October 13, 2011.
Childress, Erik. *eFilmcritic.com*. October 14, 2011.
Ebert, Roger. *Chicago Sun-Times*. October 13, 2011.
McCarthy, Todd. *Hollywood Reporter*. October 13, 2011.
Nelson, Rob. *Variety*. October 13, 2011.
Pais, Mat. *RedEye*. October 13, 2011.
Robinson, Tasha. *AV Club*. October 13, 2011.
Snider, Eric D. *Film.com*. October 14, 2011.
Verniere, James. *Boston Herald*. October 14, 2011.
Weinberg, Scott. *FEAR.net*. October 13, 2011.

QUOTES

Colin: "You think they're gonna pay a bonus for bringing home an alien instead of core samples?"

TRIVIA

The character of Kate Lloyd was patterned after Ellen Ripley from the Alien films moreso than R.J. MacReady from the original *The Thing*.

13 ASSASSINS
(Jusan-nin no shikaku)

Take Up Your Sword.
—Movie tagline

It is the 1830s and the noble tradition of the samurai is fast fading into the modern era. But when Lord Matsudaira Naritsugu (Goro Inagaki), a sadistic and politically ambitious relative of the Shogunate, sets his sights on embroiling the nation on a disastrous path towards war, those eager to see the peace kept appeal to Shinzaemon Shimada (Kôji Yakusho), an older samurai, who, after hearing a litany of Naritsuga's sins and meeting one of the despot's victims, sets about gathering together a secret assassination force. From the beginning, it is a suicide mission; a dozen men against hundreds. But Shimada, sure of the worthiness of his cause, sets out with his men, including nephew Shinroukuro (Takayuki Yamada).

Along the way, the band meets and rescues Koyata (Yûsuke Iseya), a decidedly eccentric vagabond who joins them for mysterious reasons of his own. Koyata speaks of the human world as if it is somewhat beneath him and daydreams constantly of his lost love Upashi, who was last seen squatting by a stream eating raw meat. The film does a masterful job of intimating that he may be a God or demon in disguise and his scenes in the final battle are some of the most enjoyable in the film.

Arriving at the town chosen for the ambush, Shimada and his men prepare their last stand devising a number of ingenious traps and weapons. Shimada himself knows that the real battle will be between his men and the powerful body guards of Naritsuga, especially Hanbei, Shimada's old friend, a master samurai. The battle commences and surely it must be one of the epic battles in film history. What *13 Assassins* lacks in scope it makes up for in a dizzying display of swordplay, pyrotechnics and mano-a-mano showdowns.

Hugely entertaining and often deeply moving, *13 Assassins* is no mere stab at the katana genre by the prolific Takashi Miike, it is very nearly the masterpiece of his wildly-varied career. To understand the true importance of *13 Assassins*, a little history is in order. This is a film born of a mixed parentage not only of cross-cultural influences but of the two solidly different strains of samurai film itself. The first type of samurai cinema, "chanbara," is action-oriented, concentrating on dazzling swordplay and elaborate fighting scenarios and tends to be hyper-violent, playing out like B-movie Westerns. The style is known for having a devoted following not just among martial arts cinema fans but exploitation fans as well. Such films were popularized in the west via the huge influx of martial arts cinema in general in the mid-to-late sixties.

The second type, "jidai-geki," is typified by being more invested in the historical and philosophical history of the samurai which became nationally mythologized in the east. Akira Kurasawa, whose *Seven Samurai* (1954) introduced Western audiences to the form, is considered the master of it, a fact buttressed by his masterful late period films *Kagemusha* (1980) and *Ran* (1985), which set in stone the standards for Japanese period cinema. Of course, such jidai-geki films, especially those involving large scale battle sequences, are expensive and labor-intensive to produce. Thus, samurai movies have always occupied a strange cultural locus somewhere between the extremes of arthouse and grindhouse.

How odd then that Takashi Miike, who is not at all known for samurai films, should write and direct a near perfect hybrid of the two styles. Clearly *13 Assassins* is a jidai-geki, full of finely-drawn, gradually-developed characters and conflicts, based on a true story, and shot through with interesting period details. But Miike, who has always leaned toward the grindhouse, brings his transgressive tendencies to bear often not only in terms of embracing chanbara sensibility but adding to it exactly the sort of ghoulish touches that fans of *Audition* (1999)and *Ichi The Killer* (2003) would expect. In one sequence a woman whose arms, legs and tongue have been cut off squawks and gags out a cry for justice. It is the moment of decision for Shimada, who is so taken aback by the perfection of the opportunity to use his sword for justice that he laughs. It is a moment of pure Miike mayhem. So is a booby trap of burning bulls sent stampeding down a narrow street as a battle tactic. But amidst the drawn out bloodletting and gruesome deaths is an urgent story every bit as compelling as any genre element.

Dave Canfield

CREDITS

Shinzaemon Shimada: Koji Yakusho
Lord Naritsugu Matsudaira: Goro Inagaki
Sir Doi: Mikijiro Hira

Hanbei Kitou: Masachika Ichimura
Shinrouko: Takayuki Yamada
Hirayama: Tsuyoski Ihara
Sahara: Arata Furuta
Koyata: Yusuke Iseya
Origin: Japan, United Kingdom
Language: Japanese
Released: 2010
Production: Michihirko Umezawa, Minami Ichikawa, Tochiro Shiraishi, Hirotsugu Yoshida; Sedic International, Recorded Pictures Company; released by Magnet Releasing
Directed by: Takashi Miike
Written by: Daisuke Tengan
Cinematography by: Nobuyasu Kita
Music by: Koji Endo
Sound: Jun Nakamura
Editing: Enji Yamashita
Art Direction: Yuji Hayashida
Costumes: Kazuhiro Sawataishi
MPAA rating: R
Running time: 126 minutes

REVIEWS

Aldridge, David. *Radio Times.* May 5, 2011.
Anderson, Jeffrey M. *Combustible Celluloid.* May 13, 2011.
Burr, Ty. *Boston Globe.* May 5, 2011.
Dargis, Manhola. *New York Times.* April 28, 2011.
Ebert, Roger. *Chicago Sun-Times.* May 26, 2011.
Edelstein, David. *New York Magazine.* May 2, 2011.
Felperin, Leslie. *Variety.* September 13, 2011.
Hubert, Christoph. *Sight and Sound.* May 10, 2011.
O'Hehir, Andrew. *Salon.com.* May 28, 2011.
Zacharek, Stephanie. *Movieline.* April 28, 2011.

QUOTES

Shinzaemon Shimada: "He who values his life dies a dog's death."

30 MINUTES OR LESS

Box Office: $37.1 million

Ruben Fleischer's debut *Zombieland* (2009) was a fast-paced comedy with a lot of action, and a cheerful spirit that had a lot of fun playing off the usual clichés of flesh-eating attackers. One of the greatest pleasures of all was in the casting and the nature of the protagonists played by the four leads. They made an impression on an audience as one of the rare groups that practically demanded another adventure at the end of their eighty minutes on-screen just to see these characters again. Fleischer's sophomore follow-up, *30 Minutes or Less*, feels like the *Zombieland* of an alternate dimension. It is just as short, revolves around a pair of partners with competing motivations, and contains a well-liked character actor facing the consequences of an invasion in his palatial mansion. But all the manic energy of Fleischer's previous film is filtered through characters so exceedingly dumb or unlikable that audiences are happy to bid them adieu by the time the credits roll.

Nick (Jesse Eisenberg) is a pizza delivery boy who works for a company noted for its titular guarantee (...or its free). Nick is in his mid-twenties with no greater prospects than watching action movies or his best friend, Chet (Aziz Ansari), receive sexual gratification in his car outside his apartment. Then there is Dwayne (Danny McBride), who would appear to have it made. He is another man-child without a job, mooching off his father referred to as The Major (Fred Ward), a former Marine who hit ten million in the lottery and has been living the good life since. Dwayne wastes time with his best pal, Travis (Nick Swardson), an explosives expert who at least has a skill, but only puts it to use blowing up watermelons.

Dwayne does have a master plan up his sleeve. His dream of opening up a tanning salon/prostitution service in Grand Rapids, Michigan requires some capital. Instead of waiting around for an inheritance of whatever The Major has left, Dwayne and Travis concoct an arrangement to have dad killed. Except this also requires some green. So in order to hire the boyfriend (Michael Peña) of a stripper (Bianca Kajlich) that Dwayne is sweet on, he further conspires with Travis to kidnap someone to rob a bank for them. The simplest part of their plot is choosing their mark, a simple pizza delivery boy whom they knock out, strap a bomb to and give him ten hours to get their money or he goes boom.

30 Minutes or Less makes no qualms about these two criminals being as dumb as a box of rocks, even if Dwayne talks a good game. The propensity to then saddle another average Joe with a task almost doomed to failure adds another layer of stupidity that in the right hands could turn into a farce of unprecedented opportunities. Michael Diliberti's debut screenplay, however, steps wrong as the first second ticks off the bomb's red counter. Nick is established in the very first scene as not being particularly dim in his ability to turn the tables on a couple young punks who refuse to tip him. Instead of using those same skills to decipher a way out of his predicament, he immediately jumps into the endgame of how to rob this bank. Panic is a natural reaction, but with ten hours to spare he could spend one or two trying to figure out how to involve the police without Dwayne and Travis ever being aware.

Diliberti's script takes a further lapse into gob smacking idiocy by involving Chet in the matter. Failing to ever recognize that the situation is miles removed from the villain of *Die Hard with a Vengeance* (1995) forcing his task runner to now involve an unwilling partner, Chet jumps in with two feet all too quickly. The bomb vest will not come off and can be triggered by Dwayne's cell phone. Under threat of being watched, Nick and Chet could be best served by doing a little counter-surveillance, losing their tail, and get a bomb squad to a secure location. Of course, this means an even shorter film. Therefore, Chet instantly succumbs to risking his new school teaching gig to commit a grand felony and all for someone with whom he just ended a friendship.

Ruben Fleischer's direction is also at major fault here. This is the same guy who allowed *Zombieland*'s two most cautious characters to naively attract attention to themselves by turning on a whole amusement park's worth of lights, so logic may not be his best selling point. However, Fleischer with his truncated running time never once stresses the urgency of Nick's situation. Ten hours gives him plenty of time to enlist Chet and buy the necessary supplies, but also to tell off his boss and reveal his feelings to Kate (Dilshad Vadsaria), the very girl that caused his brief estrangement to his pal in the first place. Nine hours and fifty-six minutes later, the final ticks provide no greater rush nor any sense of suspense.

30 Minutes or Less never reveals itself to be anything more than a comedy, despite some occasional lapses into action and bloodshed. All but Nick Swardson have proven themselves in film and television to be very capable comedic actors. Surprisingly enough, Swardson plays his part with the most level-headed sincerity. He is still not funny, but is less annoying than usual. McBride's usual motor-mouth shtick, put to great use on HBO's *Eastbound and Down,* loses luster here in a character not endearing enough to overcome his thick-headed planning. To see McBride at his best, one need look no further than *Pineapple Express* (2008), which Fleischer's film would love to pretend it is emulating but is miles removed from in sheer wit and skill in maximizing its mounting comic obstacles.

Every now and again a joke or a situation sticks, mostly from Ansari and Eisenberg, who having played Mark Zuckerberg in *The Social Network* (2010), again gets to make a Facebook joke in a Fleischer film. The parallels between Nick and Dwayne appear all too clear to completely avoid making a more purposeful irony of the slacker culture; one coming from found money and the other from pure laziness. Any such social statement of the rich using the poor to rob the banks of America en route to eliminating those who served for their country is lost through barrage of incompetent actions that seem far more drawn out than its 78-minutes suggest. This is the kind of loud, disjointed comedy that replaces its screwball plotting and farcical pacing with overplayed vulgarity and a lack of intelligent drive that makes one rather just order in some pizza and watch the classic action comedies. But not invite over Nick, Chet, Dwayne or Travis.

Erik Childress

CREDITS

Nick: Jesse Eisenberg
Dwayne: Danny McBride
Travis: Nick Swardson
Chet: Aziz Ansari
Juicy: Bianca Kajlich
Chango: Michael Pena
Kate: Dilshad Vadsaria
Origin: USA
Language: English
Released: 2011
Production: Stuart Cornfeld, Jeremy Kramer, Ben Stiller; Columbia Pictures, Media Rights Capital, Red Hour Films; released by Columbia Pictures
Directed by: Ruben Fleischer
Written by: Michael Diliberti, Matthew Sullivan
Cinematography by: Jess Hall
Music by: Ludwig Goransson
Sound: Kami Asgar
Music Supervisor: Isac Walter
Editing: Alan Baumgarten
Costumes: Christie Wittenborn
Production Design: Maher Ahmad
MPAA rating: R
Running time: 83 minutes

REVIEWS

Bell, Josh. *Las Vegas Weekly*. August 10, 2011.
Ebert, Roger. *Chicago Sun-Times*. August 11, 2011.
Fine, Marshall. *Hollywood & Fine*. August 11, 2011.
Gonzalez, Ed. *Slant Magazine*. August 11, 2011.
Larsen, Josh. *Larsen On Film*. August 10, 2011.
McWeeny, Drew. *Hitfix*. August 5, 2011.
Phillips, Michael. *Chicago Tribune*. August 11, 2011.
Rabin, Nathan. *AV Club*. August 11, 2011.
Rich, Katey. *CinemaBlend.com*. August 5, 2011.
Roeper, Richard. *RichardRoeper.com*. August 11, 2011.

QUOTES

Nick: "Guess what? You just brought a gun to a bombfight, officer!"

THOR

Two worlds. One hero.
—Movie tagline

Courage is immortal.
—Movie tagline

Box Office: $181 million

Issue #380 of Marvel Comic's *The Mighty Thor* was released in June 1987. Titled "Mjolnir's Song," issue #380 was the climax of a multiple issue arc in which the Norse god of Thunder Thor finally took on the Migard Serpent, Jormungand, a dragon who he is destined one day to die in combat with. Featuring captions in rhythmic verse and gloriously over the top dialogue like "Farewell, hero! No seat in Valhalla for you! The valkyries shall never find the body of Thor and bear it hence! Enter the jaws of Jormungand and dispair!" Thor and Jormugand go head to head for twenty-seven glorious, action-packed pages. Enduring fang and flame, Thor hurls his mighty hammer Mjolnir into the dragon again and again, flying above, beneath and behind his city block-sized foe looking for a chink in his armor. When Jormugand sucks Thor into his mouth and snaps his mighty mouth shut, the battle appears to be at its end. That is until Thor hurls his hammer through the dragon's teeth and bursts to freedom through a shower of bone fragments. Epic, fantastic and ridiculous, this is what *Thor* is all about. Reinforcing the epic nature of the showdown was the issue's format. A splash page uses an entire page for a single panel and a typical comic features one splash page, typically the first page of the book, and then the rest of the book is broken down into panels, six or seven to a page. In issue # 380, *every page* in the entire issue was a splash page. Cinema is the ultimate splash page and in the perfect *Thor* film adaptation every frame would be a splash page. Kenneth Branagh's *Thor* is not the perfect *Thor* film. The fault does not lie with Branagh, however, but rather with an unambitious, play-it-safe script that lacks both a Jormungand-esque villain worthy of its mighty protagonist and, for a significant portion of the film, the fantastic and otherworldly setting that makes Thor unique.

Indeed, a grim dichotomy reveals itself quickly in *Thor*: Everything set in Thor's home world of Asgard is fantastic and everything set on earth is dreadfully dull. The film opens promisingly in Asgard, which is fabulously realized by the film's superb art direction and CGI. The film's Asgard is full of vivid, vibrant colors, futuristic Norse inspired architecture, spiraled towers stretching seemingly into infinity, and, most dazzlingly, Bifröst, a bridge made out of rainbow linking Asgard to the rest of the universe. Thor's (Chris Helmsworth) father, Odin (Anthony Hopkins), rules Asgard and watches disapprovingly as his arrogant, hedonistic son saunters about exuding impudent entitlement to the throne he will someday inherit. Odin's disapproval deepens when, after frost giants sneak into Asgard and steal a powerful artifact, Thor, against his father's wishes, sets off with his companions Fandral (Josh Dallas), Volstagg (Ray Stevenson), Sif (Jamie Alexander), Hogun (Tadanobu Asano) and his magician brother Loki (Tom Hiddleson) to wrest it back from the frost giants in the forbidding, frosty realm of Jotunheim.

The frost giants' world is as beautiful and richly imagined as Asgard, full of ice blanketed ruins and 20 foot tall frost giants with glowing coal-red eyes and electric blue bodies. When the giants, unsurprisingly, resist surrendering the artifact, Thor and his companions attack, despite being outnumbered by the hundreds. In a move that would make Stan Lee smile with approval, Thor hurls his hammer and takes out a dozen frost giants with one sweeping toss. If the film delivered two hours of this kind of thing it would have been absolutely fantastic. Unfortunately, the viewer quickly discovers that sequences like this are the exception rather than the rule and that the best part of the movie is already over with after the first fifteen minutes of the film.

Cut to the extremely boring story of a group of research scientists who are studying weather patterns in New Mexico. Scientists Jane Foster and Erik Selvig are played by Natalie Portman and Stellan Skarsgård , excellent actors both, who are utterly wasted by a script that gives them nothing memorable to say or do. Into this boring dynamic falls (literally) Thor after he has been exiled from Asgard by his disappointed and angry father following his unauthorized pursuance of the stolen artifact. Thor befriends the scientists (with an utterly perfunctory romance, of course, blossoming between Helmsworth and Portman). Soon, he is tangling with the CIA-like government agency SHIELD, which has been alerted to his presence and that of his hammer (which he can no longer lift because he is now mortal).

Odin's decision to exile Thor turns out to have been a bad decision as Thor's brother Loki promptly decides to take advantage of Thor's absence and take over Asgard. Soon Odin is in a celestial coma and The Destroyer (a robot designed by Odin) has been dispatched to earth by Loki to finish off Thor and his friends. Alerted to Loki's betrayal, Thor and his companions must figure out a way to return to Asgard and defeat Loki. Unfortunately, the viewer is not much invested in Thor's retribution against his brother as the film's script fails to make its villain sufficiently villainous (a far cry from *Captain America: The First Avenger's* thoroughly sinister Red Skull). Loki is, of course, Thor's eternal nemesis and an entirely appropriate villain for him. But as generically written by *Thor's* five (never a good sign) screen writers, he is simply not very interesting or menacing. (One can only hope that a better job is done with him in 2012's *The Avengers*).

The film's other great disappointment, also attributable to its script, is its Scrooge-like doling out of the mythical settings and epic face-offs which are the main reasons to make a Thor film in the first place. Although the film opens on Asgard and closes on Asgard, the vast middle of the film is confined to modern-day New Mexico. The adventures of most super heroes (and thus the movies based on them) are set on modern day earth and audiences' fatigue with this setting can be sensed in the other two Marvel films of 2011 (*X-Men: First Class*; *Captain America: The First Avenger*) which, though required by their characters' histories to be set on earth, attempted to distinguish themselves by at least setting their stories in a different era, the 1940s and 1960s. Why rob *Thor* of the rich and unique setting established over the course of nearly fifty years of comic books that distinguishes him from all of his fellow super heroes? The answer is presumably to save some money and to accommodate audiences unfamiliar with the comic who might be alienated by an entire film set in a quasi Wagnerian universe of Norse mythology. This is a short-sighted approach as it is guaranteed to disappoint fans of the comic and because there is little evidence that wider audiences lack the adventurousness to embrace stories set in fantastical settings (the unprecedented success of *Avatar* (2009), set wholly in an alien world and principally featuring alien characters, belies this supposed alienation).

If the viewer is to be stranded on earth with Thor, the one thing that could have at least made the earth time entertaining would be a funny, fish-out-of-water script. How does an arrogant deity accustomed to immortality and universal adulation respond to being mortal and just another joe in a world that does not even know he exists? The film does a little of this (there is an amusing scene where Thor awakens in the custody of SHIELD and is offended that mere mortals—which he is now one of—would dare to touch his godly personage and another funny sequence featuring a wildly one-sided drinking contest between Thor and Selvig) but not enough to warrant the amount of dull screen time spent on planet earth

Thor belongs in the mystical realms of Asgard, Jötunheimr and Álfheimr going head to head with gods, giants and dragons. For the relatively brief periods of time the film puts him in those places it is great fun. Branagh has a terrific eye for the material and his direction, channeling the epic grandeur of *Mary Shelly's Frankenstein* (1994) and *Hamlet* (1996), suits it perfectly. *Thor*, like another recent adaptation of a celebrated literary character, *Sherlock Holmes* (2009) is a near-miss. As with *Sherlock Holmes*, *Thor* gets enough things right that if it prioritizes the appropriate elements in its sequel it will be a film worth watching. If, for *Holmes*, that means a mystery worthy of its master detective then for *Thor,* it means a villain and cosmic milieu worthy of its god hero.

Nate Vercauteren

CREDITS

Thor: Chris Hemsworth
Jane Foster: Natalie Portman
Odin: Anthony Hopkins
Professor Andrews: Stellan Skarsgard
Darcy: Kat Dennings
Frigga: Rene Russo
Volstagg: Ray Stevenson
Heimdall: Idris Elba
Loki: Tom Hiddleston
Ymir: Colm Feore
Phil Coulson: Clark Gregg
Origin: USA
Language: English
Released: 2011
Production: Kevin Feige; Marvel Entertainment, Paramount Pictures; released by Paramount Pictures
Directed by: Kenneth Branagh
Written by: Zack Stentz, Ashley Edward Miller, Don Payne
Cinematography by: Haris Zambarloukos
Music by: Patrick Doyle
Sound: Richard King
Music Supervisor: Dave Jordan
Editing: Paul Rubell
Art Direction: Maya Shimoguchi
Costumes: Alexandra Byrne
Production Design: Bo Welch
MPAA rating: PG-13
Running time: 115 minutes

REVIEWS

Burr, Ty. *Boston Globe.* May 5, 2011.
Ebert, Roger. *Chicago Sun-Times.* July 29, 2011.
Edelstein, David. *New York Magazine.* May 9, 2011.
Hiltbrand, David. *Philadelphia Inquirer.* May 5, 2011.
Hynes, Eric. *Village Voice.* May 4, 2011.
Kuipers, Richard. *Variety.* April 26, 2011.
O'Sullivan, Michael. *Washington Post.* May 5, 2011.
Phipps, Keith. *AV Club.* May 5, 2011.
Savloc, Marc. *Austin Chronicle.* May 5, 2011.
Scott, A.O. *New York Times.* May 5, 2011.

QUOTES

Thor: "This mortal form grows weak. I require sustenance!"

In 2005, Matthew Vaughn was attached to direct this film, describing it as "the birth of a hero, interweaving *Gladiator* with Norse mythology."

THE THREE MUSKETEERS

Every legend has a new beginning.
—Movie tagline

Box Office: $20.4 million

There have been so many screen adaptations of *The Three Musketeers,* the literary warhorse from Alexandre Dumas, over the years that one might wonder why Paul W.S. Anderson, the filmmaker who has inspired much scorn over the years as the man behind such things as *Event Horizon* (1997), *Soldier* (1998), *Alien Vs. Predator* (2004) and wife Milla Jovovich, would want to go where so many others have ventured. As it turns out, his desire to put the legendary swashbucklers through their paces once again was borne less out of having a fresh and inspired notion of revitalizing the property as out of a desire to capitalize on the worldwide success of *Sherlock Holmes* (2009) by taking another venerable property and goosing it with overblown special effects, martial arts mayhem and a storyline that bears only the vaguest resemblance to the original material. The end result is a film that is, aside from a couple of high points, a relentlessly mediocre effort that is certainly not the worst *Three Musketeers* movie ever made but it is nowhere close to being the best either.

As the film opens, the titular trio—Athos (Matthew Macfadyen), Aramis (Luke Evans) and Porthos (Ray Stevenson)—along with ass-kicking eye candy Milady de Winter (Jovovich) carry out a daring raid to steal the plans devised by Leonardo Da Vinci himself for a flying warship in the name of France. Alas, Milady betrays them by turning the plans over to the oily Duke of Buckingham (Orlando Bloom in a performance so demically overstated that even his hairdo chews the scenery at certain points) and leaving them in disgrace. A year later, still stewing in the juices of their shame, they encounter D'Artagnan (Logan Lerman), a brash country lad who yearns to be a musketeer himself. After the four of them soundly defeat a large number of guards belonging to Cardinal Richelieu (Christoph Waltz), the chief advisor of the youthful King Louis XIII (Freddie Fox) and a man with ambitions of ruling France himself, they are once again in the favor of the court, much to the consternation of Richelieu and the delight of Queen Anne (Juno Temple) and lady-in-waiting Constance (Gabriella Wilde). Nevertheless, Richelieu embarks on a plan to seize the throne that involves Milady stealing a necklace from the Queen and planting it on Buckingham in order to create a scandal that will plunge France and England into war and push him into power once and for all. When the musketeers get wind of the plan, they bravely set off to England in an effort to retrieve the necklace, restore the honor of the Queen and prevent war via equal parts swashbuckling, derring-do and giant limps adorned with huge guns and *slightly* anachronistic flamethrowers.

To give *The Three Musketeers* a little bit of due, it does get a couple of things right. Although the version of Milady depicted here may seem closer to the standard action babe roles that she has essayed in the likes of *The Fifth Element* (1997) or the *Resident Evil* (2002-2012) franchise that Anderson has been the guiding hand behind, Milla Jovovich is such a funny and sexy blast in the part that few are likely to complain as she goes about her duties of kissing and jumping and drinking and humping (to steal a phrase from *My Favorite Year* [1982], another film featuring a travesty of the Musketeers, though a more deliberate one in that particular case) with loads of enthusiasm and panache. Likewise, Christoph Waltz is amusingly hammy as Richelieu, and while his turn here will not have anyone forgetting his star-making one in *Inglourious Basterds* (2009), he sleazes up the proceedings in such a cheerfully loathsome manner that he is practically his own twirling moustache. When Jovovich and Waltz are on the screen, things liven up considerably but when they are away from the action, their absence leaves a void that the film is unable to fill. They make such an impact, in fact, that it is strange that Anderson and screenwriter Andrew Davies did not simply choose to create a version of the story told entirely from the perspective of the villains, especially Milady, since those are the only characters in which they seem to have any interest.

Unfortunately, they are absent too often, especially in the concluding reels, and when they are gone, what is left packs all the punch of a cardboard sword left out in the rain. Part of this is because the ostensible heroes are pretty much worthless—the elder musketeers are total stiffs and, in the form of the repellent Lerman, D'Artagnan is a loathsome little twerp. Part of it is because the promised spectacle turns out to be pretty much anything but spectacular. Anderson utilizes the same quick-cut approach to the fight scenes that he deployed on the *Resident Evil* films and while that may work in regards to zombie killing, it is much less effective in regards to sword-fighting, the kind of thing that works because of intricate choreography instead of Avid-related hysteria. As for the elaborate special effects, they are fairly underwhelming as well thanks to their occasionally chintzy-looking nature and a singular lack of

verve on the part of Anderson. The notion of giant flying warships battling over the skies of Paris may sound promising in theory but is executed in such an unimaginative manner that many viewers will find their attention drifting away from the proceedings in order to wonder in frustration what such an idea might have been like in the hands of someone like Terry Gilliam or a fantasist on his level.

As insubstantial as the candy bar that it shares a name with (though nowhere near as nutritious), *The Three Musketeers* is nonsense from start to finish and not even the aforementioned contributions from Jovovich and Waltz can quite manage to save it from utter disposability. It is so negligible, in fact, that it is too innocuous to really get worked up over. For most contemporary audiences, it will come and go without a thought, but for those who still cherish the Dumas original, take heart—this is a property that has survived treatment at the hands of people as varied as the Ritz Brothers, Gene Kelly, Oliver Reed, Charlie Sheen and Peter Hyams and it will survive this incarnation as well, and, like the characters themselves, will no doubt return one day stronger and grander than ever.

Peter Sobczynski

CREDITS

D'Artagnan: Logan Lerman
Athos: Matthew MacFadyen
Porthos: Ray Stevenson
Aramis: Luke Evans
Cardinal Richelieu: Christoph Waltz
Milady De Winter: Milla Jovovich
Duke of Buckingham: Orlando Bloom
Queen Anne: Juno Temple
Cagliostro: Til Schweiger
Rochefort: Mads Mikkelsen
Origin: USA
Language: English
Released: 2011
Production: Paul W.S. Anderson, Jeremy Bolt, Robert Kulzer; Constantin Film, Impact Pictures; released by Summit Entertainment
Directed by: Paul W.S. Anderson
Written by: Andrew Davies, Alex Litvak
Cinematography by: Glen MacPherson
Music by: Paul Haslinger
Sound: Stefan Busch
Editing: Alexander Berner
Art Direction: Nigel Churcher
Costumes: Pierre-Yves Gayraud
Production Design: Paul Denham Austerberry

MPAA rating: PG-13
Running time: 110 minutes

REVIEWS

Gibron, Bill. *Filmcritic.com.* October 20, 2011.

Holden, Stephen. *New York Times.* October 21, 2011.

Kenigsberg, Ben. *Time Out New York.* October 18, 2011.

Orndorf, Brian. *BrianOrndorf.com.* October 20, 2011.

Phillips, Michael. *Chicago Tribune.* October 20, 2011.

Phipps, Keith. *AV Club.* October 21, 2011.

Snider, Eric D. *Film.com.* October 21, 2011.

Tallerico, Brian. *HollywoodChicago.com.* October 21, 2011.

Weinberg, Scott. *Twitch.* October 21, 2011.

Wilmington, Michael. *Chicago Reader.* October 20, 2011.

QUOTES

D'Artagnan: "Enjoying the show?"

Constance: "Are you always this cocky?"

D'Artagnan: "Only on Tuesdays and whenever beautiful women are involved."

Constance: "So, you think I'm beautiful?"

D'Artagnan: "Actually, it's Tuesday."

TRIVIA

The substitute for Versailles in the movie is a German palace in Bavaria.

TINKER TAILOR SOLDIER SPY

How do you find an enemy who is hidden right before your eyes?
　—Movie tagline

The secret is out.
　—Movie tagline

Trust no one. Suspect everyone.
　—Movie tagline

The enemy is within.
　—Movie tagline

At the height of the Cold War, only a master spy could be trusted to expose one of their own.
　—Movie tagline

Box Office: $22.8 million

Adapting John Le Carre's dense 400-page book, one that had already been adapted into a legendary five-hour mini-series starring Alec Guinness, into a coherent drama with a reasonable running time seemed almost impossible when it was announced that husband and wife writing team Bridget O'Connor and Peter Straughan

would tackle the high-caliber project (O'Connor would pass away from cancer before seeing the success of her film and even earned a posthumous Oscar® nomination for her stellar work here). Given the pedigree of the source material and the beloved reputation of the mini-series (at least in the U.K.), it made sense that A-list actors would jump at the opportunity, especially if given the chance to play the timeless George Smiley, a man brought back into the spy game just when he is most needed. Smiley is an amazing character in spy fiction history, one who would anchor future Le Carre books and the kind of part that actors kill to get. Luckily for the cinematic world, the great Gary Oldman was chosen for the role and it proved to be a stroke of casting genius, even earning the living legend his first Oscar® nomination. With stellar production values and one of the best ensembles of the year, this version of *Tinker Tailor Soldier Spy* falters mostly by virtue of its incredibly abridged storytelling. There are times when the film feels too cold for its own good (especially in the first act) and other times when it feels too hurried over major plot points. However, one cannot dismiss what the filmmakers and ensemble did right here, arguably as well as anyone could have produced given the restrictions of an average cinematic running time.

Tinker Tailor Soldier Spy opens with a flurry of spy activity. One named Jim Prideaux (Mark Strong) is on a mission in Hungary, trying to find a general who wants to sell some information. It is a set-up. Prideaux is shot in the back and the men who sent him there, a leader known as Control (John Hurt) and his most supportive voice, George Smiley (Gary Oldman), are forced into retirement. A regime change at the top of British Intelligence, referred to often as "The Circus" allows some skeletons to escape the closet and it becomes clear that there is a mole in the agency, right near the top. It is clearly someone who has been there for some time and so it will take a 100% pure, trustworthy agent to find him. Smiley comes back into the fray and begins an international investigation, even learning that the betrayal at the Circus leads back to the legendary Karla, Smiley's (and British Intelligence) nemesis. As he gets deeper into his investigation, Smiley learns that Prideaux is not dead and that he may hold the key to finding the spy. Before he left, Control named the potential candidates in the pending spygate—Percy "Tinker" Alleline (Toby Jones), Bill "Tailor" Haydon (Colin Firth), Roy "Soldier" Bland (Ciaran Hinds), Toby "Poorman" Esterhase (David Dencik), and even George "Beggarman" Smiley himself.

While this may sound like more than enough plot for one spy thriller, it is merely the tip of a giant espionage iceberg in Le Carre's novel and the adaptation of it. Tom Hardy steals nearly every scene he is in as

Ricki Tarr (Tom Hardy), a key piece of the mole puzzle. Benedict Cumberbatch is front and center during the tensest scene in the film as he tries to infiltrate British Intelligence and leave with something he is not supposed to have. Russians, missing spies, and more clutter a very-crowded screenplay that often relies on exposition to the fault of any potential development of character. And all of this activity is couched in a story of the changing face of espionage in the '70s. As wiretapping and more technology took actual spies out of the spy game (making them watchers and listeners more than active participants), things changed, an element of this story that is perhaps the most interesting part of Alfredson's take on the material here.

And yet, like every part of Le Carre's vision, it feels barely tapped by this version. Director Tomas Alfredson (*Let the Right One In* [2009]) has made a film that does not just require a lot of concentration on the part of the viewer, it nearly requires them to connect thematic dots and not purely plot ones. While there is something to be said for delivering complex stories to appreciative adults, there is no denying that the density of this story sometimes gets in the way of what it is trying to deliver. However, there is no such criticism to be levied at the cast. Cumberbatch and Hardy excel in the ensemble, but the film belongs to Mr. Oldman, an actor who finally gets to turn down the volume from years of larger-than-life characters and play one whose monologue is almost entirely internal. While this film may not be a home run, his performance absolutely is one and it makes a viewer long for its success, critically and commercially, just in the hope that Oldman gets to play George Smiley again.

Brian Tallerico

CREDITS

George Smiley: Gary Oldman
Bill Haydon: Colin Firth
Roy Bland: Ciaran Hinds
Ricki Tarr: Tom Hardy
Jim Prideaux: Mark Strong
Peter Guillam: Benedict Cumberbatch
Percy Alleline: Toby Jones
Control: John Hurt
Oliver Lacon: Simon McBurney
Jerry Westerby: Stephen Graham
Ann Smiley: Katrina Vasilieva
Toby Esterhase: David Dencik
Connie Sachs: Kathy Burke
Origin: United Kingdom
Language: English

Released: 2011
Production: Tim Bevan, Eric Fellner, Robin Slovo; Focus Features Intl., Working Title, Karla Films, Paradis Film, Kilowelt Filmproduktion; released by Universal Pictures
Directed by: Tomas Alfredson
Written by: Bridget O'Connor, Peter Straughan
Cinematography by: Hoyte Van Hoytema
Music by: Alberto Iglesias
Sound: John Casali
Music Supervisor: Nick Angel
Editing: Dino Jonsater
Art Direction: Pilar Foy
Costumes: Jacqueline Durran
Production Design: Maria Djurkovic
MPAA rating: R
Running time: 127 minutes

REVIEWS

Corliss, Richard. *Time.* November 29, 2011.
Dargis, Manohla. *New York Times.* December 8, 2011.
Ebert, Roger. *Chicago Sun-Times.* December 14, 2011.
Edelstein, David. *New York Magazine.* December 12, 2011.
Gleiberman, Owen. *Entertainment Weekly.* December 7, 2011.
Phipps, Keith. *AV Club.* December 7, 2011.
Schenker, Andrew. *Slant Magazine.* December 3, 2011.
Stevens, Dana. *Slate.* December 8, 2011.
Turan, Kenneth. *Los Angeles Times.* December 8, 2011.
Zacharek, Stephanie. *Movieline.* December 8, 2011.

QUOTES

Roy Bland: "For twenty-five years we've been the only thing standing between Moscow and the Third World War!"

TRIVIA

Michael Fassbender was originally cast as Ricki Tarr, but had to back out because he was filming *X-Men: First Class* and the part fell to Tom Hardy.

AWARDS

British Acad. 2011: Adapt. Screenplay, Outstanding British Film
Nomination:
Oscars 2011: Actor (Oldman), Adapt. Screenplay, Orig. Score
British Acad. 2011: Actor (Oldman), Costume Des., Director (Alfredson), Film, Film Editing, Sound, Orig. Score, Prod. Des., Cinematog.

TOWER HEIST

It's not just a robbery. It's payback.
—Movie tagline

Ordinary guys. An extraordinary robbery.
  —Movie tagline

Box Office: $78 million

In many ways, Brett Ratner is the antithesis of the modern music video director turned feature filmmaker. Michael Bay and McG have splashed their rapid-fire editing onto the big screen favoring broad humor and flashy pyrotechnics to tell stories to those with attention deficit disorder. More critically-accepted auteurs like David Fincher, Spike Jonze and Michel Gondry have incorporated their visual styles into fanciful and riveting narratives, but never lost sight that the extended medium required a different sensibility and the basic skills inherit in a Freshman film school class. In the middle of these two extremes is Ratner, a director who has found a way to bridge from both a muted concoction of space-filling nothingness. His films sort of contain a story with actors but he has never shown the ability to tell that story. A lot appears to be happening but the editing never stresses the urgency of any of it. Ratner does not aggressively offend in the manner that Bay does, because one has to pay attention to notice when he is actually offending. And who wants to really pay attention to a Brett Ratner film? And how can one, really?

In the latest of Ratner's "how-did-he-get-THAT-cast" movies, Ben Stiller stars as Josh Kovacs, the staff manager at an upscale New York high-rise. He has security and all the patron's needs down to an inexact science that his co-workers have not all fully grasped. Charlie (Casey Affleck), worried about his sister's impending pregnancy, is late a lot. New elevator operator Enrique Dev'Reaux (Michael Pena) is being pushed on Kovacs by his own boss, Mr. Simon (Judd Hirsch). Maid Odessa (Gabourey Sidibe) is having green card issues, another is studying for the bar on the side, and no one seems to know that Code Black means a robbery-in-progress. The most stress-free relationship Josh seems to incur on a daily basis is that with penthouse owner, Arthur Shaw (Alan Alda), whom he even plays chess with on his off-hours. Little does Kovacs know that a Code Black has been going on for years under his watch.

Shaw is accused of a Ponzi scheme that has also lost the entire pension fund of the tower staff; a lapse in judgment by Kovacs who tried to triple their portfolio through his assumed friend. When the 29-year veteran doorman tries to kill himself on the verge of a retirement he may never see now, Kovacs is outraged and gets fired—along with Charlie & Enrique —for vandalizing Shaw's prized Steve McQueen automobile. Inspired by a thought from lead FBI agent on the case, Claire Denham (Tea Leoni), to "storm the castle," Josh enlists help from neighborhood criminal—and former daycare playmate—Slide (Eddie Murphy) to organize a scheme

to find the missing $20 million that Shaw has hid from the authorities. He even wrangles in the disgraced members of his staff as well as Mr. Fitzhugh (Matthew Broderick)—a recently evicted tenant from the tower who was also once a hotshot Wall Street trader —for a daring Thanksgiving day heist.

The heist film has a long and storied history in cinema from classics like John Huston's *The Asphalt Jungle* (1950) and Jules Dassin's *Rififi* (1955) to entertaining trifles such as *Ocean's Eleven* (1960), *The Italian Job* (1969), and their subsequent remakes. Little has changed through time as they normally involve a group of men — with diversity in skills if not always ethnicity—who gather to rip off the more privileged. Though *Tower Heist* was initially conceived as a counterbalanced all-black heist film, Ratner eventually had to work with a cast representative of the very class structure that has taken a beating throughout his career. Racial and sexual stereotypes are a standard in Ratner's brand of comedy. Where Steven Soderbergh did manage to mix up his crew's background—and slyly satirized elements of it—Ratner has changed the tower's staff into a racially diverse mix that is not nearly as elite as Stiller's Josh would make them out to be. Two-thirds of them seem to either not do their job well or do their job at all. Plus, during a key security breach they are all either preoccupied by Playboy magazine or running out in numbers to look at a Snoopy balloon.

Stripped bare of its economics, the heist film left is a scattered collection of half-baked ideas and double-crosses that constantly loses focus due to its illogical construction. Forget for a moment that the FBI has failed to do a scorched earth search of Shaw's penthouse for the missing money or even a safe. Disregard why Mr. Simon would hire back Charlie for a position which he is clearly unqualified—after campaigning for his firing for much of the first act —for no other reason than the plot requires his presence for a robbery he is not keen on participating in. Never mind that Odessa the maid has laced a piece of cake designed to neutralize a guard and when she no longer needs it, eats the cake herself to absolutely no effect later on. None of it as is important though as suspending one's disbelief that a ragtag group of hotel service workers and a petty thief can pull off what they are ultimately forced into doing. As their somewhat-OK laid plans come up empty they must find an impromptu beat-the-clock method of dangling a ton-plus of solid gold, sometimes with their bare hands, from one floor to another while not being spotted by anyone below at the Macys Thanksgiving parade all looking for something to put up on YouTube.

Tower Heist is a lot more fun when trying to connect Ben Stiller to his cast mates from *Flirting With Disaster* (1996) and *The Cable Guy* (1996) then letting

Casey Affleck's appearance remind viewers of how slick and professional Soderbergh's Ocean's trilogy seem by comparison. Those films (the first written by *Tower Heist* co-scribe Ted Griffin) had a lot of fun in establishing their outlandish plots while still keeping the audience in the dark enough to surprise them. Stiller may have the George Clooney role here, but he plays it well-too-straight for someone dealing with a group of amateur incompetents. When Ratner is finished, there is a film and he has made it, but the end result is inconsistent in both tone and the entertainment value one should absolutely expect within the bare minimum of a very average idea. Failing within the boundaries of such minor accomplishments is what makes Ratner more contemptible than even the worst of his contemporaries.

Erik Childress

CREDITS

Josh Kovacs: Ben Stiller
Slide: Eddie Murphy
Arthur Shaw: Alan Alda
Chase Fitzhugh: Matthew Broderick
Special Agent Claire Denham: Tea Leoni
Odessa Montero: Gabourney "Gabby" Sidibe
Charlie: Casey Affleck
Enrique Dev'Reaux: Michael Pena
Mr. Simon: Judd Hirsch
Lester: Stephen Henderson
Origin: USA
Language: English
Released: 2011
Production: Brian Grazer, Eddie Murphy; Universal Pictures, Imagine Entertainment, Relativity Media, Rat Entertainment; released by Universal Pictures
Directed by: Brett Ratner
Written by: Ted Griffin, Jeff Nathanson
Cinematography by: Dante Spinotti
Music by: Christophe Beck
Sound: Warren Shaw
Editing: Mark Helfrich
Art Direction: Nicholas Lundy
Costumes: Sarah Edwards
Production Design: Kristi Zea
MPAA rating: PG-13
Running time: 104 minutes

REVIEWS

Bayer, Jeff. *Scorecard Review.* November 14, 2011.
Hornaday, Ann. *Washington Post.* November 4, 2011.
Howell, Peter. *Toronto Star.* November 4, 2011.
Levy, Shawn. *Oregonian.* November 3, 2011.
McGranaghan, Mike. *Aisle Seat.* November 4, 2011.
McWeeny, Drew. *Hitfix.* November 3, 2011.
Scott, A.O.. *New York Times.* November 3, 2011.
Snider, Eric D.. *Film.com.* November 4, 2011.
Tobias, Scott. *NPR.* November 4, 2011.
Vaux, Rob. *Mania.com.* November 4, 2011.

QUOTES

Mr. Fitzhugh: "Shouldn't we be avoiding law enforcement? I never saw an episode of *Matlock* where the criminal banged Matlock!"

TRIVIA

Robert Redford was offered the role of Arthur Shaw, but turned it down.

TRANSFORMERS: DARK OF THE MOON

Mankind's finest achievement. Our nation's proudest moment. A secret hidden for forty years.
—Movie tagline

Earth goes dark.
—Movie tagline

The invasion we always feared. An enemy we never expected.
—Movie tagline

Box Office: $352.4 million

There is a point where almost any moviegoer gags on excess. Michael Bay has been pushing the envelope on that point for fifteen years managing to make one absolutely spectacular film (*The Rock* [1996]), spectacularly bad but watchable films (*Armageddon* [1998], *Pearl Harbor* [2001], and spectacularly offensive films (*Bad Boys II* [2003], *Transformers: Revenge of the Fallen* [2009]). Even the "spectacular" Michael Bay fails to bring life to this bloated cinematic mélange. *Transformers Dark Side of the Moon* plays like a badly-written overlong miniseries aired in one sitting at too high a volume.

Initially, the story takes viewers back to the battle that almost destroyed Cybertron, as a ship called The Ark, piloted by Autobot leader Sentinel Prime (voiced by Leonard Nimoy) is hit by enemy missiles attempting to escape. The Ark's crash landing on the moon is detected by NASA which investigates the wreckage during Apollo 11. Jumping forward to the present day, the Autobots, led by Optimus Prime (voiced by Peter

Cullen), discover a fuel cell from The Ark and a dangerous piece of Autobot technology while investigating strange goings-on at the now abandoned Chernobyl nuclear plant. Fending off a surprise attack from the Decepticon Shockwave (voiced by Frank Welker), the Autobots return home, demanding to know why information about their planet was withheld from them all these years. Secretary of Defense Charlotte Mearing (Frances McDormand) explains that humans only recently became aware of the artifact (though they did travel to the moon specifically to comb thru the crash). Unsure of who they can now trust, the Autobots led by Optimus set out to investigate, discovering the almost dead Sentinel Prime and a number of mysterious tech pillars that when activated will create a gateway for a Decepticon invasion.

The story finally shifts to the protagonist of the first two films, Sam Witwicky (Shia LeBeouf), who has found his life stalled after his last adventure with the Autobots. Taken out of the loop by the government, and unable to find a good job, he even fears his new ultra-hot girlfriend Carly (Rosie Huntington-Whiteley) will leave him, especially when he meets her high-powered, condescending hunk of a boss, multi-millionaire Dylan Gould (Patrick Dempsey). But when a job interview with eccentric CEO Bruce Bezos (John Malkovich) results in an attempt on his life by the Decepticon agent Laserbeak (Keith Szarabajka), he storms the Autobot home base demanding answers.

From here, the plot just gets more convoluted and mind-numbing. Far too many characters (robot and human), and a plethora of double-crosses and ancient secrets are brought together via a disjointed series of action set pieces that, while occasionally breathtaking, are more often than not simply obnoxiously hyper and impossible to follow. At best, it can be said that, at two-and-a-half hours, the film is simply boring, but in IMAX 3D it is grotesque and lumbering. This is a film to hold as an example of what is wrong with the ecology of the big American action movie, which is, typically, machined into narrative nonexistence until viewers have no other role than to buy tickets and leave the theater with no memory of what they saw. Thus they are prepped for the sequel. Essentially what Bay has done is to strip mine his own filmmaking process. In one sense, of course, he is smart. It is far easier to make a bad movie that seems fun to watch and is completely forgettable than one that offers a compelling mix of storytelling craft as well as slam-bang action and special effects. Directors need not shoot for the moon every time they make a tentpole film. But Bay shoots at the moon, destroying it and everything else in the frame. In the process, he also sears even the most jaded movie goer's ability to follow the story or even individual scenes with

sturm und drang, turning in one action sequence after another until there is no possibility that any one set piece will stand out. The resulting cacophony is, without hyperbole, one of the most unpleasant sensations a film has induced in recent memory.

To comment here on the cast seems almost superfluous. Shia LaBeouf is charming in a rough-cut way but severely limited by a role that that demands constant histrionics. Hopefully, he stops making movies like this before they wipe his promising skill set. The main problem is that the character of Witwicky does not grow, develop, or change in any way. He has grown tougher since the first film, but not believably or likably so. There is no sense of the righteous cause in his actions, only the stopwatch rhythm of beats demanded by the screenplay. He is the protagonist but his behavior is so completely antagonistic viewers should be aching to see him shut up rather than get a great job or hang on to his super hot girl. The rest of the cast is simply there, trying to make something out of roles that could have come off the back of carded action figures. For a film with far too many human characters these come off wholly robotic, essentially because of the way they are written, or to put it better, not written.

The first film in this franchise, *Transformers* (2007) offered viewers the chance to open a mental toy box and remember the first time they played with the toys on which it was based. The second film, *Transformers Revenge of the Fallen* (2009) squandered the good will of that favor by introducing elements of profound misogyny and racism into a movie that was promoted using children's coloring book giveaways at the theater in preview screenings. This movie makes up for a lack of offensive subject matter with a dumbness so pervasive that any further commentary would give the people responsible for its creation possible credit for attempting to do anything but sell tickets, toys, and prep the way for another entry in the series.

Dave Canfield

CREDITS

Sam Witwicky: Shia LaBeouf
Major William Lennox: Josh Duhamel
Robert Epps: Tyrese Gibson
Ron Witwicky: Kevin Dunn
Marissa Faireborn: Frances McDormand
Dylan: Patrick Dempsey
Dutch: Alan Tudyk
Simmons: John Turturro
Julie Witwicky: Julie White
Carly: Rosie Huntington-Whiteley

Jerry Wang: Ken Jeong
Bruce Brazos: John Malkovich
Megatron: Hugo Weaving (Voice)
Optimus Prime: Peter Cullen (Voice)
Silverbolt: James Avery (Voice)
Soundwave: Frank Welker (Voice)
Ratchet: Robert Foxworth (Voice)
Sideswipe: James Remar (Voice)
Dino: Francesco Quinn (Voice)
Sentinel Prime: Leonard Nimoy (Voice)
Origin: USA
Language: English
Released: 2011
Production: Ian Bryce, Tom DeSanto, Lorenzo di Bonaventura, Don Murphy; DreamWorks SKG, Paramount Pictures, Hasbro, Inc., di Bonaventura Pictures; released by Paramount Pictures
Directed by: Michael Bay
Written by: Ehren Kruger
Cinematography by: Amir M. Mokri
Music by: Steve Jablonsky
Sound: Peter J. Devlin
Editing: Roger Barton, William Goldenberg, Joel Negron
Art Direction: Richard Johnson
Costumes: Deborah L. Scott
Production Design: Nigel Phelps
MPAA rating: PG-13
Running time: 157 minutes

REVIEWS

Beiffuss, John. *Commercial Appeal.* July 1, 2011.
Corliss, Richard. *Time Magazine* June 30, 2011.
Ebert, Roger. *Chicago Sun-Times.* June 28, 2011.
Germain, David. *Ascoiated Press.* June 28, 2011.
Kenny, Glenn. *MSN Movies.* June 28, 2011.
Martain, Tim. *The Mercury.* July 7, 2011.
Puig, Claudia. *USA Today.* June 28, 2011.
Rainer, Peter. *Christian Science Monitor.* June 29, 2011.
Thomas, Rob. *Capital Times* July 29, 2011.
Weitzman, Elizabeth. *New York Daily News* June 28, 2011.

QUOTES

Sentinel Prime: "How doomed you are, Autobots. You simply fail to understand, that the needs of the many outweigh the needs of the few."

TRIVIA

Michael Bay reused a car crash scene from his earlier film *The Island* after an extra was seriously injured while shooting the scene for this film.

AWARDS

Nomination:
Oscars 2011: Sound, Sound FX Editing, Visual FX

Golden Raspberries 2011: Worst Ensemble Cast, Worst Picture, Worst Support. Actor (Dempsey, Jeong), Worst Support. Actress (Huntington-Whiteley), Worst Director (Bay), Worst Screenplay, Worst Screen Couple (LaBeouf and Huntington-Whiteley)
Screen Actors Guild 2011: Stunt Ensemble.

THE TREE OF LIFE

Box Office: $13.3 million

When the word "epic" is used in reference to a movie these days, it is usually meant to describe a film filled to the brim with insane action sequences, over-the-top special effects or star-studded casts gadding about in exchange for hefty paychecks. Although *The Tree of Life,* the latest effort from acclaimed filmmaker Terrence Malick, only the fifth in a career spanning almost forty years, contains a couple of big-name stars and one extended special effects sequence destined to be talked for years to come, it is essentially an epic of ideas and ambition of a scale rarely seen in the annals of American film. Instead of a straightforward narrative with easily deciphered themes aimed at the broadest audience possible, the film is a haunting and often mystifying cinematic tone poem dealing with the biggest and most basic questions about life and death on a canvas that stretches from the beginning of the universe to mid-1950's Texas and beyond in ways that are both personal and abstract in equal measure.

Disregarding conventional narrative structure right from the start, *The Tree of Life* offers up an impressionistic series of images that sets up the basic underlying philosophical principle—that every facet of life is the subject of a never-ending battle between the harsh and cruel way of nature and the loving and forgiving way of grace—and offers a few brief looks at the life of central character Jack O'Brien from his days as a young boy growing up in a small Texas town in the mid-1950's (Hunter McCracken) and in contemporary times (Sean Penn) where he is a successful Houston architect still haunted by those long-ago days, particularly by the tragic death of one of his two younger brothers. This goes on for approximately the entire first reel and at this point, Malick goes for broke with an extended sequence that takes viewers back to chronicle nothing less than the dawn of time itself in a series of extraordinary images (for which Malick enlisted the aid of special effects legend Douglas Trumbull as visual consultant) ranging from a nebula expanding in deepest space and cells multiplying to primordial ooze to the brief appearances of a couple of dinosaurs. Although one could theoretically debate its usefulness in regards to the rest of the story, it is as stunning and rapturously beautiful a stretch of pure filmmaking as has ever been presented on the silver screen.

From the infinite, the film settles back into the comparatively mundane, if no less confusing and potentially volatile, existence of the ten-year-old Jack, his younger brothers R.L. (Laramie Eppler) and Steve (Tye Sheridan), and his otherwise unnamed father (Brad Pitt) and mother (Jessica Chastain). It soon becomes clear that Jack's parents are meant to represent the aforementioned struggle between nature and grace for his very existence—his dad, a would-be musician who instead settled for a life as an engineer and whose only outlet for his former artistic dreams come via playing the organ in church, is a stern taskmaster who loves his children but who is nevertheless strict and unyielding with them because of his belief that doing so will properly prepare them for life in the real world while his mother strives to demonstrate that the world can also be filled with beauty and peace for those willing and able to open themselves up to it. As time passes by, Jack and his brothers play and goof around in the neighborhood and begin to get their first intimations of sex (via a piece of lingerie stolen from a neighbor's house), race (a visit to a barbecue shack that offers up virtually to only glimpse of African-Americans in the entire film) and death, both small (a thoughtless bit of childish cruelty involving a frog and some spare fireworks) and large (a death at a local pool that harshly reveals that the seemingly all-knowing and all-perfect adults are, in the end, just ordinary people in the end). Eventually, a sort of battle of wills begins to develop between Jack and his father—although he most likely doesn't quite realize it at that point, Jack is clearly afraid that he will one day grow up to be like his father at his worst moments. Ironically, there are times in which Jack's father seems to have the exact same fear but lacks the ability to change behavior that has been ingrained in him since he himself was a child.

Malick himself grew up in Texas in the mid-1950s and also had a younger brother who died at an early age but even if you went into *The Tree of Life* without knowing those details, you would still get the sense that he was working with material this time around that he connected with on a far more personal level than in the past. While his earlier films have all used the eternal conflict of nature vs. grace as their jumping-off points, this is the first time that Malick has deployed them in the service of a story that didn't also have a solid foundation based either in history or literature that also served as a sort of distancing element to boot. As a result, there is a sense of absolute authenticity to this story that is so palpable throughout that even those who weren't raised at the same time under the same circumstances will nevertheless find themselves taken back to similar mo-

ments from their own childhoods, a time when ordinary play could suddenly develop into moments of pure joy or terror depending on the circumstances and when a family dinner could erupt into frightening chaos on the basis of a single word or gesture.

That said, this is not simply another tale of a poor innocent child being raised by a cruel and heartless father and an angelic mother along the lines of *The Great Santini*(1980) and its ilk. Malick is too smart for that and instead provides us with characters that are a little more complex than that and are a little more relatable as a result. Some of the early reviews of the film suggested that the father was little more than an abusive brute but that is not the case. Yes, there are moments when he flies off the handle in a terrifying manner towards both his children and his wife and yes, there are times when his approach to parenting has an unnecessarily harsh edge, such as when he teaches Jack to punch him in the face or simply asks him "Do you love your father?"—the proper answer, of course, being "Yes, sir!" At the same time, it is clear that he does love his wife and children and deep down regrets some of his actions—at one key moment, he even confesses his flaws by admitting "I dishonored it all and didn't notice the glory." For his part, Jack grows to recognize his father not as a god or as a monster but as an ordinary person with ordinary foibles and when he hears his father's aforementioned admission, his response is one that is surprisingly empathic without relying on cheap sentiment or an unlikely burst of forgiveness to move things along. As for the mother, she is largely presented as an ethereal and saint-like creature devoted to balancing out her husband's harshness with unlimited peace, love and devotion (an extended idyll between her and her children while Father is away on business is painted in such blissful terms that it could almost be subtitled *Days of Heaven*) but at the same time, there is the sense that she sticks with her husband even through his dark moments because he is able to provide the necessary sense of discipline that she is constitutionally unable to provide herself.

When the films of Terrence Malick are written about or discussed, they are usually done so from the perspective that he is the ultimate star of them and with the possible exception of his stellar debut *Badlands* (1973) they are rarely examined from an acting perspective. This is a shame because over the course of his five films, Malick has demonstrated an unusually keen method of working with actors and that is certainly the case here. Brad Pitt deploys his often-underrated acting chops here in an alternately touching and frightening performance that is one of the very best things that he has ever done—instead of given us just another variation of the stern taskmaster cliché, he manages to humanize the character in ways that make his actions both scary and strangely understandable given his circumstances. As the mother, newcomer Jessica Chastain faces the challenge of working with a part that seems to have less on-screen dialogue than any lead female role in a major film this side of *The Piano*(1993) but she too manages to create an indelible impression that should help supercharge her blossoming career. However, the true star of the film is Hunter McCracken as the young Jack and in a role that is far more complex and nuanced than the type usually given to child actors and it is the highest compliment that whenever he is on the screen, which is more often than not, there is never the sense of "acting" per se—he instead comes across just as a normal kid, the kind familiar to the viewer's childhood as well. As the older version of Jack, Sean Penn is barely in the finished film and if he ultimately does not make the same kind of impact as his fellow cast mates, he does offer a brief and effective sketch of a man who is paradoxically torn between his conflicting childhood memories and his realization that he can never go back to those seemingly simple times again.

When *The Tree of Life* finally premiered after years of rumors and mysterious release delays (it was originally due to come out in 2009), critical response was sharply divided between those who praised it to the skies and those who dismissed it as another pretentious wank from an overrated director whose already tenuous ability to tell a straightforward story had completely atrophied from disuse. And yet, if there is any movie of late that deserves to be called an instant masterpiece, it is this one, an audacious and powerful work that is aesthetically gorgeous, thematically fascinating and emotionally devastating in equal measure and which not only lives up to the intense expectations that it has generated during its long gestation period, it manages to exceed them. Like Stanley Kubrick's *2001: A Space Odyssey* (1968), one of the very few movies that it begins to compare to in terms its ambition, scope and complete refusal to play by the rules of conventional cinema, *The Tree of Life* is a film that is destined to be analyzed, admired and argued over for as long as people are still around to do such things and long after today's box-office behemoths have long since been forgotten.

Peter Sobczynski

CREDITS

Mr. O'Brien: Brad Pitt
Jack O'Brien: Sean Penn
Mrs. O'Brien: Jessica Chastain
Uncle Ray: Jackson Hurst
Grandmother: Fiona Shaw

Jack's Wife: Joanna Going
Origin: USA
Language: English
Released: 2011
Production: Dede Gardner, Sarah Green, Grant Hill, Brad Pitt, Bill Pohlad; Brace Cove Productions; released by Fox Searchlight
Directed by: Terrence Malick
Written by: Terrence Malick
Cinematography by: Emmanuel Lubezki
Music by: Alexandre Desplat
Editing: Hank Corwin, Jay Rabinowitz, Daniel Rezende, Billy Weber, Mark Yoshikawa
Sound: Erik Aadahl, Craig Berkey
Costumes: Jacqueline West
Production Design: Jack Fisk
MPAA rating: PG-13
Running time: 138 minutes

REVIEWS

Chang, Justin. *Variety*. May 16, 2011.
Childress, Erik. *EFilmcritic.com*. June 3, 2011.
Dujsik, Mark. *Mark Reviews Movies*. June 2, 2011.
Ebert, Roger. *Chicago Sun-Times*. May 18, 2011.
Phillips, Michael. *Chicago Tribune*. June 2, 2011.
Reed, Rex. *New York Observer*. May 25, 2011.
Scott, A.O. *New York Times*. May 26, 2011.
Tallerico, Brian. *HollywoodChicago.com*. May 27, 2011.
Tobias, Scott. *AV Club*. May 26, 2011.
White, Armond. *New York Press*. May 24, 2011.

QUOTES

Mrs. O'Brien: "The nuns taught us there were two ways through life—the way of nature and the way of grace. You have to choose which one you'll follow."

TRIVIA

Heath Ledger was originally supposed to play the role that Brad Pitt eventually took over.

AWARDS

Nomination:

Oscars 2011: Cinematog., Director (Malick), Film.

TRESPASS

When terror is at your door, you can run, or you can fight.
—Movie tagline

Home invasion films take on a special resonance these days that makes them even more compelling than they were during, say, the Cold War when Marlon Brando and company took over the town in *The Wild Ones* (1962), or James Caan terrorized Olivia de Havilland in her home in *Lady in a Cage* (1964). Even Sam Peckinpah's *Straw Dogs* (1971), which devastated audiences at the time, pales before today's home invasion cinema which is colored by a near constant flow of true crime reporting on TVs, phones, and computers. Films as diverse as Michael Haneke's *Funny Games* (1997/2007) , the horror thriller *The Strangers* (2008), and straight-up thriller *Panic Room* (2002) offer powerhouse thrills, social commentary and expertly carried off cinematic suspense. So when talents like Joel Schumacher, Nicole Kidman and Nicolas Cage get together, viewers should at least expect to be interested in their efforts in this creatively fruitful sub-genre. Instead, the resulting film is a paint-by-numbers, watered-down suspense film.

Nicolas Cage plays independent diamond broker Kyle Miller, who is introduced pulling into the driveway of his luxurious mansion. All is not as it seems. In fact, nothing is ever what it seems for more than five minutes in this absurdly-plotted storyline. Miller's family is dysfunctional. Viewers will know this because when refused permission to go to a party by Mrs. Miller (Nicole Kidman) their daughter Avery (Liana Liberato) locks herself in her room only to later sneak out of the house to meet her ride on the road. A potentially boring scene consisting of a spoiled dinner and subsequent argument is interrupted when the house is invaded by a masked gang.

The gang is brutal, and, although they seem professional at first, things start to unravel quickly. It becomes pointless to hide their identities and a battle of wills ensues between captors and captives over opening a safe in the home that the thieves believe contains a large amount of uncut diamonds. Soon, gang leader Elias (Ben Mendelsohn) is arguing with menacing second-in-command Ty (Dash Mihok) while his younger brother Jonah (Cam Gigandet) and his junkie girlfriend Petal (Jordana Spiro) fall prey to their own demons.

This is the point in the film where it becomes very difficult to talk about *Trespass* without spoiling its limited entertainment value. But it is safe to say that writer Karl Gajdusek, whose only other screenwriting credit is the 2004 TV series *Dead Like Me,* is guilty of ham-fistedness in the first degree. Twists and turns abound but many of them are so implausible that they lack any power at all. The twists and turns are hardly the only problem. This is a screenplay full of dialogue clunkers and dumb ideas. The combination to a safe supposedly full of diamonds is…wait for it…"diamonds." The junkie girlfriend starts the heist off by wandering up the stairs in a haze where she starts watching the family's home movies and trying on dresses, oh, and shooting up in the middle of the job. The list of implausible plot points is almost as long as there are scenes in the film.

Director Joel Schumacher copes with the bad source material by splashing a vibrant palette and maintaining an energetic camera style but he fails to generate the same sort of energy that worked so well for *Phone Booth* (2002). *Trespass* feels simultaneously tired and hyperactive, not unlike another failed Schumacher thriller, *The Number 23* (2007). This is mostly because, while the screenplay is over-the-top, key performances are even less restrained. Cage is adrift yet again in yet another cardboard cartoony characterization. His worst moments here bring to mind the sort of hysteria that helped ruin *The Wicker Man* (2006), which is a shame since he recently turned in great work in *Kick Ass* (2009) and *The Bad Lieutenant: Port of Call - New Orleans* (2010).

Nicole Kidman is serviceable in the thankless role of wife Sarah, who has secrets that are almost completely revealed in one glance in one scene even though the movie spends nearly forever stretching out the revelation. But viewers will only feel sorry for the talented Jordana Spiro who gives Cage a run for the money in the crazy eyes department. The role of Petal is abysmal, calling on the actress to display a near constant paranoia that would be unsustainable for almost any actor. Spiro tries gamely but ultimately fails. Of the leads only Ben Mendelsohn (*Animal Kingdom* [2010]) manages to wring any pathos out his role as the gang leader caught between his junkie girlfriend and the men who have betrayed him. Liana Liberato (*Trust* [2011]) remains an actress to watch but not here. While the character of Avery does give her the chance to wax tough and rebellious it feels like type and for an actress on the verge of serious attention for her role as an abused teen in *Trust* this feels like a misstep.

Trespass may seem like a minor cinematic violation. But given the talent involved it is a wonder how lifeless and lethargic it is, in spite of so many pointed guns, explosions, threats and recriminations. It could be a perfect reflection of how bored viewers are in a world where almost any home invasion story pulled from the headlines (of section B) would be more memorable or interesting than this.

Dave Canfield

CREDITS

Kyle Miller: Nicolas Cage
Sarah Miller: Nicole Kidman
Jonah: Cam Gigandet

Avery Miller: Liana Liberato
Jake: Nico Tortorella
Elias: Ben Mendelsohn
Petal: Jordana Spiro
Ty: Dash Mihok
Kendra: Emily Meade
Origin: USA
Language: English
Released: 2011
Production: Millennium Films, Nu Image Films; released by Millennium Films
Directed by: Joel Schumacher
Written by: Karl Gajdusek
Cinematography by: Andrzej Bartkowiak
Music by: David Buckley
Sound: Jay Meagher
Editing: Bill Pankow
Art Direction: William Budge
Costumes: Judianna Makovsky
Production Design: Nathan Amondson
MPAA rating: R
Running time: 91 minutes

REVIEWS

Anderson, Melissa. *Village Voice*. October 11, 2011.
Berkshire, Geoff. *Metromix.com*. October 13, 2011.
Ebert, Roger. *Chicago Sun-Times*. October 13, 2011.
Holden, Stephen. *New York Times*. October 13, 2011.
Howell, Peter. *Toronto Star*. October 6, 2011.
Johnston, Trevor. *Time Out*. November 8, 2011.
Rosen, Neil. *NY1-TV*. October 13, 2011.
Simon, Brent. *Shared Darkness*. November 1, 2011.
Weinberg, Scott. *Twitch*. October 14, 2011.
White, Dave. *Movies.com*. October 14, 2011.

QUOTES

Kyle Miller: "I don't understand why we can't continue construction."

TRIVIA

Is currently the holder of the fastest-ever-from-theaters-to-Home-Video record with just eighteen days.

AWARDS

Nomination:
Golden Raspberries 2011: Worst Actor (Cage).

THE TRIP

Eat, drink and try not to kill each other.
—Movie tagline

Box Office: $2 million

Michael Winterbottom's *The Trip* is the definition of a film in which the parts are greater than the whole. However those parts, like the amazing meals consumed in the film by its two leads, are so delicious that it makes the whole worthy of consumption.

The inspiration for *The Trip* is Winterbottoms's delirious 2005 adaptation of *Tristram Shandy*. In that film, real-world comedians Steve Coogan and Rob Brydon played themselves playing characters in a film adaptation of Laurence Sterne's classic meta-novel. Films within films are very risky business but Winterbottom pulled it off, making one of that year's best and funniest films. *Shandy*'s most hilarious moments came from Coogan and Brydon's improvised dressing room sparing (Brydon, worried that his teeth are too yellow, hypothesizes as to the precise shade of yellow they are: "Barley meadow? Tuscan sunset?" "Pub ceiling," Coogan dryly responds) and intensely competitive impressions of famous actors, perhaps most memorably their dueling Al Pacino's from the credit sequence ("That's Columbo!" Brydon retorts dismissively as Coogan finishes his best Pacino impression). Coogan and Brydon's hilarious, improvised interactions were the best part of a very funny film and in *The Trip* Winterbottom, Coogan, and Brydon reunite with the intent of making those parts into a full length feature film of their own.

This time the excuse for Coogan and Brydon to get together and riff comedically off one another is not the filming of a movie but rather Coogan being invited to do a restaurant tour of The Lakeside District and Yorkshire Dales. His girlfriend cancels at the last minute and, scrambling, Coogan reluctantly invites third tier, fifth choice friend Rob Brydon to accompany him. As in *Shandy,* the comic actors play fictitious versions of themselves. Coogan (in what can only be hope is a very fictitious version of himself) is a bitter, self-centered, self-pitying, womanizing, commitment-phobic, moderately-successful comic actor who longs for prestige projects that will validate his deep artistic merits to the world. Brydon is his exact opposite: a cheerful, small fry comic who adores his wife and baby, has no aspirations to artistic greatness, and is content to be a low-brow comedian making his living off of ring tones based on a silly and ridiculously popular catch-phrase character he has created. With this odd couple dynamic established, the two travel from restaurant to restaurant, enjoying exquisite looking meals (the viewer is well advised to eat before watching the film, particularly if he or she is partial to scallops which are filmed to near pornographic dimensions by Winterbottom) while merrily and mercilessly sniping at one another and engaging in dueling impressions of a huge cast of famous actors.

The only drag on the fun is an unwise dramatic subplot chronicling Coogan's self-pitying graspings for artistic and sexual fulfillment that takes hold when Brydon and Coogan are away from the dinner table. Coogan's subplot is unfortunate because the dramatic aspect of *The Trip* simply does not work. *The Trip* is a 107-minute American theatrical release chopped down from a 6-part, three-hour BBC television series and it is hard to say whether the failure of the film's dramatic aspirations derives from that truncation or if it was present in the whole series. Whatever the reason, the viewer is never made to care about Coogan's wallowing in self pity because his fame is not based on sufficiently prestigious artistic achievements and the time the film devotes to his empty one-night stands with incongruously beautiful women and self pitying phone calls to his long suffering girlfriend, agents and son are a boring grind. Whenever the Coogan subplot kicks in, the viewer just wishes Coogan were back at the table sparring with Brydon. (Ironically, it seems likely that the only reason Coogan's dramatic subplot exists at all is to convince the real-world Coogan, as with his prestige seeking self in the film, to agree to do the film in the first place). Winterbottom would have been better off scrapping the dramatic aspect of the film and just making a straight up documentary of Coogan and Brydon eating amazing meals and doing their hysterically funny impressions. As it stands, *The Trip* feels like a hilarious documentary with an unconvincing dramatic subplot tacked on.

Fortunately for the viewer, most of what made it into the 107-minute feature is the hysterically funny improvisation, not the failed drama. Imagine *My Dinner With Andre* (1981) if the two diners were both stand up comedians at the top of their game. Their gut-bustingly funny impressions include Woody Allen, Al Pacino, Anthony Hopkins, Richard Burton, Ian McKellen, Tom Jones, Hugh Grant, Dustin Hoffman, Billy Connelly, Roger Moore, and Sean Connery among others. Their impressions are hilarious not only because they are spot on but also because they reflect a not so passive-aggressive competition between the two comics: "Let me finish" warns an annoyed Brydon at least three times during a 90-second Michael Caine impression that Coogan tries repeatedly to interrupt with his own, and in his own mind vastly superior, Caine impression. Fortunately for the viewer Coogan accedes to Brydon's request and the resulting Caine impressions produced by the duo are the funniest part of the film, producing rich, deep belly laughter even after a half dozen viewings. When they engage in a back and forth James Bond villain impression consisting of the single line, "Come, come, Mr. Bond, you derive as much pleasure from killing as I do," they repeat the phrase to one another so many times that it becomes a work of performance art. The film's

humor extends beyond their excellent impressions as well, featuring a hilarious improvised *Braveheart*-style period epic, a mock funeral for Brydon conducted by Coogan ("Would you go to my funeral?" asks Brydon. "Of course I would," replies Coogan, "If only to pad out the numbers") and an inspiring collaborative rendition of ABBA's "The Winner Takes It All" to name just a few.

The Trip does not really work as a conventional film and is at its best when it does not try to be one and instead simply allows its two immensely talented and funny leads to hang out and improvise. Winterbottom, Brydon and Coogan have succeeded in making one of the funniest movies of the year.

Nate Vercauteren

CREDITS

Steve: Steve Coogan
Rob: Rob Brydon
Emma: Claire Keelan
Mischa: Margo Stilley
Sally: Rebecca Johnson
Magda: Dolya Gavanski
Origin: United Kingdom
Language: English
Released: 2010
Production: Andrew Eaton, Melissa Parmenter; British Broadcasting Corporation (BBC), Revolution Films; released by IFC Films
Directed by: Michael Winterbottom
Cinematography by: Ben Smithard
Sound: Joakim Sundstrom
Costumes: Celia Yau
MPAA rating: Unrated
Running time: 107 minutes

REVIEWS

Anderson, John. *Variety*. June 6, 2011.
Burr, Ty. *Boston Globe*. June 16, 2011.
Dargis, Manohla. *New York Times*. June 9, 2011.
Ebert, Roger. *Chicago Sun-Times*. July 16, 2011.
Hoberman, J. *Village Voice*. June 7, 2011.
Hornaday, Ann. *Washington Post*. June 23, 2011.
Jones, Kimberly. *Austin Chronicle*. July 14, 2011.
Murray, Noel. *AV Club*. June 10, 2011.
Rea, Steven. *Philadelphia Inquirer*. June 16, 2011.
Smith, Kyle. *New York Post*. June 10, 2011.

QUOTES

Steve: "Death is but a moment...cowardice is a lifetime of affliction."

TROLLHUNTER
(The Trol Hunter)
(Trolljegeren)

You'll believe it when you see it!
—Movie tagline

Found footage meets Scandinavian folklore meets dark comedy in this wildly entertaining genre piece, an impressive achievement that works especially well for anyone who has ever enjoyed the work of Ray Harryhausen. André Øvredal only has one other feature to his credit, *Future Murder* (2000), which, like *Trollhunter,* credits him as co-writer. Here he is writing with Håvard S. Johansen who is listed as a story contributor as well as a creature concept designer on the film. Both should be mighty proud of their work here. Minor flaws hardly distract from this minor gem.

A trio of Norwegian students—Thomas (Glenn Erland Tosterud), Johanna (Johanna Mørck), and Kalle (Tomas Alf Larsen)—think they have found a perfect subject for their documentary on bear poaching when they hear about a suspicious character who roams the woods at night named Hans (Otto Jesperson). But after tracking him to the site of his disheveled, stinking trailer they find him completely unwilling to participate in their project, even threatening. To make matters even more complicated the students are assured by local hunters at the site of an illegally bagged bear that the animal was in fact killed somewhere else and dumped at that spot, despite the objections of Finn Haugen (Hans Morten Hansen), head of the Norwegian Wildlife Board, who insists that the hunters are wrong. With nowhere else to go for a story they turn back to Hans, deciding to secretly follow him on one of his late night sorties. While creeping silently through the woods with their equipment, they hear horrendous noises and suddenly encounter a terrified Hans who races up to them yelling "Troll!" In the ensuing melee, Thomas is attacked and bitten by something and the group narrowly escapes in Han's Land Rover, discovering their own vehicle squashed flat and missing all its tires. Hans relents. He will allow the group to film his activities. Still skeptical about the existence of trolls, the students are nonetheless ecstatic and agree to do everything Hans says for the chance to discover what is really going on.

Trollhunter is engaging on every level, often hilariously poking fun at everything from government conspiracies and bureaucracy, to religion, and even the idea of making a found footage movie that tracks imaginary animals. It is no small accomplishment for a film to inspire laughter, awe, childlike wonder and not a little fright. This is an impeccably mounted piece of cinema, though it does tell, perhaps, too simple a story

for a feature. Visually it offers breathtaking scenery, taking viewers on a virtual travelogue of Norway as a winter wasteland; a deep forest; rural farmland. Action sequences too, are exceedingly well staged if a bit harried at times. And the found footage element of the film is used to every possible advantage, particularly in establishing tension.

The special effects here are truly outstanding, often offering a near-complete, very eerie photorealism. The trolls themselves are initially reminiscent of the Muppets, large galloomping creatures that would be almost cute if they were not so lethal. Viewers see several types each with their own names, habitats, and habits. Some have multiple heads, others are roly-poly creatures living under bridges, and some are impossibly huge. But one thing that all trolls, whether Tosserlad, Ringlefinch Mountain Kings, or Jotnars have in common, is the sanction placed on them to stay within the boundaries established by the TSS (Troll Security Service).

The film does an extraordinary job bringing the pseudoscience of troll hunting to life filling in viewer's mental blanks with one ingenious bit of business after another that explains what trolls really are, how they are kept in check by the TSS system, and what must be done to successfully control and if necessary kill them. Troll hunting is not as exciting as it sounds. Underpaid, living completely under the radar, Hans has completely dedicated his life to his profession despite having to deal with pin-headed bureaucrats, no health plan and deplorable working conditions. Otto Jespersen plays Hans with straight-faced world weariness and nails the part completely. As the students stand by in awe and childlike wonder and terror, he sets about the tasks at hand with a stolid, crankiness eventually warming up to the idea of the documentary as a way out of his oppressive responsibilities.

One of the major themes of *Trollhunter* is governmental incompetence and the lengths that governments will go in hiding malfeasance and secret keeping. At first Hans Morten Hansen plays government official Finn Haugen as just another official twit, petty and intent on order for its own sake. But as the film progresses, and especially by its end, viewers get a stark reminder that such men, no matter how ridiculous they seem, often run the show from behind. *Trollhunter* could have developed its theme of conspiracy more fully but somehow the sight of a 200-foot Jotnar roaring at a little hunter becomes positively Lovecraftian no matter who wins that particular battle, a metaphor for man confronting and pretending to control something vastly bigger and ultimately untamable. Perhaps most frightening is the undefined role of Hans himself. His role in the conspiracy and the exposing of it seems blurred at best. What he is truly vested in, if anything, remains hidden like the trolls themselves. In a larger-than-life monster movie he may be the ultimate symbol of the monstrous—a good man doing too little too late to keep evil at bay.

Dave Canfield

CREDITS

Thomas: Glenn Erland Tosterud
Johanna: Johanna Morch
Kalle: Tomas Alf Larsen
Hans: Otto Jerpersen
Finn: Hans Morten Mansen
Origin: Norway
Language: Norwegian
Released: 2011
Production: Sveinung Golimo, John M. Jacobsen; Filmkameratene; released by Magnet Releasing
Directed by: Andre Ovredal
Written by: Andre Ovredal
Cinematography by: Hallvard Braein
Sound: Baard H. Ingebretsen
Music Supervisor: Henrik Hawor
Editing: Per-Erik Eriksen
Costumes: Stina Lunde
Production Design: Martin Gant
MPAA rating: PG-13
Running time: 103 minutes

REVIEWS

Abele, Robert. *Los Angeles Times.* June 24, 2011.
Clifford, Laura. *Reeling Reviews.* April 28, 2011.
Covert, Collin. *Minneapolis Star Tribune.* June 30, 2011.
Debruge, Peter. *Village Voice.* June 7, 2011.
Ebert, Roger. *Chicago Sun-Times.* June 23, 2011.
Hale, Mike *New York Times.* June 9, 2011.
Hartlaub, Peter. *San Francisco Chronicle.* June 16, 2011.
Newman, Kim. *Empire Magazine.* September 5, 2011.
O'Hehir, Andrew. *Salon.com.* June 12, 2011.
Savlov, Marc. *Austin Chronicle.* June 17, 2011.

QUOTES

Thomas: "Do you think Michael Moore gave up after the first try?"

TRIVIA

Summit Entertainment bought the rights to an American remake before this version was even released.

TRUST

What took her family years to build, a stranger stole in an instant.
—Movie tagline

Big screen dramas involving the impacts of poor teen decision-making and naiveté—even, or maybe especially those attempting to capitalize on faddish trends and emergent technology—so rarely offer up a complete portrait of how teenagers actually fit, at once comfortably and awkwardly, within a broader family system. If not depicted in breezy shorthand, they typically either condescend, making a hearty play for more adult filmgoers, or they unfold in worlds entirely absent of parents and guardians or ones in which no teenager wants or needs any form of adult guidance or advice—none of which is really true.

Trust is a rare and pleasant exception. Well, pleasant on the inside, when one reflects on its range and smarts, because its narrative shell—in which an unwanted sexual contact foisted upon a young teenage girl is but the first domino in a painful series of interfamilial reverberations—is rather grim and disagreeable. The sophomore feature film directorial effort from former sitcom star David Schwimmer, *Trust* never received a fair shake in theaters, suffering from a release by indie distributor Millennium Entertainment that never expanded beyond twenty-eight screens. Consensus critical reaction was more positive, however, and young star Liana Liberato was honored with the Best Actress Award at the 2010 Chicago International Film Festival.

Trust centers on Annie Cameron (Liberato), a sweet-natured and naïve fourteen-year-old suburban girl, and the middle child of a loving family headed by white-collar parents Will and Lynn (Clive Owen and Catherine Keener). Weeks of chatting in an online volleyball forum with an out-of-town boy she thinks is seventeen years old leads to an in-person meeting where Annie discovers Charlie (Chris Henry Coffey) is actually considerably older than he represented. She is coerced into a sexual liaison, which has ruinous consequences for her and her family. As cop Doug Tate (Jason Clarke) pours over transcripts of sexually lurid IM chats and tries to track down Charlie, Will and Lynn struggle both to find the appropriate care for their daughter and deal with their own anger and guilt over "letting it happen."

Trust bears certain thematic similarities to movies like *Hard Candy* (2006), *Downloading Nancy* (2009) and even *Rabbit Hole* (2010), which is more literally about a set of parents' grief at the loss of their child. Here, Will and Lynn mourn the loss of their daughter's innocence—both the idealized version they had in their minds, and the one spoiled by the very real physical violation that has occurred. In telling the events from both perspectives and giving full credence to each character's conflicting feelings, the movie provides an achingly honest portrait of how families share (and cope with) pain, loss, and harm, regardless of the initially impacted party.

Benefitting the material most directly is the fact that Schwimmer knows of what he oversees, having been charitably involved with and on the Board of Directors of the Rape Foundation in Santa Monica, California, for over ten years. There, he experienced firsthand the stories of those victimized by online predators, as well as, quite memorably, one father who had a lot of trouble coping with feelings of rage and vengeance, Schwimmer related in an April interview with *H Magazine.* Years later, Schwimmer work-shopped *Trust*'s script with Andy Bellin, one of the movie's writers (Robert Festinger being the other), and also co-authored a same-named stage version of the story that debuted in Chicago in 2010. There are a few notable exclusions, but this layered attention to detail, and the time spent ruminating on the topic and how it impacts families moving forward, shows throughout the movie, in ways both big and small.

Because it trades more in shades of grey and its conclusions and catharsis are not so pat, *Trust* is not always smooth in the way in which some scenes abut and fit together. But it is trying to kick up dirt from a sandbox that most films (and certainly no Hollywood-style treatment of the same subject matter) would dare focus as much time on: Annie's deep identification with her abuser, and her lashing out at her parents and the friend that reported the incident. As the movie progresses, her mood darkens and, owing in large part to the overwhelming nature of the physical experience and the psychological bonding it elicits, she refuses in treatment to characterize what has happened to her as rape. Her parents just do not understand. The nature of these scenes with psychologist Gail Friedman (Viola Davis) is honest about the sort of breakthroughs that occur in therapy, and take on the heartbreaking quality of a slow-dawning re-traumatization that is every bit as queasy as the actual rape sequence.

The easiest (and least imaginative) criticism to levy against the film is that it treads "after-school special" territory, and is just another cautionary tale about all the harm that can befall kids in the Big Bad World. That ill-considered line of attack ignores, however, the movie's social relevance with respect to its inclusion of new (and psychologically intense) modes of communication that parents cannot always effectively oversee. And it discounts, too, the skill and quality with which *Trust* is rendered.

If the metaphorical parallels of Will's work in advertising—in which his company oversees a sexually suggestive, American Apparel-type campaign with models who look awfully young—are a bit overdrawn, it is thought-provoking to see the movie confront rape bias, as when a work colleague (Noah Emmerich) ham-fistedly expresses relief to Will over the fact that Annie knew her attacker. The implication, of course, is that this gross and willful manipulation is somehow less real or traumatizing than other types of rape—a sentiment perhaps understandable on a certain level, but one that raises some difficult and uncomfortable questions for an audience and the broader culture at large, particularly men.

Mostly, though, *Trust* is populated with real, three-dimensional characters, and it captures the manner in which adolescent judgment is reasonably fallible. The film is also heartrending in its depiction of the gulf between the female teenage victim of such an assault and especially her father. More than just about anything else, males like to feel utility, and the particular emasculation and patriarchal helplessness on display in *Trust* is both rare in modern American cinema, and strikingly devastating.

To that end, it goes almost without saying that the performances here are uniformly superb. Owen summons a tremendous amount of pathos and swallowed rage as Will; he seems to literally age and crack long prior to any cathartic breakdown. As a woman striving to keep her family together, Keener movingly has no use for or deeper understanding of her husband's dangerously growing blood-thirst. Davis, meanwhile, is a perfectly modulated and sympathetic sounding board as Annie's therapist, leading her to conclusions slowly but not foisting them upon her fragile patient.

Trust is ultimately about its youngest star. Liberato gives an extraordinarily affecting and yet still natural performance, the type of which few actresses of her age would be capable. *Trust* marks her as a young actress to watch, and will appropriately be the calling card that lands her many more films.

Brent Simon

CREDITS
Will Cameron: Clive Owen
Lynn Cameron: Catherine Keener
Annie Cameron: Liana Liberato
Gail Friedman: Viola Davis
Charlie: Chris Henry Coffey
Doug Tate: Jason Clarke
Al Hart: Noah Emmerich
Peter Cameron: Spencer Curnutt
Origin: USA
Language: English
Released: 2010
Production: Ed Cathell III, Dana Golomb, Robert Greenhut, Tom Hodges, Avi Lerner; Millennium Films, Nu Image Films, Dark Harbor Stories; released by Millennium Entertainment

Directed by: David Schwimmer
Written by: Andy Bellin, Rob Festinger
Cinematography by: Andrzej Sekula
Music by: Nathan Larson
Sound: David Obermeyer
Editing: Douglas Crise
Art Direction: Kerry Sanders
Costumes: Ellen Lutter
Production Design: Michael Shaw
MPAA rating: R
Running time: 106 minutes

REVIEWS

Catsoulis, Jeannette. *New York Times*. March 31, 2011.
Chang, Justin. *Variety*. March 28, 2011.
Ebert, Roger. *Chicago Sun-Times*. March 31, 2011.
Levy, Shawn. *Oregonian*. May 5, 2011.
Neumaier, Joe. *New York Daily News*. April 1, 2011.
Phillips, Michael. *Chicago Tribune*. March 31, 2011.
Pinkerton, Nick. *Village Voice*. March 29, 2011.
Smith, Kyle. *New York Post*. April 1, 2011.
Schwarzbaum, Lisa. *Entertainment Weekly*. April 6, 2011.
Tallerico, Brian. *HollywoodChicago.com*. October 13, 2010.

QUOTES

Gail Friedman: "People get hurt. There's only so much we can do to protect ourselves, our children. The only thing we can do is be there for each other when we do fall down to pick each other up."

TUCKER & DALE VS. EVIL

Evil just messed with the wrong hillbillies.
—Movie tagline

The perfect love story…with a high body count…
—Movie tagline

Horror/comedy is a tough tightrope of a genre that has produced at least five creative failures (*Fido* [2006], *Severance* [2006], etc.) for every international hit (*Shaun of the Dead* [2004], the movies that made Sam Raimi a genre icon, etc.). A film that can be surprisingly added to the latter group is Eli Craig's smart, fun, twisted feature film debut, a movie that takes a common archetype of the horror genre and turns it on its overdone head. With the stellar comic timing of Alan Tudyk and Tyler Labine, two spectacular TV actors (from *Firefly* and *Reaper,* respectively), finally finding a home on the big screen after years of failed efforts and supporting roles, *Tucker & Dale vs. Evil* is the kind of low-budget genre film that is guaranteed a long-term audience as word-of-mouth always spread for horror movies as clever as this one.

It is almost surprising that the redneck horror movie (*The Texas Chainsaw Massacre* [1974], *Cabin Fever* [2002], *Wrong Turn* [2003], etc.) has not been parodied before (at least not in a successful enough way that anyone noticed and, no, *Hatchet* [2006] does not count). Horror writers have long played off the common fear of the hillbilly horror—the deadly, inbred people who live in the woods just waiting for innocent, beautiful suburbanites who try to take a shortcut, visit an old family cabin, or just choose the wrong exit ramp on a freeway. *Tucker & Dale vs. Evil* works from the fear icon of men in cabins, wearing overalls, going fishing, and slicing human flesh in their free time. Of course, in the real world, said fear is totally unfounded, despite the urban legends that cloud outsider's perceptions of people like Tucker (Tudyk) and Dale (Labine), a pair of lifelong friends who just happen to be, well, hillbillies.

These sweet, normal guys have travelled to a cabin that they hope to renovate (and fail to notice the bulletin board filled with newspaper clippings of all the homicidal carnage that has befallen the area in the past). They happen to be night-fishing when they stumble upon a group of young people (including Katrina Bowden of *30 Rock* and Brandon McLaren of *The Killing*) skinny dipping as so many hapless horror heroes have done in the past. Allison (Bowden) spots the overall-wearing pair, gets startled, and falls into the water and needs to be rescued by Tucker & Dale. While the gentlemen are just rescuing the waterlogged girl in her underwear, her friends, already hopped up on the paranoia created by urban legends of redneck horrors, think that they are kidnapping their friend and are probably going to eat her and wear her skin as a costume. Of course, they are just going to make her pancakes.

When Allison's friends approach the cabin, Tucker happens to be using a chainsaw when he accidentally unleashes a swarm of bees. Swinging the deadly weapon at the insects around his head, he bears a strong resemblance to Leatherface, convincing Allison's posse even further that she has been captured by pure evil. In the ensuing chaos, one of the snobby, elitist brats ends up impaled on a branch and the gang's horror paranoia turns up another notch. What unfolds is essentially a series of freak accidents and random events in which really stupid college kids get themselves killed in the company of two understandably freaked-out rednecks. The gore is not for the faint of heart but it is all choreographed with tongue firmly in bloody cheek and, consequently, should probably be more accurately classified as a comedy than a horror film.

Craig proves to have a strong ear for clever dialogue and expertly plot and paces his piece, flavoring it all with the kind of genre expertise that only comes from someone who is not just a filmmaker but a horror fan. The result is a much smarter film than the horror/comedy genre has seen in some time. It gets a bit a repetitive in the final act, but only minorly so and Craig wisely ends his piece before it could have become overcooked. Viewers should be warned that the piece is remarkably gory, such as when a cop shows up to see the two gentlemen trying to remove the aforementioned fellow from the wood chipper. None of the gore is remotely genuine and it takes on a cumulative ridiculousness due to its extreme nature, but it could turn off some viewers.

Eli Craig deserves a lot of praise and credit for walking the tightrope that has failed so many other young filmmakers in the horror/comedy category but he won half the battle when he cast Tudyk and Labine, two actors who built up large, loyal followings due to their stellar TV work and finally found material equally smart and entertaining in feature film. Sadly, few people saw their work in *Tucker & Dale vs. Evil* (it only made $224k domestically but added another, more-impressive $4 million internationally, where the hillbilly humor probably played a little differently), but it was still one of the smartest career decisions they have ever made. Films like *Tucker & Dale* always find audiences on Blu-ray and DVD. One hopes that this finds a large-enough one to warrant a sequel.

Brian Tallerico

CREDITS

Dale: Tyler Labine
Tucker: Alan Tudyk
Allison: Katrina Bowden
Chad: Jesse Moss
Jason: Brandon Jay McClaren
Naomi: Christie Laing
Chloe: Chelan Simmons
Chuck: Travis Nelson
Sheriff: Philip Granger
Origin: Canada
Language: English
Released: 2010
Production: Albert Klychak, Rosanne Milliken, Deepak Nayar, Morgan Jurgenson; Reliance Big Pictures, Loubyloo Prods., Magnet Releasing; released by Magnolia Pictures
Directed by: Eli Craig
Written by: Eli Craig, Morgan Jurgenson
Cinematography by: David Geddes

Music by: Michael Shields
Sound: Kirby Jinnah
Music Supervisor: Natasha Duprey
Editing: Bridget Durnford
Costumes: Mary Hyde-Kerr
Production Design: John Blackie
MPAA rating: R
Running time: 89 minutes

REVIEWS

Abele, Robert. *Los Angeles Times.* September 29, 2011.
Buckwalter, Ian. *NPR.* September 30, 2011.
Burr, Ty. *Boston Globe.* September 29, 2011.
DeFore, John. *Washington Post.* September 29, 2011.
Ebert, Roger. *Chicago Sun-Times.* October 5, 2011.
Genzlinger, Neil. *New York Times.* September 29, 2011.
Goodykoontz, Bill. *Arizona Republic* September 29, 2011.
Kohn, Eric. *Indiewire.* September 28, 2011.
Sachs, Ben. *Chicago Reader.* October 6, 2011.
Smith, Adam. *Empire.* September 25, 2011.

QUOTES

Tucker: "Oh hidy ho officer, we've had a doozy of a day. There we were minding our own business, just doing chores around the house, when kids started killing themselves all over my property."

TRIVIA

A rough cut of the film was leaked which unfortunately revealed various where lines were dubbed and post-production effects were used.

THE TWILIGHT SAGA: BREAKING DAWN, PART 1

Forever is only the beginning.
    —Movie tagline

Box Office: $281.3 million

There comes a time in every franchise when a series of films become "critic-proof." If it does not happen from the outset, it usually occurs after the second or third film. Usually, after a second film (if not sooner), audiences have already made up their mind whether or not they will show up for the rest of the series. They do not have to read reviews or look at a Rotten Tomatoes "tomatometer" to see if they should buy a ticket. There is either a deep investment or general indifference or disdain from the individual. If the reviews started out bad, they will most likely continue to be bad and if the audiences show up in droves for the second installment, they will likely keep showing up. Filmmakers and studios would usually rather not rock the boat with the hardcore fanbase if it means serious profitable quarterly earnings. Reviews be damned. It is strictly business at this point.

Such is the case with the *Twilight* series. Stephanie Myers' bestselling books about teenage vampires, werewolves and their warring tribes and love for the mortal teenage Bella (Kristen Stewart) have captivated mostly young teenage girls. The surface level Goth sensibilities mixed with a strangely Mormon undercurrent has mass appeal for this age group, especially now that there are real faces to go with the characters imagined in the book. By the time the second film was released (*The Twilight Saga: New Moon* [2009]), teenage girls belonged to one of two camps: "Team Edward" or "Team Jacob," the vampire and werewolf characters (respectively) fighting for Bella's heart. This became part of the vocabulary for several pop culture duals as a measure of one's taste. In this case, it is not only a question of which character is better for Bella to end up with, but more importantly for this group, who is better looking with their shirt off?

The Twilight Saga: Breaking Dawn, Part 1 is now the fourth *Twilight* film and it takes its cue from the *Harry Potter* series in breaking up the final book into two films. At this point in the story, Bella and Edward (Robert Pattinson) are about to get married. He is a vampire, she is not. They have yet to have sex. They know that if they do, there will be serious consequences if they are not married first. Bella is eighteen and it seems to be okay with her divorced parents that she is settling down so soon. She is in love, after all. Before the wedding, Edward informs Bella about his past as a murderous vampire and all whom he killed. "They were monsters," he says. "So was I." Bella does not back out. The wedding goes on as planned even after her dream that night about her wedding ending in bloodshed with a pile of corpses at the altar.

The wedding takes up a big chunk of the film's first act and carries on like a traditional wedding. Jacob (Taylor Lautner) shows up as a show of support even though he still obviously pines for Bella. Bella and Edward head off to Rio for their honeymoon where they will eventually get into bed together for the first time. They stay at a big house owned by a friend. In the moments leading up to the big event, Bella asks Edward for some "human minutes" of alone time. After some skinny dipping in the moonlight, they do what every fan has been waiting for them to do for the past three films and/or books. When Bella wakes up the next morning, the room is in shambles and there are bruises on her body.

They spend the next several days staring lovingly at each other while justifying to each other about the big decisions they have made. All seems well until Bella starts having bouts of morning sickness. She is pregnant, but with what? There is a question as to whether or not that is even possible given the circumstances. As the baby grows quickly inside her, there are more questions about what she is pregnant with and whether or not she can survive it. It is not a healthy pregnancy as Bella's body appears more and more bruised and battered with each passing day. She has no appetite until one of the vampire friends offers her a cup of blood. She takes a sip and it does the trick. She has no appetite for anything else. Many in the vampire clan try to convince her to abort the fetus, but Bella keeps it, for better or for worse. Jacob eventually shows up to help out, convinced that Edward and Bella were doomed from the start. This is clearly uncharted territory for this vampire clan, as Edward tries to find any information he can by doing a search on Yahoo for answers (what decade is this?).

Fans of the books will likely be pleased that the film is broken up into two parts so that the wedding and everything after has time to breathe and not feel too rushed. It is material that will make its fanbase swoon while the uninitiated in the audience will be waiting for something—anything—to start happening. The few action scenes that do exist in the film are too dark and muddled for anyone to really see what is happening. The war between the vampires and the werewolves, who speak *Homeward Bound*-style through laughably over the top voiceovers, is really secondary here anyway.

The directing behind the *Twilight* series may have improved a bit with this as well as its third outing, *Eclipse* (2010), but it really is for fans only at this point. Kristen Stewart still looks pouty and Taylor Lautner still cannot so much as walk without overacting. What could have been a creepy, David Cronenberg-like horror show with a complicated pregnancy is instead a PG-13 exercise in pseudo-horror without a trace of directorial personality from Bill Condon (it is still a step up from Catherine Hardwicke's ridiculously melodramatic take with the first film). Unlike the *Harry Potter* series, the *Twilight* films will enjoy its popularity in its current pop culture climate, but they certainly will not stand the test of time.

Collin Souter

CREDITS
Bella Swan: Kristen Stewart
Edward Cullen: Robert Pattinson
Jacob Black: Taylor Lautner
Dr. Carlise Cullen: Peter Facinelli

Esme Cullen: Elizabeth Reaser
Alice Cullen: Ashley Greene
Emmett Cullen: Kellan Lutz
Rosalie Hale: Nikki Reed
Jasper Hale: Jackson Rathbone
Charlie Swan: Billy Burke
Jessica Stanley: Anna Kendrick
Jane: Dakota Fanning
Aro: Michael Sheen
Origin: USA
Language: English
Released: 2011
Production: Wyck Godfrey, Karen Rosenfelt, Stephenie Meyer; Temple Hill, Sunswept Entertainment; released by Summit Entertainment
Directed by: Bill Condon
Written by: Melissa Rosenberg
Cinematography by: Guillermo Navarro
Music by: Carter Burwell
Sound: Steve Aaron
Music Supervisor: Alexandra Patsavas
Editing: Virginia Katz
Art Direction: Lorin Flemming
Costumes: Michael Wilkinson
Production Design: Richard Sherman
MPAA rating: PG-13
Running time: 117 minutes

REVIEWS

Covert, Colin. *Minneapolis Star Tribune.* November 17, 2011.
Dargis, Manohla. *New York Times.* November 17, 2011.
Ebert, Roger. *Chicago Sun-Times.* November 17, 2011.
Edelstein, David. *New Yorker Magazine.* November 20, 2011.
Guzman, Rafer. *Newsday.* November 17, 2011.
Howell, Peter. *Toronto Star.* November 18, 2011.
Kenny, Glenn. *MSN Movies.* November 17, 2011.
Morris, Wesley. *Boston Globe.* November 17, 2011.
O'Hehir, Andrew. *Salon.com.* November 17, 2011.
Whitty, Stephen. *Newark Star-Ledger.* November 17, 2011.

QUOTES

Edward Cullen: "No measure of time with you will be long enough. But we'll start with forever."

TRIVIA

Kristen Stewart has said that Taylor Lautner was in tears after seeing an unfinished cut of the film.

AWARDS

Nomination:

Golden Raspberries 2011: Worst Ensemble Cast, Worst Picture, Worst Prequel/Remake/Rip-off/Sequel, Worst Actor (Lautner), Worst Actress (Stewart), Worst Director (Condon), Worst Screenplay, Worst Screen Couple (Stewart and Lautner or Pattinson).

TYRANNOSAUR

Paddy Considine's *Tyrannosaur* opens with a scene of a dog being kicked in the gut by an abusive drunkard. The abuser instantly feels guilty about his drunken behavior and lovingly carries the pet home, where he caresses and soothes the injured beast. He feels bad about his violent decision. And yet, the next morning, the dog is still dead. All the external comfort and regret can't stop the internal bleeding. *Tyrannosaur* is a film about men and women who are internally bleeding, trying to keep up appearances for their bar-mates, customers, or neighbors, but barely keeping it together. The debut film from the talented star of *In America* (2002) and *The Red Riding Trilogy* (2009) is a gut-wrenching piece of drama that connects in large part due to the powerful performances by stars Peter Mullan, Olivia Colman, and Eddie Marsan. It is often hard to watch, but appropriately so given the bleak nature of its subject matter.

The aforementioned dog-kicking drunk is Joseph (Mullan), a widower with little left to keep him on the righteous path. His friend is dying in a hospital bed, he just killed his dog, and he begins to take down the shed in his backyard with a sledgehammer, much to the annoyance of his equally-violent neighbors. As is often the case in tales like this one, the drunk stumbles into the life of someone who first seems like a savior but turns out to have secrets just as dark if not bleaker than the man who used to call his wife "Tyrannosaur."

Joseph meets Hannah, a wide-eyed, religious, charitable woman who first appears to be the one to pull this barfly from the alley and turn his life around. By showing him some kindness, including providing him a suit for his friend's funeral, Hannah offers a little bit of light into Joseph's very-dark world. However, it is quickly revealed that Hannah has more valid reason for misery than her new friend for she is married to an absolute scumbag named James (Marsan). Hannah's alcoholic husband comes late at night and pisses on his wife while she sleeps on the couch. He punches her. He kicks her. He rapes her. And yet Hannah somehow finds a way to believe in a higher power that allows a kind believer like her to be stuck in a nightmare beyond belief for most rational people.

Considine's script for "Tyrannosaur" draws on his own history in a working class section of England and there is an authenticity to the atmosphere of the piece that would have been lost in the hands of another filmmaker. However, the personal connection may also be one of the reasons that 'Tyrannosaur" often feels overheated and underlined when another director may have been personally removed enough from the storytelling to inject it with a little more subtlety. Considine chose some challenging material for his debut directorial effort and one wonders if, given the strength of the performances on display, the film might have had more power with a more experienced filmmaker behind the helm. The film is often visually dull when a little more personality from someone not quite as attached to the melodrama could have actually made the human saga more rewarding. As is, the piece can be somewhat monotonously bleak.

These complaints are easily dismissed when one focuses on the strength of the three performances that are the true foundation of Considine's film. As is often the case, this actor-turned-director has a gift with his peers, drawing stellar work from Mullan, Colman, and Marsan. The latter has become somewhat predictable in roles such as this one but somehow digs even deeper into his bag of tricks and finds a new level of slimy evil in the role of James, one of the most disturbing creations of the year. But the film belongs to Mullan and Colman. The former brings a nearly suicidal level of depression to his lead role almost as if Hannah did not come along at just the right moment then he would surely check himself out of the land of the living. (Although, it should be noted, that the "savior" arc of Hannah & Joseph is not over-played in the slightest as it would be in many lesser films.) Mullan has long been one of the most underrated actors in the business, a true chameleon who notches another strong entry in his resume here. However, the film belongs to Colman. She takes a part that could have so easily been nothing but cliché and archetype and makes Hannah feel completely three-dimensional. She is a woman trapped between faith and the true misery of her home life. And she refuses to take the easy road, making subtle choices instead of the obvious ones. The title of *Tyrannosaur* may not refer to her character but it is Olivia Colman who has made the most impact when the credits roll.

Brian Tallerico

CREDITS

Joseph: Peter Mullan
Olivia Colman: Olivia Colman

James: Eddie Marsan
Tommy: Ned Dennehy
Marie: Sally Carman
Samuel: Samuel Bottomley
Bod: Paul Popplewell
Kelly: Sian Breckin
Origin: United Kingdom
Language: English
Released: 2011
Production: Diarmid Scrimshaw; Warp X, Inflammable Films, Optimum Releasing; released by Strand Releasing
Directed by: Paddy Considine
Written by: Paddy Considine
Cinematography by: Erik Wilson
Music by: Chris Baldwin, Dan Baker
Sound: Chris Sheedy, Billy Quinn
Music Supervisor: John Brightwood
Editing: Pia Di Ciaula
Art Direction: Andrew Ranner, Kiera Tudway
Costumes: Lance Milligan
Production Design: Simon Rogers
MPAA rating: Unrated
Running time: 91 minutes

REVIEWS

Anderson, Melissa. *Village Voice.* November 15, 2011.
Catsoulis, Jeannette. *NPR.* November 17, 2011.
Ebert, Roger. *Chicago Sun-Times.* December 1, 2011.
Neumaier, Joe. *New York Daily News.* November 17, 2011.
Pais, Matt. *RedEye.* December 1, 2011.
Phillips, Michael. *Chicago Tribune.* December 1, 2011.
Phipps, Keith. *AV Club.* November 17, 2011.
Sachs, Ben. *Chicago Reader.* December 1, 2011.
Scott, A.O. *New York Times.* November 17, 2011.
Sharkey, Betsy. *Los Angeles Times.* November 17, 2011.

AWARDS

British Acad. 2011: Outstanding Debut by a British Writer, Director, or Producer
Nomination:
Ind. Spirit 2012: Foreign Film.

U-V

UNCLE BOONMEE WHO CAN RECALL HIS PAST LIVES

(Loong Boonmee raluek chat)

Winner of the Palme D'Or at the 2010 Cannes Film Festival, writer-director Apichatpong Weerasethakul's *Uncle Boonmee Who Can Recall His Past Lives* is as unique and elliptically mesmerizing a movie as one might see all year. It is also polarizing, and decidedly not for all tastes. To describe the movie as either a psychological drama or a playful dark comedy would be fairly absurd, and yet over the course of its nearly two-hour running time *Uncle Boonmee* flirtingly, fitfully touches on exactly those emotional keys in a manner neither haughty nor false.

The story unfolds in rural Thailand, and centers on the title character (Thanapat Saisaymar), a terminally ill farmer living in the countryside with the increased assistance of his sister-in-law, Jen (Jenjira Pongpas), and young Tong (Sakda Kaewbuadee), who is brought in to cook some meals. Ho-hum domesticity gives way to intrigue when the trio is visited during dinner one evening by a couple of spirits—Boonmee's deceased wife Huay (Natthakarn Aphaiwonk), and, later, his long-missing son Boonsong (Geerasak Kulhong), who appears in the form of a red-eyed monkey. As kidney failure slowly grinds him down, Boonmee ponders why his family members returned (and indeed, whether it was really them), and what sort of changes await him in the afterlife.

Despite its seemingly otherworldly premise, *Uncle Boonmee* actually recalls less other ghost stories than a disparate group of slow-peddled cinematic exercises in ambiguity—films like Gus Van Sant's *Gerry* (2003), Wong Kar-wai's *2046* (2004), Steven Soderbergh's *Bubble* (2006), Lee Chang-dong's *Poetry* (2011) and even the docudrama *The Story of the Weeping Camel* (2004). In varying degrees, these films each deal with idealized love or relationships, karma and the possibility of reincarnation, and the sometimes dark inevitability of human frailty in the natural world.

Another common denominator of the above movies is that they all have significant script input from their directors, and therefore bear the mark of an auteur. The same is true of Weerasethakul's film. Working with a selection of mostly non-professionals, he crafts a work with a distinct and confident personality, no matter its haziness. The performances are all naturalistic and of a piece, and the costuming and effects work as it relates to especially Boonsong is impressive in its restrained simplicity.

Like a handful of other foreign filmmakers hailing from more autocratic-leaning nations, Weerasethakul (playfully known as "Joe" by many within the industry, as acknowledgment of his lengthy, almost unpronounceable name) is something of a one-man cultural export. Both because of his affection for unconventional structure and filmmaking techniques as well as his intertwined interest in unusual subject matter and the collision of Eastern ideas and Western perceptions, Weerasethakul makes his films outside the strict confines of the Thai film studio system. This has created some difficulty (*Syndromes and a Century* [2007], for instance, was banned in his home country), but also made him something of a cause célèbre within the critical community, where his films have been roundly embraced. (*Blissfully Yours* [2002] and *Tropical Malady* [2004] each also picked up awards at their respective Cannes' premieres.) While open to further interpretation and debate, this fact as much as anything else seems to have influenced the direction of Weerasethakul's development.

Even more with *Uncle Boonmee* than any of his previous works, Weerasethakul is as interested in an extra-textual reading of his work as any strict interpretation of the narrative proper. A montage of stills in the middle of the movie provides a tip of the cap to Chris Marker's *La Jetée* (1962), as well as a short movie, *A Letter To Uncle Boonmee*, that the filmmaker made with local teenagers while scouting a location in northeastern Thailand for his feature. Throughout, there are other evocations of bygone classic cinema (before he is revealed, for instance, Boonsong recalls both the Jawas from *Star Wars* (1977) and Roger Patterson and Robert Gimlin's famous 1967 photo of an alleged Bigfoot), a seeming nod to Weerasethakul's belief of a special correlative relationship between cinema and the transmigration of souls.

This is a big part of the movie's entrancing and sometimes transporting success, and also a stumbling block. The difference between being artistic-minded and willfully abstruse is often admittedly a fuzzy and rather subjective line, and there is not a sense here that Weerasethakul is being flip or overly casual. Yet by trading so exclusively in metaphor (about the intractable truth of aging and expiring, as well as reincarnation) and open-endedness instead of more fully exploring portions of the story that would seem to provide a set up for a more straightforward study of the elemental nature of fear (and particularly fear of the unknown), *Uncle Boonmee* sometimes drags. Granted, it does so in tangentially moving, unusual and sometimes even darkly amusing ways, but it drags nonetheless, and misses a crucial opportunity to tether together the ethereal and concrete.

The film's thirty-point-plus differential between its critical and user ratings on Rotten Tomatoes is no great surprise, then. *Uncle Boonmee Who Can Recall His Past Lives* is perhaps the working definition of a foreign art film, or critics' favorite. A large slice of mainstream audiences will almost certainly be merely bored, put off by a dawdling pace that yields no huge narrative twists once the element of ghosts is introduced. Even arthouse viewers more versed in foreign language films may balk, however; finding frustration in the movie's equivocations, they might be apt to label it pseudo-intellectual pap.

As with most debates couched in extremes, the truth is somewhere in between. *Uncle Boonmee* requires an active viewer, open to the possibility of shifting perspectives and different interpretations; a passive viewer of the film will inevitably be a disappointed viewer. Weerasethakul's movie is unique and tonally assured, and involving in large part because of those qualities. At the same time, in the end, its puzzle pieces feel scattered a bit too widely and arbitrarily.

Brent Simon

CREDITS

Uncle Boonmee: Thanapat Saisaymar
Jen: Jenjira Pongpas
Huay: Natthakarn Aphaiwonk
Origin: Thailand, United Kingdom, France, Spain
Language: French, Thai
Released: 2010
Production: Keith Griffiths, Simon Field, Charles de Meaux, Apichatpong Weerasethakul; Illumination Films, Kick the Machine; released by Strand Releasing
Directed by: Apichatpong Weerasethakul
Written by: Apichatpong Weerasethakul
Cinematography by: Sayombhu Mukdeeprom, Yukontorn Mingmonghon
Sound: Akritchalerm Kalayanamitr
Editing: Lee Chatametikool
Costumes: Chatchai Chaiyon
Production Design: Akekarat Homlaor
MPAA rating: Unrated
Running time: 113 minutes

REVIEWS

Chang, Justin. *Variety*. April 29, 2011.
Ebert, Roger. *Chicago Sun-Times*. April 15, 2011.
Fine, Marshall. *Hollywood & Fine*. February 28, 2011.
Levy, Shawn. *Oregonian*. April 28, 2011.
Lewis, David. *San Francisco Chronicle*. March 2, 2011.
Morgenstern, Joe. *Wall Street Journal*. March 3, 2011.
Scott, A.O. *New York Times*. March 2, 2011.
Tookey, Christopher. *Daily Mail*. November 29, 2010.
Turan, Kenneth. *Los Angeles Times*. March 3, 2011.
White, Dave. *Movies.com*. April 4, 2011.

TRIVIA

The film was inspired by the book *A Man Who Can Recall Past Lives* by Phra Sripariyattiweti.

AWARDS

Nomination:
Ind. Spirit 2011: Foreign Film.

THE UNDEFEATED

The nature of most political documentaries is to persuade the viewer to lean one way or the other. The shelf life of such films is usually short and their effectiveness is never really quantifiable. The most extreme example thus far is Michael Moore's *Fahrenheit 9/11* (2004), a film in which President George W. Bush is made out to be the enemy of the people because of how he handled the terrorist attacks on September 11, 2001. During the election year of 2004, *Fahrenheit 9/11* became the highest grossing documentary of all time, pulling in an astounding worldwide gross of $222 million. It appeared at the time that Bush's chances for re-election were looking grim if so many people had been persuaded by Moore's thesis. As it turned out, though, the film's effectiveness only went so far and Bush won the election (albeit by a slim margin).

In 2011, documentary filmmaker Stephen K. Bannon took the opposite approach to his subject, former Alaska governor and 2008 Vice Presidential candidate Sarah Palin, a divisive political figure and one of the key factors behind the burgeoning Republican-based Tea Party Movement (those who sought to take the government back to the people as President Barack Obama was pushing for health care reform, which many Tea Party members felt was too Socialist). Rather than hold Palin up for ridicule, Bannon put her on a pedestal and, thus, his movie *The Undefeated* exists as an infomercial on why Palin should be revered and not reviled. Bannon is as much a Conservative as Moore is a Liberal, so the one-sidedness of such a film should not be surprising.

What is surprising is how little time in the film is spent trying to vilify the Left. *The Undefeated* is mostly about Palin's rise to political power. With the film rooted in a three-act structure (each act getting a title and following with several chapters within that act), Bannon's film at first tries to tell a story rather than conduct a persuasive argument. The film is also based on Palin's memoir *Going Rogue: An American Life*. Palin's voiceover is heard via her audio book recording of that memoir.

Act One, dubbed "The Servant's Heart," begins by showing us "the seed" that was planted in Palin's mind about how to make effective change in her surroundings. The film chronicles her run as Mayor of Wasilla, Alaska and how the Exxon Valdez spill in 1989 served as the catalyst (or "seed") for her involvement in politics. Along with a group of advisors (known as The Magnificent Seven), Palin won adulation from the citizens of Wasilla, who gave her the confidence to run for Governor of Alaska. During her term, she brought down the greedy Alaskan oil industry, passed legislature for a long-gestating gas line project that many Governors before her never followed through on, and, of course, she cut taxes. She had an 80% approval rating in 2008 when Republican Presidential candidate John McCain asked her to be his running mate.

One would think that this is where "Act Two" would start, but this actually comes much later in the narrative. The film's title, to many, will seem foolish since she is known for losing the 2008 election, that which brought her worldwide fame. Since then, Palin has resigned from being Governor of Alaska and has instead been hired as a Fox News Correspondent and host of her own reality show. The move gives the loss of the election a short snippet in the larger story. Bannon depicts Palin as a victim of constant ethics complaints against her, all of which she had to read and respond to, which kept her from effectively governing.

But the film's third act is more about how she helped give rise to the Tea Party movement even after her electoral loss and subsequent resignation (hence the title *The Undefeated*, a title which always draws its fair share of snickering from her opponents). Here is where the narrative derails and the persuasive argument begins. Bannon is not after the Liberals. He is smart to realize that Liberals most likely will not give this movie the time of day and even if they did, they would not be anymore convinced of Palin's importance. But Republicans will see it and that is who Bannon is after. Here, the movie spends a great deal of time condemning the GOP for not being Right-wing enough and for not standing up to the President and his administration with the same zeal and principles as the Tea Party (considered by many to be a "fringe" movement). The current GOP climate is condemned by many to be a collection of political "eunuchs." The movie warns all parties that the Tea Party is here to stay and, unlike the left-leaning Green Party, will continue to fight.

Bannon's film runs almost two full hours in length and much of it is over-edited, noisy and stylistically laughable. It is put together with wall-to-wall stock music cues that demand the viewer takes everything as seriously as possible. All of the testimonials in the film (all of whom love Palin to death) are shot against a white backdrop and sound over-rehearsed, with the exception of talk show host Mark Levin, who all but takes over the third act. Every point the movie has to make about Palin's importance and how the Hollywood elite have publicly condemned her with hate speech is made ad-nauseum. Bannon's film is edited with the attention span of a newborn puppy on Red Bull. He makes the usual cuts to old stock footage (animals fighting, mushroom clouds and, of course, lots and lots of plants in the first act) as well as unintentionally hilarious reenactments of angry mobs and corporate bullies.

Love her or hate her, there is certainly an interesting movie to be made about Sarah Palin. A documentary featuring contributions from John McCain, Barack Obama, Palin herself and other key figures from the left and the right sounds like a movie that should be made many years from now, with clear heads and an interest in telling a fuller story of a truly divisive individual. A movie about a political figure does not necessarily have to be a persuasive argument on their merit in the current political spectrum. It can be a fascinating character study. *The Undefeated* is not such a movie. It is clearly a product of its time, made solely for its time. There is nothing wrong with that either, but once the movie has made its headlines, artistically speaking there is nowhere else for it to go.

Collin Souter

CREDITS

Himself: Andrew Breitbart
Himself: Gene Therriault
Herself: Judy Patrick
Himself: Con Bunde
Herself: Jamie Radtke
Herself: Sarah Palin
Origin: USA
Language: English
Released: 2011
Production: Stephen K. Bannon, Glenn Bracken Evans, Daniel Fleuette; Victory Film Groups; released by ARC Entertainment, LLC
Directed by: Stephen K. Bannon
Written by: Stephen K. Bannon
Cinematography by: Dain Valverde
Music by: David Cerbert
Editing: Dain Valverde
MPAA rating: PG-13
Running time: 113 minutes

REVIEWS

Abele, Robert. *Los Angeles Times*. July 14, 2011.
Corliss, Richard. *TIME Magazine*. July 20, 2011.
Edelstein, Davin. *New York Magazine*. July 15, 2011.
Kohn, Eric. *INDIEwire*. July 11, 2011.
Robert Levin. *The Atlantic*. July 15, 2011.
Leydon, Joe. *Variety*. July 8, 2011.
Merlan, Anna. *Village Voice*. July 12, 2011.
McCarthy, Todd. *Hollywood Reporter*. July 11, 2011.
Sobczynski, Peter. *eFilmcritic.com*. July 23, 2011.
Wilmore, Allison. *AV Club*. July 14, 2011.

AWARDS

Nomination:
Golden Raspberries 2011: Worst Actress (Palin).

UNKNOWN

Take back your life.
—Movie tagline

Box Office: $63.7 million

Based on the novel *Out of My Head* by Didier Van Cauwelaert, *Unknown* is the latest film from director Jaume Collet-Serra (*House of Wax* [2005], *Orphan* [2009]). Whereas both his horror films offered ham-fisted thrills and chills, *Unknown* offers, in the main, lots of scenes in which the lead unravels a standard genre puzzle that goes nowhere unexpected and takes too long to get there. *Unknown* certainly fails to measure up to other lost identity films like *Memento* (2000), *The Man Who Haunted Himself* (1970) or the film that it, resembles most *The Bourne Identity* (2002), which offered tightly-focused conflicts and fascinating character development to go along with expertly-utilized genre conventions. It would be easy to simply blame the writing here as neither Oliver Butcher nor Stephen Cornwell has done anything substantial or noteworthy (the sole big-screen credit between them being Cornwell's *Killing Streets* starring Michael Pare). All in all, *Unknown* plays like a reasonably-well-made-but-forgettable made-for-TV time-waster that never registers as more than the sum of its conspiratorial parts.

Dr. Martin Harris (Liam Neeson) is in East Germany with his wife Elizabeth (January Jones) to give a presentation at a conference. After his briefcase is mislaid during a taxi ride, he travels back alone to retrieve it only to have a serious car accident. Waking up days later in the hospital, he departs despite doctors warning him that his head injury could make him susceptible to hallucinations and obsessions. Arriving back at the conference he discovers that his identity, his marriage, his entire life, has been assumed by another man (Aidan Quinn). Or has it? The movie toys greatly with the notion that he might not be who he thinks he is. Begging Gina (Diane Kruger), the driver of the taxi, to help him retrace his steps, he finds himself and everyone he reaches out to exposed to trained assassins determined to keep him from uncovering his own role in a murderous espionage plot.

Unknown is well photographed, composed, etc. Collet-Serra adopts the same largely muted color palette that has served him well before in creating moody, threatening atmosphere. But here it does nothing but remind viewers how muted this whole film is. *Unknown* is well…unknowable, refusing to reveal anything about what kind of film it really is until too late. This identity crisis takes viewers through an experience that is anything but therapeutic spreading any possible emotional investment across a variety of storytelling elements. The intercut conventions of espionage thriller, psychological suspense, and action film never combine here to form anything coherent. The film plays almost as if the director and cast suffered from the same head injury that plagued the lead character, leaving it unsure of itself and where to go next.

Liam Neeson is fine in the role of Dr. Martin Harris but any viewer will quickly become bored with the stuff the screenplay forces on him, especially since, by the end of the film, he is reduced to uttering stock one-liners in the middle of a fist fight. Neeson is one of those actors that has never been afraid of appearing in whatever came his way. The results have added up, over the years, into a strange mélange of the truly great and the near maudlin. Sadly, of late, Neeson has appeared in mainly dreadful to forgettable stuff, including *After.Life* (2009), *Clash of the Titans* (2010), and *The A-Team* (2010). January Jones, best known as Betty Draper from the AMC TV series *Mad Men,* has had an undistinguished film career. A recent boost was her portrayal of Emma Frost in *X-Men: First Class* (2011) but it has yet to be seen if she can do much more than vamp her way through eye candy roles or stock character types. The gifted Diane Kruger (*National Treasure* [2004], *Inglorious Basterds* [2009]) makes a solid enough second banana side-kick. Distinguished actors Bruno Ganz (*Wings of Desire* [1987], *Downfall* [2004], *The Baader Meinhof Complex* [2008])) and Frank Langella (*Dracula* [1979], *Frost/Nixon* [2008]), *All Good Things* [2010]) have both often been tapped in the latter part of their careers to play villains and professorial types. Here, they both add some much-needed color as a pair of veteran spies engaged in a deadly game of cat and mouse. Lastly, Aidan Quinn, is a remarkably charismatic late-hour villain, but, ultimately, one that viewers have long ago relegated to the direct-to-video file in their minds. Or, like the memory-challenged hero of this disappointing film, chosen to forget entirely.

Dave Canfield

CREDITS

Dr. Martin Harris: Liam Neeson
Elizabeth Harris: January Jones
Martin B.: Aidan Quinn
Gina: Diane Kruger
Jurgen: Bruno Ganz
Rodney Cole: Frank Langella
Origin: USA
Language: English
Released: 2011
Production: Leonard Goldberg, Andrew Rona, Joel Silver; Dark Castle Entertainment, Studio Babelsberg, Studio Canal; released by Warner Bros.
Directed by: Jaume Collet-Serra
Written by: Oliver Butcher, Stephen Cornwell
Cinematography by: Flavio Labiano
Music by: John Ottman, Alexander Rudd
Sound: Oliver Tarney

Music Supervisor: Andy Ross
Editing: Tim Alverson
Art Direction: Andreas Olshausen
Costumes: Ruth Myers
Production Design: Richard Bridgland
MPAA rating: PG-13
Running time: 109 minutes

REVIEWS

Barsanti, Chris. *PopMatters.* February 18, 2011.
Catsoulis, Jeannette. *NPR.* February 18, 2011.
Ebert, Roger. *Chicago Sun-Times.* February 17, 2011.
Hoffman, Lori. *Atlantic City Weekly.* March 3, 2011.
Johnston, Trevor. *Time Out.* March 2, 2011.
Morgenstern, Joe. *Wall Street Journal.* February 17, 2011.
Puig, Claudia. *USA Today.* February 17, 2011.
Salisbury, Mark. *Total Film.* March 2, 2011.
Snider, Eric. D. *Film.com.* February 17, 2011.
Turan, Kenneth. *Los Angeles Times.* February 17, 2011.

QUOTES

Dr. Martin Harris: "Do you know what it feels like to become insane, doctor? It's like a war between being told who you are and knowing who you are. Which do you think wins?"

TRIVIA

According to his passport, Dr. Martin Harris was born on June 7th. This also happens to be the actual birthday of actor Liam Neeson.

VANISHING ON 7th STREET

Fear lives in the dark.
—Movie tagline
Stay in the light.
—Movie tagline

Vanishing on 7th Street wants to have it both ways: purposefully assigning no meaning to its supernatural events while strongly implying that there exists great significance to them. The characters' frustration with the scenario becomes the audience's, as screenwriter Anthony Jaswinski turns his bare-bones creations into mouthpieces for preaching an assortment of theories that never stick in between the times that they scramble from light source to light source.

On the surface, director Brad Anderson creates an uneasy atmosphere with his and cinematographer Uta Briesewitz' play on light and (often) digitally-manipulated shadow. Once the story begins in earnest, though, that mood of disquiet dissipates immensely due, paradoxically, to the very inexplicable quality of the mystery upon which the initial tension depends. By refusing to clarify the nature of it central disappearances, Jaswinski eventually eliminates any sensation of harm toward the movie's characters.

During the prologue, when the screenplay's ambiguity best works in its favor, the possibility of danger lurks closely for Paul (John Leguizamo), a projectionist at a movie theater and the first of the four major players in this apocalyptic situation. The sequence that follows is easily the movie's most successful, as Paul finds himself one of only two people left in the shopping mall in which his theater is located. The rest disappear after a blackout, leaving behind only their clothing, which lies cleanly on the floor where they once stood. The payoff to the sequence, after Paul and a security guard (Arthur Cartwright) explore the rest of the mall through whispering shadows only to discover the same phenomenon of clothes without their owners, is a truly chilling moment—the movie's only one—in which Anderson achieves a lot with the simple turn of a previously indiscernible head and a screech.

Also in this opening, Jaswinski establishes the story's major historical allusion, that to the lost Roanoke Colony, the great, unsolved mystery of pre-American colonization, about which Paul is reading before the lights die out and people fade away. Paul later repeats the tale to the rest of the survivors, including the legend of the single word "Croatoan" carved upon a post of the settlement's fort. That leads to further speculation—mostly about the movie's inspiration and less about the substance of the story itself—and, ultimately, a last-minute motive for one character to undergo a transition.

That character is Luke (Hayden Christensen, who is the weak link among the otherwise satisfactory performances), a television news reporter who awakens the morning after the mass disappearance (surrounded by candles from a late-night romantic encounter, keeping him safe) to an empty Detroit filled with abandoned cars and a plane that crashes into the ground for no logical reason—especially in the movie's timeline of events. Days later, he wanders the streets at night, which, he mentions, is getting longer as daylight grows shorter, scavenging for batteries for his flashlight and attempting to find a car that still works. He happens upon a brightly-lit bar, where twelve-year-old James (Jacob Latimore) waits for his mother to return and keeps a generator in the basement running. Paul, whom Luke rescues after the projectionist reappears from the darkness, and Rosemary (Thandie Newton), a mother searching for her newborn baby, soon join Luke and James at the tavern.

Two lines of plot follow. The first is the quartet debating the reason for their state of affairs. Luke assumes it is just a random occurrence, with no cause about which he cares. Paul puts forward the story of Roanoke before comparing their current survival as "the last spin on a reel [of a movie] before it's done for good." Rosemary, a religious woman, suggests the Rapture, wondering what sin or sins they may have committed to prevent them from being taken. Jaswinski seems to sympathize with Rosemary's opinion—if not the letter then certainly the spirit. Religious elements are prevalent, if only for the characters' names, which all have a biblical foundation (i.e., Paul is converted by his experience in the dark, and the second half of Rosemary's name fits in with her maternal status). The climax, set in a church with Anderson's camera holding upon iconography, is perhaps telling.

The second thrust involves a series of flashbacks for three of the characters. They only serve to reiterate information already at hand, adding nothing to the background of the characters that they have not already stated (Paul watches a video of his co-worker girlfriend vanish, Rosemary strolls through the hospital before saving herself by lighting a cigarette, and James enjoys walking through the bar while his mother is working). Paul, meanwhile, has what is revealed to be yet another episode in the gloom (The twangy opening piano notes of "Your Real Good Thing [Is About To End]" are an eerie musical echoing of the tone of the scene), which winds up being an extended bait-and-switch gag.

Along the way, even the notion of this silhouetted world as a threat comes into doubt. Jaswinski leaves "I exist," a repeated mantra throughout the movie, hanging in the air. Even whether it is a cry of pained desperation or a simple confirmation of fact is absent. Despite its effective ambiance, *Vanishing on 7th Street* is a string of questions begging for even just one answer.

Mark Dujsik

CREDITS

Luke: Hayden Christensen
Paul: John Leguizamo
Rosemary: Thandie Newton
James: Jacob Latimore
Briana: Taylor Groothius
Origin: USA
Language: English
Released: 2010
Production: Tove Christensen, Norton Herrick, Celine Rattray; Herrick Entertainment, Mandalay Vision; released by Magnet Releasing, Magnolia Pictures

Directed by: Brad Anderson
Written by: Anthony Jaswinski
Cinematography by: Uta Briesewitz
Music by: Lucas Vidal
Sound: Anton Gold
Music Supervisor: Liz Gallacher
Editing: Jeffrey Wolf
Art Direction: Scott Anderson
Costumes: Danielle Hollowell
Production Design: Stephen Beatrice
MPAA rating: R
Running time: 90 minutes

REVIEWS

Barsanti, Chris. *Filmcritic.com.* May 17, 2011.
Cogshell, Tim. *Boxoffice Magazine.* February 18, 2011.
Honeycutt, Kirk. *Hollywood Reporter.* January 6, 2011.
Hubschman, Daniel. *Hollywood.com.* February 15, 2011.
McWeeny, Drew. *HitFix.* September 19, 2010.
Murray, Noel. *AV Club.* February 17, 2011.
Putman, Dustin. *DustinPutman.com.* January 10, 2011.
Rothkopf, Joshua. *Time Out New York.* February 15, 2011.
Schager, Nick. *Slant Magazine.* February 13, 2011.
Vaux, Rob. *Mania.* February 18, 2011.

QUOTES

Luke: "I'm here because I will myself to exist."

A VERY HAROLD & KUMAR 3D CHRISTMAS

Christmas comes prematurely.
—Movie tagline

Box Office: $35.1 million

Many film comedies seem promising on paper thanks to their casts, premises, and behind-the-scenes pedigrees, but by the time they reach the screen have failed to make it all work, let alone amuse. *A Very Harold & Kumar 3D Christmas* is the opposite—on paper there is no reason any of it should work. It is the third film in a somewhat repetitive franchise about guys who like to get high. It prides itself on plumbing the crudest depths of stupid, stoner humor. The film's lead actors remain relatively unknown beyond the series, and its jokes and narrative are intentionally random and uneven. Yet, like its originator, *Harold & Kumar Go to White Castle* (2004), and even more than its immediate predecessor, *Harold & Kumar Escape from Guantanamo Bay* (2008), *A Very Harold & Kumar 3D Christmas* is not only often

very funny but impressive in its ability to keep what should be a slight, wearisome premise going.

The first two *Harold & Kumar* films played out the hazy, chaotic misadventures of a couple of post-college guys (Kal Penn's slacker Kumar and John Cho's more career-minded Harold) thrust into ridiculously R-rated journey quests involving drugs; sex; fast food; guns; Homeland Security; more drugs; and of course Neil Patrick Harris as a red-eyed, Lothario version of "himself." As it sets out with twisted affection to skewer (and pay homage to) modern Christmas movies and TV specials, the third film, *A Very Harold & Kumar 3D Christmas,* picks up several years later with the now drifted-apart lead characters older and settled—Harold into a marriage, suburban home, and financial-industry job; Kumar into drug-hazed, couch-based inertia and bachelorhood.

Soon, Harold and Kumar are reunited and head off in search of the perfect replacement Christmas tree to appease Harold's Christmas-obsessed father-in-law (Danny Trejo). Once again, along the way, there are drug jokes, body function jokes, sex jokes, snack-food fixations (a mutual love between Kumar and a semi-sentient waffle-making robot called, appropriately, Waffle Bot), violent gun play, and of course an appearance by Neil Patrick Harris. The Fourth wall is repeatedly broken, there are numerous meta-gags involving the intentionally overused 3D effects, and there is a standard fantasy land detour, this time into a bloody Claymation drug hallucination a la TV specials like *Rudolph the Red-Nosed Reindeer.*

The franchise has always championed dark, profane anarchy in the face of authority, as series creators and writers Jon Hurwitz and Hayden Schlossberg gleefully and enthusiastically charge hard in the opposite direction of "right" and "proper." *A Very Harold & Kumar 3D Christmas*, directed by newcomer Todd Strauss-Schulson, is no exception: A toddler accidentally gets high not once but three times, and few racial, ethnic, or religious groups are left un-offended—including a Jesus-in-Heaven flashback that works overtime to get an angry rise out of Christians.

Thomas Lennon provides fine comic support as a suburban square shocked by Harold and Kumar's debauched exploits, but Neil Patrick Harris remains the best example of how these films dance the line between pop-culture reality and raunchy comedy fantasy. An all-purpose showman down to his dyed roots, here Harris blends sassy 1940s cheese with edgy 1970s sleaze as he headlines a Radio City Music Hall-type Christmas stage revue. It is to the franchise's credit that Harris is never overused—he shows up just long enough to give *A Very Harold & Kumar 3D Christmas* a giddy blast of archly ironic hedonism, then is gone with a meta-winking, "See you in the next one."

For all their low-brow humor and giddy pop-culture juggling acts, the *Harold & Kumar* films continue to succeed thanks in part to smart post-ironic commentary about the very silly jokes they're making and the social structures and casual racism they're diligently undermining. *A Very Harold & Kumar 3D Christmas* gets to wallow in dumb humor and broad clichés and claim the cheap and stupid laughs, but does so with relentless weirdness and a joyfully warped warped sincerity.

The other half of the film's winning formula is the causal mastery (or masterful casualness) Cho and Penn bring to their now-familiar roles. Like many classic comedy teams, Harold and Kumar are both innocents abroad and agents of chaos, with Cho as the straight man and Penn as the anti-authority instigator. The pair's solid chemistry, poise, and deadpan timing not only smoothes over the film's hit-and-miss jokes but their laid-back likableness keeps the film's potential ugliness from feeling off-putting or hateful.

Not everything in *A Very Harold & Kumar 3D Christmas* succeeds—for every couple giggles and guffaws there is a groaner. And while end-lessons about maturity and friendship are given lip service, they are mostly here to take the edge off the film's unrelenting lunacy. Still, *A Very Harold & Kumar 3D Christmas* harbors enough overall good cheer and awareness of its own irrelevant nature to come out well ahead of its aggressive and deliberate rudeness and stupidity.

Locke Peterseim

CREDITS

Harold Lee: John Cho
Kumar Patel: Kal Penn
Maria: Paula Garces
Vanessa Fanning: Danneel Ackles
Goldstein: David Krumholtz
Todd: Thomas Lennon
Himself: Neil Patrick Harris
Mr. Perez: Danny Trejo
Sergei Katsov: Elias Koteas
Origin: USA
Language: English
Released: 2011
Production: Greg Shapiro; New Line Cinema, Mandate Pictures, Kingsgate Films; released by Warner Bros.
Directed by: Todd Strauss-Schulson
Written by: Jon Hurwitz, Hayden Schlossberg
Cinematography by: Michael Barrett
Music by: William Ross
Sound: Scott D. Smith
Music Supervisor: John Bissell
Editing: Eric Kissack
Art Direction: Ramsey Avery
Costumes: Mary Claire Hannan
Production Design: Rusty Smith
MPAA rating: R
Running time: 90 minutes

REVIEWS

Biancolli, Amy. *San Francisco Chronicle.* November 4, 2011.
Corliss, Richard. *Time.* November 3, 2011.
Ebert, Roger. *Chicago Sun-Times.* November 2, 2011.
Genzlinger, Neil. *New York Times.* November 3, 2011.
Glieberman, Owen. *Entertainment Weekly.* November 9, 2011.
Jones, Kimberly. *Austin Chronicle.* November 11, 2011.
O'Sullivan, Michael. *Washington Post.* November 3, 2011.
Phillips, Michael. *Chicago Tribune.* November 3, 2011.
Rabin, Nathan. *AV Club.* November 3, 2011.
Rocchi, James. *Box Office Magazine.* November 3, 2011.
Stevens, Dana. *Slate.* November 6, 2011.

QUOTES

Kumar: "You have a good job, you make good money, and you don't beat your wife. What more could a Latino father-in-law ask for?"

TRIVIA

At one point, Todd calls Harold "Sulu." John Cho, who plays Harold, also played Sulu in *Star Trek* (2009).

WAR HORSE

Separated by war. Tested by battle. Bound by friendship.
—Movie tagline

Box Office: $78.8 million

In much the same way that a determinedly-pulled plow is seen slicing through a sizeable stone near the beginning of *War Horse,* director Steven Spielberg likely succeeded in piercing even the hardest of hearts by his film's end. If not, it certainly was not for lack of trying throughout this adaptation of both Michael Morpurgo's 1982 young adult novel (the story comes directly from the horse's mouth) and the much-awarded stage interpretation in which puppeteers manipulated life-sized horses made from aluminum, cane and cloth as expertly as they did the audience's emotions. Spielberg was brought to tears by this story of a boy and his horse whose bond is agonizingly stretched but never broken during their separate endurance of World War I horrors. The director found himself intrigued by the challenging prospect of making a similarly-moving, cinematically-vivid version that would remain suitable for anyone in the family from middle school age on up, adding realism with beguiling horses of flesh and blood but steering clear of combat scenes that graphically, gorily depicted the same. What results is a sweeping, arrestingly-photographed film that consistently and impressively rouses and rends the heart at the PG-13 level, unabashedly bathing viewers in sentiment. Those most inclined to use the term "old-fashioned" as a compliment or gripe "They sure don't make 'em like they used to!" were especially pleased, but they were not the only ones.

Spielberg is deftly at the controls as viewers are taken soaring above resplendently-green English countryside during *War Horse*'s opening moments, and by the time they have finally swooped down into Devon and John Williams' beautiful (if often too pushy) score has welled up, anyone who has failed to be stirred must surely be in need of a hearse. Upon that truly sublime surface, teenaged Albert Narracott (promising newcomer Jeremy Irvine) watches the birth of a foal with close-up-enhanced, mesmerized wonderment. There is no mistaking that it is love at first sight. As both the young man and colt continue to grow toward maturity, Albert tentatively, tenderly, and ultimately successfully makes the horse's acquaintance.

The two ultimately become fatefully fused when Albert's father, Ted (Peter Mullan), heedlessly buys this swift, sleek, spirited thoroughbred instead of the steady, prosaic plow horse vitally needed on the family's struggling farm, the man having allowed his auction bidding to become foolishly fueled by a bitter desire to best his heartless, threatening landlord (David Thewlis). Ted's parade of pints had not helped matters either, downed to deaden the chronic pain emanating from of a gimpy leg and his wounded pride, as well as to forget his heralded but haunting service in the Boer War. A shot shows Ted standing back and silently staring at the animal in chagrined disbelief as what he has done sinks in, but his reaction is nothing compared to the incredulity of his long-suffering but devoted wife, Rosie (Emily Watson), who is the contrastingly clear-headed voice of reason and practicality. She demands this inappropriate horse be returned, although a distraught Ted attempts to simply obliterate his mistake with a gun pointed at the animal's head. However, Albert shields the four-legged friend he now calls Joey from both criticism and attack, vowing the pair will together save the farm. The gentle, perseverant persuasiveness with which Albert goes about training Joey to plow is a sweet sight. Precious little suspense but much sympathetic support is generated as the two are finally able to get in synch and the plow blade is sunk into soil softened by a conveniently-timed rain. When Ted takes his hat off to his exhausted son, a sign of not only respect but of pride and gratitude that also denotes a rite of passage, more than a few male moviegoers self-consciously hoped that dewy eyes could not be seen in the dark.

The film itself gets much darker when war is declared and Ted seizes the opportunity to make desperately-needed money by selling Joey out from under Albert. A tearful Albert can do nothing but promise his beloved horse that they will someday be together again in what seems like a touching attempt to reassure himself as much as Joey. It will take four sorely-testing years and much of *War Horse* for that to happen, and in the interim Joey winds up in multiple hands on both sides of the conflict. He is initially deemed to be a suitably-magnificent mount for noble British Capt. Nicholls (a poetic Tom Hiddleston), who quickly deems the horse remarkable and promises to treat him accordingly until compassionately returning him to Albert at the end of the war. For German soldier Gunther (David Kross), a farm boy not unlike Albert who caringly ministers to that army's horses, the capture of Joey and his stately cohort Topthorn affords serendipitous, superlative assistance with a desperately-implemented desertion dash. An ill but spirited French girl named Emilie (Celine Buckens) is then inspired to risk a ride atop solace-providing Joey despite the misgivings of her protective grandfather (memorable Niels Arestrup), and they in turn provide both horses—and the audience—with a temporary, Shangri-La safe haven from all the tumult. Finally, another German sadly gazes at what military service does to horses and expresses regret that his forces found and seized specimens as striking as Joey and Topthorn. He later mourns alongside the former when the latter dies, and soon after yells to run when a tank approaches.

The purpose of these episodic sketches that comprise Joey's often arduous and disconcerting odyssey is abundantly clear: Viewers are being reassuringly reminded that an underlying common thread of humanity continues to connect even those who, at least at present, appear to have frighteningly-little in common. It all leads up to one of the film's finest scenes, in which two soldiers—one fighting for his King and another for his Kaiser—are propelled towards each other by shared

compassion instead of enmity after a panicked, ghastly gallop leaves Joey lying injured and enmeshed in barbed wire in the midst of No Man's Land.

Speaking of land, there are contrasting images throughout *War Horse* that offer sobering commentary on man's reaping what he sows. The film's sunbathed, Edenically-verdant vistas, as well as Joey's early pulling of that plow and the resulting expanse of crops, are thought-provokingly-juxtaposed with the dark, desolate hellishness of battlefield wastelands and the titular horse being forced to later lug death-delivering artillery. Probably the film's most visually dazzling sequences is the surprise British cavalry attack on a German encampment that responds with a devastating surprise of its own. Proudly astride Joey, Capt. Nicholls and his comrades thunderously charge out from a lazily-swaying field of wheat that appears ready to be harvested and are themselves cut down by a hidden row of machineguns. Afterward, the camera pulls up to reveal a dismaying expanse of the dead. Knowing all mankind has wrought since that senseless "War to End All Wars", viewers looked down upon the lifeless bodies of soldiers from both sides and the loyal steeds that they had pressed into service and likely wondered: Which ones are the "beasts?"

Another thing that effectively gives one pause is seeing just how many of the soldiers responding to cries of "Come on, boys!" are literally just that. Although the sudden appearance of Albert in the trenches with an equally-fresh-faced but less-fortunate boyhood friend (Matt Milne) during the Second Battle of Somme in 1918 stops one short, what actually ends up hitting viewers harder is the abrupt end that a firing squad brings to young Gunther and the fourteen-year-old brother (Leonard Carow) from which he was about to be separated. It emphasizes their youth that Gunther was only trying to keep a promise made to his mother, who had wanted him to stick protectively close to Michael. At least Spielberg shows some mercy for the audience, artfully obscuring the moment they are mowed down with a rotating windmill panel.

Those who are severely allergic to either hard-to-swallow, miraculous coincidences or schmaltz were likely fumbling for their EpiPens when a temporarily-blinded Albert saves Joey's life by happening to call to him just as the wounded horse is about to be put down in fortuitously-close proximity to the young man's hospital bed. The emotions of Albert, Joey and viewers are then jerked around with what can be summed up as "You've got him back! No, you don't! Yes, you do! Wait, not so fast! Oh, forget what I said and just take him after all." The subsequent homecoming of the young man and his horse features visuals that not only hark back (as *War Horse* has on previous occasions) to films directed by

John Ford, but also obviously and specifically references the closing moments of *Gone with the Wind* (1939). Seen in silhouette against an orange-red sky, Mr. and Mrs. Narracott lovingly welcome back these two weary war veterans, and everyone is bathed in warm, golden glow signaling that everything is going to be just fine. The film closes with a close-up of Joey. It is not often that a film's horse-faced star can be termed beautiful.

War Horse received mainly positive reviews and numerous award nominations after its release just four days after Spielberg's animated *The Adventures of TinTin* (2011). It is interesting to note that the *New York Times* review of the play Spielberg enjoyed so much had described as both "steeped in...sentimentality" and "exquisite," the precise way many characterized his big-screen treatment. "Calculated" is something else often said by viewers and reviewers about the film, but the film connected enough to earn an Oscar® nomination for Best Picture. It is not hard to understand why some felt Spielberg laid the emotionalism on too thick. Still, many were able to take pleasure in what the *Times'* A.O. Scott termed the director's "strong and simple appeals to feeling. You may find yourself resisting...but my strong advice is to surrender...and allow yourself to recall, or perhaps discover, the deep pleasures of sincerity."

David L. Boxerbaum

CREDITS

Albert Narracott: Jeremy Irvine
Rose Narracott: Emily Watson
Ted Narracott: Peter Mullan
Lyons: David Thewlis
Major James Stewart: Benedict Cumberbatch
Captain Nichols: Tom Hiddleston
Geordie Soldier: Toby Kebbell
Grandfather: Niels Arestrup
Origin: USA
Language: English
Released: 2011
Production: Steven Spielberg, Kathleen Kennedy; Reliance Entertainment, Amblin Entertainment, DreamWorks SKG; released by Walt Disney Pictures
Directed by: Steven Spielberg
Written by: Lee Hall, Richard Curtis
Cinematography by: Janusz Kaminski
Music by: John Williams
Sound: Stuart Wilson
Editing: Michael Kahn
Art Direction: Neil Lamont
Costumes: Joanna Johnston
Production Design: Rick Carter

MPAA rating: PG-13
Running time: 146 minutes

REVIEWS

Burr, Ty. *Boston Globe*. December 22, 2011.
Chang, Justin. *Variety*. December 15, 2011.
Corliss, Richard. *Time*. December 19, 2011.
Denby, David. *New Yorker*. December 27, 2011.
Ebert, Roger. *Chicago Sun-Times*. December 21, 2011.
McCarthy, Todd. *Hollywood Reporter*. December 15, 2011.
Schwarzbaum, Lisa. *Entertainment Weekly*. December 16, 2011.
Scott, A.O.. *New York Times*. December 22, 2011.
Sharkey, Betsy. *Los Angeles Times*. December 26, 2011.
Travers, Peter. *Rolling Stone*. December 22, 2011.

QUOTES

Maj. Jamie Stewart: "Be brave! Be brave!"

TRIVIA

Specially designed mud was used to make the battle scenes look authentically filthy.

AWARDS

Nomination:

Oscars 2011: Art Dir./Set Dec., Cinematog., Film, Sound, Sound FX Editing, Orig. Score
British Acad. 2011: Cinematog., Sound, Visual FX, Orig. Score, Prod. Des.
Golden Globes 2012: Film—Drama, Orig. Score

THE WARD
(John Carpenter's The Ward)

Only sanity can keep you alive.
    —Movie tagline

Although it did not receive even a fraction of the hype that was accorded to Terrence Malick's return to the director's chair with *Tree of Life,* the summer of 2011 saw the long-awaited return of another revered auteur after an extended absence from the filmmaking game. That auteur was John Carpenter, the man behind such cult classics as *Halloween* (1978), *The Thing* (1982), *Big Trouble in Little China* (1986) and *They Live* (1988). After the critical and commercial failure of *Ghost of Mars*(2001), a flawed-but-entertaining attempt to restage his earlier siege classic *Assault on Precinct 13* (1976) in outer space, Carpenter laid low for the next decade and, outside of helming two episodes of the cable anthology series *Masters of Horror*, he did absolutely nothing aside from presumably cashing hefty checks from the remakes of *Assault on Precinct 13* (2005), *The Fog* (2005) and *Halloween* (2007). One might have assumed that his return to filmmaking, especially a return to the horror genre, would have generated a bunch of publicity, but when the fruit of his labors, *The Ward*, finally did open, it was only dribbled out into a handful of theaters a mere few weeks before its already announced DVD/Bluray release date, and the few reviews that it did receive were not particularly favorable. On the one hand, the tepid response is not that surprising because the film as a whole is not great—a derivative and fairly silly supernatural-themed thriller that builds to a shocking and surprising finale that will shock/surprise no one. On the other hand, it has been made with a certain care and elegance that demonstrates that even when working with weak material after a long period on the bench, Carpenter can still make a film several times more stylish than it probably deserves to be.

Set in 1966, the film opens with Kristen (Amber Heard) dazedly stumbling through the woods before setting an abandoned farmhouse on fire. This move gets her thrown into a ward at the North Bend Psychiatric Hospital, a forbidding institute that appears to be populated entirely by four fellow patients with specific and pronounced neuroses—Emily (Mamie Gummer), Iris (Lyndsey Fonseca), Sarah (Danielle Panabaker) and Zooey (Laura-Leigh)—under the care of the potentially-sinister psychiatrist Dr. Stringer (Jared Harris) aided by definitively-sinister nurses and guards.

Before long, Kristen discovers that the nefarious staff is the least of her problems—there appears to be some mysterious spirit haunting the ward that first monkeys around with her in her sleep and then attacks her in the shower. At the same time, her fellow wardmates begin to disappear one by one and while it is suggested that they are being released after a final meeting with Dr. Stringer, they are actually being brutally murdered one-by-one by someone or something. After doing some further digging, Kristen learns that the ghost is the spirit of another former inmate of the ward whom the other girls wronged and who still yearns for escape after taking her violent revenge.

The fundamental problem with *The Ward*—the basic reason why it fails to work and why it failed to even achieve a moderate theatrical release despite the presence of Carpenter and his exceptionally comely cast—is the weak screenplay by Michael & Shawn Rasmussen. If it had been stripped down to an hour and staged as an episode of *Masters of Horror*, there is a chance that it might have worked. At the very least, it presumably would have dumped all the numerous dull spots and dead ends that allow what should have been a swift and straightforward storyline to spend way too much time treading narrative water for its own good. With that extra half-hour of dramatic flab left in, viewers—even ones who are not stone-cold horror buffs—will find themselves pointing out the numerous holes and flaws in the story and remembering all the other movies that they have seen that have utilized the basic premise that the Rasmussens are playing with here. (Since to name any of those films would probably constitute a spoiler for anyone who has seen them, they will not be mentioned here but it could make for an interesting party game to watch *The Ward* with others and see who can make the longest list of probable influences.)

Of course, even if the story had been shed of the extraneous thirty minutes, it still would not overcome the even-larger problem of the singularly lame twist ending with which it concludes. Well, perhaps the Rasmussens *thought* that they were supplying a jaw-dropping twist meant to make viewers reevaluate everything that they have seen up until that point. In truth, the "twist" is so painfully obvious from so early on in the proceedings that the one thing probably keeping the interest of most viewers is the slim possibility that the story is merely playing possum with them via the obvious conclusion and that a truly knockout finale is somehow still in store for them.

And yet, while *The Ward* is not a particularly good movie by any stretch of the imagination, it is not entirely without interest and that is almost entirely due to the contributions of Carpenter. On the one hand, it is clear that for him, this is more of a going-through-the-motions project like *Christine* (1983) or *Memoirs of an Invisible Man* (1992) than one in which he has fully invested his time, energy and considerable talents into producing. That said, as going-through-the-motions pieces of hackwork go, he does make some effective contributions to help elevate the hackneyed material. Harkening back to his earlier projects in which female characters were front-and-center, he gets pretty good performances from his central actresses, all of whom play off of each other in intriguing ways. He also brings a certain style to the extended pursuit scenes that clearly separates this film from other recent genre efforts—instead of relying on quick cuts and lavish gore, he offers up long and beautifully-composed takes that actually generate some suspense. And when he gets to the bloodshed he deploys it in ways that are both minimal and memorable. While he perhaps relies a little too much here on cheap shock tactics designed to get viewers to jump out of their seats every few minutes, let it be said that few filmmakers are as skilled in that particular idiom as he once again proves to be. Though ultimately of little interest to anyone other than

Carpenter devotees, *The Ward* effectively demonstrates that his cinematic skills have not completely atrophied from a decade of idling and as soon as his skills in recognizing a good screenplay also get up to speed, he could well come up with the late-period masterpiece that his fans are hoping he still has within him.

Peter Sobczynski

CREDITS

Kristen: Amber Heard
Sarah: Danielle Panabaker
Iris: Lyndsy Fonseca
Zoey: Laura-Leigh
Emily: Mamie Gummer
Dr. Stringer: Jared Harris
Alice: Mika Boorem
Origin: USA
Language: English
Released: 2010
Production: Mike Marcus; Echo Lake Entertainment, Premier Pictures, FilmNation Entertainment; released by ARC Entertainment, LLC
Directed by: John Carpenter
Written by: Michael Rasmussen, Shawn Rasmussen
Cinematography by: Yaron Orbach
Music by: Mark Kilian
Sound: Javier Bennassar
Editing: Patrick McMahon
Art Direction: Vincent DeFelice
Costumes: Lisa Caryl
Production Design: Paul Peters
MPAA rating: R
Running time: 88 minutes

REVIEWS

Gonsalves, Rob. *eFilmcritic.com*. June 10, 2011.
Goss, William. *Film.com*. July 11, 2011.
McDonagh, Maitland. *Film Journal International*. July 8, 2011.
Newman, Kim. *Empire Magazine*. January 20, 201.
Orndorf, Brian. *BrianOrndorf.com*. June 9, 2011.
Pinkerton, Nick. *Village Voice*. July 5, 2011.
Rothkopf, Joshua. *Time Out New York*. July 6, 2011.
Tallerico, Brian. *HollywoodChicago.com*. July 7, 2011.
Tobias, Scott. *NPR*. July 8, 2011.
Weinberg, Scott. *FEARnet*. September 17, 2010.

QUOTES

Sarah: "Sorry, I don't converse with loonies."

TRIVIA

This is director John Carpenter's first feature not shot in Panavision since his debut *Dark Star* in 1974.

WARRIOR

Family is worth fighting for.
—Movie tagline

Box Office: $13.7 million

There are many different ways to make a great sports film, but one way to measure the true merit is to look at the essence of the story and question whether or not it could work without the sport. The central characters and their dilemmas should be interesting enough for the drama taking place with the sport being used merely as a means to an end. What if these characters who are facing these troubled times were not blessed with athletic ability? Would their issues still make for a compelling narrative? If the answer is yes, the film has likely done right by its story. Rocky Balboa would still be an interesting character to study for a couple hours, even if he never got in the ring. Boxing did not necessarily have to be the thing that redeemed the titular character. It is one of the reasons why the *Rocky* (1976) formula has been copied so many times, with varying degrees of success.

Warrior is that kind of sports film. The characters, whose lives are put front and center before a single punch or kick is seen, are the stuff of great tragedy and worthy of the audience's emotional investment. It is, first and foremost, a story about a broken family that has little to no chance of ever putting the past behind them and coming together again as a single unit. Many of the film's most emotional moments happen away from the sport, in this case Mixed Martial Arts. The storyline is interwoven within the sport in such a masterful way that the sport ultimately becomes a metaphor for the personal struggles between self-worth and self-loathing, forgiveness and anger, redemption and condemnation.

The film opens with Tommy Conlon (Tom Hardy), who now goes by his mother's maiden name, Tommy Riordan. Tommy has just returned home after serving in Iraq. He pays a visit to his father, Paddy (Nick Nolte), who is now 1,000 days sober and who has not seen Tommy in fourteen years. The visit is not pleasant, but one can sense the desperation on both sides. Tommy carries a grudge that is bigger and broader than his own muscular physique can handle. Old confrontations between the two are brought back to light, but Paddy is willing to try and put a good face on his situation in hopes of winning back the approval of his son. Tommy will have none of it.

In another part of town, Paddy's other son Brendan (Joel Edgerton) lives in a suburban home with his wife Tess (Jennifer Morrison) and two young daughters. He works as a high school physics teacher and is only a couple months away from possibly losing his house unless he can bring in more money. He is a good family man and has no desire to move backwards in life. Like Tommy, Brendan will have nothing to do with his father. Something happened years ago that cut Paddy off from ever seeing his son or his grandchildren.

If the story ended there, it would still be enough for a good film. The means to get this family on track to any kind of redemption is the sport that both brothers practiced back in their youth. Paddy trained his boys well in the art of Mixed Martial Arts (MMA) and, with both characters at a crossroads in their lives, it may be the one thing that can save them. Tommy never really explains why, but an upcoming tournament, The Sparta, can win him some money he desperately needs if only he could find a trainer. Reluctantly, he asks his father.

Brendan, meanwhile, also believes the tournament can help save his family's home. He tells his wife that he considered taking a job as a bouncer, but has found a far more lucrative means to an end by participating in amateur MMA fights in parking lots. It was decided long ago that Brendan would leave this life so that their kids do not have to worry about seeing their father in a hospital with life-threatening cuts and bruises. But it is either this or lose the house. To make matters worse, he has been suspended from teaching by his principal (Kevin Dunn), who is alternately outraged and fascinated by Brendan's seemingly dual existence. Brendan goes back to the gym where he originally trained with Frank (Frank Campana), an unorthodox MMA trainer who insists his fighters work out to Beethoven.

As the training goes on, the drama continues. Paddy is kept at several arms' lengths from Tommy's emotions as well as his secretive past that led him back home in the first place. Paddy, who has never been more vulnerable in his life than he is right now, maintains a degree of toughness with Bobby, reminding him that he does not have to train him; that it was Bobby who reached out to him. Paddy sees this reunion of sorts as an opportunity to try and get back in Brendan's good graciousness. When he shows up on Brendan's doorstep for the first time in four years to announce his sobriety and the fact that Tommy is back in town, he is turned away and told to leave.

It is never fully explained what happened to this family. Clues are given throughout the dialogue, but there are never any single incidents highlighted for the audience's benefit. The characters focus on the bigger picture and the major events that divided them. The screenplay by Gavin O'Connor (who also directed), Anthony Tambakis and Cliff Dorfman gives just enough without resorting to maudlin revelations about who hit who. It gets by on the notion that less is more. It is the forlorn, fatigued and scarred faces of the father and his two sons that tell the bulk of the story.

This is compounded by the performances, all of which are pitch perfect. Edgerton has the right amount of charisma and street smarts to make for a convincing teacher/street fighter. Hardy's performance is a beautiful work of subtlety, conveying the longing he feels internally as he tries to push his father further and further away. But it is Nick Nolte's performance that is the centerpiece of the film. With every pathetic, desperate quiver in his voice as he tries to win over his children, Nolte creates a character that has plenty in his deep, dark past for which to atone. It is a stunning and heartbreaking performance, one that easily solidifies it as a legitimate comeback for a great actor who fell on hard times in the last decade. It may not be a starring role, but it is definitely amongst the strongest performances of 2011.

The fight scenes are staged, shot and cut together perfectly. It is not just a series of kicks, punches and beat-downs (though there is plenty of that), but the styles of fighting are akin to the characters' personalities. Tommy punches his opponent fiercely, sometimes channeling all his rage into a single beating. Brendan wins by applying the laws of physics and rendering his opponent helpless and unmovable. There are forces pushing, pulling and beating down on these characters that are bigger than them and O'Connor keeps that conflict subtle while delivering some of the toughest, most brutal fight scenes ever filmed in a sports movie.

Warrior is a magnificent film, one that earns every tear shed by anyone who watches it. It will not be remembered for its sport so much, but for its humanity. When these fighters take to the ring, there is something truly personal at stake and the weight of every punch and body slam is felt by the audience, physically and emotionally. The ending for this film is but a moment and not a perfect resolution. There are still many demons to face and many more confrontations to be had, but there remains hope for this family that has for too long been cast adrift, lost at sea and without a real home to return to. This is a film about small, surface-level sacrifices amidst larger, more personal ones.

Collin Souter

CREDITS

Tommy Conlon: Tom Hardy
Brendan Conlon: Joel Edgerton
Paddy Conlon: Nick Nolte
Tess Conlon: Jennifer Morrison
Frank Campana: Frank Grillo

Joe Zito: Kevin Dunn
Dan Taylor: Noah Emmerich
Origin: USA
Language: English
Released: 2011
Production: Greg O'Connor; Mimran Schur Pictures, Lionsgate, Solaris Entertainment; released by Lionsgate
Directed by: Gavin O'Connor
Written by: Gavin O'Connor, Anthony Tambakis, Cliff Dorfman
Cinematography by: Masanobu Takayanagi
Music by: Mark Isham
Music Supervisor: Brian Ross
Sound: Ben Wilkins
Editing: Sean Albertson, Matt Chesse, John Gilroy, Aaron Marshall
Art Direction: James Donahue
Costumes: Abigail Murray
Production Design: Dan Leigh
MPAA rating: PG-13
Running time: 140 minutes

REVIEWS

Childress, Erik. *eFilmcritic.com.* September 6, 2011.
Ebert, Roger. *Chicago Sun-Times.* September 8, 2011.
Gleiberman, Owen. *Entertainment Weekly.* September 2, 2011.
Goodykooontz, Bill. *Arizone Republic.* September 7, 2011.
Kenny, Glenn. *MSN Movies.* September 6, 2011.
McDonagh, Maitland. *Film Journal International.* September 6, 2011.
Rea, Steven. *Philadelphia Inquirer.* September 8, 2011.
Scott, A.O. *New York Times.* September 8, 2011.
Tallerico, Brian. *HollywoodChicago.com.* August 22, 2011.
Willmore, Alison. *AV Club.* September 8, 2011.

QUOTES

Tom Conlon: "Not much of a woman's touch around here."
Paddy Conlon: "No women for me anymore, Tommy."
Tom Conlon: "Yeah. Must be tough to find a girl who could take a punch nowadays."

TRIVIA

The studio was initially resistant to casting Nolte in the film, but the writers held firm and Nolte's portrayal has subsequently won universal praise.

AWARDS

Nomination:
Oscars 2011: Support. Actor (Nolte)
Screen Actors Guild 2011: Support. Actor (Nolte).

WATER FOR ELEPHANTS

Life is the most spectacular show on earth.
—Movie tagline

Box Office: $58.7 million

Robert Pattinson's performance in *Water for Elephants* brings to mind Dorothy Parker's acerbic assessment of Katharine Hepburn in a 1933 Broadway bomb entitled *The Lake,* as he too "runs the gamut of emotions from A to B." Since the actor vaulted to fame as a cold-skinned vampire thought by scores of frenzied females to be hot stuff, many others have waited to see if the handsome *Twilight* star has anything else in his repertoire beyond brooding. Unfortunately, too much of what served to make his pasty-faced, sullen Edward Cullen so potently magnetic reappears in *Elephants* to make his Jacob Jankowski seem colorless in an equally striking but far less effective manner. Having excelled at being one of the blood-sucking, tragic undead, Pattinson unfortunately made many viewers of this film wish he had seemed less anemic and more truly alive.

That Jacob incongruously has more life in him the older he gets is due to the fact that he is played as a senior with engaging, affecting spunk by 86-year-old Hal Holbrook, whose own bag of acting tricks is so well-stocked that it could surely induce a hernia. Although only onscreen during relatively brief scenes that frame a film told mainly in flashback, Holbrook conveys infinitely more emotion in his close-ups than Pattinson does in the endless opportunities afforded him to do so. When aged Jacob begins relating his story and Holbrook's voice and visage are replaced by those of Pattinson, the latter actor's subdued presence—a hooded-eyed hollowness—initially makes perfect sense. Just before garnering a veterinary degree from Cornell that promises to give him a fighting chance against the Great Depression, Jacob learns that both of his loving Polish parents have been ripped from him in a car accident. Consequently, also gone, he learns soon after from a heartless banker, are the family's home and funds. Since Jacob has been profoundly thrown for a loop as a result of the rug being so cruelly and unexpectedly yanked out from under him, having the character gaze silently and grimly and seem so listlessly low-key is initially quite appropriate. The problem is that Pattinson's performance remains too muted throughout the film, and the repetitiveness of his looking on in angst makes those stares lose their expressiveness, seeming increasingly blank and interchangeable rather than acutely intriguing and filled with specific meaning.

It does not help matters that the circus train upon which Jacob fatefully jumps soon leads to a love story that transported few viewers of *Water for Elephants.* The character is instantly attracted to the Benzini Brothers' main attraction, a bareback rider named Marlena (Reese Witherspoon, who is a decade older than Pattinson.). A platinum blonde beauty in a sparkling sequined costume who performs atop a magnificent white horse, the woman seems set up to be Jacob's radiant savior, riding to his rescue and banishing his gloom. Although Marlena is initially a standoffish tough cookie, she does indeed grow closer to Jacob upon sensing that he is something of a kindred spirit. She appreciatively notes his deep and tender concern for animals, which is not only similar to her own but totally, mercifully different from the brutish disregard shown for them—and sometimes herself—by August (Christoph Waltz), her mercurial monster of a husband who is also the circus' owner and ringmaster. A bond forms between these two like-minded people, assessing each other to be safe havens within which their battered souls might mutually heal. Jacob and Marlena's compassionate alliance is infinitely more convincing than their resulting passionate dalliance, which is tedious instead of titillating. What is presented as the great love of their lives, a romantic flame that viewers later learn warmed the couple through decades of matrimonial bliss, unfortunately generates as much palpable heat as a furnace on the fritz. Even during the single scene in which the action takes place under the sheets, Pattinson and Witherspoon can rub together all they want, but are simply unable to create discernable sparks.

What leads up to this mere going through the motions is a crucial moment that highlights the aforementioned deficit specific to Pattinson. As the circus train starts to move, the scenery rushing by with ever-increasing rapidity, Jacob stands with Marlena before an open door—what amounts to a literal depiction of a figurative window of opportunity—and attempts to convince her to ditch everything and jump with him to freedom before it is too late. Persuading someone to take such a big leap of faith at breakneck speed calls for the potent and urgent expression of emotional conviction. Yet, as portrayed by Pattinson, Jacob makes his case with not only an expressionless face but in a somnolent monotone.

Filling the void with riveting, complex vividness is Waltz, whose August is more frightening a beast than anything growling from within the circus' holding cages. While the lion with which he takes sadistic pleasure in scaring Jacob turns out to have no bite, August himself is certainly, dangerous capable of figuratively showing some teeth. The unsettling character, whose words are emitted like staccato jabs, is by treacherously-unpredictable turns charming and churlish, complimentary and cutting, tender and tyrannical, a provider of livelihood in hard times and someone who orders pitiless, deadly dismissals. August cannot bear the thought of losing Marlena or failing to keep his financially-troubled business afloat, and so he resultantly resorts to any means necessary to establish control, perhaps most queasily when purposefully and painfully thrusting a bull hook into the hide of Rosie, Jacob and Marlena's beloved elephant upon which the owner's hopes of saving the circus are riding. Ultimately and unfortunately for August, it seems that elephants do indeed never forget.

As for moviegoers, the only other thing many were likely to remember (at least in a positive way) was the striking nature of the visuals throughout the $38 million-budgeted *Water for Elephants,* which succeeded in grossing $58.7 million but garnered mainly mixed reviews. The film manifestly benefits from a meticulous attention to evocative detail provided by production designer Jack Fisk, art director David Crank, set decorator Jim Erickson, and costume designer Jacqueline West all provided. Also laudable was the work of director of photography Rodrigo Prieto, such as his beautiful bird's-eye view of the circus train as it winds its way through the countryside at night. Other shots, such as those depicting various animals and acts, the sweaty exertion to raise massive tents or shovel reeking piles of dung, all admirably bring to life (if not quite with Gruen's grittiness and pungency) what was involved in providing escapist entertainment in an era when it was especially needed.

Too bad Pattinson could not have been effectively brought to life, as well.

David L. Boxerbaum

CREDITS

Marlena Rosenbluth: Reese Witherspoon
Jacob Jankowski: Robert Pattinson
August Rosenbluth: Christoph Waltz
Old Jacob: Hal Holbrook
Charlie O'Brien: Paul Schneider
Diamond Joe: Tim Guinee
Kinko/Walter: Mark Povinelli
Origin: USA
Language: English
Released: 2011
Production: Gil Netter, Erwin Stoff, Andrew R. Tennebaum; Fox 2000 Pictures, 3 Arts Productions, Flashback Films, Crazy Horse Effects; released by 20th Century-Fox
Directed by: Francis Lawrence
Written by: Richard LaGravenese
Cinematography by: Rodrigo Prieto
Music by: James Newton Howard
Sound: Skip Lievsay, Jeremy Peirson
Music Supervisor: Alexandra Patsavas
Editing: Alan Edward Bell
Art Direction: David Crank
Costumes: Jacqueline West

Production Design: Jack Fisk
MPAA rating: PG-13
Running time: 120 minutes

REVIEWS

Corliss, Richard. *Time*. April 21, 2011.
Debruge, Peter. *Variety*. April 21, 2011.
Ebert, Roger. *Chicago Sun-Times*. April 21, 2011.
Grady, Pam. *Boxoffice Magazine*. April 21, 2011.
Holden, Stephen. *New York Times*. April 21, 2011.
McCarthy, Todd. *Hollywood Reporter*. April 21, 2011.
Morgenstern, Joe. *Wall Street Journal*. April 21, 2011.
Morris, Wesley. *Boston Globe*. April 21, 2011.
O'Sullivan, Michael. *Washington Post*. April 21, 2011.
Phillips, Michael. *Chicago Tribune*. April 21, 2011.

QUOTES

Jacob: "I don't know if I picked that circus. But something told me that circus picked me."

TRIVIA

The role of August was originally to be played by Sean Penn until he dropped out and was replaced by Christoph Waltz.

THE WAY

Life is too big to walk it alone.
—Movie tagline

Box Office: $4.4 million

The concept of the spiritual journey is difficult at best to translate to film without seeming preachy. *The Way* is definitely a film that over-reaches but the places it does get to are really interesting, and, in its own quiet way, it sings a quiet sort of hymn over the pilgrimage journey it highlights, which is now over a thousand years old in human history. 2011 has been a remarkable year for spiritually themed American cinema. *Higher Ground* (2011), told the story of a woman who comes face-to-face with inescapable doubts after her travel thru the Jesus Movement of the 70's. *The Way* offers a polar opposite experience, in which spiritual tradition and pilgrimage form the basis for sorting through such universal themes as loss, true Christian community and the nature of faith as something fluid, lived through one day at a time, building on itself imperceptibly, and, by the end of a life, becoming a solid rock to cling to.

After his adult son Daniel (Emilio Estevez) is killed while hiking in the Pyrenees during a storm, Tom (Martin Sheen) travels to France to retrieve his body but feels compelled to finish his son's journey. Known as the Camino de Santiago, or Way of St. James, the trail offers spiritual pilgrims a walking route to the Cathedral of Santiago de Compostela. Driven by grief and a desire to understand his son better, Tom sets out.

On the way, his solitary grief is challenged by other pilgrims, all of who have been led to the journey by their own struggles. There is the large outgoing Dutchman, Joost (Yorick van Wageningen), trying to lose weight and regain his wife's passion. A kind hearted character he joins the reluctant Tom early on where they meet the Canadian divorcee Sarah (Deborah Kara Unger) whose abusive marriage and abortion have embittered her even as she claims her pilgrimage is about kicking her smoking habit. Irishman Jack (James Nesbitt) is suffering from writer's block as well as having abandoned his early dreams of becoming a great writer to pursue the safer financial path of travel writing.

It is a rewarding but arduous path, geographically and emotionally. Chance encounters with others deepen bonds, challenge assumptions, and provide opportunity for dialogue as a vast and wondrously beautiful landscape constantly unfolds around the travelers. Tom is challenged to unpack something his son said before dying, "You don't choose a life, dad. You live one." It is a phrase that takes on increased meaning as the trip takes its toll, forcing others through processes of conflict, self-discovery, and the building of community through acts of selflessness and kindness.

Estevez does struggle here with pacing. For many, the film is likely to seem an awfully long slog during which little happens. This may be especially true for people who find the idea of religious faith untenable. Enough can hardly be said here about the performance of Martin Sheen who brings nuance after nuance to the emotional arc of his character as a grieving father who finds himself unexpectedly sharing his most intimate thoughts with strangers. More importantly, Sheen provides an anchor to a story that would otherwise flounder about in its own metaphysical wanderings. As powerful as the end product is, it clearly emerged, more so than most, as a product of the process of being made rather than having been carefully conceived and written. As such, *The Way* emerges ultimately as a showcase for one of current cinema's more deeply respected Catholics actors, who, luckily, has the skill to convey his thoughts on faith with a rich good humor and equal degree of humility, creating a diary-like travelogue. This is in some sense Estevez's most accomplished film, far better than any of his recent feature work such as *Bobby* (2006).

But the list of reasons why *The Way* makes for fascinating if somewhat static viewing at times has as much to do with the real-life behind-the-scenes drama between father and son Estevez and Sheen, who make an artful statement here about the way the roles of teacher and student become interchangeable over time. The cast and crew walked some 300 to 350 kilometers over a period of forty days, using only what they could carry and the available light, giving the production an organic visual aesthetic that, when coupled with the breathtaking geography, creates a gorgeous background for the expansive view the film has of the spiritual path. It is a welcome antidote in a cinematic landscape dominated by pedantic dogmatic Christian cinema (*Fire Proof* [2008], *Soul Surfer* [2011]) and equally bland atheist fare (*The Ledge* [2011]).

Dave Canfield

CREDITS

Tom: Martin Sheen
Daniel: Emilio Estevez
Sarah: Deborah Kara Unger
Joost: Yorick van Wageningen
Jack: James Nesbitt
Captain Henn: Tchéky Karyo
Phil: Spencer Garrett
Padre Frank: Matt Clark
Origin: USA
Language: English
Released: 2010
Production: David Alexanian, Emilio Estevez, Julio Fernández; Elixir Films, Filmax Entertainment, Icon Entertainment International; released by Producers Distribution Agency
Directed by: Emilio Estevez
Written by: Emilio Estevez
Cinematography by: Juan Miguel
Music by: Tyler Bates Azpiroz
Sound: Joe Dzuban, Justin Dzuban
Editing: Raúl Dávalos
Art Direction: Victor Molero
Costumes: Tatiana Hernández
MPAA rating: PG-13
Running time: 123 minutes

REVIEWS

Ebert, Roger. *Chicago Sun-Times.* October 6, 2011.
Genzlinger, Neil. *New York Times.* October 6, 2011.
Hornaday, Ann. *Washington Post.* October 7, 2011.
Jones, Kimberley. *Austin Chronicle.* October 14, 2011.
Kohn, Eric. *IndieWIRE.* October 7, 2011.
Lasalle, Mick. *San Francisco Chronicle.* October 20, 2011.
Linden, Shari. *Los Angeles Times.* October 6, 2011.
O'Neill, Phelim. *Guardian (UK).* May 12, 2011.
Sachs, Ben. *Chicago Reader.* October 6, 2011.
Smith, Neil. *Total Film.* March 31, 2011.

QUOTES

Daniel: "You don't choose a life, dad. You live one."

TRIVIA

The film was made with a small crew of fifty people and just a couple of cameras; no trailers were used and, as director Emilio Estevez has stated, nor was there a director's chair.

W.E.

Wallis. Edward. Their affair ignited a scandal.
Their passion brought down an empire.
—Movie tagline

For fans of bizarre cinematic follies—the kind of deliriously demented project that can emerge when a production is launched with plenty of money, star power and ambition but little in the way of common sense—perhaps no film in 2011 was more eagerly anticipated than *W.E.*, a meditation on the life of Wallis Simpson, the American socialite and multiple divorcee who became one of the most infamous women in the world when England's King Edward VIII renounced his throne in order to marry her, from the mind of the equally infamous Madonna, marking her second tour of duty behind the cameras after the barely released, barely seen and barely directed *Filth & Wisdom* (2008). Indeed, when the film had its gala premiere at the Venice Film Festival, it was thoroughly decimated in the press via reviews that seemed to be trying to top each other in terms of vitriol spewed than in weighing its actual qualities. Seen in the cold light of day and taken on its own terms, those looking for a one-of-a-kind disaster will be disappointed to discover that *W.E.* is not the all-out bomb that they had been awaiting with undisguised glee. That said, it still is not very good by any stretch of the imagination and it is unlikely that anyone outside of the most rabid members of Madonna's fan base will have the patience to sit through this stylishly made but intellectually and emotionally vapid mess.

The film eschews the traditional biopic format for a dual story framework in which the familiar story of the growing relationship between Wallis (Andrea Riseborough) and Edward (James D'Arcy) and how he eventually abdicated his throne in order to be with her is intertwined with a 1998-set narrative involving one of the many people to be swept up by the romance of the tale. This storyline follows Wally Winthrop (Abbie Cornish), a New York socialite who is secretly miserable due to her marriage to a rich but abusive philanderer and her inability to conceive a child with said monster.

When a collection of items once owned by Wallis and Edward go up for sale at Sotheby's (where Wally previously worked as a research assistant before being forced to quit by the aforementioned ogre), she begins to obsess over their story and how it parallels her own. At the same time, she catches the eye of security guard Evgeni (Oscar Isaac), a Russian immigrant who is hunky, brainy and apparently very good with money since he lives in the kind of loft that most well-to-do New Yorkers would kill to possess and which even features a grand piano from which he occasionally noodles poetically. To further highlight the parallels between the two stories, there are even a few points in which Wallis appears before Wally to offer pithy observations—at one point, Wally even reciprocates by appearing during one low point in Wallis' post-marriage life but alas, the most she can offer in return of profundity is the deathless "At least you have each other."

What Madonna and co-writer Alex Keshishian (who directed the hit documentary *Madonna: Truth or Dare* (1991) are attempting here is at least somewhat ambitious but ambition does not count for very much when it lacks any clear focus or discernible point. There are times in which the film tries to play up the fairy-tale aspect of Wallis' life by lavishing viewers with so many close-ups of sparkling jewelry, designer clothes and other fancy accoutrements that they seem to get more screen time than many of the actors. At the same time, it also seems to want to dispel the myths that have surrounded this story by suggesting that not even this great romance was enough to make her happy when all was said and done. At other times, however, Madonna is still perfectly content to offer up the sugar-coated version of the story when it suits her needs, most notably in regard to Edward's documented reputation as a Nazi sympathizer, an inconvenient fact that she deals with by having it be brought up by Wally's loathsome husband and quickly dismissed as mere rumor. And yet, as dramatically uneven as these scenes may be, they are easily the best to be had in the film. This is partly because Riseborough does a fairly good job of approximating Wallis and manages to hold her own against both the swooning style and the resolutely uncharismatic D'Arcy, who utterly fails to hold up his end of the bargain in the romantic chemistry department. However, it is also due to the fact that the contemporary material is nothing more than a pretentious and borderline ridiculous bore through and through that is further done in by a performance by the usually reliable Cornish that is so utterly flat and lifeless that it seems as if she is auditioning to become an extra in the next George Romero zombie epic.

To give Madonna credit as a director, her work here is a considerable improvement over *Filth & Wisdom* and it is certainly looks good throughout. However, those hoping for any innovative flourishes on a par with her musical achievements will be disappointed to discover that, aside from the narrative gimmick, the film is almost disconcertingly straightforward—the closest thing she comes to a bold stylistic flourish is a strange sequence in which Edward and Wallis goose up a dull party with hits of speed for everyone and get them dancing to, of all things, a classic Sex Pistols tune and that merely comes across as a wan approximation of what Sofia Coppola achieved in the infinitely superior *Marie Antoinette* (2006). That film also offered viewers a not-unsympathetic view of a controversial historical figure but did so in ways that intrigued the mind as well as pleased the eye. *W.E.,* by comparison, looks good and, as year-end Oscar® bait (it did pull a solo nod for Arianne Phillips' costume design) involving 20th-century British history goes, it beats the abysmal *The Iron Lady* (2011) like a gong. Beyond that, however, let it be said that it may not be a mere coincidence that the Sex Pistols song in question is none other than "Pretty Vacant."

Peter Sobczynski

CREDITS

Wally Winthrop: Abbie Cornish
Wallis Simpson: Andrea Riseboroughe
King Edward VIII: James D'Arcy
Evgeni: Oscar Isaac
Elizabeth Bowes-Lyon: Natalie Dormer
Bertie: Laurence Fox
King George V: James Fox
William Winthrop: Richard Coyle
Queen Mary: Judy Parfitt
Stanley Baldwin: Geoffrey Palmer
Lady Thelma: Katie McGrath
Ernest: David Harbour
Origin: United Kingdom
Language: English
Released: 2011
Production: Madonna, Kris Thykier; IM Global, Semtex Films; released by Weinstein Company
Directed by: Madonna
Written by: Madonna, Alek Keshishian
Cinematography by: Hagen Bogdanski
Music by: Abel Korzeniowski
Sound: Chris Munro
Music Supervisor: Maggie Rodford
Editing: Danny Tull
Art Direction: Mark Raggett
Costumes: Arianne Phillips

Production Design: Martin Childs
MPAA rating: R
Running time: 119 minutes

REVIEWS

Bamigboye, Baz. *Daily Mail*. September 2, 2011.
Brooks, Xan. *Guardian*. September 1, 2011.
Costa, Diego. *Slant*. December 13, 2011.
Felperin, Leslie. *Variety*. September 2, 2011.
Goss, William. *Film.com*. December 23, 2011.
Gritten, David. *Daily Telegraph*. September 1, 2011.
McCarthy, Todd. *Hollywood Reporter*. September 2, 2011.
O'Hehir, Andrew. *Salon.com*. September 14, 2011.
Sharkey, Betsy. *Los Angeles Times*. December 9, 2011.
Zacharek, Stephanie. *Movieline*. December 8, 2011.

QUOTES

Wallis Simpson: "Darling, they can't hurt you if you don't let them."

TRIVIA

Director Madonna financed the majority of the film's budget herself, in addition to a UK tax credit.

AWARDS

Golden Globes 2012: Song ("Masterpiece")
Nomination:
Oscars 2011: Costume Des.
Golden Globes 2012: Orig. Score.

WE BOUGHT A ZOO

Box Office: $73.7 million

Nobody buys a zoo. It just does not happen. Ask 1,000 people on the street, and chances are none of them will say they have ever purchased an 18-acre property filled with lions, tigers and seven endangered species.

That is, however, what Benjamin Mee (Matt Damon) does in *We Bought A Zoo*, and viewers will likely be surprised that the film is based on a true story. In reality, Mee and his family purchased a zoo in England when looking for a place for his 76-year-old mother to live. Months after moving in, Mee's wife Katherine died when symptoms from a brain tumor returned. In the film, Benjamin buys a Southern California zoo for himself, his 14-year-old son Dylan (Colin Ford), and seven-year-old daughter Rosie (Maggie Elizabeth Jones) as a way of coping with the death of his wife Katherine

(Stephanie Szostak) six months before. This is not to say that Benjamin is without a support system. His brother Duncan (Thomas Haden Church) understands when Benjamin cannot bear to return to restaurants that remind him of Katherine, and, before moving, Benjamin's refrigerator is full of lasagnas given to him by neighborhood mothers out of sympathy. The suggestive comments and look on the face of one mom at his kids' school, actually, suggests that lasagna is not the only thing she wants to give Benjamin to make him feel better.

Yet Benjamin, a veteran reporter identified in an opening voiceover from Dylan as a writer who specializes in adventure, embraces the opportunity for a dramatic change of scenery to try to minimize the daily reminders of the woman with whom he no longer gets to begin and end each day. Purchasing the zoo is a deeply romantic pursuit with an undercurrent of vulnerable desperation, not so unlike Jerry Maguire (Tom Cruise) starting his own sports agency in writer-director Cameron Crowe's 1996 film named after Jerry. On that note, while viewers may be surprised to learn the true-life source of Benjamin's story—which Mee published as a memoir in 2008—few will be surprised to learn that the film comes from Crowe. Packed with deliberately chosen music and bare sentimentality, *We Bought a Zoo* has director/co-writer Crowe's name all over it.

Unfortunately, it also has co-writer Aline Brosh McKenna's (*I Don't Know How She Does It*, [2011], *27 Dresses*, [2008]) name all over it too. At times very moving, *We Bought A Zoo* also spends much of its two hours in shallow, episodic territory, whether it is zoo employee Peter MacCready (Angus Macfadyen) expressing his distaste for the zoo inspector (John Michael Higgins), Dylan opening and forgetting to close a box of snakes, or Benjamin running from a porcupine and falling over a fence onto a thorn bush. Meanwhile, several supporting characters are greatly underwritten, especially Lily (Elle Fanning), a young zoo employee who falls for Dylan simply because he comes from the city. (The zoo is in Rosemoor, California, located nine miles away from the nearest Target. This is apparently the barometer for a residence's remoteness these days.)

In fact, several of the relationships in *We Bought A Zoo* do not fully convince, including the budding flirtation between Benjamin and Lily's cousin, new head zookeeper Kelly (Scarlett Johansson). Obviously, the almost undeniably attractive Johansson was cast to give Benjamin an immediate love interest, and consequently Kelly registers equally as a valuable employee and a beautiful woman with whom Benjamin can enjoy spending time. If the plot's progressive attempts to move a widower closer to a new woman less than a year after his wife's death are successful at all, it is a result of the performances from Damon and Johansson rather than the film's examination of Benjamin's grief and when he is ready to move forward in his romantic life.

Still, *We Bought A Zoo* delivers numerous scenes in which even heart-on-sleeve emotion registers as moving and true. This comes in dialogue, such as when Benjamin, still learning how to be the only parent looking after his kids, asks them, "Did anybody even say good morning?" Or when Duncan recognizes that Benjamin may be using the zoo cages—pardon, that is enclosures, not cages—as a metaphor for everyone's desire to be free while giving him crap for making such risky decisions. (Blunt declarations like Rosie telling Benjamin, "Dylan really loves you, you know", on the other hand, just feel like lazy screenwriting.) Visually the film also effectively separates the creativity of the Mee family from a close-minded world when Dylan is expelled from school as a result of both a theft and a painting of a head bloodily becoming detached from a neck. When the principal says that he encourages creativity, it is clear that he only means art devoted to positive concepts like love, peace and the environment. Similarly, when Benjamin pitches his editor (Peter Riegert) a story called "iPocalypse", his boss turns him down and suggests that Benjamin start an online column to protect himself from possible layoffs. Benjamin's story idea is not any good, and his superior is only trying to help. Yet in this scene Crowe, always a softie for the unconventional expression of thoughts and feelings, identifies a chance for Benjamin to take an easy consolation in order to get by and shows that this is not a man who believes in that sort of thing. This becomes clear very soon when Benjamin quits, unwilling to be fired and accept the consequent health benefits, since he sees that as more unwanted sympathy.

The mix of the precise and the sappy is reflected in the film's music, normally a strength in a Crowe movie. The filmmaker misuses songs by Sigur Ros frontman Jonsi, which flutter atop the film but do not succeed in evoking a lively, playful mood as intended. Crowe also rests on tracks like Temple of the Dog's "Hunger Strike" and Neil Young's "Cinnamon Girl," which are more expected coming from the man behind the fantastic rock 'n' roll road movie *Almost Famous* (2000) and the effective rock doc *Pearl Jam Twenty* (2011). While these rock songs clash badly with the Jonsi material, they at least possess some grittier edges in a film that sometimes threatens to settle for cute when sweet works better.

That misguided cuteness certainly appears when dealing with the escape of animals, a notion Crowe presents urgently but with a coating of wonder. Anyone who remembers the massacre that resulted when wild animals escaped from an Ohio zoo in October 2011 and needed to be killed for people's safety will not take the concept of escaped zoo animals so lightly. On the other hand, Crowe excels in the warmth that exists underneath conflict between humans. Whether Benjamin and Dylan clash as a result of the way the boy reminds his father of his wife, or Benjamin grumbles about driving eighteen miles for butter but does it anyway, *We Bought A Zoo* nicely depicts a family struggling through a difficult time and unusual circumstances but knowing, deep-down, how lucky they are to still have each other.

Like Benjamin, Matt King (George Clooney) also must cope with the notion of losing his wife in Alexander Payne's *The Descendants* (2011), and Matt's struggle to reconcile difficult feelings about raising his kids alone registers more fully than it does with Benjamin in *We Bought A Zoo*. The latter film offers fewer dimensions to its young characters, even if Crowe better manages his tone of optimistic melancholy better than Payne's mix of anguish and comedy. Both films, however, tackle an experience that never gets easier no matter how many stories address it: Losing a spouse and raising kids alone. Much of the power in *We Bought A Zoo* comes from Damon's rich performance as a man attempting to handle a situation he never imagined in the only way he knows how. That makes the presence of the zoo feel not so much quirky as appropriately personal, as well as the sign of a father perhaps letting his daughter's fondness for animals overshadow his son's increasing need for support.

Even if Crowe uses love interests as a safe, unconvincing bridge from pain to comfort, *We Bought A Zoo* thrives on likable Crowe-isms that should melt even the hardest moviegoers. Besides for decrying "whatever" as the laziest word of the twentieth century, Benjamin passes on to his kids the belief that even twenty seconds of courage can accomplish a lot, and even as emotional manipulation Crowe capitalizes on this when showing how those kids would not exist if not for Benjamin's short burst of courage when meeting their mother. In a movie about protecting animals (and learning when to let them go, as Benjamin refuses to accept a tiger's approaching death), Crowe holds firmly to the importance of human connection. And the beautiful way in which Katherine looks out for Benjamin even after she passes away further shows that the only beings that can fully support and understand people are family that exist on two legs, no tail.

Matt Pais

CREDITS

Benjamin Mee: Matt Damon
Kelly Foster: Scarlett Johansson
Robin Jones: Patrick Fugit

Duncan Mee: Thomas Haden Church
Katherine Mee: Stephanie Szostak
Lily Miska: Elle Fanning
Walter Ferris: John Michael Higgins
Peter MacCready: Angus MacFadyen
Dylan Mee: Colin Ford
Rosie Mee: Maggie Elizabeth Jones
Delbert McGinty: Peter Riegert
Mr. Stevens: JB Smoove
Origin: USA
Language: English
Released: 2011
Production: Julie Yorn, Rick Yorn, Cameron Crowe; Vinyl Films, LBI Entertainment; released by 20th Century-Fox
Directed by: Cameron Crowe
Written by: Aline Brosh McKenna
Cinematography by: Rodrigo Prieto
Music by: Jonsi
Sound: Jeff Wexler
Editing: Mark Livolsi
Art Direction: Domenic Silvestri
Costumes: Deborah L. Scott
Production Design: Clay A. Griffith
MPAA rating: PG
Running time: 124 minutes

REVIEWS

Burr, Ty. *Boston Globe.* December 22, 2011.
Corliss, Richard. *Time.* December 22, 2011.
Hornaday, Ann. *Washington Post.* December 22, 2011.
Kols, Dan. *Slate.* December 22, 2011.
Phillips, Michael. *Chicago Tribune.* December 22, 2011.
Puig, Claudia. *USA Today.* December 23, 2011.
Rickey, Carrie. *Philadelphia Inquirer.* December 22, 2011.
Schager, Nick. *Slant Magazine.* December 11, 2011.
Sharkey, Betsy. *Los Angeles Times.* December 22, 2011.
Wilonsky, Robert. *Village Voice.* December 20, 2011.

QUOTES

Benjamin Mee: "You know, sometimes all you need is twenty seconds of insane courage. Just literally twenty seconds of just embarrassing bravery. And I promise you, something great will come of it."

TRIVIA

At one time, Ben Stiller was under consideration for the role of Benjamin Mee.

WE NEED TO TALK ABOUT KEVIN

Lynne Ramsay's divisive adaptation of Lionel Shriver's book about a mother's memories of her monster of a child may have split some critics and audiences but one cannot deny one universally agreed-upon fact—star Tilda Swinton has proven, yet again, that she is one of the best living actresses. After winning an Oscar® for her work in *Michael Clayton* (2007), many thought she would and should make the Academy's short list for follow-up films *Julia* (2009) and *I Am Love* (2010) but, for the third year in a row, Ms. Swinton was left out of the party for arguably the best work she has done since Tony Gilroy's film. Perhaps *We Need to Talk About Kevin* was just too dark for Academy voters as the film actually (correctly) made a few lists of the best horror films of 2011. It may not have a traditional slasher villain and may not feature found footage of kids playing with devil worship, but Ramsay's work is certainly one of horror, it just happens to be of the domestic kind. Sadly, the director's artistic excess and willingness to insert too much directorial flourish almost work as a tug of war with the realism that Swinton was so highly acclaimed for bringing to the film.

Swinton plays Eva Katchadourian and the film only works when one considers the bulk of the narrative to take place inside her head. It is a memory piece, making the exaggerated behavior of her offspring along with the dreamlike imagery on Ramsay's part more understandable (if not always dramatically forgivable). It is revealed early in the film that Eva's son Kevin (played mostly by Ezra Miller) has done something truly horrific as a teenager. How did he get there? What role did Eva's parenting play? Or the lack of it as the title may refer to in that the movie is not called *We Talked About Kevin*? Clearly, the foundation of the piece is hinting that parents often ignore significant problems with their children until the point that they do something absolutely unforgivable and it becomes too late to talk about anything.

And so Ramsay flashes back to the key moments of Kevin's life (or, at least, the ones that Eva might remember after it was too late to change the course of her son's doomed trajectory. After getting married to the relatively-nondescript Franklin (John C. Reilly), Eva gets pregnant and even that is presented as a chore. Kevin (played by Rock Duer and Jasper Newell before Miller) is a nightmare from near the very beginning. He is aggressively hard to raise, scowling like no child actually does (here is where the film must be appreciated as exaggerated memory in order to have any dramatic value at all) but Eva is no saint either. The daring question asked not quite enough by the film is whether or not a woman who does not seem to really take to parenthood might have something to do with how her son turns out should he turn out evil. Kevin cries all the time, refuses toilet training, and even breaks down Eva's patience to the point that she accidentally breaks his arm. Years later, he is doing much worse than not using the potty, mutilating his sister before going on a high school killing spree with a bow and arrow.

Frustratingly, Ramsay never connects the dots from Kevin's childhood to his teenage years. It is not a problem to make a film that presents more questions than answers, especially when it is about something as complex as parenthood, but Ramsay seems almost illogically averse to conclusions, to the point that it leaves her film hollow. She seems more interested in long shots of jelly on a coffee table or sprinklers covering the scene of a murder than she is what they mean or how they got there. There are too many flourishes in *We Need to Talk About Kevin* that are purely that—almost as if the director is showing off her skills with color and composition but sacrificing character in order to do so. *We Need to Talk About Kevin* is a cold film about a subject that just does not work if it comes off frigid and distant. Because then questions of artistic intent have to be raised—what is the point of a movie about a child murderer that is more visually resplendent than character-driven? Is it exploitation to turn the pain of real-life incidents like the ones used to inspire this film into something more reliant on imagery than emotion?

In the end, Tilda Swinton walks away from *We Need to Talk About Kevin,* even without an Oscar® nomination, not just unblemished but even more prominently at the forefront of her craft. Even through the directorial problems with the film, one can feel Swinton being genuinely in every moment of Eva's story. She is stunning yet again. One can only imagine if the film around her had lived up to her work in it.

Brian Tallerico

CREDITS

Eva: Tilda Swinton
Franklin: John C. Reilly
Teenaged Kevin: Ezra Miller
Younger Kevin: Jasper Newell
Celia: Ashley Gerasimovich
Wanda: Siobhan Fallon
Origin: USA, United Kingdom
Language: English
Released: 2011
Production: Luc Roeg, Jennifer Fox, Robert Salerno; BBC Films, U.K. Film Council; released by Oscilloscope Laboratories
Directed by: Lynne Ramsey
Written by: Lynne Ramsey, Rory Kinnear
Cinematography by: Seamus McGarvey
Music by: Johnny Greenwood

Sound: Ken Ishii
Editing: Joe Bini
Art Direction: Charles Kulsziski
Costumes: Catherine George
Production Design: Judy Becker
MPAA rating: R
Running time: 111 minutes

REVIEWS

Honeycutt, Kirk. *Hollywood Reporter.* November 29, 2011.
Jones, J.R. *Chicago Reader.* January 28, 2012.
Longworth, Karina. *Village Voice.* December 6, 2011.
Lumenick, Lou. *New York Post.* December 9, 2011.
Mondello, Bob. *NPR.* December 9, 2011.
Phillips, Michael. *Chicago Tribune.* January 26, 2012.
Reed, Rex. *New York Observer.* November 30, 2011.
Scott, A.O. *New York Times.* December 8, 2011.
Stevens, Dana. *Slate.* December 12, 2011.
Zacharek, Stephanie. *Movieline.* December 8, 2011.

QUOTES

Kevin: "It's like this: you wake and watch TV, get in your car and listen to the radio you go to your little jobs or little school, but you don't hear about that on the 6 o'clock news, why? 'Cause nothing is really happening, and you go home and watch some more TV and maybe it's a fun night and you go out and watch a movie. I mean it's got so bad that half the people on TV, inside the TV, they're watching TV. What are these people watching, people like me?"

AWARDS

Nomination:

British Acad. 2011: Actress (Swinton), Director (Ramsay), Outstanding British Film
Golden Globes 2012: Actress—Drama (Swinton)
Screen Actors Guild 2011: Actress (Swinton).

WHAT'S YOUR NUMBER?

Ally's looking for the best ex of her life.
—Movie tagline

Box Office: $14 million

There is undeniably a double standard in America (if not the world) about a person's number of sexual conquests: If a man has slept with (fill in a number with at least two digits and maybe three) women, he is a stud. If a woman has slept with that many guys, she is a slut. *What's Your Number?* recognizes this but does not have the guts to challenge this perception. Instead, it reinforces sex as something that men can do casually but women should not, which does not exactly appeal to and empower this uneven romantic comedy's target audience.

Anna Faris stars as Ally, a single woman less concerned with all the available men in Boston than with the fact that she has slept with nineteen guys, since an article in Marie Claire says that the national average for women is ten-and-a-half. And once Ally hears that a high percentage of women who sleep with twenty or more people have trouble finding a husband, her decision is made: She will not have sex with anyone until she is sure that he is the ONE.

Actually, she breaks her vow immediately, but after that, she is serious. No more sexual partners. Well, there is a loophole: Returning to old sexual partners—like *High Fidelity* (2000) without the perspective—in hopes that one of her old flames can help her recapture love without increasing her number. After all, Ally's sister Daisy (Ari Graynor) is about to marry one of her own exes (Oliver Jackson-Cohen), so Ally assumes that at least one of her guys must also deserve another chance.

If only the movie were as innocent and optimistically romantic as it sounds. Instead, Ally's just an immature fountain of desperation who lies to her mom (Blythe Danner) about multiple facets of her life and recalls her relationship with "Disgusting Donald" with no remorse whatsoever. Apparently this guy was disgusting only because he was overweight, to the extent that Ally says she learned to cook so she did not have to be seen in public with him. That Donald is played by Faris' real-life husband Chris Pratt, wearing a fat-suit during a flashback, only makes an unpleasant scene more uncomfortable.

If the act of tracking down nearly two dozen ex-boyfriends sounds taxing, fear not: Ally has help from her across-the-hall neighbor Colin (Chris Evans), who would prefer to sleep with Ally himself. Since he is not making progress in that department, he agrees to use the knowledge he gained going on stakeouts with his cop father to locate Ally's men. In return she allows him to hide in her apartment when he wants to avoid his one-night stands the next morning, a vile, cowardly habit that Ally eventually overlooks far too easily. Oh, wait: Colin is the only guy who encourages Ally's hobby of making clay sculptures, so clearly he is a good guy after all.

Not surprisingly, a movie about a woman rounding up and ultimately dismissing her exes becomes incredibly episodic, and *What's Your Number?* provides very little wit to keep itself entertaining. (No one would ever know that the film, adapted from Karyn Bosnak's 2006 novel *20 Times a Lady*, was written by former writers of *Scrubs* [2001] and *The Simpsons* [1989].) Instead, it is a dry slog through Ally's reconnections with people like Simon (Martin Freeman), whose Britishness senselessly results in Ally feigning a terrible, though sort of funny, British accent. And that is when she actually gives the guys a chance. When Ally sees that her magician/bartender ex Dave (Mike Vogel) still works as a bartender and still practices magic, she leaves without even speaking to him. This is a woman that does not want to be defined by the number of people she has slept with, but she carelessly defines the guys she encounters by traits that do not necessarily speak to the men they are. When she finally connects with her top priority, wealthy do-gooder Jake (Dave Annable), his immediate interest in her is about as believable as his availability.

With so many funny people on board (including Joel McHale, Andy Samberg and Thomas Lennon), *What's Your Number?* cannot help but register a few laughs, no matter how juvenile the material. Faris is charming and crafty enough that even her wordless gestures, such as when she tosses away hair extensions that catch on fire, can bring lightness and a chuckle to unimaginative situations. That the film features so many scenes that seem to look for excuses to depict her in her underwear can either be seen as an affirmation that women on the big screen can be both funny and sexy, or just a hypocritical way of embracing the sexuality of a character who thinks that sleeping with more people will make her damaged and unworthy of marriage.

At the center of Ally's mission is a positive goal: She no longer wants to open her heart or her goods to a man who does not deserve access. Yet the sensible, proactive nature of her quest is totally undone by the film's judgmental streak that condescends to fringe characters while saluting main characters, often simply because they are better looking, not because they are better people. The film ends with Ally learning a lesson that is certainly an important one when it comes to love: That a spouse should be someone with whom a person feels totally at ease and naked, even with all their clothes on. Of course, this message becomes shallow when applied to someone who is drawn to a not-especially nice person—while rapport is important, so is character. If anything, the biggest lesson demonstrated by Ally, who has trouble locating exes with names like Mike Miller and Jake Adams, is the Google-related caveat to dating people with generic names.

Matt Pais

CREDITS

Ally Darling: Anna Faris
Colin: Chris Evans
Jake: David Annable

Dave Hansen: Mike Vogel
Roger: Joel McHale
Barret Ingold: Thomas Lennon
Daisy Darling: Ari Gaynor
Gerry Perry: Andy Samberg
Boyfriend Rick: Zachary Quinto
Mr. Darling: Ed Begley Jr.
Ava Darling: Blythe Danner
Eddie Vogel: Oliver Jackson-Cohen
Eileen: Heather Burns
Origin: USA
Language: English
Released: 2011
Production: Beau Flynn, Tripp Vinson; Contrafilm, New Regency Pictures, Regency Enterprises, Modern VideoFilm; released by 20th Century-Fox
Directed by: Mark Mylod
Written by: Jennifer Crittenden, Gabrielle Allan
Cinematography by: J. Michael Muro
Music by: Aaron Zigman
Music Supervisor: Julia Michels
Sound: Karen Baker Landers
Editing: Julie Monroe
Art Direction: David Swayze
Costumes: Amy Westcott
Production Design: Jon Billington
MPAA rating: R
Running time: 106 minutes

REVIEWS

Bale, Miriam. *Slant Magazine.* September 29, 2011.
Chang, Justin. *Variety.* September 28, 2011.
Holden, Stephen. *New York Times.* September 29, 2011.
Morris, Wesley. *Boston Globe.* September 29, 2011.
Ogle, Connie. *Miami Herald.* September 29, 2011.
Pols, Mary. *Time.* September 29, 2011.
Puig, Claudia. *USA Today.* September 29, 2011.
Rabin, Nathan. *AV Club.* September 28, 2011.
Tobias, Scott. *NPR.* September 30, 2011.
Williams, Joe. *St. Louis Post-Dispatch.* September 29, 2011.

QUOTES

Ally Darling: "My husband is in the north pole. He's a scientist too. He's dealing with the whole ice cap situation. Yeah. He's probably going to fix it."

TRIVIA

Aziz Ansari makes a voice cameo appearance at the end of the movie on Ally's voice mail.

THE WHISTLEBLOWER

Nothing is more dangerous than the truth.
—Movie tagline

Box Office: $1.1 million

The Whistleblower, a Canadian docudrama about sex trafficking in Bosnia, is a film born in righteous anger, driven by outrage, and intended to shock and ignite. The burning passion from first-time director Larysa Kondracki and co-writer Eilis Kirwan is intended to reach out and shake the viewer, but it also somewhat flattens *The Whistleblower* as a cinematic experience. Though the filmmakers have poured a daunting and laudable amount of research into their story (which is based on real people and events), they are often too infuriated to fully embrace niceties of plotting or subtleties of character, as if slowing for a moment to consider dramatic mechanisms would be a time-wasting betrayal of their cause.

Rachel Weisz plays Kathryn Bolkovac, a true-believer Nebraskan cop who finds her dedication to her law-enforcement career trumps her custody struggles as a divorced mother. Limited in both contact with her teenage daughter and advancement at work, Bolkovac takes a job with a global security corporation contracting out to the United Nations. She soon finds herself in Sarajevo, Bosnia, in 1999, ostensibly teaching local police how to investigate crimes.

Along the way Bolkovac runs across the local brothels and the human trafficking and sex slavery that fuels their organized-crime business model. Yet when she attempts to make arrests, Bolkovac finds her efforts stymied by her fellow UN Peacekeepers—it turns out some of them are not just brothel patrons, but actively helping to keep the pipeline of terrified Eastern European girls flowing into Sarajevo.

On screen this is an infuriating subject, and Kondracki pulls no punches in showing the horrific brutality and murders committed against these young women. (Kondracki also insists she and Eilis, in working with the real Kathy Bolkovac, toned down the even more savage realities of the international sex trade.) *The Whistleblower* does not peddle in euphemistic metaphors or vague off-stage suggestions of violence—it puts it all right there, hard to stomach but demanding to be seen. There are not heroic rescues and feel-good resolutions—the film wants only to make viewers mad, and that it certainly does.

When Kondracki is not dragging Bolkovac and the audience into the Dantesque hells of sleazy sex clubs, she focuses her attention on the second half of the problem: the cover-up. Vanessa Redgrave and David Strathairn scowl appropriately with earnest gravitas as UN Human Rights officials trying to help Bolkovac. However, at every other turn they and the law officer are stonewalled, first by the security corporation, then higher-up UN officials (including Monica Bellucci), and finally (it is hinted) even the U.S. State Department. All of these players, at every level, mouth platitudes of indignation that calcify into bureaucratic regrets and eventually denials and efforts to silence. Soon what began as a gruesome crime story set in seedy brothels becomes a tale of a well-lit corporate conspiracy.

Weisz is always a formidable actress who is able to do a lot with her dauntingly attentive eyes, and she steels Bolkovac with never-quit fortitude. But perhaps out of respect to the real Bolkovac and a desire not to dilute their message with personal failings, the filmmakers only give their script's character a few broad-stroke motivations: She loves enforcing the law and cannot conceive of bending it or turning a blind eye to injustices; and her guilt over choosing her career over custody of her daughter drives her to save teenage girls halfway around the world. There are fleeting attempts to show Kathy off-duty, including a roughly sketched relationship with a fellow peacekeeper (Nikolaj Lie Kaas), but for the most part *The Whistleblower* only presents her as a crusade, which does not give Weisz much to work with in the long run. She glares, fumes, and sometimes chokes back tears, but other than Bolkovac's frustration and pain at being unable to stop the trafficking, the actress seems unable to find and share complicated, human nuances underneath the strident determination.

Kondracki and cinematographer Kieran McGuigan paint all this with grim, murky shadows and cold, gray landscapes. Pivotal scenes unfold in stark silhouette, and even the sunlight in *The Whistleblower* feels thin and strained, as if it can barely cover all the darkness below. There is no shortage of urgency or tension in the film as it pushes and pulls the viewer into Bolkovac's grim discoveries and later her heroic end-runs around the cover up, and when it comes to engaging and enraging the viewer on the subject of human trafficking, the film succeeds brutally and mightily. Though blunt, its big moments are plenty moving.

Kondracki is an issues director, *The Whistleblower* is an issues film, and Kathy Bolkovac is an issues character. The best narrative issues films, however, also have dramatic weight and cohesion beyond the horrific heft of their subjects. Kondracki admires the gritty, often paranoid films of the 1970s, but those works use compelling storytelling; rich, complex characters; and incisive dialog to create an emotional investment that runs deeper than just raw anger. The director, like her lead character, is to be commended for her passionate commitment to raising awareness about sex slavery—still a worldwide problem today. She appears to be just as dedicated to powerful filmmaking, so here is hoping her future projects rise to the impressive level of her activ-

ism, and she allows her fury to both enrich and unify her next film.

Locke Peterseim

CREDITS

Kathryn Bolkovac: Rachel Weisz
Madeleine Rees: Vanessa Redgrave
Peter Ward: David Strathairn
Laura Leviani: Monica Bellucci
Nick Kaufman: Benedict Cumberbatch
Fred Murray: David Hewlett
Bill Hynes: Liam Cunningham
Origin: Canada, Germany
Language: English
Released: 2011
Production: Amy J. Kaufman, Christina Piovesan, Celine Rattray; Samuel Goldwyn Films; released by Samuel Goldwyn Films
Directed by: Larysa Kondracki
Written by: Larysa Kondracki, Ellis Kirwan
Cinematography by: Kieran McGuigan
Music by: Mychael Danna
Sound: Mark Gingras
Music Supervisor: David Hayman
Editing: Julian Clarke
Art Direction: Vlad Vieru
Costumes: Gersha Phillips
Production Design: Caroline Foellmer
MPAA rating: R
Running time: 112 minutes

REVIEWS

Chang, Justin. *Variety.* August 2, 2011.
Gleiberman, Owen. *Entertainment Weekly.* August 3, 2011.
Holden, Stephen. *New York Times.* August 4, 2011.
Mondello, Bob. *NPR.* August 5, 2011.
Nelson, Rob. *Village Voice.* August 2, 2011.
Olsen, Mark. *Los Angele Times.* August 4, 2011.
Pols, Mary F. *TIME Magazine.* August 4, 2011.
Rechtshaffen, Michael. *Hollywood Reporter.* September 20, 2010.
Reed, Rex. *New York Observer.* August 3, 2011.
Zacharek, Stephanie. *Movieline.* August 4, 2011.

QUOTES

Blakely: "During your training you will see that peace is harder won than war. That every mornings hope is haunted by yesterday's nightmare."

TRIVIA

Rachel Weisz first read the script in 2005 when she was pregnant, but turned it down because she didn't think she could play the harsh role of Bolkovac at that time. Then, in 2009, after learning that the production hadn't moved forward, she accepted the role.

WIN WIN

In the game of life, you can't lose 'em all.
—Movie tagline

Box Office: $10.2 million

A mild-mannered, well acted, redemptive film of smartly observed humanity, *Win Win* is a dramedy whose skillful rendering expands to incorporate the full robustness of that often lazily applied hybrid descriptor. Kind of downbeat without being ponderous or melancholy, and at times funny though never in a fashion that betrays its characters, it is a movie that exudes genuine warmth, and achieves a smooth, enjoyable hold via the perfectly modulated quality of its lead performances. After premiering at the Sundance Film Festival, *Win Win* opened in mid-March, and an advertising campaign by distributor Fox Searchlight stressing the movie's somewhat unusual mentor-mentee relationship helped the film ring up over $10 million in ticket sales at the domestic box office.

The story centers around Michael Flaherty (Paul Giamatti), a small town New Jersey family man and lawyer specializing in elder care issues—not exactly the area of legal expertise in which fortunes are typically made. For additional money, he moonlights as the wrestling coach at the local high school, where he and assistant coach Stephen Vigman (Jeffrey Tambor) oversee a squad that routinely accepts their beat-downs against other schools with a sort of cheerful, shrugging aplomb.

Money also figures in Michael's decision to go beyond the norm in helping Leo Poplar (Burt Young), a client suffering from the early stages of dementia. Leo has plenty of money, so, for a court-mandated $1,500 per month stipend, Michael agrees to be his guardian, to keep Leo from becoming a ward of the state. Already overextended, though, Michael doubts his ability to adequately oversee Leo living on his own (which is his wish), and so, in a moment of weakness, exploits Leo's condition and allows him to believe that a judge has adjudicated that he must live in an assisted-care facility.

Things get complicated, however, when Leo's teenage grandson Kyle (Alex Shaffer) shows up. Unable to immediately send him back to Ohio to his mother, Cindy (Melanie Lynskey), Michael and his wife Jackie (Amy Ryan) decide to take Kyle into their home, and even enroll him in school. In short order, Kyle proves himself to be an extraordinarily gifted wrestler; he had actually gone to the state championships his freshman

year in Ohio, before eventually being kicked off the team. This talent rather naturally perks up the spirits of Michael, and somewhat unnaturally those of his friend Terry Delfino (Bobby Cannavale), a recent divorcee who latches onto Kyle's talents with the rabid enthusiasm of a parent, becoming an assistant to Michael alongside Coach Vigman (and eventually elbowing Tambor almost entirely out of the movie). When Cindy shows up and starts asking questions about the finances of her estranged father Leo, however, it sets in motion a chain of events that endangers Kyle's newly settled domesticity, and threatens to expose the moral dubiousness of Michael's choice.

In his previous movies behind the camera, *The Station Agent* (2003) and *The Visitor* (2008), writer-director Tom McCarthy has first and foremost concentrated on characters over plotting, and *Win Win* is no different. Evincing no particularly rigidly observed visual style, the movie unfolds on a fairly modest canvas, and could easily be retro-engineered into a novel given the unflashy nature of its predicaments. McCarthy and co-writer Joe Tiboni, a longtime friend and real-life attorney, float a couple dramatic trial balloons (the possibility that Cindy is a drug addict, and the fact that Michael has been ignoring shortness of breath from stress attacks for months, prioritizing his family's other financial needs over his own health), but then, for better or worse, do not do much with them in the way of typical leveraged effect. Mostly, though, *Win Win* lacks much feeling in the way of typical conflict because Kyle is so nice, well mannered and pliable. His hinted-at anger issues are so distant in the rearview mirror as to seem virtually nonexistent.

In casting Shaffer, an acting neophyte with high school wrestling experience, McCarthy also firmly establishes the parameters and priorities of his film—mostly for the good. With his placid, unflappable demeanor, and a vocal timbre that recalls comedian Brian Posehn, Shaffer is the antithesis of so many half-cocked portrayals of teen angst, which, when poorly acted, can come across as little more than vessels for overcooked energy. In counterpoint to his "edgy" platinum blonde dyed hair, Shaffer's presence is low-key and pleasant, totally of a piece with the rest of the narrative. And his athletic experience certainly gives the grappling sequences a slappy authenticity that does not extend unrealistically past the limits of what one might expect from prep-level wrestling. The only moments when Shaffer's lack of professional experience shows are in a couple sequences of more emotionally articulated anger late in the movie, but McCarthy for the most part does a good job of not placing unreasonable demands on his young star.

Win Win is really Giamatti's movie, though. With his expressive eyes, schlubby physicality and kind of naturally hangdog demeanor, Giamatti has become a something of a big screen avatar for middle-aged apprehension and emotional restriction or seclusion. When given good material, as in the Oscar®-nominated *American Splendor* (2003) and *Sideways* (2004), he especially excels in these sorts of roles because there is an inner life to his characters that shines through, and lets one know when and how he is being truthful and when he is lying or even deceiving himself. Owing to its aforementioned narrative timidity, though, *Win Win* leans a bit more heartily on this inherited offscreen impression. Giamatti's turn is not in any way a bad performance (quite the opposite), but Michael's relationships with his friends are a bit thinly drawn, so the movie leans, perhaps cannily, on an audience's recognition and acceptance of him as chiefly a vessel for middle-class struggle.

None of these critiques, however, are disqualifying, or even particularly sticky and stinging. Instead, *Win Win* draws much of its emotional connection from smart scene-to-scene interplay and the real-world relevancy of its plot focus. Like *Company Men* (2010), it concentrates on the economic difficulties of a white collar professional (albeit a tax bracket or two removed) trying to provide for his family. *Win Win* walks an interesting balance beam, however. Unlike something like *Tower Heist* (2011), it does not dip into desultory wish fulfillment; there is not a greedy scoundrel receiving comeuppance. Neither does the movie trip headlong into the emotional manipulation of a morality play. It just *is*, if that makes sense. There is no emotional overreach. *Win Win* is content to exist on a low-fi plane in which ethical considerations abut and impact the everyday tending of familial wellbeing—exactly the sort of plane on which most people exist in real life, in other words.

Within the story's third act pivots, bits of contrivance combine to drain *Win Win* of the opportunity to connect as grandly cathartic; such is the small difference between something that triumphs and something that merely succeeds. Still, the film is consistently engaging and pleasant throughout, and in its unassuming recognizability—a product, perhaps of McCarthy's ongoing working relationship with production designer John Paino, who specializes in conveying telling details in unpretentious settings—it achieves a special sort of admiration and esteem, raising legitimate questions about moral principles but not feeling it necessary to tell an audience what to think. If small, humble and innately human movies like *Win Win*, in which the biggest special effect is perhaps a noisy offscreen toilet, ever entirely disappear from theaters where they can be experienced communally, then it will truly reflect a loss, for filmgoers and filmmakers alike.

Brent Simon

CREDITS

Mike Flaherty: Paul Giamatti
Kyle Timmons: Alex Shaffer
Cindy Timmons: Melanie Lynskey
Jackie Flaherty: Amy Ryan
Terry Delfino: Bobby Cannavale
Vigman: Jeffrey Tambor
Leo Poplar: Burt Young
Shelley: Margo Martindale
Stemler: David Thompson
Origin: USA
Language: English
Released: 2011
Production: Mary Jane Skalski, Michael London, Lisa Marie Falcone; Groundswell Productions, Next Wednesday, Everest Entertainment, Dune Entertainment; released by Fox Searchlight
Directed by: Thomas McCarthy
Written by: Thomas McCarthy
Cinematography by: Oliver Brokelberg
Music by: Lyle Workman
Sound: Damian Canelos
Music Supervisor: Mary Ramos
Editing: Tom McArdle
Costumes: Melissa Toth
Production Design: John Paino, Scott Anderson
MPAA rating: R
Running time: 106 minutes

REVIEWS

Anderson, John. *Wall Street Journal*. March 17, 2011.
Berkshire, Geoff. *Metromix.com*. March 17, 2011.
Debruge, Peter. *Variety*. January 23, 2011.
Denby, David. *New Yorker*. March 14, 2011.
Kennedy, Lisa. *Denver Post*. April 1, 2011.
Lemire, Christy. *Associated Press*. March 24, 2011.
Longworth, Karina. *Village Voice*. March 15, 2011.
Scott, A.O. *New York Times*. March 17, 2011.
Tallerico, Brian. *HollywoodChicago.com*. March 25, 2011.
Turan, Kenneth. *Los Angeles Times*. March 17, 2011.

QUOTES

Jackie Flaherty: "I wanna go to Ohio and beat the crap out of his mom."
Mike Flaherty: "Oh, come on."
Jackie Flaherty: "No, I do. I want to beat the crap out of her and her stupid boyfriend."

Mike Flaherty: "Oh, okay."

Jackie Flaherty: "I'm serious."

Mike Flaherty: "I know you are. I just…I just don't think beating the crap out of everybody is the best solution, that's all."

Jackie Flaherty: "It feels like it."

AWARDS

Nomination:

Ind. Spirit 2012: Screenplay

Writers Guild 2011: Orig. Screenplay.

WINNIE THE POOH

Oh Pooh.
        —Movie tagline

Box Office: $26.7 million

Of his aft appendage, Eeyore once said, "It's not much of a tail, but I'm sort of attached to it." Take that quote, change "tail" to "tale," and one likely has the opinion of most moviegoers who saw *Winnie the Pooh*. Many people have grown up but never outgrown that beloved bear. While wee watchers in adjoining seats delightedly slurped and swallowed their way toward concession stand-administered tummy trouble, parents were themselves being filled with a comforting sense of nostalgia that led them to fondly assess this short-but-sweet feature. The sixty-three-minute film itself harkens back to simpler times, a wistful cinematic oasis of old-school coziness that provides a respite from frenetic, cacophonous CGI spectacles presented in 3D and stuffed with soon-to-be-dated cultural references. The production, which is the first time that the treasured characters have become charmingly befuddled on-screen since 2005, seems unlikely to endure in the manner of A.A. Milne's books or the three superior featurettes later combined into *The Many Adventures of Winnie the Pooh* (1977). Nevertheless, it cannot help but endear.

Whether one is of an age to have first seen Disney's classic cinematic Pooh adaptations in theaters, on videocassette, or on DVD, all viewers of this film will immediately feel reassuringly at home, not just because it begins like its prized predecessors with a live-action depiction of Christopher Robin's bedroom, but also because the scene will probably remind them of their own toy-cluttered childhood sanctuaries. A whole world can spring forth from such a niche with the help of what is described here as a "very active imagination," and what follows is supposedly emanating from that of a fellow owner of stuffed animals. Of course, it has actually sprung from the mind of Milne, who was initially inspired by his own cloth menagerie-toting Christopher Robin, and the author's charmingly-whimsical, widely-celebrated work is referenced by yet another familiar element at the outset: the depiction of an opening book that acts as a visual invitation to immerse oneself in the story about to be told. Children have been curling up with their parents to hear stories read aloud to them for about as many years as the Hundred Acre Wood has acres, and so once again a narrator (this time John Cleese) is utilized in relating and explaining what transpires during the cinematic adaptation. As in previous outings, he not only addresses viewers but also interacts with the characters, such as waking up Pooh to begin the proceedings. Also as before, not only do Milne's stories come alive on-screen but also the letters, words, sentences and paragraphs that convey them, here conking a character on the head or there helpfully assembling into a hole-extricating ladder. Finally, with Zooey Deschanel adding an only-slightly updated version of the *Winnie the Pooh* theme song, a sense of Pooh déjà vu is delightfully inescapable.

Winnie the Pooh is composed of chapters cherry-picked from Milne's Pooh output that are perhaps not the most memorable ones, and they have been combined in a way that somewhat diminishes overall focus. The new songs composed for the film do not rise to the level of those comprising the legendary Sherman Brothers' catchy canon. Yet it is exceedingly difficult to work oneself up for anything approaching real bellyaching while in the presence of this lovable, "silly old bear" whose belly, as always, is doing some potent grumbling of its own. The bulk of what happens is a tempest in a teapot, or, perhaps more appropriately, a hubbub in a honey pot. The mere leaving of a note by Christopher Robin (Jack Boulter) saying that he will be "Back Soon" leads his wholly loyal but only semi-literate forest friends to believe that he is in need of being saved from a horrifying creature called "The Backson." Thus Pooh (Jim Cummings, a fine replacement for the great Sterling Holloway), Piglet (Travis Oates), Owl (Craig Ferguson), Rabbit (*SpongeBob*'s Tom Kenny), Tigger (versatile Cummings again), Kanga (Kristen Anderson-Lopez, who also composed the aforementioned middling tunes with her husband Robert) and Roo (Wyatt Hall, son of the film's director Don Hall) get themselves needlessly wound up and then stranded down in their own Backson trap. Another plot strand involves Pooh's quest to satiate his hankering for honey. There is also a contest to find suitable derriere adornment for a temporarily-tailless Eeyore (Bud Luckey). Fittingly, things end nicely for the downcast donkey, as well as for Pooh and everyone else.

The animation in *Winnie the Pooh* is old-fashioned by choice, aiming, as art director Paul Felix put it, to "fit seamlessly with those earlier films." It is hand-drawn and two-dimensional, with backgrounds that have a lovely, pacifyingly-pastelled watercolor feel. The artwork both noticeably and effectively differs twice, once during a fear-fueled fantasy conjuring up the dreaded Backson in chalk-like detail, and then also in the sunnily-amber-saturated "Everything is Honey" sequence. The former is reminiscent of that especially memorable section in the Academy Award®-winning *Winnie the Pooh and the Blustery Day* (1968) during which characters scare themselves silly thinking about Heffalumps and Woozles.

Made on a budget of $30 million, *Winnie the Pooh* succeeded in grossing $26.6 million. Most critics were sufficiently charmed. While its titular character is prominently ample, this latest film that bears his name admittedly strikes one as slight. However, this throwback to the past is not a throwaway. Like the red balloon briefly attached to Eeyore, it is unquestionably cheer-inducing and gently buoyant. The film affords a pleasant opportunity to catch up with old friends and unabashedly introduce them to one's children. Most parents who have been looking for some suitably-soothing fare for their youngsters—not to mention themselves—agreed with Pooh that it was "time for something sweet."

David L. Boxerbaum

CREDITS

Winnie the Pooh/Tigger: Jim Cummings (Voice)
Owl: Craig Ferguson (Voice)
Rabbit: Tom Kenny (Voice)
Piglet: Travis Oates (Voice)
Eeyore: Bud Luckey (Voice)
Kanga: Kristen Anderson-Lopez (Voice)
Christopher Robin: Jack Boulter (Voice)
Roo: Wyatt Dean Hall (Voice)
Backson: Huell Howser (Voice)
Narrator: John Cleese
Origin: USA
Language: English
Released: 2011
Production: Peter Del Vecho, Clark Spencer; Walt Disney Pictures
Directed by: Stephen John Anderson, Don Hall
Written by: Stephen John Anderson, Don Hall, Clio Chiang, Don Dougherty, Kendelle Hoyer, Brian Kesinger, Nicole Mitchell, Jeremy Spears
Cinematography by: Julio Macat
Music by: Henry Jackman
Sound: Todd Toon
Music Supervisor: Tom MacDougall
Editing: Lisa Linder

Art Direction: Paul Felix, Patrick M. Sullivan Jr.
MPAA rating: G
Running time: 69 minutes

REVIEWS

Angulo Chen, Sandie. *Washington Post.* July 14, 2011.
Bowles, Scott. *USA Today.* July 14, 2011.
Chang, Justin. *Variety.* July 2, 2011.
Ebert, Roger. *Chicago Sun-Times.* July 14, 2011.
Gleiberman, Owen. *Entertainment Weekly.* July 13, 2011.
Goldstein, Gary. *Los Angeles Times.* July 14, 2011.
McCarthy, Todd. *Hollywood Reporter.* July 2, 2011.
Pols, Mary. *Time.* July 14, 2011.
Russo, Tom. *Boston Globe.* July 14, 2011.
Scott, A.O. *New York Times.* July 14, 2011.

QUOTES

Piglet: "Oh, Pooh, you went back for the honey, didn't you? But I told you the pot was empty."
Pooh: "Well, I believed you, but my tummy had to check for itself."

TRIVIA

This is only the third time that Walt Disney Animation Studios produced a sequel to one of the films from the Disney Animated Classics canon in-house.

THE WOMAN

Not every monster lives in the wild.
—Movie tagline

Lucky McKee is one of the more unique filmmaking voices of the last decade. The genre he primarily works within—horror—has existed through dichotomies of repetition designed to fulfill the needs of its blood-lusting fans. McKee is well aware of this fact, but the repetition he explores is that of human nature and repressed primal urges. Though made mostly by men, horror films are often structured around female heroines; babes surviving in the woods from the big bad wolf determined to tear their hearts out. Generally, these are caricatures that come with the formula and are too busy screaming from being stalked to examine the neuroses of individuals that have nothing to do with being chased and everything about being forced to stand alone. That is where McKee arrives. From his criminally under-seen portrait of lonely psychosis in *May* (2002) and now with *The Woman*, McKee has proven himself as maybe the preeminent auteur of feminist horror tales.

From the outside, the Cleek family looks to be an all-American Rockwell portrait. Patriarch Chris (Sean

Bridgers) is the friendly real-estate lawyer with a house in the country. He has a wife, Belle (Angela Bettis) and three children; teenager Peggy (Lauren Ashley Carter), adolescent Brian (Zach Rand), and the youngest so cute they had to name her Darlin (Shyla Molhusen). Read the body language though and it tells another story. Peggy is withdrawing herself from contact at school. Brian is in that awkward in-between stage between voyeuristic destruction and puberty. Belle is all too careful what to say in front of her husband, who is practically an android of smiles and subtle orders.

Out hunting one day, Chris comes across a woman (Pollyanna McIntosh) washing herself in the stream. Attracted first to her naked form, Chris then hits upon the idea of capturing this feral creature in an attempt to civilize her. He will even make it a family project, something to bring them together. Even if the eldest women of his own suburbanized tribe are a bit aghast, little Darlin cannot help but innocently ask "can we keep her?" The filthy woman speaks her own language and as Chris discovers a little too late, has a taste for human flesh. He will clean her up though and take no guff from Belle about it. Outside the family circle, though with no knowledge of their little social project, Peggy's teacher (Carlee Baker), suspects the secret she has been trying to hide even if she cannot fully grasp the true implications of what is happening within the Cleek household.

It is those implications that make up the forefront of the story that McKee is trying to tell. Whatever form of monster the title character is meant to represent, the true evil is not the one chained-up in the cellar but the one walking around in broad daylight. Chris Cleek is the everyday evil of the world. No supernatural powers other than the silent fear that paralyzes those closest to him from challenging or running from his control. It is a malevolence that is more terrifying because of its reality and the ability to affect and influence those around him. Bridgers' performance is a sly balance of comic audacity and startling serenity.

The dynamic of the Cleek family has the amusing baggage based in the comedies about outsiders showing up to change their world for the better. If their new guest was an alien, hobo or just a free spirit who sees the bright side to their cold demeanor, the wife would find her voice, the daughter would ask her school crush out and the son would learn his first lesson about becoming a man in typical films of this genre. Instead, the woman is an immovable object drawing out or repressing further the natural instincts of each individual. Most disturbing of all is young Brian's progression from a boy using pain to express his feelings for a girl at school to jumping right into torturous experimentation. With a father figure who chuckles off his son's behavior as "boys will be boys," the piece conveys a whole nation's worth of antiquated attitudes and prejudices.

This is still a horror film by all accounts and Lucky McKee knows how to appease those genre fans without merely condescending to their lust for gore. Adapted from the novel written by McKee and acclaimed horror novelist, Jack Ketchum, *The Woman* is actually a sequel to Ketchum's *Off Season* and *Offspring* about a family of cannibals terrorizing families. The latter was actually produced into a 2009 motion picture featuring Pollyanna McIntosh as the same unnamed character. Her cannibalistic instincts are featured throughout McKee's film, but they are really the only link to the previous stories. There is no need to walk into *The Woman* with a refresher course in Ketchum mythology as the mysteries of the character's existence provide a further psychological link between the "civilized" humans and the untamed animals that roam for pure survival. McIntosh's woman is certainly no heroine, even if one finds themselves rooting for vengeance in the shocking final scenes. She is just another part of the food chain—just as capable of cruelty towards her kind but in a more upfront and honest fashion that is sure to send the squeamish curling away from the screen.

The Woman is a wildly subversive example of modern horror that unsettles in the best possible way, providing food for thought from both sexes on the role that women play in a world guided by the male psyche. Just as McKee's May Dove Canady finally succumbed to creating the perfect man for herself, Chris Cleek applies the uneasy double standard to his own Madonna/Whore complex to achieve an endgame of a moral front disguising an immoral underbelly. *The Woman* offers brutal truth with dark humor and everything a horror fan can ask for, making it most certainly a keeper.

Erik Childress

CREDITS

Chris Cleek: Sean Bridges
Belle Cleek: Angela Bettis
The Woman: Pollyanna McIntosh
Brian Cleek: Zach Rand
Genevieve Raton: Carlee Baker
Peggy Cleek: Lauren Ashley Carter
Darlin Cleek: Shylla Molhusen
Origin: USA
Language: English
Released: 2011
Production: Andrew van den Houten, Robert Tonino; Moderncine; released by Bloody Disgusting
Directed by: Lucky McKee

Written by: Lucky McKee, Jack Ketchum
Cinematography by: Alex Vendler
Music by: Sean Spillane
Sound: Andrew Smetek
Editing: Zach Passero
Costumes: Michael Bevins, Sandra Alexandre
Production Design: Krista Gall
MPAA rating: R
Running time: 101 minutes

REVIEWS

Bitel, Anton. *Little White Lies.* August 30, 2011.
Gibron, Bill. *PopMatters.* October 14, 2011.
Gonsalves, Rob. *eFilmCritic.com.* August 9, 2011.
Goss, William. *Film.com.* October 21, 2011.
Musetto, V.A. *New York Post.* October 14, 2011.
Putman, Dustin. *DustinPutman.com.* October 18, 2011.
Rodriguez, Rene. *Miami Herald.* October 26, 2011.
Tobias, Scott. *AV Club.* October 13, 2011.
Webster, Andy. *New York Times.* October 16, 2011.
Weinberg, Scott. *FEARnet.* September 5, 2011.

QUOTES

Belle Cleek: "I never condoned what you did. Never. You just can't keep putting one thing on top of the other and expect to keep getting away with it forever. I've had it."

Chris Cleek: "Okay, so what are you gonna do, I mean what is your plan, what? I just would like to know, what the f**k you think you're going to do about it."

TRIVIA

In the film, Chris Cleek repeatedly uses the word "anophthalmia" in reference to one of his daughters. Unilateral anophthalmia is the congenital absence of one eye, and bilateral anophthalmia is the congenital absence of both eyes.

X-Z

X-MEN: FIRST CLASS

Witness the moment that will change our world.
—Movie tagline

Before he was Professor X, he was Charles. Before he was Magneto, he was Erik. Before they were enemies, they were allies.
—Movie tagline

Their powers would make [...] destiny would make the[...]
—Movie tagline

Box Office: $146.4 million

Two trends often collide in [...] superhero movie: The hiring of [...] resumes show off more attention [...] narrative than to special effects [...] then the inevitable steam-rolling [...] as studios and toy makers insis[...] scene of the film with back story, [...] CGI in order to pump the form[...] broadest possible audience consta[...] "entertainment." Watching many [...] films viewers sometimes sense the d[...] out from behind the special effects a[...] narrative, hoping to maintain some sort of idiosyncratic fingerprint on it all.

Set against a 1962 Cold War backdrop, *X-Men: First Class* is plenty over-stuffed with meddling, but it also has enough thoughtfulness and comic-book integrity to keep it out ahead of its genre's worst tendencies. That is in part due to producer Bryan Singer (whose original 2000 *X-Men* film set the mold for character over chaos

and thoughtful atmosphere over mindless action) and director Matthew Vaughn, much admired in genre circles for his energetic, stylish, and visually inventive approaches to crime films (*Layer Cake* [2004]) and superheroes (*Kick-Ass* [2010]).

In the new film, Vaughn and the usual screenwrit- [...] committee (including Singer and Vaughn's writing [...] Jane Goldman) lay out the origins of the friend- [...] ween powerful mutants Charles Xavier (James [...]) and Erik Lehnsherr (Michael Fassbender), [...] eir competing Martin Luther King Jr. and Mal- [...] proaches to mutant-human relations opened a [...] tween the unity minded Professor X and the [...] agneto. *X-Men: First Class* shows how Xavier's [...] of wealth and privilege is the source of not [...] titlement, but his compassionate empathy. Le- [...] n the extreme other hand, comes of age (and [...] mutant powers) at Auschwitz, the victim of [...] ity. Escaping the camp, he emerges into adult- [...] en by rage and vengeance.

[...]voy and Fassbender are the very best parts of *X-Me[...] First Class*—and perhaps just as much, if not more, responsible for its achievements as Singer and Vaughn. Neither man is straining his considerable acting talents here, but nor are the two lazily slumming as caricatures. McAvoy balances naïve idealism with pragmatic optimism, while using his loose charm to give Xavier a flirty twinkle. And Fassbender, looking very Richard-Burton-cool in leather jackets, puts his now-trademark deadly calm intensity to work infusing Lehnsherr with a wrath fueled by inner pain. It is a testimony to Fassbender's considerable screen presence that the actor maintains his dark, brooding dignity even when asked to don Magneto's bright maroon helmet and cape.

While *X-Men: First Class* is best in the character moments between its leads, most audiences do not want to watch a 100-minute stage play centered on Xavier and Lehnsherr playing chess and debating mutant-human morality. This is a superhero movie, after all. So atop the relatively compelling and well-essayed relationship at its core, the film piles on more mutants (good and evil) and clashes not of ideology but glowing energy blasts.

There is Kevin Bacon as villainous Sebastian Shaw, a bad guy out to use his cocky sideburns and mutant powers to play the Kennedy-Era Americans off against the Russians in hopes a Cold War nuclear showdown at the Cuban Missile Crisis will leave irradiated planet ripe for his world domination. At his side is Emma Frost, a lingerie-clad telepath who can turn her body diamond tough. Unfortunately Frost is played by January Jones, whose thespian powers are much more wooden than gemstone.

On Xavier and Lehnsherr's side is a newly formed team of mutant teenagers that feels like a collection of CGI carnival tricks—the parade of cool new superpowers becomes the primary definition of their characters. Best among the bunch are Jennifer Lawrence as the shape-shifting Mystique and Nicholas Hoult as the super-genius Hank McCoy. However, while the talented Lawrence and Hoult's characters have semi-rich backgrounds, unlike McAvoy and Fassbender, the gifted younger actors struggle to find honest emotional ground amidst the power blasts and mutant-blue make up.

Everything looks swell. Vaughn embraces the *X-Men: First Class*'s pop-art 1960s mod style with swinging enthusiasm as the story races through Vegas nightclubs and Bond-villain submarines. Nor is the director a slouch when orchestrating grand action set pieces with said submarine (plus supersonic jets and dozens of U.S. and U.S.S.R. warships and warheads).

The nature of the superhero blockbuster genre, however, never lets the film rest—the huge piles of plot demand connect-the-dot narrative shortcuts and a shorthand sketching of Xavier and Lehnsherr's pivotal friendship. Likewise, despite all his visual strengths, Vaughn never fully finds his balance amid franchise demands and summer-blockbuster effects, and potentially intriguing ideas and themes are too often reduced to speeches on beaches between super-power fights. The over-long checklist of narrative tasks *X-Men: First Class* must tick off means all that plot spills out at the finish and—after a brutally effective and chilling climax—into about three too many endings.

Despite all that, thanks to the efforts of Vaughn, McAvoy and Fassbender, *X-Men: First Class* successfully entertains and sports plenty of enjoyable, even powerful moments. That those moments are more often fueled by human (not super) powers speaks to both the film's strength and weakness: Ultimately, viewers care more about the characters than their costumed exploits. That is great for a stage play, but problematic for a super-hero movie.

Locke Peterseim

CREDITS

Charles Xavier/Professor X: James McAvoy
Erik Lensherr/Magneto: Michael Fassbender
Dr. Moira MacTaggert: Rose Byrne
Emma Frost: January Jones
Sebastian Shaw/Dr. Schmidt: Kevin Bacon
Hank McCoy/Beast: Nicholas Hoult
Alex Summers/Havok: Lucas Till
Azazel: Jason Flemyng
Man in Black: Oliver Platt
Raven Darkholme/Mystique: Jennifer Lawrence
Armando Munoz/Darwin: Edi Gathegi
Sean Cassidy/Banshee: Caleb Landry Jones
Janos Quested/Riptide: Alex Gonzales
Angel Salvadore/Wings: Zoe Kravitz
Origin: USA
Language: English
Released: 2011
Production: Gregory Goodman, Simon Kinberg, Lauren Shuler Donner, Bryan Singer; Bad Hat Production, Donners' Company, Marv Films, Marvel Enterprises, Marvel Studios; released by 20th Century-Fox
Directed by: Matthew Vaughn
Written by: Matthew Vaughn, Ashley Edward Miller, Jane Goldman, Zack Stentz
Cinematography by: John Mathieson
Music by: Henry Jackman
Sound: Simon Hayes
Editing: Lee Smith, Eddie Hamilton
Art Direction: John Frankish, Dawn Swiderski
Costumes: Sammy Sheldon
Production Design: Chris Seagers
MPAA rating: PG-13
Running time: 132 minutes

REVIEWS

Burr, Ty. *Boston Globe*. June 1, 2011.
Chang, Justin. *Variety*. May 30, 2011.
Hornaday, Ann. *Washington Post*. June 2, 2011.
Morgenstern, Joe. *Wall Street Journal*. June 2, 2011.

Puig, Claudia. *USA Today.* June 2, 2011.
Robinson, Tasha. *AV Club.* June 2, 2011.
Schwarzbaum, Lisa. *Entertainment Weekly.* June 2, 2011.
Smith, Kyle. *New York Post.* June 2, 2011.
Tobias, Scott. *NPR.* June 3, 2011.
Travers, Peter. *Rolling Stone.* June 2, 2011.

QUOTES

Professor Charles Xavier: "Listen to me very carefully, my friend: killing will not bring you peace."

TRIVIA

Amber Heard was attached to the role of Mystique before Jennifer Lawrence was cast.

AWARDS

Nomination:

Screen Actors Guild 2011: Stunt Ensemble.

YOUNG ADULT

> *Everyone gets old. Not everyone grows up.*
> —Movie tagline

Box Office: $16.3 million

With three films with increasing levels of critical success (*Thank You For Smoking* [2005], *Juno* [2007], *Up in the Air* [2009]) and four Oscar® nominations (including two for Best Director) by the time he was thirty-three, it seems safe to say that Jason Reitman was at something of a career crossroads when it came time to start production on his fourth directorial venture. It seemed likely to most that the other shoe would have to drop eventually and that Mr. Reitman would eventually deliver a film considered a critical disappointment. If that slight valley in a career of notable peaks already turns out to be *Young Adult* then Reitman can consider himself lucky. While this dramedy is flawed enough to be considered a disappointment only in comparison to his last two stellar films, it also features some daring directorial decisions in support of some of the best performances that Reitman has yet directed. While his eye for composition may not yet be fully developed and there are some screenwriting issues that allow *Young Adult* to fall below the filmmaker's recent output, his ability to draw challenging, daring performances from his actors (including Aaron Eckhart, Ellen Page, and George Clooney) remains flawless as he directs Charlize Theron to the best performance of her career and finds a perfect foil for her in the unlikeliest of places, standup comedian Patton Oswalt. They alone make *Young Adult* worthwhile.

Diablo Cody, the Oscar®-winning writer of *Juno,* reportedly crafted the story of Mavis Gary (Theron), a writer of young adult fiction (like the *Sweet Valley High* series), after questioning whether or not she herself had some issues with stunted maturity after writing primarily stories of adolescence. Mavis Gary is a Prom Queen who has never grown up. She has clearly never achieved the level of popularity and happiness that she had in high school and, therefore, has remained the calculating mean girl who sleeps around, drinks too much, and looks down on pretty much everyone around her. Gary has been understandably stuck at the maturity level in which life was easiest for her. It is later revealed that she had a marriage that went bad since high school and that her book franchise, for which she ghost writes and never receives full credit anyway, is ending. She retreats even further into her childhood, returning to her Minnesota hometown for one last attempt to rekindle high school glory.

Gary's woefully misguided plan for happiness centers around reuniting with the Prom King, high school boyfriend Buddy Slade (Patrick Wilson). She cares not that Slade is married (to Elizabeth Reaser) with a new baby. There is clearly a part of Gary's twisted mind that thinks that if she looks hot enough and flirts well enough that Buddy will realize that family life is not for him and ditch it all for the girl that got away. It seems not coincidental that Cody wrote Slade as a character making the most clear turn into adulthood—becoming a parent—as a counterpoint to someone stuck in childhood. In fact, the only person who seems to pay any attention at all to Gary upon her return home is someone else stuck at a crucial point in his life, Matt Freehauf (Patton Oswalt). Back in high school, Freehauf was so mercilessly bullied that he was physically abused to the point that he is permanently handicapped. His body is stuck in high school just as Mavis' mind is stuck there. It makes sense that Freehauf becomes something of a conscience for Gary, trying to dissuade her from going through with her homewrecking plan and forming one of the most unique duos of 2011.

Mavis Gary is a daringly unlikable character. Whereas most directors and screenwriters would have crafted an arc that asks the viewer to see through the character flaws to the eventual self-discovery that pushes the protagonist to the next level of maturity, Reitman and Cody are not interesting in telling that kind of story. They do not care if viewers do not like Mavis Gary and have crafted a risky comedy in that it eschews typical moral lessons or any sort of learning lesson. Theron was clearly inspired by the opportunity to play a character more realistically consistent than the average Hollywood creation, giving a risky, challenging, three-dimensional performance that is easily matched by one of the best supporting turns of the year from Patton Oswalt. The star of *Ratatouille* (2007) and *Big Fan* (2009) grounds the entire piece, offering the viewer's eye into the proceedings as the voice of reason against Gary's voice of bottled popularity.

Cody could have found one more plot beat, one more moment to add weight to the piece—there are really only a few moments that feel like they have any lingering power at all and they are more courtesy of smart decisions made by Theron and Oswalt than anything else—but this is a complex, daring choice for Reitman to direct at this point in his career. It is not quite the accomplishment of his last two films but it also does not seem to aspire to be so. One could argue that the film indicates that Reitman is settling into a groove—going back to a collaborator like Cody that has worked in the past and, once again, tackling immaturity in suburbia—but the tonal risks of *Young Adult* hint that this is a man who may be going home again but approaching the journey in a new way.

Brian Tallerico

CREDITS

Mavis Gary: Charlize Theron
Buddy Slade: Patrick Wilson
Matt Freehauf: Patton Oswalt
Beth Slade: Elizabeth Reaser
Mavis's Boss: J.K. Simmons
Sandra Freehauf: Collette Wolfe
Hedda Gary: Jill Eikenberry
David Gary: Richard Bekins
Jan: Mary Beth Hurt
Origin: USA
Language: English
Released: 2011
Production: Jason Reitman, Diablo Cody, Mason Novick, Lianne Halfon; Denver & Delilah Films, Mandate Pictures, Mr. Mudd; released by Paramount Pictures
Directed by: Jason Reitman
Written by: Diablo Cody
Cinematography by: Eric Steelberg
Music by: Rolfe Kent
Sound: Ken Ishii
Music Supervisor: Linda Cohen
Editing: Dana E. Glauberman
Art Direction: Michael Ahern
Costumes: David C. Robinson
Production Design: Kevin Thompson
MPAA rating: R
Running time: 94 minutes

REVIEWS

Corliss, Richard. *Time Magazine.* December 8, 2011.
Debruge, Peter. *Variety.* December 4, 2011.

Ebert, Roger. *Chicago Sun-Times.* December 7, 2011.
Hoberman, Joe. *Village Voice.* December 6, 2011.
Kois, Dan. *Slate.* December 8, 2011.
LaSalle, Mick. *San Francisco Chronicle.* December 8, 2011.
Mondello, Bob. *NPR.* December 9, 2011.
Morgenstern, Joe. *Wall Street Journal.* December 8, 2011.
Scott, A.O. *New York Times.* December 8, 2011.
Sharkey, Betsy. *Los Angeles Times.* December 8, 2011.

QUOTES

Matt Freehauf: "Guys like me are born loving women like you."

TRIVIA

On October 19, 2011, Jason Reitman and Diablo Cody hosted a sneak preview of the film at the Edina Theater in suburban Minneapolis where most of the film was made.

AWARDS

Nomination:

Golden Globes 2012: Actress—Mus./Comedy (Theron)
Writers Guild 2011: Orig. Screenplay.

YOUR HIGHNESS

> *Get your quest on.*
> —Movie tagline

> *Best. Quest. Ever.*
> —Movie tagline

Box Office: $21.6 million

Director David Gordon Green was once rightfully called "the poet of the cinema" by film critic Roger Ebert. Green's first four films had sophistication, humanity and wisdom that seemed well beyond his young age. Characters interacted with each other in a way seldom seen on American movie screens. Poetic words spoken by the actors would sound like natural conversation while his cinematographer Tim Orr would capture the sunlit and mostly unattractive details of the landscape, usually downtrodden-looking small towns or dilapidated houses. Green was able to capture the essence of a place that would compliment the characters who inhabited them. His influences were obvious (Terrence Malick and Robert Altman, to start), but his style remained his own and he was a refreshing, sincere new voice, particularly with his first film, the meditative and lyrical *George Washington* (2000).

In 2008, Green took a left turn with his career and dove into his first mainstream comedy for producer

Judd Apatow, the action-pot-comedy *Pineapple Express.* The movie was obviously his most commercially popular and yet still had his own signature touch amid the usual (and still very funny) flavoring brought by Seth Rogen and Judd Apatow. Coupled with his successful run as a director on many episodes of HBO's *Eastbound and Down,* starring his college buddy Danny McBride, made it seem as if Green was saying goodbye to his indie roots for a while and deciding to enjoy having a wider audience for his work, however different it may have been from his earlier sensibilities.

But now comes *Your Highness,* a comedy that appears to have been conceived in the same vein as *Pineapple Express* and was probably hoped to have been as successful. Many of the elements for a successful comedy were there. James Franco and Danny McBride (both stars of *Pineapple Express*) would play brothers. Zooey Deschanel and Natalie Portman would play the love interests. The film is a medieval comedy that would also be a bit of a send-up of those sword-and-sorcery quest films from the '80s (*Clash of the Titans* [1981], *The Sword and the Sorcerer* [1982] and *Dragonslayer* [1981], for example). It would be the first time Green would attempt big budget special effects after already proving himself a perfectly capable action sequence director. What resulted, however, is one of the most colossal miscalculations from one of the finest directors working today. *Your Highness* is exactly the kind of movie most directors have nightmares about being associated with for the rest of their careers.

The main culprit of this disaster, however, is its star and co-writer, Danny McBride. The story concerns Thadeous (McBride), a hapless layabout son of a king and his brother Fabious (Franco), a much more accomplished prince who returns from battle with the head of a mutant cyclops in tow. Fabious' bride Belladonna (Deschanel) suddenly gets kidnapped by the ruthless Leezar (Justin Theroux) and Fabious must convince his younger, unreliable brother Thadeous to join him and his men on a quest to rescue the princess and prove his worth. Thadeous reluctantly agrees and the quest begins.

The movie darts back and forth between the quest and Belladonna's captivity. Naturally, the men happen upon a Warrior-like woman named Isabel (Portman). She exists, of course, to become an eventual love interest for Thadeous, although there is no reason to believe anyone with an ounce of common sense in their brain would find this character appealing, but the script demands they have a love-hate thing for a while before the end credits. There are many other encounters along the way, some having to do with creatures too big for one warrior to kill, some having to do with Leezar's minions.

So many things went wrong here. There is nothing wrong with the foundation of the concept, simply its execution and insistence on being a sub-par collection of boob and pot jokes. McBride's screenplay, which he co-wrote with Ben Best, relies far too heavily on the f-word as a punchline. Yes, maybe once in a while, hearing that word come out of the mouth of a noble prince is funny, but not every single scene. It is as if Best and McBride had no other ideas for a joke. Even when the characters are smoking pot with a small, indecipherable puppet creature, the movie has no idea where to go with it.

Danny McBride has been funny before. He has always been able to pull off being an aloof and somewhat likable jerk who says things people can only dream of saying in hindsight. Here, he has written himself a role where he is trapped by an English accent and a misguided belief that everything he says is funny. He annunciates every joke in such a deliberate manner, as if he is afraid the audience will not get it unless he says it louder. Franco seems to be in good spirits and has the right idea for his role, but he, too, seems confined by the limits of the storyline and the setting (which may or may not be another planet. There are two moons. Don't ask why). Natalie Portman and Zooey Deschanel are props and nothing more. What a sad waste of talent.

As for Green himself, one of his strengths is his ability to get the best moments from his actors through improvisation and invention. Even in his darkest films, there has been a sense of freedom given to his actors to throw in a moment of levity. He is a natural choice to direct a comedy. Here, he seems all too devoted to the script as written. The actors look uninspired and Green has nothing to offer them. Perhaps the special effects and the overall scale—the biggest production of his career so far—got the best of him and did not have time to feel a scene out and see where it could really go. He and his cast mistakenly play everything straight as a way of getting laughs. The result is a movie that is not only unfunny, but also clumsy and tone-deaf.

All of this adds up to being one of the most depressing comedies in recent memory. On the page, *Your Highness* might have been conceptually funny to those who read it. The actors probably felt Green would help out with the rest and he would be great to work with. They are right in thinking that. But now it is time for Green to stop doing favors for his college buddies and to get back to what made him a great filmmaker. *Your Highness* is a major lapse in judgment for everyone involved and hopefully the poor box office take will give everyone reason to pause before pursuing another project with McBride as the author.

Collin Souter

CREDITS

Thadeous: Danny McBride
Fabious: James Franco
Isabel: Natalie Portman
Belladonna: Zooey Deschanel
Leezar: Justin Theroux
Julie: Toby Jones
Boremont: Damian Lewis
King Tallious: Charles Dance
Origin: USA
Language: English
Released: 2011
Production: Scott Stuber; Universal Pictures, Stuber
   Productions; released by Universal Pictures
Directed by: David Gordon Green
Written by: Danny McBride, Ben Best
Cinematography by: Tim Orr
Music by: Steve Jablonsky
Sound: Yann Delpuech
Music Supervisor: Becky Bentham
Editing: Craig Albert
Art Direction: Gary Freeman
Costumes: Hazel Webb-Crozier
Production Design: Mark Tildesley
MPAA rating: R
Running time: 102 minutes

REVIEWS

Covert , Colin. *Minneapolis Star Tribune.* April 7, 2011.
Biancolli, Amy. *Houston Chronicle.* April 7, 2011.
Dargis, Manohla. *New York Times.* April 7, 2011.
Ebert, Roger. *Chicago Sun-Times.* April 8, 2011.
O'Hehir, Andrew. *Salon.com.* April 7, 2011.
Pinkerton, Nick. *Village Voice.* April 6, 2011.
Rickey, Carrie. *Philadelphia Inquirer.* April 7, 2011.
Schwartzbaum, Lisa. *Entertainment Weekly.* April 6, 2011.
Sobczynski, Peter. *eFilmcritic.com.* April 8, 2011.
Whitty, Stephen. *Newark Star Ledger.* April 8, 2011.

QUOTES

Fabious: "What's your problem? Why are you being such a
   sourpuss?"
Thadeous: "I'm not being a sourpuss! I just didn't want to be
   at that celebration."
Fabious: "All I want is for you to be a part of this moment. I
   want you to be gay with me and father."
Thadeous: "I don't want to be gay with you two!"

TRIVIA

For this role, James Franco took sword training for nine
   months before and during filming.

AWARDS

Nomination:

Golden Raspberries 2011: Worst Support. Actor (Franco).

ZOOKEEPER

Welcome to his jungle.
   —Movie tagline

Box Office: $80.4 million

Zookeeper passes off pratfalls, toilet humor, and acting like an idiot and a jerk as "family" entertainment,
and those behaviors only serve to describe the movie's
main character. The incorporation of such basic and
base comic material into movies aimed at children is
nothing new, though *Zookeeper,* with its screenplay
cobbled together from an assemblage of high-concept
ideas, barely manages to form a coherent central
narrative.

As the screenplay is the collaboration of five writers
(Nick Bakay, Rock Reuben, Kevin James [who also plays
the lead], Jay Scherick, and David Ronn), the feeling
that the script has a committee mentality is justifiable.
There are broad setups for scenes and concepts, and
each of them falls by the wayside as the next arrives. In
one moment, the movie's hero has just ruined a fancy
wedding, and in the next, his entire life has changed
without even a single transitional scene to lead into the
shift. Such gaps are not only lazily written but also sloppily edited.

The opening joke is conceptually sound, based upon
Murphy's Law. In it, Griffin Keyes (James) and his
girlfriend Stephanie (Leslie Bibb) are riding on horseback
along an idyllic beach. Griffin proposes to Stephanie
(through a message in a bottle), and she turns him down
before he can even finish his verbal marriage proposal
(the golden-hour glow disappears at that instant—a
subtle gag that will be the last attempt at such humor
the movie will make). At this point, he must awkwardly
ride back along the beach with his now ex-girlfriend, as
a parade of other romantic gestures that he had set up
come along to haunt him—a mariachi band and
fireworks in the shape of a heart.

The scene is a funny concept on its own terms, but
note Bibb's performance in the sequence. Director Frank
Coraci has the actress play up her reaction of frustration
and embarrassment to the point of screeching hysteria,
thus weakening the actual foil of the joke—the bait-
and-switch effect on Griffin, whose anticipation turns to
disappointment, which, in turn, shifts to humiliation.
Coraci's distracted direction continues throughout the
movie as it lumbers through similarly rough comic

sequences. The setup to the majority of the jokes are unnecessary, as they typically result in a punch line of Griffin falling down, crashing into something or someone, or otherwise making a fool of himself.

The central plot concerns Griffin's attempt six years later to rekindle the non-existent romance between himself and Stephanie after he spots her at the engagement party for his brother (Nat Faxon) and his brother's fiancée (Steffiana De La Cruz). The party is held at the Franklin Park Zoo, where Griffin has worked as a zookeeper for nearly a decade.

The animals at the zoo can speak in and understand English, which Griffin discovers after Joe the Lion (voice of Sylvester Stallone) and Donald the Monkey (voice of Adam Sandler) concoct a plan to make their favorite zookeeper look like a hero. Instead, Griffin tumbles into the pit separating the general public from the lion's pen. After a short, frantic bit in which he believes himself to have gone insane, Griffin accepts the convention of talking animals and begins taking their advice on attracting a member of the opposite sex.

The biggest flaw (out of the many) of the comedy is that for Griffin to follow the animals' wisdom he must be incredibly, unbelievably dense. A pair of bears named Jerome and Bruce (voices of Jon Favreau and Faizon Love) teach him the "right" way to walk, which includes waving one's arms in the air and snorting. A frog (voice of Don Rickles) insists that the proper way to intimidate a foe (in this case, Gale [Joe Rogan], another of Stephanie's ex-boyfriends who is also trying to win her back) is to blow air into one's cheeks and squat down into the attack position. Sebastian the Wolf (voice of Bas Rutten) informs Griffin that females are attracted to "pee-pee" and teaches him to mark his territory with urine. His various encounters with Stephanie leading up to and at his brother's wedding give him the chance to try out these obviously anti-social behaviors to the eradication of common sense.

The voice acting is all over the place, with Cher making somewhat of an attempt at normalcy with her vocal performance of Joe's long-suffering mate Janet, while Sandler and Maya Rudolph (as Mollie the Giraffe) do over-the-top silly voices that begin to grate quickly. Indeed, the only animal performance that truly works foregoes the digital manipulation of an actual creature, and it is Bernie the Gorilla (voice of Nick Nolte), created with a man in an ape suit and an animatronic mask.

Zookeeper fails to establish any of its plot or character points, from the animals, whose participation later in the story becomes negligible, to the eventual romantic relationship between Griffin and the zoo's veterinarian Kate (Rosario Dawson), who is clearly meant to be his ultimate choice since there are no other human female characters around him. Depending on one's comic sensibilities, one might be able to forgive the movie for its low gags (a few jokes near the end that function to undermine the climactic occasion of a clichéd rush to the airport are reasonably amusing); the script's inability to develop even a fundamental dramatic arc is an entirely different matter altogether.

Mark Dujsik

CREDITS

Griffin Keyes: Kevin James
Stephanie: Leslie Bibb
Kate: Rosario Dawson
Venom: Ken Jeong
Shane: Donnie Wahlberg
Gale: Joe Rogan
Dave: Nat Faxon
Janet the Lioness: Cher (Voice)
Bernie the Gorilla: Nick Nolte (Voice)
Joe the Lion: Sylvester Stallone (Voice)
Jerome the Bear: Jon Favreau (Voice)
Barry the Elephant: Judd Apatow (Voice)
Donald the Monkey: Adam Sandler (Voice)
Bruce the Bear: Faizon Love (Voice)
Mollie the Giraffe: Maya Rudolph (Voice)
Origin: USA
Language: English
Released: 2011
Production: Todd Garner, Jack Giarraputo, Kevin James, Adam Sandler; Happy Madison Productions, Columbia Pictures, MGM, Broken Road Productions, Hey Eddie; released by Columbia Pictures, Sony Pictures Entertainment
Directed by: Frank Coraci
Written by: David Ronn, Jay Sherick, Nicky Bakay, Rock Reuben
Cinematography by: Michael J. Bennett
Music by: Rupert Gregson-Williams
Sound: David MacMillan
Music Supervisor: Michael Dilbeck
Editing: Scott Hill
Art Direction: Domenic Silvestri
Costumes: Mona May
Production Design: Kirk M. Petruccelli
MPAA rating: PG
Running time: 102 minutes

REVIEWS

Abele, Robert. *Los Angeles Times.* July 8, 2011.
Berardinelli, James. *ReelViews.* July 7, 2011.
Childress, Erik. *EfilmCritic.com.* July 8, 2011.
Ebert, Roger. *Chicago Sun-Times.* July 6, 2011.
Goodykoontz, Bill. *Arizona Republic.* July 6, 2011.
Moore, Roger. *Orlando Sentinel.* July 6, 2011.

Orndorf, Brian. *BrianOrndorf.com*. July 7, 2011.
Orange, Michelle. *Movieline*. July 7, 2011.
Putman, Dustin. *DustinPutman.com*. July 7, 2011.
Schager, Nick. *Village Voice*. July 6, 2011.

QUOTES

Griffin Keyes: "It took me five years to get over someone I don't love. I can't imagine how long it would take me to get over you."

TRIVIA

The film was shipped to theaters using the code name "The Combo."

AWARDS

Nomination:

Golden Raspberries 2011: Worst Support. Actor (Jeong).

List of Awards

Academy Awards

Film: *The Artist*

Animated Film: *Rango*

Director: Michel Hazanavicius (*The Artist*)

Actor: Jean Dujardin (*The Artist*)

Actress: Meryl Streep (*The Iron Lady*)

Supporting Actor: Christopher Plummer (*Beginners*)

Supporting Actress: Octavia Spencer (*The Help*)

Original Screenplay: Woody Allen (*Midnight in Paris*)

Adapted Screenplay: Alexander Payne, Nat Faxon, and Jim Rash (*The Descendants*)

Cinematography: Robert Richardson (*Hugo*)

Editing: Angus Wall and Kirk Baxter (*The Girl with the Dragon Tattoo*)

Art Direction: Dante Ferretti and Francesca Lo Schiavo (*Hugo*)

Visual Effects: Robert Legato, Joss Williams, Ben Grossmann, and Alex Henning (*Hugo*)

Sound: Tom Fleischman and John Midgley (*Hugo*)

Sound Editing: Philip Stockton and Eugene Gearty (*Hugo*)

Makeup: Mark Coulier and J. Roy Helland (*The Iron Lady*)

Costume Design: Mark Bridges (*The Artist*)

Original Score: Ludovic Bource (*The Artist*)

Original Song: "Man or Muppet" (Bret McKenzie *The Muppets*)

Foreign Language Film: *A Separation*

Documentary, Feature: *Undefeated*

Documentary, Short Subject: *Saving Face*

Short Film, Animated: *The Fantastic Flying Books of Mr. Morris Lessmore*

Short Film, Live Action: *The Shore*

British Academy of Film & Television Awards

Animated Film: *Rango*

Film: *The Artist*

Outstanding British Film: *Tinker Tailor Soldier Spy*

Director: Michel Hazanavicius (*The Artist*)

Original Screenplay: Michel Hazanavicius (*The Artist*)

Adapted Screenplay: Bridget O'Connor and Peter Straughan (*Tinker Tailor Soldier Spy*)

Actor: Jean Dujardin (*The Artist*)

Actress: Meryl Streep (*The Iron Lady*)

Supporting Actor: Christopher Plummer (*Beginners*)

Supporting Actress: Octavia Spencer (*The Help*)

Editing: Gregers Sall and Chris King (*Senna*)

Cinematography: Guillaume Schiffman (*The Artist*)

Production Design: Francesca Lo Schiavo and Dante Ferretti (*Hugo*)

Costume Design: Mark Bridges (*The Artist*)

Makeup: Mark Coulier, Marese Langan, and J. Roy Helland (*The Iron Lady*)

Sound: Eugene Gearty, Philip Stockton, John Midgley, and Tom Fleischman (*Hugo*)

Visual Effects: Tim Burke, John Richardson, David Vickery, and Greg Butler (*Harry Potter and the Deathly Hallows: Part 2*)

Music: Ludovic Bource (*The Artist*)

Outstanding Debut by a British Writer, Director, or Producer: Paddy Considine and Diarmid Scrimshaw (*Tyrannosaur*)

Best Documentary Film: *Senna*

Foreign Film: *The Skin I Live In*

Short Animation: *A Morning Stroll*

Short Film: *Pitch Black Heist*

Directors Guild of America Awards

Outstanding Directorial Achievement in Motion Pictures: Michel Hazanavicius (*The Artist*)

Outstanding Directorial Achievement in Documentary: James Marsh (*Project Nim*)

Golden Globes

Film, Drama: *The Descendants*
Film, Musical or Comedy: *The Artist*
Animated Film: *The Adventures of Tintin*
Director: Martin Scorsese (*Hugo*)
Actor, Drama: George Clooney (*The Descendants*)
Actor, Musical or Comedy: Jean Dujardin (*The Artist*)
Actress, Drama: Meryl Streep (*The Iron Lady*)
Actress, Musical or Comedy: Michelle Williams (*My Week with Marilyn*)
Supporting Actor: Christopher Plummer (*Beginners*)
Supporting Actress: Octavia Spencer (*The Help*)
Screenplay: Woody Allen (*Midnight in Paris*)
Score: Ludovic Bource (*The Artist*)
Song: "Masterpiece" (James Harry, Madonna, and Julie Frost, *W.E.*)
Foreign Language Film: *A Separation*

Golden Raspberry Awards

Worst Picture: *Jack and Jill*
Worst Director: Dennis Dugan (*Jack and Jill* and *Just Go with It*)
Worst Actor: Adam Sandler (*Jack and Jill* and *Just Go with It*)
Worst Actress: Adam Sandler (*Jack and Jill*)
Worst Supporting Actor: Al Pacino (*Jack and Jill*)
Worst Supporting Actress: David Spade (*Jack and Jill*)
Worst Screenplay: Steve Koren and Adam Sandler (*Jack and Jill*)
Worst Screen Couple: Adam Sandler and either Katie Holmes, Al Pacino, or Adam Sandler (*Jack and Jill*)
Worst Prequel, Remake, Rip-Off or Sequel: *Jack and Jill*
Worst Screen Ensemble: The Entire Cast *Jack and Jill*

Independent Spirit Awards

Film: *The Artist*
First Film: J.C. Chandor *Margin Call*
Director: Michel Hazanavicius (*The Artist*)
Actor: Jean Dujardin (*The Artist*)
Actress: Michelle Williams (*My Week with Marilyn*)
Supporting Actor: Christopher Plummer (*Beginners*)
Supporting Actress: Shailene Woodley (*The Descendants*)
Screenplay: Alexander Payne, Jim Rash, and Nat Faxon (*The Descendants*)

First Screenplay: Will Reiser (*50/50*)
Cinematography: Guillaume Schiffman (*The Artist*)
Foreign Film: *A Separation*
Documentary: *The Interrupters*
Truer than Fiction Award: *Where Soldiers Come From*
Robert Altman Award: *Margin Call*
John Cassavetes Award: *Pariah*

Screen Actors Guild Awards

Actor: Jean Dujardin (*The Artist*)
Actress: Viola Davis (*The Help*)
Supporting Actor: Christopher Plummer (*Beginners*)
Supporting Actress: Octavia Spencer (*The Help*)
Ensemble Cast: *The Help*
Stunt Ensemble: *Harry Potter and the Deathly Hallows: Part 2*

Writers Guild of America Awards

Original Screenplay: Woody Allen (*Midnight in Paris*)
Adapted Screenplay: Nat Faxon, Alexander Payne, and Jim Rash (*The Descendants*)
Documentary Screenplay: Katie Galloway and Kelly Duane (*Better This World*)

Obituaries

Lillian Adams (May 13, 1922–May 25, 2011). Born in New York City in 1922, Lillian Adams had an amazing film and television career that stretched over five decades, including regular commercial work and sitcom guest spots. She was never a household name or even a very recognizable face but she worked up until the very end with a film release almost a year after her passing at the age of 89. Like her TV guest star roles, her film appearances were often small ones, but she did amass credits in works like *The Jerk* (1979), *Private Benjamin* (1980), *Summer School* (1987), *Magnolia* (1999), *Little Nicky* (2000), and *Bruce Almighty* (2003). Her final credit will be the posthumous release of *Tim and Eric's Billion Dollar Movie* (2012).

Frank Alesia (January 4, 1944–February 27, 2011). Beach party film regular Frank Alesia was born in Chicago but moved to Los Angeles to climb the Hollywood ladder when he was only twenty. He ended his career as a more notable TV director (winning a daytime Emmy® for his work on *Captain Kangaroo* and directing *Laverne & Shirley* before retiring to race and breed horses but his film career peak came in the 1960s with a string of beach party movies when Frankie Avalon and Annette Funicello were two of the most popular stars in the world. The character actor appeared in *Bikini Beach* (1964), *Pajama Party* (1964), *Beach Blanket Bingo* (1965), *The Ghost in the Invisible Bikini* (1966), and *Riot on Sunset Strip* (1967).

James Arness (May 26, 1923–June 3, 2011). The iconic American actor will be best remembered for embodying one of the most legendary TV characters of all time, Marshal Matt Dillon of *Gunsmoke*. He actually played the role across four decades as the series ran from 1955 to 1975 and TV movies popped up in the 1980s and 1990s. He was born James Aurness (dropping the "u" when he decided to become an actor) in Minneapolis to Rolf Cirkler Aurness and Ruth Duesler. His younger brother was actor Peter Graves, who took a stage name from a family surname. Arness graduated from high school in 1942 and went to serve his country in World War II from 1943 to 1945, where he won the Bronze Star Medal, the Purple Heart, and more. Arness began working for RKO after the war, making his debut with Loretta Young in *The Farmer's Daughter* (1947). James Arness watched his star rise with regular sci-fi and western performances, including a number with good friend John Wayne. Arness was married twice, adopting a son in his first marriage and having two biological sons and a daughter in his second one. He died of natural causes in Brentwood at the age of 88. Notable credits include *The Thing From Another World* (1951), *Big Jim McClain* (1952), *Island in the Sky* (1953), *Them!* (1954), *Hondo* (1954), *The Sea Chase* (1955), and *Gun the Man Down* (1956).

John Barry (November 3, 1933–January 30, 2011). One of the most influential, beloved, and award-winning film composers of all time was born John Barry Prendergast in York to an English mother and an Irish father. Barry's dad worked as a projectionist in the silent movie era, introducing Barry to the power of cinema and the importance of score within it. Barry started as a classical pianist and even formed his own band in the 1950s (The John Barry Seven) before joining the staff at EMI, where he wrote compositions for Adam Faith, a singer who made his film debut in *Beat Girl* (1960) and Barry's incredible film score career had begun. In a moment of amazing serendipity, the producers of a new spy movie called *Dr. No* (1962) were looking for a theme for their soon-to-be-legendary character and John Barry's most notable composition, "James Bond Theme," was created. Over the course of his career, Barry would go on to win five Academy Awards® and four Grammy Awards. John Barry was married four times. The first three times ended in divorce until the last one, which started in 1978, lasted until his death. Overall, he has four children from the various marriages. He died of a heart attack at the age of 77 in Oyster Bay, New York. His death was memorialized five months later with a concert at Royal Albert Hall that featured the Royal Philharmonic Orchestra. Notable scores throughout John Barry's amazing career, include *Goldfinger* (1964), *Born Free* (1966–Oscar® winner), *The Lion in Winter* (1968–Oscar® winner), *Midnight Cowboy* (1969), *Diamonds Are Forever,* (1971), *King Kong* (1976), *The Deep* (1977), *Somewhere in Time* (1980), *Body Heat* (1981), *Out of Africa* (1985–Oscar® winner), *A View to a Kill* (1985), *Dances with Wolves* (1990–Oscar® winner), and *Indecent Proposal* (1993).

Frances Bay (January 23, 1919–September 15, 2011). Canadian actress Frances Bay did not really start her career until she was in her fifties but developed a nice following as a character actress late in life. She was born Frances Goffman and flirted with acting early in life, including working on the CBC's WWII radio program, before moving to Cape Town, South Africa, where she married and had one son. Her first film credit wasn't until she was nearly sixty years old when she appeared in *Foul Play* (1978) with Goldie Hawn and Chevy Chase. From there, she amassed an amazing 158 TV or film credits including notable roles in *Blue Velvet* (1986), *Twins* (1988), *The Karate Kid, Part III* (1989), *Wild at Heart* (1990), *Arachnophobia* (1990), *Twin Peaks: Fire Walk With Me* (1992), *In the Mouth of Madness* (1994), and *Happy Gilmore* (1996). She passed away from pneumonia at the age of 92.

Peter E. Berger (May 30, 1944–September 22, 2011). Academy Award®-nominated editor with dozens of film credits over decades, Peter Berger was born and died in Los Angeles, the city that he loved. His only nomination would come for *Fatal Attraction* (1987), but he had dozens of other notable productions, including several *Star Trek* films. Credits include *Star Trek IV: The Voyage Home* (1986), *Less Than Zero* (1987), *Star Trek V: The Final Frontier* (1989), *Dead Again* (1991), *Star Trek: Generations* (1994), *Star Trek: Insurrection* (1998), *Garfield* (2004), and *Alvin and the Chipmunks* (2007).

Roberts Blossom (March 25, 1924–July 8, 2011). Wonderful character actor Roberts Scott Blossom was born in New Haven, Connecticut and was raised in Cleveland. He attended Harvard University but had to give that up to join the Army and serve in World War II. His stage career did not begin until the 1950s but he won three Obie Awards over the next three decades and appeared regularly on Broadway as well. He started his film career in 1958 and would work regularly for the next four decades. He will probably be best-remembered for an emotional role in *Home Alone* (1990) but horror fans will remember him for *Deranged* (1974) and *Christine* (1983). Other notable credits include *The Great Gatsby* (1974), *Close Encounters of the Third Kind* (1977), *Escape From Alcatraz* (1979), *The Last Temptation of Christ* (1988), *Always* (1989), and *The Quick and the Dead* (1995).

Michael Cacoyannis (June 11, 1922–July 25, 2011). Born Michalis Kakogiannis in Cyprus, Director Michael Cacoyannis achieved international fame for *Zorba the Greek* and was nominated for five Oscars® overall (three for *Zorba*—Best Director, Best Adapted Screenplay, and Best Film—and two Foreign Language Film nominations for *Electra* [1962] and *Iphigenia* [1977]). He was one of the most internationally successful Greek filmmakers. His career started after moving to London to become a lawyer but ending up producing Greek programming for the BBC during World War II. He moved back to Greece and began his film career with *Windfall in Athens* (1954). Hollywood

often called, including an offer to direct Elizabeth Taylor and Marlon Brando in *Reflections in a Golden Eye* (1967) but he stuck with his Greek heritage. He was a regular on the film festival scene with many of his works playing at the Cannes Film Festival (*Elektra* won the Grand Jury Prize). Other notable credits include *The Girl in Black* (1956), *A Matter of Dignity* (1957), *The Trojan Women* (1971), and *The Cherry Orchard* (1999).

Charlie Callas (December 20, 1924–January 27, 2011). Although he would never make the kind of lasting impact in the film world as many of his contemporaries in the world of stand-up comedy, Charlie Callas was definitely a recognizable figure thanks to his ever-malleable facial features and the trademark bizarre noises that would emanate from them seemingly at random. Born Charles Callais in Brooklyn, Callas got his start in show business as a drummer who played with the likes of Tommy Dorsey and Buddy Rich before drifting into comedy. After making his television debut in 1963 on an episode of *The Hollywood Palace,* he was soon opening for Frank Sinatra in nightclubs around the country while scoring frequent appearances on such talk shows as *The Tonight Show* and *The Merv Griffin Show.* During an appearance on the latter in 1965, he caught the attention of co-panelist Jerry Lewis and that resulted in Callas making his big-screen debut in Lewis' *The Big Mouth* (1967). He would also become a favorite of fellow comedian-turned-filmmaker Mel Brooks, who cast him in *Silent Movie* (1976), *High Anxiety* (1978), *History of the World: Part I* (1981), and *Dracula: Dead and Loving It* (1995). Among other career highlights, he contributed the voice to the title character of the Disney live-action/animated hybrid *Pete's Dragon* (1977), portrayed himself in the funeral roast sequence of *Amazon Women on the Moon* (1987) and made numerous appearances on television ranging from a rare non-comedic role on the 1975-1978 series *Switch* and a too-strange-for-words appearance as comic-book villain Sinestro in the campy 1979 special *Legends of the Superheroes.* Callas passed away on January 27 at the age of 86 from natural causes, six months after the death of wife Evelyn.

John Calley (July 8, 1930–September 13, 2011). Born in Jersey City in 1930, John Calley was an American film studio executive and producer who made his biggest impact at Warner Bros. from 1968 to 1981 where he had a hand in some of the studio's biggest hits. He only received one Oscar® nomination (for *Remains of the Day* [1993]) but he was honored with the Irving G. Thalberg Memorial Award in 2009. He was close friends with Mike Nichols, with whom he collaborated on several productions. Notable credits include *The Sandpiper* (1965), *The Cincinnati Kid* (1965), *Ice Station Zebra* (1968), *Catch-22* (1970), *Fat Man and Little Boy* (1989), *Postcards From the Edge* (1990), *Closer* (2004), and *The Da Vinci Code* (2006).

Gene Cantamessa (February 17, 1931–November 8, 2011). Nominated for an Oscar® seven times, American sound engineer Gene Cantamessa won one Academy Award® for one of the most beloved films of all time, *E.T. the Extra-Terrestrial* (1982). His six other nominations were for *The Candidate* (1972), *Young Frankenstein* (1974), *Close Encounters of the Third Kind* (1977), *1941* (1979), *2010: The Year We Make Contact* (1984), and *Star Trek IV: The*

Voyage Home (1986). Other notable credits include High Anxiety (1977), *The Big Chill* (1983), *Star Trek III: The Search for Spock* (1984), *Ghostbusters* (1984), *Star Trek VI: The Undiscovered Country* (1991), *The Birdcage* (1996), and his final one, *End of Days* (1999).

Gilbert Cates (June 6, 1934–October 31, 2011). Born Gilbert Katz, Gil Cates became one of the most important people behind Hollywood's most beloved night, producing the Academy Awards® fourteen times between 1990 and 2008. Cates was a pre-med student at Syracuse University when he was asked to use his skills from the fencing team to help actors with a production of *Richard III.* He became a theater major and never looked back. He transitioned from stage to screen with a few TV movies followed by film work on *I Never Sang for My Father* (1970), *The Promise* (1979), *The Last Married Couple in America* (1980), and *Backfire* (1988).

Diane Cilento (October 5, 1933–October 6, 2011). Australian actress Diane Cilento was born in Mooloolaba, Queensland, Australia in 1933 to a pair of distinguished medical practitioners. She tried to pursue an acting career early on, winning a scholarship for the Royal Academy of Dramatic Art and moving to England in the early 1950s. She found work on stage and screen almost immediately appearing with fellow Aussie Peter Finch in *Passage Home* in 1955. She worked consistently in the 1960s but pulled out of the public eye after marrying James Bond himself, Sean Connery, in 1962. They had one son before divorcing in 1973. Notable credits include Oscar®-nominated work in *Tom Jones* (1963), *Hombre* (1967), and *The Wicker Man* (1973). She reportedly served as a stunt double in her husband's *You Only Live Twice* (1967). She died of cancer the day after her 78th birthday.

Jeff Conaway (October 5, 1950–May 27, 2011). Future generations would sadly know his battle with addiction more than his acting career thanks to his recurring appearances on VH1's *Celebrity Rehab with Dr. Drew* but there was a time when Jeff Conaway was one of the more recognizable TV and film actors in the business. Born Jeffrey Charles William Michael Conaway, the young man became an actor after accompanying his mother to a casting call for a Broadway role that he landed at the age of ten. The play would go on to win the Pulitzer and run for almost a year, during which Conaway performed the entire time. He continued as a child model and a teen rock star before attending the North Carolina School for the Arts and New York University. His film debut would not come until 1971 with *Jennifer On My Mind* (1971) and will perhaps be most-remembered for a TV role on the hit *Taxi,* which he was forced to leave after three seasons due to his drug abuse problems. His most notable film role was as Kenickie in the hit *Grease* (1978) with John Travolta and Olivia Newton-John. He would appear in dozens more straight-to-video stinkers and stands as a cautionary tale about how personal demons can derail a career. The actor passed away from pneumonia, in no small part due to the weakened immune system of a drug addict, at the age of 50.

Jackie Cooper (September 15, 1922–May 3, 2011). John Cooper Jr. was the first child actor to ever receive an Oscar® nomination for a leading role, landing an Academy Award® nomination at the age of 9 for *Skippy* (1931). He will be most-remembered as one of the members of Our Gang in the 1920s and 1930s and for his emotional performance in the classic tearjerker *The Champ* (1931) with Wallace Beery, who he would go on to work with in *The Bowery* (1933), *The Choices of Andy Purcell* (1933), *Treasure Island* (1934), and *O'Shaughnessy's Boy* (1935). Cooper would go on to serve in World War II (where he rose to the level of Captain) and defy the typical arc of the child star by actually transitioning to a successful career as an adult, although mostly on stage and the small screen. He used his experience as a TV actor to ascend to the role of Vice President of Program Development at Columbia Pictures Screen Gems TV division. The rumor is that Cooper cast Sally Field as *Gidget.* He went back to the big screen with one more legendary role as Perry White in *Superman* (1978), *Superman II* (1980), *Superman III* (1983), and *Superman IV: The Quest For Peace* (1987). He married three times and had three children. He is survived by son Russell after he passed away at the age of 88. He was interred at Arlington National Cemetery due to his service in the Navy.

Norman Corwin (May 3, 1910–October 18, 2011). Oscar®-nominated screenwriter Norman Corwin was born in Boston in 1910 and started his career as a radio drama director in the 1930s and 1940s where he worked with legends like Orson Welles and William N. Robson. He never won an Oscar® but a film about his life, *A Note of Triumph: The Golden Age of Norman Corwin* (2005) won the Academy Award® for Best Documentary Short. His nomination came for *Lust For Life* (1956), one of his few film credits.

Frank DiLeo (October 23, 1947–August 24, 2011). Frank Michael DiLeo made a much bigger mark in the music industry (both as an executive and as Michael Jackson's manager at a key time during his career in the 1980s) but played a very notable film role in Martin Scorsese's *Goodfellas* (1990). He also appeared in *Wayne's World* (1992), *Wayne's World 2* (1993), and *Kiss of Death* (1995). He died from complications after heart surgery at the age of only 63.

Peter Donaldson (October 29, 1953–January 8, 2011). Canadian actor Peter Thomas Donaldson started his career by being inspired by the performances at the legendary Stratford Festival, where he would return as one of its most notable actors for forty years of his career. He made his debut there in 1977 and spent twenty-four seasons with the festival. His stage work far outweighed his film work but he appeared in several Canadian TV series and had a memorable role in Atom Egoyan's *The Sweet Hereafter* (1997).

Marion Caroline Dougherty (February 9, 1923–December 4, 2011). Born in Pennsylvania, Marion Caroline Dougherty was a well-known and admired casting director for some of the most notable films of her era, including *Midnight Cowboy* (1969), *The Paper Chase* (1973), *Lenny* (1974), *Escape From Alcatraz* (1979), *The Killing Fields* (1984), *Lethal Weapon* (1987), *Gorillas in the Mist* (1988), *Batman* (1989), *Lethal Weapon 2* (1989), *Maverick* (1994), and *Payback* (1999), among dozens of others. She was often referred to as a "star-maker."

Paulette Dubost (October 8, 1910–September 21, 2011). Born Paulette Marie Emma Deplanque in 1910, Paulette

Dubost would go on to star in over 250 films and work with a number of legendary French directing legends including Jean Renoir, Jacques Tourneur, Preston Sturges, and Max Ophuls. Her most notable credits include *The Rules of the Game* (1939), *Viva Maria!* (1965), *The Last Metro* (1980), and *May Fools* (1990). She lived to three-days-short of 101.

William Duell (August 30, 1923–December 22, 2011). Born George William Duell (and later legally changed to Darwin William Duell), the character actor dropped his first name when he began his acting career after graduating from Green Mountain College, Illinois Wesleyan University, and Yale University. His most notable role is probably a stage one as he performed in the hit 1969 musical *1776*. He also played the role of Andrew McNair in the 1972 screen adaptation. He played Sefelt in *One Flew Over the Cuckoo's Nest* (1975) and also appeared in *The Happy Hooker* (1975), *Airplane!* (1980), *The Pope of Greenwich Village* (1984), *Ironweed* (1987), *In & Out* (1997), and *How to Lose a Guy in 10 Days* (2003).

Ryan Dunn (June 11, 1977–June 20, 2011). Professional goof-off, Ryan Dunn was a member of the Jackass crew led by Johnny Knoxville and he died after a tragic drunk driving car accident sent his Porsche into a tree. Some reports noted that the car Dunn was driving was going between 132 and 140 MPH when it veered off the road in Pennsylvania. He will be remembered for being a part of the fearless crew of performers willing to go to any physical end for a laugh in *Jackass: The Movie* (2002), *Jackass Number Two* (2006), and *Jackass 3.5* (2011). He also appeared in *The Dudesons Movie* (2006), *Blonde Ambition* (2007), and *Street Dreams* (2009).

Norma Eberhardt (July 8, 1929–September 16, 2011). Fashion model Norma Eberhardt graduated from billboard to radio, television, and film in the 1950s while also notoriously dating the legendary James Dean. She started with a small role in the Dean Martin and Jerry Lewis vehicle *Sailor Beware* (1952) (and would reportedly go on to date Lewis as well). She did another Martin & Lewis vehicle in *Jumping Jacks* (1952) and starred in *The Return of Dracula* (1958) and *Live Fast, Die Young* (1958), her two most notable roles. She moved to TV in the 1960s before essentially retiring. She passed away from a stroke at the age of 82 and was survived by her 108-year-old father and six brothers and sisters.

Peter Falk (September 16, 1927–June 23, 2011). One of the most genuinely beloved performers of his time, Peter Falk was nearly thirty years old before he began working professionally as an actor. Before then, the New York-born Falk spent time in the Merchant Marines after being rejected by the Army because of his glass eye (which replaced the right eye that had been surgically removed when he was three years old), earned a degree in Public Administration from Syracuse University and worked as an analyst with the Connecticut State Budget Bureau. Around this time, Falk began appearing in community theater projects while taking classes from noted acting teacher Eva la Gallienne and eventually moved back to New York in 1956 to make it as a full-time actor. After a few years on stage and a couple of false starts, Falk made his big-screen debut in Nicolas Ray's wild period drama *Wind Across the*

Everglades (1958). His big break came a couple of years later with his supporting turn in the low-budget gangster film *Murder, Inc.* (1960), a performance that earned him an Oscar® nomination for Best Supporting Actor, a feat he world repeat the following year with *A Pocketful of Miracles* (1961), the final work from Frank Capra. For the next few years, he would make numerous appearances on television and on the silver screen in such favorites as the Cinerama epic *It's a Mad, Mad, Mad, Mad World* (1963), the Rat Pack musical *Robin and the 7 Hoods* (1964) and the around-the-world chase comedy *The Great Race* (1965). In 1968, he appeared in the made-for-television film *Prescription Murder* as a rumpled and seemingly clueless police detective who was smarter than appearances suggested known only as Columbo. The film was such a success that it was turned into a series, part of a revolving group of titles that made up *The NBC Mystery Movie* that ran between 1971 and 1978. From the first episode (which marked one of the first professional directorial efforts of the then-unknown Steven Spielberg), the show was a hit that would earn Falk four Emmys and which he would return to for another series of TV films that appeared between 1989-2003. During his *Columbo* heyday, Falk continued to be a familiar face on the big screen as well—his friendship with filmmaker John Cassavetes led to his appearing in *Husbands* (1970), *A Woman Under the Influence* (1974) and *Opening Night* (1977), he spoofed Humphrey Bogart twice in the Neil Simon-penned farces *Murder by Death* (1976), and *The Cheap Detective* (1978), introduced the phrase "Serpentine!" into the vernacular via the cult comedy classic *The In-Laws* (1979), served as the avuncular narrator of the fairytale favorite *The Princess Bride* (1987) and even played himself (or at least an angelic variation) for Wim Wenders in *Wings of Desire* (1987) and *Faraway, So Close!* (1993). In later years, he did not work as much but still turned in memorable performances in the Walter Hill prison boxing drama *Undisputed* (2002), the family comedy-drama *The Thing About My Folks* (2005) and the sci-fi spectacular *Next* (2007) while publishing his autobiography, *Just One More Thing* in 2006. In ailing health in the last few years of his life—including rumors of dementia—he passed away on June 23rd from cardiac arrest with complications from pneumonia and Alzheimer's disease.

Margaret Field (May 10, 1922–November 6, 2011). Born Margaret Morlan in Houston, Texas, this lovely genre star was discovered by Paramount Pictures when she was just a teenager. Field studied voice training and acting at Pasadena Junior College before appearing in television westerns and sci-fi films. She married an Army officer named Richard Dryden Field and had a daughter in 1946 named Sally Field, a future legendary actress. She would act for a few more years, divorce Field and marry Jock O'Mahoney (going by Margaret O'Mahoney for much of her career in television in the 1950s and 1960s), and eventually retire to focus on family in 1968. Notable film credits include Cecil B. DeMille's *Samson and Delilah* (1949), John Farrow's *The Big Clock* (1948), and Edgar Ulmer's *The Man From Planet X* (1951).

Gunnar Fischer (November 18, 1910–June 11, 2011). Fischer was a Swedish cinematographer who made his mark working with Ingmar Bergman on several of the legend's most influential films, including *Smiles of a Summer Night* (1955) and *The Seventh Seal* (1957). Fischer studied painting for years before joining the Swedish Navy and eventually finding his way to work as an assistant camera-man. He made his debut as director of photography in 1942 earning his most acclaim for his work with Bergman. Notable credits also include *Port of Call* (1948), *Summer Interlude* (1951), *Summer with Monika* (1953), *Wild Strawberries* (1957), *The Magician* (1958), and *The Devil's Eye* (1960). Bergman's cinematographer was easily one of the most influential in the history of the film form. He was married to the same woman from 1938 until her death in 2005 and is survived by two sons—both cinematographers—six granddaughters, and five great-grandchildren.

Anne Francis (September 16, 1930–January 2, 2011). Although she would be in show business for nearly her entire life (she began working as a child model at five and made her debut on Broadway at eleven) Anne Francis would be best known for her appearance as Altaria in the science-fiction classic *Forbidden Planet* (1956), an innocent-but-alluring turn that would help jump-start the puberties of generations of pre-adolescent boys. Following her film debut in *This Time for Keeps* (1947), she appeared in supporting parts in such titles as *Susan Slept Here* (1954), *The Rocket Man* (1954), and *Bad Day at Black Rock* (1955) before scoring her first lead in the landmark juvenile delinquent drama *Blackboard Jungle* (1955). The next year found her on Altair IV in *Forbidden Planet*, a loose riff on Shakespeare's *The Tempest* that was one of the first big-budget sci-fi films to come from a major studio (MGM) and the first to be set entirely on a planet other than Earth. The film was a hit upon its initial release and would go on to be a cult favorite in the ensuing years that helped make Francis an icon of the genre as well. (She and the film would even find themselves referenced by name in the lyrics to "Science Fiction/Double Feature," the opening musical number from the fellow cult favorite *The Rocky Horror Picture Show* (1975). After that film, she would make regular appearances in films for the next couple of decades—including turns in *The Rack* (1956), *Funny Girl* (1968), the Don Knotts classic *The Love God?* (1969) and the Jerry Lewis vehicles *Don't Go Near the Water* (1967) and *Hook, Line and Sinker* (1969). In 2007, Francis was diagnosed with lung cancer but passed away on January 2nd from pancreatic cancer.

Dolores Fuller (March 10, 1923–May 9, 2011). For fans of Grade Z cinema, Dolores Fuller will always have a place in the pantheon because of her association with the infamous Edward D. Wood Jr., the low-budget filmmaker revered for being the creator of what many consider to be some of the worst movies ever made. Born Dolores Eble, Fuller made her first appearance on-screen at the age of ten in a brief and unaccredited role in Frank Capra's *It Happened One Night* (1934) and eventually began to find work on such television shows as *Queen for a Day* and *The Dinah Shore Show*. Around this time, she met Wood at a casting call for a never-produced project and they began dating. The two would appear opposite each other in Wood's directorial debut, the cross-dressing exploitation classic *Glen or Glenda* (1953) and also appeared in his follow-up *Jail Bait* (1954)

while taking small roles in other projects such as Fritz Lang's *The Blue Gardenia* (1953), the western *The Raid* (1954) and the schlock drive-in epic *Mesa of Lost Women* (1953). Her personal and professional association with Wood ended during the production of his third feature, *Bride of the Monster* (1955)—she was originally cast in the lead but, for reasons that are still disputed to this day, she was relegated to a bit part while starlet Loretta King was given the role. After a bit part in *The Opposite Sex* (1956), a lackluster remake of *The Women* (1939). Fuller would embark on an unexpected second career when she tried to convince friend Hal Wallis to cast her in the latest Elvis Presley production he was putting together, *Blue Hawaii* (1961). Instead of giving her a role, Wallis put Fuller in contact with the music publishing company charged with finding material for Presley and she began to work as a songwriter, composing twelve songs over the next few years for such Presley films as *Kid Galahad* (1962), *Roustabout* (1964), and *Change of Habit* (1969), penning tunes for the likes of Nat King Cole, Peggy Lee, and Shelly Fabares and eventually forming her own record company, Dee Dee Records (which helped to start the careers of Tanya Tucker and Johnny Rivers). A couple of decades later, when interest in Wood's life and work was revived, Fuller became a frequent subject of interviews by biographers and documentarians and even found herself being portrayed by Sarah Jessica Parker in the acclaimed biopic *Ed Wood* (1994). She passed away on May 9th in Las Vegas after what was described as a long illness.

Betty Garrett (May 23, 1919–February 12, 2011). Born in St. Joseph, Missouri in 1919, Betty Garrett was an American actress who worked on stage, TV, and screen. She was a prominent figure on two TV staples—*All in the Family* and *Laverne & Shirle*—but started her career under contract with MGM, where she appeared in a number of musical films. Garrett moved to Seattle where she was so interested in theater that she actually started her own musical productions at her school, which did not have a drama department. Her mother happened to be friends with Martha Graham, who recommended her for the Neighborhood Playhouse in New York City, where Garrett started in 1936. There, she worked with legends like Anna Sokolow, Sandy Meisner, Lehman Engel, and Margaret Webster. On stage she worked with Danny Kaye, Carol Channing, Joseph Cotten, and Orson Welles. She made her debut with MGM in 1947 in *Big City* and appeared in a number of musicals of the era for the company—*Words and Music* (1948), *On the Town* (1949), *Take Me Out to the Ball Game* (1949), and *Neptune's Daughter* (1949). She would also appear with Jack Lemmon in *My Sister Eileen* (1955) but the rest of her career was primarily on TV and stage. Her career was hurt by the fact that she was an open member of the Communist Party and so was blacklisted when HUAC began their witch hunt. She married Larry Parks in 1944 and stayed together until his death in 1975. The pair had two sons. She passed away of an aortic aneurysm on February 12th in Los Angele at the age of 91.

Annie Girardot (October 25, 1931–February 28, 2011). French actress Annie Girardot was born in Paris, France in 1931 and would go on to appear in over 150 films and win the Cesar® Award (the French equivalent of the Oscar®)

three times. Girardot graduated from the Consevatoire de la rue Blanche in 1954 and joined the prestigious Comedie Francaise after that, beginning her film career in 1955 in *Treize a Table*. She appeared in one of Jean Cocteau's plays in 1956 and really broke through in 1960 with Luchino Visconti's *Rocco and His Brothers*. While the French New Wave was crashing around the world, Girardot strayed to more popular films, serving as a box office star in her home country in films like *Vice and Virture* (1963), *Live For Life* (1967), *Love is a Funny Thing* (1969), and *Death of Love* (1970), her biggest hit in her home country and a Golden Globe nominee. Other hits from her prime box office star status include *La Ziziane* (1978), *She Does Not Drink, Smoke or Flirt But...She Talks* (1970), *Dear Inspector* (1978), and *The Ape Woman* (1964). She won her first Cesar® for *Doctor Francoise Gailland* (1977), her second for *Les Miserables,/i* (1996), and her third for Michael Haneke's amazing *The Piano Teacher* (2002). Haneke would work with her again in *Cache* (2005). She married Ranato Salvatori in 1962 and the couple had a daughter. She passed away on February 28th after a public battle with Alzheimer's Disease.

David Zelag Goodman (January 15, 1930–September 26, 2011). New York-born David Goodman was a playwright and screenwriter who made his biggest film impact co-writing *Straw Dogs* with Sam Peckinpah. He died two weeks after the release of the remake. Goodman went to Queens College and then studied at Yale Drama School. He was married to Marjorie Goodman for 61 years and the two had a daughter who teaches at UC Berkeley. Notable credits include *Lovers and Other Strangers* (1970), *Monte Walsh* (1970), *Farewell, My Lovely* (1975), *Logan's Run* (1976), *Eyes of Laura Mars* (1978), and *Fighting Back* (1982).

Michael Gough (November 23, 1916–March 17, 2011). A familiar face to several generations of genre film fans, Michael Gough originally studied at the Wye Agricultural College before leaving to pursue acting at London's famed Old Vic Theater. In 1948, he made his screen debut in the crime drama *Blanche Fury* and began working extensively in television and in film, including appearances in *The Man in the White Suit* (1952), Laurence Olivier's version of *Richard III* (1955) and *The Horse's Mouth* (1958). In 1958, he appeared as Arthur Holmwood in *Horror of Dracula* (1958), a screen version of the Bram Stoker classic produced by a fledgling new British studio named Hammer that became an international hit due to its then-shocking levels of sex and violence. After the success of that film, Gough went on to become a mainstay of the British film industry with appearances in such genre efforts as *Horrors of the Black Museum* (1959), *Konga* (1961), *The Phantom of the Opera* (1962), *The Skull* (1965), *Trog* (1970), and episodes of *Doctor Who* and *The Avengers* as well as more mainstream titles such as *Women in Love* (1969), *The Go-Between* (1970), *Savage Messiah* (1972), *The Dresser* (1983), *Top Secret* (1984), and *Out of Africa* (1985). In 1989, his career received a resurgence when Tim Burton, a longtime fan of the old Hammer films, hired Gough to play the role of loyal butler Alfred Pennyworth in his blockbuster screen version of *Batman* (1989), beginning an association that would find the actor reprising the part in *Batman Returns* (1992), *Batman Forever* (1995), and *Bat-*

man & Robin (1997) and re-teaming with Burton for *Sleepy Hollow* (1999), *Corpse Bride* (2005), and *Alice in Wonderland* (2010)—even coming out of retirement as a favor to Burton in the case of the latter. Gough passed away on March 17th after a brief illness at the age of 94.

Farley Earle Granger, Jr. (July 1, 1925–March 27, 2011). American actor Farley Granger will be most-remembered for his starring roles in two of master director Alfred Hitchcock's most notable films, *Rope* (1948) and *Strangers on a Train* (1951). He also worked with Nicholas Ray (*They Live By Night* [1949]) and Luchino Visconti (*Senso* [1953]) in that era but lost his star status, segueing into television and stage work as his Hollywood star status dimmed. Granger was born in San Jose, California and started acting when he was only five years old. He made the rounds on stage in Los Angeles and was spotted by a talent scout, appearing on the big screen when he was only eighteen (in *The North Star* [1943]). In his prime, he also appeared in *Enchantment* (1948) and *Roseanna McCoy* (1949). Between the two Hitchcock classics, Granger appeared in *Side Street* (1950), *Edge of Doom* (1950), and *Our Very Own* (1950). Rumors of homosexuality started to dog the actor and the 1950s were not kind to his career although he appeared in *Behave Yourself!* (1951), *Small Town Girl* (1953), and *The Story of Three Loves* (1953) with Leslie Caron. *Senso* took the actor overseas and he rarely returned. He appeared in *The Naked Street* (1955) and *The Girl in the Red Velvet Swing* (1955) before essentially returning to stage and eventually dabbling in television other than his unusual foreign film choices. His last credited role was in 2001's *The Next Big Thing* (2001). He had a long-term partner named Robert Calhoun who died in 2008 and he passed away himself on March 27th.

Jill Haworth (August 15, 1945–January 3, 2011). British model Jill Haworth made only one Broadway appearance but it was a landmark one, originating the role of Sally Bowles in *Cabaret*. She made her biggest impact on film working with Otto Preminger on *Exodus* (1960), *The Cardinal* (1963), and *In Harm's Way* (1965) before jumping to the stage with *Cabaret*. An interesting piece of trivia is that Stanley Kubrick wanted Haworth for the lead role in *Lolita* (1965) but Preminger held her contract and did not let her take the role. She had a non-speaking role in *The Greatest Story Ever Told* (1965) before moving on to mostly television work. She did pop up in horror films including *It!* (1966), *Horror House* (1969), and *Tower of Evil* (1972). Jill Haworth passed away of natural causes at the age of 65 in New York City on January 3rd.

Jack Hayes (February 8, 1919–August 24, 2011). American composer Jack J. Hayes was nominated twice for an Academy Award® as a part of the teams that composed the scores for *The Unsinkable Molly Brown* (1964) and *The Color Purple* (1985). He had hundreds of other credits as a member of musical departments from 1955 (*The Man with the Golden Arm*) to 2009 (*Up*).

David Hess (September 19, 1936–October 8, 2011). New York-born David Hess originally got his start in the entertainment industry as a singer-songwriter who penned tunes for the likes of Sal Mineo and the Ames Brothers, recorded a cover of the Cliff Richard number "Living Doll" that became a minor hit on the American charts in 1959 and recorded the song "All Shook Up" in 1956, a year before Elvis Presley took a crack at it. By the end of the decade, he had recorded a couple of folk albums and became the head of A&R for Mercury Records. In 1972, his career—not to mention that of the entire low-budget horror film industry—changed when he was hired to play Krug, the leader of a group of brutal psychotics who rape and murder a pair of high-school girls in the notorious Wes Craven grindhouse classic *The Last House on the Left* (1972). Despite the notoriety of the film, Hess stayed away from acting for the most part and instead found work behind the scenes in the German film industry supervising the dubbing and translations for movies by the likes of Rainer Werner Fassbender. In 1980, he returned to America to direct his sole feature, *To All a Goodnight* and began appearing in small parts in films such as *The House on the Edge of the Park* (1980), *Swamp Thing* (1982), *Armed and Dangerous* (1986) and regular television work, not to mention numerous horror films in the U.S. and Europe that traded in on the creepy persona that he still maintained from *The Last House on the Left*. In later years, he composed several pieces of music for horror fan Eli Roth for his film *Cabin Fever* (2003) and he made his last appearance in 2010 on an episode of the cable series *Royal Pains*. Hess died of a heart attack on October 8 at the age of 75.

Tim Hetherington (December 5, 1970–April 20, 2011). Born in Birkenhead, England, British-American photojournalist Tim Hetherington made his biggest waves in journalism but also delivered one of the most searing and memorable war documentaries of all time in his *Restrepo* (2010), a devastating non-fiction work co-directed with Sebastian Junger and nominated for the Academy Award® for Best Documentary Feature. Sadly, Hetherington, who made his living alongside soldiers, was killed by mortar shells covering the Libyan Civil War on April 20th. He was only 40. He was posthumously presented with the "Leadership in Entertainment Award" by the Iraq and Afghanistan Veterans of America and the Frontline Club Memorial Tribute Award.

Larry Holden (May 15, 1961–February 13, 2011). Born in Belfast in 1961, character actor Larry Holden was a regular collaborator with Christopher Nolan, appearing in his *Memento* (2000), *Insomnia* (2002), and *Batman Begins* (2005). His career was disappointingly cut short when cancer was discovered after hip surgery. He passed away on February 13th, three months before his 50th birthday.

Tresa Hughes (September 17, 1929–July 24, 2011). Tresa Hughes was primarily a stage actress, earning a Tony® nomination in 1961 for *The Devil's Advocate*. She transitioned that stage success to a small film career but she was a much-bigger stage star, appearing on Broadway for nearly thirty years. Notable film credits include *The Sentinel* (1977), *Coming Home* (1978), *Fame* (1980), *Bad Medicine* (1985), and *Don Juan DeMarco* (1995). She passed away at the age of 81 on July 21st in New York City.

Kevin Jarre (August 6, 1954–April 3, 2011). Detroit-born screenwriter, actor, and film producer Kevin Jarre was a Golden Globe Award nominee for Best Screenplay for *Glory*. Other notable screenwriting credits include *Rambo: First Blood Part II* (1985), *Tombstone* (1993), *The Devil's*

Own (1997), and *The Mummy* (1999). Jarre passed away from heart failure in Santa Monica on April 3rd at age 56.

Hal Kanter (December 18, 1918–November 6, 2011). Georgia-born screenwriter Hal Kanter arguably made his biggest influence as a writer for the Academy Awards® from 1981 to 2008 but he had an unusually diverse career before that writing for voices as diverse as Bob Hope, Jerry Lewis, Elvis Presley, and Tennessee Williams. Notable screenwriting credits include *Blue Hawaii* (1961), *Pocketful of Miracles* (1961), and *Dear Brigitte* (1965).

Paul Kent (October 13, 1930–October 7, 2011). New York-born Paul Kent is best known for playing Lieutenant Commander Beach in *Star Trek II: The Wrath of Khan* (1982). He was born in Brooklyn but his family moved to California in 1958 and Kent went with them to work with the legendary Sanford Meisner. Kent helped found Lucille Ball's Desilu Workshop and founded the Melrose Theatre in West Hollywood in 1964. Notable film credits include *Ruby* (1977), *Perfect* (1985), *A Nightmare on Elm Street 3: Dream Warriors* (1987), and *The Road Home* (2003). The actor passed away from multiple myeloma in Los Angeles on October 7th at the age of 80.

Wyatt Knight (January 20, 1955–October 25, 2011). Comedy actor Wyatt Knight was memorable as Tommy Turner in the hit 1980s franchise spawned by *Porky's* (1982)—followed by *Porky's II: The Next Day* (1983) and *Porky's 3: Revenge* (1985)—but never found fame on-screen again, sadly killing himself at the age of 56 after succumbing to painful treatments for his non-Hodgkin's Lymphoma.

Arthur Laurents (July 14, 1917–May 5, 2011). Born in Brooklyn in 1917, Arthur Levine (who changed his name to Laurents) was an acclaimed screenwriter, playwright, and stage director. Laurents graduated from Cornell University and started his career in radio, having his first script produced for the hit program *Now Playing Tomorrow*. He became a regular radio script writer but was drafted into the U.S. Army to serve in World War II but he never saw battle. After the War, Laurents became an incredibly influential playwright, writing the books for *West Side Story, Gypsy, Anyone Can Whistle,* and *La Cage Aux Folles*. He was still working in theatre very late into his life, directing a revival of *Gypsy* when he was 91. Laurent's film career was nearly as influential as he started with a controversial script for *The Snake Pit* (1948) before working with Alfred Hitchcock on *Rope* (1948) with his then-lover Farley Granger. He also wrote *Anastasia* (1956), *Bonjour Tristesse* (1958), *The Way We Were* (1973), and *The Turning Point* (1977), for which he was nominated for the Best Picture and Best Original Screenplay Academy Awards®. Like many writers of his era, Laurents suffered blacklisting under the scare spurned by HUAC. He died of pneumonia complications on May 4th at the age of 93 in New York City.

Sidney Lumet (June 25, 1924–April 9, 2011). One of the most admired, respected, and influential directors of all time was born on June 25, 1924. Some may be surprised to learn that Lumet, an actor who redefined how to shoot New York City and who was so closely associated with the city, was actually born in Philadelphia, Pennsylvania to Baruch Lumet and Eugenia Wermus, veterans of the Yiddish stage. Lumet appeared on Broadway at a very young age and even appeared in a short film in 1935 at the age of eleven. A career that could have turned into acting was interrupted when Lumet was drafted into service in World War II, spending three years in the Army. After studying at Columbia University, Lumet started a stage career with off-Broadway productions that then segued into work in television in the 1950s. He directed hundreds of episodes of television in the 1950s, including a number of films for landmark series like *Playhouse 90*, *Kraft Television Theatre*, and *Studio One*. He took the lessons he learned there and the respect as a craftsman to the world of film with one of the most notable big screen debuts of all time, *12 Angry Men* (1957) with Henry Fonda. He earned an Oscar® nomination for his debut, which was also nominated for Best Picture and Best Adapted Screenplay (losing all three awards to *The Bridge on the River Kwai* [1957]). He followed that up by working with some of the most notable actors and actresses in the history of film including Marlon Brando and Joanne Woodward (*The Fugitive Kind* [1959]), Maureen Stapleton (*A View From the Bridge* [1961]), Katherine Hepburn (*Long Day's Journey Into Night* [1962]), and Rod Steiger (*The Pawnbroker* [1964]). He would have one of the most impressively consistent directorial resumes in the history of cinema with what could be considered critical smashes in six straight decades. Other notable credits include *The Sea Gull* (1968), *Serpico* (1973), *Murder on the Orient Express* (1974), *Dog Day Afternoon* (1975), *Network* (1976), *Equus* (1977), *Prince of the City* (1981), *The Verdict* (1982), *Running on Empty* (1988), *Q & A* (1990), *Night Falls on Manhattan* (1997), and *Before the Devil Knows You're Dead* (2007). Fourteen of Lumet's films were nominated for Oscars® and the director himself was nominated for Best Director four times but never won the category. The Academy gave him an Honorary Award in 2005. Sidney Lumet was married four times, the last to Mary Gimbel from 1980 to his death, and had two children. Lumet's influence impacted everything from the way directors transition from television to film to the importance of social issues (his 1970s work was particularly cognizant of the issues of the day and arguably when Lumet was at his peak) to how a filmmaker can use a city as a more than just a setting. Lumet made the New York streets feel like characters in most of his films and his legacy will be felt for decades to come. He passed away at the age of 86 on April 9th from lymphoma.

Kenneth Mars (April 4, 1935–February 12, 2011). Chicago-born actor Kenneth Mars will be most-remembered for his work with Mel Brooks on some of his most beloved comedies including *The Producers* (1968), in which he played the lunatic playwright Franz Liebkind, and *Young Frankenstein* (1974), in which he played Police Inspector Hans Wilhelm Fredrick Kemp. Mars studies at Northwestern University in his hometown and began his acting career shortly after graduation, appearing on stage, TV, and film. He made his acting debut in 1962 on an episode of *Car 54, Where are You?* and appeared on a number of the biggest hit shows of his era. He transitioned to film late in the decade and appeared in *Butch Cassidy and the Sundance Kid* (1969), *What's Up, Doc?* (1972), *The Parallax View* (1974), *Fletch* (1985), *Radio Days* (1987), and *Shadows and Fog* (1992). With his unique voice—often stretched into an exaggerated

German accent—Mars became a staple on the animated scene, offering his talents to *The Little Mermaid* (1989), *We're Back! A Dinosaur's Story* (1993), *Thumbelina* (1994), and the entire *The Land Before Time* series (1994-2011). Kenneth Mars died from pancreatic cancer in Los Angeles on February 12th, survived by his wife of thirty-three years and two daughters.

Sue Mengers (September 2, 1932–October 15, 2011). Born in Hamburg, Germany, Sue Mengers was a talent agent who worked with dozens of notable actors and filmmakers from the 1960s through to her death at the age of seventy-nine in Beverly Hills, California. Mengers started her career as a receptionist at MCA in 1955 and dealt with agents who represented legends like Jack Benny, George Burns, Gracie Allen, Marlon Brando, and Montgomery Clift. She went from there to the legendary William Morris Agency until 1963 when she went to a newly-formed company and found future legends like Julie Harris and Anthony Perkins. She was hired by Creative Management Associates in the 1960s and worked with Paul Newman, Steve McQueen, and Robert Redford. She worked with too many cinema icons to count, including Burt Reynolds, Cher, Michael Caine, Gene Hackman, Sidney Lumet, Barbra Streisand, and many more. She passed away from pneumonia in her California home.

Harry Morgan (April 10, 1915–December 7, 2011). The Detroit-born actor will be most-remembered for his TV work on the beloved *M*A*S*H* (or arguably-as-notable work in *Dragnet*) but Harry Morgan was not just a TV legend as he also appeared in more than 100 films. Born Harry Bratsberg and raised in Muskegon, Michigan, Bratsberg would change his name to Morgan when he made his 1942 debut in *To the Shores of Tripoli*. He started his incredible string of consistent work for decades, appearing in a number of major films of the era, including *The Ox-Bow Incident* (1943), *The Big Clock* (1948), *High Noon* (1952), *The Glenn Miller Story* (1954), and *The Far Country* (1955). He swung more to radio and TV in the 1960s and beyond but still made regular film appearances, including *Inherit the Wind* (1960), *How the West Was Won* (1962), *Snowball Express* (1972), *The Shootist* (1976), and a cameo in the big screen version of *Dragnet* (1987). Morgan was married to the same woman, Eileen Detchon, from 1940 until she passed away in 1985, regularly making references to her on *M*A*S*H* and *Dragnet*. They had four sons. In 1986, Morgan remarried to Barbara Bushman Quine, who he is survived by. He passed away in his sleep on December 7th at the age of 96.

Mary Murphy (January 26, 1931–May 4, 2011). American film actress Mary Murphy was born in Washington D.C. in 1931 and would go on to become a regular cinema staple from the 1950s to the 1970s, appearing with icons like Marlon Brando, Tony Curtis, and Humphrey Bogart. She was never much of a movie star but she was a reliable performer who retired from acting in the 1980s and passed away from heart disease on May 4th in Los Angeles. Murphy's most memorable role was as good girl Kathie Bleeker in the hit *The Wild One* (1953) and she also starred in *The Desperate Hours* (1955), *Live Fast, Die Young* (1958), and *Junior Bonner* (1972).

Charles Napier (April 12, 1936–October 5, 2011). With his square jaw, growling voice and a mouth that seemed to contain twice the normal number of teeth, Charles Napier was the kind of actor who stuck in the mind of anyone who came across one of his performances. Born in Kentucky in 1936, he served in the U.S. Army and graduated from Western Kentucky University with a major in art. After returning to his alma mater to attend graduate school, he was encouraged to pursue acting and spent most of the Sixties working in community theater before finally breaking into professional show business at the end of the decade, including an appearance on the original *Star Trek* as an interstellar hippie. He eventually came to the attention of maverick independent filmmaker Russ Meyer, who cast him as a corrupt border town sheriff in the softcore sexploitation action film *Cherry, Harry & Raquel* (1970) That film was a hit and he would continue to work with Meyer in such subsequent projects as *Beyond the Valley of the Dolls* (1970), *The Seven Minutes* (1971), and the astonishingly brutal *Supervixens* (1975), in which he reprised his character from *Cherry, Harry & Raquel*. Most of these films were hits but since they were made outside of the Hollywood mainstream, they did not immediately lead to more work. As the story goes, Napier was down and out and reduced to living in his car when he was contacted by a representative of Alfred Hitchcock, who had seen and enjoyed *Supervixens*, and taken to Universal Studios, where he met Hitchcock and placed under contract to the studio. At the same time, a young filmmaker named Jonathan Demme, also a fan of the Russ Meyer filmography, hired him for his film *Citizen's Band* (1977) and began an association that would find Napier appearing in subsequent Demme projects as *Last Embrace* (1979), *Melvin and Howard* (1980), *Swing Shift* (1984), *Something Wild* (1986), *Married to the Mob* (1988), *Silence of the Lambs* (1991), *Philadelphia* (1993), *Beloved* (1998), and *The Manchurian Candidate* (2004). In addition to his work with Demme, Napier became a familiar face and voice on television (where he could be seen and/or heard in shows ranging from *The A-Team* to *The Simpsons*) and in film, where he appeared in such notable hits as *The Blues Brothers* (1980), *Rambo: First Blood Part II* (1985), *The Grifters* (1990), *Austin Powers: International Man of Mystery* (1997), and *Austin Powers: The Spy Who Shagged Me* (1999). He died on October 5th, having collapsed the previous day.

David Nelson (October 24, 1936–January 11, 2011). American actor David Oswald Nelson will forever be enshrined in TV history as the oldest son of Ozzie Nelson and Harriet Hilliard, TV's famous *Ozzie and Harriet*. Nelson appeared on the show in the 1950s and 1960s, even directing a few episodes, and continued acting, directing, and producing until his final film credit in 1990 (*Cry-Baby*). Other notable credits include *Here Come the Nelsons* (1952), *Peyton Place* (1957), *The Big Show* (1961), and *Up in Smoke* (1978). Nelson passed away from colon cancer on January 11th in Century City. He is survived by his wife of thirty-six years and four sons.

John Neville (May 2, 1925–November 19, 2011). Energetic, captivating, and consistent, British actor John Neville was arguably more accomplished on stage (he was a regular at Canada's world-famous Stratford Festival, where he was even Artistic Director for some time) but he will forever be cinematically remembered for the title character he played in Terry Gilliam's *The Adventures of Baron Munchausen* (1988). Primarily a stage actor with international acclaim until that film it gave his career a unique third act, even propelling him into the genre spotlight as he took on a recurring role on FOX's hit show *The X-Files* from 1995 to 1998 (he would also play the role in the film *X-Files: Fight the Future* (1998). Other notable credits include *The Road to Wellville* (1994), *Little Women* (1994), *The Fifth Element* (1997), *Urban Legend* (1998), *Sunshine* (1999), *Time of the Wolf* (2002), and *Spider* (2002). The actor suffered from Alzheimer's Disease later in life and passed away peacefully on November 19th, surrounded by family.

Donald Peterman (January 3, 1932–February 5, 2011). American cinematographer Donald William Peterman was not only a member of the Academy of Motion Picture Arts and Sciences and the American Society of Cinematographers but was also an Oscar® nominee himself (for *Flashdance* [1983] and *Star Trek IV: The Voyage Home* [1986]). After serving in the Army in the 1950s and shooting documentaries for them, he began a career as a clapper loader at Hal Roach Studios. He worked in TV for years, making his feature film debut in 1979 with the hit *When a Stranger Calls* and becoming one of the most prominent cinematographers of the 1980s and 1990s. Not only can his resume boast the two aforementioned Oscar® nominees but also regular work with director Ron Howard—on *Splash* (1984), *Cocoon* (1985), *Gung Ho* (1986), and *How the Grinch Stole Christmas* (2000)—and credits on *Planes, Trains & Automobiles* (1987), *She's Having a Baby* (1988), *Point Break* (1991), *Get Shorty* (1995), and *Men in Black* (1997). He passed away from myelodysplastic syndrome on February 5th, survived by his wife of fifty-four years, Sally, and his four children.

Polly Platt (January 29, 1939–July 27, 2011). American screenwriter, art director, and producer Mary Marr Platt was born in Fort Sheridan, Illinois in 1939, later changing her name to Polly. Platt started her career in summer stock, where she would meet and marry Peter Bogdanovich in 1962, starting her career on-screen by co-writing his *Targets* (1968) and going on to work as production designer on his *The Last Picture Show* (1971). The two would divorce that year (and the later film *Irreconcilable Differences* [1984] is reportedly based on their marriage problems), but she continued to work with Bogdanovich on *What's Up, Doc?* (1972) and *Paper Moon* (1973). She was the first female member of the Art Directors Guild and also handled the design for the hit *A Star is Born* (1976) and was Oscar®-nominated for her art direction of *Terms of Endearment* (1983). She would work with James L. Brooks again, co-producing for his company Gracie Films on projects like *Broadcast News* (1987), *The War of the Roses* (1989), *Say Anything...* (1989), and *Bottle Rocket* (1996). It is rumored that Platt gave Brooks the cartoon *Life is Hell* by Matt Groening and suggested that the two work on a weekly animated series. The rest is TV history. She wrote *Pretty Baby* (1978), *Good Luck, Miss Wyckoff* (1979), and *A Map of the World* (1999). Polly Platt passed away from amyotrophic lateral sclerosis on July 27th at the age of 72 and is survived by her husband of twenty-six years, Tony Wade.

Pete Postlethwaite (February 7, 1946–January 2, 2011). Taken while he was still in the prime of his career (it is not often that someone is included in the Oscar® In Memoriam montage while also being in a nominee for Best Picture that year), Pete Postlethwaite was one of the more intriguing and consistent actors of his generation. The legendary Steven Spielberg even went so far as to say that Postlethwaite was the best actor he had ever seen. Born in Warrington, England, the actor started his cinematic career relatively late in life, not really breaking through until his forties, when he appeared in *Distant Voices, Still Lives* (1988) to international acclaim. Before that, he worked at the notorious Everyman Theatre in Liverpool with Bill Nighy, Jonathan Pryce, and Julie Walters. He used that success to find work in TV before his film breakthrough in 1988. The continued and impressive string of work pretty much did not let up from that point on until his too-early death at the age of sixty-four in Shrewsbury, England. He only received one Academy Award® nomination (for *In the Name of the Father* [1993]) but he was such a consistent performer that he was made an Officer of the Order of the British Empire in 2004. Notable credits include *Hamlet* (1990), *Alien 3* (1992), *The Last of the Mohicans* (1992), *The Usual Suspects* (1995), *Romeo + Juliet* (1996), *The Lost World: Jurassic Park* (1997), *Amistad* (1997), *The Constant Gardener* (2005), *Clash of the Titans* (2010), *Inception* (2010), and *The Town* (2010). Pete Postlethwaite was diagnosed with testicular cancer as far back as 1990 and even had a testicle removed. The cancer returned and he died of the pancreatic form on January 2nd, just as *Inception* and *The Town* were earning him acclaim yet again.

Harry Redmond, Jr. (October 15, 1909–May 23, 2011). American special effects artist Harry Redmond Jr. helped change the world of cinema when he worked on the team that brought a giant ape into American theaters with the landmark film *King Kong* (1933). Born in Brooklyn but relocated to California, Redmond started his career in the prop department at First National Pictures, moving to RKO just as they were about to go through one of cinematic history's most notable phases. Not only did he work on *Kong* but he is also credited with special effects work on *The Son of Kong* (1933), *Of Human Bondage* (1934), *She* (1935), *Top Hat* (1935), *The Last Days of Pompeii* (1935), *Only Angels Have Wings* (1939), *The Secret Life of Walter Mitty* (1947), and *The Bishop's Wife* (1947). Redmond passed away at the amazing age of 101 at his Hollywood Hills home.

Cliff Robertson (September 9, 1923–September 10, 2011). A beloved and iconic actor for decades, Clifford Parker Robertson III was an American movie and TV star who won the Academy Award® for his emotionally devastating work in *Charly* (1968). Robertson was born in La Jolla, California and his mother died two years later from peritonitis, leaving Robertson to be raised by his maternal grandmother. He served in World War II after graduating from high school and attended but did not graduate from Antioch College. He started acting when he was very young but did not really begin his career until 1956's *Picnic*. Notable credits from the peak of Robertson's career (from the 1950s to the 1970s) include *The Naked and the Dead* (1958), *Gidget* (1959), *PT 109* (1963), *Charly, Three Days*

of the Condor (1975), *Midway* (1976), and *Return to Earth* (1976). In 1977, Cliff Robertson blew the whistle on an incredible embezzlement scandal at Columbia Pictures and the resulting fall-out reportedly cost him to be blacklisted for several years. He returned with a few hits in the 1980s (*Class* [1983], *Star 80* [1983], *Malone* [1987]) but nowhere near the popular appeal he had enjoyed earlier. Some bad films followed in the 1990s (*Renaissance Man* [1994], *Escape From L.A.* [1996]), but Robertson had his most notable impact late in life after he took on the iconic role of Uncle Ben Parker in Sam Raimi's *Spider-Man* movies (2002, 2004, 2007). Cliff Robertson married twice and had two children. He was an aviator who enjoyed flying his own planes and was certified as a pilot. He passed away one day after his 88th birthday on September 10th.

Jane Russell (June 21, 1921–February 28, 2011). Ernestine Jane Geraldine Russell was born in a small town in Minnesota and probably never thought that she would be one of the most desired women in the world in the 1950s and 1960s. She began her film career in 1943 and worked regularly in the music industry while trying to balance her love for acting as well. She married three times and adopted three times, making a notable philanthropic impact by founding the World Adoption International Fund. Her time in the spotlight began when Howard Hughes signed Jane Russell to a contract in 1940 and kicked off her career with a Billy the Kid story called *The Outlaw* (1943). The film caused controversy because of Russell's ample bosom and was completed in 1941 and only released on a very limited scale in 1943, not getting a wide released until 1946. A publicity still from the movie of Russell lying in hay became an iconic pin-up photo for the men fighting in World War II. Russell would not appear in another film until *Young Widow* (1946) and shortly thereafter she tried to start a career in music, even recording a song with Frank Sinatra. Film roles in Russell's career included parts in *His Kind of Woman* (1951), *Macao* (1952), *Son of Paleface* (1952), *Gentlemen Prefer Blondes* (1953), *Foxfire* (1955), *Gentleman Marry Brunettes* (1955), *The Fuzzy Pink Nightgown* (1957), *Johnny Reno* (1966), *Waco* (1966), and *Darker Than Amber* (1970). Jane Russell passed away in her home on February 28th.

Ken Russell (July 3, 1927–November 27, 2011). Perhaps the most notorious enfant terrible in the history of the British film industry, the Southampton-born Ken Russell began his career, following stints in the Royal Air Force and Merchant Navy, working in the worlds of dance and photography before moving into television. At the same time, he was making amateur documentaries as part of the English Free Cinema movement of the late 1950s and it was this work that got him a position with the BBC making groundbreaking arts documentaries. In 1963, he made his feature directorial debut with *French Dressing*, a knock-off of the Brigitte Bardot vehicle *And God Created Woman* (1956) that went nowhere but he had more success a few years later with the spy thriller *Billion Dollar Brain* (1967). He followed that with what would prove to be his first truly signature film, an adaptation of the D.H. Lawrence novel *Women in Love* (1969) that startled viewers with a frank depiction of sexuality (including male nudity) that was then unheard of in a mainstream film. The film was a critical and commercial success—Russell received his only Oscar® nomination for Best Director and Glenda Jackson won for Best Actress—and it inspired Russell to spend the next decade making a series of increasingly surreal and baroque melodramas that pushed so many buttons in such a gleeful manner. Many of these were biopics of famous artists that bore only the vaguest resemblance to their actual lives, including looks at Tchaikovsky (*The Music Lovers* [1970]), Henri Gaudier-Brzeska (*Savage Messiah* [1972]), Gustav Mahler (*Mahler* [1974]), Franz Liszt (the jaw-dropping *Lisztomania* [1975]), and Rudolph Valentino (*Valentino* [1977]). During this time, he also made *The Devils* (1971), his still-controversial adaptation of the Aldous Huxley book "The Devils of Loudon" that was heavily edited for its release in America due to imagery deemed to be sacrilegious but which nevertheless caused a sensation in both England and America, the G-rated period musical *The Boy Friend* (1971), his flamboyant cinematic take on *Tommy* (1975), the rock opera from The Who that Russell once claimed to be one of the finest works of art created in the 20th century and the hallucinatory sci-fi drama *Altered States* (1980). After the tepid response to his erotic drama *Crimes of Passion* (1984), a project heavily edited prior to its release, he returned to England to direct opera and such films as *Gothic* (1986), *The Lair of the White Worm* (1987), *Salome's Last Dance* (1987), and *The Rainbow* (1989), an adaptation of another D.H. Lawrence work that just happened to be a prequel to *Women in Love*. Following the cable docudrama *Prisoner of Honor* and the controversial drama *Whore* (1991) not to mention a turn in front of the cameras in the screen version of the John le Carre novel *The Russia House* (1990), Russell spent the next couple of decades shooting low-budget video projects that received scant distribution, served as a visiting professor at numerous universities and worked on the occasional film projects that never quite made it to fruition. In addition to his films, he also penned six novels, several books on filmmaking and the 1989 autobiography *A British Picture* (known in America as *Altered States: The Autobiography of Ken Russell*) and had been writing a column for the film section of *The Times of England* when he passed away on November 27th of natural causes.

Michael Sarrazin (May 22, 1940–April 17, 2011). Jacques Michel Andre Sarrazin was born in Quebec in 1940 and started acting from an early age, first on stage and then in TV productions in Toronto, Ontario. He caught the eye of someone from Universal and was signed to a contract, appearing in several films in the 1960s and 1970s before essentially falling off the pop culture radar. Notable credits from Michael Sarrazin's career include *Journey to Shiloh* (1968), *The Sweet Ride* (1968), *They Shoot Horses, Don't They?* (1969), *The Pursuit of Happiness* (1971), *Frankenstein: The True Story* (1973), *The Gumball Rally* (1976), and *Deadly Companion* (1980). He succumbed to a battle with cancer on April 17th and was survived by two daughters.

Tura Satana (July 10, 1938–February 4, 2011). Tura Satana may have had only one truly notable role during her screen acting career but when the role is that of Varla, the alternately sexy and terrifying force of nature at the center of Russ Meyer's cult classic *Faster, Pussycat! Kill! Kill!* (1965), one does not really require any more to make a

lasting impression with viewers. Born in Japan to a silent film actor and a circus performer, her family moved to America after World War II and eventually wound up in Chicago. After becoming a star on the burlesque circuit in its dying days, she moved to Hollywood and began make brief appearances in films like *Irma la Douce* (1963) and *Who's Been Sleeping in My Bed?* (1963) and television shows such as *Hawaiian Eye, Burke's Law,* and *The Man from U.N.C.L.E.* In 1965, she achieved screen immortality when she was hired by Meyer to star in *Faster, Pussycat! Kill! Kill!,* a violent sexploitation drama (though one without any actual nudity) in which she plays Varla, a psychotic stripper who, along with a couple of fellow go-go girls, kills a guy in the desert with her bare hands, kidnap his whiny girlfriend, and hide out at a remote ranch owned by a paralyzed and perverted old man who supposedly has hidden a fortune on the property. Bold and brash even by exploitation film standards, this no-budget, no-name exercise in weirdness is one of those movies that cannot be forgotten and much of that is due to the impact that Satana has on the viewer. In later years, Meyer would credit her for her contributions to the character and the film as a whole but they would never work together again. Instead, she did bit parts in *Our Man Flint* (1966) and the television show *The Girl from U.N.C.L.E.,* made a couple of films for schlockmeister T.V. Mikels—*The Astro-Zombies* (1969) and *The Doll Squad* (1974)—and left the entertainment industry completely and worked in a hospital and as a dispatcher for the Los Angeles Police Department. In later years, she became a cult icon—fueled by the continued popularity of *Faster, Pussycat! Kill! Kill!*—and appeared in the camp items *Sugar Boxx* (2008) and *The Haunted World of El Superbeasto* (2009) before passing away on February 4th from heart failure.

Bert Schneider (May 5, 1933–December 12, 2011). New Yorker Berton Schneider made his biggest impact on the world of film when he produced one of its most iconic and influential works in 1969's *Easy Rider*. Son of former Columbia Pictures President Abraham Schneider, Bert Schneider tried to make films that had a topical edge and was also responsible for bringing The Monkees to their most stateside popularity by producing their eponymous TV program and the controversial and totally wacky *Head* (1968), which starred the band. A young man named Jack Nicholson co-wrote *Head* and he had an idea for another film for Schneider to produce, a little road trip called *Easy Rider*. That was followed by a string of iconic 1970s films including *Five Easy Pieces* (1970), *The Last Picture Show* (1971), *The King of Marvin Gardens* (1972), *Days of Heaven* (1978), and *Hearts and Minds* (1975), the Academy Award® winner for Best Documentary. Schneider passed away from natural causes in Los Angeles at the age of 78.

Maria Schneider (March 27, 1952–February 3, 2011). Born Marie Christine Gelin, Maria Schneider made international waves when she co-starred with Marlon Brando in the controversial and explicit *Last Tango in Paris* (1972), a film that hit the cultural zeitgeist at just the right time and had an impact that resonated for decades. In fact, Schneider notoriously wrote about how the sexually explicit film impacted her emotionally, nearly accusing director Bernardo Bertolucci and Brando of sexual assault, especially in regards to the notorious butter scene, which Schneider claimed she was not informed about until she was on set. The fact that *Paris* turned Schneider into a sex symbol, especially given her emotional trauma over the film's production, somewhat derailed Schneider's career in that she wanted to be more that a sex symbol, refusing to perform nude again and never finding the fame she did with Brando. She appeared with Jack Nicholson in Michelango Antonioni's *The Passenger,* her only other truly notable film credit. She passed away at the very young age of 58 after losing a battle with cancer.

Charles Aaron "Bubba" Smith (February 28, 1945–August 3, 2011). One of the few athletes who successfully segued to acting, Bubba Smith was a defensive end for the Michigan State Spartans and played nine years in the NFL with the Baltimore Colts, Oakland Raiders, and Houston Oilers. He retired from football in 1976 after winning a Super Bowl and being named to the Pro Bowl twice and he used his experience as a commercial spokesperson for brands like Miller Lite to segue into comedies, making his largest pop cultural impact as Moses Hightower in six *Police Academy* movies (1984-1989). He also appeared in several TV films, guest starred on sitcoms, and also appeared in *Stroker Ace* (1983) with Burt Reynolds. Bubba Smith passed away at the age of 66 from heart disease and acute drug intoxication.

Patricia Smith (February 20, 1930–January 2, 2011). Born Patricia Smith Lasell, this American actress was never a monumental star herself but worked with a number of legends, including James Stewart and Jack Lemmon (supporting him in the role that won him the Oscar® for *Save the Tiger* [1973]). Her notable films include *The Bachelor Party* (1957) and *The Spirit of St. Louis* (1957), but she made her career primarily as a TV regular and guest star, working regularly all the way through into the 1990s and appearing in everything from *The Twilight Zone* to *Star Trek: The Next Generation.* Patricia Smith passed away from heart failure after suffering from diabetes for many years at the age of 80.

G.D. Spradlin (August 31, 1920–July 24, 2011). Often typecast as a bad guy, Gervase Duan Spradlin worked with so many powerhouse actors that he became one of cinema's more interesting character actors for three straight decades. Born in Pauls Valley, Oklahoma, Spradlin got his degree from the University of Oklahoma before joining the military during World War II. He was an attorney, an oil producer, and a political activist before turning to acting relatively late in life, appearing on several hit TV shows of the era for producer Fred Roos. When Roos went on to produce *The Godfather, Part II* (1974) he thought of his regular collaborator and cast him as Senator Geary. He worked consistently from that point to his retirement in 1999, memorably playing Major General Robert L. Eichelberger in *MacArthur* (1977), General Corman in *Apocalypse Now* (1979), Reverend Lemon in *Ed Wood* (1994), The President in *The Long Kiss Goodnight* (1996), and Ben Bradlee in *Dick* (1999), his final film. G.D. Spradlin passed away from natural causes at the age of 90 at his cattle ranch in San Luis Obispo, California. He was survived by his second wife, who he married in 2002, and two daughters.

Elizabeth Taylor (February 27, 1932–March 23, 2011). An international legend, Elizabeth Rosemond Taylor was, quite simply, one of the biggest movie stars of all time. She transcended pure movie stardom to become an international icon in fashion, style, and even gossip. In later years, people seemed to follow her odd personal life (including a close friendship with Michael Jackson, increasing weight problems, and multiple marriages) and it sometimes overshadowed the amazing acting ability that she used to become one of the biggest movie stars of all time. Taylor was born in London to two Americans, Francis Lenn Taylor and Sara Viola Warmbrodt, who were living there at the time. Her family moved to New York when Taylor was seven and eventually settled in Los Angeles. Taylor's father was an art dealer, which got their family into notable social circles in L.A. and Hedda Hopper introduced them to Andrea Berens, the fiancée of the chairman of Universal Pictures. Berens met Taylor and not only was Universal interested in the child star but MGM started a bidding war. Universal won and Taylor was granted a seven-year contract, making her screen debut at the age of nine in *There's One Born Every Minute* (1942). For unknown reasons, her Universal contract ended and she was soon cast in other company's child roles like *Lassie Come Home* (1943) and *Jane Eyre* (1944). Her breakthrough came with *National Velvet* (1944), which made Taylor a huge star, grossing over $4 million, a huge sum at the time. She worked regularly as a child and teen, making her first impact as an adult in the hit *Father of the Bride* (1950) with Spencer Tracy (and the awful sequel the next year). Taylor would truly make her transition with George Steven's *A Place in the Sun* (1951) with Montgomery Clift and Shelley Winters. A string of less substantial roles followed but everything changed in the mid-1950s with a string of hits, including *Giant* (1956) and four films in a row for which she would be nominated for an Oscar®—*Raintree County* (1957), *Cat on a Hot Tin Roof* (1958), *Suddenly, Last Summer* (1959), and *Butterfield 8* (1960), which finally earned her the actual Academy Award®. She became the highest paid actress at the time for the title role of *Cleopatra* (1963), where she met her future husband Richard Burton. Her notorious and tumultuous relationship with Burton would heavily impact her work with him on *Who's Afraid of Virginia Woolf?* (1966), which earned her a second Academy Award®. They would appear in six films together, making a fortune for Hollywood. She never quite found the on-screen fame that she did in the 1950s and 1960s again but she worked regularly through the 1980s, making her final appearance in *The Flintstones* (1994). Elizabeth Taylor was notoriously married eight times to seven different men, marrying and divorcing Burton twice. She often seemed to jump from one marriage to another, divorcing second husband Michael Wilding in 1957, marrying Michael Todd the same year, having him pass away tragically in 1958, and marrying Eddie Fisher in 1959. She started seeing Fisher while he was still married to Debbie Reynolds and started seeing Burton while she was still married to Fisher. Elizabeth Taylor was very vocally active in fundraising to stop HIV and AIDS, being awarded the Jean Hersholt Humanitarian Award at the Academy Awards® in 1992. Elizabeth Taylor had health problems throughout her life, having multiple operations over the years and finally succumbed to heart failure at the age of 79.

Gordon Tootoosis (October 25, 1941–July 5, 2011). Of Cree and Stoney descent, Gordon Tootoosis was born in Saskatchewan, Canada, and would go on to be one of the most notable Native American actors. Notable credits include *Alien Thunder* (1974), multiple seasons of TV's *North of 60* (1992-1997), *Legends of the Fall* (1994), *Pocahontas* (1995), *Lone Star* (1996), *The Edge* (1997), *Reindeer Games* (2000), *Open Season* (2006), and *Bury My Heart at Wounded Knee* (2007).

Theadora Van Runkle (March 27, 1928–November 4, 2011). Van Runkle was a three times Oscar®-nominated costume designer who also received a Lifetime Achievement Award from the Costume Designer's Guild in 2002. Her nominations came for her debut, *Bonnie and Clyde* (1967), *The Godfather, Part II* (1974), and *Peggy Sue Got Married* (1986). She designed for Faye Dunaway on the red carpet and also handled costume duties for *New York, New York* (1977), *The Jerk* (1979), *S.O.B.* (1981), *The Best Little Whorehouse in Texas* (1982), *Leap of Faith* (1992), *Kiss of Death* (1995), and more. She passed away on November 4th at the age of 83.

Harold William Varney (January 22, 1934–April 2, 2011). Varney was a legendary sound mixer who shared Academy Awards® for his craft for two of the most beloved films of all time—*Star Wars: Episode V–The Empire Strikes Back* (1980) and *Raiders of the Lost Ark* (1981). He would be nominated again for *Dune* (1984) and *Back to the Future* (1985). Varney worked on so many of the most notable genre films of the 1980s, including *Escape From New York* (1981), *Poltergeist* (1982), *The Thing* (1982), *Twilight Zone: The Movie* (1983), *Gremlins* (1984), *Starman* (1984), *The Goonies* (1985), and *Young Sherlock Holmes* (1985). His final film credit came on 1996's *Dragonheart*. He passed away from congestive heart failure at the age of 77 at his home in Alabama.

Yvette Vickers (August 26, 1928–2010). Born Yvette Vedder, the future B-movie sexpot originally went to UCLA to study journalism but eventually switched her major in order to study theater. During that time, she appeared in commercials and eventually went to New York City to serve as the model for White Rain shampoo before returning to California to pursue acting full-time. Under her real name, she made her screen debut in a bit part in *Sunset Boulevard* (1950) and made a few other appearances in film and television projects before being cast by James Cagney to appear in his sole directorial project, *Short Cut to Hell* (1957). After that, she found steady work for the next few years as the sultry bad girl on television and in a number of low-budget genre classics with such titles as *Reform School Girl* (1958), *Attack of the Giant Leeches* (1958), and the immortal *Attack of the 50 Ft. Woman* (1958). In 1959, she also appeared in *Playboy* in a pictorial photographed by future filmmaker Russ Meyer. Possibly as the result of her appearance in *Playboy* and other men's magazines of the period, the parts began to dry up and, outside of supporting roles in *Hud* (1963) and *What's the Matter with Helen?* (1971), she essentially left the industry altogether. She became increasingly reclusive and, in a ghoulish note reminiscent of the grisly horror films in which she made her name, her mummified body was found inside her home on April 27th after a neighbor reported having not seen her for

a while. It was determined that she died of coronary disease and it was believed that over a year may have elapsed between her death and the discovery of her body.

Gary Winick (March 31, 1961–February 27, 2011). Director Gary Winick passed away in his prime as he was still making hit films when he contracted pneumonia while trying to fight brain cancer and died at the age of only 49 in his Manhattan home. Winick made waves on the independent and festival scenes with his direction of *Tadpole* (2002) and productions of *Piece of April* (2003) and *November* (2004) and the Independent Spirit John Cassavetes Award-winning *Personal Velocity* (2003). Like so many art house directors inevitably do, Winick went mainstream and directed *13 Going on 30* (2004), *Charlotte's Web* (2006), *Bride Wars* (2009), and *Letters to Juliet* (2010), his final credit.

Dana Wynter (June 8, 1931–May 5, 2011). Born Dagmar Winter in Germany, Dana Wynter was raised in England as the daughter of a well-known surgeon and considered studying medicine herself until she decided to take a shot at acting. She made a string of brief screen appearances in British-produced films such as *The Crimson Pirate* (1952) and *Knights of the Round Table* (1953) before relocating to America on the advice of an agent, where she began making appearances on television shows and received a Golden Globe Award in 1955 for Most Promising Newcomer. The next year, she would land the part she would be most remembered for when she was cast by director Don Siegel as the female lead opposite Kevin McCarthy in the science-fiction classic *Invasion of the Body Snatchers* (1956). Over the next few years, Wynter would appear in such films as *D-Day: The Sixth of June* (1956), *In Love and War* (1958), *Sink the Bismark!* (1960), and the John Huston oddity *The List of Adrian Messenger* (1963). Although she would continue to make film appearances from time to time—most notably as Burt Lancaster's estranged wife in the box-office smash *Airport* (1970)—she was more often seen on television in guest appearances. Following a final appearance in the TV movie *The Return of Ironside* (1993), Wynter retired from acting. In her later years, she suffered from heart disease and passed away due to congestive heart failure on May 5th.

Peter Yates (July 24, 1929–January 9, 2011). Born in Aldershot, Hampshire, England in July of 1929, Peter James Yates would become one of the most notable directors of the 1960s through the 1980s, being nominated for Best Director at the Academy Awards® twice (for *Breaking Away* [1979] and *The Dresser* [1983]). Although he was not nominated for it, Yates' greatest contribution could arguably be for what he did with Steve McQueen and the car chase on the smash hit *Bullitt* (1968). Yates also directed *Robbery* (1967), *Murphy's War* (1971), *The Friends of Eddie Coyle* (1973), *Mother, Jugs & Speed* (1976), *The Deep* (1977), *Krull* (1983), *Suspect* (1987), and *An Innocent Man* (1989). Peter Yates passed away at the age of 81 on January 9th in London.

Susannah York (January 9, 1939–January 15, 2011). Born Susannah Yolande Fletcher, British actor Susannah York was Oscar®-nominated for *They Shoot Horses, Don't They?* (1969) and won Best Actress at the Cannes Film Festival for *Images* (1972). York's career started with Alec Guiness in

1960's *Tunes of Glory* and worked consistently for the next quarter-century. She co-starred with Albert Finney in the Best Picture-winning *Tom Jones* (1963) and appeared in *A Man For All Seasons* (1966), *Battle of Britain* (1969), and notoriously played Superman's mother in *Superman* (1978) and *Superman II* (1980). She played Mrs. Cratchit with George C. Scott in TV's *A Christmas Carol* (1984). She would not have many more notable credits after that but did work consistently through 2010, passing away from bone marrow cancer on January 15th in London.

Selected Film Books of 2011

Aardman Animation and Sony Pictures Animation. *The Art & Making of Arthur Christmas: An Inside Look at Behind-the-Scenes Artwork with Filmmaker Commentary.* It Books, 2011. An official tie-in for the Sony Christmas movie about the industry at the North Pole that requires hundreds of elves and a family of Santas. The book includes over 300 pieces of art including concept art, color keys, storyboards, and much more, with commentary from director/writer Sarah Smith.

Amidi, Amid. *The Art of Pixar: 25th Anniv.: The Complete Color Scripts and Select Art from 25 Years of Animation.* Chronicle Books, 2011. An updated version of a previously-available book that chronicles the success of the most important animation studio of the last quarter-century that includes behind-the-scenes details and visual accompaniment to everything from *Toy Story* (1995) to *Cars 2* (2011).

Anand, A.S. *Film: Ab Initio 1895-1909—Critiquing cinema's greatest works in chronological order.* Red Birch Publishing, 2011. An e-book that analyzes some of the earliest known films including the first ever feature film, first animated film, and first cinematic tragedy. Icons covered include the Lumiere Brothers, Georges Melies, and D.W. Griffith.

Anastasia, George, Glen Macnow, and Joe Pistone. *The Ultimate Book of Gangster Movies: Featuring the 100 Greatest Gangster Films of All Time.* Running Press, 2011. With a foreword by Joe Pistone, author of the book-turned-movie *Donnie Brasco*, this compendium not only tries to rank one of the most popular genres in the history of film but includes, trivia, sidebars, photographs, and interviews with legends of the genre, including Joe Mantegna, Michael Madsen, Chazz Palminteri, and more.

Anderson, Jack. *Shooting Movies Without Shooting Yourself in the Foot: Becoming a Cinematographer.* Focal Press, 2011. The art of cinematography is detailed with a hands-on approach to the form, starting with the fundamentals of holding a camera and shooting a scene to how to not only do it at all but do it well.

Arkin, Alan. *An Improvised Life: A Memoir.* Da Capo Press, 2011. The Oscar®-winning star of *Freebie and the Bean* (1974), *Glengarry Glen Ross* (1992), *Grosse Pointe Blank* (1997), and *Little Miss Sunshine* (2006) tells his own story in this candid and moving memoir that focuses more on a his infectious love affair with the art of acting than the specifics of his life or career.

Armour, Philip. *The 100 Greatest Western Movies of All Time: Including Five You've Never Heard Of.* TwoDot, 2011. An illustrated series of mini-essays on the title subject, including small examinations of *Once Upon a Time in the West* (1968), *High Noon* (1952), *Shane* (1953), *Unforgiven* (1992), and much more.

Armstrong, Vic, Robert Sellers, and Steven Spielberg. *The True Adventures of the World's Greatest Stuntman: My Life as Indiana Jones, James Bond, Superman and Other Movie Heroes.* Titan Books, 2011. Written by a man that millions have seen but probably never realized it, one of the most legendary stuntmen in the history of film offers from-the-set details about his experience on the sets of dozens of smash hits from *Raiders of the Lost Ark* (1981) to *Patriot Games* (1992) to *Thor* (2011).

Artis, Anthony Q. *The Shut Up and Shoot Freelance Video Guide: A Down & Dirty Production.* Focal Press, 2011. A crash course in how to become a freelance video expert that focuses on every aspect of the profession including making music videos, marketing videos, and even shooting weddings. Described as a "video cookbook," it is designed as a resource for anyone looking to turn their freelance video hobby into something more.

Banner, Lois and Mark Anderson. *MM-Personal: From the Private Archive of Marilyn Monroe.* Abrams, 2011. A compendium of over 10,000 largely unseen and heretofore unpublished pieces of memorabilia related to the legendary iconic star. Snapshots, letters, memorabilia, and more offer a glimpse into the private life of this very public figure.

Bennett, Xander. *Screenwriting Tips, You Hack: 150 Practical Pointers for Becoming a Screenwriter.* Focal Press, 2011. An in-your-face advice piece about how to improve your screenwriting with a focus on not just the basics of the form but the little things that separate one writer from another. An expansion of a successful blog website started by a script reader looking to give practical advice to the people writing the scripts he used to get paid to read.

Bernard, Susan, Jane Russell, and Lindsay Lohan. *Marilyn: Intimate Exposures.* Sterling Signature, 2011. The 50th anniversary of Marilyn Monroe's death in 2012 produced a series of collectible books in 2011 including this piece with a frameable print and photography from Hollywood legend Bruno Bernard, including her first professional sitting in 1946.

Bingen, Steven, Stephen X. Sylvester, Michael Troyan, and Debbie Reynolds. *MGM: Hollywood's Greatest Backlot.* Santa Monica Press, 2011. More than a fifth of the films produced before 1980 were on the legendary backlot at MGM and this book chronicles the golden era of one of the most important locations in cinema history.

Boman, Steve. *Film School: The True Story of a Midwestern Family Man Who Went to the World's Most Famous Film School, Fell Flat on His Face, Had a Stroke, and Sold a Television Series to CBS.* BenBella, 2011. A middle-aged reporter decided to turn his life around and applied for USC Film School, the most elite such program in the country. His book tells his unusual story from a personal perspective, offering a unique take on the value of film school education in the real world. Boman sold a TV series straight out of school.

Bosworth, Patricia. *Jane Fonda: The Private Life of a Public Woman.* Houghton Mifflin Harcourt, 2011. The controversial star of dozens of films is chronicled yet again with a focus on how her private life informed her public persona, including the statements and actions that made her persona non grata among a large, mostly conservative portion of her former fan base.

Callan, Michael Feeney. *Robert Redford: The Biography.* Knopf, 2011. Another biography of the legendary, Oscar®-winning actor. This one uses journals, script notes, and other personal papers to offer a glimpse into the life of the star of *Butch Cassidy and the Sundance Kid* (1969), *The Sting* (1973), *All the President's Men* (1976), and much more.

Castle, Alison. *Stanley Kubrick's Napoleon: The Greatest Movie Never Made.* Taschen, 2011. It seems appropriate that a book about a massive undertaking like a film about Napoleon would be called the "most grandiose book ever made" (*New York Magazine*) and clock in at over 1,000 pages. It is technically a compendium of ten books about the failed project of the legendary Stanley Kubrick culled from piles of research, correspondence, and pre-production material held by the late great director's estate for years.

Cavalier, Stephen. *The World History of Animation.* University of California Press, 2011. Betty Boop graces the cover of this self-explanatory tome, one that offers insight into much of the international animation that often gets ignored in the United States. Written by a veteran of the animation and games industries who runs Spy Pictures.

Cole, Julie Dawn and Michael Esslinger. *I Want it Now! A Memoir of Life on the Set of Willy Wonka and the Chocolate Factory.* BearManor Media, 2011. The author played the timeless role of Veruca Salt in Mel Stuart's *Willy Wonka & the Chocolate Factory* (1971) and offers her account of the making of the beloved film.

Curtis, James. *Spencer Tracy: A Biography.* Knopf, 2011. The biographer of legends like Preston Sturges and W.C. Fields tackles one of the most beloved actors of all time, the star of *Captains Courageous* (1937), *Boys Town* (1938), *Father of the Bride* (1950), *Inherit the Wind* (1960), and *Guess Who's Coming to Dinner* (1967).

Dench, Judi and John Miller. *And Furthermore.* St. Martin's Press, 2011. An autobiography of the Oscar®-winning star of *Shakespeare in Love* (1998), *Chocolat* (2000), *Iris* (2001), *Mrs. Henderson Presents* (2005), and *Notes on a Scandal* (2006), all of which she for which she was nominated.

Densham, Pen and Jay Roach. *Riding the Alligator: Strategies for a Career in Screenplay Writing (and not getting eaten).* Michael Wiese Productions, 2011. Compared to getting a screenwriting course for under $30, this book is an artist-friendly screenwriting overview from the writer of *Robin Hood: Prince of Thieves* (1991) and *Moll Flanders* (1996).

Ebert, Roger. *The Great Movies III.* University of Chicago Press, 2011. The Pulitzer Prize-winning author offers another collection of essays on what he considers to be the best films ever made.

Ebert, Roger. *Life Itself: A Memoir.* Grand Central Publishing, 2011. The Pulitzer Prize-winning author examines his own life, love of cinema and amazing courage battling cancer and refusing to give up on writing about movies.

Ebert, Roger. *Roger Ebert's Movie Yearbook 2012.* Andrews McMeel Press, 2011. The Pulitzer Prize-winning author offers his beloved annual compendium of his reviews.

Eliot, Marc. *Steve McQueen: A Biography.* Crown Archetype, 2011. Another biography of the star of *Wanted: Dead or Alive* (1958), *The Great Escape* (1963), *Bullitt* (1968), and *Papillon* (1973).

Emmerich, Roland. *Anonymous: William Shakespeare Revealed.* Newmarket Press, 2011. A visual companion to the controversial film that suggests William Shakespeare did not write the plays for which he is credited. Includes 165 color images and behind-the-scenes details about the making of *Anonymous.*

Finch, Christopher and John Lasseter. *The Art of Walt Disney: From Mickey Mouse to the Magic Kingdoms and Beyond.* Abrams, 2011. A heavily updated version of a book first published in 1973 that chronicles the achievements of arguably the most important film company of all time from the early days through Pixar.

Fisher, Carrie. *Shockaholic.* Simon & Schuster, 2011. The star of *Star Wars, Episode IV: A New Hope* (1977) continues her remarkable second career as an author and essayist.

Folkenflick, David and Participant Media. *Page One: Inside The New York Times and the Future of Journalism.* PublicAffairs, 2011. A companion to Andrew Rossi's acclaimed documentary.

Ford, Peter and Patrick McGilligan. *Glenn Ford: A Life.* University of Wisconsin Press, 2011. Another biography of the legendary star of *Gilda* (1946), *3:10 to Yuma* (1957), *Cimarron* (1960), *Pocketful of Miracles* (1961), and *The Courtship of Eddie's Father* (1963).

Franklin, DeVon and Tim Vandehey. *Produced by Faith.* Howard Books, 2011. An African-American studio executive who has worked with John Travolta, Queen Latifah, Jackie Chan, and Will Smith offers his unique take on Hollywood from the angle of a preacher and motivational speaker.

Fricke, John. *Judy: A Legendary Film Career.* Running Press, 2011. The star of two dozen of the all-time classic movie musicals, including *The Wizard of Oz* (1939), *A Star is Born* (1954), *Meet Me in St. Louis* (1944), *Easter Parade* (1948), and much more is chronicled in yet-another biography, a seemingly annual occurrence.

Garner, James, Jon Winokur, and Julie Andrews. *The Garner Files: A Memoir.* Simon & Schuster, 2011. An autobiography of the man who starred in TV's *The Rockford Files*, *Murphy's Romance* (1985), *Space Cowboys* (2000), and *The Notebook* (2004).

Gilles, D.B. *You're Funny: Turn Your Sense of Humor Into a Lucrative New Career.* Michael Wiese Productions, 2011. A lot of people think they are funny or are told they are by their friends but how do you turn that into a career?

Glintenkamp, Pamela, LucasFilm Ltd., Gore Verbinski, and Jon Favreau. *Industrial Light & Magic: The Art of Innovation.* Abrams, 2011. An extensively illustrated oral history of the company founded by George Lucas in 1975 that has been a part of such major franchises as *Star Wars*, *Indiana Jones*, and *The Terminator*.

Grant, Kevin and Franco Nero. *Any Gun Can Play: The Essential Guide to Euro-Westerns.* FAB Press, 2011. A freelance journalist focuses on the fascinating sub-genre of European Westerns, including the films of Sergio Leone, films that examined a very American setting from a distinctly European viewpoint.

Gristwood, Sarah and Hubert de Givenchy. *Breakfast at Tiffany's: The Official 50th Anniversary Companion.* Rizzoli, 2011. A companion to the beloved and iconic film starring Audrey Hepburn, George Peppard, Mickey Rooney, and Patricia Neal with new illustrations that had never been seen before.

Hansen, Miriam Bratu, and Edward Dimenberg. *Cinema and Experience: Siegfried Kracauer, Walter Benjamin, and Theodor W. Adorno (Weimar and Now: German Cultural Criticism).* University of California Press, 2011. Analysis of analysis in this book that examines the philosophical critique of three of the experts in their field.

Hearn, Marcus. *The Hammer Vault.* Titan Books, 2011. A coffee table book that examines the remarkable history of one of the most beloved B-movie studios of all time that includes props, annotated script pages, unused posters, and private correspondence. Includes hundreds of rare and previously unseen stills.

Hoberman, J. *An Army of Phantoms: American Movies and the Making of the Cold War.* New Press, 2011. The *Village Voice* critic examines film between 1946 and 1956 and how it reflected the national situation, reflecting a crucial era by the light of the silver screen.

Iglesias, Karl. *Writing for Emotional Impact: Advanced Dramatic Techniques to Attract, Engage, and Fascinate the Reader from Beginning to End.* WingSpan Publishing, 2011. UCLA screenwriting teacher offers his advice on how to connect emotionally with the viewer.

Johnson, David Kyle and William Irwin. *Inception and Philosophy: Because It's Never Just a Dream (The Blackwell Philosophy and Pop Culture Series).* Wiley, 2011. A philosophical companion to the Christopher Nolan film that examines the Oscar®-winning Leonardo DiCaprio masterpiece from a different angle.

Kael, Pauline and Sanford Schwartz. *The Age of Movies: Selected Writings of Pauline Kael.* Library of America, 2011. One of the most notable and influential film critics of all time gets another compendium of her best writing.

Keaton, Diane. *Then Again.* Random House, 2011. Another autobiographical work from the star of *The Godfather* (1972), *Annie Hall* (1977), *Manhattan* (1979), *Reds* (1981), and *The First Wives Club* (1996).

Kehr, Dave. *When Movies Mattered: Reviews from a Transformative Decade.* University of Chicago Press, 2011. A compilation of reviews from one of the most notable film critics of the 1970s and 1980s, an author for the *Chicago Reader*, *Chicago Tribune*, and the *New York Times*.

Kellow, Brian. *Pauline Kael: A Life in the Dark.* Viking Adult, 2011. Another book about one of the most legendary and influential film critics of all time from the features editor of *Opera News*.

Kenworthy, Christopher. *Master Shots Volume 2: Shooting Great Dialogue Scenes.* Michael Wiese Productions, 2011. With over 200 diagrams illustrating camera positions, the author offers detailed information on how to turn cinematography into the language of cinema.

Kessinger, Scott. *Scream Deconstructed: An Unauthorized Analysis.* Stinger Books, 2011. An examination of all four *Scream* films as to not only how and why they were as effective as they were but the impact they had on the horror genre.

Klick, Todd. *Something Startling Happens: The 120 Story Beats Every Writer Needs to Know.* Michael Wiese Productions, 2011. A screenwriting guide that approaches cinema from a beat-by-beat angle.

Landis, John. *Monsters in the Movies.* DK Adult, 2011. The fascinating horror director uses his own passion for the history of monster movies to chronicle the genre along with interviews with David Cronenberg, Christopher Lee, John Carpenter, Sam Raimi, and more. Includes over 1,000 movie stills and posters.

Laurie, Piper. *Learning to Live Out Loud: A Memoir.* Crown Archetype, 2011. An autobiography from the beloved star of *The Hustler* (1961), *Carrie* (1976), *Children of a Lesser God* (1986), and much more.

Leider, Emily W. *Myrna Loy: The Only Good Girl in Hollywood.* University of California Press, 2011. A biography of the star of *The Thin Man* (1934), *The Great Ziegfeld* (1936), *The Best Years of Our Lives* (1946), and *Mrs. Blandings Builds His Dream House* (1948).

Lennon, Thomas and Robert B. Garant. *Writing Movies for Fun and Profit.* Touchstone, 2011. The creators of TV's *Reno 911!* and *The State* and films including *Night at the Museum* (2006) and *Balls of Fury* (2007) offer their advice and tricks of the trade.

Lindsay-Hogg, Michael. *Luck and Circumstance: A Coming of Age in Hollywood, New York, and Points Beyond.* Knopf, 2011. The acclaimed director of *Let It Be* (1970) and *The Object of Beauty* (1991) remembers life with his famous mother, Geraldine Fitzgerald.

Lowe, Rob. *Stories I Only Tell My Friends: An Autobiography.* Henry Holt and Co., 2011. An autobiography of the star of *St. Elmo's Fire* (1985), *About Last Night.* (1986), *Wayne's World* (1992), and *Tommy Boy* (1995).

Lynch, Jane. *Happy Accidents.* Voice, 2011. The author is primarily known for television work, including over a hundred guest or starring credits, but has also appeared in feature films like *Best in Show* (2000), *The 40 Year Old Virgin* (2005), *Talladega Nights: The Ballad of Ricky Bobby* (2006), and *Julie & Julia* (2009).

MacLean, Fraser. *Setting the Scene: The Art & Evolution of Animation Layout.* Chronicle Books, 2011. A guide to animation from a man who has worked for Passion Pictures, Cambridges Animation Systems, Telemagination, and Walt Disney Animation Studios.

Maltin, Leonard. *Leonard Maltin's 2012 Movie Guide/* Signet, 2011. Another version of the annual reference book from the legendary critic.

Marvel Comics. *Thor: The Art of Thor the Movie.* Marvel, 2011. A companion book to the hit film directed by Kenneth Branagh and starring Chris Hemsworth.

McCabe, Bob. *Harry Potter Page to Screen: The Complete Filmmaking Journey.* Harper Design, 2011. A volume detailing the entire hit franchise and how they went from beloved books to billion dollar movies.

Meyers, Jeffrey. *John Huston: Courage and Art.* Crown Archetype, 2011. The director of iconic films including *The Maltese Falcon* (1941), *The Treasure of the Sierra Madre* (1948), *The Asphalt Jungle* (1950), and *The African Queen* (1951) gets another biography from a notable author.

Miller-Zarneke, Tracey and Dustin Hoffman. *The Art of Kung Fu Panda 2.* Insight Editions, 2011. A companion book to the hit animated film.

Nathan, Ian. *Alien Vault: The Definitive Story of the Making of the Film.* Voyageur Press, 2011. The writer, the Executive Editor of *Empire* for the last twenty years, examines the 1979 Ridley Scott film from every angle starting with its pre-production and moving all the way through to its massive influence on the sci-fi genre.

Papa, Joseph. *Elizabeth Taylor, A Passion for Life: The Wit and Wisdom of a Legend.* Harper Design, 2011. A biography of the recently-deceased icon, the star of *A Place in the Sun* (1951), *Giant* (1956), *Cat on a Hot Tin Roof* (1958), *Who's Afraid of Virginia Woolf?* (1966), and much more.

Porter, Darwin and Roy Moseley. *Damn You, Scarlett O'Hara: The Private Lives of Vivien Leigh and Laurence Olivier.* Blood Moon Productions, 2011. This dense tome chronicles the scandalous affair of "The Royal Family of the British Stage."

Queen, Ben. *The Art of Cars 2.* Chronicle Books, 2011. Another companion to a hit animated film about the production of the latest Pixar film.

Rooney, Bethany and Mary Lou Belli. *Directors tell the Story: Master the Craft of Television and Film Directing.* Focal Press, 2011. Two TV directors offer their advice on film and television with a hands-on and practical approach. The book also points reader to a companion web site for further exercises, clips in which the authors' advice is clear, and other material.

Ross, Steven J. *Hollywood Left and Right: How Movie Stars Shaped American Politics.* Oxford University Press, 2011. The author examines the role of politics in film and how the Hollywood scene has not just reflected the political one but influenced it as well.

Schechter, Jeffrey Alan. *My Story Can Beat Up Your Story: Ten Ways to Toughen Up Your Screenplay from Opening Hook to Knockout Punch.* Michael Wiese Productions, 2011. A tongue-in-cheek approach to screenwriting advice from an Emmy Award-wining and WGA Award-winning writer who has worked for Warner Bros., Universal Pictures, ABC, NBC, and much more.

Scherzer, Mark and Keith Fenimore. *Hire Me, Hollywood!: Your Behind-the-Scenes Guide to the Most Exciting—and Unexpected—Jobs in Show Business.* Adams Media, 2011. A unique approach to getting a job in Hollywood that features interviews with Hair Stylists, Senior Talent Executives, Stunt Women, and even an On-Set Tutor. Not everyone in Hollywood needs to be an actor, writer, or director.

Schickel, Richard. *Conversations with Scorsese.* Knopf, 2011. The legendary critic/writer discusses the work of Martin Scorsese with the man himself.

Seger, Linda. *Writing Subtext: What Lies Beneath.* Michael Wiese Productions, 2011. An examination of the unspoken meaning of words and exchanges that can be applied to all kinds of writing, featuring examples from not just screenplays but real life.

Shatner, William and Chris Regan. *Shatner Rules: Your Key to Understanding the Shatnerverse and the World at Large.* Dutton Adult, 2011. Another book from the man who turned his time on *Star Trek* into an amazing career.

Smith, Dwayne Alexander and A.J. Sheppard. *Ten Simple F*cking Rules for Writing a Great F*cking Screenplay.* Damn Good Idea Productions, 2011. An e-book that approaches screenwriting advice from a humorous angle.

Speiser, Lainie. *Confessions of the Hundred Hottest Porn Stars: Intimate, Funny, Outrageous, Sexy, Instructional, and Shocking Tell-Alls from the Biggest Names in the Biz.* Quiver, 2011. A publicist for *Penthouse* interviews some of the most legendary actresses in the adult film business.

Spielberg, Steven. *War Horse (Newmarket Pictorial Moviebook).* Newmarket Press, 2011. A companion book to Steven Spielberg's film, a 2011 Oscar® nominee for Best Picture.

Stanley, John. *The Gang That Shot Up Hollywood: Chronicles of a Chronicle Writer (Vol. 1).* Creatures at Large, 2011. Written by a thirty-three year veteran writer of the *San Francisco Chronicle,* this book focuses on a number of the alpha male personalities of Hollywood like Clint Eastwood, John Wayne, Chuck Norris, and Robert Mitchum.

Su, Haitao and Vincent Zhao. *Alive Character Design: For Games, Animation and Film.* Gingko Press, 2011. A study of character design for working and would-be animators.

Taylor, Matt and Steven Spielberg. *Jaws: Memories from Martha's Vineyard.* Moonrise Media, 2011. A wonderful coffee table book that examines the filming of Spielberg's timeless masterpiece through photos and interviews with the people on-set who helped turn Martha's Vineyard into one of the most impressive movie settings of all time.

Tipton, Scott. *Star Trek Vault: 40 Years from the Archives.* Abrams, 2011. The author of a number of *Star Trek* comics turns his expertise on the television episodes and films that started a phenomenon. It covers all six of the series iterations and all ten of the films.

Turner Classic Movies. *TCM Classic Movie Trivia: Featuring More Than 4,000 Questions to Test Your Trivia Smarts.* Chronicle Books, 2011. A self-explanatory trivia book about classic films from the network built around them.

Vaux, Sara Anson. *The Ethical Vision of Clint Eastwood.* Wm. B. Eerdmans Publishing Company, 2011. The Director of the Office of Fellowships at Northwestern University, where she teaches film in the religious studies department examines the career of the legendary actor and director from a unique perspective.

Vogler, Christopher and David McKenna. *Memo from the Story Department: Secrets of Structure and Character.* Michael Wiese Productions, 2011. A top story analyst and consultant for major Hollywood studios and talent offers a volume designed to generate story ideas and give writers the tools to build them into screenplays.

Webb, Clifton, David L. Smith, and Robert Wagner. *Sitting Pretty: The Life and Times of Clifton Webb.* University Press of Mississippi, 2011. Professor emeritus of telecommuni-cations at Ball State University chronicles the life of the star of *Laura* (1944), *Titanic* (1953), *Three Coins in the Fountain* (1954), and *The Man Who Never Was* (1956).

Weta Workshop. *The Art of the Adventures of Tintin.* Harper Design, 2011. A visual companion to the Steven Spielberg film with interviews, production stills, and tons of behind-the-scenes details.

White, Mindi. *Getting Past Me: A Writer's Guide to Production Company Readers.* Limelight, 2011. A small volume from a story analyst, otherwise known as the gatekeepers of production companies, and how to get a script passed them.

Wilson, Michael Henry. *Scorsese on Scorsese (Cahiers du Cinema).* Phaedon Press, 2011. Culled from over three decades of interviews with Martin Scorsese, starting with his short films and moving all the way through *Shutter Island* (2010).

Windham, Ryder and Peter Vilmur.
Star Wars: The Complete Vader. Lucasbooks, 2011. More rare memorabilia, more behind-the-scenes anecdotes, more, more, more on what is probably the most well-documented film production of all time, this time with an emphasis on the legendary villain.

Winkler, Peter.
Dennis Hopper: The Wild Ride of a Hollywood Rebel. Barricade Books, 2011. The first book to chronicle the entire life and filmography of the recently-passed legendary star of *Easy Rider* (1969), *Apocalypse Now* (1979), *True Romance* (1993), and *Speed* (1994).

Zahed, Ramin and Guillermo Del Toro.
The Art of Puss in Boots. Insight Editions, 2011. A companion book to the movie that turned Antonio Banderas' kitten character into his own action icon.

Zinoman, Jason and Pete Larkin.
Shock Value: How a Few Eccentric Outsiders Gave Us Nightmares, Conquered Hollywood, and Invented Modern Horror. Penguin Press HC, 2011. A chronicle of the 1970s horror movement led by Wes Craven, Roman Polanski, John Carpenter, and Brian De Palma.

Director Index

J.J. Abrams (1966-)
  Super 8 *358*

Salim Akil
  Jumping the Broom *209*

Tomas Alfredson (1965-)
  Tinker Tailor Soldier Spy *377*

Woody Allen (1935-)
  Midnight in Paris *248*

Pedro Almodovar (1951-)
  The Skin I Live In *335*

Brad Anderson (1964-)
  Vanishing on 7th Street *401*

Paul W.S. Anderson (1965-)
  The Three Musketeers *375*

Stephen John Anderson
  Winnie the Pooh *425*

Fred Andrews
  Creature *81*

Peter Andrews
  See Steven Soderbergh

Gregg Araki (1959-)
  Kaboom *215 *

Miguel Arteta (1965-)
  Cedar Rapids *61*

Kelly Asbury (1960-)
  Gnomeo & Juliet *139*

Richard Ayoade
  Submarine *353*

Stephen K. Bannon
  The Undefeated *398*

Daniel Barnz
  Beastly *30*

Michael Bay (1965-)
  Transformers: Dark of the
    Moon *380*

Xavier Beauvois
  Of Gods and Men *270*

Thomas Bezucha
  Monte Carlo *259*

Suzanne (Susanne) Bier (1960-)
  In a Better World *185*

Brad Bird (1957-)
  Mission: Impossible—Ghost Pro-
    tocol *253*

Lauren Bittner (1980-)
  Paranormal Activity 3 *277 *

James Bobin
  The Muppets *261*

Darren Lynn Bousman (1979-)
  11-11-11 *113*

David Bowers (1970-)
  Diary of a Wimpy Kid: Rodrick
    Rules *94*

Tom Brady
  Bucky Larson: Born to Be a
    Star *50*

Kenneth Branagh (1960-)
  Thor *373*

Michael Brandt (1968-)
  The Double *100*

Craig Brewer (1971-)
  Footloose *127*

Neil Burger
  Limitless *227*

Mike Cahill
  Another Earth *12*

Martin Campbell (1940-)
  Green Lantern *143*

Giuseepe Capotondi
  The Double Hour *102*

John Carpenter (1948-)
  The Ward *407*

D.J. Caruso (1965-)
  I Am Number Four *176*

Tim Chamber
  The Mighty Macs *250*

J.C. Chandor
  Margin Call *238*

Christian E. Christiansen
  The Roommate *316*

Jon M. Chu
  Justin Bieber: Never Say
    Never *212*

George Clooney (1961-)
  The Ides of March *181*

Jaume Collet-Serra (1974-)
  Unknown *400*

Bill Condon (1955-)
  The Twilight Saga: Breaking
    Dawn, Part 1 *392*

Paddy Considine (1974-)
  Tyrannosaur *394*

Frank Coraci (1965-)
  Zookeeper *434*

Joe Cornish
  Attack the Block *23*

Eli Craig (1972-)
  Tucker & Dale vs. Evil *391*

Wes Craven (1939-)
  Scream 4 *323*

David Cronenberg (1943-)
  A Dangerous Method *85 *

Cameron Crowe (1957-)
  Pearl Jam Twenty *283*
  We Bought a Zoo *416*

Larysa Kondracki
   The Whistleblower *421*

Shawn Ku
   Beautiful Boy *33*

John Landis (1950-)
   Burke and Hare *51*

John Lasseter (1957-)
   Cars 2 *58*

Francis Lawrence (1971-)
   Water for Elephants *411*

Chang-dong Lee
   Poetry *279*

Dennis Lee
   Fireflies in the Garden *125*

Julia Leigh
   Sleeping Beauty *337*

Jonathan Levine
   50/50 *120*

Shawn Levy (1968-)
   Real Steel *305*

Brad Lewis
   Cars 2 *58*

Jonathan Liebesman (1976-)
   Battle: Los Angeles *29*

Justin Lin (1973-)
   Fast Five *119 *

Phyllida Lloyd (1957-)
   The Iron Lady *196*

Kenneth Lonergan
   Margaret *228*

Gonzalo Lopez-Gallego
   Apollo 18 *13*

Sam Lowry
   See Steven Soderbergh

Rod Lurie (1962-)
   Straw Dogs *351*

Patrick Lussier
   Drive Angry *107*

Kevin MacDonald (1967-)
   The Eagle *111 *

John Madden (1949-)
   The Debt *88*

Madonna (1959-)
   W.E. *414*

Terrence Malick (1943-)
   The Tree of Life *382*

Ami Canaan Mann
   Texas Killing Fields *357*

James Marsh (1963-)
   Project Nim *294*

Garry Marshall (1934-)
   New Year's Eve *267 *

Rob Marshall (1960-)
   Pirates of the Caribbean: On
      Stranger Tides *287*

Tom McCarthy (1969-)
   Win Win *423*

John M. McDonagh
   The Guard *145*

Douglas McGrath (1958-)
   I Don't Know How She Does
      It *178*

Lucky McKee (1975-)
   The Woman *426*

Gary McKendry
   Killer Elite *218*

Sean McNamara (1963-)
   Soul Surfer *345*

Steve McQueen (1969-)
   Shame *329*

Cindy Meehl
   Buck *48*

Olivier Megaton
   Colombiana *66*

Jim Mickle
   Stake Land *340*

Takashi Miike (1960-)
   13 Assassins *370*

Bennett Miller (1966-)
   Moneyball *257*

Chris Miller (1975-)
   Puss in Boots *299*

George Miller (1945-)
   Happy Feet Two *152*

Mike Mills (1966)
   Beginners *36*

Mike Mitchell
   Alvin and the Chipmunks: Chip-
      wrecked *8*

Kevin Monroe
   Dylan Dog: Dead of
      Night *108*

Dito Montiel (1965-)
   The Son of No One *344*

Guillem Morales
   Julia's Eyes *200*

Errol Morris (1948-)
   Tabloid *361 *

Greg Mottola (1964-)
   Paul *281*

Oren Moverman
   Rampart *301 *

Mark Mylod
   What's Your Number? *419*

Andrew Niccol (1964-)
   In Time *188*

Jeff Nichols
   Take Shelter *364*

Marcus Nispel (1964-)
   Conan the Barbarian *69*

Troy Nixey
   Don't Be Afraid of the
      Dark *99*

George Nolfi
   The Adjustment Bureau *2*

Joe Nussbaum (1973-)
   Prom *296*

Gavin O'Connor
   Warrior *409*

Andre Ovredal
   Trollhunter *388*

Lloyd Owen (1966-)
   Apollo 18 *13*

Francois Ozon (1967-)
   Potiche *292*

Oliver Parker (1960-)
   Johnny English Reborn *205*

Alexander Payne (1961-)
   The Descendants *90*

Oren Peli
   Paranormal Activity 3 *277 *

Jesse Peretz (1968-)
   Our Idiot Brother *274*

Alexandre O. Philippe
   The People vs. George Lu-
      cas *284*

Todd Phillips (1970-)
   The Hangover Part II *149*

Roman Polanski (1933-)
   Carnage *56*

Richard Press
   Bill Cunningham New York *44*

Steven Quale
   Final Destination 5 *124*

Josh Radnor (1974-)
   Happythankyoumoreplease *153*

Lynne Ramsey
   We Need to Talk About
      Kevin *418*

Michael Rapaport (1970-)
   Beats, Rhymes & Life: The Trav-
      els of a Tribe Called
      Quest *32*

Brett Ratner (1969-)
   Tower Heist *378*

Robert Redford (1937-)
   The Conspirator *70*

Dee Rees
   Pariah *278*

Nicolas Winding Refn (1970-)
   Drive *104*

Kelly Reichardt
   Meek's Cutoff *244*

Screenwriter Index

Will Gluck
    Friends With Benefits *128*

Jean-Luc Godard (1930-)
    Film Socialisme *122*

Evan Goldberg
    The Green Hornet *142*

Michael Goldenberg (1965-)
    Green Lantern *143*

Jane Goldman (1970-)
    The Debt *88*
    X-Men: First Class *429 *

Jonathan M. Goldstein (1969-)
    Horrible Bosses *167*

Cory Goodman
    Priest *293*

Alfred Gough (1967-)
    I Am Number Four *176*

Michael Green
    Green Lantern *143*

Kathy Greenberg
    Gnomeo & Juliet *139*

Alex Gregory
    A Good Old Fashioned Orgy
        140

Ted Griffin (1970-)
    Tower Heist *378*

Marc Guggenheim
    Green Lantern *143*

James Gunn (1970-)
    Super *357*

Derek Haas (1970-)
    The Double *100*

Don Hall
    Winnie the Pooh *425*

Lee Hall (1966-)
    War Horse *405 *

Christopher Hampton (1946-)
    A Dangerous Method *85 *

Tom Hanks (1956-)
    Larry Crowne *223 *

William Hayes
    Shark Night 3D *331*

Michel Hazanavicius
    The Artist *19*

Eric Heisserer
    Final Destination 5 *124*
    The Thing *368*

Jonathan Hensleigh
    Kill the Irishman *216*

Werner Herzog (1942-)
    Cave of Forgotten Dreams *60*
    Into the Abyss *195*

Grant Heslov (1963-)
    The Ides of March *181*

Adrian Hodges
    My Week With Marilyn *263*

Sean Hood (1966-)
    Conan the Barbarian *69*

Kendelle Hoyer
    Winnie the Pooh *425*

Elizabeth Hunter
    Jumping the Broom *209*

Jon Hurwitz (1977-)
    A Very Harold & Kumar 3D
        Christmas *403*

Peter Huyek
    A Good Old Fashioned Orgy
        140

Rick Jaffa
    Rise of the Planet of the Apes
        312

Karen Janszen
    Dolphin Tale *97*

Rula Jebreal
    Miral *251*

Anders Thomas Jensen (1972-)
    In a Better World *185*

David Leslie Johnson
    Red Riding Hood *306*

Philip Johnston
    Cedar Rapids *61*

Angelina Jolie (1975-)
    In the Land of Blood and Honey
        187

Krishna Jones
    The Perfect Host *286*

Pete Jones
    Hall Pass *147 *

Todd R. Jones
    Rio *311*

Jeff Judah
    Diary of a Wimpy Kid: Rodrick
        Rules *94*

Miranda July (1974-)
    The Future *133*

Morgan Jurgenson
    Tucker & Dale vs. Evil *391*

Robert Mark Kamen
    Colombiana *66*

Jason Keller (1971-)
    Machine Gun Preacher *233 *

Alex Kendrick
    Courageous *76*

Stephen Kendrick
    Courageous *76*

Alek Keshishian (1964-)
    W.E. *414*

Brian Kesinger
    Winnie the Pooh *425*

Jack Ketchum
    The Woman *426*

Abbas Kiarostami (1940-)
    Certified Copy *63*

Kyle Killen
    The Beaver *35*

Rory Kinnear
    We Need to Talk About Kevin
        418

Ellis Kirwan
    The Whistleblower *421*

Steve Kloves (1960-)
    Harry Potter and the Deathly
        Hallows: Part 2 *155*

Larysa Kondracki
    The Whistleblower *421*

Steve Koren
    Jack and Jill *201*

Alex Kotlowitz
    The Interrupters *193*

Ehren Kruger (1972-)
    Transformers: Dark of the Moon
        380

Shawn Ku
    Beautiful Boy *33*

Alex Kurtzman (1973-)
    Cowboys & Aliens *78*

Richard LaGravenese (1959-)
    Water for Elephants *411*

Chang-dong Lee
    Poetry *279*

Dennis Lee
    Fireflies in the Garden *125*

Tony Leech
    Hoodwinked Too! Hood vs. Evil
        164

Julia Leigh
    Sleeping Beauty *337*

Jason Lew
    Restless *309*

Damon Lindelof
    Cowboys & Aliens *78*

Alex Litvak
    The Three Musketeers *375*

Paul Livingston (1956-)
    Happy Feet Two *152*

Seth Lockhead
    Hanna *150*

Allan Loeb
    The Dilemma *96*
    Just Go With It *210*

John Logan (1961-)
    Coriolanus *74*
    Hugo *169*
    Rango *303*

Cinematographer Index

Michel Abramowicz
  The Thing *368*

Thomas Ackerman
  Alvin and the Chipmunks: Chipwrecked *8*

Barry Ackroyd (1954-)
  Coriolanus *74*

Javier Aguirresarobe (1948-)
  A Better Life *39*
  Fright Night *130*

Jose Luis Alcaine (1938-)
  The Skin I Live In *335*

Juan Ruiz Anchia
  Blackthorn *46*

Peter Andrews
  See Steven Soderbergh

Francois Aragno
  Film Socialisme *122*

Florian Ballhaus (1965-)
  Mr. Popper's Penguins *255*

Michael Barrett (1970-)
  Bucky Larson: Born to Be a
  Star *50*
  Everything Must Go *114*
  A Very Harold & Kumar 3D
  Christmas *403*

Andrzej Bartkowiak (1950-)
  Trespass *384*

Jean-Paul Battaggia
  Film Socialisme *122*

Dion Beebe
  Green Lantern *143*

Robert Benavides
  Beats, Rhymes & Life: The Trav-
  els of a Tribe Called
  Quest *32*

Michael J. Bennett
  Zookeeper *434*

Ross Berryman (1954-)
  Atlas Shrugged: Part 1 *21*

Luca Bigazzi (1958-)
  Certified Copy *63*

Christopher Blauvelt
  Meek's Cutoff *244*

Sean Bobbitt
  Shame *329*

Hagen Bogdanski
  The Beaver *35*
  W.E. *414*

Hallvard Braein
  Trollhunter *388*

John Brawley (1973-)
  The Perfect Host *286*

David M. Brewer
  Insidious *191*

Uta Briesewitz
  Arthur *16*
  Vanishing on 7th Street *401*

Oliver Brokelberg
  Win Win *423*

Jonathan Brown
  Monte Carlo *259*

Bobby Bukowski
  Rampart *301 *

Don Burgess (1956-)
  The Muppets *261*
  Priest *293*
  Source Code *347*

Mike Cahill
  Another Earth *12*

Gary Capo
  Shark Night 3D *331*

Tony Cenicola
  Bill Cunningham New York *44*

Caroline Champetier (1954-)
  Of Gods and Men *270*

Robert Chappell
  Tabloid *361 *

Chuy Chavez
  Cedar Rapids *61*

Manuel Alberto Claro
  Melancholia *246*

Chuck Cohen
  The Mighty Macs *250*

Daniel Cohen
  Johnny English Reborn *205*

Peter Lyons Collister (1956-)
  Hop *165*

Jeff Cronenweth (1962-)
  The Girl With the Dragon Tattoo *135 *

Dean Cundey (1946-)
  Jack and Jill *201*

Tobias Datum
  Terri *365*

Benjamin Davis
  The Debt *88*
  The Rite *314*

Elliot Davis
  The Iron Lady *196*

Roger Deakins (1949-)
  In Time *188*

Johanne Debas
  Midnight in Paris *248*

Editor Index

Jennifer Abbott
  I Am *175*

Sandra Adair
  Everything Must Go *114*

Peter R. Adam
  Anonymous *10*

Tracy Adams
  Limitless *227*

Craig Albert
  Your Highness *432*

Jonathan Alberts
  Like Crazy *226*

Sean Albertson
  Warrior *409*

Dede Allen
  Fireflies in the Garden *125*

Craig Alpert
  The Sitter *334*

Tim Alverson
  Unknown *400*

Jonathan Amos
  Attack the Block *23*

Peter Amundson
  Alvin and the Chipmunks: Chip-
    wrecked *8*

Robert Anich Cole
  Hoodwinked Too! Hood vs.
    Evil *164*

Catherine Apple
  Gnomeo & Juliet *139*

Gregg Araki (1959-)
  Kaboom *215 *

John Axelrad
  Something Borrowed *342*

Stuart Baird (1947-)
  Green Lantern *143*

Zene Baker
  50/50 *120*

Roger Barton
  Transformers: Dark of the
    Moon *380*

Alan Baumgarten
  30 Minutes or Less *371*

Kirk Baxter
  The Girl With the Dragon Tat-
    too *135 *

Pete Beaudreau
  Margin Call *238*

Alan Edward Bell
  Water for Elephants *411*

Guy Bensley
  Johnny English Reborn *205*

Alexander Berner
  The Debt *88*
  The Three Musketeers *375*

Jill Bilcock
  Don't Be Afraid of the
    Dark *99*

Joe Bini
  Cave of Forgotten Dreams *60*
  Into the Abyss *195*
  We Need to Talk About
    Kevin *418*

Anne-Sophie Bion
  The Artist *19*

Andrew Bird
  The Future *133*

Ken Blackwell
  Conan the Barbarian *69*

Sarah Boyd
  Straw Dogs *351*

Peter Boyle
  The Thing *368*

Robert Brakey
  Fireflies in the Garden *125*

Maryann Brandon
  Kung Fu Panda 2 *220*
  Super 8 *358*

Anita Brandt-Burgoyne
  A Good Old Fashioned
    Orgy *140*

David Brenner
  Pirates of the Caribbean: On
    Stranger Tides *287*

Randy Bricker
  The Roommate *316*

Conrad Buff
  Rise of the Planet of the
    Apes *312*

Mike Cahill
  Another Earth *12*

Jeff W. Canavan
  Soul Surfer *345*

Bruce Cannon
  Abduction *1 *

Luis Carballar
  The Devil's Double *93*

John Carnochan
  Arthur Christmas *18*

Jay Cassidy
  Justin Bieber: Never Say
    Never *212*

Art Director Index

Charmian Adams
    My Week With Marilyn *263*
Michael Ahern
    Our Idiot Brother *274*
    The Son of No One *344*
    Young Adult *431*
Gustav Alsina
    Passion Play *280*
Scott Anderson
    Vanishing on 7th Street *401*
Alan Au
    Jack and Jill *201*
    Just Go With It *210*
Francois Audouy
    Green Lantern *143*
Ramsey Avery
    A Very Harold & Kumar 3D
        Christmas *403*
Abdellah Baadil
    Contagion *72*
Zach Bangma
    Drive Angry *107*
Patrick Banister
    The Thing *368*
Gary Baugh
    Kill the Irishman *216*
Annie Beauchamp
    Sleeping Beauty *337*
Curt Beech
    The Help *158*
John Bell
    Rango *303*
Gregory A. Berry
    J. Edgar *199 *
    No Strings Attached *269*

Susan Bolles
    Red State *308*
Yvonne Boudreaux
    Puncture *297*
Drew Boughton
    Pirates of the Caribbean: On
        Stranger Tides *287*
William Budge
    Drive Angry *107*
    Trespass *384*
Chris Burian-Mohr
    Cowboys & Aliens *78*
Andrew Max Cahn
    The Muppets *261*
    Priest *293*
Ryan L. Carlson
    Hoodwinked Too! Hood vs.
        Evil *164*
Shawn Carroll
    Higher Ground *161*
Stephen H. Carter
    The Adjustment Bureau *2*
Sue Chan
    Crazy, Stupid, Love *79*
John Chichester
    Pirates of the Caribbean: On
        Stranger Tides *287*
Nigel Churcher
    The Three Musketeers *375*
John Collins
    Jack and Jill *201*
    Just Go With It *210*
Gonzalo Cordoba
    Project Nim *294*

Chris Cornwell
    Footloose *127*
    The Ides of March *181*
Robert Cowper
    Pirates of the Caribbean: On
        Stranger Tides *287*
David Crank
    Water for Elephants *411*
Susie Cullen
    Albert Nobbs *6*
Douglas Cumming
    I Am Number Four *176*
Keith Cunningham
    Bridesmaids *47*
Charles Daboub Jr.
    Hop *165*
Charlo Dalli
    The Devil's Double *93*
Liba Daniels
    Abduction *1 *
Ricardo Davila
    From Prada to Nada *131*
Vincent DeFelice
    The Ward *407*
Karen DeJong
    Gnomeo & Juliet *139*
Ross Dempster
    50/50 *120*
Nick Dent
    Burke and Hare *51*
    The Iron Lady *196*
John Dexter
    Captain America: The First
        Avenger *55 *

Simon McCutcheon
Killer Elite *218*

Carlos Menendez
Larry Crowne *223 *

Rade Mihajlovic
Coriolanus *74*

Victor Molero
The Way *403*

Randy Moore
Fright Night *130*

Niall Moroney
Hanna *150*

Dan Morski
Hall Pass *147 *

Matthew Munn (1975-)
The Sitter *334*

Christa Munro
Priest *293*

Lisa Myers
Higher Ground *161*

David Nelson
Happy Feet Two *152*

Norman Newberry
Mars Needs Moms *239*

Andy Nicholson
Captain America: The First
Avenger *55 *

Jenny O'Connell
Sanctum *321 *

Andreas Olshausen
Unknown *400*

Molly Page
Snow Flower and the Secret
Fan *341*

Greg Papalia
The Green Hornet *142*

Sarah Pasquali
Submarine *353*

Tracy Perkins
Life, Above All *217*

Pierre Perrault
Source Code *347*

Boris Piot
Of Gods and Men *270*

JB Popplewell
Kaboom *215 *

Abigail Potter
Beautiful Boy *33*

Rosario Provenza
Soul Surfer *345*

Mark Raggett
W.E. *414*

Andrew Ranner
Tyrannosaur *394*

Seth Reed
Real Steel *305*

Paul Richards (1934-)
Machine Gun Preacher *233 *

Brad Ricker
Moneyball *257*

Peter Rogness
Extremely Loud and Incredibly
Close *116*

Christiane Rothe
Life, Above All *217*

Brian Rzepka
Another Earth *12*

Kerry Sanders
Trust *389*

Lorenzo Sartor
Certified Copy *63*

Christian Schellewald
Puss in Boots *299*

Denis Schnegg
One Day *272*

David Scott
Moneyball *257*
Super 8 *358*

Linda Sena
Everything Must Go *114*

Maya Shimoguchi
Thor *373*

Chris Shriver
The Smurfs *339*

Jeom-hui Sihm
Poetry *279*

Domenic Silvestri
We Bought a Zoo *416*
Zookeeper *434*

Rob Simons
Cedar Rapids *61*

Jennifer Spence
Insidious *191*

Mike Stallion
Johnny English Reborn *205*

Thomas Stefan
The Human Centipede II (Full
Sequence) *165*

James Steuart
Conan the Barbarian *69*

Gerald Sullivan
Scream 4 *323*

Patrick M. Sullivan, Jr.
Winnie the Pooh *425*

David Swayze
What's Your Number? *419*

Dawn Swiderski
The Rum Diary *317*
X-Men: First Class *429 *

David Tabbert
Martha Marcy May Mar-
lene *241*

Sandi Tanaka
Final Destination 5 *124*

Christopher Tanden
A Better Life *39*

Christopher Tandon
Drive *104*

Team Coatwolf
Bellflower *38*

Jocelyn Thomas
Sleeping Beauty *337*

Lucinda Thomson
Don't Be Afraid of the
Dark *99*

Evgeni Tomov
Arthur Christmas *18*

Chris Trujillo
Happythankyoumoreplease *153*

Kiera Tudway
Tyrannosaur *394*

Thomas Valentine
Battle: Los Angeles *29*
Fast Five *119 *

Grant Van Der Slagt
Sucker Punch *355*

Lucy van Lonkhuyzen
The Guard *145*

Charles Varga, Jr.
Hesher *159*

Mikael Varhelyi
The Girl With the Dragon Tattoo *135 *

Vlad Vieru
The Whistleblower *421*

Thomas Voth
Pirates of the Caribbean: On
Stranger Tides *287*

David Warren
Hugo *169*

Sarah White
Pariah *278*

Jeff Wisniewski
The Adventures of Tintin *4*

Patricia Woodbridge
Mr. Popper's Penguins *255*

Andrew Woodhouse
Gnomeo & Juliet *139*

Music Director Index

Matt Aberly
  The Change-Up *64*

Michael Andrews
  Bad Teacher *27 *
  Bridesmaids *47*

Mark De Gli Antoni
  Into the Abyss *195*

Craig Armstrong (1959-)
  In Time *188*

David Arnold (1962-)
  Paul *281*

Ali N. Askin
  Life, Above All *217*

Tyler Bates Azpiroz
  The Way *403*

Chris P. Bacon
  Gnomeo & Juliet *139*
  Source Code *347*

Klaus Badelt (1968-)
  Dylan Dog: Dead of
    Night *108*

Dan Baker
  Tyrannosaur *394*

Chris Baldwin
  Tyrannosaur *394*

Lorne Balfe
  The Dilemma *96*

James Edward Barker
  The Human Centipede II (Full
    Sequence) *165*

Tyler Bates
  Conan the Barbarian *69*
  The Darkest Hour *87*
  Sucker Punch *355*
  Super *357*

Christophe Beck (1972-)
  Cedar Rapids *61*
  Crazy, Stupid, Love *79*
  The Hangover Part II *149*
  The Muppets *261*
  Tower Heist *378*

Marco Beltrami (1966-)
  Don't Be Afraid of the
    Dark *99*
  Scream 4 *323*
  Soul Surfer *345*
  The Thing *368*

Danny Bensi
  Martha Marcy May Mar-
    lene *241*

Joseph Bishara
  11-11-11 *113*
  Insidious *191*

Fernand Bos
  Hall Pass *147 *

Ludovic Bource
  The Artist *19*

Jon Brion (1963-)
  The Future *133*

David Buckley
  Trespass *384*

Adam Burke
  Hobo With a Shotgun *162*

Carter Burwell (1955-)
  The Twilight Saga: Breaking
    Dawn, Part 1 *392*

Felix Buxton
  Attack the Block *23*

Brian Byrne
  Albert Nobbs *6*

Calexico
  The Guard *145*

Patrick Cassidy (1956-)
  Kill the Irishman *216*

Pasquale Catalano
  The Double Hour *102*

David Cerbert
  The Undefeated *398*

Elia Cmiral (1957-)
  Atlas Shrugged: Part 1 *21*

Harry Cohen
  Apollo 18 *13*

Jane Antonia Cornish
  Fireflies in the Garden *125*

Mychael Danna (1958-)
  Moneyball *257*
  The Whistleblower *421*

Marius De Vries (1961-)
  Sucker Punch *355*

John Debney (1956-)
  The Change-Up *64*
  The Double *100*
  Dream House *103*
  New Year's Eve *267 *
  No Strings Attached *269*

Alexandre Desplat (1961-)
  A Better Life *39*
  Carnage *56*
  Extremely Loud and Incredibly
    Close *116*
  Harry Potter and the Deathly
    Hallows: Part 2 *155*
  The Ides of March *181*
  The Tree of Life *382*

Ramin Djawadi
  Fright Night *130*

Patrick Doyle (1953-)
  Rise of the Planet of the
    Apes *312*
  Thor *373*

Clint Eastwood (1930-)
  J. Edgar *199 *

Danny Elfman (1953-)
  Real Steel *305*
  Restless *309*

Jonathan Elias
  The Son of No One *344*

Koji Endo (1964-)
  13 Assassins *370*

Harry Escott (1976-)
  Shame *329*

Ilan Eshkeri
  Coriolanus *74*
  Johnny English Reborn *205*

Fall on Your Sword
  Another Earth *12*

John (Gianni) Frizzell (1966-)
  The Roommate *316*

Ben Frost
  Sleeping Beauty *337*

Michael Giacchino (1967-)
  Cars 2 *58*
  50/50 *120*
  Mission: Impossible—Ghost Pro-
    tocol *253*
  Monte Carlo *259*
  Super 8 *358*

Richard Gibbs (1955-)
  Judy Moody and the Not Bum-
    mer Summer *206*

Lucio Godoy (1958-)
  Blackthorn *46*

Murray Gold (1969-)
  Hoodwinked Too! Hood vs.
    Evil *164*

Ludwig Goransson (1984-)
  30 Minutes or Less *371*

Jeff Grace
  Meek's Cutoff *244*
  Stake Land *340*

Johnny Greenwood
  We Need to Talk About
    Kevin *418*

Harry Gregson-Williams (1961-)
  Arthur Christmas *18*
  Cowboys & Aliens *78*

Rupert Gregson-Williams (1966-)
  Jack and Jill *201*
  Just Go With It *210*
  Zookeeper *434*

Lawrence Nash Groupe
  Straw Dogs *351*

Kevin Haskins
  Creature *81*

Paul Haslinger (1962-)
  The Three Musketeers *375*

Alex Heffes (1971-)
  Red Riding Hood *306*
  The Rite *314*

Jon Hegel
  The People vs. George Lu-
    cas *284*

Reinhold Heil (1954-)
  Killer Elite *218*

Christian Henson (1971-)
  The Devil's Double *93*

Gregoire Hetzel
  Incendies *190*

Andrew Hewitt (1976-)
  Submarine *353*

Dickon Hinchliffe
  Project Nim *294*
  Rampart *301 *
  Passion Play *280*
  Texas Killing Fields *357*

David Hirschfelder (1960-)
  Sanctum *321 *

Darius Hobert
  Hobo With a Shotgun *162*

Mandy Hoffman
  Terri *365*

Trevor Horn
  Take Me Home Tonight *362*

James Newton Howard (1951-)
  Gnomeo & Juliet *139*
  The Green Hornet *142*
  Green Lantern *143*
  Larry Crowne *223 *
  Water for Elephants *411*

Alberto Iglesias (1955-)
  The Skin I Live In *335*
  Tinker Tailor Soldier Spy *377*

Mark Isham (1951-)
  The Conspirator *70*
  Dolphin Tale *97*
  The Mechanic *243*
  Warrior *409*

Steve Jablonsky (1970-)
  Transformers: Dark of the
    Moon *380*
  Your Highness *432*

Henry Jackman
  Puss in Boots *299*
  Winnie the Pooh *425*
  X-Men: First Class *429 *

Jaymay
  Happythankyoumoreplease *153*

Elton John (1947-)
  Gnomeo & Juliet *139*

Eric Johnson
  Our Idiot Brother *274*

Jonsi (1975-)
  We Bought a Zoo *416*

Saunder Jurriaans
  Martha Marcy May Mar-
    lene *241*

David Kahne
  Magic Trip: Ken Kesey's Search
    for a Kool Place *235*

Jonathan Keevil
  Bellflower *38*

Rolfe Kent (1963-)
  Mr. Popper's Penguins *255*
  Young Adult *431*

Mark Kilian
  The Ward *407*

Johnny Klimek (1962-)
  Killer Elite *218*

Harald Kloser (1956-)
  Anonymous *10*

Abel Korzeniowski
  W.E. *414*

John Kusiak
  Tabloid *361 *

Nathan Larson (1970-)
  Margin Call *238*
  Our Idiot Brother *274*
  Trust *389*

Christopher Lennertz (1972-)
  Hop *165*
  Horrible Bosses *167*

Paul Leonard-Morgan
  Limitless *227*

Deborah Lurie
  Footloose *127*
  Justin Bieber: Never Say
    Never *212*
  Prom *296*

Dario Marianelli (1963-)
  Jane Eyre *203*

Cliff Martinez (1954-)
  Contagion *72*
  Drive *104*
  The Lincoln Lawyer *229*

Jeff McIlwain
  The Sitter *334*

Nathaniel Mechaly (1972-)
  Colombiana *66*

Trevor Morris (1970-)
  Beautiful Boy *33*
  Immortals *183*

Mark Mothersbaugh
  Alvin and the Chipmunks: Chip-
    wrecked *8*

Performer Index

Hiam Abbass (1960-)
Miral *251*

Danneel Ackles (1979-)
A Very Harold & Kumar 3D
Christmas *403*

Isabella Acres (2001-)
The Future *133*

Amy Adams (1974-)
The Muppets *261*

Jane Adams (1965-)
Restless *309*

Trace Adkins
The Lincoln Lawyer *229*

Casey Affleck (1975-)
Tower Heist *378*

Dianna Agron (1986-)
Glee: The 3D Concert
Movie *137*
I Am Number Four *176*

Nae-sang Ahn
Poetry *279*

Malin Akerman (1978-)
Happythankyoumoreplease *153*

Adewale Akinnuoye-Agbaje (1967-)
The Thing *368*

Jessica Alba (1981-)
Spy Kids: All the Time in the
World in 4D *348*

Alan Alda (1936-)
Tower Heist *378*

Fausto Russo Alesi
The Double Hour *102*

Jane Alexander (1939-)
Dream House *103*

Michael Algieri
Happythankyoumoreplease *153*

Roger Allam (1953-)
The Iron Lady *196*

Fred Allen (1894-1956)
Into the Abyss *195*

Joaquim Almeida
Fast Five *119 *

Laz Alonso
Jumping the Broom *209*
Straw Dogs *351*

Allen Altman
Incendies *190*

Bruce Altman (1955-)
The Sitter *334*

Robert Amaya
Courageous *76*

Jeff Ament
Pearl Jam Twenty *283*

Madchen Amick (1970-)
Priest *293*

Elena Anaya (1975-)
The Skin I Live In *335*

Mini Anden (1978-)
The Mechanic *243*

Anthony Anderson (1970-)
Scream 4 *323*

Gillian Anderson (1968-)
Johnny English Reborn *205*

Paul Anderson
Sherlock Holmes: A Game of
Shadows *332*

Kristen Anderson-Lopez
Winnie the Pooh (V) *425*

Michelle Ang
Big Mommas: Like Father, Like
Son *41*

Michael Angarano (1987-)
The Art of Getting By *15*
Red State *308*

Kurt Angel
Dylan Dog: Dead of
Night *108*

Bob Angelini
Project Nim *294*

Jennifer Aniston (1969-)
Horrible Bosses *167*
Just Go With It *210*

David Annable
What's Your Number? *419*

Odette Yustman Annable
The Double *100*

Aziz Ansari (1983-)
30 Minutes or Less *371*

Raymond Anthony Thomas
Pariah *278*

Judd Apatow (1967-)
Zookeeper (V) *434*

Natthakarn Aphaiwonk
Uncle Boonmee Who Can Recall
His Past Lives *397 *

Christina Applegate (1971-)
Alvin and the Chipmunks: Chip-
wrecked (V) *8*
Hall Pass *147 *

Tomas Arana (1959-)
The Roommate *316*

Michael Arden
Source Code *347*

Niels Arestrup (1949-)
War Horse *405 *

Nina Arianda
Higher Ground *161*
Midnight in Paris *248*

Sebastian Armesto
Anonymous *10*

Fred Armisen (1966-)
The Smurfs (V) *339*

Richard Armitage
Captain America: The First
Avenger *55 *

David Arquette (1971-)
Scream 4 *323*

Andrew Astor
Insidious *191*

Rowan Atkinson (1955-)
Johnny English Reborn *205*

Hayley Atwell
Captain America: The First
Avenger *55 *

Jake T. Austin (1994-)
Rio (V) *311*

James Avery (1948-)
Transformers: Dark of the Moon
(V) *380*

Lubna Azabal
Incendies *190*

Hank Azaria (1964-)
Happy Feet Two (V) *152*
Hop (V) *165*
The Smurfs (V) *339*

Kevin Bacon (1958-)
Crazy, Stupid, Love *79*
Super *357*
X-Men: First Class *429 *

Penn Badgley (1986-)
Margin Call *238*

Dominique Baffier
Cave of Forgotten Dreams *60*

Preston Bailey (2000-)
Judy Moody and the Not Bummer Summer *206*

Carlee Baker
The Woman *426*

Jordan Baker
Another Earth *12*

Kathy Baker (1950-)
Machine Gun Preacher *233 *
Take Shelter *364*

Simon Baker (1969-)
Margin Call *238*

Dato Bakhtadze
The Darkest Hour *87*

Sonya Balmores
Soul Surfer *345*

Talia Balsam (1960-)
No Strings Attached *269*

Eric Bana (1968-)
Hanna *150*

Antonio Banderas (1960-)
Puss in Boots (V) *299*
The Skin I Live In *335*
Spy Kids: All the Time in the
World in 4D *348*

Elizabeth Banks (1974-)
Our Idiot Brother *274*

Coleman Barks
I Am *175 *

Adriana Barraza (1956-)
From Prada to Nada *131*

Bill Barretta
The Muppets (V) *261*

Neill Barry (1965-)
Atlas Shrugged: Part 1 *21*

Justin Bartha (1978-)
The Hangover Part II *149*

Gary Basaraba (1959-)
The Smurfs *339*

Angela Bassett (1958-)
Green Lantern *143*
Jumping the Broom *209*

Jason Bateman (1969-)
The Change-Up *64*
Horrible Bosses *167*
Paul *281*

Nick Bateman
Hobo With a Shotgun *162*

Kathy Bates (1948-)
Midnight in Paris *248*

Sareh Bayat (1975-)
A Separation *327*

Adam Beach (1972-)
Cowboys & Aliens *78*

Simon Russell Beale (1961-)
My Week With Marilyn *263*

Jordana Beatty
Judy Moody and the Not Bummer Summer *206*

Ned Beatty (1937-)
Rampart *301 *
Rango (V) *303*

Graham Beckel (1955-)
Atlas Shrugged: Part 1 *21*

Ed Begley, Jr. (1949-)
What's Your Number? *419*

Nicole Beharie
Shame *329*

Berenice Bejo
The Artist *19*

Richard Bekins (1954-)
Young Adult *431*

Baya Belal
Incendies *190*

Emma Bell (1986-)
Final Destination 5 *124*

Jamie Bell (1986-)
The Adventures of Tintin
(V) *4*
The Eagle *111 *
Jane Eyre *203*

Kristen Bell (1980-)
Scream 4 *323*

Lake Bell
A Good Old Fashioned
Orgy *140*
No Strings Attached *269*

Marshall Bell (1944-)
Puncture *297*
The Rum Diary *317*

Camilla Belle (1986-)
From Prada to Nada *131*

Maria Bello (1967-)
Abduction *1 *
Beautiful Boy *33*

Monica Bellucci (1968-)
The Whistleblower *421*

Adel Bencherif
Of Gods and Men *270*

Landry Bender
The Sitter *334*

Beto Benites
Colombiana *66*

Haley Bennett
Kaboom *215 *

Steven Berkoff (1937-)
The Girl With the Dragon Tattoo *135 *

Jeannie Berlin
Margaret *228*

Halle Berry (1968-)
New Year's Eve *267 *

Owen Best
Diary of a Wimpy Kid: Rodrick
Rules *94*

Paul Bettany (1971-)
Margin Call *238*
Priest *293*

Angela Bettis (1975-)
The Woman *426*

Ken Bevel
Courageous *76*

Flint Beverage
　　Another Earth *12*

Victoria Bewick
　　The Iron Lady *196*

Charlie Bewley
　　Like Crazy *226*

Leslie Bibb (1974-)
　　A Good Old Fashioned
　　　　Orgy *140*
　　Zookeeper *434*

Demian Bichir (1963-)
　　A Better Life *39*

Justin Bieber (1994-)
　　Justin Bieber: Never Say
　　　　Never *212*

Michael Biehn (1956-)
　　Puncture *297*
　　Take Me Home Tonight *362*

Jessica Biel (1982-)
　　New Year's Eve *267 *

Leo Bill
　　The Girl With the Dragon Tat-
　　　　too *135 *

Juliette Binoche (1964-)
　　Certified Copy *63*
　　The Son of No One *344*

Stephen Bishop (1951-)
　　Moneyball *257*

John Bisignano
　　Senna *325*

Lauren Bittner
　　The Mighty Macs *250*

Jack Black (1969-)
　　The Big Year *42*
　　Kung Fu Panda 2 *220*

Maddi Black
　　The Human Centipede II (Full
　　　　Sequence) *165*

Michael Ian Black (1971-)
　　Take Me Home Tonight *362*

Kimberly Blair
　　The Mighty Macs *250*

Rachael Blake
　　Sleeping Beauty *337*

Roba Blal
　　Miral *251*

Rowan Blanchard
　　Spy Kids: All the Time in the
　　　　World in 4D *348*

Tammy Blanchard (1976-)
　　Moneyball *257*

Cate Blanchett (1969-)
　　Hanna *150*

Moon Bloodgood (1975-)
　　Beautiful Boy *33*

Orlando Bloom (1977-)
　　The Three Musketeers *375*

Callum Blue (1977-)
　　Colombiana *66*

Mark Blum (1950-)
　　I Don't Know How She Does
　　　　It *178*

Emily Blunt (1983-)
　　The Adjustment Bureau *2*
　　Gnomeo & Juliet *139*

Jonah Bobo (1997-)
　　Crazy, Stupid, Love *79*

Kim Bodnia
　　In a Better World *185*

Matt Bomer
　　In Time *188*

Jon Bon Jovi (1962-)
　　New Year's Eve *267 *

Helena Bonham Carter (1966-)
　　Harry Potter and the Deathly
　　　　Hallows: Part 2 *155*

Hugh Bonneville (1963-)
　　Burke and Hare *51*

Mika Boorem (1987-)
　　The Ward *407*

Keegan Boos
　　Beginners *36*

Zachary Booth
　　The Beaver *35*

David Boreanaz (1971-)
　　The Mighty Macs *250*

Jesse Borrego (1962-)
　　Colombiana *66*

Dominic Borrelli
　　The Human Centipede II (Full
　　　　Sequence) *165*

Michelle Borth
　　A Good Old Fashioned
　　　　Orgy *140*

Devon Bostick
　　Diary of a Wimpy Kid: Rodrick
　　　　Rules *94*

Kate Bosworth (1983-)
　　Straw Dogs *351*

Samuel Bottomley
　　Tyrannosaur *394*

Pierre Boulanger (1987-)
　　Monte Carlo *259*

Jack Boulter
　　Winnie the Pooh (V) *425*

Katrina Bowden
　　Tucker & Dale vs. Evil *391*

Julie Bowen (1970-)
　　Horrible Bosses *167*
　　Jumping the Broom *209*

Grant Bowler
　　Atlas Shrugged: Part 1 *21*

Sammy Boyarsky
　　Rampart *301 *

Cayden Boyd
　　Fireflies in the Garden *125*

John Boyega
　　Attack the Block *23*

Boyz II Men
　　Justin Bieber: Never Say
　　　　Never *212*

Luke Bracey
　　Monte Carlo *259*

Alice Braga (1983-)
　　The Rite *314*

Kenneth Branagh (1960-)
　　My Week With Marilyn *263*

Russell Brand (1975-)
　　Arthur *16*
　　Hop (V) *165*

Rebekah Brandes
　　Bellflower *38*

Buck Brannaman
　　Buck *48*

Creed Bratton (1943-)
　　Terri *365*

Nicholas Braun (1988-)
　　Prom *296*
　　Red State *308*

Sian Breckin
　　Tyrannosaur *394*

Andrew Breitbart
　　The Undefeated *398*

Abigail Breslin (1996-)
　　New Year's Eve *267 *
　　Rango (V) *303*

Jordana Brewster (1980-)
　　Fast Five *119 *

Beau Bridges (1941-)
　　The Descendants *90*

Chris Bridges
　　See Ludacris
　　New Year's Eve *267 *
　　No Strings Attached *269*

Sean Bridges
　　The Woman *426*

Anita Briem (1982-)
　　Dylan Dog: Dead of
　　　　Night *108*

Jim Broadbent (1949-)
　　Arthur Christmas (V) *18*
　　The Iron Lady *196*

Devin Brochu
　　Hesher *159*

Matthew Broderick (1962-)
Tower Heist *378*

Adam Brody (1980-)
Scream 4 *323*

Adrien Brody (1973-)
Midnight in Paris *248*

Albert Brooks (1947-)
Drive *104*

Mehcad Brooks
Creature *81*

Pierce Brosnan (1953-)
I Don't Know How She Does
It *178*

Clancy Brown (1959-)
Cowboys & Aliens *78*
Green Lantern (V) *143*

Eleanor Brown
Courageous *76*

Jessica Tyler Brown
Paranormal Activity 3 *277 *

Emily Browning (1988-)
Sleeping Beauty *337*
Sucker Punch *355*

Carla Bruni (1967-)
Midnight in Paris *248*

Gaetano Bruno
The Double Hour *102*

Rob Brydon (1965-)
The Trip *386*

Andy Buckley
Alvin and the Chipmunks: Chipwrecked *8*

Sandra Bullock (1964-)
Extremely Loud and Incredibly
Close *116*

Con Bunde
The Undefeated *398*

Billy Burke (1966-)
Drive Angry *107*
Red Riding Hood *306*
The Twilight Saga: Breaking
Dawn, Part 1 *392*

Kathy Burke (1964-)
Tinker Tailor Soldier Spy *377*

Robert John Burke (1961-)
Limitless *227*

Jason Burkett
Into the Abyss *195*

Dan Burman
The Human Centipede II (Full
Sequence) *165*

Heather Burns (1974-)
What's Your Number? *419*

Jere Burns (1954-)
Prom *296*

Ellen Burstyn (1932-)
The Mighty Macs *250*

Kate Burton (1957-)
Puncture *297*

Steve Buscemi (1957-)
Rampart *301 *

Gerard Butler (1969-)
Coriolanus *74*
Machine Gun Preacher *233 *

Asa Butterfield (1997-)
Hugo *169*

Norbert Lee Butz
Higher Ground *161*

P.J. Byrne
Final Destination 5 *124*

Rose Byrne (1979-)
Bridesmaids *47*
Insidious *191*
X-Men: First Class *429 *

Julia Gutierrez Caba
Julia's Eyes *200*

Nicolas Cage (1964-)
Drive Angry *107*
Season of the Witch *324*
Trespass *384*

Kevin Cahoon
Mars Needs Moms (V) *239*

Kandace Caine
The Human Centipede II (Full
Sequence) *165*

Michael Caine (1933-)
Cars 2 (V) *58*
Gnomeo & Juliet *139*

Zoe Caldwell (1933-)
Extremely Loud and Incredibly
Close *116*

Matt Cameron
Pearl Jam Twenty *283*

Christa Campbell (1973-)
The Mechanic *243*

Danielle Campbell
Prom *296*

Neve Campbell (1973-)
Scream 4 *323*

Jamie Campbell Bower
Anonymous *10*

Bobby Cannavale (1971-)
Win Win *423*

Robert Capron
Diary of a Wimpy Kid: Rodrick
Rules *94*

Linda Cardellini (1975-)
Kill the Irishman *216*

Steve Carell (1962-)
Crazy, Stupid, Love *79*

Peter Carey (1943-)
Machine Gun Preacher *233 *

Amy Carlson (1968-)
Green Lantern *143*

Chris Carmack (1980-)
Shark Night 3D *331*

Sally Carman
Tyrannosaur *394*

Keith Carradine (1951-)
Cowboys & Aliens *78*

Jim Carrey (1962-)
Mr. Popper's Penguins *255*

Madeline Carroll (1996-)
Machine Gun Preacher *233 *
Mr. Popper's Penguins *255*

Peter Carroll (1943-)
Sleeping Beauty *337*

Jim Carter (1948-)
My Week With Marilyn *263*

Lauren Ashley Carter
The Woman *426*

Katarina Cas
The Guard *145*

Dillon Casey
Creature *81*

Bryce Cass (1997-)
Battle: Los Angeles *29*

Neal Cassady (1926-68)
Magic Trip: Ken Kesey's Search
for a Kool Place *235*

Vincent Cassel (1967-)
A Dangerous Method *85 *

Katie Cassidy (1986-)
Monte Carlo *259*

Rosie Cavaliero
Jane Eyre *203*

Henry Cavill (1983-)
Immortals *183*

Cedric the Entertainer (1964-)
Larry Crowne *223 *

Michael Cerveris
Stake Land *340*

Valentina Cervi
Jane Eyre *203*

Jackie Chan (1954-)
Kung Fu Panda 2 *220*

Rohan Chand
Jack and Jill *201*

Kyle Chandler (1965-)
Super 8 *358*

Yin Chang
Prom *296*

Jeffrey Chase (1968-)
The Mechanic *243*

Jessica Chastain (1981-)
Coriolanus *74*
The Debt *88*
The Help *158*
Take Shelter *364*
Texas Killing Fields *357*
The Tree of Life *382*

Don Cheadle (1964-)
The Guard *145*

Cher (1946-)
Zookeeper (V) *434*

Jake Cherry (1996-)
The Son of No One *344*

Coco Chiang
Snow Flower and the Secret
Fan *341*

John Cho (1972-)
A Very Harold & Kumar 3D
Christmas *403*

Min-Sik Choi (1962-)
I Saw the Devil *179*

Moo-seong Choi
I Saw the Devil *179*

Noam Chomsky
I Am *175 *

Thomas Chong (1938-)
Hoodwinked Too! Hood vs. Evil
(V) *164*

Jay Chou
The Green Hornet *142*

Hayden Christensen (1981-)
Vanishing on 7th Street *401*

Jesper Christensen (1948-)
The Debt *88*
Melancholia *246*

Julie Christie (1941-)
Red Riding Hood *306*

Warren Christie
Apollo 18 *13*

Rami Chuene
Life, Above All *217*

Ho-jin Chun
I Saw the Devil *179*

Kook-haun Chun
I Saw the Devil *179*

Jamie Chung (1983-)
The Hangover Part II *149*
Sucker Punch *355*

Thomas Haden Church (1960-)
We Bought a Zoo *416*

Sam Claflin
Pirates of the Caribbean: On
Stranger Tides *287*

Matt Clark
The Way *403*

Jason Clarke
Texas Killing Fields *357*
Trust *389*

Patricia Clarkson (1959-)
Friends With Benefits *128*
One Day *272*

Jill Clayburgh (1944-2010)
Bridesmaids *47*

John Cleese (1939-)
Winnie the Pooh (N) *425*

George Clooney (1961-)
The Descendants *90*
The Ides of March *181*

Glenn Close (1947-)
Albert Nobbs *6*
Hoodwinked Too! Hood vs. Evil
(V) *164*

Jean Clottes
Cave of Forgotten Dreams *60*

Dani Codina
Julia's Eyes *200*

Chris Henry Coffey (1971-)
Trust *389*

Bern Cohen
Project Nim *294*

Sacha Baron Cohen (1971-)
Hugo *169*

Enrico Colantoni (1963-)
Contagion *72*

Gary Cole (1957-)
Hop *165*

Chris Colfer (1990-)
Glee: The 3D Concert
Movie *137*

Toni Collette (1972-)
Fright Night *130*

Lily Collins (1989-)
Abduction *1 *
Priest *293*

Pauline Collins (1940-)
Albert Nobbs *6*

Olivia Colman (1974-)
The Iron Lady *196*
Tyrannosaur *394*

Robbie Coltrane (1950-)
Harry Potter and the Deathly
Hallows: Part 2 *155*

Michaela Conlin
The Lincoln Lawyer *229*

Jennifer Connelly (1970-)
The Dilemma *96*

Harry Connick, Jr. (1967-)
Dolphin Tale *97*

Paddy Considine (1974-)
Submarine *353*

Steve Coogan (1965-)
Our Idiot Brother *274*
The Trip *386*

Mason Cook
Spy Kids: All the Time in the
World in 4D *348*

Bradley Cooper (1975-)
The Hangover Part II *149*
Limitless *227*

Chris Cooper (1951-)
The Muppets *261*

David A. Cooper
J. Edgar *199 *

Dominic Cooper (1978-)
Captain America: The First
Avenger *55 *
The Devil's Double *93*
My Week With Marilyn *263*

Brady Corbet (1988-)
Martha Marcy May Mar-
lene *241*
Melancholia *246*

Ronnie Corbett (1930-)
Burke and Hare *51*

Rob Corddry (1971-)
Cedar Rapids *61*

Chris Cornell
Pearl Jam Twenty *283*

Jan Cornet (1982-)
The Skin I Live In *335*

Abbie Cornish (1982-)
Limitless *227*
Sucker Punch *355*
W.E. *414*

Nick Corri
See Jsu Garcia

Nikolaj Coster-Waldau (1970-)
Blackthorn *46*

Marion Cotillard (1975-)
Contagion *72*
Midnight in Paris *248*

Maxwell Perry Cotton
Mr. Popper's Penguins *255*

Shamika Cotton
Pariah *278*

Joel Courtney
Super 8 *358*

Brian Cox (1946-)
Coriolanus *74*
Rise of the Planet of the
Apes *312*

Courteney Cox (1964-)
Scream 4 *323*

Richard Coyle (1972-)
W.E. *414*

Patrick Dempsey (1966-)
  Transformers: Dark of the
    Moon *380*

Judi Dench (1934-)
  J. Edgar *199 *
  Jane Eyre *203*
  My Week With Marilyn *263*
  Pirates of the Caribbean: On
    Stranger Tides *287*

David Dencik (1974-)
  The Girl With the Dragon Tat-
    too *135 *
  Tinker Tailor Soldier Spy *377*

Catherine Deneuve (1943-)
  Potiche *292*

Brian Dennehy (1939-)
  The Big Year *42*

Ned Dennehy
  Tyrannosaur *394*

Kat Dennings (1986-)
  Thor *373*

Gerard Depardieu (1948-)
  Potiche *292*

Johnny Depp (1963-)
  Pirates of the Caribbean: On
    Stranger Tides *287*
  Rango (V) *303*
  The Rum Diary *317*

Eugenio Derbez
  Jack and Jill *201*

Laura Dern (1966-)
  Everything Must Go *114*

Pablo Derqui
  Julia's Eyes *200*

Zooey Deschanel (1980-)
  Our Idiot Brother *274*
  Your Highness *432*

Melissa Desormeaux-Poulin
  Incendies *190*

Loretta Devine (1949-)
  Jumping the Broom *209*

Alyssa Diaz
  Shark Night 3D *331*

Cameron Diaz (1972-)
  Bad Teacher *27 *
  The Green Hornet *142*

Leonardo DiCaprio (1974-)
  J. Edgar *199 *

Andy Dick (1965-)
  Hoodwinked Too! Hood vs. Evil
    (V) *164*

Vin Diesel (1967-)
  Fast Five *119 *

Taye Diggs (1972-)
  Dylan Dog: Dead of
    Night *108*

Kgomotso Ditshweni
  Life, Above All *217*

Branko Djuric
  In the Land of Blood and
    Honey *187*

Nikola Djuricko
  In the Land of Blood and
    Honey *187*

Dagmara Dominczyk (1976-)
  Higher Ground *161*

Vincent D'Onofrio (1959-)
  Kill the Irishman *216*

Jeffrey Donovan (1968-)
  J. Edgar *199 *

Stephen Dorff (1973-)
  Bucky Larson: Born to Be a
    Star *50*
  Immortals *183*

Natalie Dormer (1982-)
  W.E. *414*

Portia Doubleday
  Big Mommas: Like Father, Like
    Son *41*

Gary Dourdan (1966-)
  Jumping the Broom *209*

Brad Dourif (1950-)
  Priest *293*

Kevin Downes
  Courageous *76*

Brian Downey (1044-)
  Hobo With a Shotgun *162*

Robert Downey, Jr. (1965-)
  Sherlock Holmes: A Game of
    Shadows *332*

Franz Drameh
  Attack the Block *23*

Jesse Draper
  The Mighty Macs *250*

Rachel Dratch (1966-)
  Just Go With It *210*

Josh Duhamel (1972-)
  New Year's Eve *267 *
  Transformers: Dark of the
    Moon *380*

Jean Dujardin
  The Artist *19*

Michael Clarke Duncan (1957-)
  Green Lantern (V) *143*

Kevin Dunn (1956-)
  Transformers: Dark of the
    Moon *380*
  Warrior *409*

Kirsten Dunst (1982-)
  Melancholia *246*

Molly Dunsworth
  Hobo With a Shotgun *162*

Kevin Durand (1974-)
  I Am Number Four *176*
  Real Steel *305*

James Duval (1973-)
  Kaboom *215 *

Trine Dyrholm (1972-)
  In a Better World *185*

Aaron Eckhart
  Battle: Los Angeles *29*

Aaron Eckhart (1968-)
  The Rum Diary *317*

Joel Edgerton (1974-)
  The Thing *368*
  Warrior *409*

Cory Edwards
  Hoodwinked Too! Hood vs.
    Evil *164*

Zac Efron (1987-)
  New Year's Eve *267 *

Colin Egglesfield
  Something Borrowed *342*

Jennifer Ehle (1969-)
  Contagion *72*

Jill Eikenberry (1946-)
  Young Adult *431*

Jesse Eisenberg (1983-)
  Rio (V) *311*
  30 Minutes or Less *371*

Ned Eisenberg (1957-)
  Limitless *227*

Yolanda El Karam
  Miral *251*

Yasmine El Masri
  Miral *251*

Abdelghafour Elaaziz
  Incendies *190*

Idris Elba (1972-)
  Thor *373*

Ron Eldard (1965-)
  Super 8 *358*

Jenna Elfman (1971-)
  Friends With Benefits *128*

Christine Elise (1965-)
  Prom *296*

Hector Elizondo (1936-)
  New Year's Eve *267 *

Aunjanue Ellis (1969-)
  The Help *158*

Gad Elmaleh (1971-)
  The Adventures of Tintin
    (V) *4*

Cary Elwes (1962-)
  No Strings Attached *269*

Noah Emmerich (1965-)
  Super 8 *358*
  Trust *389*
  Warrior *409*

Mike Epps (1970-)
  Jumping the Broom *209*

Arlen Escarpeta (1981-)
  Final Destination 5 *124*

Alex Esmail
  Attack the Block *23*

Emilio Estevez
  The Way *403*

Lauren Etchells
  Courageous *76*

Chris Evans (1981-)
  Captain America: The First
    Avenger *55 *
  Puncture *297*
  What's Your Number? *419*

Luke Evans (1979-)
  Immortals *183*
  The Three Musketeers *375*

Angie Everhart (1969-)
  Take Me Home Tonight *362*

Peter Facinelli (1973-)
  The Twilight Saga: Breaking
    Dawn, Part 1 *392*

Siobhan Fallon (1961-)
  We Need to Talk About
    Kevin *418*

Dakota Fanning (1994-)
  The Twilight Saga: Breaking
    Dawn, Part 1 *392*

Elle Fanning (1998-)
  Super 8 *358*
  We Bought a Zoo *416*

Sarina Farhadi
  A Separation *327*

Anna Faris (1976-)
  Alvin and the Chipmunks: Chip-
    wrecked (V) *8*
  Take Me Home Tonight *362*
  What's Your Number? *419*

Taissa Farmiga (1994-)
  Higher Ground *161*

Vera Farmiga (1973-)
  Higher Ground *161*
  Source Code *347*

Colin Farrell (1976-)
  Fright Night *130*
  Horrible Bosses *167*

Nicholas Farrell (1955-)
  The Iron Lady *196*

Michael Fassbender (1977-)
  A Dangerous Method *85 *
  Jane Eyre *203*
  Shame *329*
  X-Men: First Class *429 *

Jon Favreau (1966-)
  Zookeeper (V) *434*

Nat Faxon
  Zookeeper *434*

Katie Featherston (1982-)
  Paranormal Activity 3 *277 *

Tom Felton (1987-)
  Harry Potter and the Deathly
    Hallows: Part 2 *155*
  Rise of the Planet of the
    Apes *312*

Colm Feore (1958-)
  Thor *373*

Craig Ferguson (1962-)
  Winnie the Pooh (V) *425*

Shiloh Fernandez
  Red Riding Hood *306*

Will Ferrell (1968-)
  Everything Must Go *114*

William Fichtner (1956-)
  Drive Angry *107*

Ralph Fiennes (1962-)
  Coriolanus *74*
  Harry Potter and the Deathly
    Hallows: Part 2 *155*

Nathan Fillion (1971-)
  Super *357*

Colin Firth (1960-)
  Tinker Tailor Soldier Spy *377*

Jenna Fischer (1974-)
  Hall Pass *147 *

Andy Fischer-Price
  Kaboom *215 *

Laurence Fishburne (1963-)
  Contagion *72*

Frances Fisher (1952-)
  The Lincoln Lawyer *229*
  The Roommate *316*

Isla Fisher (1976-)
  Burke and Hare *51*
  Rango (V) *303*

Miles Fisher (1983-)
  Final Destination 5 *124*

Schuyler Fisk (1982-)
  Restless *309*

Fionnula Flanagan (1941-)
  The Guard *145*
  Kill the Irishman *216*

Jason Flemyng (1966-)
  X-Men: First Class *429 *

Margaret Anne Florence
  The Mighty Macs *250*

Patrick Flueger (1983-)
  Footloose *127*

Miriam Flynn (1952-)
  Bucky Larson: Born to Be a
    Star *50*

Dan Fogler (1976-)
  Mars Needs Moms (V) *239*
  Take Me Home Tonight *362*

Lyndsy Fonseca
  The Ward *407*

Colin Ford
  We Bought a Zoo *416*

Faith Ford (1960-)
  Prom *296*

Harrison Ford (1942-)
  Cowboys & Aliens *78*

Robert Forster (1941-)
  The Descendants *90*

Will Forte (1970-)
  A Good Old Fashioned
    Orgy *140*

Ben Foster (1980-)
  The Mechanic *243*
  Rampart *301 *

Jodie Foster (1963-)
  The Beaver *35*
  Carnage *56*

James Fox (1939-)
  W.E. *414*

Laurence Fox (1978-)
  W.E. *414*

Megan Fox (1986-)
  Passion Play *280*

Robert Foxworth (1941-)
  Transformers: Dark of the Moon
    (V) *380*

Jeff Foxworthy (1958-)
  The Smurfs (V) *339*

Jamie Foxx (1967-)
  Horrible Bosses *167*
  Rio (V) *311*

Claire Foy (1984-)
  Season of the Witch *324*

Dave Franco
  Fright Night *130*

James Franco (1978-)
  Rise of the Planet of the
    Apes *312*
  Your Highness *432*

Morgan Freeman (1937-)
  Dolphin Tale *97*

Ulf Friberg (1962-)
  The Girl With the Dragon Tat-
    too *135 *

Brenda Fricker (1944-)
  Albert Nobbs *6*

Anna Friel (1976-)
    Limitless *227*

Jean-Marie Frin
    Of Gods and Men *270*

Carole Fritz
    Cave of Forgotten Dreams *60*

Nick Frost (1972-)
    Attack the Block *23*
    Paul *281*

Stephen Fry (1957-)
    Sherlock Holmes: A Game of
        Shadows *332*

Patrick Fugit (1982-)
    We Bought a Zoo *416*

Amanda Fuller
    Creature *81*

Kurt Fuller (1952-)
    Midnight in Paris *248*

Edward Furlong (1977-)
    The Green Hornet *142*

Arata Furuta
    13 Assassins *370*

Sarah Gadon (1987-)
    A Dangerous Method *85 *

Gal Gadot
    Fast Five *119 *

Charlotte Gainsbourg (1972-)
    Melancholia *246*

Johnny Galecki (1975-)
    In Time *188*

Zach Galifianakis (1969-)
    The Hangover Part II *149*
    Puss in Boots *(V)* *299*

Bronagh Gallagher (1972-)
    Albert Nobbs *6*

Kyle Gallner (1986-)
    Beautiful Boy *33*
    Red State *308*

Nathan Gamble (1998-)
    Dolphin Tale *97*

Michael Gambon (1940-)
    Harry Potter and the Deathly
        Hallows: Part 2 *155*

Bruno Ganz (1941-)
    Unknown *400*

Romola Garai (1982-)
    One Day *272*

Victor Garber (1949-)
    Kung Fu Panda 2 *220*

Paula Garces (1974-)
    A Very Harold & Kumar 3D
        Christmas *403*

Jsu Garcia (1963-)
    Atlas Shrugged: Part 1 *21*

Jennifer Garner (1972-)
    Arthur *16*

Brad Garrett (1960-)
    Hoodwinked Too! Hood vs. Evil
        (V) *164*

Spencer Garrett
    The Way *403*

Edi Gathegi (1979-)
    Atlas Shrugged: Part 1 *21*
    X-Men: First Class *429 *

Maxim Gaudette
    Incendies *190*

Dolya Gavanski
    The Trip *386*

Ari Gaynor
    What's Your Number? *419*

Jean-Michel Geneste
    Cave of Forgotten Dreams *60*

Daniel Jude Gennis
    The Human Centipede II (Full
        Sequence) *165*

Ashley Gerasimovich (2004-)
    We Need to Talk About
        Kevin *418*

Richard Gere (1949-)
    The Double *100*

Ricky Gervais (1961-)
    Spy Kids: All the Time in the
        World in 4D *(V)* *348*

Greta Gerwig
    Arthur *16*
    No Strings Attached *269*

Paul Giamatti (1967-)
    The Hangover Part II *149*
    The Ides of March *181*
    Win Win *423*

Timothy Gibbs (1967-)
    11-11-11 *113*

Mel Gibson (1956-)
    The Beaver *35*

Tyrese Gibson (1978-)
    Fast Five *119 *
    Transformers: Dark of the
        Moon *380*

Cam Gigandet
    Priest *293*
    The Roommate *316*
    Trespass *384*

Brian Gilbert (1960-)
    The Son of No One *344*

Remy Girard (1950-)
    Incendies *190*

Brendan Gleeson (1954-)
    Albert Nobbs *6*
    The Guard *145*

Iain Glen (1961-)
    The Iron Lady *196*

Scott Glenn (1942-)
    Sucker Punch *355*

Wendy Glenn
    11-11-11 *113*

Evan Glodell
    Bellflower *38*

Griffin Gluck (2000-)
    Just Go With It *210*

Judith Godreche (1972-)
    Potiche *292*

Dave Goelz (1946-)
    The Muppets *(V)* *261*

Walton Goggins (1971-)
    Cowboys & Aliens *78*
    Straw Dogs *351*

Joanna Going (1963-)
    The Tree of Life *382*

Darren Goldstein (1974-)
    Limitless *227*

Tony Goldwyn (1960-)
    The Mechanic *243*

Ian Gomez (1964-)
    Larry Crowne *223 *

Selena Gomez (1992-)
    Monte Carlo *259*

Alex Gonzales
    X-Men: First Class *429 *

Meagan Good (1981-)
    Jumping the Broom *209*

John Goodman (1952-)
    The Artist *19*
    Extremely Loud and Incredibly
        Close *116*
    Red State *308*

Ginnifer Goodwin (1978-)
    Something Borrowed *342*

Zachary Gordon (1998-)
    Diary of a Wimpy Kid: Rodrick
        Rules *94*

Joseph Gordon-Levitt (1981-)
    50/50 *120*
    Hesher *159*

Ryan Gosling (1980-)
    Crazy, Stupid, Love *79*
    Drive *104*
    The Ides of March *181*

Stone Gossart
    Pearl Jam Twenty *283*

Elliott Gould (1938-)
    Contagion *72*

Nolan Gould
    Friends With Benefits *128*

Dakota Goyo (1999-)
  Real Steel *305*

Topher Grace (1978-)
  The Double *100*
  Take Me Home Tonight *362*

Heather Graham (1970-)
  Judy Moody and the Not Bummer Summer *206*

Stephen Graham (1973-)
  Season of the Witch *324*
  Texas Killing Fields *357*
  Tinker Tailor Soldier Spy *377*

Holliday Grainger
  Jane Eyre *203*

Kelsey Grammer (1954-)
  I Don't Know How She Does It *178*

Philip Granger
  Tucker & Dale vs. Evil *391*

Beth Grant (1949-)
  The Artist *19*

Richard E. Grant (1957-)
  The Iron Lady *196*

Vincent Grashaw
  Bellflower *38*

Sprague Grayden
  Paranormal Activity 3 *277 *

Ari Graynor (1983-)
  The Sitter *334*

Seth Green (1974-)
  Mars Needs Moms (V) *239*

Bryan Greenberg (1978-)
  Friends With Benefits *128*

Ashley Greene (1987-)
  The Twilight Saga: Breaking Dawn, Part 1 *392*

Bruce Greenwood (1956-)
  Meek's Cutoff *244*

Judy Greer (1971-)
  The Descendants *90*

Clark Gregg (1964-)
  Mr. Popper's Penguins *255*
  Thor *373*

Pam Grier (1949-)
  Larry Crowne *223 *

Richard Griffiths (1947-)
  Hugo *169*
  Pirates of the Caribbean: On Stranger Tides *287*

Riley Griffiths
  Super 8 *358*

Frank Grillo (1963-)
  Warrior *409*

Rupert Grint (1988-)
  Harry Potter and the Deathly Hallows: Part 2 *155*

Josh Groban
  Crazy, Stupid, Love *79*

Taylor Groothius
  Vanishing on 7th Street *401*

Ioan Gruffudd (1974-)
  Fireflies in the Garden *125*
  Sanctum *321 *

Matthew Gray Gubler
  Alvin and the Chipmunks: Chipwrecked (V) *8*

Carla Gugino (1971-)
  The Mighty Macs *250*
  Mr. Popper's Penguins *255*
  Sucker Punch *355*

Tim Guinee (1962-)
  Water for Elephants *411*

Mamie Gummer (1983-)
  The Ward *407*

Tim Gunn (1953-)
  The Smurfs *339*

Bob Gunton (1945-)
  The Lincoln Lawyer *229*

Luis Guzman (1956-)
  Arthur *16*

Jake Gyllenhaal (1980-)
  Source Code *347*

Lukas Haas (1976-)
  Red Riding Hood *306*

Bill Hader (1978-)
  Hoodwinked Too! Hood vs. Evil (V) *164*
  Paul *281*

Kathryn Hahn (1974-)
  Our Idiot Brother *274*

Sid Haig
  Creature *81*

Tony Hale (1970-)
  Happythankyoumoreplease *153*

Philip Baker Hall (1931-)
  Mr. Popper's Penguins *255*

Pooch Hall
  Jumping the Broom *209*

Rebecca Hall (1982-)
  Everything Must Go *114*

Wyatt Dean Hall
  Winnie the Pooh (V) *425*

Josh Hamilton (1968-)
  J. Edgar *199 *

Lisa Gay Hamilton (1964-)
  Take Shelter *364*

Jon Hamm (1971-)
  Bridesmaids *47*
  Sucker Punch *355*

Armie Hammer
  J. Edgar *199 *

Chelsea Handler
  Hop *165*

Tom Hanks (1956-)
  Extremely Loud and Incredibly Close *116*
  Larry Crowne *223 *

Lucas Hansen
  The Human Centipede II (Full Sequence) *165*

David Harbour (1974-)
  The Green Hornet *142*
  W.E. *414*

Jamie Harding
  The Devil's Double *93*

Cory Hardrict
  Battle: Los Angeles *29*

Matt Hardwick
  Courageous *76*

Tom Hardy (1977-)
  Tinker Tailor Soldier Spy *377*
  Warrior *409*

Elisabeth Harnois (1979-)
  Mars Needs Moms (V) *239*

Woody Harrelson (1962-)
  Friends With Benefits *128*
  Rampart *301 *

Danielle Harris
  Stake Land *340*

Danneel Harris (1979-)
  The Roommate *316*

Jared Harris (1961-)
  Sherlock Holmes: A Game of Shadows *332*
  The Ward *407*

Lee Nicholas Harris
  The Human Centipede II (Full Sequence) *165*

Neil Patrick Harris (1973-)
  Beastly *30*
  The Smurfs *339*
  A Very Harold & Kumar 3D Christmas *403*

Rachael Harris (1968-)
  Diary of a Wimpy Kid: Rodrick Rules *94*

Laurence R. Harvey
  The Human Centipede II (Full Sequence) *165*

Tamer Hassan (1968-)
  The Double *100*

David Hasselhoff (1952-)
  Hop *165*

Patricia Hastie
  The Descendants *90*

Vanessa Anne Hudgens (1988-)
Beastly *30*
Sucker Punch *355*

Kate Hudson (1979-)
Something Borrowed *342*

Neal Huff
Meek's Cutoff *244*

Finola Hughes (1960-)
Like Crazy *226*

Bonnie Hunt (1964-)
Cars 2 *(V)* *58*

Helen Hunt (1963-)
Soul Surfer *345*

Jumayh Hunter
Attack the Block *23*

Sam Huntington (1982-)
Dylan Dog: Dead of
Night *108*

Rosie Huntington-Whiteley
Transformers: Dark of the
Moon *380*

Jackson Hurst
The Tree of Life *382*

John Hurt (1940-)
Harry Potter and the Deathly
Hallows: Part 2 *155*
Immortals *183*
Melancholia *246*
Tinker Tailor Soldier Spy *377*

Mary Beth Hurt (1948-)
Young Adult *431*

Anjelica Huston (1951-)
The Big Year *42*
50/50 *120*

Danny Huston (1962-)
The Conspirator *70*

Bill Hutchens
The Human Centipede II (Full
Sequence) *165*

Jessica Hynes
Burke and Hare *51*

Ice Cube (1969-)
Rampart *301 *

Masachika Ichimura
13 Assassins *370*

Rhys Ifans (1968-)
Anonymous *10*
Passion Play *280*

Tsuyoski Ihara (1963-)
13 Assassins *370*

Goro Inagaki
13 Assassins *370*

Jeremy Irons (1948-)
Margin Call *238*

Max Irons
Red Riding Hood *306*

Jeremy Irvine
War Horse *405 *

Bill Irwin (1950-)
Higher Ground *161*

Oscar Isaac (1980-)
Drive *104*
Sucker Punch *355*
W.E. *414*

Jason Isaacs (1963-)
Abduction *1 *
Cars 2 *(V)* *58*

Yusuke Iseya
13 Assassins *370*

Jason Issacs
Harry Potter and the Deathly
Hallows: Part 2 *155*

Dana Ivey (1942-)
The Help *158*

Eddie Izzard (1962-)
Cars 2 *(V)* *58*

Hugh Jackman (1968-)
Real Steel *305*
Snow Flower and the Secret
Fan *341*

Brandon T. Jackson (1984-)
Big Mommas: Like Father, Like
Son *41*

Philip Jackson (1948-)
My Week With Marilyn *263*

Samuel L. Jackson (1948-)
Captain America: The First
Avenger *55 *

Oliver Jackson-Cohen (1986-)
What's Your Number? *419*

Derek Jacobi (1938-)
My Week With Marilyn *263*

Eric Jacobson (1970-)
The Muppets *(V)* *261*

Geraldine James (1950-)
Arthur *16*
The Girl With the Dragon Tat-
too *135 *
Sherlock Holmes: A Game of
Shadows *332*

Kevin James (1965-)
The Dilemma *96*
Zookeeper *434*

Lennie James (1965-)
Colombiana *66*

Allison Janney (1960-)
The Help *158*

Martin Jarvis (1941-)
The Girl With the Dragon Tattoo *135 *

Richard Jenkins (1953-)
Friends With Benefits *128*
Hall Pass *147 *
The Rum Diary *317*

Brent Jennings
Moneyball *257*

Ashley Jensen (1969-)
Arthur Christmas *(V)* *18*
Gnomeo & Juliet *139*

David Jensen
Creature *81*

Ken Jeong (1969-)
The Hangover Part II *149*
Transformers: Dark of the
Moon *380*
Zookeeper *434*

Otto Jerpersen (1954-)
Trollhunter *388*

Paul Jesson (1946-)
Coriolanus *74*

Goran Jevtic
In the Land of Blood and
Honey *187*

Salome Jimenez
11-11-11 *113*

Paul Johansson (1964-)
Atlas Shrugged: Part 1 *21*

Scarlett Johansson (1984-)
We Bought a Zoo *416*

Aaron Johnson (1990-)
Albert Nobbs *6*

Dakota Johnson (1989-)
Beastly *30*

Don Johnson (1949-)
Bucky Larson: Born to Be a
Star *50*
A Good Old Fashioned
Orgy *140*

Dwayne "The Rock" Johnson (1972-)
Fast Five *119 *

Rebecca Johnson
The Trip *386*

Angelina Jolie (1975-)
Kung Fu Panda 2 *220*

Caleb Landry Jones
X-Men: First Class *429 *

Felicity Jones (1984-)
Like Crazy *226*

January Jones (1978-)
Unknown *400*
X-Men: First Class *429 *

Leeon Jones
Attack the Block *23*

Maggie Elizabeth Jones
We Bought a Zoo *416*

Rashida Jones (1976-)
The Big Year *42*
Friends With Benefits *128*
The Muppets *261*
Our Idiot Brother *274*

Toby Jones (1967-)
The Adventures of Tintin
(V) *4*
Captain America: The First
Avenger *55 *
My Week With Marilyn *263*
The Rite *314*
Tinker Tailor Soldier Spy *377*
Your Highness *432*

Tommy Lee Jones (1946-)
Captain America: The First
Avenger *55 *

Vinnie Jones (1965-)
Kill the Irishman *216*

Christopher Jordan Wallace
Everything Must Go *114*

Milla Jovovich (1975-)
The Three Musketeers *375*

Ashley Judd (1968-)
Dolphin Tale *97*

Jose Julian
A Better Life *39*

Miranda July (1974-)
The Future *133*

Gianna Jun (1981-)
Snow Flower and the Secret
Fan *341*

Steve Kahn
Diary of a Wimpy Kid: Rodrick
Rules *94*

Bianca Kajlich (1977-)
30 Minutes or Less *371*

Patricia Kalember (1957-)
Limitless *227*

Daniel Kaluuya
Johnny English Reborn *205*

Tom Kane (1962-)
The Smurfs (N) *339*

Sung Kang (1972-)
Fast Five *119 *

John Kani
Coriolanus *74*

Archie Kao (1969-)
Snow Flower and the Secret
Fan *341*

Anil Kapoor (1959-)
Mission: Impossible—Ghost Protocol *253*

Vincent Kartheiser (1979-)
In Time *188*

Tcheky Karyo
The Way *403*

Ryo Kase (1974-)
Restless *309*

Mark Kassen (1971-)
Puncture *297*

Stana Katic
The Double *100*

William Katt (1950-)
Super *357*

Zoe Kazan (1983-)
Happythankyoumoreplease *153*
Meek's Cutoff *244*

Michael Keaton (1951-)
Cars 2 (V) *58*

Hugh Keays-Byrne (1947-)
Sleeping Beauty *337*

Toby Kebbell (1982-)
The Conspirator *70*
War Horse *405 *

Claire Keelan
The Trip *386*

Rory Keenan
The Guard *145*

Catherine Keener (1961-)
Trust *389*

Mary Page Keller (1961-)
Beginners *36*

Michael Kelly (1969-)
The Adjustment Bureau *2*

Minka Kelly (1980-)
The Roommate *316*

Ellie Kemper
Bridesmaids *47*

Alex Kendrick
Courageous *76*

Anna Kendrick (1985-)
50/50 *120*
The Twilight Saga: Breaking
Dawn, Part 1 *392*

Mimi Kennedy (1949-)
Midnight in Paris *248*

Rebekah Kennedy
Creature *81*

Tom Kenny (1962-)
Winnie the Pooh (V) *425*

Brian Kerwin (1949-)
The Help *158*

Ken Kesey (1935-2001)
Magic Trip: Ken Kesey's Search
for a Kool Place *235*

Thato Kgaladi
Life, Above All *217*

Nicole Kidman (1966-)
Just Go With It *210*
Trespass *384*

Udo Kier (1944-)
Melancholia *246*

Val Kilmer (1959-)
Kill the Irishman *216*

Hira Kim
Poetry *279*

In-seo Kim
I Saw the Devil *179*

Yoon-Seo Kim
I Saw the Devil *179*

Joey King (1999-)
Crazy, Stupid, Love *79*

Ben Kingsley (1943-)
Hugo *169*

Alex Kingston (1963-)
Like Crazy *226*

Sean Kingston (1990-)
Justin Bieber: Never Say
Never *212*

Joel Kinnaman (1979-)
The Darkest Hour *87*
The Girl With the Dragon Tat-
too *135 *

Greg Kinnear (1963-)
I Don't Know How She Does
It *178*

Michael Kitchen (1948-)
My Week With Marilyn *263*

Jurgen Klein
The Girl With the Dragon Tattoo *135 *

Kevin Kline (1947-)
The Conspirator *70*
No Strings Attached *269*

Heidi Klum (1973-)
Hoodwinked Too! Hood vs. Evil
(V) *164*

Shirley Knight (1937-)
Our Idiot Brother *274*

Keira Knightley (1985-)
A Dangerous Method *85 *

David Koechner (1962-)
Final Destination 5 *124*
Paul *281*

Goran Kostic
In the Land of Blood and
Honey *187*

Elias Koteas (1961-)
Dream House *103*
A Very Harold & Kumar 3D
Christmas *403*

John Krasinski (1979-)
Something Borrowed *342*

Nick Krause
The Descendants *90*

Blake Lively (1987-)
Green Lantern *143*

Harold Lloyd, Jr. (1931-71)
Jane Eyre *203*

Harry Lloyd (1983-)
The Iron Lady *196*

Tony Lo Bianco
Kill the Irishman *216*

Bruno Lochet
Potiche *292*

Justin Long (1978-)
Alvin and the Chipmunks: Chip-
wrecked (V) *8*
The Conspirator *70*

Robert Longstreet
Take Shelter *364*

Michael Lonsdale (1931-)
Of Gods and Men *270*

George Lopez (1961-)
Rio (V) *311*
The Smurfs (V) *339*

Richard Lopez
Into the Abyss *195*

Donal Louge (1966-)
Shark Night 3D *331*

Faizon Love (1968-)
Big Mommas: Like Father, Like
Son *41*
Zookeeper (V) *434*

Ophelia Lovibond (1986)
Mr. Popper's Penguins *255*

Chris Lowell
The Help *158*

Isabel Lucas
Immortals *183*

Jessica Lucas
Big Mommas: Like Father, Like
Son *41*

Josh(ua) Lucas (1971-)
J. Edgar *199 *
The Lincoln Lawyer *229*

Matt Lucas (1974-)
Gnomeo & Juliet *139*

Shannon Lucio (1980-)
Fireflies in the Garden *125*

Bud Luckey
Winnie the Pooh (V) *425*

Ludacris
Fast Five *119 *
Justin Bieber: Never Say
Never *212*

Fabrice Lunchini
Potiche *292*

Billy Lush
Straw Dogs *351*

Kellan Lutz (1985-)
Immortals *183*
The Twilight Saga: Breaking
Dawn, Part 1 *392*

Jane Lynch (1960-)
Paul *281*

John Lynch (1961-)
Paul *281*

John Carroll Lynch (1963-)
Hesher *159*

Kelly Lynch (1959-)
Kaboom *215 *
Passion Play *280*

Melanie Lynskey (1977-)
Win Win *423*

Andie MacDowell (1958-)
Footloose *127*
Monte Carlo *259*

Angus MacFadyen (1964-)
We Bought a Zoo *416*

Matthew MacFadyen (1974-)
The Three Musketeers *375*

Kari Machett
The Tree of Life *382*

Jacqueline MacInnes-Wood
Final Destination 5 *124*

Anthony Mackie (1979-)
The Adjustment Bureau *2*
Real Steel *305*

Laine MacNeil
Diary of a Wimpy Kid: Rodrick
Rules *94*

William H. Macy (1950-)
The Lincoln Lawyer *229*

Bailee Madison (1999-)
Don't Be Afraid of the
Dark *99*
Just Go With It *210*

Virginia Madsen (1963-)
Red Riding Hood *306*

Mohamed Majd
Incendies *190*

Keaobaka Makanyane
Life, Above All *217*

John Malkovich (1953-)
Transformers: Dark of the
Moon *380*

Jena Malone (1984-)
Sucker Punch *355*

Xavier Maly
Of Gods and Men *270*

Harriet Manamela
Life, Above All *217*

Aasif Mandvi (-1966)
Margin Call *238*

Leslie Mann (1972-)
The Change-Up *64*
Rio (V) *311*

Hans Morten Mansen
Trollhunter *388*

Joe Mantegna (1947-)
Cars 2 (V) *58*

Khomotso Manyaka
Life, Above All *217*

William Mapother (1965-)
Another Earth *12*

Kate Mara (1983-)
Happythankyoumoreplease *153*

Rooney Mara (1985-)
The Girl With the Dragon Tattoo *135 *

Constance Marie (1965-)
Puss in Boots (V) *299*

Cheech Marin (1946-)
Cars 2 (V) *58*
Hoodwinked Too! Hood vs. Evil
(V) *164*

Zana Marjanovic
In the Land of Blood and
Honey *187*

Brit Marling
Another Earth *12*

Jerry Marobyane
Life, Above All *217*

Christopher Marquette (1984-)
The Double *100*

Eddie Marsan (1968-)
Sherlock Holmes: A Game of
Shadows *332*
Tyrannosaur *394*

James Marsden (1973-)
Hop *165*
Straw Dogs *351*

Matthew Marsden (1972-)
Atlas Shrugged: Part 1 *21*

Demetri Martin
Contagion *72*
Take Me Home Tonight *362*

Jesse L. Martin (1969-)
Puncture *297*

Rusty Martin
Courageous *76*

Steve Martin (1945-)
The Big Year *42*

Margo Martindale (1951-)
Win Win *423*

Maximillian Martini (1969-)
Colombiana *66*

Vladimir Mashkov (1963-)
Mission: Impossible—Ghost Protocol *253*

Tom Mison
One Day *272*

Mr. Wiggles
See Ludacris

Katy Mixon (1981-)
Drive Angry *107*
Take Shelter *364*

Tinah Mnumzana
Life, Above All *217*

Payman Moaadi
A Separation *327*

Katherine Moenning (1977-)
The Lincoln Lawyer *229*

Shylla Molhusen
The Woman *426*

Alfred Molina (1953-)
Abduction *1 *
Rango (V) *303*

Jordi Molla (1968-)
Colombiana *66*

Jason Momoa
Conan the Barbarian *69*

Michelle Monaghan (1976-)
Machine Gun Preacher *233 *
Source Code *347*

Cory Monteith (1982-)
Glee: The 3D Concert
Movie *137*
Monte Carlo *259*

Janet Montgomery
Our Idiot Brother *274*

Alicia Moore
See Pink

Demi Moore (1962-)
Margin Call *238*

Joel David Moore (1977-)
Shark Night 3D *331*

Julianne Moore (1961-)
Crazy, Stupid, Love *79*

Mircea Moore
The Change-Up *64*

Stephan Campbell Moore (1979-)
Season of the Witch *324*

Johanna Morch
Trollhunter *388*

Chloe Grace Moretz (1997-)
Hugo *169*
Texas Killing Fields *357*

Jeffrey Dean Morgan
Texas Killing Fields *357*

Joseph Morgan
Immortals *183*

Tracy Morgan (1968-)
The Son of No One *344*

Kathryn Morris (1969-)
Moneyball *257*

Jennifer Morrison (1979-)
Warrior *409*

Temuera Morrison (1961-)
Green Lantern *143*

David Morse (1953-)
Drive Angry *107*

Glenn Morshower (1959-)
Moneyball *257*

Viggo Mortensen (1958-)
A Dangerous Method *85 *

Emily Mortimer (1971-)
Cars 2 (V) *58*
Hugo *169*
Our Idiot Brother *274*

Carrie-Anne Moss (1970-)
Fireflies in the Garden *125*

Jesse Moss (1983-)
Tucker & Dale vs. Evil *391*

Ebon Moss-Bachrach (1978-)
Higher Ground *161*

Ido Mosseri
Bucky Larson: Born to Be a
Star *50*

Parris Mosteller
Judy Moody and the Not Bummer Summer *206*

Abdallah Moundy
Of Gods and Men *270*

Anson Mount (1973-)
Straw Dogs *351*

Stephen Moyer (1969-)
The Double *100*
Priest *293*

Bridget Moynahan (1972-)
Battle: Los Angeles *29*

Ali Shaheed Muhammad (1970-)
Beats, Rhymes & Life: The Trav-
els of a Tribe Called
Quest *32*

Oliver Muirhead
Like Crazy *226*

Peter Mullan (1954-)
Tyrannosaur *394*
War Horse *405 *

Carey Mulligan (1985-)
Drive *104*
Shame *329*

Dermot Mulroney (1963-)
J. Edgar *199 *

Olivia Munn (1980-)
I Don't Know How She Does
It *178*

Cillian Murphy (1976-)
In Time *188*

Donna Murphy (1958-)
Higher Ground *161*

Eddie Murphy (1961-)
Tower Heist *378*

Bill Murray (1950-)
Passion Play *280*

Lerato Mvelase
Life, Above All *217*

Per Myrberg
The Girl With the Dragon Tattoo *135 *

Ne-Yo (1982-)
Battle: Los Angeles *29*

Kevin Nealon (1953-)
Bucky Larson: Born to Be a
Star *50*
Just Go With It *210*

Liam Neeson (1952-)
The Hangover Part II *149*
Unknown *400*

Angelica Nelsom
Courageous *76*

Craig T. Nelson (1946-)
Soul Surfer *345*

Sean Nelson
Stake Land *340*

Tommy Nelson
Meek's Cutoff *244*

Travis Nelson (1990-)
Tucker & Dale vs. Evil *391*

James Nesbitt (1966-)
Coriolanus *74*
The Way *403*

George Newbern (1964-)
Fireflies in the Garden *125*

Jasper Newell
We Need to Talk About
Kevin *418*

Thandie Newton (1972-)
Vanishing on 7th Street *401*

Wayne Newton (1942-)
Hoodwinked Too! Hood vs. Evil
(V) *164*

Austin Nichols
Beautiful Boy *33*

Rachel Nichols (1980-)
Conan the Barbarian *69*

Lorraine Nicholson (1990-)
Soul Surfer *345*

William Johnk Nielsen
In a Better World *185*

Michael Pena (1976-)
Battle: Los Angeles *29*
Everything Must Go *114*
The Lincoln Lawyer *229*
30 Minutes or Less *371*
Tower Heist *378*

Kal Penn (1977-)
A Very Harold & Kumar 3D
Christmas *403*

Sean Penn (1960-)
The Tree of Life *382*

Wayne Pere
Creature *81*

Elizabeth Perkins (1960-)
Hop *165*

Ron Perlman (1950-)
Conan the Barbarian *69*
Drive *104*
Season of the Witch *324*

Olivier Perrier (1940-)
Of Gods and Men *270*

Katy Perry
The Smurfs (V) *339*

Megahn Perry (1977-)
The Perfect Host *286*

Mikael Persbrandt (1963-)
In a Better World *185*

Alex Pettyfer (1990-)
Beastly *30*
I Am Number Four *176*
In Time *188*

Michelle Pfeiffer (1957-)
New Year's Eve *267 *

Busy Philips (1979-)
I Don't Know How She Does
It *178*

Ryan Phillippe (1974-)
The Lincoln Lawyer *229*

Loic Pichon
Of Gods and Men *270*

David Hyde Pierce (1959-)
The Perfect Host *286*

Geoffrey Pierson (1949-)
J. Edgar *199 *

Rosamund Pike (1979-)
The Big Year *42*

Alison Pill (1985-)
Midnight in Paris *248*

Dzana Pinjo
In the Land of Blood and
Honey *187*

Pink (1979-)
Happy Feet Two (V) *152*

Freida Pinto
Immortals *183*
Miral *251*
Rise of the Planet of the
Apes *312*

Brad Pitt (1963-)
Happy Feet Two (V) *152*
Moneyball *257*
The Tree of Life *382*

Jeremy Piven (1965-)
Spy Kids: All the Time in the
World in 4D *348*

Oliver Platt (1960-)
X-Men: First Class *429 *

Jesse Plemons (1988-)
Paul *281*

Christopher Plummer (1927-)
Beginners *36*
The Girl With the Dragon Tat-
too *135 *
Priest *293*

Amy Poehler (1971-)
Alvin and the Chipmunks: Chip-
wrecked (V) *8*
Hoodwinked Too! Hood vs. Evil
(V) *164*

Lucia Poli
The Double Hour *102*

Jon Polito (1950-)
Atlas Shrugged: Part 1 *21*

Kevin Pollak (1958-)
The Big Year *42*

Jenjira Pongpas
Uncle Boonmee Who Can Recall
His Past Lives *397 *

Aubrey Poolo
Life, Above All *217*

Imogen Poots
Fright Night *130*
Jane Eyre *203*

Paul Popplewell (1977-)
Tyrannosaur *394*

Natalie Portman (1981-)
Hesher *159*
No Strings Attached *269*
Thor *373*
Your Highness *432*

Mark Povinelli
Water for Elephants *411*

Chris Pratt
Moneyball *257*
Take Me Home Tonight *362*

Alain Prost
Senna *325*

Lucy Punch (1977-)
Bad Teacher *27 *
A Good Old Fashioned
Orgy *140*
Take Me Home Tonight *362*

Dominic Purcell (1970-)
Killer Elite *218*
Straw Dogs *351*

Joe Putterlik
The Future *133*

Missi Pyle (1973-)
The Artist *19*

Maggie Q (1979-)
Priest *293*

Q-Tip
Beats, Rhymes & Life: The Trav-
els of a Tribe Called
Quest *32*

Dennis Quaid (1954-)
Footloose *127*
Soul Surfer *345*

Philip Quast (1957-)
The Devil's Double *93*

Aidan Quinn (1959-)
Unknown *400*

Francesco Quinn (1963-2011)
Transformers: Dark of the Moon
(V) *380*

Zachary Quinto (1977-)
Margin Call *238*
What's Your Number? *419*

Olivier Rabourdin
Of Gods and Men *270*

Daniel Radcliffe (1989-)
Harry Potter and the Deathly
Hallows: Part 2 *155*

Josh Radnor (1974-)
Happythankyoumoreplease *153*

Jamie Radtke
The Undefeated *398*

Denis Rafter
11-11-11 *113*

Miranda Raison (1980-)
My Week With Marilyn *263*

Charlotte Rampling (1945-)
Melancholia *246*

Laura Ramsey (1982-)
Kill the Irishman *216*

Zach Rand
The Woman *426*

James Ransone (1979-)
The Son of No One *344*

Noomi Rapace (1979-)
Sherlock Holmes: A Game of
Shadows *332*

Kseniya Rappoport (1974-)
The Double Hour *102*

Jackson Rathbone (1984-)
The Twilight Saga: Breaking
Dawn, Part 1 *392*

John Ratzenberger (1947-)
Cars 2 (V) *58*

Boris Ruiz
Julia's Eyes *200*

Geoffrey Rush (1951-)
Green Lantern (V) *143*
Pirates of the Caribbean: On
Stranger Tides *287*

Grayson Russell (1998-)
Diary of a Wimpy Kid: Rodrick
Rules *94*

Rene Russo (1954-)
Thor *373*

Amy Ryan (1970-)
Win Win *423*

Winona Ryder (1971-)
The Dilemma *96*

Markus Rygaard
In a Better World *185*

Daryl Sabara (1992-)
Spy Kids: All the Time in the
World in 4D *348*

Ludivine Sagnier (1979-)
The Devil's Double *93*

Thanapat Saisaymar
Uncle Boonmee Who Can Recall
His Past Lives *397 *

Zoe Saldana (1978-)
Colombiana *66*

Andy Samberg (1978-)
Friends With Benefits *128*
What's Your Number? *419*

Angus Sampson
Insidious *191*

Xavier Samuel
Anonymous *10*

Jay O. Sanders (1953-)
Green Lantern *143*

Adam Sandler (1966-)
Jack and Jill *201*
Just Go With It *210*
Zookeeper (V) *434*

Julian Sands (1958-)
The Girl With the Dragon Tattoo *135 *

Peter Sarsgaard (1971-)
Green Lantern *143*

Eddie Lee Sausage
Into the Abyss *195*

Souleymane Sy Savane
Machine Gun Preacher *233 *

Nadim Sawalha (1935-)
Incendies *190*

Tom Schanley (1961-)
A Better Life *39*

Richard Schiff (1959-)
Johnny English Reborn *205*

Taylor Schilling (1984-)
Atlas Shrugged: Part 1 *21*

Steve Schirripa (1958-)
Kill the Irishman *216*

Stella Schnabel
Miral *251*

Lauren Schneider
Creature *81*

Paul Schneider (1973-)
Water for Elephants *411*

Pablo Schreiber (1978-)
Happythankyoumoreplease *153*

Matt Schulze (1972-)
Fast Five *119 *

Til Schweiger (1963-)
New Year's Eve *267 *
The Three Musketeers *375*

Adam Scott (1973-)
Our Idiot Brother *274*

Dougray Scott (1965-)
My Week With Marilyn *263*

Tom Everett Scott (1970-)
Mars Needs Moms (V) *239*

Amy Sedaris (1961-)
Puss in Boots (V) *299*

Jason Segel (1980-)
Bad Teacher *27 *
The Muppets *261*

Ayrton Senna (1960-94)
Senna *325*

Rade Serbedzija (1946-)
In the Land of Blood and
Honey *187*

Andy Serkis (1964-)
The Adventures of Tintin
(V) *4*
Burke and Hare *51*
Rise of the Planet of the
Apes *312*

John Sessions (1953-)
The Iron Lady *196*

Corey Sevier (1984-)
Immortals *183*

Lea Seydoux (1985-)
Mission: Impossible—Ghost Protocol *253*

Amanda Seyfried (1985-)
In Time *188*
Red Riding Hood *306*

Tom Shadyac (1960-)
I Am *175 *

Alex Shaffer
Win Win *423*

Sarah Shahi (1980-)
I Don't Know How She Does
It *178*

Tony Shalhoub (1953-)
Cars 2 (V) *58*

Michael Shanks (1970-)
Red Riding Hood *306*

Michael Shannon (1974-)
Machine Gun Preacher *233 *
Take Shelter *364*

Fiona Shaw (1958-)
The Tree of Life *382*

Vinessa Shaw (1976-)
Puncture *297*

Alia Shawkat (1989-)
Cedar Rapids *61*

Lin Shaye (1944-)
A Good Old Fashioned
Orgy *140*
Insidious *191*

Martin Sheen (1940-)
The Double *100*
The Way *403*

Michael Sheen (1969-)
Beautiful Boy *33*
Midnight in Paris *248*
The Twilight Saga: Breaking
Dawn, Part 1 *392*

Marley Shelton (1974-)
The Mighty Macs *250*
Scream 4 *323*

Sam Shepard (1943-)
Blackthorn *46*

Rade Sherbedgia
See Rade Serbedzija

William Shimell
Certified Copy *63*

Martin Short (1950-)
Hoodwinked Too! Hood vs. Evil
(V) *164*

Alexander Siddig (1965-)
Miral *251*

Gabourney "Gabby" Sidibe
Tower Heist *378*

Alicia Silverstone (1976-)
The Art of Getting By *15*

Chelan Simmons (1982-)
Tucker & Dale vs. Evil *391*

J.K. Simmons (1955-)
Young Adult *431*

Johnny Simmons
The Conspirator *70*

Ty Simpkins
Insidious *191*

Nirut Sirichanya
The Hangover Part II *149*

Alexander Skarsgard (1976-)
Melancholia *246*
Straw Dogs *351*

George Takei (1940-)
Larry Crowne *223 *

Jeffrey Tambor (1944-)
Mr. Popper's Penguins *255*
Paul *281*
Win Win *423*

Catherine Tate (1968-)
Monte Carlo *259*

Channing Tatum (1980-)
The Dilemma *96*
The Eagle *111 *
The Son of No One *344*

Buck Taylor (1938-)
Cowboys & Aliens *78*

Noah Taylor (1969-)
Submarine *353*

Rachael Taylor (1984-)
The Darkest Hour *87*

Aimee Teegaarden
Prom *296*

Miles Teller
Footloose *127*

Juno Temple
Kaboom *215 *
The Three Musketeers *375*

David Tennant (1971-)
Fright Night *130*

Jon Tenney (1961-)
Green Lantern *143*

Alma Terzic
In the Land of Blood and
Honey *187*

Charlize Theron (1975-)
Young Adult *431*

Justin Theroux (1971-)
Your Highness *432*

Gene Therriault
The Undefeated *398*

David Thewlis (1963-)
Anonymous *10*
Harry Potter and the Deathly
Hallows: Part 2 *155*
War Horse *405 *

Olivia Thirlby (1986-)
The Darkest Hour *87*
No Strings Attached *269*

Ross Thomas
Soul Surfer *345*

Riley Thomas Stewart
The Beaver *35*

David Thompson
Win Win *423*

Emma Thompson (1959-)
Harry Potter and the Deathly
Hallows: Part 2 *155*

Jack Thompson (1940-)
Don't Be Afraid of the
Dark *99*

Kenan Thompson (1978-)
The Smurfs *(V)* *339*

Lea Thompson (1962-)
J. Edgar *199 *

Ulrich Thomsen (1963-)
In a Better World *185*
Season of the Witch *324*
The Thing *368*

Billy Bob Thornton (1955-)
Puss in Boots *(V)* *299*

Lucas Till (1990-)
Battle: Los Angeles *29*
X-Men: First Class *429 *

Justin Timberlake (1981-)
Bad Teacher *27 *
Friends With Benefits *128*
In Time *188*

Filippo Timi
The Double Hour *102*

Milos Timotijevic
In the Land of Blood and
Honey *187*

Analeigh Tipton
Crazy, Stupid, Love *79*

Tony Todd (1954-)
Final Destination 5 *124*

Marisa Tomei (1964-)
Crazy, Stupid, Love *79*
The Ides of March *181*
The Lincoln Lawyer *229*

Pip Torrens (1960-)
My Week With Marilyn *263*

Nico Tortorella
Scream 4 *323*
Trespass *384*

Gilles Tosello
Cave of Forgotten Dreams *60*

Glenn Erland Tosterud
Trollhunter *388*

Elodie Tougne
Jack and Jill *201*

Michelle Trachtenberg (1985-)
Take Me Home Tonight *362*

Luke Treadway
Attack the Block *23*

Danny Trejo (1944-)
Spy Kids: All the Time in the
World in 4D *348*
A Very Harold & Kumar 3D
Christmas *403*

Joe Lo Truglio
Paul *281*

Antonia Truppo
The Double Hour *102*

Stanley Tucci (1960-)
Captain America: The First
Avenger *55 *
Magic Trip: Ken Kesey's Search
for a Kool Place *(N)* *235*
Margin Call *238*

Alan Tudyk (1971-)
Transformers: Dark of the
Moon *380*
Tucker & Dale vs. Evil *391*

John Turturro (1957-)
Cars 2 *(V)* *58*
Transformers: Dark of the
Moon *380*

Desmond Tutu (1931-)
I Am *175 *

Liv Tyler (1977-)
Super *357*

Tyrese
See Tyrese Gibson

Cicely Tyson (1933-)
The Help *158*

Blair Underwood (1964-)
The Art of Getting By *15*

Carrie Underwood (1983-)
Soul Surfer *345*

Deborah Kara Unger
The Way *403*

Karl Urban (1972-)
Priest *293*

Usher
See Usher Raymond

Dilshad Vadsaria
30 Minutes or Less *371*

Wilmer Valderrama (1980-)
From Prada to Nada *131*
Larry Crowne *223 *

Jean-Claude Van Damme (1961-)
Kung Fu Panda 2 *220*

Luis van Rooten (1906-73)
Contagion *72*

Pierre van Vliet
Senna *325*

Yorick Van Wageningen (1964-)
The Girl With the Dragon Tat-
too *135 *
The Way *403*

Courtney B. Vance (1960-)
Final Destination 5 *124*

Janet Varney
Judy Moody and the Not Bummer Summer *206*

Michael Vartan (1968-)
Colombiana *66*

Katrina Vasilieva
  Tinker Tailor Soldier Spy *377*

Vince Vaughn (1970-)
  The Dilemma *96*

Edward Vedder
  Pearl Jam Twenty *283*

Alexa Vega (1988-)
  From Prada to Nada *131*
  Spy Kids: All the Time in the
    World in 4D *348*

Sofia Vergara (1972-)
  Happy Feet Two (V) *152*
  New Year's Eve *267 *
  The Smurfs (V) *339*

Veronika Vernadskaya
  The Darkest Hour *87*

Karin Viard (1966-)
  Potiche *292*

Pruitt Taylor Vince (1960-)
  Creature *81*
  Drive Angry *107*

Goran Visnjic (1972-)
  Beginners *36*
  The Girl With the Dragon Tat-
    too *135 *

Mike Vogel (1979-)
  The Help *158*
  What's Your Number? *419*

Max von Sydow (1929-)
  Extremely Loud and Incredibly
    Close *116*

Julian Wadham (1958-)
  The Iron Lady *196*

Donnie Wahlberg (1969-)
  Zookeeper *434*

Rhys Wakefield
  Sanctum *321 *

Christopher Walken (1943-)
  Kill the Irishman *216*

Paul Walker (1973-)
  Fast Five *119 *

Pernell Walker
  Pariah *278*

Sinqua Walls
  Shark Night 3D *331*

Julie Walters
  Gnomeo & Juliet *139*

Christoph Waltz
  Carnage *56*
  The Green Hornet *142*
  The Three Musketeers *375*
  Water for Elephants *411*

Zoe Wanamaker (1949-)
  My Week With Marilyn *263*

Patrick Warburton (1964-)
  Hoodwinked Too! Hood vs. Evil
    (V) *164*

Gemma Ward (1987-)
  Pirates of the Caribbean: On
    Stranger Tides *287*

Sophie Ward (1965-)
  Jane Eyre *203*

Jennifer Lynn Warren
  Creature *81*

David Warshofsky (1959-)
  The Future *133*

Mia Wasikowska (1989-)
  Albert Nobbs *6*
  Jane Eyre *203*
  Restless *309*

Emily Watson (1967-)
  Fireflies in the Garden *125*
  War Horse *405 *

Emma Watson (1990-)
  Harry Potter and the Deathly
    Hallows: Part 2 *155*
  My Week With Marilyn *263*

Naomi Watts (1968-)
  Dream House *103*
  J. Edgar *199 *

Tony Way
  The Girl With the Dragon Tat-
    too *135 *

Kim Wayans (1961-)
  Pariah *278*

Sigourney Weaver (1949-)
  Abduction *1 *
  Cedar Rapids *61*
  Paul *281*
  Rampart *301 *

Hugo Weaving (1959-)
  Captain America: The First
    Avenger *55 *
  Happy Feet Two (V) *152*
  Transformers: Dark of the Moon
    (V) *380*

Rachel Weisz (1971-)
  Dream House *103*
  The Whistleblower *421*

Frank Welker (1946-)
  The Smurfs (V) *339*
  Transformers: Dark of the Moon
    (V) *380*

Dominic West (1969-)
  Johnny English Reborn *205*

Ed Westwick (1987-)
  J. Edgar *199 *

Leigh Whannell (1977-)
  Insidious *191*

Shea Whigham (1969-)
  The Lincoln Lawyer *229*
  Take Shelter *364*

Jodie Whitaker
  Attack the Block *23*
  One Day *272*

Jaleel White (1976-)
  Judy Moody and the Not Bum-
    mer Summer *206*

Jarobi White
  Beats, Rhymes & Life: The Trav-
    els of a Tribe Called
    Quest *32*

Julie White
  Our Idiot Brother *274*
  Transformers: Dark of the
    Moon *380*

Isiah Whitlock, Jr. (1954-)
  Cedar Rapids *61*

Steve Whitmire (1959-)
  The Muppets (V) *261*

Daniel Lawrence Whitney
  See Larry the Cable Guy

Johnny Whitworth (1975-)
  Limitless *227*

Dianne Wiest (1948-)
  The Big Year *42*

Kristen Wiig (1973-)
  Bridesmaids *47*
  Paul *281*

Olivia Wilde (1984-)
  The Change-Up *64*
  Cowboys & Aliens *78*
  In Time *188*

Tom Wilkinson (1948-)
  Burke and Hare *51*
  The Conspirator *70*
  The Debt *88*
  The Green Hornet *142*
  Mission: Impossible—Ghost Pro-
    tocol *253*

Will I Am
  Rio (V) *311*

Ashley Williams
  Margin Call *238*
  Something Borrowed *342*

Frank Williams
  Senna *325*

JoBeth Williams (1953-)
  The Big Year *42*

Mark Williams (1959-)
  Albert Nobbs *6*

Michelle Williams (1980-)
  Meek's Cutoff *244*
  My Week With Marilyn *263*

Richard Williams
  Senna *325*

Robin Williams (1952-)
  Happy Feet Two (V) *152*

David Wilmot
  The Guard *145*

Lambert Wilson (1959-)
Of Gods and Men *270*

Owen Wilson (1968-)
The Big Year *42*
Cars 2 *(V)* *58*
Hall Pass *147 *
Midnight in Paris *248*

Patrick Wilson (1973-)
Insidious *191*
Young Adult *431*

Rainn Wilson (1968-)
Hesher *159*
Super *357*

Rita Wilson (1958-)
The Art of Getting By *15*
Larry Crowne *223 *

Kate Winslet (1975-)
Carnage *56*
Contagion *72*

Mary Elizabeth Winstead (1984-)
The Thing *368*

Ray Winstone (1957-)
Happy Feet Two *(V)* *152*
Hugo *169*
Rango *(V)* *303*

Jonathan Winters (1925-)
The Smurfs *(V)* *339*

Kristoffer Ryan Winters (1978-)
Judy Moody and the Not Bummer Summer *206*

Jessie Wiseman
Bellflower *38*

Rebecca Wisocky
Atlas Shrugged: Part 1 *21*

Reese Witherspoon (1976-)
Water for Elephants *411*

Collette Wolfe (1980-)
Young Adult *431*

Russell Wong (1963-)
Snow Flower and the Secret Fan *341*

Elijah Wood (1981-)
Happy Feet Two *(V)* *152*

Evan Rachel Wood (1987-)
The Ides of March *181*
The Conspirator *70*

Shailene Woodley
The Descendants *90*

James Woods (1947-)
Straw Dogs *351*

Kenny Wormald
Footloose *127*

Sam Worthington (1976-)
The Debt *88*
Texas Killing Fields *357*

Bonnie Wright (1991-)
Harry Potter and the Deathly Hallows: Part 2 *155*

Gunner Wright (1973-)
J. Edgar *199 *

Jeffrey Wright (1965-)
Extremely Loud and Incredibly Close *116*
Source Code *347*

Robin Wright
The Conspirator *70*
The Girl With the Dragon Tattoo *135 *
Moneyball *257*
Rampart *301 *

Ellen Wroe
Final Destination 5 *124*

Jiang Wu
Snow Flower and the Secret Fan *341*

Vivian Wu (1966-)
Snow Flower and the Secret Fan *341*

Daniel Wyllie
Sanctum *321 *

Jacob Wysocki
Terri *365*

Koji Yakusho (1956-)
13 Assassins *370*

Takayuki Yamada
13 Assassins *370*

Adam "MCA" Yauch (1964-)
Beats, Rhymes & Life: The Travels of a Tribe Called Quest *32*

Anton Yelchin (1989-)
The Beaver *35*
Fright Night *130*
Like Crazy *226*
The Smurfs *(V)* *339*

Ashlynn Yennie
The Human Centipede II (Full Sequence) *165*

Michelle Yeoh (1962-)
Kung Fu Panda 2 *220*

Ben York-Jones
Like Crazy *226*

Burt Young (1940-)
Win Win *423*

Jeong-hie Yun
Poetry *279*

Karl Yune
Real Steel *305*

Bridger Zadina (1994-)
Terri *365*

Billy Zane (1966-)
The Roommate *316*

Howard Zinn
I Am *175 *

Rob Zombie (1966-)
Super *(V)* *357*

Cozi Zuehlsdorff
Dolphin Tale *97*

Chris Zylka
Kaboom *215 *
Shark Night 3D *331*

Subject Index

3-D Movies

The Adventures of Tintin *4*
Arthur Christmas *18*
Cars 2 *58*
Conan the Barbarian *69*
The Darkest Hour *87*
Dolphin Tale *97*
Drive Angry *107*
Final Destination 5 *124*
The Green Hornet *142*
Green Lantern *143*
Happy Feet Two *152*
Harry Potter and the Deathly
    Hallows, Part 2 *155*
Hoodwinked Too! Hood vs.
    Evil *164*
Hugo *169*
Immortals *183*
Mars Needs Moms *239*
Pirates of the Caribbean: On
    Stranger Tides *287*
Priest *293*
Puss in Boots *299*
Rio *311*
Sanctum *321 *
Shark Night 3D *331*
The Smurfs *339*
Spy Kids: All the Time in the
    World in 4D *348*
Thor *373*
The Three Musketeers *375*
Transformers: Dark of the
    Moon *380*
A Very Harold & Kumar Christ-
    mas *403*

Action-Adventure

Abduction *1 *

Alvin and the Chipmunks: Chip-
    wrecked *8*
Battle: Los Angeles *29*
Bellflower *38*
Contagion *72*
The Debt *88*
The Devil's Double *93*
The Double *100*
The Double Hour *102*
Drive *104*
Drive Angry *107*
The Eagle *111 *
11-11-11 *113*
Fast Five *119 *
The Green Hornet *142*
Hanna *150*
Hugo *169*
Immortals *183*
Kill the Irishman *216*
Killer Elite *218*
Limitless *227*
Machine Gun Preacher *233 *
The Mechanic *243*
Mission: Impossible—Ghost Pro-
    tocol *253*
Priest *293*
Puss in Boots *299*
Real Steel *305*
Sanctum *321 *
Sherlock Holmes: A Game of
    Shadows *332*
Source Code *347*
13 Assassins *370*
30 Minutes or Less *371*
The Three Musketeers *375*
Unknown *400*
Warrior *409*
X-Men: First Class *429 *

Action-Comedy

Attack the Block *23*
Johnny English Reborn *205*
Pirates of the Caribbean: On
    Stranger Tides *287*
Season of the Witch *324*
Your Highness *432*

Adapted from a Book

The Adjustment Bureau *2*
From Prada to Nada *131*
The Three Musketeers *375*
Tinker Tailor Soldier Spy *377*

Adapted from a Fairy Tale

Hoodwinked Too! Hood vs.
    Evil *164*
Puss in Boots *299*

Adapted from a Play

Coriolanus *74*
Gnomeo & Juliet *139*
The Ides of March *181*
Incendies *190*
Potiche *292*
Restless *309*

Adapted from a Story

Everything Must Go *114*

Adapted from Comics

The Adventures of Tintin *4*
The Smurfs *339*

Adapted from Memoirs or
Diaries

The Big Year *42*
Higher Ground *161*

Business or Industry
Atlas Shrugged: Part 1 *21*
Margin Call *238*

Cannibalism
The Woman *426*

Carnivals or Circuses
Passion Play *280*
Water for Elephants *411*

Cats
The Future *133*
Puss in Boots *299*
The Smurfs *339*

Chicago
The Interrupters *193*
Louder Than a Bomb *231*
Source Code *347*
Transformers: Dark of the
Moon *380*
Trust *389*

Child Abuse
Fireflies in the Garden *125*

Childhood
Dolphin Tale *97*
Extremely Loud and Incredibly
Close *116*
Hugo *169*
Judy Moody and the Not Bum-
mer Summer *206*
Life, Above All *225*
Paranormal Activity 3 *277 *
A Separation *327*

China
Kung Fu Panda 2 *220*
Snow Flower and the Secret
Fan *341*

Christianity
Higher Ground *161*

Christmas
Arthur Christmas *18*
A Very Harold & Kumar Christ-
mas *403*

Civil War
The Conspirator *70*

Clergymen
Footloose *127*
Red State *308*

Clothing or Fashion
Bill Cunningham New York *44*

College
Kaboom *215 *
Larry Crowne *223 *
The Roommate *316*

Coma
Insidious *191*
Snow Flower and the Secret
Fan *341*

Comedy
Burke & Hare *51*
From Prada to Nada *131*
Monte Carlo *259*
Prom *296*
Submarine *353*
Super *357*
Young Adult *431*

Comedy-Drama
The Beaver *35*
Everything Must Go *114*
50/50 *120*
Happythankyoumoreplease *153*
Take Me Home Tonight *362*

Coming of Age
The Art of Getting By *15*
Pariah *278*
Submarine *353*
Terri *365*
The Tree of Life *382*

Concert Films
Glee: The 3D Concert
Movie *137*
Pearl Jam Twenty *283*

**Conspiracies or Conspiracy
Theories**
Apollo 18 *13*
The Girl With the Dragon Tat-
too *135 *

Contract Killers
Hanna *150*
Johnny English Reborn *205*
Killer Elite *218*
The Mechanic *243*

Crime Drama
Fast Five *119 *
The Girl With the Dragon Tat-
too *135 *
I Saw the Devil *179*
The Lincoln Lawyer *229*
Rampart *301 *
The Son of No One *344*
Texas Killing Fields *367*

Trespass *384*
The Woman *426*

Crime or Criminals
Drive *104*
Trespass *384*

Cults
Drive Angry *107*
Kaboom *215 *
Martha Marcy May Mar-
lene *241*

Dance
Footloose *127*

Deadly Viruses
Contagion *72*

Death & the Afterlife
11-11-11 *113*
Final Destination 5 *124*
Into the Abyss *195*

Demons or Wizards
Harry Potter and the Deathly
Hallows, Part 2 *155*
Paranormal Activity 3 *277 *
The Smurfs *339*
Your Highness *432*

Dentists or Dentistry
Horrible Bosses *167*

Detroit
Vanishing on 7th Street *401*

Diseases or Illness
50/50 *120*
Poetry *289*

Divorce
Crazy, Stupid, Love. *79*
Just Go With It *210*

Doctors
The Debt *88*
The Skin I Live In *335*
The Ward *407*

Doctors or Nurses
Attack the Block *23*
Burke & Hare *51*
Contagion *72*
In a Better World *185*
Unknown *400*

Documentary Films
Beats, Rhymes and Life: The
Travels of a Tribe Called
Quest *32*

Fires

Bellflower *38*

Flashback

Blackthorn *46*
The Debt *88*
Fireflies in the Garden *125*
Green Lantern *143*
Incendies *190*
Jane Eyre *203*
Martha Marcy May Marlene *241*
Potiche *292*
The Skin I Live In *335*
Snow Flower and the Secret Fan *341*
The Son of No One *344*
Trespass *384*
The Way *413*
W.E. *414*
X-Men: First Class *429 *

Folklore or Legends

Red Riding Hood *306*
Thor *373*
The Troll Hunter *388*

Food or Food Industry

The Perfect Host *286*
The Trip *386*

Foreign: Australian

Sleeping Beauty *337*

Foreign: Belgian

Certified Copy *63*
The Devil's Double *93*
Potiche *292*

Foreign: British

Arthur Christmas *18*
Attack the Block *23*
Burke & Hare *51*
The Debt *88*
Harry Potter and the Deathly Hallows, Part 2 *155*
The Human Centipede 2 (Full Sequence) *171*
Jane Eyre *203*
Johnny English Reborn *205*
Paul *281*
Project Nim *294*
Senna *325*
Shame *329*
Submarine *353*
13 Assassins *370*
Tinker Tailor Soldier Spy *377*
The Trip *386*
Tyrannosaur *394*
Uncle Boonmee Who Can Recall His Past Lives *397 *
We Need to Talk About Kevin *418*

Foreign: Canadian

Incendies *190*
Tucker & Dale vs. Evil *391*
The Whistleblower *421*

Foreign: Danish

In a Better World *185*
Melancholia *246*

Foreign: French

The Artist *19*
Certified Copy *63*
Incendies *190*
Kaboom *215 *
Melancholia *246*
Miral *251*
Of Gods and Men *270*
Potiche *292*
Uncle Boonmee Who Can Recall His Past Lives *397 *

Foreign: German

The Future *133*
Life, Above All *225*
Melancholia *246*
The Whistleblower *421*

Foreign: Indian

Miral *251*

Foreign: Iranian

A Separation *327*

Foreign: Irish

Albert Nobbs *6*
The Guard *145*

Foreign: Isreali

Miral *251*

Foreign: Italian

Certified Copy *63*
The Double Hour *102*
Miral *251*

Foreign: Japanese

13 Assassins *370*

Foreign: Korean

I Saw the Devil *179*
Poetry *289*

Foreign: Norwegian

Trollhunter *388*

Foreign: South African

Life, Above All *225*

Foreign: Spanish

Blackthorn *46*
Julia's Eyes *208*

Foreign: Spanish

Melancholia *246*
The Skin I Live In *335*
Uncle Boonmee Who Can Recall His Past Lives *397 *

Foreign: Swiss

Film Socialisme *122*

Forests or Trees

Winnie the Pooh *425*

Framed

In Time *188*
Mission: Impossible—Ghost Protocol *253*

France

Cave of Forgotten Dreams *60*
War Horse *405 *

Friends or Friendship

Bellflower *38*
The Change-Up *64*
Crazy, Stupid, Love. *79*
The Dilemma *96*
50/50 *120*
A Good Old Fashioned Orgy *140*
Hall Pass *147 *
The Hangover, Part 2 *149*
Hesher *159*
Horrible Bosses *167*
Paul *281*
The Trip *386*
Tucker & Dale vs. Evil *391*
A Very Harold & Kumar Christmas *403*

Fugitives

In Time *188*
Paul *281*

Funerals

Fireflies in the Garden *125*

Gays or Lesbians

Beginners *36*
Colombiana *66*
Kaboom *215 *
Our Idiot Brother *274*
Pariah *278*

Gender Confusion

Big Mommas: Like Father, Like Son *41*

Genetics

Rise of the Planet of the
Apes *312*
X-Men: First Class *429 *

Genre Parody

Johnny English Reborn *205*
Tucker & Dale vs. Evil *391*

Ghosts or Spirits

Insidious *191*
Uncle Boonmee Who Can Recall
His Past Lives *397 *
The Ward *407*

Great Britain

The Iron Lady *196*
The Trip *386*
W.E. *414*

Hackers

The Girl With the Dragon Tattoo *135 *

Handicapped

Beastly *30*
The Debt *88*
Dolphin Tale *97*
Passion Play *280*
Soul Surfer *345*

Hawaii

The Descendants *90*
Just Go With It *210*
Soul Surfer *345*

Heists

Tower Heist *378*

Hispanic Culture

From Prada to Nada *131*

Holidays

Hop *165*
Take Me Home Tonight *362*

Homeless

Hobo With a Shotgun *162*

Honeymoons

The Twilight Saga: Breaking
Dawn, Part 1 *392*

Hong Kong

Contagion *72*

Horror

Don't Be Afraid of the
Dark *99*
Dream House *103*
11-11-11 *113*
Insidious *191*
Jane Eyre *203*
Paranormal Activity 3 *277 *
The Rite *314*
Scream 4 *323*
The Skin I Live In *335*
The Twilight Saga: Breaking
Dawn, Part 1 *392*
Vanishing on 7th Street *401*

Horror Comedy

Burke & Hare *51*
Dylan Dog: Dead of
Night *108*
Fright Night *130*
The Troll Hunter *388*
Tucker & Dale vs. Evil *391*

Horses

Buck *48*
War Horse *405 *

Hospitals or Medicine

Insidious *191*

Hostages

The Human Centipede 2 (Full
Sequence) *171*
The Perfect Host *286*
Red State *308*
Trespass *384*

Hotels or Motels

Albert Nobbs *6*
Cedar Rapids *61*
The Double Hour *102*

Houston

Puncture *297*

Infants

Spy Kids 4: All the Time in the
World *348*

Insurance

Cedar Rapids *61*

Inteligence Service Agencies

The Double *100*
X-Men: First Class *429 *

Interviews

Bill Cunningham New York *44*
The People vs. George Lu-
cas *284*
Project Nim *294*
Senna *325*
Tabloid *361 *

Inventors or Inventions

Atlas Shrugged: Part 1 *21*

Ireland

The Guard *145*

Islam

In the Land of Blood and
Honey *187*
Of Gods and Men *270*

Islands

Alvin and the Chipmunks: Chipwrecked *8*

Isreal

The Debt *88*

Italy

Certified Copy *63*

Japan

13 Assassins *370*

Journalism

The Adventures of Tintin *4*
The Girl With the Dragon Tat-
too *135 *
The Rum Diary *317*
The Son of No One *344*

Kidnappers or Kidnappings

Mars Needs Moms *239*
Of Gods and Men *270*
Priest *293*
Super 8 *358*
The Woman *426*
Your Highness *432*

Labor or Unions

Potiche *292*

Law or Lawyers

The Conspirator *70*
Hobo With a Shotgun *162*
I Saw the Devil *179*
The Lincoln Lawyer *229*
Puncture *297*
A Separation *327*
Something Borrowed *342*
Win Win *423*

Live Action/Animation Combinations

Alvin and the Chipmunks: Chip-
wrecked *8*
Hop *165*
The Smurfs *339*

Writers

Anonymous *10*
Colombiana *66*
11-11-11 *113*
Fireflies in the Garden *125*
The Help *158*
Limitless *227*
Our Idiot Brother *274*
Young Adult *431*

Zombies

Dylan Dog: Dead of
Night *108*

Zoos

We Bought a Zoo *416*
Zookeeper *434*

Title Index

This cumulative index is an alphabetical list of all films covered in the volumes of the *Magill's Cinema Annual.* Film titles are indexed on a word-by-word basis, including articles and prepositions. English leading articles (A, An, The) are ignored, as are foreign leading articles (El, Il, La, Las, Le, Les, Los). Acronyms appear alphabetically as if regular words. Common abbreviations in titles file as if they are spelled out. Proper names in titles are alphabetized beginning with the individual's first name. Titles with numbers are alphabetized as if the numbers were spelled out. When numeric titles gather in close proximity to each other, the titles will be arranged in a low-to-high numeric sequence. Films reviewed in this volume are cited in bold with an Arabic number indicating the page number on which the review begins; films reviewed in past volumes are cited with the *Annual* year in which the review was published. Original and alternate titles are cross-referenced to the American release title. Titles of retrospective films are followed by the year, in brackets, of their original release.

A

A corps perdu. *See* Straight for the Heart.

A. I.: *Artificial Intelligence* 2002

A la Mode (Fausto) 1995

A Lot Like Love 2006

A Ma Soeur. *See* Fat Girl.

A nos amours 1984

Abandon 2003

ABCD 2002

Abduction pg. 1

Abgeschminkt! *See* Making Up!.

About a Boy 2003

About Adam 2002

About Last Night... 1986

About Schmidt 2003

Above the Law 1988

Above the Rim 1995

Abrazos rotos, Los. *See* Broken Embraces.

Abre Los Ojos. *See* Open Your Eyes.

Abril Despedacado. *See* Behind the Sun.

Absence of Malice 1981

Absolute Beginners 1986

Absolute Power 1997

Absolution 1988

Abyss, The 1989

Accepted 2007

Accidental Tourist, The 1988

Accompanist, The 1993

Accordeur de tremblements de terre, L'. *See* Piano Tuner of Earthquakes, The.

Accused, The 1988

Ace in the Hole [1951] 1986, 1991

Ace Ventura: Pet Detective 1995

Ace Ventura: When Nature Calls 1996

Aces: Iron Eagle III 1992

Acid House, The 2000

Acqua e sapone. *See* Water and Soap.

Across the Tracks 1991

Across the Universe 2008

Acting on Impulse 1995

Action Jackson 1988

Actress 1988

Adam 2010

Adam Sandler's 8 Crazy Nights 2003

Adam's Rib [1950] 1992

Adaptation 2003

Addams Family, The 1991

Addams Family Values 1993

Addicted to Love 1997

Addiction, The 1995

Addition, L'. *See* Patsy, The.

Adjo, Solidaritet. *See* Farewell Illusion.

Adjuster, The 1992

Adjustment Bureau, The pg. 2

Adolescente, L' 1982

Adoration 2010

Adventureland 2010

Big Momma's House 2 2007

Big Mommas: Like Father, Like Son pg. 41

Big Night 1996

Big One, The 1999

Big Picture, The 1989

Big Shots 1987

Big Squeeze, The 1996

Big Tease, The 2001

Big Time 1988

Big Top Pee-Wee 1988

Big Town, The 1987

Big Trouble (Cassavetes) 1986

Big Trouble (Sonnenfeld) 2003

Big Trouble in Little China 1986

Big Year, The pg. 42

Biker Boyz 2004

Bikur Ha-Tizmoret. *See* Band's Visit, The.

Bill and Ted's Bogus Journey 1991

Bill and Ted's Excellent Adventure 1989

Billy Bathgate 1991

Bill Cunningham New York pg. 44

Billy Budd [1962] 1981

Billy Elliot 2001

Billy Madison 1995

Billy's Hollywood Screen Kiss 1999

Biloxi Blues 1988

Bin-jip. *See* 3-Iron.

Bingo 1991

BINGO 2000

Bio-Dome 1996

Bird 1988

Bird on a Wire 1990

Birdcage, The 1996

Birdy 1984

Birth 2005

Birth of a Nation, The [1915] 1982, 1992

Birthday Girl 2003

Bitter Moon 1995

Bittere Ernte. *See* Angry Harvest.

Biutiful 2011

Bix (1990) 1995

Bix (1991) 1995

Bizet's Carmen 1984

Black and White 2001

Black Beauty 1995

Black Book 2008

Black Cat, The (Fulci) 1984

Black Cat (Shin) 1993

Black Cat, White Cat 2000

Black Cauldron, The 1985

Black Christmas 2007

Black Dahlia, The 2007

Black Dog 1999

Black Dynamite 2010

Black Harvest 1995

Black Hawk Down 2002

Black Joy 1986

Black Knight 2002

Black Lizard 1995

Black Mask 2000

Black Moon Rising 1986

Black Peter [1964] 1985

Black Rain (Imamura) 1990

Black Rain (Scott) 1989

Black Robe 1991

Black Sheep 1996

Black Snake Moan 2008

Black Stallion Returns, The 1983

Black Swan 2011

Black Widow 1987

Blackboard Jungle [1955] 1986, 1992

Blackout 1988

Blackout. *See* I Like It Like That.

Blackthorn pg. 46

Blade 1999

Blade II 2003

Blade Runner 1982

Blade: Trinity 2005

Blades of Glory 2008

Blair Witch Project, The 2000

Blame It on Night 1984

Blame It on Rio 1984

Blame It on the Bellboy 1992

Blank Check 1995

Blankman 1995

Blassblaue Frauenschrift, Eine. *See* Woman's Pale Blue Handwriting, A.

Blast 'em 1995

Blast from the Past 2000

Blaze 1989

Bless the Child 2001

Bless Their Little Hearts 1991

Blessures Assassines, Les. *See* Murderous Maids.

Blind Date 1987

Blind Fairies *See* Ignorant Fairies

Blind Fury 1990

Blind Side, The 2010

Blind Swordsman: Zatoichi, The. *See* Zatoichi.

Blindness 2009

Blink 1995

Bliss 1986

Bliss 1997

Blob, The 1988

Blood and Chocolate 2008

Blood and Concrete 1991

Blood and Wine 1997

Blood Diamond 2007

Blood Diner 1987

Blood in Blood Out 1995

Blood, Guts, Bullets and Octane 2001

Blood Money 1988

Blood of Heroes, The 1990

Blood Salvage 1990

Blood Simple 1985

Blood Wedding 1982

Blood Work 2003

Bloodfist 1989

Bloodhounds of Broadway 1989

BloodRayne 2007

Bloodsport 1988

Bloody Sunday 2003

Blow 2002

Blow Dry 2002

Blow Out 1981

Blown Away 1995

Blue (Jarman) 1995

Blue (Kieslowski) 1993

Blue Car 2004

Blue Chips 1995

Blue City 1986

Blue Crush 2003

Blue Desert 1991

Blue Ice 1995

Blue Iguana, The 1988

Blue in the Face 1995

Blue Kite, The 1995

Blue Monkey 1987

Blue Skies Again 1983

Blue Sky 1995

Blue Steel 1990

Blue Streak 2000

Blue Thunder 1983

Blue Valentine 2011

Blue Velvet 1986

Blue Villa, The 1995

Bluebeard's Eighth Wife [1938] 1986

Blues Brothers 2000 1999

Blues Lahofesh Hagadol. *See* Late Summer Blues.

Boat, The. *See* Boot, Das.

Boat is Full, The 1982

Boat That Rocked, The. *See* Pirate Radio.

Boat Trip 2004

Bob le Flambeur [1955] 1983

Bob Marley: Time Will Tell. *See* Time Will Tell.

Bob Roberts 1992

Bobby 2007

Bobby Jones: Stroke of Genius 2005

Bodies, Rest, and Motion 1993

Body, The 2002

Body and Soul 1982

Body Chemistry 1990

Body Double 1984

Body Heat 1981

Body Melt 1995

Body of Evidence 1993

Body of Lies 2009

Body Parts 1991

Body Rock 1984

Body Shots 2000

Body Slam 1987

Body Snatchers 1995

Bodyguard, The 1992

Bodyguards, The. *See* La Scorta.

Boesman & Lena 2001

Bogus 1996

Boheme, La [1926] 1982

Boiler Room 2001

Boiling Point 1993

Bolero (Derek) 1984

Bolero (Lelouch) 1982

Bollywood/Hollywood 2003

Bolt 2009

Bom Yeorum Gaeul Gyeoul Geurigo…Bom. *See* Spring, Summer, Autumn, Winter…And Spring.

Bon Plaisir, Le 1984

Bon Voyage 1995

Bon Voyage (Rappenaeau) 2005

Bone Collector, The 2000

Bonfire of the Vanities, The 1990

Bongwater 1999

Bonne Route. *See* Latcho Drom.

Boogeyman 2006

Boogie Nights 1997

Book of Eli, The 2011

Book of Love 1991

Book of Shadows: Blair Witch 2 2001

Boomerang 1992

Boondock Saints: All Saints Day, The 2010

Boost, The 1988

Boot, Das 1982

Boot Ist Voll, Das. *See* Boat Is Full, The.

Bootmen 2001

Booty Call 1997

Booye Kafoor, Atre Yas. *See* Smell of Camphor, Fragrance of Jasmine.

Bopha! 1993

Borat: Cultural Learnings of America for Make Benefit Glorious Nation of Kazakhstan 2007

Border, The 1982

Boricua's Bond 2001

Born American 1986

Born in East L.A. 1987

Born Into Brothels: Calcutta's Red Light Kids 2006

Born on the Fourth of July 1989

Born Romantic 2002

Born to Be a Star. *See* Bucky Larson: Born to Be a Star.

Born to Be Wild 1996

Born to Race 1988

Born Yesterday 1993

Borrowers, The 1999

Borstal Boy 2003

Bose Zellen. *See* Free Radicals.

Bossa Nova 2001

Bostonians, The 1984

Bottle Rocket 1996

Bottle Shock 2009

Boum, La 1983

Bounce 2001

Bound 1996

Bound and Gagged 1993

Bound by Honor 1993

Bounty, The 1984

Bounty Hunter, The 2011

Bourne Identity, The 2003

Bourne Supremacy, The 2005

Bourne Ultimatum, The 2008

Bowfinger 2000

Box, The 2010

Box of Moonlight 1997

Boxer, The 1997

Boxer and Death, The 1988

Boxing Helena 1993

Boy in Blue, The 1986

Boy in the Striped Pajamas, The 2009

Boy Who Could Fly, The 1986

Boy Who Cried Bitch, The 1991

Boyfriend School, The. *See* Don't Tell Her It's Me.

Boyfriends 1997

Boyfriends and Girlfriends 1988

Boynton Beach Bereavement Club, The. *See* Boynton Beach Club, The.

Boynton Beach Club, The 2007

Boys 1996

Chase, The 1995

Chasers 1995

Chasing Amy 1988

Chasing Liberty 2005

Chasing Papi 2004

Chateau, The 2003

Chateau de ma mere, Le. *See* My Mother's Castle.

Chattahoochee 1990

Chattanooga Choo Choo 1984

Che 2010

Cheap Shots 1991

Cheaper by the Dozen 2004

Cheaper by the Dozen 2 2006

Cheatin' Hearts 1993

Check Is in the Mail, The 1986

Checking Out 1989

Cheech & Chong Still Smokin' 1983

Cheech & Chong's The Corsican Brothers 1984

Cheetah 1989

Chef in Love, A 1997

Chelsea Walls 2003

Chere Inconnue. *See* I Sent a Letter to My Love.

Chéri 2010

Cherish 2003

Cherry Orchard, The 2003

Cherry Pink. *See* Just Looking.

Chevre, La. *See* Goat, The.

Chi bi. *See* Red Cliff.

Chicago 2003

Chicago Joe and the Showgirl 1990

Chicago 10 2009

Chicken Hawk: Men Who Love Boys 1995

Chicken Little 2006

Chicken Run 2001

Chief Zabu 1988

Chihwaseon: Painted Fire 2003

Child, The 2007

Child's Play 1988

Child's Play II 1990

Child's Play III 1991

Children of a Lesser God 1986

Children of Heaven, The 2000

Children of Men 2007

Children of Nature 1995

Children of the Corn II 1993

Children of the Revolution 1997

Chile, la Memoria Obstinada. *See* Chile, Obstinate Memory.

Chile, Obstinate Memory 1999

Chill Factor 2000

Chilled in Miami. *See* New In Town.

Chimes at Midnight. *See* Falstaff.

China Cry 1990

China Girl 1987

China Moon 1995

China, My Sorrow 1995

China Syndrome, The [1979] 1988

Chinese Box 1999

Chinese Ghost Story II, A 1990

Chinese Ghost Story III, A 1991

Chipmunk Adventure, The 1987

Chloe 2011

Chocolat (Denis) 1989

Chocolat (Hallstrom) 2001

Chocolate War, The 1988

Choke 2009

Choke Canyon 1986

Choose Me 1984, 1985

Chopper 2002

Chopper Chicks in Zombie Town 1991

Chopping Mall 1986

Choristes, Les. *See* Chorus, The.

Chorus, The 2006

Chorus Line, A 1985

Chorus of Disapproval, A 1989

Chosen, The 1982

Christine 1983

Christine F. 1982

Christmas Carol, A 2010

Christmas Story, A 1983

Christmas Tale, A 2009

Christmas with the Kranks 2005

Christopher Columbus: The Discovery 1992

Chronicles of Narnia: Prince Caspian, The 2009

Chronicles of Narnia: The Lion, the Witch and the Wardrobe, The 2006

Chronicles of Narnia: The Voyage of the Dawn Treader, The 2011

Chronicles of Riddick, The 2005

Chronos 1985

Chuck & Buck 2001

Chuck Berry: Hail! Hail! Rock 'n' Roll 1987

C.H.U.D. 1984

Chungking Express 1996

Chunhyang 2001

Chutney Popcorn 2001

Ciao, Professore! 1995

Cidade des homens. *See* City of Men.

Cider House Rules, The 2000

Cienaga, La 2002

Cinderella Man 2006

Cinderella Story, A 2005

Cinema Paradiso 1989

Cinema Verite: Defining the Moment 2001

Circle, The 2002

Circle of Deceit 1982

Circle of Friends 1995

Circuitry Man 1990

Cirque du Freak: The Vampire's Assistant 2010

Citizen Ruth 1996

Citta della donne, La. *See* City of Women.

City by the Sea 2003

City Girl, The 1984

City Hall 1996

City Heat 1984

City Limits 1985

City of Angels 1999

City of Ember 2009

City of Ghosts 2004

City of God 2004

City of Hope 1991

City of Industry 1997

City Island 2011

City of Joy 1992

City of Lost Children 1996

City of Men 2009

Dance Maker, The 2000

Dance of the Damned 1989

Dance with a Stranger 1985

Dance with Me 1999

Dancer in the Dark 2001

Dancer, Texas Pop. 81 1999

Dancer Upstairs, The 2004

Dancers 1987

Dances with Wolves 1990

Dancing at Lughnasa 1999

Dancing in the Dark 1986

Dangerous Beauty 1999

Dangerous Game (Ferrara) 1995

Dangerous Game (Hopkins) 1988

Dangerous Ground 1997

Dangerous Liaisons 1988

Dangerous Lives of Altar Boys, The 2003

Dangerous Love 1988

Dangerous Method, A pg. 85

Dangerous Minds 1995

Dangerous Moves 1985

Dangerous Woman, A 1993

Dangerously Close 1986

Daniel 1983

Danny Boy 1984

Danny Deckchair 2005

Danny the Dog. *See* Unleashed.

Dante's Peak 1997

Danton 1983

Danzon 1992

Daredevil 2004

Darfur Now 2008

Darjeeling Limited, The 2008

Dark Backward, The 1991

Dark Before Dawn 1988

Dark Blue 2004

Dark Blue World 2002

Dark City

Dark Crystal, The 1982

Dark Days 2001

Dark Eyes 1987

Dark Half, The 1993

Dark Knight, The 2009

Dark Obsession 1991

Dark of the Night 1986

Dark Star [1975] 1985

Dark Water 2006

Dark Wind, The 1995

Darkest Hour, The pg. 87

Darkman 1990

Darkness 2005

Darkness, Darkness. *See* South of Reno.

Darkness Falls 2004

D.A.R.Y.L. 1985

Date Movie 2007

Date Night 2011

Date with an Angel 1987

Daughter of the Nile 1988

Daughters of the Dust 1992

Daughters of the Sun 2001

Dauntaun Herozu. *See* Hope and Pain.

Dave 1993

Dave Chappelle's Block Party 2007

Dawn of the Dead 2005

Day After Tomorrow, The 2005

Day I Became a Woman, The 2002

Day in October, A 1992

Day of the Dead 1985

Day the Earth Stood Still, The 2009

Daybreakers 2011

Dayereh. *See* Circle, The.

Daylight 1996

Days of Glory 2008

Days of Thunder 1990

Days of Wine and Roses [1962] 1988

Daytrippers, The 1997

Dazed and Confused 1993

D.C. Cab 1983

De Eso No Se Habla. *See* I Don't Want to Talk About It.

De-Lovely 2005

De Poolse Bruid. *See* Polish Bride, The.

Dead, The 1987

Dead Again 1991

Dead Alive 1993

Dead Bang 1989

Dead Calm 1989

Dead Heat 1988

Dead Man 1996

Dead Man on Campus 1999

Dead Man Walking 1995

Dead Man's Curve 2000

Dead Men Don't Wear Plaid 1982

Dead of Winter 1987

Dead Poets Society 1989

Dead Pool, The 1988

Dead Presidents 1995

Dead Ringers 1988

Dead Silence 2008

Dead Snow 2010

Dead Space 1991

Dead Women in Lingerie 1991

Dead Zone, The 1983

Dead-end Drive-in 1986

Deadfall 1995

Deadline 1987

Deadly Eyes 1982

Deadly Friend 1986

Deadly Illusion 1987

Deadly Intent 1988

Deal, The 2006

Deal of the Century 1983

Dealers 1989

Dear American 1987

Dear Diary. *See* Caro Diario.

Dear Frankie 2006

Dear God 1996

Dear John 2011

Death and the Maiden 1995

Death at a Funeral 2008

Death at a Funeral 2011

Death Becomes Her 1992

Death Before Dishonor 1987

Death of a Soldier 1986

Death of an Angel 1986

Death of Mario Ricci, The 1985

Death of Mr. Lazarescu, The 2007

Death Proof. *See* Grindhouse.

Death Race 2009

Death Sentence 2008

Death to Smoochy 2003

Death Valley 1982

Dick Tracy 1990

Dickie Roberts: Former Child Star 2004

Did You Hear About the Morgans? 2010

Die Another Day 2003

Die Fetten Jahre sind vorbei. *See* Edukators, The.

Die Hard 1988

Die Hard II 1990

Die Hard with a Vengeance 1995

Die Mommie Die! 2004

Die Story Von Monty Spinneratz. *See* A Rat's Story.

Dieu Est Grand, Je Suis Tout Petite. *See* God Is Great, I'm Not.

Different for Girls 1997

DIG! 2005

Digging to China 1999

Diggstown 1992

Dilemma, The pg. 96

Dim Sum 1985

Dimanche a la Campagne, Un. *See* A Sunday in the Country.

Diminished Capacity 2009

Diner 1982

Dinner for Schmucks 2011

Dinner Game, The 2000

Dinner Rush 2002

Dinosaur 2001

Dinosaur's Story, A. *See* We're Back.

Dirty Cop No Donut 2003

Dirty Dancing 1987

Dirty Dancing: Havana Nights 2005

Dirty Dishes 1983

Dirty Harry [1971] 1982

Dirty Love 2006

Dirty Pretty Things 2004

Dirty Rotten Scoundrels 1988

Dirty Shame, A 2005

Dirty Work 1999

Disappearance of Alice Creed, The 2011

Disappearance of Garcia Lorca, The 1997

Disaster Movie 2009

Disclosure 1995

Discreet Charm of the Bourgeoisie, The [1972] 2001

Discrete, La 1992

Disgrace 2010

Dish, The 2002

Disney's A Christmas Carol. *See* Christmas Carol, A.

Disney's Teacher's Pet 2005

Disney's The Kid 2001

Disorderlies 1987

Disorganized Crime 1989

Disraeli [1929] 1981

Distant Harmony 1988

Distant Thunder 1988

Distant Voices, Still Lives 1988

Distinguished Gentleman, The 1992

District 9 2010

District 13: Ultimatum 2011

Divo, Il 2010

Distribution of Lead, The 1989

Disturbed 1990

Disturbia 2008

Disturbing Behavior 1999

Diva 1982

Divan 2005

Divided Love. *See* Maneuvers.

Divided We Fall 2002

Divine Intervention: A Chronicle of Love and Pain 2004

Divine Secrets of the Ya-Ya Sisterhood, The 2003

Diving Bell and the Butterfly, The 2008

Diving In 1990

Divorce, Le 2004

Divorcee, The [1930] 1981

Djomeh 2002

Do or Die 1995

Do the Right Thing 1989

D.O.A. 1988

DOA: Dead or Alive 2008

Doc Hollywood 1991

Doc's Kingdom 1988

Docteur Petiot 1995

Doctor, The 1991

Dr. Agaki 2000

Doctor and the Devils, The 1985

Dr. Bethune 1995

Dr. Butcher, M.D. 1982

Doctor Detroit 1983

Dr. Dolittle 1999

Dr. Dolittle 2 2002

Dr. Giggles 1992

Dr. Jekyll and Ms. Hyde 1995

Dr. Petiot. *See* Docteur Petiot.

Dr. Seuss' Horton Hears a Who! 2009

Dr. Seuss' How the Grinch Stole Christmas 2001

Dr. Seuss' The Cat in the Hat 2004

Dr. Sleep. *See* Close Your Eyes.

Dr. T and the Women 2001

Doctor Zhivago [1965] 1990

Dodgeball: A True Underdog Story 2005

Dog of Flanders, A 2000

Dog Park 2000

Dogfight 1991

Dogma 2000

Dogtooth 2011

Dogville 2005

Doin' Time on Planet Earth 1988

Dolls 1987

Dolls 2006

Dolly Dearest 1992

Dolly In. *See* Travelling Avant.

Dolores Claiborne 1995

Dolphin Tale pg. 97

Domestic Disturbance 2002

Dominick and Eugene 1988

Dominion: Prequel to the Exorcist 2006

Domino 2006

Don Juan DeMarco 1995

Don Juan, My Love 1991

Don McKay 2011

Dona Herlinda and Her Son 1986

Donkey Who Drank the Moon, The 1988

Donna della luna, La. *See* Woman in the Moon.

Donnie Brasco 1997

Experience Preferred...but Not Essential 1983

Explorers 1985

Exposed 1983

Express, The 2009

Extract 2010

Extramuros 1995

Extraordinary Measures 2011

Extreme Measures 1996

Extreme Ops 2003

Extreme Prejudice 1987

Extremely Loud and Incredibly Close pg. 116

Extremities 1986

Eye for an Eye, An 1996

Eye of God 1997

Eye of the Beholder 2001

Eye of the Needle 1981

Eye of the Tiger, The 1986

Eye, The 2009

Eyes of Tammy Faye, The 2001

Eyes Wide Shut 2000

F

F/X 1986

F/X II 1991

Fabulous Baker Boys, The 1989

Fabulous Destiny of Amelie Poulain, The. *See* Amelie.

Face/Off 1997

Faces of Women 1987

Facing Windows 2005

Factory Girl 2008

Factotum 2007

Faculty, The 1999

Fahrenheit 9/11 2005

Failure to Launch 2007

Fair Game 1995

Fair Game 2011

Fairytale—A True Story 1997

Faithful 1996

Faithless 2002

Fakebook 1989

Falcon and the Snowman, The 1985

Fall 1997

Fallen 1999

Fallen Angels 1999

Falling, The. *See* Alien Predator.

Falling Down 1993

Falling from Grace 1992

Falling in Love 1984

Fälscher, Die. *See* Counterfeiters, The.

Falstaff [1966] 1982

Fame 2010

Family, The 1988

Family Business 1989

Family Man 2001

Family Prayers 1993

Family Stone, The 2006

Family Thing, A 1996

Famine Within, The 1992

Fan, The 1996

Fanboys 2010

Fandango 1985

Fanny and Alexander 1983

Fanny och Alexander. *See* Fanny and Alexander.

Fantasies [1973] 1982

Fantastic Four 2006

Fantastic Four: Rise of the Silver Surfer 2008

Fantastic Mr. Fox 2010

Fantomes des Trois Madeleines, Les. *See* Three Madeleines, The.

Fantome D'henri Langlois, Le. *See* Henri Langlois: The Phantom of the Cinematheque.

Far and Away 1992

Far from Heaven 2003

Far from Home 1989

Far From Home: The Adventures of Yellow Dog 1995

Far North 1988

Far Off Place, A 1993

Far Out Man 1990

Faraway, So Close 1993

Farewell Illusion 1986

Farewell My Concubine 1993

Farewell to the King 1989

Fargo 1996

Farinelli 1995

Farmer and Chase 1997

Fast & Furious 2010

Fast and the Furious, The 2002

Fast and the Furious: Tokyo Drift, The 2007

Fast, Cheap & Out of Control 1997

Fast Five pg. 119

Fast Food 1989

Fast Food, Fast Women 2002

Fast Forward 1985

Fast Talking 1986

Fast Times at Ridgemont High 1982

Faster 2011

Fat Albert 2005

Fat City [1972] 1983

Fat Girl 2002

Fat Guy Goes Nutzoid 1987

Fat Man and Little Boy 1989

Fatal Attraction 1987

Fatal Beauty 1987

Fatal Instinct 1993

Fate Ignoranti. *See* Ignorant Fairies.

Father 1995

Father Hood 1993

Father of the Bride (Minnelli) [1950] 1993

Father of the Bride (Shyer) 1991

Father of the Bride Part II 1995

Fathers and Sons 1992

Father's Day 1997

Fausto. *See* A la Mode.

Fauteuils d'orchestre. *See* Avenue Montaigne.

Favor, The 1995

Favour, the Watch, and the Very Big Fish, The 1992

Fay Grim 2008

Fear 1988

Fear 1996

Fear and Loathing in Las Vegas 1999

Fear, Anxiety and Depression 1989

Fear of a Black Hat 1995

Feardotcom 2003

Fearless 1993

Fearless. *See* Jet Li's Fearless.

Feast of July 1995

Feast of Love 2008

Glamazon: A Different Kind of Girl 1995

Glamour 2002

Glaneurs et la Glaneuse, Les. *See* Gleaners and I, The.

Glass House, The 2002

Glass Menagerie, The 1987

Glass Shield, The 1995

Gleaming the Cube 1989

Gleaners and I, The 2002

Glee: The 3D Concert Movie pg. 137

Glengarry Glen Ross 1992

Glimmer Man, The 1996

Glitter 2002

Gloire de mon pere, La. *See* My Father's Glory.

Gloomy Sunday 2004

Gloria (Cassavetes) [1980] 1987

Gloria (Lumet) 2000

Glory 1989

Glory Road 2007

Gnomeo & Juliet pg. 139

Go 2000

Go Fish 1995

Go Now 1999

Goal! The Dream Begins 2007

Goat, The 1985

Gobots 1986

God Doesn't Believe in Us Anymore 1988

God Grew Tired of Us 2008

God Is Great, I'm Not 2003

God Is My Witness 1993

God Said "Ha"! 2000

Goddess of 1967, The 2003

Godfather, Part III, The 1990

Gods and Generals 2004

Gods and Monsters 1999

Gods Must Be Crazy, The 1984

Gods Must Be Crazy II, The 1990

God's Will 1989

Godsend 2005

Godzilla 1985 1985

Godzilla 1997

Godzilla 2000 2001

Gohatto. *See* Taboo.

Goin' to Chicago 1991

Going All the Way 1997

Going Berserk 1983

Going the Distance 2011

Going Undercover 1988

Goin' South 1978

Gold Diggers: The Secret of Bear Mountain 1995

Golden Bowl, The 2002

Golden Child, The 1986

Golden Compass, The 2008

Golden Gate 1995

Golden Seal 1983

Goldeneye 1995

Gomorrah 2010

Gone Baby Gone 2008

Gone Fishin' 1997

Gone in Sixty Seconds 2001

Gone With the Wind [1939] 1981, 1982, 1997

Gong fu. *See* Kung Fu Hustle.

Gonza the Spearman 1988

Good Boy! 2004

Good Burger 1997

Good Bye Cruel World 1984

Good Bye, Lenin! 2005

Good Evening, Mr. Wallenberg 1995

Good German, The 2007

Good Girl, The 2003

Good Hair 2010

Good Luck Chuck 2008

Good Man in Africa, A 1995

Good Marriage, A. *See* Beau Mariage, Le.

Good Morning, Babylon 1987

Good Morning, Vietnam 1987

Good Mother, The 1988

Good Night, and Good Luck 2006

Good Old Fashioned Orgy, A pg. 140

Good Shepherd, The 2007

Good Son, The 1993

Good, the Bad, the Weird, The 2011

Good Thief, The 2004

Good Weather, But Stormy Late This Afternoon 1987

Good Will Hunting 1997

Good Woman, A 2007

Good Woman of Bangkok, The 1992

Good Work. *See* Beau Travail.

Good Year, A 2007

Goodbye, Children. *See* Au Revoir les Enfants.

Goodbye Lover 2000

Goodbye, New York 1985

Goodbye People, The 1986

Goodbye Solo 2010

GoodFellas 1990

Goods: Live Hard, Sell Hard, The 2010

Goods: The Don Ready Story, The. *See* Goods: Live Hard, Sell Hard, The.

Goofy Movie, A 1995

Goonies, The 1985

Gordy 1995

Gorillas in the Mist 1988

Gorky Park 1983

Gorky Triology, The. *See* Among People.

Gosford Park 2002

Gospel 1984

Gospel According to Vic 1986

Gossip 2001

Gossip (Nutley) 2003

Gost 1988

Gotcha! 1985

Gothic 1987

Gothika 2004

Gout des Autres, Le. *See* Taste of Others, The.

Gouttes d'Eau sur Pierres Brulantes. *See* Water Drops on Burning Rocks.

Governess 1999

Goya in Bordeaux 2001

Grace Is Gone 2008

Grace of My Heart 1996

Grace Quigley 1985

Gracie 2008

Graffiti Bridge 1990

Gran Fiesta, La 1987

Gran Torino 2009

Grand Bleu, Le. *See* Big Blue, The (Besson).

Grand Canyon 1991

Grand Canyon: The Hidden Secrets 1987

Grand Chemin, Le. *See* Grand Highway, The.

Grand Highway, The 1988

Grand Illusion, The 2000

Grand Isle 1995

Grande Cocomero, Il. *See* Great Pumpkin, The.

Grandfather, The 2000

Grandma's Boy 2007

Grandview, U.S.A. 1984

Grass Harp, The 1996

Gravesend 1997

Graveyard Shift. *See* Stephen King's Graveyard Shift.

Gray Matters 2008

Gray's Anatomy 1997

Grease [1978] 1997

Grease II 1982

Great Balls of Fire! 1989

Great Barrier Reef, The 1990

Great Buck Howard, The 2010

Great Day In Harlem, A 1995

Great Debaters, The 2008

Great Expectations 1999

Great Mouse Detective, The 1986

Great Muppet Caper, The 1981

Great Outdoors, The 1988

Great Pumpkin, The 1993

Great Raid, The 2006

Great Wall, A 1986

Great White Hype, The 1996

Greatest, The 2011

Greatest Game Ever Played, The 2006

Greatest Movie Ever Sold, The. *See* POM Wonderful Presents: The Greatest Movie Ever Sold.

Greedy 1995

Green Card 1990

Green Desert 2001

Green Hornet, The pg. 142

Green Lantern pg. 143

Green Mile, The 2000

Green Zone 2011

Greenberg 2011

Greenfingers 2002

Greenhouse, The 1996

Gregory's Girl 1982

Gremlins 1984

Gremlins II 1990

Grey Fox, The 1983

Grey Zone, The 2003

Greystoke 1984

Gridlock'd 1988

Grief 1995

Grievous Bodily Harm 1988

Grifters, The 1990

Grim Prairie Tales 1990

Grind 2004

Grindhouse 2008

Gringo 1985

Grizzly Man 2006

Grizzly Mountain 1997

Groomsmen, The 2007

Groove 2001

Gross Anatomy 1989

Grosse Fatigue 1995

Grosse Pointe Blank 1997

Ground Truth, The 2008

Ground Zero 1987, 1988

Groundhog Day 1993

Grown Ups 2011

Grudge, The 2005

Grudge 2, The 2007

Grumpier Old Men 1995

Grumpy Old Men 1993

Grune Wuste. *See* Green Desert.

Guard, The pg. 145

Guardian, The 1990

Guardian, The 2007

Guarding Tess 1995

Guatanamera 1997

Guelwaar 1995

Guerre du Feu, La. *See* Quest for Fire.

Guess Who 2006

Guess Who's Coming to Dinner? [1967] 1992

Guest, The 1984

Guests of Hotel Astoria, The 1989

Guilty as Charged 1992

Guilty as Sin 1993

Guilty by Suspicion 1991

Guinevere 2000

Gulliver's Travels 2011

Gummo 1997

Gun in Betty Lou's Handbag, The 1992

Gun Shy 2001

Gunbus. *See* Sky Bandits.

Guncrazy 1993

Gunfighter, The [1950] 1989

Gung Ho 1986

Gunmen 1995

Gunner Palace 2006

Guru, The 2004

Guy Named Joe, A [1943] 1981

Guy Thing, A 2004

Guys, The 2003

Gwendoline 1984

Gwoemul. *See* Host, The.

Gyakufunsha Kazoku. *See* Crazy Family, The.

Gymkata 1985

H

H. M. Pulham, Esq. [1941] 1981

Hable con Ella. *See* Talk to Her.

Hackers 1995

Hadesae: The Final Incident 1992

Hadley's Rebellion 1984

Haevnen. *See* In a Better World.

Hail Mary 1985

Hairdresser's Husband, The 1992

Hairspray 1988

Hairspray 2008

Haizi wang. *See* King of the Children.

Hak hap. *See* Black Mask

Hak mau. *See* Black Cat.

Half-Baked 1999

Half Moon Street 1986

M

Mr. Deeds 2003

Mr. Deeds Goes to Town [1936] 1982

Mr. Destiny 1990

Mr. Frost 1990

Mr. Holland's Opus 1995

Mr. Jealousy 1999

Mister Johnson 1991

Mr. Jones 1993

Mr. Love 1986

Mr. Magoo 1997

Mr. Magorium's Wonder Emporium 2008

Mr. Mom 1983

Mr. Nanny 1993

Mr. Nice Guy 1999

Mr. North 1988

Mr. Payback 1995

Mr. Poppers Penguins pg. 255

Mister Roberts [1955] 1988

Mr. Saturday Night 1992

Mr. Smith Goes to Washington [1939] 1982

Mr. 3000 2005

Mr. Wonderful 1993

Mr. Woodcock 2008

Mr. Write 1995

Mr. Wrong 1996

Mistress 1992

Mrs. Brown 1997

Mrs. Dalloway 1999

Mrs. Doubtfire 1993

Mrs. Henderson Presents 2006

Mrs. Palfrey at the Claremont 2007

Mrs. Parker and the Vicious Circle 1995

Mrs. Soffel 1984

Mrs. Winterbourne 1996

Misunderstood 1984

Mit Liv som Hund. *See* My Life as a Dog.

Mitad del cielo, La. *See* Half of Heaven.

Mixed Blood 1985

Mixed Nuts 1995

Mo' Better Blues 1990

Mo' Money 1992

Moartea domnului Lazarescu. *See* Death of Mr. Lazarescu, The.

Mobsters 1991

Mod Squad, The 2000

Modern Girls 1986

Modern Romance 1981

Moderns, The 1988

Mogan Do. *See* Infernal Affairs.

Mois d'avril sont meurtriers, Les. *See* April Is a Deadly Month.

Moitie Gauche du Frigo, La. *See* Left Hand Side of the Fridge, The.

Moll Flanders 1996

Molly 2000

Mom and Dad Save the World 1992

Môme, La. *See* Vie en Rose, La.

Mommie Dearest 1981

Mon bel Amour, Ma Dechirure. *See* My True Love, My Wound.

Mon meilleur ami. *See* My Best Friend.

Mona Lisa 1986

Mona Lisa Smile 2004

Mondays in the Sun 2004

Mondo New York 1988

Mondovino 2006

Money for Nothing 1993

Money Man 1995

Money Pit, The 1986

Money Talks 1997

Money Train 1995

Money Tree, The 1992

Moneyball pg. 257

Mongol 2009

Mongolian Tale, A 1997

Monkey Shines 1988

Monkey Trouble 1995

Monkeybone 2002

Monsieur Hire 1990

Monsieur Ibrahim 2004

Monsieur N 2006

Monsignor 1982

Monsoon Wedding 2003

Monster 2004

Monster, The 1996

Monster House 2007

Monster in a Box 1992

Monster-in-Law 2006

Monster in the Closet 1987

Monster Squad, The 1987

Monsters 2011

Monster's Ball 2002

Monsters, Inc. 2002

Monsters vs. Aliens 2010

Montana Run 1992

Monte Carlo pg. 259

Montenegro 1981

Month by the Lake, A 1995

Month in the Country, A 1987

Monty Python's The Meaning of Life 1983

Monument Ave. 1999

Moolaade 2005

Moon 2010

Moon in the Gutter 1983

Moon Over Broadway 1999

Moon over Parador 1988

Moon Shadow [1995] 2001

Moonlight and Valentino 1995

Moonlight Mile 2003

Moonlighting 1982

Moonstruck 1987

More Than A Game 2010

Morgan Stewart's Coming Home 1987

Moriarty. *See* Sherlock Holmes.

Morning After, The 1986

Morning Glory 1993

Morning Glory 2011

Morons from Outer Space 1985

Mort de Mario Ricci, La. *See* Death of Mario Ricci, The.

Mortal Kombat 1995

Mortal Kombat II: Annihilation 1997

Mortal Thoughts 1991

Mortuary Academy 1988

Morvern Callar 2003

Mosca addio. *See* Moscow Farewell.

Moscow Farewell 1987

Moscow on the Hudson 1984

Mosquito Coast, The 1986

Purple Haze 1983

Purple Hearts 1984

Purple Noon [1960] 1996

Purple People Eaters, The 1988

Purple Rain 1984

Purple Rose of Cairo, The 1985

Pursuit of Happyness, The 2007

Push 2010

Pushing Tin 2000

Puss in Boots pg. 299

Pyromaniac's Love Story, A 1995

Q

Q & A 1990

Qianxi Mambo. *See* Millennium mambo.

Qimsong. *See* Emperor's Shadow, The.

Qiu Ju Da Guansi. *See* Story of Qiu Ju, The.

Quantum of Solace 2009

Quarantine 2009

Quarrel, The 1992

Quartet 1981

Quatre Aventures de Reinette et Mirabelle. *See* Four Adventures of Reinette and Mirabelle.

Queen, The 2007

Queen City Rocker 1987

Queen Margot 1995

Queen of Diamonds 1995

Queen of Hearts 1989

Queen of the Damned 2003

Queens Logic 1991

Quelques Jours avec moi. *See* Few Days with Me, A.

Querelle 1983

Quest, The 1996

Quest for Camelot 1999

Quest for Fire 1982

Question of Silence, The 1984

Quick and the Dead, The 1995

Quick Change 1990

Quiet, The 2007

Quiet American, The 2003

Quiet Earth, The 1985

Quiet Man, The [1952] 1981

Quiet Room, The 1997

Quigley Down Under 1990

Quills 2001

Quitting 2003

Quiz Show 1995

R

Rabbit Hole 2011

Rabbit-Proof Fence 2003

Race for Glory 1989

Race the Sun 1996

Race to Witch Mountain 2010

Rachel Getting Married 2009

Rachel Papers, The 1989

Rachel River 1987

Racing Stripes 2006

Racing with the Moon 1984

Radio 2004

Radio Days 1987

Radio Flyer 1992

Radioland Murders 1995

Radium City 1987

Rage: Carrie 2 2000

Rage in Harlem, A 1991

Rage of Honor 1987

Raggedy Man 1981

Raggedy Rawney, The 1988

Raging Angels 1995

Raging Fury. *See* Hell High.

Ragtime 1981

Raiders of the Lost Ark 1981

Rain 2003

Rain. *See* Baran.

Rain Killer, The 1990

Rain Man 1988

Rain Without Thunder 1993

Rainbow Brite and the Star Stealer 1985

Rainbow, The 1989

Raining Stones 1995

Raintree County [1957] 1993

Rainy Day Friends 1985

Raise the Red Lantern 1992

Raise Your Voice 2005

Raisin in the Sun, A [1961] 1992

Raising Arizona 1987

Raising Cain 1992

Raising Helen 2005

Raising Victor Vargas 2004

Rambling Rose 1991

Rambo 2009

Rambo: First Blood Part II 1985

Rambo III 1988

Ramona 1995

Ramona and Beezus 2011

Rampage 1987, 1992

Rampart pg. 301

Ran 1985

Random Hearts 2000

Rango pg. 303

Ransom 1996

Rapa Nui 1995

Rapid Fire 1992

Rappin' 1985

Rapture, The 1991

Raspad 1992

Rasputin [1975] 1985

Rat Race 2002

Ratatouille 2008

Ratboy 1986

Rat's Tale, A 1999

Ratcatcher 2001

Rate It X 1986

Ravenous 2000

Raw Deal 1986

Rawhead Rex 1987

Ray 2005

Rayon vert, Le. *See* Summer.

Razorback 1985

Razor's Edge, The 1984

Re-Animator 1985

Read My Lips 2003

Reader, The 1988, 1989

Reader, The 2009

Ready to Rumble 2001

Ready to Wear 1995

Real Blonde, The 1999

Real Genius 1985

Real McCoy, The 1993

Real Men 1987

Shipwrecked 1991

Shiqisuide Danche. *See* Beijing Bicycle.

Shirley Valentine 1989

Shiza. *See* Shizo.

Shoah 1985

Shock to the System, A 1990

Shocker 1989

Shoot 'Em Up 2008

Shoot the Moon 1982

Shoot to Kill 1988

Shooter 2008

Shooting, The [1966] 1995

Shooting Dogs. *See* Beyond the Gates.

Shooting Fish 1999

Shooting Party, The 1985

Shootist, The [1976] 1982

Shopgirl 2006

Short Circuit 1986

Short Circuit II 1988

Short Cuts 1993

Short Film About Love, A 1995

Short Time 1990

Shorts: The Adventures of the Wishing Rock 2010

Shot, The 1996

Shout 1991

Show, The 1995

Show Me Love 2000

Show of Force, A 1990

Showdown in Little Tokyo 1991

Shower, The 2001

Showgirls 1995

Showtime 2003

Shrek 2002

Shrek Forever After 2011

Shrek the Third 2008

Shrek 2 2005

Shrimp on the Barbie, The 1990

Shutter 2009

Shutter Island 2011

Shvitz, The. *See* New York in Short: The Shvitz and Let's Fall in Love.

Shy People 1987

Siberiade 1982

Sibling Rivalry 1990

Sicilian, The 1987

Sick: The Life and Death of Bob Flanagan, Supermasochist 1997

Sicko 2008

Sid and Nancy 1986

Side Out 1990

Sidekicks 1993

Sidewalk Stories 1989

Sidewalks of New York, The 2002

Sideways 2005

Siege, The 1999

Siesta 1987

Sign o' the Times 1987

Sign of the Cross, The [1932] 1984

Signal Seven 1986

Signs 2003

Signs & Wonders 2002

Signs of Life 1989

Silence, The 2001

Silence After the Shot, The. *See* Legend of Rita, The.

Silence at Bethany, The 1988

Silence of the Lambs, The 1991

Silencer, The 1995

Silent Fall 1995

Silent Hill 2007

Silent Madness, The 1984

Silent Night 1988

Silent Night, Deadly Night 1984

Silent Night, Deadly Night II 1987

Silent Night, Deadly Night III 1989

Silent Rage 1982

Silent Tongue 1995

Silent Touch, The 1995

Silent Victim 1995

Silk Road, The 1992

Silkwood 1983

Silver City (Sayles) 2005

Silver City (Turkiewicz) 1985

Silverado 1985

Simon Birch 1999

Simon Magnus 2002

Simon the Magician 2001

Simone 2003

Simpatico 2000

Simple Men 1992

Simple Plan, A 1999

Simple Twist of Fate, A 1995

Simple Wish, A 1997

Simply Irresistible 2000

Simpsons Movie, The 2008

Sin City 2006

Sin Nombre 2010

Sin Noticias de Dios. *See* No News from God.

Sinbad: Legend of the Seven Seas 2004

Since Otar Left 2005

Sincerely Charlotte 1986

Sinful Life, A 1989

Sing 1989

Singin' in the Rain [1952] 1985

Singing Detective, The 2004

Singing the Blues in Red 1988

Single Man, A 2010

Single White Female 1992

Singles 1992

Sioux City 1995

Sirens 1995

Sister Act 1992

Sister Act II 1993

Sister, My Sister 1995

Sister, Sister 1987

Sisterhood of the Traveling Pants, The 2006

Sisterhood of the Traveling Pants 2, The 2009

Sisters. *See* Some Girls.

Sitcom 2000

Sitter, The pg. 334

Siu lam juk kau. *See* Shaolin Soccer.

Siulam Chukkau. *See* Shaolin Soccer.

Six Days, Seven Nights 1999

Six Days, Six Nights 1995

Six Degrees of Separation 1993

Six Pack 1982

Six-String Samurai 1999

Six Ways to Sunday 2000

Six Weeks 1982

16 Blocks 2007

Sixteen Candles 1984

Sixteen Days of Glory 1986

Sixth Day, The 2001

Sixth Man, The 1997

Sixth Sense, The 2000

Sixty Glorious Years [1938] 1983

'68 1987

Skeleton Key, The 2006

Ski Country 1984

Ski Patrol 1990

Skin Deep 1989

Skin I Live In, The pg. 335

Skins 2003

Skinwalkers 2008

Skipped Parts 2002

Skulls, The 2001

Sky Bandits 1986

Sky Blue 2006

Sky Captain and the World of To-morrow 2005

Sky High 2006

Sky of Our Childhood, The 1988

Skyline 1984

Skyline 2011

Slacker 1991

Slackers 2003

Slam 1997

Slam Dance 1987

Slap Shot [1977] 1981

Slapstick 1984

Slate, Wyn, and Me 1987

Slave Coast. *See* Cobra Verde.

Slave Girls from Beyond Infinity 1987

Slaves of New York 1989

Slaves to the Underground 1997

Slayground 1984

SLC Punk 2000

Sleazy Uncle, The 1991

Sleep With Me 1995

Sleepers 1996

Sleeping Beauty pg. 337

Sleeping with the Enemy 1991

Sleepless in Seattle 1993

Sleepover 2005

Sleepwalkers. *See* Stephen King's Sleepwalkers.

Sleepwalking 2009

Sleepy Hollow 2000

Sleepy Time Gal, The 2002

Sleuth 2008

Sliding Doors 1999

Sling Blade 1996

Slingshot, The 1995

Slipping Down Life, A 2005

Slither 2007

Sliver 1993

Slow Burn 2008

Slugs 1988

Slumdog Millionaire 2009

Slums of Beverly Hills 1999

Small Faces 1996

Small Soldiers 1999

Small Time Crooks 2001

Small Wonders 1996

Smart People 2009

Smash Palace 1982

Smell of Camphor, Fragrance of Jas-mine 2001

Smile Like Yours, A 1997

Smiling Fish and Goat on Fire 2001

Smilla's Sense of Snow 1997

Smithereens 1982, 1985

Smoke 1995

Smoke Signals 1999

Smokey and the Bandit, Part 3 1983

Smokin' Aces 2008

Smoking/No Smoking [1995] 2001

Smooth Talk 1985

Smurfs, The pg. 339

Smurfs and the Magic Flute, The 1983

Snake Eyes 1999

Snake Eyes. *See* Dangerous Game.

Snakes on a Plane 2007

Snapper, The 1993

Snatch 2002

Sneakers 1992

Sniper 1993

Snow Angels 2009

Snow Day 2001

Snow Dogs 2003

Snow Falling in Cedars 2000

Snow Flower and the Secret Fan pg. 341

Snows of Kilimanjaro, The [1952] 1982

S.O.B. 1981

So I Married an Axe Murderer 1993

Soapdish 1991

Sobibor, October 14, 1943, 4 p.m. 2002

Social Network, The 2011

Society 1992

Sofie 1993

Soft Fruit 2001

Soft Shell Man 2003

Softly Softly 1985

Sokhout. *See* Silence, The.

Sol del Membrillo, El. *See* Dream of Light.

Solarbabies 1986

Solaris 2003

Solas 2001

Soldier 1999

Soldier, The 1982

Soldier's Daughter Never Cries, A 1999

Soldier's Story, A 1984

Soldier's Tale, A 1988

Solid Gold Cadillac, The [1956] 1984

Solitary Man 2011

Solo 1996

Soloist, The 2010

Solomon and Gaenor 2001

Some Girls 1988

Some Kind of Hero 1982

Some Kind of Wonderful 1987

Some Like It Hot [1959] 1986, 1988

Some Mother's Son 1996

Someone Else's America 1996

Someone Like You 2002

Someone to Love 1987, 1988

Someone to Watch Over Me 1987

Somersault 2007

Something Borrowed pg. 342

World of Henry Orient, The [1964] 1983

World Trade Center 2007

World Traveler 2003

World's Fastest Indian, The 2007

World's Greatest Dad 2010

Worth Winning 1989

Wraith, The 1986

Wrestler, The 2009

Wrestling Ernest Hemingway 1993

Wristcutters: A Love Story 2008

Wrong Couples, The 1987

Wrong Guys, The 1988

Wrong Is Right 1982

Wrong Man, The 1995

Wrong Turn 2004

Wrongfully Accused 1999

Wu ji. *See* Promise, The.

Wu jian dao. *See* Infernal Affairs.

Wyatt Earp 1995

X

X. *See* Malcolm X.

X-Files, The 1999

X-Files: I Want to Believe, The 2009

X-Men, The 2001

X-Men: First Class pg. 429

X-Men: The Last Stand 2007

X-Men Origins: Wolverine 2010

X2: X-Men United 2004

Xero. *See* Home Remedy.

Xiao cai feng. *See* Balzac and the Little Chinese Seamstress.

Xica [1976] 1982

Xica da Silva. *See* Xica.

Xingfu Shiguang. *See* Happy Times.

Xiu Xiu, The Sent Down Girl 2000

Xizao. *See* Shower, The.

XX/XY 2004

XXX 2003

XXX: State of the Union 2006

Y

Y tu mama tambien 2003

Yaaba 1990

Yards, The 2001

Yari No Gonza Kasane Katabira. *See* Gonza the Spearman.

Yatgo Ho Yan. *See* Mr. Nice Guy.

Year My Voice Broke, The 1987, 1988

Year of Comet 1992

Year of Living Dangerously, The 1983

Year of the Dog 2008

Year of the Dragon 1985

Year of the Gun 1991

Year of the Horse 1997

Year of the Quiet Sun, A 1986

Year One 2010

Yearling, The [1946] 1989

Yella 2009

Yellowbeard 1983

Yen Family 1988, 1990

Yentl 1983

Yes 2006

Yes, Giorgio 1982

Yes Man 2009

Yesterday. *See* Quitting.

Yi Yi 2001

Yihe yuan. *See* Summer Palace.

Ying xiong. *See* Hero.

Yogi Bear 2011

Yol 1982

Yor: The Hunter from the Future 1983

You Again 2011

You, Me and Dupree 2007

You Can Count on Me 2001

You Can't Hurry Love 1988

You Don't Mess with the Zohan 2009

You Got Served 2005

You Kill Me 2008

You So Crazy 1995

You Talkin' to Me? 1987

You Toscanini 1988

You Will Meet a Tall Dark Stranger 2011

Young Adam 2005

Young Adult pg. 431

YoungHeart 2009

Young Dr. Kildare [1938] 1985

Young Doctors in Love 1982

Young Einstein 1988

Young Guns 1988

Young Guns II 1990

Young Poisoner's Handbook, The 1996

Young Sherlock Holmes 1985

Young Soul Rebels 1991

Young Victoria, The 2010

Youngblood 1986

Your Friends & Neighbors 1999

Your Highness pg. 432

Yours, Mine & Ours 2006

Youth in Revolt 2011

Youth Without Youth 2008

You've Got Mail 1999

Yu-Gi-Oh! The Movie 2005

Z

Zack and Miri Make a Porno 2009

Zappa 1984

Zapped! 1982

Zathura 2006

Zatoichi 2005

Zebdegi Edame Darad. *See* And Life Goes On.

Zebrahead 1992

Zegen. *See* Pimp, The.

Zelary 2005

Zelig 1983

Zelly and Me 1988

Zentropa 1992

Zero Degrees Kelvin 1996

Zero Effect 1999

Zero Patience 1995

Zeus and Roxanne 1997

Zhou Yu's Train 2005

Zir-e Poust-e Shahr. *See* Under the Skin of the City.

Zjoek 1987

Zodiac 2008

Zombie and the Ghost Train 1995

Zombie High 1987

Zombieland 2010

Zookeeper pg.434

Zoolander 2002

Zoom 2007

Zoot Suit 1981

Zuotian. *See* Quitting.

Zus & Zo 2004

Zwartboek. *See* Black Book.

For Reference

Not to be taken from this room